Operating System Concepts

Eighth Edition

International Student Version

ABRAHAM SILBERSCHATZ
Yale University

PETER BAER GALVIN
Corporate Technologies, Inc.

GREG GAGNE
Westminster College

WILEY-INDIA

OPERATING SYSTEM CONCEPTS
INTERNATIONAL STUDENT VERSION
Eighth Edition

Authorized reprint by Wiley India (P.) Ltd., 4435/7, Ansari Road, Daryaganj, New Delhi 110 002.

Reprint: 2013

Printed at : Nisha Enterprises, Sahibabad

ISBN : 978-81-265-2051-0

To my children, Lemor, Sivan, and Aaron
and my Nicolette

Avi Silberschatz

To my wife, Carla,
and my children, Gwen, Owen, and Maddie

Peter Baer Galvin

To my wife, Pat,
and our sons, Tom and Jay

Greg Gagne

Abraham Silberschatz is the Sidney J. Weinberg Professor & Chair of Computer Science at Yale University. Prior to joining Yale, he was the Vice President of the Information Sciences Research Center at Bell Laboratories. Prior to that, he held a chaired professorship in the Department of Computer Sciences at the University of Texas at Austin.

Professor Silberschatz is an ACM Fellow and an IEEE Fellow. He received the 2002 IEEE Taylor L. Booth Education Award, the 1998 ACM Karl V. Karlstrom Outstanding Educator Award, and the 1997 ACM SIGMOD Contribution Award. In recognition of his outstanding level of innovation and technical excellence, he was awarded the Bell Laboratories President's Award for three different projects—the QTM Project (1998), the DataBlitz Project (1999), and the NetInventory Project (2004).

Professor Silberschatz' writings have appeared in numerous ACM and IEEE publications and other professional conferences and journals. He is a coauthor of the textbook *Database System Concepts*. He has also written Op-Ed articles for the New York Times, the Boston Globe, and the Hartford Courant, among others.

Peter Baer Galvin is the chief technologist for Corporate Technologies (www.cptech.com), a computer facility reseller and integrator. Before that, Mr. Galvin was the systems manager for Brown University's Computer Science Department. He is also Sun columnist for *;login:* magazine. Mr. Galvin has written articles for *Byte* and other magazines, and has written columns for *SunWorld* and *SysAdmin* magazines. As a consultant and trainer, he has given talks and taught tutorials on security and system administration worldwide.

Greg Gagne is chair of the Computer Science department at Westminster College in Salt Lake City where he has been teaching since 1990. In addition to teaching operating systems, he also teaches computer networks, distributed systems, and software engineering. He also provides workshops to computer science educators and industry professionals.

Preface

Operating systems are an essential part of any computer system. Similarly, a course on operating systems is an essential part of any computer-science education. This field is undergoing rapid change, as computers are now prevalent in virtually every application, from games for children through the most sophisticated planning tools for governments and multinational firms. Yet the fundamental concepts remain fairly clear, and it is on these that we base this book.

We wrote this book as a text for an introductory course in operating systems at the junior or senior undergraduate level or at the first-year graduate level. We hope that practitioners will also find it useful. It provides a clear description of the *concepts* that underlie operating systems. As prerequisites, we assume that the reader is familiar with basic data structures, computer organization, and a high-level language, such as C or Java. The hardware topics required for an understanding of operating systems are included in Chapter 1. For code examples, we use predominantly C, with some Java, but the reader can still understand the algorithms without a thorough knowledge of these languages.

Concepts are presented using intuitive descriptions. Important theoretical results are covered, but formal proofs are omitted. The bibliographical notes at the end of each chapter contain pointers to research papers in which results were first presented and proved, as well as references to material for further reading. In place of proofs, figures and examples are used to suggest why we should expect the result in question to be true.

The fundamental concepts and algorithms covered in the book are often based on those used in existing commercial operating systems. Our aim is to present these concepts and algorithms in a general setting that is not tied to one particular operating system. We present a large number of examples that pertain to the most popular and the most innovative operating systems, including Sun Microsystems' Solaris; Linux; Microsoft Windows Vista, Windows 2000, and Windows XP; and Apple Mac OS X. When we refer to Windows XP as an example operating system, we are implying Windows Vista, Windows XP, and Windows 2000. If a feature exists in a specific release, we state this explicitly.

Organization of This Book

The organization of this text reflects our many years of teaching courses on operating systems. Consideration was also given to the feedback provided by the reviewers of the text, as well as comments submitted by readers of earlier editions. In addition, the content of the text corresponds to the suggestions from *Computing Curricula 2005* for teaching operating systems, published by the Joint Task Force of the IEEE Computing Society and the Association for Computing Machinery (ACM).

On the supporting Web site for this text, we provide several sample syllabi that suggest various approaches for using the text in both introductory and advanced courses. As a general rule, we encourage readers to progress sequentially through the chapters, as this strategy provides the most thorough study of operating systems. However, by using the sample syllabi, a reader can select a different ordering of chapters (or subsections of chapters).

On-line support for the text is provided by WileyPLUS. On this site, students can find sample exercises and programming problems, and instructors can assign and grade problems. In addition, in WileyPLUS, students can access new operating-system simulators, which are used to work through exercises and hands-on lab activities. References to the simulators and associated activities appear at the ends of several chapters in the text.

Content of This Book

The text is organized in eight major parts:

- **Overview**. Chapters 1 and 2 explain what operating systems *are,* what they *do,* and how they are *designed* and *constructed*. These chapters discuss what the common features of an operating system are, what an operating system does for the user, and what it does for the computer-system operator. The presentation is motivational and explanatory in nature. We have avoided a discussion of how things are done internally in these chapters. Therefore, they are suitable for individual readers or for students in lower-level classes who want to learn what an operating system is without getting into the details of the internal algorithms.

- **Process management**. Chapters 3 through 7 describe the process concept and concurrency as the heart of modern operating systems. A *process* is the unit of work in a system. Such a system consists of a collection of *concurrently* executing processes, some of which are operating-system processes (those that execute system code) and the rest of which are user processes (those that execute user code). These chapters cover methods for process scheduling, interprocess communication, process synchronization, and deadlock handling. Also included is a discussion of threads, as well as an examination of issues related to multicore systems.

- **Memory management**. Chapters 8 and 9 deal with the management of main memory during the execution of a process. To improve both the utilization of the CPU and the speed of its response to its users, the computer must keep several processes in memory. There are many different memory-management schemes, reflecting various approaches to memory management, and the effectiveness of a particular algorithm depends on the situation.

- **Storage management**. Chapters 10 through 13 describe how the file system, mass storage, and I/O are handled in a modern computer system. The file system provides the mechanism for on-line storage of and access to both data and programs. We describe the classic internal algorithms and structures of storage management and provide a firm practical understanding of the algorithms used—their properties, advantages, and disadvantages. Our discussion of storage also includes matters related to secondary and tertiary storage. Since the I/O devices that attach to a computer vary widely, the operating system needs to provide a wide range of functionality to applications to allow them to control all aspects of these devices. We discuss system I/O in depth, including I/O system design, interfaces, and internal system structures and functions. In many ways, I/O devices are the slowest major components of the computer. Because they represent a performance bottleneck, we also examine performance issues associated with I/O devices.

- **Protection and security**. Chapters 14 and 15 discuss the mechanisms necessary for the protection and security of computer systems. The processes in an operating system must be protected from one another's activities, and to provide such protection, we must ensure that only processes that have gained proper authorization from the operating system can operate on the files, memory, CPU, and other resources of the system. Protection is a mechanism for controlling the access of programs, processes, or users to the resources defined by a computer system. This mechanism must provide a means of specifying the controls to be imposed, as well as a means of enforcement. Security protects the integrity of the information stored in the system (both data and code), as well as the physical resources of the system, from unauthorized access, malicious destruction or alteration, and accidental introduction of inconsistency.

- **Distributed systems**. Chapters 16 through 18 deal with a collection of processors that do not share memory or a clock—a *distributed system.* By providing the user with access to the various resources that it maintains, a distributed system can improve computation speed and data availability and reliability. Such a system also provides the user with a distributed file system, which is a file-service system whose users, servers, and storage devices are dispersed among the sites of a distributed system. A distributed system must provide various mechanisms for process synchronization and communication, as well as for dealing with deadlock problems and a variety of failures that are not encountered in a centralized system.

- **Special-purpose systems**. Chapters 19 and 20 deal with systems used for specific purposes, including real-time systems and multimedia systems. These systems have specific requirements that differ from those of the general-purpose systems that are the focus of the remainder of the text. Real-time systems may require not only that computed results be "correct" but also that the results be produced within a specified deadline period. Multimedia systems require quality-of-service guarantees ensuring that the multimedia data are delivered to clients within a specific time frame.

- **Case studies**. Chapters 21 through 23 in the book, and Appendices A through C (which are available on www.wiley.com/go/global/silberschatz and in WileyPLUS), integrate the concepts described in the earlier chapters by describing real operating systems. These systems include Linux, Windows XP, FreeBSD, Mach, and Windows 2000. We chose Linux and FreeBSD because UNIX—at one time—was almost small enough to understand yet was not a "toy" operating system. Most of its internal algorithms were selected for *simplicity*, rather than for speed or sophistication. Both Linux and FreeBSD are readily available to computer-science departments, so many students have access to these systems. We chose Windows XP and Windows 2000 because they provide an opportunity for us to study a modern operating system with a design and implementation drastically different from those of UNIX. Chapter 23 briefly describes a few other influential operating systems.

Operating-System Environments

This book uses examples of many real-world operating systems to illustrate fundamental operating-system concepts. However, particular attention is paid to the Microsoft family of operating systems (including Windows Vista, Windows 2000, and Windows XP) and various versions of UNIX (including Solaris, BSD, and Mac OS X). We also provide a significant amount of coverage of the Linux operating system reflecting the most recent version of the kernel —Version 2.6—at the time this book was written.

The text also provides several example programs written in C and Java. These programs are intended to run in the following programming environments:

- **Windows systems**. The primary programming environment for Windows systems is the Win32 API (**a**pplication **p**rogramming **i**nterface), which provides a comprehensive set of functions for managing processes, threads, memory, and peripheral devices. We provide several C programs illustrating the use of the Win32 API. Example programs were tested on systems running Windows Vista, Windows 2000, and Windows XP.

- **POSIX**. POSIX (which stands for *Portable Operating System Interface*) represents a set of standards implemented primarily for UNIX-based operating systems. Although Windows Vista, Windows XP, and Windows 2000 systems can also run certain POSIX programs, our coverage of POSIX focuses primarily on UNIX and Linux systems. POSIX-compliant systems must implement the POSIX core standard (POSIX.1): Linux, Solaris, and Mac OS X are examples of POSIX-compliant systems. POSIX also defines several extensions to the standards, including real-time extensions (POSIX1.b) and an extension for a threads library (POSIX1.c, better known as Pthreads). We provide several programming examples written in C illustrating the POSIX base API, as well as Pthreads and the extensions for real-time programming. These example programs were tested on Debian Linux 2.4 and 2.6 systems, Mac OS X 10.5, and Solaris 10 using the gcc 3.3 and 4.0 compilers.

- **Java**. Java is a widely used programming language with a rich API and built-in language support for thread creation and management. Java programs run on any operating system supporting a Java virtual machine (or JVM). We illustrate various operating system and networking concepts with several Java programs tested using the Java 1.5 JVM.

We have chosen these three programming environments because it is our opinion that they best represent the two most popular models of operating systems: Windows and UNIX/Linux, along with the widely used Java environment. Most programming examples are written in C, and we expect readers to be comfortable with this language; readers familiar with both the C and Java languages should easily understand most programs provided in this text.

In some instances—such as thread creation—we illustrate a specific concept using all three programming environments, allowing the reader to contrast the three different libraries as they address the same task. In other situations, we may use just one of the APIs to demonstrate a concept. For example, we illustrate shared memory using just the POSIX API; socket programming in TCP/IP is highlighted using the Java API.

The Eighth Edition

As we wrote the Eighth Edition of *Operating System Concepts*, we were guided by the many comments and suggestions we received from readers of our previous editions, as well as by our own observations about the rapidly changing fields of operating systems and networking. We have rewritten material in most of the chapters by bringing older material up to date and removing material that was no longer of interest or relevance.

We have made substantive revisions and organizational changes in many of the chapters. Most importantly, we have added coverage of open-source operating systems in Chapter 1. We have also added more practice exercises for students and included solutions in WileyPLUS, which also includes new simulators to provide demonstrations of operating-system operation. Below, we provide a brief outline of the major changes to the various chapters:

- **Chapter 1, Introduction,** has been expanded to include multicore CPUs, clustered computers, and open-source operating systems.
- **Chapter 2, System Structures,** provides significantly updated coverage of virtual machines, as well as multicore CPUs, the GRUB boot loader, and operating-system debugging.
- **Chapter 3, Process Concept,** provides new coverage of pipes as a form of interprocess communication.
- **Chapter 4, Multithreaded Programming,** adds new coverage of programming for multicore systems.
- **Chapter 5, Process Scheduling,** adds coverage of virtual machine scheduling and multithreaded, multicore architectures.
- **Chapter 6, Synchronization,** adds a discussion of mutual exclusion locks, priority inversion, and transactional memory.
- **Chapter 8, Memory-Management Strategies,** includes discussion of NUMA.

- **Chapter 9, Virtual-Memory Management,** updates the Solaris example to include Solaris 10 memory management.
- **Chapter 10, File System,** is updated with current technologies and capacities.
- **Chapter 11, Implementing File Systems,** includes a full description of Sun's ZFS file system and expands the coverage of volumes and directories.
- **Chapter 12, Secondary-Storage Structure,** adds coverage of iSCSI, volumes, and ZFS pools.
- **Chapter 13, I/O Systems,** adds coverage of PCIX PCI Express, and HyperTransport.
- **Chapter 16, Distributed Operating Systems,** adds coverage of 802.11 wireless networks.
- **Chapter 21, The Linux System,** has been updated to cover the latest version of the Linux kernel.
- **Chapter 23, Influential Operating Systems,** increases coverage of very early computers as well as TOPS-20, CP/M, MS-DOS, Windows, and the original Mac OS.

Programming Problems and Projects

To emphasize the concepts presented in the text, we have added several programming problems and projects that use the POSIX and Win32 APIs, as well as Java. We have added more than 15 new programming problems, which emphasize processes, threads, shared memory, process synchronization, and networking. In addition, we have added or modified several programming projects that are more involved than standard programming exercises. These projects include adding a system call to the Linux kernel, using pipes on both UNIX and Windows systems, using UNIX message queues, creating multithreaded applications, and solving the producer–consumer problem using shared memory.

The Eighth Edition also incorporates a set of operating-system simulators designed by Steven Robbins of the University of Texas at San Antonio. The simulators are intended to model the behavior of an operating system as it performs various tasks, such as CPU and disk-head scheduling, process creation and interprocess communication, starvation, and address translation. These simulators are written in Java and will run on any computer system with Java 1.4. Students can download the simulators from WileyPLUS and observe the behavior of several operating system concepts in various scenarios. In addition, each simulator includes several exercises that ask students to set certain parameters of the simulator, observe how the system behaves, and then explain this behavior. These exercises can be assigned through WileyPLUS. The WileyPLUS course also includes algorithmic problems and tutorials developed by Scott M. Pike of Texas A&M University.

Teaching Supplements

The following teaching supplements are available in WileyPLUS and on www.wiley.com/go/global/silberschatz: a set of slides to accompany the book, model course syllabi, all C and Java source code, up-to-date errata, three case study appendices and the Distributed Communication appendix. The WileyPLUS course also contains the simulators and associated exercises, additional practice exercises (with solutions) not found in the text, and a testbank of additional problems. Students are encouraged to solve the practice exercises on their own and then use the provided solutions to check their own answers.

To obtain restricted supplements, such as the solution guide to the exercises in the text, contact your local John Wiley & Sons sales representative. Note that these supplements are available only to faculty who use this text.

Mailing List

We use the mailman system for communication among the users of *Operating System Concepts.* If you wish to use this facility, please visit the following URL and follow the instructions there to subscribe:

http://mailman.cs.yale.edu/mailman/listinfo/os-book

The mailman mailing-list system provides many benefits, such as an archive of postings, as well as several subscription options, including digest and Web only. To send messages to the list, send e-mail to:

os-book@cs.yale.edu

Depending on the message, we will either reply to you personally or forward the message to everyone on the mailing list. The list is moderated, so you will receive no inappropriate mail.

Students who are using this book as a text for class should not use the list to ask for answers to the exercises. They will not be provided.

Suggestions

We have attempted to clean up every error in this new edition, but—as happens with operating systems—a few obscure bugs may remain. We would appreciate hearing from you about any textual errors or omissions that you identify.

If you would like to suggest improvements or to contribute exercises, we would also be glad to hear from you. Please send correspondence to os-book-authors@cs.yale.edu.

Acknowledgments

This book is derived from the previous editions, the first three of which were coauthored by James Peterson. Others who helped us with previous editions include Hamid Arabnia, Rida Bazzi, Randy Bentson, David Black,

Joseph Boykin, Jeff Brumfield, Gael Buckley, Roy Campbell, P. C. Capon, John Carpenter, Gil Carrick, Thomas Casavant, Bart Childs, Ajoy Kumar Datta, Joe Deck, Sudarshan K. Dhall, Thomas Doeppner, Caleb Drake, M. Racsit Eskicioğlu, Hans Flack, Robert Fowler, G. Scott Graham, Richard Guy, Max Hailperin, Rebecca Hartman, Wayne Hathaway, Christopher Haynes, Don Heller, Bruce Hillyer, Mark Holliday, Dean Hougen, Michael Huangs, Ahmed Kamel, Morty Kewstel, Richard Kieburtz, Carol Kroll, Morty Kwestel, Thomas LeBlanc, John Leggett, Jerrold Leichter, Ted Leung, Gary Lippman, Carolyn Miller, Michael Molloy, Euripides Montagne, Yoichi Muraoka, Jim M. Ng, Banu Özden, Ed Posnak, Boris Putanec, Charles Qualline, John Quarterman, Mike Reiter, Gustavo Rodriguez-Rivera, Carolyn J. C. Schauble, Thomas P. Skinner, Yannis Smaragdakis, Jesse St. Laurent, John Stankovic, Adam Stauffer, Steven Stepanek, John Sterling, Hal Stern, Louis Stevens, Pete Thomas, David Umbaugh, Steve Vinoski, Tommy Wagner, Larry L. Wear, John Werth, James M. Westall, J. S. Weston, and Yang Xiang

Parts of Chapter 12 were derived from a paper by Hillyer and Silberschatz [1996]. Parts of Chapter 17 were derived from a paper by Levy and Silberschatz [1990]. Chapter 21 was derived from an unpublished manuscript by Stephen Tweedie. Chapter 22 was derived from an unpublished manuscript by Dave Probert, Cliff Martin, and Avi Silberschatz. Appendix C was derived from an unpublished manuscript by Cliff Martin. Cliff Martin also helped with updating the UNIX appendix to cover FreeBSD. Some of the exercises and accompanying solutions were supplied by Arvind Krishnamurthy.

Mike Shapiro, Bryan Cantrill, and Jim Mauro answered several Solaris-related questions. Bryan Cantrill from Sun Microsystems helped with the ZFS coverage. Steve Robbins of the University of Texas at San Antonio designed the set of simulators that we incorporate in WileyPLUS. Reece Newman of Westminster College initially explored this set of simulators and their appropriateness for this text. Josh Dees and Rob Reynolds contributed coverage of Microsoft's .NET. The project for POSIX message queues was contributed by John Trono of Saint Michael's College in Colchester, Vermont.

Marilyn Turnamian helped generate figures and presentation slides. Mark Wogahn has made sure that the software to produce the book (e.g., Latex macros, fonts) works properly.

Our Associate Publisher, Dan Sayre, provided expert guidance as we prepared this edition. He was assisted by Carolyn Weisman, who managed many details of this project smoothly. The Senior Production Editor Ken Santor, was instrumental in handling all the production details. Lauren Sapira and Cindy Johnson have been very helpful with getting material ready and available for WileyPlus.

Beverly Peavler copy-edited the manuscript. The freelance proofreader was Katrina Avery; the freelance indexer was WordCo, Inc.

Abraham Silberschatz, New Haven, CT, 2008
Peter Baer Galvin, Burlington, MA, 2008
Greg Gagne, Salt Lake City, UT, 2008

Contents

PART ONE ■ OVERVIEW

Chapter 1 Introduction

Chapter 2 System Structures

PART TWO ■ PROCESS MANAGEMENT

Chapter 3 Process Concept

Chapter 4 Multithreaded Programming

Chapter 5 Process Scheduling

PART THREE ■ PROCESS COORDINATION

Chapter 6 Synchronization

Chapter 7 Deadlocks

PART FOUR ■ MEMORY MANAGEMENT

Chapter 8 Memory-Management Strategies

Chapter 9 Virtual-Memory Management

PART FIVE ■ STORAGE MANAGEMENT

Chapter 10 File System

Chapter 11 Implementing File Systems

Chapter 12 Secondary-Storage Structure

Chapter 13 I/O Systems

PART SIX ■ PROTECTION AND SECURITY

Chapter 14 System Protection

Chapter 15 System Security

PART SEVEN ■ DISTRIBUTED SYSTEMS

Chapter 16 Distributed Operating Systems

Chapter 17 Distributed File Systems

Chapter 18 Distributed Synchronization

PART EIGHT ■ SPECIAL PURPOSE SYSTEMS

Chapter 19 Real-Time Systems

Chapter 20 Multimedia Systems

PART NINE ■ CASE STUDIES

Chapter 21 The Linux System

Chapter 22 Windows XP

Chapter 23 Influential Operating Systems

Chapter A BSD UNIX

Appendix B The Mach System

Appendix C Windows 2000

Part One

Overview

An *operating system* acts as an intermediary between the user of a computer and the computer hardware. The purpose of an operating system is to provide an environment in which a user can execute programs in a *convenient* and *efficient* manner.

An operating system is software that manages the computer hardware. The hardware must provide appropriate mechanisms to ensure the correct operation of the computer system and to prevent user programs from interfering with the proper operation of the system.

Internally, operating systems vary greatly in their makeup, since they are organized along many different lines. The design of a new operating system is a major task. It is important that the goals of the system be well defined before the design begins. These goals form the basis for choices among various algorithms and strategies.

Because an operating system is large and complex, it must be created piece by piece. Each of these pieces should be a well delineated portion of the system, with carefully defined inputs, outputs, and functions.

CHAPTER 1

Introduction

An operating system is a program that manages the computer hardware. It also provides a basis for application programs and acts as an intermediary between the computer user and the computer hardware. An amazing aspect of operating systems is how varied they are in accomplishing these tasks. Mainframe operating systems are designed primarily to optimize utilization of hardware. Personal computer (PC) operating systems support complex games, business applications, and everything in between. Operating systems for handheld computers are designed to provide an environment in which a user can easily interface with the computer to execute programs. Thus, some operating systems are designed to be *convenient*, others to be *efficient*, and others some combination of the two.

Before we can explore the details of computer system operation, we need to know something about system structure. We begin by discussing the basic functions of system startup, I/O, and storage. We also describe the basic computer architecture that makes it possible to write a functional operating system.

Because an operating system is large and complex, it must be created piece by piece. Each of these pieces should be a well-delineated portion of the system, with carefully defined inputs, outputs, and functions. In this chapter, we provide a general overview of the major components of an operating system.

CHAPTER OBJECTIVES

- To provide a grand tour of the major components of operating systems.
- To describe the basic organization of computer systems.

1.1 What Operating Systems Do

We begin our discussion by looking at the operating system's role in the overall computer system. A computer system can be divided roughly into

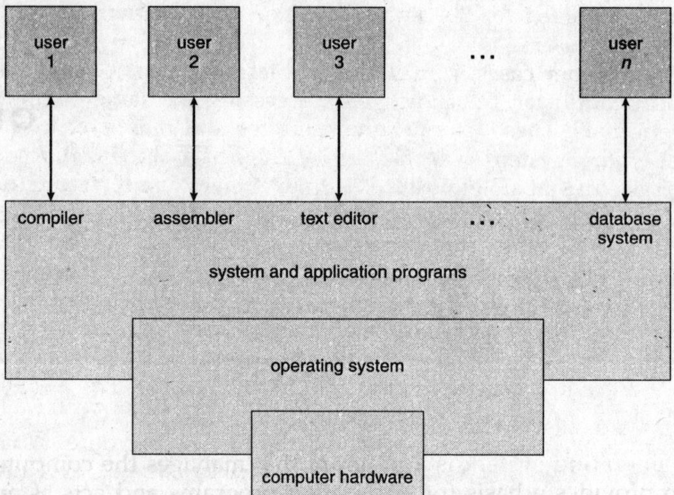

Figure 1.1 Abstract view of the components of a computer system.

four components: the *hardware*, the *operating system*, the *application programs*, and the *users* (Figure 1.1).

The **hardware**—the **central processing unit (CPU)**, the **memory**, and the **input/output (I/O) devices**—provides the basic computing resources for the system. The **application programs**—such as word processors, spreadsheets, compilers, and Web browsers—define the ways in which these resources are used to solve users' computing problems. The operating system controls the hardware and coordinates its use among the various application programs for the various users.

We can also view a computer system as consisting of hardware, software, and data. The operating system provides the means for proper use of these resources in the operation of the computer system. An operating system is similar to a *government*. Like a government, it performs no useful function by itself. It simply provides an *environment* within which other programs can do useful work.

To understand more fully the operating system's role, we next explore operating systems from two viewpoints: that of the user and that of the system.

1.1.1 User View

The user's view of the computer varies according to the interface being used. Most computer users sit in front of a PC, consisting of a monitor, keyboard, mouse, and system unit. Such a system is designed for one user to monopolize its resources. The goal is to maximize the work (or play) that the user is performing. In this case, the operating system is designed mostly for **ease of use**, with some attention paid to performance and none paid to **resource utilization**—how various hardware and software resources are shared. Performance is, of course, important to the user; but such systems are optimized for the single-user experience rather than the requirements of multiple users.

In other cases, a user sits at a terminal connected to a **mainframe** or a **minicomputer**. Other users are accessing the same computer through other terminals. These users share resources and may exchange information. The operating system in such cases is designed to maximize resource utilization—to assure that all available CPU time, memory, and I/O are used efficiently and that no individual user takes more than her fair share.

In still other cases, users sit at **workstations** connected to networks of other workstations and **servers**. These users have dedicated resources at their disposal, but they also share resources such as networking and servers—file, compute, and print servers. Therefore, their operating system is designed to compromise between individual usability and resource utilization.

Recently, many varieties of handheld computers have come into fashion. Most of these devices are standalone units for individual users. Some are connected to networks, either directly by wire or (more often) through wireless modems and networking. Because of power, speed, and interface limitations, they perform relatively few remote operations. Their operating systems are designed mostly for individual usability, but performance per unit of battery life is important as well.

Some computers have little or no user view. For example, embedded computers in home devices and automobiles may have numeric keypads and may turn indicator lights on or off to show status, but they and their operating systems are designed primarily to run without user intervention.

1.1.2 System View

From the computer's point of view, the operating system is the program most intimately involved with the hardware. In this context, we can view an operating system as a **resource allocator**. A computer system has many resources that may be required to solve a problem: CPU time, memory space, file-storage space, I/O devices, and so on. The operating system acts as the manager of these resources. Facing numerous and possibly conflicting requests for resources, the operating system must decide how to allocate them to specific programs and users so that it can operate the computer system efficiently and fairly. As we have seen, resource allocation is especially important where many users access the same mainframe or minicomputer.

A slightly different view of an operating system emphasizes the need to control the various I/O devices and user programs. An operating system is a control program. A **control program** manages the execution of user programs to prevent errors and improper use of the computer. It is especially concerned with the operation and control of I/O devices.

1.1.3 Defining Operating Systems

We have looked at the operating system's role from the views of the user and of the system. How, though, can we define what an operating system is? In general, we have no completely adequate definition of an operating system. Operating systems exist because they offer a reasonable way to solve the problem of creating a usable computing system. The fundamental goal of computer systems is to execute user programs and to make solving user

STORAGE DEFINITIONS AND NOTATION

A **bit** is the basic unit of computer storage. It can contain one of two values, zero and one. All other storage in a computer is based on collections of bits. Given enough bits, it is amazing how many things a computer can represent: numbers, letters, images, movies, sounds, documents, and programs, to name a few. A **byte** is 8 bits, and on most computers it is the smallest convenient chunk of storage. For example, most computers don't have an instruction to move a bit but do have one to move a byte. A less common term is **word**, which is a given computer architecture's native storage unit. A word is generally made up of one or more bytes. For example, a computer may have instructions to move 64-bit (8-byte) words.

A kilobyte, or KB, is 1,024 bytes; a megabyte, or MB, is $1{,}024^2$ bytes; and a gigabyte, or GB, is $1{,}024^3$ bytes. Computer manufacturers often round off these numbers and say that a megabyte is 1 million bytes and a gigabyte is 1 billion bytes.

problems easier. Toward this goal, computer hardware is constructed. Since bare hardware alone is not particularly easy to use, application programs are developed. These programs require certain common operations, such as those controlling the I/O devices. The common functions of controlling and allocating resources are then brought together into one piece of software: the operating system.

In addition, we have no universally accepted definition of what is part of the operating system. A simple viewpoint is that it includes everything a vendor ships when you order "the operating system." The features included, however, vary greatly across systems. Some systems take up less than 1 megabyte of space and lack even a full-screen editor, whereas others require gigabytes of space and are entirely based on graphical windowing systems. A more common definition, and the one that we usually follow, is that the operating system is the one program running at all times on the computer—usually called the **kernel**. (Along with the kernel, there are two other types of programs: **systems programs**, which are associated with the operating system but are not part of the kernel, and **application programs**, which include all programs not associated with the operation of the system.)

The matter of what constitutes an operating system has become increasingly important. In 1998, the United States Department of Justice filed suit against Microsoft, in essence claiming that Microsoft included too much functionality in its operating systems and thus prevented application vendors from competing. For example, a Web browser was an integral part of the operating systems. As a result, Microsoft was found guilty of using its operating-system monopoly to limit competition.

1.2 Computer-System Organization

Before we can explore the details of how computer systems operate, we need general knowledge of the structure of a computer system. In this section, we look at several parts of this structure. The section is mostly concerned

THE STUDY OF OPERATING SYSTEMS

There has never been a more interesting time to study operating systems, and it has never been easier. The open-source movement has overtaken operating systems, causing many of them to be made available in both source and binary (executable) format. This list includes Linux, BSD UNIX, Solaris, and part of Mac OS X. The availability of source code allows us to study operating systems from the inside out. Questions that previously could only be answered by looking at documentation or the behavior of an operating system can now be answered by examining the code itself.

In addition, the rise of virtualization as a mainstream (and frequently free) computer function makes it possible to run many operating systems on top of one core system. For example, VMware (`http://www.vmware.com`) provides a free "player" on which hundreds of free "virtual appliances" can run. Using this method, students can try out hundreds of operating systems within their existing operating systems at no cost.

Operating systems that are no longer commercially viable have been open-sourced as well, enabling us to study how systems operated in a time of fewer CPU, memory, and storage resources. An extensive but not complete list of open-source operating-system projects is available from `http://dmoz.org/Computers/Software/Operating_Systems/Open_Source/`. Simulators of specific hardware are also available in some cases, allowing the operating system to run on "native" hardware, all within the confines of a modern computer and modern operating system. For example, a DECSYSTEM-20 simulator running on Mac OS X can boot TOPS-20, load the source tapes, and modify and compile a new TOPS-20 kernel. An interested student can search the Internet to find the original papers that describe the operating system and the original manuals.

The advent of open-source operating systems also makes it easy to make the move from student to operating-system developer. With some knowledge, some effort, and an Internet connection, a student can even create a new operating-system distribution! Just a few years, ago it was difficult or impossible to get access to source code. Now that access is limited only by how much time and disk space a student has.

with computer-system organization, so you can skim or skip it if you already understand the concepts.

1.2.1 Computer-System Operation

A modern general-purpose computer system consists of one or more CPUs and a number of device controllers connected through a common bus that provides access to shared memory (Figure 1.2). Each device controller is in charge of a specific type of device (for example, disk drives, audio devices, and video displays). The CPU and the device controllers can execute concurrently, competing for memory cycles. To ensure orderly access to the shared memory, a memory controller is provided whose function is to synchronize access to the memory.

For a computer to start running—for instance, when it is powered up or rebooted—it needs to have an initial program to run. This initial

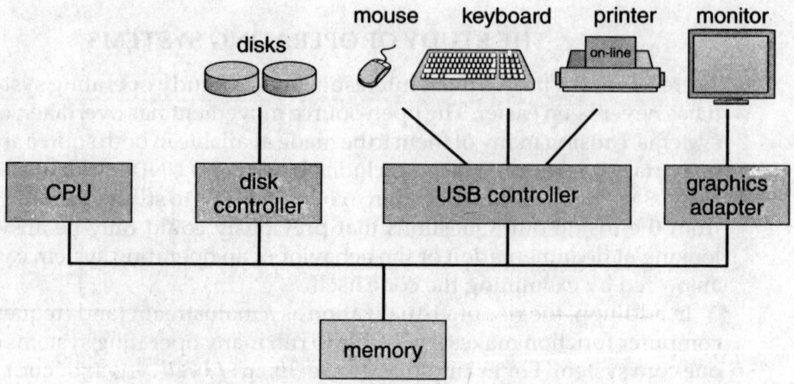

Figure 1.2 A modern computer system.

program, or **bootstrap program**, tends to be simple. Typically, it is stored in read-only memory (**ROM**) or electrically erasable programmable read-only memory (**EEPROM**), known by the general term **firmware**, within the computer hardware. It initializes all aspects of the system, from CPU registers to device controllers to memory contents. The bootstrap program must know how to load the operating system and how to start executing that system. To accomplish this goal, the bootstrap program must locate and load into memory the operating-system kernel. The operating system then starts executing the first process, such as "init," and waits for some event to occur.

The occurrence of an event is usually signaled by an **interrupt** from either the hardware or the software. Hardware may trigger an interrupt at any time by sending a signal to the CPU, usually by way of the system bus. Software may trigger an interrupt by executing a special operation called a **system call** (also called a **monitor call**).

When the CPU is interrupted, it stops what it is doing and immediately transfers execution to a fixed location. The fixed location usually contains the starting address where the service routine for the interrupt is located. The interrupt service routine executes; on completion, the CPU resumes the interrupted computation. A time line of this operation is shown in Figure 1.3.

Interrupts are an important part of a computer architecture. Each computer design has its own interrupt mechanism, but several functions are common. The interrupt must transfer control to the appropriate interrupt service routine. The straightforward method for handling this transfer would be to invoke a generic routine to examine the interrupt information; the routine, in turn, would call the interrupt-specific handler. However, interrupts must be handled quickly. Since only a predefined number of interrupts is possible, a table of pointers to interrupt routines can be used instead to provide the necessary speed. The interrupt routine is called indirectly through the table, with no intermediate routine needed. Generally, the table of pointers is stored in low memory (the first hundred or so locations). These locations hold the addresses of the interrupt service routines for the various devices. This array, or **interrupt vector**, of addresses is then indexed by a unique device number, given with the interrupt request, to provide the address of the interrupt service routine for

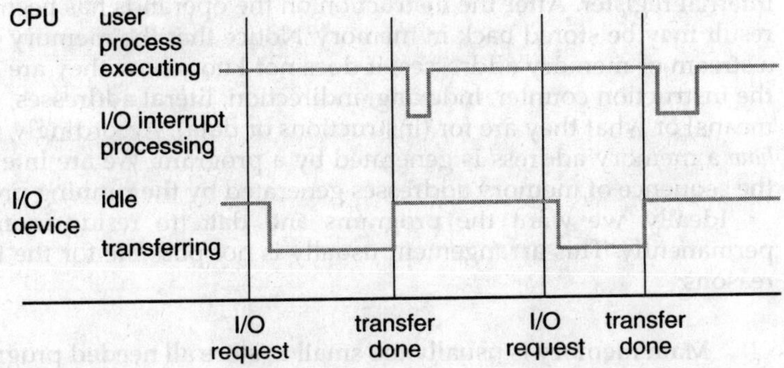

Figure 1.3 Interrupt time line for a single process doing output.

the interrupting device. Operating systems as different as Windows and UNIX dispatch interrupts in this manner.

The interrupt architecture must also save the address of the interrupted instruction. Many old designs simply stored the interrupt address in a fixed location or in a location indexed by the device number. More recent architectures store the return address on the system stack. If the interrupt routine needs to modify the processor state—for instance, by modifying register values—it must explicitly save the current state and then restore that state before returning. After the interrupt is serviced, the saved return address is loaded into the program counter, and the interrupted computation resumes as though the interrupt had not occurred.

1.2.2 Storage Structure

The CPU can load instructions only from memory, so any programs to run must be stored there. General-purpose computers run most of their programs from rewriteable memory, called main memory (also called **random-access memory** or **RAM**). Main memory commonly is implemented in a semiconductor technology called **dynamic random-access memory (DRAM)**. Computers use other forms of memory as well. Because the read-only memory (ROM) cannot be changed, only static programs are stored there. The immutability of ROM is of use in game cartridges. EEPROM cannot be changed frequently and so contains mostly static programs. For example, smartphones have EEPROM to store their factory-installed programs.

All forms of memory provide an array of words. Each word has its own address. Interaction is achieved through a sequence of `load` or `store` instructions to specific memory addresses. The `load` instruction moves a word from main memory to an internal register within the CPU, whereas the `store` instruction moves the content of a register to main memory. Aside from explicit loads and stores, the CPU automatically loads instructions from main memory for execution.

A typical instruction–execution cycle, as executed on a system with a **von Neumann architecture**, first fetches an instruction from memory and stores that instruction in the **instruction register**. The instruction is then decoded and may cause operands to be fetched from memory and stored in some internal register. After the instruction on the operands has been executed, the result may be stored back in memory. Notice that the memory unit sees only a stream of memory addresses; it does not know how they are generated (by the instruction counter, indexing, indirection, literal addresses, or some other means) or what they are for (instructions or data). Accordingly, we can ignore *how* a memory address is generated by a program. We are interested only in the sequence of memory addresses generated by the running program.

Ideally, we want the programs and data to reside in main memory permanently. This arrangement usually is not possible for the following two reasons:

1. Main memory is usually too small to store all needed programs and data permanently.
2. Main memory is a *volatile* storage device that loses its contents when power is turned off or otherwise lost.

Thus, most computer systems provide **secondary storage** as an extension of main memory. The main requirement for secondary storage is that it be able to hold large quantities of data permanently.

The most common secondary-storage device is a **magnetic disk**, which provides storage for both programs and data. Most programs (system and application) are stored on a disk until they are loaded into memory. Many programs then use the disk as both the source and the destination of their processing. Hence, the proper management of disk storage is of central importance to a computer system, as we discuss in Chapter 12.

In a larger sense, however, the storage structure that we have described—consisting of registers, main memory, and magnetic disks—is only one of many possible storage systems. Others include cache memory, CD-ROM, magnetic tapes, and so on. Each storage system provides the basic functions of storing a datum and holding that datum until it is retrieved at a later time. The main differences among the various storage systems lie in speed, cost, size, and volatility.

The wide variety of storage systems in a computer system can be organized in a hierarchy (Figure 1.4) according to speed and cost. The higher levels are expensive, but they are fast. As we move down the hierarchy, the cost per bit generally decreases, whereas the access time generally increases. This trade-off is reasonable; if a given storage system were both faster and less expensive than another—other properties being the same—then there would be no reason to use the slower, more expensive memory. In fact, many early storage devices, including paper tape and core memories, are relegated to museums now that magnetic tape and **semiconductor memory** have become faster and cheaper. The top four levels of memory in Figure 1.4 may be constructed using semiconductor memory.

In addition to differing in speed and cost, the various storage systems are either volatile or nonvolatile. As mentioned earlier, **volatile storage** loses its contents when the power to the device is removed. In the absence of expensive battery and generator backup systems, data must be written to **nonvolatile storage** for safekeeping. In the hierarchy shown in Figure 1.4, the storage systems above the electronic disk are volatile, whereas those below

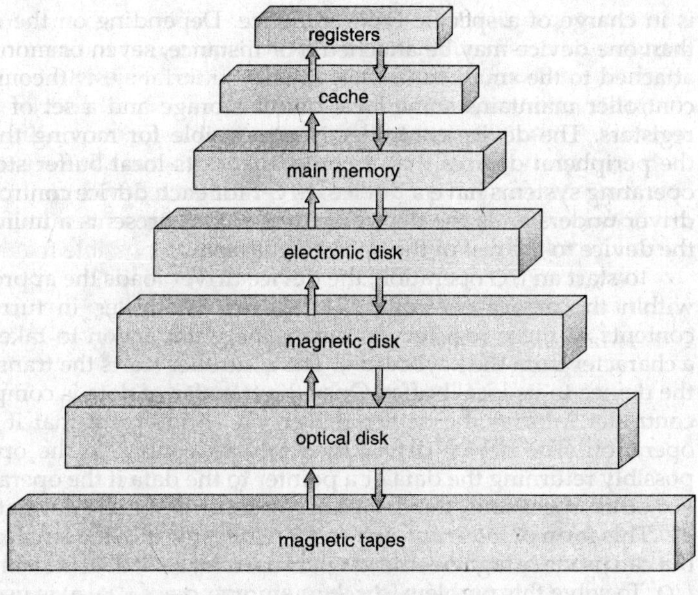

Figure 1.4 Storage-device hierarchy.

are nonvolatile. An **electronic disk** can be designed to be either volatile or nonvolatile. During normal operation, the electronic disk stores data in a large DRAM array, which is volatile. But many electronic-disk devices contain a hidden magnetic hard disk and a battery for backup power. If external power is interrupted, the electronic-disk controller copies the data from RAM to the magnetic disk. When external power is restored, the controller copies the data back into RAM. Another form of electronic disk is flash memory, which is popular in cameras and **personal digital assistants** (**PDAs**), in robots, and increasingly as removable storage on general-purpose computers. Flash memory is slower than DRAM but needs no power to retain its contents. Another form of nonvolatile storage is **NVRAM**, which is DRAM with battery backup power. This memory can be as fast as DRAM and (as long as the battery lasts) is nonvolatile.

The design of a complete memory system must balance all the factors just discussed: it must use only as much expensive memory as necessary while providing as much inexpensive, nonvolatile memory as possible. Caches can be installed to improve performance where a large access-time or transfer-rate disparity exists between two components.

1.2.3 I/O Structure

Storage is only one of many types of I/O devices within a computer. A large portion of operating system code is dedicated to managing I/O, both because of its importance to the reliability and performance of a system and because of the varying nature of the devices. Next, we provide an overview of I/O.

A general-purpose computer system consists of CPUs and multiple device controllers that are connected through a common bus. Each device controller is in charge of a specific type of device. Depending on the controller, more than one device may be attached. For instance, seven or more devices can be attached to the **small computer-systems interface (SCSI)** controller. A device controller maintains some local buffer storage and a set of special-purpose registers. The device controller is responsible for moving the data between the peripheral devices that it controls and its local buffer storage. Typically, operating systems have a **device driver** for each device controller. This device driver understands the device controller and presents a uniform interface to the device to the rest of the operating system.

To start an I/O operation, the device driver loads the appropriate registers within the device controller. The device controller, in turn, examines the contents of these registers to determine what action to take (such as "read a character from the keyboard"). The controller starts the transfer of data from the device to its local buffer. Once the transfer of data is complete, the device controller informs the device driver via an interrupt that it has finished its operation. The device driver then returns control to the operating system, possibly returning the data or a pointer to the data if the operation was a read. For other operations, the device driver returns status information.

This form of interrupt-driven I/O is fine for moving small amounts of data but can produce high overhead when used for bulk data movement such as disk I/O. To solve this problem, **direct memory access (DMA)** is used. After setting up buffers, pointers, and counters for the I/O device, the device controller transfers an entire block of data directly to or from its own buffer storage to memory, with no intervention by the CPU. Only one interrupt is generated per block, to tell the device driver that the operation has completed, rather than the one interrupt per byte generated for low-speed devices. While the device controller is performing these operations, the CPU is available to accomplish other work.

Some high-end systems use switch rather than bus architecture. On these systems, multiple components can talk to other components concurrently, rather than competing for cycles on a shared bus. In this case, DMA is even more effective. Figure 1.5 shows the interplay of all components of a computer system.

1.3 Computer-System Architecture

In Section 1.2, we introduced the general structure of a typical computer system. A computer system may be organized in a number of different ways, which we can categorize roughly according to the number of general-purpose processors used.

1.3.1 Single-Processor Systems

Most systems use a single processor. The variety of single-processor systems may be surprising, however, since these systems range from PDAs through mainframes. On a single-processor system, there is one main CPU capable of executing a general-purpose instruction set, including instructions from user processes. Almost all systems have other special-purpose processors as well. They may come in the form of device-specific processors, such as disk,

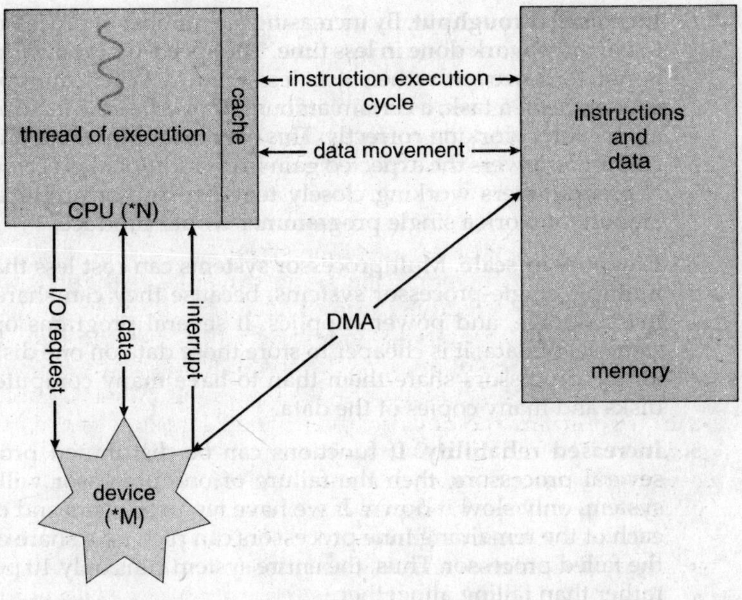

Figure 1.5 How a modern computer system works.

keyboard, and graphics controllers; or, on mainframes, they may come in the form of more general-purpose processors, such as I/O processors that move data rapidly among the components of the system.

All of these special-purpose processors run a limited instruction set and do not run user processes. Sometimes they are managed by the operating system, in that the operating system sends them information about their next task and monitors their status. For example, a disk-controller microprocessor receives a sequence of requests from the main CPU and implements its own disk queue and scheduling algorithm. This arrangement relieves the main CPU of the overhead of disk scheduling. PCs contain a microprocessor in the keyboard to convert the keystrokes into codes to be sent to the CPU. In other systems or circumstances, special-purpose processors are low-level components built into the hardware. The operating system cannot communicate with these processors; they do their jobs autonomously. The use of special-purpose microprocessors is common and does not turn a single-processor system into a multiprocessor. If there is only one general-purpose CPU, then the system is a single-processor system.

1.3.2 Multiprocessor Systems

Although single-processor systems are most common, **multiprocessor systems** (also known as **parallel systems** or **tightly coupled systems**) are growing in importance. Such systems have two or more processors in close communication, sharing the computer bus and sometimes the clock, memory, and peripheral devices.

Multiprocessor systems have three main advantages:

1. **Increased throughput**. By increasing the number of processors, we expect to get more work done in less time. The speed-up ratio with *N* processors is not *N*, however; rather, it is less than *N*. When multiple processors cooperate on a task, a certain amount of overhead is incurred in keeping all the parts working correctly. This overhead, plus contention for shared resources, lowers the expected gain from additional processors. Similarly, *N* programmers working closely together do not produce *N* times the amount of work a single programmer would produce.

2. **Economy of scale**. Multiprocessor systems can cost less than equivalent multiple single-processor systems, because they can share peripherals, mass storage, and power supplies. If several programs operate on the same set of data, it is cheaper to store those data on one disk and to have all the processors share them than to have many computers with local disks and many copies of the data.

3. **Increased reliability**. If functions can be distributed properly among several processors, then the failure of one processor will not halt the system, only slow it down. If we have ten processors and one fails, then each of the remaining nine processors can pick up a share of the work of the failed processor. Thus, the entire system runs only 10 percent slower, rather than failing altogether.

Increased reliability of a computer system is crucial in many applications. The ability to continue providing service proportional to the level of surviving hardware is called **graceful degradation**. Some systems go beyond graceful degradation and are called **fault tolerant**, because they can suffer a failure of any single component and still continue operation. Note that fault tolerance requires a mechanism to allow the failure to be detected, diagnosed, and, if possible, corrected. The HP NonStop (formerly Tandem) system uses both hardware and software duplication to ensure continued operation despite faults. The system consists of multiple pairs of CPUs, working in lockstep. Both processors in the pair execute each instruction and compare the results. If the results differ, then one CPU of the pair is at fault, and both are halted. The process that was being executed is then moved to another pair of CPUs, and the instruction that failed is restarted. This solution is expensive, since it involves special hardware and considerable hardware duplication.

The multiple-processor systems in use today are of two types. Some systems use **asymmetric multiprocessing**, in which each processor is assigned a specific task. A master processor controls the system; the other processors either look to the master for instruction or have predefined tasks. This scheme defines a master–slave relationship. The master processor schedules and allocates work to the slave processors.

The most common systems use **symmetric multiprocessing (SMP)**, in which each processor performs all tasks within the operating system. SMP means that all processors are peers; no master–slave relationship exists between processors. Figure 1.6 illustrates a typical SMP architecture. Notice that each processor has its own set of registers, as well as a private—or local—cache; however, all processors share physical memory. An example of the SMP system is Solaris, a commercial version of UNIX designed by Sun Microsystems. A Solaris system can be configured to employ dozens of processors, all running

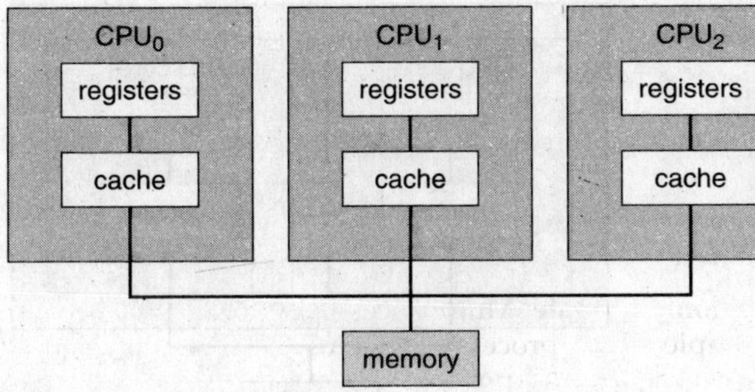

Figure 1.6 Symmetric multiprocessing architecture.

Solaris. The benefit of this model is that many processes can run simultaneously —*N* processes can run if there are *N* CPUs—without causing a significant deterioration of performance. However, we must carefully control I/O to ensure that the data reach the appropriate processor. Also, since the CPUs are separate, one may be sitting idle while another is overloaded, resulting in inefficiencies. These inefficiencies can be avoided if the processors share certain data structures. A multiprocessor system of this form will allow processes and resources—such as memory—to be shared dynamically among the various processors and can lower the variance among the processors. Such a system must be written carefully, as we shall see in Chapter 6. Virtually all modern operating systems—including Windows, Windows XP, Mac OS X, and Linux —now provide support for SMP.

The difference between symmetric and asymmetric multiprocessing may result from either hardware or software. Special hardware can differentiate the multiple processors, or the software can be written to allow only one master and multiple slaves. For instance, Sun's operating system SunOS Version 4 provided asymmetric multiprocessing, whereas Version 5 (Solaris) is symmetric on the same hardware.

Multiprocessing adds CPUs to increase computing power. If the CPU has an integrated memory controller, then adding CPUs can also increase the amount of memory addressable in the system. Either way, multiprocessing can cause a system to change its memory access model from uniform memory access (**UMA**) to non-uniform memory access (**NUMA**). UMA is defined as the situation in which access to any RAM from any CPU takes the same amount of time. With NUMA, some parts of memory may take longer to access than other parts, creating a performance penalty. Operating systems can minimize the NUMA penalty through resource management, as discussed in Section 9.5.4.

A recent trend in CPU design is to include multiple computing **cores** on a single chip. In essence, these are multiprocessor chips. They can be more efficient than multiple chips with single cores because on-chip communication is faster than between-chip communication. In addition, one chip with multiple cores uses significantly less power than multiple single-core chips. As a result, multicore systems are especially well suited for server systems such as database and Web servers.

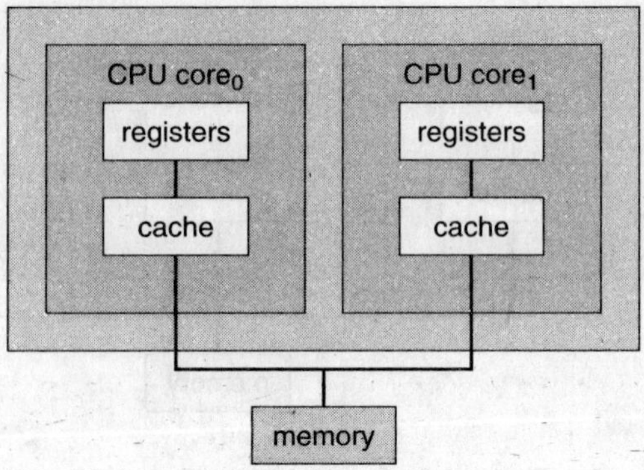

Figure 1.7 A dual-core design with two cores placed on the same chip.

In Figure 1.7, we show a dual-core design with two cores on the same chip. In this design, each core has its own register set as well as its own local cache; other designs might use a shared cache or a combination of local and shared caches. Aside from architectural considerations, such as cache, memory, and bus contention, these multicore CPUs appear to the operating system as *N* standard processors. This tendency puts pressure on operating system designers—and application programmers—to make use of those CPUs.

Finally, **blade servers** are a recent development in which multiple processor boards, I/O boards, and networking boards are placed in the same chassis. The difference between these and traditional multiprocessor systems is that each blade-processor board boots independently and runs its own operating system. Some blade-server boards are multiprocessor as well, which blurs the lines between types of computers. In essence, these servers consist of multiple independent multiprocessor systems.

1.3.3 Clustered Systems

Another type of multiple-CPU system is the **clustered system**. Like multiprocessor systems, clustered systems gather together multiple CPUs to accomplish computational work. Clustered systems differ from multiprocessor systems, however, in that they are composed of two or more individual systems—or nodes—joined together. The definition of the term *clustered* is not concrete; many commercial packages wrestle with what a clustered system is and why one form is better than another. The generally accepted definition is that clustered computers share storage and are closely linked via a **local-area network (LAN)** (as described in Section 1.10) or a faster interconnect, such as InfiniBand.

Clustering is usually used to provide **high-availability** service; that is, service will continue even if one or more systems in the cluster fail. High availability is generally obtained by adding a level of redundancy in the system. A layer of cluster software runs on the cluster nodes. Each node can monitor one or more of the others (over the LAN). If the monitored machine fails, the monitoring machine can take ownership of its storage and restart the applications that were running on the failed machine. The users and clients of the applications see only a brief interruption of service.

BEOWULF CLUSTERS

Beowulf clusters are designed for solving high-performance computing tasks. These clusters are built using commodity hardware—such as personal computers—that are connected via a simple local area network. Interestingly, a Beowulf cluster uses no one specific software package but rather consists of a set of open-source software libraries that allow the computing nodes in the cluster to communicate with one another. Thus, there are a variety of approaches for constructing a Beowulf cluster, although Beowulf computing nodes typically run the Linux operating system. Since Beowulf clusters require no special hardware and operate using open-source software that is freely available, they offer a low-cost strategy for building a high-performance computing cluster. In fact, some Beowulf clusters built from collections of discarded personal computers are using hundreds of computing nodes to solve computationally expensive problems in scientific computing.

Clustering can be structured asymmetrically or symmetrically. In **asymmetric clustering**, one machine is in **hot-standby mode** while the other is running the applications. The hot-standby host machine does nothing but monitor the active server. If that server fails, the hot-standby host becomes the active server. In **symmetric mode**, two or more hosts are running applications and are monitoring each other. This mode is obviously more efficient, as it uses all of the available hardware. It does require that more than one application be available to run.

As a cluster consists of several computer systems connected via a network, clusters may also be used to provide **high-performance computing** environments. Such systems can supply significantly greater computational power than single-processor or even SMP systems because they are capable of running an application concurrently on all computers in the cluster. However, applications must be written specifically to take advantage of the cluster by using a technique known as **parallelization**, which consists of dividing a program into separate components that run in parallel on individual computers in the cluster. Typically, these applications are designed so that once each computing node in the cluster has solved its portion of the problem, the results from all the nodes are combined into a final solution.

Other forms of clusters include parallel clusters and clustering over a wide-area network (WAN) (as described in Section 1.10). Parallel clusters allow multiple hosts to access the same data on the shared storage. Because most operating systems lack support for simultaneous data access by multiple hosts, parallel clusters are usually accomplished by use of special versions of software and special releases of applications. For example, Oracle Real Application Cluster is a version of Oracle's database that has been designed to run on a parallel cluster. Each machine runs Oracle, and a layer of software tracks access to the shared disk. Each machine has full access to all data in the database. To provide this shared access to data, the system must also supply access control and locking to ensure that no conflicting operations occur. This function, commonly known as a **distributed lock manager (DLM)**, is included in some cluster technology.

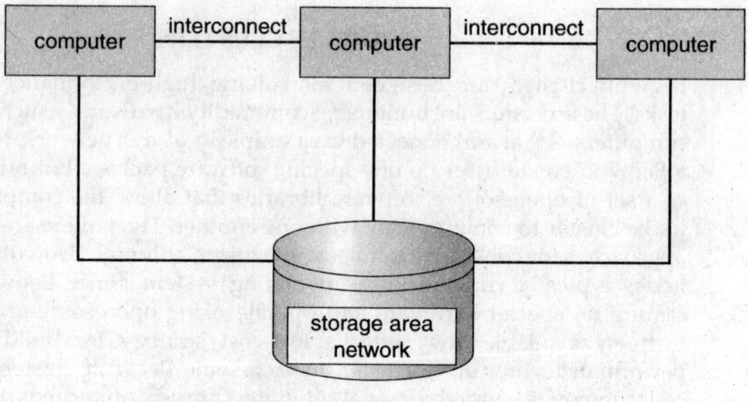

Figure 1.8 General structure of a clustered system.

Cluster technology is changing rapidly. Some cluster products support dozens of systems in a cluster, as well as clustered nodes that are separated by miles. Many of these improvements are made possible by **storage-area networks (SANs)**, as described in Section 12.3.3, which allow many systems to attach to a pool of storage. If the applications and their data are stored on the SAN, then the cluster software can assign the application to run on any host that is attached to the SAN. If the host fails, then any other host can take over. In a database cluster, dozens of hosts can share the same database, greatly increasing performance and reliability. Figure 1.8 depicts the general structure of a clustered system.

1.4 Operating-System Structure

Now that we have discussed basic information about computer-system organization and architecture, we are ready to talk about operating systems. An operating system provides the environment within which programs are executed. Internally, operating systems vary greatly in their makeup, since they are organized along many different lines. There are, however, many commonalities, which we consider in this section.

One of the most important aspects of operating systems is the ability to multiprogram. A single program cannot, in general, keep either the CPU or the I/O devices busy at all times. Single users frequently have multiple programs running. **Multiprogramming** increases CPU utilization by organizing jobs (code and data) so that the CPU always has one to execute.

The idea is as follows: The operating system keeps several jobs in memory simultaneously (Figure 1.9). Since, in general, main memory is too small to accommodate all jobs, the jobs are kept initially on the disk in the **job pool**. This pool consists of all processes residing on disk awaiting allocation of main memory.

The set of jobs in memory can be a subset of the jobs kept in the job pool. The operating system picks and begins to execute one of the jobs in memory. Eventually, the job may have to wait for some task, such as an I/O operation,

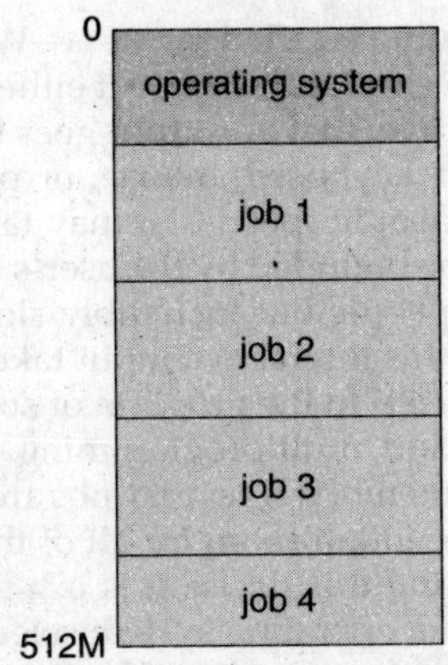

Figure 1.9 Memory layout for a multiprogramming system.

to complete. In a non-multiprogrammed system, the CPU would sit idle. In a multiprogrammed system, the operating system simply switches to, and executes, another job. When *that* job needs to wait, the CPU is switched to *another* job, and so on. Eventually, the first job finishes waiting and gets the CPU back. As long as at least one job needs to execute, the CPU is never idle.

This idea is common in other life situations. A lawyer does not work for only one client at a time, for example. While one case is waiting to go to trial or have papers typed, the lawyer can work on another case. If he has enough clients, the lawyer will never be idle for lack of work. (Idle lawyers tend to become politicians, so there is a certain social value in keeping lawyers busy.)

Multiprogrammed systems provide an environment in which the various system resources (for example, CPU, memory, and peripheral devices) are utilized effectively, but they do not provide for user interaction with the computer system. **Time sharing** (or **multitasking**) is a logical extension of multiprogramming. In time-sharing systems, the CPU executes multiple jobs by switching among them, but the switches occur so frequently that the users can interact with each program while it is running.

Time sharing requires an **interactive** (or **hands-on**) **computer system**, which provides direct communication between the user and the system. The user gives instructions to the operating system or to a program directly, using a input device such as a keyboard or a mouse, and waits for immediate results on an output device. Accordingly, the **response time** should be short—typically less than one second.

A time-shared operating system allows many users to share the computer simultaneously. Since each action or command in a time-shared system tends to be short, only a little CPU time is needed for each user. As the system switches rapidly from one user to the next, each user is given the impression that the entire computer system is dedicated to his use, even though it is being shared among many users

A time-shared operating system uses CPU scheduling and multiprogramming to provide each user with a small portion of a time-shared computer. Each user has at least one separate program in memory. A program loaded into memory and executing is called a **process**. When a process executes, it typically executes for only a short time before it either finishes or needs to perform I/O. I/O may be interactive; that is, output goes to a display for the user, and input comes from a user keyboard, mouse, or other device. Since interactive I/O typically runs at "people speeds," it may take a long time to complete. Input, for example, may be bounded by the user's typing speed; seven characters per second is fast for people but incredibly slow for computers. Rather than let the CPU sit idle as this interactive input takes place, the operating system will rapidly switch the CPU to the program of some other user.

Time sharing and multiprogramming require that several jobs be kept simultaneously in memory. If several jobs are ready to be brought into memory, and if there is not enough room for all of them, then the system must choose among them. Making this decision is **job scheduling**, which is discussed in Chapter 5. When the operating system selects a job from the job pool, it loads that job into memory for execution. Having several programs in memory at the same time requires some form of memory management, which is covered in Chapters 8 and 9. In addition, if several jobs are ready to run at the same time, the system must choose among them. Making this decision is **CPU scheduling**, which is discussed in Chapter 5. Finally, running multiple jobs concurrently requires that their ability to affect one another be limited in all phases of the operating system, including process scheduling, disk storage, and memory management. These considerations are discussed throughout the text.

In a time-sharing system, the operating system must ensure reasonable response time, which is sometimes accomplished through **swapping**, where processes are swapped in and out of main memory to the disk. A more common method for achieving this goal is **virtual memory**, a technique that allows the execution of a process that is not completely in memory (Chapter 9). The main advantage of the virtual-memory scheme is that it enables users to run programs that are larger than actual **physical memory**. Further, it abstracts main memory into a large, uniform array of storage, separating **logical memory** as viewed by the user from physical memory. This arrangement frees programmers from concern over memory-storage limitations.

Time-sharing systems must also provide a file system (Chapters 10 and 11). The file system resides on a collection of disks; hence, disk management must be provided (Chapter 12). Also, time-sharing systems provide a mechanism for protecting resources from inappropriate use (Chapter 14). To ensure orderly execution, the system must provide mechanisms for job synchronization and communication (Chapter 6), and it may ensure that jobs do not get stuck in a deadlock, forever waiting for one another (Chapter 7).

1.5 Operating-System Operations

As mentioned earlier, modern operating systems are **interrupt driven**. If there are no processes to execute, no I/O devices to service, and no users to whom to respond, an operating system will sit quietly, waiting for something to happen. Events are almost always signaled by the occurrence of an interrupt or a trap. A **trap** (or an **exception**) is a software-generated interrupt caused either by an error (for example, division by zero or invalid memory access) or by a specific request from a user program that an operating-system service be performed. The interrupt-driven nature of an operating system defines that system's general structure. For each type of interrupt, separate segments of code in the operating system determine what action should be taken. An interrupt service routine is provided that is responsible for dealing with the interrupt.

Since the operating system and the users share the hardware and software resources of the computer system, we need to make sure that an error in a user program could cause problems only for the one program running. With sharing, many processes could be adversely affected by a bug in one program. For example, if a process gets stuck in an infinite loop, this loop could prevent the correct operation of many other processes. More subtle errors can occur in a multiprogramming system, where one erroneous program might modify another program, the data of another program, or even the operating system itself.

Without protection against these sorts of errors, either the computer must execute only one process at a time or all output must be suspect. A properly designed operating system must ensure that an incorrect (or malicious) program cannot cause other programs to execute incorrectly.

1.5.1 Dual-Mode Operation

In order to ensure the proper execution of the operating system, we must be able to distinguish between the execution of operating-system code and user-defined code. The approach taken by most computer systems is to provide hardware support that allows us to differentiate among various modes of execution.

At the very least, we need two separate **modes** of operation: **user mode** and **kernel mode** (also called **supervisor mode**, **system mode**, or **privileged mode**). A bit, called the **mode bit**, is added to the hardware of the computer to indicate the current mode: kernel (0) or user (1). With the mode bit, we are able to distinguish between a task that is executed on behalf of the operating system and one that is executed on behalf of the user. When the computer system is executing on behalf of a user application, the system is in user mode. However, when a user application requests a service from the operating system (via a system call), it must transition from user to kernel mode to fulfill the request. This is shown in Figure 1.10. As we shall see, this architectural enhancement is useful for many other aspects of system operation as well.

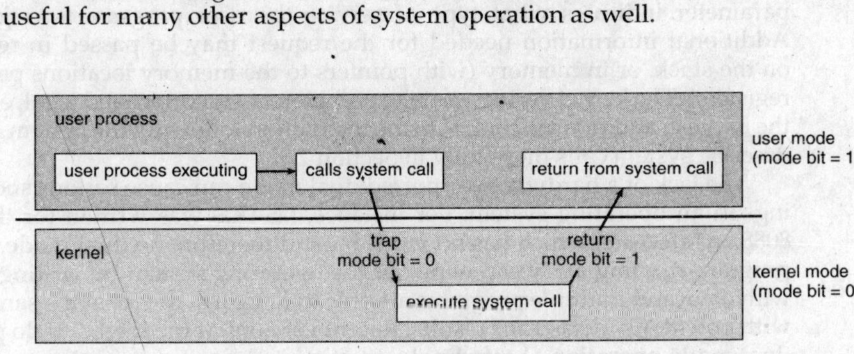

Figure 1.10 Transition from user to kernel mode.

At system boot time, the hardware starts in kernel mode. The operating system is then loaded and starts user applications in user mode. Whenever a trap or interrupt occurs, the hardware switches from user mode to kernel mode (that is, changes the state of the mode bit to 0). Thus, whenever the operating system gains control of the computer, it is in kernel mode. The system always switches to user mode (by setting the mode bit to 1) before passing control to a user program.

The dual mode of operation provides us with the means for protecting the operating system from errant users—and errant users from one another. We accomplish this protection by designating some of the machine instructions that may cause harm as **privileged instructions**. The hardware allows privileged instructions to be executed only in kernel mode. If an attempt is made to execute a privileged instruction in user mode, the hardware does not execute the instruction but rather treats it as illegal and traps it to the operating system.

The instruction to switch to kernel mode is an example of a privileged instruction. Some other examples include I/O control, timer management, and interrupt management. As we shall see throughout the text, there are many additional privileged instructions.

We can now see the life cycle of instruction execution in a computer system. Initial control resides in the operating system, where instructions are executed in kernel mode. When control is given to a user application, the mode is set to user mode. Eventually, control is switched back to the operating system via an interrupt, a trap, or a system call.

System calls provide the means for a user program to ask the operating system to perform tasks reserved for the operating system on the user program's behalf. A system call is invoked in a variety of ways, depending on the functionality provided by the underlying processor. In all forms, it is the method used by a process to request action by the operating system. A system call usually takes the form of a trap to a specific location in the interrupt vector. This trap can be executed by a generic `trap` instruction, although some systems (such as the MIPS R2000 family) have a specific `syscall` instruction.

When a system call is executed, it is treated by the hardware as a software interrupt. Control passes through the interrupt vector to a service routine in the operating system, and the mode bit is set to kernel mode. The system-call service routine is a part of the operating system. The kernel examines the interrupting instruction to determine what system call has occurred; a parameter indicates what type of service the user program is requesting. Additional information needed for the request may be passed in registers, on the stack, or in memory (with pointers to the memory locations passed in registers). The kernel verifies that the parameters are correct and legal, executes the request, and returns control to the instruction following the system call. We describe system calls more fully in Section 2.3.

The lack of a hardware-supported dual mode can cause serious shortcomings in an operating system. For instance, MS-DOS was written for the Intel 8088 architecture, which has no mode bit and therefore no dual mode. A user program running awry can wipe out the operating system by writing over it with data; and multiple programs are able to write to a device at the same time, with potentially disastrous results. Recent versions of the Intel CPU do provide dual-mode operation. Accordingly, most contemporary operating systems—such as Microsoft Vista and Windows XP, as well as Unix, Linux, and Solaris

—take advantage of this dual-mode feature and provide greater protection for the operating system.

Once hardware protection is in place, it detects errors that violate modes. These errors are normally handled by the operating system. If a user program fails in some way—such as by making an attempt either to execute an illegal instruction or to access memory that is not in the user's address space—then the hardware traps to the operating system. The trap transfers control through the interrupt vector to the operating system, just as an interrupt does. When a program error occurs, the operating system must terminate the program abnormally. This situation is handled by the same code as a user-requested abnormal termination. An appropriate error message is given, and the memory of the program may be dumped. The memory dump is usually written to a file so that the user or programmer can examine it and perhaps correct it and restart the program.

1.5.2 Time

We must ensure that the operating system maintains control over the CPU. We cannot allow a user program to get stuck in an infinite loop or to fail to call system services and never return control to the operating system. To accomplish this goal, we can use a **timer**. A timer can be set to interrupt the computer after a specified period. The period may be fixed (for example, 1/60 second) or variable (for example, from 1 millisecond to 1 second). A **variable timer** is generally implemented by a fixed-rate clock and a counter. The operating system sets the counter. Every time the clock ticks, the counter is decremented. When the counter reaches 0, an interrupt occurs. For instance, a 10-bit counter with a 1-millisecond clock allows interrupts at intervals from 1 millisecond to 1,024 milliseconds, in steps of 1 millisecond.

Before turning over control to the user, the operating system ensures that the timer is set to interrupt. If the timer interrupts, control transfers automatically to the operating system, which may treat the interrupt as a fatal error or may give the program more time. Clearly, instructions that modify the content of the timer are privileged.

Thus, we can use the timer to prevent a user program from running too long. A simple technique is to initialize a counter with the amount of time that a program is allowed to run. A program with a 7-minute time limit, for example, would have its counter initialized to 420. Every second, the timer interrupts and the counter is decremented by 1. As long as the counter is positive, control is returned to the user program. When the counter becomes negative, the operating system terminates the program for exceeding the assigned time limit.

1.6 Process Management

A program does nothing unless its instructions are executed by a CPU. A program in execution, as mentioned, is a process. A time-shared user program such as a compiler is a process. A word-processing program being run by an individual user on a PC is a process. A system task, such as sending output to a printer, can also be a process (or at least part of one). For now, you can consider a process to be a job or a time-shared program, but later you will learn that the concept is more general. As we shall see in Chapter 3, it is possible to provide system calls that allow processes to create subprocesses to execute concurrently.

A process needs certain resources—including CPU time, memory, files, and I/O devices—to accomplish its task. These resources are either given to the process when it is created or allocated to it while it is running. In addition to the various physical and logical resources that a process obtains when it is created, various initialization data (input) may be passed along. For example, consider a process whose function is to display the status of a file on the screen of a terminal. The process will be given as an input the name of the file and will execute the appropriate instructions and system calls to obtain and display on the terminal the desired information. When the process terminates, the operating system will reclaim any reusable resources.

We emphasize that a program by itself is not a process; a program is a *passive* entity, like the contents of a file stored on disk, whereas a process is an *active* entity. A single-threaded process has one **program counter** specifying the next instruction to execute. (Threads are covered in Chapter 4.) The execution of such a process must be sequential. The CPU executes one instruction of the process after another, until the process completes. Further, at any time, one instruction at most is executed on behalf of the process. Thus, although two processes may be associated with the same program, they are nevertheless considered two separate execution sequences. A multithreaded process has multiple program counters, each pointing to the next instruction to execute for a given thread.

A process is the unit of work in a system. Such a system consists of a collection of processes, some of which are operating-system processes (those that execute system code) and the rest of which are user processes (those that execute user code). All these processes can potentially execute concurrently—by multiplexing on a single CPU, for example.

The operating system is responsible for the following activities in connection with process management:

- Scheduling processes and threads on the CPUs
- Creating and deleting both user and system processes
- Suspending and resuming processes
- Providing mechanisms for process synchronization
- Providing mechanisms for process communication

We discuss process-management techniques in Chapters 3 through 6.

1.7 Memory Management

As we discussed in Section 1.2.2, the main memory is central to the operation of a modern computer system. Main memory is a large array of words or bytes, ranging in size from hundreds of thousands to billions. Each word or byte has its own address. Main memory is a repository of quickly accessible data shared by the CPU and I/O devices. The central processor reads instructions from main memory during the instruction-fetch cycle and both reads and writes data from main memory during the data-fetch cycle (on a von Neumann architecture). As noted earlier, the main memory is generally the only large storage device that the CPU is able to address and access directly. For example, for the CPU to process data from disk, those data must first be transferred to main memory by CPU-generated I/O calls. In the same way, instructions must be in memory for the CPU to execute them.

For a program to be executed, it must be mapped to absolute addresses and loaded into memory. As the program executes, it accesses program instructions and data from memory by generating these absolute addresses. Eventually, the program terminates, its memory space is declared available, and the next program can be loaded and executed.

To improve both the utilization of the CPU and the speed of the computer's response to its users, general-purpose computers must keep several programs in memory, creating a need for memory management. Many different memory-management schemes are used. These schemes reflect various approaches, and the effectiveness of any given algorithm depends on the situation. In selecting a memory-management scheme for a specific system, we must take into account many factors—especially the *hardware* design of the system. Each algorithm requires its own hardware support.

The operating system is responsible for the following activities in connection with memory management:

- Keeping track of which parts of memory are currently being used and by whom
- Deciding which processes (or parts thereof) and data to move into and out of memory
- Allocating and deallocating memory space as needed

Memory-management techniques are discussed in Chapters 8 and 9.

1.8 Storage Management

To make the computer system convenient for users, the operating system provides a uniform, logical view of information storage. The operating system abstracts from the physical properties of its storage devices to define a logical storage unit, the **file**. The operating system maps files onto physical media and accesses these files via the storage devices.

1.8.1 File-System Management

File management is one of the most visible components of an operating system. Computers can store information on several different types of physical media. Magnetic disk, optical disk, and magnetic tape are the most common. Each of these media has its own characteristics and physical organization. Each medium is controlled by a device, such as a disk drive or tape drive, that also has its own unique characteristics. These properties include access speed, capacity, data-transfer rate, and access method (sequential or random).

A file is a collection of related information defined by its creator. Commonly, files represent programs (both source and object forms) and data. Data files may be numeric, alphabetic, alphanumeric, or binary. Files may be free-form (for example, text files), or they may be formatted rigidly (for example, fixed fields). Clearly, the concept of a file is an extremely general one.

The operating system implements the abstract concept of a file by managing mass-storage media, such as tapes and disks, and the devices that control them. Also, files are normally organized into directories to make them easier to use. Finally, when multiple users have access to files, it may be desirable to control by whom and in what ways (for example, read, write, append) files may be accessed.

The operating system is responsible for the following activities in connection with file management:

- Creating and deleting files
- Creating and deleting directories to organize files
- Supporting primitives for manipulating files and directories
- Mapping files onto secondary storage
- Backing up files on stable (nonvolatile) storage media

File-management techniques are discussed in Chapters 10 and 11.

1.8.2 Mass-Storage Management

As we have already seen, because main memory is too small to accommodate all data and programs, and because the data that it holds are lost when power is lost, the computer system must provide secondary storage to back up main memory. Most modern computer systems use disks as the principal on-line storage medium for both programs and data. Most programs—including compilers, assemblers, word processors, editors, and formatters—are stored on a disk until loaded into memory and then use the disk as both the source and destination of their processing. Hence, the proper management of disk storage is of central importance to a computer system. The operating system is responsible for the following activities in connection with disk management:

- Free-space management
- Storage allocation
- Disk scheduling

Because secondary storage is used frequently, it must be used efficiently. The entire speed of operation of a computer may hinge on the speeds of the disk subsystem and the algorithms that manipulate that subsystem.

There are, however, many uses for storage that is slower and lower in cost (and sometimes of higher capacity) than secondary storage. Backups of disk data, seldom-used data, and long-term archival storage are some examples. Magnetic tape drives and their tapes and CD and DVD drives and platters are typical **tertiary storage** devices. The media (tapes and optical platters) vary between WORM (write-once, read-many-times) and RW (read–write) formats.

Tertiary storage is not crucial to system performance, but it still must be managed. Some operating systems take on this task, while others leave tertiary-storage management to application programs. Some of the functions that operating systems can provide include mounting and unmounting media in devices, allocating and freeing the devices for exclusive use by processes, and migrating data from secondary to tertiary storage.

Techniques for secondary and tertiary storage management are discussed in Chapter 12.

1.8.3 Caching

Caching is an important principle of computer systems. Information is normally kept in some storage system (such as main memory). As it is used, it is copied into a faster storage system—the cache—on a temporary basis. When we need a particular piece of information, we first check whether it is in the cache. If it is, we use the information directly from the cache; if it is not, we use the information from the source, putting a copy in the cache under the assumption that we will need it again soon.

In addition, internal programmable registers, such as index registers, provide a high-speed cache for main memory. The programmer (or compiler) implements the register-allocation and register-replacement algorithms to decide which information to keep in registers and which to keep in main memory. There are also caches that are implemented totally in hardware. For instance, most systems have an instruction cache to hold the instructions expected to be executed next. Without this cache, the CPU would have to wait several cycles while an instruction was fetched from main memory. For similar reasons, most systems have one or more high-speed data caches in the memory hierarchy. We are not concerned with these hardware-only caches in this text, since they are outside the control of the operating system.

Because caches have limited size, **cache management** is an important design problem. Careful selection of the cache size and of a replacement policy can result in greatly increased performance. Figure 1.11 compares storage performance in large workstations and small servers. Various replacement algorithms for software-controlled caches are discussed in Chapter 9.

Level	1	2	3	4
Name	registers	cache	main memory	disk storage
Typical size	< 1 KB	< 16 MB	< 64 GB	> 100 GB
Implementation technology	custom memory with multiple ports, CMOS	on-chip or off-chip CMOS SRAM	CMOS DRAM	magnetic disk
Access time (ns)	0.25 – 0.5	0.5 – 25	80 – 250	5,000.000
Bandwidth (MB/sec)	20,000 – 100,000	5000 – 10,000	1000 – 5000	20 – 150
Managed by	compilor	hardware	operating system	operating system
Backed by	cache	main memory	disk	CD or tape

Figure 1.11 Performance of various levels of storage.

Main memory can be viewed as a fast cache for secondary storage, since data in secondary storage must be copied into main memory for use, and data must be in main memory before being moved to secondary storage for safekeeping. The file-system data, which resides permanently on secondary storage, may appear on several levels in the storage hierarchy. At the highest level, the operating system may maintain a cache of file-system data in main memory. In addition, electronic RAM disks (also known as **solid-state disks**) may be used for high-speed storage that is accessed through the file-system interface. The bulk of secondary storage is on magnetic disks. The magnetic-disk storage, in turn, is often backed up onto magnetic tapes or removable disks to protect against data loss in case of a hard-disk failure. Some systems automatically archive old file data from secondary storage to tertiary storage, such as tape jukeboxes, to lower the storage cost (see Chapter 12).

The movement of information between levels of a storage hierarchy may be either explicit or implicit, depending on the hardware design and the controlling operating-system software. For instance, data transfer from cache to CPU and registers is usually a hardware function, with no operating-system intervention. In contrast, transfer of data from disk to memory is usually controlled by the operating system.

In a hierarchical storage structure, the same data may appear in different levels of the storage system. For example, suppose that an integer A that is to be incremented by 1 is located in file B, and file B resides on magnetic disk. The increment operation proceeds by first issuing an I/O operation to copy the disk block on which A resides to main memory. This operation is followed by copying A to the cache and to an internal register. Thus, the copy of A appears in several places: on the magnetic disk, in main memory, in the cache, and in an internal register (see Figure 1.12). Once the increment takes place in the internal register, the value of A differs in the various storage systems. The value of A becomes the same only after the new value of A is written from the internal register back to the magnetic disk.

In a computing environment where only one process executes at a time, this arrangement poses no difficulties, since an access to integer A will always be to the copy at the highest level of the hierarchy. However, in a multitasking environment, where the CPU is switched back and forth among various processes, extreme care must be taken to ensure that, if several processes wish to access A, then each of these processes will obtain the most recently updated value of A.

The situation becomes more complicated in a multiprocessor environment where, in addition to maintaining internal registers, each of the CPUs also contains a local cache (Figure 1.6). In such an environment, a copy of A may exist simultaneously in several caches. Since the various CPUs can all execute concurrently, we must make sure that an update to the value of A in one cache

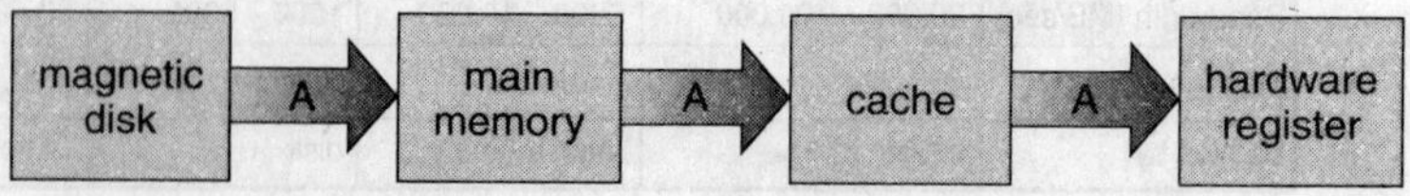

Figure 1.12 Migration of integer A from disk to register.

is immediately reflected in all other caches where A resides. This situation is called cache coherency, and it is usually a hardware problem (handled below the operating-system level).

In a distributed environment, the situation becomes even more complex. In this environment, several copies (or replicas) of the same file can be kept on different computers that are distributed in space. Since the various replicas may be accessed and updated concurrently, some distributed systems ensure that, when a replica is updated in one place, all other replicas are brought up to date as soon as possible. There are various ways to achieve this guarantee, as we discuss in Chapter 17.

1.8.4 I/O Systems

One of the purposes of an operating system is to hide the peculiarities of specific hardware devices from the user. For example, in UNIX, the peculiarities of I/O devices are hidden from the bulk of the operating system itself by the **I/O subsystem**. The I/O subsystem consists of several components:

- A memory-management component that includes buffering, caching, and spooling
- A general device-driver interface
- Drivers for specific hardware devices

Only the device driver knows the peculiarities of the specific device to which it is assigned.

We discussed in Section 1.2.3 how interrupt handlers and device drivers are used in the construction of efficient I/O subsystems. In Chapter 13, we discuss how the I/O subsystem interfaces to the other system components, manages devices, transfers data, and detects I/O completion.

1.9 Protection and Security

If a computer system has multiple users and allows the concurrent execution of multiple processes, then access to data must be regulated. For that purpose, mechanisms ensure that files, memory segments, CPU, and other resources can be operated on by only those processes that have gained proper authorization from the operating system. For example, memory-addressing hardware ensures that a process can execute only within its own address space. The timer ensures that no process can gain control of the CPU without eventually relinquishing control. Device-control registers are not accessible to users, so the integrity of the various peripheral devices is protected.

Protection, then, is any mechanism for controlling the access of processes or users to the resources defined by a computer system. This mechanism must provide means to specify the controls to be imposed and means to enforce the controls.

Protection can improve reliability by detecting latent errors at the interfaces between component subsystems. Early detection of interface errors can often prevent contamination of a healthy subsystem by another subsystem that is malfunctioning. Furthermore, an unprotected resource cannot defend against use (or misuse) by an unauthorized or incompetent user. A protection-oriented system provides a means to distinguish between authorized and unauthorized usage, as we discuss in Chapter 14.

A system can have adequate protection but still be prone to failure and allow inappropriate access. Consider a user whose authentication information (her means of identifying herself to the system) is stolen. Her data could be copied or deleted, even though file and memory protection are working. It is the job of **security** to defend a system from external and internal attacks. Such attacks spread across a huge range and include viruses and worms, denial-of-service attacks (which use all of a system's resources and so keep legitimate users out of the system), identity theft, and theft of service (unauthorized use of a system). Prevention of some of these attacks is considered an operating-system function on some systems, while other systems leave the prevention to policy or additional software. Due to the alarming rise in security incidents, operating-system security features represent a fast-growing area of research and implementation. Security is discussed in Chapter 15.

Protection and security require the system to be able to distinguish among all its users. Most operating systems maintain a list of user names and associated **user identifiers (user IDs)**. In Windows Vista parlance, this is a **security ID (SID)**. These numerical IDs are unique, one per user. When a user logs in to the system, the authentication stage determines the appropriate user ID for the user. That user ID is associated with all of the user's processes and threads. When an ID needs to be user readable, it is translated back to the user name via the user name list.

In some circumstances, we wish to distinguish among sets of users rather than individual users. For example, the owner of a file on a UNIX system may be allowed to issue all operations on that file, whereas a selected set of users may only be allowed to read the file. To accomplish this, we need to define a group name and the set of users belonging to that group. Group functionality can be implemented as a system-wide list of group names and **group identifiers**. A user can be in one or more groups, depending on operating-system design decisions. The user's group IDs are also included in every associated process and thread.

In the course of normal use of a system, the user ID and group ID for a user are sufficient. However, a user sometimes needs to **escalate privileges** to gain extra permissions for an activity. The user may need access to a device that is restricted, for example. Operating systems provide various methods to allow privilege escalation. On UNIX, for example, the `setuid` attribute on a program causes that program to run with the user ID of the owner of the file, rather than the current user's ID. The process runs with this **effective UID** until it turns off the extra privileges or terminates.

1.10 Distributed Systems

A distributed system is a collection of physically separate, possibly heterogeneous, computer systems that are networked to provide the users with access to the various resources that the system maintains. Access to a shared resource increases computation speed, functionality, data availability, and reliability. Some operating systems generalize network access as a form of file access, with the details of networking contained in the network interface's device driver. Others make users specifically invoke network functions. Generally, systems contain a mix of the two modes—for example FTP and NFS. The protocols that create a distributed system can greatly affect that system's utility and popularity.

A **network**, in the simplest terms, is a communication path between two or more systems. Distributed systems depend on networking for their functionality. Networks vary by the protocols used, the distances between nodes, and the transport media. TCP/IP is the most common network protocol, although ATM and other protocols are in widespread use. Likewise, operating-system support of protocols varies. Most operating systems support TCP/IP, including the Windows and UNIX operating systems. Some systems support proprietary protocols to suit their needs. To an operating system, a network protocol simply needs an interface device--a network adapter, for example—with a device driver to manage it, as well as software to handle data. These concepts are discussed throughout this book.

Networks are characterized based on the distances between their nodes. A **local-area network (LAN)** connects computers within a room, a floor, or a building. A **wide-area network (WAN)** usually links buildings, cities, or countries. A global company may have a WAN to connect its offices worldwide. These networks may run one protocol or several protocols. The continuing advent of new technologies brings about new forms of networks. For example, a **metropolitan-area network (MAN)** could link buildings within a city. BlueTooth and 802.11 devices use wireless technology to communicate over a distance of several feet, in essence creating a **small-area network** such as might be found in a home.

The media to carry networks are equally varied. They include copper wires, fiber strands, and wireless transmissions between satellites, microwave dishes, and radios. When computing devices are connected to cellular phones, they create a network. Even very short-range infrared communication can be used for networking. At a rudimentary level, whenever computers communicate, they use or create a network. These networks also vary in their performance and reliability.

Some operating systems have taken the concept of networks and distributed systems further than the notion of providing network connectivity. A **network operating system** is an operating system that provides features such as file sharing across the network and that includes a communication scheme that allows different processes on different computers to exchange messages. A computer running a network operating system acts autonomously from all other computers on the network, although it is aware of the network and is able to communicate with other networked computers. A distributed operating system provides a less autonomous environment: The different operating systems communicate closely enough to provide the illusion that only a single operating system controls the network.

We cover computer networks and distributed systems in Chapters 16 through 18.

1.11 Special-Purpose Systems

The discussion thus far has focused on the general-purpose computer systems that we are all familiar with. There are, however, other classes of computer systems whose functions are more limited and whose objective is to deal with limited computation domains.

1.11.1 Real-Time Embedded Systems

Embedded computers are the most prevalent form of computers in existence. These devices are found everywhere, from car engines and manufacturing robots to DVDs and microwave ovens. They tend to have very specific tasks. The systems they run on are usually primitive, and so the operating systems provide limited features. Usually, they have little or no user interface, preferring to spend their time monitoring and managing hardware devices, such as automobile engines and robotic arms.

These embedded systems vary considerably. Some are general-purpose computers, running standard operating systems—such as UNIX—with special-purpose applications to implement the functionality. Others are hardware devices with a special-purpose embedded operating system providing just the functionality desired. Yet others are hardware devices with application-specific integrated circuits (**ASICs**) that perform their tasks without an operating system.

The use of embedded systems continues to expand. The power of these devices, both as standalone units and as elements of networks and the Web, is sure to increase as well. Even now, entire houses can be computerized, so that a central computer—either a general-purpose computer or an embedded system—can control heating and lighting, alarm systems, and even coffee makers. Web access can enable a home owner to tell the house to heat up before she arrives home. Someday, the refrigerator may call the grocery store when it notices the milk is gone.

Embedded systems almost always run **real-time operating systems**. A real-time system is used when rigid time requirements have been placed on the operation of a processor or the flow of data; thus, it is often used as a control device in a dedicated application. Sensors bring data to the computer. The computer must analyze the data and possibly adjust controls to modify the sensor inputs. Systems that control scientific experiments, medical imaging systems, industrial control systems, and certain display systems are real-time systems. Some automobile-engine fuel-injection systems, home-appliance controllers, and weapon systems are also real-time systems.

A real-time system has well-defined, fixed time constraints. Processing *must* be done within the defined constraints, or the system will fail. For instance, it would not do for a robot arm to be instructed to halt *after* it had smashed into the car it was building. A real-time system functions correctly only if it returns the correct result within its time constraints. Contrast this system with a time-sharing system, where it is desirable (but not mandatory) to respond quickly, or a batch system, which may have no time constraints at all.

In Chapter 19, we cover real-time embedded systems in great detail. In Chapter 5, we consider the scheduling facility needed to implement real-time functionality in an operating system. In Chapter 9, we describe the design of memory management for real-time computing. Finally, in Chapter 22, we describe the real-time components of the Windows XP operating system.

1.11.2 Multimedia Systems

Most operating systems are designed to handle conventional data such as text files, programs, word-processing documents, and spreadsheets. However, a recent trend in technology is the incorporation of **multimedia data** into computer systems. Multimedia data consist of audio and video files as well as conventional files. These data differ from conventional data in that multimedia data—such as frames of video—must be delivered (streamed) according to certain time restrictions (for example, 30 frames per second).

Multimedia describes a wide range of applications in popular use today. These include audio files such as MP3, DVD movies, video conferencing, and short video clips of movie previews or news stories downloaded over the Internet. Multimedia applications may also include live webcasts (broadcasting over the World Wide Web) of speeches or sporting events and even live webcams that allow a viewer in Manhattan to observe customers at a cafe in Paris. Multimedia applications need not be either audio or video; rather, a multimedia application often includes a combination of both. For example, a movie may consist of separate audio and video tracks. Nor must multimedia applications be delivered only to desktop personal computers. Increasingly, they are being directed toward smaller devices, including PDAs and cellular telephones. For example, a stock trader may have stock quotes delivered wirelessly and in real time to his PDA.

In Chapter 20, we explore the demands of multimedia applications, describe how multimedia data differ from conventional data, and explain how the nature of these data affects the design of operating systems that support the requirements of multimedia systems.

1.11.3 Handheld Systems

Handheld systems include personal digital assistants (PDAs), such as Palm and Pocket-PCs, and cellular telephones, many of which use special-purpose embedded operating systems. Developers of handheld systems and applications face many challenges, most of which are due to the limited size of such devices. For example, a PDA is typically about 5 inches in height and 3 inches in width, and it weighs less than one-half pound. Because of their size, most handheld devices have small amounts of memory, slow processors, and small display screens. We take a look now at each of these limitations.

The amount of physical memory in a handheld depends on the device, but typically it is somewhere between 1 MB and 1 GB. (Contrast this with a typical PC or workstation, which may have several gigabytes of memory.) As a result, the operating system and applications must manage memory efficiently. This includes returning all allocated memory to the memory manager when the memory is not being used. In Chapter 9, we explore virtual memory, which allows developers to write programs that behave as if the system has more memory than is physically available. Currently, not many handheld devices use virtual memory techniques, so program developers must work within the confines of limited physical memory.

A second issue of concern to developers of handheld devices is the speed of the processor used in the devices. Processors for most handheld devices run at a fraction of the speed of a processor in a PC. Faster processors require more power. To include a faster processor in a handheld device would require a larger battery, which would take up more space and would have to be replaced (or recharged) more frequently. Most handheld devices use smaller, slower processors that consume less power. Therefore, the operating system and applications must be designed not to tax the processor.

The last issue confronting program designers for handheld devices is I/O. A lack of physical space limits input methods to small keyboards, handwriting recognition, or small screen-based keyboards. The small display screens limit output options. Whereas a monitor for a home computer may measure up to 30 inches, the display for a handheld device is often no more than 3 inches square. Familiar tasks, such as reading e-mail and browsing Web pages, must be condensed into smaller displays. One approach for displaying the content in Web pages is **Web clipping**, where only a small subset of a Web page is delivered and displayed on the handheld device.

Some handheld devices use wireless technology, such as BlueTooth or 802.11, allowing remote access to e-mail and Web browsing. Cellular telephones with connectivity to the Internet fall into this category. However, for PDAs that do not provide wireless access, downloading data typically requires the user first to download the data to a PC or workstation and then download the data to the PDA. Some PDAs allow data to be directly copied from one device to another using an infrared link.

Generally, the limitations in the functionality of PDAs are balanced by their convenience and portability. Their use continues to expand as network connections become more available and other options, such as digital cameras and MP3 players, expand their utility.

1.12 Computing Environments

So far, we have provided an overview of computer-system organization and major operating-system components. We conclude with a brief overview of how these are used in a variety of computing environments.

1.12.1 Traditional Computing

As computing matures, the lines separating many of the traditional computing environments are blurring. Consider the "typical office environment." Just a few years ago, this environment consisted of PCs connected to a network, with servers providing file and print services. Remote access was awkward, and portability was achieved by use of laptop computers. Terminals attached to mainframes were prevalent at many companies as well, with even fewer remote access and portability options.

The current trend is toward providing more ways to access these computing environments. Web technologies are stretching the boundaries of traditional computing. Companies establish **portals**, which provide Web accessibility to their internal servers. **Network computers** are essentially terminals that understand Web-based computing. Handheld computers can synchronize with

PCs to allow very portable use of company information. Handheld PDAs can also connect to **wireless networks** to use the company's Web portal (as well as the myriad other Web resources).

At home, most users had a single computer with a slow modem connection to the office, the Internet, or both. Today, network-connection speeds once available only at great cost are relatively inexpensive, giving home users more access to more data. These fast data connections are allowing home computers to serve up Web pages and to run networks that include printers, client PCs, and servers. Some homes even have **firewalls** to protect their networks from security breaches. Those firewalls cost thousands of dollars a few years ago and did not even exist a decade ago.

In the latter half of the previous century, computing resources were scarce. (Before that, they were nonexistent!) For a period of time, systems were either batch or interactive. Batch systems processed jobs in bulk, with predetermined input (from files or other sources of data). Interactive systems waited for input from users. To optimize the use of the computing resources, multiple users shared time on these systems. Time-sharing systems used a timer and scheduling algorithms to rapidly cycle processes through the CPU, giving each user a share of the resources.

Today, traditional time-sharing systems are uncommon. The same scheduling technique is still in use on workstations and servers, but frequently the processes are all owned by the same user (or a single user and the operating system). User processes, and system processes that provide services to the user, are managed so that each frequently gets a slice of computer time. Consider the windows created while a user is working on a PC, for example, and the fact that they may be performing different tasks at the same time.

1.12.2 Client–Server Computing

As PCs have become faster, more powerful, and cheaper, designers have shifted away from centralized system architecture. Terminals connected to centralized systems are now being supplanted by PCs. Correspondingly, user-interface functionality once handled directly by centralized systems is increasingly being handled by PCs. As a result, many of today's systems act as **server systems** to satisfy requests generated by **client systems**. This form of specialized distributed system, called a **client–server** system, has the general structure depicted in Figure 1.13.

Server systems can be broadly categorized as compute servers and file servers:

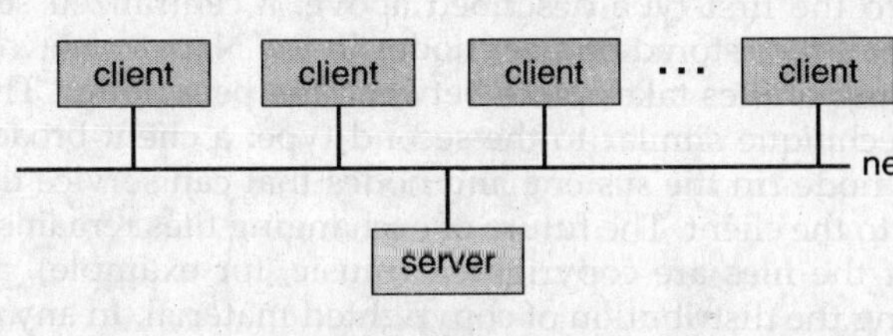

Figure 1.13 General structure of a client–server system.

- The **compute-server system** provides an interface to which a client can send a request to perform an action (for example, read data); in response, the server executes the action and sends back results to the client. A server running a database that responds to client requests for data is an example of such a system.

- The **file-server system** provides a file-system interface where clients can create, update, read, and delete files. An example of such a system is a Web server that delivers files to clients running Web browsers.

1.12.3 Peer-to-Peer Computing

Another structure for a distributed system is the peer-to-peer (P2P) system model. In this model, clients and servers are not distinguished from one another; instead, all nodes within the system are considered peers, and each may act as either a client or a server, depending on whether it is requesting or providing a service. Peer-to-peer systems offer an advantage over traditional client-server systems. In a client-server system, the server is a bottleneck; but in a peer-to-peer system, services can be provided by several nodes distributed throughout the network.

To participate in a peer-to-peer system, a node must first join the network of peers. Once a node has joined the network, it can begin providing services to and requesting services from—other nodes in the network. Determining what services are available is accomplished in one of two general ways:

- When a node joins a network, it registers its service with a centralized lookup service on the network. Any node desiring a specific service first contacts this centralized lookup service to determine which node provides the service. The remainder of the communication takes place between the client and the service provider.

- A peer acting as a client must first discover what node provides a desired service by broadcasting a request for the service to all other nodes in the network. The node (or nodes) providing that service responds to the peer making the request. To support this approach, a *discovery protocol* must be provided that allows peers to discover services provided by other peers in the network.

Peer-to-peer networks gained widespread popularity in the late 1990s with several file-sharing services, such as Napster and Gnutella, that enable peers to exchange files with one another. The Napster system uses an approach similar to the first type described above: a centralized server maintains an index of all files stored on peer nodes in the Napster network, and the actual exchanging of files takes place between the peer nodes. The Gnutella system uses a technique similar to the second type: a client broadcasts file requests to other nodes in the system, and nodes that can service the request respond directly to the client. The future of exchanging files remains uncertain because many of the files are copyrighted (music, for example), and there are laws governing the distribution of copyrighted material. In any case, though, peer-to-peer technology undoubtedly will play a role in the future of many services, such as searching, file exchange, and e-mail.

1.12.4 Web-Based Computing

The Web has become ubiquitous, leading to more access by a wider variety of devices than was dreamt of a few years ago. PCs are still the most prevalent access devices, with workstations, handheld PDAs, and even cell phones also providing access.

Web computing has increased the emphasis on networking. Devices that were not previously networked now include wired or wireless access. Devices that were networked now have faster network connectivity, provided by either improved networking technology, optimized network implementation code, or both.

The implementation of Web-based computing has given rise to new categories of devices, such as **load balancers**, which distribute network connections among a pool of similar servers. Operating systems like Windows 95, which acted as Web clients, have evolved into Linux and Windows XP, which can act as Web servers as well as clients. Generally, the Web has increased the complexity of devices because their users require them to be Web-enabled.

1.13 Open-Source Operating Systems

The study of operating systems, as noted earlier, is made easier by the availability of a vast number of open-source releases. **Open-source operating systems** are those made available in source-code format rather than as compiled binary code. Linux is the most famous open- source operating system, while Microsoft Windows is a well-known example of the opposite **closed-source** approach. Starting with the source code allows the programmer to produce binary code that can be executed on a system. Doing the opposite—**reverse engineering** the source code from the binaries—is quite a lot of work, and useful items such as comments are never recovered. Learning operating systems by examining the actual source code, rather than reading summaries of that code, can be extremely useful. With the source code in hand, a student can modify the operating system and then compile and run the code to try out those changes, which is another excellent learning tool. This text includes projects that involve modifying operating system source code, while also describing algorithms at a high level to be sure all important operating system topics are covered. Throughout the text, we provide pointers to examples of open-source code for deeper study.

There are many benefits to open-source operating systems, including a community of interested (and usually unpaid) programmers who contribute to the code by helping to debug it, analyze it, provide support, and suggest changes. Arguably, open-source code is more secure than closed-source code because many more eyes are viewing the code. Certainly open-source code has bugs, but open-source advocates argue that bugs tend to be found and fixed faster owing to the number of people using and viewing the code. Companies that earn revenue from selling their programs tend to be hesitant to open-source their code, but Red Hat, SUSE, Sun, and a myriad of other companies are doing just that and showing that commercial companies benefit, rather than suffer, when they open-source their code. Revenue can be generated through support contracts and the sale of hardware on which the software runs, for example.

1.13.1 History

In the early days of modern computing (that is, the 1950s), a great deal of software was available in open-source format. The original hackers (computer enthusiasts) at MIT's Tech Model Railroad Club left their programs in drawers for others to work on. "Homebrew" user groups exchanged code during their meetings. Later, company-specific user groups, such as Digital Equipment Corporation's DEC, accepted contributions of source-code programs, collected them onto tapes, and distributed the tapes to interested members.

Computer and software companies eventually sought to limit the use of their software to authorized computers and paying customers. Releasing only the binary files compiled from the source code, rather than the source code itself, helped them to achieve this goal, as well as protecting their code and their ideas from their competitors. Another issue involved copyrighted material. Operating systems and other programs can limit the ability to play back movies and music or display electronic books to authorized computers. Such **copy protection** or **Digital Rights Management (DRM)** would not be effective if the source code that implemented these limits were published. Laws in many countries, including the U.S. Digital Millennium Copyright Act (DMCA), make it illegal to reverse-engineer DRM code or otherwise try to circumvent copy protection.

To counter the move to limit software use and redistribution, Richard Stallman in 1983 started the GNU project to create a free, open-source UNIX-compatible operating system. In 1985, he published the GNU Manifesto, which argues that all software should be free and open-sourced. He also formed the **Free Software Foundation (FSF)** with the goal of encouraging the free exchange of software source code and the free use of that software. Rather than copyright its software, the FSF "copylefts" the software to encourage sharing and improvement. The **GNU General Public License (GPL)** codifies copylefting and is a common license under which free software is released. Fundamentally, GPL requires that the source code be distributed with any binaries and that any changes made to the source code be released under the same GPL license.

1.13.2 Linux

As an example of an open-source operating system, consider **GNU/Linux**. The GNU project produced many UNIX-compatible tools, including compilers, editors, and utilities, but never released a kernel. In 1991, a student in Finland, Linus Torvalds, released a rudimentary UNIX-like kernel using the GNU compilers and tools and invited contributions worldwide. The advent of the Internet meant that anyone interested could download the source code, modify it, and submit changes to Torvalds. Releasing updates once a week allowed this so-called Linux operating system to grow rapidly, enhanced by several thousand programmers.

The resulting GNU/Linux operating system has spawned hundreds of unique **distributions**, or custom builds, of the system. Major distributions include RedHat, SUSE, Fedora, Debian, Slackware, and Ubuntu. Distributions vary in function, utility, installed applications, hardware support, user interface, and purpose. For example, RedHat Enterprise Linux is geared to large commercial use. PCLinuxOS is a **LiveCD**—an operating system that can be booted and run from a CD-ROM without being installed on a system's hard disk. One variant of PCLinuxOS, "PCLinuxOS Supergamer DVD," is a **LiveDVD** that includes graphics drivers and games. A gamer can run it on any compatible system simply by booting from the DVD. When the gamer is finished, a reboot of the system resets it to its installed operating system.

Access to the Linux source code varies by release. Here, we consider Ubuntu Linux. Ubuntu is a popular Linux distribution that comes in a variety of types, including those tuned for desktops, servers, and students. Its founder pays for the printing and mailing of DVDs containing the binary and source code (which helps to make it popular). The following steps outline a way to explore the Ubuntu kernel source code on systems that support the free "VMware Player" tool:

- Download the player from `http://www.vmware.com/download/player/` and install it on your system.
- Download a virtual machine containing Ubuntu. Hundreds of "appliances", or virtual machine images, pre-installed with operating systems and applications, are available from VMware at `http://www.vmware.com/appliances/`.
- Boot the virtual machine within VMware Player.
- Get the source code of the kernel release of interest, such as 2.6, by executing `wget http://www.kernel.org/pub/linux/kernel/v2.6/linux-2.6.18.1.tar.bz2` within the Ubuntu virtual machine.
- Uncompress and untar the downloaded file via `tar xjf linux-2.6.18.1.tar.bz2`.
- Explore the source code of the Ubuntu kernel, which is now in `./linux-2.6.18.1`.

For more about Linux, see Chapter 21. For more about virtual machines, see Section 2.8.

1.13.3 BSD UNIX

BSD UNIX has a longer and more complicated history than Linux. It started in 1978 as a derivative of AT&T's UNIX. Releases from the University of California at Berkeley (UCB) came in source and binary form, but they were not open-source because a license from AT&T was required. BSD UNIX's development was slowed by a lawsuit by AT&T, but eventually a fully functional, open-source version, 4.4BSD-lite, was released in 1994.

Just as with Linux, there are many distributions of BSD UNIX, including FreeBSD, NetBSD, OpenBSD, and DragonflyBSD. To explore the source code of FreeBSD, simply download the virtual machine image of the version of interest and boot it within VMware, as described above for Ubuntu Linux. The source code comes with the distribution and is stored in `/usr/src/`. The kernel source code is in `/usr/src/sys`. For example, to examine the virtual-memory implementation code in the FreeBSD kernel, see the files in `/usr/src/sys/vm`.

Darwin, the core kernel component of MAC, is based on BSD UNIX and is open-sourced as well. That source code is available from `http://www.opensource.apple.com/darwinsource/`. Every MAC release has its open-source components posted at that site. The name of the package that contains the kernel is "xnu." The source code for MAC kernel revision 1228 (the source code to MAC Leopard) can be found at www.opensource.apple.com/darwinsource/tarballs/apsl/xnu-1228.tar.gz. Apple also provides extensive developer tools, documentation, and support at `http://connect.apple.com`. For more information, see Appendix A.

1.13.4 Solaris

Solaris is the commercial UNIX-based operating system of Sun Microsystems. Originally, Sun's **SunOS** operating system was based on BSD UNIX. Sun moved to AT&T's System V UNIX as its base in 1991. In 2005, Sun open-sourced some of the Solaris code, and over time, the company has added more and more to that open-source code base. Unfortunately, not all of Solaris is open-sourced, because some of the code is still owned by AT&T and other companies. However, Solaris can be compiled from the open source and linked with binaries of the close-sourced components, so it can still be explored, modified, compiled, and tested.

The source code is available from `http://opensolaris.org/os/downloads/`. Also available there are pre-compiled distributions based on the source code, documentation, and discussion groups. It is not necessary to download the entire source-code bundle from the site, because Sun allows visitors to explore the source code on-line via a source code browser.

1.13.5 Utility

The free software movement is driving legions of programmers to create thousands of open-source projects, including operating systems. Sites like `http://freshmeat.net/` and `http://distrowatch.com/` provide portals to many of these projects. Open-source projects enable students to use source code as a learning tool. They can modify programs and test them, help find and fix bugs, and otherwise explore mature, full-featured operating systems, compilers, tools, user interfaces, and other types of programs. The availability of source code for historic projects, such as Multics, can help students to understand those projects and to build knowledge that will help in the implementation of new projects.

GNU/Linux, BSD UNIX, and Solaris are all open-source operating systems, but each has its own goals, utility, licensing, and purpose. Sometimes licenses are not mutually exclusive and cross-pollination occurs, allowing rapid improvements in operating-system projects. For example, several major components of Solaris have been ported to BSD UNIX. The advantages of free software and open sourcing are likely to increase the number and quality of open-source projects, leading to an increase in the number of individuals and companies that use these projects.

1.14 Summary

An operating system is software that manages the computer hardware, as well as providing an environment for application programs to run. Perhaps the most visible aspect of an operating system is the interface to the computer system it provides to the human user.

For a computer to do its job of executing programs, the programs must be in main memory. Main memory is the only large storage area that the processor can access directly. It is an array of words or bytes, ranging in size from millions to billions. Each word in memory has its own address. The main memory is usually a volatile storage device that loses its contents when power is turned off or lost. Most computer systems provide secondary storage as an extension of main memory. Secondary storage provides a form of nonvolatile storage that is capable of holding large quantities of data permanently. The most common secondary-storage device is a magnetic disk, which provides storage of both programs and data.

The wide variety of storage systems in a computer system can be organized in a hierarchy according to speed and cost. The higher levels are expensive, but they are fast. As we move down the hierarchy, the cost per bit generally decreases, whereas the access time generally increases.

There are several different strategies for designing a computer system. Uniprocessor systems have only a single processor, while multiprocessor systems contain two or more processors that share physical memory and peripheral devices. The most common multiprocessor design is symmetric multiprocessing (or SMP), where all processors are considered peers and run independently of one another. Clustered systems are a specialized form of multiprocessor systems and consist of multiple computer systems connected by a local area network.

To best utilize the CPU, modern operating systems employ multiprogramming, which allows several jobs to be in memory at the same time, thus ensuring that the CPU always has a job to execute. Time-sharing systems are an extension of multiprogramming wherein CPU scheduling algorithms rapidly switch between jobs, thus providing the illusion that each job is running concurrently.

The operating system must ensure correct operation of the computer system. To prevent user programs from interfering with the proper operation of the system, the hardware has two modes: user mode and kernel mode. Various instructions (such as I/O instructions and halt instructions) are privileged and can be executed only in kernel mode. The memory in which the operating system resides must also be protected from modification by the user. A timer prevents infinite loops. These facilities (dual mode, privileged instructions, memory protection, and timer interrupt) are basic building blocks used by operating systems to achieve correct operation.

A process (or job) is the fundamental unit of work in an operating system. Process management includes creating and deleting processes and providing mechanisms for processes to communicate and synchronize with each other. An operating system manages memory by keeping track of what parts of memory are being used and by whom. The operating system is also responsible for dynamically allocating and freeing memory space. Storage space is also managed by the operating system; this includes providing file systems for representing files and directories and managing space on mass-storage devices.

Operating systems must also be concerned with protecting and securing the operating system and users. Protection measures are mechanisms that control the access of processes or users to the resources made available by the computer system. Security measures are responsible for defending a computer system from external or internal attacks.

Distributed systems allow users to share resources on geographically dispersed hosts connected via a computer network. Services may be provided through either the client–server model or the peer-to-peer model. In a clustered system, multiple machines can perform computations on data residing on shared storage, and computing can continue even when some subset of cluster members fails.

LANs and WANs are the two basic types of networks. LANs enable processors distributed over a small geographical area to communicate, whereas WANs allow processors distributed over a larger area to communicate. LANs typically are faster than WANs.

There are several computer systems that serve specific purposes. These include real-time operating systems designed for embedded environments such as consumer devices, automobiles, and robotics. Real-time operating systems have well-defined, fixed-time constraints. Processing *must* be done within the defined constraints, or the system will fail. Multimedia systems involve the delivery of multimedia data and often have special requirements of displaying or playing audio, video, or synchronized audio and video streams.

Recently, the influence of the Internet and the World Wide Web has encouraged the development of operating systems that include Web browsers and networking and communication software as integral features.

The free software movement has created thousands of open-source projects, including operating systems. Because of these projects, students are able to use source code as a learning tool. They can modify programs and test them, help find and fix bugs, and otherwise explore mature, full-featured operating systems, compilers, tools, user interfaces, and other types of programs.

GNU/Linux, BSD UNIX, and Solaris are all open-source operating systems. The advantages of free software and open sourcing are likely to increase the number and quality of open-source projects, leading to an increase in the number of individuals and companies that use these projects.

Exercises

1.1 How are network computers different from traditional personal computers? Describe some usage scenarios in which it is advantageous to use network computers.

1.2 What network configuration would best suit the following environments?

a. A dormitory floor

b. A university campus

c. A state

d. A nation

1.3 Give two reasons why caches are useful. What problems do they solve? What problems do they cause? If a cache can be made as large as the device for which it is caching (for instance, a cache as large as a disk), why not make it that large and eliminate the device?

1.4 Under what circumstances would a user be better off using a time-sharing system rather than a PC or a single-user workstation?

1.5 List the four steps that are necessary to run a program on a completely dedicated machine—a computer that is running only that program.

1.6 How does the distinction between kernel mode and user mode function as a rudimentary form of protection (security) system?

1.7 In a multiprogramming and time-sharing environment, several users share the system simultaneously. This situation can result in various security problems.

a. What are two such problems?

b. Can we ensure the same degree of security in a time-shared machine as in a dedicated machine? Explain your answer.

1.8 Describe a mechanism for enforcing memory protection in order to prevent a program from modifying the memory associated with other programs.

1.9 What are the tradeoffs inherent in handheld computers?

1.10 Distinguish between the client–server and peer-to-peer models of distributed systems.

1.11 Some computer systems do not provide a privileged mode of operation in hardware. Is it possible to construct a secure operating system for these computer systems? Give arguments both that it is and that it is not possible.

1.12 What are the main differences between operating systems for mainframe computers and personal computers?

1.13 Which of the following instructions should be privileged?

a. Set value of timer.

b. Read the clock.

c. Clear memory.

d. Issue a trap instruction.

e. Turn off interrupts.

f. Modify entries in device-status table.

g. Switch from user to kernel mode.

h. Access I/O device.

1.14 Discuss, with examples, how the problem of maintaining coherence of cached data manifests itself in the following processing environments:

a. Single-processor systems

b. Multiprocessor systems

c. Distributed systems

1.15 Identify several advantages and several disadvantages of open-source operating systems. Include the types of people who would find each aspect to be an advantage or a disadvantage.

1.16 How do clustered systems differ from multiprocessor systems? What is required for two machines belonging to a cluster to cooperate to provide a highly available service?

1.17 What is the main difficulty that a programmer must overcome in writing an operating system for a real-time environment?

1.18 Direct memory access is used for high-speed I/O devices in order to avoid increasing the CPU's execution load.

a. How does the CPU interface with the device to coordinate the transfer?

b. How does the CPU know when the memory operations are complete?

c. The CPU is allowed to execute other programs while the DMA controller is transferring data. Does this process interfere with the execution of the user programs? If so, describe what forms of interference are caused.

1.19 Identify which of the functionalities listed below need to be supported by the operating system for (a) handheld devices and (b) real-time systems.

a. Batch programming

b. Virtual memory

c. Time sharing

1.20 Some CPUs provide for more than two modes of operation. What are two possible uses of these multiple modes?

1.21 Define the essential properties of the following types of operating systems:

a. Batch

b. Interactive

c. Time sharing

d. Real time

e. Network

f. Parallel

g. Distributed

h. Clustered

i. Handheld

1.22 Describe the differences between symmetric and asymmetric multiprocessing. What are three advantages and one disadvantage of multiprocessor systems?

1.23 The issue of resource utilization shows up in different forms in different types of operating systems. List what resources must be managed carefully in the following settings:

a. Mainframe or minicomputer systems

b. Workstations connected to servers

c. Handheld computers

1.24 What is the purpose of interrupts? What are the differences between a trap and an interrupt? Can traps be generated intentionally by a user program? If so, for what purpose?

1.25 Consider an SMP system similar to what is shown in Figure 1.6. Illustrate with an example how data residing in memory could in fact have two different values in each of the local caches.

1.26 Consider a computing cluster consisting of two nodes running a database. Describe two ways in which the cluster software can manage access to the data on the disk Discuss the benefits and disadvantages of each.

Bibliographical Notes

Brookshear [2003] provides an overview of computer science in general.

An overview of the Linux operating system is presented in Bovet and Cesati [2006]. Solomon and Russinovich [2000] give an overview of Microsoft Windows and considerable technical detail about the system internals and components. Russinovich and Solomon [2005] update this information to Windows Server 2003 and Windows XP. McDougall and Mauro [2007] cover the internals of the Solaris operating system. Mac OS X is presented at `http://www.apple.com/macosx`. Mac OS X internals are discussed in Singh [2007].

Coverage of peer-to-peer systems includes Parameswaran et al. [2001], Gong [2002], Ripeanu et al. [2002], Agre [2003], Balakrishnan et al. [2003], and Loo [2003]. A discussion of peer-to-peer file-sharing systems can be found in Lee [2003]. Good coverage of cluster computing is provided by Buyya [1999]. Recent advances in cluster computing are described by Ahmed [2000]. A survey of issues relating to operating-system support for distributed systems can be found in Tanenbaum and Van Renesse [1985].

Many general textbooks cover operating systems, including Stallings [2000b], Nutt [2004], and Tanenbaum [2001].

Hamacher et al. [2002] describe computer organization, and McDougall and Laudon [2006] discuss multicore processors. Hennessy and Patterson [2007] provide coverage of I/O systems and buses, and of system architecture in general. Blaauw and Brooks [1997] describe details of the architecture of many computer systems, including several from IBM. Stokes [2007] provides an illustrated introduction to microprocessors and computer architecture.

Cache memories, including associative memory, are described and analyzed by Smith [1982]. That paper also includes an extensive bibliography on the subject.

Discussions concerning magnetic-disk technology are presented by Freedman [1983] and by Harker et al. [1981]. Optical disks are covered by Kenville [1982], Fujitani [1984], O'Leary and Kitts [1985], Gait [1988], and Olsen and Kenley [1989]. Discussions of floppy disks are offered by Pechura and Schoeffler [1983] and by Sarisky [1983]. General discussions concerning mass-storage technology are offered by Chi [1982] and by Hoagland [1985].

Kurose and Ross [2005] and Tanenbaum [2003] provide general overviews of computer networks. Fortier [1989] presents a detailed discussion of networking hardware and software. Kozierok [2005] discuss TCP in detail. Mullender [1993] provides an overview of distributed systems. Wolf [2003] discusses recent developments in developing embedded systems. Issues related to handheld devices can be found in Myers and Beigl [2003] and Di Pietro and Mancini [2003].

A full discussion of the history of open sourcing and its benefits and challenges is found in Raymond [1999]. The history of hacking is discussed in Levy [1994]. The Free Software Foundation has published its philosophy on its Web site: `http://www.gnu.org/philosophy/free-software-for-freedom.html`. Detailed instructions on how to build the Ubuntu Linux kernel are on http://www.howtoforge.com/kernel_compilation_ubuntu. The open-source components of MAC are available from http://developer.apple.com/opensource/index.html.

Wikipedia (http://en.wikipedia.org/wiki/Richard_Stallman) has an informative entry about Richard Stallman.

The source code of Multics is available at http://web.mit.edu/multics-history/source/Multics_Internet_Server/Multics_sources.html.

CHAPTER 2

System Structures

An operating system provides the environment within which programs are executed. Internally, operating systems vary greatly in their makeup, since they are organized along many different lines. The design of a new operating system is a major task. It is important that the goals of the system be well defined before the design begins. These goals form the basis for choices among various algorithms and strategies.

We can view an operating system from several vantage points. One view focuses on the services that the system provides; another, on the interface that it makes available to users and programmers; a third, on its components and their interconnections. In this chapter, we explore all three aspects of operating systems, showing the viewpoints of users, programmers, and operating-system designers. We consider what services an operating system provides, how they are provided, how they are debugged, and what the various methodologies are for designing such systems. Finally, we describe how operating systems are created and how a computer starts its operating system.

CHAPTER OBJECTIVES

- To describe the services an operating system provides to users, processes, and other systems.
- To discuss the various ways of structuring an operating system.
- To explain how operating systems are installed and customized and how they boot.

2.1 Operating-System Services

An operating system provides an environment for the execution of programs. It provides certain services to programs and to the users of those programs. The specific services provided, of course, differ from one operating system to another, but we can identify common classes. These operating-system services are provided for the convenience of the programmer, to make the programming

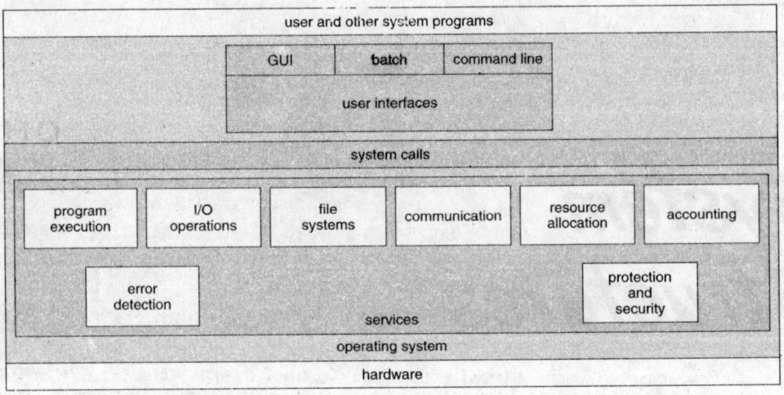

Figure 2.1 A view of operating system services.

task easier. Figure 2.1 shows one view of the various operating-system services and how they interrelate.

One set of operating-system services provides functions that are helpful to the user.

- **User interface**. Almost all operating systems have a **user interface (UI)**. This interface can take several forms. One is a **DTrace command-line interface (CLI)**, which uses text commands and a method for entering them (say, a program to allow entering and editing of commands). Another is a **batch interface**, in which commands and directives to control those commands are entered into files, and those files are executed. Most commonly, a **graphical user interface (GUI)** is used. Here, the interface is a window system with a pointing device to direct I/O, choose from menus, and make selections and a keyboard to enter text. Some systems provide two or all three of these variations.

- **Program execution**. The system must be able to load a program into memory and to run that program. The program must be able to end its execution, either normally or abnormally (indicating error).

- **I/O operations**. A running program may require I/O, which may involve a file or an I/O device. For specific devices, special functions may be desired (such as recording to a CD or DVD drive or blanking a display screen). For efficiency and protection, users usually cannot control I/O devices directly. Therefore, the operating system must provide a means to do I/O.

- **File-system manipulation**. The file system is of particular interest. Obviously, programs need to read and write files and directories. They also need to create and delete them by name, search for a given file, and list file information. Finally, some programs include permissions management to allow or deny access to files or directories based on file ownership. Many operating systems provide a variety of file systems, sometimes to allow personal choice, and sometimes to provide specific features or performance characteristics.

- **Communications**. There are many circumstances in which one process needs to exchange information with another process. Such communication may occur between processes that are executing on the same computer or between processes that are executing on different computer systems tied together by a computer network. Communications may be implemented via *shared memory* or through *message passing*, in which packets of information are moved between processes by the operating system.

- **Error detection**. The operating system needs to be constantly aware of possible errors. Errors may occur in the CPU and memory hardware (such as a memory error or a power failure), in I/O devices (such as a parity error on tape, a connection failure on a network, or lack of paper in the printer), and in the user program (such as an arithmetic overflow, an attempt to access an illegal memory location, or a too-great use of CPU time). For each type of error, the operating system should take the appropriate action to ensure correct and consistent computing. Of course, there is variation in how operating systems react to and correct errors. Debugging facilities can greatly enhance the user's and programmer's abilities to use the system efficiently.

Another set of operating-system functions exists not for helping the user but rather for ensuring the efficient operation of the system itself. Systems with multiple users can gain efficiency by sharing the computer resources among the users.

- **Resource allocation**. When there are multiple users or multiple jobs running at the same time, resources must be allocated to each of them. Many different types of resources are managed by the operating system. Some (such as CPU cycles, main memory, and file storage) may have special allocation code, whereas others (such as I/O devices) may have much more general request and release code. For instance, in determining how best to use the CPU, operating systems have CPU-scheduling routines that take into account the speed of the CPU, the jobs that must be executed, the number of registers available, and other factors. There may also be routines to allocate printers, modems, USB storage drives, and other peripheral devices.

- **Accounting**. We want to keep track of which users use how much and what kinds of computer resources. This record keeping may be used for accounting (so that users can be billed) or simply for accumulating usage statistics. Usage statistics may be a valuable tool for researchers who wish to reconfigure the system to improve computing services.

- **Protection and security**. The owners of information stored in a multiuser or networked computer system may want to control use of that information. When several separate processes execute concurrently, it should not be possible for one process to interfere with the others or with the operating system itself. Protection involves ensuring that all access to system resources is controlled. Security of the system from outsiders is also important. Such security starts with requiring each user to authenticate himself or herself to the system, usually by means of a password, to gain access to system resources. It extends to defending external I/O devices, including modems and network adapters, from invalid access attempts and to recording all such connections for detection of break-ins. If a system is to be protected and secure, precautions must be instituted throughout it. A chain is only as strong as its weakest link.

2.2 User Operating-System Interface

We mentioned earlier that there are several ways for users to interface with the operating system. Here, we discuss two fundamental approaches. One provides a command-line interface, or **command interpreter**, that allows users to directly enter commands to be performed by the operating system. The other allows users to interface with the operating system via a graphical user interface, or GUI.

2.2.1 Command Interpreter

Some operating systems include the command interpreter in the kernel. Others, such as Windows XP and UNIX, treat the command interpreter as a special program that is running when a job is initiated or when a user first logs on (on interactive systems). On systems with multiple command interpreters to choose from, the interpreters are known as **shells**. For example, on UNIX and Linux systems, a user may choose among several different shells, including the *Bourne shell*, *C shell*, *Bourne-Again shell*, *Korn shell*, and others. Third-party shells and free user-written shells are also available. Most shells provide similar functionality, and a user's choice of which shell to use is generally based on personal preference. Figure 2.2 shows the Bourne shell command interpreter being used on Solaris 10.

The main function of the command interpreter is to get and execute the next user-specified command. Many of the commands given at this level manipulate files: create, delete, list, print, copy, execute, and so on. The MS-DOS and UNIX shells operate in this way. These commands can be implemented in two general ways.

In one approach, the command interpreter itself contains the code to execute the command. For example, a command to delete a file may cause the command interpreter to jump to a section of its code that sets up the parameters and makes the appropriate system call. In this case, the number of commands that can be given determines the size of the command interpreter, since each command requires its own implementing code.

An alternative approach—used by UNIX, among other operating systems—implements most commands through system programs. In this case, the command interpreter does not understand the command in any way; it merely uses the command to identify a file to be loaded into memory and executed. Thus, the UNIX command to delete a file

```
rm file.txt
```

would search for a file called `rm`, load the file into memory, and execute it with the parameter `file.txt`. The function associated with the `rm` command would be defined completely by the code in the file `rm`. In this way, programmers can add new commands to the system easily by creating new files with the proper

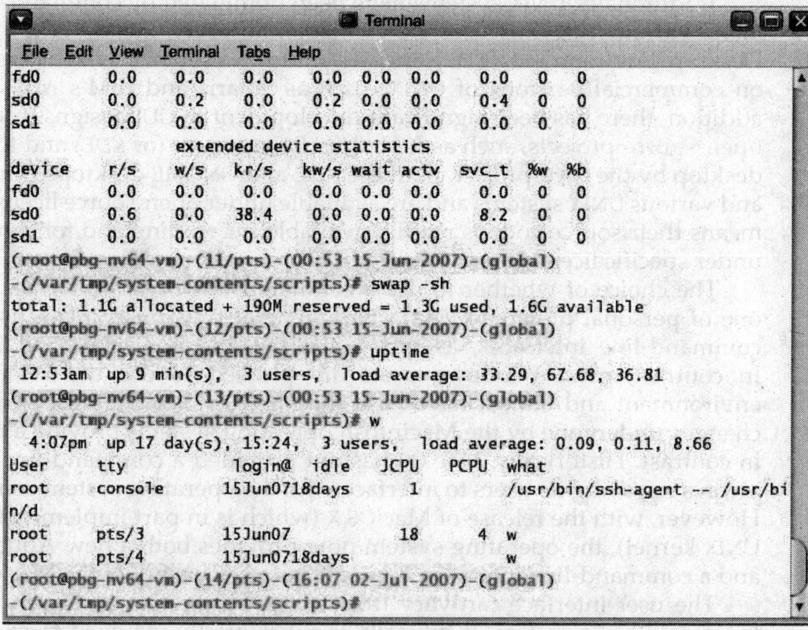

Figure 2.2 The Bourne shell command interpreter in Solaris 10.

names. The command-interpreter program, which can be small, does not have to be changed for new commands to be added.

2.2.2 Graphical User Interfaces

A second strategy for interfacing with the operating system is through a user-friendly graphical user interface, or GUI. Here, rather than entering commands directly via a command-line interface, users employ a mouse-based window-and-menu system characterized by a **desktop** metaphor. The user moves the mouse to position its pointer on images, or **icons**, on the screen (the desktop) that represent programs, files, directories, and system functions. Depending on the mouse pointer's location, clicking a button on the mouse can invoke a program, select a file or directory—known as a **folder**—or pull down a menu that contains commands.

Graphical user interfaces first appeared due in part to research taking place in the early 1970s at Xerox PARC research facility. The first GUI appeared on the Xerox Alto computer in 1973. However, graphical interfaces became more widespread with the advent of Apple Macintosh computers in the 1980s. The user interface for the Macintosh operating system (Mac OS) has undergone various changes over the years, the most significant being the adoption of the *Aqua* interface that appeared with Mac OS X. Microsoft's first version of Windows—Version 1.0—was based on the addition of a GUI interface to the MS-DOS operating system. Later versions of Windows have made cosmetic changes in the appearance of the GUI along with several enhancements in its functionality, including Windows Explorer.

Traditionally, UNIX systems have been dominated by command-line interfaces. Various GUI interfaces are available, however, including the Common Desktop Environment (CDE) and X-Windows systems, which are common on commercial versions of UNIX, such as Solaris and IBM's AIX system. In addition, there has been significant development in GUI designs from various **open-source** projects, such as *K Desktop Environment* (or *KDE*) and the *GNOME* desktop by the GNU project. Both the KDE and GNOME desktops run on Linux and various UNIX systems and are available under open-source licenses, which means their source code is readily available for reading and for modification under specific license terms.

The choice of whether to use a command-line or GUI interface is mostly one of personal preference. As a very general rule, many UNIX users prefer command-line interfaces, as they often provide powerful shell interfaces. In contrast, most Windows users are pleased to use the Windows GUI environment and almost never use the MS-DOS shell interface. The various changes undergone by the Macintosh operating systems provide a nice study in contrast. Historically, Mac OS has not provided a command-line interface, always requiring its users to interface with the operating system using its GUI. However, with the release of Mac OS X (which is in part implemented using a UNIX kernel), the operating system now provides both a new Aqua interface and a command-line interface. Figure 2.3 is a screenshot of the Mac OS X GUI.

The user interface can vary from system to system and even from user to user within a system. It typically is substantially removed from the actual system structure. The design of a useful and friendly user interface is therefore

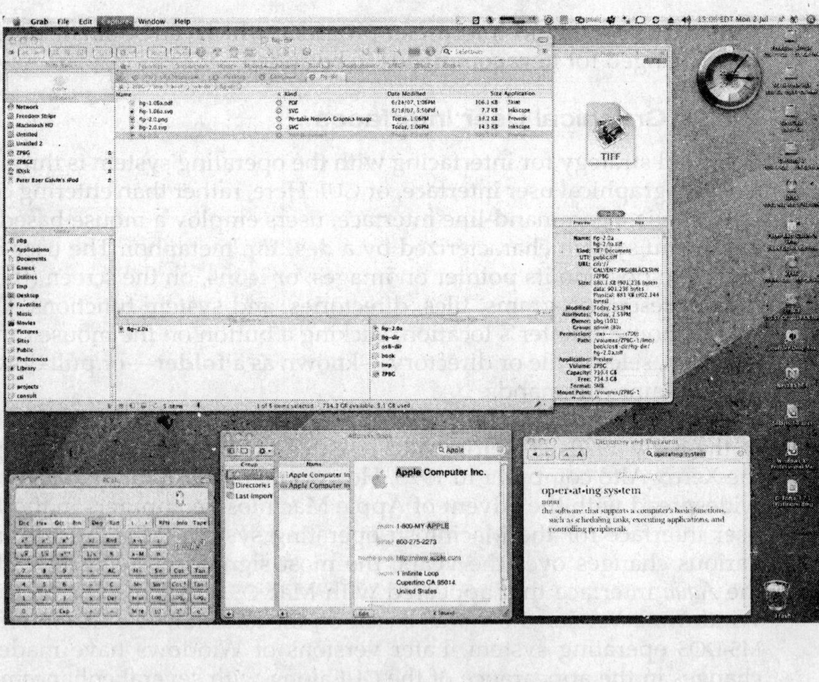

Figure 2.3 The Mac OS X GUI.

not a direct function of the operating system. In this book, we concentrate on the fundamental problems of providing adequate service to user programs. From the point of view of the operating system, we do not distinguish between user programs and system programs.

2.3 System Calls

System calls provide an interface to the services made available by an operating system. These calls are generally available as routines written in C and C++, although certain low-level tasks (for example, tasks where hardware must be accessed directly), may need to be written using assembly-language instructions.

Before we discuss how an operating system makes system calls available, let's first use an example to illustrate how system calls are used: writing a simple program to read data from one file and copy them to another file. The first input that the program will need is the names of the two files: the input file and the output file. These names can be specified in many ways, depending on the operating-system design. One approach is for the program to ask the user for the names of the two files. In an interactive system, this approach will require a sequence of system calls, first to write a prompting message on the screen and then to read from the keyboard the characters that define the two files. On mouse-based and icon-based systems, a menu of file names is usually displayed in a window. The user can then use the mouse to select the source name, and a window can be opened for the destination name to be specified. This sequence requires many I/O system calls.

Once the two file names are obtained, the program must open the input file and create the output file. Each of these operations requires another system call. There are also possible error conditions for each operation. When the program tries to open the input file, it may find that there is no file of that name or that the file is protected against access. In these cases, the program should print a message on the console (another sequence of system calls) and then terminate abnormally (another system call). If the input file exists, then we must create a new output file. We may find that there is already an output file with the same name. This situation may cause the program to abort (a system call), or we may delete the existing file (another system call) and create a new one (another system call). Another option, in an interactive system, is to ask the user (via a sequence of system calls to output the prompting message and to read the response from the terminal) whether to replace the existing file or to abort the program.

Now that both files are set up, we enter a loop that reads from the input file (a system call) and writes to the output file (another system call). Each read and write must return status information regarding various possible error conditions. On input, the program may find that the end of the file has been reached or that there was a hardware failure in the read (such as a parity error). The write operation may encounter various errors, depending on the output device (no more disk space, printer out of paper, and so on).

Finally, after the entire file is copied, the program may close both files (another system call), write a message to the console or window (more system calls), and finally terminate normally (the final system call). As we can see, even simple programs may make heavy use of the operating system. Frequently, systems execute thousands of system calls per second. This system-call sequence is shown in Figure 2.4.

Most programmers never see this level of detail, however. Typically, application developers design programs according to an **application programming interface (API)**. The API specifies a set of functions that are available to an application programmer, including the parameters that are passed to each function and the return values the programmer can expect. Three of the most common APIs available to application programmers are the Win32 API for Windows systems, the POSIX API for POSIX-based systems (which include virtually all versions of UNIX, Linux, and Mac OS X), and the Java API for designing programs that run on the Java virtual machine. Note that—unless specified—the system-call names used throughout this text are generic examples. Each operating system has its own name for each system call.

Behind the scenes, the functions that make up an API typically invoke the actual system calls on behalf of the application programmer. For example, the Win32 function `CreateProcess()` (which unsurprisingly is used to create a new process) actually calls the `NTCreateProcess()` system call in the Windows kernel. Why would an application programmer prefer programming according to an API rather than invoking actual system calls? There are several reasons for doing so. One benefit of programming according to an API concerns program portability: An application programmer designing a program using an API can expect her program to compile and run on any system that supports the same API (although in reality, architectural differences often make this more difficult than it may appear). Furthermore, actual system calls can often be more detailed and difficult to work with than the API available to an application programmer. Regardless, there often exists a strong correlation between a function in the API and its associated system call within the kernel.

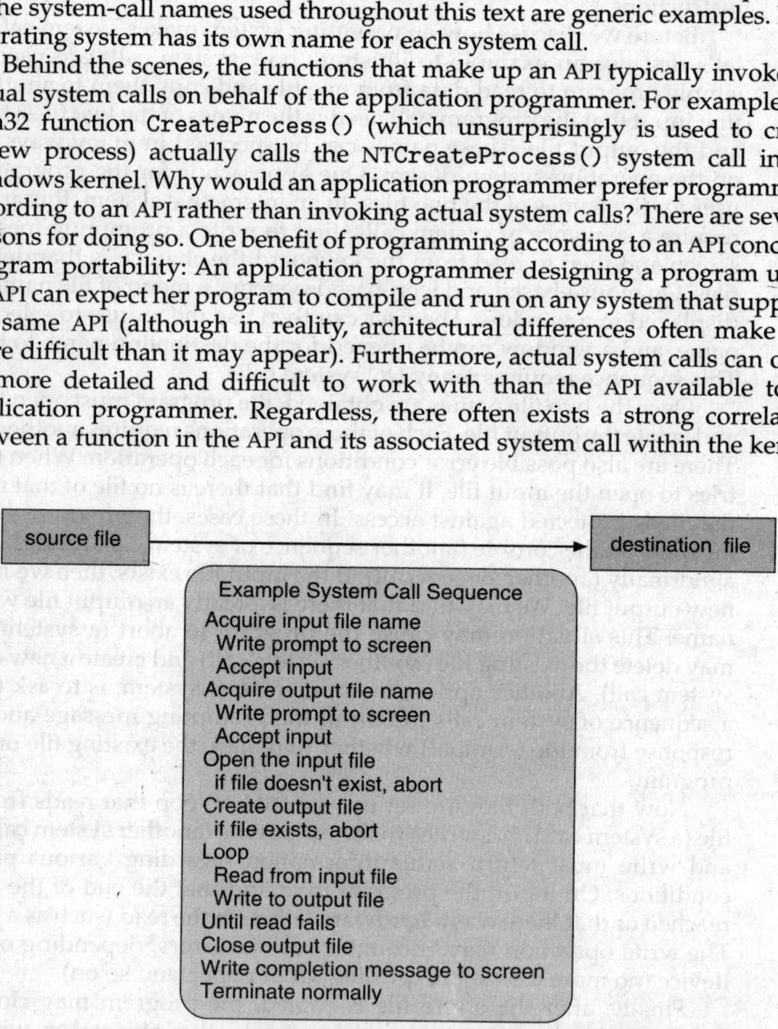

Figure 2.4 Example of how system calls are used.

EXAMPLE OF STANDARD API

As an example of a standard API, consider the `ReadFile()` function in the Win32 API—a function for reading from a file. The API for this function appears in Figure 2.5.

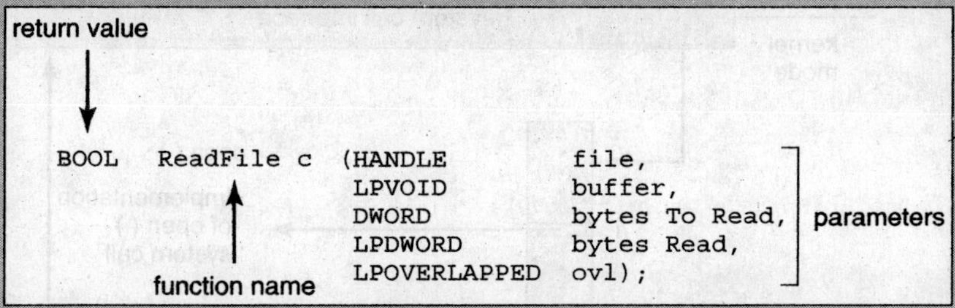

Figure 2.5 The API for the `ReadFile()` function.

A description of the parameters passed to `ReadFile()` is as follows:

- HANDLE file—the file to be read
- LPVOID buffer—a buffer where the data will be read into and written from
- DWORD bytesToRead—the number of bytes to be read into the buffer
- LPDWORD bytesRead—the number of bytes read during the last read
- LPOVERLAPPED ovl—indicates if overlapped I/O is being used

In fact, many of the POSIX and Win32 APIs are similar to the native system calls provided by the UNIX, Linux, and Windows operating systems.

The run-time support system (a set of functions built into libraries included with a compiler) for most programming languages provides a **system-call interface** that serves as the link to system calls made available by the operating system. The system-call interface intercepts function calls in the API and invokes the necessary system calls within the operating system. Typically, a number is associated with each system call, and the system-call interface maintains a table indexed according to these numbers. The system call interface then invokes the intended system call in the operating-system kernel and returns the status of the system call and any return values.

The caller need know nothing about how the system call is implemented or what it does during execution. Rather, it need only obey the API and understand what the operating system will do as a result of the execution of that system call. Thus, most of the details of the operating-system interface are hidden from the programmer by the API and are managed by the run-time support library. The relationship between an API, the system-call interface, and the operating

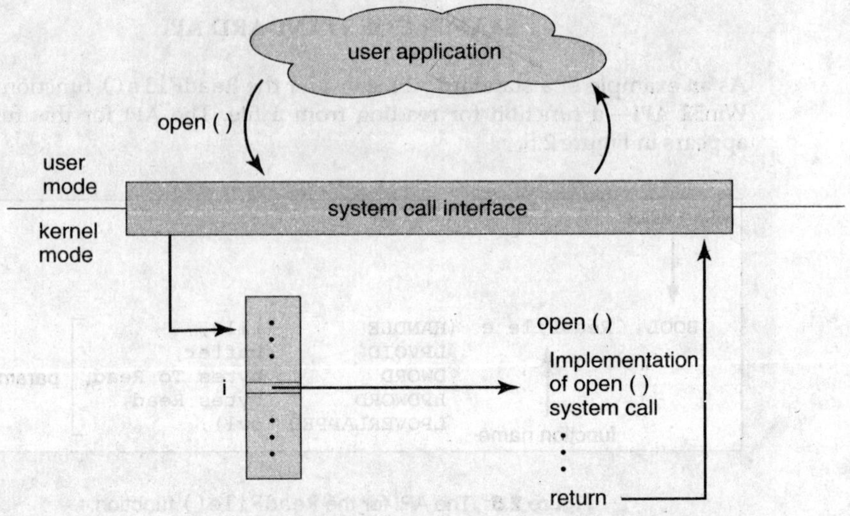

Figure 2.6 The handling of a user application invoking the `open()` system call.

system is shown in Figure 2.6, which illustrates how the operating system handles a user application invoking the `open()` system call.

System calls occur in different ways, depending on the computer in use. Often, more information is required than simply the identity of the desired system call. The exact type and amount of information vary according to the particular operating system and call. For example, to get input, we may need to specify the file or device to use as the source, as well as the address and length of the memory buffer into which the input should be read. Of course, the device or file and length may be implicit in the call.

Three general methods are used to pass parameters to the operating system. The simplest approach is to pass the parameters in *registers*. In some cases, however, there may be more parameters than registers. In these cases, the parameters are generally stored in a *block*, or table, in memory, and the address of the block is passed as a parameter in a register (Figure 2.7). This is the approach taken by Linux and Solaris. Parameters also can be placed, or *pushed*, onto the *stack* by the program and *popped* off the stack by the operating system. Some operating systems prefer the block or stack method because those approaches do not limit the number or length of parameters being passed.

2.4 Types of System Calls

System calls can be grouped roughly into six major categories: **process control**, **file manipulation**, **device manipulation**, **information maintenance**, **communications**, and **protection**. In Sections 2.4.1 through 2.4.6, we discuss briefly the types of system calls that may be provided by an operating system. Most of these system calls support, or are supported by, concepts and functions

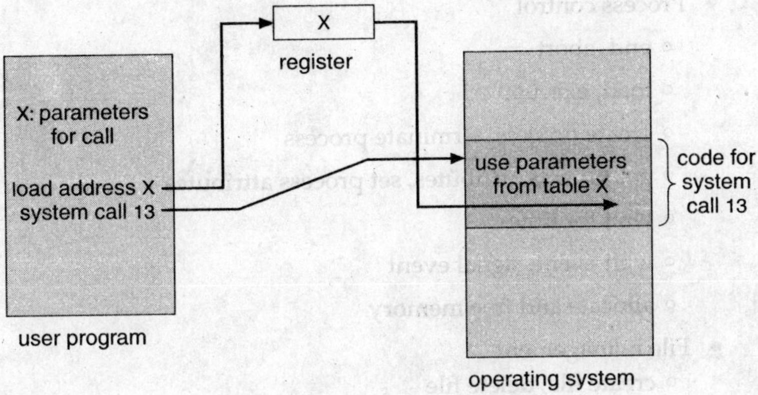

Figure 2.7 Passing of parameters as a table.

that are discussed in later chapters. Figure 2.8 summarizes the types of system calls normally provided by an operating system.

2.4.1 Process Control

A running program needs to be able to halt its execution either normally (end) or abnormally (`abort`). If a system call is made to terminate the currently running program abnormally, or if the program runs into a problem and causes an error trap, a dump of memory is sometimes taken and an error message generated. The dump is written to disk and may be examined by a **debugger**—a system program designed to aid the programmer in finding and correcting bugs—to determine the cause of the problem. Under either normal or abnormal circumstances, the operating system must transfer control to the invoking command interpreter. The command interpreter then reads the next command. In an interactive system, the command interpreter simply continues with the next command; it is assumed that the user will issue an appropriate command to respond to any error. In a GUI system, a pop-up window might alert the user to the error and ask for guidance. In a batch system, the command interpreter usually terminates the entire job and continues with the next job. Some systems allow control cards to indicate special recovery actions in case an error occurs. A **control card** is a batch-system concept. It is a command to manage the execution of a process. If the program discovers an error in its input and wants to terminate abnormally, it may also want to define an error level. More severe errors can be indicated by a higher-level error parameter. It is then possible to combine normal and abnormal termination by defining a normal termination as an error at level 0. The command interpreter or a following program can use this error level to determine the next action automatically.

A process or job executing one program may want to `load` and `execute` another program. This feature allows the command interpreter to execute a program as directed by, for example, a user command, the click of a mouse, or a batch command. An interesting question is where to return control when the loaded program terminates. This question is related to the problem of

- Process control
  - end, abort
  - load, execute
  - create process, terminate process
  - get process attributes, set process attributes
  - wait for time
  - wait event, signal event
  - allocate and free memory
- File management
  - create file, delete file
  - open, close
  - read, write, reposition
  - get file attributes, set file attributes
- Device management
  - request device, release device
  - read, write, reposition
  - get device attributes, set device attributes
  - logically attach or detach devices
- Information maintenance
  - get time or date, set time or date
  - get system data, set system data
  - get process, file, or device attributes
  - set process, file, or device attributes
- Communications
  - create, delete communication connection
  - send, receive messages
  - transfer status information
  - attach or detach remote devices

Figure 2.8 Types of system calls.

whether the existing program is lost, saved, or allowed to continue execution concurrently with the new program.

If control returns to the existing program when the new program terminates, we must save the memory image of the existing program; thus, we have effectively created a mechanism for one program to call another program. If both programs continue concurrently, we have created a new job or process to

EXAMPLES OF WINDOWS AND UNIX SYSTEM CALLS

	Windows	Unix
Process Control	`CreateProcess()`	`fork()`
	`ExitProcess()`	`exit()`
	`WaitForSingleObject()`	`wait()`
File Manipulation	`CreateFile()`	`open()`
	`ReadFile()`	`read()`
	`WriteFile()`	`write()`
	`CloseHandle()`	`close()`
Device Manipulation	`SetConsoleMode()`	`ioctl()`
	`ReadConsole()`	`read()`
	WriteConsole()	write()
Information Maintenance	`GetCurrentProcessID()`	`getpid()`
	`SetTimer()`	`alarm()`
	`Sleep()`	`sleep()`
Communication	`CreatePipe()`	`pipe()`
	`CreateFileMapping()`	`shmget()`
	`MapViewOfFile()`	`mmap()`
Protection	`SetFileSecurity()`	`chmod()`
	`InitlializeSecurityDescriptor()`	`umask()`
	`SetSecurityDescriptorGroup()`	`chown()`

be multiprogrammed. Often, there is a system call specifically for this purpose (`create process` or `submit job`).

If we create a new job or process, or perhaps even a set of jobs or processes, we should be able to control its execution. This control requires the ability to determine and reset the attributes of a job or process, including the job's priority, its maximum allowable execution time, and so on (`get process attributes` and `set process attributes`). We may also want to terminate a job or process that we created (`terminate process`) if we find that it is incorrect or is no longer needed.

Having created new jobs or processes, we may need to wait for them to finish their execution. We may want to wait for a certain amount of time to pass (`wait time`); more probably, we will want to wait for a specific event to occur (`wait event`). The jobs or processes should then signal when that event has occurred (`signal event`). Quite often, two or more processes may share data. To ensure the integrity of the data being shared, operating systems often provide system calls allowing a process to **lock** shared data, thus preventing another process from accessing the data while it is locked. Typically such system calls include `acquire lock` and `release lock`. System calls of these

EXAMPLE OF STANDARD C LIBRARY

The standard C library provides a portion of the system-call interface for many versions of UNIX and Linux. As an example, let's assume a C program invokes the `printf()` statement. The C library intercepts this call and invokes the necessary system call(s) in the operating system—in this instance, the `write()` system call. The C library takes the value returned by `write()` and passes it back to the user program. This is shown in Figure 2.9.

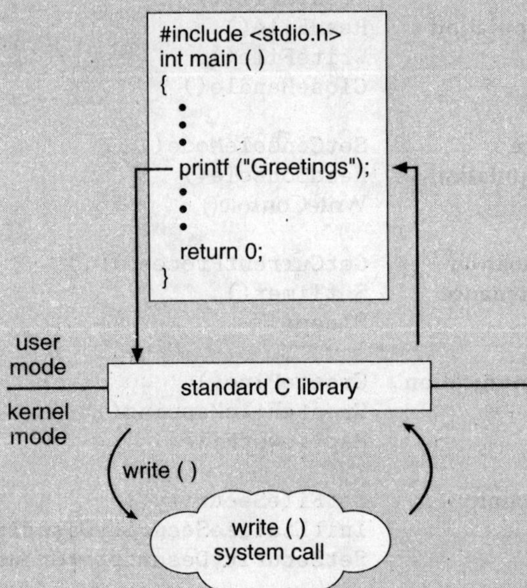

Figure 2.9 Standard C library handling of `write()`.

types, dealing with the coordination of concurrent processes, are discussed in great detail in Chapter 6.

There are so many facets of and variations in process and job control that we next use two examples—one involving a single-tasking system and the other a multitasking system—to clarify these concepts. The MS-DOS operating system is an example of a single-tasking system. It has a command interpreter that is invoked when the computer is started (Figure 2.10(a)). Because MS-DOS is single-tasking, it uses a simple method to run a program and does not create a new process. It loads the program into memory, writing over most of itself to give the program as much memory as possible (Figure 2.10(b)). Next, it sets the instruction pointer to the first instruction of the program. The program then runs, and either an error causes a trap, or the program executes a system call to terminate. In either case, the error code is saved in the system memory for later use. Following this action, the small portion of the command interpreter that was not overwritten resumes execution. Its first task is to reload the rest

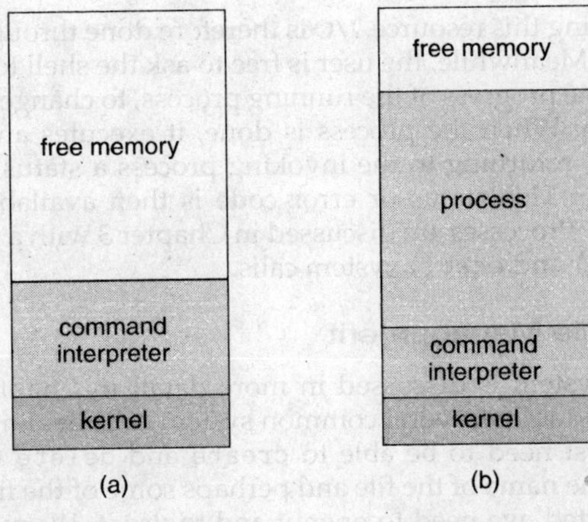

Figure 2.10 MS-DOS execution. (a) At system startup. (b) Running a program.

of the command interpreter from disk. Then the command interpreter makes the previous error code available to the user or to the next program.

FreeBSD (derived from Berkeley UNIX) is an example of a multitasking system. When a user logs on to the system, the shell of the user's choice is run. This shell is similar to the MS-DOS shell in that it accepts commands and executes programs that the user requests. However, since FreeBSD is a multitasking system, the command interpreter may continue running while another program is executed (Figure 2.11). To start a new process, the shell executes a `fork()` system call. Then, the selected program is loaded into memory via an `exec()` system call, and the program is executed. Depending on the way the command was issued, the shell then either waits for the process to finish or runs the process "in the background." In the latter case, the shell immediately requests another command. When a process is running in the background, it cannot receive input directly from the keyboard, because the

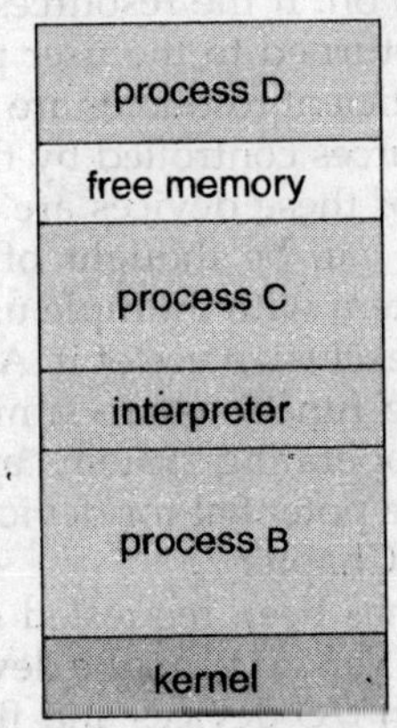

Figure 2.11 FreeBSD running multiple programs.

shell is using this resource. I/O is therefore done through files or through a GUI interface. Meanwhile, the user is free to ask the shell to run other programs, to monitor the progress of the running process, to change that program's priority, and so on. When the process is done, it executes an `exit()` system call to terminate, returning to the invoking process a status code of 0 or a nonzero error code. This status or error code is then available to the shell or other programs. Processes are discussed in Chapter 3 with a program example using the `fork()` and `exec()` system calls.

2.4.2 File Management

The file system is discussed in more detail in Chapters 10 and 11. We can, however, identify several common system calls dealing with files.

We first need to be able to `create` and `delete` files. Either system call requires the name of the file and perhaps some of the file's attributes. Once the file is created, we need to `open` it and to use it. We may also `read`, `write`, or `reposition` (rewinding or skipping to the end of the file, for example). Finally, we need to `close` the file, indicating that we are no longer using it.

We may need these same sets of operations for directories if we have a directory structure for organizing files in the file system. In addition, for either files or directories, we need to be able to determine the values of various attributes and perhaps to reset them if necessary. File attributes include the file name, file type, protection codes, accounting information, and so on. At least two system calls, `get file attribute` and `set file attribute`, are required for this function. Some operating systems provide many more calls, such as calls for file `move` and `copy`. Others might provide an API that performs those operations using code and other system calls, and others might just provide system programs to perform those tasks. If the system programs are callable by other programs, then each can be considered an API by other system programs.

2.4.3 Device Management

A process may need several resources to execute—main memory, disk drives, access to files, and so on. If the resources are available, they can be granted, and control can be returned to the user process. Otherwise, the process will have to wait until sufficient resources are available.

The various resources controlled by the operating system can be thought of as devices. Some of these devices are physical devices (for example, disk drives), while others can be thought of as abstract or virtual devices (for example, files). A system with multiple users may require us to first `request` the device, to ensure exclusive use of it. After we are finished with the device, we `release` it. These functions are similar to the `open` and `close` system calls for files. Other operating systems allow unmanaged access to devices. The hazard then is the potential for device contention and perhaps deadlock, which is described in Chapter 7.

Once the device has been requested (and allocated to us), we can `read`, `write`, and (possibly) `reposition` the device, just as we can with files. In fact, the similarity between I/O devices and files is so great that many operating systems, including UNIX, merge the two into a combined file–device structure. In this case, a set of system calls is used on both files and devices. Sometimes,

I/O devices are identified by special file names, directory placement, or file attributes.

The user interface can also make files and devices appear to be similar, even though the underlying system calls are dissimilar. This is another example of the many design decisions that go into building an operating system and user interface.

2.4.4 Information Maintenance

Many system calls exist simply for the purpose of transferring information between the user program and the operating system. For example, most systems have a system call to return the current `time` and `date`. Other system calls may return information about the system, such as the number of current users, the version number of the operating system, the amount of free memory or disk space, and so on.

Another set of system calls is helpful in debugging a program. Many systems provide system calls to `dump` memory. This provision is useful for debugging. A program `trace` lists each system call as it is executed. Even microprocessors provide a CPU mode known as *single step,* in which a trap is executed by the CPU after every instruction. The trap is usually caught by a debugger.

Many operating systems provide a time profile of a program to indicate the amount of time that the program executes at a particular location or set of locations. A time profile requires either a tracing facility or regular timer interrupts. At every occurrence of the timer interrupt, the value of the program counter is recorded. With sufficiently frequent timer interrupts, a statistical picture of the time spent on various parts of the program can be obtained.

In addition, the operating system keeps information about all its processes, and system calls are used to access this information. Generally, calls are also used to reset the process information (`get process attributes` and `set process attributes`). In Section 3.1.3, we discuss what information is normally kept.

2.4.5 Communication

There are two common models of interprocess communication: the message-passing model and the shared-memory model. In the **message-passing model**, the communicating processes exchange messages with one another to transfer information. Messages can be exchanged between the processes either directly or indirectly through a common mailbox. Before communication can take place, a connection must be opened. The name of the other communicator must be known, be it another process on the same system or a process on another computer connected by a communications network. Each computer in a network has a *host name* by which it is commonly known. A host also has a network identifier, such as an IP address. Similarly, each process has a *process name,* and this name is translated into an identifier by which the operating system can refer to the process. The `get hostid` and `get processid` system calls do this translation. The identifiers are then passed to the general-purpose `open` and `close` calls provided by the file system or to specific `open connection` and `close connection` system calls, depending on the system's model of communication. The recipient process usually must give its permission for communication to take place with an `accept connection` call. Most processes that will be receiving connections are special-purpose *daemons*, which are systems programs provided for that purpose. They execute a `wait for connection` call and are awakened when a connection is made. The source of the communication, known as the *client*, and the receiving daemon, known as a *server*, then exchange messages by using `read message` and `write message` system calls. The `close connection` call terminates the communication.

In the **shared-memory model**, processes use `shared memory create` and `shared memory attach` system calls to create and gain access to regions of memory owned by other processes. Recall that, normally, the operating system tries to prevent one process from accessing another process's memory. Shared memory requires that two or more processes agree to remove this restriction. They can then exchange information by reading and writing data in the shared areas. The form of the data is determined by the processes and are not under the operating system's control. The processes are also responsible for ensuring that they are not writing to the same location simultaneously. Such mechanisms are discussed in Chapter 6. In Chapter 4, we look at a variation of the process scheme—threads—in which memory is shared by default.

Both of the models just discussed are common in operating systems, and most systems implement both. Message passing is useful for exchanging smaller amounts of data, because no conflicts need be avoided. It is also easier to implement than is shared memory for intercomputer communication. Shared memory allows maximum speed and convenience of communication, since it can be done at memory transfer speeds when it takes place within a computer. Problems exist, however, in the areas of protection and synchronization between the processes sharing memory.

2.4.6 Protection

Protection provides a mechanism for controlling access to the resources provided by a computer system. Historically, protection was a concern only on multiprogrammed computer systems with several users. However, with the advent of networking and the Internet, all computer systems, from servers to PDAs, must be concerned with protection.

Typically, system calls providing protection include `set permission` and `get permission`, which manipulate the permission settings of resources such as files and disks. The `allow user` and `deny user` system calls specify whether particular users can—or cannot—be allowed access to certain resources.

We cover protection in Chapter 14 and the much larger issue of security in Chapter 15.

2.5 System Programs

Another aspect of a modern system is the collection of system programs. Recall Figure 1.1, which depicted the logical computer hierarchy. At the lowest level is hardware. Next is the operating system, then the system programs, and finally the application programs. **System programs**, also known as **system utilities**, provide a convenient environment for program development and execution.

Some of them are simply user interfaces to system calls; others are considerably more complex. They can be divided into these categories:

- **File management**. These programs create, delete, copy, rename, print, dump, list, and generally manipulate files and directories.
- **Status information**. Some programs simply ask the system for the date, time, amount of available memory or disk space, number of users, or similar status information. Others are more complex, providing detailed performance, logging, and debugging information. Typically, these programs format and print the output to the terminal or other output devices or files or display it in a window of the GUI. Some systems also support a **registry**, which is used to store and retrieve configuration information.
- **File modification**. Several text editors may be available to create and modify the content of files stored on disk or other storage devices. There may also be special commands to search contents of files or perform transformations of the text.
- **Programming-language support**. Compilers, assemblers, debuggers, and interpreters for common programming languages (such as C, C++, Java, Visual Basic, and PERL) are often provided to the user with the operating system.
- **Program loading and execution**. Once a program is assembled or compiled, it must be loaded into memory to be executed. The system may provide absolute loaders, relocatable loaders, linkage editors, and overlay loaders. Debugging systems for either higher-level languages or machine language are needed as well.
- **Communications**. These programs provide the mechanism for creating virtual connections among processes, users, and computer systems. They allow users to send messages to one another's screens, to browse Web pages, to send electronic-mail messages, to log in remotely, or to transfer files from one machine to another.

In addition to systems programs, most operating systems are supplied with programs that are useful in solving common problems or performing common operations. Such **application programs** include Web browsers, word processors and text formatters, spreadsheets, database systems, compilers, plotting and statistical-analysis packages, and games.

The view of the operating system seen by most users is defined by the application and system programs, rather than by the actual system calls. Consider a user's PC. When a user's computer is running the Mac OS X operating system, the user might see the GUI, featuring a mouse-and-windows interface. Alternatively, or even in one of the windows, the user might have a command-line UNIX shell. Both use the same set of system calls, but the system calls look different and act in different ways. Further confusing the user view, consider the user dual-booting from Mac OS X into Windows Vista. Now the same user on the same hardware has two entirely different interfaces and two sets of applications using the same physical resources. On the same hardware, then, a user can be exposed to multiple user interfaces sequentially or concurrently.

2.6 Operating-System Design and Implementation

In this section, we discuss problems we face in designing and implementing an operating system. There are, of course, no complete solutions to such problems, but there are approaches that have proved successful.

2.6.1 Design Goals

The first problem in designing a system is to define goals and specifications. At the highest level, the design of the system will be affected by the choice of hardware and the type of system: batch, time shared, single user, multiuser, distributed, real time, or general purpose.

Beyond this highest design level, the requirements may be much harder to specify. The requirements can, however, be divided into two basic groups: *user* goals and *system* goals.

Users desire certain obvious properties in a system. The system should be convenient to use, easy to learn and to use, reliable, safe, and fast. Of course, these specifications are not particularly useful in the system design, since there is no general agreement on how to achieve them.

A similar set of requirements can be defined by those people who must design, create, maintain, and operate the system. The system should be easy to design, implement, and maintain; and it should be flexible, reliable, error free, and efficient. Again, these requirements are vague and may be interpreted in various ways.

There is, in short, no unique solution to the problem of defining the requirements for an operating system. The wide range of systems in existence shows that different requirements can result in a large variety of solutions for different environments. For example, the requirements for VxWorks, a real-time operating system for embedded systems, must have been substantially different from those for MVS, a large multiuser, multiaccess operating system for IBM mainframes.

Specifying and designing an operating system is a highly creative task. Although no textbook can tell you how to do it, general principles have been developed in the field of **software engineering**, and we turn now to a discussion of some of these principles.

2.6.2 Mechanisms and Policies

One important principle is the separation of **policy** from **mechanism**. Mechanisms determine *how* to do something; policies determine *what* will be done. For example, the timer construct (see Section 1.5.2) is a mechanism for ensuring CPU protection, but deciding how long the timer is to be set for a particular user is a policy decision.

The separation of policy and mechanism is important for flexibility. Policies are likely to change across places or over time. In the worst case, each change in policy would require a change in the underlying mechanism. A general mechanism insensitive to changes in policy would be more desirable. A change in policy would then require redefinition of only certain parameters of the system. For instance, consider a mechanism for giving priority to certain types of programs over others. If the mechanism is properly separated from policy, it can be used either to support a policy decision that I/O-intensive programs should have priority over CPU-intensive ones or to support the opposite policy.

Microkernel-based operating systems (Section 2.7.3) take the separation of mechanism and policy to one extreme by implementing a basic set of primitive building blocks. These blocks are almost policy free, allowing more advanced mechanisms and policies to be added via user-created kernel modules or via user programs themselves. As an example, consider the history of UNIX. At first, it had a time-sharing scheduler. In the latest version of Solaris, scheduling is controlled by loadable tables. Depending on the table currently loaded, the system can be time shared, batch processing, real time, fair share, or any combination. Making the scheduling mechanism general purpose allows vast policy changes to be made with a single `load-new-table` command. At the other extreme is a system such as Windows, in which both mechanism and policy are encoded in the system to enforce a global look and feel. All applications have similar interfaces, because the interface itself is built into the kernel and system libraries. The Mac OS X operating system has similar functionality.

Policy decisions are important for all resource allocation. Whenever it is necessary to decide whether or not to allocate a resource, a policy decision must be made. Whenever the question is *how* rather than *what*, it is a mechanism that must be determined.

2.6.3 Implementation

Once an operating system is designed, it must be implemented. Traditionally, operating systems have been written in assembly language. Now, however, they are most commonly written in higher-level languages such as C or C++.

The first system that was not written in assembly language was probably the Master Control Program (MCP) for Burroughs computers. MCP was written in a variant of ALGOL. MULTICS, developed at MIT, was written mainly in PL/1. The Linux and Windows XP operating systems are written mostly in C, although there are some small sections of assembly code for device drivers and for saving and restoring the state of registers.

The advantages of using a higher-level language, or at least a systems-implementation language, for implementing operating systems are the same as those accrued when the language is used for application programs: the code can be written faster, is more compact, and is easier to understand and debug. In addition, improvements in compiler technology will improve the generated code for the entire operating system by simple recompilation. Finally, an operating system is far easier to *port*—to move to some other hardware—if it is written in a higher-level language. For example, MS-DOS was written in Intel 8088 assembly language. Consequently, it runs natively only on the Intel X86 family of CPUs. (Although MS-DOS runs natively only on Intel X86, emulators of the X86 instruction set allow the operating system to run non-natively—slower, with more resource use—on other CPUs. **Emulators** are programs that duplicate the functionality of one system with another system.) The Linux operating system, in contrast, is written mostly in C and is available natively on a number of different CPUs, including Intel X86, Sun SPARC, and IBMPowerPC.

The only possible disadvantages of implementing an operating system in a higher-level language are reduced speed and increased storage requirements. This, however, is no longer a major issue in today's systems. Although an expert assembly-language programmer can produce efficient small routines, for large programs a modern compiler can perform complex analysis and apply sophisticated optimizations that produce excellent code. Modern processors have deep pipelining and multiple functional units that can handle the details of complex dependencies much more easily than can the human mind.

As is true in other systems, major performance improvements in operating systems are more likely to be the result of better data structures and algorithms than of excellent assembly-language code. In addition, although operating systems are large, only a small amount of the code is critical to high performance; the memory manager and the CPU scheduler are probably the most critical routines. After the system is written and is working correctly, bottleneck routines can be identified and can be replaced with assembly-language equivalents.

2.7 Operating-System Structure

A system as large and complex as a modern operating system must be engineered carefully if it is to function properly and be modified easily. A common approach is to partition the task into small components rather than have one monolithic system. Each of these modules should be a well-defined portion of the system, with carefully defined inputs, outputs, and functions. We have already discussed briefly in Chapter 1 the common components of operating systems. In this section, we discuss how these components are interconnected and melded into a kernel.

2.7.1 Simple Structure

Many commercial operating systems do not have well-defined structures. Frequently, such systems started as small, simple, and limited systems and then grew beyond their original scope. MS-DOS is an example of such a system. It was originally designed and implemented by a few people who had no idea that it would become so popular. It was written to provide the most functionality in the least space, so it was not divided into modules carefully. Figure 2.12 shows its structure.

In MS-DOS, the interfaces and levels of functionality are not well separated. For instance, application programs are able to access the basic I/O routines to write directly to the display and disk drives. Such freedom leaves MS-DOS vulnerable to errant (or malicious) programs, causing entire system crashes when user programs fail. Of course, MS-DOS was also limited by the hardware of its era. Because the Intel 8088 for which it was written provides no dual mode and no hardware protection, the designers of MS-DOS had no choice but to leave the base hardware accessible.

Another example of limited structuring is the original UNIX operating system. Like MS-DOS, UNIX initially was limited by hardware functionality. It consists of two separable parts: the kernel and the system programs. The kernel

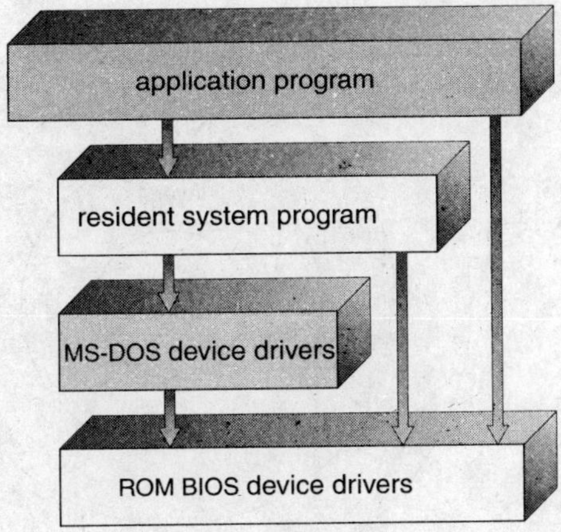

Figure 2.12 MS-DOS layer structure.

is further separated into a series of interfaces and device drivers, which have been added and expanded over the years as UNIX has evolved. We can view the traditional UNIX operating system as being layered, as shown in Figure 2.13. Everything below the system-call interface and above the physical hardware is the kernel. The kernel provides the file system, CPU scheduling, memory management, and other operating-system functions through system calls. Taken in sum, that is an enormous amount of functionality to be combined into one level. This monolithic structure was difficult to implement and maintain.

2.7.2 Layered Approach

With proper hardware support, operating systems can be broken into pieces that are smaller and more appropriate than those allowed by the original

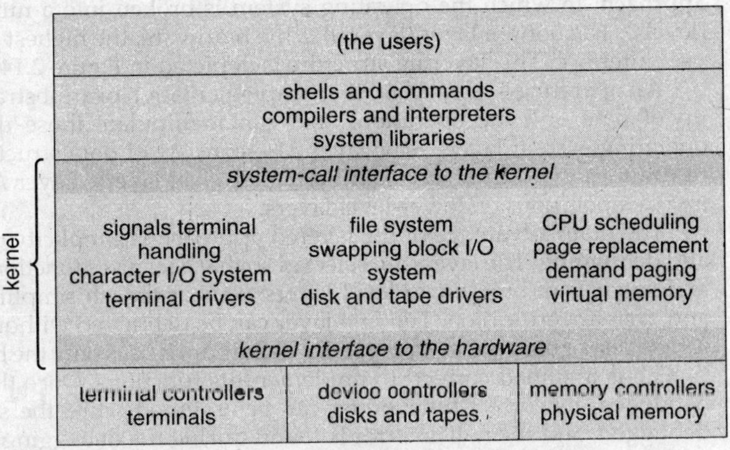

Figure 2.13 Traditional UNIX system structure.

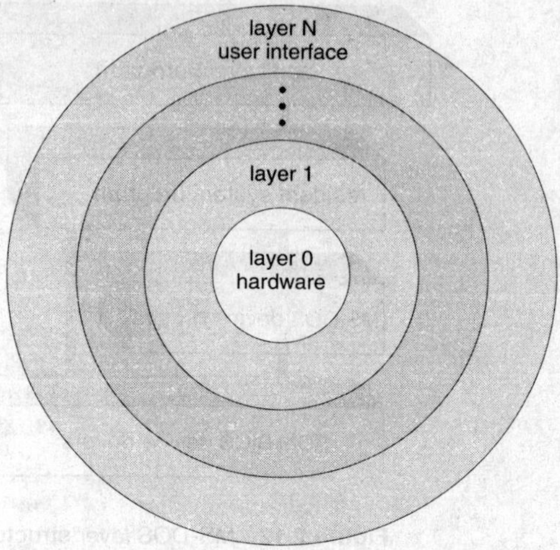

Figure 2.14 A layered operating system.

MS-DOS and UNIX systems. The operating system can then retain much greater control over the computer and over the applications that make use of that computer. Implementers have more freedom in changing the inner workings of the system and in creating modular operating systems. Under a top-down approach, the overall functionality and features are determined and are separated into components. Information hiding is also important, because it leaves programmers free to implement the low-level routines as they see fit, provided that the external interface of the routine stays unchanged and that the routine itself performs the advertised task.

A system can be made modular in many ways. One method is the **layered approach**, in which the operating system is broken into a number of layers (levels). The bottom layer (layer 0) is the hardware; the highest (layer *N*) is the user interface. This layering structure is depicted in Figure 2.14.

An operating-system layer is an implementation of an abstract object made up of data and the operations that can manipulate those data. A typical operating-system layer—say, layer *M*—consists of data structures and a set of routines that can be invoked by higher-level layers. Layer *M*, in turn, can invoke operations on lower-level layers.

The main advantage of the layered approach is simplicity of construction and debugging. The layers are selected so that each uses functions (operations) and services of only lower-level layers. This approach simplifies debugging and system verification. The first layer can be debugged without any concern for the rest of the system, because, by definition, it uses only the basic hardware (which is assumed correct) to implement its functions. Once the first layer is debugged, its correct functioning can be assumed while the second layer is debugged, and so on. If an error is found during the debugging of a particular layer, the error must be on that layer, because the layers below it are already debugged. Thus, the design and implementation of the system are simplified.

Each layer is implemented with only those operations provided by lower-level layers. A layer does not need to know how these operations are implemented; it needs to know only what these operations do. Hence, each layer hides the existence of certain data structures, operations, and hardware from higher-level layers.

The major difficulty with the layered approach involves appropriately defining the various layers. Because a layer can use only lower-level layers, careful planning is necessary. For example, the device driver for the backing store (disk space used by virtual-memory algorithms) must be at a lower level than the memory-management routines, because memory management requires the ability to use the backing store.

Other requirements may not be so obvious. The backing-store driver would normally be above the CPU scheduler, because the driver may need to wait for I/O and the CPU can be rescheduled during this time. However, on a large system, the CPU scheduler may have more information about all the active processes than can fit in memory. Therefore, this information may need to be swapped in and out of memory, requiring the backing-store driver routine to be below the CPU scheduler.

A final problem with layered implementations is that they tend to be less efficient than other types. For instance, when a user program executes an I/O operation, it executes a system call that is trapped to the I/O layer, which calls the memory-management layer, which in turn calls the CPU-scheduling layer, which is then passed to the hardware. At each layer, the parameters may be modified, data may need to be passed, and so on. Each layer adds overhead to the system call; the net result is a system call that takes longer than does one on a nonlayered system.

These limitations have caused a small backlash against layering in recent years. Fewer layers with more functionality are being designed, providing most of the advantages of modularized code while avoiding the difficult problems of layer definition and interaction.

2.7.3 Microkernels

We have already seen that as UNIX expanded, the kernel became large and difficult to manage. In the mid-1980s, researchers at Carnegie Mellon University developed an operating system called **Mach** that modularized the kernel using the **microkernel** approach. This method structures the operating system by removing all nonessential components from the kernel and implementing them as system and user-level programs. The result is a smaller kernel. There is little consensus regarding which services should remain in the kernel and which should be implemented in user space. Typically, however, microkernels provide minimal process and memory management, in addition to a communication facility.

The main function of the microkernel is to provide a communication facility between the client program and the various services that are also running in user space. Communication is provided by *message passing*, which was described in Section 2.4.5. For example, if the client program wishes to access a file, it must interact with the file server. The client program and service never interact directly. Rather, they communicate indirectly by exchanging messages with the microkernel.

One benefit of the microkernel approach is ease of extending the operating system. All new services are added to user space and consequently do not require modification of the kernel. When the kernel does have to be modified, the changes tend to be fewer, because the microkernel is a smaller kernel. The resulting operating system is easier to port from one hardware design to another. The microkernel also provides more security and reliability, since most services are running as user—rather than kernel—processes. If a service fails, the rest of the operating system remains untouched.

Several contemporary operating systems have used the microkernel approach. Tru64 UNIX (formerly Digital UNIX) provides a UNIX interface to the user, but it is implemented with a Mach kernel. The Mach kernel maps UNIX system calls into messages to the appropriate user-level services. The Mac OS X kernel (also known as *Darwin*) is also based on the Mach microkernel.

Another example is QNX, a real-time operating system. The QNX microkernel provides services for message passing and process scheduling. It also handles low-level network communication and hardware interrupts. All other services in QNX are provided by standard processes that run outside the kernel in user mode.

Unfortunately, microkernels can suffer from performance decreases due to increased system function overhead. Consider the history of Windows NT. The first release had a layered microkernel organization. However, this version delivered low performance compared with that of Windows 95. Windows NT 4.0 partially redressed the performance problem by moving layers from user space to kernel space and integrating them more closely. By the time Windows XP was designed, its architecture was more monolithic than microkernel.

2.7.4 Modules

Perhaps the best current methodology for operating-system design involves using object-oriented programming techniques to create a modular kernel. Here, the kernel has a set of core components and links in additional services either during boot time or during run time. Such a strategy uses dynamically loadable modules and is common in modern implementations of UNIX, such as Solaris, Linux, and Mac OS X. For example, the Solaris operating system structure, shown in Figure 2.15, is organized around a core kernel with seven types of loadable kernel modules:

1. Scheduling classes
2. File systems
3. Loadable system calls
4. Executable formats
5. STREAMS modules
6. Miscellaneous
7. Device and bus drivers

Such a design allows the kernel to provide core services yet also allows certain features to be implemented dynamically. For example, device and

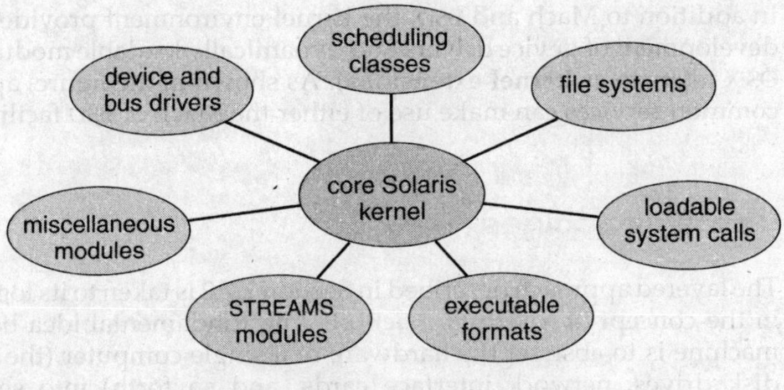

Figure 2.15 Solaris loadable modules.

bus drivers for specific hardware can be added to the kernel, and support for different file systems can be added as loadable modules. The overall result resembles a layered system in that each kernel section has defined, protected interfaces; but it is more flexible than a layered system in that any module can call any other module. Furthermore, the approach is like the microkernel approach in that the primary module has only core functions and knowledge of how to load and communicate with other modules; but it is more efficient, because modules do not need to invoke message passing in order to communicate.

The Apple Mac OS X operating system uses a hybrid structure. It is a layered system in which one layer consists of the Mach microkernel. The structure of Mac OS X appears in Figure 2.16. The top layers include application environments and a set of services providing a graphical interface to applications. Below these layers is the kernel environment, which consists primarily of the Mach microkernel and the BSD kernel. Mach provides memory management; support for remote procedure calls (RPCs) and interprocess communication (IPC) facilities, including message passing; and thread scheduling. The BSD component provides a BSD command line interface, support for networking and file systems, and an implementation of POSIX APIs, including Pthreads.

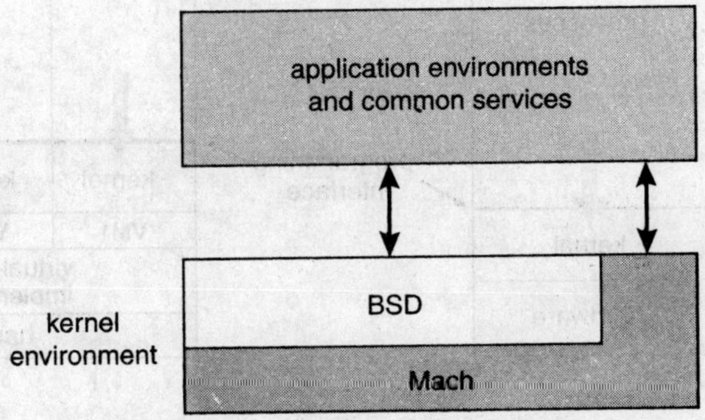

Figure 2.16 The Mac OS X structure.

In addition to Mach and BSD, the kernel environment provides an I/O kit for development of device drivers and dynamically loadable modules (which Mac OS X refers to as **kernel extensions**). As shown in the figure, applications and common services can make use of either the Mach or BSD facilities directly.

2.8 Virtual Machines

The layered approach described in Section 2.7.2 is taken to its logical conclusion in the concept of a **virtual machine**. The fundamental idea behind a virtual machine is to abstract the hardware of a single computer (the CPU, memory, disk drives, network interface cards, and so forth) into several different execution environments, thereby creating the illusion that each separate execution environment is running its own private computer.

By using CPU scheduling (Chapter 5) and virtual-memory techniques (Chapter 9), an operating system **host** can create the illusion that a process has its own processor with its own (virtual) memory. The virtual machine provides an interface that is *identical* to the underlying bare hardware. Each **guest** process is provided with a (virtual) copy of the underlying computer (Figure 2.17). Usually, the guest process is in fact an operating system, and that is how a single physical machine can run multiple operating systems concurrently, each in its own virtual machine.

2.8.1 History

Virtual machines first appeared commercially on IBM mainframes via the VM operating system in 1972. VM has evolved and is still available, and many of

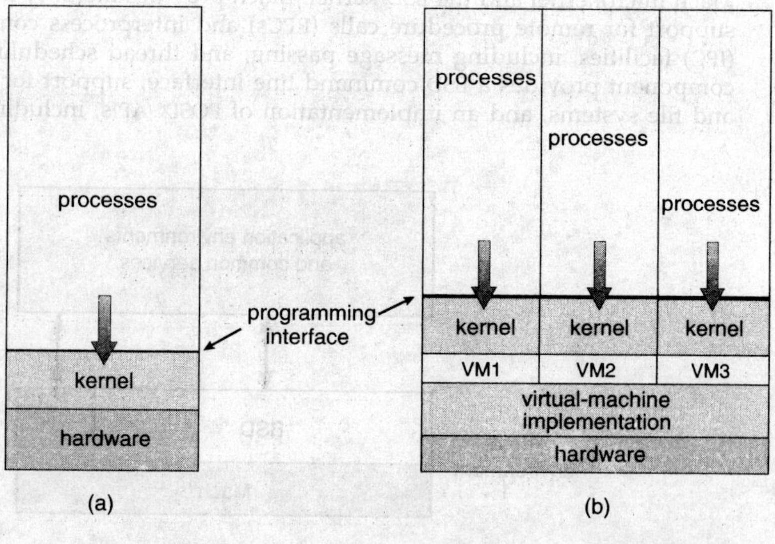

Figure 2.17 System models. (a) Nonvirtual machine. (b) Virtual machine.

the original concepts are found in other systems, making this facility worth exploring.

IBM VM370 divided a mainframe into multiple virtual machines, each running its own operating system. A major difficulty with the VM virtual-machine approach involved disk systems. Suppose that the physical machine had three disk drives but wanted to support seven virtual machines. Clearly, it could not allocate a disk drive to each virtual machine, because the virtual-machine software itself needed substantial disk space to provide virtual memory and spooling. The solution was to provide virtual disks—termed *minidisks* in IBM's VM operating system—that are identical in all respects except size. The system implemented each minidisk by allocating as many tracks on the physical disks as the minidisk needed.

Once these virtual machines were created, users could run any of the operating systems or software packages that were available on the underlying machine. For the IBM VM system, a user normally ran CMS—a single-user interactive operating system.

2.8.2 Benefits

There are several reasons for creating a virtual machine. Most of them are fundamentally related to being able to share the same hardware yet run several different execution environments (that is, different operating systems) concurrently.

One important advantage is that the host system is protected from the virtual machines, just as the virtual machines are protected from each other. A virus inside a guest operating system might damage that operating system but is unlikely to affect the host or the other guests. Because each virtual machine is completely isolated from all other virtual machines, there are no protection problems. At the same time, however, there is no direct sharing of resources. Two approaches to provide sharing have been implemented. First, it is possible to share a file-system volume and thus to share files. Second, it is possible to define a network of virtual machines, each of which can send information over the virtual communications network. The network is modeled after physical communication networks but is implemented in software.

A virtual-machine system is a perfect vehicle for operating-systems research and development. Normally, changing an operating system is a difficult task. Operating systems are large and complex programs, and it is difficult to be sure that a change in one part will not cause obscure bugs to appear in some other part. The power of the operating system makes changing it particularly dangerous. Because the operating system executes in kernel mode, a wrong change in a pointer could cause an error that would destroy the entire file system. Thus, it is necessary to test all changes to the operating system carefully.

The operating system, however, runs on and controls the entire machine. Therefore, the current system must be stopped and taken out of use while changes are made and tested. This period is commonly called *system development time*. Since it makes the system unavailable to users, system-development time is often scheduled late at night or on weekends, when system load is low.

A virtual-machine system can eliminate much of this problem. System programmers are given their own virtual machine, and system development is done on the virtual machine instead of on a physical machine. Normal system operation seldom needs to be disrupted for system development.

Another advantage of virtual machines for developers is that multiple operating systems can be running on the developer's workstation concurrently. This virtualized workstation allows for rapid porting and testing of programs in varying environments. Similarly, quality-assurance engineers can test their applications in multiple environments without buying, powering, and maintaining a computer for each environment.

A major advantage of virtual machines in production data-center use is system **consolidation**, which involves taking two or more separate systems and running them in virtual machines on one system. Such physical-to-virtual conversions result in resource optimization, as many lightly used systems can be combined to create one more heavily used system.

If the use of virtual machines continues to spread, application deployment will evolve accordingly. If a system can easily add, remove, and move a virtual machine, then why install applications on that system directly? Instead, application developers would pre-install the application on a tuned and customized operating system in a virtual machine. That virtual environment would be the release mechanism for the application. This method would be an improvement for application developers; application management would become easier, less tuning would required, and technical support of the application would be more straightforward. System administrators would find the environment easier to manage as well. Installation would be simple, and redeploying the application to another system would be much easier than the usual steps of uninstalling and reinstalling. For widespread adoption of this methodology to occur, though, the format of virtual machines must be standardized so that any virtual machine will run on any virtualization platform. The "Open Virtual Machine Format" is an attempt to do just that, and it could succeed in unifying virtual-machine formats.

2.8.3 Simulation

System virtualization as discussed so far is just one of many system-emulation methodologies. Virtualization is the most common because it makes guest operating systems and applications "believe" they are running on native hardware. Because only the system's resources need to be virtualized, these guests run at almost full speed.

Another methodology is **simulation**, in which the host system has one system architecture and the guest system was compiled for a different architecture. For example, suppose a company has replaced its outdated computer system with a new system but would like to continue to run certain important programs that were compiled for the old system. The programs could be run in an emulator that translates each of the outdated system's instructions into the native instruction set of the new system. Emulation can increase the life of programs and allow us to explore old architectures without having an actual old machine, but its major challenge is performance. Instruction-set emulation can run an order of magnitude slower than native instructions. Thus, unless the new machine is ten times faster than the old, the program running on the new machine will run slower than it did on its native hardware. Another challenge is that it is difficult to create a correct emulator because, in essence, this involves writing an entire CPU in software.

2.8.4 Para-virtualization

Para-virtualization is another variation on this theme. Rather than try to trick a guest operating system into believing it has a system to itself, para-virtualization presents the guest with a system that is similar but not identical to the guest's preferred system. The guest must be modified to run on the paravirtualized hardware. The gain for this extra work is more efficient use of resources and a smaller virtualization layer.

Solaris 10 includes **containers**, or **zones**, that create a virtual layer between the operating system and the applications. In this system, only one kernel is installed, and the hardware is not virtualized. Rather, the operating system and its devices are virtualized, providing processes within a container with the impression that they are the only processes on the system. One or more containers can be created, and each can have its own applications, network stacks, network address and ports, user accounts, and so on. CPU resources can be divided up among the containers and the systemwide processes. Figure 2.18 shows a Solaris 10 system with two containers and the standard "global" user space.

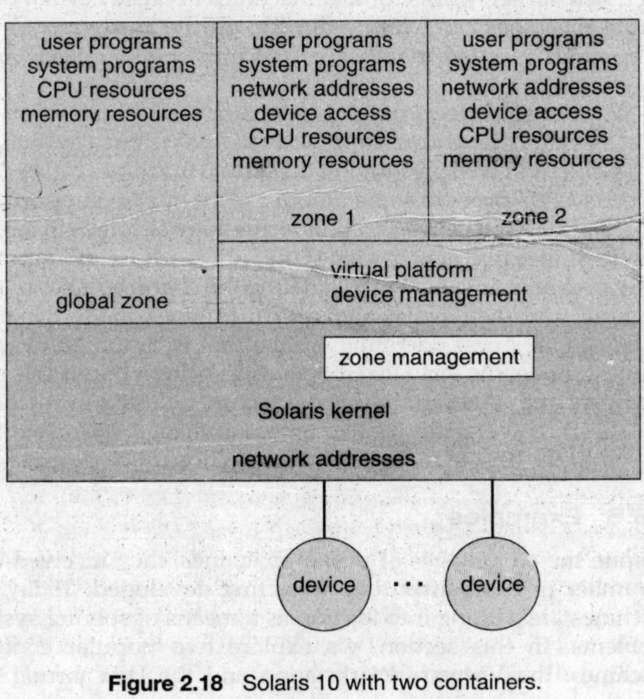

Figure 2.18 Solaris 10 with two containers.

2.8.5 Implementation

Although the virtual-machine concept is useful, it is difficult to implement. Much work is required to provide an *exact* duplicate of the underlying machine. Remember that the underlying machine typically has two modes: user mode and kernel mode. The virtual-machine software can run in kernel mode, since it is the operating system. The virtual machine itself can execute in only user mode. Just as the physical machine has two modes, however, so must the virtual machine. Consequently, we must have a virtual user mode and a virtual kernel mode, both of which run in a physical user mode. Those actions that cause a transfer from user mode to kernel mode on a real machine (such as a system call or an attempt to execute a privileged instruction) must also cause a transfer from virtual user mode to virtual kernel mode on a virtual machine.

Such a transfer can be accomplished as follows. When a system call, for example, is made by a program running on a virtual machine in virtual user mode, it will cause a transfer to the virtual-machine monitor in the real machine. When the virtual-machine monitor gains control, it can change the register contents and program counter for the virtual machine to simulate the effect of the system call. It can then restart the virtual machine, noting that it is now in virtual kernel mode.

The major difference, of course, is time. Whereas the real I/O might have taken 100 milliseconds, the virtual I/O might take less time (because it is spooled) or more time (because it is interpreted). In addition, the CPU is being multiprogrammed among many virtual machines, further slowing down the virtual machines in unpredictable ways. In the extreme case, it may be necessary to simulate all instructions to provide a true virtual machine. VM, discussed earlier, works for IBM machines because normal instructions for the virtual machines can execute directly on the hardware. Only the privileged instructions (needed mainly for I/O) must be simulated and hence execute more slowly.

Without some level of hardware support, virtualization would be impossible. The more hardware support available within a system, the more feature rich, stable, and well performing the virtual machines can be. All major general-purpose CPUs provide some amount of hardware support for virtualization. For example, AMD virtualization technology is found in several AMD processors. It defines two new modes of operation—host and guest. Virtual machine software can enable host mode, define the characteristics of each guest virtual machine, and then switch the system to guest mode, passing control of the system to the guest operating system that is running in the virtual machine. In guest mode, the virtualized operating system thinks it is running on native hardware and sees certain devices (those included in the host's definition of the guest). If the guest tries to access a virtualized resource, then control is passed to the host to manage that interaction.

2.8.6 Examples

Despite the advantages of virtual machines, they received little attention for a number of years after they were first developed. Today, however, virtual machines are coming into fashion as a means of solving system compatibility problems. In this section, we explore two popular contemporary virtual machines: the VMware Workstation and the Java virtual machine. As you will see, these virtual machines can typically run on top of operating systems of any of the design types discussed earlier. Thus, operating system design methods—simple layers, microkernels, modules, and virtual machines—are not mutually exclusive.

2.8.6.1 VMware

Most of the virtualization techniques discussed in this section require virtualization to be supported by the kernel. Another method involves writing the virtualization tool to run in user mode as an application on top of the operating system. Virtual machines running within this tool believe they are running on bare hardware but in fact are running inside a user-level application.

VMware Workstation is a popular commercial application that abstracts Intel X86 and compatible hardware into isolated virtual machines. VMware Workstation runs as an application on a host operating system such as Windows or Linux and allows this host system to concurrently run several different guest operating systems as independent virtual machines.

The architecture of such a system is shown in Figure 2.19. In this scenario, Linux is running as the host operating system; and FreeBSD, Windows NT, and Windows XP are running as guest operating systems. The virtualization layer is the heart of VMware, as it abstracts the physical hardware into isolated virtual machines running as guest operating systems. Each virtual machine has its own virtual CPU, memory, disk drives, network interfaces, and so forth.

The physical disk the guest owns and manages is really just a file within the file system of the host operating system. To create an identical guest instance, we can simply copy the file. Copying the file to another location protects the guest instance against a disaster at the original site. Moving the file to another

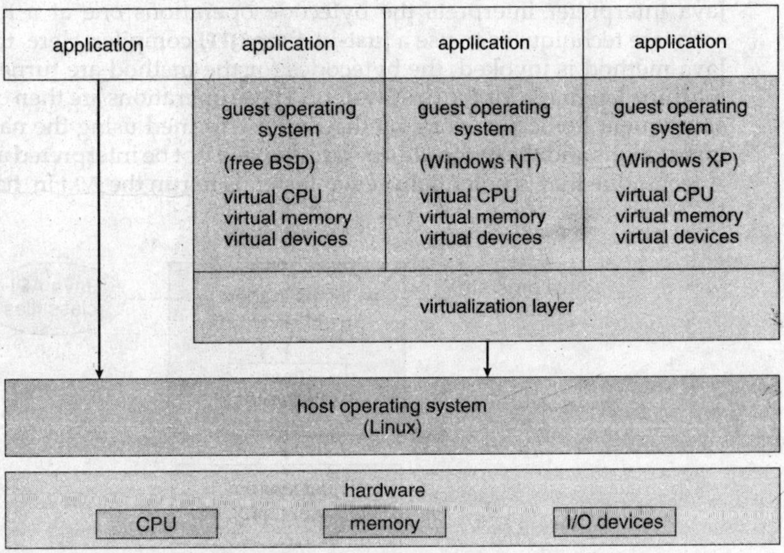

Figure 2.19 VMware architecture.

location moves the guest system. These scenarios show how virtualization can improve the efficiency of system administration as well as system resource use.

2.8.6.2 The Java Virtual Machine

Java is a popular object-oriented programming language introduced by Sun Microsystems in 1995. In addition to a language specification and a large API library, Java also provides a specification for a Java virtual machine—or JVM.

Java objects are specified with the `class` construct; a Java program consists of one or more classes. For each Java class, the compiler produces an architecture-neutral **bytecode** output (`.class`) file that will run on any implementation of the JVM.

The JVM is a specification for an abstract computer. It consists of a **class loader** and a Java interpreter that executes the architecture-neutral bytecodes, as diagrammed in Figure 2.20. The class loader loads the compiled `.class` files from both the Java program and the Java API for execution by the Java interpreter. After a class is loaded, the verifier checks that the `.class` file is valid Java bytecode and does not overflow or underflow the stack. It also ensures that the bytecode does not perform pointer arithmetic, which could provide illegal memory access. If the class passes verification, it is run by the Java interpreter. The JVM also automatically manages memory by performing **garbage collection**—the practice of reclaiming memory from objects no longer in use and returning it to the system. Much research focuses on garbage collection algorithms for increasing the performance of Java programs in the virtual machine.

The JVM may be implemented in software on top of a host operating system, such as Windows, Linux, or Mac OS X, or as part of a Web browser. Alternatively, the JVM may be implemented in hardware on a chip specifically designed to run Java programs. If the JVM is implemented in software, the Java interpreter interprets the bytecode operations one at a time. A faster software technique is to use a **just-in-time (JIT)** compiler. Here, the first time a Java method is invoked, the bytecodes for the method are turned into native machine language for the host system. These operations are then cached so that subsequent invocations of a method are performed using the native machine instructions and the bytecode operations need not be interpreted all over again. A technique that is potentially even faster is to run the JVM in hardware on a

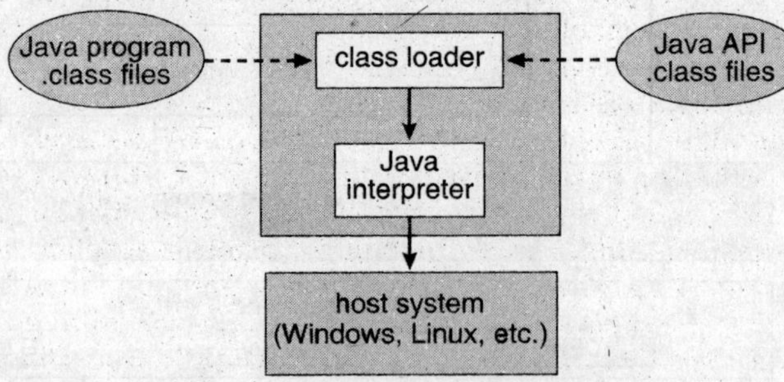

Figure 2.20 The Java virtual machine.

THE .NET FRAMEWORK

The .NET Framework is a collection of technologies, including a set of class libraries, and an execution environment that come together to provide a platform for developing software. This platform allows programs to be written to target the .NET Framework instead of a specific architecture. A program written for the .NET Framework need not worry about the specifics of the hardware or the operating system on which it will run. Thus, any architecture implementing .NET will be able to successfully execute the program. This is because the execution environment abstracts these details and provides a virtual machine as an intermediary between the executing program and the underlying architecture.

At the core of the .NET Framework is the Common Language Runtime (CLR). The CLR is the implementation of the .NET virtual machine. It provides an environment for execution of programs written in any of the languages targeted at the .NET Framework. Programs written in languages such as C# (pronounced *C-sharp*) and VB.NET are compiled into an intermediate, architecture-independent language called Microsoft Intermediate Language (MS-IL). These compiled files, called assemblies, include MS-IL instructions and metadata. They have file extensions of either .EXE or .DLL. Upon execution of a program, the CLR loads assemblies into what is known as the **Application Domain**. As instructions are requested by the executing program, the CLR converts the MS-IL instructions inside the assemblies into native code that is specific to the underlying architecture using just-in-time compilation. Once instructions have been converted to native code, they are kept and will continue to run as native code for the CPU. The architecture of the CLR for the .NET framework is shown in Figure 2.21.

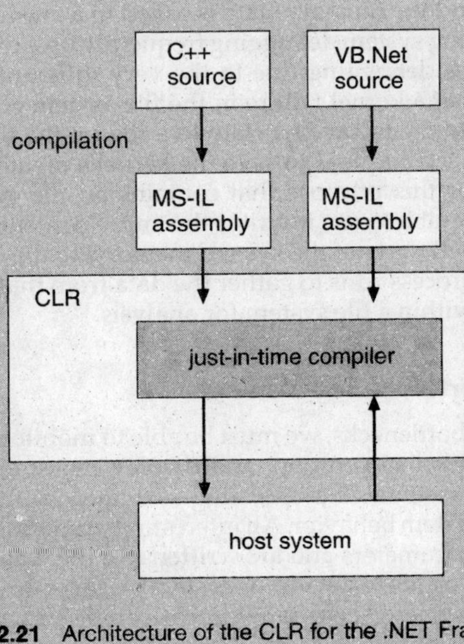

Figure 2.21 Architecture of the CLR for the .NET Framework.

special Java chip that executes the Java bytecode operations as native code, thus bypassing the need for either a software interpreter or a just-in-time compiler.

2.9 Operating-System Debugging

Broadly, **debugging** is the activity of finding and fixing errors, or **bugs**, in a system. Debugging seeks to find and fix errors in both hardware and software. Performance problems are considered bugs, so debugging can also include **performance tuning**, which seeks to improve performance by removing **bottlenecks** in the processing taking place within a system. A discussion of hardware debugging is outside of the scope of this text. In this section, we explore debugging kernel and process errors and performance problems.

2.9.1 Failure Analysis

If a process fails, most operating systems write the error information to a **log file** to alert system operators or users that the problem occurred. The operating system can also take a **core dump**—a capture of the memory (referred to as the "core" in the early days of computing) of the process. This core image is stored in a file for later analysis. Running programs and core dumps can be probed by a **debugger**, a tool designed to allow a programmer to explore the code and memory of a process.

Debugging user-level process code is a challenge. Operating system kernel debugging even more complex because of the size and complexity of the kernel, its control of the hardware, and the lack of user-level debugging tools. A kernel failure is called a **crash**. As with a process failure, error information is saved to a log file, and the memory state is saved to a **crash dump**.

Operating system debugging frequently uses different tools and techniques than process debugging due to the very different nature of these two tasks. Consider that a kernel failure in the file-system code would make it risky for the kernel to try to save its state to a file on the file system before rebooting. A common technique is to save the kernel's memory state to a section of disk set aside for this purpose that contains no file system. If the kernel detects an unrecoverable error, it writes the entire contents of memory, or at least the kernel-owned parts of the system memory, to the disk area. When the system reboots, a process runs to gather the data from that area and write it to a crash dump file within a file system for analysis.

2.9.2 Performance Tuning

To identify bottlenecks, we must be able to monitor system performance. Code must be added to compute and display measures of system behavior. In a number of systems, the operating system does this task by producing trace listings of system behavior. All interesting events are logged with their time and important parameters and are written to a file. Later, an analysis program can process the log file to determine system performance and to identify bottlenecks and inefficiencies. These same traces can be run as input for a simulation of a suggested improved system. Traces also can help people to find errors in operating-system behavior.

Kernighan's Law

"Debugging is twice as hard as writing the code in the first place. Therefore, if you write the code as cleverly as possible, you are, by definition, not smart enough to debug it."

Another approach to performance tuning is to include interactive tools with the system that allow users and administrators to question the state of various components of the system to look for bottlenecks. The UNIX command `top` displays resources used on the system, as well as a sorted list of the "top" resource-using processes. Other tools display the state of disk I/O, memory allocation, and network traffic. The authors of these single-purpose tools try to guess what a user would want to see while analyzing a system and to provide that information.

Making running operating systems easier to understand, debug, and tune is an active area of operating system research and implementation. The cycle of enabling tracing as system problems occur and analyzing the traces later is being broken by a new generation of kernel-enabled performance analysis tools. Further, these tools are not single-purpose or merely for sections of code that were written to emit debugging data. The Solaris 10 DTrace dynamic tracing facility is a leading example of such a tool.

2.9.3 DTrace

DTrace is a facility that dynamically adds probes to a running system, both in user processes and in the kernel. These probes can be queried via the D programming language to determine an astonishing amount about the kernel, the system state, and process activities. For example, Figure 2.22 follows an application as it executes a system call (`ioctl`) and further shows the functional calls within the kernel as they execute to perform the system call. Lines ending with "U" are executed in user mode, and lines ending in "K" in kernel mode.

Debugging the interactions between user-level and kernel code is nearly impossible without a toolset that understands both sets of code and can instrument the interactions. For that toolset to be truly useful, it must be able to debug any area of a system, including areas that were not written with debugging in mind, and do so without affecting system reliability. This tool must also have a minimum performance impact—ideally it should have no impact when not in use and a proportional impact during use. The DTrace tool meets these requirements and provides a dynamic, safe, low-impact debugging environment.

Until the DTrace framework and tools became available with Solaris 10, kernel debugging was usually shrouded in mystery and accomplished via happenstance and archaic code and tools. For example, CPUs have a breakpoint feature that will halt execution and allow a debugger to examine the state of the system. Then execution can continue until the next breakpoint or termination. This method cannot be used in a multiuser operating system kernel without negatively affecting all of the users on the system. **Profiling**, which periodically samples the instruction pointer to determine which code is being executed, can show statistical trends but not individual activities. Code can be included in the kernel to emit specific data under specific circumstances, but that code

```
# ./all.d 'pgrep xclock' XEventsQueued
dtrace: script './all.d' matched 52377 probes
CPU FUNCTION
  0 -> XEventsQueued                          U
  0   -> _XEventsQueued                       U
  0     -> _X11TransBytesReadable             U
  0     <- _X11TransBytesReadable             U
  0     -> _X11TransSocketBytesReadable U
  0     <- _X11TransSocketBytesreadable U
  0     -> ioctl                              U
  0       -> ioctl                            K
  0         -> getf                           K
  0           -> set_active_fd                K
  0           <- set_active_fd                K
  0         <- getf                           K
  0         -> get_udatamodel                 K
  0         <- get_udatamodel                 K
...
  0         -> releasef                       K
  0           -> clear_active_fd              K
  0           <- clear_active_fd              K
  0           -> cv_broadcast                 K
  0           <- cv_broadcast                 K
  0         <- releasef                       K
  0       <- ioctl                            K
  0     <- ioctl                              U
  0   <- _XEventsQueued                       U
  0 <- XEventsQueued                          U
```

Figure 2.22 Solaris 10 dtrace follows a system call within the kernel.

slows down the kernel and tends not to be included in the part of the kernel where the specific problem being debugged is occurring.

In contrast, DTrace runs on production systems—systems that are running important or critical applications—and causes no harm to the system. It slows activities while enabled, but after execution it resets the system to its pre-debugging state. It is also a broad and deep tool. It can broadly debug everything happening in the system (both at the user and kernel levels and between the user and kernel layers). DTrace can also delve deeply into code, showing individual CPU instructions or kernel subroutine activities.

DTrace is composed of a compiler, a framework, **providers** of **probes** written within that framework, and **consumers** of those probes. DTrace providers create probes. Kernel structures exist to keep track of all probes that the providers have created. The probes are stored in a hash table data structure that is hashed by name and indexed according to unique probe identifiers. When a probe is enabled, a bit of code in the area to be probed is rewritten to call `dtrace_probe(probe identifier)` and then continue with the code's original operation. Different providers create different kinds of probes. For example, a kernel system-call probe works differently from a user-process probe, and that is different from an I/O probe.

DTrace features a compiler that generates a byte code that is run in the kernel. This code is assured to be "safe" by the compiler. For example, no loops are allowed, and only specific kernel state modifications are allowed when specifically requested. Only users with the DTrace "privileges" (or "root" users) are allowed to use DTrace, as it can retrieve private kernel data (and modify data if requested). The generated code runs in the kernel and enables probes. It also enables consumers in user mode and enables communications between the two.

A DTrace consumer is code that is interested in a probe and its results. A consumer requests that the provider create one or more probes. When a probe fires, it emits data that are managed by the kernel. Within the kernel, actions called **enabling control blocks**, or **ECBs**, are performed when probes fire. One probe can cause multiple ECBs to execute if more than one consumer is interested in that probe. Each ECB contains a predicate ("if statement") that can filter out that ECB. Otherwise, the list of actions in the ECB is executed. The most usual action is to capture some bit of data, such as a variable's value at that point of the probe execution. By gathering such data, a complete picture of a user or kernel action can be built. Further, probes firing from both user space and the kernel can show how a user-level action caused kernel-level reactions. Such data are invaluable for performance monitoring and code optimization.

Once the probe consumer terminates, its ECBs are removed. If there are no ECBs consuming a probe, the probe is removed. That involves rewriting the code to remove the dtrace_probe call and put back the original code. Thus, before a probe is created and after it is destroyed, the system is exactly the same, as if no probing occurred.

DTrace takes care to assure that probes do not use too much memory or CPU capacity, which could harm the running system. The buffers used to hold the probe results are monitored for exceeding default and maximum limits. CPU time for probe execution is monitored as well. If limits are exceeded, the consumer is terminated, along with the offending probes. Buffers are allocated per CPU to avoid contention and data loss.

An example of D code and its output shows some of its utility. The following program shows the DTrace code to enable scheduler probes and record the amount of CPU time of each process running with user ID 101 while those probes are enabled (that is, while the program runs):

```
sched:::on-cpu
uid == 101
{
     self->ts = timestamp;
}

sched:::off-cpu
self->ts
{
     @time[execname] = sum(timestamp - self->ts);
     self->ts = 0;
}
```

The output of the program, showing the processes and how much time (in nanoseconds) they spend running on the CPUs, is shown in Figure 2.23.

```
# dtrace -s sched.d
dtrace: script 'sched.d' matched 6 probes
^C
    gnome-settings-d          142354
    gnome-vfs-daemon          158243
    dsdm                      189804
    wnck-applet               200030
    gnome-panel               277864
    clock-applet              374916
    mapping-daemon            385475
    xscreensaver              514177
    metacity                  539281
    Xorg                     2579646
    gnome-terminal           5007269
    mixer_applet2            7388447
    java                    10769137
```

Figure 2.23 Output of the D code.

Because DTrace is part of the open-source Solaris 10 operating system, it is being added to other operating systems when those systems do not have conflicting license agreements. For example, DTrace has been added to Mac OS X 10.5 and FreeBSD and will likely spread further due to its unique capabilities. Other operating systems, especially the Linux derivatives, are adding kernel-tracing functionality as well. Still other operating systems are beginning to include performance and tracing tools fostered by research at various institutions, including the Paradyn project.

2.10 Operating-System Generation

It is possible to design, code, and implement an operating system specifically for one machine at one site. More commonly, however, operating systems are designed to run on any of a class of machines at a variety of sites with a variety of peripheral configurations. The system must then be configured or generated for each specific computer site, a process sometimes known as **system generation (SYSGEN)**.

The operating system is normally distributed on disk, on CD-ROM or DVD-ROM, or as an "ISO" image, which is a file in the format of a CD-ROM or DVD-ROM. To generate a system, we use a special program. This SYSGEN program reads from a given file, or asks the operator of the system for information concerning the specific configuration of the hardware system, or probes the hardware directly to determine what components are there. The following kinds of information must be determined.

- What CPU is to be used? What options (extended instruction sets, floating-point arithmetic, and so on) are installed? For multiple CPU systems, each CPU may be described.

- How will the boot disk be formatted? How many sections, or "partitions," will it be separated into, and what will go into each partition?
- How much memory is available? Some systems will determine this value themselves by referencing memory location after memory location until an "illegal address" fault is generated. This procedure defines the final legal address and hence the amount of available memory.
- What devices are available? The system will need to know how to address each device (the device number), the device interrupt number, the device's type and model, and any special device characteristics.
- What operating-system options are desired, or what parameter values are to be used? These options or values might include how many buffers of which sizes should be used, what type of CPU-scheduling algorithm is desired, what the maximum number of processes to be supported is, and so on.

Once this information is determined, it can be used in several ways. At one extreme, a system administrator can use it to modify a copy of the source code of the operating system. The operating system then is completely compiled. Data declarations, initializations, and constants, along with conditional compilation, produce an output-object version of the operating system that is tailored to the system described.

At a slightly less tailored level, the system description can lead to the creation of tables and the selection of modules from a precompiled library. These modules are linked together to form the generated operating system. Selection allows the library to contain the device drivers for all supported I/O devices, but only those needed are linked into the operating system. Because the system is not recompiled, system generation is faster, but the resulting system may be overly general.

At the other extreme, it is possible to construct a system that is completely table driven. All the code is always part of the system, and selection occurs at execution time, rather than at compile or link time. System generation involves simply creating the appropriate tables to describe the system.

The major differences among these approaches are the size and generality of the generated system and the ease of modifying it as the hardware configuration changes. Consider the cost of modifying the system to support a newly acquired graphics terminal or another disk drive. Balanced against that cost, of course, is the frequency (or infrequency) of such changes.

2.11 System Boot

After an operating system is generated, it must be made available for use by the hardware. But how does the hardware know where the kernel is or how to load that kernel? The procedure of starting a computer by loading the kernel is known as *booting* the system. On most computer systems, a small piece of code known as the **bootstrap program** or **bootstrap loader** locates the kernel, loads it into main memory, and starts its execution. Some computer systems, such as PCs, use a two-step process in which a simple bootstrap loader fetches a more complex boot program from disk, which in turn loads the kernel.

When a CPU receives a reset event—for instance, when it is powered up or rebooted—the instruction register is loaded with a predefined memory location, and execution starts there. At that location is the initial bootstrap program. This program is in the form of **read-only memory (ROM)**, because the RAM is in an unknown state at system startup. ROM is convenient because it needs no initialization and cannot easily be infected by a computer virus.

The bootstrap program can perform a variety of tasks. Usually, one task is to run diagnostics to determine the state of the machine. If the diagnostics pass, the program can continue with the booting steps. It can also initialize all aspects of the system, from CPU registers to device controllers and the contents of main memory. Sooner or later, it starts the operating system.

Some systems—such as cellular phones, PDAs, and game consoles—store the entire operating system in ROM. Storing the operating system in ROM is suitable for small operating systems, simple supporting hardware, and rugged operation. A problem with this approach is that changing the bootstrap code requires changing the ROM hardware chips. Some systems resolve this problem by using **erasable programmable read-only memory (EPROM)**, which is read-only except when explicitly given a command to become writable. All forms of ROM are also known as **firmware**, since their characteristics fall somewhere between those of hardware and those of software. A problem with firmware in general is that executing code there is slower than executing code in RAM. Some systems store the operating system in firmware and copy it to RAM for fast execution. A final issue with firmware is that it is relatively expensive, so usually only small amounts are available.

For large operating systems (including most general-purpose operating systems like Windows, Mac OS X, and UNIX) or for systems that change frequently, the bootstrap loader is stored in firmware, and the operating system is on disk. In this case, the bootstrap runs diagnostics and has a bit of code that can read a single block at a fixed location (say block zero) from disk into memory and execute the code from that boot block. The program stored in the boot block may be sophisticated enough to load the entire operating system into memory and begin its execution. More typically, it is simple code (as it fits in a single disk block) and knows only the address on disk and length of the remainder of the bootstrap program. GRUB is an example of an open-source bootstrap program for Linux systems. All of the disk-bound bootstrap, and the operating system itself, can be easily changed by writing new versions to disk. A disk that has a boot partition (more on that in Section 12.5.1) is called a **boot disk** or **system disk**.

Now that the full bootstrap program has been loaded, it can traverse the file system to find the operating system kernel, load it into memory, and start its execution. It is only at this point that the system is said to be **running**.

2.12 Summary

Operating systems provide a number of services. At the lowest level, system calls allow a running program to make requests from the operating system directly. At a higher level, the command interpreter or shell provides a mechanism for a user to issue a request without writing a program. Commands may come from files during batch-mode execution or directly from a terminal when in an interactive or time-shared mode. System programs are provided to satisfy many common user requests.

The types of requests vary according to level. The system-call level must provide the basic functions, such as process control and file and device manipulation. Higher-level requests, satisfied by the command interpreter or system programs, are translated into a sequence of system calls. System services can be classified into several categories: program control, status requests, and I/O requests. Program errors can be considered implicit requests for service.

Once the system services are defined, the structure of the operating system can be developed. Various tables are needed to record the information that defines the state of the computer system and the status of the system's jobs.

The design of a new operating system is a major task. It is important that the goals of the system be well defined before the design begins. The type of system desired is the foundation for choices among various algorithms and strategies that will be needed.

Since an operating system is large, modularity is important. Designing a system as a sequence of layers or using a microkernel is considered a good technique. The virtual-machine concept takes the layered approach and treats both the kernel of the operating system and the hardware as though they were hardware. Even other operating systems may be loaded on top of this virtual machine.

Throughout the entire operating-system design cycle, we must be careful to separate policy decisions from implementation details (mechanisms). This separation allows maximum flexibility if policy decisions are to be changed later.

Operating systems are now almost always written in a systems-implementation language or in a higher-level language. This feature improves their implementation, maintenance, and portability. To create an operating system for a particular machine configuration, we must perform system generation.

Debugging process and kernel failures can be accomplished through the use of debuggers and other tools that analyze core dumps. Tools such as DTrace analyze production systems to find bottlenecks and understand other system behavior.

For a computer system to begin running, the CPU must initialize and start executing the bootstrap program in firmware. The bootstrap can execute the operating system directly if the operating system is also in the firmware, or it can complete a sequence in which it loads progressively smarter programs from firmware and disk until the operating system itself is loaded into memory and executed.

Exercises

2.1 What are the five major activities of an operating system with regard to file management?

2.2 What are the three major activities of an operating system with regard to memory management?

2.3 Why is a just-in-time compiler useful for executing Java programs?

2.4 The services and functions provided by an operating system can be divided into two main categories. Briefly describe the two categories and discuss how they differ.

2.5 Why is the separation of mechanism and policy desirable?

2.6 Would it be possible for the user to develop a new command interpreter using the system-call interface provided by the operating system?

2.7 What is the purpose of the command interpreter? Why is it usually separate from the kernel?

2.8 What is the main advantage for an operating-system designer of using a virtual-machine architecture? What is the main advantage for a user?

2.9 It is sometimes difficult to achieve a layered approach if two components of the operating system are dependent on each other. Identify a scenario in which it is unclear how to layer two system components that require tight coupling of their functionalities.

2.10 What is the main advantage of the layered approach to system design? What are the disadvantages of using the layered approach?

2.11 What is the relationship between a guest operating system and a host operating system in a system like VMware? What factors need to be considered in choosing the host operating system?

2.12 Describe three general methods for passing parameters to the operating system.

2.13 What is the main advantage of the microkernel approach to system design? How do user programs and system services interact in a microkernel architecture? What are the disadvantages of using the microkernel approach?

2.14 What system calls have to be executed by a command interpreter or shell in order to start a new process?

2.15 What are the two models of interprocess communication? What are the strengths and weaknesses of the two approaches?

2.16 The experimental Synthesis operating system has an assembler incorporated in the kernel. To optimize system-call performance, the kernel assembles routines within kernel space to minimize the path that the system call must take through the kernel. This approach is the antithesis of the layered approach, in which the path through the kernel is extended to make building the operating system easier. Discuss the pros and cons of the Synthesis approach to kernel design and system-performance optimization.

2.17 In what ways is the modular kernel approach similar to the layered approach? In what ways does it differ from the layered approach?

2.18 How could a system be designed to allow a choice of operating systems from which to boot? What would the bootstrap program need to do?

2.19 What are the advantages and disadvantages of using the same system-call interface for manipulating both files and devices?

2.20 Describe how you could obtain a statistical profile of the amount of time spent by a program executing different sections of its code. Discuss the importance of obtaining such a statistical profile.

2.21 Why do some systems store the operating system in firmware, while others store it on disk?

Programming Problems

2.22 In Section 2.3, we described a program that copies the contents of one file to a destination file. This program works by first prompting the user for the name of the source and destination files. Write this program using either the Win32 or POSIX API. Be sure to include all necessary error checking, including ensuring that the source file exists.

Once you have correctly designed and tested the program, if you used a system that supports it, run the program using a utility that traces system calls. Linux systems provide the `ptrace` utility, and Solaris systems use the `truss` or `dtrace` command. On Mac OS X, the `ktrace` facility provides similar functionality. As Windows systems do not provide such features, you will have to trace through the Win32 version of this program using a debugger.

Programming Projects

2.23 Adding a system call to the Linux Kernel.

In this project, you will study the system-call interface provided by the Linux operating system and learn how user programs communicate with the operating system kernel via this interface. Your task is to incorporate a new system call into the kernel, thereby expanding the functionality of the operating system.

Part 1: Getting Started

A user-mode procedure call is performed by passing arguments to the called procedure either on the stack or through registers, saving the current state and the value of the program counter, and jumping to the beginning of the code corresponding to the called procedure. The process continues to have the same privileges as before.

System calls appear as procedure calls to user programs but result in a change in execution context and privileges. In Linux on the Intel 386 architecture, a system call is accomplished by storing the system-call number into the EAX register, storing arguments to the system call in other hardware registers, and executing a trap instruction (which is the

INT 0x80 assembly instruction). After the trap is executed, the system-call number is used to index into a table of code pointers to obtain the starting address for the handler code implementing the system call. The process then jumps to this address, and the privileges of the process are switched from user to kernel mode. With the expanded privileges, the process can now execute kernel code, which may include privileged instructions that cannot be executed in user mode. The kernel code can then carry out the requested services, such as interacting with I/O devices, and can perform process management and other activities that cannot be performed in user mode.

The system call numbers for recent versions of the Linux kernel are listed in `/usr/src/linux-2.x/include/asm-i386/unistd.h`. (For instance, `__NR_close` corresponds to the system call `close()`, which is invoked for closing a file descriptor, and is defined as value 6.) The list of pointers to system-call handlers is typically stored in the file `/usr/src/linux-2.x/arch/i386/kernel/entry.S` under the heading `ENTRY(sys_call_table)`. Notice that `sys_close` is stored at entry number 6 in the table to be consistent with the system-call number defined in the `unistd.h` file. (The keyword `.long` denotes that the entry will occupy the same number of bytes as a data value of type `long`.)

Part 2: Building a New Kernel

Before adding a system call to the kernel, you must familiarize yourself with the task of building the binary for a kernel from its source code and booting the machine with the newly built kernel. This activity comprises the following tasks, some of which depend on the particular installation of the Linux operating system in use.

- Obtain the kernel source code for the Linux distribution. If the source code package has already been installed on your machine, the corresponding files might be available under `/usr/src/linux` or `/usr/src/linux-2.x` (where the suffix corresponds to the kernel version number). If the package has not yet been installed, it can be downloaded from the provider of your Linux distribution or from `http://www.kernel.org`.
- Learn how to configure, compile, and install the kernel binary. This will vary among the different kernel distributions, but some typical commands for building the kernel (after entering the directory where the kernel source code is stored) include:
  - `make xconfig`
  - `make dep`
  - `make bzImage`
- Add a new entry to the set of bootable kernels supported by the system. The Linux operating system typically uses utilities such as `lilo` and `grub` to maintain a list of bootable kernels from which the

user can choose during machine boot-up. If your system supports `lilo`, add an entry to `lilo.conf`, such as:

```
image=/boot/bzImage.mykernel
label=mykernel
root=/dev/hda5
read-only
```

where `/boot/bzImage.mykernel` is the kernel image and `mykernel` is the label associated with the new kernel. This step will allow you to choose the new kernel during the boot-up process. You will then have the option of either booting the new kernel or booting the unmodified kernel if the newly built kernel does not function properly.

Part 3: Extending the Kernel Source

You can now experiment with adding a new file to the set of source files used for compiling the kernel. Typically, the source code is stored in the `/usr/src/linux-2.x/kernel` directory, although that location may differ in your Linux distribution. There are two options for adding the system call. The first is to add the system call to an existing source file in this directory. The second is to create a new file in the source directory and modify `/usr/src/linux-2.x/kernel/Makefile` to include the newly created file in the compilation process. The advantage of the first approach is that when you modify an existing file that is already part of the compilation process, the Makefile need not be modified.

Part 4: Adding a System Call to the Kernel

Now that you are familiar with the various background tasks corresponding to building and booting Linux kernels, you can begin the process of adding a new system call to the Linux kernel. In this project, the system call will have limited functionality; it will simply transition from user mode to kernel mode, print a message that is logged with the kernel messages, and transition back to user mode. We will call this the *helloworld* system call. While it has only limited functionality, it illustrates the system-call mechanism and sheds light on the interaction between user programs and the kernel.

- Create a new file called `helloworld.c` to define your system call. Include the header files `linux/linkage.h` and `linux/kernel.h`. Add the following code to this file:

```
#include <linux/linkage.h>
#include <linux/kernel.h>
asmlinkage int sys_helloworld() {
  printk(KERN_EMERG "hello world!");

  return 1;
}
```

This creates a system call with the name sys_helloworld(). If you choose to add this system call to an existing file in the source directory, all that is necessary is to add the sys_helloworld() function to the file you choose. In the code, asmlinkage is a remnant from the days when Linux used both C++ and C code and is used to indicate that the code is written in C. The printk() function is used to print messages to a kernel log file and therefore may be called only from the kernel. The kernel messages specified in the parameter to printk() are logged in the file /var/log/kernel/warnings. The function prototype for the printk() call is defined in /usr/include/linux/kernel.h.

- Define a new system call number for __NR_helloworld in /usr/src/linux-2.x/include/asm-i386/unistd.h. A user program can use this number to identify the newly added system call. Also be sure to increment the value for __NR_syscalls, which is stored in the same file. This constant tracks the number of system calls currently defined in the kernel.
- Add an entry .long sys_helloworld to the sys_call_table defined in the /usr/src/linux-2.x/arch/i386/kernel/entry.S file. As discussed earlier, the system-call number is used to index into this table to find the position of the handler code for the invoked system call.
- Add your file helloworld.c to the Makefile (if you created a new file for your system call.) Save a copy of your old kernel binary image (in case there are problems with your newly created kernel). You can now build the new kernel, rename it to distinguish it from the unmodified kernel, and add an entry to the loader configuration files (such as lilo.conf). After completing these steps, you can boot either the old kernel or the new kernel that contains your system call.

Part 5: Using the System Call from a User Program

When you boot with the new kernel, it will support the newly defined system call; you now simply need to invoke this system call from a user program. Ordinarily, the standard C library supports an interface for system calls defined for the Linux operating system. As your new system call is not linked into the standard C library, however, invoking your system call will require manual intervention.

As noted earlier, a system call is invoked by storing the appropriate value in a hardware register and performing a trap instruction. Unfortunately, these low-level operations cannot be performed using C language statements and instead require assembly instructions. Fortunately, Linux provides macros for instantiating wrapper functions that contain the appropriate assembly instructions. For instance, the following C program uses the _syscall0() macro to invoke the newly defined system call:

```
#include <linux/errno.h>
#include <sys/syscall.h>
#include <linux/unistd.h>

_syscall0(int, helloworld);

main()
{
  helloworld();
}
```

- The `_syscall0` macro takes two arguments. The first specifies the type of the value returned by the system call; the second is the name of the system call. The name is used to identify the system-call number that is stored in the hardware register before the trap instruction is executed. If your system call requires arguments, then a different macro (such as `_syscall0`, where the suffix indicates the number of arguments) could be used to instantiate the assembly code required for performing the system call.

- Compile and execute the program with the newly built kernel. There should be a message "`hello world!`" in the kernel log file `/var/log/kernel/warnings` to indicate that the system call has executed.

As a next step, consider expanding the functionality of your system call. How would you pass an integer value or a character string to the system call and have it printed into the kernel log file? What are the implications of passing pointers to data stored in the user program's address space as opposed to simply passing an integer value from the user program to the kernel using hardware registers?

Bibliographical Notes

Dijkstra [1968] advocated the layered approach to operating-system design. Brinch-Hansen [1970] was an early proponent of constructing an operating system as a kernel (or nucleus) on which more complete systems can be built.

System instrumentation and dynamic tracing are described in Tamches and Miller [1999]. DTrace is discussed in Cantrill et al. [2004]. The DTrace source code is available at `http://src.opensolaris.org/source/`. Cheung and Loong [1995] explore issues of operating-system structure from microkernel to extensible systems.

MS-DOS, Version 3.1, is described in Microsoft [1986]. Windows NT and Windows 2000 are described by Solomon [1998] and Solomon and Russinovich [2000]. Windows 2003 and Windows XP internals are described in Russinovich and Solomon [2005]. Hart [2005] covers Windows systems programming in detail. BSD UNIX is described in McKusick et al. [1996]. Bovet and Cesati [2006] thoroughly discuss the Linux kernel. Several UNIX systems—including Mach—are treated in detail in Vahalia [1996]. Mac OS X is presented at http://www.apple.com/macosx and in Singh [2007]. Solaris is fully described in McDougall and Mauro [2007].

The first operating system to provide a virtual machine was the CP/67 on an IBM 360/67. The commercially available IBM VM/370 operating system was derived from CP/67. Details regarding Mach, a microkernel-based operating system, can be found in Young et al. [1987]. Kaashoek et al. [1997] present details regarding exokernel operating systems, wherein the architecture separates management issues from protection, thereby giving untrusted software the ability to exercise control over hardware and software resources.

The specifications for the Java language and the Java virtual machine are presented by Gosling et al. [1996] and by Lindholm and Yellin [1999], respectively. The internal workings of the Java virtual machine are fully described by Venners [1998]. Golm et al. [2002] highlight the JX operating system; Back et al. [2000] cover several issues in the design of Java operating systems. More information on Java is available on the Web at http://www.javasoft.com. Details about the implementation of VMware can be found in Sugerman et al. [2001]. Information about the Open Virtual Machine Format can be found at http://www.vmware.com/appliances/learn/ovf.html.

Part Two

Process Management

A *process* can be thought of as a program in execution. A process will need certain resources—such as CPU time, memory, files, and I/O devices—to accomplish its task. These resources are allocated to the process either when it is created or while it is executing.

A process is the unit of work in most systems. Systems consist of a collection of processes: Operating-system processes execute system code, and user processes execute user code. All these processes may execute concurrently.

Although traditionally a process contained only a single *thread* of control as it ran, most modern operating systems now support processes that have multiple threads.

The operating system is responsible for the following activities in connection with process and thread management: the creation and deletion of both user and system processes; the scheduling of processes; and the provision of mechanisms for synchronization, communication, and deadlock handling for processes.

CHAPTER 3

Process Concept

Early computer systems allowed only one program to be executed at a time. This program had complete control of the system and had access to all the system's resources. In contrast, current-day computer systems allow multiple programs to be loaded into memory and executed concurrently. This evolution required firmer control and more compartmentalization of the various programs; and these needs resulted in the notion of a **process**, which is a program in execution. A process is the unit of work in a modern time-sharing system.

The more complex the operating system is, the more it is expected to do on behalf of its users. Although its main concern is the execution of user programs, it also needs to take care of various system tasks that are better left outside the kernel itself. A system therefore consists of a collection of processes: operating-system processes executing system code and user processes executing user code. Potentially, all these processes can execute concurrently, with the CPU (or CPUs) multiplexed among them. By switching the CPU between processes, the operating system can make the computer more productive. In this chapter, you will read about what processes are and how they work.

CHAPTER OBJECTIVES

- To introduce the notion of a process — a program in execution, which forms the basis of all computation.
- To describe the various features of processes, including scheduling, creation and termination, and communication.
- To describe communication in client–server systems.

3.1 Process Concept

A question that arises in discussing operating systems involves what to call all the CPU activities. A batch system executes *jobs,* whereas a time-shared system has *user programs,* or *tasks.* Even on a single-user system such as Microsoft

Windows, a user may be able to run several programs at one time: a word processor, a Web browser, and an e-mail package. And even if the user can execute only one program at a time, the operating system may need to support its own internal programmed activities, such as memory management. In many respects, all these activities are similar, so we call all of them *processes*.

The terms *job* and *process* are used almost interchangeably in this text. Although we personally prefer the term *process*, much of operating-system theory and terminology was developed during a time when the major activity of operating systems was job processing. It would be misleading to avoid the use of commonly accepted terms that include the word *job* (such as *job scheduling*) simply because *process* has superseded *job*.

3.1.1 The Process

Informally, as mentioned earlier, a process is a program in execution. A process is more than the program code, which is sometimes known as the **text section**. It also includes the current activity, as represented by the value of the **program counter** and the contents of the processor's registers. A process generally also includes the process **stack**, which contains temporary data (such as function parameters, return addresses, and local variables), and a **data section**, which contains global variables. A process may also include a **heap**, which is memory that is dynamically allocated during process run time. The structure of a process in memory is shown in Figure 3.1.

We emphasize that a program by itself is not a process; a program is a *passive* entity, such as a file containing a list of instructions stored on disk (often called an **executable file**), whereas a process is an *active* entity, with a program counter specifying the next instruction to execute and a set of associated resources. A program becomes a process when an executable file is loaded into memory. Two common techniques for loading executable files are double-clicking an icon representing the executable file and entering the name of the executable file on the command line (as in `prog.exe` or `a.out`.)

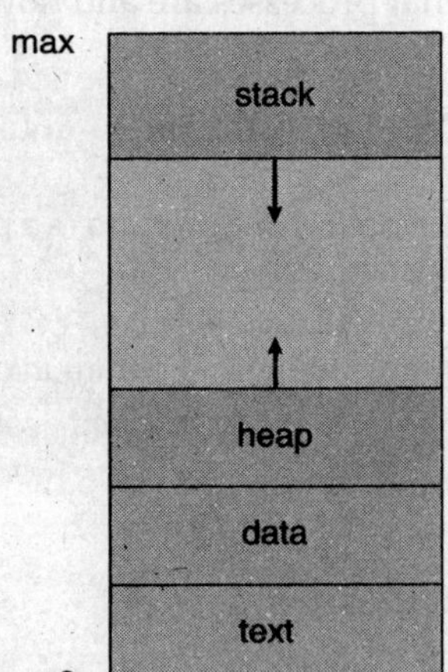

Figure 3.1 Process in memory.

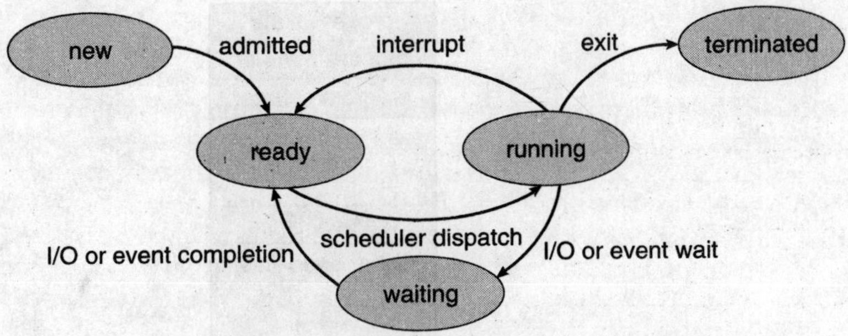

Figure 3.2 Diagram of process state.

Although two processes may be associated with the same program, they are nevertheless considered two separate execution sequences. For instance, several users may be running different copies of the mail program, or the same user may invoke many copies of the Web browser program. Each of these is a separate process; and although the text sections are equivalent, the data, heap, and stack sections vary. It is also common to have a process that spawns many processes as it runs. We discuss such matters in Section 3.4.

3.1.2 Process State

As a process executes, it changes **state**. The state of a process is defined in part by the current activity of that process. Each process may be in one of the following states:

- **New**. The process is being created.
- **Running**. Instructions are being executed.
- **Waiting**. The process is waiting for some event to occur (such as an I/O completion or reception of a signal).
- **Ready**. The process is waiting to be assigned to a processor.
- **Terminated**. The process has finished execution.

These names are arbitrary, and they vary across operating systems. The states that they represent are found on all systems, however. Certain operating systems also more finely delineate process states. It is important to realize that only one process can be *running* on any processor at any instant. Many processes may be *ready* and *waiting*, however. The state diagram corresponding to these states is presented in Figure 3.2.

3.1.3 Process Control Block

Each process is represented in the operating system by a **process control block (PCB)**—also called a *task control block*. A PCB is shown in Figure 3.3. It contains many pieces of information associated with a specific process, including these:

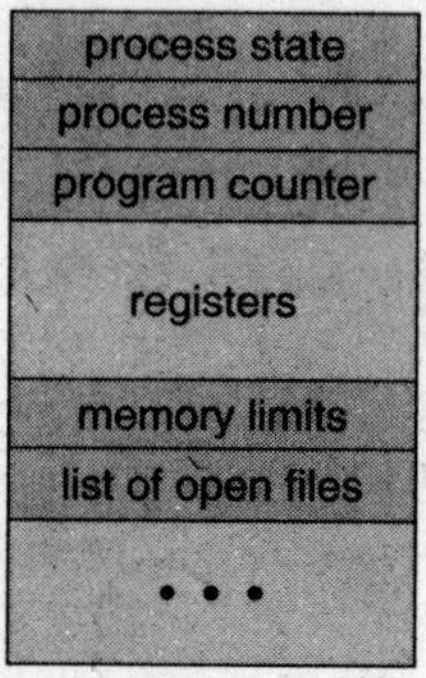

Figure 3.3 Process control block (PCB).

- **Process state**. The state may be new, ready, running, waiting, halted, and so on.
- **Program counter**. The counter indicates the address of the next instruction to be executed for this process.
- **CPU registers**. The registers vary in number and type, depending on the computer architecture. They include accumulators, index registers, stack pointers, and general-purpose registers, plus any condition-code information. Along with the program counter, this state information must be saved when an interrupt occurs, to allow the process to be continued correctly afterward (Figure 3.4).
- **CPU-scheduling information**. This information includes a process priority, pointers to scheduling queues, and any other scheduling parameters. (Chapter 5 describes process scheduling.)
- **Memory-management information**. This information may include such information as the value of the base and limit registers, the page tables, or the segment tables, depending on the memory system used by the operating system (Chapter 8).
- **Accounting information**. This information includes the amount of CPU and real time used, time limits, account numbers, job or process numbers, and so on.
- **I/O status information**. This information includes the list of I/O devices allocated to the process, a list of open files, and so on.

In brief, the PCB simply serves as the repository for any information that may vary from process to process.

3.1.4 Threads

The process model discussed so far has implied that a process is a program that performs a single **thread** of execution. For example, when a process is running a word-processor program, a single thread of instructions is being executed. This single thread of control allows the process to perform only one

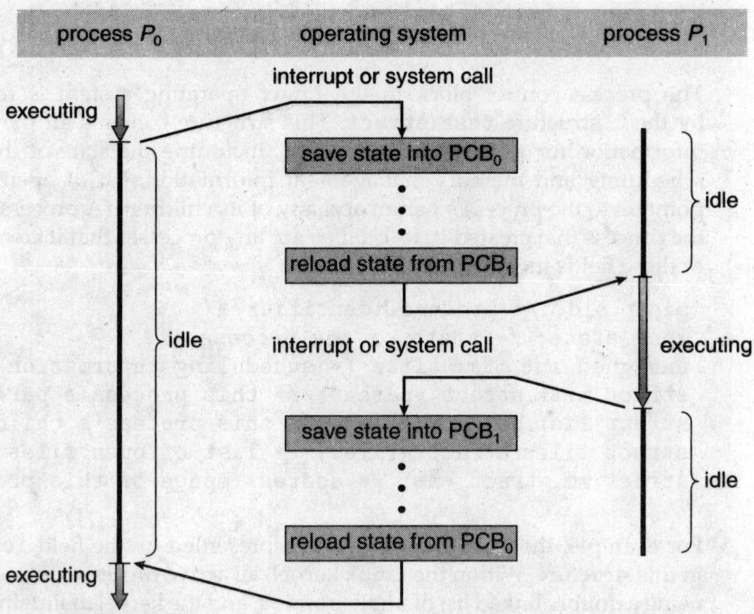

Figure 3.4 Diagram showing CPU switch from process to process.

task at one time. The user cannot simultaneously type in characters and run the spell checker within the same process, for example. Many modern operating systems have extended the process concept to allow a process to have multiple threads of execution and thus to perform more than one task at a time. On a system that supports threads, the PCB is expanded to include information for each thread. Other changes throughout the system are also needed to support threads. Chapter 4 explores multithreaded processes in detail.

3.2 Process Scheduling

The objective of multiprogramming is to have some process running at all times, to maximize CPU utilization. The objective of time sharing is to switch the CPU among processes so frequently that users can interact with each program while it is running. To meet these objectives, the **process scheduler** selects an available process (possibly from a set of several available processes) for program execution on the CPU. For a single-processor system, there will never be more than one running process. If there are more processes, the rest will have to wait until the CPU is free and can be rescheduled.

3.2.1 Scheduling Queues

As processes enter the system, they are put into a **job queue**, which consists of all processes in the system. The processes that are residing in main memory and are ready and waiting to execute are kept on a list called the **ready queue**.

PROCESS REPRESENTATION IN LINUX

The process control block in the Linux operating system is represented by the C structure `task_struct`. This structure contains all the necessary information for representing a process, including the state of the process, scheduling and memory-management information, list of open files, and pointers to the process's parent and any of its children. (A process's *parent* is the process that created it; its *children* are any processes that it creates.) Some of these fields include:

```
pid_t pid; /* process identifier */
long state; /* state of the process */
unsigned int time_slice /* scheduling information */
struct task_struct *parent; /* this process's parent */
struct list_head children; /* this process's children */
struct files_struct *files; /* list of open files */
struct mm_struct *mm; /* address space of this process */
```

For example, the state of a process is represented by the field `long state` in this structure. Within the Linux kernel, all active processes are represented using a doubly linked list of `task_struct`, and the kernel maintains a pointer —`current`—to the process currently executing on the system. This is shown in Figure 3.5.

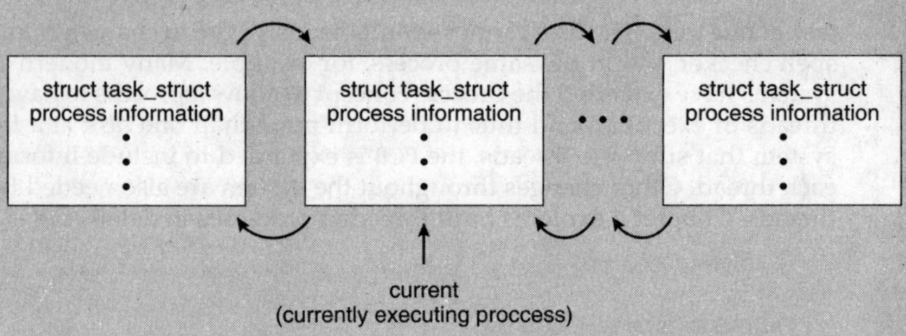

Figure 3.5 Active processes in Linux.

As an illustration of how the kernel might manipulate one of the fields in the `task_struct` for a specified process, let's assume the system would like to change the state of the process currently running to the value `new_state`. If `current` is a pointer to the process currently executing, its state is changed with the following:

```
current->state = new_state;
```

This queue is generally stored as a linked list. A ready-queue header contains pointers to the first and final PCBs in the list. Each PCB includes a pointer field that points to the next PCB in the ready queue.

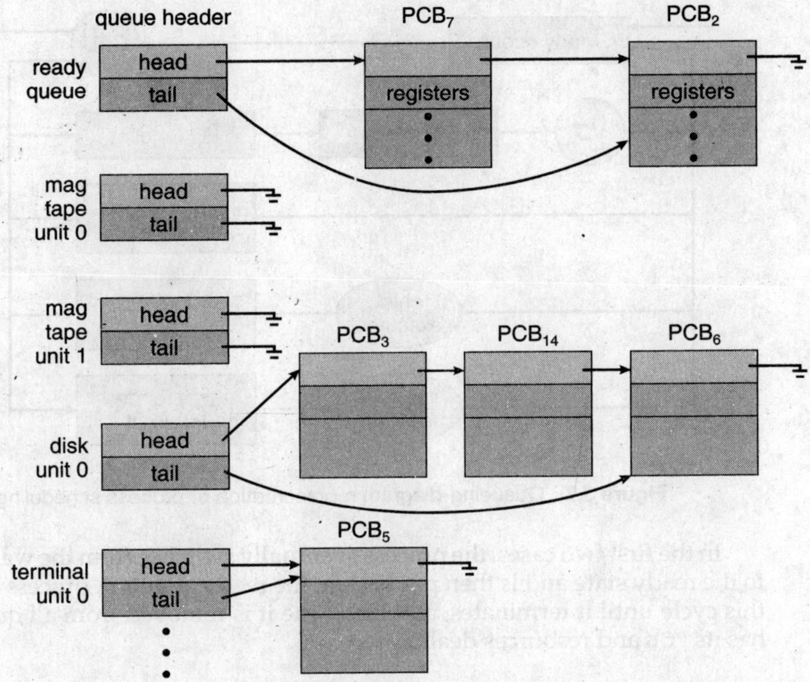

Figure 3.6 The ready queue and various I/O device queues.

The system also includes other queues. When a process is allocated the CPU, it executes for a while and eventually quits, is interrupted, or waits for the occurrence of a particular event, such as the completion of an I/O request. Suppose the process makes an I/O request to a shared device, such as a disk. Since there are many processes in the system, the disk may be busy with the I/O request of some other process. The process therefore may have to wait for the disk. The list of processes waiting for a particular I/O device is called a **device queue**. Each device has its own device queue (Figure 3.6).

A common representation of process scheduling is a **queueing diagram**, such as that in Figure 3.7. Each rectangular box represents a queue. Two types of queues are present: the ready queue and a set of device queues. The circles represent the resources that serve the queues, and the arrows indicate the flow of processes in the system.

A new process is initially put in the ready queue. It waits there until it is selected for execution, or is **dispatched**. Once the process is allocated the CPU and is executing, one of several events could occur:

- The process could issue an I/O request and then be placed in an I/O queue.
- The process could create a new subprocess and wait for the subprocess's termination.
- The process could be removed forcibly from the CPU, as a result of an interrupt, and be put back in the ready queue.

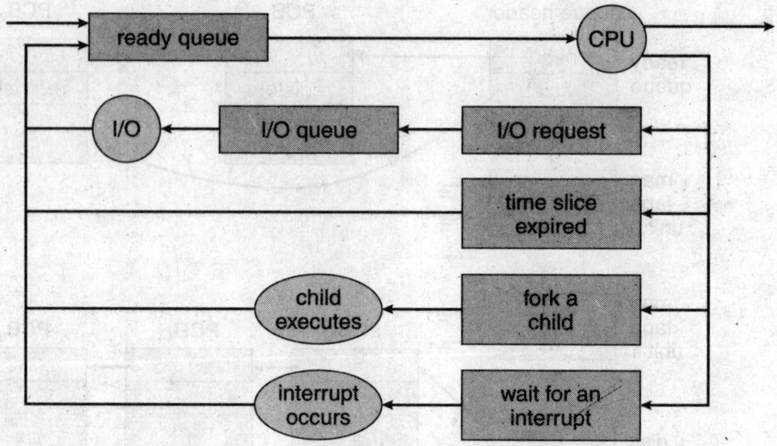

Figure 3.7 Queueing-diagram representation of process scheduling.

In the first two cases, the process eventually switches from the waiting state to the ready state and is then put back in the ready queue. A process continues this cycle until it terminates, at which time it is removed from all queues and has its PCB and resources deallocated.

3.2.2 Schedulers

A process migrates among the various scheduling queues throughout its lifetime. The operating system must select, for scheduling purposes, processes from these queues in some fashion. The selection process is carried out by the appropriate **scheduler**.

Often, in a batch system, more processes are submitted than can be executed immediately. These processes are spooled to a mass-storage device (typically a disk), where they are kept for later execution. The **long-term scheduler**, or **job scheduler**, selects processes from this pool and loads them into memory for execution. The **short-term scheduler**, or **CPU scheduler**, selects from among the processes that are ready to execute and allocates the CPU to one of them.

The primary distinction between these two schedulers lies in frequency of execution. The short-term scheduler must select a new process for the CPU frequently. A process may execute for only a few milliseconds before waiting for an I/O request. Often, the short-term scheduler executes at least once every 100 milliseconds. Because of the short time between executions, the short-term scheduler must be fast. If it takes 10 milliseconds to decide to execute a process for 100 milliseconds, then 10/(100 + 10) = 9 percent of the CPU is being used (wasted) simply for scheduling the work.

The long-term scheduler executes much less frequently; minutes may separate the creation of one new process and the next. The long-term scheduler controls the **degree of multiprogramming** (the number of processes in memory). If the degree of multiprogramming is stable, then the average rate of process creation must be equal to the average departure rate of processes leaving the system. Thus, the long-term scheduler may need to be invoked only when a process leaves the system. Because of the longer interval between executions, the long-term scheduler can afford to take more time to decide which process should be selected for execution.

It is important that the long-term scheduler make a careful selection. In general, most processes can be described as either I/O bound or CPU bound. An **I/O-bound process** is one that spends more of its time doing I/O than it spends doing computations. A **CPU-bound process**, in contrast, generates I/O requests infrequently, using more of its time doing computations. It is important that the long-term scheduler select a good **process mix** of I/O-bound and CPU-bound processes. If all processes are I/O bound, the ready queue will almost always be empty, and the short-term scheduler will have little to do. If all processes are CPU bound, the I/O waiting queue will almost always be empty, devices will go unused, and again the system will be unbalanced. The system with the best performance will thus have a combination of CPU-bound and I/O-bound processes.

On some systems, the long-term scheduler may be absent or minimal. For example, time-sharing systems such as UNIX and Microsoft Windows systems often have no long-term scheduler but simply put every new process in memory for the short-term scheduler. The stability of these systems depends either on a physical limitation (such as the number of available terminals) or on the self-adjusting nature of human users. If performance declines to unacceptable levels on a multiuser system, some users will simply quit.

Some operating systems, such as time-sharing systems, may introduce an additional, intermediate level of scheduling. This **medium-term scheduler** is diagrammed in Figure 3.8. The key idea behind a medium-term scheduler is that sometimes it can be advantageous to remove processes from memory (and from active contention for the CPU) and thus reduce the degree of multiprogramming. Later, the process can be reintroduced into memory, and its execution can be continued where it left off. This scheme is called **swapping**. The process is swapped out, and is later swapped in, by the medium-term scheduler. Swapping may be necessary to improve the process mix or because a change in memory requirements has overcommitted available memory, requiring memory to be freed up. Swapping is discussed in Chapter 8.

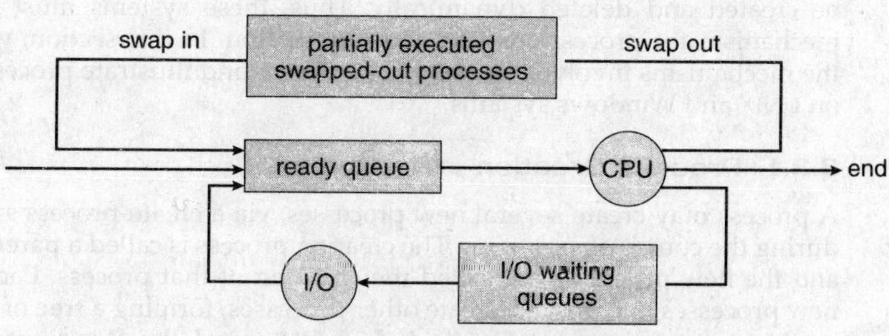

Figure 3.8 Addition of medium-term scheduling to the queueing diagram.

3.2.3 Context Switch

As mentioned in Section 1.2.1, interrupts cause the operating system to change a CPU from its current task and to run a kernel routine. Such operations happen frequently on general-purpose systems. When an interrupt occurs, the system needs to save the current **context** of the process running on the CPU so that it can restore that context when its processing is done, essentially suspending the process and then resuming it. The context is represented in the PCB of the process; it includes the value of the CPU registers, the process state (see Figure 3.2), and memory-management information. Generically, we perform a **state save** of the current state of the CPU, be it in kernel or user mode, and then a **state restore** to resume operations.

Switching the CPU to another process requires performing a state save of the current process and a state restore of a different process. This task is known as a **context switch**. When a context switch occurs, the kernel saves the context of the old process in its PCB and loads the saved context of the new process scheduled to run. Context-switch time is pure overhead, because the system does no useful work while switching. Its speed varies from machine to machine, depending on the memory speed, the number of registers that must be copied, and the existence of special instructions (such as a single instruction to load or store all registers). Typical speeds are a few milliseconds.

Context-switch times are highly dependent on hardware support. For instance, some processors (such as the Sun UltraSPARC) provide multiple sets of registers. A context switch here simply requires changing the pointer to the current register set. Of course, if there are more active processes than there are register sets, the system resorts to copying register data to and from memory, as before. Also, the more complex the operating system, the more work must be done during a context switch. As we will see in Chapter 8, advanced memory-management techniques may require extra data to be switched with each context. For instance, the address space of the current process must be preserved as the space of the next task is prepared for use. How the address space is preserved, and what amount of work is needed to preserve it, depend on the memory-management method of the operating system.

3.3 Operations on Processes

The processes in most systems can execute concurrently, and they may be created and deleted dynamically. Thus, these systems must provide a mechanism for process creation and termination. In this section, we explore the mechanisms involved in creating processes and illustrate process creation on UNIX and Windows systems.

3.3.1 Process Creation

A process may create several new processes, via a create-process system call, during the course of execution. The creating process is called a **parent** process, and the new processes are called the **children** of that process. Each of these new processes may in turn create other processes, forming a **tree** of processes.

Most operating systems (including UNIX and the Windows family of operating systems) identify processes according to a unique **process identifier** (or **pid**), which is typically an integer number. Figure 3.9 illustrates a typical process tree for the Solaris operating system, showing the name of each process and its pid. In Solaris, the process at the top of the tree is the `sched` process, with pid of 0. The `sched` process creates several children processes—including `pageout` and `fsflush`. These processes are responsible for managing memory and file systems. The `sched` process also creates the `init` process, which serves as the root parent process for all user processes. In Figure 3.9, we see two children of `init`—`inetd` and `dtlogin`. `inetd` is responsible for networking services such as `telnet` and `ftp`; `dtlogin` is the process representing a user login screen. When a user logs in, `dtlogin` creates an X-windows session (`Xsession`), which in turns creates the `sdt_shel` process. Below `sdt_shel`, a user's command-line shell—the C-shell or `csh`—is created. In this command-line interface, the user can then invoke various child processes, such as the `ls` and `cat` commands. We also see a `csh` process with pid of 7778 representing a user who has logged onto the system using `telnet`. This user has started the Netscape browser (pid of 7785) and the emacs editor (pid of 8105).

On UNIX, we can obtain a listing of processes by using the ps command. For example, the command `ps -el` will list complete information for all processes currently active in the system. It is easy to construct a process tree similar to what is shown in Figure 3.9 by recursively tracing parent processes all the way to the `init` process.

In general, a process will need certain resources (CPU time, memory, files, I/O devices) to accomplish its task. When a process creates a subprocess, that

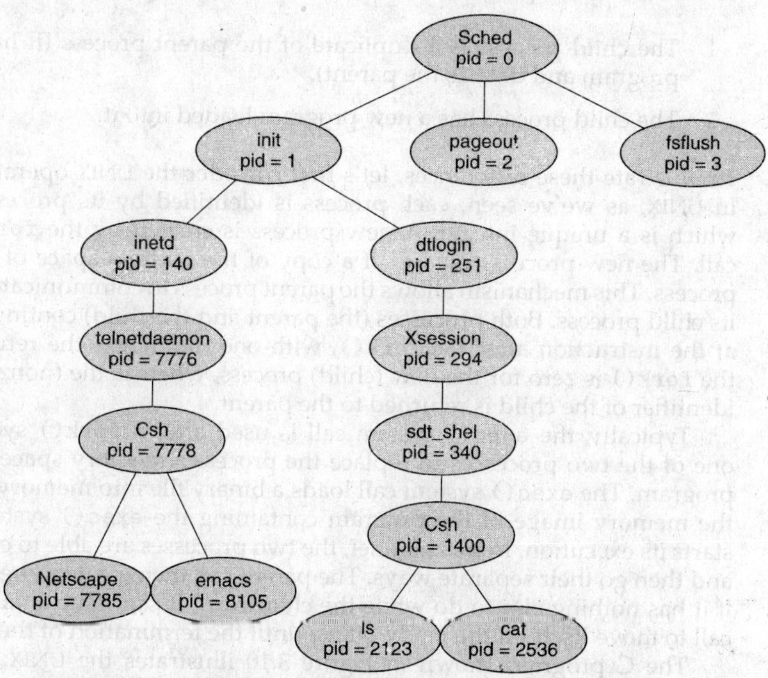

Figure 3.9 A tree of processes on a typical Solaris system.

subprocess may be able to obtain its resources directly from the operating system, or it may be constrained to a subset of the resources of the parent process. The parent may have to partition its resources among its children, or it may be able to share some resources (such as memory or files) among several of its children. Restricting a child process to a subset of the parent's resources prevents any process from overloading the system by creating too many subprocesses.

In addition to the various physical and logical resources that a process obtains when it is created, initialization data (input) may be passed along by the parent process to the child process. For example, consider a process whose function is to display the contents of a file—say, *img.jpg*—on the screen of a terminal. When it is created, it will get, as an input from its parent process, the name of the file *img.jpg*, and it will use that file name, open the file, and write the contents out. It may also get the name of the output device. Some operating systems pass resources to child processes. On such a system, the new process may get two open files, *img.jpg* and the terminal device, and may simply transfer the datum between the two.

When a process creates a new process, two possibilities exist in terms of execution:

1. The parent continues to execute concurrently with its children.
2. The parent waits until some or all of its children have terminated.

There are also two possibilities in terms of the address space of the new process:

1. The child process is a duplicate of the parent process (it has the same program and data as the parent).
2. The child process has a new program loaded into it.

To illustrate these differences, let's first consider the UNIX operating system. In UNIX, as we've seen, each process is identified by its process identifier, which is a unique integer. A new process is created by the `fork()` system call. The new process consists of a copy of the address space of the original process. This mechanism allows the parent process to communicate easily with its child process. Both processes (the parent and the child) continue execution at the instruction after the `fork()`, with one difference: the return code for the `fork()` is zero for the new (child) process, whereas the (nonzero) process identifier of the child is returned to the parent.

Typically, the `exec()` system call is used after a `fork()` system call by one of the two processes to replace the process's memory space with a new program. The `exec()` system call loads a binary file into memory (destroying the memory image of the program containing the `exec()` system call) and starts its execution. In this manner, the two processes are able to communicate and then go their separate ways. The parent can then create more children; or, if it has nothing else to do while the child runs, it can issue a `wait()` system call to move itself off the ready queue until the termination of the child.

The C program shown in Figure 3.10 illustrates the UNIX system calls previously described. We now have two different processes running copies of the same program. The only difference is that the value of `pid` (the process

```
#include <sys/types.h>
#include <stdio.h>
#include <unistd.h>

int main()
{
pid_t pid;

   /* fork a child process */
   pid = fork();

   if (pid < 0) { /* error occurred */
      fprintf(stderr, "Fork Failed");
      return 1;
   }
   else if (pid == 0) { /* child process */
      execlp("/bin/ls","ls",NULL);
   }
   else { /* parent process */
      /* parent will wait for the child to complete */
      wait(NULL);
      printf("Child Complete");
   }

   return 0;
}
```

Figure 3.10 Creating a separate process using the UNIX `fork()` system call.

identifier) for the child process is zero, while that for the parent is an integer value greater than zero (in fact, it is the actual pid of the child process). The child process inherits privileges and scheduling attributes from the parent, as well certain resources, such as open files. The child process then overlays its address space with the UNIX command `/bin/ls` (used to get a directory listing) using the `execlp()` system call (`execlp()` is a version of the `exec()` system call). The parent waits for the child process to complete with the `wait()` system call. When the child process completes (by either implicitly or explicitly invoking `exit()`) the parent process resumes from the call to `wait()`, where it completes using the `exit()` system call. This is also illustrated in Figure 3.11.

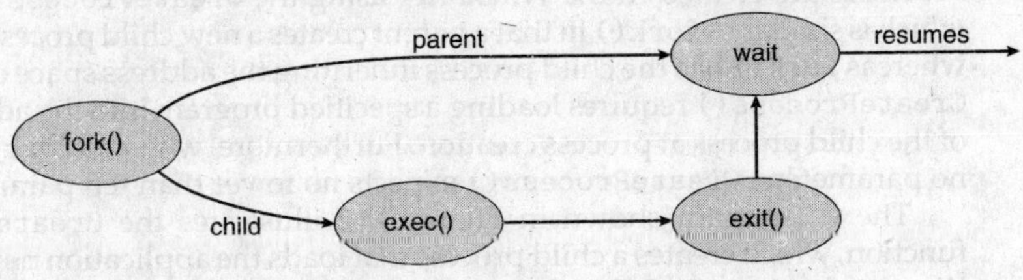

Figure 3.11 Process creation using `fork()` system call.

```
#include <stdio.h>
#include <windows.h>

int main(VOID)
{
STARTUPINFO si;
PROCESS_INFORMATION pi;

   // allocate memory
   ZeroMemory(&si, sizeof(si));
   si.cb = sizeof(si);
   ZeroMemory(&pi, sizeof(pi));

   // create child process
   if (!CreateProcess(NULL, // use command line
     "C:\\WINDOWS\\system32\\mspaint.exe", // command line
     NULL, // don't inherit process handle
     NULL, // don't inherit thread handle
     FALSE, // disable handle inheritance
     0, // no creation flags
     NULL, // use parent's environment block
     NULL, // use parent's existing directory
     &si,
     &pi))
   {
      fprintf(stderr, "Create Process Failed");
      return -1;
   }
   // parent will wait for the child to complete
   WaitForSingleObject(pi.hProcess, INFINITE);
   printf("Child Complete");

   // close handles
   CloseHandle(pi.hProcess);
   CloseHandle(pi.hThread);
}
```

Figure 3.12 Creating a separate process using the Win32 API.

As an alternative example, we next consider process creation in Windows. Processes are created in the Win32 API using the `CreateProcess()` function, which is similar to `fork()` in that a parent creates a new child process. However, whereas `fork()` has the child process inheriting the address space of its parent, `CreateProcess()` requires loading a specified program into the address space of the child process at process creation. Furthermore, whereas `fork()` is passed no parameters, `CreateProcess()` expects no fewer than ten parameters.

The C program shown in Figure 3.12 illustrates the `CreateProcess()` function, which creates a child process that loads the application `mspaint.exe`. We opt for many of the default values of the ten parameters passed to `CreateProcess()`. Readers interested in pursuing the details of process creation and management in the Win32 API are encouraged to consult the bibliographical notes at the end of this chapter.

Two parameters passed to `CreateProcess()` are instances of the STARTUPINFO and PROCESS_INFORMATION structures. STARTUPINFO specifies many properties of the new process, such as window size and appearance and handles to standard input and output files. The PROCESS_INFORMATION structure contains a handle and the identifiers to the newly created process and its thread. We invoke the `ZeroMemory()` function to allocate memory for each of these structures before proceeding with `CreateProcess()`.

The first two parameters passed to `CreateProcess()` are the application name and command-line parameters. If the application name is NULL (as it is in this case), the command-line parameter specifies the application to load. In this instance, we are loading the Microsoft Windows *mspaint.exe* application. Beyond these two initial parameters, we use the default parameters for inheriting process and thread handles as well as specifying no creation flags. We also use the parent's existing environment block and starting directory. Last, we provide two pointers to the STARTUPINFO and PROCESS_INFORMATION structures created at the beginning of the program. In Figure 3.10, the parent process waits for the child to complete by invoking the `wait()` system call. The equivalent of this in Win32 is `WaitForSingleObject()`, which is passed a handle of the child process—`pi.hProcess`—and waits for this process to complete. Once the child process exits, control returns from the `WaitForSingleObject()` function in the parent process.

3.3.2 Process Termination

A process terminates when it finishes executing its final statement and asks the operating system to delete it by using the `exit()` system call. At that point, the process may return a status value (typically an integer) to its parent process (via the `wait()` system call). All the resources of the process—including physical and virtual memory, open files, and I/O buffers—are deallocated by the operating system.

Termination can occur in other circumstances as well. A process can cause the termination of another process via an appropriate system call (for example, `TerminateProcess()` in Win32). Usually, such a system call can be invoked only by the parent of the process that is to be terminated. Otherwise, users could arbitrarily kill each other's jobs. Note that a parent needs to know the identities of its children. Thus, when one process creates a new process, the identity of the newly created process is passed to the parent.

A parent may terminate the execution of one of its children for a variety of reasons, such as these:

- The child has exceeded its usage of some of the resources that it has been allocated. (To determine whether this has occurred, the parent must have a mechanism to inspect the state of its children.)
- The task assigned to the child is no longer required.
- The parent is exiting, and the operating system does not allow a child to continue if its parent terminates.

Some systems, including VMS, do not allow a child to exist if its parent has terminated. In such systems, if a process terminates (either normally or abnormally), then all its children must also be terminated. This phenomenon, referred to as **cascading termination**, is normally initiated by the operating system.

To illustrate process execution and termination, consider that, in UNIX, we can terminate a process by using the `exit()` system call; its parent process may wait for the termination of a child process by using the `wait()` system call. The `wait()` system call returns the process identifier of a terminated child so that the parent can tell which of its children has terminated. If the parent terminates, however, all its children have assigned as their new parent the `init` process. Thus, the children still have a parent to collect their status and execution statistics.

3.4 Interprocess Communication

Processes executing concurrently in the operating system may be either independent processes or cooperating processes. A process is **independent** if it cannot affect or be affected by the other processes executing in the system. Any process that does not share data with any other process is independent. A process is **cooperating** if it can affect or be affected by the other processes executing in the system. Clearly, any process that shares data with other processes is a cooperating process.

There are several reasons for providing an environment that allows process cooperation:

- **Information sharing**. Since several users may be interested in the same piece of information (for instance, a shared file), we must provide an environment to allow concurrent access to such information.
- **Computation speedup**. If we want a particular task to run faster, we must break it into subtasks, each of which will be executing in parallel with the others. Notice that such a speedup can be achieved only if the computer has multiple processing elements (such as CPUs or I/O channels).
- **Modularity**. We may want to construct the system in a modular fashion, dividing the system functions into separate processes or threads, as we discussed in Chapter 2.
- **Convenience**. Even an individual user may work on many tasks at the same time. For instance, a user may be editing, printing, and compiling in parallel.

Cooperating processes require an **interprocess communication** (IPC) mechanism that will allow them to exchange data and information. There are two fundamental models of interprocess communication: (1) **shared memory** and (2) **message passing**. In the shared-memory model, a region of memory that is shared by cooperating processes is established. Processes can then exchange information by reading and writing data to the shared region. In the message-passing model, communication takes place by means of messages exchanged

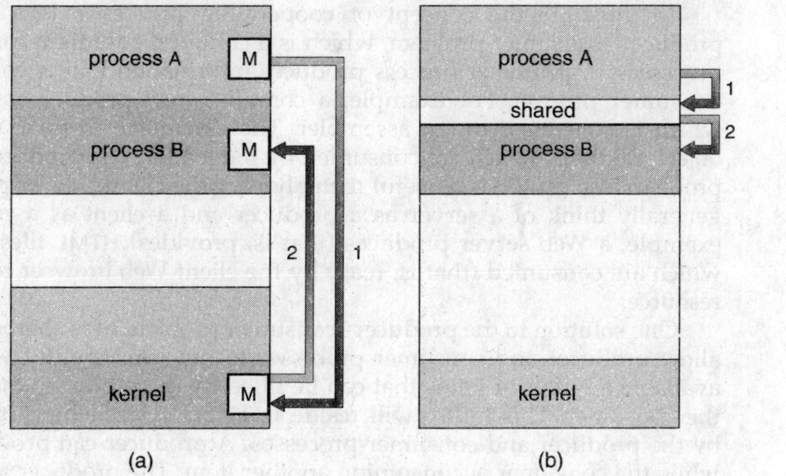

Figure 3.13 Communications models. (a) Message passing. (b) Shared memory.

between the cooperating processes. The two communications models are contrasted in Figure 3.13.

Both of the models just discussed are common in operating systems, and many systems implement both. Message passing is useful for exchanging smaller amounts of data, because no conflicts need be avoided. Message passing is also easier to implement than is shared memory for intercomputer communication. Shared memory allows maximum speed and convenience of communication. Shared memory is faster than message passing, as message-passing systems are typically implemented using system calls and thus require the more time-consuming task of kernel intervention. In contrast, in shared-memory systems, system calls are required only to establish shared-memory regions. Once shared memory is established, all accesses are treated as routine memory accesses, and no assistance from the kernel is required. In the remainder of this section, we explore each of these IPC models in more detail.

3.4.1 Shared-Memory Systems

Interprocess communication using shared memory requires communicating processes to establish a region of shared memory. Typically, a shared-memory region resides in the address space of the process creating the shared-memory segment. Other processes that wish to communicate using this shared-memory segment must attach it to their address space. Recall that, normally, the operating system tries to prevent one process from accessing another process's memory. Shared memory requires that two or more processes agree to remove this restriction. They can then exchange information by reading and writing data in the shared areas. The form of the data and the location are determined by these processes and are not under the operating system's control. The processes are also responsible for ensuring that they are not writing to the same location simultaneously.

To illustrate the concept of cooperating processes, let's consider the producer–consumer problem, which is a common paradigm for cooperating processes. A **producer** process produces information that is consumed by a **consumer** process. For example, a compiler may produce assembly code, which is consumed by an assembler. The assembler, in turn, may produce object modules, which are consumed by the loader. The producer–consumer problem also provides a useful metaphor for the client–server paradigm. We generally think of a server as a producer and a client as a consumer. For example, a Web server produces (that is, provides) HTML files and images, which are consumed (that is, read) by the client Web browser requesting the resource.

One solution to the producer–consumer problem uses shared memory. To allow producer and consumer processes to run concurrently, we must have available a buffer of items that can be filled by the producer and emptied by the consumer. This buffer will reside in a region of memory that is shared by the producer and consumer processes. A producer can produce one item while the consumer is consuming another item. The producer and consumer must be synchronized, so that the consumer does not try to consume an item that has not yet been produced.

Two types of buffers can be used. The **unbounded buffer** places no practical limit on the size of the buffer. The consumer may have to wait for new items, but the producer can always produce new items. The **bounded buffer** assumes a fixed buffer size. In this case, the consumer must wait if the buffer is empty, and the producer must wait if the buffer is full.

Let's look more closely at how the bounded buffer can be used to enable processes to share memory. The following variables reside in a region of memory shared by the producer and consumer processes:

```
#define BUFFER_SIZE 10

typedef struct {
    . . .
}item;

item buffer[BUFFER_SIZE];
int in = 0;
int out = 0;
```

The shared buffer is implemented as a circular array with two logical pointers: `in` and `out`. The variable `in` points to the next free position in the buffer; `out` points to the first full position in the buffer. The buffer is empty when `in == out`; the buffer is full when ((`in` + 1) % BUFFER_SIZE) == `out`.

The code for the producer and consumer processes is shown in Figures 3.14 and 3.15, respectively. The producer process has a local variable `nextProduced` in which the new item to be produced is stored. The consumer process has a local variable `nextConsumed` in which the item to be consumed is stored.

This scheme allows at most BUFFER_SIZE – 1 items in the buffer at the same time. We leave it as an exercise for you to provide a solution where BUFFER_SIZE items can be in the buffer at the same time. In Section 3.5.1, we illustrate the POSIX API for shared memory.

```
item nextProduced;

while (true) {
        /* produce an item in nextProduced */
        while (((in + 1) % BUFFER_SIZE) == out)
          ; /* do nothing */
        buffer[in] = nextProduced;
        in = (in + 1) % BUFFER_SIZE;
}
```

Figure 3.14 The producer process.

One issue this illustration does not address concerns the situation in which both the producer process and the consumer process attempt to access the shared buffer concurrently. In Chapter 6, we discuss how synchronization among cooperating processes can be implemented effectively in a shared-memory environment.

3.4.2 Message-Passing Systems

In Section 3.4.1, we showed how cooperating processes can communicate in a shared-memory environment. The scheme requires that these processes share a region of memory and that the code for accessing and manipulating the shared memory be written explicitly by the application programmer. Another way to achieve the same effect is for the operating system to provide the means for cooperating processes to communicate with each other via a message-passing facility.

Message passing provides a mechanism to allow processes to communicate and to synchronize their actions without sharing the same address space and is particularly useful in a distributed environment, where the communicating processes may reside on different computers connected by a network. For example, a **chat** program used on the World Wide Web could be designed so that chat participants communicate with one another by exchanging messages.

A message-passing facility provides at least two operations: send(message) and receive(message). Messages sent by a process can be of either fixed or variable size. If only fixed-sized messages can be sent, the system-level implementation is straightforward. This restriction, however, makes the task

```
item nextConsumed;

while (true) {
        while (in == out)
             ; // do nothing

        nextConsumed = buffer[out];
        out = (out + 1) % BUFFER_SIZE;
        /* consume the item in nextConsumed */
}
```

Figure 3.15 The consumer process.

of programming more difficult. Conversely, variable-sized messages require a more complex system-level implementation, but the programming task becomes simpler. This is a common kind of tradeoff seen throughout operating-system design.

If processes *P* and *Q* want to communicate, they must send messages to and receive messages from each other; a **communication link** must exist between them. This link can be implemented in a variety of ways. We are concerned here not with the link's physical implementation (such as shared memory, hardware bus, or network, which are covered in Chapter 16) but rather with its logical implementation. Here are several methods for logically implementing a link and the `send()/receive()` operations:

- Direct or indirect communication
- Synchronous or asynchronous communication
- Automatic or explicit buffering

We look at issues related to each of these features next.

3.4.2.1 Naming

Processes that want to communicate must have a way to refer to each other. They can use either direct or indirect communication.

Under **direct communication**, each process that wants to communicate must explicitly name the recipient or sender of the communication. In this scheme, the `send()` and `receive()` primitives are defined as:

- `send(P, message)`—Send a `message` to process `P`.
- `receive(Q, message)`—Receive a `message` from process `Q`.

A communication link in this scheme has the following properties:

- A link is established automatically between every pair of processes that want to communicate. The processes need to know only each other's identity to communicate.
- A link is associated with exactly two processes.
- Between each pair of processes, there exists exactly one link.

This scheme exhibits *symmetry* in addressing; that is, both the sender process and the receiver process must name the other to communicate. A variant of this scheme employs *asymmetry* in addressing. Here, only the sender names the recipient; the recipient is not required to name the sender. In this scheme, the `send()` and `receive()` primitives are defined as follows:

- `send(P, message)`—Send a `message` to process `P`.
- `receive(id, message)`—Receive a `message` from any process; the variable *id* is set to the name of the process with which communication has taken place.

The disadvantage in both of these schemes (symmetric and asymmetric) is the limited modularity of the resulting process definitions. Changing the identifier of a process may necessitate examining all other process definitions. All references to the old identifier must be found, so that they can be modified to the new identifier. In general, any such **hard-coding** techniques, where identifiers must be explicitly stated, are less desirable than techniques involving indirection, as described next.

With **indirect communication**, the messages are sent to and received from **mailboxes**, or **ports**. A mailbox can be viewed abstractly as an object into which messages can be placed by processes and from which messages can be removed. Each mailbox has a unique identification. For example, POSIX message queues use an integer value to identify a mailbox. In this scheme, a process can communicate with some other process via a number of different mailboxes. Two processes can communicate only if the processes have a shared mailbox, however. The `send()` and `receive()` primitives are defined as follows:

- `send(A, message)`—Send a `message` to mailbox `A`.
- `receive(A, message)`—Receive a `message` from mailbox `A`.

In this scheme, a communication link has the following properties:

- A link is established between a pair of processes only if both members of the pair have a shared mailbox.
- A link may be associated with more than two processes.
- Between each pair of communicating processes, there may be a number of different links, with each link corresponding to one mailbox.

Now suppose that processes P_1, P_2, and P_3 all share mailbox A. Process P_1 sends a message to A, while both P_2 and P_3 execute a `receive()` from A. Which process will receive the message sent by P_1? The answer depends on which of the following methods we choose:

- Allow a link to be associated with two processes at most.
- Allow at most one process at a time to execute a `receive()` operation.
- Allow the system to select arbitrarily which process will receive the message (that is, either P_2 or P_3, but not both, will receive the message). The system also may define an algorithm for selecting which process will receive the message (that is, *round robin*, where processes take turns receiving messages). The system may identify the receiver to the sender.

A mailbox may be owned either by a process or by the operating system. If the mailbox is owned by a process (that is, the mailbox is part of the address space of the process), then we distinguish between the owner (which can only receive messages through this mailbox) and the user (which can only send messages to the mailbox). Since each mailbox has a unique owner, there can be no confusion about which process should receive a message sent to this mailbox. When a process that owns a mailbox terminates, the mailbox disappears. Any process that subsequently sends a message to this mailbox must be notified that the mailbox no longer exists.

In contrast, a mailbox that is owned by the operating system has an existence of its own. It is independent and is not attached to any particular process. The operating system then must provide a mechanism that allows a process to do the following:

- Create a new mailbox.
- Send and receive messages through the mailbox.
- Delete a mailbox.

The process that creates a new mailbox is that mailbox's owner by default. Initially, the owner is the only process that can receive messages through this mailbox. However, the ownership and receiving privilege may be passed to other processes through appropriate system calls. Of course, this provision could result in multiple receivers for each mailbox.

3.4.2.2 Synchronization

Communication between processes takes place through calls to `send()` and `receive()` primitives. There are different design options for implementing each primitive. Message passing may be either **blocking** or **nonblocking**—also known as **synchronous** and **asynchronous**.

- **Blocking send**. The sending process is blocked until the message is received by the receiving process or by the mailbox.
- **Nonblocking send**. The sending process sends the message and resumes operation.
- **Blocking receive**. The receiver blocks until a message is available.
- **Nonblocking receive**. The receiver retrieves either a valid message or a null.

Different combinations of `send()` and `receive()` are possible. When both `send()` and `receive()` are blocking, we have a **rendezvous** between the sender and the receiver. The solution to the producer–consumer problem becomes trivial when we use blocking `send()` and `receive()` statements. The producer merely invokes the blocking `send()` call and waits until the message is delivered to either the receiver or the mailbox. Likewise, when the consumer invokes `receive()`, it blocks until a message is available.

Note that the concepts of synchronous and asynchronous occur frequently in operating-system I/O algorithms, as you will see throughout this text.

3.4.2.3 Buffering

Whether communication is direct or indirect, messages exchanged by communicating processes reside in a temporary queue. Basically, such queues can be implemented in three ways:

- **Zero capacity**. The queue has a maximum length of zero; thus, the link cannot have any messages waiting in it. In this case, the sender must block until the recipient receives the message.
- **Bounded capacity**. The queue has finite length *n;* thus, at most *n* messages can reside in it. If the queue is not full when a new message is sent, the message is placed in the queue (either the message is copied or a pointer to the message is kept), and the sender can continue execution without

waiting. The link's capacity is finite, however. If the link is full, the sender must block until space is available in the queue.

- **Unbounded capacity**. The queue's length is potentially infinite; thus, any number of messages can wait in it. The sender never blocks.

The zero-capacity case is sometimes referred to as a message system with no buffering; the other cases are referred to as systems with automatic buffering.

3.5 Examples of IPC Systems

In this section, we explore three different IPC systems. We first cover the POSIX API for shared memory and then discuss message passing in the Mach operating system. We conclude with Windows XP, which interestingly uses shared memory as a mechanism for providing certain types of message passing.

3.5.1 An Example: POSIX Shared Memory

Several IPC mechanisms are available for POSIX systems, including shared memory and message passing. Here, we explore the POSIX API for shared memory.

A process must first create a shared memory segment using the `shmget()` system call (`shmget()` is derived from `SHared Memory GET`). The following example illustrates the use of `shmget()`:

```
segment_id = shmget(IPC_PRIVATE, size, S_IRUSR | S_IWUSR);
```

This first parameter specifies the key (or identifier) of the shared-memory segment. If this is set to IPC_PRIVATE, a new shared-memory segment is created. The second parameter specifies the size (in bytes) of the shared-memory segment. Finally, the third parameter identifies the mode, which indicates how the shared-memory segment is to be used—that is, for reading, writing, or both. By setting the mode to S_IRUSR | S_IWUSR, we are indicating that the owner may read or write to the shared-memory segment. A successful call to `shmget()` returns an integer identifier for the shared-memory segment. Other processes that want to use this region of shared memory must specify this identifier.

Processes that wish to access a shared-memory segment must attach it to their address space using the `shmat()` (`SHared Memory ATtach`) system call. The call to `shmat()` expects three parameters as well. The first is the integer identifier of the shared-memory segment being attached, and the second is a pointer location in memory indicating where the shared memory will be attached. If we pass a value of NULL, the operating system selects the location on the user's behalf. The third parameter identifies a flag that allows the shared-memory region to be attached in read-only or read-write mode; by passing a parameter of `0`, we allow both reads and writes to the shared region. We attach a region of shared memory using `shmat()` as follows:

```
shared_memory = (char *) shmat(id, NULL, 0);
```

If successful, `shmat()` returns a pointer to the beginning location in memory where the shared-memory region has been attached.

Once the region of shared memory is attached to a process's address space, the process can access the shared memory as a routine memory access using the pointer returned from `shmat()`. In this example, `shmat()` returns a pointer to a character string. Thus, we could write to the shared-memory region as follows:

```
sprintf(shared_memory, "Writing to shared memory");
```

Other processes sharing this segment would see the updates to the shared-memory segment.

Typically, a process using an existing shared-memory segment first attaches the shared-memory region to its address space and then accesses (and possibly updates) the region of shared memory. When a process no longer requires access to the shared-memory segment, it detaches the segment from its address space. To detach a region of shared memory, the process can pass the pointer of the shared-memory region to the `shmdt()` system call, as follows:

```
shmdt(shared_memory);
```

Finally, a shared-memory segment can be removed from the system with the `shmctl()` system call, which is passed the identifier of the shared segment along with the flag IPC_RMID.

The program shown in Figure 3.16 illustrates the POSIX shared-memory API just discussed. This program creates a 4,096-byte shared-memory segment. Once the region of shared memory is attached, the process writes the message `Hi There!` to shared memory. After outputting the contents of the updated memory, it detaches and removes the shared-memory region. We provide further exercises using the POSIX shared-memory API in the programming exercises at the end of this chapter.

3.5.2 An Example: Mach

As an example of a message-based operating system, we next consider the Mach operating system, developed at Carnegie Mellon University. We introduced Mach in Chapter 2 as part of the Mac OS X operating system. The Mach kernel supports the creation and destruction of multiple tasks, which are similar to processes but have multiple threads of control. Most communication in Mach—including most of the system calls and all intertask information—is carried out by *messages*. Messages are sent to and received from mailboxes, called *ports* in Mach.

Even system calls are made by messages. When a task is created, two special mailboxes—the Kernel mailbox and the Notify mailbox—are also created. The Kernel mailbox is used by the kernel to communicate with the task. The kernel sends notification of event occurrences to the Notify port. Only three system calls are needed for message transfer. The `msg_send()` call sends a message to a mailbox. A message is received via `msg_receive()`. Remote procedure calls (RPCs) are executed via `msg_rpc()`, which sends a message and waits for exactly one return message from the sender. In this way, the RPC models a typical subroutine procedure call but can work between systems—hence the term *remote*.

The `port_allocate()` system call creates a new mailbox and allocates space for its queue of messages. The maximum size of the message queue

```
#include <stdio.h>
#include <sys/shm.h>
#include <sys/stat.h>

int main()
{
/* the identifier for the shared memory segment */
int segment_id;
/* a pointer to the shared memory segment */
char *shared_memory;
/* the size (in bytes) of the shared memory segment */
const int size = 4096;

   /* allocate a shared memory segment */
   segment_id = shmget(IPC_PRIVATE, size, S_IRUSR | S_IWUSR);

   /* attach the shared memory segment */
   shared_memory = (char *) shmat(segment_id, NULL, 0);

   /* write a message to the shared memory segment */
   sprintf(shared_memory, "Hi there!");

   /* now print out the string from shared memory */
   printf("*%s\n", shared_memory);

   /* now detach the shared memory segment */
   shmdt(shared_memory);

   /* now remove the shared memory segment */
   shmctl(segment_id, IPC_RMID, NULL);

   return 0;
}
```

Figure 3.16 C program illustrating POSIX shared-memory API.

defaults to eight messages. The task that creates the mailbox is that mailbox's owner. The owner is also allowed to receive from the mailbox. Only one task at a time can either own or receive from a mailbox, but these rights can be sent to other tasks if desired.

The mailbox's message queue is initially empty. As messages are sent to the mailbox, the messages are copied into the mailbox. All messages have the same priority. Mach guarantees that multiple messages from the same sender are queued in first-in, first-out (FIFO) order but does not guarantee an absolute ordering. For instance, messages from two senders may be queued in any order.

The messages themselves consist of a fixed-length header followed by a variable-length data portion. The header indicates the length of the message and includes two mailbox names. One mailbox name is the mailbox to which the message is being sent. Commonly, the sending thread expects a reply; so the mailbox name of the sender is passed on to the receiving task, which can use it as a "return address."

The variable part of a message is a list of typed data items. Each entry in the list has a type, size, and value. The type of the objects specified in the message is important, since objects defined by the operating system—such as ownership or receive access rights, task states, and memory segments—may be sent in messages.

The send and receive operations themselves are flexible. For instance, when a message is sent to a mailbox, the mailbox may be full. If the mailbox is not full, the message is copied to the mailbox, and the sending thread continues. If the mailbox is full, the sending thread has four options:

1. Wait indefinitely until there is room in the mailbox.
2. Wait at most *n* milliseconds.
3. Do not wait at all but rather return immediately.
4. Temporarily cache a message. One message can be given to the operating system to keep, even though the mailbox to which that message is being sent is full. When the message can be put in the mailbox, a message is sent back to the sender; only one such message to a full mailbox can be pending at any time for a given sending thread.

The final option is meant for server tasks, such as a line-printer driver. After finishing a request, such tasks may need to send a one-time reply to the task that had requested service; but they must also continue with other service requests, even if the reply mailbox for a client is full.

The receive operation must specify the mailbox or mailbox set from which a message is to be received. A **mailbox set** is a collection of mailboxes, as declared by the task, which can be grouped together and treated as one mailbox for the purposes of the task. Threads in a task can receive only from a mailbox or mailbox set for which the task has receive access. A `port_status()` system call returns the number of messages in a given mailbox. The receive operation attempts to receive from (1) any mailbox in a mailbox set or (2) a specific (named) mailbox. If no message is waiting to be received, the receiving thread can either wait at most *n* milliseconds or not wait at all.

The Mach system was especially designed for distributed systems, which we discuss in Chapters 16 through 18, but Mach is also suitable for single-processor systems, as evidenced by its inclusion in the Mac OS X system. The major problem with message systems has generally been poor performance caused by double copying of messages; the message is copied first from the sender to the mailbox and then from the mailbox to the receiver. The Mach message system attempts to avoid double-copy operations by using virtual-memory-management techniques (Chapter 9). Essentially, Mach maps the address space containing the sender's message into the receiver's address space. The message itself is never actually copied. This message-management technique provides a large performance boost but works for only intrasystem messages. The Mach operating system is discussed in an extra chapter posted on our website.

3.5.3 An Example: Windows XP

The Windows XP operating system is an example of modern design that employs modularity to increase functionality and decrease the time needed to implement new features. Windows XP provides support for multiple operating environments, or *subsystems,* with which application programs communicate via a message-passing mechanism. The application programs can be considered clients of the Windows XP subsystem server.

The message-passing facility in Windows XP is called the **local procedure-call (LPC)** facility. The LPC in Windows XP communicates between two processes on the same machine. It is similar to the standard RPC mechanism that is widely used, but it is optimized for and specific to Windows XP. Like Mach, Windows XP uses a port object to establish and maintain a connection between two processes. Every client that calls a subsystem needs a communication channel, which is provided by a port object and is never inherited. Windows XP uses two types of ports: connection ports and communication ports. They are really the same but are given different names according to how they are used.

Connection ports are named *objects* and are visible to all processes; they give applications a way to set up communication channels (Chapter 22). The communication works as follows:

- The client opens a handle to the subsystem's connection port object.
- The client sends a connection request.
- The server creates two private communication ports and returns the handle to one of them to the client.
- The client and server use the corresponding port handle to send messages or callbacks and to listen for replies.

Windows XP uses two types of message-passing techniques over a port that the client specifies when it establishes the channel. The simplest, which is used for small messages, uses the port's message queue as intermediate storage and copies the message from one process to the other. Under this method, messages of up to 256 bytes can be sent.

If a client needs to send a larger message, it passes the message through a **section object**, which sets up a region of shared memory. The client has to decide when it sets up the channel whether or not it will need to send a large message. If the client determines that it does want to send large messages, it asks for a section object to be created. Similarly, if the server decides that replies will be large, it creates a section object. So that the section object can be used, a small message is sent that contains a pointer and size information about the section object. This method is more complicated than the first method, but it avoids data copying. In both cases, a callback mechanism can be used when either the client or the server cannot respond immediately to a request. The callback mechanism allows them to perform asynchronous message handling. The structure of local procedure calls in Windows XP is shown in Figure 3.17.

It is important to note that the LPC facility in Windows XP is not part of the Win32 API and hence is not visible to the application programmer. Rather, applications using the Win32 API invoke standard remote procedure calls.

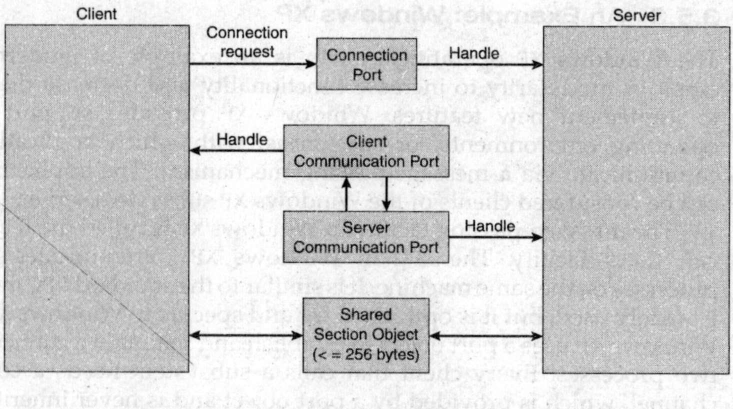

Figure 3.17 Local procedure calls in Windows XP.

When the RPC is being invoked on a process on the same system, the RPC is indirectly handled through a local procedure call. LPCs are also used in a few other functions that are part of the Win32 API.

3.6 Communication in Client–Server Systems

In Section 3.4, we described how processes can communicate using shared memory and message passing. These techniques can be used for communication in client–server systems (Section 1.12.2) as well. In this section, we explore three other strategies for communication in client–server systems: sockets, remote procedure calls (RPCs), and pipes.

3.6.1 Sockets

A **socket** is defined as an endpoint for communication. A pair of processes communicating over a network employ a pair of sockets—one for each process. A socket is identified by an IP address concatenated with a port number. In general, sockets use a client–server architecture. The server waits for incoming client requests by listening to a specified port. Once a request is received, the server accepts a connection from the client socket to complete the connection. Servers implementing specific services (such as telnet, FTP, and HTTP) listen to well-known ports (a telnet server listens to port 23; an FTP server listens to port 21; and a Web, or HTTP, server listens to port 80). All ports below 1024 are considered *well known;* we can use them to implement standard services.

When a client process initiates a request for a connection, it is assigned a port by its host computer. This port is some arbitrary number greater than 1024. For example, if a client on host X with IP address 146.86.5.20 wishes to establish a connection with a Web server (which is listening on port 80) at address 161.25.19.8, host X may be assigned port 1625. The connection will consist of a pair of sockets: (146.86.5.20:1625) on host X and (161.25.19.8:80) on the Web server. This situation is illustrated in Figure 3.18. The packets traveling between the hosts are delivered to the appropriate process based on the destination port number.

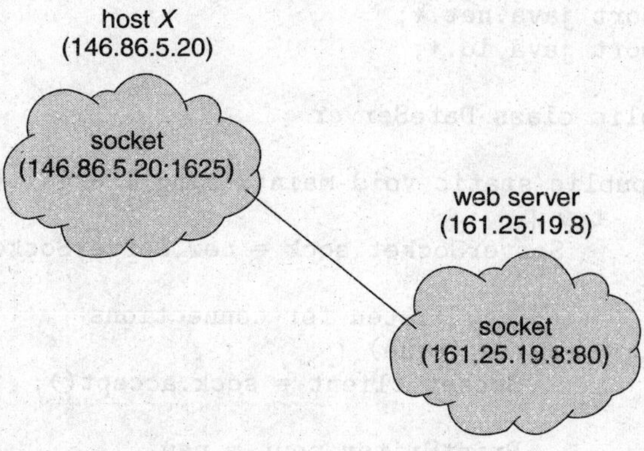

Figure 3.18 Communication using sockets.

All connections must be unique. Therefore, if another process also on host X wished to establish another connection with the same Web server, it would be assigned a port number greater than 1024 and not equal to 1625. This ensures that all connections consist of a unique pair of sockets.

Although most program examples in this text use C, we will illustrate sockets using Java, as it provides a much easier interface to sockets and has a rich library for networking utilities. Those interested in socket programming in C or C++ should consult the bibliographical notes at the end of the chapter.

Java provides three different types of sockets. **Connection-oriented (TCP) sockets** are implemented with the `Socket` class. **Connectionless (UDP) sockets** use the `DatagramSocket` class. Finally, the `MulticastSocket` class is a subclass of the `DatagramSocket` class. A multicast socket allows data to be sent to multiple recipients.

Our example describes a date server that uses connection-oriented TCP sockets. The operation allows clients to request the current date and time from the server. The server listens to port 6013, although the port could have any arbitrary number greater than 1024. When a connection is received, the server returns the date and time to the client.

The date server is shown in Figure 3.19. The server creates a `ServerSocket` that specifies it will listen to port 6013. The server then begins listening to the port with the `accept()` method. The server blocks on the `accept()` method waiting for a client to request a connection. When a connection request is received, `accept()` returns a socket that the server can use to communicate with the client.

The details of how the server communicates with the socket are as follows. The server first establishes a `PrintWriter` object that it will use to communicate with the client. A `PrintWriter` object allows the server to write to the socket using the routine `print()` and `println()` methods for output. The server process sends the date to the client, calling the method `println()`. Once it has written the date to the socket, the server closes the socket to the client and resumes listening for more requests.

A client communicates with the server by creating a socket and connecting to the port on which the server is listening. We implement such a client in the

```
import java.net.*;
import java.io.*;

public class DateServer
{
   public static void main(String[] args) {
      try {
         ServerSocket sock = new ServerSocket(6013);

         // now listen for connections
         while (true) {
            Socket client = sock.accept();

            PrintWriter pout = new
             PrintWriter(client.getOutputStream(), true);

            // write the Date to the socket
            pout.println(new java.util.Date().toString());

            // close the socket and resume
            // listening for connections
            client.close();
         }
      }
      catch (IOException ioe) {
        System.err.println(ioe);
      }
   }
}
```

Figure 3.19 Date server.

Java program shown in Figure 3.20. The client creates a Socket and requests a connection with the server at IP address 127.0.0.1 on port 6013. Once the connection is made, the client can read from the socket using normal stream I/O statements. After it has received the date from the server, the client closes the socket and exits. The IP address 127.0.0.1 is a special IP address known as the **loopback**. When a computer refers to IP address 127.0.0.1, it is referring to itself. This mechanism allows a client and server on the same host to communicate using the TCP/IP protocol. The IP address 127.0.0.1 could be replaced with the IP address of another host running the date server. In addition to an IP address, an actual host name, such as *www.westminstercollege.edu*, can be used as well.

Communication using sockets—although common and efficient—is considered a low-level form of communication between distributed processes. One reason is that sockets allow only an unstructured stream of bytes to be exchanged between the communicating threads. It is the responsibility of the client or server application to impose a structure on the data. In the next two subsections, we look at two higher-level methods of communication: remote procedure calls (RPCs) and pipes.

```
import java.net.*;
import java.io.*;

public class DateClient
{
  public static void main(String[] args) {
    try {
      //make connection to server socket
      Socket sock = new Socket("127.0.0.1",6013);

      InputStream in = sock.getInputStream();
      BufferedReader bin = new
        BufferedReader(new InputStreamReader(in));

      // read the date from the socket
      String line;
      while ( (line = bin.readLine()) != null)
        System.out.println(line);

      // close the socket connection
      sock.close();
    }
    catch (IOException ioe) {
      System.err.println(ioe);
    }
  }
}
```

Figure 3.20 Date client.

3.6.2 Remote Procedure Calls

One of the most common forms of remote service is the RPC paradigm, which we discussed briefly in Section 3.5.2. The RPC was designed as a way to abstract the procedure-call mechanism for use between systems with network connections. It is similar in many respects to the IPC mechanism described in Section 3.4, and it is usually built on top of such a system. Here, however, because we are dealing with an environment in which the processes are executing on separate systems, we must use a message-based communication scheme to provide remote service. In contrast to the IPC facility, the messages exchanged in RPC communication are well structured and are thus no longer just packets of data. Each message is addressed to an RPC daemon listening to a port on the remote system, and each contains an identifier of the function to execute and the parameters to pass to that function. The function is then executed as requested, and any output is sent back to the requester in a separate message.

A *port* is simply a number included at the start of a message packet. Whereas a system normally has one network address, it can have many ports within that address to differentiate the many network services it supports. If a remote process needs a service, it addresses a message to the proper port. For instance, if a system wished to allow other systems to be able to list its current users, it would have a daemon supporting such an RPC attached to a port—say, port 3027. Any remote system could obtain the needed information (that is, the list of current users) by sending an RPC message to port 3027 on the server; the data would be received in a reply message.

The semantics of RPCs allow a client to invoke a procedure on a remote host as it would invoke a procedure locally. The RPC system hides the details that allow communication to take place by providing a **stub** on the client side. Typically, a separate stub exists for each separate remote procedure. When the client invokes a remote procedure, the RPC system calls the appropriate stub, passing it the parameters provided to the remote procedure. This stub locates the port on the server and *marshals* the parameters. Parameter marshalling involves packaging the parameters into a form that can be transmitted over a network. The stub then transmits a message to the server using message passing. A similar stub on the server side receives this message and invokes the procedure on the server. If necessary, return values are passed back to the client using the same technique.

One issue that must be dealt with concerns differences in data representation on the client and server machines. Consider the representation of 32-bit integers. Some systems (known as *big-endian*) store the most significant byte first, while other systems (known as *little-endian*) store the least significant byte first. Neither order is "better" per se; rather, the choice is arbitrary within a computer architecture. To resolve differences like this, many RPC systems define a machine-independent representation of data. One such representation is known as **external data representation (XDR)**. On the client side, parameter marshalling involves converting the machine-dependent data into XDR before they are sent to the server. On the server side, the XDR data are unmarshalled and converted to the machine-dependent representation for the server.

Another important issue involves the semantics of a call. Whereas local procedure calls fail only under extreme circumstances, RPCs can fail, or be duplicated and executed more than once, as a result of common network errors. One way to address this problem is for the operating system to ensure that messages are acted on *exactly once*, rather than *at most once*. Most local procedure calls have the "exactly once" functionality, but it is more difficult to implement.

First, consider "at most once". This semantic can be implemented by attaching a timestamp to each message. The server must keep a history of all the timestamps of messages it has already processed or a history large enough to ensure that repeated messages are detected. Incoming messages that have a timestamp already in the history are ignored. The client can then send a message one or more times and be assured that it only executes once. (Generation of these timestamps is discussed in Section 18.1.)

For "exactly once," we need to remove the risk that the server will never receive the request. To accomplish this, the server must implement the "at most once" protocol described above but must also acknowledge to the client that the RPC call was received and executed. These ACK messages are common throughout networking. The client must resend each RPC call periodically until it receives the ACK for that call.

Another important issue concerns the communication between a server and a client. With standard procedure calls, some form of binding takes place during link, load, or execution time (Chapter 8) so that a procedure call's name is replaced by the memory address of the procedure call. The RPC scheme requires a similar binding of the client and the server port, but how does a client know the port numbers on the server? Neither system has full information about the other because they do not share memory.

Two approaches are common. First, the binding information may be predetermined, in the form of fixed port addresses. At compile time, an RPC call has a fixed port number associated with it. Once a program is compiled, the server cannot change the port number of the requested service. Second, binding can be done dynamically by a rendezvous mechanism. Typically, an operating system provides a rendezvous (also called a **matchmaker**) daemon on a fixed RPC port. A client then sends a message containing the name of the RPC to the rendezvous daemon requesting the port address of the RPC it needs to execute. The port number is returned, and the RPC calls can be sent to that port until the process terminates (or the server crashes). This method requires the extra overhead of the initial request but is more flexible than the first approach. Figure 3.21 shows a sample interaction.

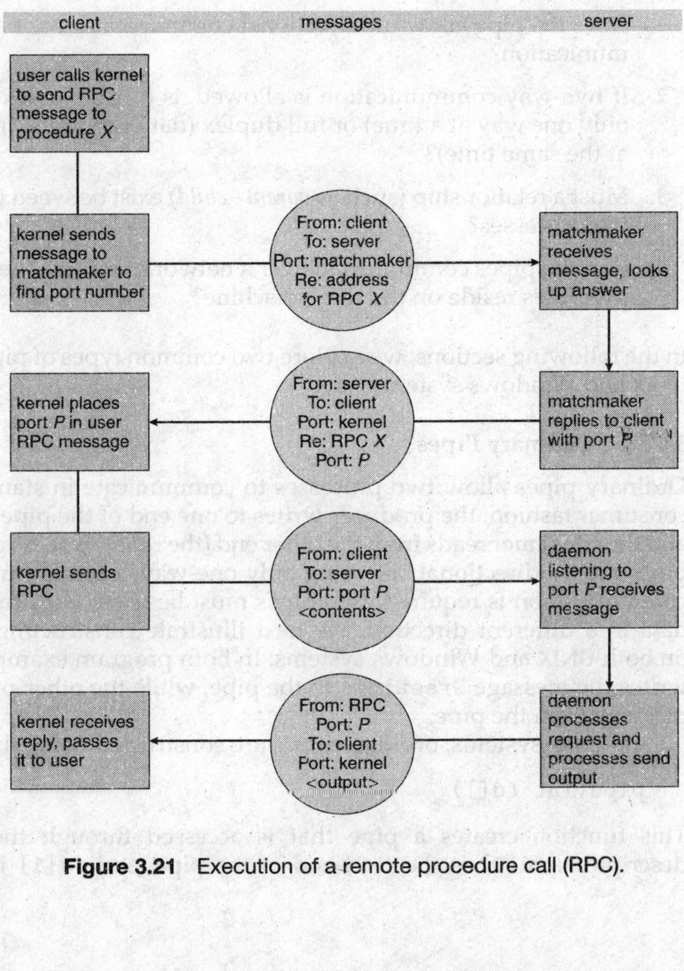

Figure 3.21 Execution of a remote procedure call (RPC).

The RPC scheme is useful in implementing a distributed file system (Chapter 17). Such a system can be implemented as a set of RPC daemons and clients. The messages are addressed to the distributed file system port on a server on which a file operation is to take place. The message contains the disk operation to be performed. The disk operation might be `read`, `write`, `rename`, `delete`, or `status`, corresponding to the usual file-related system calls. The return message contains any data resulting from that call, which is executed by the DFS daemon on behalf of the client. For instance, a message might contain a request to transfer a whole file to a client or be limited to a simple block request. In the latter case, several such requests may be needed if a whole file is to be transferred.

3.6.3 Pipes

A **pipe** acts as a conduit allowing two processes to communicate. Pipes were one of the first IPC mechanisms in early UNIX systems and typically provide one of the simpler ways for processes to communicate with one another, although they also have some limitations. In implementing a pipe, four issues must be considered:

1. Does the pipe allow unidirectional communication or bidirectional communication?
2. If two-way communication is allowed, is it half duplex (data can travel only one way at a time) or full duplex (data can travel in both directions at the same time)?
3. Must a relationship (such as *parent–child*) exist between the communicating processes?
4. Can the pipes communicate over a network, or must the communicating processes reside on the same machine?

In the following sections, we explore two common types of pipes used on both UNIX and Windows systems.

3.6.3.1 Ordinary Pipes

Ordinary pipes allow two processes to communicate in standard producer–consumer fashion; the producer writes to one end of the pipe (the **write-end**), and the consumer reads from the other end (the **read-end**). As a result, ordinary pipes are unidirectional, allowing only one-way communication. If two-way communication is required, two pipes must be used, with each pipe sending data in a different direction. We next illustrate constructing ordinary pipes on both UNIX and Windows systems. In both program examples, one process writes the message `Greetings` to the pipe, while the other process reads this message from the pipe.

On UNIX systems, ordinary pipes are constructed using the function

```
pipe(int fd[])
```

This function creates a pipe that is accessed through the `int fd[]` file descriptors: `fd[0]` is the read-end of the pipe, and `fd[1]` is the write end.

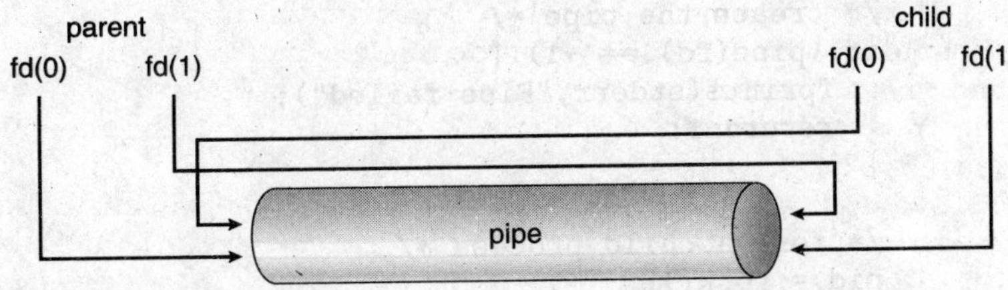

Figure 3.22 File descriptors for an ordinary pipe.

UNIX treats a pipe as a special type of file; thus, pipes can be accessed using ordinary `read()` and `write()` system calls.

An ordinary pipe cannot be accessed from outside the process that creates it. Thus, typically a parent process creates a pipe and uses it to communicate with a child process it creates via `fork()`. Recall from Section 3.3.1 that a child process inherits open files from its parent. Since a pipe is a special type of file, the child inherits the pipe from its parent process. Figure 3.22 illustrates the relationship of the file descriptor `fd` to the parent and child processes.

In the UNIX program shown in Figure 3.23, the parent process creates a pipe and then sends a `fork()` call creating the child process. What occurs after the `fork()` call depends on how the data are to flow through the pipe. In this instance, the parent writes to the pipe and the child reads from it. It is important to notice that both the parent process and the child process initially close their unused ends of the pipe. Although the program shown in Figure 3.23 does not require this action, it is an important step to ensure that a process reading from the pipe can detect end-of-file (`read()` returns 0) when the writer has closed its end of the pipe.

```
#include <sys/types.h>
#include <stdio.h>
#include <string.h>
#include <unistd.h>

#define BUFFER_SIZE 25
#define READ_END 0
#define WRITE_END 1

int main(void)
{
char write_msg[BUFFER_SIZE] = "Greetings";
char read_msg[BUFFER_SIZE];
int fd[2];
pid_t pid;
```

program continues in Figure 3.24

Figure 3.23 Ordinary pipes in UNIX.

```
    /* create the pipe */
    if (pipe(fd) == -1) {
      fprintf(stderr,"Pipe failed");
      return 1;
    }

    /* fork a child process */
    pid = fork();

    if (pid < 0) { /* error occurred */
      fprintf(stderr, "Fork Failed");
      return 1;
    }

    if (pid > 0) { /* parent process */
      /* close the unused end of the pipe */
      close(fd[READ_END]);

      /* write to the pipe */
      write(fd[WRITE_END], write_msg, strlen(write_msg)+1);

      /* close the write end of the pipe */
      close(fd[WRITE_END]);
    }
    else { /* child process */
      /* close the unused end of the pipe */
      close(fd[WRITE_END]);

      /* read from the pipe */
      read(fd[READ_END], read_msg, BUFFER_SIZE);
      printf("read %s",read_msg);

      /* close the write end of the pipe */
      close(fd[READ_END]);
    }

    return 0;
}
```

Figure 3.24 Continuation of Figure 3.23 program.

Ordinary pipes on Windows systems are termed **anonymous pipes**, and they behave similarly to their UNIX counterparts: they are unidirectional and employ parent–child relationships between the communicating processes. In addition, reading and writing to the pipe can be accomplished with the ordinary `ReadFile()` and `WriteFile()` functions. The Win32 API for creating pipes is the `CreatePipe()` function, which is passed four parameters: separate handles for (1) reading and (2) writing to the pipe, as well as (3) an instance of the STARTUPINFO structure, which is used to specify that the child process is to

```
#include <stdio.h>
#include <stdlib.h>
#include <windows.h>

#define BUFFER_SIZE 25

int main(VOID)
{
HANDLE ReadHandle, WriteHandle;
STARTUPINFO si;
PROCESS_INFORMATION pi;
char message[BUFFER_SIZE] = "Greetings";
DWORD written;
```

program continues in Figure 3.26

Figure 3.25 Windows anonymous pipes — parent process.

inherit the handles of the pipe. Furthermore, (4) the size of the pipe (in bytes) may be specified.

Figure 3.25 illustrates a parent process creating an anonymous pipe for communicating with its child. Unlike UNIX systems, in which a child process automatically inherits a pipe created by its parent, Windows requires the programmer to specify which attributes the child process will inherit. This is accomplished by first initializing the SECURITY_ATTRIBUTES structure to allow handles to be inherited and then redirecting the child process's handles for standard input or standard output to the read or write handle of the pipe. Since the child will be reading from the pipe, the parent must redirect the child's standard input to the read handle of the pipe. Furthermore, as the pipes are half duplex, it is necessary to prohibit the child from inheriting the write end of the pipe. Creating the child process is similar to the program in Figure 3.12, except that the fifth parameter is set to TRUE, indicating that the child process is to inherit designated handles from its parent. Before writing to the pipe, the parent first closes its unused read end of the pipe. The child process that reads from the pipe is shown in Figure 3.27. Before reading from the pipe, this program obtains the read handle to the pipe by invoking `GetStdHandle()`.

Note that ordinary pipes require a parent–child relationship between the communicating processes on both UNIX and Windows systems. This means that these pipes can be used only for communication between processes on the same machine.

3.6.3.2 Named Pipes

Ordinary pipes provide a simple communication mechanism between a pair of processes. However, ordinary pipes exist only while the processes are communicating with one another. On both UNIX and Windows systems, once the processes have finished communicating and terminated, the ordinary pipe ceases to exist.

```
    /* set up security attributes allowing pipes to be inherited */
    SECURITY_ATTRIBUTES sa = {sizeof(SECURITY_ATTRIBUTES),NULL,TRUE};
    /* allocate memory */
    ZeroMemory(&pi, sizeof(pi));

    /* create the pipe */
    if (!CreatePipe(&ReadHandle, &WriteHandle, &sa, 0)) {
      fprintf(stderr, "Create Pipe Failed");
      return 1;
    }

    /* establish the START_INFO structure for the child process */
    GetStartupInfo(&si);
    si.hStdOutput = GetStdHandle(STD_OUTPUT_HANDLE);

    /* redirect standard input to the read end of the pipe */
    si.hStdInput = ReadHandle;
    si.dwFlags = STARTF_USESTDHANDLES;

    /* don't allow the child to inherit the write end of pipe */
    SetHandleInformation(WriteHandle, HANDLE_FLAG_INHERIT, 0);

    /* create the child process */
    CreateProcess(NULL, "child.exe", NULL, NULL,
     TRUE, /* inherit handles */
     0, NULL, NULL, &si, &pi);

    /* close the unused end of the pipe */
    CloseHandle(ReadHandle);

    /* the parent writes to the pipe */
    if (!WriteFile(WriteHandle, message,BUFFER_SIZE,&written,NULL))
      fprintf(stderr, "Error writing to pipe.");

    /* close the write end of the pipe */
    CloseHandle(WriteHandle);

    /* wait for the child to exit */
    WaitForSingleObject(pi.hProcess, INFINITE);
    CloseHandle(pi.hProcess);
    CloseHandle(pi.hThread);
    return 0;
    }
```

Figure 3.26 Continuation of Figure 3.25 program.

Named pipes provide a much more powerful communication tool; communication can be bidirectional, and no parent–child relationship is required. Once a named pipe is established, several processes can use it for

```
#include <stdio.h>
#include <windows.h>

#define BUFFER_SIZE 25

int main(VOID)
{
HANDLE Readhandle;
CHAR buffer[BUFFER_SIZE];
DWORD read;

   /* get the read handle of the pipe */
   ReadHandle = GetStdHandle(STD_INPUT_HANDLE);

   /* the child reads from the pipe */
   if (ReadFile(ReadHandle, buffer, BUFFER_SIZE, &read, NULL))
     printf("child read %s",buffer);
   else
     fprintf(stderr, "Error reading from pipe");

   return 0;
}
```

Figure 3.27 Windows anonymous pipes — child process.

communication. In fact, in a typical scenario, a named pipe has several writers. Additionally, named pipes continue to exist after communicating processes have finished. Both UNIX and Windows systems support named pipes, although the details of implementation vary greatly. Next, we explore named pipes in each of these systems.

Named pipes are referred to as FIFOs in UNIX systems. Once created, they appear as typical files in the file system. A FIFO is created with the `mkfifo()` system call and manipulated with the ordinary `open()`, `read()`, `write()`, and `close()` system calls. It will continue to exist until it is explicitly deleted from the file system. Although FIFOs allow bidirectional communication, only half-duplex transmission is permitted. If data must travel in both directions, two FIFOs are typically used. Additionally, the communicating processes must reside on the same machine; sockets (Section 3.6.1) must be used if intermachine communication is required.

Named pipes on Windows systems provide a richer communication mechanism than their UNIX counterparts. Full-duplex communication is allowed, and the communicating processes may reside on either the same or different machines. Additionally, only byte-oriented data may be transmitted across a UNIX FIFO, whereas Windows systems allow either byte- or message-oriented data. Named pipes are created with the `CreateNamedPipe()` function, and a client can connect to a named pipe using `ConnectNamedPipe()`. Communication over the named pipe can be accomplished using the `ReadFile()` and `WriteFile()` functions.

PIPES IN PRACTICE

Pipes are used quite often in the UNIX command-line environment for situations in which the output of one command serves as input to the second. For example, the UNIX `ls` command produces a directory listing. For especially long directory listings, the output may scroll through several screens. The command `more` manages output by displaying only one screen of output at a time; the user must press the space bar to move from one screen to the next. Setting up a pipe between the `ls` and `more` commands (which are running as individual processes) allows the output of `ls` to be delivered as the input to `more`, enabling the user to display a large directory listing a screen at a time. A pipe can be constructed on the command line using the | character. The complete command is

```
ls | more
```

In this scenario, the `ls` command serves as the producer, and its output is consumed by the `more` command.

Windows systems provide a `more` command for the DOS shell with functionality similar to that of its UNIX counterpart. The DOS shell also uses the | character for establishing a pipe. The only difference is that to get a directory listing, DOS uses the `dir` command rather than `ls`. The equivalent command in DOS to what is shown above is

```
dir | more
```

3.7 Summary

A process is a program in execution. As a process executes, it changes state. The state of a process is defined by that process's current activity. Each process may be in one of the following states: new, ready, running, waiting, or terminated. Each process is represented in the operating system by its own process control block (PCB).

A process, when it is not executing, is placed in some waiting queue. There are two major classes of queues in an operating system: I/O request queues and the ready queue. The ready queue contains all the processes that are ready to execute and are waiting for the CPU. Each process is represented by a PCB, and the PCBs can be linked together to form a ready queue. Long-term (job) scheduling is the selection of processes that will be allowed to contend for the CPU. Normally, long-term scheduling is heavily influenced by resource-allocation considerations, especially memory management. Short-term (CPU) scheduling is the selection of one process from the ready queue.

Operating systems must provide a mechanism for parent processes to create new child processes. The parent may wait for its children to terminate before proceeding, or the parent and children may execute concurrently. There are several reasons for allowing concurrent execution: information sharing, computation speedup, modularity, and convenience.

The processes executing in the operating system may be either independent processes or cooperating processes. Cooperating processes require an interprocess communication mechanism to communicate with each other. Principally, communication is achieved through two schemes: shared memory and message passing. The shared-memory method requires communicating processes to share some variables. The processes are expected to exchange information through the use of these shared variables. In a shared-memory system, the responsibility for providing communication rests with the application programmers; the operating system needs to provide only the shared memory. The message-passing method allows the processes to exchange messages. The responsibility for providing communication may rest with the operating system itself. These two schemes are not mutually exclusive and can be used simultaneously within a single operating system.

Communication in client–server systems may use (1) sockets, (2) remote procedure calls (RPCs), or (3) pipes. A socket is defined as an endpoint for communication. A connection between a pair of applications consists of a pair of sockets, one at each end of the communication channel. RPCs are another form of distributed communication. An RPC occurs when a process (or thread) calls a procedure on a remote application. Ordinary pipes allow communication between parent and child processes, while named pipes permit unrelated processes to communicate with one another.

Exercises

3.1 What are the benefits and the disadvantages of each of the following? Consider both the system level and the programmer level.

a. Synchronous and asynchronous communication

b. Automatic and explicit buffering

c. Send by copy and send by reference

d. Fixed-sized and variable-sized messages

3.2 Consider the RPC mechanism. Describe the undesirable consequences that could arise from not enforcing either the "at most once" or "exactly once" semantic. Describe possible uses for a mechanism that has neither of these guarantees.

3.3 With respect to the RPC mechanism, consider the "exactly once" semantic. Does the algorithm for implementing this semantic execute correctly even if the ACK message back to the client is lost due to a network problem? Describe the sequence of messages and discuss whether "exactly once" is still preserved.

3.4 Palm OS provides no means of concurrent processing. Discuss three major complications that concurrent processing adds to an operating system.

3.5 Describe the actions taken by a kernel to context-switch between processes.

3.6 The Sun UltraSPARC processor has multiple register sets. Describe what happens when a context switch occurs if the new context is already loaded into one of the register sets. What happens if the new context is in memory rather than in a register set and all the register sets are in use?

3.7 Construct a process tree similar to Figure 3.9. To obtain process information for the UNIX or Linux system, use the command `ps -ael`. Use the command `man ps` to get more information about the ps command. On Windows systems, you will have to use the task manager.

3.8 Give an example of a situation in which ordinary pipes are more suitable than named pipes and an example of a situation in which named pipes are more suitable than ordinary pipes.

3.9 Describe the differences among short-term, medium-term, and long-term scheduling.

3.10 Including the initial parent process, how many processes are created by the program shown in Figure 3.28?

3.11 Using the program in Figure 3.29, identify the values of `pid` at lines `A`, `B`, `C`, and `D`. (Assume that the actual pids of the parent and child are 2600 and 2603, respectively.)

```
#include <stdio.h>
#include <unistd.h>

int main()
{
   /* fork a child process */
   fork();

   /* fork another child process */
   fork();

   /* and fork another */
   fork();

   return 0;
}
```

Figure 3.28 How many processes are created?

```
#include <sys/types.h>
#include <stdio.h>
#include <unistd.h>

int main()
{
pid_t pid, pid1;

   /* fork a child process */
   pid = fork();

   if (pid < 0) { /* error occurred */
     fprintf(stderr, "Fork Failed");
     return 1;
   }
   else if (pid == 0) { /* child process */
     pid1 = getpid();
     printf("child: pid = %d",pid); /* A */
     printf("child: pid1 = %d",pid1); /* B */
   }
   else { /* parent process */
     pid1 = getpid();
     printf("parent: pid = %d",pid); /* C */
     printf("parent: pid1 = %d",pid1); /* D */
     wait(NULL);
   }

   return 0;
}
```

Figure 3.29 What are the pid values?

3.12 Using the program shown in Figure 3.30, explain what the output will be at Line A.

Programming Problems

3.13 The Fibonacci sequence is the series of numbers 0, 1, 1, 2, 3, 5, 8, ... Formally, it can be expressed as:

$$
\begin{aligned}
fib_0 &= 0 \\
fib_1 &= 1 \\
fib_n &= fib_{n-1} + fib_{n-2}
\end{aligned}
$$

Write a C program using the `fork()` system call that generates the Fibonacci sequence in the child process. The number of the sequence will be provided in the command line. For example, if 5 is provided, the first five numbers in the Fibonacci sequence will be output by the child

```
#include <sys/types.h>
#include <stdio.h>
#include <unistd.h>

int value = 5;

int main()
{
pid_t pid;

   pid = fork();

   if (pid == 0) { /* child process */
      value += 15;
      return 0;
   }
   else if (pid > 0) { /* parent process */
      wait(NULL);
      printf("PARENT: value = %d",value); /* LINE A */
      return 0;
   }
}
```

Figure 3.30 What output will be at Line A?

process. Because the parent and child processes have their own copies of the data, it will be necessary for the child to output the sequence. Have the parent invoke the `wait()` call to wait for the child process to complete before exiting the program. Perform necessary error checking to ensure that a non-negative number is passed on the command line.

3.14 Repeat the preceding exercise, this time using the `CreateProcess()` function in the Win32 API. In this instance, you will need to specify a separate program to be invoked from `CreateProcess()`. It is this separate program that will run as a child process outputting the Fibonacci sequence. Perform necessary error checking to ensure that a non-negative number is passed on the command line.

3.15 Modify the date server shown in Figure 3.19 so that it delivers random jokes rather than the current date. Allow the jokes to contain multiple lines. The date client shown in Figure 3.20 can be used to read the multi-line jokes returned by the joke server.

3.16 An echo server echoes back whatever it receives from a client. For example, if a client sends the server the string *Hello there!* the server will respond with the exact data it received from the client—that is, *Hello there!*

Write an echo server using the Java networking API described in Section 3.6.1. This server will wait for a client connection using the `accept()` method. When a client connection is received, the server will loop, performing the following steps:

- Read data from the socket into a buffer.
- Write the contents of the buffer back to the client.

The server will break out of the loop only when it has determined that the client has closed the connection.

The server shown in Figure 3.19 uses the `java.io.BufferedReader` class. `BufferedReader` extends the `java.io.Reader` class, which is used for reading character streams. However, the echo server cannot guarantee that it will read characters from clients; it may receive binary data as well. The class `java.io.InputStream` deals with data at the byte level rather than the character level. Thus, this echo server must use an object that extends `java.io.InputStream`. The `read()` method in the `java.io.InputStream` class returns −1 when the client has closed its end of the socket connection.

3.17 In Exercise 3.13, the child process must output the Fibonacci sequence, since the parent and child have their own copies of the data. Another approach to designing this program is to establish a shared-memory segment between the parent and child processes. This technique allows the child to write the contents of the Fibonacci sequence to the shared-memory segment and has the parent output the sequence when the child completes. Because the memory is shared, any changes the child makes will be reflected in the parent process as well.

This program will be structured using POSIX shared memory as described in Section 3.5.1. The program first requires creating the data structure for the shared-memory segment. This is most easily accomplished using a `struct`. This data structure will contain two items: (1) a fixed-sized array of size `MAX_SEQUENCE` that will hold the Fibonacci values and (2) the size of the sequence the child process is to generate—`sequence_size`, where `sequence_size` ≤ `MAX_SEQUENCE`. These items can be represented in a `struct` as follows:

```
#define MAX_SEQUENCE 10

typedef struct {
   long fib_sequence[MAX_SEQUENCE];
   int sequence_size;
} shared_data;
```

The parent process will progress through the following steps:

a. Accept the parameter passed on the command line and perform error checking to ensure that the parameter is ≤ MAX_SEQUENCE.

b. Create a shared-memory segment of size `shared_data`.

c. Attach the shared-memory segment to its address space.

d. Set the value of `sequence_size` to the parameter on the command line.

e. Fork the child process and invoke the `wait()` system call to wait for the child to finish.

f. Output the value of the Fibonacci sequence in the shared-memory segment.

g. Detach and remove the shared-memory segment.

Because the child process is a copy of the parent, the shared-memory region will be attached to the child's address space as well as the parent's. The child process will then write the Fibonacci sequence to shared memory and finally will detach the segment.

One issue of concern with cooperating processes involves synchronization issues. In this exercise, the parent and child processes must be synchronized so that the parent does not output the Fibonacci sequence until the child finishes generating the sequence. These two processes will be synchronized using the `wait()` system call; the parent process will invoke `wait()`, which will cause it to be suspended until the child process exits.

3.18 Design a program using ordinary pipes in which one process sends a string message to a second process, and the second process reverses the case of each character in the message and sends it back to the first process. For example, if the first process sends the message `Hi There`, the second process will return `hI tHERE`. This will require using two pipes, one for sending the original message from the first to the second process, and the other for sending the modified message from the second back to the first process. You may write this program using either UNIX or Windows pipes.

3.19 Design a file-copying program named `FileCopy` using ordinary pipes. This program will be passed two parameters: the first is the name of the file to be copied, and the second is the name of the copied file. The program will then create an ordinary pipe and write the contents of the file to be copied to the pipe. The child process will read this file from the pipe and write it to the destination file. For example, if we invoke the program as follows:

```
FileCopy input.txt copy.txt
```

the file `input.txt` will be written to the pipe. The child process will read the contents of this file and write it to the destination file `copy.txt`. You may write this program using either UNIX or Windows pipes.

3.20 Most UNIX and Linux systems provide the `ipcs` command. This command lists the status of various POSIX interprocess communication mechanisms, including shared-memory segments. Much of the information for the command comes from the data structure `struct shmid_ds`, which is available in the /usr/include/sys/shm.h file. Some of the fields in this structure include:

- int shm_segsz—size of the shared-memory segment
- short shm_nattch—number of attaches to the shared-memory segment
- struct ipc_perm shm_perm—permission structure of the shared-memory segment

The struct ipc_perm data structure (which is available in the file /usr/include/sys/ipc.h) contains the fields:

- unsigned short uid—identifier of the user of the shared-memory segment
- unsigned short mode—permission modes
- key_t key (on Linux systems, __key)—user-specified key identifier

The permission modes are set according to how the shared-memory segment is established with the shmget() system call. Permissions are identified according to the following:

mode	meaning
0400	Read permission of owner.
0200	Write permission of owner.
0040	Read permission of group.
0020	Write permission of group.
0004	Read permission of world.
0002	Write permission of world.

Permissions can be accessed by using the bitwise *AND* operator &. For example, if the statement mode & 0400 evaluates to "true," the permission mode gives read permission to the owner of the shared-memory segment.

A shared-memory segment can be identified according to a user-specified key or according to the integer value returned from the shmget() system call, which represents the integer identifier of the shared-memory segment created. The shm_ds structure for a given integer segment identifier can be obtained with the following shmctl() system call:

```
/* identifier of the shared memory segment*/
int segment_id;
shm_ds shmbuffer;

shmctl(segment_id, IPC_STAT, &shmbuffer);
```

If successful, shmctl() returns 0; otherwise, it returns −1 indicating an error condition (the global variable errno can be accessed to determine the error condition).

Write a C program that is passed an identifier for a shared-memory segment. This program will invoke the shmctl() function to obtain its shm_ds structure. It will then output the following values of the shared-memory segment:

- Segment ID
- Key
- Mode
- Owner UID
- Size
- Number of attaches

Programming Projects

3.21 POSIX Message Passing.

This project consists of using POSIX message queues for communicating temperatures between each of four external processes and a central process. The project can be completed on systems that support POSIX message passing, such as UNIX, Linux, and Mac OS X.

Part 1: Overview

Four external processes will communicate temperatures to a central process, which in turn will reply with its own temperature and will indicate whether the entire system has stabilized. Each process will receive its initial temperature upon creation and will recalculate a new temperature according to two formulas:

new external temp =
*(myTemp * 3 + 2 * centralTemp) / 5;*

new central temp =
*(2 * centralTemp + four temps received from external processes) / 6;*

Initially, each external process will send its temperature to the mailbox for the central process. If all four temperatures are exactly the same as those sent by the four processes during the last iteration, the system has stabilized. In this case, the central process will notify each external process that it is now finished (along with the central process itself), and each process will output the final stabilized temperature. If the system has not yet become stable, the central process will send its new temperature to the mailbox for each of the outer processes and await their replies. The processes will continue to run until the temperature has stabilized.

Part 2: The Message Passing System

Processes can exchange messages by using four system calls: `msgget()`, `msgsnd()`, `msgrcv()`, and `msgctl()`. The `msgget()` function converts a mailbox name to a message queue id, `msqid`. (A mailbox name is an externally known message queue name that is shared among the cooperating processes.) `msqid`, the internal identifier returned by `msgget()`, must be passed to all subsequent system calls using this message queue to facilitate interprocess communication. A typical invocation of `msgget()`is seen below:

```
msqid = msgget(1234, 0600 | IPC_CREAT);
```

The first parameter is the name of the mailbox, and the second parameter instructs the operating system to create the message queue if it does not already exist, with read and write privileges only for processes with the same user id as this process. If a message queue already exists for this mailbox name, `msgget()` returns the `msqid` of the existing mailbox. To avoid attaching to an existing message queue, a process can first attempt to attach to the mailbox by omitting `IPC_CREAT` and then checking the return value from `msgget()`. If `msqid` is negative, an error has occurred during the system call, and the globally accessible variable `errno` can be consulted to determine whether the error occurred because the message queue already exists or for some other reason. If the process determines that the mailbox does not currently exist, it can then create it by including `IPC_CREAT`. (For the current project, this strategy should not be necessary if students are using standalone PCs or are assigned unique ranges of mailbox names by the instructor.)

Once a valid `msqid` has been established, a process can begin to use `msgsnd()` to send messages and `msgrcv()` to receive messages. The messages being sent and received are similar in format to those described in Section 3.5.2, as they include a fixed-length portion at the beginning followed by a variable-length portion. Obviously, the senders and receivers must agree on the format of the messages being exchanged. Since the operating system specifies one field in the fixed-length portion of every message format, and at least one piece of information will be sent to the receiving process, it is logical to create a data aggregate for each type of message using a `struct`. The first field of any such `struct` must be a `long`, and it will contain the priority of the message. (This project does not use this functionality; we recommend that you simply make the first field in every message equal to the same integral value, such as 2.) Other fields in the messages contain the information to be shared between the communicating processes. Three additional fields are recommended: (1) the temperature being sent, (2) the process number of the external process sending the message (0 for the central process), and (3) a flag that is set to 0 but that the central process will set to 1 when it notices stability. A recommended `struct` appears as follows:

```
struct {
        long priority;
        int temp;
        int pid;
        int stable;
} msgp;
```

Assuming the msqid has been established, examples of msgsnd() and msgrcv() appear as such:

```
int stat, msqid;

stat = msgsnd(msqid, &msgp,
               sizeof(msgp)-sizeof(long), 0);

stat = msgrcv(msqid, &msgp,
               sizeof(msgp)-sizeof(long), 2, 0);
```

The first parameter in both system calls must be a valid msqid; otherwise a negative value is returned. (Both functions return the number of bytes sent or received upon successful completion of the operation.) The second parameter is the address of where to find or store the message to be sent or received, followed by the number of information bytes to be sent or received. The final parameter of 0 indicates that the operations will be synchronous and that the sender will block if the message queue is full. (IPC_NOWAIT would be used if asynchronous, or nonblocking, operations were desired. Each individual message queue can hold a maximum number of messages—or bytes—so it is possible for the queue to become filled, which is one reason a sender may block when attempting to transmit a message.) The 2 that appears before this final parameter in msgrcv() indicates the minimum priority level of the messages the process wishes to receive; the receiver will wait until a message of that priority (or higher) is sent to the msqid if this is a synchronous operation.

Once a process is finished using a message queue, it must be removed so that the mailbox can be reused by other processes. Unless it is removed, the message queue—and any messages that have not yet been received—will remain in the storage space that has been provided for this mailbox by the kernel. To remove the message queue, and delete any unread messages therein, it is necessary to invoke msgctl(), as follows:

```
struct msgid_ds dummyParam;
status = msgctl(msqid, IPC_RMID, &dummyParam);
```

The third parameter is necessary because this function requires it, but it is used only if it the programmer wishes to collect some statistics about the usage of the message queue. This is accomplished by substituting IPC_STAT as the second parameter.

All programs should include the following three header files, which are found in /usr/include/sys: ipc.h, types.h, and msg.h. One possibly confusing artifact of the message queue implementation bears mentioning at this point. After a mailbox is removed via `msgctl()`, any subsequent attempts to create another mailbox with that same name using `msgget()` will typically generate a different `msqid`.

Part 3: Creating the Processes

Each external process, as well as the central server, will create its own mailbox with the name $X + i$, where i is a numeric identifier of the external process 1..4 or zero for the central process. Thus, if X were 70, then the central process would receive messages in the mailbox named 70, and it would send its replies to mailboxes 71–74. Outer process 2 would receive in mailbox 72 and would send to mailbox 70, and so forth. Thus, each external process will attach to two mailboxes, and the central process will attach to five. If each process specifies `IPC_CREAT` when invoking `msgget()`, the first process that invokes `msgget()` actually creates the mailbox; subsequent calls to `msgget()` attach to the existing mailbox. The protocol for removal should be that the mailbox/message queue that each process is listening to should be the only one it removes —via `msgctl()`.)

Each external process will be uniquely identified by a command-line parameter. The first parameter to each external process will be its initial temperature, and the second parameter will be its unique number: 1, 2, 3, or 4. The central server will be passed one parameter—its initial temperature. Assuming the executable name of the external process is `external` and the central server is `central`, invoking all five processes will be done as follows:

```
./external 100 1 &
./external 22 2 &
./external 50 3 &
./external 40 4 &
./central 60 &
```

Part 4: Implementation Hints

It might be best to start by sending one message successfully from the central process to a single outer process, and vice versa, before trying to write all the code to solve this problem. It is also wise to check all the return values from the four message queue system calls for possible failed requests and to output a message to the screen after each one successfully completes. The message should indicate what was accomplished and by whom—for instance, "mailbox 71 has been created by outer process 1," "message received by central process from external process 2," and so forth. These messages can be removed or commented out after the problem is solved. Processes should also verify that they were passed the correct number of command-line parameters (via the `argc` parameter in `main()`). Finally, extraneous messages residing in a queue can cause a collection of cooperating processes that function correctly to appear erroneous. For that reason, it is wise to remove all mailboxes relevant to this project to ensure that mailboxes are empty before the processes begin. The easiest way to do this is to use the ipcs command to list all message queues and the ipcrm command to remove existing message queues. The ipcs command lists the msqid of all message queues on the system. Use ipcrm to remove message queues according to their msqid. For example, if msqid 163845 appears with the output of ipcs, it can be deleted with the following command:

```
ipcrm -q 163845
```

Bibliographical Notes

Interprocess communication in the RC 4000 system is discussed by Brinch-Hansen [1970]. Schlichting and Schneider [1982] discuss asynchronous message-passing primitives. The IPC facility implemented at the user level is described by Bershad et al. [1990].

Details of interprocess communication in UNIX systems are presented by Gray [1997]. Barrera [1991] and Vahalia [1996] describe interprocess communication in the Mach system. Russinovich and Solomon [2005], Solomon and Russinovich [2000], and Stevens [1999] outline interprocess communication in Windows 2003, Windows 2000 and UNIX respectively. Hart [2005] covers Windows systems programming in detail.

The implementation of RPCs is discussed by Birrell and Nelson [1984]. Shrivastava and Panzieri [1982] describes the design of a reliable RPC mechanism, and Tay and Ananda [1990] presents a survey of RPCs. Stankovic [1982] and Staunstrup [1982] discuss procedure calls versus message-passing communication. Harold [2005] provides coverage of socket programming in Java. Hart [2005] and Robbins and Robbins [2003] cover pipes in Windows and UNIX systems, respectively.

CHAPTER 4

Multithreaded Programming

The process model introduced in Chapter 3 assumed that a process was an executing program with a single thread of control. Most modern operating systems now provide features enabling a process to contain multiple threads of control. This chapter introduces many concepts associated with multithreaded computer systems, including a discussion of the APIs for the Pthreads, Win32, and Java thread libraries. We look at many issues related to multithreaded programming and its effect on the design of operating systems. Finally, we explore how the Windows XP and Linux operating systems support threads at the kernel level.

CHAPTER OBJECTIVES

- To introduce the notion of a thread — a fundamental unit of CPU utilization that forms the basis of multithreaded computer systems.
- To discuss the APIs for the Pthreads, Win32, and Java thread libraries.
- To examine issues related to multithreaded programming.

4.1 Overview

A thread is a basic unit of CPU utilization; it comprises a thread ID, a program counter, a register set, and a stack. It shares with other threads belonging to the same process its code section, data section, and other operating-system resources, such as open files and signals. A traditional (or **heavyweight**) process has a single thread of control. If a process has multiple threads of control, it can perform more than one task at a time. Figure 4.1 illustrates the difference between a traditional **single-threaded** process and a **multithreaded** process.

4.1.1 Motivation

Many software packages that run on modern desktop PCs are multithreaded. An application typically is implemented as a separate process with several threads of control. A Web browser might have one thread display images or

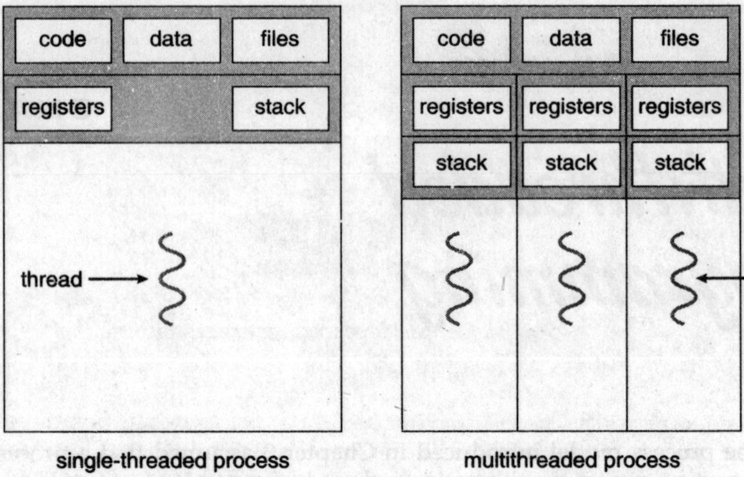

Figure 4.1 Single-threaded and multithreaded processes.

text while another thread retrieves data from the network, for example. A word processor may have a thread for displaying graphics, another thread for responding to keystrokes from the user, and a third thread for performing spelling and grammar checking in the background.

In certain situations, a single application may be required to perform several similar tasks. For example, a Web server accepts client requests for Web pages, images, sound, and so forth. A busy Web server may have several (perhaps thousands of) clients concurrently accessing it. If the Web server ran as a traditional single-threaded process, it would be able to service only one client at a time, and a client might have to wait a very long time for its request to be serviced.

One solution is to have the server run as a single process that accepts requests. When the server receives a request, it creates a separate process to service that request. In fact, this process-creation method was in common use before threads became popular. Process creation is time consuming and resource intensive, however. If the new process will perform the same tasks as the existing process, why incur all that overhead? It is generally more efficient to use one process that contains multiple threads. If the Web-server process is multithreaded, the server will create a separate thread that listens for client requests. When a request is made, rather than creating another process, the server will create a new thread to service the request and resume listening for additional requests. This is illustrated in Figure 4.2.

Threads also play a vital role in remote procedure call (RPC) systems. Recall from Chapter 3 that RPCs allow interprocess communication by providing a communication mechanism similar to ordinary function or procedure calls. Typically, RPC servers are multithreaded. When a server receives a message, it services the message using a separate thread. This allows the server to service several concurrent requests.

Finally, most operating system kernels are now multithreaded; several threads operate in the kernel, and each thread performs a specific task, such

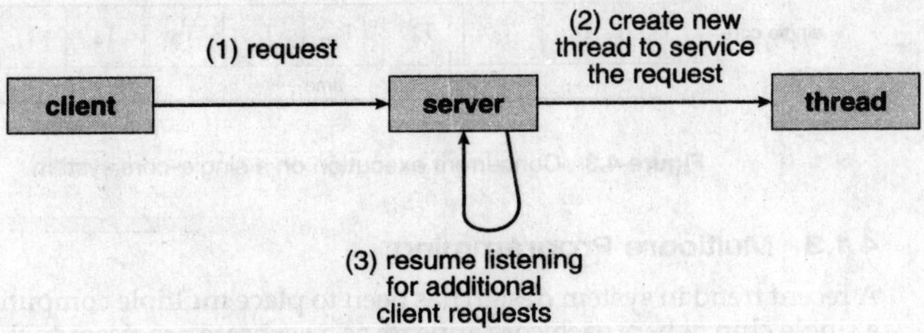

Figure 4.2 Multithreaded server architecture.

as managing devices or interrupt handling. For example, Solaris creates a set of threads in the kernel specifically for interrupt handling; Linux uses a kernel thread for managing the amount of free memory in the system.

4.1.2 Benefits

The benefits of multithreaded programming can be broken down into four major categories:

1. **Responsiveness**. Multithreading an interactive application may allow a program to continue running even if part of it is blocked or is performing a lengthy operation, thereby increasing responsiveness to the user. For instance, a multithreaded Web browser could allow user interaction in one thread while an image was being loaded in another thread.

2. **Resource sharing**. Processes may only share resources through techniques such as shared memory or message passing. Such techniques must be explicitly arranged by the programmer. However, threads share the memory and the resources of the process to which they belong by default. The benefit of sharing code and data is that it allows an application to have several different threads of activity within the same address space.

3. **Economy**. Allocating memory and resources for process creation is costly. Because threads share the resources of the process to which they belong, it is more economical to create and context-switch threads. Empirically gauging the difference in overhead can be difficult, but in general it is much more time consuming to create and manage processes than threads. In Solaris, for example, creating a process is about thirty times slower than is creating a thread, and context switching is about five times slower.

4. **Scalability**. The benefits of multithreading can be greatly increased in a multiprocessor architecture, where threads may be running in parallel on different processors. A single-threaded process can only run on one processor, regardless how many are available. Multithreading on a multi-CPU machine increases parallelism. We explore this issue further in the following section.

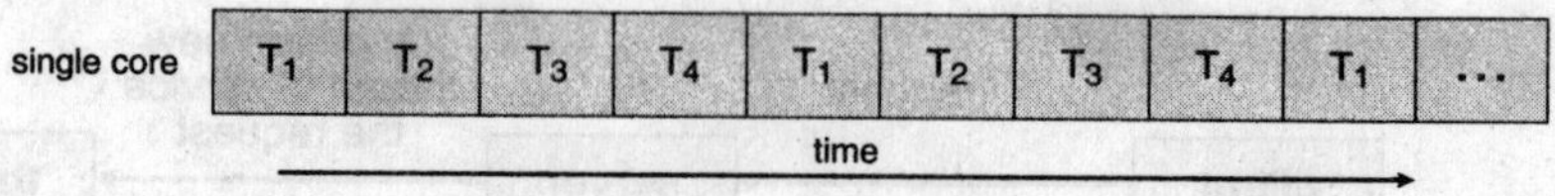

Figure 4.3 Concurrent execution on a single-core system.

4.1.3 Multicore Programming

A recent trend in system design has been to place multiple computing cores on a single chip, where each core appears as a separate processor to the operating system (Section 1.3.2). Multithreaded programming provides a mechanism for more efficient use of multiple cores and improved concurrency. Consider an application with four threads. On a system with a single computing core, concurrency merely means that the execution of the threads will be interleaved over time (Figure 4.3), as the processing core is capable of executing only one thread at a time. On a system with multiple cores, however, concurrency means that the threads can run in parallel, as the system can assign a separate thread to each core (Figure 4.4).

The trend towards multicore systems has placed pressure on system designers as well as application programmers to make better use of the multiple computing cores. Designers of operating systems must write scheduling algorithms that use multiple processing cores to allow the parallel execution shown in Figure 4.4. For application programmers, the challenge is to modify existing programs as well as design new programs that are multithreaded to take advantage of multicore systems. In general, five areas present challenges in programming for multicore systems:

1. **Dividing activities.** This involves examining applications to find areas that can be divided into separate, concurrent tasks and thus can run in parallel on individual cores.

2. **Balance.** While identifying tasks that can run in parallel, programmers must also ensure that the tasks perform equal work of equal value. In some instances, a certain task may not contribute as much value to the overall process as other tasks; using a separate execution core to run that task may not be worth the cost.

3. **Data splitting.** Just as applications are divided into separate tasks, the data accessed and manipulated by the tasks must be divided to run on separate cores.

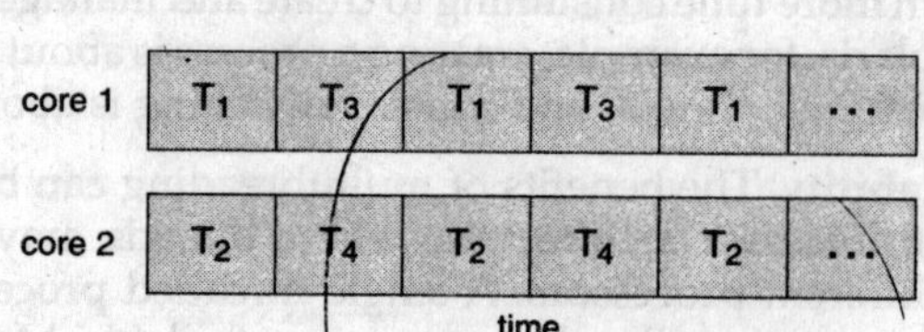

Figure 4.4 Parallel execution on a multicore system.

4. **Data dependency**. The data accessed by the tasks must be examined for dependencies between two or more tasks. In instances where one task depends on data from another, programmers must ensure that the execution of the tasks is synchronized to accommodate the data dependency. We examine such strategies in Chapter 6.
5. **Testing and debugging**. When a program is running in parallel on multiple cores, there are many different execution paths. Testing and debugging such concurrent programs is inherently more difficult than testing and debugging single-threaded applications.

Because of these challenges, many software developers argue that the advent of multicore systems will require an entirely new approach to designing software systems in the future.

4.2 Multithreading Models

Our discussion so far has treated threads in a generic sense. However, support for threads may be provided either at the user level, for **user threads**, or by the kernel, for **kernel threads**. User threads are supported above the kernel and are managed without kernel support, whereas kernel threads are supported and managed directly by the operating system. Virtually all contemporary operating systems—including Windows XP, Linux, Mac OS X, Solaris, and Tru64 UNIX (formerly Digital UNIX)—support kernel threads.

Ultimately, a relationship must exist between user threads and kernel threads. In this section, we look at three common ways of establishing such a relationship.

4.2.1 Many-to-One Model

The many-to-one model (Figure 4.5) maps many user-level threads to one kernel thread. Thread management is done by the thread library in user

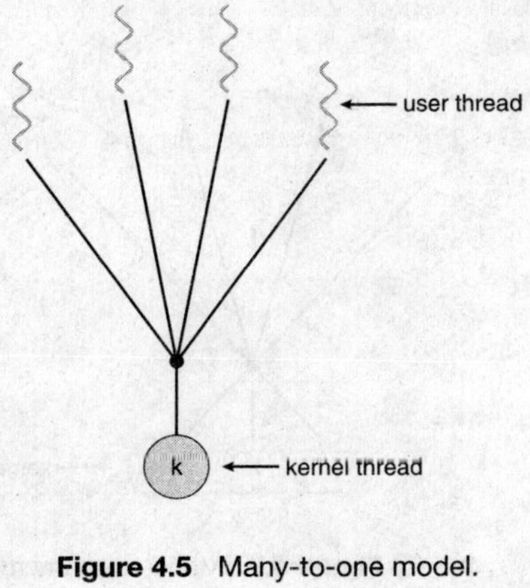

Figure 4.5 Many-to-one model.

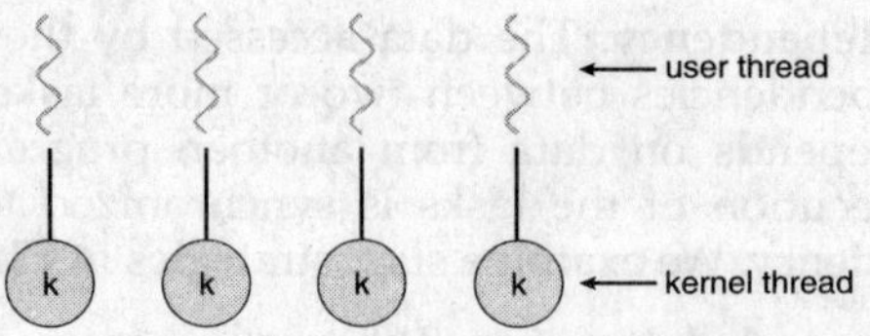

Figure 4.6 One-to-one model.

space, so it is efficient; but the entire process will block if a thread makes a blocking system call. Also, because only one thread can access the kernel at a time, multiple threads are unable to run in parallel on multiprocessors. Green threads—a thread library available for Solaris—uses this model, as does GNU Portable Threads.

4.2.2 One-to-One Model

The one-to-one model (Figure 4.6) maps each user thread to a kernel thread. It provides more concurrency than the many-to-one model by allowing another thread to run when a thread makes a blocking system call; it also allows multiple threads to run in parallel on multiprocessors. The only drawback to this model is that creating a user thread requires creating the corresponding kernel thread. Because the overhead of creating kernel threads can burden the performance of an application, most implementations of this model restrict the number of threads supported by the system. Linux, along with the family of Windows operating systems, implement the one-to-one model.

4.2.3 Many-to-Many Model

The many-to-many model (Figure 4.7) multiplexes many user-level threads to a smaller or equal number of kernel threads. The number of kernel threads may be specific to either a particular application or a particular machine (an application may be allocated more kernel threads on a multiprocessor than on a uniprocessor). Whereas the many-to-one model allows the developer to

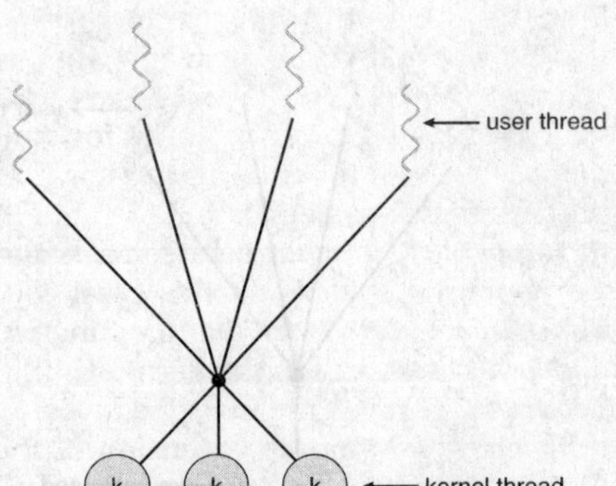

Figure 4.7 Many-to-many model.

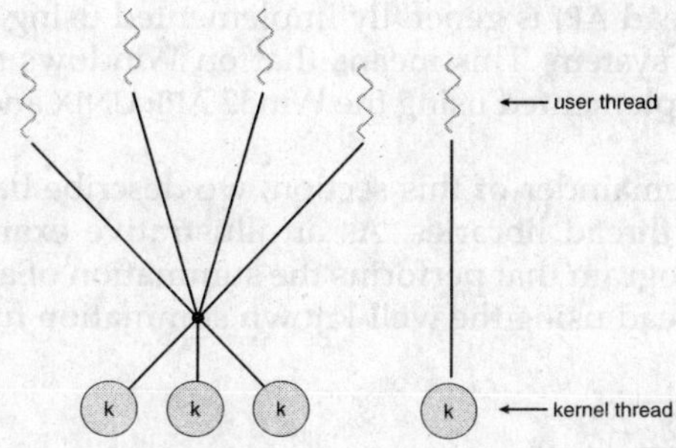

Figure 4.8 Two-level model.

create as many user threads as she wishes, true concurrency is not gained because the kernel can schedule only one thread at a time. The one-to-one model allows for greater concurrency, but the developer has to be careful not to create too many threads within an application (and in some instances may be limited in the number of threads she can create). The many-to-many model suffers from neither of these shortcomings: developers can create as many user threads as necessary, and the corresponding kernel threads can run in parallel on a multiprocessor. Also, when a thread performs a blocking system call, the kernel can schedule another thread for execution.

One popular variation on the many-to-many model still multiplexes many user-level threads to a smaller or equal number of kernel threads but also allows a user-level thread to be bound to a kernel thread. This variation, sometimes referred to as the *two-level model* (Figure 4.8), is supported by operating systems such as IRIX, HP-UX, and Tru64 UNIX. The Solaris operating system supported the two-level model in versions older than Solaris 9. However, beginning with Solaris 9, this system uses the one-to-one model.

4.3 Thread Libraries

A **thread library** provides the programmer with an API for creating and managing threads. There are two primary ways of implementing a thread library. The first approach is to provide a library entirely in user space with no kernel support. All code and data structures for the library exist in user space. This means that invoking a function in the library results in a local function call in user space and not a system call.

The second approach is to implement a kernel-level library supported directly by the operating system. In this case, code and data structures for the library exist in kernel space. Invoking a function in the API for the library typically results in a system call to the kernel.

Three main thread libraries are in use today: (1) POSIX Pthreads, (2) Win32, and (3) Java. Pthreads, the threads extension of the POSIX standard, may be provided as either a user- or kernel-level library. The Win32 thread library is a kernel-level library available on Windows systems. The Java thread API allows threads to be created and managed directly in Java programs. However, because in most instances the JVM is running on top of a host operating system, the Java thread API is generally implemented using a thread library available on the host system. This means that on Windows systems, Java threads are typically implemented using the Win32 API; UNIX and Linux systems often use Pthreads.

In the remainder of this section, we describe basic thread creation using these three thread libraries. As an illustrative example, we design a multithreaded program that performs the summation of a non-negative integer in a separate thread using the well-known summation function:

$$sum = \sum_{i=0}^{N} i$$

For example, if N were 5, this function would represent the summation of integers from 0 to 5, which is 15. Each of the three programs will be run with the upper bounds of the summation entered on the command line; thus, if the user enters 8, the summation of the integer values from 0 to 8 will be output.

4.3.1 Pthreads

Pthreads refers to the POSIX standard (IEEE 1003.1c) defining an API for thread creation and synchronization. This is a *specification* for thread behavior, not an *implementation*. Operating system designers may implement the specification in any way they wish. Numerous systems implement the Pthreads specification, including Solaris, Linux, Mac OS X, and Tru64 UNIX. *Shareware* implementations are available in the public domain for the various Windows operating systems as well.

The C program shown in Figure 4.9 demonstrates the basic Pthreads API for constructing a multithreaded program that calculates the summation of a non-negative integer in a separate thread. In a Pthreads program, separate threads begin execution in a specified function. In Figure 4.9, this is the `runner()` function. When this program begins, a single thread of control begins in `main()`. After some initialization, `main()` creates a second thread that begins control in the `runner()` function. Both threads share the global data `sum`.

Let's look more closely at this program. All Pthreads programs must include the `pthread.h` header file. The statement `pthread_t tid` declares the identifier for the thread we will create. Each thread has a set of attributes, including stack size and scheduling information. The `pthread_attr_t attr` declaration represents the attributes for the thread. We set the attributes in the function call `pthread_attr_init(&attr)`. Because we did not explicitly set any attributes, we use the default attributes provided. (In Chapter 5, we discuss some of the scheduling attributes provided by the Pthreads API.) A separate thread is created with the `pthread_create()` function call. In addition to passing the thread identifier and the attributes for the thread, we also pass the name of the function where the new thread will begin execution—in this case, the `runner()` function. Last, we pass the integer parameter that was provided on the command line, `argv[1]`.

At this point, the program has two threads: the initial (or parent) thread in `main()` and the summation (or child) thread performing the summation

```
#include <pthread.h>
#include <stdio.h>

int sum; /* this data is shared by the thread(s) */
void *runner(void *param); /* the thread */

int main(int argc, char *argv[])
{
  pthread_t tid; /* the thread identifier */
  pthread_attr_t attr; /* set of thread attributes */

  if (argc != 2) {
    fprintf(stderr,"usage: a.out <integer value>\n");
    return -1;
  }
  if (atoi(argv[1]) < 0) {
    fprintf(stderr,"%d must be >= 0\n",atoi(argv[1]));
    return -1;
  }

  /* get the default attributes */
  pthread_attr_init(&attr);
  /* create the thread */
  pthread_create(&tid,&attr,runner,argv[1]);
  /* wait for the thread to exit */
  pthread_join(tid,NULL);

  printf("sum = %d\n",sum);
}

/* The thread will begin control in this function */
void *runner(void *param)
{
  int i, upper = atoi(param);
  sum = 0;

  for (i = 1; i <= upper; i++)
    sum += i;

  pthread_exit(0);
}
```

Figure 4.9 Multithreaded C program using the Pthreads API.

operation in the runner() function. After creating the summation thread, the parent thread will wait for it to complete by calling the pthread_join() function. The summation thread will complete when it calls the function pthread_exit(). Once the summation thread has returned, the parent thread will output the value of the shared data sum.

4.3.2 Win32 Threads

The technique for creating threads using the Win32 thread library is similar to the Pthreads technique in several ways. We illustrate the Win32 thread API in the C program shown in Figure 4.10. Notice that we must include the `windows.h` header file when using the Win32 API.

Just as in the Pthreads version shown in Figure 4.9, data shared by the separate threads—in this case, `Sum`—are declared globally (the `DWORD` data type is an unsigned 32-bit integer). We also define the `Summation()` function that is to be performed in a separate thread. This function is passed a pointer to a `void`, which Win32 defines as LPVOID. The thread performing this function sets the global data `Sum` to the value of the summation from 0 to the parameter passed to `Summation()`.

Threads are created in the Win32 API using the `CreateThread()` function, and—just as in Pthreads—a set of attributes for the thread is passed to this function. These attributes include security information, the size of the stack, and a flag that can be set to indicate if the thread is to start in a suspended state. In this program, we use the default values for these attributes (which do not initially set the thread to a suspended state and instead make it eligible to be run by the CPU scheduler). Once the summation thread is created, the parent must wait for it to complete before outputting the value of `Sum`, as the value is set by the summation thread. Recall that the Pthread program (Figure 4.9) had the parent thread wait for the summation thread using the `pthread_join()` statement. We perform the equivalent of this in the Win32 API using the `WaitForSingleObject()` function, which causes the creating thread to block until the summation thread has exited. (We cover synchronization objects in more detail in Chapter 6.)

4.3.3 Java Threads

Threads are the fundamental model of program execution in a Java program, and the Java language and its API provide a rich set of features for the creation and management of threads. All Java programs comprise at least a single thread of control—even a simple Java program consisting of only a `main()` method runs as a single thread in the JVM.

There are two techniques for creating threads in a Java program. One approach is to create a new class that is derived from the `Thread` class and to override its `run()` method. An alternative—and more commonly used—technique is to define a class that implements the `Runnable` interface. The `Runnable` interface is defined as follows:

```
public interface Runnable
{
    public abstract void run();
}
```

When a class implements `Runnable`, it must define a `run()` method. The code implementing the `run()` method is what runs as a separate thread.

Figure 4.11 shows the Java version of a multithreaded program that determines the summation of a non-negative integer. The `Summation` class implements the `Runnable` interface. Thread creation is performed by creating

```
#include <windows.h>
#include <stdio.h>
DWORD Sum; /* data is shared by the thread(s) */
/* the thread runs in this separate function */

DWORD WINAPI Summation(LPVOID Param)
{
  DWORD Upper = *(DWORD*)Param;
  for (DWORD i = 0; i <= Upper; i++)
    Sum += i;
  return 0;
}

int main(int argc, char *argv[])
{
  DWORD ThreadId;
  HANDLE ThreadHandle;
  int Param;
  /* perform some basic error checking */
  if (argc != 2) {
    fprintf(stderr,"An integer parameter is required\n");
    return -1;
  }
  Param = atoi(argv[1]);
  if (Param < 0) {
    fprintf(stderr,"An integer >= 0 is required\n");
    return -1;
  }

  // create the thread
  ThreadHandle = CreateThread(
    NULL, // default security attributes
    0, // default stack size
    Summation, // thread function
    &Param, // parameter to thread function
    0, // default creation flags
    &ThreadId); // returns the thread identifier

  if (ThreadHandle != NULL) {
    // now wait for the thread to finish
    WaitForSingleObject(ThreadHandle,INFINITE);

    // close the thread handle
    CloseHandle(ThreadHandle);

    printf("sum = %d\n",Sum);
  }
}
```

Figure 4.10 Multithreaded C program using the Win32 API.

```
class Sum
{
   private int sum;

   public int getSum() {
    return sum;
   }

   public void setSum(int sum) {
    this.sum = sum;
   }
}

class Summation implements Runnable
{
   private int upper;
   private Sum sumValue;

   public Summation(int upper, Sum sumValue) {
    this.upper = upper;
    this.sumValue = sumValue;
   }

   public void run() {
    int sum = 0;
    for (int i = 0; i <= upper; i++)
      sum += i;
    sumValue.setSum(sum);
   }
}

public class Driver
{
   public static void main(String[] args) {
    if (args.length > 0) {
     if (Integer.parseInt(args[0]) < 0)
      System.err.println(args[0] + " must be >= 0.");
     else {
      // create the object to be shared
      Sum sumObject = new Sum();
      int upper = Integer.parseInt(args[0]);
      Thread thrd = new Thread(new Summation(upper, sumObject));
      thrd.start();
      try {
        thrd.join();
        System.out.println
              ("The sum of "+upper+" is "+sumObject.getSum());
     } catch (InterruptedException ie) { }
     }
    }
    else
     System.err.println("Usage: Summation <integer value>"); }
}
```

Figure 4.11 Java program for the summation of a non-negative integer.

an object instance of the Thread class and passing the constructor a Runnable object.

Creating a Thread object does not specifically create the new thread; rather, it is the start() method that creates the new thread. Calling the start() method for the new object does two things:

1. It allocates memory and initializes a new thread in the JVM.

2. It calls the run() method, making the thread eligible to be run by the JVM. (Note that we never call the run() method directly. Rather, we call the start() method, and it calls the run() method on our behalf.)

When the summation program runs, two threads are created by the JVM. The first is the parent thread, which starts execution in the main() method. The second thread is created when the start() method on the Thread object is invoked. This child thread begins execution in the run() method of the Summation class. After outputting the value of the summation, this thread terminates when it exits from its run() method.

Sharing of data between threads occurs easily in Win32 and Pthreads, since shared data are simply declared globally. As a pure object-oriented language, Java has no such notion of global data; if two or more threads are to share data in a Java program, the sharing occurs by passing references to the shared object to the appropriate threads. In the Java program shown in Figure 4.11, the main thread and the summation thread share the object instance of the Sum class. This shared object is referenced through the appropriate getSum() and setSum() methods. (You might wonder why we don't use an Integer object rather than designing a new sum class. The reason is that the Integer class is **immutable**—that is, once its value is set, it cannot change.)

Recall that the parent threads in the Pthreads and Win32 libraries use pthread_join() and WaitForSingleObject() (respectively) to wait for the summation threads to finish before proceeding. The join() method in Java provides similar functionality. (Notice that join() can throw an InterruptedException, which we choose to ignore.)

4.4 Threading Issues

In this section, we discuss some of the issues to consider with multithreaded programs.

4.4.1 The fork() and exec() System Calls

In Chapter 3, we described how the fork() system call is used to create a separate, duplicate process. The semantics of the fork() and exec() system calls change in a multithreaded program.

If one thread in a program calls fork(), does the new process duplicate all threads, or is the new process single-threaded? Some UNIX systems have chosen to have two versions of fork(), one that duplicates all threads and another that duplicates only the thread that invoked the fork() system call.

The exec() system call typically works in the same way as described in Chapter 3. That is, if a thread invokes the exec() system call, the program

The JVM and the Host Operating System

The JVM is typically implemented on top of a host operating system (see Figure 2.20). This setup allows the JVM to hide the implementation details of the underlying operating system and to provide a consistent, abstract environment that allows Java programs to operate on any platform that supports a JVM. The specification for the JVM does not indicate how Java threads are to be mapped to the underlying operating system, instead leaving that decision to the particular implementation of the JVM. For example, the Windows XP operating system uses the one-to-one model; therefore, each Java thread for a JVM running on such a system maps to a kernel thread. On operating systems that use the many-to-many model (such as Tru64 UNIX), a Java thread is mapped according to the many-to-many model. Solaris initially implemented the JVM using the many-to-one model (the green threads library, mentioned earlier). Later releases of the JVM were implemented using the many-to-many model. Beginning with Solaris 9, Java threads were mapped using the one-to-one model. In addition, there may be a relationship between the Java thread library and the thread library on the host operating system. For example, implementations of a JVM for the Windows family of operating systems might use the Win32 API when creating Java threads; Linux, Solaris, and Mac OS X systems might use the Pthreads API.

specified in the parameter to `exec()` will replace the entire process—including all threads.

Which of the two versions of `fork()` to use depends on the application. If `exec()` is called immediately after forking, then duplicating all threads is unnecessary, as the program specified in the parameters to `exec()` will replace the process. In this instance, duplicating only the calling thread is appropriate. If, however, the separate process does not call `exec()` after forking, the separate process should duplicate all threads.

4.4.2 Cancellation

Thread cancellation is the task of terminating a thread before it has completed. For example, if multiple threads are concurrently searching through a database and one thread returns the result, the remaining threads might be canceled. Another situation might occur when a user presses a button on a Web browser that stops a Web page from loading any further. Often, a Web page is loaded using several threads—each image is loaded in a separate thread. When a user presses the *stop* button on the browser, all threads loading the page are canceled.

A thread that is to be canceled is often referred to as the **target thread**. Cancellation of a target thread may occur in two different scenarios:

1. **Asynchronous cancellation**. One thread immediately terminates the target thread.

2. **Deferred cancellation**. The target thread periodically checks whether it should terminate, allowing it an opportunity to terminate itself in an orderly fashion.

The difficulty with cancellation occurs in situations where resources have been allocated to a canceled thread or where a thread is canceled while in the midst of updating data it is sharing with other threads. This becomes especially troublesome with asynchronous cancellation. Often, the operating system will reclaim system resources from a canceled thread but will not reclaim all resources. Therefore, canceling a thread asynchronously may not free a necessary system-wide resource.

With deferred cancellation, in contrast, one thread indicates that a target thread is to be canceled, but cancellation occurs only after the target thread has checked a flag to determine whether or not it should be canceled. The thread can perform this check at a point at which it can be canceled safely. Pthreads refers to such points as **cancellation points**.

4.4.3 Signal Handling

A **signal** is used in UNIX systems to notify a process that a particular event has occurred. A signal may be received either synchronously or asynchronously, depending on the source of and the reason for the event being signaled. All signals, whether synchronous or asynchronous, follow the same pattern:

1. A signal is generated by the occurrence of a particular event.
2. A generated signal is delivered to a process.
3. Once delivered, the signal must be handled.

Examples of synchronous signals include illegal memory access and division by 0. If a running program performs either of these actions, a signal is generated. Synchronous signals are delivered to the same process that performed the operation that caused the signal (that is the reason they are considered synchronous).

When a signal is generated by an event external to a running process, that process receives the signal asynchronously. Examples of such signals include terminating a process with specific keystrokes (such as `<control><C>`) and having a timer expire. Typically, an asynchronous signal is sent to another process.

A signal may be *handled* by one of two possible handlers:

1. A default signal handler
2. A user-defined signal handler

Every signal has a **default signal handler** that is run by the kernel when handling that signal. This default action can be overridden by a **user-defined signal handler** that is called to handle the signal. Signals are handled in different ways. Some signals (such as changing the size of a window) are simply ignored; others (such as an illegal memory access) are handled by terminating the program.

Handling signals in single-threaded programs is straightforward: signals are always delivered to a process. However, delivering signals is more complicated in multithreaded programs, where a process may have several threads. Where, then, should a signal be delivered?

In general, the following options exist:

1. Deliver the signal to the thread to which the signal applies.
2. Deliver the signal to every thread in the process.
3. Deliver the signal to certain threads in the process.
4. Assign a specific thread to receive all signals for the process.

The method for delivering a signal depends on the type of signal generated. For example, synchronous signals need to be delivered to the thread causing the signal and not to other threads in the process. However, the situation with asynchronous signals is not as clear. Some asynchronous signals—such as a signal that terminates a process (`<control><C>`, for example)—should be sent to all threads.

Most multithreaded versions of UNIX allow a thread to specify which signals it will accept and which it will block. Therefore, in some cases, an asynchronous signal may be delivered only to those threads that are not blocking it. However, because signals need to be handled only once, a signal is typically delivered only to the first thread found that is not blocking it. The standard UNIX function for delivering a signal is `kill(pid_t pid, int signal)`, which specifies the process (`pid`) to which a particular signal is to be delivered. POSIX Pthreads provides the `pthread_kill(pthread_t tid, int signal)` function, which allows a signal to be delivered to a specified thread (`tid`).

Although Windows does not explicitly provide support for signals, they can be emulated using **asynchronous procedure calls (APCs)**. The APC facility allows a user thread to specify a function that is to be called when the user thread receives notification of a particular event. As indicated by its name, an APC is roughly equivalent to an asynchronous signal in UNIX. However, whereas UNIX must contend with how to deal with signals in a multithreaded environment, the APC facility is more straightforward, since an APC is delivered to a particular thread rather than a process.

4.4.4 Thread Pools

In Section 4.1, we mentioned multithreading in a Web server. In this situation, whenever the server receives a request, it creates a separate thread to service the request. Whereas creating a separate thread is certainly superior to creating a separate process, a multithreaded server nonetheless has potential problems. The first issue concerns the amount of time required to create the thread prior to servicing the request, together with the fact that this thread will be discarded once it has completed its work. The second issue is more troublesome: if we allow all concurrent requests to be serviced in a new thread, we have not placed a bound on the number of threads concurrently active in the system. Unlimited threads could exhaust system resources, such as CPU time or memory. One solution to this problem is to use a **thread pool**.

The general idea behind a thread pool is to create a number of threads at process startup and place them into a *pool,* where they sit and wait for work. When a server receives a request, it awakens a thread from this pool—if one is available—and passes it the request for service. Once the thread completes its service, it returns to the pool and awaits more work. If the pool contains no available thread, the server waits until one becomes free.

Thread pools offer these benefits:

1. Servicing a request with an existing thread is usually faster than waiting to create a thread.
2. A thread pool limits the number of threads that exist at any one point. This is particularly important on systems that cannot support a large number of concurrent threads.

The number of threads in the pool can be set heuristically based on factors such as the number of CPUs in the system, the amount of physical memory, and the expected number of concurrent client requests. More sophisticated thread-pool architectures can dynamically adjust the number of threads in the pool according to usage patterns. Such architectures provide the further benefit of having a smaller pool—thereby consuming less memory—when the load on the system is low.

The Win32 API provides several functions related to thread pools. Using the thread pool API is similar to creating a thread with the `Thread Create()` function, as described in Section 4.3.2. Here, a function that is to run as a separate thread is defined. Such a function may appear as follows:

```
DWORD WINAPI PoolFunction(AVOID Param) {
   /**
   * this function runs as a separate thread.
   **/
}
```

A pointer to `PoolFunction()` is passed to one of the functions in the thread pool API, and a thread from the pool executes this function. One such member in the thread pool API is the `QueueUserWorkItem()` function, which is passed three parameters:

- `LPTHREAD_START_ROUTINE Function`—a pointer to the function that is to run as a separate thread
- `PVOID Param`—the parameter passed to `Function`
- `ULONG Flags`—flags indicating how the thread pool is to create and manage execution of the thread

An example of invoking a function is:

```
QueueUserWorkItem(&PoolFunction, NULL, 0);
```

This causes a thread from the thread pool to invoke `PoolFunction()` on behalf of the programmer. In this instance, we pass no parameters to

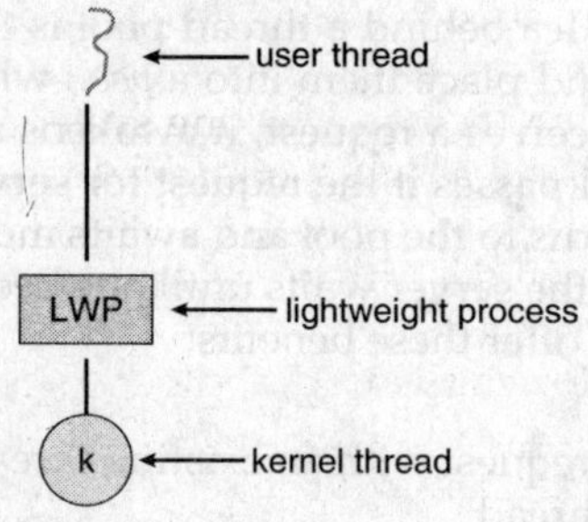

Figure 4.12 Lightweight process (LWP).

PoolFunction(). Because we specify 0 as a flag, we provide the thread pool with no special instructions for thread creation.

Other members in the Win32 thread pool API include utilities that invoke functions at periodic intervals or when an asynchronous I/O request completes. The `java.util.concurrent` package in Java 1.5 provides a thread pool utility as well.

4.4.5 Thread-Specific Data

Threads belonging to a process share the data of the process. Indeed, this sharing of data provides one of the benefits of multithreaded programming. However, in some circumstances, each thread might need its own copy of certain data. We will call such data **thread-specific data**. For example, in a transaction-processing system, we might service each transaction in a separate thread. Furthermore, each transaction might be assigned a unique identifier. To associate each thread with its unique identifier, we could use thread-specific data. Most thread libraries—including Win32 and Pthreads—provide some form of support for thread-specific data. Java provides support as well.

4.4.6 Scheduler Activations

A final issue to be considered with multithreaded programs concerns communication between the kernel and the thread library, which may be required by the many-to-many and two-level models discussed in Section 4.2.3. Such coordination allows the number of kernel threads to be dynamically adjusted to help ensure the best performance.

Many systems implementing either the many-to-many or the two-level model place an intermediate data structure between the user and kernel threads. This data structure—typically known as a lightweight process, or LWP—is shown in Figure 4.12. To the user-thread library, the LWP appears to be a *virtual processor* on which the application can schedule a user thread to run. Each LWP is attached to a kernel thread, and it is kernel threads that the operating system schedules to run on physical processors. If a kernel thread blocks (such as while waiting for an I/O operation to complete), the LWP blocks as well. Up the chain, the user-level thread attached to the LWP also blocks.

An application may require any number of LWPs to run efficiently. Consider a CPU-bound application running on a single processor. In this scenario, only one thread can run at once, so one LWP is sufficient. An application that is I/O-intensive may require multiple LWPs to execute, however. Typically, an LWP is required for each concurrent blocking system call. Suppose, for example, that five different file-read requests occur simultaneously. Five LWPs are needed, because all could be waiting for I/O completion in the kernel. If a process has only four LWPs, then the fifth request must wait for one of the LWPs to return from the kernel.

One scheme for communication between the user-thread library and the kernel is known as **scheduler activation**. It works as follows: The kernel provides an application with a set of virtual processors (LWPs), and the application can schedule user threads onto an available virtual processor. Furthermore, the kernel must inform an application about certain events. This procedure is known as an **upcall**. Upcalls are handled by the thread library with an **upcall handler**, and upcall handlers must run on a virtual processor. One event that triggers an upcall occurs when an application thread is about to block. In this scenario, the kernel makes an upcall to the application informing it that a thread is about to block and identifying the specific thread. The kernel then allocates a new virtual processor to the application. The application runs an upcall handler on this new virtual processor, which saves the state of the blocking thread and relinquishes the virtual processor on which the blocking thread is running. The upcall handler then schedules another thread that is eligible to run on the new virtual processor. When the event that the blocking thread was waiting for occurs, the kernel makes another upcall to the thread library informing it that the previously blocked thread is now eligible to run. The upcall handler for this event also requires a virtual processor, and the kernel may allocate a new virtual processor or preempt one of the user threads and run the upcall handler on its virtual processor. After marking the unblocked thread as eligible to run, the application schedules an eligible thread to run on an available virtual processor.

4.5 Operating-System Examples

In this section, we explore how threads are implemented in Windows XP and Linux systems.

4.5.1 Windows XP Threads

Windows XP implements the Win32 API, which is the primary API for the family of Microsoft operating systems (Windows 95, 98, NT, 2000, and XP). Indeed, much of what is mentioned in this section applies to this entire family of operating systems.

A Windows XP application runs as a separate process, and each process may contain one or more threads. The Win32 API for creating threads is covered in Section 4.3.2. Windows XP uses the one-to-one mapping described in Section 4.2.2, where each user-level thread maps to an associated kernel thread. However, Windows XP also provides support for a **fiber** library, which provides the functionality of the many-to-many model (Section 4.2.3). By using the thread library, any thread belonging to a process can access the address space of the process.

The general components of a thread include:

- A thread ID uniquely identifying the thread
- A register set representing the status of the processor
- A user stack, employed when the thread is running in user mode, and a kernel stack, employed when the thread is running in kernel mode
- A private storage area used by various run-time libraries and dynamic link libraries (DLLs)

The register set, stacks, and private storage area are known as the **context** of the thread. The primary data structures of a thread include:

- ETHREAD—executive thread block
- KTHREAD—kernel thread block
- TEB—thread environment block

The key components of the ETHREAD include a pointer to the process to which the thread belongs and the address of the routine in which the thread starts control. The ETHREAD also contains a pointer to the corresponding KTHREAD.

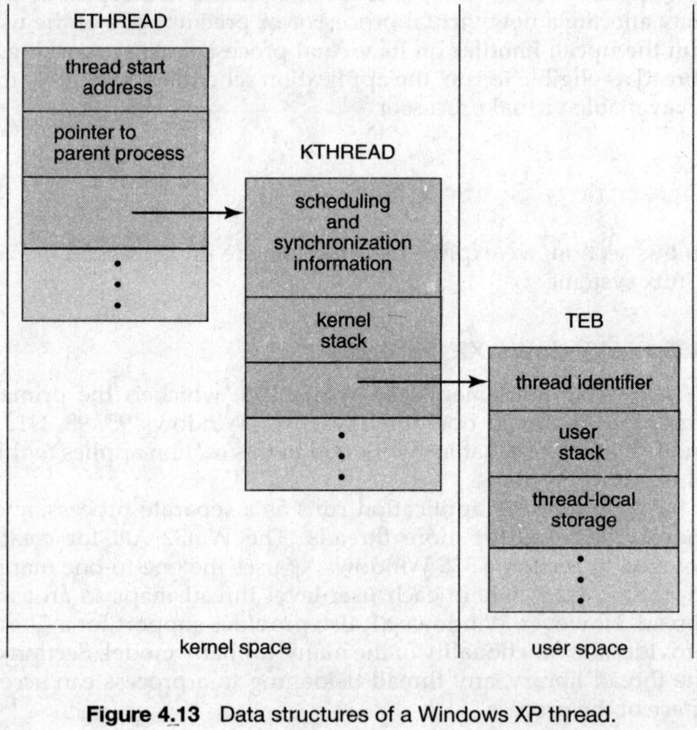

Figure 4.13 Data structures of a Windows XP thread.

The KTHREAD includes scheduling and synchronization information for the thread. In addition, the KTHREAD includes the kernel stack (used when the thread is running in kernel mode) and a pointer to the TEB.

The ETHREAD and the KTHREAD exist entirely in kernel space; this means that only the kernel can access them. The TEB is a user-space data structure that is accessed when the thread is running in user mode. Among other fields, the TEB contains the thread identifier, a user-mode stack, and an array for thread-specific data (which Windows XP terms **thread-local storage**). The structure of a Windows XP thread is illustrated in Figure 4.13.

4.5.2 Linux Threads

Linux provides the `fork()` system call with the traditional functionality of duplicating a process, as described in Chapter 3. Linux also provides the ability to create threads using the `clone()` system call. However, Linux does not distinguish between processes and threads. In fact, Linux generally uses the term *task*—rather than *process* or *thread*—when referring to a flow of control within a program.

When `clone()` is invoked, it is passed a set of flags, which determine how much sharing is to take place between the parent and child tasks. Some of these flags are listed below:

flag	meaning
CLONE_FS	File-system information is shared.
CLONE_VM	The same memory space is shared.
CLONE_SIGHAND	Signal handlers are shared.
CLONE_FILES	The set of open files is shared.

For example, if `clone()` is passed the flags CLONE_FS, CLONE_VM, CLONE_SIGHAND, and CLONE_FILES, the parent and child tasks will share the same file-system information (such as the current working directory), the same memory space, the same signal handlers, and the same set of open files. Using `clone()` in this fashion is equivalent to creating a thread as described in this chapter, since the parent task shares most of its resources with its child task. However, if none of these flags is set when `clone()` is invoked, no sharing takes place, resulting in functionality similar to that provided by the `fork()` system call.

The varying level of sharing is possible because of the way a task is represented in the Linux kernel. A unique kernel data structure (specifically, `struct task_struct`) exists for each task in the system. This data structure, instead of storing data for the task, contains pointers to other data structures where these data are stored—for example, data structures that represent the list of open files, signal-handling information, and virtual memory. When `fork()` is invoked, a new task is created, along with a *copy* of all the associated data structures of the parent process. A new task is also created when the `clone()` system call is made. However, rather than copying all data structures, the new task *points* to the data structures of the parent task, depending on the set of flags passed to `clone()`.

Several distributions of the Linux kernel now include the NPTL thread library. NPTL (which stands for Native POSIX Thread Library) provides a POSIX-compliant thread model for Linux systems along with several other features, such as better support for SMP systems, as well as taking advantage of NUMA support. In addition, the start-up cost for creating a thread is lower with NPTL than with traditional Linux threads. Finally, with NPTL, the system has the potential to support hundreds of thousands of threads. Such support becomes more important with the growth of multicore and other SMP systems.

4.6 Summary

A thread is a flow of control within a process. A multithreaded process contains several different flows of control within the same address space. The benefits of multithreading include increased responsiveness to the user, resource sharing within the process, economy, and scalability issues such as more efficient use of multiple cores.

User-level threads are threads that are visible to the programmer and are unknown to the kernel. The operating-system kernel supports and manages kernel-level threads. In general, user-level threads are faster to create and manage than are kernel threads, as no intervention from the kernel is required. Three different types of models relate user and kernel threads: The many-to-one model maps many user threads to a single kernel thread. The one-to-one model maps each user thread to a corresponding kernel thread. The many-to-many model multiplexes many user threads to a smaller or equal number of kernel threads.

Most modern operating systems provide kernel support for threads; among these are Windows 98, NT, 2000, and XP, as well as Solaris and Linux.

Thread libraries provide the application programmer with an API for creating and managing threads. Three primary thread libraries are in common use: POSIX Pthreads, Win32 threads for Windows systems, and Java threads.

Multithreaded programs introduce many challenges for the programmer, including the semantics of the `fork()` and `exec()` system calls. Other issues include thread cancellation, signal handling, and thread-specific data.

Exercises

4.1 Provide two programming examples in which multithreading does *not* provide better performance than a single-threaded solution.

4.2 Write a multithreaded Java, Pthreads, or Win32 program that outputs prime numbers. This program should work as follows: The user will run the program and will enter a number on the command line. The program will then create a separate thread that outputs all the prime numbers less than or equal to the number entered by the user.

4.3 Which of the following components of program state are shared across threads in a multithreaded process?

a. Register values

b. Heap memory

c. Global variables

d. Stack memory

4.4 The program shown in Figure 4.14 uses the Pthreads API. What would be the output from the program at LINE C and LINE P?

```
#include <pthread.h>
#include <stdio.h>

int value = 0;
void *runner(void *param); /* the thread */

int main(int argc, char *argv[])
{
int pid;
pthread_t tid;
pthread_attr_t attr;

  pid = fork();

  if (pid == 0) { /* child process */
    pthread_attr_init(&attr);
    pthread_create(&tid,&attr,runner,NULL);
    pthread_join(tid,NULL);
    printf("CHILD: value = %d",value); /* LINE C */
  }
  else if (pid > 0) { /* parent process */
    wait(NULL);
    printf("PARENT: value = %d",value); /* LINE P */
  }
}

void *runner(void *param) {
  value = 5;
  pthread_exit(0);
}
```

Figure 4.14 C program for Exercise 4.4.

4.5 Consider a multiprocessor system and a multithreaded program written using the many-to-many threading model. Let the number of user-level threads in the program be more than the number of processors in the system. Discuss the performance implications of the following scenarios.

a. The number of kernel threads allocated to the program is less than the number of processors.

b. The number of kernel threads allocated to the program is equal to the number of processors.

c. The number of kernel threads allocated to the program is greater than the number of processors but less than the number of user-level threads.

4.6 What are two differences between user-level threads and kernel-level threads? Under what circumstances is one type better than the other?

4.7 Exercise 3.16 in Chapter 3 involves designing an echo server using the Java threading API. However, this server is single-threaded, meaning that the server cannot respond to concurrent echo clients until the current client exits. Modify the solution to Exercise 3.16 so that the echo server services each client in a separate request.

4.8 Modify the socket-based date server (Figure 3.19) in Chapter 3 so that the server services each client request in a separate thread.

4.9 Can a multithreaded solution using multiple user-level threads achieve better performance on a multiprocessor system than on a single-processor system? Explain.

4.10 What resources are used when a thread is created? How do they differ from those used when a process is created?

4.11 Under what circumstances does a multithreaded solution using multiple kernel threads provide better performance than a single-threaded solution on a single-processor system?

4.12 The Fibonacci sequence is the series of numbers 0, 1, 1, 2, 3, 5, 8, ... Formally, it can be expressed as:

$$fib_0 = 0$$
$$fib_1 = 1$$
$$fib_n = fib_{n-1} + fib_{n-2}$$

Write a multithreaded program that generates the Fibonacci sequence using either the Java, Pthreads, or Win32 thread library. This program should work as follows: The user will enter on the command line the number of Fibonacci numbers that the program is to generate. The program will then create a separate thread that will generate the Fibonacci numbers, placing the sequence in data that can be shared by the threads (an array is probably the most convenient data structure). When the thread finishes execution, the parent thread will output the sequence generated by the child thread. Because the parent thread cannot begin outputting the Fibonacci sequence until the child thread finishes, this will require having the parent thread wait for the child thread to finish, using the techniques described in Section 4.3.

4.13 A Pthread program that performs the summation function was provided in Section 4.3.1. Rewrite this program in Java.

4.14 As described in Section 4.5.2, Linux does not distinguish between processes and threads. Instead, Linux treats both in the same way, allowing a task to be more akin to a process or a thread depending on the set of flags passed to the `clone()` system call. However, many operating systems—such as Windows XP and Solaris—treat processes and threads differently. Typically, such systems use a notation wherein the data structure for a process contains pointers to the separate threads belonging to the process. Contrast these two approaches for modeling processes and threads within the kernel.

4.15 Describe the actions taken by a thread library to context-switch between user-level threads.

Projects

The set of projects below deal with two distinct topics—naming service and matrix muliplication.

Project 1: Naming Service Project

A naming service such as DNS (for domain name system) can be used to resolve IP names to IP addresses. For example, when someone accesses the host `www.westminstercollege.edu`, a naming service is used to determine the IP address that is mapped to the IP name `www.westminstercollege.edu`. This assignment consists of writing a multithreaded naming service in Java using sockets (see Section 3.6.1).

The `java.net` API provides the following mechanism for resolving IP names:

```
InetAddress hostAddress =
   InetAddress.getByName("www.westminstercollege.edu");
String IPaddress = hostAddress.getHostAddress();
```

where `getByName()` throws an `UnknownHostException` if it is unable to resolve the host name.

The Server

The server will listen to port 6052 waiting for client connections. When a client connection is made, the server will service the connection in a separate thread and will resume listening for additional client connections. Once a client makes a connection to the server, the client will write the IP name it wishes the server to resolve—such as `www.westminstercollege.edu`—to the socket. The server thread will read this IP name from the socket and either resolve its IP address or, if it cannot locate the host address, catch an `UnknownHostException`. The server will write the IP address back to the client or, in the case of an `UnknownHostException`, will write the message "`Unable to resolve host <host name>`." Once the server has written to the client, it will close its socket connection.

The Client

Initially, write just the server application and connect to it via telnet. For example, assuming the server is running on the localhost, a telnet session would appear as follows. (Client responses appear in blue.)

```
telnet localhost 6052
Connected to localhost.
Escape character is '^]'.
www.westminstercollege.edu
146.86.1.17
Connection closed by foreign host.
```

By initially having telnet act as a client, you can more easily debug any problems you may have with your server. Once you are convinced your server is working properly, you can write a client application. The client will be passed the IP name that is to be resolved as a parameter. The client will open a socket connection to the server and then write the IP name that is to be resolved. It will then read the response sent back by the server. As an example, if the client is named `NSClient`, it is invoked as follows:

```
java NSClient www.westminstercollege.edu
```

and the server will respond with the corresponding IP address or "unknown host" message. Once the client has output the IP address, it will close its socket connection.

Project 2: Matrix Multiplication Project

Given two matrices, A and B, where matrix A contains M rows and K columns and matrix B contains K rows and N columns, the **matrix product** of A and B is matrix C, where C contains M rows and N columns. The entry in matrix C for row i, column j ($C_{i,j}$) is the sum of the products of the elements for row i in matrix A and column j in matrix B. That is,

$$C_{i,j} = \sum_{n=1}^{K} A_{i,n} \times B_{n,j}$$

For example, if A is a 3-by-2 matrix and B is a 2-by-3 matrix, element $C_{3,1}$ is the sum of $A_{3,1} \times B_{1,1}$ and $A_{3,2} \times B_{2,1}$.

For this project, calculate each element $C_{i,j}$ in a separate *worker* thread. This will involve creating $M \times N$ worker threads. The main—or parent—thread will initialize the matrices A and B and allocate sufficient memory for matrix C, which will hold the product of matrices A and B. These matrices will be declared as global data so that each worker thread has access to A, B, and C.

Matrices A and B can be initialized statically, as shown below:

```
#define M 3
#define K 2
#define N 3

int A [M][K] = { {1,4}, {2,5}, {3,6} };
int B [K][N] = { {8,7,6}, {5,4,3} };
int C [M] [N];
```

Alternatively, they can be populated by reading in values from a file.

Passing Parameters to Each Thread

The parent thread will create $M \times N$ worker threads, passing each worker the values of row i and column j that it is to use in calculating the matrix product. This requires passing two parameters to each thread. The easiest approach with Pthreads and Win32 is to create a data structure using a `struct`. The members of this structure are i and j, and the structure appears as follows:

```
/* structure for passing data to threads */
struct v
{
   int i; /* row */
   int j; /* column */
};
```

Both the Pthreads and Win32 programs will create the worker threads using a strategy similar to that shown below:

```
/* We have to create M * N worker threads */
for (i = 0; i < M, i++)
   for (j = 0; j < N; j++ ) {
      struct v *data = (struct v *) malloc(sizeof(struct v));
      data->i = i;
      data->j = j;
      /* Now create the thread passing it data as a parameter */
   }
}
```

```
public class WorkerThread implements Runnable
{
    private int row;
    private int col;
    private int[][] A;
    private int[][] B;
    private int[][] C;

    public WorkerThread(int row, int col, int[][] A,
     int[][] B, int[][] C) {
      this.row = row;
      this.col = col;
      this.A = A;
      this.B = B;
      this.C = C;
    }
    public void run() {
      /* calculate the matrix product in C[row] [col] */
    }
}
```

Figure 4.15 Worker thread in Java.

The data pointer will be passed to either the `pthread_create()` (Pthreads) function or the `CreateThread()` (Win32) function, which in turn will pass it as a parameter to the function that is to run as a separate thread.

Sharing of data between Java threads is different from sharing between threads in Pthreads or Win32. One approach is for the main thread to create and initialize the matrices A, B, and C. This main thread will then create the worker threads, passing the three matrices—along with row i and column j—to the constructor for each worker. Thus, the outline of a worker thread appears in Figure 4.15.

Waiting for Threads to Complete

Once all worker threads have completed, the main thread will output the product contained in matrix C. This requires the main thread to wait for all worker threads to finish before it can output the value of the matrix product. Several different strategies can be used to enable a thread to wait for other threads to finish. Section 4.3 describes how to wait for a child thread to complete using the Win32, Pthreads, and Java thread libraries. Win32 provides the `WaitForSingleObject()` function, whereas Pthreads and Java use `pthread_join()` and `join()`, respectively. However, in these programming examples, the parent thread waits for a single child thread to finish; completing this exercise will require waiting for multiple threads.

In Section 4.3.2, we describe the `WaitForSingleObject()` function, which is used to wait for a single thread to finish. However, the Win32 API also provides the `WaitForMultipleObjects()` function, which is used when waiting for multiple threads to complete. `WaitForMultipleObjects()` is passed four parameters:

```
#define NUM_THREADS 10

/* an array of threads to be joined upon */
pthread_t workers[NUM_THREADS];

for (int i = 0; i < NUM_THREADS; i++)
   pthread_join(workers[i], NULL);
```

Figure 4.16 Pthread code for joining ten threads.

1. The number of objects to wait for
2. A pointer to the array of objects
3. A flag indicating if all objects have been signaled
4. A timeout duration (or INFINITE)

For example, if THandles is an array of thread HANDLE objects of size N, the parent thread can wait for all its child threads to complete with the statement:

```
WaitForMultipleObjects(N, THandles, TRUE, INFINITE);
```

A simple strategy for waiting on several threads using the Pthreads pthread_join() or Java's join() is to enclose the join operation within a simple for loop. For example, you could join on ten threads using the Pthread code depicted in Figure 4.16. The equivalent code using Java threads is shown in Figure 4.17.

```
final static int NUM_THREADS = 10;

/* an array of threads to be joined upon */
Thread[] workers = new Thread[NUM_THREADS];

for (int i = 0; i < NUM_THREADS; i++) {
   try {
      workers[i].join();
    } catch (InterruptedException ie) { }
}
```

Figure 4.17 Java code for joining ten threads.

Bibliographical Notes

Threads have had a long evolution, starting as "cheap concurrency" in programming languages and moving to "lightweight processes", with early examples that included the Thoth system (Cheriton et al. [1979]) and the Pilot system (Redell et al. [1980]). Binding [1985] described moving threads into the UNIX kernel. Mach (Accetta et al. [1986], Tevanian et al. [1987a]) and V (Cheriton [1988]) made extensive use of threads, and eventually almost all major operating systems implemented them in some form or another.

Thread performance issues were discussed by Anderson et al. [1989], who continued their work in Anderson et al. [1991] by evaluating the performance of user-level threads with kernel support. Bershad et al. [1990] describe combining threads with RPC. Engelschall [2000] discusses a technique for supporting user-level threads. An analysis of an optimal thread-pool size can be found in Ling et al. [2000]. Scheduler activations were first presented in Anderson et al. [1991], and Williams [2002] discusses scheduler activations in the NetBSD system. Other mechanisms by which the user-level thread library and the kernel cooperate with each other are discussed in Marsh et al. [1991], Govindan and Anderson [1991], Draves et al. [1991], and Black [1990]. Zabatta and Young [1998] compare Windows NT and Solaris threads on a symmetric multiprocessor. Pinilla and Gill [2003] compare Java thread performance on Linux, Windows, and Solaris.

Vahalia [1996] covers threading in several versions of UNIX. McDougall and Mauro [2007] describe recent developments in threading the Solaris kernel. Russinovich and Solomon [2005] discuss threading in the Windows operating system family. Bovet and Cesati [2006] and Love [2004] explain how Linux handles threading and Singh [2007] covers threads in Mac OS X.

Information on Pthreads programming is given in Lewis and Berg [1998] and Butenhof [1997]. Oaks and Wong [1999], Lewis and Berg [2000], and Holub [2000] discuss multithreading in Java. Goetz et al. [2006] present a detailed discussion of concurrent programming in Java. Beveridge and Wiener [1997] and Cohen and Woodring [1997] describe multithreading using Win32.

CHAPTER 5

Process Scheduling

CPU scheduling is the basis of multiprogrammed operating systems. By switching the CPU among processes, the operating system can make the computer more productive. In this chapter, we introduce basic CPU-scheduling concepts and present several CPU-scheduling algorithms. We also consider the problem of selecting an algorithm for a particular system.

In Chapter 4, we introduced threads to the process model. On operating systems that support them, it is kernel-level threads—not processes—that are in fact being scheduled by the operating system. However, the terms **process scheduling** and **thread scheduling** are often used interchangeably. In this chapter, we use *process scheduling* when discussing general scheduling concepts and *thread scheduling* to refer to thread-specific ideas.

CHAPTER OBJECTIVES

- To introduce CPU scheduling, which is the basis for multiprogrammed operating systems.
- To describe various CPU-scheduling algorithms.
- To discuss evaluation criteria for selecting a CPU-scheduling algorithm for a particular system.

5.1 Basic Concepts

In a single-processor system, only one process can run at a time; any others must wait until the CPU is free and can be rescheduled. The objective of multiprogramming is to have some process running at all times, to maximize CPU utilization. The idea is relatively simple. A process is executed until it must wait, typically for the completion of some I/O request. In a simple computer system, the CPU then just sits idle. All this waiting time is wasted; no useful work is accomplished. With multiprogramming, we try to use this time productively. Several processes are kept in memory at one time. When one process has to wait, the operating system takes the CPU away from that

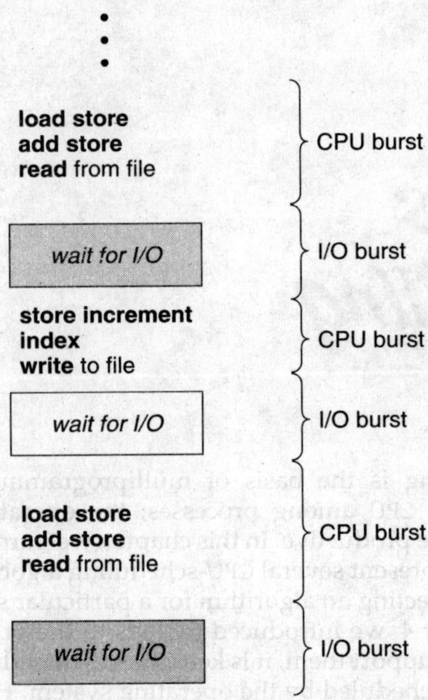

Figure 5.1 Alternating sequence of CPU and I/O bursts.

process and gives the CPU to another process. This pattern continues. Every time one process has to wait, another process can take over use of the CPU.

Scheduling of this kind is a fundamental operating-system function. Almost all computer resources are scheduled before use. The CPU is, of course, one of the primary computer resources. Thus, its scheduling is central to operating-system design.

5.1.1 CPU–I/O Burst Cycle

The success of CPU scheduling depends on an observed property of processes: process execution consists of a **cycle** of CPU execution and I/O wait. Processes alternate between these two states. Process execution begins with a **CPU burst**. That is followed by an **I/O burst**, which is followed by another CPU burst, then another I/O burst, and so on. Eventually, the final CPU burst ends with a system request to terminate execution (Figure 5.1).

The durations of CPU bursts have been measured extensively. Although they vary greatly from process to process and from computer to computer, they tend to have a frequency curve similar to that shown in Figure 5.2. The curve is generally characterized as exponential or hyperexponential, with a large number of short CPU bursts and a small number of long CPU bursts. An I/O-bound program typically has many short CPU bursts. A CPU-bound

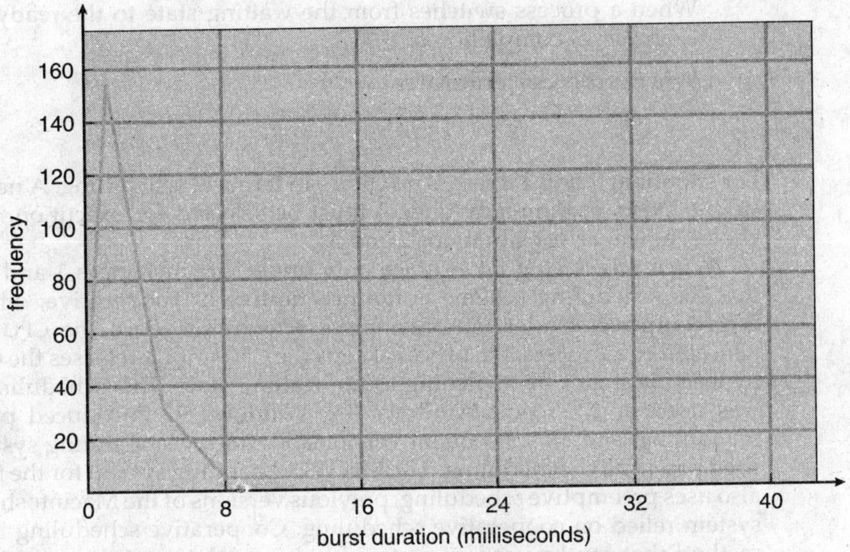

Figure 5.2 Histogram of CPU-burst durations.

program might have a few long CPU bursts. This distribution can be important in the selection of an appropriate CPU-scheduling algorithm.

5.1.2 CPU Scheduler

Whenever the CPU becomes idle, the operating system must select one of the processes in the ready queue to be executed. The selection process is carried out by the **short-term scheduler** (or CPU scheduler). The scheduler selects a process from the processes in memory that are ready to execute and allocates the CPU to that process.

Note that the ready queue is not necessarily a first-in, first-out (FIFO) queue. As we shall see when we consider the various scheduling algorithms, a ready queue can be implemented as a FIFO queue, a priority queue, a tree, or simply an unordered linked list. Conceptually, however, all the processes in the ready queue are lined up waiting for a chance to run on the CPU. The records in the queues are generally process control blocks (PCBs) of the processes.

5.1.3 Preemptive Scheduling

CPU-scheduling decisions may take place under the following four circumstances:

1. When a process switches from the running state to the waiting state (for example, as the result of an I/O request or an invocation of `wait` for the termination of one of the child processes)
2. When a process switches from the running state to the ready state (for example, when an interrupt occurs)

3. When a process switches from the waiting state to the ready state (for example, at completion of I/O)
4. When a process terminates

For situations 1 and 4, there is no choice in terms of scheduling. A new process (if one exists in the ready queue) must be selected for execution. There is a choice, however, for situations 2 and 3.

When scheduling takes place only under circumstances 1 and 4, we say that the scheduling scheme is **nonpreemptive** or **cooperative**; otherwise, it is **preemptive**. Under nonpreemptive scheduling, once the CPU has been allocated to a process, the process keeps the CPU until it releases the CPU either by terminating or by switching to the waiting state. This scheduling method was used by Microsoft Windows 3.x; Windows 95 introduced preemptive scheduling, and all subsequent versions of Windows operating systems have used preemptive scheduling. The Mac OS X operating system for the Macintosh also uses preemptive scheduling; previous versions of the Macintosh operating system relied on cooperative scheduling. Cooperative scheduling is the only method that can be used on certain hardware platforms, because it does not require the special hardware (for example, a timer) needed for preemptive scheduling.

Unfortunately, preemptive scheduling incurs a cost associated with access to shared data. Consider the case of two processes that share data. While one is updating the data, it is preempted so that the second process can run. The second process then tries to read the data, which are in an inconsistent state. In such situations, we need new mechanisms to coordinate access to shared data; we discuss this topic in Chapter 6.

Preemption also affects the design of the operating-system kernel. During the processing of a system call, the kernel may be busy with an activity on behalf of a process. Such activities may involve changing important kernel data (for instance, I/O queues). What happens if the process is preempted in the middle of these changes and the kernel (or the device driver) needs to read or modify the same structure? Chaos ensues. Certain operating systems, including most versions of UNIX, deal with this problem by waiting either for a system call to complete or for an I/O block to take place before doing a context switch. This scheme ensures that the kernel structure is simple, since the kernel will not preempt a process while the kernel data structures are in an inconsistent state. Unfortunately, this kernel-execution model is a poor one for supporting real-time computing and multiprocessing. These problems, and their solutions, are described in Sections 5.5 and 19.5.

Because interrupts can, by definition, occur at any time, and because they cannot always be ignored by the kernel, the sections of code affected by interrupts must be guarded from simultaneous use. The operating system needs to accept interrupts at almost all times; otherwise, input might be lost or output overwritten. So that these sections of code are not accessed concurrently by several processes, they disable interrupts at entry and reenable interrupts at exit. It is important to note that sections of code that disable interrupts do not occur very often and typically contain few instructions.

5.1.4 Dispatcher

Another component involved in the CPU-scheduling function is the **dispatcher**. The dispatcher is the module that gives control of the CPU to the process selected by the short-term scheduler. This function involves the following:

- Switching context
- Switching to user mode
- Jumping to the proper location in the user program to restart that program

The dispatcher should be as fast as possible, since it is invoked during every process switch. The time it takes for the dispatcher to stop one process and start another running is known as the **dispatch latency**.

5.2 Scheduling Criteria

Different CPU-scheduling algorithms have different properties, and the choice of a particular algorithm may favor one class of processes over another. In choosing which algorithm to use in a particular situation, we must consider the properties of the various algorithms.

Many criteria have been suggested for comparing CPU-scheduling algorithms. Which characteristics are used for comparison can make a substantial difference in which algorithm is judged to be best. The criteria include the following:

- **CPU utilization**. We want to keep the CPU as busy as possible. Conceptually, CPU utilization can range from 0 to 100 percent. In a real system, it should range from 40 percent (for a lightly loaded system) to 90 percent (for a heavily used system).
- **Throughput**. If the CPU is busy executing processes, then work is being done. One measure of work is the number of processes that are completed per time unit, called *throughput*. For long processes, this rate may be one process per hour; for short transactions, it may be ten processes per second.
- **Turnaround time**. From the point of view of a particular process, the important criterion is how long it takes to execute that process. The interval from the time of submission of a process to the time of completion is the *turnaround time.* Turnaround time is the sum of the periods spent waiting to get into memory, waiting in the ready queue, executing on the CPU, and doing I/O.
- **Waiting time**. The CPU-scheduling algorithm does not affect the amount of time during which a process executes or does I/O; it affects only the amount of time that a process spends waiting in the ready queue. *Waiting time* is the sum of the periods spent waiting in the ready queue.
- **Response time**. In an interactive system, turnaround time may not be the best criterion. Often, a process can produce some output fairly early and can continue computing new results while previous results are being

output to the user. Thus, another measure is the time from the submission of a request until the first response is produced. This measure, called *response time*, is the time it takes to start responding, not the time it takes to output the response. The turnaround time is generally limited by the speed of the output device.

It is desirable to maximize CPU utilization and throughput and to minimize turnaround time, waiting time, and response time. In most cases, we optimize the average measure. However, under some circumstances, it is desirable to optimize the minimum or maximum values rather than the average. For example, to guarantee that all users get good service, we may want to minimize the maximum response time.

Investigators have suggested that, for interactive systems (such as time-sharing systems), it is more important to minimize the *variance* in the response time than to minimize the average response time. A system with reasonable and *predictable* response time may be considered more desirable than a system that is faster on the average but is highly variable. However, little work has been done on CPU-scheduling algorithms that minimize variance.

As we discuss various CPU-scheduling algorithms in the following section, we illustrate their operation. An accurate illustration should involve many processes, each a sequence of several hundred CPU bursts and I/O bursts. For simplicity, though, we consider only one CPU burst (in milliseconds) per process in our examples. Our measure of comparison is the average waiting time. More elaborate evaluation mechanisms are discussed in Section 5.7.

5.3 Scheduling Algorithms

CPU scheduling deals with the problem of deciding which of the processes in the ready queue is to be allocated the CPU. There are many different CPU-scheduling algorithms. In this section, we describe several of them.

5.3.1 First-Come, First-Served Scheduling

By far the simplest CPU-scheduling algorithm is the **first-come, first-served (FCFS) scheduling algorithm**. With this scheme, the process that requests the CPU first is allocated the CPU first. The implementation of the FCFS policy is easily managed with a FIFO queue. When a process enters the ready queue, its PCB is linked onto the tail of the queue. When the CPU is free, it is allocated to the process at the head of the queue. The running process is then removed from the queue. The code for FCFS scheduling is simple to write and understand.

On the negative side, the average waiting time under the FCFS policy is often quite long. Consider the following set of processes that arrive at time 0, with the length of the CPU burst given in milliseconds:

Process	Burst Time
P_1	24
P_2	3
P_3	3

If the processes arrive in the order P_1, P_2, P_3, and are served in FCFS order, we get the result shown in the following **Gantt chart**, which is a bar chart that illustrates a particular schedule, including the start and finish times of each of the participating processes:

The waiting time is 0 milliseconds for process P_1, 24 milliseconds for process P_2, and 27 milliseconds for process P_3. Thus, the average waiting time is (0 + 24 + 27)/3 = 17 milliseconds. If the processes arrive in the order P_2, P_3, P_1, however, the results will be as shown in the following Gantt chart:

The average waiting time is now (6 + 0 + 3)/3 = 3 milliseconds. This reduction is substantial. Thus, the average waiting time under an FCFS policy is generally not minimal and may vary substantially if the processes CPU burst times vary greatly.

In addition, consider the performance of FCFS scheduling in a dynamic situation. Assume we have one CPU-bound process and many I/O-bound processes. As the processes flow around the system, the following scenario may result. The CPU-bound process will get and hold the CPU. During this time, all the other processes will finish their I/O and will move into the ready queue, waiting for the CPU. While the processes wait in the ready queue, the I/O devices are idle. Eventually, the CPU-bound process finishes its CPU burst and moves to an I/O device. All the I/O-bound processes, which have short CPU bursts, execute quickly and move back to the I/O queues. At this point, the CPU sits idle. The CPU-bound process will then move back to the ready queue and be allocated the CPU. Again, all the I/O processes end up waiting in the ready queue until the CPU-bound process is done. There is a **convoy effect** as all the other processes wait for the one big process to get off the CPU. This effect results in lower CPU and device utilization than might be possible if the shorter processes were allowed to go first.

Note also that the FCFS scheduling algorithm is nonpreemptive. Once the CPU has been allocated to a process, that process keeps the CPU until it releases the CPU, either by terminating or by requesting I/O. The FCFS algorithm is thus particularly troublesome for time-sharing systems, where it is important that each user get a share of the CPU at regular intervals. It would be disastrous to allow one process to keep the CPU for an extended period.

5.3.2 Shortest-Job-First Scheduling

A different approach to CPU scheduling is the **shortest-job-first (SJF) scheduling algorithm**. This algorithm associates with each process the length of the process's next CPU burst. When the CPU is available, it is assigned to the process that has the smallest next CPU burst. If the next CPU bursts of two processes are the same, FCFS scheduling is used to break the tie. Note that a more appropriate term for this scheduling method would be the *shortest-next-CPU-burst algorithm,* because scheduling depends on the length of the next CPU burst of a process, rather than its total length. We use the term SJF because most people and textbooks use this term to refer to this type of scheduling.

As an example of SJF scheduling, consider the following set of processes, with the length of the CPU burst given in milliseconds:

Process	Burst Time
P_1	6
P_2	8
P_3	7
P_4	3

Using SJF scheduling, we would schedule these processes according to the following Gantt chart:

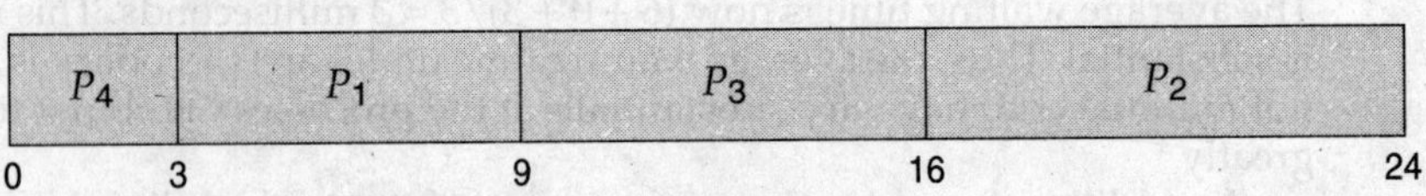

The waiting time is 3 milliseconds for process P_1, 16 milliseconds for process P_2, 9 milliseconds for process P_3, and 0 milliseconds for process P_4. Thus, the average waiting time is $(3 + 16 + 9 + 0)/4 = 7$ milliseconds. By comparison, if we were using the FCFS scheduling scheme, the average waiting time would be 10.25 milliseconds.

The SJF scheduling algorithm is provably *optimal,* in that it gives the minimum average waiting time for a given set of processes. Moving a short process before a long one decreases the waiting time of the short process more than it increases the waiting time of the long process. Consequently, the *average* waiting time decreases.

The real difficulty with the SJF algorithm is knowing the length of the next CPU request. For long-term (job) scheduling in a batch system, we can use as the length the process time limit that a user specifies when he submits the job. Thus, users are motivated to estimate the process time limit accurately, since a lower value may mean faster response. (Too low a value will cause a time-limit-exceeded error and require resubmission.) SJF scheduling is used frequently in long-term scheduling.

Although the SJF algorithm is optimal, it cannot be implemented at the level of short-term CPU scheduling. With short-term scheduling, there is no way to know the length of the next CPU burst. One approach is to try to approximate SJF scheduling. We may not *know* the length of the next CPU burst, but we may be able to *predict* its value. We expect that the next CPU burst will be similar in length to the previous ones. By computing an approximation of the length of the next CPU burst, we can pick the process with the shortest predicted CPU burst.

The next CPU burst is generally predicted as an **exponential average** of the measured lengths of previous CPU bursts. We can define the exponential average with the following formula. Let t_n be the length of the nth CPU burst, and let τ_{n+1} be our predicted value for the next CPU burst. Then, for α, $0 \le \alpha \le 1$, define

$$\tau_{n+1} = \alpha\, t_n + (1 - \alpha)\tau_n.$$

The value of t_n contains our most recent information; τ_n stores the past history. The parameter α controls the relative weight of recent and past history in our prediction. If $\alpha = 0$, then $\tau_{n+1} = \tau_n$, and recent history has no effect (current conditions are assumed to be transient). If $\alpha = 1$, then $\tau_{n+1} = t_n$, and only the most recent CPU burst matters (history is assumed to be old and irrelevant). More commonly, $\alpha = 1/2$, so recent history and past history are equally weighted. The initial τ_0 can be defined as a constant or as an overall system average. Figure 5.3 shows an exponential average with $\alpha = 1/2$ and $\tau_0 = 10$.

To understand the behavior of the exponential average, we can expand the formula for τ_{n+1} by substituting for τ_n, to find

$$\tau_{n+1} = \alpha t_n + (1 - \alpha)\alpha t_{n-1} + \cdots + (1-\alpha)^j \alpha t_{n-j} + \cdots + (1-\alpha)^{n+1}\tau_0.$$

Since both α and $(1 - \alpha)$ are less than or equal to 1, each successive term has less weight than its predecessor.

The SJF algorithm can be either preemptive or nonpreemptive. The choice arises when a new process arrives at the ready queue while a previous process is still executing. The next CPU burst of the newly arrived process may be shorter

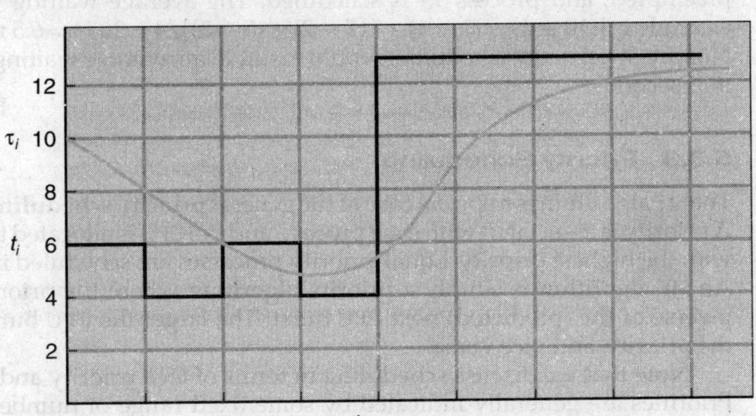

CPU burst (t_i)	6	4	6	4	13	13	13	...
"guess" (τ_i)	10	8	6	6	5	9	11	12	...

Figure 5.3 Prediction of the length of the next CPU burst.

than what is left of the currently executing process. A preemptive SJF algorithm will preempt the currently executing process, whereas a nonpreemptive SJF algorithm will allow the currently running process to finish its CPU burst. Preemptive SJF scheduling is sometimes called **shortest-remaining-time-first scheduling**.

As an example, consider the following four processes, with the length of the CPU burst given in milliseconds:

Process	Arrival Time	Burst Time
P_1	0	8
P_2	1	4
P_3	2	9
P_4	3	5

If the processes arrive at the ready queue at the times shown and need the indicated burst times, then the resulting preemptive SJF schedule is as depicted in the following Gantt chart:

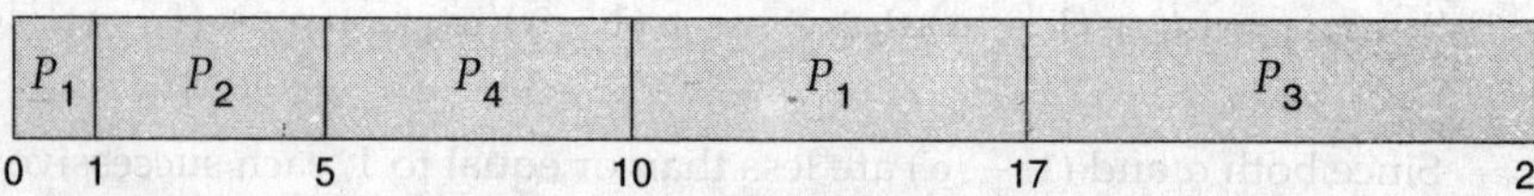

Process P_1 is started at time 0, since it is the only process in the queue. Process P_2 arrives at time 1. The remaining time for process P_1 (7 milliseconds) is larger than the time required by process P_2 (4 milliseconds), so process P_1 is preempted, and process P_2 is scheduled. The average waiting time for this example is $[(10 - 1) + (1 - 1) + (17 - 2) + (5 - 3)]/4 = 26/4 = 6.5$ milliseconds. Nonpreemptive SJF scheduling would result in an average waiting time of 7.75 milliseconds.

5.3.3 Priority Scheduling

The SJF algorithm is a special case of the general **priority scheduling algorithm**. A priority is associated with each process, and the CPU is allocated to the process with the highest priority. Equal-priority processes are scheduled in FCFS order. An SJF algorithm is simply a priority algorithm where the priority (p) is the inverse of the (predicted) next CPU burst. The larger the CPU burst, the lower the priority, and vice versa.

Note that we discuss scheduling in terms of *high* priority and *low* priority. Priorities are generally indicated by some fixed range of numbers, such as 0 to 7 or 0 to 4,095. However, there is no general agreement on whether 0 is the highest or lowest priority. Some systems use low numbers to represent low priority; others use low numbers for high priority. This difference can lead to confusion. In this text, we assume that low numbers represent high priority.

As an example, consider the following set of processes, assumed to have arrived at time 0 in the order $P_1, P_2, \cdots, P_5$, with the length of the CPU burst given in milliseconds:

Process	Burst Time	Priority
P_1	10	3
P_2	1	1
P_3	2	4
P_4	1	5
P_5	5	2

Using priority scheduling, we would schedule these processes according to the following Gantt chart:

The average waiting time is 8.2 milliseconds.

Priorities can be defined either internally or externally. Internally defined priorities use some measurable quantity or quantities to compute the priority of a process. For example, time limits, memory requirements, the number of open files, and the ratio of average I/O burst to average CPU burst have been used in computing priorities. External priorities are set by criteria outside the operating system, such as the importance of the process, the type and amount of funds being paid for computer use, the department sponsoring the work, and other, often political, factors.

Priority scheduling can be either preemptive or nonpreemptive. When a process arrives at the ready queue, its priority is compared with the priority of the currently running process. A preemptive priority scheduling algorithm will preempt the CPU if the priority of the newly arrived process is higher than the priority of the currently running process. A nonpreemptive priority scheduling algorithm will simply put the new process at the head of the ready queue.

A major problem with priority scheduling algorithms is **indefinite blocking**, or **starvation**. A process that is ready to run but waiting for the CPU can be considered blocked. A priority scheduling algorithm can leave some low-priority processes waiting indefinitely. In a heavily loaded computer system, a steady stream of higher-priority processes can prevent a low-priority process from ever getting the CPU. Generally, one of two things will happen. Either the process will eventually be run (at 2 A.M. Sunday, when the system is finally lightly loaded), or the computer system will eventually crash and lose all unfinished low-priority processes. (Rumor has it that, when they shut down the IBM 7094 at MIT in 1973, they found a low-priority process that had been submitted in 1967 and had not yet been run.)

A solution to the problem of indefinite blockage of low-priority processes is **aging**. Aging is a technique of gradually increasing the priority of processes that wait in the system for a long time. For example, if priorities range from 127 (low) to 0 (high), we could increase the priority of a waiting process by 1 every 15 minutes. Eventually, even a process with an initial priority of 127 would have the highest priority in the system and would be executed. In fact, it would take no more than 32 hours for a priority-127 process to age to a priority-0 process.

5.3.4 Round-Robin Scheduling

The **round-robin (RR) scheduling algorithm** is designed especially for time-sharing systems. It is similar to FCFS scheduling, but preemption is added to enable the system to switch between processes. A small unit of time, called a **time quantum** or time slice, is defined. A time quantum is generally from 10 to 100 milliseconds in length. The ready queue is treated as a circular queue. The CPU scheduler goes around the ready queue, allocating the CPU to each process for a time interval of up to 1 time quantum.

To implement RR scheduling, we keep the ready queue as a FIFO queue of processes. New processes are added to the tail of the ready queue. The CPU scheduler picks the first process from the ready queue, sets a timer to interrupt after 1 time quantum, and dispatches the process.

One of two things will then happen. The process may have a CPU burst of less than 1 time quantum. In this case, the process itself will release the CPU voluntarily. The scheduler will then proceed to the next process in the ready queue. Otherwise, if the CPU burst of the currently running process is longer than 1 time quantum, the timer will go off and will cause an interrupt to the operating system. A context switch will be executed, and the process will be put at the **tail** of the ready queue. The CPU scheduler will then select the next process in the ready queue.

The average waiting time under the RR policy is often long. Consider the following set of processes that arrive at time 0, with the length of the CPU burst given in milliseconds:

Process	Burst Time
P_1	24
P_2	3
P_3	3

If we use a time quantum of 4 milliseconds, then process P_1 gets the first 4 milliseconds. Since it requires another 20 milliseconds, it is preempted after the first time quantum, and the CPU is given to the next process in the queue, process P_2. Process P_2 does not need 4 milliseconds, so it quits before its time quantum expires. The CPU is then given to the next process, process P_3. Once each process has received 1 time quantum, the CPU is returned to process P_1 for an additional time quantum. The resulting RR schedule is as follows:

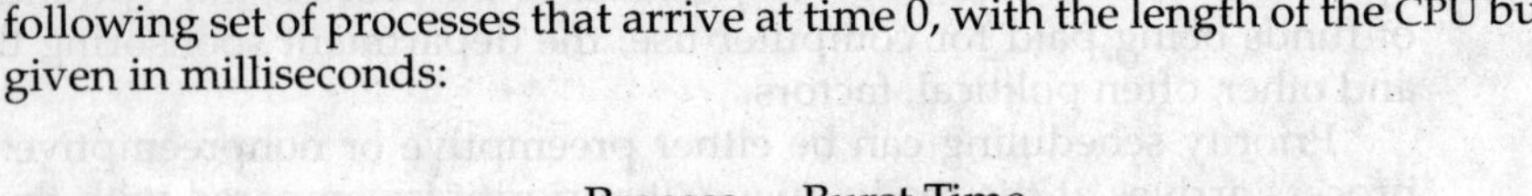

Let's calculate the average waiting time for the above schedule. P_1 waits for 6 millisconds (10 - 4), P_2 waits for 4 millisconds, and P_3 waits for 7 millisconds. Thus, the average waiting time is 17/3 = 5.66 milliseconds.

In the RR scheduling algorithm, no process is allocated the CPU for more than 1 time quantum in a row (unless it is the only runnable process). If a process's CPU burst exceeds 1 time quantum, that process is preempted and is put back in the ready queue. The RR scheduling algorithm is thus preemptive.

If there are n processes in the ready queue and the time quantum is q, then each process gets $1/n$ of the CPU time in chunks of at most q time units. Each process must wait no longer than $(n - 1) \times q$ time units until its next time quantum. For example, with five processes and a time quantum of 20 milliseconds, each process will get up to 20 milliseconds every 100 milliseconds.

The performance of the RR algorithm depends heavily on the size of the time quantum. At one extreme, if the time quantum is extremely large, the RR policy is the same as the FCFS policy. In contrast, if the time quantum is extremely small (say, 1 millisecond), the RR approach is called **processor sharing** and (in theory) creates the appearance that each of n processes has its own processor running at $1/n$ the speed of the real processor. This approach was used in Control Data Corporation (CDC) hardware to implement ten peripheral processors with only one set of hardware and ten sets of registers. The hardware executes one instruction for one set of registers, then goes on to the next. This cycle continues, resulting in ten slow processors rather than one fast one. (Actually, since the processor was much faster than memory and each instruction referenced memory, the processors were not much slower than ten real processors would have been.)

In software, we need also to consider the effect of context switching on the performance of RR scheduling. Assume, for example, that we have only one process of 10 time units. If the quantum is 12 time units, the process finishes in less than 1 time quantum, with no overhead. If the quantum is 6 time units, however, the process requires 2 quanta, resulting in a context switch. If the time quantum is 1 time unit, then nine context switches will occur, slowing the execution of the process accordingly (Figure 5.4).

Thus, we want the time quantum to be large with respect to the context-switch time. If the context-switch time is approximately 10 percent of the time quantum, then about 10 percent of the CPU time will be spent in context switching. In practice, most modern systems have time quanta ranging from 10 to 100 milliseconds. The time required for a context switch is typically less than 10 microseconds; thus, the context-switch time is a small fraction of the time quantum.

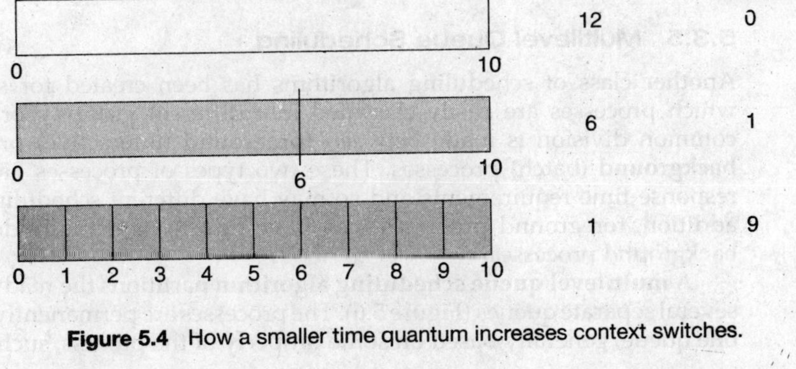

Figure 5.4 How a smaller time quantum increases context switches.

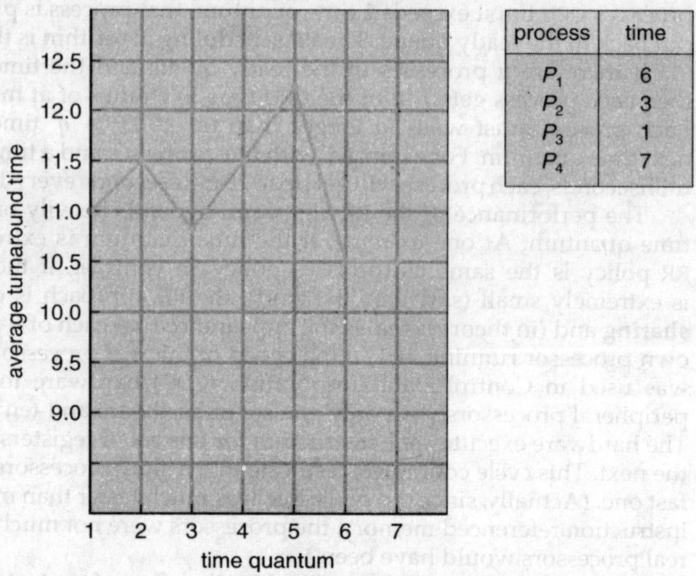

Figure 5.5 How turnaround time varies with the time quantum.

Turnaround time also depends on the size of the time quantum. As we can see from Figure 5.5, the average turnaround time of a set of processes does not necessarily improve as the time-quantum size increases. In general, the average turnaround time can be improved if most processes finish their next CPU burst in a single time quantum. For example, given three processes of 10 time units each and a quantum of 1 time unit, the average turnaround time is 29. If the time quantum is 10, however, the average turnaround time drops to 20. If context-switch time is added in, the average turnaround time increases even more for a smaller time quantum, since more context switches are required.

Although the time quantum should be large compared with the context-switch time, it should not be too large. If the time quantum is too large, RR scheduling degenerates to an FCFS policy. A rule of thumb is that 80 percent of the CPU bursts should be shorter than the time quantum.

5.3.5 Multilevel Queue Scheduling

Another class of scheduling algorithms has been created for situations in which processes are easily classified into different groups. For example, a common division is made between **foreground** (interactive) processes and **background** (batch) processes. These two types of processes have different response-time requirements and so may have different scheduling needs. In addition, foreground processes may have priority (externally defined) over background processes.

A **multilevel queue scheduling algorithm** partitions the ready queue into several separate queues (Figure 5.6). The processes are permanently assigned to one queue, generally based on some property of the process, such as memory

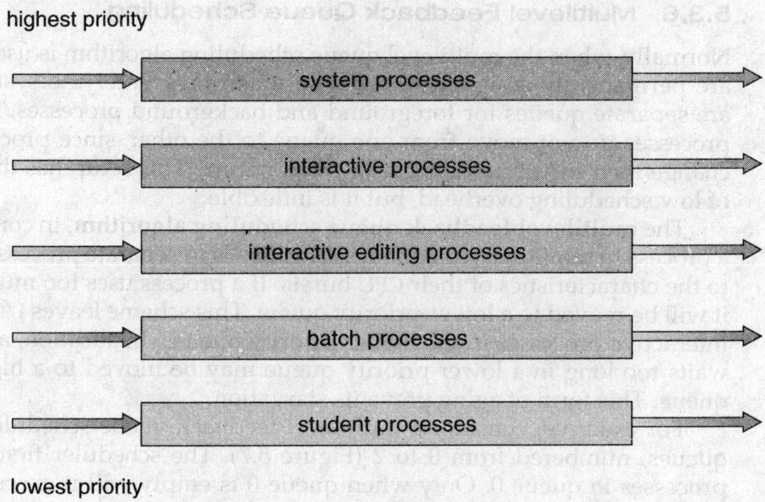

Figure 5.6 Multilevel queue scheduling.

size, process priority, or process type. Each queue has its own scheduling algorithm. For example, separate queues might be used for foreground and background processes. The foreground queue might be scheduled by an RR algorithm, while the background queue is scheduled by an FCFS algorithm.

In addition, there must be scheduling among the queues, which is commonly implemented as fixed-priority preemptive scheduling. For example, the foreground queue may have absolute priority over the background queue.

Let's look at an example of a multilevel queue scheduling algorithm with five queues, listed below in order of priority:

1. System processes
2. Interactive processes
3. Interactive editing processes
4. Batch processes
5. Student processes

Each queue has absolute priority over lower-priority queues. No process in the batch queue, for example, could run unless the queues for system processes, interactive processes, and interactive editing processes were all empty. If an interactive editing process entered the ready queue while a batch process was running, the batch process would be preempted.

Another possibility is to time-slice among the queues. Here, each queue gets a certain portion of the CPU time, which it can then schedule among its various processes. For instance, in the foreground–background queue example, the foreground queue can be given 80 percent of the CPU time for RR scheduling among its processes, whereas the background queue receives 20 percent of the CPU to give to its processes on an FCFS basis.

5.3.6 Multilevel Feedback Queue Scheduling

Normally, when the multilevel queue scheduling algorithm is used, processes are permanently assigned to a queue when they enter the system. If there are separate queues for foreground and background processes, for example, processes do not move from one queue to the other, since processes do not change their foreground or background nature. This setup has the advantage of low scheduling overhead, but it is inflexible.

The **multilevel feedback queue scheduling algorithm**, in contrast, allows a process to move between queues. The idea is to separate processes according to the characteristics of their CPU bursts. If a process uses too much CPU time, it will be moved to a lower-priority queue. This scheme leaves I/O-bound and interactive processes in the higher-priority queues. In addition, a process that waits too long in a lower-priority queue may be moved to a higher-priority queue. This form of aging prevents starvation.

For example, consider a multilevel feedback queue scheduler with three queues, numbered from 0 to 2 (Figure 5.7). The scheduler first executes all processes in queue 0. Only when queue 0 is empty will it execute processes in queue 1. Similarly, processes in queue 2 will only be executed if queues 0 and 1 are empty. A process that arrives for queue 1 will preempt a process in queue 2. A process in queue 1 will in turn be preempted by a process arriving for queue 0.

A process entering the ready queue is put in queue 0. A process in queue 0 is given a time quantum of 8 milliseconds. If it does not finish within this time, it is moved to the tail of queue 1. If queue 0 is empty, the process at the head of queue 1 is given a quantum of 16 milliseconds. If it does not complete, it is preempted and is put into queue 2. Processes in queue 2 are run on an FCFS basis but are run only when queues 0 and 1 are empty.

This scheduling algorithm gives highest priority to any process with a CPU burst of 8 milliseconds or less. Such a process will quickly get the CPU, finish its CPU burst, and go off to its next I/O burst. Processes that need more than 8 but less than 24 milliseconds are also served quickly, although with lower priority than shorter processes. Long processes automatically sink to queue 2 and are served in FCFS order with any CPU cycles left over from queues 0 and 1.

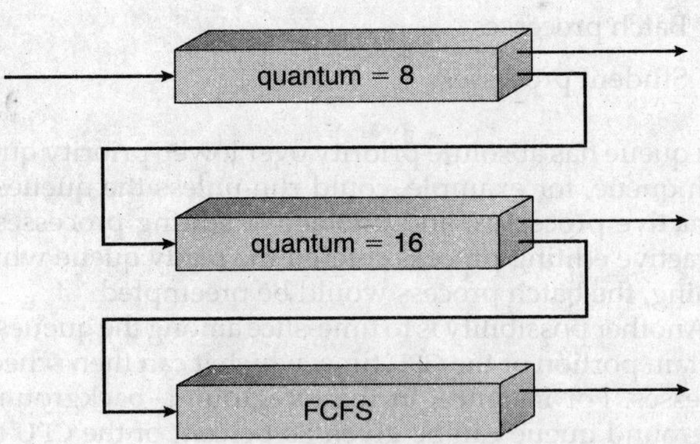

Figure 5.7 Multilevel feedback queues.

In general, a multilevel feedback queue scheduler is defined by the following parameters:

- The number of queues
- The scheduling algorithm for each queue
- The method used to determine when to upgrade a process to a higher-priority queue
- The method used to determine when to demote a process to a lower-priority queue
- The method used to determine which queue a process will enter when that process needs service

The definition of a multilevel feedback queue scheduler makes it the most general CPU-scheduling algorithm. It can be configured to match a specific system under design. Unfortunately, it is also the most complex algorithm, since defining the best scheduler requires some means by which to select values for all the parameters.

5.4 Thread Scheduling

In Chapter 4, we introduced threads to the process model, distinguishing between *user-level* and *kernel-level* threads. On operating systems that support them, it is kernel-level threads—not processes—that are being scheduled by the operating system. User-level threads are managed by a thread library, and the kernel is unaware of them. To run on a CPU, user-level threads must ultimately be mapped to an associated kernel-level thread, although this mapping may be indirect and may use a lightweight process (LWP). In this section, we explore scheduling issues involving user-level and kernel-level threads and offer specific examples of scheduling for Pthreads.

5.4.1 Contention Scope

One distinction between user-level and kernel-level threads lies in how they are scheduled. On systems implementing the many-to-one (Section 4.2.1) and many-to-many (Section 4.2.3) models, the thread library schedules user-level threads to run on an available LWP, a scheme known as **process-contention scope (PCS)**, since competition for the CPU takes place among threads belonging to the same process. When we say the thread library *schedules* user threads onto available LWPs, we do not mean that the thread is actually running on a CPU; this would require the operating system to schedule the kernel thread onto a physical CPU. To decide which kernel thread to schedule onto a CPU, the kernel uses **system-contention scope (SCS)**. Competition for the CPU with SCS scheduling takes place among all threads in the system. Systems using the one-to-one model (Section 4.2.2), such as Windows XP, Solaris, and Linux, schedule threads using only SCS.

Typically, PCS is done according to priority—the scheduler selects the runnable thread with the highest priority to run. User-level thread priorities are set by the programmer and are not adjusted by the thread library, although some thread libraries may allow the programmer to change the priority of a thread. It is important to note that PCS will typically preempt the thread currently running in favor of a higher-priority thread; however, there is no guarantee of time slicing (Section 5.3.4) among threads of equal priority.

5.4.2 Pthread Scheduling

We provided a sample POSIX Pthread program in Section 4.3.1, along with an introduction to thread creation with Pthreads. Now, we highlight the POSIX Pthread API that allows specifying either PCS or SCS during thread creation. Pthreads identifies the following contention scope values:

- PTHREAD_SCOPE_PROCESS schedules threads using PCS scheduling.
- PTHREAD_SCOPE_SYSTEM schedules threads using SCS scheduling.

On systems implementing the many-to-many model, the PTHREAD_SCOPE_PROCESS policy schedules user-level threads onto available LWPs. The number of LWPs is maintained by the thread library, perhaps using scheduler activations (Section 4.4.6). The PTHREAD_SCOPE_SYSTEM scheduling policy will create and bind an LWP for each user-level thread on many-to-many systems, effectively mapping threads using the one-to-one policy.

The Pthread IPC provides two functions for getting—and setting—the contention scope policy:

- `pthread_attr_setscope(pthread_attr_t *attr, int scope)`
- `pthread_attr_getscope(pthread_attr_t *attr, int *scope)`

The first parameter for both functions contains a pointer to the attribute set for the thread. The second parameter for the `pthread_attr_setscope()` function is passed either the PTHREAD_SCOPE_SYSTEM or the PTHREAD_SCOPE_PROCESS value, indicating how the contention scope is to be set. In the case of `pthread_attr_getscope()`, this second parameter contains a pointer to an `int` value that is set to the current value of the contention scope. If an error occurs, each of these functions returns a non-zero value.

In Figure 5.8, we illustrate a Pthread scheduling API. The program first determines the existing contention scope and sets it to PTHREAD_SCOPE_PROCESS. It then creates five separate threads that will run using the SCS scheduling policy. Note that on some systems, only certain contention scope values are allowed. For example, Linux and Mac OS X systems allow only PTHREAD_SCOPE_SYSTEM.

5.5 Multiple-Processor Scheduling

Our discussion thus far has focused on the problems of scheduling the CPU in a system with a single processor. If multiple CPUs are available, **load sharing** becomes possible; however, the scheduling problem becomes correspondingly

```
#include <pthread.h>
#include <stdio.h>
#define NUM_THREADS 5

int main(int argc, char *argv[])
{
  int i, scope;
  pthread_t tid[NUM_THREADS];
  pthread_attr_t attr;

  /* get the default attributes */
  pthread_attr_init(&attr);

  /* first inquire on the current scope */
  if (pthread_attr_getscope(&attr, &scope) != 0)
    fprintf(stderr, "Unable to get scheduling scope\n");
  else {
    if (scope == PTHREAD_SCOPE_PROCESS)
     printf("PTHREAD_SCOPE_PROCESS");
    else if (scope == PTHREAD_SCOPE_SYSTEM)
     printf("PTHREAD_SCOPE_SYSTEM");
    else
     fprintf(stderr, "Illegal scope value.\n");
  }

  /* set the scheduling algorithm to PCS or SCS */
  pthread_attr_setscope(&attr, PTHREAD_SCOPE_SYSTEM);

  /* create the threads */
  for (i = 0; i < NUM_THREADS; i++)
     pthread_create(&tid[i],&attr,runner,NULL);

  /* now join on each thread */
  for (i = 0; i < NUM_THREADS; i++)
     pthread_join(tid[i], NULL);
}

/* Each thread will begin control in this function */
void *runner(void *param)
{
  /* do some work ... */

  pthread_exit(0);
}
```

Figure 5.8 Pthread scheduling API.

more complex. Many possibilities have been tried; and as we saw with single-processor CPU scheduling, there is no one best solution. Here, we discuss several concerns in multiprocessor scheduling. We concentrate on systems in which the processors are identical—**homogeneous**—in terms of their functionality; we can then use any available processor to run any process in the queue. (Note, however, that even with homogeneous multiprocessors, there are sometimes limitations on scheduling. Consider a system with an I/O device attached to a private bus of one processor. Processes that wish to use that device must be scheduled to run on that processor.)

5.5.1 Approaches to Multiple-Processor Scheduling

One approach to CPU scheduling in a multiprocessor system has all scheduling decisions, I/O processing, and other system activities handled by a single processor—the master server. The other processors execute only user code. This **asymmetric multiprocessing** is simple because only one processor accesses the system data structures, reducing the need for data sharing.

A second approach uses **symmetric multiprocessing (SMP)**, where each processor is self-scheduling. All processes may be in a common ready queue, or each processor may have its own private queue of ready processes. Regardless, scheduling proceeds by having the scheduler for each processor examine the ready queue and select a process to execute. As we shall see in Chapter 6, if we have multiple processors trying to access and update a common data structure, the scheduler must be programmed carefully. We must ensure that two processors do not choose the same process and that processes are not lost from the queue. Virtually all modern operating systems support SMP, including Windows XP, Windows 2000, Solaris, Linux, and Mac OS X. In the remainder of this section, we discuss issues concerning SMP systems.

5.5.2 Processor Affinity

Consider what happens to cache memory when a process has been running on a specific processor. The data most recently accessed by the process populate the cache for the processor; and as a result, successive memory accesses by the process are often satisfied in cache memory. Now consider what happens if the process migrates to another processor. The contents of cache memory must be invalidated for the first processor, and the cache for the second processor must be repopulated. Because of the high cost of invalidating and repopulating caches, most SMP systems try to avoid migration of processes from one processor to another and instead attempt to keep a process running on the same processor. This is known as **processor affinity**—that is, a process has an affinity for the processor on which it is currently running.

Processor affinity takes several forms. When an operating system has a policy of attempting to keep a process running on the same processor—but not guaranteeing that it will do so—we have a situation known as **soft affinity**. Here, it is possible for a process to migrate between processors. Some systems —such as Linux—also provide system calls that support **hard affinity**, thereby allowing a process to specify that it is not to migrate to other processors. Solaris allows processes to be assigned to processor sets, limiting which processes can run on which CPUs. It also implements soft affinity.

The main-memory architecture of a system can affect processor affinity issues. Figure 5.9 illustrates an architecture featuring non-uniform memory access (NUMA), in which a CPU has faster access to some parts of main memory than to other parts. Typically, this occurs in systems containing combined CPU

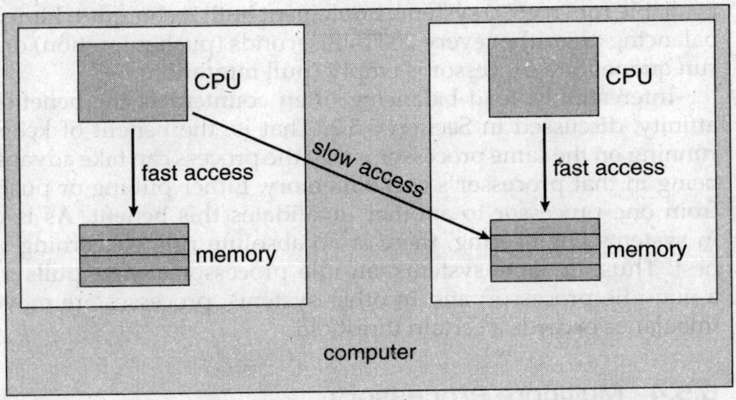

Figure 5.9 NUMA and CPU scheduling.

and memory boards. The CPUs on a board can access the memory on that board with less delay than they can access memory on other boards in the system. If the operating system's CPU scheduler and memory-placement algorithms work together, then a process that is assigned affinity to a particular CPU can be allocated memory on the board where that CPU resides. This example also shows that operating systems are frequently not as cleanly defined and implemented as described in operating-system textbooks. Rather, the "solid lines" between sections of an operating system are frequently only "dotted lines," with algorithms creating connections in ways aimed at optimizing performance and reliability.

5.5.3 Load Balancing

On SMP systems, it is important to keep the workload balanced among all processors to fully utilize the benefits of having more than one processor. Otherwise, one or more processors may sit idle while other processors have high workloads, along with lists of processes awaiting the CPU. **Load balancing** attempts to keep the workload evenly distributed across all processors in an SMP system. It is important to note that load balancing is typically only necessary on systems where each processor has its own private queue of eligible processes to execute. On systems with a common run queue, load balancing is often unnecessary, because once a processor becomes idle, it immediately extracts a runnable process from the common run queue. It is also important to note, however, that in most contemporary operating systems supporting SMP, each processor does have a private queue of eligible processes.

There are two general approaches to load balancing: **push migration** and **pull migration**. With push migration, a specific task periodically checks the load on each processor and—if it finds an imbalance—evenly distributes the load by moving (or pushing) processes from overloaded to idle or less-busy processors. Pull migration occurs when an idle processor pulls a waiting task from a busy processor. Push and pull migration need not be mutually exclusive and are in fact often implemented in parallel on load-balancing systems. For example, the Linux scheduler (described in Section 5.6.3) and the ULE scheduler available for FreeBSD systems implement both techniques. Linux runs its load-balancing algorithm every 200 milliseconds (push migration) or whenever the run queue for a processor is empty (pull migration).

Interestingly, load balancing often counteracts the benefits of processor affinity, discussed in Section 5.5.2. That is, the benefit of keeping a process running on the same processor is that the process can take advantage of its data being in that processor's cache memory. Either pulling or pushing a process from one processor to another invalidates this benefit. As is often the case in systems engineering, there is no absolute rule concerning what policy is best. Thus, in some systems, an idle processor always pulls a process from a non-idle processor; and in other systems, processes are moved only if the imbalance exceeds a certain threshold.

5.5.4 Multicore Processors

Traditionally, SMP systems have allowed several threads to run concurrently by providing multiple physical processors. However, a recent trend in computer hardware has been to place multiple processor cores on the same physical chip, resulting in a **multicore processor**. Each core has a register set to maintain its architectural state and thus appears to the operating system to be a separate physical processor. SMP systems that use multicore processors are faster and consume less power than systems in which each processor has its own physical chip.

Multicore processors may complicate scheduling issues. Let's consider how this can happen. Researchers have discovered that when a processor accesses memory, it spends a significant amount of time waiting for the data to become available. This situation, known as a **memory stall**, may occur for various reasons, such as a cache miss (accessing data that is not in cache memory). Figure 5.10 illustrates a memory stall. In this scenario, the processor can spend up to 50 percent of its time waiting for data to become available from memory. To remedy this situation, many recent hardware designs have implemented multithreaded processor cores in which two (or more) hardware threads are assigned to each core. That way, if one thread stalls while waiting for memory, the core can switch to another thread. Figure 5.11 illustrates a dual-threaded processor core on which the execution of thread 0 and the execution of thread 1 are interleaved. From an operating-system perspective, each hardware thread appears as a logical processor that is available to run a software thread. Thus, on a dual-threaded, dual-core system, four logical processors are presented to the operating system. The UltraSPARC T1 CPU has eight cores per chip and four

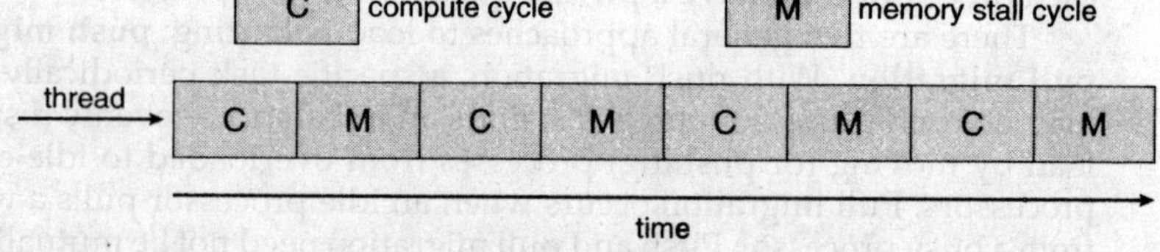

Figure 5.10 Memory stall.

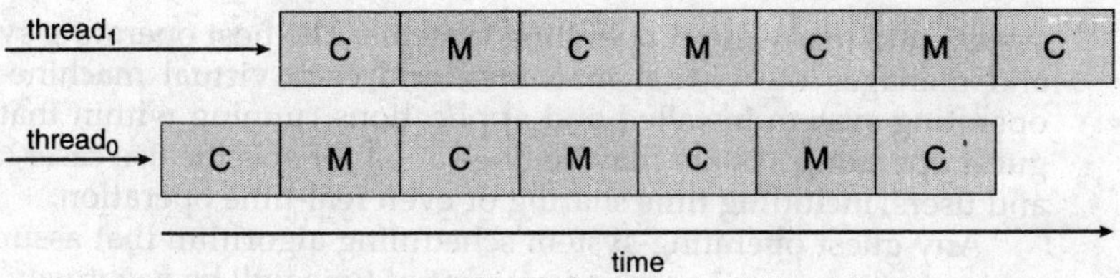

Figure 5.11 Multithreaded multicore system.

hardware threads per core; from the perspective of the operating system, there appear to be 32 logical processors.

In general, there are two ways to multithread a processor: **coarse-grained** and **fine-grained** multithreading. With coarse-grained multithreading, a thread executes on a processor until a long-latency event such as a memory stall occurs. Because of the delay caused by the long-latency event, the processor must switch to another thread to begin execution. However, the cost of switching between threads is high, as the instruction pipeline must be flushed before the other thread can begin execution on the processor core. Once this new thread begins execution, it begins filling the pipeline with its instructions. Fine-grained (or interleaved) multithreading switches between threads at a much finer level of granularity—typically at the boundary of an instruction cycle. However, the architectural design of fine-grained systems includes logic for thread switching. As a result, the cost of switching between threads is small.

Notice that a multithreaded multicore processor actually requires two different levels of scheduling. On one level are the scheduling decisions that must be made by the operating system as it chooses which software thread to run on each hardware thread (logical processor). For this level of scheduling, the operating system may choose any scheduling algorithm, such as those described in Section 5.3. A second level of scheduling specifies how each core decides which hardware thread to run. There are several strategies to adopt in this situation. The UltraSPARC T1, mentioned earlier, uses a simple round-robin algorithm to schedule the four hardware threads to each core. Another example, the Intel Itanium, is a dual-core processor with two hardware-managed threads per core. Assigned to each hardware thread is a dynamic *urgency* value ranging from 0 to 7, with 0 representing the lowest urgency, and 7 the highest. The Itanium identifies five different events that may trigger a thread switch. When one of these events occurs, the thread-switching logic compares the urgency of the two threads and selects the thread with the highest urgency value to execute on the processor core.

5.5.5 Virtualization and Scheduling

A system with virtualization, even a single-CPU system, frequently acts like a multiprocessor system. The virtualization software presents one or more virtual CPUs to each of the virtual machines running on the system and then schedules the use of the physical CPUs among the virtual machines. The significant variations between virtualization technologies make it difficult to summarize the effect of virtualization on scheduling (see Section 2.8). In general, though, most virtualized environments have one host operating system and many guest operating systems. The host operating system creates and manages the virtual machines, and each virtual machine has a guest operating system installed and applications running within that guest. Each guest operating system may be fine-tuned for specific use cases, applications, and users, including time sharing or even real-time operation.

Any guest operating-system scheduling algorithm that assumes a certain amount of progress in a given amount of time will be negatively impacted by virtualization. Consider a time-sharing operating system that tries to allot 100 milliseconds to each time slice to give users a reasonable response time. Within a virtual machine, this operating system is at the mercy of the virtualization system as to what CPU resources it actually receives. A given 100-millisecond time slice may take much more than 100 milliseconds of virtual CPU time. Depending on how busy the system is, the time slice may take a second or more, resulting in very poor response times for users logged into that virtual machine. The effect on a real-time operating system would be even more catastrophic.

The net effect of such scheduling layering is that individual virtualized operating systems receive only a portion of the available CPU cycles, even though they believe they are receiving all of the cycles and indeed that they are scheduling all of those cycles. Commonly, the time-of-day clocks in virtual machines are incorrect because timers take longer to trigger than they would on dedicated CPUs. Virtualization can thus undo the good scheduling-algorithm efforts of the operating systems within virtual machines.

5.6 Operating System Examples

We turn next to a description of the scheduling policies of the Solaris, Windows XP, and Linux operating systems. It is important to remember that we are describing the scheduling of kernel threads with Solaris and Windows XP. Recall that Linux does not distinguish between processes and threads; thus, we use the term *task* when discussing the Linux scheduler.

5.6.1 Example: Solaris Scheduling

Solaris uses priority-based thread scheduling where each thread belongs to one of six classes:

1. Time sharing (TS)
2. Interactive (IA)
3. Real time (RT)
4. System (SYS)
5. Fair share (FSS)
6. Fixed priority (FP)

Within each class there are different priorities and different scheduling algorithms.

The default scheduling class for a process is time sharing. The scheduling policy for the time-sharing class dynamically alters priorities and assigns time

priority	time quantum	time quantum expired	return from sleep
0	200	0	50
5	200	0	50
10	160	0	51
15	160	5	51
20	120	10	52
25	120	15	52
30	80	20	53
35	80	25	54
40	40	30	55
45	40	35	56
50	40	40	58
55	40	45	58
59	20	49	59

Figure 5.12 Solaris dispatch table for time-sharing and interactive threads.

slices of different lengths using a multilevel feedback queue. By default, there is an inverse relationship between priorities and time slices. The higher the priority, the smaller the time slice; and the lower the priority, the larger the time slice. Interactive processes typically have a higher priority; CPU-bound processes, a lower priority. This scheduling policy gives good response time for interactive processes and good throughput for CPU-bound processes. The interactive class uses the same scheduling policy as the time-sharing class, but it gives windowing applications—such as those created by the KDE or GNOME window managers—a higher priority for better performance.

Figure 5.12 shows the dispatch table for scheduling time-sharing and interactive threads. These two scheduling classes include 60 priority levels, but for brevity, we display only a handful. The dispatch table shown in Figure 5.12 contains the following fields:

- **Priority**. The class-dependent priority for the time-sharing and interactive classes. A higher number indicates a higher priority.

- **Time quantum**. The time quantum for the associated priority. This illustrates the inverse relationship between priorities and time quanta: the lowest priority (priority 0) has the highest time quantum (200 milliseconds), and the highest priority (priority 59) has the lowest time quantum (20 milliseconds).

- **Time quantum expired**. The new priority of a thread that has used its entire time quantum without blocking. Such threads are considered

CPU-intensive. As shown in the table, these threads have their priorities lowered.

- **Return from sleep**. The priority of a thread that is returning from sleeping (such as waiting for I/O). As the table illustrates, when I/O is available for a waiting thread, its priority is boosted to between 50 and 59, thus supporting the scheduling policy of providing good response time for interactive processes.

Threads in the real-time class are given the highest priority. This assignment allows a real-time process to have a guaranteed response from the system within a bounded period of time. A real-time process will run before a process in any other class. In general, however, few processes belong to the real-time class.

Solaris uses the system class to run kernel threads, such as the scheduler and paging daemon. Once established, the priority of a system thread does not change. The system class is reserved for kernel use (user processes running in kernel mode are not in the system class).

The fixed-priority and fair-share classes were introduced with Solaris 9. Threads in the fixed-priority class have the same priority range as those in the time-sharing class; however, their priorities are not dynamically adjusted. The fair-share scheduling class uses CPU **shares** instead of priorities to make scheduling decisions. CPU shares indicate entitlement to available CPU resources and are allocated to a set of processes (known as a **project**).

Each scheduling class includes a set of priorities. However, the scheduler converts the class-specific priorities into global priorities and selects the thread with the highest global priority to run. The selected thread runs on the CPU until it (1) blocks, (2) uses its time slice, or (3) is preempted by a higher-priority thread. If there are multiple threads with the same priority, the scheduler uses a round-robin queue. Figure 5.13 illustrates how the six scheduling classes relate to one another and how they map to global priorities. Notice that the kernel maintains 10 threads for servicing interrupts. These threads do not belong to any scheduling class and execute at the highest priority (160–169). As mentioned, Solaris has traditionally used the many-to-many model (Section 4.2.3) but switched to the one-to-one model (Section 4.2.2) beginning with Solaris 9.

5.6.2 Example: Windows XP Scheduling

Windows XP schedules threads using a priority-based, preemptive scheduling algorithm. The Windows XP scheduler ensures that the highest-priority thread will always run. The portion of the Windows XP kernel that handles scheduling is called the *dispatcher*. A thread selected to run by the dispatcher will run until it is preempted by a higher-priority thread, until it terminates, until its time quantum ends, or until it calls a blocking system call, such as for I/O. If a higher-priority real-time thread becomes ready while a lower-priority thread is running, the lower-priority thread will be preempted. This preemption gives a real-time thread preferential access to the CPU when the thread needs such access.

The dispatcher uses a 32-level priority scheme to determine the order of thread execution. Priorities are divided into two classes. The **variable class**

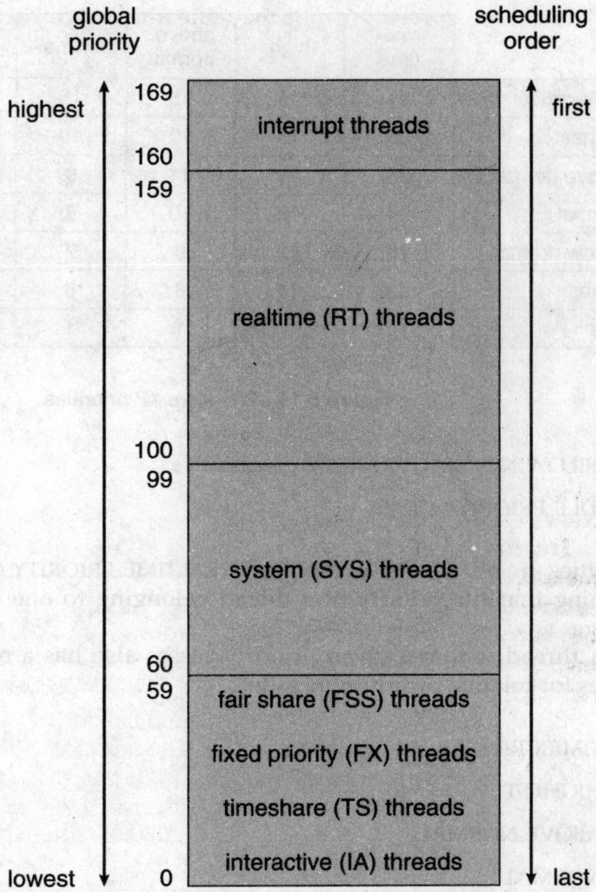

Figure 5.13 Solaris scheduling.

contains threads having priorities from 1 to 15, and the real-time class contains threads with priorities ranging from 16 to 31. (There is also a thread running at priority 0 that is used for memory management.) The dispatcher uses a queue for each scheduling priority and traverses the set of queues from highest to lowest until it finds a thread that is ready to run. If no ready thread is found, the dispatcher will execute a special thread called the idle thread.

There is a relationship between the numeric priorities of the Windows XP kernel and the Win32 API. The Win32 API identifies several priority classes to which a process can belong. These include:

- REALTIME_PRIORITY_CLASS
- HIGH_PRIORITY_CLASS
- ABOVE_NORMAL_PRIORITY_CLASS
- NORMAL_PRIORITY_CLASS

	real-time	high	above normal	normal	below normal	idle priority
time-critical	31	15	15	15	15	15
highest	26	15	12	10	8	6
above normal	25	14	11	9	7	5
normal	24	13	10	8	6	4
below normal	23	12	9	7	5	3
lowest	22	11	8	6	4	2
idle	16	1	1	1	1	1

Figure 5.14 Windows XP priorities.

- BELOW_NORMAL_PRIORITY_CLASS
- IDLE_PRIORITY_CLASS

Priorities in all classes except the REALTIME_PRIORITY_CLASS are variable, meaning that the priority of a thread belonging to one of these classes can change

A thread within a given priority classes also has a relative priority. The values for relative priorities include:

- TIME_CRITICAL
- HIGHEST
- ABOVE_NORMAL
- NORMAL
- BELOW_NORMAL
- LOWEST
- IDLE

The priority of each thread is based on both the priority class it belongs to and its relative priority within that class. This relationship is shown in Figure 5.14. The values of the priority classes appear in the top row. The left column contains the values for the relative priorities. For example, if the relative priority of a thread in the ABOVE_NORMAL_PRIORITY_CLASS is NORMAL, the numeric priority of that thread is 10.

Furthermore, each thread has a base priority representing a value in the priority range for the class the thread belongs to. By default, the base priority is the value of the NORMAL relative priority for that class. The base priorities for each priority class are:

- REALTIME_PRIORITY_CLASS—24
- HIGH_PRIORITY_CLASS—13

- ABOVE_NORMAL_PRIORITY_CLASS—10
- NORMAL_PRIORITY_CLASS—8
- BELOW_NORMAL_PRIORITY_CLASS—6
- IDLE_PRIORITY_CLASS—4

Processes are typically members of the NORMAL_PRIORITY_CLASS. A process belongs to this class unless the parent of the process was of the IDLE_PRIORITY_CLASS or unless another class was specified when the process was created. The initial priority of a thread is typically the base priority of the process the thread belongs to.

When a thread's time quantum runs out, that thread is interrupted; if the thread is in the variable-priority class, its priority is lowered. The priority is never lowered below the base priority, however. Lowering the priority tends to limit the CPU consumption of compute-bound threads. When a variable-priority thread is released from a wait operation, the dispatcher boosts the priority. The amount of the boost depends on what the thread was waiting for; for example, a thread that was waiting for keyboard I/O would get a large increase, whereas a thread waiting for a disk operation would get a moderate one. This strategy tends to give good response times to interactive threads that are using the mouse and windows. It also enables I/O-bound threads to keep the I/O devices busy while permitting compute-bound threads to use spare CPU cycles in the background. This strategy is used by several time-sharing operating systems, including UNIX. In addition, the window with which the user is currently interacting receives a priority boost to enhance its response time.

When a user is running an interactive program, the system needs to provide especially good performance. For this reason, Windows XP has a special scheduling rule for processes in the NORMAL_PRIORITY_CLASS. Windows XP distinguishes between the *foreground process* that is currently selected on the screen and the *background processes* that are not currently selected. When a process moves into the foreground, Windows XP increases the scheduling quantum by some factor—typically by 3. This increase gives the foreground process three times longer to run before a time-sharing preemption occurs.

5.6.3 Example: Linux Scheduling

Prior to Version 2.5, the Linux kernel ran a variation of the traditional UNIX scheduling algorithm. Two problems with the traditional UNIX scheduler are that it does not provide adequate support for SMP systems and that it does not scale well as the number of tasks on the system grows. With Version 2.5, the scheduler was overhauled, and the kernel now provides a scheduling algorithm that runs in constant time—known as $O(1)$—regardless of the number of tasks on the system. The new scheduler also provides increased support for SMP, including processor affinity and load balancing, as well as providing fairness and support for interactive tasks.

The Linux scheduler is a preemptive, priority-based algorithm with two separate priority ranges: a **real-time** range from 0 to 99 and a **nice** value ranging from 100 to 140. These two ranges map into a global priority scheme wherein numerically lower values indicate higher priorities.

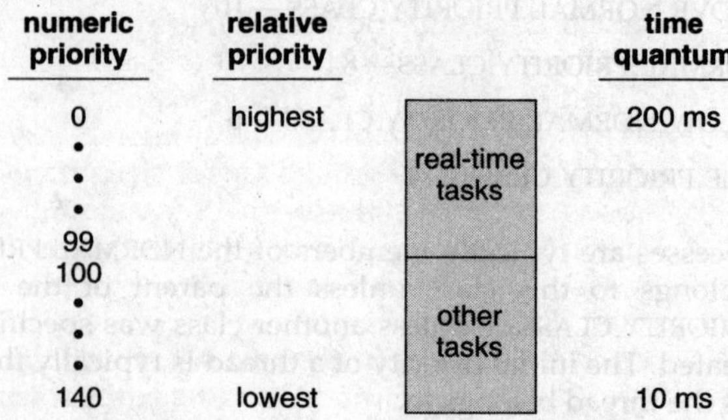

Figure 5.15 The relationship between priorities and time-slice length.

Unlike schedulers for many other systems, including Solaris (Section 5.6.1) and Windows XP (Section 5.6.2), Linux assigns higher-priority tasks longer time quanta and lower-priority tasks shorter time quanta. The relationship between priorities and time-slice length is shown in Figure 5.15.

A runnable task is considered eligible for execution on the CPU as long as it has time remaining in its time slice. When a task has exhausted its time slice, it is considered expired and is not eligible for execution again until all other tasks have also exhausted their time quanta. The kernel maintains a list of all runnable tasks in a **runqueue** data structure. Because of its support for SMP, each processor maintains its own runqueue and schedules itself independently. Each runqueue contains two priority arrays: **active** and **expired**. The active array contains all tasks with time remaining in their time slices, and the expired array contains all expired tasks. Each of these priority arrays contains a list of tasks indexed according to priority (Figure 5.16). The scheduler chooses the task with the highest priority from the active array for execution on the CPU. On multiprocessor machines, this means that each processor is scheduling the highest-priority task from its own runqueue structure. When all tasks have exhausted their time slices (that is, the active array is empty), the two priority arrays are exchanged; the expired array becomes the active array, and vice versa.

Linux implements real-time scheduling as defined by POSIX.1b, which is described in Section 5.4.2. Real-time tasks are assigned static priorities. All

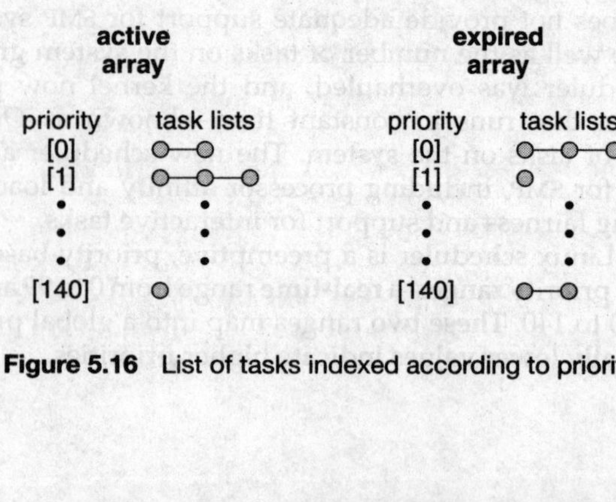

Figure 5.16 List of tasks indexed according to priority.

other tasks have dynamic priorities that are based on their *nice* values plus or minus the value 5. The interactivity of a task determines whether the value 5 will be added to or subtracted from the *nice* value. A task's interactivity is determined by how long it has been sleeping while waiting for I/O. Tasks that are more interactive typically have longer sleep times and therefore are more likely to have adjustments closer to −5, as the scheduler favors interactive tasks. The result of such adjustments will be higher priorities for these tasks. Conversely, tasks with shorter sleep times are often more CPU-bound and thus will have their priorities lowered.

A task's dynamic priority is recalculated when the task has exhausted its time quantum and is to be moved to the expired array. Thus, when the two arrays are exchanged, all tasks in the new active array have been assigned new priorities and corresponding time slices.

5.7 Algorithm Evaluation

How do we select a CPU-scheduling algorithm ror a particular system? As we saw in Section 5.3, there are many scheduling algorithms, each with its own parameters. As a result, selecting an algorithm can be difficult.

The first problem is defining the criteria to be used in selecting an algorithm. As we saw in Section 5.2, criteria are often defined in terms of CPU utilization, response time, or throughput. To select an algorithm, we must first define the relative importance of these elements. Our criteria may include several measures, such as:

- Maximizing CPU utilization under the constraint that the maximum response time is 1 second
- Maximizing throughput such that turnaround time is (on average) linearly proportional to total execution time

Once the selection criteria have been defined, we want to evaluate the algorithms under consideration. We next describe the various evaluation methods we can use.

5.7.1 Deterministic Modeling

One major class of evaluation methods is **analytic evaluation**. Analytic evaluation uses the given algorithm and the system workload to produce a formula or number that evaluates the performance of the algorithm for that workload.

Deterministic modeling is one type of analytic evaluation. This method takes a particular predetermined workload and defines the performance of each algorithm for that workload. For example, assume that we have the workload shown below. All five processes arrive at time 0, in the order given, with the length of the CPU burst given in milliseconds:

Process	Burst Time
P_1	10
P_2	29
P_3	3
P_4	7
P_5	12

Consider the FCFS, SJF, and RR (quantum = 10 milliseconds) scheduling algorithms for this set of processes. Which algorithm would give the minimum average waiting time?

For the FCFS algorithm, we would execute the processes as

The waiting time is 0 milliseconds for process P_1, 10 milliseconds for process P_2, 39 milliseconds for process P_3, 42 milliseconds for process P_4, and 49 milliseconds for process P_5. Thus, the average waiting time is (0 + 10 + 39 + 42 + 49)/5 = 28 milliseconds.

With nonpreemptive SJF scheduling, we execute the processes as

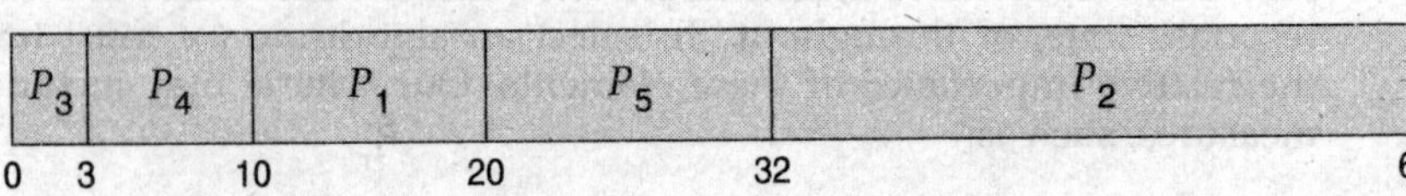

The waiting time is 10 milliseconds for process P_1, 32 milliseconds for process P_2, 0 milliseconds for process P_3, 3 milliseconds for process P_4, and 20 milliseconds for process P_5. Thus, the average waiting time is (10 + 32 + 0 + 3 + 20)/5 = 13 milliseconds.

With the RR algorithm, we execute the processes as

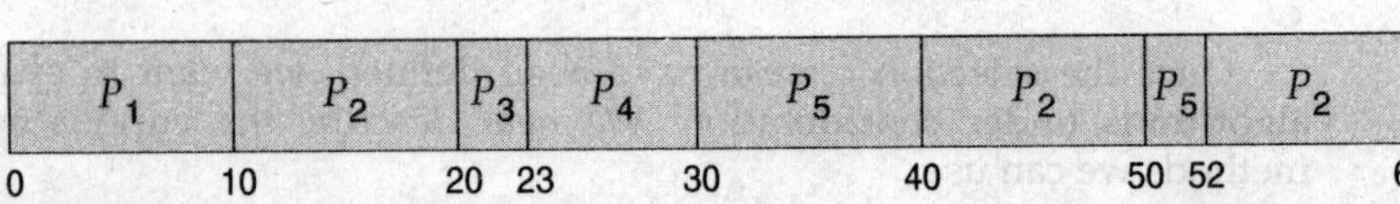

The waiting time is 0 milliseconds for process P_1, 32 milliseconds for process P_2, 20 milliseconds for process P_3, 23 milliseconds for process P_4, and 40 milliseconds for process P_5. Thus, the average waiting time is (0 + 32 + 20 + 23 + 40)/5 = 23 milliseconds.

We see that, *in this case,* the average waiting time obtained with the SJF policy is less than half that obtained with FCFS scheduling; the RR algorithm gives us an intermediate value.

Deterministic modeling is simple and fast. It gives us exact numbers, allowing us to compare the algorithms. However, it requires exact numbers for input, and its answers apply only to those cases. The main uses of deterministic modeling are in describing scheduling algorithms and providing examples. In cases where we are running the same program over and over again and can measure the program's processing requirements exactly, we may be able to use deterministic modeling to select a scheduling algorithm. Furthermore, over a set of examples, deterministic modeling may indicate trends that can then be analyzed and proved separately. For example, it can be shown that, for the environment described (all processes and their times available at time 0), the SJF policy will always result in the minimum waiting time.

5.7.2 Queueing Models

On many systems, the processes that are run vary from day to day, so there is no static set of processes (or times) to use for deterministic modeling. What can be determined, however, is the distribution of CPU and I/O bursts. These distributions can be measured and then approximated or simply estimated. The result is a mathematical formula describing the probability of a particular CPU burst. Commonly, this distribution is exponential and is described by its mean. Similarly, we can describe the distribution of times when processes arrive in the system (the arrival-time distribution). From these two distributions, it is possible to compute the average throughput, utilization, waiting time, and so on for most algorithms.

The computer system is described as a network of servers. Each server has a queue of waiting processes. The CPU is a server with its ready queue, as is the I/O system with its device queues. Knowing arrival rates and service rates, we can compute utilization, average queue length, average wait time, and so on. This area of study is called **queueing-network analysis**.

As an example, let n be the average queue length (excluding the process being serviced), let W be the average waiting time in the queue, and let λ be the average arrival rate for new processes in the queue (such as three processes per second). We expect that during the time W that a process waits, $\lambda \times W$ new processes will arrive in the queue. If the system is in a steady state, then the number of processes leaving the queue must be equal to the number of processes that arrive. Thus,

$$n = \lambda \times W.$$

This equation, known as **Little's formula**, is particularly useful because it is valid for any scheduling algorithm and arrival distribution.

We can use Little's formula to compute one of the three variables if we know the other two. For example, if we know that 7 processes arrive every second (on average), and that there are normally 14 processes in the queue, then we can compute the average waiting time per process as 2 seconds.

Queueing analysis can be useful in comparing scheduling algorithms, but it also has limitations. At the moment, the classes of algorithms and distributions that can be handled are fairly limited. The mathematics of complicated algorithms and distributions can be difficult to work with. Thus, arrival and service distributions are often defined in mathematically tractable —but unrealistic—ways. It is also generally necessary to make a number of independent assumptions, which may not be accurate. As a result of these difficulties, queueing models are often only approximations of real systems, and the accuracy of the computed results may be questionable.

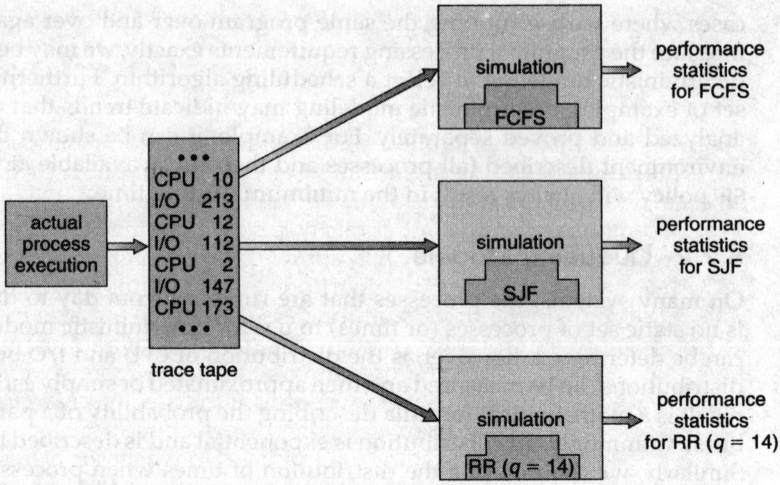

Figure 5.17 Evaluation of CPU schedulers by simulation.

5.7.3 Simulations

To get a more accurate evaluation of scheduling algorithms, we can use **simulations**. Running simulations involves programming a model of the computer system. Software data structures represent the major components of the system. The simulator has a variable representing a clock; as this variable's value is increased, the simulator modifies the system state to reflect the activities of the devices, the processes, and the scheduler. As the simulation executes, statistics that indicate algorithm performance are gathered and printed.

The data to drive the simulation can be generated in several ways. The most common method uses a random-number generator that is programmed to generate processes, CPU burst times, arrivals, departures, and so on, according to probability distributions. The distributions can be defined mathematically (uniform, exponential, Poisson) or empirically. If a distribution is to be defined empirically, measurements of the actual system under study are taken. The results define the distribution of events in the real system; this distribution can then be used to drive the simulation.

A distribution-driven simulation may be inaccurate, however, because of relationships between successive events in the real system. The frequency distribution indicates only how many instances of each event occur; it does not indicate anything about the order of their occurrence. To correct this problem, we can use **trace tapes**. We create a trace tape by monitoring the real system and recording the sequence of actual events (Figure 5.17). We then use this sequence to drive the simulation. Trace tapes provide an excellent way to compare two algorithms on exactly the same set of real inputs. This method can produce accurate results for its inputs.

Simulations can be expensive, often requiring hours of computer time. A more detailed simulation provides more accurate results, but it also takes more computer time. In addition, trace tapes can require large amounts of storage space. Finally, the design, coding, and debugging of the simulator can be a major task.

5.7.4 Implementation

Even a simulation is of limited accuracy. The only completely accurate way to evaluate a scheduling algorithm is to code it up, put it in the operating system, and see how it works. This approach puts the actual algorithm in the real system for evaluation under real operating conditions.

The major difficulty with this approach is the high cost. The expense is incurred not only in coding the algorithm and modifying the operating system to support it (along with its required data structures) but also in the reaction of the users to a constantly changing operating system. Most users are not interested in building a better operating system; they merely want to get their processes executed and use their results. A constantly changing operating system does not help the users to get their work done.

Another difficulty is that the environment in which the algorithm is used will change. The environment will change not only in the usual way, as new programs are written and the types of problems change, but also as a result of the performance of the scheduler. If short processes are given priority, then users may break larger processes into sets of smaller processes. If interactive processes are given priority over noninteractive processes, then users may switch to interactive use.

For example, researchers designed one system that classified interactive and noninteractive processes automatically by looking at the amount of terminal I/O. If a process did not input or output to the terminal in a 1-second interval, the process was classified as noninteractive and was moved to a lower-priority queue. In response to this policy, one programmer modified his programs to write an arbitrary character to the terminal at regular intervals of less than 1 second. The system gave his programs a high priority, even though the terminal output was completely meaningless.

The most flexible scheduling algorithms are those that can be altered by the system managers or by the users so that they can be tuned for a specific application or set of applications. A workstation that performs high-end graphical applications, for instance, may have scheduling needs different from those of a Web server or file server. Some operating systems—particularly several versions of UNIX—allow the system manager to fine-tune the scheduling parameters for a particular system configuration. For example, Solaris provides the `dispadmin` command to allow the system administrator to modify the parameters of the scheduling classes described in Section 5.6.1.

Another approach is to use APIs that modify the priority of a process or thread. The Java, /POSIX, and /WinAPI/ provide such functions. The downfall of this approach is that performance-tuning a system or application most often does not result in improved performance in more general situations.

5.8 Summary

CPU scheduling is the task of selecting a waiting process from the ready queue and allocating the CPU to it. The CPU is allocated to the selected process by the dispatcher.

First-come, first-served (FCFS) scheduling is the simplest scheduling algorithm, but it can cause short processes to wait for very long processes. Shortest-job-first (SJF) scheduling is provably optimal, providing the shortest average waiting time. Implementing SJF scheduling is difficult, however, because predicting the length of the next CPU burst is difficult. The SJF algorithm is a special case of the general priority scheduling algorithm, which simply allocates the CPU to the highest-priority process. Both priority and SJF scheduling may suffer from starvation. Aging is a technique to prevent starvation.

Round-robin (RR) scheduling is more appropriate for a time-shared (interactive) system. RR scheduling allocates the CPU to the first process in the ready queue for q time units, where q is the time quantum. After q time units, if the process has not relinquished the CPU, it is preempted, and the process is put at the tail of the ready queue. The major problem is the selection of the time quantum. If the quantum is too large, RR scheduling degenerates to FCFS scheduling; if the quantum is too small, scheduling overhead in the form of context-switch time becomes excessive.

The FCFS algorithm is nonpreemptive; the RR algorithm is preemptive. The SJF and priority algorithms may be either preemptive or nonpreemptive.

Multilevel queue algorithms allow different algorithms to be used for different classes of processes. The most common model includes a foreground interactive queue that uses RR scheduling and a background batch queue that uses FCFS scheduling. Multilevel feedback queues allow processes to move from one queue to another.

Many contemporary computer systems support multiple processors and allow each processor to schedule itself independently. Typically, each processor maintains its own private queue of processes (or threads), all of which are available to run. Additional issues related to multiprocessor scheduling include processor affinity, load balancing, and multicore processing as well as scheduling on virtualization systems.

Operating systems supporting threads at the kernel level must schedule threads—not processes—for execution. This is the case with Solaris and Windows XP. Both of these systems schedule threads using preemptive, priority-based scheduling algorithms, including support for real-time threads. The Linux process scheduler uses a priority-based algorithm with real-time support as well. The scheduling algorithms for these three operating systems typically favor interactive over batch and CPU-bound processes.

The wide variety of scheduling algorithms demands that we have methods to select among algorithms. Analytic methods use mathematical analysis to determine the performance of an algorithm. Simulation methods determine performance by imitating the scheduling algorithm on a "representative" sample of processes and computing the resulting performance. However, simulation can at best provide an approximation of actual system performance; the only reliable technique for evaluating a scheduling algorithm is to implement the algorithm on an actual system and monitor its performance in a "real-world" environment.

Exercises

5.1 Why is it important for the scheduler to distinguish I/O-bound programs from CPU-bound programs?

5.2 A CPU-scheduling algorithm determines an order for the execution of its scheduled processes. Given *n* processes to be scheduled on one processor, how many different schedules are possible? Give a formula in terms of *n*.

5.3 Consider a system running ten I/O-bound tasks and one CPU-bound task. Assume that the I/O-bound tasks issue an I/O operation once for every millisecond of CPU computing and that each I/O operation takes 10 milliseconds to complete. Also assume that the context-switching overhead is 0.1 millisecond and that all processes are long-running tasks. Describe the CPU utilization for a round-robin scheduler when:

a. The time quantum is 1 millisecond

b. The time quantum is 10 milliseconds

5.4 What advantage is there in having different time-quantum sizes at different levels of a multilevel queueing system?

5.5 Consider a system implementing multilevel queue scheduling. What strategy can a computer user employ to maximize the amount of CPU time allocated to the user's process?

5.6 Consider the scheduling algorithm in the Solaris operating system for time-sharing threads.

a. What is the time quantum (in milliseconds) for a thread with priority 10? With priority 55?

b. Assume that a thread with priority 35 has used its entire time quantum without blocking. What new priority will the scheduler assign this thread?

c. Assume that a thread with priority 35 blocks for I/O before its time quantum has expired. What new priority will the scheduler assign this thread?

5.7 Explain the differences in how much the following scheduling algorithms discriminate in favor of short processes:

a. FCFS

b. RR

c. Multilevel feedback queues

5.8 Consider the exponential average formula used to predict the length of the next CPU burst. What are the implications of assigning the following values to the parameters used by the algorithm?

a. $\alpha = 0$ and $\tau_0 = 100$ milliseconds

b. $\alpha = 0.99$ and $\tau_0 = 10$ milliseconds

5.9 Which of the following scheduling algorithms could result in starvation?

a. First-come, first-served

b. Shortest job first

c. Round robin

d. Priority

5.10 Suppose that a scheduling algorithm (at the level of short-term CPU scheduling) favors those processes that have used the least processor time in the recent past. Why will this algorithm favor I/O-bound programs and yet not permanently starve CPU-bound programs?

5.11 Using the Windows XP scheduling algorithm, determine the numeric priority of each of the following threads.

a. A thread in the REALTIME_PRIORITY_CLASS with a relative priority of HIGHEST

b. A thread in the NORMAL_PRIORITY_CLASS with a relative priority of NORMAL

c. A thread in the HIGH_PRIORITY_CLASS with a relative priority of ABOVE_NORMAL

5.12 Consider a variant of the RR scheduling algorithm in which the entries in the ready queue are pointers to the PCBs.

a. What would be the effect of putting two pointers to the same process in the ready queue?

b. What would be two major advantages and two disadvantages of this scheme?

c. How would you modify the basic RR algorithm to achieve the same effect without the duplicate pointers?

5.13 Consider the following set of processes, with the length of the CPU burst given in milliseconds:

Process	Burst Time	Priority
P_1	10	3
P_2	1	1
P_3	2	3
P_4	1	4
P_5	5	2

The processes are assumed to have arrived in the order P_1, P_2, P_3, P_4, P_5, all at time 0.

a. Draw four Gantt charts that illustrate the execution of these processes using the following scheduling algorithms: FCFS, SJF, nonpreemptive priority (a smaller priority number implies a higher priority), and RR (quantum = 1).

b. What is the turnaround time of each process for each of the scheduling algorithms in part a?

c. What is the waiting time of each process for each of these scheduling algorithms?

d. Which of the algorithms results in the minimum average waiting time (over all processes)?

5.14 The traditional UNIX scheduler enforces an inverse relationship between priority numbers and priorities: the higher the number, the lower the priority. The scheduler recalculates process priorities once per second using the following function:

Priority = (recent CPU usage / 2) + base

where base = 60 and *recent CPU usage* refers to a value indicating how often a process has used the CPU since priorities were last recalculated.

Assume that recent CPU usage for process P_1 is 40, for process P_2 is 18, and for process P_3 is 10. What will be the new priorities for these three processes when priorities are recalculated? Based on this information, does the traditional UNIX scheduler raise or lower the relative priority of a CPU-bound process?

5.15 Discuss how the following pairs of scheduling criteria conflict in certain settings.

a. CPU utilization and response time

b. Average turnaround time and maximum waiting time

c. I/O device utilization and CPU utilization

5.16 Consider a preemptive priority scheduling algorithm based on dynamically changing priorities. Larger priority numbers imply higher priority. When a process is waiting for the CPU (in the ready queue, but not running), its priority changes at a rate α; when it is running, its priority changes at a rate β. All processes are given a priority of 0 when they enter the ready queue. The parameters α and β can be set to give many different scheduling algorithms.

a. What is the algorithm that results from $\beta > \alpha > 0$?

b. What is the algorithm that results from $\alpha < \beta < 0$?

5.17 Suppose that the following processes arrive for execution at the times indicated. Each process will run for the amount of time listed. In answering the questions, use nonpreemptive scheduling, and base all decisions on the information you have at the time the decision must be made.

Process	Arrival Time	Burst Time
P_1	0.0	8
P_2	0.4	4
P_3	1.0	1

a. What is the average turnaround time for these processes with the FCFS scheduling algorithm?

b. What is the average turnaround time for these processes with the SJF scheduling algorithm?

c. The SJF algorithm is supposed to improve performance, but notice that we chose to run process P_1 at time 0 because we did not know that two shorter processes would arrive soon. Compute what the average turnaround time will be if the CPU is left idle for the first 1 unit and then SJF scheduling is used. Remember that processes P_1 and P_2 are waiting during this idle time, so their waiting time may increase. This algorithm could be known as future-knowledge scheduling.

Bibliographical Notes

Feedback queues were originally implemented on the CTSS system described in Corbato et al. [1962]. This feedback queue scheduling system was analyzed by Schrage [1967]. The preemptive priority scheduling algorithm of Exercise 5.16 was suggested by Kleinrock [1975].

Anderson et al. [1989], Lewis and Berg [1998], and Philbin et al. [1996] discuss thread scheduling. Multicore scheduling is examined in McNairy and Bhatia [2005] and Kongetira et al. [2005].

Scheduling techniques that take into account information regarding process execution times from previous runs are described in Fisher [1981], Hall et al. [1996], and Lowney et al. [1993].

Fair-share schedulers are covered by Henry [1984], Woodside [1986], and Kay and Lauder [1988].

Scheduling policies used in the UNIX V operating system are described by Bach [1987]; those for UNIX FreeBSD 5.2 are presented by McKusick and Neville-Neil [2005]; and those for the Mach operating system are discussed by Black [1990]. Love [2005] covers scheduling in Linux. Details of the ULE scheduler can be found in Roberson [2003]. Solaris scheduling is described by Mauro and McDougall [2007]. Solomon [1998], Solomon and Russinovich [2000], and Russinovich and Solomon [2005] discuss scheduling in Windows internals. Butenhof [1997] and Lewis and Berg [1998] describe scheduling in Pthreads systems. Siddha et al. [2007] discuss scheduling challenges on multicore systems.

Part Three

Process Coordination

CHAPTER 6

Synchronization

A cooperating process is one that can affect or be affected by other processes executing in the system. Cooperating processes can either directly share a logical address space (that is, both code and data) or be allowed to share data only through files or messages. The former case is achieved through the use of threads, discussed in Chapter 4. Concurrent access to shared data may result in data inconsistency, however. In this chapter, we discuss various mechanisms to ensure the orderly execution of cooperating processes that share a logical address space, so that data consistency is maintained.

CHAPTER OBJECTIVES

- To introduce the critical-section problem, whose solutions can be used to ensure the consistency of shared data.
- To present both software and hardware solutions of the critical-section problem.
- To introduce the concept of an atomic transaction and describe mechanisms to ensure atomicity.

6.1 Background

In Chapter 3, we developed a model of a system consisting of cooperating sequential processes or threads, all running asynchronously and possibly sharing data. We illustrated this model with the producer–consumer problem, which is representative of operating systems. Specifically, in Section 3.4.1, we described how a bounded buffer could be used to enable processes to share memory.

Let's return to our consideration of the bounded buffer. As we pointed out, our original solution allowed at most BUFFER_SIZE − 1 items in the buffer at the same time. Suppose we want to modify the algorithm to remedy this deficiency. One possibility is to add an integer variable `counter`, initialized to 0. `counter` is incremented every time we add a new item to the buffer and is decremented every time we remove one item from the buffer. The code for the producer process can be modified as follows:

```
while (true) {
        /* produce an item in nextProduced */
        while (counter == BUFFER_SIZE)
            ; /* do nothing */
        buffer[in] = nextProduced;
        in = (in + 1) % BUFFER_SIZE;
        counter++;
}
```

The code for the consumer process can be modified as follows:

```
while (true) {
        while (counter == 0)
            ; /* do nothing */
        nextConsumed = buffer[out];
        out = (out + 1) % BUFFER_SIZE;
        counter--;
        /* consume the item in nextConsumed */
}
```

Although both the producer and consumer routines shown above are correct separately, they may not function correctly when executed concurrently. As an illustration, suppose that the value of the variable counter is currently 5 and that the producer and consumer processes execute the statements "counter++" and "counter--" concurrently. Following the execution of these two statements, the value of the variable counter may be 4, 5, or 6! The only correct result, though, is counter == 5, which is generated correctly if the producer and consumer execute separately.

We can show that the value of counter may be incorrect as follows. Note that the statement "counter++" may be implemented in machine language (on a typical machine) as

$$\begin{aligned}&register_1 = \texttt{counter}\\&register_1 = register_1 + 1\\&\texttt{counter} = register_1\end{aligned}$$

where $register_1$ is one of the local CPU registers. Similarly, the statement $register_2$"counter--" is implemented as follows:

$$\begin{aligned}&register_2 = \texttt{counter}\\&register_2 = register_2 - 1\\&\texttt{counter} = register_2\end{aligned}$$

where again $register_2$ is on eof the local CPU registers. Even though $register_1$ and $register_2$ may be the same physical register (an accumulator, say), remember that the contents of this register will be saved and restored by the interrupt handler (Section 1.2.3).

The concurrent execution of "`counter++`" and "`counter--`" is equivalent to a sequential execution in which the lower-level statements presented previously are interleaved in some arbitrary order (but the order within each high-level statement is preserved). One such interleaving is

T_0:	*producer*	execute	$register_1$ = `counter`	$\{register_1 = 5\}$
T_1:	*producer*	execute	$register_1 = register_1 + 1$	$\{register_1 = 6\}$
T_2:	*consumer*	execute	$register_2$ = `counter`	$\{register_2 = 5\}$
T_3:	*consumer*	execute	$register_2 = register_2 - 1$	$\{register_2 = 4\}$
T_4:	*producer*	execute	`counter` = $register_1$	$\{counter = 6\}$
T_5:	*consumer*	execute	`counter` = $register_2$	$\{counter = 4\}$

Notice that we have arrived at the incorrect state "`counter == 4`", indicating that four buffers are full, when, in fact, five buffers are full. If we reversed the order of the statements at T_4 and T_5, we would arrive at the incorrect state "`counter == 6`".

We would arrive at this incorrect state because we allowed both processes to manipulate the variable `counter` concurrently. A situation like this, where several processes access and manipulate the same data concurrently and the outcome of the execution depends on the particular order in which the access takes place, is called a **race condition**. To guard against the race condition above, we need to ensure that only one process at a time can be manipulating the variable `counter`. To make such a guarantee, we require that the processes be synchronized in some way.

Situations such as the one just described occur frequently in operating systems as different parts of the system manipulate resources. Furthermore, with the growth of multicore systems, there is an increased emphasis on developing multithreaded applications wherein several threads—which are quite possibly sharing data—are running in parallel on different processing cores. Clearly, we want any changes that result from such activities not to interfere with one another. Because of the importance of this issue, a major portion of this chapter is concerned with **process synchronization** and **coordination** amongst cooperating processes.

6.2 The Critical-Section Problem

Consider a system consisting of n processes $\{P_0, P_1, ..., P_{n-1}\}$. Each process has a segment of code, called a **critical section**, in which the process may be changing common variables, updating a table, writing a file, and so on. The important feature of the system is that, when one process is executing in its critical section, no other process is to be allowed to execute in its critical section. That is, no two processes are executing in their critical sections at the same time. The *critical-section problem* is to design a protocol that the processes can use to cooperate. Each process must request permission to enter its critical section. The section of code implementing this request is the **entry section**. The critical section may be followed by an **exit section**. The remaining code is the **remainder section**. The general structure of a typical process P_i is shown in

```
do {

    | entry section |

        critical section

    | exit section |

        remainder section

} while (TRUE);
```

Figure 6.1 General structure of a typical process P_i.

Figure 6.1. The entry section and exit section are enclosed in boxes to highlight these important segments of code.

A solution to the critical-section problem must satisfy the following three requirements:

1. **Mutual exclusion**. If process P_i is executing in its critical section, then no other processes can be executing in their critical sections.

2. **Progress**. If no process is executing in its critical section and some processes wish to enter their critical sections, then only those processes that are not executing in their remainder sections can participate in deciding which will enter its critical section next, and this selection cannot be postponed indefinitely.

3. **Bounded waiting**. There exists a bound, or limit, on the number of times that other processes are allowed to enter their critical sections after a process has made a request to enter its critical section and before that request is granted.

We assume that each process is executing at a nonzero speed. However, we can make no assumption concerning the **relative speed** of the *n* processes.

At a given point in time, many kernel-mode processes may be active in the operating system. As a result, the code implementing an operating system (*kernel code*) is subject to several possible race conditions. Consider as an example a kernel data structure that maintains a list of all open files in the system. This list must be modified when a new file is opened or closed (adding the file to the list or removing it from the list). If two processes were to open files simultaneously, the separate updates to this list could result in a race condition. Other kernel data structures that are prone to possible race conditions include structures for maintaining memory allocation, for maintaining process lists, and for interrupt handling. It is up to kernel developers to ensure that the operating system is free from such race conditions.

Two general approaches are used to handle critical sections in operating systems: (1) **preemptive kernels** and (2) **nonpreemptive kernels**. A preemptive kernel allows a process to be preempted while it is running in kernel mode. A nonpreemptive kernel does not allow a process running in kernel mode to be preempted; a kernel-mode process will run until it exits kernel mode, blocks, or voluntarily yields control of the CPU. Obviously, a nonpreemptive kernel is essentially free from race conditions on kernel data structures, as only one process is active in the kernel at a time. We cannot say the same about preemptive kernels, so they must be carefully designed to ensure that shared kernel data are free from race conditions. Preemptive kernels are especially difficult to design for SMP architectures, since in these environments it is possible for two kernel-mode processes to run simultaneously on different processors.

Why, then, would anyone favor a preemptive kernel over a nonpreemptive one? A preemptive kernel is more suitable for real-time programming, as it will allow a real-time process to preempt a process currently running in the kernel. Furthermore, a preemptive kernel may be more responsive, since there is less risk that a kernel-mode process will run for an arbitrarily long period before relinquishing the processor to waiting processes. Of course, this effect can be minimized by designing kernel code that does not behave in this way. Later in this chapter, we explore how various operating systems manage preemption within the kernel.

6.3 Peterson's Solution

Next, we illustrate a classic software-based solution to the critical-section problem known as **Peterson's solution**. Because of the way modern computer architectures perform basic machine-language instructions, such as `load` and `store`, there are no guarantees that Peterson's solution will work correctly on such architectures. However, we present the solution because it provides a good algorithmic description of solving the critical-section problem and illustrates some of the complexities involved in designing software that addresses the requirements of mutual exclusion, progress, and bounded waiting.

Peterson's solution is restricted to two processes that alternate execution between their critical sections and remainder sections. The processes are numbered P_0 and P_1. For convenience, when presenting P_i, we use P_j to denote the other process; that is, `j` equals 1 − `i`.

Peterson's solution requires the two processes to share two data items:

```
int turn;
boolean flag[2];
```

The variable `turn` indicates whose turn it is to enter its critical section. That is, if `turn == i`, then process P_i is allowed to execute in its critical section. The `flag` array is used to indicate if a process *is ready* to enter its critical section. For example, if `flag[i]` is `true`, this value indicates that P_i is ready to enter its critical section. With an explanation of these data structures complete, we are now ready to describe the algorithm shown in Figure 6.2.

To enter the critical section, process P_i first sets `flag[i]` to be `true` and then sets `turn` to the value `j`, thereby asserting that if the other process wishes to enter the critical section, it can do so. If both processes try to enter at the same time, `turn` will be set to both `i` and `j` at roughly the same time. Only one of these assignments will last; the other will occur but will be overwritten immediately.

```
do {

    flag[i] = TRUE;
    turn = j;
    while (flag[j] && turn == j);

        critical section

    flag[i] = FALSE;

        remainder section

} while (TRUE);
```

Figure 6.2 The structure of process P_i in Peterson's solution.

The eventual value of `turn` determines which of the two processes is allowed to enter its critical section first.

We now prove that this solution is correct. We need to show that:

1. Mutual exclusion is preserved.
2. The progress requirement is satisfied.
3. The bounded-waiting requirement is met.

To prove property 1, we note that each P_i enters its critical section only if either `flag[j] == false` or `turn == i`. Also note that, if both processes can be executing in their critical sections at the same time, then `flag[0] == flag[1] == true`. These two observations imply that P_0 and P_1 could not have successfully executed their `while` statements at about the same time, since the value of `turn` can be either 0 or 1 but cannot be both. Hence, one of the processes —say, P_j—must have successfully executed the while statement, whereas P_i had to execute at least one additional statement ("`turn == j`"). However, at that time, `flag[j] == true` and `turn == j`, and this condition will persist as long as P_j is in its critical section; as a result, mutual exclusion is preserved.

To prove properties 2 and 3, we note that a process P_i can be prevented from entering the critical section only if it is stuck in the while loop with the condition `flag[j] == true` and `turn == j`; this loop is the only one possible. If P_j is not ready to enter the critical section, then `flag[j] == false`, and P_i can enter its critical section. If P_j has set `flag[j]` to `true` and is also executing in its `while` statement, then either `turn == i` or `turn == j`. If `turn == i`, then P_i will enter the critical section. If `turn == j`, then P_j will enter the critical section. However, once P_j exits its critical section, it will reset `flag[j]` to `false`, allowing P_i to enter its critical section. If P_j resets `flag[j]` to `true`, it must also set `turn` to `i`. Thus, since P_i does not change the value of the variable `turn` while executing the `while` statement, P_i will enter the critical section (progress) after at most one entry by P_j (bounded waiting).

```
do {
    | acquire lock |

        critical section

    | release lock |

        remainder section

} while (TRUE);
```

Figure 6.3 Solution to the critical-section problem using locks.

6.4 Synchronization Hardware

We have just described one software-based solution to the critical-section problem. However, as mentioned, software-based solutions such as Peterson's are not guaranteed to work on modern computer architectures. Instead, we can generally state that any solution to the critical-section problem requires a simple tool—a **lock**. Race conditions are prevented by requiring that critical regions be protected by locks. That is, a process must acquire a lock before entering a critical section; it releases the lock when it exits the critical section. This is illustrated in Figure 6.3.

In the following discussions, we explore several more solutions to the critical-section problem using techniques ranging from hardware to software-based APIs available to application programmers. All these solutions are based on the premise of locking; however, as we shall see, the designs of such locks can be quite sophisticated.

We start by presenting some simple hardware instructions that are available on many systems and showing how they can be used effectively in solving the critical-section problem. Hardware features can make any programming task easier and improve system efficiency.

The critical-section problem could be solved simply in a uniprocessor environment if we could prevent interrupts from occurring while a shared variable was being modified. In this manner, we could be sure that the current sequence of instructions would be allowed to execute in order without preemption. No other instructions would be run, so no unexpected modifications could be made to the shared variable. This is often the approach taken by nonpreemptive kernels.

Unfortunately, this solution is not as feasible in a multiprocessor environment. Disabling interrupts on a multiprocessor can be time consuming, as the

```
boolean TestAndSet(boolean *target) {
    boolean rv = *target;
    *target = TRUE;
    return rv;
}
```

Figure 6.4 The definition of the `TestAndSet()` instruction.

```
do {
   while (TestAndSet(&lock))
      ; // do nothing

      // critical section

   lock = FALSE;

      // remainder section
} while (TRUE);
```

Figure 6.5 Mutual-exclusion implementation with TestAndSet().

message is passed to all the processors. This message passing delays entry into each critical section, and system efficiency decreases. Also consider the effect on a system's clock if the clock is kept updated by interrupts.

Many modern computer systems therefore provide special hardware instructions that allow us either to test and modify the content of a word or to swap the contents of two words **atomically**—that is, as one uninterruptible unit. We can use these special instructions to solve the critical-section problem in a relatively simple manner. Rather than discussing one specific instruction for one specific machine, we abstract the main concepts behind these types of instructions by describing the `TestAndSet()` and `Swap()` instructions.

The `TestAndSet()` instruction can be defined as shown in Figure 6.4. The important characteristic of this instruction is that it is executed atomically. Thus, if two `TestAndSet()` instructions are executed simultaneously (each on a different CPU), they will be executed sequentially in some arbitrary order. If the machine supports the `TestAndSet()` instruction, then we can implement mutual exclusion by declaring a Boolean variable `lock`, initialized to `false`. The structure of process P_i is shown in Figure 6.5.

The `Swap()` instruction, in contrast to the `TestAndSet()` instruction, operates on the contents of two words; it is defined as shown in Figure 6.6. Like the `TestAndSet()` instruction, it is executed atomically. If the machine supports the `Swap()` instruction, then mutual exclusion can be provided as follows. A global Boolean variable `lock` is declared and is initialized to `false`. In addition, each process has a local Boolean variable `key`. The structure of process P_i is shown in Figure 6.7.

Although these algorithms satisfy the mutual-exclusion requirement, they do not satisfy the bounded-waiting requirement. In Figure 6.8, we present another algorithm using the `TestAndSet()` instruction that satisfies all the critical-section requirements. The common data structures are

```
void Swap(boolean *a, boolean *b) {
   boolean temp = *a;
   *a = *b;
   *b = temp;
}
```

Figure 6.6 The definition of the Swap() instruction.

```
do {
   key = TRUE;
   while (key == TRUE)
      Swap(&lock, &key);

         // critical section

   lock = FALSE;

         // remainder section
} while (TRUE);
```

Figure 6.7 Mutual-exclusion implementation with the Swap() instruction.

```
boolean waiting[n];
boolean lock;
```

These data structures are initialized to false. To prove that the mutual-exclusion requirement is met, we note that process P_i can enter its critical section only if either waiting[i] == false or key == false. The value of key can become false only if the TestAndSet() is executed. The first process to execute the TestAndSet() will find key == false; all others must wait. The variable waiting[i] can become false only if another process leaves its critical section; only one waiting[i] is set to false, maintaining the mutual-exclusion requirement.

```
do {
   waiting[i] = TRUE;
   key = TRUE;
   while (waiting[i] && key)
      key = TestAndSet(&lock);
   waiting[i] = FALSE;

      // critical section

   j = (i + 1) % n;
   while ((j != i) && !waiting[j])
      j = (j + 1) % n;

   if (j == i)
      lock = FALSE;
   else
      waiting[j] = FALSE;

      // remainder section
} while (TRUE);
```

Figure 6.8 Bounded-waiting mutual exclusion with TestAndSet().

To prove that the progress requirement is met, we note that the arguments presented for mutual exclusion also apply here, since a process exiting the critical section either sets `lock` to `false` or sets `waiting[j]` to `false`. Both allow a process that is waiting to enter its critical section to proceed.

To prove that the bounded-waiting requirement is met, we note that, when a process leaves its critical section, it scans the array `waiting` in the cyclic ordering ($i + 1, i + 2, ..., n - 1, 0, ..., i - 1$). It designates the first process in this ordering that is in the entry section (`waiting[j] == true`) as the next one to enter the critical section. Any process waiting to enter its critical section will thus do so within $n - 1$ turns.

Unfortunately for hardware designers, implementing atomic `TestAndSet()` instructions on multiprocessors is not a trivial task. Such implementations are discussed in books on computer architecture.

6.5 Semaphores

The hardware-based solutions to the critical-section problem presented in Section 6.4 are complicated for application programmers to use. To overcome this difficulty, we can use a synchronization tool called a **semaphore**.

A semaphore `S` is an integer variable that, apart from initialization, is accessed only through two standard atomic operations: `wait()` and `signal()`. The `wait()` operation was originally termed `P` (from the Dutch *proberen*, "to test"); `signal()` was originally called `V` (from *verhogen*, "to increment"). The definition of `wait()` is as follows:

```
wait(S) {
   while S <= 0
      ; // no-op
   S--;
}
```

The definition of `signal()` is as follows:

```
signal(S) {
   S++;
}
```

All modifications to the integer value of the semaphore in the `wait()` and `signal()` operations must be executed indivisibly. That is, when one process modifies the semaphore value, no other process can simultaneously modify that same semaphore value. In addition, in the case of `wait(S)`, the testing of the integer value of `S` ($S \leq 0$), as well as its possible modification (`S--`), must be executed without interruption. We shall see how these operations can be implemented in Section 6.5.2; first, let us see how semaphores can be used.

6.5.1 Usage

Operating systems often distinguish between counting and binary semaphores. The value of a **counting semaphore** can range over an unrestricted domain. The value of a **binary semaphore** can range only between 0 and 1. On some systems, binary semaphores are known as **mutex locks**, as they are locks that provide *mut*ual *ex*clusion.

We can use binary semaphores to deal with the critical-section problem for multiple processes. The *n* processes share a semaphore, `mutex`, initialized to 1. Each process P_i is organized as shown in Figure 6.9.

Counting semaphores can be used to control access to a given resource consisting of a finite number of instances. The semaphore is initialized to the number of resources available. Each process that wishes to use a resource performs a `wait()` operation on the semaphore (thereby decrementing the count). When a process releases a resource, it performs a `signal()` operation (incrementing the count). When the count for the semaphore goes to 0, all resources are being used. After that, processes that wish to use a resource will block until the count becomes greater than 0.

We can also use semaphores to solve various synchronization problems. For example, consider two concurrently running processes: P_1 with a statement S_1 and P_2 with a statement S_2. Suppose we require that S_2 be executed only after S_1 has completed. We can implement this scheme readily by letting P_1 and P_2 share a common semaphore `synch`, initialized to 0, and by inserting the statements

```
S1;
signal(synch);
```

in process P_1 and the statements

```
wait(synch);
S2;
```

in process P_2. Because `synch` is initialized to 0, P_2 will execute S_2 only after P_1 has invoked `signal(synch)`, which is after statement S_1 has been executed.

6.5.2 Implementation

The main disadvantage of the semaphore definition given here is that it requires busy waiting. While a process is in its critical section, any other process that tries to enter its critical section must loop continuously in the entry code. This continual looping is clearly a problem in a real multiprogramming system,

```
do {
   wait(mutex);

      // critical section

   signal(mutex);

      // remainder section
} while (TRUE);
```

Figure 6.9 Mutual-exclusion implementation with semaphores.

where a single CPU is shared among many processes. Busy waiting wastes CPU cycles that some other process might be able to use productively. This type of semaphore is also called a **spinlock** because the process "spins" while waiting for the lock. (Spinlocks do have an advantage in that no context switch is required when a process must wait on a lock, and a context switch may take considerable time. Thus, when locks are expected to be held for short times, spinlocks are useful; they are often employed on multiprocessor systems where one thread can "spin" on one processor while another thread performs its critical section on another processor.)

To overcome the need for busy waiting, we can modify the definition of the `wait()` and `signal()` semaphore operations. When a process executes the `wait()` operation and finds that the semaphore value is not positive, it must wait. However, rather than engaging in busy waiting, the process can *block* itself. The block operation places a process into a waiting queue associated with the semaphore, and the state of the process is switched to the waiting state. Then control is transferred to the CPU scheduler, which selects another process to execute.

A process that is blocked, waiting on a semaphore `S`, should be restarted when some other process executes a `signal()` operation. The process is restarted by a `wakeup()` operation, which changes the process from the waiting state to the ready state. The process is then placed in the ready queue. (The CPU may or may not be switched from the running process to the newly ready process, depending on the CPU-scheduling algorithm.)

To implement semaphores under this definition, we define a semaphore as a "C" struct:

```
typedef struct {
    int value;
    struct process *list;
} semaphore;
```

Each semaphore has an integer `value` and a list of processes `list`. When a process must wait on a semaphore, it is added to the list of processes. A `signal()` operation removes one process from the list of waiting processes and awakens that process.

The `wait()` semaphore operation can now be defined as

```
wait(semaphore *S) {
        S->value--;
        if (S->value < 0) {
                add this process to S->list;
                block();
        }
}
```

The `signal()` semaphore operation can now be defined as

```
signal(semaphore *S) {
        S->value++;
        if (S->value <= 0) {
                remove a process P from S->list;
                wakeup(P);
        }
}
```

The `block()` operation suspends the process that invokes it. The `wakeup(P)` operation resumes the execution of a blocked process P. These two operations are provided by the operating system as basic system calls.

Note that in this implementation, semaphore values may be negative, although semaphore values are never negative under the classical definition of semaphores with busy waiting. If a semaphore value is negative, its magnitude is the number of processes waiting on that semaphore. This fact results from switching the order of the decrement and the test in the implementation of the `wait()` operation.

The list of waiting processes can be easily implemented by a link field in each process control block (PCB). Each semaphore contains an integer value and a pointer to a list of PCBs. One way to add and remove processes from the list so as to ensure bounded waiting is to use a FIFO queue, where the semaphore contains both head and tail pointers to the queue. In general, however, the list can use *any* queueing strategy. Correct usage of semaphores does not depend on a particular queueing strategy for the semaphore lists.

It is critical that semaphores be executed atomically. We must guarantee that no two processes can execute `wait()` and `signal()` operations on the same semaphore at the same time. This is a critical-section problem; and in a single-processor environment (that is, where only one CPU exists), we can solve it by simply inhibiting interrupts during the time the `wait()` and `signal()` operations are executing. This scheme works in a single-processor environment because, once interrupts are inhibited, instructions from different processes cannot be interleaved. Only the currently running process executes until interrupts are reenabled and the scheduler can regain control.

In a multiprocessor environment, interrupts must be disabled on every processor; otherwise, instructions from different processes (running on different processors) may be interleaved in some arbitrary way. Disabling interrupts on every processor can be a difficult task and furthermore can seriously diminish performance. Therefore, SMP systems must provide alternative locking techniques—such as spinlocks—to ensure that `wait()` and `signal()` are performed atomically.

It is important to admit that we have not completely eliminated busy waiting with this definition of the `wait()` and `signal()` operations. Rather, we have moved busy waiting from the entry section to the critical sections of application programs. Furthermore, we have limited busy waiting to the critical sections of the `wait()` and `signal()` operations, and these sections are short (if properly coded, they should be no more than about ten instructions). Thus, the critical section is almost never occupied, and busy waiting occurs rarely, and then for only a short time. An entirely different situation exists with application programs whose critical sections may be long (minutes or even hours) or may almost always be occupied. In such cases, busy waiting is extremely inefficient.

6.5.3 Deadlocks and Starvation

The implementation of a semaphore with a waiting queue may result in a situation where two or more processes are waiting indefinitely for an event that can be caused only by one of the waiting processes. The event in question is the execution of a `signal()` operation. When such a state is reached, these processes are said to be **deadlocked**.

To illustrate this, we consider a system consisting of two processes, P_0 and P_1, each accessing two semaphores, S and Q, set to the value 1:

```
      P0              P1

   wait(S);        wait(Q);
   wait(Q);        wait(S);
      .               .
      .               .
      .               .
   signal(S);      signal(Q);
   signal(Q);      signal(S);
```

Suppose that P_0 executes `wait(S)` and then P_1 executes `wait(Q)`. When P_0 executes `wait(Q)`, it must wait until P_1 executes `signal(Q)`. Similarly, when P_1 executes `wait(S)`, it must wait until P_0 executes `signal(S)`. Since these `signal()` operations cannot be executed, P_0 and P_1 are deadlocked.

We say that a set of processes is in a deadlock state when every process in the set is waiting for an event that can be caused only by another process in the set. The events with which we are mainly concerned here are *resource acquisition and release*. However, other types of events may result in deadlocks, as we show in Chapter 7. In that chapter, we describe various mechanisms for dealing with the deadlock problem.

Another problem related to deadlocks is **indefinite blocking**, or **starvation**, a situation in which processes wait indefinitely within the semaphore. Indefinite blocking may occur if we remove processes from the list associated with a semaphore in LIFO (last-in, first-out) order.

6.5.4 Priority Inversion

A scheduling challenge arises when a higher-priority process needs to read or modify kernel data that are currently being accessed by a lower-priority process—or a chain of lower-priority processes. Since kernel data are typically protected with a lock, the higher-priority process will have to wait for a lower-priority one to finish with the resource. The situation becomes more complicated if the lower-priority process is preempted in favor of another process with a higher priority. As an example, assume we have three processes, L, M, and H, whose priorities follow the order $L < M < H$. Assume that process H requires resource R, which is currently being accessed by process L. Ordinarily, process H would wait for L to finish using resource R. However, now suppose that process M becomes runnable, thereby preempting process

PRIORITY INVERSION AND THE MARS PATHFINDER

Priority inversion can be more than a scheduling inconvenience. On systems with tight time constraints (such as real-time systems—see Chapter 19), priority inversion can cause a process to take longer than it should to accomplish a task. When that happens, other failures can cascade, resulting in system failure.

Consider the Mars Pathfinder, a NASA space probe that landed a robot, the Sojourner rover, on Mars in 1997 to conduct experiments. Shortly after the Sojourner began operating, it started to experience frequent computer resets. Each reset reinitialized all hardware and software, including communications. If the problem had not been solved, the Sojourner would have failed in its mission.

The problem was caused by the fact that one high-priority task, "bc_dist," was taking longer than expected to complete its work. This task was being forced to wait for a shared resource that was held by the lower-priority "ASI/MET" task, which in turn was preempted by multiple medium-priority tasks. The "bc_dist" task would stall waiting for the shared resource, and ultimately the "bc_sched" task would discover the problem and perform the reset. The Sojourner was suffering from a typical case of priority inversion.

The operating system on the Sojourner was VxWorks (see Section 19.6), which had a global variable to enable priority inheritance on all semaphores. After testing, the variable was set on the Sojourner (on Mars!), and the problem was solved.

A full description of the problem, its detection, and its solution was written by the software team lead and is available at research.microsoft.com/mbj/Mars_Pathfinder/Authoritative_Account.html.

L. Indirectly, a process with a lower priority—process *M*—has affected how long process *H* must wait for *L* to relinquish resource *R*.

This problem is known as **priority inversion**. It occurs only in systems with more than two priorities, so one solution is to have only two priorities. That is insufficient for most general-purpose operating systems, however. Typically these systems solve the problem by implementing a **priority-inheritance protocol**. According to this protocol, all processes that are accessing resources needed by a higher-priority process inherit the higher priority until they are finished with the resources in question. When they are finished, their priorities revert to their original values. In the example above, a priority-inheritance protocol would allow process *L* to temporarily inherit the priority of process *H*, thereby preventing process *M* from preempting its execution. When process *L* had finished using resource *R*, it would relinquish its inherited priority from *H* and assume its original priority. Because resource *R* would now be available, process *H*—not *M*—would run next.

6.6 Classic Problems of Synchronization

In this section, we present a number of synchronization problems as examples of a large class of concurrency-control problems. These problems are used for

```
do {
   . . .
   // produce an item in nextp
   . . .
   wait(empty);
   wait(mutex);
   . . .
   // add nextp to buffer
   . . .
   signal(mutex);
   signal(full);
} while (TRUE);
```

Figure 6.10 The structure of the producer process.

testing nearly every newly proposed synchronization scheme. In our solutions to the problems, we use semaphores for synchronization.

6.6.1 The Bounded-Buffer Problem

The *bounded-buffer problem* was introduced in Section 6.1; it is commonly used to illustrate the power of synchronization primitives. Here, we present a general structure of this scheme without committing ourselves to any particular implementation; we provide a related programming project in the exercises at the end of the chapter.

We assume that the pool consists of *n* buffers, each capable of holding one item. The mutex semaphore provides mutual exclusion for accesses to the buffer pool and is initialized to the value 1. The empty and full semaphores count the number of empty and full buffers. The semaphore empty is initialized to the value n; the semaphore full is initialized to the value 0.

The code for the producer process is shown in Figure 6.10; the code for the consumer process is shown in Figure 6.11. Note the symmetry between the producer and the consumer. We can interpret this code as the producer producing full buffers for the consumer or as the consumer producing empty buffers for the producer.

```
do {
   wait(full);
   wait(mutex);
   . . .
   // remove an item from buffer to nextc
   . . .
   signal(mutex);
   signal(empty);
   . . .
   // consume the item in nextc
   . . .
} while (TRUE);
```

Figure 6.11 The structure of the consumer process.

6.6.2 The Readers–Writers Problem

Suppose that a database is to be shared among several concurrent processes. Some of these processes may want only to read the database, whereas others may want to update (that is, to read and write) the database. We distinguish between these two types of processes by referring to the former as **readers** and to the latter as **writers**. Obviously, if two readers access the shared data simultaneously, no adverse effects will result. However, if a writer and some other process (either a reader or a writer) access the database simultaneously, chaos may ensue.

To ensure that these difficulties do not arise, we require that the writers have exclusive access to the shared database while writing to the database. This synchronization problem is referred to as the *readers–writers problem*. Since it was originally stated, it has been used to test nearly every new synchronization primitive. The readers–writers problem has several variations, all involving priorities. The simplest one, referred to as the *first* readers–writers problem, requires that no reader be kept waiting unless a writer has already obtained permission to use the shared object. In other words, no reader should wait for other readers to finish simply because a writer is waiting. The *second* readers–writers problem requires that, once a writer is ready, that writer performs its write as soon as possible. In other words, if a writer is waiting to access the object, no new readers may start reading.

A solution to either problem may result in starvation. In the first case, writers may starve; in the second case, readers may starve. For this reason, other variants of the problem have been proposed. Next, we present a solution to the first readers–writers problem. Refer to the bibliographical notes at the end of the chapter for references describing starvation-free solutions to the second readers–writers problem.

In the solution to the first readers–writers problem, the reader processes share the following data structures:

```
semaphore mutex, wrt;
int readcount;
```

The semaphores `mutex` and `wrt` are initialized to 1; `readcount` is initialized to 0. The semaphore `wrt` is common to both reader and writer processes. The `mutex` semaphore is used to ensure mutual exclusion when the variable `readcount` is updated. The `readcount` variable keeps track of how many processes are currently reading the object. The semaphore `wrt` functions as a mutual-exclusion semaphore for the writers. It is also used by the first or last reader that enters or exits the critical section. It is not used by readers who enter or exit while other readers are in their critical sections.

The code for a writer process is shown in Figure 6.12; the code for a reader process is shown in Figure 6.13. Note that, if a writer is in the critical section and n readers are waiting, then one reader is queued on `wrt`, and $n - 1$ readers are queued on `mutex`. Also observe that, when a writer executes `signal(wrt)`, we may resume the execution of either the waiting readers or a single waiting writer. The selection is made by the scheduler.

The readers–writers problem and its solutions have been generalized to provide reader–writer locks on some systems. Acquiring a reader–writer lock

```
do {
    wait(wrt);
        . . .
    // writing is performed
        . . .
    signal(wrt);
} while (TRUE);
```

Figure 6.12 The structure of a writer process.

requires specifying the mode of the lock: either *read* or *write* access. When a process wishes only to read shared data, it requests the reader–writer lock in read mode; a process wishing to modify the shared data must request the lock in write mode. Multiple processes are permitted to concurrently acquire a reader–writer lock in read mode, but only one process may acquire the lock for writing, as exclusive access is required for writers.

Reader–writer locks are most useful in the following situations:

- In applications where it is easy to identify which processes only read shared data and which processes only write shared data.
- In applications that have more readers than writers. This is because reader–writer locks generally require more overhead to establish than semaphores or mutual-exclusion locks. The increased concurrency of allowing multiple readers compensates for the overhead involved in setting up the reader–writer lock.

6.6.3 The Dining-Philosophers Problem

Consider five philosophers who spend their lives thinking and eating. The philosophers share a circular table surrounded by five chairs, each belonging

```
do {
    wait(mutex);
    readcount++;
    if (readcount == 1)
        wait(wrt);
    signal(mutex);
        . . .
    // reading is performed
        . . .
    wait(mutex);
    readcount--;
    if (readcount == 0)
        signal(wrt);
    signal(mutex);
} while (TRUE);
```

Figure 6.13 The structure of a reader process.

Figure 6.14 The situation of the dining philosophers.

to one philosopher. In the center of the table is a bowl of rice, and the table is laid with five single chopsticks (Figure 6.14). When a philosopher thinks, she does not interact with her colleagues. From time to time, a philosopher gets hungry and tries to pick up the two chopsticks that are closest to her (the chopsticks that are between her and her left and right neighbors). A philosopher may pick up only one chopstick at a time. Obviously, she cannot pick up a chopstick that is already in the hand of a neighbor. When a hungry philosopher has both her chopsticks at the same time, she eats without releasing her chopsticks. When she is finished eating, she puts down both of her chopsticks and starts thinking again.

The *dining-philosophers problem* is considered a classic synchronization problem neither because of its practical importance nor because computer scientists dislike philosophers but because it is an example of a large class of concurrency-control problems. It is a simple representation of the need to allocate several resources among several processes in a deadlock-free and starvation-free manner.

One simple solution is to represent each chopstick with a semaphore. A philosopher tries to grab a chopstick by executing a `wait()` operation on that semaphore; she releases her chopsticks by executing the `signal()` operation on the appropriate semaphores. Thus, the shared data are

```
semaphore chopstick[5];
```

where all the elements of `chopstick` are initialized to 1. The structure of philosopher *i* is shown in Figure 6.15.

Although this solution guarantees that no two neighbors are eating simultaneously, it nevertheless must be rejected because it could create a deadlock. Suppose that all five philosophers become hungry simultaneously and each grabs her left chopstick. All the elements of `chopstick` will now be equal to 0. When each philosopher tries to grab her right chopstick, she will be delayed forever.

Several possible remedies to the deadlock problem are listed next.

- Allow at most four philosophers to be sitting simultaneously at the table.

```
do {
   wait(chopstick[i]);
   wait(chopstick[(i+1) % 5]);
      . . .
   // eat
      . . .
   signal(chopstick[i]);
   signal(chopstick[(i+1) % 5]);
      . . .
   // think
      . . .
} while (TRUE);
```

Figure 6.15 The structure of philosopher *i*.

- Allow a philosopher to pick up her chopsticks only if both chopsticks are available (to do this, she must pick them up in a critical section).
- Use an asymmetric solution; that is, an odd philosopher picks up first her left chopstick and then her right chopstick, whereas an even philosopher picks up her right chopstick and then her left chopstick.

In Section 6.7, we present a solution to the dining-philosophers problem that ensures freedom from deadlocks. Note, however, that any satisfactory solution to the dining-philosophers problem must guard against the possibility that one of the philosophers will starve to death. A deadlock-free solution does not necessarily eliminate the possibility of starvation.

6.7 Monitors

Although semaphores provide a convenient and effective mechanism for process synchronization, using them incorrectly can result in timing errors that are difficult to detect, since these errors happen only if some particular execution sequences take place and these sequences do not always occur.

We have seen an example of such errors in the use of counters in our solution to the producer–consumer problem (Section 6.1). In that example, the timing problem happened only rarely, and even then the counter value appeared to be reasonable—off by only 1. Nevertheless, the solution is obviously not an acceptable one. It is for this reason that semaphores were introduced in the first place.

Unfortunately, such timing errors can still occur when semaphores are used. To illustrate how, we review the semaphore solution to the critical-section problem. All processes share a semaphore variable `mutex`, which is initialized to 1. Each process must execute `wait(mutex)` before entering the critical section and `signal(mutex)` afterward. If this sequence is not observed, two processes may be in their critical sections simultaneously. Next, we examine the various difficulties that may result. Note that these difficulties will arise even if a *single* process is not well behaved. This situation may be caused by an honest programming error or an uncooperative programmer.

- Suppose that a process interchanges the order in which the `wait()` and `signal()` operations on the semaphore `mutex` are executed, resulting in the following execution:

```
signal(mutex);
    ...
  critical section
    ...
wait(mutex);
```

  In this situation, several processes may be executing in their critical sections simultaneously, violating the mutual-exclusion requirement. This error may be discovered only if several processes are simultaneously active in their critical sections. Note that this situation may not always be reproducible.

- Suppose that a process replaces `signal(mutex)` with `wait(mutex)`. That is, it executes

```
wait(mutex);
    ...
  critical section
    ...
wait(mutex);
```

  In this case, a deadlock will occur.

- Suppose that a process omits the `wait(mutex)`, or the `signal(mutex)`, or both. In this case, either mutual exclusion is violated or a deadlock will occur.

These examples illustrate that various types of errors can be generated easily when programmers use semaphores incorrectly to solve the critical-section problem. Similar problems may arise in the other synchronization models discussed in Section 6.6.

To deal with such errors, researchers have developed high-level language constructs. In this section, we describe one fundamental high-level synchronization construct—the **monitor** type.

6.7.1 Usage

A *abstract data type* — or ADT — encapsulates private data with public methods to operate on that data. A *monitor type* is an ADT which presents a set of programmer-defined operations that are provided mutual exclusion within the monitor. The monitor type also contains the declaration of variables whose values define the state of an instance of that type, along with the bodies of procedures or functions that operate on those variables. The syntax of a monitor type is shown in Figure 6.16. The representation of a monitor type cannot be used directly by the various processes. Thus, a procedure defined within a monitor can access only those variables declared locally within the monitor and its formal parameters. Similarly, the local variables of a monitor can be accessed by only the local procedures.

```
monitor monitor name
{
    // shared variable declarations

    procedure P1 ( . . . ) {
        . . .
    }

    procedure P2 ( . . . ) {
        . . .
    }
        .
        .
        .
    procedure Pn ( . . . ) {
        . . .
    }

    initialization code ( . . . ) {
        . . .
    }
}
```

Figure 6.16 Syntax of a monitor.

The monitor construct ensures that only one process at a time is active within the monitor. Consequently, the programmer does not need to code this synchronization constraint explicitly (Figure 6.17). However, the monitor construct, as defined so far, is not sufficiently powerful for modeling some synchronization schemes. For this purpose, we need to define additional synchronization mechanisms. These mechanisms are provided by the `condition` construct. A programmer who needs to write a tailor-made synchronization scheme can define one or more variables of type *condition*:

```
condition x, y;
```

The only operations that can be invoked on a condition variable are `wait()` and `signal()`. The operation

```
x.wait();
```

means that the process invoking this operation is suspended until another process invokes

```
x.signal();
```

The `x.signal()` operation resumes exactly one suspended process. If no process is suspended, then the `signal()` operation has no effect; that is, the state of `x` is the same as if the operation had never been executed (Figure

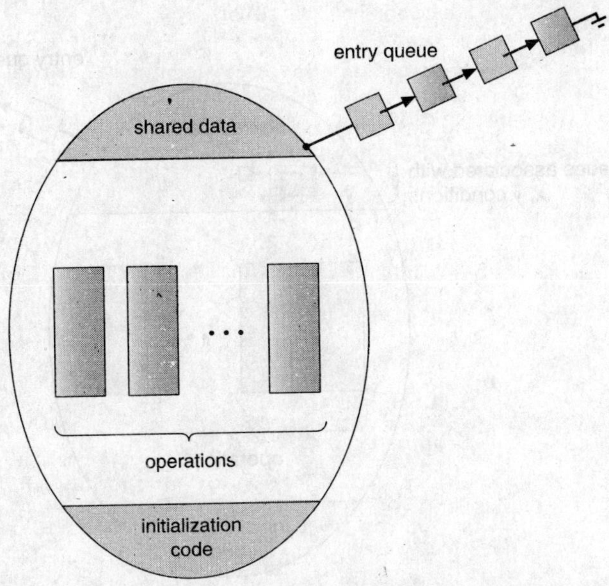

Figure 6.17 Schematic view of a monitor.

6.18). Contrast this operation with the `signal()` operation associated with semaphores, which always affects the state of the semaphore.

Now suppose that, when the `x.signal()` operation is invoked by a process `P`, there exists a suspended process `Q` associated with condition `x`. Clearly, if the suspended process `Q` is allowed to resume its execution, the signaling process `P` must wait. Otherwise, both `P` and `Q` would be active simultaneously within the monitor. Note, however, that both processes can conceptually continue with their execution. Two possibilities exist:

1. **Signal and wait**. *P* either waits until *Q* leaves the monitor or waits for another condition.
2. **Signal and continue.** *Q* either waits until *P* leaves the monitor or waits for another condition.

There are reasonable arguments in favor of adopting either option. On the one hand, since *P* was already executing in the monitor, the *signal-and-continue* method seems more reasonable. On the other hand, if we allow thread *P* to continue, then by the time *Q* is resumed, the logical condition for which *Q* was waiting may no longer hold. A compromise between these two choices was adopted in the language Concurrent Pascal. When thread *P* executes the signal operation, it immediately leaves the monitor. Hence, *Q* is immediately resumed.

Many programming languages have incorporated the idea of the monitor as described in this section, including Concurrent Pascal, Mesa, C# (pronounced *C-sharp*), and Java. Other languages—such as Erlang—provide some type of concurrency support using a similar mechanism.

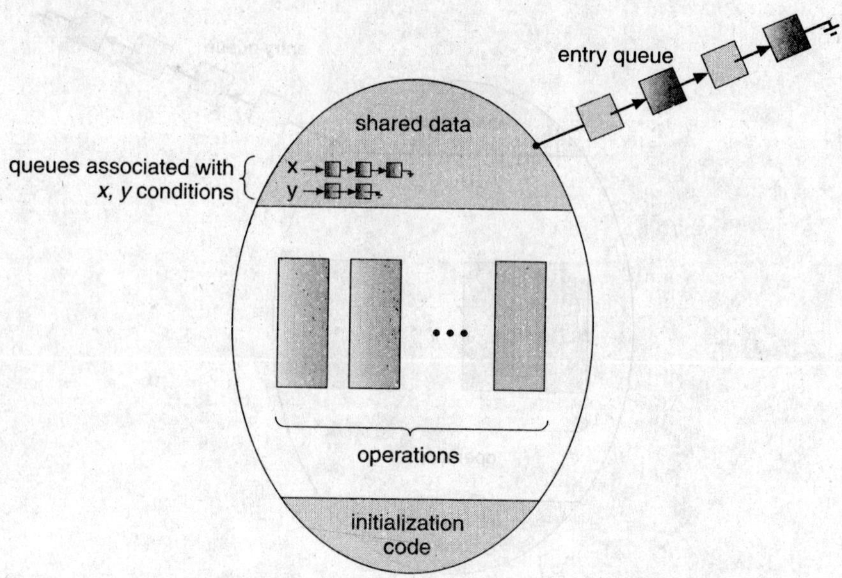

Figure 6.18 Monitor with condition variables.

6.7.2 Dining-Philosophers Solution Using Monitors

Next, we illustrate monitor concepts by presenting a deadlock-free solution to the dining-philosophers problem. This solution imposes the restriction that a philosopher may pick up her chopsticks only if both of them are available. To code this solution, we need to distinguish among three states in which we may find a philosopher. For this purpose, we introduce the following data structure:

```
enum {THINKING, HUNGRY, EATING} state[5];
```

Philosopher *i* can set the variable `state[i] = EATING` only if her two neighbors are not eating: (`state[(i+4) % 5] != EATING`) and (`state[(i+1) % 5] != EATING`).

We also need to declare

```
condition self[5];
```

in which philosopher *i* can delay herself when she is hungry but is unable to obtain the chopsticks she needs.

We are now in a position to describe our solution to the dining-philosophers problem. The distribution of the chopsticks is controlled by the monitor `DiningPhilosophers`, whose definition is shown in Figure 6.19. Each philosopher, before starting to eat, must invoke the operation `pickup()`. This act may result in the suspension of the philosopher process. After the successful completion of the operation, the philosopher may eat. Following this, the philosopher invokes

```
monitor dp
{
  enum {THINKING, HUNGRY, EATING} state[5];
  condition self[5];

  void pickup(int i) {
    state[i] = HUNGRY;
    test(i);
    if (state[i] != EATING)
      self[i].wait();
  }

  void putdown(int i) {
    state[i] = THINKING;
    test((i + 4) % 5);
    test((i + 1) % 5);
  }

  void test(int i) {
    if ((state[(i + 4) % 5] != EATING) &&
     (state[i] == HUNGRY) &&
     (state[(i + 1) % 5] != EATING)) {
       state[i] = EATING;
       self[i].signal();
    }
  }

  initialization_code() {
    for (int i = 0; i < 5; i++)
      state[i] = THINKING;
  }
}
```

Figure 6.19 A monitor solution to the dining-philosopher problem.

the putdown() operation. Thus, philosopher *i* must invoke the operations pickup() and putdown() in the following sequence:

```
DiningPhilosophers.pickup(i);
                ...
               eat
                ...
DiningPhilosophers.putdown(i);
```

It is easy to show that this solution ensures that no two neighbors are eating simultaneously and that no deadlocks will occur. We note, however, that it is possible for a philosopher to starve to death. We do not present a solution to this problem but rather leave it as an exercise for you.

6.7.3 Implementing a Monitor Using Semaphores

We now consider a possible implementation of the monitor mechanism using semaphores. For each monitor, a semaphore `mutex` (initialized to 1) is provided. A process must execute `wait(mutex)` before entering the monitor and must execute `signal(mutex)` after leaving the monitor.

Since a signaling process must wait until the resumed process either leaves or waits, an additional semaphore, `next`, is introduced, initialized to 0. The signaling processes can use `next` to suspend themselves. An integer variable `next_count` is also provided to count the number of processes suspended on `next`. Thus, each external procedure F is replaced by

```
wait(mutex);
   ...
   body of F
   ...
if (next_count > 0)
   signal(next);
else
   signal(mutex);
```

Mutual exclusion within a monitor is ensured.

We can now describe how condition variables are implemented as well. For each condition `x`, we introduce a semaphore `x_sem` and an integer variable `x_count`, both initialized to 0. The operation `x.wait()` can now be implemented as

```
x_count++;
if (next_count > 0)
   signal(next);
else
   signal(mutex);
wait(x_sem);
x_count--;
```

The operation `x.signal()` can be implemented as

```
if (x_count > 0) {
   next_count++;
   signal(x_sem);
   wait(next);
   next_count--;
}
```

This implementation is applicable to the definitions of monitors given by both Hoare and Brinch-Hansen. In some cases, however, the generality of the implementation is unnecessary, and a significant improvement in efficiency is possible. We leave this problem to you in Exercise 6.35.

6.7.4 Resuming Processes within a Monitor

We turn now to the subject of process-resumption order within a monitor. If several processes are suspended on condition `x`, and an `x.signal()` operation

```
monitor ResourceAllocator
{
   boolean busy;
   condition x;

   void acquire(int time) {
      if (busy)
         x.wait(time);
      busy = TRUE;
   }

   void release() {
      busy = FALSE;
      x.signal();
   }

   initialization_code() {
      busy = FALSE;
   }
}
```

Figure 6.20 A monitor to allocate a single resource.

is executed by some process, then how do we determine which of the suspended processes should be resumed next? One simple solution is to use an FCFS ordering, so that the process that has been waiting the longest is resumed first. In many circumstances, however, such a simple scheduling scheme is not adequate. For this purpose, the **conditional-wait** construct can be used; it has the form

```
x.wait(c);
```

where c is an integer expression that is evaluated when the `wait()` operation is executed. The value of c, which is called a **priority number**, is then stored with the name of the process that is suspended. When `x.signal()` is executed, the process with the smallest priority number is resumed next.

To illustrate this new mechanism, consider the `ResourceAllocator` monitor shown in Figure 6.20, which controls the allocation of a single resource among competing processes. Each process, when requesting an allocation of this resource, specifies the maximum time it plans to use the resource. The monitor allocates the resource to the process that has the shortest time-allocation request. A process that needs to access the resource in question must observe the following sequence:

```
R.acquire(t);
   ...
 access the resource;
   ...
R.release();
```

where R is an instance of type `ResourceAllocator`.

Unfortunately, the monitor concept cannot guarantee that the preceding access sequence will be observed. In particular, the following problems can occur:

- A process might access a resource without first gaining access permission to the resource.
- A process might never release a resource once it has been granted access to the resource.
- A process might attempt to release a resource that it never requested.
- A process might request the same resource twice (without first releasing the resource).

The same difficulties are encountered with the use of semaphores, and these difficulties are similar in nature to those that encouraged us to develop the monitor constructs in the first place. Previously, we had to worry about the correct use of semaphores. Now, we have to worry about the correct use of higher-level programmer-defined operations, with which the compiler can no longer assist us.

One possible solution to the current problem is to include the resource-access operations within the `ResourceAllocator` monitor. However, using this solution will mean that scheduling is done according to the built-in monitor-scheduling algorithm rather than the one we have coded.

To ensure that the processes observe the appropriate sequences, we must inspect all the programs that make use of the `ResourceAllocator` monitor and its managed resource. We must check two conditions to establish the correctness of this system. First, user processes must always make their calls on the monitor in a correct sequence. Second, we must be sure that an uncooperative process does not simply ignore the mutual-exclusion gateway provided by the monitor and try to access the shared resource directly, without using the access protocols. Only if these two conditions can be ensured can we guarantee that no time-dependent errors will occur and that the scheduling algorithm will not be defeated.

Although this inspection may be possible for a small, static system, it is not reasonable for a large system or a dynamic system. This access-control problem can be solved only through the use of additional mechanisms that are described in Chapter 14.

Many programming languages have incorporated the idea of the monitor as described in this section, including Concurrent Pascal, Mesa, C# (pronounced *C-sharp*), and Java. Other languages—such as Erlang—provide some type of concurrency support using a similar mechanism.

6.8 Synchronization Examples

We next describe the synchronization mechanisms provided by the Solaris, Windows XP, and Linux operating systems, as well as the Pthreads API. We have chosen these three operating systems because they provide good examples of different approaches for synchronizing the kernel, and we have included the

JAVA MONITORS

Java provides a monitor-like concurrency mechanism for thread synchronization. Every object in Java has associated with it a single lock. When a method is declared to be synchronized, calling the method requires owning the lock for the object. We declare a synchronized method by placing the synchronized keyword in the method definition. The following defines the safeMethod() as synchronized, for example:

```
public class SimpleClass {
    . . .
    public synchronized void safeMethod() {
      /* Implementation of safeMethod() */
      . . .
    }
}
```

Next, assume we create an object instance of SimpleClass, such as:

```
SimpleClass sc = new SimpleClass();
```

Invoking the sc.safeMethod() method requires owning the lock on the object instance sc. If the lock is already owned by another thread, the thread calling the synchronized method blocks and is placed in the **entry set** for the object's lock. The entry set represents the set of threads waiting for the lock to become available. If the lock is available when a synchronized method is called, the calling thread becomes the owner of the object's lock and can enter the method. The lock is released when the thread exits the method; a thread from the entry set is then selected as the new owner of the lock.

Java also provides wait() and notify() methods, which are similar in function to the wait() and signal() statements for a monitor. Release 1.5 of the Java language provides API support for semaphores, condition variables, and mutex locks (among other concurrency mechanisms) in the java.util.concurrent package.

Pthreads API because it is widely used for thread creation and synchronization by developers on UNIX and Linux systems. As you will see in this section, the synchronization methods available in these differing systems vary in subtle and significant ways.

6.8.1 Synchronization in Solaris

To control access to critical sections, Solaris provides adaptive mutexes, condition variables, semaphores, reader–writer locks, and turnstiles. Solaris implements semaphores and condition variables essentially as they are presented in Sections 6.5 and 6.7. In this section, we describe adaptive mutexes, reader–writer locks, and turnstiles.

An **adaptive mutex** protects access to every critical data item. On a multiprocessor system, an adaptive mutex starts as a standard semaphore implemented as a spinlock. If the data are locked and therefore already in use, the adaptive mutex does one of two things. If the lock is held by a thread that is currently running on another CPU, the thread spins while waiting for the lock to become available, because the thread holding the lock is likely to finish soon. If the thread holding the lock is not currently in run state, the thread blocks, going to sleep until it is awakened by the release of the lock. It is put to sleep so that it will not spin while waiting, since the lock will not be freed very soon. A lock held by a sleeping thread is likely to be in this category. On a single-processor system, the thread holding the lock is never running if the lock is being tested by another thread, because only one thread can run at a time. Therefore, on this type of system, threads always sleep rather than spin if they encounter a lock.

Solaris uses the adaptive-mutex method to protect only data that are accessed by short code segments. That is, a mutex is used if a lock will be held for less than a few hundred instructions. If the code segment is longer than that, the spin-waiting method is exceedingly inefficient. For these longer code segments, condition variables and semaphores are used. If the desired lock is already held, the thread issues a wait and sleeps. When a thread frees the lock, it issues a signal to the next sleeping thread in the queue. The extra cost of putting a thread to sleep and waking it, and of the associated context switches, is less than the cost of wasting several hundred instructions waiting in a spinlock.

Reader–writer locks are used to protect data that are accessed frequently but are usually accessed in a read-only manner. In these circumstances, reader–writer locks are more efficient than semaphores, because multiple threads can read data concurrently, whereas semaphores always serialize access to the data. Reader–writer locks are relatively expensive to implement, so again they are used only on long sections of code.

Solaris uses turnstiles to order the list of threads waiting to acquire either an adaptive mutex or a reader–writer lock. A **turnstile** is a queue structure containing threads blocked on a lock. For example, if one thread currently owns the lock for a synchronized object, all other threads trying to acquire the lock will block and enter the turnstile for that lock. When the lock is released, the kernel selects a thread from the turnstile as the next owner of the lock. Each synchronized object with at least one thread blocked on the object's lock requires a separate turnstile. However, rather than associating a turnstile with each synchronized object, Solaris gives each kernel thread its own turnstile. Because a thread can be blocked only on one object at a time, this is more efficient than having a turnstile for each object.

The turnstile for the first thread to block on a synchronized object becomes the turnstile for the object itself. Threads subsequently blocking on the lock will be added to this turnstile. When the initial thread ultimately releases the lock, it gains a new turnstile from a list of free turnstiles maintained by the kernel. To prevent a priority inversion, turnstiles are organized according to a **priority-inheritance protocol**. This means that if a lower-priority thread currently holds a lock on which a higher-priority thread is blocked, the thread with the lower priority will temporarily inherit the priority of the higher-priority thread. Upon releasing the lock, the thread will revert to its original priority.

Note that the locking mechanisms used by the kernel are implemented for user-level threads as well, so the same types of locks are available inside and outside the kernel. A crucial implementation difference is the priority-inheritance protocol. Kernel-locking routines adhere to the kernel priority-inheritance methods used by the scheduler, as described in Section 19.4; user-level thread-locking mechanisms do not provide this functionality.

To optimize Solaris performance, developers have refined and fine-tuned the locking methods. Because locks are used frequently and typically are used for crucial kernel functions, tuning their implementation and use can produce great performance gains.

6.8.2 Synchronization in Windows XP

The Windows XP operating system is a multithreaded kernel that provides support for real-time applications and multiple processors. When the Windows XP kernel accesses a global resource on a uniprocessor system, it temporarily masks interrupts for all interrupt handlers that may also access the global resource. On a multiprocessor system, Windows XP protects access to global resources using spinlocks. Just as in Solaris, the kernel uses spinlocks only to protect short code segments. Furthermore, for reasons of efficiency, the kernel ensures that a thread will never be preempted while holding a spinlock.

For thread synchronization outside the kernel, Windows XP provides **dispatcher objects**. Using a dispatcher object, threads synchronize according to several different mechanisms, including mutexes, semaphores, events, and timers. The system protects shared data by requiring a thread to gain ownership of a mutex to access the data and to release ownership when it is finished. Semaphores behave as described in Section 6.5. **Events** are similar to condition variables; that is, they may notify a waiting thread when a desired condition occurs. Finally, timers are used to notify one (or more than one) thread that a specified amount of time has expired.

Dispatcher objects may be in either a signaled state or a nonsignaled state. A **signaled state** indicates that an object is available and a thread will not block when acquiring the object. A **nonsignaled state** indicates that an object is not available and a thread will block when attempting to acquire the object. We illustrate the state transitions of a mutex lock dispatcher object in Figure 6.21.

A relationship exists between the state of a dispatcher object and the state of a thread. When a thread blocks on a nonsignaled dispatcher object, its state changes from ready to waiting, and the thread is placed in a waiting queue for that object. When the state for the dispatcher object moves to signaled, he kernel checks whether any threads are waiting on the object. If so, the

Figure 6.21 Mutex dispatcher object.

kernel moves one thread—or possibly more threads—from the waiting state to the ready state, where they can resume executing. The number of threads the kernel selects from the waiting queue depends on the type of dispatcher object for which it is waiting. The kernel will select only one thread from the waiting queue for a mutex, since a mutex object may be "owned" by only a single thread. For an event object, the kernel will select all threads that are waiting for the event.

We can use a mutex lock as an illustration of dispatcher objects and thread states. If a thread tries to acquire a mutex dispatcher object that is in a nonsignaled state, that thread will be suspended and placed in a waiting queue for the mutex object. When the mutex moves to the signaled state (because another thread has released the lock on the mutex), the thread waiting at the front of the queue will be moved from the waiting state to the ready state and will acquire the mutex lock.

We provide a programming project at the end of this chapter that uses mutex locks and semaphores in the Win32 API.

6.8.3 Synchronization in Linux

Prior to Version 2.6, Linux was a nonpreemptive kernel, meaning that a process running in kernel mode could not be preempted—even if a higher-priority process became available to run. Now, however, the Linux kernel is fully preemptive, so a task can be preempted when it is running in the kernel.

The Linux kernel provides spinlocks and semaphores (as well as reader–writer versions of these two locks) for locking in the kernel. On SMP machines, the fundamental locking mechanism is a spinlock, and the kernel is designed so that the spinlock is held only for short durations. On single-processor machines, spinlocks are inappropriate for use and are replaced by enabling and disabling kernel preemption. That is, on single-processor machines, rather than holding a spinlock, the kernel disables kernel preemption; and rather than releasing the spinlock, it enables kernel preemption. This is summarized below:

single processor	multiple processors
Disable kernel preemption.	Acquire spin lock.
Enable kernel preemption.	Release spin lock.

Linux uses an interesting approach to disable and enable kernel preemption. It provides two simple system calls—`preempt_disable()` and `preempt_enable()`—for disabling and enabling kernel preemption. In addition, however, the kernel is not preemptible if a kernel-mode task is holding a lock. To enforce this rule, each task in the system has a `thread-info` structure containing a counter, `preempt_count`, to indicate the number of locks being held by the task. When a lock is acquired, `preempt_count` is incremented. It is decremented when a lock is released. If the value of `preempt_count` for the task currently running is greater than zero, it is not safe to preempt the kernel, as this task currently holds a lock. If the count is zero, the kernel can safely be interrupted (assuming there are no outstanding calls to `preempt_disable()`).

Spinlocks—along with enabling and disabling kernel preemption—are used in the kernel only when a lock (or disabling kernel preemption) is held for a short duration. When a lock must be held for a longer period, semaphores are appropriate for use.

6.8.4 Synchronization in Pthreads

The Pthreads API provides mutex locks, condition variables, and read–write locks for thread synchronization. This API is available for programmers and is not part of any particular kernel. Mutex locks represent the fundamental synchronization technique used with Pthreads. A mutex lock is used to protect critical sections of code—that is, a thread acquires the lock before entering a critical section and releases it upon exiting the critical section. Condition variables in Pthreads behave much as described in Section 6.7. Read–write locks behave similarly to the locking mechanism described in Section 6.6.2. Many systems that implement Pthreads also provide semaphores, although they are not part of the Pthreads standard and instead belong to the POSIX SEM extension. Other extensions to the Pthreads API include spinlocks, but not all extensions are considered portable from one implementation to another. We provide a programming project at the end of this chapter that uses Pthreads mutex locks and semaphores.

6.9 Atomic Transactions

The mutual exclusion of critical sections ensures that the critical sections are executed atomically—that is, as one uninterruptible unit. If two critical sections are instead executed concurrently, the result is equivalent to their sequential execution in some unknown order. Although this property is useful in many application domains, in many cases we would like to make sure that a critical section forms a single logical unit of work that either is performed in its entirety or is not performed at all. An example is funds transfer, in which one account is debited and another is credited. Clearly, it is essential for data consistency either that both the credit and debit occur or that neither occurs.

Consistency of data, along with storage and retrieval of data, is a concern often associated with **database systems**. Recently, there has been an upsurge of interest in using database-systems techniques in operating systems. Operating systems can be viewed as manipulators of data; as such, they can benefit from the advanced techniques and models available from database research. For instance, many of the ad hoc techniques used in operating systems to manage files could be more flexible and powerful if more formal database methods were used in their place. In Sections 6.9.2 to 6.9.4, we describe some of these database techniques and explain how they can be used by operating systems. First, however, we deal with the general issue of transaction atomicity. It is this property that the database techniques are meant to address.

6.9.1 System Model

A collection of instructions (or operations) that performs a single logical function is called a **transaction**. A major issue in processing transactions is the preservation of atomicity despite the possibility of failures within the computer system.

We can think of a transaction as a program unit that accesses and perhaps updates various data items that reside on a disk within some files. From our point of view, such a transaction is simply a sequence of `read` and `write` operations terminated by either a `commit` operation or an `abort` operation. A `commit` operation signifies that the transaction has terminated its execution successfully, whereas an `abort` operation signifies that the transaction has

TRANSACTIONAL MEMORY

With the emergence of multicore systems has come increased pressure to develop multithreaded applications that take advantage of multiple processing cores. However, multithreaded applications present an increased risk of race conditions and deadlocks. Traditionally, techniques such as locks, semaphores, and monitors have been used to address these issues. However, **transactional memory** provides an alternative strategy for developing thread-safe concurrent applications.

A **memory transaction** is a sequence of memory read–write operations that are atomic. If all operations in a transaction are completed, the memory transaction is committed; otherwise, the operations must be aborted and rolled back. The benefits of transactional memory can be obtained through features added to a programming language.

Consider an example. Suppose we have a function `update()` that modifies shared data. Traditionally, this function would be written using locks such as the following:

```
update () {
   acquire();
   /* modify shared data */
   release();
}
```

However, using synchronization mechanisms such as locks and semaphores involves many potential problems, including deadlocks. Additionally, as the number of threads increases, traditional locking does not scale well.

As an alternative to traditional methods, new features that take advantage of transactional memory can be added to a programming language. In our example, suppose we add the construct `atomic{S}`, which ensures that the operations in `S` execute as a transaction. This allows us to rewrite the `update()` method as follows:

```
update () {
   atomic {
      /* modify shared data */
   }
}
```

Continued on following page.

TRANSACTIONAL MEMORY (Continued)

The advantage of using such a mechanism rather than locks is that the transactional memory system—not the developer—is responsible for guaranteeing atomicity. Additionally, the system can identify which statements in atomic blocks can be executed concurrently, such as concurrent read access to a shared variable. It is, of course, possible for a programmer to identify these situations and use reader–writer locks, but the task becomes increasingly difficult as the number of threads within an application grows.

Transactional memory can be implemented in either software or hardware. Software transactional memory (STM), as the name suggests, implements transactional memory exclusively in software—no special hardware is needed. STM works by inserting instrumentation code inside transaction blocks. The code is inserted by a compiler and manages each transaction by examining where statements may run concurrently and where specific low-level locking is required. Hardware transactional memory (small HTM) uses hardware cache hierarchies and cache coherency protocols to manage and resolve conflicts involving shared data residing in separate processors caches. HTM requires no special code instrumentation and thus has less overhead than STM. However, HTM does require that existing cache hierarchies and cache coherency protocols be modified to support transactional memory.

Transactional memory has existed for several years without widespread implementation. However, the growth of multicore systems and the associated emphasis on concurrent programming have prompted a significant amount of research in this area on the part of both academics and hardware vendors, including Intel and Sun Microsystems.

ended its normal execution due to some logical error or a system failure. If a terminated transaction has completed its execution successfully, it is **committed**; otherwise, it is **aborted**.

Since an aborted transaction may already have modified the data that it has accessed, the state of these data may not be the same as it would have been if the transaction had executed atomically. So that atomicity is ensured, an aborted transaction must have no effect on the state of the data that it has already modified. Thus, the state of the data accessed by an aborted transaction must be restored to what it was just before the transaction started executing. We say that such a transaction has been **rolled back**. It is part of the responsibility of the system to ensure this property.

To determine how the system should ensure atomicity, we need first to identify the properties of devices used for storing the various data accessed by the transactions. Various types of storage media are distinguished by their relative speed, capacity, and resilience to failure.

- **Volatile storage**. Information residing in volatile storage does not usually survive system crashes. Examples of such storage are main and cache memory. Access to volatile storage is extremely fast, both because of the speed of the memory access itself and because it is possible to access directly any data item in volatile storage.

- **Nonvolatile storage**. Information residing in nonvolatile storage usually survives system crashes. Examples of media for such storage are disks and magnetic tapes. Disks are more reliable than main memory but less reliable than magnetic tapes. Both disks and tapes, however, are subject to failure, which may result in loss of information. Currently, nonvolatile storage is slower than volatile storage by several orders of magnitude, because disk and tape devices are electromechanical and require physical motion to access data.

- **Stable storage**. Information residing in stable storage is *never* lost (*never* should be taken with a grain of salt, since theoretically such absolutes cannot be guaranteed). To implement an approximation of such storage, we need to replicate information in several nonvolatile storage caches (usually disk) with independent failure modes and to update the information in a controlled manner (Section 12.8).

Here, we are concerned only with ensuring transaction atomicity in an environment where failures result in the loss of information on volatile storage.

6.9.2 Log-Based Recovery

One way to ensure atomicity is to record, on stable storage, information describing all the modifications made by the transaction to the various data it accesses. The most widely used method for achieving this form of recording is write-ahead logging. Here, the system maintains, on stable storage, a data structure called the log. Each log record describes a single operation of a transaction write and has the following fields:

- **Transaction name**. The unique name of the transaction that performed the `write` operation
- **Data item name**. The unique name of the data item written
- **Old value**. The value of the data item prior to the `write` operation
- **New value**. The value that the data item will have after the write

Other special log records exist to record significant events during transaction processing, such as the start of a transaction and the commit or abort of a transaction.

Before a transaction T_i starts its execution, the record $< T_i$ `starts`$>$ is written to the log. During its execution, any `write` operation by T_i is *preceded* by the writing of the appropriate new record to the log. When T_i commits, the record $< T_i$ `commits`$>$ is written to the log.

Because the information in the log is used in reconstructing the state of the data items accessed by the various transactions, we cannot allow the actual update to a data item to take place before the corresponding log record is written out to stable storage. We therefore require that, prior to execution of a `write`(X) operation, the log records corresponding to X be written onto stable storage.

Note the performance penalty inherent in this system. Two physical writes are required for every logical write requested. Also, more storage is needed, both for the data themselves and for the log recording the changes. In cases where the data are extremely important and fast failure recovery is necessary, however, the functionality is worth the price.

Using the log, the system can handle any failure that does not result in the loss of information on nonvolatile storage. The recovery algorithm uses two procedures:

- undo(T_i), which restores the value of all data updated by transaction T_i to the old values
- redo(T_i), which sets the value of all data updated by transaction T_i to the new values

The set of data updated by T_i and the appropriate old and new values can be found in the log. Note that the undo and redo operations must be idempotent (that is, multiple executions must have the same result as does one execution) to guarantee correct behavior even if a failure occurs during the recovery process.

If a transaction T_i aborts, then we can restore the state of the data that it has updated by simply executing undo(T_i). If a system failure occurs, we restore the state of all updated data by consulting the log to determine which transactions need to be redone and which need to be undone. This classification of transactions is accomplished as follows:

- Transaction T_i needs to be undone if the log contains the < T_i starts> record but does not contain the < T_i commits> record.
- Transaction T_i needs to be redone if the log contains both the < T_i starts> and the < T_i commits> records.

6.9.3 Checkpoints

When a system failure occurs, we must consult the log to determine which transactions need to be redone and which need to be undone. In principle, we need to search the entire log to make these determinations. There are two major drawbacks to this approach:

1. The searching process is time consuming.
2. Most of the transactions that, according to our algorithm, need to be redone have already actually updated the data that the log says they need to modify. Although redoing the data modifications will cause no harm (due to idempotency), it will nevertheless cause recovery to take longer.

To reduce these types of overhead, we introduce the concept of **checkpoints**. During execution, the system maintains the write-ahead log. In addition, the system periodically performs checkpoints that require the following sequence of actions to take place:

1. Output all log records currently residing in volatile storage (usually main memory) onto stable storage.
2. Output all modified data residing in volatile storage to the stable storage.
3. Output a log record <checkpoint> onto stable storage.

The presence of a `<checkpoint>` record in the log allows the system to streamline its recovery procedure. Consider a transaction T_i that committed prior to the checkpoint. The $< T_i$ `commits`$>$ record appears in the log before the `<checkpoint>` record. Any modifications made by T_i must have been written to stable storage either prior to the checkpoint or as part of the checkpoint itself. Thus, at recovery time, there is no need to perform a `redo` operation on T_i.

This observation allows us to refine our previous recovery algorithm. After a failure has occurred, the recovery routine examines the log to determine the most recent transaction T_i that started executing before the most recent checkpoint took place. It finds such a transaction by searching the log backward to find the first `<checkpoint>` record and then finding the subsequent $< T_i$ `start`$>$ record.

Once transaction T_i has been identified, the `redo` and `undo` operations need be applied only to transaction T_i and all transactions T_j that started executing after transaction T_i. We'll call these transactions set T. The remainder of the log can be ignored. The recovery operations that are required are as follows:

- For all transactions T_k in T for which the record $< T_k$ `commits`$>$ appears in the log, execute `redo`(T_k).
- For all transactions T_k in T that have no $< T_k$ `commits`$>$ record in the log, execute undo(T_k).

6.9.4 Concurrent Atomic Transactions

We have been considering an environment in which only one transaction can be executing at a time. We now turn to the case where multiple transactions are active simultaneously. Because each transaction is atomic, the concurrent execution of transactions must be equivalent to the case where these transactions are executed serially in some arbitrary order. This property, called **serializability**, can be maintained by simply executing each transaction within a critical section. That is, all transactions share a common semaphore *mutex*, which is initialized to 1. When a transaction starts executing, its first action is to execute `wait`(*mutex*). After the transaction either commits or aborts, it executes `signal`(*mutex*).

Although this scheme ensures the atomicity of all concurrently executing transactions, it is nevertheless too restrictive. As we shall see, in many cases we can allow transactions to overlap their execution while maintaining serializability. A number of different **concurrency-control algorithms** ensure serializability, and we describe these algorithms next.

6.9.4.1 Serializability

Consider a system with two data items, A and B, that are both read and written by two transactions, T_0 and T_1. Suppose that these transactions are executed atomically in the order T_0 followed by T_1. This execution sequence, which is called a **schedule**, is represented in Figure 6.22. In schedule 1 of Figure 6.22, the sequence of instruction steps is in chronological order from top to bottom, with instructions of T_0 appearing in the left column and instructions of T_1 appearing in the right column.

T_0	T_1
read(A)	
write(A)	
read(B)	
write(B)	
	read(A)
	write(A)
	read(B)
	write(B)

Figure 6.22 Schedule 1: A serial schedule in which T_0 is followed by T_1.

A schedule in which each transaction is executed atomically is called a **serial schedule**. A serial schedule consists of a sequence of instructions from various transactions wherein the instructions belonging to a particular transaction appear together. Thus, for a set of n transactions, there exist $n!$ different valid serial schedules. Each serial schedule is correct, because it is equivalent to the atomic execution of the various participating transactions in some arbitrary order.

If we allow the two transactions to overlap their execution, then the resulting schedule is no longer serial. A **nonserial schedule** does not necessarily imply an incorrect execution (that is, an execution that is not equivalent to one represented by a serial schedule). To see that this is the case, we need to define the notion of **conflicting operations**.

Consider a schedule S in which there are two consecutive operations O_i and O_j of transactions T_i and T_j, respectively. We say that O_i and O_j *conflict* if they access the same data item and at least one of them is a `write` operation. To illustrate the concept of conflicting operations, we consider the nonserial schedule 2 of Figure 6.23. The `write`(A) operation of T_0 conflicts with the `read`(A) operation of T_1. However, the `write`(A) operation of T_1 does not conflict with the `read`(B) operation of T_0, because the two operations access different data items.

T_0	T_1
read(A)	
write(A)	
	read(A)
	write(A)
read(B)	
write(B)	
	read(B)
	write(B)

Figure 6.23 Schedule 2: A concurrent serializable schedule.

Let O_i and O_j be consecutive operations of a schedule S. If O_i and O_j are operations of different transactions and O_i and O_j do not conflict, then we can swap the order of O_i and O_j to produce a new schedule S'. We expect S to be equivalent to S', as all operations appear in the same order in both schedules, except for O_i and O_j, whose order does not matter.

We can illustrate the swapping idea by considering again schedule 2 of Figure 6.23. As the `write`(A) operation of T_1 does not conflict with the `read`(B) operation of T_0, we can swap these operations to generate an equivalent schedule. Regardless of the initial system state, both schedules produce the same final system state. Continuing with this procedure of swapping nonconflicting operations, we get:

- Swap the `read`(B) operation of T_0 with the `read`(A) operation of T_1.
- Swap the `write`(B) operation of T_0 with the `write`(A) operation of T_1.
- Swap the `write`(B) operation of T_0 with the `read`(A) operation of T_1.

The final result of these swaps is schedule 1 in Figure 6.22, which is a serial schedule. Thus, we have shown that schedule 2 is equivalent to a serial schedule. This result implies that, regardless of the initial system state, schedule 2 will produce the same final state as will some serial schedule.

If a schedule S can be transformed into a serial schedule S' by a series of swaps of nonconflicting operations, we say that a schedule S is **conflict serializable**. Thus, schedule 2 is conflict serializable, because it can be transformed into the serial schedule 1.

6.9.4.2 Locking Protocol

One way to ensure serializability is to associate a lock with each data item and to require that each transaction follow a **locking protocol** that governs how locks are acquired and released. There are various modes in which a data item can be locked. In this section, we restrict our attention to two modes:

- **Shared**. If a transaction T_i has obtained a shared-mode lock (denoted by S) on data item Q, then T_i can read this item but cannot write Q.
- **Exclusive**. If a transaction T_i has obtained an exclusive-mode lock (denoted by X) on data item Q, then T_i can both read and write Q.

We require that every transaction request a lock in an appropriate mode on data item Q, depending on the type of operations it will perform on Q.

To access data item Q, transaction T_i must first lock Q in the appropriate mode. If Q is not currently locked, then the lock is granted, and T_i can now access it. However, if the data item Q is currently locked by some other transaction, then T_i may have to wait. More specifically, suppose that T_i requests an exclusive lock on Q. In this case, T_i must wait until the lock on Q is released. If T_i requests a shared lock on Q, then T_i must wait if Q is locked in exclusive mode. Otherwise, it can obtain the lock and access Q. Notice that this scheme is quite similar to the readers–writers algorithm discussed in Section 6.6.2.

A transaction may unlock a data item that it locked at an earlier point. It must, however, hold a lock on a data item as long as it accesses that item.

Moreover, it is not always desirable for a transaction to unlock a data item immediately after its last access of that data item, because serializability may not be ensured.

One protocol that ensures serializability is the **two-phase locking protocol**. This protocol requires that each transaction issue lock and unlock requests in two phases:

- **Growing phase**. A transaction may obtain locks but may not release any locks.
- **Shrinking phase**. A transaction may release locks but may not obtain any new locks.

Initially, a transaction is in the growing phase. The transaction acquires locks as needed. Once the transaction releases a lock, it enters the shrinking phase, and no more lock requests can be issued.

The two-phase locking protocol ensures conflict serializability (Exercise 6.14). It does not, however, ensure freedom from deadlock. In addition, it is possible that, for a given set of transactions, there are conflict-serializable schedules that cannot be obtained by use of the two-phase locking protocol. To improve performance over two-phase locking, we need either to have additional information about the transactions or to impose some structure or ordering on the set of data.

6.9.4.3 Timestamp-Based Protocols

In the locking protocols described above, the order followed by pairs of conflicting transactions is determined at execution time. Another method for determining the serializability order is to select an order in advance. The most common method for doing so is to use a **timestamp** ordering scheme.

With each transaction T_i in the system, we associate a unique fixed timestamp, denoted by TS(T_i). This timestamp is assigned by the system before the transaction T_i starts execution. If a transaction T_i has been assigned timestamp TS(T_i), and later a new transaction T_j enters the system, then TS(T_i) $<$ TS(T_j). There are two simple methods for implementing this scheme:

- Use the value of the system clock as the timestamp; that is, a transaction's timestamp is equal to the value of the clock when the transaction enters the system. This method will not work for transactions that occur on separate systems or for processors that do not share a clock.
- Use a logical counter as the timestamp; that is, a transaction's timestamp is equal to the value of the counter when the transaction enters the system. The counter is incremented after a new timestamp is assigned.

The timestamps of the transactions determine the serializability order. Thus, if TS(T_i) $<$ TS(T_j), then the system must ensure that the schedule produced is equivalent to a serial schedule in which transaction T_i appears before transaction T_j.

To implement this scheme, we associate with each data item Q two timestamp values:

- **W-timestamp**(Q) denotes the largest timestamp of any transaction that successfully executed `write`(Q).
- **R-timestamp**(Q) denotes the largest timestamp of any transaction that successfully executed `read`(Q).

These timestamps are updated whenever a new `read`(Q) or `write`(Q) instruction is executed.

The timestamp ordering protocol ensures that any conflicting `read` and `write` operations are executed in timestamp order. This protocol operates as follows:

- Suppose that transaction T_i issues `read`(Q):
  - If TS(T_i) < W-timestamp(), then T_i needs to read a value of Q that was already overwritten. Hence, the `read` operation is rejected, and T_i is rolled back.
  - If TS(T_i) ≥ W-timestamp(Q), then the `read` operation is executed, and R-timestamp(Q) is set to the maximum of R-timestamp(Q) and TS(T_i).
- Suppose that transaction T_i issues `write`(Q):
  - If TS(T_i) < R-timestamp(Q), then the value of Q that T_i is producing was needed previously and T_i assumed that this value would never be produced. Hence, the `write` operation is rejected, and T_i is rolled back.
  - If TS(T_i) < W-timestamp(Q), then T_i is attempting to write an obsolete value of Q. Hence, this `write` operation is rejected, and T_i is rolled back.
  - Otherwise, the `write` operation is executed.

A transaction T_i that is rolled back as a result of either a `read` or `write` operation is assigned a new timestamp and is restarted.

To illustrate this protocol, consider schedule 3 in Figure 6.24, which includes transactions T_2 and T_3. We assume that a transaction is assigned a timestamp immediately before its first instruction. Thus, in schedule 3, TS(T_2) < TS(T_3), and the schedule is possible under the timestamp protocol.

This execution can also be produced by the two-phase locking protocol. However, some schedules are possible under the two-phase locking protocol but not under the timestamp protocol, and vice versa.

T_2	T_3
read(B)	
	read(B)
	write(B)
read(A)	
	read(A)
	write(A)

Figure 6.24 Schedule 3: A schedule possible under the timestamp protocol.

The timestamp protocol ensures conflict serializability. This capability follows from the fact that conflicting operations are processed in timestamp order. The protocol also ensures freedom from deadlock, because no transaction ever waits.

6.10 Summary

Given a collection of cooperating sequential processes that share data, mutual exclusion must be provided to ensure that a critical section of code is used by only one process or thread at a time. Typically, computer hardware provides several operations that ensure mutual exclusion. However, such hardware-based solutions are too complicated for most developers to use. Semaphores overcome this obstacle. Semaphores can be used to solve various synchronization problems and can be implemented efficiently, especially if hardware support for atomic operations is available.

Various synchronization problems (such as the bounded-buffer problem, the readers–writers problem, and the dining-philosophers problem) are important mainly because they are examples of a large class of concurrency-control problems. These problems are used to test nearly every newly proposed synchronization scheme.

The operating system must provide the means to guard against timing errors. Several language constructs have been proposed to deal with these problems. Monitors provide the synchronization mechanism for sharing abstract data types. A condition variable provides a method by which a monitor procedure can block its execution until it is signaled to continue.

Operating systems also provide support for synchronization. For example, Solaris, Windows XP, and Linux provide mechanisms such as semaphores, mutexes, spinlocks, and condition variables to control access to shared data. The Pthreads API provides support for mutexes and condition variables.

A transaction is a program unit that must be executed atomically; that is, either all the operations associated with it are executed to completion, or none are performed. To ensure atomicity despite system failure, we can use a write-ahead log. All updates are recorded on the log, which is kept in stable storage. If a system crash occurs, the information in the log is used in restoring the state of the updated data items, which is accomplished by use of the undo and `redo` operations. To reduce the overhead in searching the log after a system failure has occurred, we can use a checkpoint scheme.

To ensure serializability when the execution of several transactions overlaps, we must use a concurrency-control scheme. Various concurrency-control schemes ensure serializability by delaying an operation or aborting the transaction that issued the operation. The most common ones are locking protocols and timestamp ordering schemes.

Exercises

6.1 The first known correct software solution to the critical-section problem for two processes was developed by Dekker. The two processes, P_0 and P_1, share the following variables:

```
boolean flag[2]; /* initially false */
int turn;
```

```
do {
    flag[i] = TRUE;

    while (flag[j]) {
        if (turn == j) {
            flag[i] = false;
            while (turn == j)
                ; // do nothing
            flag[i] = TRUE;
        }
    }

        // critical section

    turn = j;
    flag[i] = FALSE;

        // remainder section
} while (TRUE);
```

Figure 6.25 The structure of process P_i in Dekker's algorithm.

The structure of process P_i (i == 0 or 1) is shown in Figure 6.25; the other process is P_j (j == 1 or 0). Prove that the algorithm satisfies all three requirements for the critical-section problem.

6.2 Explain why interrupts are not appropriate for implementing synchronization primitives in multiprocessor systems.

6.3 The first known correct software solution to the critical-section problem for n processes with a lower bound on waiting of $n - 1$ turns was presented by Eisenberg and McGuire. The processes share the following variables:

```
enum pstate {idle, want_in, in_cs};
pstate flag[n];
int turn;
```

All the elements of `flag` are initially `idle`; the initial value of `turn` is immaterial (between 0 and `n-1`). The structure of process P_i is shown in Figure 6.26. Prove that the algorithm satisfies all three requirements for the critical-section problem.

6.4 Write a monitor that implements an *alarm clock* that enables a calling program to delay itself for a specified number of time units (*ticks*). You may assume the existence of a real hardware clock that invokes a procedure *tick* in your monitor at regular intervals.

6.5 A file is to be shared among different processes, each of which has a unique number. The file can be accessed simultaneously by several processes, subject to the following constraint: The sum of all unique

```
do {
   while (TRUE) {
      flag[i] = want_in;
      j = turn;

      while (j != i) {
         if (flag[j] != idle) {
            j = turn;
         else
            j = (j + 1) % n;
      }

      flag[i] = in_cs;
      j = 0;

      while ( (j < n) && (j == i || flag[j] != in_cs))
         j++;

      if ( (j >= n) && (turn == i || flag[turn] == idle))
         break;
   }

      // critical section

   j = (turn + 1) % n;

   while (flag[j] == idle)
      j = (j + 1) % n;

   turn = j;
   flag[i] = idle;

      // remainder section
} while (TRUE);
```

Figure 6.26 The structure of process P_i in Eisenberg and McGuire's algorithm.

numbers associated with all the processes currently accessing the file must be less than *n*. Write a monitor to coordinate access to the file.

6.6 The decrease_count() function in the previous exercise currently returns 0 if sufficient resources are available and −1 otherwise. This leads to awkward programming for a process that wishes to obtain a number of resources:

```
while (decrease_count(count) == 1)
   ;
```

Rewrite the resource-manager code segment using a monitor and condition variables so that the decrease_count() function suspends the process until sufficient resources are available. This will allow a process to invoke `decrease_count()` by simply calling

```
decrease_count(count);
```

The process will return from this function call only when sufficient resources are available.

6.7 Exercise 4.12 requires the parent thread to wait for the child thread to finish its execution before printing out the computed values. If we let the parent thread access the Fibonacci numbers as soon as they have been computed by the child thread — rather than waiting for the child thread to terminate — Explain what changes would be necessary to the solution for this exercise? Implement your modified solution.

6.8 In Section 6.4, we mentioned that disabling interrupts frequently can affect the system's clock. Explain why this can occur and how such effects can be minimized.

6.9 Servers can be designed to limit the number of open connections. For example, a server may wish to have only *N* socket connections at any point in time. As soon as *N* connections are made, the server will not accept another incoming connection until an existing connection is released. Explain how semaphores can be used by a server to limit the number of concurrent connections.

6.10 Why do Solaris, Linux, and Windows XP use spinlocks as a synchronization mechanism only on multiprocessor systems and not on single-processor systems?

6.11 Show that, if the `wait()` and `signal()` semaphore operations are not executed atomically, then mutual exclusion may be violated.

6.12 Show how to implement the `wait()` and `signal()` semaphore operations in multiprocessor environments using the `TestAndSet()` instruction. The solution should exhibit minimal busy waiting.

6.13 Suppose we replace the `wait()` and `signal()` operations of monitors with a single construct `await(B)`, where `B` is a general Boolean expression that causes the process executing it to wait until `B` becomes `true`.

a. Write a monitor using this scheme to implement the readers–writers problem.

b. Explain why, in general, this construct cannot be implemented efficiently.

c. What restrictions need to be put on the `await` statement so that it can be implemented efficiently? (Hint: Restrict the generality of `B`; see Kessels [1977].)

6.14 Show that the two-phase locking protocol ensures conflict serializability.

6.15 How does the `signal()` operation associated with monitors differ from the corresponding operation defined for semaphores?

6.16 Describe how volatile, nonvolatile, and stable storage differ in cost.

6.17 Explain why implementing synchronization primitives by disabling interrupts is not appropriate in a single-processor system if the synchronization primitives are to be used in user-level programs.

6.18 Consider a system consisting of processes $P_1, P_2, \ldots, P_n$, each of which has a unique priority number. Write a monitor that allocates three identical line printers to these processes, using the priority numbers for deciding the order of allocation.

6.19 Describe two kernel data structures in which race conditions are possible. Be sure to include a description of how a race condition can occur.

6.20 Assume that a finite number of resources of a single resource type must be managed. Processes may ask for a number of these resources and —once finished—will return them. As an example, many commercial software packages provide a given number of **licenses**, indicating the number of applications that may run concurrently. When the application is started, the license count is decremented. When the application is terminated, the license count is incremented. If all licenses are in use, requests to start the application are denied. Such requests will only be granted when an existing license holder terminates the application and a license is returned.

The following program segment is used to manage a finite number of instances of an available resource. The maximum number of resources and the number of available resources are declared as follows:

```
#define MAX_RESOURCES 5
int available_resources = MAX_RESOURCES;
```

When a process wishes to obtain a number of resources, it invokes the `decrease_count()` function:

```
/* decrease available_resources by count resources */
/* return 0 if sufficient resources available, */
/* otherwise return -1 */
int decrease_count(int count) {
  if (available_resources < count)
    return -1;
  else {
    available_resources -= count;

    return 0;
  }
}
```

When a process wants to return a number of resources, it calls the `increase_count()` function:

```
/* increase available_resources by count */
int increase_count(int count) {
    available_resources += count;

    return 0;
}
```

The preceding program segment produces a race condition. Do the following:

a. Identify the data involved in the race condition.

b. Identify the location (or locations) in the code where the race condition occurs.

c. Using a semaphore, fix the race condition. It is ok to modify the `decrease_count()` function so that the calling process is blocked until sufficient resources are available.

6.21 Explain why spinlocks are not appropriate for single-processor systems yet are often used in multiprocessor systems.

6.22 **The Cigarette-Smokers Problem**. Consider a system with three *smoker* processes and one *agent* process. Each smoker continuously rolls a cigarette and then smokes it. But to roll and smoke a cigarette, the smoker needs three ingredients: tobacco, paper, and matches. One of the smoker processes has paper, another has tobacco, and the third has matches. The agent has an infinite supply of all three materials. The agent places two of the ingredients on the table. The smoker who has the remaining ingredient then makes and smokes a cigarette, signaling the agent on completion. The agent then puts out another two of the three ingredients, and the cycle repeats. Write a program to synchronize the agent and the smokers using Java synchronization.

6.23 Describe how the `Swap()` instruction can be used to provide mutual exclusion that satisfies the bounded-waiting requirement.

6.24 Windows Vista provides a new lightweight synchronization tool called **slim reader–writer** locks. Whereas most implementations of reader–writer locks favor either readers or writers, or perhaps order waiting threads using a FIFO policy, slim reader–writer locks favor neither readers nor writers, nor are waiting threads ordered in a FIFO queue. Explain the benefits of providing such a synchronization tool.

6.25 What are the implications of assigning a new timestamp to a transaction that is rolled back? How does the system process transactions that were issued after the rolled-back transaction but that have timestamps smaller than the new timestamp of the rolled-back transaction?

6.26 Discuss the tradeoff between fairness and throughput of operations in the readers–writers problem. Propose a method for solving the readers–writers problem without causing starvation.

6.27 When a signal is performed on a condition inside a monitor, the signaling process can either continue its execution or transfer control to the process that is signaled. How would the solution to 6.5 differ with these two different ways in which signaling can be performed?

6.28 What is the meaning of the term *busy waiting*? What other kinds of waiting are there in an operating system? Can busy waiting be avoided altogether? Explain your answer.

6.29 Demonstrate that monitors and semaphores are equivalent insofar as they can be used to implement the same types of synchronization problems.

6.30 In log-based systems that provide support for transactions, updates to data items cannot be performed before the corresponding entries are logged. Why is this restriction necessary?

6.31 Explain the purpose of the checkpoint mechanism. How often should checkpoints be performed? Describe how the frequency of checkpoints affects:

- System performance when no failure occurs
- The time it takes to recover from a system crash
- The time it takes to recover from a disk crash

6.32 Write a bounded-buffer monitor in which the buffers (portions) are embedded within the monitor itself.

6.33 The strict mutual exclusion within a monitor makes the bounded-buffer monitor of Exercise 6.32 mainly suitable for small portions.

a. Explain why this is true.

b. Design a new scheme that is suitable for larger portions.

6.34 Race conditions are possible in many computer systems. Consider a banking system with two functions: `deposit(amount)` and `withdraw(amount)`. These two functions are passed the `amount` that is to be deposited or withdrawn from a bank account. Assume a shared bank account exists between a husband and wife and concurrently the husband calls the `withdraw()` function and the wife calls `deposit()`. Describe how a race condition is possible and what might be done to prevent the race condition from occurring.

6.35 Suppose the `signal()` statement can appear only as the last statement in a monitor procedure. Suggest how the implementation described in Section 6.7 can be simplified in this situation.

Programming Problems

6.36 **The Sleeping-Barber Problem**. A barbershop consists of a waiting room with *n* chairs and a barber room with one barber chair. If there are no customers to be served, the barber goes to sleep. If a customer enters the barbershop and all chairs are occupied, then the customer leaves the shop. If the barber is busy but chairs are available, then the customer sits in one of the free chairs. If the barber is asleep, the customer wakes up the barber. Write a program to coordinate the barber and the customers.

Programming Projects

6.37 **Producer–Consumer Problem**

In Section 6.6.1, we had presented a semaphore-based solution to the producer–consumer problem using a bounded buffer. In this project, we will design a programming solution to the bounded-buffer problem using the producer and consumer processes shown in Figures 6.10 and 6.11. The solution presented in Section 6.6.1 uses three semaphores: `empty` and `full`, which count the number of empty and full slots in the buffer, and `mutex`, which is a binary (or mutual-exclusion) semaphore that protects the actual insertion or removal of items in the buffer. For this project, standard counting semaphores will be used for `empty` and `full`, and a mutex lock, rather than a binary semaphore, will be used to represent `mutex`. The producer and consumer—running as separate threads—will move items to and from a buffer that is synchronized with these `empty`, `full`, and `mutex` structures. You can solve this problem using either Pthreads or the Win32 API.

The Buffer

Internally, the buffer will consist of a fixed-size array of type `buffer_item` (which will be defined using a `typedef`). The array of `buffer_item` objects will be manipulated as a circular queue. The definition of `buffer_item`, along with the size of the buffer, can be stored in a header file such as the following:

```
/* buffer.h */
typedef int buffer_item;
#define BUFFER_SIZE 5
```

The buffer will be manipulated with two functions, `insert_item()` and `remove_item()`, which are called by the producer and consumer threads, respectively. A skeleton outlining these functions appears in Figure 6.27.

```
#include "buffer.h"

/* the buffer */
buffer_item buffer[BUFFER_SIZE];

int insert_item(buffer_item item) {
   /* insert item into buffer
     return 0 if successful, otherwise
     return -1 indicating an error condition */
}

int remove_item(buffer_item *item) {
   /* remove an object from buffer
     placing it in item
     return 0 if successful, otherwise
     return -1 indicating an error condition */
}
```

Figure 6.27 A skeleton program.

The insert_item() and remove_item() functions will synchronize the producer and consumer using the algorithms outlined in Figures 6.10 and 6.11. The buffer will also require an initialization function that initializes the mutual-exclusion object mutex along with the empty and full semaphores.

The main() function will initialize the buffer and create the separate producer and consumer threads. Once it has created the producer and consumer threads, the main() function will sleep for a period of time and, upon awakening, will terminate the application. The main() function will be passed three parameters on the command line:

a. How long to sleep before terminating

b. The number of producer threads

c. The number of consumer threads

A skeleton for this function appears in Figure 6.28.

```
#include "buffer.h"

int main(int argc, char *argv[]) {
  /* 1. Get command line arguments argv[1],argv[2],argv[3] */
  /* 2. Initialize buffer */
  /* 3. Create producer thread(s) */
  /* 4. Create consumer thread(s) */
  /* 5. Sleep */
  /* 6. Exit */
}
```

Figure 6.28 A skeleton program.

Producer and Consumer Threads

The producer thread will alternate between sleeping for a random period of time and inserting a random integer into the buffer. Random numbers will be produced using the rand() function, which produces random integers between 0 and RAND_MAX. The consumer will also sleep for a random period of time and, upon awakening, will attempt to remove an item from the buffer. An outline of the producer and consumer threads appears in Figure 6.29.

In the following sections, we first cover details specific to Pthreads and then describe details of the Win32 API.

Pthreads Thread Creation

Creating threads using the Pthreads API is discussed in Chapter 4. Please refer to that chapter for specific instructions regarding creation of the producer and consumer using Pthreads.

```
#include <stdlib.h> /* required for rand() */
#include "buffer.h"

void *producer(void *param) {
   buffer_item item;

   while (TRUE) {
      /* sleep for a random period of time */
      sleep(...);
      /* generate a random number */
      item = rand();
      if (insert_item(item))
         fprintf("report error condition");
      else
         printf("producer produced %d\n",item);
}

void *consumer(void *param) {
   buffer_item item;

   while (TRUE) {
      /* sleep for a random period of time */
      sleep(...);
      if (remove_item(&item))
         fprintf("report error condition");
      else
         printf("consumer consumed %d\n",item);
}
```

Figure 6.29 An outline of the producer and consumer threads.

```
#include <pthread.h>
pthread_mutex_t mutex;

/* create the mutex lock */
pthread_mutex_init(&mutex,NULL);

/* acquire the mutex lock */
pthread_mutex_lock(&mutex);

/*** critical section ***/

/* release the mutex lock */
pthread_mutex_unlock(&mutex);
```

Figure 6.30 Code sample.

Pthreads Mutex Locks

The code sample depicted in Figure 6.30 illustrates how mutex locks available in the Pthread API can be used to protect a critical section.

Pthreads uses the `pthread_mutex_t` data type for mutex locks. A mutex is created with the `pthread_mutex_init(&mutex,NULL)` function, with the first parameter being a pointer to the mutex. By passing `NULL` as a second parameter, we initialize the mutex to its default attributes. The mutex is acquired and released with the `pthread_mutex_lock()` and `pthread_mutex_unlock()` functions. If the mutex lock is unavailable when `pthread_mutex_lock()` is invoked, the calling thread is blocked until the owner invokes `pthread_mutex_unlock()`. All mutex functions return a value of 0 with correct operation; if an error occurs, these functions return a nonzero error code.

Pthreads Semaphores

Pthreads provides two types of semaphores—named and unnamed. For this project, we use unnamed semaphores. The code below illustrates how a semaphore is created:

```
#include <semaphore.h>
sem_t sem;

/* Create the semaphore and initialize it to 5 */
sem_init(&sem, 0, 5);
```

The `sem_init()` creates and initializes a semaphore. This function is passed three parameters:

a. A pointer to the semaphore

b. A flag indicating the level of sharing

c. The semaphore's initial value

```
#include <semaphore.h>
sem_t mutex;

/* create the semaphore */
sem_init(&mutex, 0, 1);

/* acquire the semaphore */
sem_wait(&mutex);

/*** critical section ***/

/* release the semaphore */
sem_post(&mutex);
```

Figure 6.31 AAA5.

In this example, by passing the flag 0, we are indicating that this semaphore can only be shared by threads belonging to the same process that created the semaphore. A nonzero value would allow other processes to access the semaphore as well. In this example, we initialize the semaphore to the value 5.

In Section 6.5, we described the classical `wait()` and `signal()` semaphore operations. Pthreads names the `wait()` and `signal()` operations `sem_wait()` and `sem_post()`, respectively. The code example shown in Figure 6.31 creates a binary semaphore `mutex` with an initial value of 1 and illustrates its use in protecting a critical section.

Win32

Details concerning thread creation using the Win32 API are available in Chapter 4. Please refer to that chapter for specific instructions.

Win32 Mutex Locks

Mutex locks are a type of dispatcher object, as described in Section 6.8.2. The following illustrates how to create a mutex lock using the `CreateMutex()` function:

```
#include <windows.h>

HANDLE Mutex;
Mutex = CreateMutex(NULL, FALSE, NULL);
```

The first parameter refers to a security attribute for the mutex lock. By setting this attribute to `NULL`, we are disallowing any children of the process creating this mutex lock to inherit the handle of the mutex. The second parameter indicates whether the creator of the mutex is the initial owner of the mutex lock. Passing a value of `FALSE` indicates that the thread creating the mutex is not the initial owner; we shall soon see how mutex locks are acquired. The third parameter allows naming of the mutex. However, because we provide a value of NULL, we do not name the mutex. If successful, CreateMutex() returns a HANDLE to the mutex lock; otherwise, it returns NULL.

In Section 6.8.2, we identified dispatcher objects as being either *signaled* or *nonsignaled*. A signaled object is available for ownership; once a dispatcher object (such as a mutex lock) is acquired, it moves to the nonsignaled state. When the object is released, it returns to signaled. Mutex locks are acquired by invoking the WaitForSingleObject() function, passing the function the HANDLE to the lock and a flag indicating how long to wait. The following code demonstrates how the mutex lock created above can be acquired:

```
WaitForSingleObject(Mutex, INFINITE);
```

The parameter value INFINITE indicates that we will wait an infinite amount of time for the lock to become available. Other values could be used that would allow the calling thread to time out if the lock did not become available within a specified time. If the lock is in a signaled state, WaitForSingleObject() returns immediately, and the lock becomes nonsignaled. A lock is released (moves to the signaled state) by invoking ReleaseMutex(), such as:

```
ReleaseMutex(Mutex);
```

Win32 Semaphores

Semaphores in the Win32 API are also dispatcher objects and thus use the same signaling mechanism as mutex locks. Semaphores are created as follows:

```
#include <windows.h>

HANDLE Sem;
Sem = CreateSemaphore(NULL, 1, 5, NULL);
```

The first and last parameters identify a security attribute and a name for the semaphore, similar to what was described for mutex locks. The second and third parameters indicate the initial value and maximum value of the semaphore. In this instance, the initial value of the semaphore is 1, and its maximum value is 5. If successful, CreateSemaphore() returns a HANDLE to the mutex lock; otherwise, it returns NULL.

Semaphores are acquired with the same WaitForSingleObject() function as mutex locks. We acquire the semaphore Sem created in this example by using the statement:

```
WaitForSingleObject(Semaphore, INFINITE);
```

If the value of the semaphore is > 0, the semaphore is in the signaled state and thus is acquired by the calling thread. Otherwise, the calling thread blocks indefinitely—as we are specifying INFINITE—until the semaphore becomes signaled.

The equivalent of the `signal()` operation on Win32 semaphores is the `ReleaseSemaphore()` function. This function is passed three parameters:

a. The HANDLE of the semaphore

b. The amount by which to increase the value of the semaphore

c. A pointer to the previous value of the semaphore

We can increase `Sem` by 1 using the following statement:

```
ReleaseSemaphore(Sem, 1, NULL);
```

Both `ReleaseSemaphore()` and `ReleaseMutex()` return nonzero if successful and zero otherwise.

Bibliographical Notes

The mutual-exclusion problem was first discussed in a classic paper by Dijkstra [1965a]. Dekker's algorithm (Exercise 6.1)—the first correct software solution to the two-process mutual-exclusion problem—was developed by the Dutch mathematician T. Dekker. This algorithm also was discussed by Dijkstra [1965a]. A simpler solution to the two-process mutual-exclusion problem has since been presented by Peterson [1981] (Figure 6.2).

Dijkstra [1965b] presented the first solution to the mutual-exclusion problem for n processes. This solution, however, does not have an upper bound on the amount of time a process must wait before it is allowed to enter the critical section. Knuth [1966] presented the first algorithm with a bound; his bound was 2^n turns. A refinement of Knuth's algorithm by deBruijn [1967] reduced the waiting time to n^2 turns, after which Eisenberg and McGuire [1972] succeeded in reducing the time to the lower bound of $n-1$ turns. Another algorithm that also requires $n-1$ turns but is easier to program and to understand is the bakery algorithm, which was developed by Lamport [1974]. Burns [1978] developed the hardware-solution algorithm that satisfies the bounded-waiting requirement.

General discussions concerning the mutual-exclusion problem were offered by Lamport [1986] and Lamport [1991]. A collection of algorithms for mutual exclusion was given by Raynal [1986].

The semaphore concept was suggested by Dijkstra [1965a]. Patil [1971] examined the question of whether semaphores can solve all possible synchronization problems. Parnas [1975] discussed some of the flaws in Patil's arguments. Kosaraju [1973] followed up on Patil's work to produce a problem that cannot be solved by `wait()` and `signal()` operations. Lipton [1974] discussed the limitations of various synchronization primitives.

The classic process-coordination problems that we have described are paradigms for a large class of concurrency-control problems. The bounded-buffer problem, the dining-philosophers problem, and the sleeping-barber problem (Exercise 6.36) were suggested by Dijkstra [1965a] and Dijkstra [1971]. The cigarette-smokers problem (Exercise 6.22 was developed by Patil [1971]. The readers–writers problem was suggested by Courtois et al. [1971]. The issue of concurrent reading and writing was discussed by Lamport [1977]. The problem of synchronization of independent processes was discussed by Lamport [1976].

The critical-region concept was suggested by Hoare [1972] and by Brinch-Hansen [1972]. The monitor concept was developed by Brinch-Hansen [1973]. A complete description of the monitor was given by Hoare [1974]. Kessels [1977] proposed an extension to the monitor to allow automatic signaling. Experience obtained from the use of monitors in concurrent programs was discussed by Lampson and Redell [1979]. They also examined the priority inversion problem. General discussions concerning concurrent programming were offered by Ben-Ari [1990] and Birrell [1989].

Optimizing the performance of locking primitives has been discussed in many works, such as Lamport [1987], Mellor-Crummey and Scott [1991], and Anderson [1990]. The use of shared objects that do not require the use of critical sections was discussed in Herlihy [1993], Bershad [1993], and Kopetz and Reisinger [1993]. Novel hardware instructions and their utility in implementing synchronization primitives have been described in works such as Culler et al. [1998], Goodman et al. [1989], Barnes [1993], and Herlihy and Moss [1993].

Some details of the locking mechanisms used in Solaris were presented in Mauro and McDougall [2007]. Note that the locking mechanisms used by the kernel are implemented for user-level threads as well, so the same types of locks are available inside and outside the kernel. Details of Windows 2000 synchronization can be found in Solomon and Russinovich [2000]. Goetz et al. [2006] presents a detailed discussion of concurrent programming in Java as well as the `java.util.concurrent` package.

The write-ahead log scheme was first introduced in System R by Gray et al. [1981]. The concept of serializability was formulated by Eswaran et al. [1976] in connection with their work on concurrency control for System R. The two-phase locking protocol was introduced by Eswaran et al. [1976]. The timestamp-based concurrency-control scheme was provided by Reed [1983]. Various timestamp-based concurrency-control algorithms were explained by Bernstein and Goodman [1980]. Adl-Tabatabai et al. [2007] discusses transactional memory.

CHAPTER 7

Deadlocks

In a multiprogramming environment, several processes may compete for a finite number of resources. A process requests resources; if the resources are not available at that time, the process enters a waiting state. Sometimes, a waiting process is never again able to change state, because the resources it has requested are held by other waiting processes. This situation is called a **deadlock**. We discussed this issue briefly in Chapter 6 in connection with semaphores.

Perhaps the best illustration of a deadlock can be drawn from a law passed by the Kansas legislature early in the 20th century. It said, in part: "When two trains approach each other at a crossing, both shall come to a full stop and neither shall start up again until the other has gone."

In this chapter, we describe methods that an operating system can use to prevent or deal with deadlocks. Although some applications can identify programs that may deadlock, operating systems typically do not provide deadlock-prevention facilities, and it remains the responsibility of programmers to ensure that they design deadlock-free programs. Deadlock problems can only become more common, given current trends, including larger numbers of processes, multithreaded programs, many more resources within a system, and an emphasis on long-lived file and database servers rather than batch systems.

CHAPTER OBJECTIVES

- To develop a description of deadlocks, which prevent sets of concurrent processes from completing their tasks.
- To present a number of different methods for preventing or avoiding deadlocks in a computer system.

7.1 System Model

A system consists of a finite number of resources to be distributed among a number of competing processes. The resources are partitioned into several types, each consisting of some number of identical instances. Memory space, CPU cycles, files, and I/O devices (such as printers and DVD drives) are examples of resource types. If a system has two CPUs, then the resource type *CPU* has two instances. Similarly, the resource type *printer* may have five instances.

If a process requests an instance of a resource type, the allocation of *any* instance of the type will satisfy the request. If it will not, then the instances are not identical, and the resource type classes have not been defined properly. For example, a system may have two printers. These two printers may be defined to be in the same resource class if no one cares which printer prints which output. However, if one printer is on the ninth floor and the other is in the basement, then people on the ninth floor may not see both printers as equivalent, and separate resource classes may need to be defined for each printer.

A process must request a resource before using it and must release the resource after using it. A process may request as many resources as it requires to carry out its designated task. Obviously, the number of resources requested may not exceed the total number of resources available in the system. In other words, a process cannot request three printers if the system has only two.

Under the normal mode of operation, a process may utilize a resource in only the following sequence:

1. **Request**. The process requests the resource. If the request cannot be granted immediately (for example, if the resource is being used by another process), then the requesting process must wait until it can acquire the resource.

2. **Use**. The process can operate on the resource (for example, if the resource is a printer, the process can print on the printer).

3. **Release**. The process releases the resource.

The request and release of resources are system calls, as explained in Chapter 2. Examples are the `request()` and `release()` device, `open()` and `close()` file, and `allocate()` and `free()` memory system calls. Request and release of resources that are not managed by the operating system can be accomplished through the `wait()` and `signal()` operations on semaphores or through acquisition and release of a mutex lock. For each use of a kernel-managed resource by a process or thread, the operating system checks to make sure that the process has requested and has been allocated the resource. A system table records whether each resource is free or allocated; for each resource that is allocated, the table also records the process to which it is allocated. If a process requests a resource that is currently allocated to another process, it can be added to a queue of processes waiting for this resource.

A set of processes is in a deadlocked state when every process in the set is waiting for an event that can be caused only by another process in the set. The events with which we are mainly concerned here are resource acquisition and release. The resources may be either physical resources (for example, printers, tape drives, memory space, and CPU cycles) or logical resources (for example, files, semaphores, and monitors). However, other types of events may result in deadlocks (for example, the IPC facilities discussed in Chapter 3).

To illustrate a deadlocked state, consider a system with three CD RW drives. Suppose each of three processes holds one of these CD RW drives. If each process now requests another drive, the three processes will be in a deadlocked state. Each is waiting for the event "CD RW is released," which can be caused only by one of the other waiting processes. This example illustrates a deadlock involving the same resource type.

Deadlocks may also involve different resource types. For example, consider a system with one printer and one DVD drive. Suppose that process P_i is holding the DVD and process P_j is holding the printer. If P_i requests the printer and P_j requests the DVD drive, a deadlock occurs.

A programmer who is developing multithreaded applications must pay particular attention to this problem. Multithreaded programs are good candidates for deadlock because multiple threads can compete for shared resources.

7.2 Deadlock Characterization

In a deadlock, processes never finish executing, and system resources are tied up, preventing other jobs from starting. Before we discuss the various methods for dealing with the deadlock problem, we look more closely at features that characterize deadlocks.

7.2.1 Necessary Conditions

A deadlock situation can arise if the following four conditions hold simultaneously in a system:

1. **Mutual exclusion**. At least one resource must be held in a nonsharable mode; that is, only one process at a time can use the resource. If another

DEADLOCK WITH MUTEX LOCKS

Let's see how deadlock can occur in a multithreaded Pthread program using mutex locks. The `pthread_mutex_init()` function initializes an unlocked mutex. Mutex locks are acquired and released using `pthread_mutex_lock()` and `pthread_mutex_unlock()`, respectively. If a thread attempts to acquire a locked mutex, the call to `pthread_mutex_lock()` blocks the thread until the owner of the mutex lock invokes `pthread_mutex_unlock()`.

Two mutex locks are created in the following code example:

```
/* Create and initialize the mutex locks */
pthread_mutex_t first_mutex;
pthread_mutex_t second_mutex;

pthread_mutex_init(&first_mutex,NULL);
pthread_mutex_init(&second_mutex,NULL);
```

Next, two threads—`thread_one` and `thread_two`—are created, and both these threads have access to both mutex locks. `thread_one` and `thread_two` run in the functions `do_work_one()` and `do_work_two()`, respectively, as shown in Figure 7.1.

DEADLOCK WITH MUTEX LOCKS (Continued)

```
/* thread_one runs in this function */
void *do_work_one(void *param)
{
    pthread_mutex_lock(&first_mutex);
    pthread_mutex_lock(&second_mutex);
    /**
     * Do some work
     */
    pthread_mutex_unlock(&second_mutex);
    pthread_mutex_unlock(&first_mutex);

    pthread_exit(0);
}

/* thread_two runs in this function */
void *do_work_two(void *param)
{
    pthread_mutex_lock(&second_mutex);
    pthread_mutex_lock(&first_mutex);
    /**
     * Do some work
     */
    pthread_mutex_unlock(&first_mutex);
    pthread_mutex_unlock(&second_mutex);

    pthread_exit(0);
}
```

Figure 7.1 Deadlock example.

In this example, `thread_one` attempts to acquire the mutex locks in the order (1) `first_mutex`, (2) `second_mutex`, while `thread_two` attempts to acquire the mutex locks in the order (1) `second_mutex`, (2) `first_mutex`. Deadlock is possible if `thread_one` acquires `first_mutex` while `thread_two` aacquites `second_mutex`.

Note that, even though deadlock is possible, it will not occur if `thread_one` is able to acquire and release the mutex locks for `first_mutex` and `second_mutex` before `thread_two` attempts to acquire the locks. This example illustrates a problem with handling deadlocks: it is difficult to identify and test for deadlocks that may occur only under certain circumstances.

process requests that resource, the requesting process must be delayed until the resource has been released.

2. **Hold and wait**. A process must be holding at least one resource and waiting to acquire additional resources that are currently being held by other processes.

3. **No preemption**. Resources cannot be preempted; that is, a resource can be released only voluntarily by the process holding it, after that process has completed its task.

4. **Circular wait**. A set $\{P_0, P_1, ..., P_n\}$ of waiting processes must exist such that P_0 is waiting for a resource held by P_1, P_1 is waiting for a resource held by P_2, ..., P_{n-1} is waiting for a resource held by P_n, and P_n is waiting for a resource held by P_0.

We emphasize that all four conditions must hold for a deadlock to occur. The circular-wait condition implies the hold-and-wait condition, so the four conditions are not completely independent. We shall see in Section 7.4, however, that it is useful to consider each condition separately.

7.2.2 Resource-Allocation Graph

Deadlocks can be described more precisely in terms of a directed graph called a system resource-allocation graph. This graph consists of a set of vertices V and a set of edges E. The set of vertices V is partitioned into two different types of nodes: $P = \{P_1, P_2, ..., P_n\}$, the set consisting of all the active processes in the system, and $R = \{R_1, R_2, ..., R_m\}$, the set consisting of all resource types in the system.

A directed edge from process P_i to resource type R_j is denoted by $P_i \rightarrow R_j$; it signifies that process P_i has requested an instance of resource type R_j and is currently waiting for that resource. A directed edge from resource type R_j to process P_i is denoted by $R_j \rightarrow P_i$; it signifies that an instance of resource type R_j has been allocated to process P_i. A directed edge $P_i \rightarrow R_j$ is called a request edge; a directed edge $R_j \rightarrow P_i$ is called an assignment edge.

Pictorially, we represent each process P_i as a circle and each resource type R_j as a rectangle. Since resource type R_j may have more than one instance, we represent each such instance as a dot within the rectangle. Note that a request edge points to only the rectangle R_j, whereas an assignment edge must also designate one of the dots in the rectangle.

When process P_i requests an instance of resource type R_j, a request edge is inserted in the resource-allocation graph. When this request can be fulfilled, the request edge is *instantaneously* transformed to an assignment edge. When the process no longer needs access to the resource, it releases the resource; as a result, the assignment edge is deleted.

The resource-allocation graph shown in Figure 7.2 depicts the following situation.

- The sets P, R, and E:
  - $P = \{P_1, P_2, P_3\}$
  - $R = \{R_1, R_2, R_3, R_4\}$
  - $E = \{P_1 \rightarrow R_1, P_2 \rightarrow R_3, R_1 \rightarrow P_2, R_2 \rightarrow P_2, R_2 \rightarrow P_1, R_3 \rightarrow P_3\}$
- Resource instances:
  - One instance of resource type R_1
  - Two instances of resource type R_2

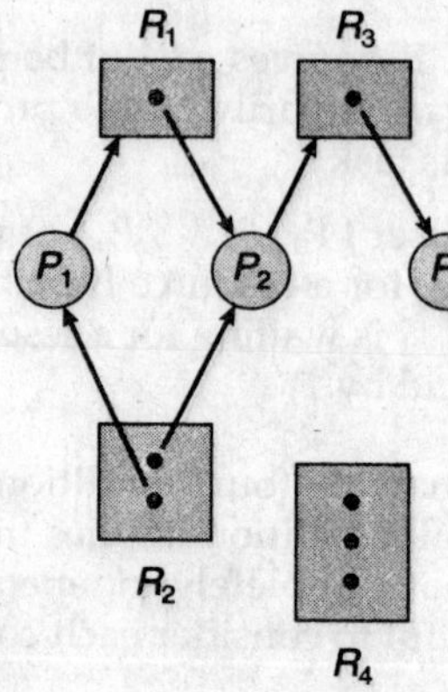

Figure 7.2 Resource-allocation graph.

- One instance of resource type R_3
- Three instances of resource type R_4

- Process states:
  - Process P_1 is holding an instance of resource type R_2 and is waiting for an instance of resource type R_1.
  - Process P_2 is holding an instance of R_1 and an instance of R_2 and is waiting for an instance of R_3.
  - Process P_3 is holding an instance of R_3.

Given the definition of a resource-allocation graph, it can be shown that, if the graph contains no cycles, then no process in the system is deadlocked. If the graph does contain a cycle, then a deadlock may exist.

If each resource type has exactly one instance, then a cycle implies that a deadlock has occurred. If the cycle involves only a set of resource types, each of which has only a single instance, then a deadlock has occurred. Each process involved in the cycle is deadlocked. In this case, a cycle in the graph is both a necessary and a sufficient condition for the existence of deadlock.

If each resource type has several instances, then a cycle does not necessarily imply that a deadlock has occurred. In this case, a cycle in the graph is a necessary but not a sufficient condition for the existence of deadlock.

To illustrate this concept, we return to the resource-allocation graph depicted in Figure 7.2. Suppose that process P_3 requests an instance of resource type R_2. Since no resource instance is currently available, a request edge $P_3 \rightarrow R_2$ is added to the graph (Figure 7.3). At this point, two minimal cycles exist in the system:

$$P_1 \rightarrow R_1 \rightarrow P_2 \rightarrow R_3 \rightarrow P_3 \rightarrow R_2 \rightarrow P_1$$
$$P_2 \rightarrow R_3 \rightarrow P_3 \rightarrow R_2 \rightarrow P_2$$

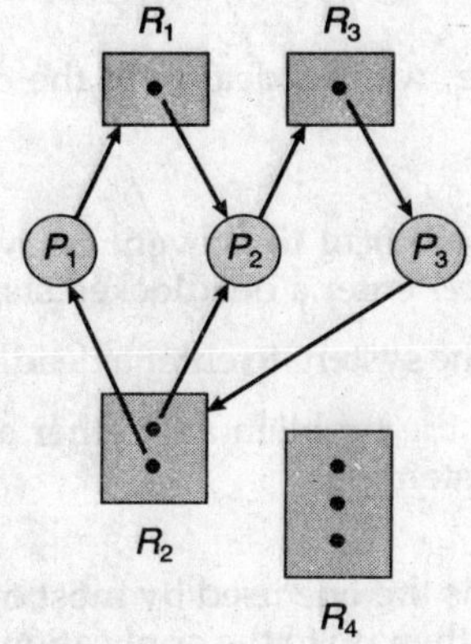

Figure 7.3 Resource-allocation graph with a deadlock.

Processes P_1, P_2, and P_3 are deadlocked. Process P_2 is waiting for the resource R_3, which is held by process P_3. Process P_3 is waiting for either process P_1 or process P_2 to release resource R_2. In addition, process P_1 is waiting for process P_2 to release resource R_1.

Now consider the resource-allocation graph in Figure 7.4. In this example, we also have a cycle:

$$P_1 \rightarrow R_1 \rightarrow P_3 \rightarrow R_2 \rightarrow P_1$$

However, there is no deadlock. Observe that process P_4 may release its instance of resource type R_2. That resource can then be allocated to P_3, breaking the cycle.

In summary, if a resource-allocation graph does not have a cycle, then the system is *not* in a deadlocked state. If there is a cycle, then the system may or may not be in a deadlocked state. This observation is important when we deal with the deadlock problem.

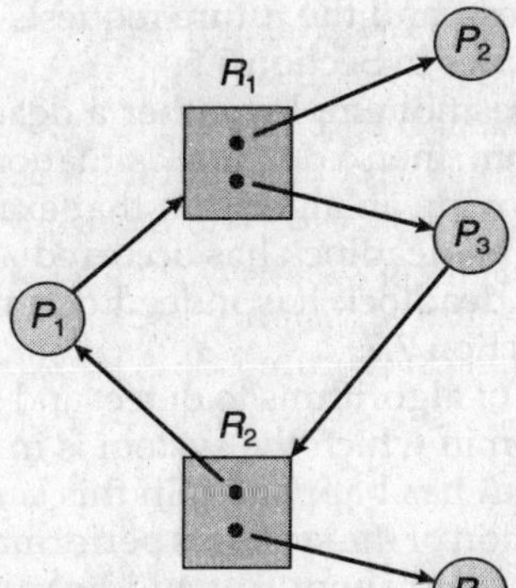

Figure 7.4 Resource-allocation graph with a cycle but no deadlock.

7.3 Methods for Handling Deadlocks

Generally speaking, we can deal with the deadlock problem in one of three ways:

- We can use a protocol to prevent or avoid deadlocks, ensuring that the system will *never* enter a deadlocked state.
- We can allow the system to enter a deadlocked state, detect it, and recover.
- We can ignore the problem altogether and pretend that deadlocks never occur in the system.

The third solution is the one used by most operating systems, including UNIX and Windows; it is then up to the application developer to write programs that handle deadlocks.

Next, we elaborate briefly on each of the three methods for handling deadlocks. Then, in Sections 7.4 through 7.7, we present detailed algorithms. Before proceeding, we should mention that some researchers have argued that none of the basic approaches alone is appropriate for the entire spectrum of resource-allocation problems in operating systems. The basic approaches can be combined, however, allowing us to select an optimal approach for each class of resources in a system.

To ensure that deadlocks never occur, the system can use either a deadlock-prevention or a deadlock-avoidance scheme. **Deadlock prevention** provides a set of methods for ensuring that at least one of the necessary conditions (Section 7.2.1) cannot hold. These methods prevent deadlocks by constraining how requests for resources can be made. We discuss these methods in Section 7.4.

Deadlock avoidance requires that the operating system be given in advance additional information concerning which resources a process will request and use during its lifetime. With this additional knowledge, it can decide for each request whether or not the process should wait. To decide whether the current request can be satisfied or must be delayed, the system must consider the resources currently available, the resources currently allocated to each process, and the future requests and releases of each process. We discuss these schemes in Section 7.5.

If a system does not employ either a deadlock-prevention or a deadlock-avoidance algorithm, then a deadlock situation may arise. In this environment, the system can provide an algorithm that examines the state of the system to determine whether a deadlock has occurred and an algorithm to recover from the deadlock (if a deadlock has indeed occurred). We discuss these issues in Section 7.6 and Section 7.7.

In the absence of algorithms to detect and recover from deadlocks, we may arrive at a situation in which the system is in a deadlock state yet has no way of recognizing what has happened. In this case, the undetected deadlock will result in deterioration of the system's performance, because resources are being held by processes that cannot run and because more and more processes, as they make requests for resources, will enter a deadlocked state. Eventually, the system will stop functioning and will need to be restarted manually.

Although this method may not seem to be a viable approach to the deadlock problem, it is nevertheless used in most operating systems, as mentioned earlier. In many systems, deadlocks occur infrequently (say, once per year); thus, this method is cheaper than the prevention, avoidance, or detection and recovery methods, which must be used constantly. Also, in some circumstances, a system is in a frozen state but not in a deadlocked state. We see this situation, for example, with a real-time process running at the highest priority (or any process running on a nonpreemptive scheduler) and never returning control to the operating system. The system must have manual recovery methods for such conditions and may simply use those techniques for deadlock recovery.

7.4 Deadlock Prevention

As we noted in Section 7.2.1, for a deadlock to occur, each of the four necessary conditions must hold. By ensuring that at least one of these conditions cannot hold, we can *prevent* the occurrence of a deadlock. We elaborate on this approach by examining each of the four necessary conditions separately.

7.4.1 Mutual Exclusion

The mutual-exclusion condition must hold for nonsharable resources. For example, a printer cannot be simultaneously shared by several processes. Sharable resources, in contrast, do not require mutually exclusive access and thus cannot be involved in a deadlock. Read-only files are a good example of a sharable resource. If several processes attempt to open a read-only file at the same time, they can be granted simultaneous access to the file. A process never needs to wait for a sharable resource. In general, however, we cannot prevent deadlocks by denying the mutual-exclusion condition, because some resources are intrinsically nonsharable.

7.4.2 Hold and Wait

To ensure that the hold-and-wait condition never occurs in the system, we must guarantee that, whenever a process requests a resource, it does not hold any other resources. One protocol that can be used requires each process to request and be allocated all its resources before it begins execution. We can implement this provision by requiring that system calls requesting resources for a process precede all other system calls.

An alternative protocol allows a process to request resources only when it has none. A process may request some resources and use them. Before it can request any additional resources, however, it must release all the resources that it is currently allocated.

To illustrate the difference between these two protocols, we consider a process that copies data from a DVD drive to a file on disk, sorts the file, and then prints the results to a printer. If all resources must be requested at the beginning of the process, then the process must initially request the DVD drive, disk file, and printer. It will hold the printer for its entire execution, even though it needs the printer only at the end.

The second method allows the process to request initially only the DVD drive and disk file. It copies from the DVD drive to the disk and then releases both the DVD drive and the disk file. The process must then again request the disk file and the printer. After copying the disk file to the printer, it releases these two resources and terminates.

Both these protocols have two main disadvantages. First, resource utilization may be low, since resources may be allocated but unused for a long period. In the example given, for instance, we can release the DVD drive and disk file, and then again request the disk file and printer, only if we can be sure that our data will remain on the disk file. Otherwise, we must request all resources at the beginning for both protocols.

Second, starvation is possible. A process that needs several popular resources may have to wait indefinitely, because at least one of the resources that it needs is always allocated to some other process.

7.4.3 No Preemption

The third necessary condition for deadlocks is that there be no preemption of resources that have already been allocated. To ensure that this condition does not hold, we can use the following protocol. If a process is holding some resources and requests another resource that cannot be immediately allocated to it (that is, the process must wait), then all resources the process is currently holding are preempted. In other words, these resources are implicitly released. The preempted resources are added to the list of resources for which the process is waiting. The process will be restarted only when it can regain its old resources, as well as the new ones that it is requesting.

Alternatively, if a process requests some resources, we first check whether they are available. If they are, we allocate them. If they are not, we check whether they are allocated to some other process that is waiting for additional resources. If so, we preempt the desired resources from the waiting process and allocate them to the requesting process. If the resources are neither available nor held by a waiting process, the requesting process must wait. While it is waiting, some of its resources may be preempted, but only if another process requests them. A process can be restarted only when it is allocated the new resources it is requesting and recovers any resources that were preempted while it was waiting.

This protocol is often applied to resources whose state can be easily saved and restored later, such as CPU registers and memory space. It cannot generally be applied to such resources as printers and tape drives.

7.4.4 Circular Wait

The fourth and final condition for deadlocks is the circular-wait condition. One way to ensure that this condition never holds is to impose a total ordering of all resource types and to require that each process requests resources in an increasing order of enumeration.

To illustrate, we let $R = \{R_1, R_2, ..., R_m\}$ be the set of resource types. We assign to each resource type a unique integer number, which allows us to compare two resources and to determine whether one precedes another in our ordering. Formally, we define a one-to-one function $F: R \rightarrow N$, where N is the set of natural numbers. For example, if the set of resource types R includes tape drives, disk drives, and printers, then the function F might be defined as follows:

$$F(\text{tape drive}) = 1$$
$$F(\text{disk drive}) = 5$$
$$F(\text{printer}) = 12$$

We can now consider the following protocol to prevent deadlocks: Each process can request resources only in an increasing order of enumeration. That is, a process can initially request any number of instances of a resource type —say, R_i. After that, the process can request instances of resource type R_j if and only if $F(R_j) > F(R_i)$. For example, using the function defined previously, a process that wants to use the tape drive and printer at the same time must first request the tape drive and then request the printer. Alternatively, we can require that a process requesting an instance of resource type R_j must have released any resources R_i such that $F(R_i) \geq F(R_j)$. It must also be noted that if several instances of the same resource type are needed, a *single* request for all of them must be issued.

If these two protocols are used, then the circular-wait condition cannot hold. We can demonstrate this fact by assuming that a circular wait exists (proof by contradiction). Let the set of processes involved in the circular wait be $\{P_0, P_1, ..., P_n\}$, where P_i is waiting for a resource R_i, which is held by process P_{i+1}. (Modulo arithmetic is used on the indexes, so that P_n is waiting for a resource R_n held by P_0.) Then, since process P_{i+1} is holding resource R_i while requesting resource R_{i+1}, we must have $F(R_i) < F(R_{i+1})$ for all i. But this condition means that $F(R_0) < F(R_1) < ... < F(R_n) < F(R_0)$. By transitivity, $F(R_0) < F(R_0)$, which is impossible. Therefore, there can be no circular wait.

We can accomplish this scheme in an application program by developing an ordering among all synchronization objects in the system. All requests for synchronization objects must be made in increasing order. For example, if the lock ordering in the Pthread program shown in Figure 7.1 was

$$F(\texttt{first\_mutex}) = 1$$
$$F(\texttt{second\_mutex}) = 5$$

then `thread_two` could not request the locks out of order.

Keep in mind that developing an ordering, or hierarchy, does not in itself prevent deadlock. It is up to application developers to write programs that follow the ordering. Also note that the function F should be defined according to the normal order of usage of the resources in a system. For example, because the tape drive is usually needed before the printer, it would be reasonable to define $F(\text{tape drive}) < F(\text{printer})$.

Although ensuring that resources are acquired in the proper order is the responsibility of application developers, certain software can be used to verify that locks are acquired in the proper order and to give appropriate warnings when locks are acquired out of order and deadlock is possible. One lock-order verifier, which works on BSD versions of UNIX such as FreeBSD, is known as **witness**. Witness uses mutual-exclusion locks to protect critical sections, as described in Chapter 6; it works by dynamically maintaining the relationship of lock orders in a system. Let's use the program shown in Figure 7.1 as an example. Assume that `thread_one` is the first to acquire the locks and does so in the order (1) `first_mutex`, (2) `second_mutex`. Witness records the relationship that `first_mutex` must be acquired before `second_mutex`. If `thread_two` later acquires the locks out of order, witness generates a warning message on the system console.

It is also important to note that imposing a lock ordering does not guarantee deadlock prevention if locks can be acquired dynamically. For example, assume we have a function that transfers funds between two accounts. To prevent a race condition, each account has an associated semaphore that is obtained from a `getLock()` function such as the following:

```
void transaction(Account from, Account to, double amount)
{
    Semaphore lock1, lock2;
    lock1 = getLock(from);
    lock2 = getLock(to);

    wait(lock1);
      wait(lock2);

        withdraw(from, amount);
        deposit(to, amount);

      signal(lock2);
    signal(lock1);
}
```

Deadlock is possible if two threads simultaneously invoke the `transaction()` function, transposing different accounts. That is, one thread might invoke

```
transaction(checkingAccount, savingsAccount, 25);
```

and another might invoke

```
transaction(savingsAccount, checkingAccount, 50);
```

We leave it as an exercise for students to fix this situation.

7.5 Deadlock Avoidance

Deadlock-prevention algorithms, as discussed in Section 7.4, prevent deadlocks by restraining how requests can be made. The restraints ensure that at least one of the necessary conditions for deadlock cannot occur and, hence, that deadlocks cannot hold. Possible side effects of preventing deadlocks by this method, however, are low device utilization and reduced system throughput.

An alternative method for avoiding deadlocks is to require additional information about how resources are to be requested. For example, in a system with one tape drive and one printer, the system might need to know that process *P* will request first the tape drive and then the printer before releasing both resources, whereas process *Q* will request first the printer and then the tape drive. With this knowledge of the complete sequence of requests and releases for each process, the system can decide for each request whether or not the process should wait in order to avoid a possible future deadlock. Each request requires that in making this decision the system consider the resources currently available, the resources currently allocated to each process, and the future requests and releases of each process.

The various algorithms that use this approach differ in the amount and type of information required. The simplest and most useful model requires that each process declare the *maximum number* of resources of each type that it may need. Given this a priori information, it is possible to construct an algorithm that ensures that the system will never enter a deadlocked state. Such an algorithm defines the deadlock-avoidance approach. A deadlock-avoidance algorithm dynamically examines the resource-allocation state to ensure that a circular-wait condition can never exist. The resource-allocation *state* is defined by the number of available and allocated resources and the maximum demands of the processes. In the following sections, we explore two deadlock-avoidance algorithms.

7.5.1 Safe State

A state is *safe* if the system can allocate resources to each process (up to its maximum) in some order and still avoid a deadlock. More formally, a system is in a safe state only if there exists a **safe sequence**. A sequence of processes $<P_1, P_2, ..., P_n>$ is a safe sequence for the current allocation state if, for each P_i, the resource requests that P_i can still make can be satisfied by the currently available resources plus the resources held by all P_j, with $j < i$. In this situation, if the resources that P_i needs are not immediately available, then P_i can wait until all P_j have finished. When they have finished, P_i can obtain all of its needed resources, complete its designated task, return its allocated resources, and terminate. When P_i terminates, P_{i+1} can obtain its needed resources, and so on. If no such sequence exists, then the system state is said to be *unsafe*.

A safe state is not a deadlocked state. Conversely, a deadlocked state is an unsafe state. Not all unsafe states are deadlocks, however (Figure 7.5). An unsafe state *may* lead to a deadlock. As long as the state is safe, the operating system can avoid unsafe (and deadlocked) states. In an unsafe state, the operating system cannot prevent processes from requesting resources in such a way that a deadlock occurs. The behavior of the processes controls unsafe states.

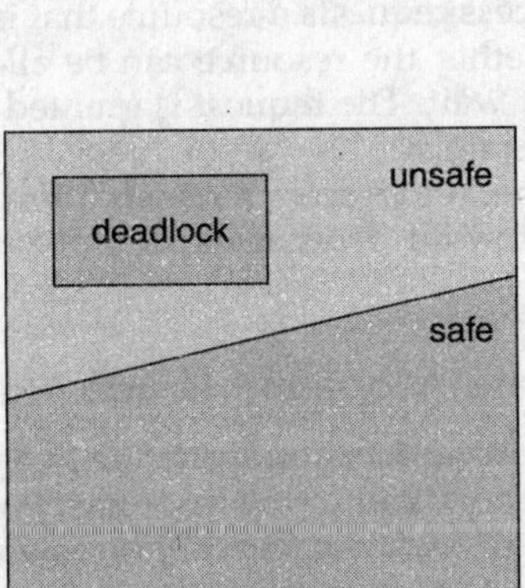

Figure 7.5 Safe, unsafe, and deadlocked state spaces.

To illustrate, we consider a system with twelve magnetic tape drives and three processes: P_0, P_1, and P_2. Process P_0 requires ten tape drives, process P_1 may need as many as four tape drives, and process P_2 may need up to nine tape drives. Suppose that, at time t_0, process P_0 is holding five tape drives, process P_1 is holding two tape drives, and process P_2 is holding two tape drives. (Thus, there are three free tape drives.)

	Maximum Needs	Current Needs
P_0	10	5
P_1	4	2
P_2	9	2

At time t_0, the system is in a safe state. The sequence $<P_1, P_0, P_2>$ satisfies the safety condition. Process P_1 can immediately be allocated all its tape drives and then return them (the system will then have five available tape drives); then process P_0 can get all its tape drives and return them (the system will then have ten available tape drives); and finally process P_2 can get all its tape drives and return them (the system will then have all twelve tape drives available).

A system can go from a safe state to an unsafe state. Suppose that, at time t_1, process P_2 requests and is allocated one more tape drive. The system is no longer in a safe state. At this point, only process P_1 can be allocated all its tape drives. When it returns them, the system will have only four available tape drives. Since process P_0 is allocated five tape drives but has a maximum of ten, it may request five more tape drives. If it does so, it will have to wait, because they are unavailable. Similarly, process P_2 may request six additional tape drives and have to wait, resulting in a deadlock. Our mistake was in granting the request from process P_2 for one more tape drive. If we had made P_2 wait until either of the other processes had finished and released its resources, then we could have avoided the deadlock.

Given the concept of a safe state, we can define avoidance algorithms that ensure that the system will never deadlock. The idea is simply to ensure that the system will always remain in a safe state. Initially, the system is in a safe state. Whenever a process requests a resource that is currently available, the system must decide whether the resource can be allocated immediately or whether the process must wait. The request is granted only if the allocation leaves the system in a safe state.

In this scheme, if a process requests a resource that is currently available, it may still have to wait. Thus, resource utilization may be lower than it would otherwise be.

7.5.2 Resource-Allocation-Graph Algorithm

If we have a resource-allocation system with only one instance of each resource type, we can use a variant of the resource-allocation graph defined in Section 7.2.2 for deadlock avoidance. In addition to the request and assignment edges already described, we introduce a new type of edge, called a **claim edge**. A claim edge $P_i \rightarrow R_j$ indicates that process P_i may request resource R_j at some time in the future. This edge resembles a request edge in direction but is represented in the graph by a dashed line. When process P_i requests resource

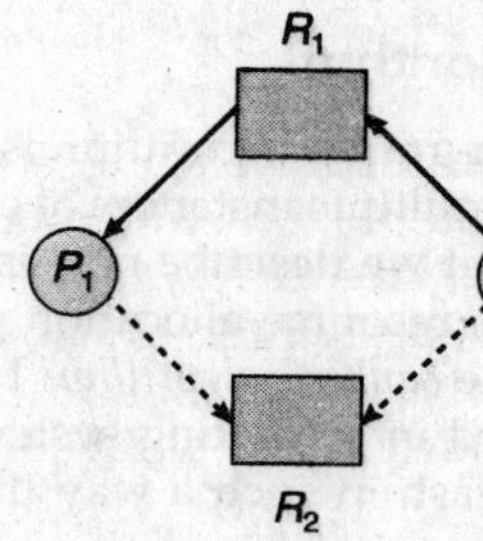

Figure 7.6 Resource-allocation graph for deadlock avoidance.

R_j, the claim edge $P_i \rightarrow R_j$ is converted to a request edge. Similarly, when a resource R_j is released by P_i, the assignment edge $R_j \rightarrow P_i$ is reconverted to a claim edge $P_i \rightarrow R_j$.

We note that the resources must be claimed a priori in the system. That is, before process P_i starts executing, all its claim edges must already appear in the resource-allocation graph. We can relax this condition by allowing a claim edge $P_i \rightarrow R_j$ to be added to the graph only if all the edges associated with process P_i are claim edges.

Now suppose that process P_i requests resource R_j. The request can be granted only if converting the request edge $P_i \rightarrow R_j$ to an assignment edge $R_j \rightarrow P_i$ does not result in the formation of a cycle in the resource-allocation graph. We check for safety by using a cycle-detection algorithm. An algorithm for detecting a cycle in this graph requires an order of n^2 operations, where n is the number of processes in the system.

If no cycle exists, then the allocation of the resource will leave the system in a safe state. If a cycle is found, then the allocation will put the system in an unsafe state. In that case, process P_i will have to wait for its requests to be satisfied.

To illustrate this algorithm, we consider the resource-allocation graph of Figure 7.6. Suppose that P_2 requests R_2. Although R_2 is currently free, we cannot allocate it to P_2, since this action will create a cycle in the graph (Figure 7.7). A cycle, as mentioned, indicates that the system is in an unsafe state. If P_1 requests R_2, and P_2 requests R_1, then a deadlock will occur.

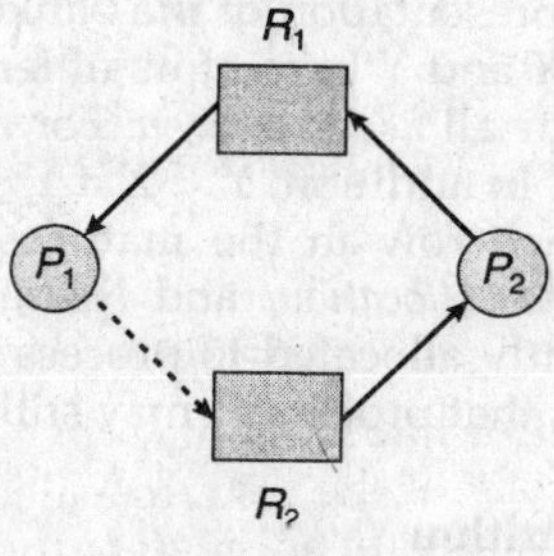

Figure 7.7 An unsafe state in a resource-allocation graph.

7.5.3 Banker's Algorithm

The resource-allocation-graph algorithm is not applicable to a resource-allocation system with multiple instances of each resource type. The deadlock-avoidance algorithm that we describe next is applicable to such a system but is less efficient than the resource-allocation graph scheme. This algorithm is commonly known as the *banker's algorithm*. The name was chosen because the algorithm could be used in a banking system to ensure that the bank never allocated its available cash in such a way that it could no longer satisfy the needs of all its customers.

When a new process enters the system, it must declare the maximum number of instances of each resource type that it may need. This number may not exceed the total number of resources in the system. When a user requests a set of resources, the system must determine whether the allocation of these resources will leave the system in a safe state. If it will, the resources are allocated; otherwise, the process must wait until some other process releases enough resources.

Several data structures must be maintained to implement the banker's algorithm. These data structures encode the state of the resource-allocation system. We need the following data structures, where n is the number of processes in the system and m is the number of resource types:

- **Available**. A vector of length m indicates the number of available resources of each type. If *Available*[*j*] equals *k*, then *k* instances of resource type R_j are available.

- **Max**. An $n \times m$ matrix defines the maximum demand of each process. If *Max*[*i*][*j*] equals *k*, then process P_i may request at most *k* instances of resource type R_j.

- **Allocation**. An $n \times m$ matrix defines the number of resources of each type currently allocated to each process. If *Allocation*[*i*][*j*] equals *k*, then process P_i is currently allocated *k* instances of resource type R_j.

- **Need**. An $n \times m$ matrix indicates the remaining resource need of each process. If *Need*[*i*][*j*] equals *k*, then process P_i may need *k* more instances of resource type R_j to complete its task. Note that *Need*[*i*][*j*] equals *Max*[*i*][*j*] – *Allocation*[*i*][*j*].

These data structures vary over time in both size and value.

To simplify the presentation of the banker's algorithm, we next establish some notation. Let X and Y be vectors of length n. We say that $X \leq Y$ if and only if $X[i] \leq Y[i]$ for all $i = 1, 2, ..., n$. For example, if $X = (1,7,3,2)$ and $Y = (0,3,2,1)$, then $Y \leq X$. In addition, $Y < X$ if $Y \leq X$ and $Y \neq X$.

We can treat each row in the matrices *Allocation* and *Need* as vectors and refer to them as $Allocation_i$ and $Need_i$. The vector $Allocation_i$ specifies the resources currently allocated to process P_i; the vector $Need_i$ specifies the additional resources that process P_i may still request to complete its task.

7.5.3.1 Safety Algorithm

We can now present the algorithm for finding out whether or not a system is in a safe state. This algorithm can be described as follows:

1. Let *Work* and *Finish* be vectors of length m and n, respectively. Initialize *Work* = *Available* and *Finish*[*i*] = *false* for $i = 0, 1, \ldots, n-1$.

2. Find an index i such that both

   a. *Finish*[*i*] == *false*

   b. $Need_i \leq Work$

   If no such i exists, go to step 4.

3. $Work = Work + Allocation_i$
   Finish[*i*] = *true*
   Go to step 2.

4. If *Finish*[*i*] == *true* for all i, then the system is in a safe state.

This algorithm may require an order of $m \times n^2$ operations to determine whether a state is safe.

7.5.3.2 Resource-Request Algorithm

Next, we describe the algorithm for determining whether requests can be safely granted.

Let $Request_i$ be the request vector for process P_i. If $Request_i\,[j] == k$, then process P_i wants k instances of resource type R_j. When a request for resources is made by process P_i, the following actions are taken:

1. If $Request_i \leq Need_i$, go to step 2. Otherwise, raise an error condition, since the process has exceeded its maximum claim.

2. If $Request_i \leq Available$, go to step 3. Otherwise, P_i must wait, since the resources are not available.

3. Have the system pretend to have allocated the requested resources to process P_i by modifying the state as follows:

$$Available = Available - Request_i;$$
$$Allocation_i = Allocation_i + Request_i;$$
$$Need_i = Need_i - Request_i;$$

   If the resulting resource-allocation state is safe, the transaction is completed, and process P_i is allocated its resources. However, if the new state is unsafe, then P_i must wait for $Request_i$, and the old resource-allocation state is restored.

7.5.3.3 An Illustrative Example

To illustrate the use of the banker's algorithm, consider a system with five processes P_0 through P_4 and three resource types *A*, *B*, and *C*. Resource type *A* has ten instances, resource type *B* has five instances, and resource type *C* has seven instances. Suppose that, at time T_0, the following snapshot of the system has been taken:

	Allocation	Max	Available
	A B C	A B C	A B C
P_0	0 1 0	7 5 3	3 3 2
P_1	2 0 0	3 2 2	
P_2	3 0 2	9 0 2	
P_3	2 1 1	2 2 2	
P_4	0 0 2	4 3 3	

The content of the matrix *Need* is defined to be *Max* − *Allocation* and is as follows:

	Need
	A B C
P_0	7 4 3
P_1	1 2 2
P_2	6 0 0
P_3	0 1 1
P_4	4 3 1

We claim that the system is currently in a safe state. Indeed, the sequence $<P_1, P_3, P_4, P_2, P_0>$ satisfies the safety criteria. Suppose now that process P_1 requests one additional instance of resource type A and two instances of resource type C, so $Request_1 = (1,0,2)$. To decide whether this request can be immediately granted, we first check that $Request_1 \leq Available$—that is, that $(1,0,2) \leq (3,3,2)$, which is true. We then pretend that this request has been fulfilled, and we arrive at the following new state:

	Allocation	Need	Available
	A B C	A B C	A B C
P_0	0 1 0	7 4 3	2 3 0
P_1	3 0 2	0 2 0	
P_2	3 0 2	6 0 0	
P_3	2 1 1	0 1 1	
P_4	0 0 2	4 3 1	

We must determine whether this new system state is safe. To do so, we execute our safety algorithm and find that the sequence $<P_1, P_3, P_4, P_0, P_2>$ satisfies the safety requirement. Hence, we can immediately grant the request of process P_1.

You should be able to see, however, that when the system is in this state, a request for (3,3,0) by P_4 cannot be granted, since the resources are not available. Furthermore, a request for (0,2,0) by P_0 cannot be granted, even though the resources are available, since the resulting state is unsafe.

We leave it as a programming exercise for students to implement the banker's algorithm.

7.6 Deadlock Detection

If a system does not employ either a deadlock-prevention or a deadlock-avoidance algorithm, then a deadlock situation may occur. In this environment, the system may provide:

- An algorithm that examines the state of the system to determine whether a deadlock has occurred
- An algorithm to recover from the deadlock

In the following discussion, we elaborate on these two requirements as they pertain to systems with only a single instance of each resource type, as well as to systems with several instances of each resource type. At this point, however, we note that a detection-and-recovery scheme requires overhead that includes not only the run-time costs of maintaining the necessary information and executing the detection algorithm but also the potential losses inherent in recovering from a deadlock.

7.6.1 Single Instance of Each Resource Type

If all resources have only a single instance, then we can define a deadlock-detection algorithm that uses a variant of the resource-allocation graph, called a *wait-for* graph. We obtain this graph from the resource-allocation graph by removing the resource nodes and collapsing the appropriate edges.

More precisely, an edge from P_i to P_j in a wait-for graph implies that process P_i is waiting for process P_j to release a resource that P_i needs. An edge $P_i \rightarrow P_j$ exists in a wait-for graph if and only if the corresponding resource-allocation graph contains two edges $P_i \rightarrow R_q$ and $R_q \rightarrow P_j$ for some resource R_q. For example, in Figure 7.8, we present a resource-allocation graph and the corresponding wait-for graph.

As before, a deadlock exists in the system if and only if the wait-for graph contains a cycle. To detect deadlocks, the system needs to *maintain* the wait-for graph and periodically *invoke an algorithm* that searches for a cycle in the graph. An algorithm to detect a cycle in a graph requires an order of n^2 operations, where n is the number of vertices in the graph.

7.6.2 Several Instances of a Resource Type

The wait-for graph scheme is not applicable to a resource-allocation system with multiple instances of each resource type. We turn now to a deadlock-detection algorithm that is applicable to such a system. The algorithm employs several time-varying data structures that are similar to those used in the banker's algorithm (Section 7.5.3):

- **Available**. A vector of length m indicates the number of available resources of each type.
- **Allocation**. An $n \times m$ matrix defines the number of resources of each type currently allocated to each process.

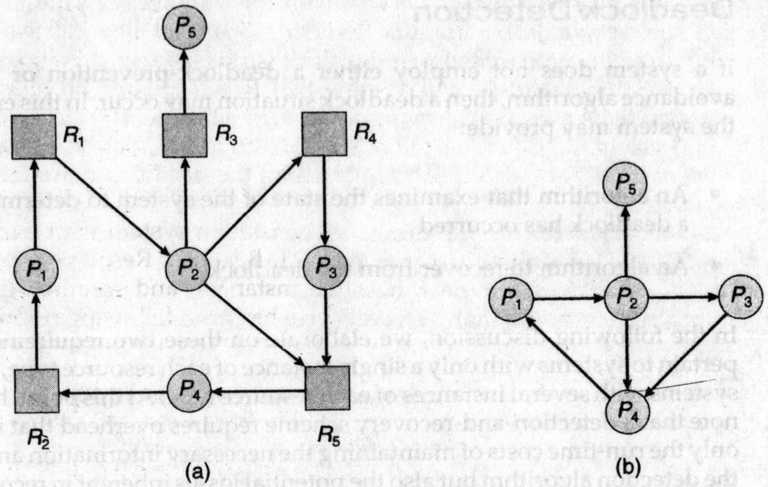

Figure 7.8 (a) Resource-allocation graph. (b) Corresponding wait-for graph.

- **Request**. An $n \times m$ matrix indicates the current request of each process. If *Request*[*i*][*j*] equals *k*, then process P_i is requesting *k* more instances of resource type R_j.

The $\leq$ relation between two vectors is defined as in Section 7.5.3. To simplify notation, we again treat the rows in the matrices *Allocation* and *Request* as vectors; we refer to them as $Allocation_i$ and $Request_i$. The detection algorithm described here simply investigates every possible allocation sequence for the processes that remain to be completed. Compare this algorithm with the banker's algorithm of Section 7.5.3.

1. Let *Work* and *Finish* be vectors of length *m* and *n*, respectively. Initialize *Work* = *Available*. For *i* = 0, 1, ..., *n*-1, if $Allocation_i \neq 0$, then *Finish*[*i*] = *false*; otherwise, *Finish*[*i*] = *true*.
2. Find an index *i* such that both
   a. *Finish*[*i*] == *false*
   b. $Request_i \leq Work$

   If no such *i* exists, go to step 4.
3. *Work* = *Work* + $Allocation_i$
   Finish[*i*] = *true*
   Go to step 2.
4. If *Finish*[*i*] == *false* for some *i*, $0 \leq i < n$, then the system is in a deadlocked state. Moreover, if *Finish*[*i*] == *false*, then process P_i is deadlocked.

This algorithm requires an order of $m \times n^2$ operations to detect whether the system is in a deadlocked state.

You may wonder why we reclaim the resources of process P_i (in step 3) as soon as we determine that $Request_i \leq Work$ (in step 2b). We know that P_i is currently *not* involved in a deadlock (since $Request_i \leq Work$). Thus, we take an optimistic attitude and assume that P_i will require no more resources to complete its task; it will thus soon return all currently allocated resources to the system. If our assumption is incorrect, a deadlock may occur later. That deadlock will be detected the next time the deadlock-detection algorithm is invoked.

To illustrate this algorithm, we consider a system with five processes P_0 through P_4 and three resource types *A, B,* and *C*. Resource type *A* has seven instances, resource type *B* has two instances, and resource type *C* has six instances. Suppose that, at time T_0, we have the following resource-allocation state:

	Allocation	*Request*	*Available*
	A B C	*A B C*	*A B C*
P_0	0 1 0	0 0 0	0 0 0
P_1	2 0 0	2 0 2	
P_2	3 0 3	0 0 0	
P_3	2 1 1	1 0 0	
P_4	0 0 2	0 0 2	

We claim that the system is not in a deadlocked state. Indeed, if we execute our algorithm, we will find that the sequence $<P_0, P_2, P_3, P_1, P_4>$ results in *Finish*[*i*] == *true* for all *i*.

Suppose now that process P_2 makes one additional request for an instance of type *C*. The *Request* matrix is modified as follows:

	Request
	A B C
P_0	0 0 0
P_1	2 0 2
P_2	0 0 1
P_3	1 0 0
P_4	0 0 2

We claim that the system is now deadlocked. Although we can reclaim the resources held by process P_0, the number of available resources is not sufficient to fulfill the requests of the other processes. Thus, a deadlock exists, consisting of processes P_1, P_2, P_3, and P_4.

7.6.3 Detection-Algorithm Usage

When should we invoke the detection algorithm? The answer depends on two factors:

1. How *often* is a deadlock likely to occur?
2. How *many* processes will be affected by deadlock when it happens?

If deadlocks occur frequently, then the detection algorithm should be invoked frequently. Resources allocated to deadlocked processes will be idle until the deadlock can be broken. In addition, the number of processes involved in the deadlock cycle may grow.

Deadlocks occur only when some process makes a request that cannot be granted immediately. This request may be the final request that completes a chain of waiting processes. In the extreme, then, we can invoke the deadlock-detection algorithm every time a request for allocation cannot be granted immediately. In this case, we can identify not only the deadlocked set of processes but also the specific process that "caused" the deadlock. (In reality, each of the deadlocked processes is a link in the cycle in the resource graph, so all of them, jointly, caused the deadlock.) If there are many different resource types, one request may create many cycles in the resource graph, each cycle completed by the most recent request and "caused" by the one identifiable process.

Of course, invoking the deadlock-detection algorithm for every resource request will incur considerable overhead in computation time. A less expensive alternative is simply to invoke the algorithm at defined intervals—for example, once per hour or whenever CPU utilization drops below 40 percent. (A deadlock eventually cripples system throughput and causes CPU utilization to drop.) If the detection algorithm is invoked at arbitrary points in time, the resource graph may contain many cycles. In this case, we generally cannot tell which of the many deadlocked processes "caused" the deadlock.

7.7 Recovery from Deadlock

When a detection algorithm determines that a deadlock exists, several alternatives are available. One possibility is to inform the operator that a deadlock has occurred and to let the operator deal with the deadlock manually. Another possibility is to let the system *recover* from the deadlock automatically. There are two options for breaking a deadlock. One is simply to abort one or more processes to break the circular wait. The other is to preempt some resources from one or more of the deadlocked processes.

7.7.1 Process Termination

To eliminate deadlocks by aborting a process, we use one of two methods. In both methods, the system reclaims all resources allocated to the terminated processes.

- **Abort all deadlocked processes.** This method clearly will break the deadlock cycle, but at great expense; the deadlocked processes may have computed for a long time, and the results of these partial computations must be discarded and probably will have to be recomputed later.
- **Abort one process at a time until the deadlock cycle is eliminated.** This method incurs considerable overhead, since after each process is aborted, a deadlock-detection algorithm must be invoked to determine whether any processes are still deadlocked.

Aborting a process may not be easy. If the process was in the midst of updating a file, terminating it will leave that file in an incorrect state. Similarly, if the process was in the midst of printing data on a printer, the system must reset the printer to a correct state before printing the next job.

If the partial termination method is used, then we must determine which deadlocked process (or processes) should be terminated. This determination is a policy decision, similar to CPU-scheduling decisions. The question is basically an economic one; we should abort those processes whose termination will incur the minimum cost. Unfortunately, the term *minimum cost* is not a precise one. Many factors may affect which process is chosen, including:

1. What the priority of the process is
2. How long the process has computed and how much longer the process will compute before completing its designated task
3. How many and what types of resources the process has used (for example, whether the resources are simple to preempt)
4. How many more resources the process needs in order to complete
5. How many processes will need to be terminated
6. Whether the process is interactive or batch

7.7.2 Resource Preemption

To eliminate deadlocks using resource preemption, we successively preempt some resources from processes and give these resources to other processes until the deadlock cycle is broken.

If preemption is required to deal with deadlocks, then three issues need to be addressed:

1. **Selecting a victim**. Which resources and which processes are to be preempted? As in process termination, we must determine the order of preemption to minimize cost. Cost factors may include such parameters as the number of resources a deadlocked process is holding and the amount of time the process has thus far consumed during its execution.

2. **Rollback**. If we preempt a resource from a process, what should be done with that process? Clearly, it cannot continue with its normal execution; it is missing some needed resource. We must roll back the process to some safe state and restart it from that state.

   Since, in general, it is difficult to determine what a safe state is, the simplest solution is a total rollback: abort the process and then restart it. Although it is more effective to roll back the process only as far as necessary to break the deadlock, this method requires the system to keep more information about the state of all running processes.

3. **Starvation**. How do we ensure that starvation will not occur? That is, how can we guarantee that resources will not always be preempted from the same process?

In a system where victim selection is based primarily on cost factors, it may happen that the same process is always picked as a victim. As a result, this process never completes its designated task, a starvation situation that must be dealt with in any practical system. Clearly, we must ensure that a process can be picked as a victim only a (small) finite number of times. The most common solution is to include the number of rollbacks in the cost factor.

7.8 Summary

A deadlocked state occurs when two or more processes are waiting indefinitely for an event that can be caused only by one of the waiting processes. There are three principal methods for dealing with deadlocks:

- Use some protocol to prevent or avoid deadlocks, ensuring that the system will never enter a deadlocked state.
- Allow the system to enter a deadlocked state, detect it, and then recover.
- Ignore the problem altogether and pretend that deadlocks never occur in the system.

The third solution is the one used by most operating systems, including UNIX and Windows.

A deadlock can occur only if four necessary conditions hold simultaneously in the system: mutual exclusion, hold and wait, no preemption, and circular wait. To prevent deadlocks, we can ensure that at least one of the necessary conditions never holds.

A method for avoiding deadlocks, rather than preventing them, requires that the operating system have a priori information about how each process will utilize system resources. The banker's algorithm, for example, requires a priori information about the maximum number of each resource class that each process may request. Using this information, we can define a deadlock-avoidance algorithm.

If a system does not employ a protocol to ensure that deadlocks will never occur, then a detection-and-recovery scheme may be employed. A deadlock-detection algorithm must be invoked to determine whether a deadlock has occurred. If a deadlock is detected, the system must recover either by terminating some of the deadlocked processes or by preempting resources from some of the deadlocked processes.

Where preemption is used to deal with deadlocks, three issues must be addressed: selecting a victim, rollback, and starvation. In a system that selects victims for rollback primarily on the basis of cost factors, starvation may occur, and the selected process can never complete its designated task.

Researchers have argued that none of the basic approaches alone is appropriate for the entire spectrum of resource-allocation problems in operating systems. The basic approaches can be combined, however, allowing us to select an optimal approach for each class of resources in a system.

Exercises

7.1 A single-lane bridge connects the two Vermont villages of North Tunbridge and South Tunbridge. Farmers in the two villages use this bridge to deliver their produce to the neighboring town. The bridge can become deadlocked if a northbound and a southbound farmer get on the bridge at the same time (Vermont farmers are stubborn and are unable to back up.) Using semaphores, design an algorithm that prevents deadlock. Initially, do not be concerned about starvation (the situation in which northbound farmers prevent southbound farmers from using the bridge, or vice versa).

7.2 Modify your solution to Exercise 7.1 so that it is starvation-free.

7.3 Consider a system consisting of four resources of the same type that are shared by three processes, each of which needs at most two resources. Show that the system is deadlock free.

7.4 Consider the traffic deadlock depicted in Figure 7.9.

a. Show that the four necessary conditions for deadlock hold in this example.

b. State a simple rule for avoiding deadlocks in this system.

7.5 In a real computer system, neither the resources available nor the demands of processes for resources are consistent over long periods (months). Resources break or are replaced, new processes come and go, and new resources are bought and added to the system. If deadlock is controlled by the banker's algorithm, which of the following changes

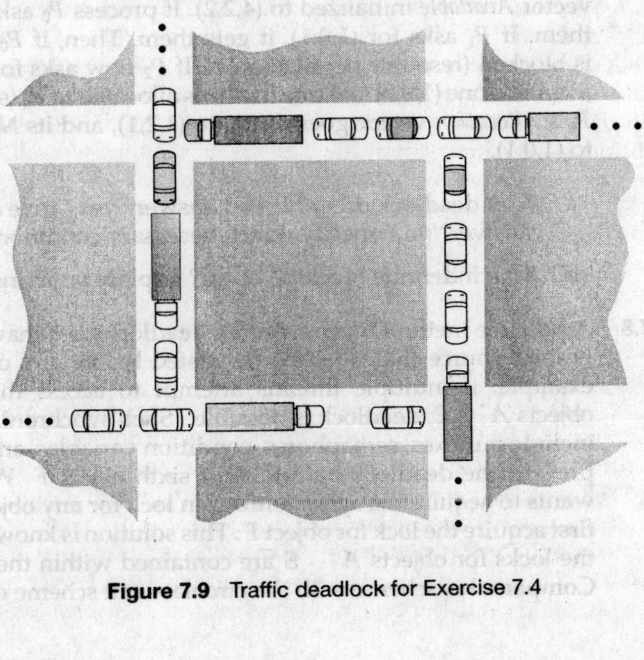

Figure 7.9 Traffic deadlock for Exercise 7.4

can be made safely (without introducing the possibility of deadlock), and under what circumstances?

a. Increase *Available* (new resources added).

b. Decrease *Available* (resource permanently removed from system).

c. Increase *Max* for one process (the process needs or wants more resources than allowed).

d. Decrease *Max* for one process (the process decides it does not need that many resources).

e. Increase the number of processes.

f. Decrease the number of processes.

7.6 We can obtain the banker's algorithm for a single resource type from the general banker's algorithm simply by reducing the dimensionality of the various arrays by 1. Show through an example that we cannot implement the multiple-resource-type banker's scheme by applying the single-resource-type scheme to each resource type individually.

7.7 Consider the following resource-allocation policy. Requests for and releases of resources are allowed at any time. If a request for resources cannot be satisfied because the resources are not available, then we check any processes that are blocked waiting for resources. If a blocked process has the desired resources, then these resources are taken away from it and are given to the requesting process. The vector of resources for which the blocked process is waiting is increased to include the resources that were taken away.

For example, consider a system with three resource types and the vector *Available* initialized to (4,2,2). If process P_0 asks for (2,2,1), it gets them. If P_1 asks for (1,0,1), it gets them. Then, if P_0 asks for (0,0,1), it is blocked (resource not available). If P_2 now asks for (2,0,0), it gets the available one (1,0,0) and one that was allocated to P_0 (since P_0 is blocked). P_0's *Allocation* vector goes down to (1,2,1), and its *Need* vector goes up to (1,0,1).

a. Can deadlock occur? If you answer "yes," give an example. If you answer "no," specify which necessary condition cannot occur.

b. Can indefinite blocking occur? Explain your answer.

7.8 A possible method for preventing deadlocks is to have a single, higher-order resource that must be requested before any other resource. For example, if multiple threads attempt to access the synchronization objects $A \cdots E$, deadlock is possible. (Such synchronization objects may include mutexes, semaphores, condition variables, and the like.) We can prevent the deadlock by adding a sixth object F. Whenever a thread wants to acquire the synchronization lock for any object $A \cdots E$, it must first acquire the lock for object F. This solution is known as **containment**: the locks for objects $A \cdots E$ are contained within the lock for object F. Compare this scheme with the circular-wait scheme of Section 7.4.4.

7.9 Compare the circular-wait scheme with the various deadlock-avoidance schemes (like the banker's algorithm) with respect to the following issues:

a. Runtime overheads

b. System throughput

7.10 Consider the following snapshot of a system:

	Allocation	*Max*	*Available*
	A B C D	*A B C D*	*A B C D*
P_0	0 0 1 2	0 0 1 2	1 5 2 0
P_1	1 0 0 0	1 7 5 0	
P_2	1 3 5 4	2 3 5 6	
P_3	0 6 3 2	0 6 5 2	
P_4	0 0 1 4	0 6 5 6	

Answer the following questions using the banker's algorithm:

a. What is the content of the matrix *Need*?

b. Is the system in a safe state?

c. If a request from process P_1 arrives for (0,4,2,0), can the request be granted immediately?

7.11 Consider a system consisting of m resources of the same type being shared by n processes. A process can request or release only one resource at a time. Show that the system is deadlock free if the following two conditions hold:

a. The maximum need of each process is between one resource and m resources.

b. The sum of all maximum needs is less than $m + n$.

7.12 Consider a computer system that runs 5,000 jobs per month and has no deadlock-prevention or deadlock-avoidance scheme. Deadlocks occur about twice per month, and the operator must terminate and rerun about 10 jobs per deadlock. Each job is worth about $2 (in CPU time), and the jobs terminated tend to be about half-done when they are aborted.

A systems programmer has estimated that a deadlock-avoidance algorithm (like the banker's algorithm) could be installed in the system with an increase in the average execution time per job of about 10 percent. Since the machine currently has 30 percent idle time, all 5,000 jobs per month could still be run, although turnaround time would increase by about 20 percent on average.

a. What are the arguments for installing the deadlock-avoidance algorithm?

b. What are the arguments against installing the deadlock-avoidance algorithm?

7.13 Consider the deadlock situation that can occur in the dining-philosophers problem when the philosophers obtain the chopsticks one at a time. Discuss how the four necessary conditions for deadlock hold in this setting. Discuss how deadlocks could be avoided by eliminating any one of the four necessary conditions.

7.14 What is the optimistic assumption made in the deadlock-detection algorithm? How can this assumption be violated?

7.15 Consider the version of the dining-philosophers problem in which the chopsticks are placed at the center of the table and any two of them can be used by a philosopher. Assume that requests for chopsticks are made one at a time. Describe a simple rule for determining whether a particular request can be satisfied without causing deadlock given the current allocation of chopsticks to philosophers.

7.16 Is it possible to have a deadlock involving only a single process? Explain your answer.

7.17 Consider again the setting in the preceding question. Assume now that each philosopher requires three chopsticks to eat. Resource requests are still issued one at a time. Describe some simple rules for determining whether a particular request can be satisfied without causing deadlock given the current allocation of chopsticks to philosophers.

7.18 In Section 7.4.4, we describe a situation in which we prevent deadlock by ensuring that all locks are acquired in a certain order. However, we also point out that deadlock is possible in this situation if two threads simultaneously invoke the `transaction()` function. Fix the `transaction()` function to prevent deadlocks.

Programming Problems

7.19 Write a multithreaded program that implements the banker's algorithm discussed in Section 7.5.3. Create *n* threads that request and release resources from the bank. The banker will grant the request only if it leaves the system in a safe state. You may write this program using either Pthreads or Win32 threads. It is important that shared data be safe from concurrent access. To ensure safe access to shared data, you can use mutex locks, which are available in both the Pthreads and Win32 APIs. The use of mutex locks in both of these libraries is described in the project entitled "Producer–Consumer Problem" at the end of Chapter 6.

Bibliographical Notes

Dijkstra [1965a] was one of the first and most influential contributors in the deadlock area. Holt [1972] was the first person to formalize the notion of deadlocks in terms of an allocation-graph model similar to the one presented in this chapter. Starvation was also covered by Holt [1972]. Hyman [1985] provided the deadlock example from the Kansas legislature. A recent study of deadlock handling is provided in Levine [2003].

The various prevention algorithms were suggested by Havender [1968], who devised the resource-ordering scheme for the IBM OS/360 system.

The banker's algorithm for avoiding deadlocks was developed for a single resource type by Dijkstra [1965a] and was extended to multiple resource types by Habermann [1969]. Exercises 7.3 and 7.11 are from Holt [1971].

The deadlock-detection algorithm for multiple instances of a resource type, which is described in Section 7.6.2, was presented by Coffman et al. [1971].

Bach [1987] describes how many of the algorithms in the traditional UNIX kernel handle deadlock. Solutions to deadlock problems in networks are discussed in works such as Culler et al. [1998] and Rodeheffer and Schroeder [1991].

The witness lock-order verifier is presented in Baldwin [2002].

Part Four

Memory Management

The main purpose of a computer system is to execute programs. These programs, together with the data they access, must be at least partially in main memory during execution.

To improve both the utilization of the CPU and the speed of its response to users, a general-purpose computer must keep several processes in memory. Many memory-management schemes exist, reflecting various approaches, and the effectiveness of each algorithm depends on the situation. Selection of a memory-management scheme for a system depends on many factors, especially on the *hardware* design of the system. Most algorithms require hardware support.

Memory Management Strategies

CHAPTER 8

In Chapter 5, we showed how the CPU can be shared by a set of processes. As a result of CPU scheduling, we can improve both the utilization of the CPU and the speed of the computer's response to its users. To realize this increase in performance, however, we must keep several processes in memory; that is, we must *share* memory.

In this chapter, we discuss various ways to manage memory. The memory-management algorithms vary from a primitive bare-machine approach to paging and segmentation strategies. Each approach has its own advantages and disadvantages. Selection of a memory-management method for a specific system depends on many factors, especially on the *hardware* design of the system. As we shall see, many algorithms require hardware support, although recent designs have closely integrated the hardware and operating system.

CHAPTER OBJECTIVES

- To provide a detailed description of various ways of organizing memory hardware.
- To discuss various memory-management techniques, including paging and segmentation.
- To provide a detailed description of the Intel Pentium, which supports both pure segmentation and segmentation with paging.

8.1 Background

As we saw in Chapter 1, memory is central to the operation of a modern computer system. Memory consists of a large array of words or bytes, each with its own address. The CPU fetches instructions from memory according to the value of the program counter. These instructions may cause additional loading from and storing to specific memory addresses.

A typical instruction-execution cycle, for example, first fetches an instruction from memory. The instruction is then decoded and may cause operands to be fetched from memory. After the instruction has been executed on the operands, results may be stored back in memory. The memory unit sees only a stream of memory addresses; it does not know how they are generated (by the instruction counter, indexing, indirection, literal addresses, and so on) or what they are for (instructions or data). Accordingly, we can ignore *how* a program generates a memory address. We are interested only in the sequence of memory addresses generated by the running program.

We begin our discussion by covering several issues that are pertinent to the various techniques for managing memory. This coverage includes an overview of basic hardware issues, the binding of symbolic memory addresses to actual physical addresses, and the distinction between logical and physical addresses. We conclude the section with a discussion of dynamically loading and linking code and shared libraries.

8.1.1 Basic Hardware

Main memory and the registers built into the processor itself are the only storage that the CPU can access directly. There are machine instructions that take memory addresses as arguments, but none that take disk addresses. Therefore, any instructions in execution, and any data being used by the instructions, must be in one of these direct-access storage devices. If the data are not in memory, they must be moved there before the CPU can operate on them.

Registers that are built into the CPU are generally accessible within one cycle of the CPU clock. Most CPUs can decode instructions and perform simple operations on register contents at the rate of one or more operations per clock tick. The same cannot be said of main memory, which is accessed via a transaction on the memory bus. Completing a memory access may take many cycles of the CPU clock. In such cases, the processor normally needs to stall, since it does not have the data required to complete the instruction that it is executing. This situation is intolerable because of the frequency of memory accesses. The remedy is to add fast memory between the CPU and

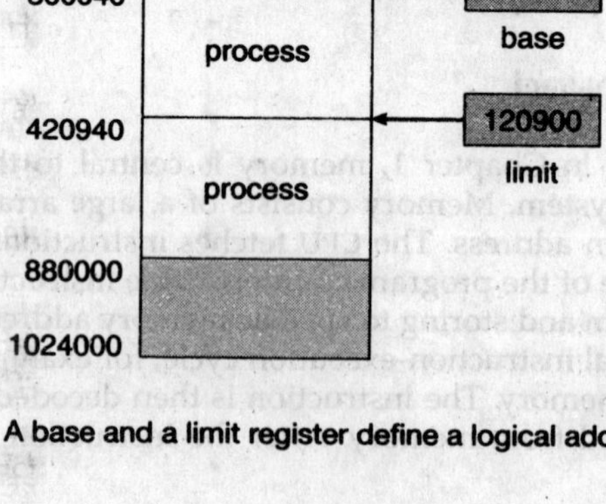

Figure 8.1 A base and a limit register define a logical address space.

main memory. A memory buffer used to accommodate a speed differential, called a **cache**, is described in Section 1.8.3.

Not only are we concerned with the relative speed of accessing physical memory, but we also must ensure correct operation to protect the operating system from access by user processes and, in addition, to protect user processes from one another. This protection must be provided by the hardware. It can be implemented in several ways, as we shall see throughout the chapter. In this section, we outline one possible implementation.

We first need to make sure that each process has a separate memory space. To do this, we need the ability to determine the range of legal addresses that the process may access and to ensure that the process can access only these legal addresses. We can provide this protection by using two registers, usually a base and a limit, as illustrated in Figure 8.1. The **base register** holds the smallest legal physical memory address; the **limit register** specifies the size of the range. For example, if the base register holds 300040 and the limit register is 120900, then the program can legally access all addresses from 300040 through 420939 (inclusive).

Protection of memory space is accomplished by having the CPU hardware compare *every* address generated in user mode with the registers. Any attempt by a program executing in user mode to access operating-system memory or other users' memory results in a trap to the operating system, which treats the attempt as a fatal error (Figure 8.2). This scheme prevents a user program from (accidentally or deliberately) modifying the code or data structures of either the operating system or other users.

The base and limit registers can be loaded only by the operating system, which uses a special privileged instruction. Since privileged instructions can be executed only in kernel mode, and since only the operating system executes in kernel mode, only the operating system can load the base and limit registers. This scheme allows the operating system to change the value of the registers but prevents user programs from changing the registers' contents.

The operating system, executing in kernel mode, is given unrestricted access to both operating system memory and users' memory. This provision allows the operating system to load users' programs into users' memory, to

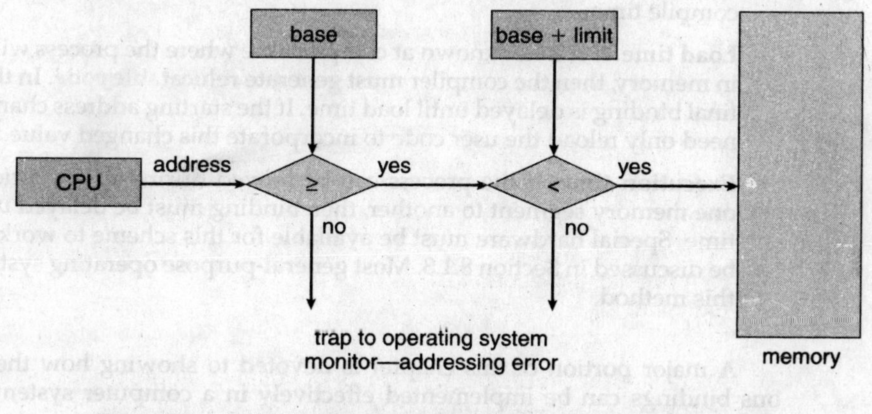

Figure 8.2 Hardware address protection with base and limit registers.

dump out those programs in case of errors, to access and modify parameters of system calls, and so on.

8.1.2 Address Binding

Usually, a program resides on a disk as a binary executable file. To be executed, the program must be brought into memory and placed within a process. Depending on the memory management in use, the process may be moved between disk and memory during its execution. The processes on the disk that are waiting to be brought into memory for execution form the **input queue**.

The normal procedure is to select one of the processes in the input queue and to load that process into memory. As the process is executed, it accesses instructions and data from memory. Eventually, the process terminates, and its memory space is declared available.

Most systems allow a user process to reside in any part of the physical memory. Thus, although the address space of the computer starts at 00000, the first address of the user process need not be 00000. This approach affects the addresses that the user program can use. In most cases, a user program will go through several steps—some of which may be optional—before being executed (Figure 8.3). Addresses may be represented in different ways during these steps. Addresses in the source program are generally symbolic (such as *count*). A compiler will typically **bind** these symbolic addresses to relocatable addresses (such as "14 bytes from the beginning of this module"). The linkage editor or loader will in turn bind the relocatable addresses to absolute addresses (such as 74014). Each binding is a mapping from one address space to another.

Classically, the binding of instructions and data to memory addresses can be done at any step along the way:

- **Compile time**. If you know at compile time where the process will reside in memory, then **absolute code** can be generated. For example, if you know that a user process will reside starting at location *R*, then the generated compiler code will start at that location and extend up from there. If, at some later time, the starting location changes, then it will be necessary to recompile this code. The MS-DOS .COM-format programs are bound at compile time.

- **Load time**. If it is not known at compile time where the process will reside in memory, then the compiler must generate **relocatable code**. In this case, final binding is delayed until load time. If the starting address changes, we need only reload the user code to incorporate this changed value.

- **Execution time**. If the process can be moved during its execution from one memory segment to another, then binding must be delayed until run time. Special hardware must be available for this scheme to work, as will be discussed in Section 8.1.3. Most general-purpose operating systems use this method.

A major portion of this chapter is devoted to showing how these various bindings can be implemented effectively in a computer system and to discussing appropriate hardware support.

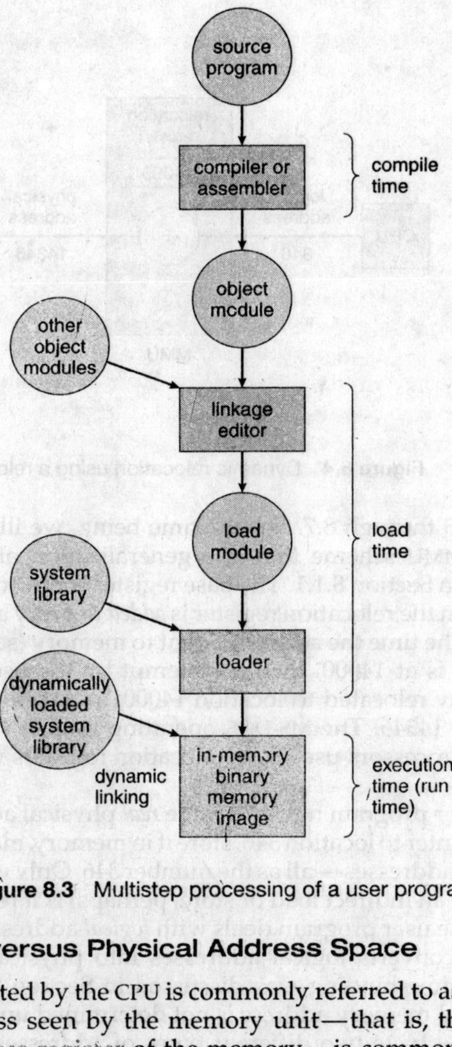

Figure 8.3 Multistep processing of a user program.

8.1.3 Logical versus Physical Address Space

An address generated by the CPU is commonly referred to as a **logical address**, whereas an address seen by the memory unit—that is, the one loaded into the **memory-address register** of the memory—is commonly referred to as a **physical address**.

The compile-time and load-time address-binding methods generate identical logical and physical addresses. However, the execution-time address-binding scheme results in differing logical and physical addresses. In this case, we usually refer to the logical address as a **virtual address**. We use *logical address* and *virtual address* interchangeably in this text. The set of all logical addresses generated by a program is a **logical address space**; the set of all physical addresses corresponding to these logical addresses is a **physical address space**. Thus, in the execution-time address-binding scheme, the logical and physical address spaces differ.

The run-time mapping from virtual to physical addresses is done by a hardware device called the **memory-management unit** (**MMU**). We can choose from many different methods to accomplish such mapping, as we discuss in

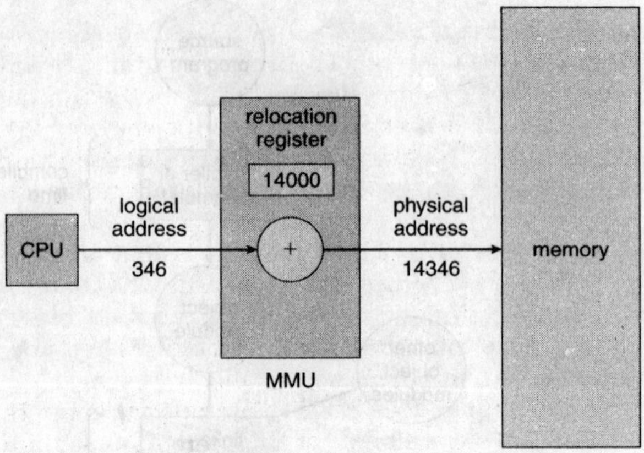

Figure 8.4 Dynamic relocation using a relocation register.

Sections 8.3 through 8.7. For the time being, we illustrate this mapping with a simple MMU scheme that is a generalization of the base-register scheme described in Section 8.1.1. The base register is now called a **relocation register**. The value in the relocation register is *added* to every address generated by a user process at the time the address is sent to memory (see Figure 8.4). For example, if the base is at 14000, then an attempt by the user to address location 0 is dynamically relocated to location 14000; an access to location 346 is mapped to location 14346. The MS-DOS operating system running on the Intel 80x86 family of processors used four relocation registers when loading and running processes.

The user program never sees the *real* physical addresses. The program can create a pointer to location 346, store it in memory, manipulate it, and compare it with other addresses—all as the number 346. Only when it is used as a memory address (in an indirect load or store, perhaps) is it relocated relative to the base register. The user program deals with *logical* addresses. The memory-mapping hardware converts logical addresses into physical addresses. This form of execution-time binding was discussed in Section 8.1.2. The final location of a referenced memory address is not determined until the reference is made.

We now have two different types of addresses: logical addresses (in the range 0 to *max*) and physical addresses (in the range $R + 0$ to $R + max$ for a base value R). The user generates only logical addresses and thinks that the process runs in locations 0 to *max*. The user program generates only logical addresses and thinks that the process runs in locations 0 to *max*. However, these logical addresses must be mapped to physical addresses before they are used.

The concept of a *logical address space* that is bound to a separate *physical address space* is central to proper memory management.

8.1.4 Dynamic Loading

In our discussion so far, it has been necessary for the entire program and all data of a process to be in physical memory for the process to execute. The size of a process has thus been limited to the size of physical memory. To obtain better memory-space utilization, we can use **dynamic loading**. With dynamic loading, a routine is not loaded until it is called. All routines are kept on disk in a relocatable load format. The main program is loaded into memory and is executed. When a routine needs to call another routine, the calling routine first checks to see whether the other routine has been loaded. If it has not, the relocatable linking loader is called to load the desired routine into memory and to update the program's address tables to reflect this change. Then control is passed to the newly loaded routine.

The advantage of dynamic loading is that an unused routine is never loaded. This method is particularly useful when large amounts of code are needed to handle infrequently occurring cases, such as error routines. In this case, although the total program size may be large, the portion that is used (and hence loaded) may be much smaller.

Dynamic loading does not require special support from the operating system. It is the responsibility of the users to design their programs to take advantage of such a method. Operating systems may help the programmer, however, by providing library routines to implement dynamic loading.

8.1.5 Dynamic Linking and Shared Libraries

Figure 8.3 also shows **dynamically linked libraries**. Some operating systems support only **static linking**, in which system language libraries are treated like any other object module and are combined by the loader into the binary program image. Dynamic linking, in contrast, is similar to dynamic loading. Here, though, linking, rather than loading, is postponed until execution time. This feature is usually used with system libraries, such as language subroutine libraries. Without this facility, each program on a system must include a copy of its language library (or at least the routines referenced by the program) in the executable image. This requirement wastes both disk space and main memory.

With dynamic linking, a *stub* is included in the image for each library-routine reference. The stub is a small piece of code that indicates how to locate the appropriate memory-resident library routine or how to load the library if the routine is not already present. When the stub is executed, it checks to see whether the needed routine is already in memory. If it is not, the program loads the routine into memory. Either way, the stub replaces itself with the address of the routine and executes the routine. Thus, the next time that particular code segment is reached, the library routine is executed directly, incurring no cost for dynamic linking. Under this scheme, all processes that use a language library execute only one copy of the library code.

This feature can be extended to library updates (such as bug fixes). A library may be replaced by a new version, and all programs that reference the library will automatically use the new version. Without dynamic linking, all such programs would need to be relinked to gain access to the new library. So that programs will not accidentally execute new, incompatible versions of libraries, version information is included in both the program and the library. More than one version of a library may be loaded into memory, and each program uses its version information to decide which copy of the library to use. Versions with minor changes retain the same version number, whereas versions with major changes increment the number. Thus, only programs that are compiled with the new library version are affected by any incompatible changes incorporated in it. Other programs linked before the new library was installed will continue using the older library. This system is also known as **shared libraries**.

Unlike dynamic loading, dynamic linking generally requires help from the operating system. If the processes in memory are protected from one another, then the operating system is the only entity that can check to see whether the needed routine is in another process's memory space or that can allow multiple processes to access the same memory addresses. We elaborate on this concept when we discuss paging in Section 8.4.4.

8.2 Swapping

A process must be in memory to be executed. A process, however, can be **swapped** temporarily out of memory to a **backing store** and then brought back into memory for continued execution. For example, assume a multiprogramming environment with a round-robin CPU-scheduling algorithm. When a quantum expires, the memory manager will start to swap out the process that just finished and to swap another process into the memory space that has been freed (Figure 8.5). In the meantime, the CPU scheduler will allocate a time slice to some other process in memory. When each process finishes its quantum, it will be swapped with another process. Ideally, the memory manager can swap processes fast enough that some processes will be in memory, ready to execute, when the CPU scheduler wants to reschedule the CPU. In addition, the quantum must be large enough to allow reasonable amounts of computing to be done between swaps.

A variant of this swapping policy is used for priority-based scheduling algorithms. If a higher-priority process arrives and wants service, the memory manager can swap out the lower-priority process and then load and execute the higher-priority process. When the higher-priority process finishes, the

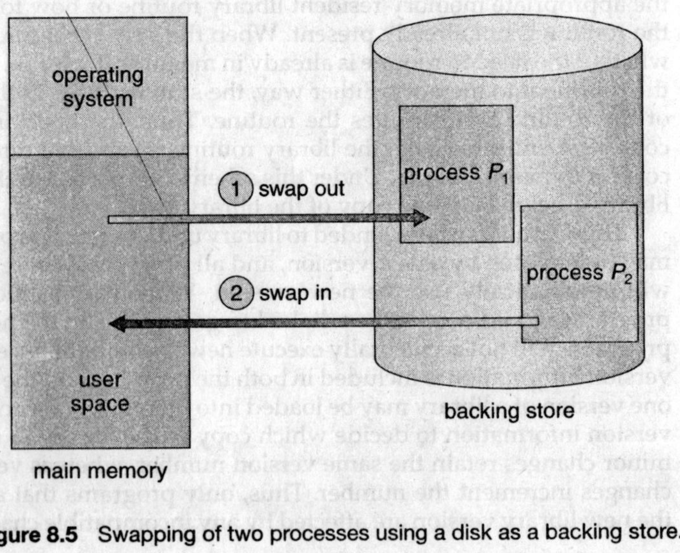

Figure 8.5 Swapping of two processes using a disk as a backing store.

lower-priority process can be swapped back in and continued. This variant of swapping is sometimes called roll out, roll in.

Normally, a process that is swapped out will be swapped back into the same memory space it occupied previously. This restriction is dictated by the method of address binding. If binding is done at assembly or load time, then the process cannot be easily moved to a different location. If execution-time binding is being used, however, then a process can be swapped into a different memory space, because the physical addresses are computed during execution time.

Swapping requires a backing store. The backing store is commonly a fast disk. It must be large enough to accommodate copies of all memory images for all users, and it must provide direct access to these memory images. The system maintains a `ready queue` consisting of all processes whose memory images are on the backing store or in memory and are ready to run. Whenever the CPU scheduler decides to execute a process, it calls the dispatcher. The dispatcher checks to see whether the next process in the queue is in memory. If it is not, and if there is no free memory region, the dispatcher swaps out a process currently in memory and swaps in the desired process. It then reloads registers and transfers control to the selected process.

The context-switch time in such a swapping system is fairly high. To get an idea of the context-switch time, let us assume that the user process is 100 MB in size and the backing store is a standard hard disk with a transfer rate of 50 MB per second. The actual transfer of the 100-MB process to or from main memory takes

$$100 \text{ MB}/50 \text{ MB per second} = 2 \text{ seconds}.$$

Assuming an average latency of 8 milliseconds, the swap time is 2008 milliseconds. Since we must both swap out and swap in, the total swap time is about 4016 milliseconds.

Notice that the major part of the swap time is transfer time. The total transfer time is directly proportional to the *amount* of memory swapped. If we have a computer system with 4 GB of main memory and a resident operating system taking 1 GB, the maximum size of the user process is 3 GB. However, many user processes may be much smaller than this—say, 100 MB. A 100-MB process could be swapped out in 2 seconds, compared with the 60 seconds required for swapping 3 GB. Clearly, it would be useful to know exactly how much memory a user process *is* using, not simply how much it *might be* using. Then we would need to swap only what is actually used, reducing swap time. For this method to be effective, the user must keep the system informed of any changes in memory requirements. Thus, a process with dynamic memory requirements will need to issue system calls (`request memory` and `release memory`) to inform the operating system of its changing memory needs.

Swapping is constrained by other factors as well. If we want to swap a process, we must be sure that it is completely idle. Of particular concern is any pending I/O. A process may be waiting for an I/O operation when we want to swap that process to free up memory. However, if the I/O is asynchronously accessing the user memory for I/O buffers, then the process cannot be swapped. Assume that the I/O operation is queued because the device is busy. If we were to swap out process P_1 and swap in process P_2, the

I/O operation might then attempt to use memory that now belongs to process P_2. There are two main solutions to this problem: never swap a process with pending I/O, or execute I/O operations only into operating-system buffers. Transfers between operating-system buffers and process memory then occur only when the process is swapped in.

The assumption, mentioned earlier, that swapping requires few, if any, head seeks needs further explanation. We postpone discussing this issue until Chapter 12, where secondary-storage structure is covered. Generally, swap space is allocated as a chunk of disk, separate from the file system, so that its use is as fast as possible.

Currently, standard swapping is used in few systems. It requires too much swapping time and provides too little execution time to be a reasonable memory-management solution. Modified versions of swapping, however, are found on many systems.

A modification of swapping is used in many versions of UNIX. Swapping is normally disabled but will start if many processes are running and are using a threshold amount of memory. Swapping is again halted when the load on the system is reduced. Memory management in UNIX is described fully in Sections 21.7 and A.6.

Early PCs—which lacked the sophistication to implement more advanced memory-management methods—ran multiple large processes by using a modified version of swapping. A prime example is the Microsoft Windows 3.1 operating system, which supports concurrent execution of processes in memory. If a new process is loaded and there is insufficient main memory, an old process is swapped to disk. This operating system does not provide full swapping, however, because the user, rather than the scheduler, decides when it is time to preempt one process for another. Any swapped-out process remains swapped out (and not executing) until the user selects that process to run. Subsequent versions of Microsoft operating systems take advantage of the advanced MMU features now found in PCs. We explore such features in Section 8.4 and in Chapter 9, where we cover virtual memory.

8.3 Contiguous Memory Allocation

The main memory must accommodate both the operating system and the various user processes. We therefore need to allocate main memory in the most efficient way possible. This section explains one common method, contiguous memory allocation.

The memory is usually divided into two partitions: one for the resident operating system and one for the user processes. We can place the operating system in either low memory or high memory. The major factor affecting this decision is the location of the interrupt vector. Since the interrupt vector is often in low memory, programmers usually place the operating system in low memory as well. Thus, in this text, we discuss only the situation in which the operating system resides in low memory. The development of the other situation is similar.

We usually want several user processes to reside in memory at the same time. We therefore need to consider how to allocate available memory to the processes that are in the input queue waiting to be brought into memory.

In **contiguous memory allocation**, each process is contained in a single contiguous section of memory.

8.3.1 Memory Mapping and Protection

Before discussing memory allocation further, we must discuss the issue of memory mapping and protection. We can provide these features by using a relocation register, as discussed in Section 8.1.3, together with a limit register, as discussed in Section 8.1.1. The relocation register contains the value of the smallest physical address; the limit register contains the range of logical addresses (for example, relocation = 100040 and limit = 74600). With relocation and limit registers, each logical address must be less than the limit register; the MMU maps the logical address *dynamically* by adding the value in the relocation register. This mapped address is sent to memory (Figure 8.6).

When the CPU scheduler selects a process for execution, the dispatcher loads the relocation and limit registers with the correct values as part of the context switch. Because every address generated by a CPU is checked against these registers, we can protect both the operating system and the other users' programs and data from being modified by this running process.

The relocation-register scheme provides an effective way to allow the operating system's size to change dynamically. This flexibility is desirable in many situations. For example, the operating system contains code and buffer space for device drivers. If a device driver (or other operating-system service) is not commonly used, we do not want to keep the code and data in memory, as we might be able to use that space for other purposes. Such code is sometimes called transient operating-system code; it comes and goes as needed. Thus, using this code changes the size of the operating system during program execution.

8.3.2 Memory Allocation

Now we are ready to turn to memory allocation. One of the simplest methods for allocating memory is to divide memory into several fixed-sized partitions. Each partition may contain exactly one process. Thus, the degree

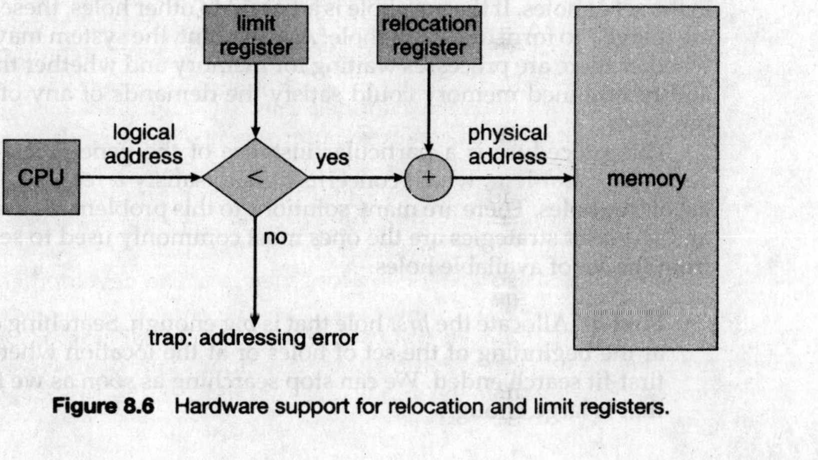

Figure 8.6 Hardware support for relocation and limit registers.

of multiprogramming is bound by the number of partitions. In this multiple-partition method, when a partition is free, a process is selected from the input queue and is loaded into the free partition. When the process terminates, the partition becomes available for another process. This method was originally used by the IBM OS/360 operating system (called MFT); it is no longer in use. The method described next is a generalization of the fixed-partition scheme (called MVT); it is used primarily in batch environments. Many of the ideas presented here are also applicable to a time-sharing environment in which pure segmentation is used for memory management (Section 8.6).

In the variable-partition scheme, the operating system keeps a table indicating which parts of memory are available and which are occupied. Initially, all memory is available for user processes and is considered one large block of available memory, a hole. Eventually, as you will see, memory contains a set of holes of various sizes.

As processes enter the system, they are put into an input queue. The operating system takes into account the memory requirements of each process and the amount of available memory space in determining which processes are allocated memory. When a process is allocated space, it is loaded into memory, and it can then compete for CPU time. When a process terminates, it releases its memory, which the operating system may then fill with another process from the input queue.

At any given time, then, we have a list of available block sizes and an input queue. The operating system can order the input queue according to a scheduling algorithm. Memory is allocated to processes until, finally, the memory requirements of the next process cannot be satisfied—that is, no available block of memory (or hole) is large enough to hold that process. The operating system can then wait until a large enough block is available, or it can skip down the input queue to see whether the smaller memory requirements of some other process can be met.

In general, as mentioned, the memory blocks available comprise a *set* of holes of various sizes scattered throughout memory. When a process arrives and needs memory, the system searches the set for a hole that is large enough for this process. If the hole is too large, it is split into two parts. One part is allocated to the arriving process; the other is returned to the set of holes. When a process terminates, it releases its block of memory, which is then placed back in the set of holes. If the new hole is adjacent to other holes, these adjacent holes are merged to form one larger hole. At this point, the system may need to check whether there are processes waiting for memory and whether this newly freed and recombined memory could satisfy the demands of any of these waiting processes.

This procedure is a particular instance of the general dynamic storage-allocation problem, which concerns how to satisfy a request of size n from a list of free holes. There are many solutions to this problem. The first-fit, best-fit, and worst-fit strategies are the ones most commonly used to select a free hole from the set of available holes.

- **First fit**. Allocate the *first* hole that is big enough. Searching can start either at the beginning of the set of holes or at the location where the previous first-fit search ended. We can stop searching as soon as we find a free hole that is large enough.

- **Best fit**. Allocate the *smallest* hole that is big enough. We must search the entire list, unless the list is ordered by size. This strategy produces the smallest leftover hole.
- **Worst fit**. Allocate the *largest* hole. Again, we must search the entire list, unless it is sorted by size. This strategy produces the largest leftover hole, which may be more useful than the smaller leftover hole from a best-fit approach.

Simulations have shown that both first fit and best fit are better than worst fit in terms of decreasing time and storage utilization. Neither first fit nor best fit is clearly better than the other in terms of storage utilization, but first fit is generally faster.

8.3.3 Fragmentation

Both the first-fit and best-fit strategies for memory allocation suffer from external fragmentation. As processes are loaded and removed from memory, the free memory space is broken into little pieces. External fragmentation exists when there is enough total memory space to satisfy a request but the available spaces are not contiguous; storage is fragmented into a large number of small holes. This fragmentation problem can be severe. In the worst case, we could have a block of free (or wasted) memory between every two processes. If all these small pieces of memory were in one big free block instead, we might be able to run several more processes.

Whether we are using the first-fit or best-fit strategy can affect the amount of fragmentation. (First fit is better for some systems, whereas best fit is better for others.) Another factor is which end of a free block is allocated. (Which is the leftover piece—the one on the top or the one on the bottom?) No matter which algorithm is used, however, external fragmentation will be a problem.

Depending on the total amount of memory storage and the average process size, external fragmentation may be a minor or a major problem. Statistical analysis of first fit, for instance, reveals that, even with some optimization, given N allocated blocks, another 0.5 N blocks will be lost to fragmentation. That is, one-third of memory may be unusable! This property is known as the 50-percent rule.

Memory fragmentation can be internal as well as external. Consider a multiple-partition allocation scheme with a hole of 18,464 bytes. Suppose that the next process requests 18,462 bytes. If we allocate exactly the requested block, we are left with a hole of 2 bytes. The overhead to keep track of this hole will be substantially larger than the hole itself. The general approach to avoiding this problem is to break the physical memory into fixed-sized blocks and allocate memory in units based on block size. With this approach, the memory allocated to a process may be slightly larger than the requested memory. The difference between these two numbers is internal fragmentation—unused memory that is internal to a partition.

One solution to the problem of external fragmentation is compaction. The goal is to shuffle the memory contents so as to place all free memory together in one large block. Compaction is not always possible, however. If relocation is static and is done at assembly or load time, compaction cannot be done; compaction is possible *only* if relocation is dynamic and is done at execution time. If addresses are relocated dynamically, relocation requires only moving the program and data and then changing the base register to reflect the new base address. When compaction is possible, we must determine its cost. The simplest compaction algorithm is to move all processes toward one end of memory; all holes move in the other direction, producing one large hole of available memory. This scheme can be expensive.

Another possible solution to the external-fragmentation problem is to permit the logical address space of the processes to be noncontiguous, thus allowing a process to be allocated physical memory wherever such memory is available. Two complementary techniques achieve this solution: paging (Section 8.4) and segmentation (Section 8.6). These techniques can also be combined (Section 8.7).

8.4 Paging

Paging is a memory-management scheme that permits the physical address space of a process to be noncontiguous. Paging avoids external fragmentation and the need for compaction. It also solves the considerable problem of fitting memory chunks of varying sizes onto the backing store; most memory-management schemes used before the introduction of paging suffered from this problem. The problem arises because, when some code fragments or data residing in main memory need to be swapped out, space must be found on the backing store. The backing store has the same fragmentation problems discussed in connection with main memory, but access is much slower, so compaction is impossible. Because of its advantages over earlier methods, paging in its various forms is used in most operating systems.

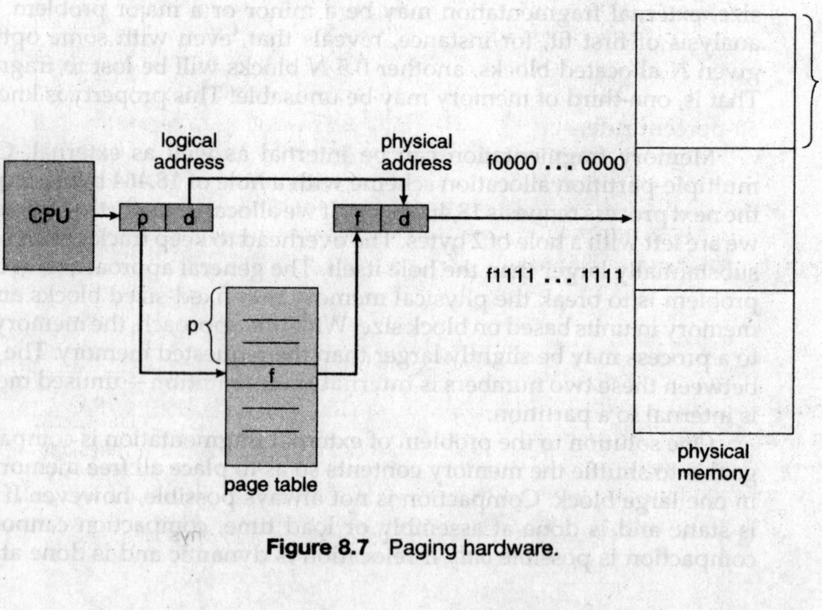

Figure 8.7 Paging hardware.

Traditionally, support for paging has been handled by hardware. However, recent designs have implemented paging by closely integrating the hardware and operating system, especially on 64-bit microprocessors.

8.4.1 Basic Method

The basic method for implementing paging involves breaking physical memory into fixed-sized blocks called **frames** and breaking logical memory into blocks of the same size called **pages**. When a process is to be executed, its pages are loaded into any available memory frames from their source (a file system or the backing store). The backing store is divided into fixed-sized blocks that are of the same size as the memory frames.

The hardware support for paging is illustrated in Figure 8.7. Every address generated by the CPU is divided into two parts: a **page number (p)** and a **page offset (d)**. The page number is used as an index into a **page table**. The page table contains the base address of each page in physical memory. This base address is combined with the page offset to define the physical memory address that is sent to the memory unit. The paging model of memory is shown in Figure 8.8.

The page size (like the frame size) is defined by the hardware. The size of a page is typically a power of 2, varying between 512 bytes and 16 MB per page, depending on the computer architecture. The selection of a power of 2 as a page size makes the translation of a logical address into a page number and page offset particularly easy. If the size of the logical address space is 2^m, and a page size is 2^n addressing units (bytes or words), then the high-order $m - n$ bits of a logical address designate the page number, and the n low-order bits designate the page offset. Thus, the logical address is as follows:

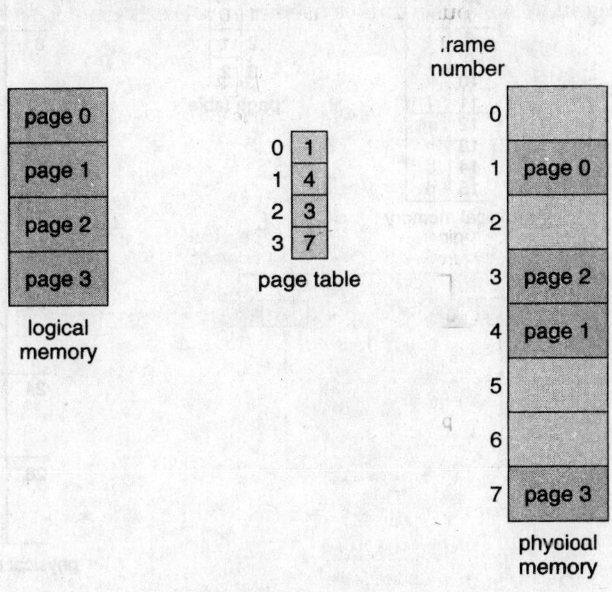

Figure 8.8 Paging model of logical and physical memory.

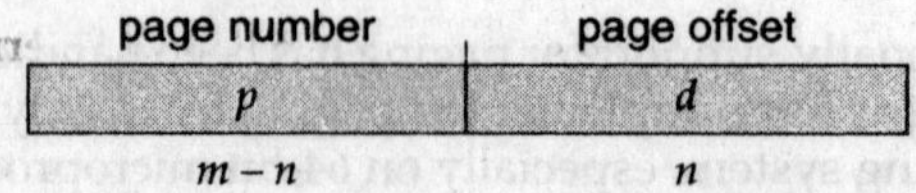

where p is an index into the page table and d is the displacement within the page.

As a concrete (although minuscule) example, consider the memory in Figure 8.9. Here, in the logical address, $n= 2$ and $m = 4$. Using a page size of 4 bytes and a physical memory of 32 bytes (8 pages), we show how the user's view of memory can be mapped into physical memory. Logical address 0 is page 0, offset 0. Indexing into the page table, we find that page 0 is in frame 5. Thus, logical address 0 maps to physical address 20 [$= (5 \times 4) + 0$]. Logical address 3 (page 0, offset 3) maps to physical address 23 [$= (5 \times 4) + 3$]. Logical address 4 is page 1, offset 0; according to the page table, page 1 is mapped to frame 6. Thus, logical address 4 maps to physical address 24 [$= (6 \times 4) + 0$]. Logical address 13 maps to physical address 9.

You may have noticed that paging itself is a form of dynamic relocation. Every logical address is bound by the paging hardware to some physical address. Using paging is similar to using a table of base (or relocation) registers, one for each frame of memory.

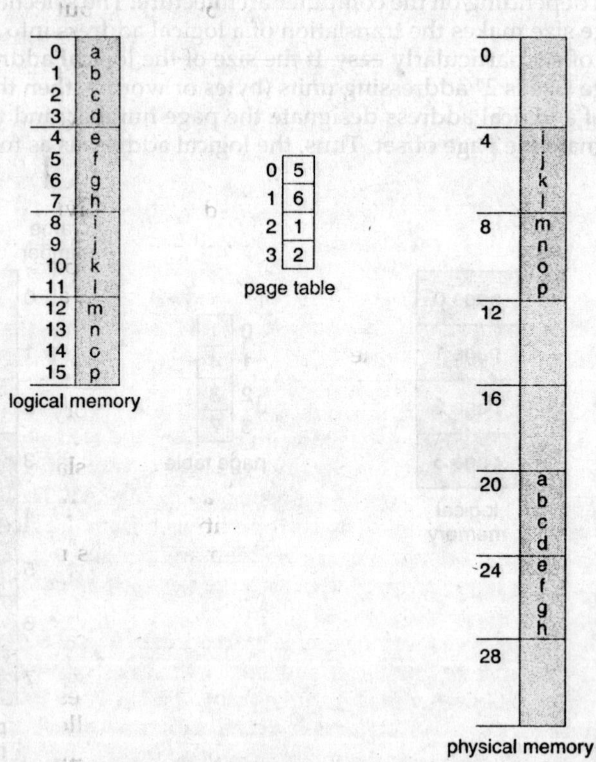

Figure 8.9 Paging example for a 32-byte memory with 4-byte pages.

When we use a paging scheme, we have no external fragmentation: *any* free frame can be allocated to a process that needs it. However, we may have some internal fragmentation. Notice that frames are allocated as units. If the memory requirements of a process do not happen to coincide with page boundaries, the *last* frame allocated may not be completely full. For example, if page size is 2,048 bytes, a process of 72,766 bytes will need 35 pages plus 1,086 bytes. It will be allocated 36 frames, resulting in internal fragmentation of 2,048 − 1,086 = 962 bytes. In the worst case, a process would need n pages plus 1 byte. It would be allocated $n + 1$ frames, resulting in internal fragmentation of almost an entire frame.

If process size is independent of page size, we expect internal fragmentation to average one-half page per process. This consideration suggests that small page sizes are desirable. However, overhead is involved in each page-table entry, and this overhead is reduced as the size of the pages increases. Also, disk I/O is more efficient when the amount data being transferred is larger (Chapter 12). Generally, page sizes have grown over time as processes, data sets, and main memory have become larger. Today, pages typically are between 4 KB and 8 KB in size, and some systems support even larger page sizes. Some CPUs and kernels even support multiple page sizes. For instance, Solaris uses page sizes of 8 KB and 4 MB, depending on the data stored by the pages. Researchers are now developing support for variable on-the-fly page size.

Usually, each page-table entry is 4 bytes long, but that size can vary as well. A 32-bit entry can point to one of 2^{32} physical page frames. If frame size is 4 KB, then a system with 4-byte entries can address 2^{44} bytes (or 16 TB) of physical memory.

When a process arrives in the system to be executed, its size, expressed in pages, is examined. Each page of the process needs one frame. Thus, if the process requires n pages, at least n frames must be available in memory. If n frames are available, they are allocated to this arriving process. The first page of the process is loaded into one of the allocated frames, and the frame number is put in the page table for this process. The next page is loaded into another frame, its frame number is put into the page table, and so on (Figure 8.10).

An important aspect of paging is the clear separation between the user's view of memory and the actual physical memory. The user program views memory as one single space, containing only this one program. In fact, the user program is scattered throughout physical memory, which also holds other programs. The difference between the user's view of memory and the actual physical memory is reconciled by the address-translation hardware. The logical addresses are translated into physical addresses. This mapping is hidden from the user and is controlled by the operating system. Notice that the user process by definition is unable to access memory it does not own. It has no way of addressing memory outside of its page table, and the table includes only those pages that the process owns.

Since the operating system is managing physical memory, it must be aware of the allocation details of physical memory—which frames are allocated, which frames are available, how many total frames there are, and so on. This information is generally kept in a data structure called a frame table. The frame table has one entry for each physical page frame, indicating whether the latter is free or allocated and, if it is allocated, to which page of which process or processes.

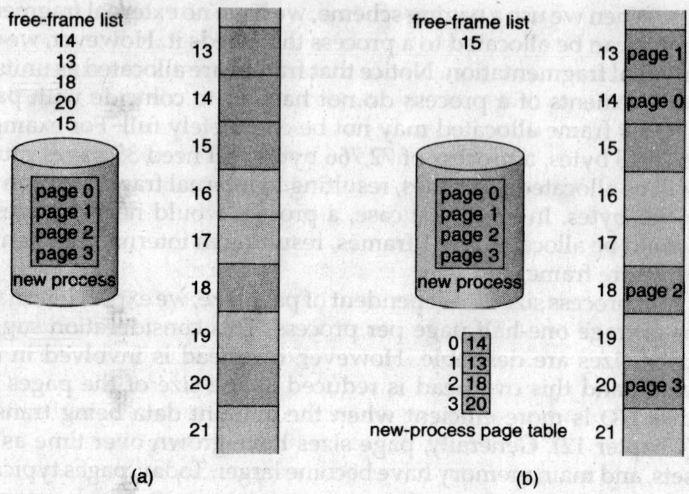

Figure 8.10 Free frames (a) before allocation and (b) after allocation.

In addition, the operating system must be aware that user processes operate in user space, and all logical addresses must be mapped to produce physical addresses. If a user makes a system call (to do I/O, for example) and provides an address as a parameter (a buffer, for instance), that address must be mapped to produce the correct physical address. The operating system maintains a copy of the page table for each process, just as it maintains a copy of the instruction counter and register contents. This copy is used to translate logical addresses to physical addresses whenever the operating system must map a logical address to a physical address manually. It is also used by the CPU dispatcher to define the hardware page table when a process is to be allocated the CPU. Paging therefore increases the context-switch time.

8.4.2 Hardware Support

Each operating system has its own methods for storing page tables. Most allocate a page table for each process. A pointer to the page table is stored with the other register values (like the instruction counter) in the process control block. When the dispatcher is told to start a process, it must reload the user registers and define the correct hardware page-table values from the stored user page table.

The hardware implementation of the page table can be done in several ways. In the simplest case, the page table is implemented as a set of dedicated registers. These registers should be built with very high-speed logic to make the paging-address translation efficient. Every access to memory must go through the paging map, so efficiency is a major consideration. The CPU dispatcher reloads these registers, just as it reloads the other registers. Instructions to load or modify the page-table registers are, of course, privileged, so that only the operating system can change the memory map. The DEC PDP-11 is an example of such an architecture. The address consists of 16 bits, and the page size is 8 KB. The page table thus consists of eight entries that are kept in fast registers.

The use of registers for the page table is satisfactory if the page table is reasonably small (for example, 256 entries). Most contemporary computers, however, allow the page table to be very large (for example, 1 million entries). For these machines, the use of fast registers to implement the page table is not feasible. Rather, the page table is kept in main memory, and a **page-table base register (PTBR)** points to the page table. Changing page tables requires changing only this one register, substantially reducing context-switch time.

The problem with this approach is the time required to access a user memory location. If we want to access location *i*, we must first index into the page table, using the value in the PTBR offset by the page number for *i*. This task requires a memory access. It provides us with the frame number, which is combined with the page offset to produce the actual address. We can then access the desired place in memory. With this scheme, *two* memory accesses are needed to access a byte (one for the page-table entry, one for the byte). Thus, memory access is slowed by a factor of 2. This delay would be intolerable under most circumstances. We might as well resort to swapping!

The standard solution to this problem is to use a special, small, fast-lookup hardware cache, called a **translation look-aside buffer (TLB)**. The TLB is associative, high-speed memory. Each entry in the TLB consists of two parts: a key (or tag) and a value. When the associative memory is presented with an item, the item is compared with all keys simultaneously. If the item is found, the corresponding value field is returned. The search is fast; the hardware, however, is expensive. Typically, the number of entries in a TLB is small, often numbering between 64 and 1,024.

The TLB is used with page tables in the following way. The TLB contains only a few of the page-table entries. When a logical address is generated by the CPU, its page number is presented to the TLB. If the page number is found, its frame number is immediately available and is used to access memory. The whole task may take less than 10 percent longer than it would if an unmapped memory reference were used.

If the page number is not in the TLB (known as a **TLB miss**), a memory reference to the page table must be made. When the frame number is obtained, we can use it to access memory (Figure 8.11). In addition, we add the page number and frame number to the TLB, so that they will be found quickly on the next reference. If the TLB is already full of entries, the operating system must select one for replacement. Replacement policies range from least recently used (LRU) to random. Furthermore, some TLBs allow certain entries to be **wired down**, meaning that they cannot be removed from the TLB. Typically, TLB entries for kernel code are wired down.

Some TLBs store **address-space identifiers (ASIDs)** in each TLB entry. An ASID uniquely identifies each process and is used to provide address-space protection for that process. When the TLB attempts to resolve virtual page numbers, it ensures that the ASID for the currently running process matches the ASID associated with the virtual page. If the ASIDs do not match, the attempt is treated as a TLB miss. In addition to providing address-space protection, an ASID allows the TLB to contain entries for several different processes simultaneously. If the TLB does not support separate ASIDs, then every time a new page table is selected (for instance, with each context switch), the TLB must be flushed (or erased) to ensure that the next executing process does not use the wrong translation information. Otherwise, the TLB could include old entries that

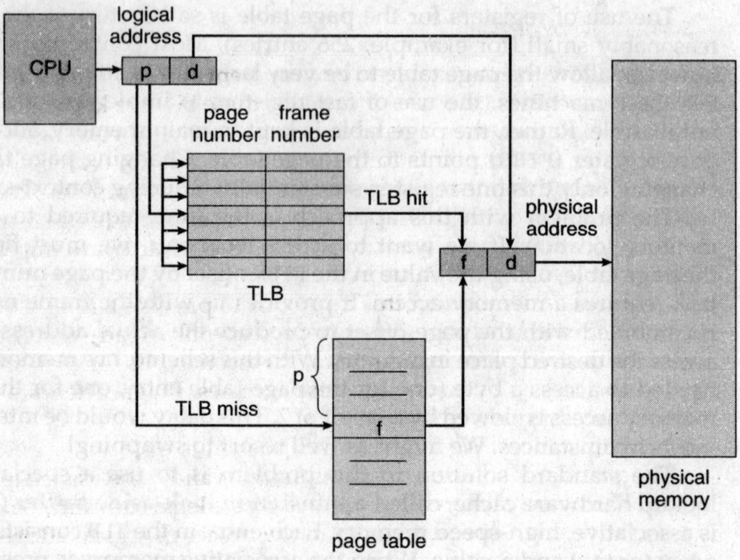

Figure 8.11 Paging hardware with TLB.

contain valid virtual addresses but have incorrect or invalid physical addresses left over from the previous process.

The percentage of times that a particular page number is found in the TLB is called the **hit ratio**. An 80-percent hit ratio, for example, means that we find the desired page number in the TLB 80 percent of the time. If it takes 20 nanoseconds to search the TLB and 100 nanoseconds to access memory, then a mapped-memory access takes 120 nanoseconds when the page number is in the TLB. If we fail to find the page number in the TLB (20 nanoseconds), then we must first access memory for the page table and frame number (100 nanoseconds) and then access the desired byte in memory (100 nanoseconds), for a total of 220 nanoseconds. To find the **effective memory-access time**, we weight the case by its probability:

$$\begin{aligned}\text{effective access time} &= 0.80 \times 120 + 0.20 \times 220 \\ &= 140 \text{ nanoseconds.}\end{aligned}$$

In this example, we suffer a 40-percent slowdown in memory-access time (from 100 to 140 nanoseconds).

For a 98-percent hit ratio, we have

$$\begin{aligned}\text{effective access time} &= 0.98 \times 120 + 0.02 \times 220 \\ &= 122 \text{ nanoseconds.}\end{aligned}$$

This increased hit rate produces only a 22 percent slowdown in access time. We will further explore the impact of the hit ratio on the TLB in Chapter 9.

8.4.3 Protection

Memory protection in a paged environment is accomplished by protection bits associated with each frame. Normally, these bits are kept in the page table.

One bit can define a page to be read–write or read-only. Every reference to memory goes through the page table to find the correct frame number. At the same time that the physical address is being computed, the protection bits can be checked to verify that no writes are being made to a read-only page. An attempt to write to a read-only page causes a hardware trap to the operating system (or memory-protection violation).

We can easily expand this approach to provide a finer level of protection. We can create hardware to provide read-only, read–write, or execute-only protection; or, by providing separate protection bits for each kind of access, we can allow any combination of these accesses. Illegal attempts will be trapped to the operating system.

One additional bit is generally attached to each entry in the page table: a **valid–invalid** bit. When this bit is set to "valid," the associated page is in the process's logical address space and is thus a legal (or valid) page. When the bit is set to"invalid," the page is not in the process's logical address space. Illegal addresses are trapped by use of the valid–invalid bit. The operating system sets this bit for each page to allow or disallow access to the page.

Suppose, for example, that in a system with a 14-bit address space (0 to 16383), we have a program that should use only addresses 0 to 10468. Given a page size of 2 KB, we have the situation shown in Figure 8.12. Addresses in

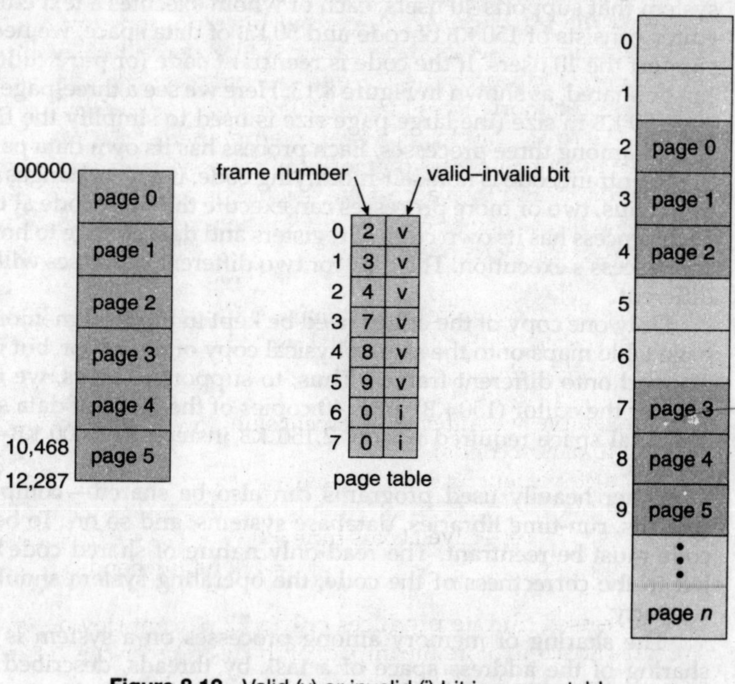

Figure 8.12 Valid (v) or invalid (i) bit in a page table.

pages 0, 1, 2, 3, 4, and 5 are mapped normally through the page table. Any attempt to generate an address in pages 6 or 7, however, will find that the valid–invalid bit is set to invalid, and the computer will trap to the operating system (invalid page reference).

Notice that this scheme has created a problem. Because the program extends only to address 10468, any reference beyond that address is illegal. However, references to page 5 are classified as valid, so accesses to addresses up to 12287 are valid. Only the addresses from 12288 to 16383 are invalid. This problem is a result of the 2-KB page size and reflects the internal fragmentation of paging.

Rarely does a process use all its address range. In fact, many processes use only a small fraction of the address space available to them. It would be wasteful in these cases to create a page table with entries for every page in the address range. Most of this table would be unused but would take up valuable memory space. Some systems provide hardware, in the form of a **page-table length register (PTLR)**, to indicate the size of the page table. This value is checked against every logical address to verify that the address is in the valid range for the process. Failure of this test causes an error trap to the operating system.

8.4.4 Shared Pages

An advantage of paging is the possibility of *sharing* common code. This consideration is particularly important in a time-sharing environment. Consider a system that supports 40 users, each of whom executes a text editor. If the text editor consists of 150 KB of code and 50 KB of data space, we need 8,000 KB to support the 40 users. If the code is **reentrant code** (or **pure code**), however, it can be shared, as shown in Figure 8.13. Here we see a three-page editor—each page 50 KB in size (the large page size is used to simplify the figure)—being shared among three processes. Each process has its own data page.

Reentrant code is non-self-modifying code: it never changes during execution. Thus, two or more processes can execute the same code at the same time. Each process has its own copy of registers and data storage to hold the data for the process's execution. The data for two different processes will, of course, be different.

Only one copy of the editor need be kept in physical memory. Each user's page table maps onto the same physical copy of the editor, but data pages are mapped onto different frames. Thus, to support 40 users, we need only one copy of the editor (150 KB), plus 40 copies of the 50 KB of data space per user. The total space required is now 2,150 KB instead of 8,000 KB—a significant savings.

Other heavily used programs can also be shared—compilers, window systems, run-time libraries, database systems, and so on. To be sharable, the code must be reentrant. The read-only nature of shared code should not be left to the correctness of the code; the operating system should enforce this property.

The sharing of memory among processes on a system is similar to the sharing of the address space of a task by threads, described in Chapter 4. Furthermore, recall that in Chapter 3 we described shared memory as a method

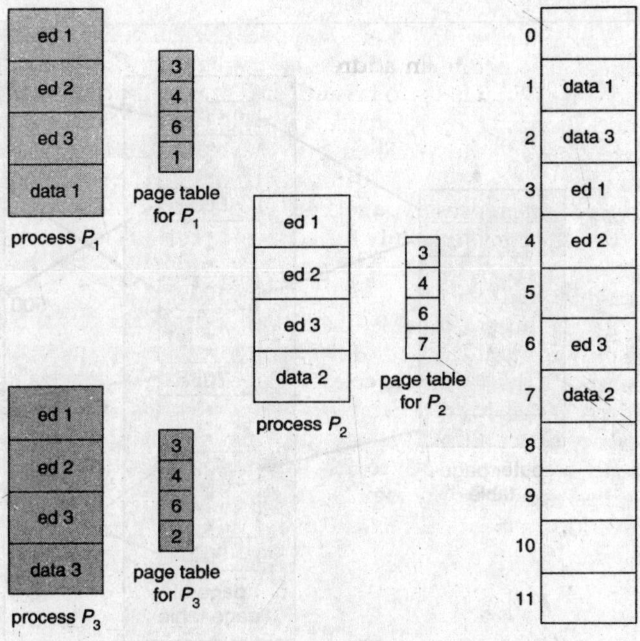

Figure 8.13 Sharing of code in a paging environment.

of interprocess communication. Some operating systems implement shared memory using shared pages.

Organizing memory according to pages provides numerous benefits in addition to allowing several processes to share the same physical pages. We cover several other benefits in Chapter 9.

8.5 Structure of the Page Table

In this section, we explore some of the most common techniques for structuring the page table.

8.5.1 Hierarchical Paging

Most modern computer systems support a large logical address space (2^{32} to 2^{64}). In such an environment, the page table itself becomes excessively large. For example, consider a system with a 32-bit logical address space. If the page size in such a system is 4 KB (2^{12}), then a page table may consist of up to 1 million entries ($2^{32}/2^{12}$). Assuming that each entry consists of 4 bytes, each process may need up to 4 MB of physical address space for the page table alone. Clearly, we would not want to allocate the page table contiguously in main memory. One simple solution to this problem is to divide the page table into smaller pieces. We can accomplish this division in several ways.

One way is to use a two-level paging algorithm, in which the page table itself is also paged (Figure 8.14). For example, consider again the system with

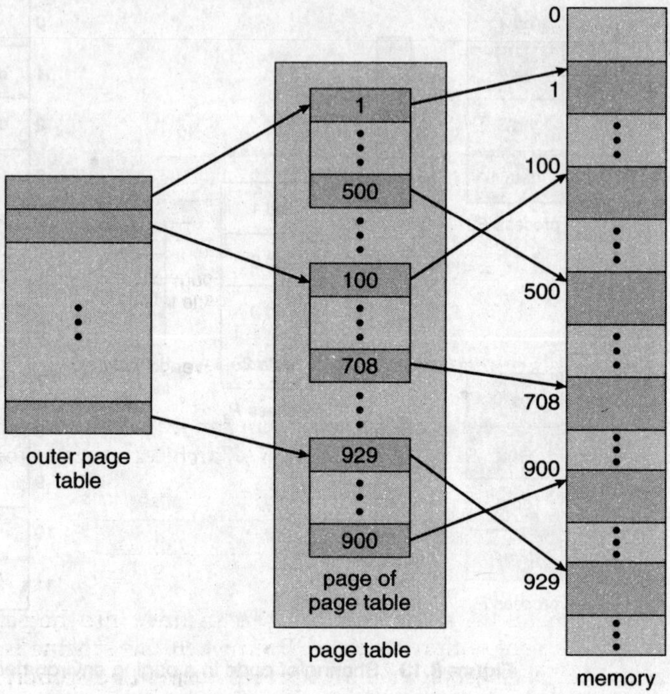

Figure 8.14 A two-level page-table scheme.

a 32-bit logical address space and a page size of 4 KB. A logical address is divided into a page number consisting of 20 bits and a page offset consisting of 12 bits. Because we page the page table, the page number is further divided into a 10-bit page number and a 10-bit page offset. Thus, a logical address is as follows:

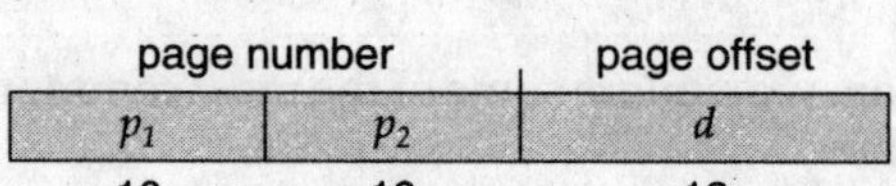

where p_1 is an index into the outer page table and p_2 is the displacement within the page of the outer page table. The address-translation method for this architecture is shown in Figure 8.15. Because address translation works from the outer page table inward, this scheme is also known as a **forward-mapped page table**.

The VAX architecture supports a variation of two-level paging. The VAX is a 32-bit machine with a page size of 512 bytes. The logical address space of a process is divided into four equal sections, each of which consists of 2^{30} bytes. Each section represents a different part of the logical address space of a process. The first 2 high-order bits of the logical address designate the appropriate section. The next 21 bits represent the logical page number of that section, and the final 9 bits represent an offset in the desired page. By partitioning the page

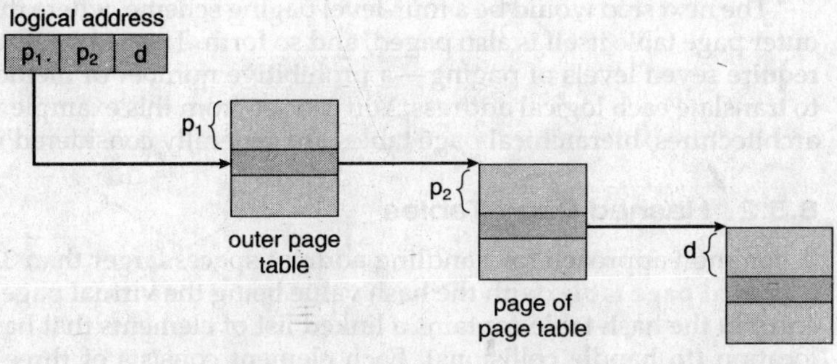

Figure 8.15 Address translation for a two-level 32-bit paging architecture.

table in this manner, the operating system can leave partitions unused until a process needs them. An address on the VAX architecture is as follows:

section	page	offset
s	p	d
2	21	9

where s designates the section number, p is an index into the page table, and d is the displacement within the page. Even when this scheme is used, the size of a one-level page table for a VAX process using one section is 2^{21} bits $*$ 4 bytes per entry = 8 MB. To further reduce main-memory use, the VAX pages the user-process page tables.

For a system with a 64-bit logical address space, a two-level paging scheme is no longer appropriate. To illustrate this point, let us suppose that the page size in such a system is 4 KB (2^{12}). In this case, the page table consists of up to 2^{52} entries. If we use a two-level paging scheme, then the inner page tables can conveniently be one page long, or contain 2^{10} 4-byte entries. The addresses look like this:

outer page	inner page	offset
p_1	p_2	d
42	10	12

The outer page table consists of 2^{42} entries, or 2^{44} bytes. The obvious way to avoid such a large table is to divide the outer page table into smaller pieces. (This approach is also used on some 32-bit processors for added flexibility and efficiency.)

We can divide the outer page table in various ways. We can page the outer page table, giving us a three-level paging scheme. Suppose that the outer page table is made up of standard-size pages (2^{10} entries, or 2^{12} bytes). In this case, a 64-bit address space is still daunting:

2nd outer page	outer page	inner page	offset
p_1	p_2	p_3	d
32	10	10	12

The outer page table is still 2^{34} bytes in size.

The next step would be a four-level paging scheme, where the second-level outer page table itself is also paged, and so forth. The 64-bit UltraSPARC would require seven levels of paging—a prohibitive number of memory accesses—to translate each logical address. You can see from this example why, for 64-bit architectures, hierarchical page tables are generally considered inappropriate.

8.5.2 Hashed Page Tables

A common approach for handling address spaces larger than 32 bits is to use a **hashed page table**, with the hash value being the virtual page number. Each entry in the hash table contains a linked list of elements that hash to the same location (to handle collisions). Each element consists of three fields: (1) the virtual page number, (2) the value of the mapped page frame, and (3) a pointer to the next element in the linked list.

The algorithm works as follows: The virtual page number in the virtual address is hashed into the hash table. The virtual page number is compared with field 1 in the first element in the linked list. If there is a match, the corresponding page frame (field 2) is used to form the desired physical address. If there is no match, subsequent entries in the linked list are searched for a matching virtual page number. This scheme is shown in Figure 8.16.

A variation of this scheme that is favorable for 64-bit address spaces has been proposed. This variation uses **clustered page tables**, which are similar to hashed page tables except that each entry in the hash table refers to several pages (such as 16) rather than a single page. Therefore, a single page-table entry can store the mappings for multiple physical-page frames. Clustered page tables are particularly useful for **sparse** address spaces, where memory references are noncontiguous and scattered throughout the address space.

8.5.3 Inverted Page Tables

Usually, each process has an associated page table. The page table has one entry for each page that the process is using (or one slot for each virtual

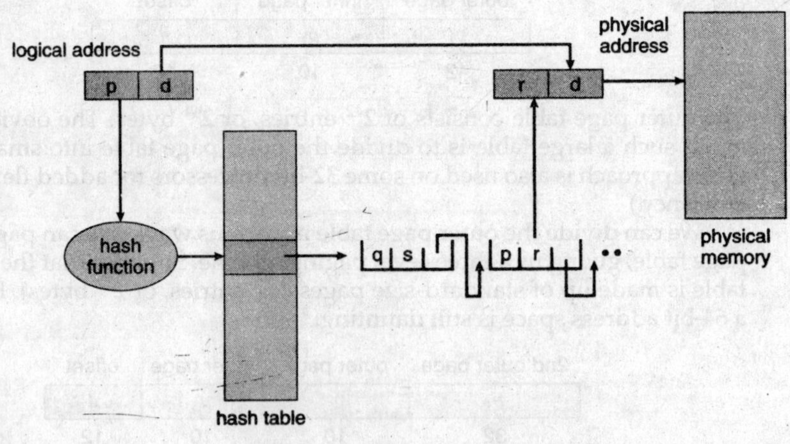

Figure 8.16 Hashed page table.

address, regardless of the latter's validity). This table representation is a natural one, since processes reference pages through the pages' virtual addresses. The operating system must then translate this reference into a physical memory address. Since the table is sorted by virtual address, the operating system is able to calculate where in the table the associated physical address entry is located and to use that value directly. One of the drawbacks of this method is that each page table may consist of millions of entries. These tables may consume large amounts of physical memory just to keep track of how other physical memory is being used.

To solve this problem, we can use an **inverted page table**. An inverted page table has one entry for each real page (or frame) of memory. Each entry consists of the virtual address of the page stored in that real memory location, with information about the process that owns the page. Thus, only one page table is in the system, and it has only one entry for each page of physical memory. Figure 8.17 shows the operation of an inverted page table. Compare it with Figure 8.7, which depicts a standard page table in operation. Inverted page tables often require that an address-space identifier (Section 8.4.2) be stored in each entry of the page table, since the table usually contains several different address spaces mapping physical memory. Storing the address-space identifier ensures that a logical page for a particular process is mapped to the corresponding physical page frame. Examples of systems using inverted page tables include the 64-bit UltraSPARC and PowerPC.

To illustrate this method, we describe a simplified version of the inverted page table used in the IBM RT. Each virtual address in the system consists of a triple:

<process-id, page-number, offset>.

Each inverted page-table entry is a pair <process-id, page-number> where the process-id assumes the role of the address-space identifier. When a memory

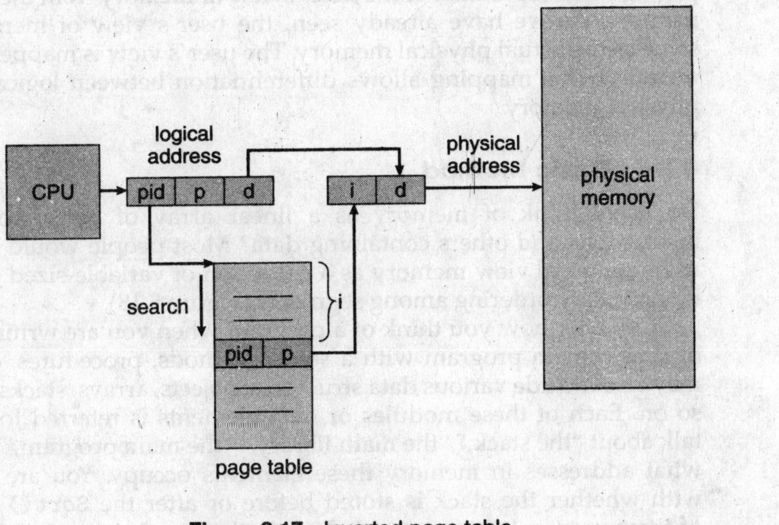

Figure 8.17 Inverted page table.

reference occurs, part of the virtual address, consisting of <process-id, page-number>, is presented to the memory subsystem. The inverted page table is then searched for a match. If a match is found—say, at entry *i*—then the physical address <*i*, offset> is generated. If no match is found, then an illegal address access has been attempted.

Although this scheme decreases the amount of memory needed to store each page table, it increases the amount of time needed to search the table when a page reference occurs. Because the inverted page table is sorted by physical address, but lookups occur on virtual addresses, the whole table might need to be searched for a match. This search would take far too long. To alleviate this problem, we use a hash table, as described in Section 8.5.2, to limit the search to one—or at most a few—page-table entries. Of course, each access to the hash table adds a memory reference to the procedure, so one virtual memory reference requires at least two real memory reads—one for the hash-table entry and one for the page table. (Recall that the TLB is searched first, before the hash table is consulted, offering some performance improvement.)

Systems that use inverted page tables have difficulty implementing shared memory. Shared memory is usually implemented as multiple virtual addresses (one for each process sharing the memory) that are mapped to one physical address. This standard method cannot be used with inverted page tables; because there is only one virtual page entry for every physical page, one physical page cannot have two (or more) shared virtual addresses. A simple technique for addressing this issue is to allow the page table to contain only one mapping of a virtual address to the shared physical address. This means that references to virtual addresses that are not mapped result in page faults.

8.6 Segmentation

An important aspect of memory management that became unavoidable with paging is the separation of the user's view of memory from the actual physical memory. As we have already seen, the user's view of memory is not the same as the actual physical memory. The user's view is mapped onto physical memory. This mapping allows differentiation between logical memory and physical memory.

8.6.1 Basic Method

Do users think of memory as a linear array of bytes, some containing instructions and others containing data? Most people would say no. Rather, users prefer to view memory as a collection of variable-sized segments, with no necessary ordering among segments (Figure 8.18).

Consider how you think of a program when you are writing it. You think of it as a main program with a set of methods, procedures, or functions. It may also include various data structures: objects, arrays, stacks, variables, and so on. Each of these modules or data elements is referred to by name. You talk about "the stack," "the math library," "the main program," without caring what addresses in memory these elements occupy. You are not concerned with whether the stack is stored before or after the `Sqrt()` function. Each of these segments is of variable length; the length is intrinsically defined by

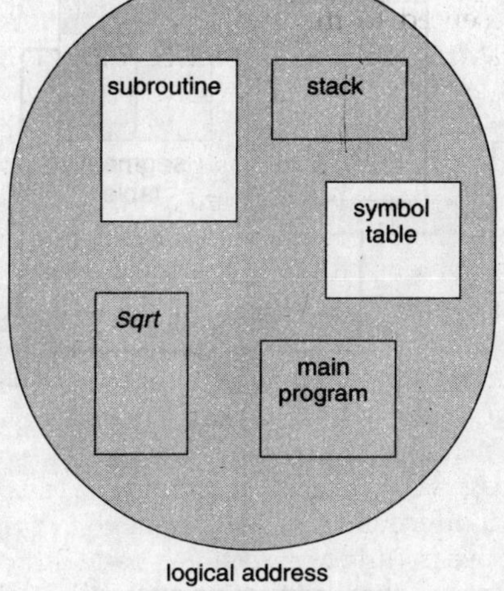

Figure 8.18 User's view of a program.

the purpose of the segment in the program. Elements within a segment are identified by their offset from the beginning of the segment: the first statement of the program, the seventh stack frame entry in the stack, the fifth instruction of the `Sqrt()`, and so on.

Segmentation is a memory-management scheme that supports this user view of memory. A logical address space is a collection of segments. Each segment has a name and a length. The addresses specify both the segment name and the offset within the segment. The user therefore specifies each address by two quantities: a segment name and an offset. (Contrast this scheme with the paging scheme, in which the user specifies only a single address, which is partitioned by the hardware into a page number and an offset, all invisible to the programmer.)

For simplicity of implementation, segments are numbered and are referred to by a segment number, rather than by a segment name. Thus, a logical address consists of a *two tuple:*

<segment-number, offset>.

Normally, the user program is compiled, and the compiler automatically constructs segments reflecting the input program.

A C compiler might create separate segments for the following:

1. The code
2. Global variables
3. The heap, from which memory is allocated
4. The stacks used by each thread
5. The standard C library

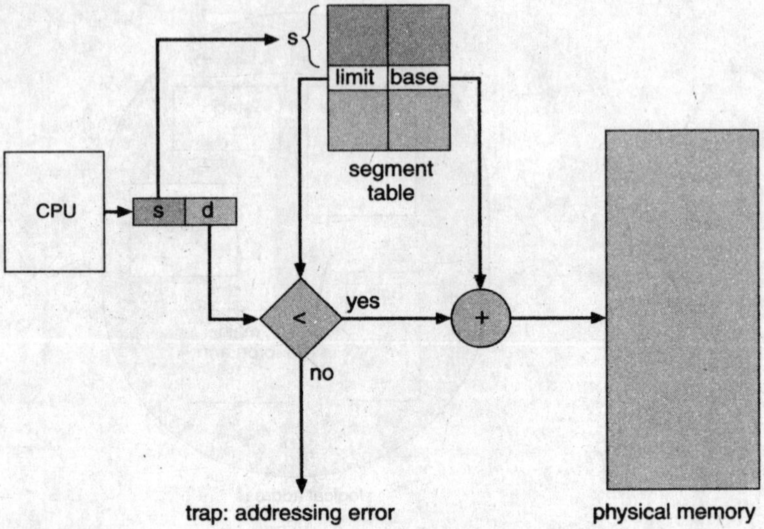

Figure 8.19 Segmentation hardware.

Libraries that are linked in during compile time might be assigned separate segments. The loader would take all these segments and assign them segment numbers.

8.6.2 Hardware

Although the user can now refer to objects in the program by a two-dimensional address, the actual physical memory is still, of course, a one-dimensional sequence of bytes. Thus, we must define an implementation to map two-dimensional user-defined addresses into one-dimensional physical addresses. This mapping is effected by a **segment table**. Each entry in the segment table has a *segment base* and a *segment limit*. The segment base contains the starting physical address where the segment resides in memory, and the segment limit specifies the length of the segment.

The use of a segment table is illustrated in Figure 8.19. A logical address consists of two parts: a segment number, *s*, and an offset into that segment, *d*. The segment number is used as an index to the segment table. The offset *d* of the logical address must be between 0 and the segment limit. If it is not, we trap to the operating system (logical addressing attempt beyond end of segment). When an offset is legal, it is added to the segment base to produce the address in physical memory of the desired byte. The segment table is thus essentially an array of base–limit register pairs.

As an example, consider the situation shown in Figure 8.20. We have five segments numbered from 0 through 4. The segments are stored in physical memory as shown. The segment table has a separate entry for each segment, giving the beginning address of the segment in physical memory (or base) and the length of that segment (or limit). For example, segment 2 is 400 bytes long and begins at location 4300. Thus, a reference to byte 53 of segment 2 is mapped

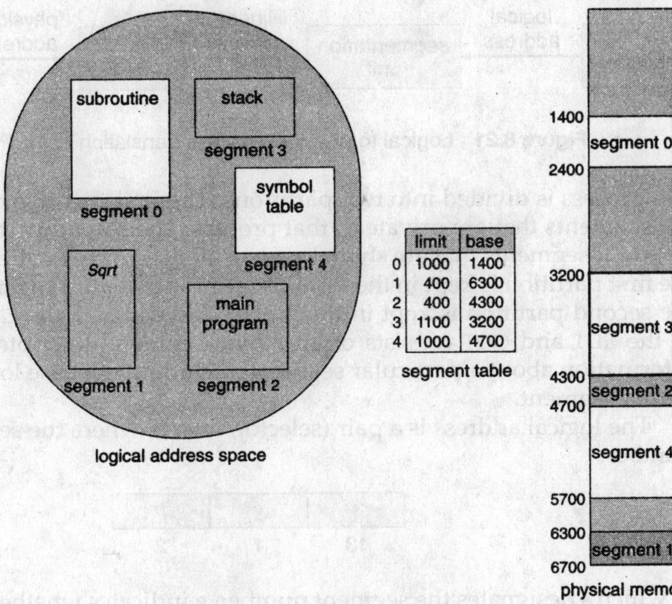

Figure 8.20 Example of segmentation.

onto location 4300 + 53 = 4353. A reference to segment 3, byte 852, is mapped to 3200 (the base of segment 3) + 852 = 4052. A reference to byte 1222 of segment 0 would result in a trap to the operating system, as this segment is only 1,000 bytes long.

8.7 Example: The Intel Pentium

Both paging and segmentation have advantages and disadvantages. In fact, some architectures provide both. In this section, we discuss the Intel Pentium architecture, which supports both pure segmentation and segmentation with paging. We do not give a complete description of the memory-management structure of the Pentium in this text. Rather, we present the major ideas on which it is based. We conclude our discussion with an overview of Linux address translation on Pentium systems.

In Pentium systems, the CPU generates logical addresses, which are given to the segmentation unit. The segmentation unit produces a linear address for each logical address. The linear address is then given to the paging unit, which in turn generates the physical address in main memory. Thus, the segmentation and paging units form the equivalent of the memory-management unit (MMU). This scheme is shown in Figure 8.21.

8.7.1 Pentium Segmentation

The Pentium architecture allows a segment to be as large as 4 GB, and the maximum number of segments per process is 16 K. The logical-address space

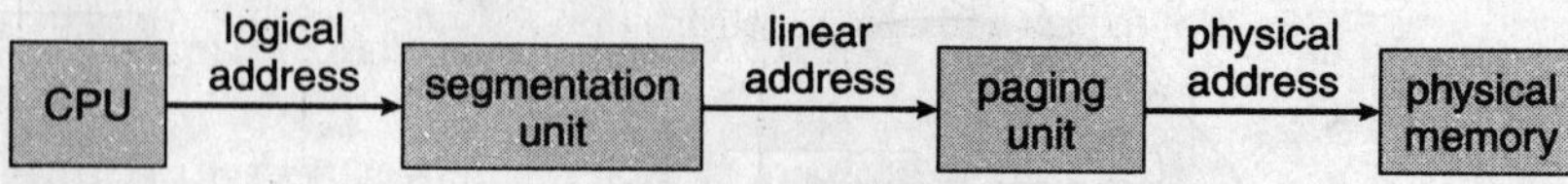

Figure 8.21 Logical to physical address translation in the Pentium.

of a process is divided into two partitions. The first partition consists of up to 8 K segments that are private to that process. The second partition consists of up to 8 K segments that are shared among all the processes. Information about the first partition is kept in the **local descriptor table** (LDT); information about the second partition is kept in the **global descriptor table** (GDT). Each entry in the LDT and GDT consists of an 8-byte segment descriptor with detailed information about a particular segment, including the base location and limit of that segment.

The logical address is a pair (selector, offset), where the selector is a 16-bit number:

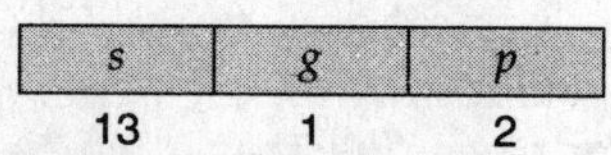

in which s designates the segment number, g indicates whether the segment is in the GDT or LDT, and p deals with protection. The offset is a 32-bit number specifying the location of the byte (or word) within the segment in question.

The machine has six segment registers, allowing six segments to be addressed at any one time by a process. It also has six 8-byte microprogram registers to hold the corresponding descriptors from either the LDT or GDT. This cache lets the Pentium avoid having to read the descriptor from memory for every memory reference.

The linear address on the Pentium is 32 bits long and is formed as follows. The segment register points to the appropriate entry in the LDT or GDT. The base and limit information about the segment in question is used to generate a **linear address**. First, the limit is used to check for address validity. If the address is not valid, a memory fault is generated, resulting in a trap to the operating system. If it is valid, then the value of the offset is added to the value of the base, resulting in a 32-bit linear address. This is shown in Figure 8.22. In the following section, we discuss how the paging unit turns this linear address into a physical address.

8.7.2 Pentium Paging

The Pentium architecture allows a page size of either 4 KB or 4 MB. For 4-KB pages, the Pentium uses a two-level paging scheme in which the division of the 32-bit linear address is as follows:

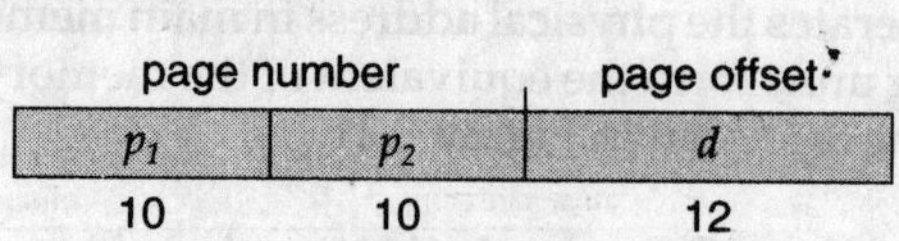

The address-translation scheme for this architecture is similar to the scheme shown in Figure 8.15. The Intel Pentium address translation is shown in more

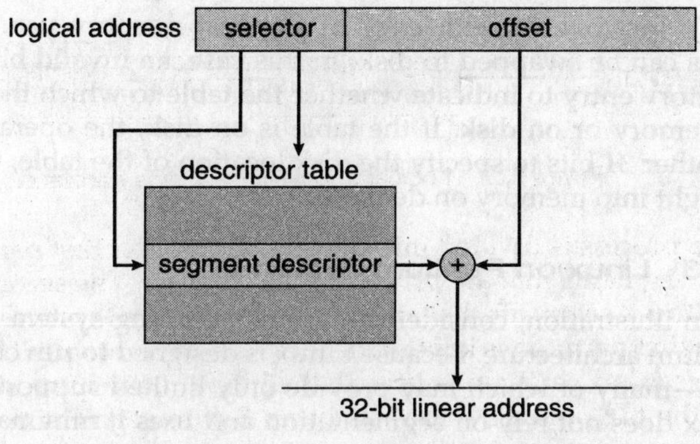

Figure 8.22 Intel Pentium segmentation.

detail in Figure 8.23. The 10 high-order bits reference an entry in the outermost page table, which the Pentium terms the **page directory**. (The CR3 register points to the page directory for the current process.) The page directory entry points to an inner page table that is indexed by the contents of the innermost 10 bits in the linear address. Finally, the low-order bits 0–11 refer to the offset in the 4-KB page pointed to in the page table.

One entry in the page directory is the Page Size flag, which—if set—indicates that the size of the page frame is 4 MB and not the standard 4 KB. If this flag is set, the page directory points directly to the 4-MB page frame, bypassing the inner page table; and the 22 low-order bits in the linear address refer to the offset in the 4-MB page frame.

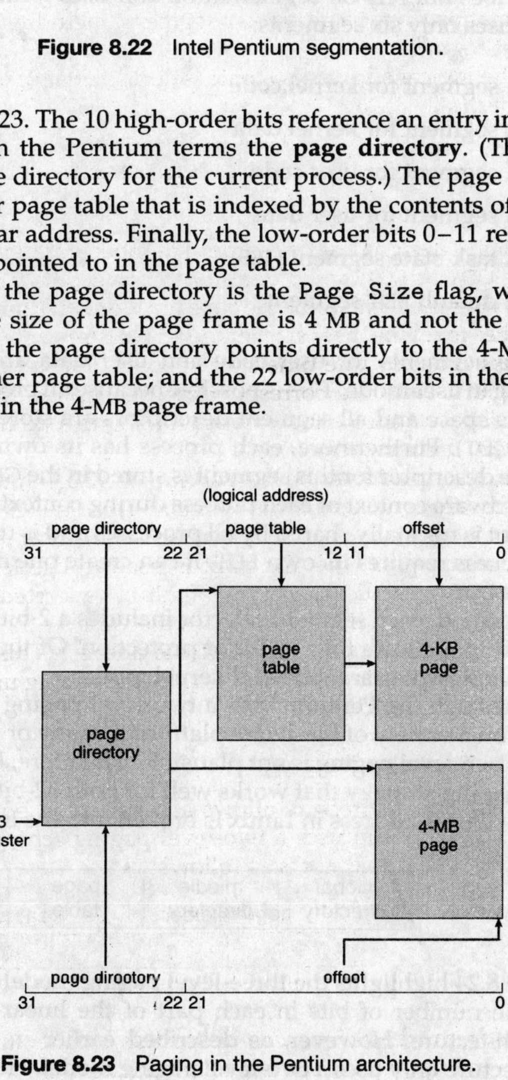

Figure 8.23 Paging in the Pentium architecture.

To improve the efficiency of physical memory use, Intel Pentium page tables can be swapped to disk. In this case, an invalid bit is used in the page directory entry to indicate whether the table to which the entry is pointing is in memory or on disk. If the table is on disk, the operating system can use the other 31 bits to specify the disk location of the table; the table then can be brought into memory on demand.

8.7.3 Linux on Pentium Systems

As an illustration, consider the Linux operating system running on the Intel Pentium architecture. Because Linux is designed to run on a variety of processors—many of which may provide only limited support for segmentation—Linux does not rely on segmentation and uses it minimally. On the Pentium, Linux uses only six segments:

1. A segment for kernel code
2. A segment for kernel data
3. A segment for user code
4. A segment for user data
5. A task-state segment (TSS)
6. A default LDT segment

The segments for user code and user data are shared by all processes running in user mode. This is possible because all processes use the same logical address space and all segment descriptors are stored in the global descriptor table (GDT). Furthermore, each process has its own task-state segment (TSS), and the descriptor for this segment is stored in the GDT. The TSS is used to store the hardware context of each process during context switches. The default LDT segment is normally shared by all processes and is usually not used. However, if a process requires its own LDT, it can create one and use that instead of the default LDT.

As noted, each segment selector includes a 2-bit field for protection. Thus, the Pentium allows four levels of protection. Of these four levels, Linux only recognizes two: user mode and kernel mode.

Although the Pentium uses a two-level paging model, Linux is designed to run on a variety of hardware platforms, many of which are 64-bit platforms where two-level paging is not plausible. Therefore, Linux has adopted a three-level paging strategy that works well for both 32-bit and 64-bit architectures.

The linear address in Linux is broken into the following four parts:

global directory	middle directory	page table	offset

Figure 8.24 highlights the three-level paging model in Linux.

The number of bits in each part of the linear address varies according to architecture. However, as described earlier in this section, the Pentium architecture only uses a two-level paging model. How, then, does Linux apply

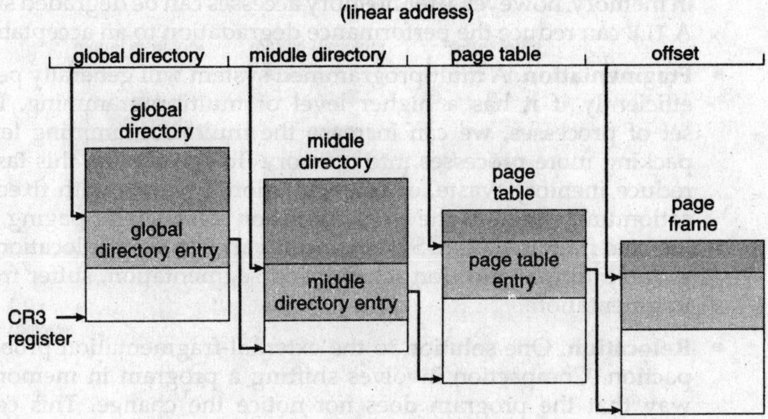

Figure 8.24 Three-level paging in Linux.

its three-level model on the Pentium? In this situation, the size of the middle directory is zero bits, effectively bypassing the middle directory.

Each task in Linux has its own set of page tables and—just as in Figure 8.23—the CR3 register points to the global directory for the task currently executing. During a context switch, the value of the CR3 register is saved and restored in the TSS segments of the tasks involved in the context switch.

8.8 Summary

Memory-management algorithms for multiprogrammed operating systems range from the simple single-user system approach to paged segmentation. The most important determinant of the method used in a particular system is the hardware provided. Every memory address generated by the CPU must be checked for legality and possibly mapped to a physical address. The checking cannot be implemented (efficiently) in software. Hence, we are constrained by the hardware available.

The various memory-management algorithms (contiguous allocation, paging, segmentation, and combinations of paging and segmentation) differ in many aspects. In comparing different memory-management strategies, we use the following considerations:

- **Hardware support**. A simple base register or a base–limit register pair is sufficient for the single- and multiple-partition schemes, whereas paging and segmentation need mapping tables to define the address map.
- **Performance**. As the memory-management algorithm becomes more complex, the time required to map a logical address to a physical address increases. For the simple systems, we need only compare or add to the logical address—operations that are fast. Paging and segmentation can be as fast if the mapping table is implemented in fast registers. If the table is

in memory, however, user memory accesses can be degraded substantially. A TLB can reduce the performance degradation to an acceptable level.

- **Fragmentation**. A multiprogrammed system will generally perform more efficiently if it has a higher level of multiprogramming. For a given set of processes, we can increase the multiprogramming level only by packing more processes into memory. To accomplish this task, we must reduce memory waste, or fragmentation. Systems with fixed-sized allocation units, such as the single-partition scheme and paging, suffer from internal fragmentation. Systems with variable-sized allocation units, such as the multiple-partition scheme and segmentation, suffer from external fragmentation.

- **Relocation**. One solution to the external-fragmentation problem is compaction. Compaction involves shifting a program in memory in such a way that the program does not notice the change. This consideration requires that logical addresses be relocated dynamically, at execution time. If addresses are relocated only at load time, we cannot compact storage.

- **Swapping**. Swapping can be added to any algorithm. At intervals determined by the operating system, usually dictated by CPU-scheduling policies, processes are copied from main memory to a backing store and later are copied back to main memory. This scheme allows more processes to be run than can be fit into memory at one time.

- **Sharing**. Another means of increasing the multiprogramming level is to share code and data among different users. Sharing generally requires that either paging or segmentation be used to provide small packets of information (pages or segments) that can be shared. Sharing is a means of running many processes with a limited amount of memory, but shared programs and data must be designed carefully.

- **Protection**. If paging or segmentation is provided, different sections of a user program can be declared execute-only, read-only, or read–write. This restriction is necessary with shared code or data and is generally useful in any case to provide simple run-time checks for common programming errors.

Exercises

8.1 Explain the difference between internal and external fragmentation.

8.2 Compare the memory organization schemes of contiguous memory allocation, pure segmentation, and pure paging with respect to the following issues:

a. External fragmentation

b. Internal fragmentation

c. Ability to share code across processes

8.3 Why are segmentation and paging sometimes combined into one scheme?

8.4 Most systems allow a program to allocate more memory to its address space during execution. Allocation of data in the heap segments of programs is an example of such allocated memory. What is required to support dynamic memory allocation in the following schemes?

a. Contiguous memory allocation

b. Pure segmentation

c. Pure paging

8.5 Consider the Intel address-translation scheme shown in Figure 8.22.

a. Describe all the steps taken by the Intel Pentium in translating a logical address into a physical address.

b. What are the advantages to the operating system of hardware that provides such complicated memory translation?

c. Are there any disadvantages to this address-translation system? If so, what are they? If not, why is this scheme not used by every manufacturer?

8.6 What is the purpose of paging the page tables?

8.7 Explain why sharing a reentrant module is easier when segmentation is used than when pure paging is used.

8.8 On a system with paging, a process cannot access memory that it does not own. Why? How could the operating system allow access to other memory? Why should it or should it not?

8.9 Compare the segmented paging scheme with the hashed page table scheme for handling large address spaces. Under what circumstances is one scheme preferable to the other?

8.10 Consider a paging system with the page table stored in memory.

a. If a memory reference takes 200 nanoseconds, how long does a paged memory reference take?

b. If we add TLBs, and 75 percent of all page-table references are found in the TLBs, what is the effective memory reference time? (Assume that finding a page-table entry in the TLBs takes zero time, if the entry is there.)

8.11 Compare paging with segmentation with respect to the amount of memory required by the address translation structures in order to convert virtual addresses to physical addresses.

8.12 Consider a system in which a program can be separated into two parts: code and data. The CPU knows whether it wants an instruction (instruction fetch) or data (data fetch or store). Therefore, two base–limit register pairs are provided: one for instructions and one for data. The instruction base–limit register pair is automatically read-only, so programs can be shared among different users. Discuss the advantages and disadvantages of this scheme.

8.13 Consider the following process for generating binaries. A compiler is used to generate the object code for individual modules, and a linkage editor is used to combine multiple object modules into a single program binary. How does the linkage editor change the binding of instructions and data to memory addresses? What information needs to be passed from the compiler to the linkage editor to facilitate the memory-binding tasks of the linkage editor?

8.14 Consider a logical address space of 64 pages of 1,024 words each, mapped onto a physical memory of 32 frames.

a. How many bits are there in the logical address?

b. How many bits are there in the physical address?

8.15 Consider the hierarchical paging scheme used by the VAX architecture. How many memory operations are performed when a user program executes a memory-load operation?

8.16 Given five memory partitions of 100 KB, 500 KB, 200 KB, 300 KB, and 600 KB (in order), how would the first-fit, best-fit, and worst-fit algorithms place processes of 212 KB, 417 KB, 112 KB, and 426 KB (in order)? Which algorithm makes the most efficient use of memory?

8.17 Describe a mechanism by which one segment could belong to the address space of two different processes.

8.18 Consider a computer system with a 32-bit logical address and 4-KB page size. The system supports up to 512 MB of physical memory. How many entries are there in each of the following?

a. A conventional single-level page table

b. An inverted page table

8.19 Assuming a 1-KB page size, what are the page numbers and offsets for the following address references (provided as decimal numbers):

a. 2375

b. 19366

c. 30000

d. 256

e. 16385

8.20 Program binaries in many systems are typically structured as follows. Code is stored starting with a small, fixed virtual address, such as 0. The code segment is followed by the data segment that is used for storing the program variables. When the program starts executing, the stack is allocated at the other end of the virtual address space and is allowed to grow toward lower virtual addresses. What is the significance of this structure for the following schemes?

a. Contiguous memory allocation

b. Pure segmentation

c. Pure paging

8.21 Consider the following segment table:

Segment	Base	Length
0	219	600
1	2300	14
2		
90	100	
3	1327	580
4	1952	96

What are the physical addresses for the following logical addresses?

a. 0,430

b. 1,10

c. 2,500

d. 3,400

e. 4,112

8.22 Consider a logical address space of 32 pages with 1,024 words per page, mapped onto a physical memory of 16 frames.

a. How many bits are required in the logical address?

b. How many bits are required in the physical address?

8.23 Sharing segments among processes without requiring that they have the same segment number is possible in a dynamically linked segmentation system.

a. Define a system that allows static linking and sharing of segments without requiring that the segment numbers be the same.

b. Describe a paging scheme that allows pages to be shared without requiring that the page numbers be the same.

Programming Problems

8.24 Assume that a system has a 32-bit virtual address with a 4-KB page size. Write a C program that is passed a virtual address (in decimal) on the command line and have it output the page number and offset for the given address. As an example, your program would run as follows:

```
./a.out 19986
```

Your program would output:

```
The address 19986 contains:
page number = 4
offset = 3602
```

Writing this program will require using the appropriate data type to store 32 bits. We encourage you to use `unsigned` data types as well.

Bibliographical Notes

Dynamic storage allocation was discussed by Knuth [1973] (Section 2.5), who found through simulation results that first fit is generally superior to best fit. Knuth [1973] also discussed the 50-percent rule.

The concept of paging can be credited to the designers of the Atlas system, which has been described by Kilburn et al. [1961] and by Howarth et al. [1961]. The concept of segmentation was first discussed by Dennis [1965]. Paged segmentation was first supported in the GE 645, on which MULTICS was originally implemented (Organick [1972] and Daley and Dennis [1967]).

Inverted page tables are discussed in an article about the IBM RT storage manager by Chang and Mergen [1988].

Address translation in software is covered in Jacob and Mudge [1997].

Hennessy and Patterson [2002] explains the hardware aspects of TLBs, caches, and MMUs. Talluri et al. [1995] discusses page tables for 64-bit address spaces. Alternative approaches to enforcing memory protection are proposed and studied in Wahbe et al. [1993a], Chase et al. [1994], Bershad et al. [1995], and Thorn [1997]. Dougan et al. [1999] and Jacob and Mudge [2001] discuss techniques for managing the TLB. Fang et al. [2001] evaluate support for large pages.

Tanenbaum [2001] discusses Intel 80386 paging. Memory management for several architectures—such as the Pentium II, PowerPC, and UltraSPARC—are described by Jacob and Mudge [1998a]. Segmentation on Linux systems is presented in Bovet and Cesati [2002].

CHAPTER 9

Virtual-Memory Management

In Chapter 8, we discussed various memory-management strategies used in computer systems. All these strategies have the same goal: to keep many processes in memory simultaneously to allow multiprogramming. However, they tend to require that an entire process be in memory before it can execute.

Virtual memory is a technique that allows the execution of processes that are not completely in memory. One major advantage of this scheme is that programs can be larger than physical memory. Further, virtual memory abstracts main memory into an extremely large, uniform array of storage, separating logical memory as viewed by the user from physical memory. This technique frees programmers from the concerns of memory-storage limitations. Virtual memory also allows processes to share files easily and to implement shared memory. In addition, it provides an efficient mechanism for process creation. Virtual memory is not easy to implement, however, and may substantially decrease performance if it is used carelessly. In this chapter, we discuss virtual memory in the form of demand paging and examine its complexity and cost.

CHAPTER OBJECTIVES

- To describe the benefits of a virtual memory system.
- To explain the concepts of demand paging, page-replacement algorithms, and allocation of page frames.
- To discuss the principles of the working-set model.

9.1 Background

The memory-management algorithms outlined in Chapter 8 are necessary because of one basic requirement: The instructions being executed must be in physical memory. The first approach to meeting this requirement is to place the entire logical address space in physical memory. Dynamic loading can help to ease this restriction, but it generally requires special precautions and extra work by the programmer.

The requirement that instructions must be in physical memory to be executed seems both necessary and reasonable; but it is also unfortunate, since it limits the size of a program to the size of physical memory. In fact, an examination of real programs shows us that, in many cases, the entire program is not needed. For instance, consider the following:

- Programs often have code to handle unusual error conditions. Since these errors seldom, if ever, occur in practice, this code is almost never executed.
- Arrays, lists, and tables are often allocated more memory than they actually need. An array may be declared 100 by 100 elements, even though it is seldom larger than 10 by 10 elements. An assembler symbol table may have room for 3,000 symbols, although the average program has less than 200 symbols.
- Certain options and features of a program may be used rarely. For instance, the routines on U.S. government computers that balance the budget have not been used in many years.

Even in those cases where the entire program is needed, it may not all be needed at the same time.

The ability to execute a program that is only partially in memory would confer many benefits:

- A program would no longer be constrained by the amount of physical memory that is available. Users would be able to write programs for an extremely large *virtual* address space, simplifying the programming task.

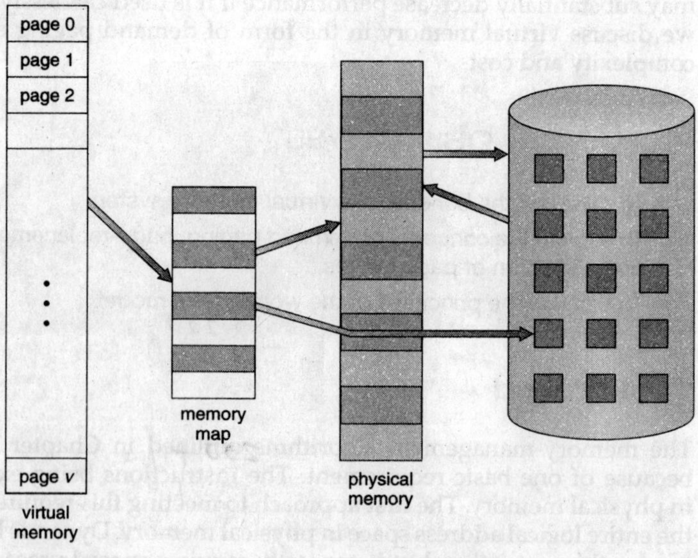

Figure 9.1 Diagram showing virtual memory that is larger than physical memory.

- Because each user program could take less physical memory, more programs could be run at the same time, with a corresponding increase in CPU utilization and throughput but with no increase in response time or turnaround time.
- Less I/O would be needed to load or swap user programs into memory, so each user program would run faster.

Thus, running a program that is not entirely in memory would benefit both the system and the user.

Virtual memory involves the separation of logical memory as perceived by users from physical memory. This separation allows an extremely large virtual memory to be provided for programmers when only a smaller physical memory is available (Figure 9.1). Virtual memory makes the task of programming much easier, because the programmer no longer needs to worry about the amount of physical memory available; she can concentrate instead on the problem to be programmed.

The **virtual address space** of a process refers to the logical (or virtual) view of how a process is stored in memory. Typically, this view is that a process begins at a certain logical address—say, address 0—and exists in contiguous memory, as shown in Figure 9.2. Recall from Chapter 8, though, that in fact physical memory may be organized in page frames and that the physical page frames assigned to a process may not be contiguous. It is up to the memory-management unit (MMU) to map logical pages to physical page frames in memory.

Note in Figure 9.2 that we allow for the heap to grow upward in memory as it is used for dynamic memory allocation. Similarly, we allow for the stack to grow downward in memory through successive function calls. The large blank space (or hole) between the heap and the stack is part of the virtual address

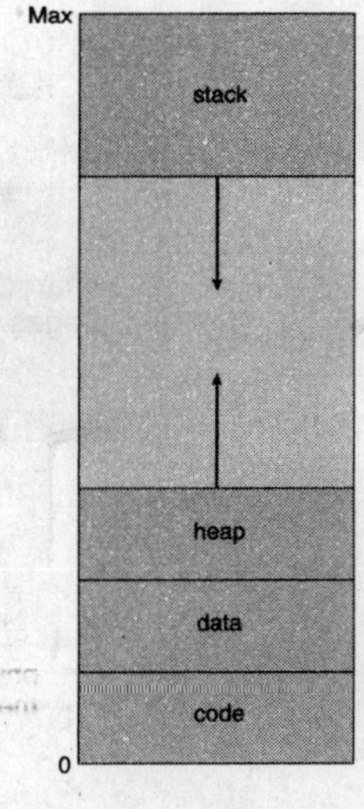

Figure 9.2 Virtual address space.

space but will require actual physical pages only if the heap or stack grows. Virtual address spaces that include holes are known as sparse address spaces. Using a sparse address space is beneficial because the holes can be filled as the stack or heap segments grow or if we wish to dynamically link libraries (or possibly other shared objects) during program execution.

In addition to separating logical memory from physical memory, virtual memory allows files and memory to be shared by two or more processes through page sharing (Section 8.4.4). This leads to the following benefits:

- System libraries can be shared by several processes through mapping of the shared object into a virtual address space. Although each process considers the shared libraries to be part of its virtual address space, the actual pages where the libraries reside in physical memory are shared by all the processes (Figure 9.3). Typically, a library is mapped read-only into the space of each process that is linked with it.
- Similarly, virtual memory enables processes to share memory. Recall from Chapter 3 that two or more processes can communicate through the use of shared memory. Virtual memory allows one process to create a region of memory that it can share with another process. Processes sharing this region consider it part of their virtual address space, yet the actual physical pages of memory are shared, much as is illustrated in Figure 9.3.
- Virtual memory can allow pages to be shared during process creation with the `fork()` system call, thus speeding up process creation.

We further explore these—and other—benefits of virtual memory later in this chapter. First, though, we discuss implementing virtual memory through demand paging.

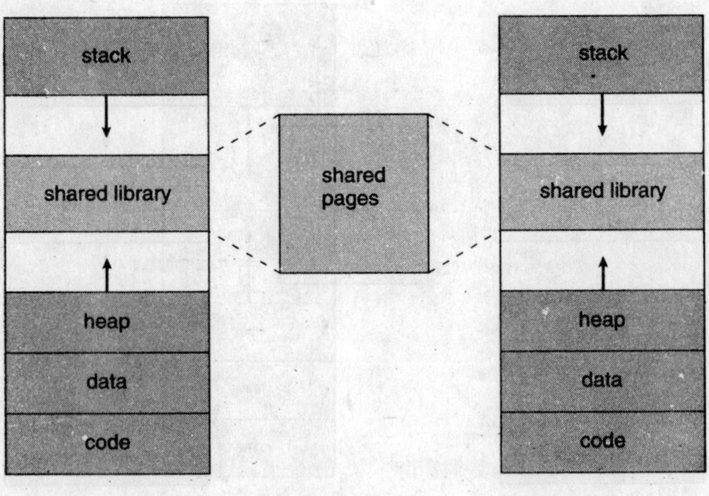

Figure 9.3 Shared library using virtual memory.

9.2 Demand Paging

Consider how an executable program might be loaded from disk into memory. One option is to load the entire program in physical memory at program execution time. However, a problem with this approach is that we may not initially *need* the entire program in memory. Suppose a program starts with a list of available options from which the user is to select. Loading the entire program into memory results in loading the executable code for *all* options, regardless of whether an option is ultimately selected by the user or not. An alternative strategy is to load pages only as they are needed. This technique is known as demand paging and is commonly used in virtual memory systems. With demand-paged virtual memory, pages are only loaded when they are demanded during program execution; pages that are never accessed are thus never loaded into physical memory.

A demand-paging system is similar to a paging system with swapping (Figure 9.4) where processes reside in secondary memory (usually a disk). When we want to execute a process, we swap it into memory. Rather than swapping the entire process into memory, however, we use a lazy swapper. A lazy swapper never swaps a page into memory unless that page will be needed. Since we are now viewing a process as a sequence of pages, rather than as one large contiguous address space, use of the term *swapper* is technically incorrect. A swapper manipulates entire processes, whereas a pager is concerned with the individual pages of a process. We thus use *pager,* rather than *swapper,* in connection with demand paging.

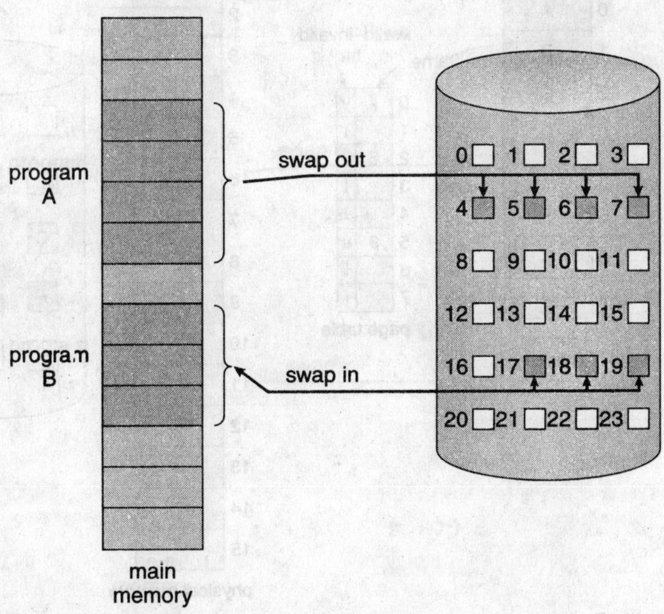

Figure 9.4 Transfer of a paged memory to contiguous disk space.

9.2.1 Basic Concepts

When a process is to be swapped in, the pager guesses which pages will be used before the process is swapped out again. Instead of swapping in a whole process, the pager brings only those pages into memory. Thus, it avoids reading into memory pages that will not be used anyway, decreasing the swap time and the amount of physical memory needed.

With this scheme, we need some form of hardware support to distinguish between the pages that are in memory and the pages that are on the disk. The valid–invalid bit scheme described in Section 8.4.3 can be used for this purpose. This time, however, when this bit is set to "valid," the associated page is both legal and in memory. If the bit is set to "invalid," the page either is not valid (that is, not in the logical address space of the process) or is valid but is currently on the disk. The page-table entry for a page that is brought into memory is set as usual, but the page-table entry for a page that is not currently in memory is either simply marked invalid or contains the address of the page on disk. This situation is depicted in Figure 9.5.

Notice that marking a page invalid will have no effect if the process never attempts to access that page. Hence, if we guess right and page in all and only those pages that are actually needed, the process will run exactly as though we had brought in all pages. While the process executes and accesses pages that are **memory resident**, execution proceeds normally.

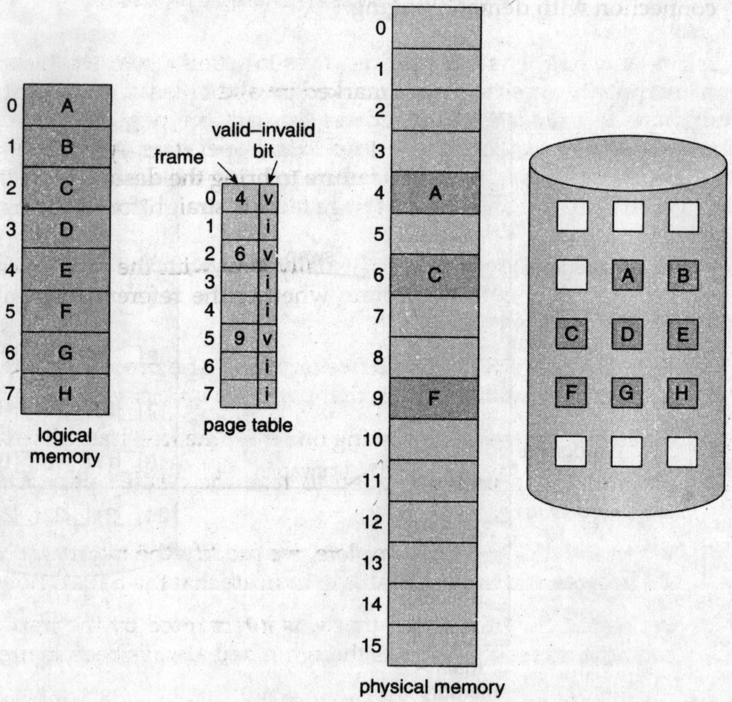

Figure 9.5 Page table when some pages are not in main memory.

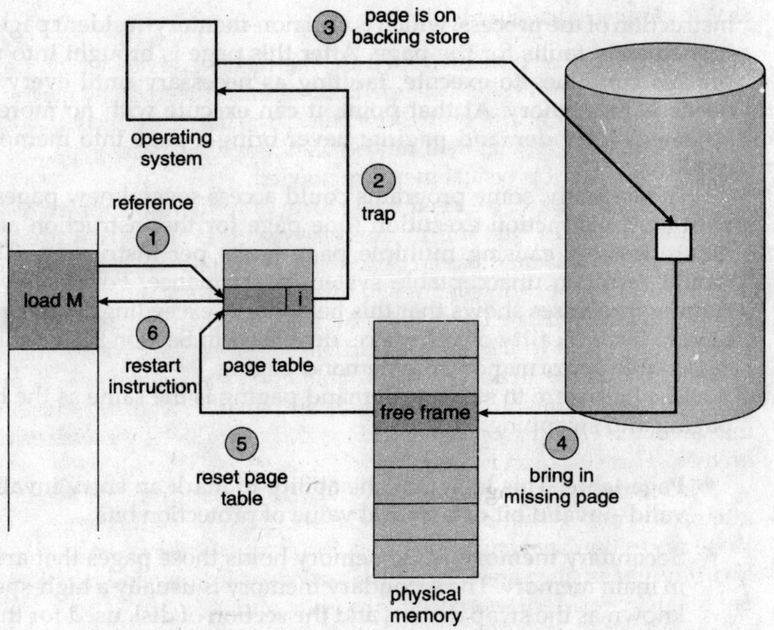

Figure 9.6 Steps in handling a page fault.

But what happens if the process tries to access a page that was not brought into memory? Access to a page marked invalid causes a page fault. The paging hardware, in translating the address through the page table, will notice that the invalid bit is set, causing a trap to the operating system. This trap is the result of the operating system's failure to bring the desired page into memory. The procedure for handling this page fault is straightforward (Figure 9.6):

1. We check an internal table (usually kept with the process control block) for this process to determine whether the reference was a valid or an invalid memory access.
2. If the reference was invalid, we terminate the process. If it was valid, but we have not yet brought in that page, we now page it in.
3. We find a free frame (by taking one from the free-frame list, for example).
4. We schedule a disk operation to read the desired page into the newly allocated frame.
5. When the disk read is complete, we modify the internal table kept with the process and the page table to indicate that the page is now in memory.
6. We restart the instruction that was interrupted by the trap. The process can now access the page as though it had always been in memory.

In the extreme case, we can start executing a process with *no* pages in memory. When the operating system sets the instruction pointer to the first instruction of the process, which is on a non-memory-resident page, the process immediately faults for the page. After this page is brought into memory, the process continues to execute, faulting as necessary until every page that it needs is in memory. At that point, it can execute with no more faults. This scheme is pure demand paging: never bring a page into memory until it is required.

Theoretically, some programs could access several new pages of memory with each instruction execution (one page for the instruction and many for data), possibly causing multiple page faults per instruction. This situation would result in unacceptable system performance. Fortunately, analysis of running processes shows that this behavior is exceedingly unlikely. Programs tend to have locality of reference, described in Section 9.6.1, which results in reasonable performance from demand paging.

The hardware to support demand paging is the same as the hardware for paging and swapping:

- **Page table**. This table has the ability to mark an entry invalid through a valid–invalid bit or a special value of protection bits.
- **Secondary memory**. This memory holds those pages that are not present in main memory. The secondary memory is usually a high-speed disk. It is known as the swap device, and the section of disk used for this purpose is known as swap space. Swap-space allocation is discussed in Chapter 12.

A crucial requirement for demand paging is the ability to restart any instruction after a page fault. Because we save the state (registers, condition code, instruction counter) of the interrupted process when the page fault occurs, we must be able to restart the process in *exactly* the same place and state, except that the desired page is now in memory and is accessible. In most cases, this requirement is easy to meet. A page fault may occur at any memory reference. If the page fault occurs on the instruction fetch, we can restart by fetching the instruction again. If a page fault occurs while we are fetching an operand, we must fetch and decode the instruction again and then fetch the operand.

As a worst-case example, consider a three-address instruction such as ADD the content of A to B, placing the result in C. These are the steps to execute this instruction:

1. Fetch and decode the instruction (ADD).
2. Fetch A.
3. Fetch B.
4. Add A and B.
5. Store the sum in C.

If we fault when we try to store in C (because C is in a page not currently in memory), we will have to get the desired page, bring it in, correct the page table, and restart the instruction. The restart will require fetching the instruction again, decoding it again, fetching the two operands again, and then adding again. However, there is not much repeated work (less than one complete instruction), and the repetition is necessary only when a page fault occurs.

The major difficulty arises when one instruction may modify several different locations. For example, consider the IBM System 360/370 MVC (move character) instruction, which can move up to 256 bytes from one location to another (possibly overlapping) location. If either block (source or destination) straddles a page boundary, a page fault might occur after the move is partially done. In addition, if the source and destination blocks overlap, the source block may have been modified, in which case we cannot simply restart the instruction.

This problem can be solved in two different ways. In one solution, the microcode computes and attempts to access both ends of both blocks. If a page fault is going to occur, it will happen at this step, before anything is modified. The move can then take place; we know that no page fault can occur, since all the relevant pages are in memory. The other solution uses temporary registers to hold the values of overwritten locations. If there is a page fault, all the old values are written back into memory before the trap occurs. This action restores memory to its state before the instruction was started, so that the instruction can be repeated.

This is by no means the only architectural problem resulting from adding paging to an existing architecture to allow demand paging, but it illustrates some of the difficulties involved. Paging is added between the CPU and the memory in a computer system. It should be entirely transparent to the user process. Thus, people often assume that paging can be added to any system. Although this assumption is true for a non-demand-paging environment, where a page fault represents a fatal error, it is not true where a page fault means only that an additional page must be brought into memory and the process restarted.

9.2.2 Performance of Demand Paging

Demand paging can significantly affect the performance of a computer system. To see why, let's compute the **effective access time** for a demand-paged memory. For most computer systems, the memory-access time, denoted *ma*, ranges from 10 to 200 nanoseconds. As long as we have no page faults, the effective access time is equal to the memory access time. If, however, a page fault occurs, we must first read the relevant page from disk and then access the desired word.

Let p be the probability of a page fault ($0 \leq p \leq 1$). We would expect p to be close to zero—that is, we would expect to have only a few page faults. The **effective access time** is then

$$\text{effective access time} = (1 - p) \times ma + p \times \text{page fault time}.$$

To compute the effective access time, we must know how much time is needed to service a page fault. A page fault causes the following sequence to occur:

1. Trap to the operating system.
2. Save the user registers and process state.

3. Determine that the interrupt was a page fault.
4. Check that the page reference was legal and determine the location of the page on the disk.
5. Issue a read from the disk to a free frame:
   a. Wait in a queue for this device until the read request is serviced.
   b. Wait for the device seek and/or latency time.
   c. Begin the transfer of the page to a free frame.
6. While waiting, allocate the CPU to some other user (CPU scheduling, optional).
7. Receive an interrupt from the disk I/O subsystem (I/O completed).
8. Save the registers and process state for the other user (if step 6 is executed).
9. Determine that the interrupt was from the disk.
10. Correct the page table and other tables to show that the desired page is now in memory.
11. Wait for the CPU to be allocated to this process again.
12. Restore the user registers, process state, and new page table, and then resume the interrupted instruction.

Not all of these steps are necessary in every case. For example, we are assuming that, in step 6, the CPU is allocated to another process while the I/O occurs. This arrangement allows multiprogramming to maintain CPU utilization but requires additional time to resume the page-fault service routine when the I/O transfer is complete.

In any case, we are faced with three major components of the page-fault service time:

1. Service the page-fault interrupt.
2. Read in the page.
3. Restart the process.

The first and third tasks can be reduced, with careful coding, to several hundred instructions. These tasks may take from 1 to 100 microseconds each. The page-switch time, however, will probably be close to 8 milliseconds. (A typical hard disk has an average latency of 3 milliseconds, a seek of 5 milliseconds, and a transfer time of 0.05 milliseconds. Thus, the total paging time is about 8 milliseconds, including hardware and software time.) Remember also that we are looking at only the device-service time. If a queue of processes is waiting for the device, we have to add device-queueing time as we wait for the paging device to be free to service our request, increasing even more the time to swap.

With an average page-fault service time of 8 milliseconds and a memory-access time of 200 nanoseconds, the effective access time in nanoseconds is

$$\begin{aligned}\text{effective access time} &= (1 - p) \times (200) + p\ (8\text{ milliseconds})\\ &= (1 - p) \times 200 + p \times 8{,}000{,}000\\ &= 200 + 7{,}999{,}800 \times p.\end{aligned}$$

We see, then, that the effective access time is directly proportional to the **page-fault rate**. If one access out of 1,000 causes a page fault, the effective access time is 8.2 microseconds. The computer will be slowed down by a factor of 40 because of demand paging! If we want performance degradation to be less than 10 percent, we need

$$\begin{aligned}220 &> 200 + 7{,}999{,}800 \times p,\\ 20 &> 7{,}999{,}800 \times p,\\ p &< 0.0000025.\end{aligned}$$

That is, to keep the slowdown due to paging at a reasonable level, we can allow fewer than one memory access out of 399,990 to page-fault. In sum, it is important to keep the page-fault rate low in a demand-paging system. Otherwise, the effective access time increases, slowing process execution dramatically.

An additional aspect of demand paging is the handling and overall use of swap space. Disk I/O to swap space is generally faster than that to the file system. It is faster because swap space is allocated in much larger blocks, and file lookups and indirect allocation methods are not used (Chapter 12). The system can therefore gain better paging throughput by copying an entire file image into the swap space at process startup and then performing demand paging from the swap space. Another option is to demand pages from the file system initially but to write the pages to swap space as they are replaced. This approach will ensure that only needed pages are read from the file system but that all subsequent paging is done from swap space.

Some systems attempt to limit the amount of swap space used through demand paging of binary files. Demand pages for such files are brought directly from the file system. However, when page replacement is called for, these frames can simply be overwritten (because they are never modified), and the pages can be read in from the file system again if needed. Using this approach, the file system itself serves as the backing store. However, swap space must still be used for pages not associated with a file; these pages include the stack and heap for a process. This method appears to be a good compromise and is used in several systems, including Solaris and BSD UNIX.

9.3 Copy-on-Write

In Section 9.2, we illustrated how a process can start quickly by merely demand-paging in the page containing the first instruction. However, process creation using the `fork()` system call may initially bypass the need for demand paging by using a technique similar to page sharing (covered in Section 8.4.4). This technique provides for rapid process creation and minimizes the number of new pages that must be allocated to the newly created process.

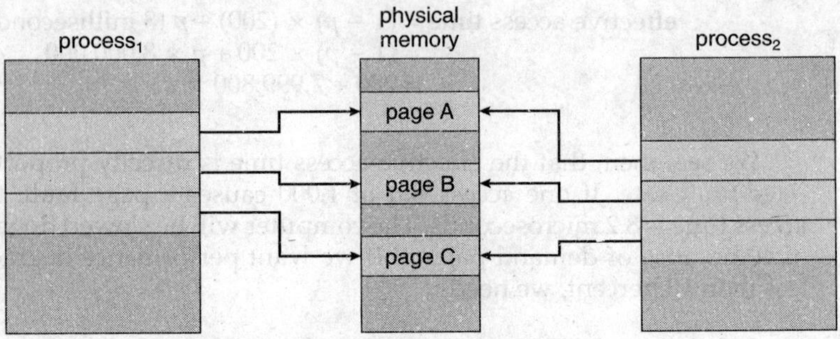

Figure 9.7 Before process 1 modifies page C.

Recall that the `fork()` system call creates a child process that is a duplicate of its parent. Traditionally, `fork()` worked by creating a copy of the parent's address space for the child, duplicating the pages belonging to the parent. However, considering that many child processes invoke the `exec()` system call immediately after creation, the copying of the parent's address space may be unnecessary. Instead, we can use a technique known as **copy-on-write**, which works by allowing the parent and child processes initially to share the same pages. These shared pages are marked as copy-on-write pages, meaning that if either process writes to a shared page, a copy of the shared page is created. Copy-on-write is illustrated in Figures 9.7 and Figure 9.8, which show the contents of the physical memory before and after process 1 modifies page C.

For example, assume that the child process attempts to modify a page containing portions of the stack, with the pages set to be copy-on-write. The operating system will create a copy of this page, mapping it to the address space of the child process. The child process will then modify its copied page and not the page belonging to the parent process. Obviously, when the copy-on-write technique is used, only the pages that are modified by either process are copied; all unmodified pages can be shared by the parent and child processes. Note, too,

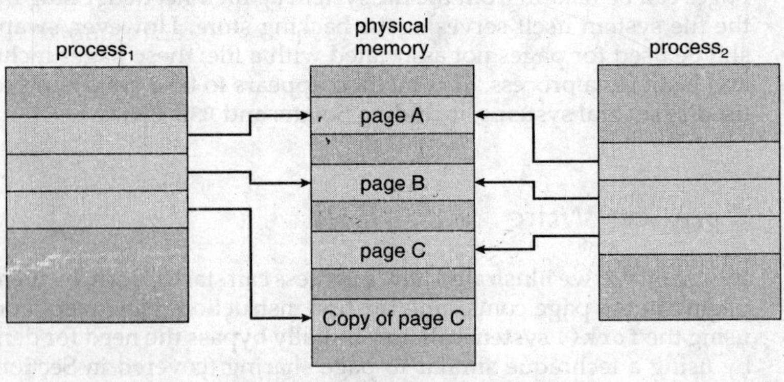

Figure 9.8 After process 1 modifies page C.

that only pages that can be modified need be marked as copy-on-write. Pages that cannot be modified (pages containing executable code) can be shared by the parent and child. Copy-on-write is a common technique used by several operating systems, including Windows XP, Linux, and Solaris.

When it is determined that a page is going to be duplicated using copy-on-write, it is important to note the location from which the free page will be allocated. Many operating systems provide a **pool** of free pages for such requests. These free pages are typically allocated when the stack or heap for a process must expand or when there are copy-on-write pages to be managed. Operating systems typically allocate these pages using a technique known as **zero-fill-on-demand**. Zero-fill-on-demand pages have been zeroed-out before being allocated, thus erasing the previous contents.

Several versions of UNIX (including Solaris and Linux) provide a variation of the `fork()` system call—`vfork()` (for **virtual memory fork**)— that operates differently from `fork()` with copy-on-write. With `vfork()`, the parent process is suspended, and the child process uses the address space of the parent. Because `vfork()` does not use copy-on-write, if the child process changes any pages of the parent's address space, the altered pages will be visible to the parent once it resumes. Therefore, `vfork()` must be used with caution to ensure that the child process does not modify the address space of the parent. `vfork()` is intended to be used when the child process calls `exec()` immediately after creation. Because no copying of pages takes place, `vfork()` is an extremely efficient method of process creation and is sometimes used to implement UNIX command-line shell interfaces.

9.4 Page Replacement

In our earlier discussion of the page-fault rate, we assumed that each page faults at most once, when it is first referenced. This representation is not strictly accurate, however. If a process of ten pages actually uses only half of them, then demand paging saves the I/O necessary to load the five pages that are never used. We could also increase our degree of multiprogramming by running twice as many processes. Thus, if we had forty frames, we could run eight processes, rather than the four that could run if each required ten frames (five of which were never used).

If we increase our degree of multiprogramming, we are **over-allocating** memory. If we run six processes, each of which is ten pages in size but actually uses only five pages, we have higher CPU utilization and throughput, with ten frames to spare. It is possible, however, that each of these processes, for a particular data set, may suddenly try to use all ten of its pages, resulting in a need for sixty frames when only forty are available.

Further, consider that system memory is not used only for holding program pages. Buffers for I/O also consume a considerable amount of memory. This use can increase the strain on memory-placement algorithms. Deciding how much memory to allocate to I/O and how much to program pages is a significant challenge. Some systems allocate a fixed percentage of memory for I/O buffers, whereas others allow both user processes and the I/O subsystem to compete for all system memory.

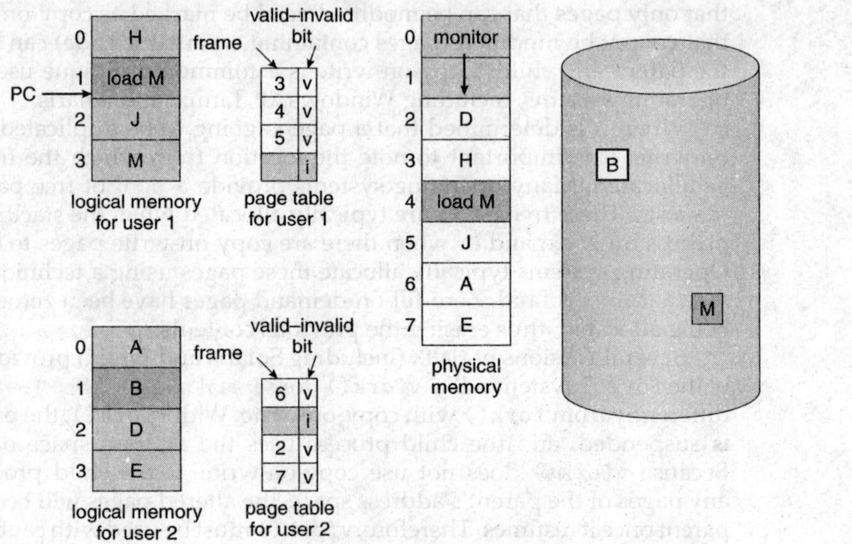

Figure 9.9 Need for page replacement.

Over-allocation of memory manifests itself as follows. While a user process is executing, a page fault occurs. The operating system determines where the desired page is residing on the disk but then finds that there are *no* free frames on the free-frame list; all memory is in use (Figure 9.9).

The operating system has several options at this point. It could terminate the user process. However, demand paging is the operating system's attempt to improve the computer system's utilization and throughput. Users should not be aware that their processes are running on a paged system—paging should be logically transparent to the user. So this option is not the best choice.

The operating system could instead swap out a process, freeing all its frames and reducing the level of multiprogramming. This option is a good one in certain circumstances, and we consider it further in Section 9.6. Here, we discuss the most common solution: **page replacement**.

9.4.1 Basic Page Replacement

Page replacement takes the following approach. If no frame is free, we find one that is not currently being used and free it. We can free a frame by writing its contents to swap space and changing the page table (and all other tables) to indicate that the page is no longer in memory (Figure 9.10). We can now use the freed frame to hold the page for which the process faulted. We modify the page-fault service routine to include page replacement:

1. Find the location of the desired page on the disk.

2. Find a free frame:

    a. If there is a free frame, use it.

b. If there is no free frame, use a page-replacement algorithm to select a **victim frame**.

c. Write the victim frame to the disk; change the page and frame tables accordingly.

3. Read the desired page into the newly freed frame; change the page and frame tables.

4. Restart the user process.

Notice that, if no frames are free, *two* page transfers (one out and one in) are required. This situation effectively doubles the page-fault service time and increases the effective access time accordingly.

We can reduce this overhead by using a **modify bit** (or **dirty bit**). When this scheme is used, each page or frame has a modify bit associated with it in the hardware. The modify bit for a page is set by the hardware whenever any word or byte in the page is written into, indicating that the page has been modified. When we select a page for replacement, we examine its modify bit. If the bit is set, we know that the page has been modified since it was read in from the disk. In this case, we must write the page to the disk. If the modify bit is not set, however, the page has *not* been modified since it was read into memory. In this case, we need not write the memory page to the disk: it is already there. This technique also applies to read-only pages (for example, pages of binary code). Such pages cannot be modified; thus, they may be discarded when desired. This scheme can significantly reduce the time required to service a page fault, since it reduces I/O time by one-half *if* the page has not been modified.

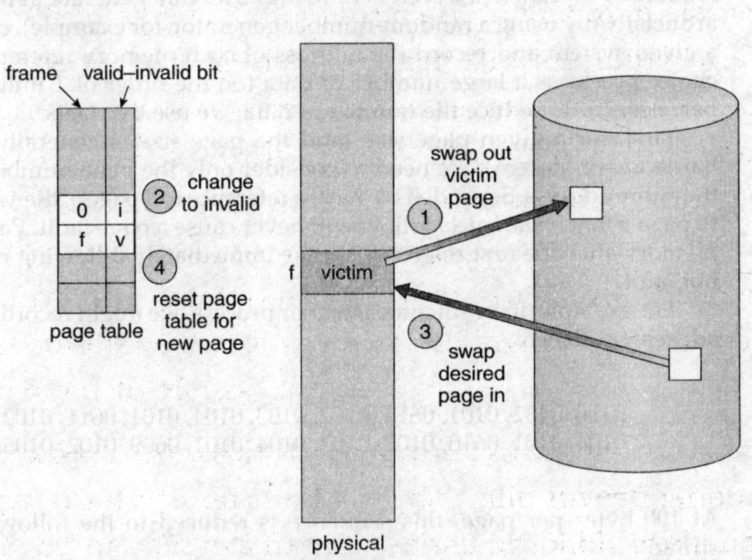

Figure 9.10 Page replacement.

Page replacement is basic to demand paging. It completes the separation between logical memory and physical memory. With this mechanism, an enormous virtual memory can be provided for programmers on a smaller physical memory. With no demand paging, user addresses are mapped into physical addresses, so the two sets of addresses can be different. All the pages of a process still must be in physical memory, however. With demand paging, the size of the logical address space is no longer constrained by physical memory. If we have a user process of twenty pages, we can execute it in ten frames simply by using demand paging and using a replacement algorithm to find a free frame whenever necessary. If a page that has been modified is to be replaced, its contents are copied to the disk. A later reference to that page will cause a page fault. At that time, the page will be brought back into memory, perhaps replacing some other page in the process.

We must solve two major problems to implement demand paging: we must develop a **frame-allocation algorithm** and a **page-replacement algorithm**. That is, if we have multiple processes in memory, we must decide how many frames to allocate to each process; and when page replacement is required, we must select the frames that are to be replaced. Designing appropriate algorithms to solve these problems is an important task, because disk I/O is so expensive. Even slight improvements in demand-paging methods yield large gains in system performance.

There are many different page-replacement algorithms. Every operating system probably has its own replacement scheme. How do we select a particular replacement algorithm? In general, we want the one with the lowest page-fault rate.

We evaluate an algorithm by running it on a particular string of memory references and computing the number of page faults. The string of memory references is called a **reference string**. We can generate reference strings artificially (by using a random-number generator, for example), or we can trace a given system and record the address of each memory reference. The latter choice produces a large number of data (on the order of 1 million addresses per second). To reduce the number of data, we use two facts.

First, for a given page size (and the page size is generally fixed by the hardware or system), we need to consider only the page number, rather than the entire address. Second, if we have a reference to a page p, then any references to page p that *immediately* follow will never cause a page fault. Page p will be in memory after the first reference, so the immediately following references will not fault.

For example, if we trace a particular process, we might record the following address sequence:

0100, 0432, 0101, 0612, 0102, 0103, 0104, 0101, 0611, 0102, 0103,
0104, 0101, 0610, 0102, 0103, 0104, 0101, 0609, 0102, 0105

At 100 bytes per page, this sequence is reduced to the following reference string:

1, 4, 1, 6, 1, 6, 1, 6, 1, 6, 1

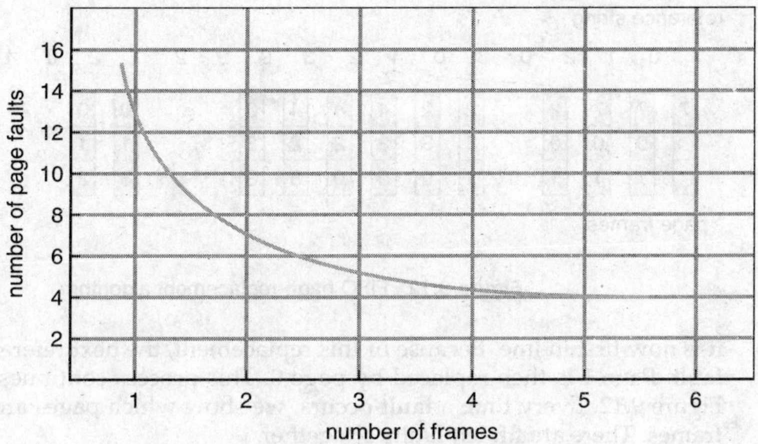

Figure 9.11 Graph of page faults versus number of frames.

To determine the number of page faults for a particular reference string and page-replacement algorithm, we also need to know the number of page frames available. Obviously, as the number of frames available increases, the number of page faults decreases. For the reference string considered previously, for example, if we had three or more frames, we would have only three faults—one fault for the first reference to each page. In contrast, with only one frame available, we would have a replacement with every reference, resulting in eleven faults. In general, we expect a curve such as that in Figure 9.11. As the number of frames increases, the number of page faults drops to some minimal level. Of course, adding physical memory increases the number of frames.

We next illustrate several page-replacement algorithms. In doing so, we use the reference string

7, 0, 1, 2, 0, 3, 0, 4, 2, 3, 0, 3, 2, 1, 2, 0, 1, 7, 0, 1

for a memory with three frames.

9.4.2 FIFO Page Replacement

The simplest page-replacement algorithm is a first-in, first-out (FIFO) algorithm. A FIFO replacement algorithm associates with each page the time when that page was brought into memory. When a page must be replaced, the oldest page is chosen. Notice that it is not strictly necessary to record the time when a page is brought in. We can create a FIFO queue to hold all pages in memory. We replace the page at the head of the queue. When a page is brought into memory, we insert it at the tail of the queue.

For our example reference string, our three frames are initially empty. The first three references (7, 0, 1) cause page faults and are brought into these empty frames. The next reference (2) replaces page 7, because page 7 was brought in first. Since 0 is the next reference and 0 is already in memory, we have no fault for this reference. The first reference to 3 results in replacement of page 0, since

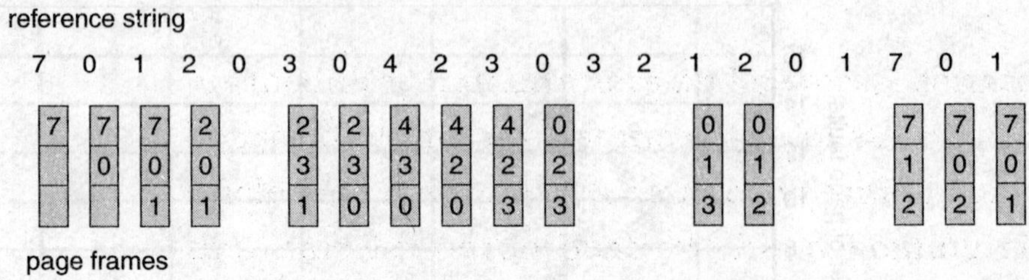

Figure 9.12 FIFO page-replacement algorithm.

it is now first in line. Because of this replacement, the next reference, to 0, will fault. Page 1 is then replaced by page 0. This process continues as shown in Figure 9.12. Every time a fault occurs, we show which pages are in our three frames. There are fifteen faults altogether.

The FIFO page-replacement algorithm is easy to understand and program. However, its performance is not always good. On the one hand, the page replaced may be an initialization module that was used a long time ago and is no longer needed. On the other hand, it could contain a heavily used variable that was initialized early and is in constant use.

Notice that, even if we select for replacement a page that is in active use, everything still works correctly. After we replace an active page with a new one, a fault occurs almost immediately to retrieve the active page. Some other page must be replaced to bring the active page back into memory. Thus, a bad replacement choice increases the page-fault rate and slows process execution. It does not, however, cause incorrect execution.

To illustrate the problems that are possible with a FIFO page-replacement algorithm, we consider the following reference string:

1, 2, 3, 4, 1, 2, 5, 1, 2, 3, 4, 5

Figure 9.13 shows the curve of page faults for this reference string versus the number of available frames. Notice that the number of faults for four frames (ten) is *greater* than the number of faults for three frames (nine)! This most unexpected result is known as **Belady's anomaly**: for some page-replacement algorithms, the page-fault rate may *increase* as the number of allocated frames increases. We would expect that giving more memory to a process would improve its performance. In some early research, investigators noticed that this assumption was not always true. Belady's anomaly was discovered as a result.

9.4.3 Optimal Page Replacement

One result of the discovery of Belady's anomaly was the search for an **optimal page-replacement algorithm**, which has the lowest page-fault rate of all algorithms and will never suffer from Belady's anomaly. Such an algorithm does exist and has been called OPT or MIN. It is simply this:

Replace the page that will not be used
for the longest period of time.

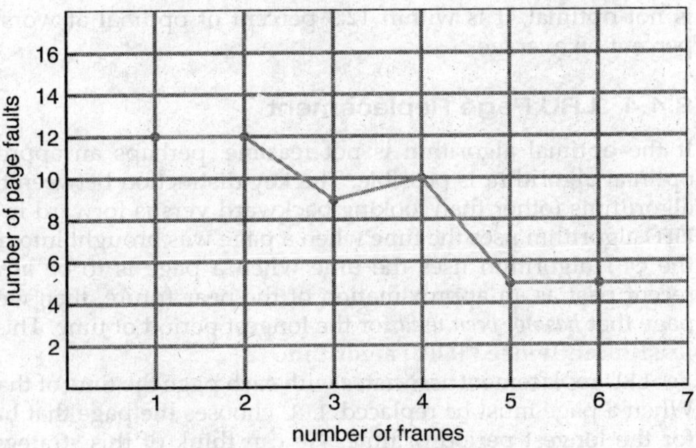

Figure 9.13 Page-fault curve for FIFO replacement on a reference string.

Use of this page-replacement algorithm guarantees the lowest possible page-fault rate for a fixed number of frames.

For example, on our sample reference string, the optimal page-replacement algorithm would yield nine page faults, as shown in Figure 9.14. The first three references cause faults that fill the three empty frames. The reference to page 2 replaces page 7, because page 7 will not be used until reference 18, whereas page 0 will be used at 5, and page 1 at 14. The reference to page 3 replaces page 1, as page 1 will be the last of the three pages in memory to be referenced again. With only nine page faults, optimal replacement is much better than a FIFO algorithm, which results in fifteen faults. (If we ignore the first three, which all algorithms must suffer, then optimal replacement is twice as good as FIFO replacement.) In fact, no replacement algorithm can process this reference string in three frames with fewer than nine faults.

Unfortunately, the optimal page-replacement algorithm is difficult to implement, because it requires future knowledge of the reference string. (We encountered a similar situation with the SJF CPU-scheduling algorithm in Section 5.3.2.) As a result, the optimal algorithm is used mainly for comparison studies. For instance, it may be useful to know that, although a new algorithm

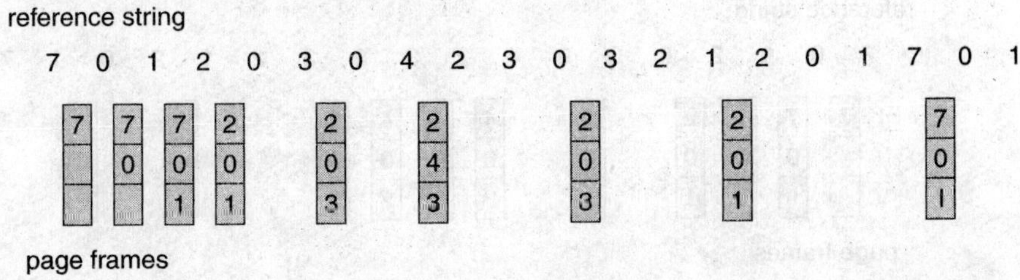

Figure 9.14 Optimal page-replacement algorithm.

is not optimal, it is within 12.3 percent of optimal at worst and within 4.7 percent on average.

9.4.4 LRU Page Replacement

If the optimal algorithm is not feasible, perhaps an approximation of the optimal algorithm is possible. The key distinction between the FIFO and OPT algorithms (other than looking backward versus forward in time) is that the FIFO algorithm uses the time when a page was brought into memory, whereas the OPT algorithm uses the time when a page is to be *used.* If we use the recent past as an approximation of the near future, then we can replace the page that *has not been used* for the longest period of time. This approach is the **least-recently-used (LRU) algorithm.**

LRU replacement associates with each page the time of that page's last use. When a page must be replaced, LRU chooses the page that has not been used for the longest period of time. We can think of this strategy as the optimal page-replacement algorithm looking backward in time, rather than forward. (Strangely, if we let S^R be the reverse of a reference string S, then the page-fault rate for the OPT algorithm on S is the same as the page-fault rate for the OPT algorithm on S^R. Similarly, the page-fault rate for the LRU algorithm on S is the same as the page-fault rate for the LRU algorithm on S^R.)

The result of applying LRU replacement to our example reference string is shown in Figure 9.15. The LRU algorithm produces twelve faults. Notice that the first five faults are the same as those for optimal replacement. When the reference to page 4 occurs, however, LRU replacement sees that, of the three frames in memory, page 2 was used least recently. Thus, the LRU algorithm replaces page 2, not knowing that page 2 is about to be used. When it then faults for page 2, the LRU algorithm replaces page 3, since it is now the least recently used of the three pages in memory. Despite these problems, LRU replacement with twelve faults is much better than FIFO replacement with fifteen.

The LRU policy is often used as a page-replacement algorithm and is considered to be good. The major problem is *how* to implement LRU replacement. An LRU page-replacement algorithm may require substantial hardware assistance. The problem is to determine an order for the frames defined by the time of last use. Two implementations are feasible:

- **Counters**. In the simplest case, we associate with each page-table entry a time-of-use field and add to the CPU a logical clock or counter. The clock is

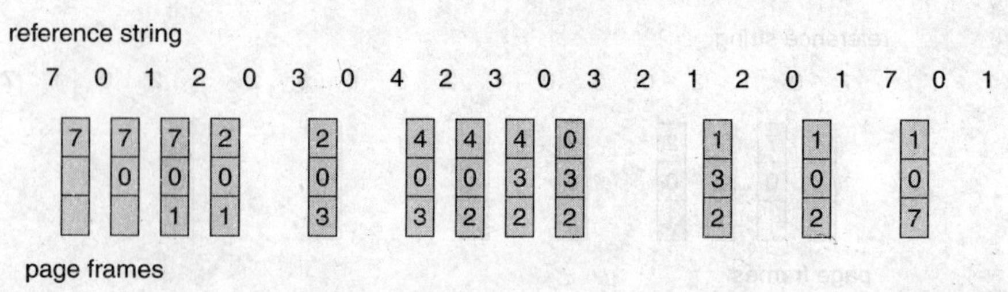

Figure 9.15 LRU page-replacement algorithm.

incremented for every memory reference. Whenever a reference to a page is made, the contents of the clock register are copied to the time-of-use field in the page-table entry for that page. In this way, we always have the "time" of the last reference to each page. We replace the page with the smallest time value. This scheme requires a search of the page table to find the LRU page and a write to memory (to the time-of-use field in the page table) for each memory access. The times must also be maintained when page tables are changed (due to CPU scheduling). Overflow of the clock must be considered.

- **Stack**. Another approach to implementing LRU replacement is to keep a stack of page numbers. Whenever a page is referenced, it is removed from the stack and put on the top. In this way, the most recently used page is always at the top of the stack and the least recently used page is always at the bottom (Figure 9.16). Because entries must be removed from the middle of the stack, it is best to implement this approach by using a doubly linked list with a head pointer and a tail pointer. Removing a page and putting it on the top of the stack then requires changing six pointers at worst. Each update is a little more expensive, but there is no search for a replacement; the tail pointer points to the bottom of the stack, which is the LRU page. This approach is particularly appropriate for software or microcode implementations of LRU replacement.

Like optimal replacement, LRU replacement does not suffer from Belady's anomaly. Both belong to a class of page-replacement algorithms, called **stack algorithms**, that can never exhibit Belady's anomaly. A stack algorithm is an algorithm for which it can be shown that the set of pages in memory for n frames is always a *subset* of the set of pages that would be in memory with $n + 1$ frames. For LRU replacement, the set of pages in memory would be the n most recently referenced pages. If the number of frames is increased, these n pages will still be the most recently referenced and so will still be in memory.

Note that neither implementation of LRU would be conceivable without hardware assistance beyond the standard TLB registers. The updating of the

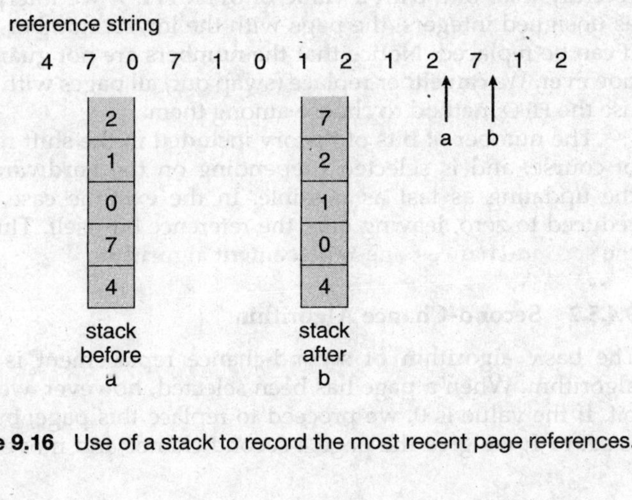

Figure 9.16 Use of a stack to record the most recent page references.

clock fields or stack must be done for *every* memory reference. If we were to use an interrupt for every reference to allow software to update such data structures, it would slow every memory reference by a factor of at least ten, hence slowing every user process by a factor of ten. Few systems could tolerate that level of overhead for memory management.

9.4.5 LRU-Approximation Page Replacement

Few computer systems provide sufficient hardware support for true LRU page replacement. Some systems provide no hardware support, and other page-replacement algorithms (such as a FIFO algorithm) must be used. Many systems provide some help, however, in the form of a **reference bit**. The reference bit for a page is set by the hardware whenever that page is referenced (either a read or a write to any byte in the page). Reference bits are associated with each entry in the page table.

Initially, all bits are cleared (to 0) by the operating system. As a user process executes, the bit associated with each page referenced is set (to 1) by the hardware. After some time, we can determine which pages have been used and which have not been used by examining the reference bits, although we do not know the *order* of use. This information is the basis for many page-replacement algorithms that approximate LRU replacement.

9.4.5.1 Additional-Reference-Bits Algorithm

We can gain additional ordering information by recording the reference bits at regular intervals. We can keep an 8-bit byte for each page in a table in memory. At regular intervals (say, every 100 milliseconds), a timer interrupt transfers control to the operating system. The operating system shifts the reference bit for each page into the high-order bit of its 8-bit byte, shifting the other bits right by 1 bit and discarding the low-order bit. These 8-bit shift registers contain the history of page use for the last eight time periods. If the shift register contains 00000000, for example, then the page has not been used for eight time periods; a page that is used at least once in each period has a shift register value of 11111111. A page with a history register value of 11000100 has been used more recently than one with a value of 01110111. If we interpret these 8-bit bytes as unsigned integers, the page with the lowest number is the LRU page, and it can be replaced. Notice that the numbers are not guaranteed to be unique, however. We can either replace (swap out) all pages with the smallest value or use the FIFO method to choose among them.

The number of bits of history included in the shift register can be varied, of course, and is selected (depending on the hardware available) to make the updating as fast as possible. In the extreme case, the number can be reduced to zero, leaving only the reference bit itself. This algorithm is called the **second-chance page-replacement algorithm**.

9.4.5.2 Second-Chance Algorithm

The basic algorithm of second-chance replacement is a FIFO replacement algorithm. When a page has been selected, however, we inspect its reference bit. If the value is 0, we proceed to replace this page; but if the reference bit is set to 1, we give the page a second chance and move on to select the next

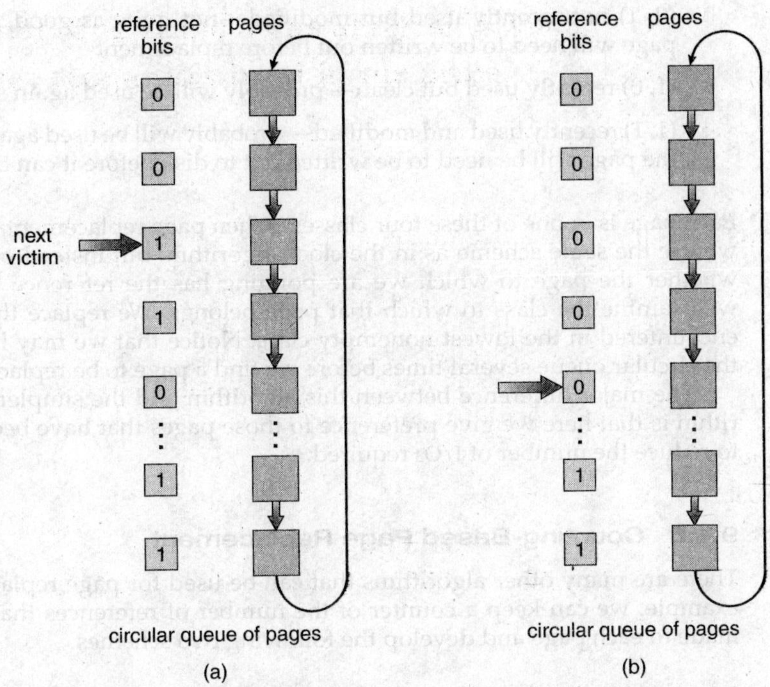

Figure 9.17 Second-chance (clock) page-replacement algorithm.

FIFO page. When a page gets a second chance, its reference bit is cleared, and its arrival time is reset to the current time. Thus, a page that is given a second chance will not be replaced until all other pages have been replaced (or given second chances). In addition, if a page is used often enough to keep its reference bit set, it will never be replaced.

One way to implement the second-chance algorithm (sometimes referred to as the *clock* algorithm) is as a circular queue. A pointer (that is, a hand on the clock) indicates which page is to be replaced next. When a frame is needed, the pointer advances until it finds a page with a 0 reference bit. As it advances, it clears the reference bits (Figure 9.17). Once a victim page is found, the page is replaced, and the new page is inserted in the circular queue in that position. Notice that, in the worst case, when all bits are set, the pointer cycles through the whole queue, giving each page a second chance. It clears all the reference bits before selecting the next page for replacement. Second-chance replacement degenerates to FIFO replacement if all bits are set.

9.4.5.3 Enhanced Second-Chance Algorithm

We can enhance the second-chance algorithm by considering the reference bit and the modify bit (described in Section 9.4.1) as an ordered pair. With these two bits, we have the following four possible classes:

1. (0, 0) neither recently used nor modified—best page to replace

2. (0, 1) not recently used but modified—not quite as good, because the page will need to be written out before replacement
3. (1, 0) recently used but clean—probably will be used again soon
4. (1, 1) recently used and modified—probably will be used again soon, and the page will be need to be written out to disk before it can be replaced

Each page is in one of these four classes. When page replacement is called for, we use the same scheme as in the clock algorithm; but instead of examining whether the page to which we are pointing has the reference bit set to 1, we examine the class to which that page belongs. We replace the first page encountered in the lowest nonempty class. Notice that we may have to scan the circular queue several times before we find a page to be replaced.

The major difference between this algorithm and the simpler clock algorithm is that here we give preference to those pages that have been modified to reduce the number of I/Os required.

9.4.6 Counting-Based Page Replacement

There are many other algorithms that can be used for page replacement. For example, we can keep a counter of the number of references that have been made to each page and develop the following two schemes.

- The **least frequently used (LFU) page-replacement algorithm** requires that the page with the smallest count be replaced. The reason for this selection is that an actively used page should have a large reference count. A problem arises, however, when a page is used heavily during the initial phase of a process but then is never used again. Since it was used heavily, it has a large count and remains in memory even though it is no longer needed. One solution is to shift the counts right by 1 bit at regular intervals, forming an exponentially decaying average usage count.
- The **most frequently used (MFU) page-replacement algorithm** is based on the argument that the page with the smallest count was probably just brought in and has yet to be used.

As you might expect, neither MFU nor LFU replacement is common. The implementation of these algorithms is expensive, and they do not approximate OPT replacement well.

9.4.7 Page-Buffering Algorithms

Other procedures are often used in addition to a specific page-replacement algorithm. For example, systems commonly keep a pool of free frames. When a page fault occurs, a victim frame is chosen as before. However, the desired page is read into a free frame from the pool before the victim is written out. This procedure allows the process to restart as soon as possible, without waiting for the victim page to be written out. When the victim is later written out, its frame is added to the free-frame pool.

An expansion of this idea is to maintain a list of modified pages. Whenever the paging device is idle, a modified page is selected and is written to the disk. Its modify bit is then reset. This scheme increases the probability that a page will be clean when it is selected for replacement and will not need to be written out.

Another modification is to keep a pool of free frames but to remember which page was in each frame. Since the frame contents are not modified when a frame is written to the disk, the old page can be reused directly from the free-frame pool if it is needed before that frame is reused. No I/O is needed in this case. When a page fault occurs, we first check whether the desired page is in the free-frame pool. If it is not, we must select a free frame and read into it.

This technique is used in the VAX/VMS system along with a FIFO replacement algorithm. When the FIFO replacement algorithm mistakenly replaces a page that is still in active use, that page is quickly retrieved from the free-frame pool, and no I/O is necessary. The free-frame buffer provides protection against the relatively poor, but simple, FIFO replacement algorithm. This method is necessary because the early versions of VAX did not implement the reference bit correctly.

Some versions of the UNIX system use this method in conjunction with the second-chance algorithm. It can be a useful augmentation to any page-replacement algorithm, to reduce the penalty incurred if the wrong victim page is selected.

9.4.8 Applications and Page Replacement

In certain cases, applications accessing data through the operating system's virtual memory perform worse than if the operating system provided no buffering at all. A typical example is a database, which provides its own memory management and I/O buffering. Applications like this understand their memory use and disk use better than does an operating system that is implementing algorithms for general-purpose use. If the operating system is buffering I/O, and the application is doing so as well, then twice the memory is being used for a set of I/O.

In another example, data warehouses frequently perform massive sequential disk reads, followed by computations and writes. The LRU algorithm would be removing old pages and preserving new ones, while the application would more likely be reading older pages than newer ones (as it starts its sequential reads again). Here, MFU would actually be more efficient than LRU.

Because of such problems, some operating systems give special programs the ability to use a disk partition as a large sequential array of logical blocks, without any file-system data structures. This array is sometimes called the **raw disk**, and I/O to this array is termed raw I/O. Raw I/O bypasses all the file-system services, such as file I/O demand paging, file locking, prefetching, space allocation, file names, and directories. Note that although certain applications are more efficient when implementing their own special-purpose storage services on a raw partition, most applications perform better when they use the regular file-system services.

9.5 Allocation of Frames

We turn next to the issue of allocation. How do we allocate the fixed amount of free memory among the various processes? If we have 93 free frames and two processes, how many frames does each process get?

The simplest case is the single-user system. Consider a single-user system with 128 KB of memory composed of pages 1 KB in size. This system has 128 frames. The operating system may take 35 KB, leaving 93 frames for the user process. Under pure demand paging, all 93 frames would initially be put on the free-frame list. When a user process started execution, it would generate a sequence of page faults. The first 93 page faults would all get free frames from the free-frame list. When the free-frame list was exhausted, a page-replacement algorithm would be used to select one of the 93 in-memory pages to be replaced with the 94th, and so on. When the process terminated, the 93 frames would once again be placed on the free-frame list.

There are many variations on this simple strategy. We can require that the operating system allocate all its buffer and table space from the free-frame list. When this space is not in use by the operating system, it can be used to support user paging. We can try to keep three free frames reserved on the free-frame list at all times. Thus, when a page fault occurs, there is a free frame available to page into. While the page swap is taking place, a replacement can be selected, which is then written to the disk as the user process continues to execute. Other variants are also possible, but the basic strategy is clear: the user process is allocated any free frame.

9.5.1 Minimum Number of Frames

Our strategies for the allocation of frames are constrained in various ways. We cannot, for example, allocate more than the total number of available frames (unless there is page sharing). We must also allocate at least a minimum number of frames. Here, we look more closely at the latter requirement.

One reason for allocating at least a minimum number of frames involves performance. Obviously, as the number of frames allocated to each process decreases, the page-fault rate increases, slowing process execution. In addition, remember that, when a page fault occurs before an executing instruction is complete, the instruction must be restarted. Consequently, we must have enough frames to hold all the different pages that any single instruction can reference.

For example, consider a machine in which all memory-reference instructions may reference only one memory address. In this case, we need at least one frame for the instruction and one frame for the memory reference. In addition, if one-level indirect addressing is allowed (for example, a `load` instruction on page 16 can refer to an address on page 0, which is an indirect reference to page 23), then paging requires at least three frames per process. Think about what might happen if a process had only two frames.

The minimum number of frames is defined by the computer architecture. For example, the move instruction for the PDP-11 includes more than one word for some addressing modes, and thus the instruction itself may straddle two pages. In addition, each of its two operands may be indirect references, for a total of six frames. Another example is the IBM 370 MVC instruction. Since the instruction is from storage location to storage location, it takes 6 bytes and can straddle two pages. The block of characters to move and the area to which it is to be moved can each also straddle two pages. This situation would require six frames. The worst case occurs when the MVC instruction is the operand of an EXECUTE instruction that straddles a page boundary; in this case, we need eight frames.

The worst-case scenario occurs in computer architectures that allow multiple levels of indirection (for example, each 16-bit word could contain a 15-bit address plus a 1-bit indirect indicator). Theoretically, a simple load instruction could reference an indirect address that could reference an indirect address (on another page) that could also reference an indirect address (on yet another page), and so on, until every page in virtual memory had been touched. Thus, in the worst case, the entire virtual memory must be in physical memory. To overcome this difficulty, we must place a limit on the levels of indirection (for example, limit an instruction to at most 16 levels of indirection). When the first indirection occurs, a counter is set to 16; the counter is then decremented for each successive indirection for this instruction. If the counter is decremented to 0, a trap occurs (excessive indirection). This limitation reduces the maximum number of memory references per instruction to 17, requiring the same number of frames.

Whereas the minimum number of frames per process is defined by the architecture, the maximum number is defined by the amount of available physical memory. In between, we are still left with significant choice in frame allocation.

9.5.2 Allocation Algorithms

The easiest way to split m frames among n processes is to give everyone an equal share, m/n frames. For instance, if there are 93 frames and five processes, each process will get 18 frames. The three leftover frames can be used as a free-frame buffer pool. This scheme is called **equal allocation**.

An alternative is to recognize that various processes will need differing amounts of memory. Consider a system with a 1-KB frame size. If a small student process of 10 KB and an interactive database of 127 KB are the only two processes running in a system with 62 free frames, it does not make much sense to give each process 31 frames. The student process does not need more than 10 frames, so the other 21 are, strictly speaking, wasted.

To solve this problem, we can use **proportional allocation**, in which we allocate available memory to each process according to its size. Let the size of the virtual memory for process p_i be s_i, and define

$$S = \sum s_i.$$

Then, if the total number of available frames is m, we allocate a_i frames to process p_i, where a_i is approximately

$$a_i = s_i / S \times m.$$

Of course, we must adjust each a_i to be an integer that is greater than the minimum number of frames required by the instruction set, with a sum not exceeding *m*.

With proportional allocation, we would split 62 frames between two processes, one of 10 pages and one of 127 pages, by allocating 4 frames and 57 frames, respectively, since

$$10/137 \times 62 \approx 4, \text{ and}$$
$$127/137 \times 62 \approx 57.$$

In this way, both processes share the available frames according to their "needs," rather than equally.

In both equal and proportional allocation, of course, the allocation may vary according to the multiprogramming level. If the multiprogramming level is increased, each process will lose some frames to provide the memory needed for the new process. Conversely, if the multiprogramming level decreases, the frames that were allocated to the departed process can be spread over the remaining processes.

Notice that, with either equal or proportional allocation, a high-priority process is treated the same as a low-priority process. By its definition, however, we may want to give the high-priority process more memory to speed its execution, to the detriment of low-priority processes. One solution is to use a proportional allocation scheme wherein the ratio of frames depends not on the relative sizes of processes but rather on the priorities of processes or on a combination of size and priority.

9.5.3 Global versus Local Allocation

Another important factor in the way frames are allocated to the various processes is page replacement. With multiple processes competing for frames, we can classify page-replacement algorithms into two broad categories: **global replacement** and **local replacement**. Global replacement allows a process to select a replacement frame from the set of all frames, even if that frame is currently allocated to some other process; that is, one process can take a frame from another. Local replacement requires that each process select from only its own set of allocated frames.

For example, consider an allocation scheme wherein we allow high-priority processes to select frames from low-priority processes for replacement. A process can select a replacement from among its own frames or the frames of any lower-priority process. This approach allows a high-priority process to increase its frame allocation at the expense of a low-priority process. With a local replacement strategy, the number of frames allocated to a process does not change. With global replacement, a process may happen to select only frames allocated to other processes, thus increasing the number of frames allocated to it (assuming that other processes do not choose *its* frames for replacement).

One problem with a global replacement algorithm is that a process cannot control its own page-fault rate. The set of pages in memory for a process depends not only on the paging behavior of that process but also on the paging behavior of other processes. Therefore, the same process may perform quite differently (for example, taking 0.5 seconds for one execution and 10.3 seconds for the next execution) because of totally external circumstances. Such is not the case with a local replacement algorithm. Under local replacement, the set of pages in memory for a process is affected by the paging behavior of only that process. Local replacement might hinder a process, however, by not making available to it other, less used pages of memory. Thus, global replacement generally results in greater system throughput and is therefore the more common method.

9.5.4 Non-Uniform Memory Access

Thus far in our coverage of virtual memory, we have assumed that all main memory is created equal—or at least that it is accessed equally. On many computer systems, that is not the case. Often, in systems with multiple CPUs (Section 1.3.2), a given CPU can access some sections of main memory faster than it can access others. These performance differences are caused by how CPUs and memory are interconnected in the system. Frequently, such a system is made up of several system boards, each containing multiple CPUs and some memory. The system boards are interconnected in various ways, ranging from system busses to high-speed network connections like InfiniBand. As you might expect, the CPUs on a particular board can access the memory on that board with less delay than they can access memory on other boards in the system. Systems in which memory access times vary significantly are known collectively as **non-uniform memory access** (**NUMA**) systems, and without exception, they are slower than systems in which memory and CPUs are located on the same motherboard.

Managing which page frames are stored at which locations can significantly affect performance in NUMA systems. If we treat memory as uniform in such a system, CPUs may wait significantly longer for memory access than if we modify memory allocation algorithms to take NUMA into account. Similar changes must be made to the scheduling system. The goal of these changes is to have memory frames allocated "as close as possible" to the CPU on which the process is running. The definition of "close" is "with minimum latency," which typically means on the same system board as the CPU.

The algorithmic changes consist of having the scheduler track the last CPU on which each process ran. If the scheduler tries to schedule each process onto its previous CPU, and the memory-management system tries to allocate frames for the process close to the CPU on which it is being scheduled, then improved cache hits and decreased memory access times will result.

The picture is more complicated once threads are added. For example, a process with many running threads may end up with those threads scheduled on many different system boards. How is the memory to be allocated in this case? Solaris solves the problem by creating an **lgroup** entity in the kernel. Each lgroup gathers together close CPUs and memory. In fact, there is a hierarchy of lgroups based on the amount of latency between the groups. Solaris tries to schedule all threads of a process and allocate all memory of a process within an lgroup. If that is not possible, it picks nearby lgroups for the rest of the resources needed. In this manner, overall memory latency is minimized, and CPU cache hit rates are maximized.

9.6 Thrashing

If the number of frames allocated to a low-priority process falls below the minimum number required by the computer architecture, we must suspend that process's execution. We should then page out its remaining pages, freeing all its allocated frames. This provision introduces a swap-in, swap-out level of intermediate CPU scheduling.

In fact, look at any process that does not have "enough" frames. If the process does not have the number of frames it needs to support pages in active use, it will quickly page-fault. At this point, it must replace some page. However, since all its pages are in active use, it must replace a page that will be needed again right away. Consequently, it quickly faults again, and again, and again, replacing pages that it must bring back in immediately.

This high paging activity is called **thrashing**. A process is thrashing if it is spending more time paging than executing.

9.6.1 Cause of Thrashing

Thrashing results in severe performance problems. Consider the following scenario, which is based on the actual behavior of early paging systems.

The operating system monitors CPU utilization. If CPU utilization is too low, we increase the degree of multiprogramming by introducing a new process to the system. A global page-replacement algorithm is used; it replaces pages without regard to the process to which they belong. Now suppose that a process enters a new phase in its execution and needs more frames. It starts faulting and taking frames away from other processes. These processes need those pages, however, and so they also fault, taking frames from other processes. These faulting processes must use the paging device to swap pages in and out. As they queue up for the paging device, the ready queue empties. As processes wait for the paging device, CPU utilization decreases.

The CPU scheduler sees the decreasing CPU utilization and *increases* the degree of multiprogramming as a result. The new process tries to get started by taking frames from running processes, causing more page faults and a longer queue for the paging device. As a result, CPU utilization drops even further, and the CPU scheduler tries to increase the degree of multiprogramming even more. Thrashing has occurred, and system throughput plunges. The page-fault rate increases tremendously. As a result, the effective memory-access time increases. No work is getting done, because the processes are spending all their time paging.

This phenomenon is illustrated in Figure 9.18, in which CPU utilization is plotted against the degree of multiprogramming. As the degree of multiprogramming increases, CPU utilization also increases, although more slowly, until a maximum is reached. If the degree of multiprogramming is increased even further, thrashing sets in, and CPU utilization drops sharply. At this point, to increase CPU utilization and stop thrashing, we must *decrease* the degree of multiprogramming.

We can limit the effects of thrashing by using a **local replacement algorithm** (or **priority replacement algorithm**). With local replacement, if one process starts thrashing, it cannot steal frames from another process and cause the latter to thrash as well. However, the problem is not entirely solved. If processes are

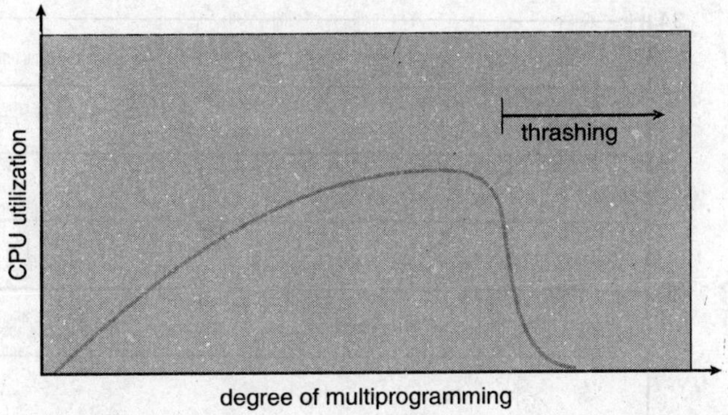

Figure 9.18 Thrashing.

thrashing, they will be in the queue for the paging device most of the time. The average service time for a page fault will increase because of the longer average queue for the paging device. Thus, the effective access time will increase even for a process that is not thrashing.

To prevent thrashing, we must provide a process with as many frames as it needs. But how do we know how many frames it "needs"? There are several techniques. The working-set strategy (Section 9.6.2) starts by looking at how many frames a process is actually using. This approach defines the **locality model** of process execution.

The locality model states that, as a process executes, it moves from locality to locality. A locality is a set of pages that are actively used together (Figure 9.19). A program is generally composed of several different localities, which may overlap.

For example, when a function is called, it defines a new locality. In this locality, memory references are made to the instructions of the function call, its local variables, and a subset of the global variables. When we exit the function, the process leaves this locality, since the local variables and instructions of the function are no longer in active use. We may return to this locality later.

Thus, we see that localities are defined by the program structure and its data structures. The locality model states that all programs will exhibit this basic memory reference structure. Note that the locality model is the unstated principle behind the caching discussions so far in this book. If accesses to any types of data were random rather than patterned, caching would be useless.

Suppose we allocate enough frames to a process to accommodate its current locality. It will fault for the pages in its locality until all these pages are in memory; then, it will not fault again until it changes localities. If we do not allocate enough frames to accommodate the size of the current locality, the process will thrash, since it cannot keep in memory all the pages that it is actively using.

9.6.2 Working-Set Model

As mentioned, the **working-set model** is based on the assumption of locality. This model uses a parameter, Δ, to define the **working-set window**. The idea

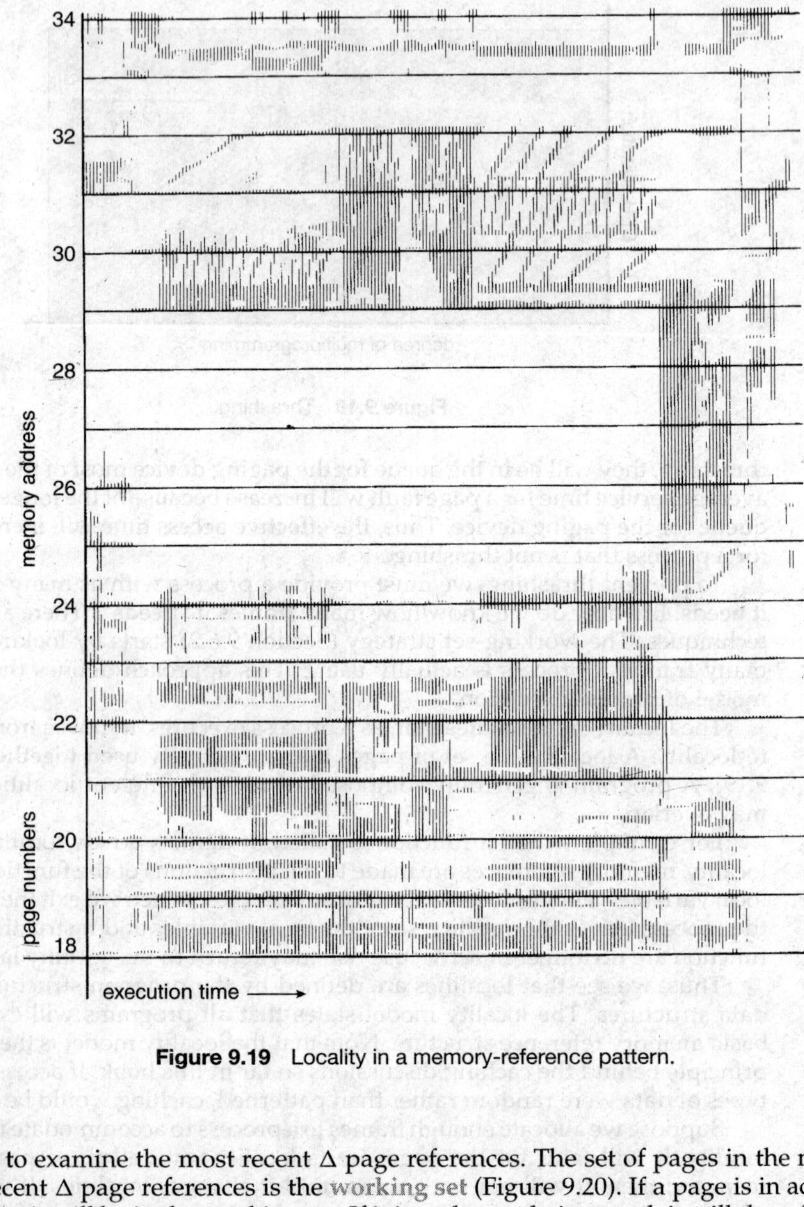

Figure 9.19 Locality in a memory-reference pattern.

is to examine the most recent Δ page references. The set of pages in the most recent Δ page references is the **working set** (Figure 9.20). If a page is in active use, it will be in the working set. If it is no longer being used, it will drop from the working set Δ time units after its last reference. Thus, the working set is an approximation of the program's locality.

For example, given the sequence of memory references shown in Figure 9.20, if Δ = 10 memory references, then the working set at time t_1 is {1, 2, 5, 6, 7}. By time t_2, the working set has changed to {3, 4}.

The accuracy of the working set depends on the selection of Δ. If Δ is too small, it will not encompass the entire locality; if Δ is too large, it may overlap

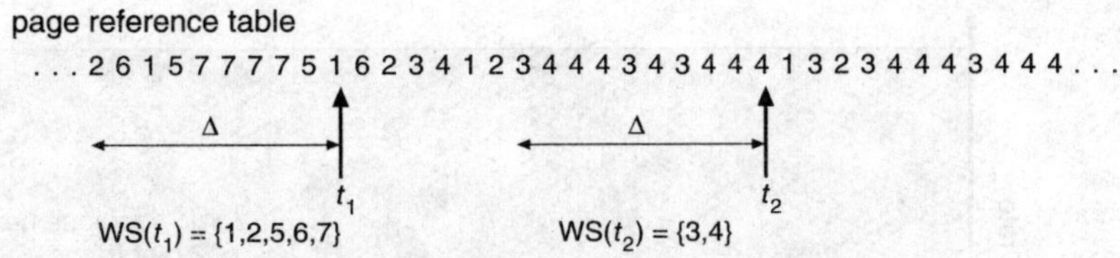

Figure 9.20 Working-set model.

several localities. In the extreme, if Δ is infinite, the working set is the set of pages touched during the process execution.

The most important property of the working set, then, is its size. If we compute the working-set size, WSS_i, for each process in the system, we can then consider that

$$D = \sum WSS_i,$$

where D is the total demand for frames. Each process is actively using the pages in its working set. Thus, process i needs WSS_i frames. If the total demand is greater than the total number of available frames ($D > m$), thrashing will occur, because some processes will not have enough frames.

Once Δ has been selected, use of the working-set model is simple. The operating system monitors the working set of each process and allocates to that working set enough frames to provide it with its working-set size. If there are enough extra frames, another process can be initiated. If the sum of the working-set sizes increases, exceeding the total number of available frames, the operating system selects a process to suspend. The process's pages are written out (swapped), and its frames are reallocated to other processes. The suspended process can be restarted later.

This working-set strategy prevents thrashing while keeping the degree of multiprogramming as high as possible. Thus, it optimizes CPU utilization.

The difficulty with the working-set model is keeping track of the working set. The working-set window is a moving window. At each memory reference, a new reference appears at one end and the oldest reference drops off the other end. A page is in the working set if it is referenced anywhere in the working-set window.

We can approximate the working-set model with a fixed-interval timer interrupt and a reference bit. For example, assume that Δ equals 10,000 references and that we can cause a timer interrupt every 5,000 references. When we get a timer interrupt, we copy and clear the reference-bit values for each page. Thus, if a page fault occurs, we can examine the current reference bit and two in-memory bits to determine whether a page was used within the last 10,000 to 15,000 references. If it was used, at least one of these bits will be on. If it has not been used, these bits will be off. Those pages with at least one bit on will be considered to be in the working set. Note that this arrangement is not entirely accurate, because we cannot tell where, within an interval of 5,000, a reference occurred. We can reduce the uncertainty by increasing the number of history bits and the frequency of interrupts (for example, 10 bits and interrupts every 1,000 references). However, the cost to service these more frequent interrupts will be correspondingly higher.

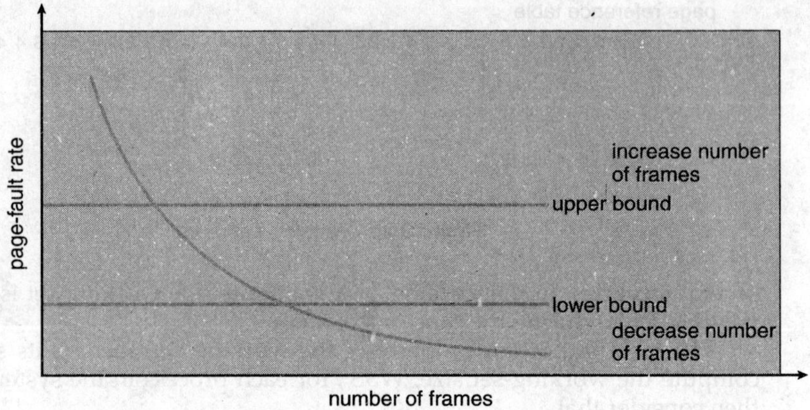

Figure 9.21 Page-fault frequency.

9.6.3 Page-Fault Frequency

The working-set model is successful, and knowledge of the working set can be useful for prepaging (Section 9.9.1), but it seems a clumsy way to control thrashing. A strategy that uses the **page-fault frequency** (PFF) takes a more direct approach.

The specific problem is how to prevent thrashing. Thrashing has a high page-fault rate. Thus, we want to control the page-fault rate. When it is too high, we know that the process needs more frames. Conversely, if the page-fault rate is too low, then the process may have too many frames. We can establish upper and lower bounds on the desired page-fault rate (Figure 9.21). If the actual page-fault rate exceeds the upper limit, we allocate the process another frame; if the page-fault rate falls below the lower limit, we remove a frame from the process. Thus, we can directly measure and control the page-fault rate to prevent thrashing.

As with the working-set strategy, we may have to suspend a process. If the page-fault rate increases and no free frames are available, we must select some process and suspend it. The freed frames are then distributed to processes with high page-fault rates.

9.7 Memory-Mapped Files

Consider a sequential read of a file on disk using the standard system calls `open()`, `read()`, and `write()`. Each file access requires a system call and disk access. Alternatively, we can use the virtual memory techniques discussed so far to treat file I/O as routine memory accesses. This approach, known as **memory mapping** a file, allows a part of the virtual address space to be logically associated with the file. As we shall see, this can lead to significant performance increases when performing I/O.

WORKING SETS AND PAGE FAULT RATES

There is a direct relationship between the working set of a process and its page-fault rate. Typically, as shown in Figure 9.20, the working set of a process changes over time as references to data and code sections move from one locality to another. Assuming there is sufficient memory to store the working set of a process (that is, the process is not thrashing), the page-fault rate of the process will transition between peaks and valleys over time. This general behavior is shown in Figure 9.22.

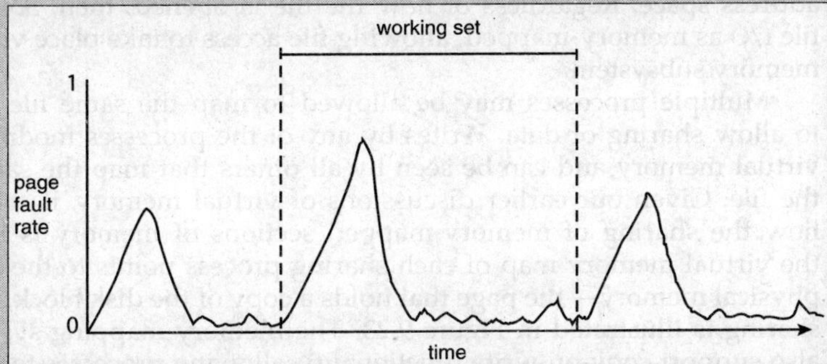

Figure 9.22 Page fault rate over time.

A peak in the page-fault rate occurs when we begin demand-paging a new locality. However, once the working set of this new locality is in memory, the page-fault rate falls. When the process moves to a new working set, the page-fault rate rises toward a peak once again, returning to a lower rate once the new working set is loaded into memory. The span of time between the start of one peak and the start of the next peak represents the transition from one working set to another.

9.7.1 Basic Mechanism

Memory mapping a file is accomplished by mapping a disk block to a page (or pages) in memory. Initial access to the file proceeds through ordinary demand paging, resulting in a page fault. However, a page-sized portion of the file is read from the file system into a physical page (some systems may opt to read in more than a page-sized chunk of memory at a time). Subsequent reads and writes to the file are handled as routine memory accesses, thereby simplifying file access and usage by allowing the system to manipulate files through memory rather than incurring the overhead of using the `read()` and `write()` system calls. Similarly, as file I/O is done in memory — as opposed to using system calls that involve disk I/O — file access is much faster as well.

Note that writes to the file mapped in memory are not necessarily immediate (synchronous) writes to the file on disk. Some systems may choose to update the physical file when the operating system periodically checks whether the page in memory has been modified. When the file is closed, all the memory-mapped data are written back to disk and removed from the virtual memory of the process.

Some operating systems provide memory mapping only through a specific system call and use the standard system calls to perform all other file I/O. However, some systems choose to memory-map a file regardless of whether the file was specified as memory-mapped. Let's take Solaris as an example. If a file is specified as memory-mapped (using the `mmap()` system call), Solaris maps the file into the address space of the process. If a file is opened and accessed using ordinary system calls, such as `open()`, `read()`, and `write()`, Solaris still memory-maps the file; however, the file is mapped to the kernel address space. Regardless of how the file is opened, then, Solaris treats all file I/O as memory-mapped, allowing file access to take place via the efficient memory subsystem.

Multiple processes may be allowed to map the same file concurrently, to allow sharing of data. Writes by any of the processes modify the data in virtual memory and can be seen by all others that map the same section of the file. Given our earlier discussions of virtual memory, it should be clear how the sharing of memory-mapped sections of memory is implemented: the virtual memory map of each sharing process points to the same page of physical memory—the page that holds a copy of the disk block. This memory sharing is illustrated in Figure 9.23. The memory-mapping system calls can also support copy-on-write functionality, allowing processes to share a file in read-only mode but to have their own copies of any data they modify. So that

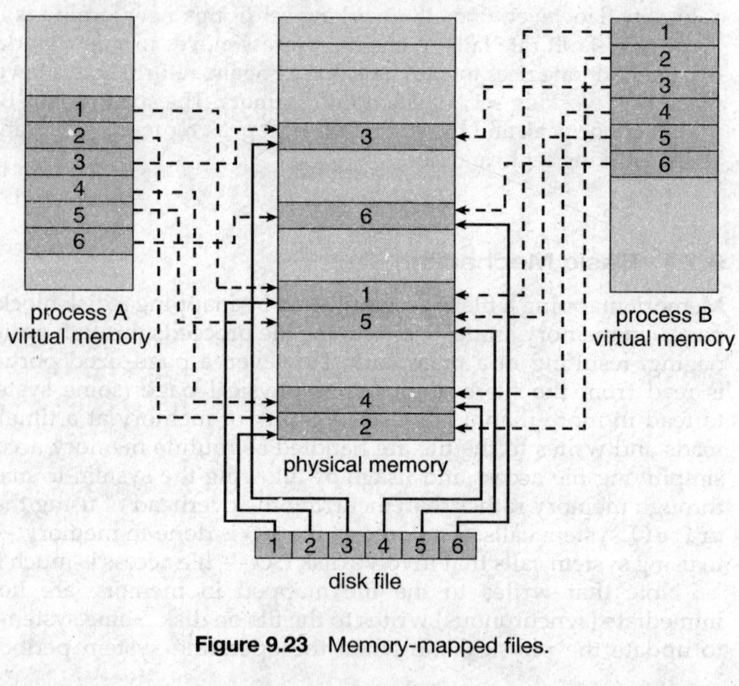

Figure 9.23 Memory-mapped files.

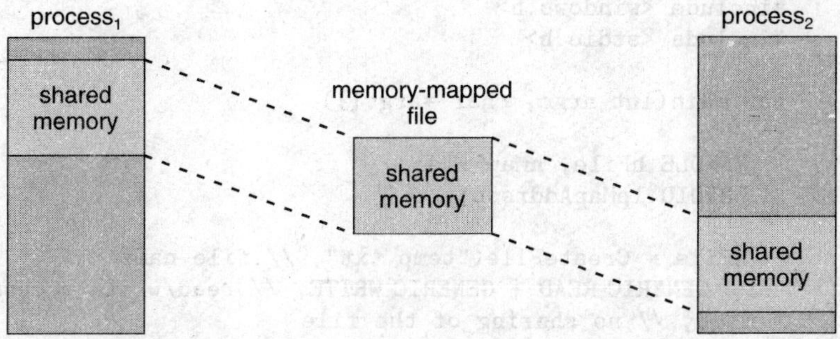

Figure 9.24 Shared memory in Windows using memory-mapped I/O.

access to the shared data is coordinated, the processes involved might use one of the mechanisms for achieving mutual exclusion described in Chapter 6.

In many ways, the sharing of memory-mapped files is similar to shared memory as described in Section 3.4.1. Not all systems use the same mechanism for both; on UNIX and Linux systems, for example, memory mapping is accomplished with the `mmap()` system call, whereas shared memory is achieved with the POSIX-compliant `shmget()` and `shmat()` systems calls (Section 3.5.1). On Windows NT, 2000, and XP systems, however, shared memory is accomplished by memory mapping files. On these systems, processes can communicate using shared memory by having the communicating processes memory-map the same file into their virtual address spaces. The memory-mapped file serves as the region of shared memory between the communicating processes (Figure 9.24). In the following section, we illustrate support in the Win32 API for shared memory using memory-mapped files.

9.7.2 Shared Memory in the Win32 API

The general outline for creating a region of shared memory using memory-mapped files in the Win32 API involves first creating a **file mapping** for the file to be mapped and then establishing a *view* of the mapped file in a process's virtual address space. A second process can then open and create a view of the mapped file in its virtual address space. The mapped file represents the shared-memory object that will enable communication to take place between the processes.

We next illustrate these steps in more detail. In this example, a producer process first creates a shared-memory object using the memory-mapping features available in the Win32 API. The producer then writes a message to shared memory. After that, a consumer process opens a mapping to the shared-memory object and reads the message written by the consumer.

To establish a memory-mapped file, a process first opens the file to be mapped with the `CreateFile()` function, which returns a `HANDLE` to the opened file. The process then creates a mapping of this file `HANDLE` using the `CreateFileMapping()` function. Once the file mapping is established, the process then establishes a view of the mapped file in its virtual address space with the `MapViewOfFile()` function. The view of the mapped file represents the portion of the file being mapped in the virtual address space of the process

```
#include <windows.h>
#include <stdio.h>

int main(int argc, char *argv[])
{
   HANDLE hFile, hMapFile;
   LPVOID lpMapAddress;

   hFile = CreateFile("temp.txt", // file name
      GENERIC_READ | GENERIC_WRITE, // read/write access
      0, // no sharing of the file
      NULL, // default security
      OPEN_ALWAYS, // open new or existing file
      FILE_ATTRIBUTE_NORMAL, // routine file attributes
      NULL); // no file template

   hMapFile = CreateFileMapping(hFile, // file handle
      NULL, // default security
      PAGE_READWRITE, // read/write access to mapped pages
      0, // map entire file
      0,
      TEXT("SharedObject")); // named shared memory object

   lpMapAddress = MapViewOfFile(hMapFile, // mapped object handle
      FILE_MAP_ALL_ACCESS, // read/write access
      0, // mapped view of entire file
      0,
      0);

   // write to shared memory
   sprintf(lpMapAddress,"Shared memory message");

   UnmapViewOfFile(lpMapAddress);
   CloseHandle(hFile);
   CloseHandle(hMapFile);
}
```

Figure 9.25 Producer writing to shared memory using the Win32 API.

—the entire file or only a portion of it may be mapped. We illustrate this sequence in the program shown in Figure 9.25. (We eliminate much of the error checking for code brevity.)

The call to `CreateFileMapping()` creates a **named shared-memory object** called `SharedObject`. The consumer process will communicate using this shared-memory segment by creating a mapping to the same named object. The producer then creates a view of the memory-mapped file in its virtual address space. By passing the last three parameters the value 0, it indicates that the mapped view is the entire file. It could instead have passed values specifying an offset and size, thus creating a view containing only a subsection of the file. (It is important to note that the entire mapping may not be loaded

```
#include <windows.h>
#include <stdio.h>

int main(int argc, char *argv[])
{
   HANDLE hMapFile;
   LPVOID lpMapAddress;

   hMapFile = OpenFileMapping(FILE_MAP_ALL_ACCESS, // R/W access
      FALSE, // no inheritance
      TEXT("SharedObject")); // name of mapped file object

   lpMapAddress = MapViewOfFile(hMapFile, // mapped object handle
      FILE_MAP_ALL_ACCESS, // read/write access
      0, // mapped view of entire file
      0,
      0);

   // read from shared memory
   printf("Read message %s", lpMapAddress);

   UnmapViewOfFile(lpMapAddress);
   CloseHandle(hMapFile);
}
```

Figure 9.26 Consumer reading from shared memory using the Win32 API.

into memory when the mapping is established. Rather, the mapped file may be demand-paged, thus bringing pages into memory only as they are accessed.) The `MapViewOfFile()` function returns a pointer to the shared-memory object; any accesses to this memory location are thus accesses to the memory-mapped file. In this instance, the producer process writes the message "`Shared memory message`" to shared memory.

A program illustrating how the consumer process establishes a view of the named shared-memory object is shown in Figure 9.26. This program is somewhat simpler than the one shown in Figure 9.25, as all that is necessary is for the process to create a mapping to the existing named shared-memory object. The consumer process must also create a view of the mapped file, just as the producer process did in the program in Figure 9.25. The consumer then reads from shared memory the message "`Shared memory message`" that was written by the producer process.

Finally, both processes remove the view of the mapped file with a call to `UnmapViewOfFile()`. We provide a programming exercise at the end of this chapter using shared memory with memory mapping in the Win32 API.

9.7.3 Memory-Mapped I/O

In the case of I/O, as mentioned in Section 1.2.1, each I/O controller includes registers to hold commands and the data being transferred. Usually, special I/O instructions allow data transfers between these registers and system memory.

To allow more convenient access to I/O devices, many computer architectures provide **memory-mapped I/O**. In this case, ranges of memory addresses are set aside and are mapped to the device registers. Reads and writes to these memory addresses cause the data to be transferred to and from the device registers. This method is appropriate for devices that have fast response times, such as video controllers. In the IBM PC, each location on the screen is mapped to a memory location. Displaying text on the screen is almost as easy as writing the text into the appropriate memory-mapped locations.

Memory-mapped I/O is also convenient for other devices, such as the serial and parallel ports used to connect modems and printers to a computer. The CPU transfers data through these kinds of devices by reading and writing a few device registers, called an I/O **port**. To send out a long string of bytes through a memory-mapped serial port, the CPU writes one data byte to the data register and sets a bit in the control register to signal that the byte is available. The device takes the data byte and then clears the bit in the control register to signal that it is ready for the next byte. Then the CPU can transfer the next byte. If the CPU uses polling to watch the control bit, constantly looping to see whether the device is ready, this method of operation is called **programmed I/O (PIO)**. If the CPU does not poll the control bit, but instead receives an interrupt when the device is ready for the next byte, the data transfer is said to be **interrupt driven**.

9.8 Allocating Kernel Memory

When a process running in user mode requests additional memory, pages are allocated from the list of free page frames maintained by the kernel. This list is typically populated using a page-replacement algorithm such as those discussed in Section 9.4 and most likely contains free pages scattered throughout physical memory, as explained earlier. Remember, too, that if a user process requests a single byte of memory, internal fragmentation will result, as the process will be granted an entire page frame.

Kernel memory, however, is often allocated from a free-memory pool different from the list used to satisfy ordinary user-mode processes. There are two primary reasons for this:

1. The kernel requests memory for data structures of varying sizes, some of which are less than a page in size. As a result, the kernel must use memory conservatively and attempt to minimize waste due to fragmentation. This is especially important because many operating systems do not subject kernel code or data to the paging system.
2. Pages allocated to user-mode processes do not necessarily have to be in contiguous physical memory. However, certain hardware devices interact directly with physical memory—without the benefit of a virtual memory interface—and consequently may require memory residing in physically contiguous pages.

In the following sections, we examine two strategies for managing free memory that is assigned to kernel processes: the "buddy system" and slab allocation.

9.8.1 Buddy System

The buddy system allocates memory from a fixed-size segment consisting of physically contiguous pages. Memory is allocated from this segment using a **power-of-2 allocator**, which satisfies requests in units sized as a power of 2 (4 KB, 8 KB, 16 KB, and so forth). A request in units not appropriately sized is rounded up to the next highest power of 2. For example, if a request for 11 KB is made, it is satisfied with a 16-KB segment.

Let's consider a simple example. Assume the size of a memory segment is initially 256 KB and the kernel requests 21 KB of memory. The segment is initially divided into two *buddies*—which we will call A_L and A_R—each 128 KB in size. One of these buddies is further divided into two 64-KB buddies—B_L and B_R. However, the next-highest power of 2 from 21 KB is 32 KB so either B_L or B_R is again divided into two 32-KB buddies, C_L and C_R. One of these buddies is used to satisfy the 21-KB request. This scheme is illustrated in Figure 9.27, where C_L is the segment allocated to the 21 KB request.

An advantage of the buddy system is how quickly adjacent buddies can be combined to form larger segments using a technique known as **coalescing**. In Figure 9.27, for example, when the kernel releases the C_L unit it was allocated, the system can coalesce C_L and C_R into a 64-KB segment. This segment, B_L, can in turn be coalesced with its buddy B_R to form a 128-KB segment. Ultimately, we can end up with the original 256-KB segment.

The obvious drawback to the buddy system is that rounding up to the next highest power of 2 is very likely to cause fragmentation within allocated segments. For example, a 33-KB request can only be satisfied with a 64-KB segment. In fact, we cannot guarantee that less than 50 percent of the allocated unit will be wasted due to internal fragmentation. In the following section, we explore a memory allocation scheme where no space is lost due to fragmentation.

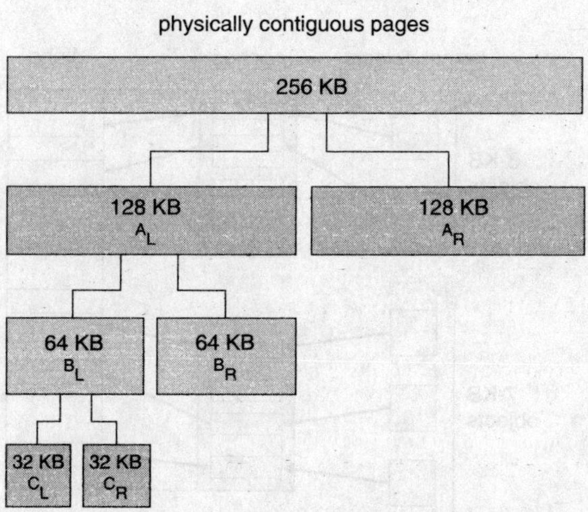

Figure 9.27 Buddy system allocation.

9.8.2 Slab Allocation

A second strategy for allocating kernel memory is known as **slab allocation**. A **slab** is made up of one or more physically contiguous pages. A **cache** consists of one or more slabs. There is a single cache for each unique kernel data structure —for example, a separate cache for the data structure representing process descriptors, a separate cache for file objects, a separate cache for semaphores, and so forth. Each cache is populated with **objects** that are instantiations of the kernel data structure the cache represents. For example, the cache representing semaphores stores instances of semaphore objects, the cache representing process descriptors stores instances of process descriptor objects, and so forth. The relationship between slabs, caches, and objects is shown in Figure 9.28. The figure shows two kernel objects 3 KB in size and three objects 7 KB in size. These objects are stored in their respective caches.

The slab-allocation algorithm uses caches to store kernel objects. When a cache is created, a number of objects—which are initially marked as **free**—are allocated to the cache. The number of objects in the cache depends on the size of the associated slab. For example, a 12-KB slab (made up of three continguous 4-KB pages) could store six 2-KB objects. Initially, all objects in the cache are marked as free. When a new object for a kernel data structure is needed, the allocator can assign any free object from the cache to satisfy the request. The object assigned from the cache is marked as **used**.

Let's consider a scenario in which the kernel requests memory from the slab allocator for an object representing a process descriptor. In Linux systems, a process descriptor is of the type `struct task_struct`, which requires approximately 1.7 KB of memory. When the Linux kernel creates a new task, it requests the necessary memory for the `struct task_struct` object from its cache. The cache will fulfill the request using a `struct task_struct` object that has already been allocated in a slab and is marked as free.

In Linux, a slab may be in one of three possible states:

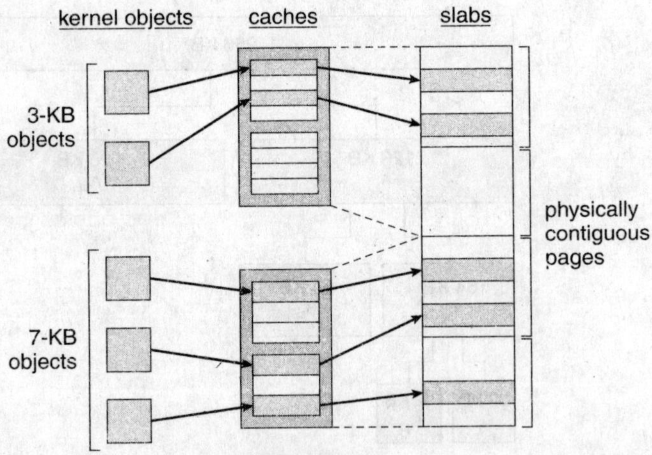

Figure 9.28 Slab allocation.

1. **Full**. All objects in the slab are marked as used.
2. **Empty**. All objects in the slab are marked as free.
3. **Partial**. The slab consists of both used and free objects.

The slab allocator first attempts to satisfy the request with a free object in a partial slab. If none exist, a free object is assigned from an empty slab. If no empty slabs are available, a new slab is allocated from contiguous physical pages and assigned to a cache; memory for the object is allocated from this slab.

The slab allocator provides two main benefits:

1. No memory is wasted due to fragmentation. Fragmentation is not an issue because each unique kernel data structure has an associated cache, and each cache is made up of one or more slabs that are divided into chunks the size of the objects being represented. Thus, when the kernel requests memory for an object, the slab allocator returns the exact amount of memory required to represent the object.

2. Memory requests can be satisfied quickly. The slab allocation scheme is thus particularly effective for managing memory when objects are frequently allocated and deallocated, as is often the case with requests from the kernel. The act of allocating—and releasing—memory can be a time-consuming process. However, objects are created in advance and thus can be quickly allocated from the cache. Furthermore, when the kernel has finished with an object and releases it, it is marked as free and returned to its cache, thus making it immediately available for subsequent requests from the kernel.

The slab allocator first appeared in the Solaris 2.4 kernel. Because of its general-purpose nature, this allocator is now also used for certain user-mode memory requests in Solaris. Linux originally used the buddy system; however, beginning with Version 2.2, the Linux kernel adopted the slab allocator.

9.9 Other Considerations

The major decisions that we make for a paging system are the selections of a replacement algorithm and an allocation policy, which we discussed earlier in this chapter. There are many other considerations as well, and we discuss several of them here.

9.9.1 Prepaging

An obvious property of pure demand paging is the large number of page faults that occur when a process is started. This situation results from trying to get the initial locality into memory. The same situation may arise at other times. For instance, when a swapped-out process is restarted, all its pages are on the disk, and each must be brought in by its own page fault. **Prepaging** is an attempt to prevent this high level of initial paging. The strategy is to bring into memory at one time all the pages that will be needed. Some operating systems—notably Solaris—prepage the page frames for small files.

In a system using the working-set model, for example, we keep with each process a list of the pages in its working set. If we must suspend a process (due to an I/O wait or a lack of free frames), we remember the working set for that process. When the process is to be resumed (because I/O has finished or enough free frames have become available), we automatically bring back into memory its entire working set before restarting the process.

Prepaging may offer an advantage in some cases. The question is simply whether the cost of using prepaging is less than the cost of servicing the corresponding page faults. It may well be the case that many of the pages brought back into memory by prepaging will not be used.

Assume that s pages are prepaged and a fraction α of these s pages is actually used ($0 \leq \alpha \leq 1$). The question is whether the cost of the $s * \alpha$ saved page faults is greater or less than the cost of prepaging $s * (1 - \alpha)$ unnecessary pages. If α is close to 0, prepaging loses; if α is close to 1, prepaging wins.

9.9.2 Page Size

The designers of an operating system for an existing machine seldom have a choice concerning the page size. However, when new machines are being designed, a decision regarding the best page size must be made. As you might expect, there is no single best page size. Rather, there is a set of factors that support various sizes. Page sizes are invariably powers of 2, generally ranging from 4,096 (2^{12}) to 4,194,304 (2^{22}) bytes.

How do we select a page size? One concern is the size of the page table. For a given virtual memory space, decreasing the page size increases the number of pages and hence the size of the page table. For a virtual memory of 4 MB (2^{22}), for example, there would be 4,096 pages of 1,024 bytes but only 512 pages of 8,192 bytes. Because each active process must have its own copy of the page table, a large page size is desirable.

Memory is better utilized with smaller pages, however. If a process is allocated memory starting at location 00000 and continuing until it has as much as it needs, it probably will not end exactly on a page boundary. Thus, a part of the final page must be allocated (because pages are the units of allocation) but will be unused (creating internal fragmentation). Assuming independence of process size and page size, we can expect that, on the average, half of the final page of each process will be wasted. This loss is only 256 bytes for a page of 512 bytes but is 4,096 bytes for a page of 8,192 bytes. To minimize internal fragmentation, then, we need a small page size.

Another problem is the time required to read or write a page. I/O time is composed of seek, latency, and transfer times. Transfer time is proportional to the amount transferred (that is, the page size)—a fact that would seem to argue for a small page size. However, as we shall see in Section 12.1.1, latency and seek time normally dwarf transfer time. At a transfer rate of 2 MB per second, it takes only 0.2 milliseconds to transfer 512 bytes. Latency time, though, is perhaps 8 milliseconds and seek time 20 milliseconds. Of the total I/O time (28.2 milliseconds), therefore, only 1 percent is attributable to the actual transfer. Doubling the page size increases I/O time to only 28.4 milliseconds. It takes 28.4 milliseconds to read a single page of 1,024 bytes but

56.4 milliseconds to read the same amount as two pages of 512 bytes each. Thus, a desire to minimize I/O time argues for a larger page size.

With a smaller page size, though, total I/O should be reduced, since locality will be improved. A smaller page size allows each page to match program locality more accurately. For example, consider a process 200 KB in size, of which only half (100 KB) is actually used in an execution. If we have only one large page, we must bring in the entire page, a total of 200 KB transferred and allocated. If instead we had pages of only 1 byte, then we could bring in only the 100 KB that are actually used, resulting in only 100 KB transferred and allocated. With a smaller page size, we have better **resolution**, allowing us to isolate only the memory that is actually needed. With a larger page size, we must allocate and transfer not only what is needed but also anything else that happens to be in the page, whether it is needed or not. Thus, a smaller page size should result in less I/O and less total allocated memory.

But did you notice that with a page size of 1 byte, we would have a page fault for *each* byte? A process of 200 KB that used only half of that memory would generate only one page fault with a page size of 200 KB but 102,400 page faults with a page size of 1 byte. Each page fault generates the large amount of overhead needed for processing the interrupt, saving registers, replacing a page, queueing for the paging device, and updating tables. To minimize the number of page faults, we need to have a large page size.

Other factors must be considered as well (such as the relationship between page size and sector size on the paging device). The problem has no best answer. As we have seen, some factors (internal fragmentation, locality) argue for a small page size, whereas others (table size, I/O time) argue for a large page size. However, the historical trend is toward larger page sizes. Indeed, the first edition of *Operating System Concepts* (1983) used 4,096 bytes as the upper bound on page sizes, and this value was the most common page size in 1990. Modern systems may now use much larger page sizes, as we will see in the following section.

9.9.3 TLB Reach

In Chapter 8, we introduced the **hit ratio** of the TLB. Recall that the hit ratio for the TLB refers to the percentage of virtual address translations that are resolved in the TLB rather than the page table. Clearly, the hit ratio is related to the number of entries in the TLB, and the way to increase the hit ratio is by increasing the number of entries in the TLB. This, however, does not come cheaply, as the associative memory used to construct the TLB is both expensive and power hungry.

Related to the hit ratio is a similar metric: the **TLB reach**. The TLB reach refers to the amount of memory accessible from the TLB and is simply the number of entries multiplied by the page size. Ideally, the working set for a process is stored in the TLB. If it is not, the process will spend a considerable amount of time resolving memory references in the page table rather than the TLB. If we double the number of entries in the TLB, we double the TLB reach. However, for some memory-intensive applications, this may still prove insufficient for storing the working set.

Another approach for increasing the TLB reach is to either increase the size of the page or provide multiple page sizes. If we increase the page size—say, from 8 KB to 32 KB—we quadruple the TLB reach. However, this may lead to an increase in fragmentation for some applications that do not require such a large page size as 32 KB. Alternatively, an operating system may provide several different page sizes. For example, the UltraSPARC supports page sizes of 8 KB, 64 KB, 512 KB, and 4 MB. Of these available pages sizes, Solaris uses both 8-KB and 4-MB page sizes. And with a 64-entry TLB, the TLB reach for Solaris ranges from 512 KB with 8-KB pages to 256 MB with 4-MB pages. For the majority of applications, the 8-KB page size is sufficient, although Solaris maps the first 4 MB of kernel code and data with two 4-MB pages. Solaris also allows applications—such as databases—to take advantage of the large 4-MB page size.

Providing support for multiple page sizes requires the operating system —not hardware—to manage the TLB. For example, one of the fields in a TLB entry must indicate the size of the page frame corresponding to the TLB entry. Managing the TLB in software and not hardware comes at a cost in performance. However, the increased hit ratio and TLB reach offset the performance costs. Indeed, recent trends indicate a move toward software-managed TLBs and operating-system support for multiple page sizes. The UltraSPARC, MIPS, and Alpha architectures employ software-managed TLBs. The PowerPC and Pentium manage the TLB in hardware.

9.9.4 Inverted Page Tables

Section 8.5.3 introduced the concept of the inverted page table. The purpose of this form of page management is to reduce the amount of physical memory needed to track virtual-to-physical address translations. We accomplish this savings by creating a table that has one entry per page of physical memory, indexed by the pair <process-id, page-number>.

Because they keep information about which virtual memory page is stored in each physical frame, inverted page tables reduce the amount of physical memory needed to store this information. However, the inverted page table no longer contains complete information about the logical address space of a process, and that information is required if a referenced page is not currently in memory. Demand paging requires this information to process page faults. For the information to be available, an external page table (one per process) must be kept. Each such table looks like the traditional per-process page table and contains information on where each virtual page is located.

But do external page tables negate the utility of inverted page tables? Since these tables are referenced only when a page fault occurs, they do not need to be available quickly. Instead, they are themselves paged in and out of memory as necessary. Unfortunately, a page fault may now cause the virtual memory manager to generate another page fault as it pages in the external page table it needs to locate the virtual page on the backing store. This special case requires careful handling in the kernel and a delay in the page-lookup processing.

9.9.5 Program Structure

Demand paging is designed to be transparent to the user program. In many cases, the user is completely unaware of the paged nature of memory. In other cases, however, system performance can be improved if the user (or compiler) has an awareness of the underlying demand paging.

Let's look at a contrived but informative example. Assume that pages are 128 words in size. Consider a C program whose function is to initialize to 0 each element of a 128-by-128 array. The following code is typical:

```
int i, j;
int[128][128] data;

for (j = 0; j < 128; j++)
    for (i = 0; i < 128; i++)
        data[i][j] = 0;
```

Notice that the array is stored row major; that is, the array is stored `data[0][0]`, `data[0][1]`, ···, `data[0][127]`, `data[1][0]`, `data[1][1]`, ···, `data[127][127]`. For pages of 128 words, each row takes one page. Thus, the preceding code zeros one word in each page, then another word in each page, and so on. If the operating system allocates fewer than 128 frames to the entire program, then its execution will result in $128 \times 128 = 16{,}384$ page faults. In contrast, suppose we change the code to

```
int i, j;
int[128][128] data;

for (i = 0; i < 128; i++)
    for (j = 0; j < 128; j++)
        data[i][j] = 0;
```

This code zeros all the words on one page before starting the next page, reducing the number of page faults to 128.

Careful selection of data structures and programming structures can increase locality and hence lower the page-fault rate and the number of pages in the working set. For example, a stack has good locality, since access is always made to the top. A hash table, in contrast, is designed to scatter references, producing bad locality. Of course, locality of reference is just one measure of the efficiency of the use of a data structure. Other heavily weighted factors include search speed, total number of memory references, and total number of pages touched.

At a later stage, the compiler and loader can have a significant effect on paging. Separating code and data and generating reentrant code means that code pages can be read-only and hence will never be modified. Clean pages do not have to be paged out to be replaced. The loader can avoid placing routines across page boundaries, keeping each routine completely in one page. Routines that call each other many times can be packed into the same page. This packaging is a variant of the bin-packing problem of operations research: try to pack the variable-sized load segments into the fixed-sized pages so that interpage references are minimized. Such an approach is particularly useful for large page sizes.

The choice of programming language can affect paging as well. For example, C and C++ use pointers frequently, and pointers tend to randomize access to memory, thereby potentially diminishing a process's locality. Some studies have shown that object-oriented programs also tend to have a poor locality of reference.

9.9.6 I/O Interlock

When demand paging is used, we sometimes need to allow some of the pages to be **locked** in memory. One such situation occurs when I/O is done to or from user (virtual) memory. I/O is often implemented by a separate I/O processor. For example, a controller for a USB storage device is generally given the number of bytes to transfer and a memory address for the buffer (Figure 9.29). When the transfer is complete, the CPU is interrupted.

We must be sure the following sequence of events does not occur: A process issues an I/O request and is put in a queue for that I/O device. Meanwhile, the CPU is given to other processes. These processes cause page faults; and one of them, using a global replacement algorithm, replaces the page containing the memory buffer for the waiting process. The pages are paged out. Some time later, when the I/O request advances to the head of the device queue, the I/O occurs to the specified address. However, this frame is now being used for a different page belonging to another process.

There are two common solutions to this problem. One solution is never to execute I/O to user memory. Instead, data are always copied between system memory and user memory. I/O takes place only between system memory and the I/O device. To write a block on tape, we first copy the block to system memory and then write it to tape. This extra copying may result in unacceptably high overhead.

Another solution is to allow pages to be locked into memory. Here, a lock bit is associated with every frame. If the frame is locked, it cannot be selected for replacement. Under this approach, to write a block on tape, we lock into memory the pages containing the block. The system can then continue as usual. Locked pages cannot be replaced. When the I/O is complete, the pages are unlocked.

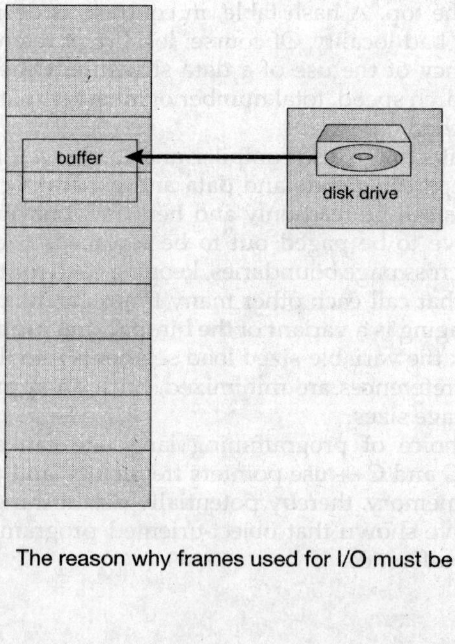

Figure 9.29 The reason why frames used for I/O must be in memory.

Lock bits are used in various situations. Frequently, some or all of the operating-system kernel is locked into memory, as many operating systems cannot tolerate a page fault caused by the kernel.

Another use for a lock bit involves normal page replacement. Consider the following sequence of events: A low-priority process faults. Selecting a replacement frame, the paging system reads the necessary page into memory. Ready to continue, the low-priority process enters the ready queue and waits for the CPU. Since it is a low-priority process, it may not be selected by the CPU scheduler for a time. While the low-priority process waits, a high-priority process faults. Looking for a replacement, the paging system sees a page that is in memory but has not been referenced or modified: it is the page that the low-priority process just brought in. This page looks like a perfect replacement: it is clean and will not need to be written out, and it apparently has not been used for a long time.

Whether the high-priority process should be able to replace the low-priority process is a policy decision. After all, we are simply delaying the low-priority process for the benefit of the high-priority process. However, we are wasting the effort spent to bring in the page for the low-priority process. If we decide to prevent replacement of a newly brought-in page until it can be used at least once, then we can use the lock bit to implement this mechanism. When a page is selected for replacement, its lock bit is turned on; it remains on until the faulting process is again dispatched.

Using a lock bit can be dangerous: The lock bit may get turned on but never turned off. Should this situation occur (because of a bug in the operating system, for example), the locked frame becomes unusable. On a single-user system, the overuse of locking would hurt only the user doing the locking. Multiuser systems must be less trusting of users. For instance, Solaris allows locking "hints," but it is free to disregard these hints if the free-frame pool becomes too small or if an individual process requests that too many pages be locked in memory.

9.10 Operating-System Examples

In this section, we describe how Windows XP and Solaris implement virtual memory.

9.10.1 Windows XP

Windows XP implements virtual memory using demand paging with **clustering**. Clustering handles page faults by bringing in not only the faulting page but also several pages following the faulting page. When a process is first created, it is assigned a working-set minimum and maximum. The **working-set minimum** is the minimum number of pages the process is guaranteed to have in memory. If sufficient memory is available, a process may be assigned as many pages as its **working-set maximum**. For most applications, the value of working-set minimum and working-set maximum is 50 and 345 pages, respectively. (In some circumstances, a process may be allowed to exceed its working-set maximum.) The virtual memory manager maintains a list of free page frames. Associated with this list is a threshold value that is used to indicate whether sufficient free memory is available. If a page fault occurs for a process that is below its working-set maximum, the virtual memory manager allocates a page from this list of free pages. If a process that is at its working-set maximum incurs a page fault, it must select a page for replacement using a local page-replacement policy.

When the amount of free memory falls below the threshold, the virtual memory manager uses a tactic known as **automatic working-set trimming** to restore the value above the threshold. Automatic working-set trimming works by evaluating the number of pages allocated to processes. If a process has been allocated more pages than its working-set minimum, the virtual memory manager removes pages until the process reaches its working-set minimum. A process that is at its working-set minimum may be allocated pages from the free-page-frame list once sufficient free memory is available.

The algorithm used to determine which page to remove from a working set depends on the type of processor. On single-processor 80x86 systems, Windows XP uses a variation of the *clock* algorithm discussed in Section 9.4.5.2. On Alpha and multiprocessor x86 systems, clearing the reference bit may require invalidating the entry in the translation look-aside buffer on other processors. Rather than incurring this overhead, Windows XP uses a variation on the FIFO algorithm discussed in Section 9.4.2.

9.10.2 Solaris

In Solaris, when a thread incurs a page fault, the kernel assigns a page to the faulting thread from the list of free pages it maintains. Therefore, it is imperative that the kernel keep a sufficient amount of free memory available. Associated with this list of free pages is a parameter—*lotsfree*—that represents a threshold to begin paging. The *lotsfree* parameter is typically set to 1/64 the size of the physical memory. Four times per second, the kernel checks whether the amount of free memory is less than *lotsfree*. If the number of free pages falls below *lotsfree*, a process known as a **pageout** starts up. The pageout process is similar to the second-chance algorithm described in Section 9.4.5.2, except that it uses two hands while scanning pages, rather than one. The pageout process works as follows: The front hand of the clock scans all pages in memory, setting the reference bit to 0. Later, the back hand of the clock examines the reference bit for the pages in memory, appending each page whose reference bit is still set to 0 to the free list and writing to disk its contents if modified. Solaris maintains a cache list of pages that have been "freed" but have not yet been overwritten. The free list contains frames that have invalid contents. Pages can be **reclaimed** from the cache list if they are accessed before being moved to the free list.

The pageout algorithm uses several parameters to control the rate at which pages are scanned (known as the *scanrate*). The scanrate is expressed in pages per second and ranges from *slowscan* to *fastscan*. When free memory falls below *lotsfree*, scanning occurs at *slowscan* pages per second and progresses to *fastscan*, depending on the amount of free memory available. The default value of *slowscan* is 100 pages per second; *fastscan* is typically set to the value (total physical pages)/2 pages per second, with a maximum of 8,192 pages per second. This is shown in Figure 9.30 (with *fastscan* set to the maximum).

The distance (in pages) between the hands of the clock is determined by a system parameter, *handspread*. The amount of time between the front hand's

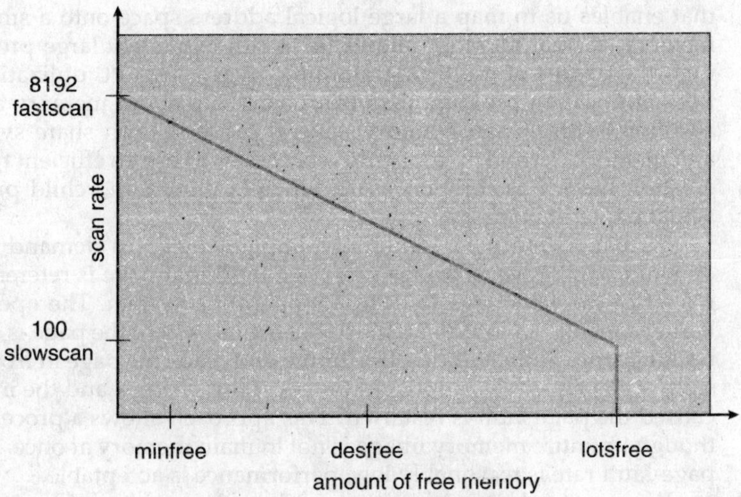

Figure 9.30 Solaris page scanner.

clearing a bit and the back hand's investigating its value depends on the *scanrate* and the *handspread*. If *scanrate* is 100 pages per second and *handspread* is 1,024 pages, 10 seconds can pass between the time a bit is set by the front hand and the time it is checked by the back hand. However, because of the demands placed on the memory system, a *scanrate* of several thousand is not uncommon. This means that the amount of time between clearing and investigating a bit is often a few seconds.

As mentioned above, the pageout process checks memory four times per second. However, if free memory falls below *desfree* (Figure 9.30), pageout will run 100 times per second with the intention of keeping at least *desfree* free memory available. If the pageout process is unable to keep the amount of free memory at *desfree* for a 30-second average, the kernel begins swapping processes, thereby freeing all pages allocated to swapped processes. In general, the kernel looks for processes that have been idle for long periods of time. If the system is unable to maintain the amount of free memory at *minfree*, the pageout process is called for every request for a new page.

Recent releases of the Solaris kernel have provided enhancements of the paging algorithm. One such enhancement involves recognizing pages from shared libraries. Pages belonging to libraries that are being shared by several processes—even if they are eligible to be claimed by the scanner—are skipped during the page-scanning process. Another enhancement concerns distinguishing pages that have been allocated to processes from pages allocated to regular files. This is known as **priority paging** and is covered in Section 11.6.2.

9.11 Summary

It is desirable to be able to execute a process whose logical address space is larger than the available physical address space. Virtual memory is a technique that enables us to map a large logical address space onto a smaller physical memory. Virtual memory allows us to run extremely large processes and to raise the degree of multiprogramming, increasing CPU utilization. Further, it frees application programmers from worrying about memory availability. In addition, with virtual memory, several processes can share system libraries and memory. Virtual memory also enables us to use an efficient type of process creation known as copy-on-write, wherein parent and child processes share actual pages of memory.

Virtual memory is commonly implemented by demand paging. Pure demand paging never brings in a page until that page is referenced. The first reference causes a page fault to the operating system. The operating-system kernel consults an internal table to determine where the page is located on the backing store. It then finds a free frame and reads the page in from the backing store. The page table is updated to reflect this change, and the instruction that caused the page fault is restarted. This approach allows a process to run even though its entire memory image is not in main memory at once. As long as the page-fault rate is reasonably low, performance is acceptable.

We can use demand paging to reduce the number of frames allocated to a process. This arrangement can increase the degree of multiprogramming (allowing more processes to be available for execution at one time) and—in theory, at least—the CPU utilization of the system. It also allows processes to be run even though their memory requirements exceed the total available physical memory. Such processes run in virtual memory.

If total memory requirements exceed the capacity of physical memory, then it may be necessary to replace pages from memory to free frames for new pages. Various page-replacement algorithms are used. FIFO page replacement is easy to program but suffers from Belady's anomaly. Optimal page replacement requires future knowledge. LRU replacement is an approximation of optimal page replacement, but even it may be difficult to implement. Most page-replacement algorithms, such as the second-chance algorithm, are approximations of LRU replacement.

In addition to a page-replacement algorithm, a frame-allocation policy is needed. Allocation can be fixed, suggesting local page replacement, or dynamic, suggesting global replacement. The working-set model assumes that processes execute in localities. The working set is the set of pages in the current locality. Accordingly, each process should be allocated enough frames for its current working set. If a process does not have enough memory for its working set, it will thrash. Providing enough frames to each process to avoid thrashing may require process swapping and scheduling.

Most operating systems provide features for memory mapping files, thus allowing file I/O to be treated as routine memory access. The Win32 API implements shared memory through memory mapping files.

Kernel processes typically require memory to be allocated using pages that are physically contiguous. The buddy system allocates memory to kernel processes in units sized according to a power of 2, which often results in fragmentation. Slab allocators assign kernel data structures to caches associated with slabs, which are made up of one or more physically contiguous pages. With slab allocation, no memory is wasted due to fragmentation, and memory requests can be satisfied quickly.

In addition to requiring that we solve the major problems of page replacement and frame allocation, the proper design of a paging system requires that we consider prepaging, page size, TLB reach, inverted page tables, program structure, I/O interlock, and other issues.

Exercises

9.1 Assume there is a 1,024-KB segment where memory is allocated using the buddy system. Using Figure 9.27 as a guide, draw a tree illustrating how the following memory requests are allocated:

- Request 240 bytes
- Request 120 bytes
- Request 60 bytes
- Request 130 bytes

Next, modify the tree for the following releases of memory. Perform coalescing whenever possible:

- Release 240 bytes
- Release 60 bytes
- Release 120 bytes

9.2 Consider the page table for a system with 12-bit virtual and physical addresses with 256-byte pages. The list of free page frames is *D*, *E*, *F* (that is, *D* is at the head of the list, *E* is second, and *F* is last).

Page	Page Frame
0	–
1	2
2	C
3	A
4	–
5	4
6	3
7	–
8	B
9	0

Convert the following virtual addresses to their equivalent physical addresses in hexadecimal. All numbers are given in hexadecimal. (A dash for a page frame indicates that the page is not in memory.)

- 9EF
- 111
- 700
- 0FF

9.3 A page-replacement algorithm should minimize the number of page faults. We can achieve this minimization by distributing heavily used pages evenly over all of memory, rather than having them compete for a small number of page frames. We can associate with each page frame a counter of the number of pages associated with that frame. Then, to replace a page, we can search for the page frame with the smallest counter.

a. Define a page-replacement algorithm using this basic idea. Specifically address these problems:
   i. What is the initial value of the counters?
   ii. When are counters increased?
   iii. When are counters decreased?
   iv. How is the page to be replaced selected?

b. How many page faults occur for your algorithm for the following reference string with four page frames?

   1, 2, 3, 4, 5, 3, 4, 1, 6, 7, 8, 7, 8, 9, 7, 8, 9, 5, 4, 5, 4, 2.

c. What is the minimum number of page faults for an optimal page-replacement strategy for the reference string in part b with four page frames?

9.4 Consider a demand-paging system with the following time-measured utilizations:

CPU utilization	20%
Paging disk	97.7%
Other I/O devices	5%

For each of the following, say whether it will (or is likely to) improve CPU utilization. Explain your answers.

a. Install a faster CPU.

b. Install a bigger paging disk.

c. Increase the degree of multiprogramming.

d. Decrease the degree of multiprogramming.

e. Install more main memory.

f. Install a faster hard disk or multiple controllers with multiple hard disks.

g. Add prepaging to the page-fetch algorithms.

h. Increase the page size.

9.5 Consider a demand-paged computer system where the degree of multiprogramming is currently fixed at four. The system was recently measured to determine utilization of the CPU and the paging disk. The results are one of the following alternatives. For each case, what is happening? Can the degree of multiprogramming be increased to increase the CPU utilization? Is the paging helping?

a. CPU utilization 13 percent; disk utilization 97 percent

b. CPU utilization 87 percent; disk utilization 3 percent

c. CPU utilization 13 percent; disk utilization 3 percent

9.6 Consider a demand-paging system with a paging disk that has an average access and transfer time of 20 milliseconds. Addresses are translated through a page table in main memory, with an access time of 1 microsecond per memory access. Thus, each memory reference through the page table takes two accesses. To improve this time, we have added an associative memory that reduces access time to one memory reference if the page-table entry is in the associative memory.

Assume that 80 percent of the accesses are in the associative memory and that, of those remaining, 10 percent (or 2 percent of the total) cause page faults. What is the effective memory access time?

9.7 A simplified view of thread states is **Ready**, **Running**, and **Blocked**, where a thread is either ready and waiting to be scheduled, is running on the processor, or is blocked (i.e. is waiting for I/O.) This is illustrated in Figure 9.31. Assuming a thread is in the Running state, answer the following questions: (Be sure to explain your answer.)

a. Will the thread change state if it incurs a page fault? If so, to what new state?

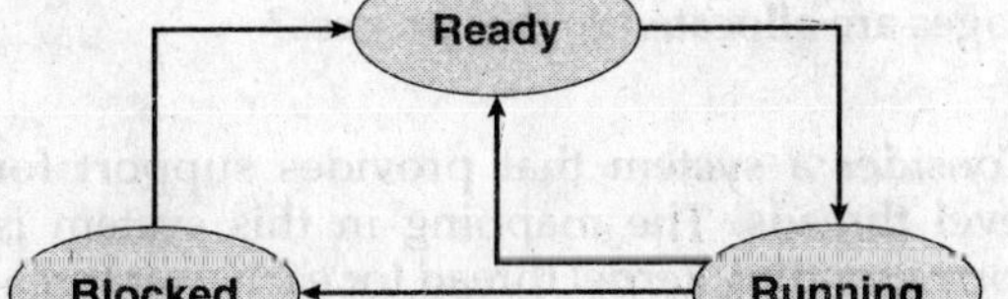

Figure 9.31 Thread state diagram for Exercise 9.7.

b. Will the thread change state if it generates a TLB miss that is resolved in the page table? If so, to what new state?

c. Will the thread change state if an address reference is resolved in the page table? If so, to what new state?

9.8 Discuss the hardware support required to support demand paging.

9.9 Consider the following page reference string:

1, 2, 3, 4, 2, 1, 5, 6, 2, 1, 2, 3, 7, 6, 3, 2, 1, 2, 3, 6.

How many page faults would occur for the following replacement algorithms, assuming one, two, three, four, five, six, and seven frames? Remember that all frames are initially empty, so your first unique pages will cost one fault each.

- LRU replacement
- FIFO replacement
- Optimal replacement

9.10 Consider a system that allocates pages of different sizes to its processes. What are the advantages of such a paging scheme? What modifications to the virtual memory system provide this functionality?

9.11 Discuss situations in which the most frequently used page-replacement algorithm generates fewer page faults than the least recently used page-replacement algorithm. Also discuss under what circumstances the opposite holds.

9.12 Under what circumstances do page faults occur? Describe the actions taken by the operating system when a page fault occurs.

9.13 Suppose that a machine provides instructions that can access memory locations using the one-level indirect addressing scheme. What sequence of page faults is incurred when all of the pages of a program are currently nonresident and the first instruction of the program is an indirect memory-load operation? What happens when the operating system is using a per-process frame allocation technique and only two pages are allocated to this process?

9.14 Consider a system that provides support for user-level and kernel-level threads. The mapping in this system is one to one (there is a corresponding kernel thread for each user thread). Does a multithreaded process consist of (a) a working set for the entire process or (b) a working set for each thread? Explain.

9.15 What is the copy-on-write feature, and under what circumstances is it beneficial to use this feature? What hardware support is required to implement this feature?

9.16 Consider the two-dimensional array A:

```
int A[][] = new int[100][100];
```

where `A[0][0]` is at location 200 in a paged memory system with pages of size 200. A small process that manipulates the matrix resides in page 0 (locations 0 to 199). Thus, every instruction fetch will be from page 0.

For three page frames, how many page faults are generated by the following array-initialization loops, using LRU replacement and assuming that page frame 1 contains the process and the other two are initially empty?

a.
```
for (int j = 0; j < 100; j++)
    for (int i = 0; i < 100; i++)
        A[i][j] = 0;
```

b.
```
for (int i = 0; i < 100; i++)
    for (int j = 0; j < 100; j++)
        A[i][j] = 0;
```

9.17 Discuss situations in which the least frequently used page-replacement algorithm generates fewer page faults than the least recently used page-replacement algorithm. Also discuss under what circumstances the opposite holds.

9.18 What is the cause of thrashing? How does the system detect thrashing? Once it detects thrashing, what can the system do to eliminate this problem?

9.19 Assume that you are monitoring the rate at which the pointer in the clock algorithm (which indicates the candidate page for replacement) moves. What can you say about the system if you notice the following behavior:

a. Pointer is moving fast.

b. Pointer is moving slow.

9.20 The VAX/VMS system uses a FIFO replacement algorithm for resident pages and a free-frame pool of recently used pages. Assume that the free-frame pool is managed using the least recently used replacement policy. Answer the following questions:

a. If a page fault occurs and if the page does not exist in the free-frame pool, how is free space generated for the newly requested page?

b. If a page fault occurs and if the page exists in the free-frame pool, how is the resident page set and the free-frame pool managed to make space for the requested page?

c. What does the system degenerate to if the number of resident pages is set to one?

d. What does the system degenerate to if the number of pages in the free-frame pool is zero?

9.21 The slab-allocation algorithm uses a separate cache for each different object type. Assuming there is one cache per object type, explain why this scheme doesn't scale well with multiple CPUs. What could be done to address this scalability issue?

9.22 Assume that we have a demand-paged memory. The page table is held in registers. It takes 8 milliseconds to service a page fault if an empty frame is available or if the replaced page is not modified and 20 milliseconds if the replaced page is modified. Memory-access time is 100 nanoseconds.

Assume that the page to be replaced is modified 70 percent of the time. What is the maximum acceptable page-fault rate for an effective access time of no more than 200 nanoseconds?

9.23 Segmentation is similar to paging but uses variable-sized "pages." Define two segment-replacement algorithms based on FIFO and LRU page-replacement schemes. Remember that since segments are not the same size, the segment that is chosen to be replaced may not be big enough to leave enough consecutive locations for the needed segment. Consider strategies for systems where segments cannot be relocated and strategies for systems where they can.

9.24 Which of the following programming techniques and structures are "good" for a demand-paged environment ? Which are "not good"? Explain your answers.

a. Stack

b. Hashed symbol table

c. Sequential search

d. Binary search

e. Pure code

f. Vector operations

g. Indirection

9.25 When a page fault occurs, the process requesting the page must block while waiting for the page to be brought from disk into physical memory. Assume that there exists a process with five user-level threads and that the mapping of user threads to kernel threads is many to one. If one user thread incurs a page fault while accessing its stack, would the other user threads belonging to the same process also be affected by the page fault—that is, would they also have to wait for the faulting page to be brought into memory? Explain.

9.26 Consider a system that uses pure demand paging.

a. When a process first starts execution, how would you characterize the page fault rate?

b. Once the working set for a process is loaded into memory, how would you characterize the page fault rate?

c. Assume that a process changes its locality and the size of the new working set is too large to be stored in available free memory. Identify some options system designers could choose from to handle this situation.

9.27 Assume that a program has just referenced an address in virtual memory. Describe a scenario in which each of the following can occur. (If no such scenario can occur, explain why.)

- TLB miss with no page fault
- TLB miss and page fault
- TLB hit and no page fault
- TLB hit and page fault

9.28 A certain computer provides its users with a virtual memory space of 2^{32} bytes. The computer has 2^{18} bytes of physical memory. The virtual memory is implemented by paging, and the page size is 4,096 bytes. A user process generates the virtual address 11123456. Explain how the system establishes the corresponding physical location. Distinguish between software and hardware operations.

9.29 When virtual memory is implemented in a computing system, there are certain costs associated with the technique and certain benefits. List the costs and the benefits. Is it possible for the costs to exceed the benefits? If it is, what measures can be taken to ensure that this does not happen?

9.30 Give an example that illustrates the problem with restarting the move character instruction (MVC) on the IBM 360/370 when the source and destination regions are overlapping.

9.31 Consider the parameter Δ used to define the working-set window in the working-set model. What is the effect of setting Δ to a small value on the page-fault frequency and the number of active (nonsuspended) processes currently executing in the system? What is the effect when Δ is set to a very high value?

9.32 Is it possible for a process to have two working sets, one representing data and another representing code? Explain.

9.33 Suppose that your replacement policy (in a paged system) is to examine each page regularly and to discard that page if it has not been used since the last examination. What would you gain and what would you lose by using this policy rather than LRU or second-chance replacement?

Programming Problems

9.34 Write a program that implements the FIFO and LRU page-replacement algorithms presented in this chapter. First, generate a random page-reference string where page numbers range from 0 to 9. Apply the random page-reference string to each algorithm, and record the number of page faults incurred by each algorithm. Implement the replacement algorithms so that the number of page frames can vary from 1 to 7. Assume that demand paging is used.

9.35 The *Catalan* numbers are an integer sequence C_n that appear in tree-enumeration problems. The first Catalan numbers for $n = 1, 2, 3, \ldots$ are $1, 2, 5, 14, 42, 132, \ldots$. A formula generating C_n is

$$C_n = \frac{1}{(n+1)}\binom{2n}{n} = \frac{(2n)!}{(n+1)!n!}$$

Design two programs that communicate with shared memory using the Win32 API as outlined in Section 9.7.2. The producer process will generate the Catalan sequence and write it to a shared memory object. The consumer process will then read and output the sequence from shared memory.

In this instance, the producer process will be passed an integer parameter on the command line specifying how many Catalan numbers to produce (for example, providing 5 on the command line means the producer process will generate the first five Catalan numbers).

Bibliographical Notes

Demand paging was first used in the Atlas system, implemented on the Manchester University MUSE computer around 1960 (Kilburn et al. [1961]). Another early demand-paging system was MULTICS, implemented on the GE 645 system (Organick [1972]).

Belady et al. [1969] were the first researchers to observe that the FIFO replacement strategy may produce the anomaly that bears Belady's name. Mattson et al. [1970] demonstrated that stack algorithms are not subject to Belady's anomaly.

The optimal replacement algorithm was presented by Belady [1966] and was proved to be optimal by Mattson et al. [1970]. Belady's optimal algorithm is for a fixed allocation; Prieve and Fabry [1976] presented an optimal algorithm for situations in which the allocation can vary.

The enhanced clock algorithm was discussed by Carr and Hennessy [1981].

The working-set model was developed by Denning [1968]. Discussions concerning the working-set model were presented by Denning [1980].

The scheme for monitoring the page-fault rate was developed by Wulf [1969], who successfully applied this technique to the Burroughs B5500 computer system.

Wilson et al. [1995] presented several algorithms for dynamic memory allocation. Johnstone and Wilson [1998] described various memory-fragmentation issues. Buddy system memory allocators were described in Knowlton [1965], Peterson and Norman [1977], and Purdom, Jr. and Stigler [1970]. Bonwick [1994] discussed the slab allocator, and Bonwick and Adams [2001] extended the discussion to multiple processors. Other memory-fitting algorithms can be found in Stephenson [1983], Bays [1977], and Brent [1989]. A survey of memory-allocation strategies can be found in Wilson et al. [1995].

Solomon and Russinovich [2000] and Russinovich and Solomon [2005] described how Windows implements virtual memory. McDougall and Mauro [2007] discussed virtual memory in Solaris. Virtual memory techniques in Linux and BSD were described by Bovet and Cesati [2002] and McKusick et al. [1996], respectively. Ganapathy and Schimmel [1998] and Navarro et al. [2002] discussed operating system support for multiple page sizes. Ortiz [2001] described virtual memory used in a real-time embedded operating system.

Jacob and Mudge [1998b] compared implementations of virtual memory in the MIPS, PowerPC, and Pentium architectures. A companion article (Jacob and Mudge [1998a]) described the hardware support necessary for implementation of virtual memory in six different architectures, including the UltraSPARC.

Part Five

Storage Management

Since main memory is usually too small to accommodate all the data and programs permanently, the computer system must provide secondary storage to back up main memory. Modern computer systems use disks as the primary on-line storage medium for information (both programs and data). The file system provides the mechanism for on-line storage of and access to both data and programs residing on the disks. A file is a collection of related information defined by its creator. The files are mapped by the operating system onto physical devices. Files are normally organized into directories for ease of use.

The devices that attach to a computer vary in many aspects. Some devices transfer a character or a block of characters at a time. Some can be accessed only sequentially, others randomly. Some transfer data synchronously, others asynchronously. Some are dedicated, some shared. They can be read-only or read–write. They vary greatly in speed. In many ways, they are also the slowest major component of the computer.

Because of all this device variation, the operating system needs to provide a wide range of functionality to applications, to allow them to control all aspects of the devices. One key goal of an operating system's I/O subsystem is to provide the simplest interface possible to the rest of the system. Because devices are a performance bottleneck, another key is to optimize I/O for maximum concurrency.

CHAPTER 10

File System

For most users, the file system is the most visible aspect of an operating system. It provides the mechanism for on-line storage of and access to both data and programs of the operating system and all the users of the computer system. The file system consists of two distinct parts: a collection of *files,* each storing related data, and a *directory structure,* which organizes and provides information about all the files in the system. File systems live on devices, which we explore fully in the following chapters but touch upon here. In this chapter, we consider the various aspects of files and the major directory structures. We also discuss the semantics of sharing files among multiple processes, users, and computers. Finally, we discuss ways to handle *file protection,* necessary when we have multiple users and we want to control who may access files and how files may be accessed.

CHAPTER OBJECTIVES

- To explain the function of file systems.
- To describe the interfaces to file systems.
- To discuss file-system design tradeoffs, including access methods, file sharing, file locking, and directory structures.
- To explore file-system protection.

10.1 File Concept

Computers can store information on various storage media, such as magnetic disks, magnetic tapes, and optical disks. So that the computer system will be convenient to use, the operating system provides a uniform logical view of information storage. The operating system abstracts from the physical properties of its storage devices to define a logical storage unit, the *file.* Files are mapped by the operating system onto physical devices. These storage devices are usually nonvolatile, so the contents are persistent through power failures and system reboots.

A file is a named collection of related information that is recorded on secondary storage. From a user's perspective, a file is the smallest allotment of logical secondary storage; that is, data cannot be written to secondary storage unless they are within a file. Commonly, files represent programs (both source and object forms) and data. Data files may be numeric, alphabetic, alphanumeric, or binary. Files may be free form, such as text files, or may be formatted rigidly. In general, a file is a sequence of bits, bytes, lines, or records, the meaning of which is defined by the file's creator and user. The concept of a file is thus extremely general.

The information in a file is defined by its creator. Many different types of information may be stored in a file—source programs, object programs, executable programs, numeric data, text, payroll records, graphic images, sound recordings, and so on. A file has a certain defined **structure**, which depends on its type. A *text* file is a sequence of characters organized into lines (and possibly pages). A *source* file is a sequence of subroutines and functions, each of which is further organized as declarations followed by executable statements. An *object* file is a sequence of bytes organized into blocks understandable by the system's linker. An *executable* file is a series of code sections that the loader can bring into memory and execute.

10.1.1 File Attributes

A file is named, for the convenience of its human users, and is referred to by its name. A name is usually a string of characters, such as *example.c*. Some systems differentiate between uppercase and lowercase characters in names, whereas other systems do not. When a file is named, it becomes independent of the process, the user, and even the system that created it. For instance, one user might create the file *example.c,* and another user might edit that file by specifying its name. The file's owner might write the file to a floppy disk, send it in an e-mail, or copy it across a network, and it could still be called *example.c* on the destination system.

A file's attributes vary from one operating system to another but typically consist of these:

- **Name**. The symbolic file name is the only information kept in human-readable form.
- **Identifier**. This unique tag, usually a number, identifies the file within the file system; it is the non-human-readable name for the file.
- **Type**. This information is needed for systems that support different types of files.
- **Location**. This information is a pointer to a device and to the location of the file on that device.
- **Size**. The current size of the file (in bytes, words, or blocks) and possibly the maximum allowed size are included in this attribute.
- **Protection**. Access-control information determines who can do reading, writing, executing, and so on.

- **Time, date, and user identification**. This information may be kept for creation, last modification, and last use. These data can be useful for protection, security, and usage monitoring.

The information about all files is kept in the directory structure, which also resides on secondary storage. Typically, a directory entry consists of the file's name and its unique identifier. The identifier in turn locates the other file attributes. It may take more than a kilobyte to record this information for each file. In a system with many files, the size of the directory itself may be megabytes. Because directories, like files, must be nonvolatile, they must be stored on the device and brought into memory piecemeal, as needed.

10.1.2 File Operations

A file is an **abstract data type**. To define a file properly, we need to consider the operations that can be performed on files. The operating system can provide system calls to create, write, read, reposition, delete, and truncate files. Let's examine what the operating system must do to perform each of these six basic file operations. It should then be easy to see how other similar operations, such as renaming a file, can be implemented.

- **Creating a file**. Two steps are necessary to create a file. First, space in the file system must be found for the file. We discuss how to allocate space for the file in Chapter 11. Second, an entry for the new file must be made in the directory.

- **Writing a file**. To write a file, we make a system call specifying both the name of the file and the information to be written to the file. Given the name of the file, the system searches the directory to find the file's location. The system must keep a *write* pointer to the location in the file where the next write is to take place. The write pointer must be updated whenever a write occurs.

- **Reading a file**. To read from a file, we use a system call that specifies the name of the file and where (in memory) the next block of the file should be put. Again, the directory is searched for the associated entry, and the system needs to keep a *read* pointer to the location in the file where the next read is to take place. Once the read has taken place, the read pointer is updated. Because a process is usually either reading from or writing to a file, the current operation location can be kept as a per-process **current-file-position pointer**. Both the read and write operations use this same pointer, saving space and reducing system complexity.

- **Repositioning within a file**. The directory is searched for the appropriate entry, and the current-file-position pointer is repositioned to a given value. Repositioning within a file need not involve any actual I/O. This file operation is also known as a file *seek*.

- **Deleting a file**. To delete a file, we search the directory for the named file. Having found the associated directory entry, we release all file space, so that it can be reused by other files, and erase the directory entry.

- **Truncating a file**. The user may want to erase the contents of a file but keep its attributes. Rather than forcing the user to delete the file and then recreate it, this function allows all attributes to remain unchanged—except for file length—but lets the file be reset to length zero and its file space released.

These six basic operations comprise the minimal set of required file operations. Other common operations include *appending* new information to the end of an existing file and *renaming* an existing file. These primitive operations can then be combined to perform other file operations. For instance, we can create a *copy* of a file, or copy the file to another I/O device, such as a printer or a display, by creating a new file and then reading from the old and writing to the new. We also want to have operations that allow a user to get and set the various attributes of a file. For example, we may want to have operations that allow a user to determine the status of a file, such as the file's length, and to set file attributes, such as the file's owner.

Most of the file operations mentioned involve searching the directory for the entry associated with the named file. To avoid this constant searching, many systems require that an `open()` system call be made before a file is first used actively. The operating system keeps a small table, called the **open-file table**, containing information about all open files. When a file operation is requested, the file is specified via an index into this table, so no searching is required. When the file is no longer being actively used, it is *closed* by the process, and the operating system removes its entry from the open-file table. `create` and `delete` are system calls that work with closed rather than open files.

Some systems implicitly open a file when the first reference to it is made. The file is automatically closed when the job or program that opened the file terminates. Most systems, however, require that the programmer open a file explicitly with the `open()` system call before that file can be used. The `open()` operation takes a file name and searches the directory, copying the directory entry into the open-file table. The `open()` call can also accept access-mode information—create, read-only, read–write, append-only, and so on. This mode is checked against the file's permissions. If the request mode is allowed, the file is opened for the process. The `open()` system call typically returns a pointer to the entry in the open-file table. This pointer, not the actual file name, is used in all I/O operations, avoiding any further searching and simplifying the system-call interface.

The implementation of the `open()` and `close()` operations is more complicated in an environment where several processes may open the file simultaneously. This may occur in a system where several different applications open the same file at the same time. Typically, the operating system uses two levels of internal tables: a per-process table and a system-wide table. The per-process table tracks all files that a process has open. Stored in this table is information regarding the use of the file by the process. For instance, the current file pointer for each file is found here. Access rights to the file and accounting information can also be included.

Each entry in the per-process table in turn points to a system-wide open-file table. The system-wide table contains process-independent information, such as the location of the file on disk, access dates, and file size. Once a file has been opened by one process, the system-wide table includes an entry for the file.

When another process executes an `open()` call, a new entry is simply added to the process's open-file table pointing to the appropriate entry in the system-wide table. Typically, the open-file table also has an *open count* associated with each file to indicate how many processes have the file open. Each `close()` decreases this *open count*, and when the *open count* reaches zero, the file is no longer in use, and the file's entry is removed from the open-file table.

In summary, several pieces of information are associated with an open file.

- **File pointer**. On systems that do not include a file offset as part of the `read()` and `write()` system calls, the system must track the last read–write location as a current-file-position pointer. This pointer is unique to each process operating on the file and therefore must be kept separate from the on-disk file attributes.
- **File-open count**. As files are closed, the operating system must reuse its open-file table entries, or it could run out of space in the table. Because multiple processes may have opened a file, the system must wait for the last file to close before removing the open-file table entry. The file-open counter tracks the number of opens and closes and reaches zero on the last close. The system can then remove the entry.
- **Disk location of the file**. Most file operations require the system to modify data within the file. The information needed to locate the file on disk is kept in memory so that the system does not have to read it from disk for each operation.
- **Access rights**. Each process opens a file in an access mode. This information is stored on the per-process table so the operating system can allow or deny subsequent I/O requests.

Some operating systems provide facilities for locking an open file (or sections of a file). File locks allow one process to lock a file and prevent other processes from gaining access to it. File locks are useful for files that are shared by several processes—for example, a system log file that can be accessed and modified by a number of processes in the system.

FILE LOCKING IN JAVA

In the Java API, acquiring a lock requires first obtaining the `FileChannel` for the file to be locked. The `lock()` method of the `FileChannel` is used to acquire the lock. The API of the `lock()` method is

```
FileLock lock(long begin, long end, boolean shared)
```

where `begin` and `end` are the beginning and ending positions of the region being locked. Setting **`shared`** to `true` is for shared locks; setting `shared` to `false` acquires the lock exclusively. The lock is released by invoking the `release()` of the `FileLock` returned by the `lock()` operation.

The program in Figure 10.1 illustrates file locking in Java. This program acquires two locks on the file *file.txt*. The first half of the file is acquired as an exclusive lock; the lock for the second half is a shared lock.

FILE LOCKING IN JAVA (Continued)

```
import java.io.*;
import java.nio.channels.*;

public class LockingExample {
  public static final boolean EXCLUSIVE = false;
  public static final boolean SHARED = true;

  public static void main(String args[]) throws IOException {
   FileLock sharedLock = null;
   FileLock exclusiveLock = null;

   try {
    RandomAccessFile raf = new RandomAccessFile("file.txt","rw");

    // get the channel for the file
    FileChannel ch = raf.getChannel();

    // this locks the first half of the file - exclusive
    exclusiveLock = ch.lock(0, raf.length()/2, EXCLUSIVE);

    /** Now modify the data . . . */

    // release the lock
    exclusiveLock.release();

    // this locks the second half of the file - shared
    sharedLock = ch.lock(raf.length()/2+1,raf.length(),SHARED);

    /** Now read the data . . . */

    // release the lock
    sharedLock.release();
   } catch (java.io.IOException ioe) {
    System.err.println(ioe);
   }
   finally {
    if (exclusiveLock != null)
         exclusiveLock.release();
    if (sharedLock != null)
         sharedLock.release();
   }
  }
}
```

Figure 10.1 File-locking example in Java.

File locks provide functionality similar to reader–writer locks, covered in Section 6.6.2. A **shared lock** is akin to a reader lock in that several processes can acquire the lock concurrently. An **exclusive lock** behaves like a writer lock; only one process at a time can acquire such a lock. It is important to note that not all operating systems provide both types of locks; some systems only provide exclusive file locking.

Furthermore, operating systems may provide either **mandatory** or **advisory** file-locking mechanisms. If a lock is mandatory, then once a process acquires an exclusive lock, the operating system will prevent any other process from accessing the locked file. For example, assume a process acquires an exclusive lock on the file `system.log`. If we attempt to open `system.log` from another process—for example, a text editor—the operating system will prevent access until the exclusive lock is released. This occurs even if the text editor is not written explicitly to acquire the lock. Alternatively, if the lock is advisory, then the operating system will not prevent the text editor from acquiring access to `system.log`. Rather, the text editor must be written so that it manually acquires the lock before accessing the file. In other words, if the locking scheme is mandatory, the operating system ensures locking integrity. For advisory locking, it is up to software developers to ensure that locks are appropriately acquired and released. As a general rule, Windows operating systems adopt mandatory locking, and UNIX systems employ advisory locks.

The use of file locks requires the same precautions as ordinary process synchronization. For example, programmers developing on systems with mandatory locking must be careful to hold exclusive file locks only while they are accessing the file; otherwise, they will prevent other processes from accessing the file as well. Furthermore, some measures must be taken to ensure that two or more processes do not become involved in a deadlock while trying to acquire file locks.

10.1.3 File Types

When we design a file system—indeed, an entire operating system—we always consider whether the operating system should recognize and support file types. If an operating system recognizes the type of a file, it can then operate on the file in reasonable ways. For example, a common mistake occurs when a user tries to print the binary-object form of a program. This attempt normally produces garbage; however, the attempt can succeed *if* the operating system has been told that the file is a binary-object program.

A common technique for implementing file types is to include the type as part of the file name. The name is split into two parts—a name and an *extension*, usually separated by a period character (Figure 10.2). In this way, the user and the operating system can tell from the name alone what the type of a file is. For example, most operating systems allow users to specify a file name as a sequence of characters followed by a period and terminated by an extension of additional characters. File name examples include *resume.doc*, *Server.java*, and *ReaderThread.c*.

The system uses the extension to indicate the type of the file and the type of operations that can be done on that file. Only a file with a *.com*, *.exe*, or *.bat* extension can be *executed*, for instance. The *.com* and *.exe* files are two forms of binary executable files, whereas a *.bat* file is a **batch file** containing, in ASCII format, commands to the operating system. MS-DOS recognizes only a few extensions, but application programs also use extensions to indicate file types in which they are interested. For example, assemblers expect source files to have an *.asm* extension, and the Microsoft Word word processor expects its files to

file type	usual extension	function
executable	exe, com, bin or none	ready-to-run machine-language program
object	obj, o	compiled, machine language, not linked
source code	c, cc, java, pas, asm, a	source code in various languages
batch	bat, sh	commands to the command interpreter
text	txt, doc	textual data, documents
word processor	wp, tex, rtf, doc	various word-processor formats
library	lib, a, so, dll	libraries of routines for programmers
print or view	ps, pdf, jpg	ASCII or binary file in a format for printing or viewing
archive	arc, zip, tar	related files grouped into one file, sometimes compressed, for archiving or storage
multimedia	mpeg, mov, rm, mp3, avi	binary file containing audio or A/V information

Figure 10.2 Common file types.

end with a *.doc* extension. These extensions are not required, so a user may specify a file without the extension (to save typing), and the application will look for a file with the given name and the extension it expects. Because these extensions are not supported by the operating system, they can be considered as "hints" to the applications that operate on them.

Another example of the utility of file types comes from the TOPS-20 operating system. If the user tries to execute an object program whose source file has been modified (or edited) since the object file was produced, the source file will be recompiled automatically. This function ensures that the user always runs an up-to-date object file. Otherwise, the user could waste a significant amount of time executing the old object file. For this function to be possible, the operating system must be able to discriminate the source file from the object file, to check the time that each file was created or last modified, and to determine the language of the source program (in order to use the correct compiler).

Consider, too, the Mac OS X operating system. In this system, each file has a type, such as *TEXT* (for text file) or *APPL* (for application). Each file also has a creator attribute containing the name of the program that created it. This attribute is set by the operating system during the `create()` call, so its use is enforced and supported by the system. For instance, a file produced by a word processor has the word processor's name as its creator. When the user opens that file, by double-clicking the mouse on the icon representing the file, the word processor is invoked automatically, and the file is loaded, ready to be edited.

The UNIX system uses a crude magic number stored at the beginning of some files to indicate roughly the type of the file—executable program, batch file (or shell script), PostScript file, and so on. Not all files have magic numbers, so system features cannot be based solely on this information. UNIX does not record the name of the creating program, either. UNIX does allow file-name-extension hints, but these extensions are neither enforced nor depended on by the operating system; they are meant mostly to aid users in determining what type of contents the file contains. Extensions can be used or ignored by a given application, but that is up to the application's programmer.

10.1.4 File Structure

File types also can be used to indicate the internal structure of the file. As mentioned in Section 10.1.3, source and object files have structures that match the expectations of the programs that read them. Further, certain files must conform to a required structure that is understood by the operating system. For example, the operating system requires that an executable file have a specific structure so that it can determine where in memory to load the file and what the location of the first instruction is. Some operating systems extend this idea into a set of system-supported file structures, with sets of special operations for manipulating files with those structures. For instance, DEC's VMS operating system has a file system that supports three defined file structures.

This point brings us to one of the disadvantages of having the operating system support multiple file structures: the resulting size of the operating system is cumbersome. If the operating system defines five different file structures, it needs to contain the code to support these file structures. In addition, it may be necessary to define every file as one of the file types supported by the operating system. When new applications require information structured in ways not supported by the operating system, severe problems may result.

For example, assume that a system supports two types of files: text files (composed of ASCII characters separated by a carriage return and line feed) and executable binary files. Now, if we (as users) want to define an encrypted file to protect the contents from being read by unauthorized people, we may find neither file type to be appropriate. The encrypted file is not ASCII text lines but rather is (apparently) random bits. Although it may appear to be a binary file, it is not executable. As a result, we may have to circumvent or misuse the operating system's file-type mechanism or abandon our encryption scheme.

Some operating systems impose (and support) a minimal number of file structures. This approach has been adopted in UNIX, MS-DOS, and others. UNIX considers each file to be a sequence of 8-bit bytes; no interpretation of these bits is made by the operating system. This scheme provides maximum flexibility but little support. Each application program must include its own code to interpret an input file as to the appropriate structure. However, all operating systems must support at least one structure—that of an executable file—so that the system is able to load and run programs.

The Macintosh operating system also supports a minimal number of file structures. It expects files to contain two parts: a resource fork and a data fork. The resource fork contains information of interest to the user. For instance, it holds the labels of any buttons displayed by the program. A foreign user may want to re-label these buttons in his own language, and the Macintosh operating system provides tools to allow modification of the data in the resource fork. The data fork contains program code or data—the traditional file contents. To accomplish the same task on a UNIX or MS-DOS system, the programmer would need to change and recompile the source code, unless she created her own user-changeable data file. Clearly, it is useful for an operating system to support structures that will be used frequently and that will save the programmer substantial effort. Too few structures make programming inconvenient, whereas too many cause operating-system bloat and programmer confusion.

10.1.5 Internal File Structure

Internally, locating an offset within a file can be complicated for the operating system. Disk systems typically have a well-defined block size determined by the size of a sector. All disk I/O is performed in units of one block (physical record), and all blocks are the same size. It is unlikely that the physical record size will exactly match the length of the desired logical record. Logical records may even vary in length. **Packing** a number of logical records into physical blocks is a common solution to this problem.

For example, the UNIX operating system defines all files to be simply streams of bytes. Each byte is individually addressable by its offset from the beginning (or end) of the file. In this case, the logical record size is 1 byte. The file system automatically packs and unpacks bytes into physical disk blocks—say, 512 bytes per block—as necessary.

The logical record size, physical block size, and packing technique determine how many logical records are in each physical block. The packing can be done either by the user's application program or by the operating system. In either case, the file may be considered a sequence of blocks. All the basic I/O functions operate in terms of blocks. The conversion from logical records to physical blocks is a relatively simple software problem.

Because disk space is always allocated in blocks, some portion of the last block of each file is generally wasted. If each block were 512 bytes, for example, then a file of 1,949 bytes would be allocated four blocks (2,048 bytes); the last 99 bytes would be wasted. The waste incurred to keep everything in units of blocks (instead of bytes) is **internal fragmentation**. All file systems suffer from internal fragmentation; the larger the block size, the greater the internal fragmentation.

10.2 Access Methods

Files store information. When it is used, this information must be accessed and read into computer memory. The information in the file can be accessed in several ways. Some systems provide only one access method for files. Other systems, such as those of IBM, support many access methods, and choosing the right one for a particular application is a major design problem.

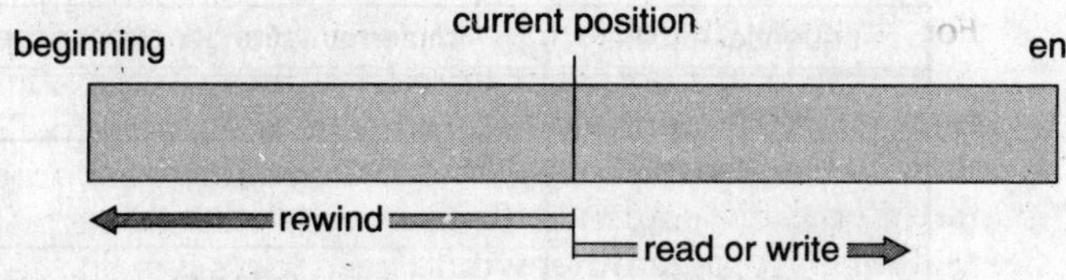

Figure 10.3 Sequential-access file.

10.2.1 Sequential Access

The simplest access method is **sequential access**. Information in the file is processed in order, one record after the other. This mode of access is by far the most common; for example, editors and compilers usually access files in this fashion.

Reads and writes make up the bulk of the operations on a file. A read operation—*read next*—reads the next portion of the file and automatically advances a file pointer, which tracks the I/O location. Similarly, the write operation—*write next*—appends to the end of the file and advances to the end of the newly written material (the new end of file). Such a file can be reset to the beginning; and on some systems, a program may be able to skip forward or backward *n* records for some integer *n*—perhaps only for *n* = 1. Sequential access, which is depicted in Figure 10.3, is based on a tape model of a file and works as well on sequential-access devices as it does on random-access ones.

10.2.2 Direct Access

Another method is **direct access** (or **relative access**). A file is made up of fixed-length **logical records** that allow programs to read and write records rapidly in no particular order. The direct-access method is based on a disk model of a file, since disks allow random access to any file block. For direct access, the file is viewed as a numbered sequence of blocks or records. Thus, we may read block 14, then read block 53, and then write block 7. There are no restrictions on the order of reading or writing for a direct-access file.

Direct-access files are of great use for immediate access to large amounts of information. Databases are often of this type. When a query concerning a particular subject arrives, we compute which block contains the answer and then read that block directly to provide the desired information.

As a simple example, on an airline-reservation system, we might store all the information about a particular flight (for example, flight 713) in the block identified by the flight number. Thus, the number of available seats for flight 713 is stored in block 713 of the reservation file. To store information about a larger set, such as people, we might compute a hash function on the people's names or search a small in-memory index to determine a block to read and search.

For the direct-access method, the file operations must be modified to include the block number as a parameter. Thus, we have *read n*, where *n* is the block number, rather than *read next*, and *write n* rather than *write next*. An alternative approach is to retain *read next* and *write next*, as with sequential

sequential access	implementation for direct access
reset	*cp = 0;*
read next	*read cp;* *cp = cp + 1;*
write next	*write cp;* *cp = cp + 1;*

Figure 10.4 Simulation of sequential access on a direct-access file.

access, and to add an operation *position file to n*, where *n* is the block number. Then, to effect a *read n*, we would *position to n* and then *read next*.

The block number provided by the user to the operating system is normally a relative block number. A relative block number is an index relative to the beginning of the file. Thus, the first relative block of the file is 0, the next is 1, and so on, even though the absolute disk address may be 14703 for the first block and 3192 for the second. The use of relative block numbers allows the operating system to decide where the file should be placed (called the *allocation problem*, as discussed in Chapter 11) and helps to prevent the user from accessing portions of the file system that may not be part of her file. Some systems start their relative block numbers at 0; others start at 1.

How, then, does the system satisfy a request for record *N* in a file? Assuming we have a logical record length *L*, the request for record *N* is turned into an I/O request for *L* bytes starting at location $L * (N)$ within the file (assuming the first record is $N = 0$). Since logical records are of a fixed size, it is also easy to read, write, or delete a record.

Not all operating systems support both sequential and direct access for files. Some systems allow only sequential file access; others allow only direct access. Some systems require that a file be defined as sequential or direct when it is created; such a file can be accessed only in a manner consistent with its declaration. We can easily simulate sequential access on a direct-access file by simply keeping a variable *cp* that defines our current position, as shown in Figure 10.4. Simulating a direct-access file on a sequential-access file, however, is extremely inefficient and clumsy.

10.2.3 Other Access Methods

Other access methods can be built on top of a direct-access method. These methods generally involve the construction of an index for the file. The index, like an index in the back of a book, contains pointers to the various blocks. To find a record in the file, we first search the index and then use the pointer to access the file directly and to find the desired record.

For example, a retail-price file might list the universal product codes (UPCs) for items, with the associated prices. Each record consists of a 10-digit UPC and a 6-digit price, for a 16-byte record. If our disk has 1,024 bytes per block, we can store 64 records per block. A file of 120,000 records would occupy about 2,000 blocks (2 million bytes). By keeping the file sorted by UPC, we can define an index consisting of the first UPC in each block. This index would have 2,000 entries of 10 digits each, or 20,000 bytes, and thus could be kept in memory. To

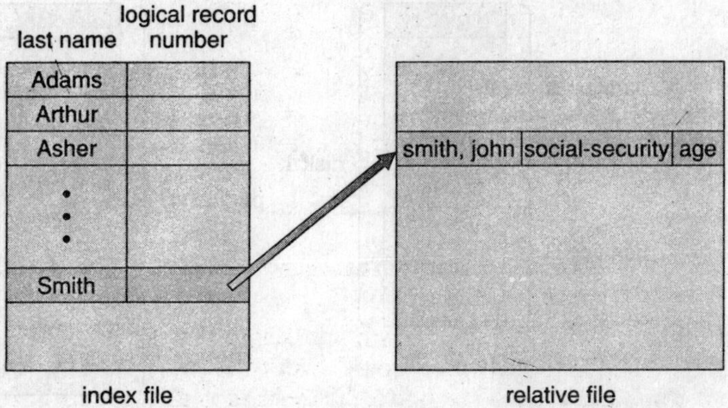

Figure 10.5 Example of index and relative files.

find the price of a particular item, we can make a binary search of the index. From this search, we learn exactly which block contains the desired record and access that block. This structure allows us to search a large file doing little I/O.

With large files, the index file itself may become too large to be kept in memory. One solution is to create an index for the index file. The primary index file would contain pointers to secondary index files, which would point to the actual data items.

For example, IBM's indexed sequential-access method (ISAM) uses a small master index that points to disk blocks of a secondary index. The secondary index blocks point to the actual file blocks. The file is kept sorted on a defined key. To find a particular item, we first make a binary search of the master index, which provides the block number of the secondary index. This block is read in, and again a binary search is used to find the block containing the desired record. Finally, this block is searched sequentially. In this way, any record can be located from its key by at most two direct-access reads. Figure 10.5 shows a similar situation as implemented by VMS index and relative files.

10.3 Directory and Disk Structure

Next, we consider how to store files. Certainly, no general-purpose computer stores just one file. There are typically thousand, millions, and even billions of files within a computer. Files are stored on random-access storage devices, including hard disks, optical disks, and solid state (memory-based) disks.

A storage device can be used in its entirety for a file system. It can also be subdivided for finer-grained control. For example, a disk can be **partitioned** into quarters, and each quarter can hold a file system. Storage devices can also be collected together into RAID sets that provide protection from the failure of a single disk (as described in Section 12.7). Sometimes, disks are subdivided and also collected into RAID sets.

Partitioning is useful for limiting the sizes of individual file systems, putting multiple file-system types on the same device, or leaving part of the device available for other uses, such as swap space or unformatted (**raw**) disk

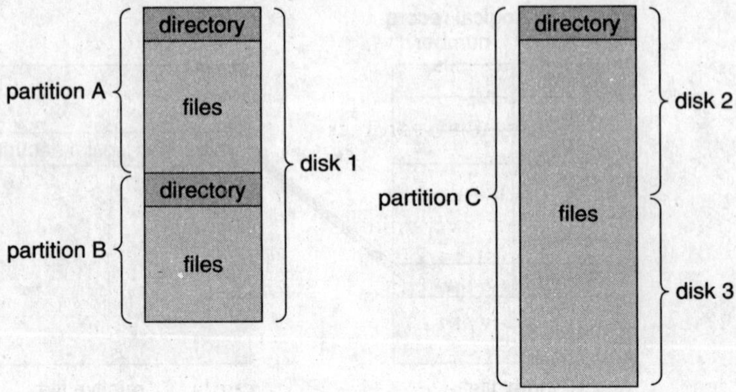

Figure 10.6 A typical file-system organization.

space. Partitions are also known as **slices** or (in the IBM world) **minidisks**. A file system can be created on each of these parts of the disk. Any entity containing a file system is generally known as a **volume**. The volume may be a subset of a device, a whole device, or multiple devices linked together into a RAID set. Each volume can be thought of as a virtual disk. Volumes can also store multiple operating systems, allowing a system to boot and run more than one operating system.

Each volume that contains a file system must also contain information about the files in the system. This information is kept in entries in a **device directory** or **volume table of contents**. The device directory (more commonly known simply as that **directory**) records information—such as name, location, size, and type—for all files on that volume. Figure 10.6 shows a typical file-system organization.

10.3.1 Storage Structure

As we have just seen, a general-purpose computer system has multiple storage devices, and those devices can be sliced up into volumes that hold file systems. Computer systems may have zero or more file systems, and the file systems may be of varying types. For example, a typical Solaris system may have dozens of file systems of a dozen different types, as shown in the file system list in Figure 10.7.

In this book, we consider only general-purpose file systems. It is worth noting, though, that there are many special-purpose file systems. Consider the types of file systems in the Solaris example mentioned above:

- **tmpfs**—a "temporary" file system that is created in volatile main memory and has its contents erased if the system reboots or crashes
- **objfs**—a "virtual" file system (essentially an interface to the kernel that looks like a file system) that gives debuggers access to kernel symbols
- **ctfs**—a virtual file system that maintains "contract" information to manage which processes start when the system boots and must continue to run during operation

/	ufs
/devices	devfs
/dev	dev
/system/contract	ctfs
/proc	proc
/etc/mnttab	mntfs
/etc/svc/volatile	tmpfs
/system/object	objfs
/lib/libc.so.1	lofs
/dev/fd	fd
/var	ufs
/tmp	tmpfs
/var/run	tmpfs
/opt	ufs
/zpbge	zfs
/zpbge/backup	zfs
/export/home	zfs
/var/mail	zfs
/var/spool/mqueue	zfs
/zpbg	zfs
/zpbg/zones	zfs

Figure 10.7 Solaris File System.

- **lofs**—a "loop back" file system that allows one file system to be accessed in place of another one
- **procfs**—a virtual file system that presents information on all processes as a file system
- **ufs, zfs**—general-purpose file systems

The file systems of computers, then, can be extensive. Even within a file system, it is useful to segregate files into groups and manage and act on those groups. This organization involves the use of directories. In the remainder of this section, we explore the topic of directory structure.

10.3.2 Directory Overview

The directory can be viewed as a symbol table that translates file names into their directory entries. If we take such a view, we see that the directory itself can be organized in many ways. We want to be able to insert entries, to delete entries, to search for a named entry, and to list all the entries in the directory. In this section, we examine several schemes for defining the logical structure of the directory system.

When considering a particular directory structure, we need to keep in mind the operations that are to be performed on a directory:

- **Search for a file**. We need to be able to search a directory structure to find the entry for a particular file. Since files have symbolic names, and similar names may indicate a relationship between files, we may want to be able to find all files whose names match a particular pattern.

- **Create a file**. New files need to be created and added to the directory.
- **Delete a file**. When a file is no longer needed, we want to be able to remove it from the directory.
- **List a directory**. We need to be able to list the files in a directory and the contents of the directory entry for each file in the list.
- **Rename a file**. Because the name of a file represents its contents to its users, we must be able to change the name when the contents or use of the file changes. Renaming a file may also allow its position within the directory structure to be changed.
- **Traverse the file system**. We may wish to access every directory and every file within a directory structure. For reliability, it is a good idea to save the contents and structure of the entire file system at regular intervals. Often, we do this by copying all files to magnetic tape. This technique provides a backup copy in case of system failure. In addition, if a file is no longer in use, the file can be copied to tape and the disk space of that file released for reuse by another file.

In the following sections, we describe the most common schemes for defining the logical structure of a directory.

10.3.3 Single-Level Directory

The simplest directory structure is the single-level directory. All files are contained in the same directory, which is easy to support and understand (Figure 10.8).

A single-level directory has significant limitations, however, when the number of files increases or when the system has more than one user. Since all files are in the same directory, they must have unique names. If two users call their data file *test*, then the unique-name rule is violated. For example, in one programming class, 23 students called the program for their second assignment *prog2*; another 11 called it *assign2*. Although file names are generally selected to reflect the content of the file, they are often limited in length, complicating the task of making file names unique. The MS-DOS operating system allows only 11-character file names; UNIX, in contrast, allows 255 characters.

Even a single user on a single-level directory may find it difficult to remember the names of all the files as the number of files increases. It is not

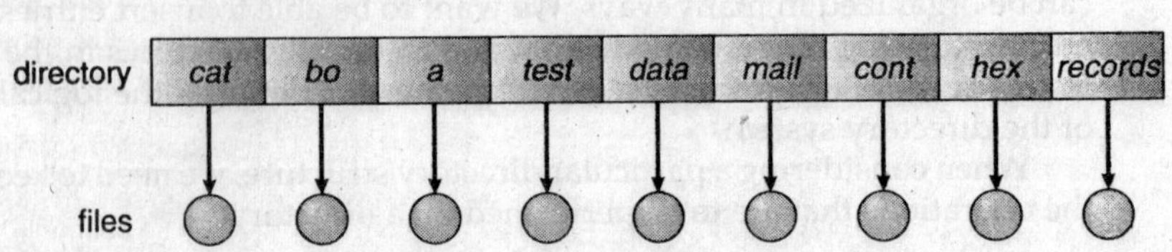

Figure 10.8 Single-level directory.

uncommon for a user to have hundreds of files on one computer system and an equal number of additional files on another system. Keeping track of so many files is a daunting task.

10.3.4 Two-Level Directory

As we have seen, a single-level directory often leads to confusion of file names among different users. The standard solution is to create a *separate* directory for each user.

In the two-level directory structure, each user has his own **user file directory (UFD)**. The UFDs have similar structures, but each lists only the files of a single user. When a user job starts or a user logs in, the system's **master file directory (MFD)** is searched. The MFD is indexed by user name or account number, and each entry points to the UFD for that user (Figure 10.9).

When a user refers to a particular file, only his own UFD is searched. Thus, different users may have files with the same name, as long as all the file names within each UFD are unique. To create a file for a user, the operating system searches only that user's UFD to ascertain whether another file of that name exists. To delete a file, the operating system confines its search to the local UFD; thus, it cannot accidentally delete another user's file that has the same name.

The user directories themselves must be created and deleted as necessary. A special system program is run with the appropriate user name and account information. The program creates a new UFD and adds an entry for it to the MFD. The execution of this program might be restricted to system administrators. The allocation of disk space for user directories can be handled with the techniques discussed in Chapter 11 for files themselves.

Although the two-level directory structure solves the name-collision problem, it still has disadvantages. This structure effectively isolates one user from another. Isolation is an advantage when the users are completely independent but is a disadvantage when the users *want* to cooperate on some task and to access one another's files. Some systems simply do not allow local user files to be accessed by other users.

If access is to be permitted, one user must have the ability to name a file in another user's directory. To name a particular file uniquely in a two-level directory, we must give both the user name and the file name. A two-level directory can be thought of as a tree, or an inverted tree, of height 2. The root of the tree is the MFD. Its direct descendants are the UFDs. The descendants of

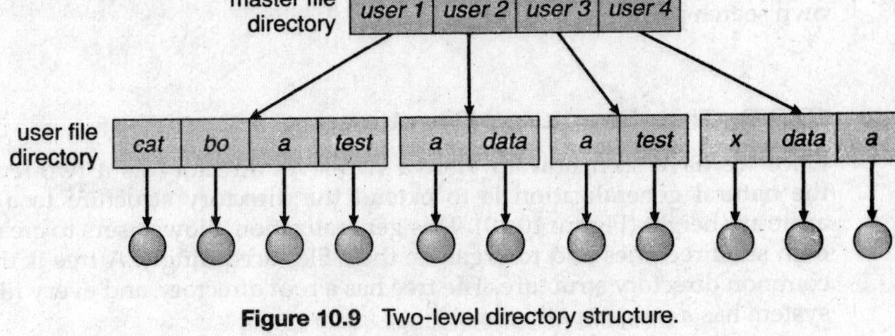

Figure 10.9 Two-level directory structure.

the UFDs are the files themselves. The files are the leaves of the tree. Specifying a user name and a file name defines a path in the tree from the root (the MFD) to a leaf (the specified file). Thus, a user name and a file name define a *path name*. Every file in the system has a path name. To name a file uniquely, a user must know the path name of the file desired.

For example, if user A wishes to access her own test file named *test*, she can simply refer to *test*. To access the file named *test* of user B (with directory-entry name *userb*), however, she might have to refer to */userb/test*. Every system has its own syntax for naming files in directories other than the user's own.

Additional syntax is needed to specify the volume of a file. For instance, in MS-DOS a volume is specified by a letter followed by a colon. Thus, a file specification might be *C:\userb\test*. Some systems go even further and separate the volume, directory name, and file name parts of the specification. For instance, in VMS, the file *login.com* might be specified as: *u:[sst.jdeck]login.com;1*, where *u* is the name of the volume, *sst* is the name of the directory, *jdeck* is the name of the subdirectory, and *1* is the version number. Other systems simply treat the volume name as part of the directory name. The first name given is that of the volume, and the rest is the directory and file. For instance, */u/pbg/test* might specify volume *u*, directory *pbg*, and file *test*.

A special case of this situation occurs with the system files. Programs provided as part of the system—loaders, assemblers, compilers, utility routines, libraries, and so on—are generally defined as files. When the appropriate commands are given to the operating system, these files are read by the loader and executed. Many command interpreters simply treat such a command as the name of a file to load and execute. As the directory system is defined presently, this file name would be searched for in the current UFD. One solution would be to copy the system files into each UFD. However, copying all the system files would waste an enormous amount of space. (If the system files require 5 MB, then supporting 12 users would require $5 \times 12 = 60$ MB just for copies of the system files.)

The standard solution is to complicate the search procedure slightly. A special user directory is defined to contain the system files (for example, user 0). Whenever a file name is given to be loaded, the operating system first searches the local UFD. If the file is found, it is used. If it is not found, the system automatically searches the special user directory that contains the system files. The sequence of directories searched when a file is named is called the **search path**. The search path can be extended to contain an unlimited list of directories to search when a command name is given. This method is the one most used in UNIX and MS-DOS. Systems can also be designed so that each user has his own search path.

10.3.5 Tree-Structured Directories

Once we have seen how to view a two-level directory as a two-level tree, the natural generalization is to extend the directory structure to a tree of arbitrary height (Figure 10.10). This generalization allows users to create their own subdirectories and to organize their files accordingly. A tree is the most common directory structure. The tree has a root directory, and every file in the system has a unique path name.

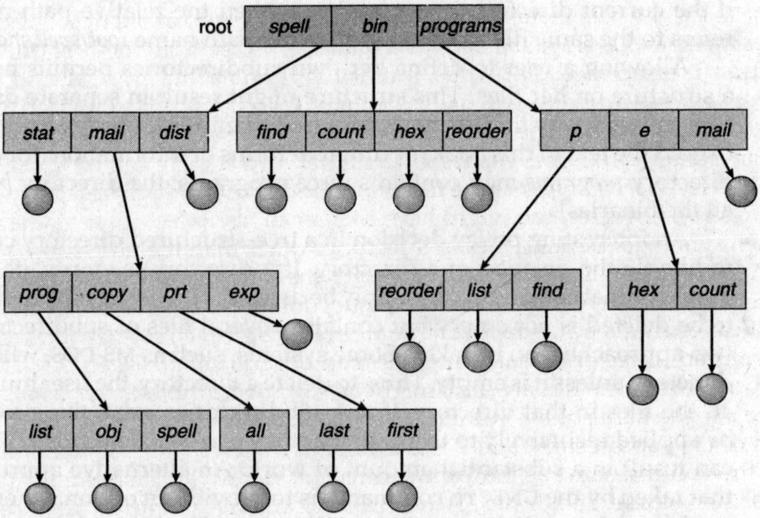

Figure 10.10 Tree-structured directory structure.

A directory (or subdirectory) contains a set of files or subdirectories. A directory is simply another file, but it is treated in a special way. All directories have the same internal format. One bit in each directory entry defines the entry as a file (0) or as a subdirectory (1). Special system calls are used to create and delete directories.

In normal use, each process has a current directory. The **current directory** should contain most of the files that are of current interest to the process. When reference is made to a file, the current directory is searched. If a file is needed that is not in the current directory, then the user usually must either specify a path name or change the current directory to be the directory holding that file. To change directories, a system call is provided that takes a directory name as a parameter and uses it to redefine the current directory. Thus, the user can change his current directory whenever he desires. From one change `directory` system call to the next, all open system calls search the current directory for the specified file. Note that the search path may or may not contain a special entry that stands for "the current directory."

The initial current directory of the login shell of a user is designated when the user job starts or the user logs in. The operating system searches the accounting file (or some other predefined location) to find an entry for this user (for accounting purposes). In the accounting file is a pointer to (or the name of) the user's initial directory. This pointer is copied to a local variable for this user that specifies the user's initial current directory. From that shell, other processes can be spawned. The current directory of any subprocess is usually the current directory of the parent when it was spawned.

Path names can be of two types: *absolute* and *relative*. An **absolute path name** begins at the root and follows a path down to the specified file, giving the directory names on the path. A **relative path name** defines a path from the current directory. For example, in the tree-structured file system of Figure 10.10, if the current directory is *root/spell/mail,* then the relative path name *prt/first* refers to the same file as does the absolute path name *root/spell/mail/prt/first.*

Allowing a user to define her own subdirectories permits her to impose a structure on her files. This structure might result in separate directories for files associated with different topics (for example, a subdirectory was created to hold the text of this book) or different forms of information (for example, the directory *programs* may contain source programs; the directory *bin* may store all the binaries).

An interesting policy decision in a tree-structured directory concerns how to handle the deletion of a directory. If a directory is empty, its entry in the directory that contains it can simply be deleted. However, suppose the directory to be deleted is not empty but contains several files or subdirectories. One of two approaches can be taken. Some systems, such as MS-DOS, will not delete a directory unless it is empty. Thus, to delete a directory, the user must first delete all the files in that directory. If any subdirectories exist, this procedure must be applied recursively to them, so that they can be deleted also. This approach can result in a substantial amount of work. An alternative approach, such as that taken by the UNIX `rm` command, is to provide an option: when a request is made to delete a directory, all that directory's files and subdirectories are also to be deleted. Either approach is fairly easy to implement; the choice is one of policy. The latter policy is more convenient, but it is also more dangerous, because an entire directory structure can be removed with one command. If that command is issued in error, a large number of files and directories will need to be restored (assuming a backup exists).

With a tree-structured directory system, users can be allowed to access, in addition to their files, the files of other users. For example, user B can access a file of user A by specifying its path names. User B can specify either an absolute or a relative path name. Alternatively, user B can change her current directory to be user A's directory and access the file by its file names.

A path to a file in a tree-structured directory can be longer than a path in a two-level directory. To allow users to access programs without having to remember these long paths, the Macintosh operating system automates the search for executable programs. One method it uses is to maintain a file, called the *Desktop File,* containing the metadata code and the name and location of all executable programs it has seen. When a new hard disk is added to the system, or the network is accessed, the operating system traverses the directory structure, searching for executable programs on the device and recording the pertinent information. This mechanism supports the double-click execution functionality described previously. A double-click on a file causes its creator-attribute data to be read and the *Desktop File* to be searched for a match. Once the match is found, the appropriate executable program is started with the clicked-on file as its input.

10.3.6 Acyclic-Graph Directories

Consider two programmers who are working on a joint project. The files associated with that project can be stored in a subdirectory, separating them from other projects and files of the two programmers. But since both programmers are equally responsible for the project, both want the subdirectory to be in

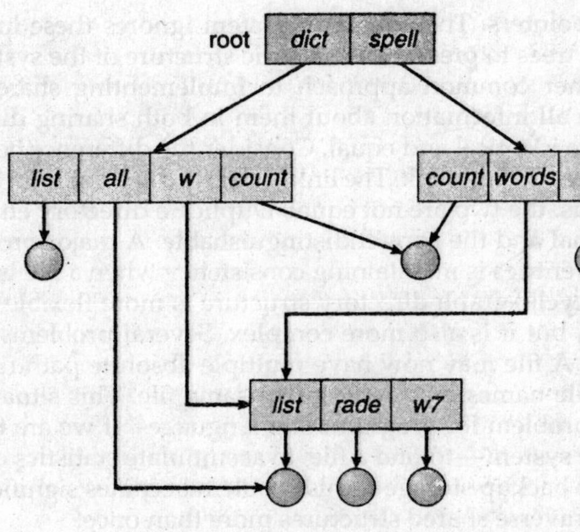

Figure 10.11 Acyclic-graph directory structure.

their own directories. The common subdirectory should be *shared*. A shared directory or file will exist in the file system in two (or more) places at once.

A tree structure prohibits the sharing of files or directories. An acyclic graph —that is, a graph with no cycles—allows directories to share subdirectories and files (Figure 10.11). The *same* file or subdirectory may be in two different directories. The acyclic graph is a natural generalization of the tree-structured directory scheme.

It is important to note that a shared file (or directory) is not the same as two copies of the file. With two copies, each programmer can view the copy rather than the original, but if one programmer changes the file, the changes will not appear in the other's copy. With a shared file, only *one* actual file exists, so any changes made by one person are immediately visible to the other. Sharing is particularly important for subdirectories; a new file created by one person will automatically appear in all the shared subdirectories.

When people are working as a team, all the files they want to share can be put into one directory. The UFD of each team member will contain this directory of shared files as a subdirectory. Even in the case of a single user, the user's file organization may require that some file be placed in different subdirectories. For example, a program written for a particular project should be both in the directory of all programs and in the directory for that project.

Shared files and subdirectories can be implemented in several ways. A common way, exemplified by many of the UNIX systems, is to create a new directory entry called a link. A **link** is effectively a pointer to another file or subdirectory. For example, a link may be implemented as an absolute or a relative path name. When a reference to a file is made, we search the directory. If the directory entry is marked as a link, then the name of the real file is included in the link information. We **resolve** the link by using that path name to locate the real file. Links are easily identified by their format in the directory entry (or by having a special type on sy ms that support types) and are effectively indirect pointers. The operating system ignores these links when traversing directory trees to preserve the acyclic structure of the system.

Another common approach to implementing shared files is simply to duplicate all information about them in both sharing directories. Thus, both entries are identical and equal. Consider the difference between this approach and the creation of a link. The link is clearly different from the original directory entry; thus, the two are not equal. Duplicate directory entries, however, make the original and the copy indistinguishable. A major problem with duplicate directory entries is maintaining consistency when a file is modified.

An acyclic-graph directory structure is more flexible than is a simple tree structure, but it is also more complex. Several problems must be considered carefully. A file may now have multiple absolute path names. Consequently, distinct file names may refer to the same file. This situation is similar to the aliasing problem for programming languages. If we are trying to traverse the entire file system—to find a file, to accumulate statistics on all files, or to copy all files to backup storage—this problem becomes significant, since we do not want to traverse shared structures more than once.

Another problem involves deletion. When can the space allocated to a shared file be deallocated and reused? One possibility is to remove the file whenever anyone deletes it, but this action may leave dangling pointers to the now-nonexistent file. Worse, if the remaining file pointers contain actual disk addresses, and the space is subsequently reused for other files, these dangling pointers may point into the middle of other files.

In a system where sharing is implemented by symbolic links, this situation is somewhat easier to handle. The deletion of a link need not affect the original file; only the link is removed. If the file entry itself is deleted, the space for the file is deallocated, leaving the links dangling. We can search for these links and remove them as well, but unless a list of the associated links is kept with each file, this search can be expensive. Alternatively, we can leave the links until an attempt is made to use them. At that time, we can determine that the file of the name given by the link does not exist and can fail to resolve the link name; the access is treated just as with any other illegal file name. (In this case, the system designer should consider carefully what to do when a file is deleted and another file of the same name is created, before a symbolic link to the original file is used.) In the case of UNIX, symbolic links are left when a file is deleted, and it is up to the user to realize that the original file is gone or has been replaced. Microsoft Windows (all flavors) uses the same approach.

Another approach to deletion is to preserve the file until all references to it are deleted. To implement this approach, we must have some mechanism for determining that the last reference to the file has been deleted. We could keep a list of all references to a file (directory entries or symbolic links). When a link or a copy of the directory entry is established, a new entry is added to the file-reference list. When a link or directory entry is deleted, we remove its entry on the list. The file is deleted when its file-reference list is empty.

The trouble with this approach is the variable and potentially large size of the file-reference list. However, we really do not need to keep the entire list —we need to keep only a count of the *number* of references. Adding a new link or directory entry increments the reference count; deleting a link or entry decrements the count. When the count is 0, the file can be deleted; there are no remaining references to it. The UNIX operating system uses this approach for nonsymbolic links (or **hard links**), keeping a reference count in the file information block (or *inode;* see Appendix A.7.2). By effectively prohibiting multiple references to directories, we maintain an acyclic-graph structure.

To avoid problems such as the ones just discussed, some systems do not allow shared directories or links. For example, in MS-DOS, the directory structure is a tree structure rather than an acyclic graph.

10.3.7 General Graph Directory

A serious problem with using an acyclic-graph structure is ensuring that there are no cycles. If we start with a two-level directory and allow users to create subdirectories, a tree-structured directory results. It should be fairly easy to see that simply adding new files and subdirectories to an existing tree-structured directory preserves the tree-structured nature. However, when we add links, the tree structure is destroyed, resulting in a simple graph structure (Figure 10.12).

The primary advantage of an acyclic graph is the relative simplicity of the algorithms to traverse the graph and to determine when there are no more references to a file. We want to avoid traversing shared sections of an acyclic graph twice, mainly for performance reasons. If we have just searched a major shared subdirectory for a particular file without finding it, we want to avoid searching that subdirectory again; the second search would be a waste of time.

If cycles are allowed to exist in the directory, we likewise want to avoid searching any component twice, for reasons of correctness as well as performance. A poorly designed algorithm might result in an infinite loop continually searching through the cycle and never terminating. One solution is to limit arbitrarily the number of directories that will be accessed during a search.

A similar problem exists when we are trying to determine when a file can be deleted. With acyclic-graph directory structures, a value of 0 in the reference count means that there are no more references to the file or directory,

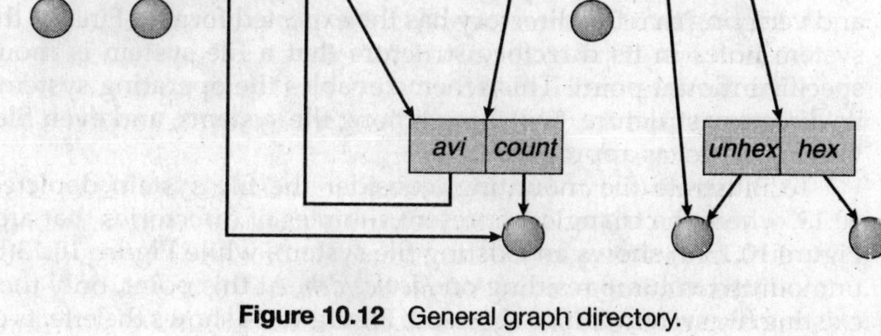

Figure 10.12 General graph directory.

and the file can be deleted. However, when cycles exist, the reference count may not be 0 even when it is no longer possible to refer to a directory or file. This anomaly results from the possibility of self-referencing (or a cycle) in the directory structure. In this case, we generally need to use a garbage-collection scheme to determine when the last reference has been deleted and the disk space can be reallocated. Garbage collection involves traversing the entire file system, marking everything that can be accessed. Then, a second pass collects everything that is not marked onto a list of free space. (A similar marking procedure can be used to ensure that a traversal or search will cover everything in the file system once and only once.) Garbage collection for a disk-based file system, however, is extremely time consuming and is thus seldom attempted.

Garbage collection is necessary only because of possible cycles in the graph. Thus, an acyclic-graph structure is much easier to work with. The difficulty is to avoid cycles as new links are added to the structure. How do we know when a new link will complete a cycle? There are algorithms to detect cycles in graphs; however, they are computationally expensive, especially when the graph is on disk storage. A simpler algorithm in the special case of directories and links is to bypass links during directory traversal. Cycles are avoided, and no extra overhead is incurred.

10.4 File-System Mounting

Just as a file must be *opened* before it is used, a file system must be *mounted* before it can be available to processes on the system. More specifically, the directory structure may be built out of multiple volumes, which must be mounted to make them available within the file-system name space.

The mount procedure is straightforward. The operating system is given the name of the device and the mount point—the location within the file structure where the file system is to be attached. Some operating systems require that a file system type be provided, while others inspect the structures of the device and determine the type of file system. Typically, a mount point is an empty directory. For instance, on a UNIX system, a file system containing a user's home directories might be mounted as */home;* then, to access the directory structure within that file system, we could precede the directory names with */home*, as in */home/jane*. Mounting that file system under */users* would result in the path name */users/jane*, which we could use to reach the same directory.

Next, the operating system verifies that the device contains a valid file system. It does so by asking the device driver to read the device directory and verifying that the directory has the expected format. Finally, the operating system notes in its directory structure that a file system is mounted at the specified mount point. This scheme enables the operating system to traverse its directory structure, switching among file systems, and even file systems of varying types, as appropriate.

To illustrate file mounting, consider the file system depicted in Figure 10.13, where the triangles represent subtrees of directories that are of interest. Figure 10.13(a) shows an existing file system, while Figure 10.13(b) shows an unmounted volume residing on */device/dsk*. At this point, only the files on the existing file system can be accessed. Figure 10.14 shows the effects of mounting

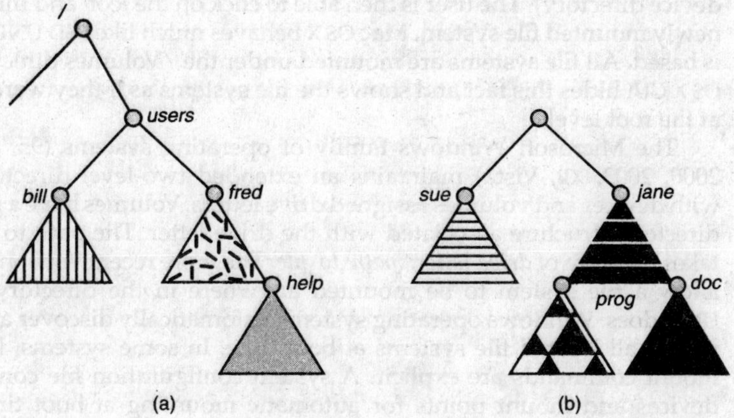

Figure 10.13 File system. (a) Existing system. (b) Unmounted volume.

the volume residing on */device/dsk* over */users*. If the volume is unmounted, the file system is restored to the situation depicted in Figure 10.13.

Systems impose semantics to clarify functionality. For example, a system may disallow a mount over a directory that contains files; or it may make the mounted file system available at that directory and obscure the directory's existing files until the file system is unmounted, terminating the use of the file system and allowing access to the original files in that directory. As another example, a system may allow the same file system to be mounted repeatedly, at different mount points; or it may only allow one mount per file system.

Consider the actions of the classic Macintosh operating system. Whenever the system encounters a disk for the first time (hard disks are found at boot time, and optical disks are seen when they are inserted into the drive), the Macintosh operating system searches for a file system on the device. If it finds one, it automatically mounts the file system at the root level, adding a folder icon on the screen labeled with the name of the file system (as stored in the

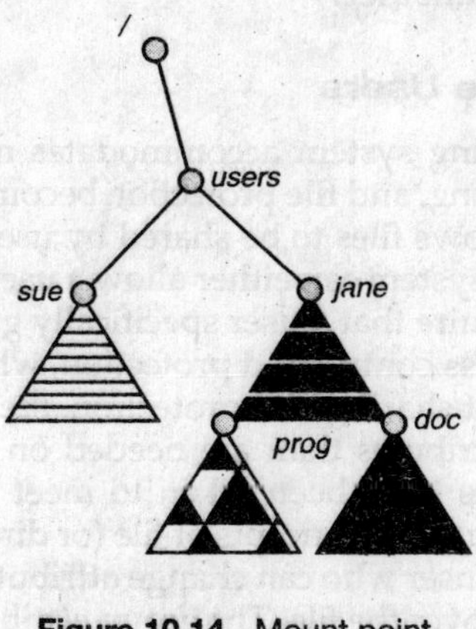

Figure 10.14 Mount point.

device directory). The user is then able to click on the icon and thus display the newly mounted file system. Mac OS X behaves much like BSD UNIX, on which it is based. All file systems are mounted under the /Volumes directory. The Mac OS X GUI hides this fact and shows the file systems as if they were all mounted at the root level.

The Microsoft Windows family of operating systems (95, 98, NT, small 2000, 2003, XP, Vista) maintains an extended two-level directory structure, with devices and volumes assigned drive letters. Volumes have a general graph directory structure associated with the drive letter. The path to a specific file takes the form of *drive-letter:\path\to\file*. The more recent versions of Windows allow a file system to be mounted anywhere in the directory tree, just as UNIX does. Windows operating systems automatically discover all devices and mount all located file systems at boot time. In some systems, like UNIX, the mount commands are explicit. A system configuration file contains a list of devices and mount points for automatic mounting at boot time, but other mounts may be executed manually.

Issues concerning file system mounting are further discussed in Section 11.2.2 and in Appendix A.7.5.

10.5 File Sharing

In the previous sections, we explored the motivation for file sharing and some of the difficulties involved in allowing users to share files. Such file sharing is very desirable for users who want to collaborate and to reduce the effort required to achieve a computing goal. Therefore, user-oriented operating systems must accommodate the need to share files in spite of the inherent difficulties.

In this section, we examine more aspects of file sharing. We begin by discussing general issues that arise when multiple users share files. Once multiple users are allowed to share files, the challenge is to extend sharing to multiple file systems, including remote file systems; we discuss that challenge as well. Finally, we consider what to do about conflicting actions occurring on shared files. For instance, if multiple users are writing to a file, should all the writes be allowed to occur, or should the operating system protect the users' actions from one another?

10.5.1 Multiple Users

When an operating system accommodates multiple users, the issues of file sharing, file naming, and file protection become preeminent. Given a directory structure that allows files to be shared by users, the system must mediate the file sharing. The system can either allow a user to access the files of other users by default or require that a user specifically grant access to the files. These are the issues of access control and protection, which are covered in Section 10.6.

To implement sharing and protection, the system must maintain more file and directory attributes than are needed on a single-user system. Although many approaches have been taken to meet this requirement, most systems have evolved to use the concepts of file (or directory) *owner* (or *user*) and *group*. The owner is the user who can change attributes and grant access and who has the most control over the file. The group attribute defines a subset of users who can share access to the file. For example, the owner of a file on a UNIX system can issue all operations on a file, while members of the file's group can execute one subset of those operations, and all other users can execute another subset of operations. Exactly which operations can be executed by group members and other users is definable by the file's owner. More details on permission attributes are included in the next section.

The owner and group IDs of a given file (or directory) are stored with the other file attributes. When a user requests an operation on a file, the user ID can be compared with the owner attribute to determine if the requesting user is the owner of the file. Likewise, the group IDs can be compared. The result indicates which permissions are applicable. The system then applies those permissions to the requested operation and allows or denies it.

Many systems have multiple local file systems, including volumes of a single disk or multiple volumes on multiple attached disks. In these cases, the ID checking and permission matching are straightforward, once the file systems are mounted.

10.5.2 Remote File Systems

With the advent of networks (Chapter 16), communication among remote computers became possible. Networking allows the sharing of resources spread across a campus or even around the world. One obvious resource to share is data in the form of files.

Through the evolution of network and file technology, remote file-sharing methods have changed. The first implemented method involves manually transferring files between machines via programs like `ftp`. The second major method uses a **distributed file system (DFS)** in which remote directories are visible from a local machine. In some ways, the third method, the **World Wide Web**, is a reversion to the first. A browser is needed to gain access to the remote files, and separate operations (essentially a wrapper for `ftp`) are used to transfer files.

`ftp` is used for both anonymous and authenticated access. **Anonymous access** allows a user to transfer files without having an account on the remote system. The World Wide Web uses anonymous file exchange almost exclusively. DFS involves a much tighter integration between the machine that is accessing the remote files and the machine providing the files. This integration adds complexity, which we describe in this section.

10.5.2.1 The Client–Server Model

Remote file systems allow a computer to mount one or more file systems from one or more remote machines. In this case, the machine containing the files is the *server,* and the machine seeking access to the files is the *client.* The client–server relationship is common with networked machines. Generally, the server declares that a resource is available to clients and specifies exactly which resource (in this case, which files) and exactly which clients. A server can serve multiple clients, and a client can use multiple servers, depending on the implementation details of a given client–server facility.

The server usually specifies the available files on a volume or directory level. Client identification is more difficult. A client can be specified by a network name or other identifier, such as an *IP address,* but these can be **spoofed,** or imitated. As a result of spoofing, an unauthorized client could be allowed access to the server. More secure solutions include secure authentication of the client via encrypted keys. Unfortunately, with security come many challenges, including ensuring compatibility of the client and server (they must use the same encryption algorithms) and security of key exchanges (intercepted keys could again allow unauthorized access). Because of the difficulty of solving these problems, unsecure authentication methods are most commonly used.

In the case of UNIX and its network file system (NFS), authentication takes place via the client networking information, by default. In this scheme, the user's IDs on the client and server must match. If they do not, the server will be unable to determine access rights to files. Consider the example of a user who has an ID of 1000 on the client and 2000 on the server. A request from the client to the server for a specific file will not be handled appropriately, as the server will determine if user 1000 has access to the file rather than basing the determination on the *real* user ID of 2000. Access is thus granted or denied based on incorrect authentication information. The server must trust the client to present the correct user ID. Note that the NFS protocols allow many-to-many relationships. That is, many servers can provide files to many clients. In fact, a given machine can be both a server to some NFS clients and a client of other NFS servers.

Once the remote file system is mounted, file operation requests are sent on behalf of the user across the network to the server via the DFS protocol. Typically, a file-open request is sent along with the ID of the requesting user. The server then applies the standard access checks to determine if the user has credentials to access the file in the mode requested. The request is either allowed or denied. If it is allowed, a file handle is returned to the client application, and the application then can perform read, write, and other operations on the file. The client closes the file when access is completed. The operating system may apply semantics similar to those for a local file-system mount or may use different semantics.

10.5.2.2 Distributed Information Systems

To make client–server systems easier to manage, **distributed information systems**, also known as **distributed naming services**, provide unified access to the information needed for remote computing. The **domain name system (DNS)** provides host-name-to-network-address translations for the entire Internet (including the World Wide Web). Before DNS became widespread, files containing the same information were sent via e-mail or `ftp` between all networked hosts. This methodology was not scalable. DNS is further discussed in Section 16.5.1.

Other distributed information systems provide *user name/password/user ID/group ID* space for a distributed facility. UNIX systems have employed a wide variety of distributed-information methods. Sun Microsystems introduced *yellow pages* (since renamed **network information service**, or **NIS**), and most of the industry adopted its use. It centralizes storage of user names, host names, printer information, and the like. Unfortunately, it uses unsecure authentication methods, including sending user passwords unencrypted (in *clear text*) and identifying hosts by IP address. Sun's NIS+ is a much more secure replacement for NIS but is also much more complicated and has not been widely adopted.

In the case of Microsoft's common Internet file system (CIFS), network information is used in conjunction with user authentication (user name and password) to create a network login that the server uses to decide whether to allow or deny access to a requested file system. For this authentication to be valid, the user names must match from machine to machine (as with NFS). Microsoft uses two distributed naming structures to provide a single name space for users. The older naming technology is domains. The newer technology, available in Windows XP and Windows 2000, is active directory. Once established, the distributed naming facility is used by all clients and servers to authenticate users.

The industry is moving toward use of the lightweight directory-access protocol (LDAP) as a secure distributed naming mechanism. In fact, active directory is based on LDAP. Sun Microsystems includes LDAP with the operating system and allows it to be employed for user authentication as well as system-wide retrieval of information, such as availability of printers. Conceivably, one distributed LDAP directory could be used by an organization to store all user and resource information for all the organization's computers. The result would be secure single sign-on for users, who would enter their authentication information once for access to all computers within the organization. It would also ease system-administration efforts by combining, in one location, information that is currently scattered in various files on each system or in different distributed information services.

10.5.2.3 Failure Modes

Local file systems can fail for a variety of reasons, including failure of the disk containing the file system, corruption of the directory structure or other disk-management information (collectively called metadata), disk-controller failure, cable failure, and host-adapter failure. User or system-administrator failure can also cause files to be lost or entire directories or volumes to be deleted. Many of these failures will cause a host to crash and an error condition to be displayed, and human intervention will be required to repair the damage.

Remote file systems have even more failure modes. Because of the complexity of network systems and the required interactions between remote machines, many more problems can interfere with the proper operation of remote file systems. In the case of networks, the network can be interrupted between two hosts. Such interruptions can result from hardware failure, poor hardware configuration, or networking implementation issues. Although some networks have built-in resiliency, including multiple paths between hosts, many do not. Any single failure can thus interrupt the flow of DFS commands.

Consider a client in the midst of using a remote file system. It has files open from the remote host; among other activities, it may be performing directory lookups to open files, reading or writing data to files, and closing files. Now consider a partitioning of the network, a crash of the server, or even a scheduled shutdown of the server. Suddenly, the remote file system is no longer reachable. This scenario is rather common, so it would not be appropriate for the client system to act as it would if a local file system were lost. Rather, the system can either terminate all operations to the lost server or delay operations until the server is again reachable. These failure semantics are defined and implemented as part of the remote-file-system protocol. Termination of all operations can result in users' losing data—and patience. Thus, most DFS protocols either enforce or allow delaying of file-system operations to remote hosts, with the hope that the remote host will become available again.

To implement this kind of recovery from failure, some kind of **state information** may be maintained on both the client and the server. If both server and client maintain knowledge of their current activities and open files, then they can seamlessly recover from a failure. In the situation where the server crashes but must recognize that it has remotely mounted exported file systems and opened files, NFS takes a simple approach, implementing a **stateless** DFS. In essence, it assumes that a client request for a file read or write would not have occurred unless the file system had been remotely mounted and the file had been previously open. The NFS protocol carries all the information needed to locate the appropriate file and perform the requested operation. Similarly, it does not track which clients have the exported volumes mounted, again assuming that if a request comes in, it must be legitimate. While this stateless approach makes NFS resilient and rather easy to implement, it also makes it unsecure. For example, forged read or write requests could be allowed by an NFS server even though the requisite mount request and permission check had not taken place. These issues are addressed in the industry standard NFS Version 4, in which NFS is made stateful to improve its security, performance, and functionality.

10.5.3 Consistency Semantics

Consistency semantics represent an important criterion for evaluating any file system that supports file sharing. These semantics specify how multiple users of a system are to access a shared file simultaneously. In particular, they specify when modifications of data by one user will be observable by other users. These semantics are typically implemented as code with the file system.

Consistency semantics are directly related to the process-synchronization algorithms of Chapter 6. However, the complex algorithms of that chapter tend not to be implemented in the case of file I/O because of the great latencies and slow transfer rates of disks and networks. For example, performing an atomic transaction to a remote disk could involve several network communications, several disk reads and writes, or both. Systems that attempt such a full set of functionalities tend to perform poorly. A successful implementation of complex sharing semantics can be found in the Andrew file system.

For the following discussion, we assume that a series of file accesses (that is, reads and writes) attempted by a user to the same file is always enclosed between the `open()` and `close()` operations. The series of accesses between the `open()` and `close()` operations makes up a **file session**. To illustrate the concept, we sketch several prominent examples of consistency semantics.

10.5.3.1 UNIX Semantics

The UNIX file system (Chapter 17) uses the following consistency semantics:

- Writes to an open file by a user are visible immediately to other users who have this file open.

- One mode of sharing allows users to share the pointer of current location into the file. Thus, the advancing of the pointer by one user affects all sharing users. Here, a file has a single image that interleaves all accesses, regardless of their origin.

In the UNIX semantics, a file is associated with a single physical image that is accessed as an exclusive resource. Contention for this single image causes delays in user processes.

10.5.3.2 Session Semantics

The Andrew file system (AFS) (Chapter 17) uses the following consistency semantics:

- Writes to an open file by a user are not visible immediately to other users that have the same file open.
- Once a file is closed, the changes made to it are visible only in sessions starting later. Already open instances of the file do not reflect these changes.

According to these semantics, a file may be associated temporarily with several (possibly different) images at the same time. Consequently, multiple users are allowed to perform both read and write accesses concurrently on their images of the file, without delay. Almost no constraints are enforced on scheduling accesses.

10.5.3.3 Immutable-Shared-Files Semantics

A unique approach is that of **immutable shared files**. Once a file is declared as *shared* by its creator, it cannot be modified. An immutable file has two key properties: its name may not be reused, and its contents may not be altered. Thus, the name of an immutable file signifies that the contents of the file are fixed. The implementation of these semantics in a distributed system (Chapter 17) is simple, because the sharing is disciplined (read-only).

10.6 Protection

When information is stored in a computer system, we want to keep it safe from physical damage (the issue of *reliability*) and improper access (the issue of *protection*).

Reliability is generally provided by duplicate copies of files. Many computers have systems programs that automatically (or through computer-operator intervention) copy disk files to tape at regular intervals (once per day or week or month) to maintain a copy should a file system be accidentally destroyed. File systems can be damaged by hardware problems (such as errors in reading or writing), power surges or failures, head crashes, dirt, temperature extremes, and vandalism. Files may be deleted accidentally. Bugs in the file-system software can also cause file contents to be lost. Reliability is covered in more detail in Chapter 12.

Protection can be provided in many ways. For a small single-user system, we might provide protection by physically removing the floppy disks and locking them in a desk drawer or file cabinet. In a multiuser system, however, other mechanisms are needed.

10.6.1 Types of Access

The need to protect files is a direct result of the ability to access files. Systems that do not permit access to the files of other users do not need protection. Thus, we could provide complete protection by prohibiting access. Alternatively, we could provide free access with no protection. Both approaches are too extreme for general use. What is needed is **controlled access**.

Protection mechanisms provide controlled access by limiting the types of file access that can be made. Access is permitted or denied depending on several factors, one of which is the type of access requested. Several different types of operations may be controlled:

- **Read**. Read from the file.
- **Write**. Write or rewrite the file.
- **Execute**. Load the file into memory and execute it.
- **Append**. Write new information at the end of the file.
- **Delete**. Delete the file and free its space for possible reuse.
- **List**. List the name and attributes of the file.

Other operations, such as renaming, copying, and editing the file, may also be controlled. For many systems, however, these higher-level functions may be implemented by a system program that makes lower-level system calls. Protection is provided at only the lower level. For instance, copying a file may be implemented simply by a sequence of read requests. In this case, a user with read access can also cause the file to be copied, printed, and so on.

Many protection mechanisms have been proposed. Each has advantages and disadvantages and must be appropriate for its intended application. A small computer system that is used by only a few members of a research group, for example, may not need the same types of protection as a large corporate computer that is used for research, finance, and personnel operations. We discuss some approaches to protection in the following sections and present a more complete treatment in Chapter 14.

10.6.2 Access Control

The most common approach to the protection problem is to make access dependent on the identity of the user. Different users may need different types of access to a file or directory. The most general scheme to implement identity-dependent access is to associate with each file and directory an **access-control list (ACL)** specifying user names and the types of access allowed for each user. When a user requests access to a particular file, the operating system checks the access list associated with that file. If that user is listed for the requested access, the access is allowed. Otherwise, a protection violation occurs, and the user job is denied access to the file.

This approach has the advantage of enabling complex access methodologies. The main problem with access lists is their length. If we want to allow everyone to read a file, we must list all users with read access. This technique has two undesirable consequences:

- Constructing such a list may be a tedious and unrewarding task, especially if we do not know in advance the list of users in the system.
- The directory entry, previously of fixed size, now must be of variable size, resulting in more complicated space management.

These problems can be resolved by use of a condensed version of the access list.

To condense the length of the access-control list, many systems recognize three classifications of users in connection with each file:

- **Owner**. The user who created the file is the owner.
- **Group**. A set of users who are sharing the file and need similar access is a group, or work group.
- **Universe**. All other users in the system constitute the universe.

The most common recent approach is to combine access-control lists with the more general (and easier to implement) owner, group, and universe access-control scheme just described. For example, Solaris 2.6 and beyond use the three categories of access by default but allow access-control lists to be added to specific files and directories when more fine-grained access control is desired.

To illustrate, consider a person, Sara, who is writing a new book. She has hired three graduate students (Jim, Dawn, and Jill) to help with the project. The text of the book is kept in a file named *book*. The protection associated with this file is as follows:

- Sara should be able to invoke all operations on the file.
- Jim, Dawn, and Jill should be able only to read and write the file; they should not be allowed to delete the file.
- All other users should be able to read, but not write, the file. (Sara is interested in letting as many people as possible read the text so that she can obtain feedback.)

To achieve such protection, we must create a new group—say, *text*—with members Jim, Dawn, and Jill. The name of the group, *text*, must then be associated with the file *book*, and the access rights must be set in accordance with the policy we have outlined.

Now consider a visitor to whom Sara would like to grant temporary access to Chapter 1. The visitor cannot be added to the *text* group because that would give him access to all chapters. Because a file can only be in one group, Sara cannot add another group to Chapter 1. With the addition of access-control-list functionality, though, the visitor can be added to the access control list of Chapter 1.

For this scheme to work properly, permissions and access lists must be controlled tightly. This control can be accomplished in several ways. For example, in the UNIX system, groups can be created and modified only by the manager of the facility (or by any superuser). Thus, control is achieved through human interaction. In the VMS system, the owner of the file can create and modify the access-control list. Access lists are discussed further in Section 14.5.2.

With the more limited protection classification, only three fields are needed to define protection. Often, each field is a collection of bits, and each bit either allows or prevents the access associated with it. For example, the UNIX system defines three fields of 3 bits each—`rwx`, where `r` controls read access, `w` controls write access, and `x` controls execution. A separate field is kept for the file owner, for the file's group, and for all other users. In this scheme, 9 bits per file are needed to record protection information. Thus, for our example, the protection fields for the file *book* are as follows: for the owner Sara, all bits are set; for the group *text*, the `r` and `w` bits are set; and for the universe, only the `r` bit is set.

One difficulty in combining approaches comes in the user interface. Users must be able to tell when the optional ACL permissions are set on a file. In the Solaris example, a "+" appends the regular permissions, as in:

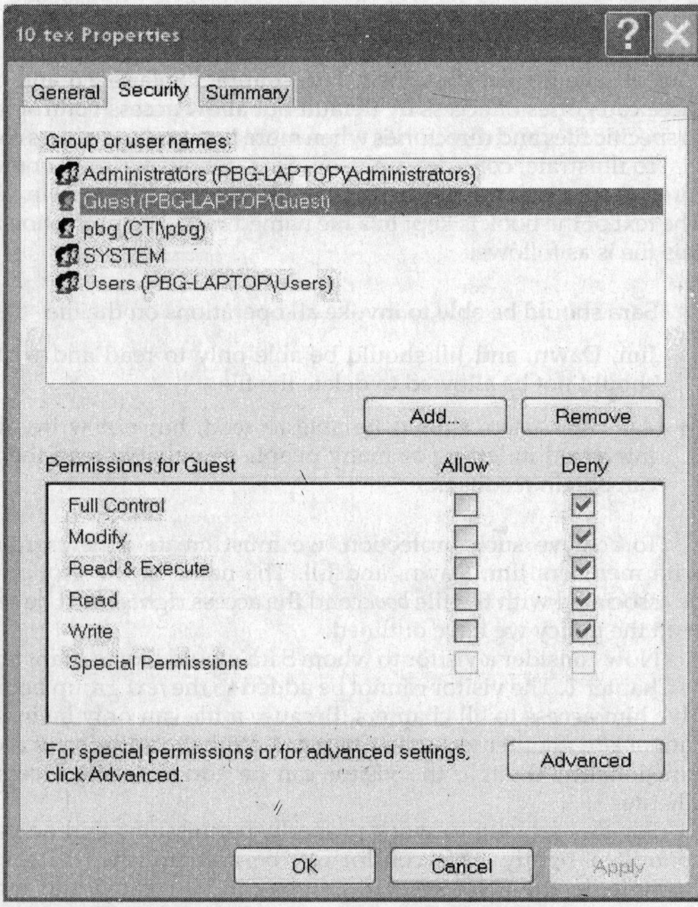

Figure 10.15 Windows XP access-control list management.

```
19 -rw-r--r--+ 1 jim staff 130 May 25 22:13 file1
```

A separate set of commands, `setfacl` and `getfacl`, is used to manage the ACLs.

Windows XP users typically manage access-control lists via the GUI. Figure 10.15 shows a file-permission window on Windows XP's NTFS file system. In this example, user "guest" is specifically denied access to the file *10.tex*.

Another difficulty is assigning precedence when permission and ACLs conflict. For example, if Joe is in a file's group, which has read permission, but the file has an ACL granting Joe read and write permission, should a write by Joe be granted or denied? Solaris gives ACLs precedence (as they are more fine-grained and are not assigned by default). This follows the general rule that specificity should have priority.

10.6.3 Other Protection Approaches

Another approach to the protection problem is to associate a password with each file. Just as access to the computer system is often controlled by a password, access to each file can be controlled in the same way. If the passwords are chosen randomly and changed often, this scheme may be effective in limiting access to a file. The use of passwords has a few disadvantages, however. First, the number of passwords that a user needs to remember may

PERMISSIONS IN A UNIX SYSTEM

In the UNIX system, directory protection and file protection are handled similarly. Associated with each subdirectory are three fields—owner, group, and universe—each consisting of the three bits `rwx`. Thus, a user can list the content of a subdirectory only if the `r` bit is set in the appropriate field. Similarly, a user can change his current directory to another current directory (say, *foo*) only if the `x` bit associated with the *foo* subdirectory is set in the appropriate field.

A sample directory listing from a UNIX environment is shown in Figure 10.16. The first field describes the protection of the file or directory. A `d` as the first character indicates a subdirectory. Also shown are the number of links to the file, the owner's name, the group's name, the size of the file in bytes, the date of last modification, and finally the file's name (with optional extension).

-rw-rw-r--	1 pbg	staff	31200	Sep 3 08:30	intro.ps
drwx------	5 pbg	staff	512	Jul 8 09.33	private/
drwxrwxr-x	2 pbg	staff	512	Jul 8 09:35	doc/
drwxrwx---	2 pbg	student	512	Aug 3 14:13	student-proj/
-rw-r--r--	1 pbg	staff	9423	Feb 24 2003	program.c
-rwxr-xr-x	1 pbg	staff	20471	Feb 24 2003	program
drwx--x--x	4 pbg	faculty	512	Jul 31 10:31	lib/
drwx------	3 pbg	staff	1024	Aug 29 06:52	mail/
drwxrwxrwx	3 pbg	staff	512	Jul 8 09:35	test/

Figure 10.16 A sample directory listing.

become large, making the scheme impractical. Second, if only one password is used for all the files, then once it is discovered, all files are accessible; protection is on an all-or-none basis. Some systems (for example, TOPS-20) allow a user to associate a password with a subdirectory, rather than with an individual file, to deal with this problem. The IBMVM/CMS operating system allows three passwords for a minidisk—one each for read, write, and multiwrite access.

Some single-user operating systems—such as MS-DOS and versions of the Macintosh operating system prior to Mac OS X—provide little in terms of file protection. In scenarios where these older systems are now being placed on networks requiring file sharing and communication, protection mechanisms must be retrofitted into them. Designing a feature for a new operating system is almost always easier than adding a feature to an existing one. Such updates are usually less effective and are not seamless.

In a multilevel directory structure, we need to protect not only individual files but also collections of files in subdirectories; that is, we need to provide a mechanism for directory protection. The directory operations that must be protected are somewhat different from the file operations. We want to control the creation and deletion of files in a directory. In addition, we probably want to control whether a user can determine the existence of a file in a directory. Sometimes, knowledge of the existence and name of a file is significant in itself. Thus, listing the contents of a directory must be a protected operation. Similarly, if a path name refers to a file in a directory, the user must be allowed access to both the directory and the file. In systems where files may have numerous path names (such as acyclic or general graphs), a given user may have different access rights to a particular file, depending on the path name used.

10.7 Summary

A file is an abstract data type defined and implemented by the operating system. It is a sequence of logical records. A logical record may be a byte, a line (of fixed or variable length), or a more complex data item. The operating system may specifically support various record types or may leave that support to the application program.

The major task for the operating system is to map the logical file concept onto physical storage devices such as magnetic tape or disk. Since the physical record size of the device may not be the same as the logical record size, it may be necessary to order logical records into physical records. Again, this task may be supported by the operating system or left for the application program.

Each device in a file system keeps a volume table of contents or a device directory listing the location of the files on the device. In addition, it is useful to create directories to allow files to be organized. A single-level directory in a multiuser system causes naming problems, since each file must have a unique name. A two-level directory solves this problem by creating a separate directory for each users files. The directory lists the files by name and includes the file's location on the disk, length, type, owner, time of creation, time of last use, and so on.

The natural generalization of a two-level directory is a tree-structured directory. A tree-structured directory allows a user to create subdirectories to organize files. Acyclic-graph directory structures enable users to share subdirectories and files but complicate searching and deletion. A general graph structure allows complete flexibility in the sharing of files and directories but sometimes requires garbage collection to recover unused disk space.

Disks are segmented into one or more volumes, each containing a file system or left "raw." File systems may be mounted into the system's naming structures to make them available. The naming scheme varies by operating system. Once mounted, the files within the volume are available for use. File systems may be unmounted to disable access or for maintenance.

File sharing depends on the semantics provided by the system. Files may have multiple readers, multiple writers, or limits on sharing. Distributed file systems allow client hosts to mount volumes or directories from servers, as long as they can access each other across a network. Remote file systems present challenges in reliability, performance, and security. Distributed information systems maintain user, host, and access information so that clients and servers can share state information to manage use and access.

Since files are the main information-storage mechanism in most computer systems, file protection is needed. Access to files can be controlled separately for each type of access—read, write, execute, append, delete, list directory, and so on. File protection can be provided by access lists, passwords, or other techniques.

Exercises

10.1 Some systems provide file sharing by maintaining a single copy of a file; other systems maintain several copies, one for each of the users sharing the file. Discuss the relative merits of each approach.

10.2 Some systems automatically open a file when it is referenced for the first time and close the file when the job terminates. Discuss the advantages and disadvantages of this scheme compared with the more traditional one, where the user has to open and close the file explicitly.

10.3 In some systems, a subdirectory can be read and written by an authorized user, just as ordinary files can be.

a. Describe the protection problems that could arise.

b. Suggest a scheme for dealing with each of these protection problems.

10.4 Why do some systems keep track of the type of a file, while others leave it to the user and others simply do not implement multiple file types? Which system is "better?"

10.5 Consider a system that supports 5,000 users. Suppose that you want to allow 4,990 of these users to be able to access one file.

a. How would you specify this protection scheme in UNIX?

b. Can you suggest another protection scheme that can be used more effectively for this purpose than the scheme provided by UNIX?

10.6 What are the advantages and disadvantages of providing mandatory locks instead of advisory locks whose usage is left to users' discretion?

10.7 Explain the purpose of the `open()` and `close()` operations.

10.8 The open-file table is used to maintain information about files that are currently open. Should the operating system maintain a separate table for each user or just maintain one table that contains references to files that are currently being accessed by all users? If the same file is being accessed by two different programs or users, should there be separate entries in the open-file table?

10.9 Give an example of an application that could benefit from operating-system support for random access to indexed files.

10.10 Discuss the advantages and disadvantages of associating with remote file systems (stored on file servers) a set of failure semantics different from that associated with local file systems.

10.11 Could you simulate a multilevel directory structure with a single-level directory structure in which arbitrarily long names can be used? If your answer is yes, explain how you can do so, and contrast this scheme with the multilevel directory scheme. If your answer is no, explain what prevents your simulation's success. How would your answer change if file names were limited to seven characters?

10.12 What are the implications of supporting UNIX consistency semantics for shared access for files stored on remote file systems?

10.13 If the operating system knew that a certain application was going to access file data in a sequential manner, how could it exploit this information to improve performance?

10.14 Consider a file system in which a file can be deleted and its disk space reclaimed while links to that file still exist. What problems may occur if a new file is created in the same storage area or with the same absolute path name? How can these problems be avoided?

10.15 Discuss the advantages and disadvantages of supporting links to files that cross mount points (that is, the file link refers to a file that is stored in a different volume).

10.16 What are the advantages and disadvantages of recording the name of the creating program with the file's attributes (as is done in the Macintosh operating system)?

Bibliographical Notes

General discussions concerning file systems are offered by Grosshans [1986]. Golden and Pechura [1986] describe the structure of microcomputer file systems. Database systems and their file structures are described in full in Silberschatz et al. [2001].

A multilevel directory structure was first implemented on the MULTICS system (Organick [1972]). Most operating systems now implement multilevel directory structures. These include Linux (Bovet and Cesati [2002]), Mac OS X (http://www.apple.com/macosx/), Solaris (McDougall and Mauro [2007]), and all versions of Windows (Russinovich and Solomon [2005]).

The network file system (NFS), designed by Sun Microsystems, allows directory structures to be spread across networked computer systems. NFS is fully described in Chapter 17. NFS Version 4 is described in RFC3505 (http://www.ietf.org/rfc/rfc3530.txt). General discussion of Solaris file systems is found in the Sun *System Administration Guide: Devices and File Systems* (http://docs.sun.com/app/docs/doc/817-5093).

DNS was first proposed by Su [1982] and has gone through several revisions since, with Mockapetris [1987] adding several major features. Eastlake [1999] has proposed security extensions to let DNS hold security keys.

LDAP, also known as X.509, is a derivative subset of the X.500 distributed directory protocol. It was defined by Yeong et al. [1995] and has been implemented on many operating systems.

Interesting research is ongoing in the area of file-system interfaces—in particular, on issues relating to file naming and attributes. For example, the Plan 9 operating system from Bell Laboratories (Lucent Technology) makes all objects look like file systems. Thus, to display a list of processes on a system, a user simply lists the contents of the */proc* directory. Similarly, to display the time of day, a user need only type the file */dev/time*.

CHAPTER 11

Implementing File Systems

As we saw in Chapter 10, the file system provides the mechanism for on-line storage and access to file contents, including data and programs. The file system resides permanently on *secondary storage*, which is designed to hold a large amount of data permanently. This chapter is primarily concerned with issues surrounding file storage and access on the most common secondary-storage medium, the disk. We explore ways to structure file use, to allocate disk space, to recover freed space, to track the locations of data, and to interface other parts of the operating system to secondary storage. Performance issues are considered throughout the chapter.

CHAPTER OBJECTIVES

- To describe the details of implementing local file systems and directory structures.
- To describe the implementation of remote file systems.
- To discuss block allocation and free-block algorithms and trade-offs.

11.1 File-System Structure

Disks provide the bulk of secondary storage on which a file system is maintained. They have two characteristics that make them a convenient medium for storing multiple files:

1. A disk can be rewritten in place; it is possible to read a block from the disk, modify the block, and write it back into the same place.
2. A disk can access directly any block of information it contains. Thus, it is simple to access any file either sequentially or randomly, and switching from one file to another requires only moving the read–write heads and waiting for the disk to rotate.

We discuss disk structure in great detail in Chapter 12.

To improve I/O efficiency, I/O transfers between memory and disk are performed in units of *blocks*. Each block has one or more sectors. Depending on the disk drive, sector size varies from 32 bytes to 4,096 bytes; the usual size is 512 bytes.

File systems provide efficient and convenient access to the disk by allowing data to be stored, located, and retrieved easily. A file system poses two quite different design problems. The first problem is defining how the file system should look to the user. This task involves defining a file and its attributes, the operations allowed on a file, and the directory structure for organizing files. The second problem is creating algorithms and data structures to map the logical file system onto the physical secondary-storage devices.

The file system itself is generally composed of many different levels. The structure shown in Figure 11.1 is an example of a layered design. Each level in the design uses the features of lower levels to create new features for use by higher levels.

The lowest level, the *I/O control,* consists of **device drivers** and interrupt handlers to transfer information between the main memory and the disk system. A device driver can be thought of as a translator. Its input consists of high-level commands such as "retrieve block 123." Its output consists of low-level, hardware-specific instructions that are used by the hardware controller, which interfaces the I/O device to the rest of the system. The device driver usually writes specific bit patterns to special locations in the I/O controller's memory to tell the controller which device location to act on and what actions to take. The details of device drivers and the I/O infrastructure are covered in Chapter 13.

The **basic file system** needs only to issue generic commands to the appropriate device driver to read and write physical blocks on the disk. Each physical block is identified by its numeric disk address (for example, drive 1, cylinder 73, track 2, sector 10). This layer also manages the memory buffers and caches that hold various file-system, directory, and data blocks. A block

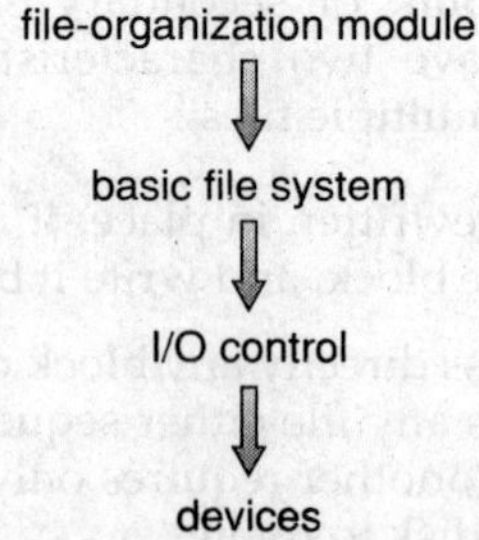

Figure 11.1 Layered file system.

in the buffer is allocated before the transfer of a disk block can occur. When the buffer is full, the buffer manager must find more buffer memory or free up buffer space to allow a requested I/O to complete. Caches are used to hold frequently used file-system metadata to improve performance, so managing their contents is critical for optimum system performance.

The **file-organization module** knows about files and their logical blocks, as well as physical blocks. By knowing the type of file allocation used and the location of the file, the file-organization module can translate logical block addresses to physical block addresses for the basic file system to transfer. Each file's logical blocks are numbered from 0 (or 1) through N. Since the physical blocks containing the data usually do not match the logical numbers, a translation is needed to locate each block. The file-organization module also includes the free-space manager, which tracks unallocated blocks and provides these blocks to the file-organization module when requested.

Finally, the **logical file system** manages metadata information. Metadata includes all of the file-system structure except the actual *data* (or contents of the files). The logical file system manages the directory structure to provide the file-organization module with the information the latter needs, given a symbolic file name. It maintains file structure via file-control blocks. A **file-control block (FCB)** (an **inode** in most UNIX file systems) contains information about the file, including ownership, permissions, and location of the file contents. The logical file system is also responsible for protection and security, as discussed in Chapters 10 and 14.

When a layered structure is used for file-system implementation, duplication of code is minimized. The I/O control and sometimes the basic file-system code can be used by multiple file systems. Each file system can then have its own logical file-system and file-organization modules. Unfortunately, layering can introduce more operating system overhead, which may result in decreased performance. The use of layering, including the decision about how many layers to use and what each layer should do, is a major challenge in designing new systems.

Many file systems are in use today. Most operating systems support more than one. For example, most CD-ROMs are written in the ISO 9660 format, a standard format agreed on by CD-ROM manufacturers. In addition to removable-media file systems, each operating system has one or more disk-based file systems. UNIX uses the **UNIX file system (UFS)**, which is based on the Berkeley Fast File System (FFS). Windows NT, 2000, and XP support disk file-system formats of FAT, FAT32, and NTFS (or Windows NT File System), as well as CD-ROM, DVD, and floppy-disk file-system formats. Although Linux supports over forty different file systems, the standard Linux file system is known as the **extended file system**, with the most common versions being ext2 and ext3. There are also distributed file systems in which a file system on a server is mounted by one or more client computers across a network.

File-system research continues to be an active area of operating-system design and implementation. Google created its own file system to meet the company's specific storage and retrieval needs. Another interesting project is the FUSE file-system, which provides flexibility in file-system use by implementing and executing file systems as user-level rather than kernel-level code. Using FUSE, a user can add a new file system to a variety of operating systems and can use that file system to manage her files.

11.2 File-System Implementation

As was described in Section 10.1.2, operating systems implement `open()` and `close()` systems calls for processes to request access to file contents. In this section, we delve into the structures and operations used to implement file-system operations.

11.2.1 Overview

Several on-disk and in-memory structures are used to implement a file system. These structures vary depending on the operating system and the file system, but some general principles apply.

On disk, the file system may contain information about how to boot an operating system stored there, the total number of blocks, the number and location of free blocks, the directory structure, and individual files. Many of these structures are detailed throughout the remainder of this chapter; here, we describe them briefly:

- A **boot control block** (per volume) can contain information needed by the system to boot an operating system from that volume. If the disk does not contain an operating system, this block can be empty. It is typically the first block of a volume. In UFS, it is called the **boot block**; in NTFS, it is the **partition boot sector**.
- A **volume control block** (per volume) contains volume (or partition) details, such as the number of blocks in the partition, the size of the blocks, a free-block count and free-block pointers, and a free-FCB count and FCB pointers. In UFS, this is called a **superblock**; in NTFS, it is stored in the **master file table**.
- A directory structure (per file system) is used to organize the files. In UFS, this includes file names and associated inode numbers. In NTFS, it is stored in the master file table.
- A per-file FCB contains many details about the file. It has a unique identifier number to allow association with a directory entry. In NTFS, this information is actually stored within the master file table, which uses a relational database structure, with a row per file.

The in-memory information is used for both file-system management and performance improvement via caching. The data are loaded at mount time, updated during file-system operations, and discarded at dismount. Several types of structures may be included.

- An in-memory **mount table** contains information about each mounted volume.
- An in-memory directory-structure cache holds the directory information of recently accessed directories. (For directories at which volumes are mounted, it can contain a pointer to the volume table.)
- The **system-wide open-file table** contains a copy of the FCB of each open file, as well as other information.

file permissions
file dates (create, access, write)
file owner, group, ACL
file size
file data blocks or pointers to file data blocks

Figure 11.2 A typical file-control block.

- The **per-process open-file table** contains a pointer to the appropriate entry in the system-wide open-file table, as well as other information.
- Buffers hold file-system blocks when they are being read from disk or written to disk.

To create a new file, an application program calls the logical file system. The logical file system knows the format of the directory structures. To create a new file, it allocates a new FCB. (Alternatively, if the file-system implementation creates all FCBs at file-system creation time, an FCB is allocated from the set of free FCBs.) The system then reads the appropriate directory into memory, updates it with the new file name and FCB, and writes it back to the disk. A typical FCB is shown in Figure 11.2.

Some operating systems, including UNIX, treat a directory exactly the same as a file—one with a "type" field indicating that it is a directory. Other operating systems, including Windows NT, implement separate system calls for files and directories and treat directories as entities separate from files. Whatever the larger structural issues, the logical file system can call the file-organization module to map the directory I/O into disk-block numbers, which are passed on to the basic file system and I/O control system.

Now that a file has been created, it can be used for I/O. First, though, it must be *opened*. The `open()` call passes a file name to the logical file system. The `open()` system call first searches the system-wide open-file table to see if the file is already in use by another process. If it is, a per-process open-file table entry is created pointing to the existing system-wide open-file table. This algorithm can save substantial overhead. If the file is not already open, the directory structure is searched for the given file name. Parts of the directory structure are usually cached in memory to speed directory operations. Once the file is found, the FCB is copied into a system-wide open-file table in memory. This table not only stores the FCB but also tracks the number of processes that have the file open.

Next, an entry is made in the per-process open-file table, with a pointer to the entry in the system-wide open-file table and some other fields. These other fields may include a pointer to the current location in the file (for the next `read()` or `write()` operation) and the access mode in which the file is open. The `open()` call returns a pointer to the appropriate entry in the per-process

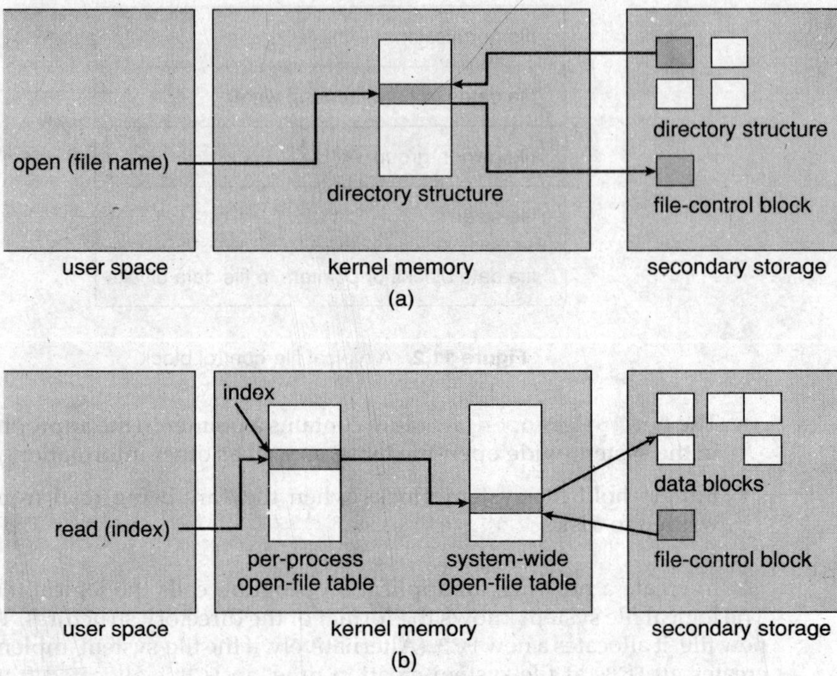

Figure 11.3 In-memory file-system structures. (a) File open. (b) File read.

file-system table. All file operations are then performed via this pointer. The file name may not be part of the open-file table, as the system has no use for it once the appropriate FCB is located on disk. It could be cached, though, to save time on subsequent opens of the same file. The name given to the entry varies. UNIX systems refer to it as a **file descriptor**; Windows refers to it as a **file handle**.

When a process closes the file, the per-process table entry is removed, and the system-wide entry's open count is decremented. When all users that have opened the file close it, any updated metadata is copied back to the disk-based directory structure, and the system-wide open-file table entry is removed.

Some systems complicate this scheme further by using the file system as an interface to other system aspects, such as networking. For example, in UFS, the system-wide open-file table holds the inodes and other information for files and directories. It also holds similar information for network connections and devices. In this way, one mechanism can be used for multiple purposes.

The caching aspects of file-system structures should not be overlooked. Most systems keep all information about an open file, except for its actual data blocks, in memory. The BSD UNIX system is typical in its use of caches wherever disk I/O can be saved. Its average cache hit rate of 85 percent shows that these techniques are well worth implementing. The BSD UNIX system is described fully in Appendix A.

The operating structures of a file-system implementation are summarized in Figure 11.3.

11.2.2 Partitions and Mounting

The layout of a disk can have many variations, depending on the operating system. A disk can be sliced into multiple partitions, or a volume can span multiple partitions on multiple disks. The former layout is discussed here, while the latter, which is more appropriately considered a form of RAID, is covered in Section 12.7.

Each partition can be either "raw," containing no file system, or "cooked," containing a file system. **Raw disk** is used where no file system is appropriate. UNIX swap space can use a raw partition, for example, as it uses its own format on disk and does not use a file system. Likewise, some databases use raw disk and format the data to suit their needs. Raw disk can also hold information needed by disk RAID systems, such as bit maps indicating which blocks are mirrored and which have changed and need to be mirrored. Similarly, raw disk can contain a miniature database holding RAID configuration information, such as which disks are members of each RAID set. Raw disk use is further discussed in Section 12.5.1.

Boot information can be stored in a separate partition. Again, it has its own format, because at boot time the system does not have the file-system code loaded and therefore cannot interpret the file-system format. Rather, boot information is usually a sequential series of blocks, loaded as an image into memory. Execution of the image starts at a predefined location, such as the first byte. This **boot loader** in turn knows enough about the file-system structure to be able to find and load the kernel and start it executing. It can contain more than the instructions for how to boot a specific operating system. For instance, PCs and other systems can be **dual-booted**. Multiple operating systems can be installed on such a system. How does the system know which one to boot? A boot loader that understands multiple file systems and multiple operating systems can occupy the boot space. Once loaded, it can boot one of the operating systems available on the disk. The disk can have multiple partitions, each containing a different type of file system and a different operating system.

The **root partition**, which contains the operating-system kernel and sometimes other system files, is mounted at boot time. Other volumes can be automatically mounted at boot or manually mounted later, depending on the operating system. As part of a successful mount operation, the operating system verifies that the device contains a valid file system. It does so by asking the device driver to read the device directory and verifying that the directory has the expected format. If the format is invalid, the partition must have its consistency checked and possibly corrected, either with or without user intervention. Finally, the operating system notes in its in-memory mount table that a file system is mounted, along with the type of the file system. The details of this function depend on the operating system. Microsoft Windows–based systems mount each volume in a separate name space, denoted by a letter and a colon. To record that a file system is mounted at `F:`, for example, the operating system places a pointer to the file system in a field of the device structure corresponding to `F:`. When a process specifies the driver letter, the operating system finds the appropriate file-system pointer and traverses the directory structures on that device to find the specified file or directory. Later versions of Windows can mount a file system at any point within the existing directory structure.

On UNIX, file systems can be mounted at any directory. Mounting is implemented by setting a flag in the in-memory copy of the inode for that directory. The flag indicates that the directory is a mount point. A field then points to an entry in the mount table, indicating which device is mounted there. The mount table entry contains a pointer to the superblock of the file system on that device. This scheme enables the operating system to traverse its directory structure, switching seamlessly among file systems of varying types.

11.2.3 Virtual File Systems

The previous section makes it clear that modern operating systems must concurrently support multiple types of file systems. But how does an operating system allow multiple types of file systems to be integrated into a directory structure? And how can users seamlessly move between file-system types as they navigate the file-system space? We now discuss some of these implementation details.

An obvious but suboptimal method of implementing multiple types of file systems is to write directory and file routines for each type. Instead, however, most operating systems, including UNIX, use object-oriented techniques to simplify, organize, and modularize the implementation. The use of these methods allows very dissimilar file-system types to be implemented within the same structure, including network file systems, such as NFS. Users can access files that are contained within multiple file systems on the local disk or even on file systems available across the network.

Data structures and procedures are used to isolate the basic system-call functionality from the implementation details. Thus, the file-system implementation consists of three major layers, as depicted schematically in Figure 11.4. The first layer is the file-system interface, based on the `open()`, `read()`, `write()`, and `close()` calls and on file descriptors.

The second layer is called the **virtual file system (VFS)** layer. The VFS layer serves two important functions:

1. It separates file-system-generic operations from their implementation by defining a clean VFS interface. Several implementations for the VFS interface may coexist on the same machine, allowing transparent access to different types of file systems mounted locally.
2. It provides a mechanism for uniquely representing a file throughout a network. The VFS is based on a file-representation structure, called a **vnode**, that contains a numerical designator for a network-wide unique file. (UNIX inodes are unique within only a single file system.) This network-wide uniqueness is required for support of network file systems. The kernel maintains one vnode structure for each active node (file or directory).

Thus, the VFS distinguishes local files from remote ones, and local files are further distinguished according to their file-system types.

The VFS activates file-system-specific operations to handle local requests according to their file-system types and calls the NFS protocol procedures for remote requests. File handles are constructed from the relevant vnodes and are passed as arguments to these procedures. The layer implementing the

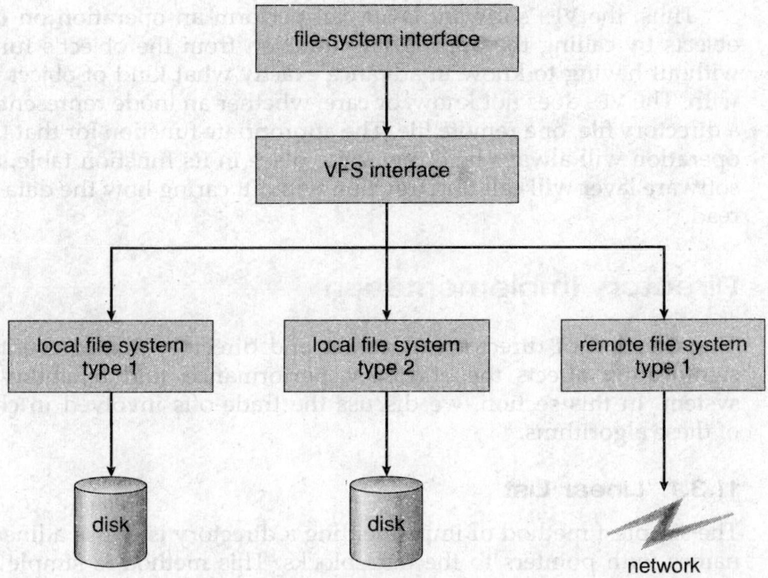

Figure 11.4 Schematic view of a virtual file system.

file-system type or the remote-file-system protocol is the third layer of the architecture.

Let's briefly examine the VFS architecture in Linux. The four main object types defined by the Linux VFS are:

- The **inode object**, which represents an individual file
- The **file object**, which represents an open file
- The **superblock object**, which represents an entire file system
- The **dentry object**, which represents an individual directory entry

For each of these four object types, the VFS defines a set of operations that must be implemented. Every object of one of these types contains a pointer to a function table. The function table lists the addresses of the actual functions that implement the defined operations for that particular object. For example, an abbreviated API for some of the operations for the file object include:

- `int open(. . .)`—Open a file.
- `ssize_t read(. . .)`—Read from a file.
- `ssize_t write(. . .)`—Write to a file.
- `int mmap(. . .)`—Memory-map a file.

An implementation of the file object for a specific file type is required to implement each function specified in the definition of the file object. (The complete definition of the file object is specified in the `struct file_operations`, which is located in the file `/usr/include/linux/fs.h`.)

Thus, the VFS software layer can perform an operation on one of these objects by calling the appropriate function from the object's function table, without having to know in advance exactly what kind of object it is dealing with. The VFS does not know, or care, whether an inode represents a disk file, a directory file, or a remote file. The appropriate function for that file's `read()` operation will always be at the same place in its function table, and the VFS software layer will call that function without caring how the data are actually read.

11.3 Directory Implementation

The selection of directory-allocation and directory-management algorithms significantly affects the efficiency, performance, and reliability of the file system. In this section, we discuss the trade-offs involved in choosing one of these algorithms.

11.3.1 Linear List

The simplest method of implementing a directory is to use a linear list of file names with pointers to the data blocks. This method is simple to program but time-consuming to execute. To create a new file, we must first search the directory to be sure that no existing file has the same name. Then, we add a new entry at the end of the directory. To delete a file, we search the directory for the named file and then release the space allocated to it. To reuse the directory entry, we can do one of several things. We can mark the entry as unused (by assigning it a special name, such as an all-blank name, or with a used–unused bit in each entry), or we can attach it to a list of free directory entries. A third alternative is to copy the last entry in the directory into the freed location and to decrease the length of the directory. A linked list can also be used to decrease the time required to delete a file.

The real disadvantage of a linear list of directory entries is that finding a file requires a linear search. Directory information is used frequently, and users will notice if access to it is slow. In fact, many operating systems implement a software cache to store the most recently used directory information. A cache hit avoids the need to constantly reread the information from disk. A sorted list allows a binary search and decreases the average search time. However, the requirement that the list be kept sorted may complicate creating and deleting files, since we may have to move substantial amounts of directory information to maintain a sorted directory. A more sophisticated tree data structure, such as a B-tree, might help here. An advantage of the sorted list is that a sorted directory listing can be produced without a separate sort step.

11.3.2 Hash Table

Another data structure used for a file directory is a **hash table**. With this method, a linear list stores the directory entries, but a hash data structure is also used. The hash table takes a value computed from the file name and returns a pointer to the file name in the linear list. Therefore, it can greatly decrease the directory search time. Insertion and deletion are also fairly straightforward, although some provision must be made for **collisions**—situations in which two file names hash to the same location.

The major difficulties with a hash table are its generally fixed size and the dependence of the hash function on that size. For example, assume that we make a linear-probing hash table that holds 64 entries. The hash function converts file names into integers from 0 to 63, for instance, by using the remainder of a division by 64. If we later try to create a 65th file, we must enlarge the directory hash table—say, to 128 entries. As a result, we need a new hash function that must map file names to the range 0 to 127, and we must reorganize the existing directory entries to reflect their new hash-function values.

Alternatively, a chained-overflow hash table can be used. Each hash entry can be a linked list instead of an individual value, and we can resolve collisions by adding the new entry to the linked list. Lookups may be somewhat slowed, because searching for a name might require stepping through a linked list of colliding table entries. Still, this method is likely to be much faster than a linear search through the entire directory.

11.4 Allocation Methods

The direct-access nature of disks allows us flexibility in the implementation of files. In almost every case, many files are stored on the same disk. The main problem is how to allocate space to these files so that disk space is utilized effectively and files can be accessed quickly. Three major methods of allocating disk space are in wide use: contiguous, linked, and indexed. Each method has advantages and disadvantages. Some systems (such as Data General's RDOS for its Nova line of computers) support all three. More commonly, a system uses one method for all files within a file-system type.

11.4.1 Contiguous Allocation

Contiguous allocation requires that each file occupy a set of contiguous blocks on the disk. Disk addresses define a linear ordering on the disk. With this ordering, assuming that only one job is accessing the disk, accessing block $b + 1$ after block b normally requires no head movement. When head movement is needed (from the last sector of one cylinder to the first sector of the next cylinder), the head need only move from one track to the next. Thus, the number of disk seeks required for accessing contiguously allocated files is minimal, as is seek time when a seek is finally needed. The IBM VM/CMS operating system uses contiguous allocation because it provides such good performance.

Contiguous allocation of a file is defined by the disk address and length (in block units) of the first block. If the file is n blocks long and starts at location b, then it occupies blocks $b, b + 1, b + 2, ..., b + n - 1$. The directory entry for each file indicates the address of the starting block and the length of the area allocated for this file (Figure 11.5).

Accessing a file that has been allocated contiguously is easy. For sequential access, the file system remembers the disk address of the last block referenced and, when necessary, reads the next block. For direct access to block i of a file that starts at block b, we can immediately access block $b + i$. Thus, both sequential and direct access can be supported by contiguous allocation.

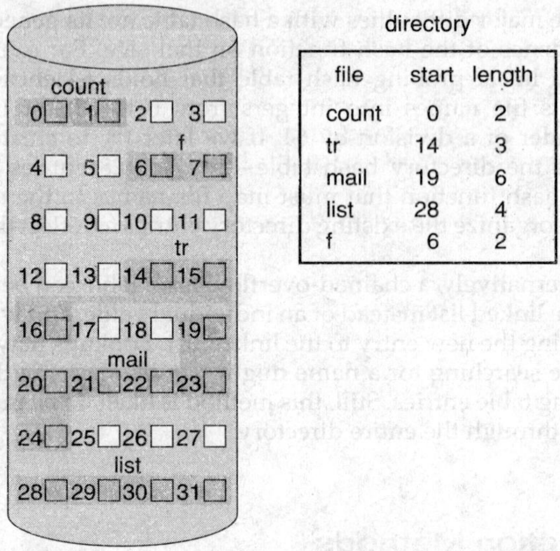

Figure 11.5 Contiguous allocation of disk space.

Contiguous allocation has some problems, however. One difficulty is finding space for a new file. The system chosen to manage free space determines how this task is accomplished; these management systems are discussed in Section 11.5. Any management system can be used, but some are slower than others.

The contiguous-allocation problem can be seen as a particular application of the general **dynamic storage-allocation** problem discussed in Section 8.3, which involves how to satisfy a request of size *n* from a list of free holes. First fit and best fit are the most common strategies used to select a free hole from the set of available holes. Simulations have shown that both first fit and best fit are more efficient than worst fit in terms of both time and storage utilization. Neither first fit nor best fit is clearly best in terms of storage utilization, but first fit is generally faster.

All these algorithms suffer from the problem of **external fragmentation**. As files are allocated and deleted, the free disk space is broken into little pieces. External fragmentation exists whenever free space is broken into chunks. It becomes a problem when the largest contiguous chunk is insufficient for a request; storage is fragmented into a number of holes, none of which is large enough to store the data. Depending on the total amount of disk storage and the average file size, external fragmentation may be a minor or a major problem.

One strategy for preventing loss of significant amounts of disk space to external fragmentation is to copy an entire file system onto another disk or tape. The original disk is then freed completely, creating one large contiguous free space. We then copy the files back onto the original disk by allocating contiguous space from this one large hole. This scheme effectively **compacts** all free space into one contiguous space, solving the fragmentation problem. However, the cost of this compaction is time and it can be particularly severe for large hard disks that use contiguous allocation, where compacting all the space may take hours and may be necessary on a weekly basis. Some systems require that this function be done **off-line**, with the file system unmounted. During this **down time**, normal system operation generally cannot be permitted, so such compaction is avoided at all costs on production machines. Most modern systems that need defragmentation can perform it **on-line** during normal system operations, but the performance penalty can be substantial.

Another problem with contiguous allocation is determining how much space is needed for a file. When the file is created, the total amount of space it will need must be found and allocated. How does the creator (program or person) know the size of the file to be created? In some cases, this determination may be fairly simple (copying an existing file, for example); in general, however, the size of an output file may be difficult to estimate.

If we allocate too little space to a file, we may find that the file cannot be extended. Especially with a best-fit allocation strategy, the space on both sides of the file may be in use. Hence, we cannot make the file larger in place. Two possibilities then exist. First, the user program can be terminated, with an appropriate error message. The user must then allocate more space and run the program again. These repeated runs may be costly. To prevent them, the user will normally overestimate the amount of space needed, resulting in considerable wasted space. The other possibility is to find a larger hole, copy the contents of the file to the new space, and release the previous space. This series of actions can be repeated as long as space exists, although it can be time consuming. However, the user need never be informed explicitly about what is happening; the system continues despite the problem, although more and more slowly.

Even if the total amount of space needed for a file is known in advance, preallocation may be inefficient. A file that will grow slowly over a long period (months or years) must be allocated enough space for its final size, even though much of that space will be unused for a long time. The file therefore has a large amount of internal fragmentation.

To minimize these drawbacks, some operating systems use a modified contiguous-allocation scheme. Here, a contiguous chunk of space is allocated initially; then, if that amount proves not to be large enough, another chunk of contiguous space, known as an **extent**, is added. The location of a file's blocks is then recorded as a location and a block count, plus a link to the first block of the next extent. On some systems, the owner of the file can set the extent size, but this setting results in inefficiencies if the owner is incorrect. Internal fragmentation can still be a problem if the extents are too large, and external fragmentation can become a problem as extents of varying sizes are allocated and deallocated. The commercial Veritas file system uses extents to optimize performance. It is a high-performance replacement for the standard UNIX UFS.

11.4.2 Linked Allocation

Linked allocation solves all problems of contiguous allocation. With linked allocation, each file is a linked list of disk blocks; the disk blocks may be scattered anywhere on the disk. The directory contains a pointer to the first and last blocks of the file. For example, a file of five blocks might start at block 9 and continue at block 16, then block 1, then block 10, and finally block 25 (Figure 11.6). Each block contains a pointer to the next block. These pointers

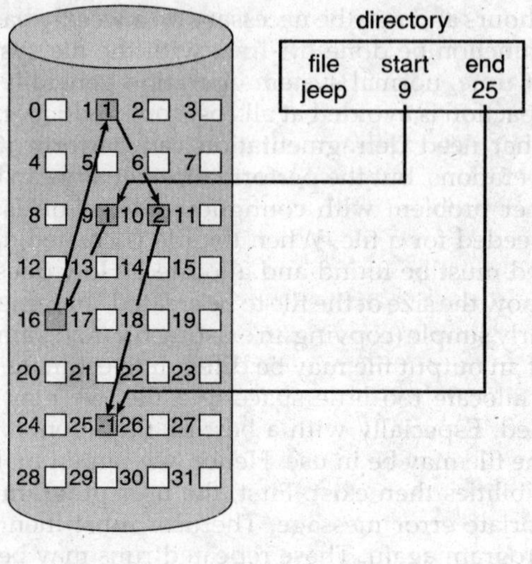

Figure 11.6 Linked allocation of disk space.

are not made available to the user. Thus, if each block is 512 bytes in size, and a disk address (the pointer) requires 4 bytes, then the user sees blocks of 508 bytes.

To create a new file, we simply create a new entry in the directory. With linked allocation, each directory entry has a pointer to the first disk block of the file. This pointer is initialized to *nil* (the end-of-list pointer value) to signify an empty file. The size field is also set to 0. A write to the file causes the free-space management system to find a free block, and this new block is written to and is linked to the end of the file. To read a file, we simply read blocks by following the pointers from block to block. There is no external fragmentation with linked allocation, and any free block on the free-space list can be used to satisfy a request. The size of a file need not be declared when that file is created. A file can continue to grow as long as free blocks are available. Consequently, it is never necessary to compact disk space.

Linked allocation does have disadvantages, however. The major problem is that it can be used effectively only for sequential-access files. To find the *i*th block of a file, we must start at the beginning of that file and follow the pointers until we get to the *i*th block. Each access to a pointer requires a disk read, and some require a disk seek. Consequently, it is inefficient to support a direct-access capability for linked-allocation files.

Another disadvantage is the space required for the pointers. If a pointer requires 4 bytes out of a 512-byte block, then 0.78 percent of the disk is being used for pointers, rather than for information. Each file requires slightly more space than it would otherwise.

The usual solution to this problem is to collect blocks into multiples, called **clusters**, and to allocate clusters rather than blocks. For instance, the file system may define a cluster as four blocks and operate on the disk only in cluster units. Pointers then use a much smaller percentage of the file's disk space. This method allows the logical-to-physical block mapping to remain simple but improves disk throughput (because fewer disk-head seeks are required) and decreases the space needed for block allocation and free-list management. The cost of this approach is an increase in internal fragmentation, because more space is wasted when a cluster is partially full than when a block is partially full. Clusters can be used to improve the disk-access time for many other algorithms as well, so they are used in most file systems.

Yet another problem of linked allocation is reliability. Recall that the files are linked together by pointers scattered all over the disk, and consider what would happen if a pointer were lost or damaged. A bug in the operating-system software or a disk hardware failure might result in picking up the wrong pointer. This error could in turn result in linking into the free-space list or into another file. One partial solution is to use doubly linked lists, and another is to store the file name and relative block number in each block; however, these schemes require even more overhead for each file.

An important variation on linked allocation is the use of a **file-allocation table (FAT)**. This simple but efficient method of disk-space allocation is used by the MS-DOS and OS/2 operating systems. A section of disk at the beginning of each volume is set aside to contain the table. The table has one entry for each disk block and is indexed by block number. The FAT is used in much the same way as a linked list. The directory entry contains the block number of the first block of the file. The table entry indexed by that block number contains the block number of the next block in the file. This chain continues until it reaches the last block, which has a special end-of-file value as the table entry. An unused block is indicated by a table value of 0. Allocating a new block to a file is a simple matter of finding the first 0-valued table entry and replacing the previous end-of-file value with the address of the new block. The 0 is then replaced with the end-of-file value. An illustrative example is the FAT structure shown in Figure 11.7 for a file consisting of disk blocks 217, 618, and 339.

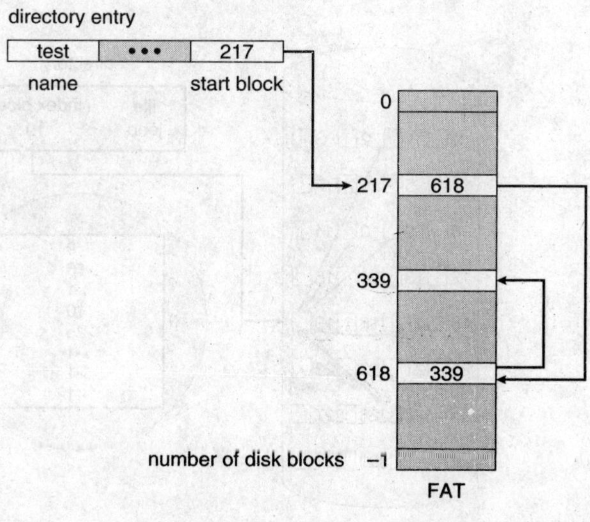

Figure 11.7 File-allocation table.

The FAT allocation scheme can result in a significant number of disk head seeks, unless the FAT is cached. The disk head must move to the start of the volume to read the FAT and find the location of the block in question, then move to the location of the block itself. In the worst case, both moves occur for each of the blocks. A benefit is that random-access time is improved, because the disk head can find the location of any block by reading the information in the FAT.

11.4.3 Indexed Allocation

Linked allocation solves the external-fragmentation and size-declaration problems of contiguous allocation. However, in the absence of a FAT, linked allocation cannot support efficient direct access, since the pointers to the blocks are scattered with the blocks themselves all over the disk and must be retrieved in order. **Indexed allocation** solves this problem by bringing all the pointers together into one location: the **index block**.

Each file has its own index block, which is an array of disk-block addresses. The ith entry in the index block points to the ith block of the file. The directory contains the address of the index block (Figure 11.8). To find and read the ith block, we use the pointer in the ith index-block entry. This scheme is similar to the paging scheme described in Section 8.4.

When the file is created, all pointers in the index block are set to *nil*. When the *i*th block is first written, a block is obtained from the free-space manager, and its address is put in the *i*th index-block entry.

Indexed allocation supports direct access, without suffering from external fragmentation, because any free block on the disk can satisfy a request for more space. Indexed allocation does suffer from wasted space, however. The pointer overhead of the index block is generally greater than the pointer overhead of linked allocation. Consider a common case in which we have a file of only one or two blocks. With linked allocation, we lose the space of only one pointer per

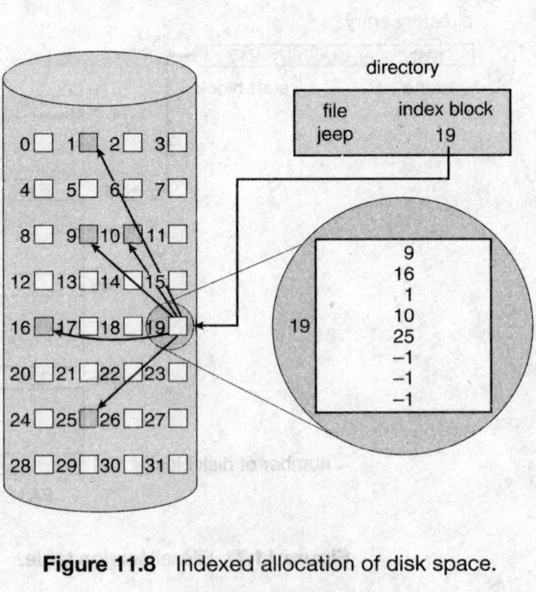

Figure 11.8 Indexed allocation of disk space.

block. With indexed allocation, an entire index block must be allocated, even if only one or two pointers will be non-*nil*.

This point raises the question of how large the index block should be. Every file must have an index block, so we want the index block to be as small as possible. If the index block is too small, however, it will not be able to hold enough pointers for a large file, and a mechanism will have to be available to deal with this issue. Mechanisms for this purpose include the following:

- **Linked scheme**. An index block is normally one disk block. Thus, it can be read and written directly by itself. To allow for large files, we can link together several index blocks. For example, an index block might contain a small header giving the name of the file and a set of the first 100 disk-block addresses. The next address (the last word in the index block) is *nil* (for a small file) or is a pointer to another index block (for a large file).

- **Multilevel index**. A variant of linked representation uses a first-level index block to point to a set of second-level index blocks, which in turn point to the file blocks. To access a block, the operating system uses the first-level index to find a second-level index block and then uses that block to find the desired data block. This approach could be continued to a third or fourth level, depending on the desired maximum file size. With 4,096-byte blocks, we could store 1,024 four-byte pointers in an index block. Two levels of indexes allow 1,048,576 data blocks and a file size of up to 4 GB.

- **Combined scheme**. Another alternative, used in the UFS, is to keep the first, say, 15 pointers of the index block in the file's inode. The first 12 of these pointers point to **direct blocks**; that is, they contain addresses of blocks that contain data of the file. Thus, the data for small files (of no more than 12 blocks) do not need a separate index block. If the block size is 4 KB, then up to 48 KB of data can be accessed directly. The next three pointers point to **indirect blocks**. The first points to a **single indirect block**, which is an index block containing not data but the addresses of blocks that do contain data. The second points to a **double indirect block**, which contains the address of a block that contains the addresses of blocks that contain pointers to the actual data blocks. The last pointer contains the address of a **triple indirect block**. Under this method, the number of blocks that can be allocated to a file exceeds the amount of space addressable by the four-byte file pointers used by many operating systems. A 32-bit file pointer reaches only 2^{32} bytes, or 4 GB. Many UNIX implementations, including Solaris and IBM's AIX, now support up to 64-bit file pointers. Pointers of this size allow files and file systems to be terabytes in size. A UNIX inode is shown in Figure 11.9.

Indexed-allocation schemes suffer from some of the same performance problems as does linked allocation. Specifically, the index blocks can be cached in memory, but the data blocks may be spread all over a volume.

11.4.4 Performance

The allocation methods that we have discussed vary in their storage efficiency and data-block access times. Both are important criteria in selecting the proper method or methods for an operating system to implement.

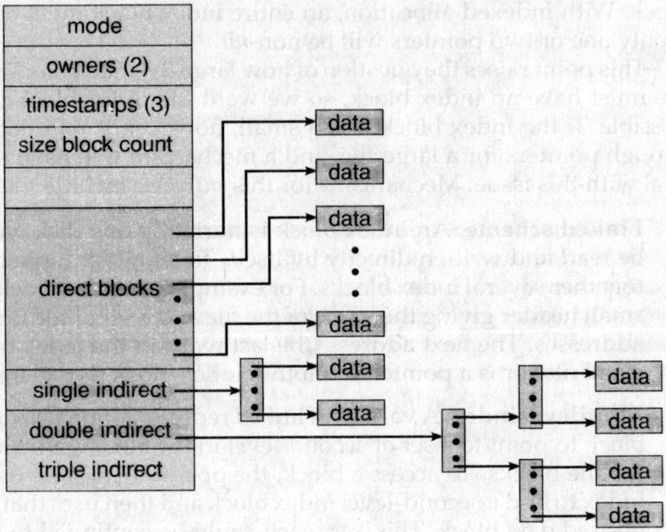

Figure 11.9 The UNIX inode.

Before selecting an allocation method, we need to determine how the systems will be used. A system with mostly sequential access should not use the same method as a system with mostly random access.

For any type of access, contiguous allocation requires only one access to get a disk block. Since we can easily keep the initial address of the file in memory, we can calculate immediately the disk address of the *i*th block (or the next block) and read it directly.

For linked allocation, we can also keep the address of the next block in memory and read it directly. This method is fine for sequential access; for direct access, however, an access to the *i*th block might require *i* disk reads. This problem indicates why linked allocation should not be used for an application requiring direct access.

As a result, some systems support direct-access files by using contiguous allocation and sequential-access files by using linked allocation. For these systems, the type of access to be made must be declared when the file is created. A file created for sequential access will be linked and cannot be used for direct access. A file created for direct access will be contiguous and can support both direct access and sequential access, but its maximum length must be declared when it is created. In this case, the operating system must have appropriate data structures and algorithms to support *both* allocation methods. Files can be converted from one type to another by the creation of a new file of the desired type, into which the contents of the old file are copied. The old file may then be deleted and the new file renamed.

Indexed allocation is more complex. If the index block is already in memory, then the access can be made directly. However, keeping the index block in memory requires considerable space. If this memory space is not available, then we may have to read first the index block and then the desired data block. For a two-level index, two index-block reads might be necessary. For an extremely large file, accessing a block near the end of the file would require reading in all the index blocks before the needed data block finally could be read. Thus, the performance of indexed allocation depends on the index structure, on the size of the file, and on the position of the block desired.

Some systems combine contiguous allocation with indexed allocation by using contiguous allocation for small files (up to three or four blocks) and automatically switching to an indexed allocation if the file grows large. Since most files are small, and contiguous allocation is efficient for small files, average performance can be quite good.

For instance, the version of the UNIX operating system from Sun Microsystems was changed in 1991 to improve performance in the file-system allocation algorithm. The performance measurements indicated that the maximum disk throughput on a typical workstation (a 12-MIPS SPARCstation1) took 50 percent of the CPU and produced a disk bandwidth of only 1.5 MB per second. To improve performance, Sun made changes to allocate space in clusters of 56 KB whenever possible (56 KB was the maximum size of a DMA transfer on Sun systems at that time). This allocation reduced external fragmentation, and thus seek and latency times. In addition, the disk-reading routines were optimized to read in these large clusters. The inode structure was left unchanged. As a result of these changes, plus the use of read-ahead and free-behind (discussed in Section 11.6.2), 25 percent less CPU was used, and throughput substantially improved.

Many other optimizations are in use. Given the disparity between CPU speed and disk speed, it is not unreasonable to add thousands of extra instructions to the operating system to save just a few disk-head movements. Furthermore, this disparity is increasing over time, to the point where hundreds of thousands of instructions reasonably could be used to optimize head movements.

11.5 Free-Space Management

Since disk space is limited, we need to reuse the space from deleted files for new files, if possible. (Write-once optical disks only allow one write to any given sector, and thus such reuse is not physically possible.) To keep track of free disk space, the system maintains a **free-space list**. The free-space list records all *free* disk blocks—those not allocated to some file or directory. To create a file, we search the free-space list for the required amount of space and allocate that space to the new file. This space is then removed from the free-space list. When a file is deleted, its disk space is added to the free-space list. The free-space list, despite its name, might not be implemented as a list, as we discuss next.

11.5.1 Bit Vector

Frequently, the free-space list is implemented as a **bit map** or **bit vector**. Each block is represented by 1 bit. If the block is free, the bit is 1; if the block is allocated, the bit is 0.

For example, consider a disk where blocks 2, 3, 4, 5, 8, 9, 10, 11, 12, 13, 17, 18, 25, 26, and 27 are free and the rest of the blocks are allocated. The free-space bit map would be

001111001111110001100000011100000 ...

The main advantage of this approach is its relative simplicity and its efficiency in finding the first free block or n consecutive free blocks on the disk. Indeed, many computers supply bit-manipulation instructions that can be used effectively for that purpose. For example, the Intel family starting with the 80386 and the Motorola family starting with the 68020 have instructions that return the offset in a word of the first bit with the value 1 (these processors have powered PCs and Macintosh systems, respectively). One technique for finding the first free block on a system that uses a bit-vector to allocate disk space is to sequentially check each word in the bit map to see whether that value is not 0, since a 0-valued word contains only 0 bits and represents a set of allocated blocks. The first non-0 word is scanned for the first 1 bit, which is the location of the first free block. The calculation of the block number is

(number of bits per word) × (number of 0-value words) + offset of first 1 bit.

Again, we see hardware features driving software functionality. Unfortunately, bit vectors are inefficient unless the entire vector is kept in main memory (and is written to disk occasionally for recovery needs). Keeping it in main memory is possible for smaller disks but not necessarily for larger ones. A 1.3-GB disk with 512-byte blocks would need a bit map of over 332 KB to track its free blocks, although clustering the blocks in groups of four reduces this number to around 83 KB per disk. A 1-TB disk with 4-KB blocks requires 32 MB to store its bit map. Given that disk size constantly increases, the problem with bit vectors will continue to escalate. A 1-PB file system would take a 32-GB bitmap just to manage its free space.

11.5.2 Linked List

Another approach to free-space management is to link together all the free disk blocks, keeping a pointer to the first free block in a special location on the disk and caching it in memory. This first block contains a pointer to the next free disk block, and so on. Recall our earlier example (Section 11.5.1), in which blocks 2, 3, 4, 5, 8, 9, 10, 11, 12, 13, 17, 18, 25, 26, and 27 were free and the rest of the blocks were allocated. In this situation, we would keep a pointer to block 2 as the first free block. Block 2 would contain a pointer to block 3, which would point to block 4, which would point to block 5, which would point to block 8, and so on (Figure 11.10). This scheme is not efficient; to traverse the list, we must read each block, which requires substantial I/O time. Fortunately, however, traversing the free list is not a frequent action. Usually, the operating system simply needs a free block so that it can allocate that block to a file, so the first block in the free list is used. The FAT method incorporates free-block accounting into the allocation data structure. No separate method is needed.

11.5.3 Grouping

A modification of the free-list approach stores the addresses of n free blocks in the first free block. The first $n-1$ of these blocks are actually free. The last block contains the addresses of another n free blocks, and so on. The addresses

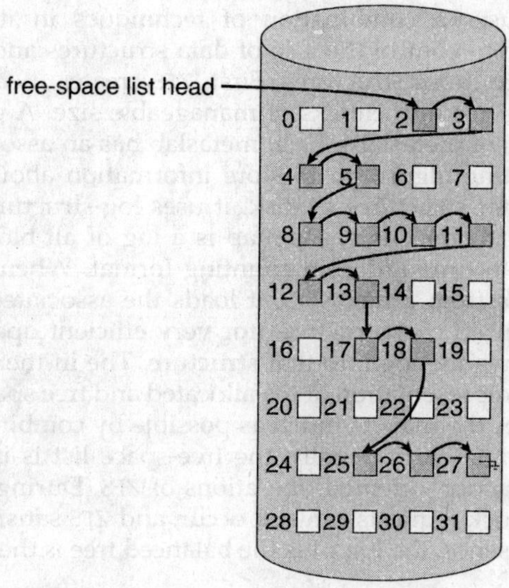

Figure 11.10 Linked free-space list on disk.

of a large number of free blocks can now be found quickly, unlike the situation when the standard linked-list approach is used.

11.5.4 Counting

Another approach takes advantage of the fact that, generally, several contiguous blocks may be allocated or freed simultaneously, particularly when space is allocated with the contiguous-allocation algorithm or through clustering. Thus, rather than keeping a list of *n* free disk addresses, we can keep the address of the first free block and the number (*n*) of free contiguous blocks that follow the first block. Each entry in the free-space list then consists of a disk address and a count. Although each entry requires more space than would a simple disk address, the overall list is shorter, as long as the count is generally greater than 1. Note that this method of tracking free space is similar to the extent method of allocating blocks. These entries can be stored in a B-tree, rather than a linked list, for efficient lookup, insertion, and deletion.

11.5.5 Space Maps

Sun's ZFS file system was designed to encompass huge numbers of files, directories, and even file systems (in ZFS, we can create file-system hierarchies). The resulting data structures could have been large and inefficient if they had not been designed and implemented properly. On these scales, metadata I/O can have a large performance impact. Consider, for example, that if the free-space list is implemented as a bit map, bit maps must be modified both when blocks are allocated and when they are freed. Freeing 1 GB of data on a 1-TB disk could cause thousands of blocks of bit maps to be updated, because those data blocks could be scattered over the entire disk.

ZFS uses a combination of techniques in its free-space management algorithm to control the size of data structures and minimize the I/O needed to manage those structures. First, ZFS creates **metaslabs** to divide the space on the device into chucks of manageable size. A given volume may contain hundreds of metaslabs. Each metaslab has an associated space map. ZFS uses the counting algorithm to store information about free blocks. Rather than write count structures to disk, it uses log-structured file- system techniques to record them. The space map is a log of all block activity (allocating and freeing), in time order, in counting format. When ZFS decides to allocate or free space from a metaslab, it loads the associated space map into memory in a balanced-tree structure (for very efficient operation), indexed by offset, and replays the log into that structure. The in-memory space map is then an accurate representation of the allocated and free space in the metaslab. ZFS also condenses the map as much as possible by combining contiguous free blocks into a single entry. Finally, the free-space list is updated on disk as part of the transaction-oriented operations of ZFS. During the collection and sorting phase, block requests can still occur, and ZFS satisfies these requests from the log. In essence, the log plus the balanced tree *is* the free list.

11.6 Efficiency and Performance

Now that we have discussed various block-allocation and directory-management options, we can further consider their effect on performance and efficient disk use. Disks tend to represent a major bottleneck in system performance, since they are the slowest main computer component. In this section, we discuss a variety of techniques used to improve the efficiency and performance of secondary storage.

11.6.1 Efficiency

The efficient use of disk space depends heavily on the disk allocation and directory algorithms in use. For instance, UNIX inodes are preallocated on a volume. Even an "empty" disk has a percentage of its space lost to inodes. However, by preallocating the inodes and spreading them across the volume, we improve the file system's performance. This improved performance results from the UNIX allocation and free-space algorithms, which try to keep a file's data blocks near that file's inode block to reduce seek time.

As another example, let's reconsider the clustering scheme discussed in Section 11.4, which aids in file-seek and file-transfer performance at the cost of internal fragmentation. To reduce this fragmentation, BSD UNIX varies the cluster size as a file grows. Large clusters are used where they can be filled, and small clusters are used for small files and the last cluster of a file. This system is described in Appendix A.

The types of data normally kept in a file's directory (or inode) entry also require consideration. Commonly, a "last write date" is recorded to supply information to the user and to determine whether the file needs to be backed up. Some systems also keep a "last access date," so that a user can determine when the file was last read. The result of keeping this information is that, whenever the file is read, a field in the directory structure must be written to. That means the block must be read into memory, a section changed, and the block written back out to disk, because operations on disks occur only in block (or cluster) chunks. So any time a file is opened for reading, its directory entry must be read and written as well. This requirement can be inefficient for frequently accessed files, so we must weigh its benefit against its performance cost when designing a file system. Generally, *every* data item associated with a file needs to be considered for its effect on efficiency and performance.

As an example, consider how efficiency is affected by the size of the pointers used to access data. Most systems use either 16- or 32-bit pointers throughout the operating system. These pointer sizes limit the length of a file to either 2^{16} (64 KB) or 2^{32} bytes (4 GB). Some systems implement 64-bit pointers to increase this limit to 2^{64} bytes, which is a very large number indeed. However, 64-bit pointers take more space to store and in turn make the allocation and free-space-management methods (linked lists, indexes, and so on) use more disk space.

One of the difficulties in choosing a pointer size, or indeed any fixed allocation size within an operating system, is planning for the effects of changing technology. Consider that the IBM PC XT had a 10-MB hard drive and an MS-DOS file system that could support only 32 MB. (Each FAT entry was 12 bits, pointing to an 8-KB cluster.) As disk capacities increased, larger disks had to be split into 32-MB partitions, because the file system could not track blocks beyond 32 MB. As hard disks with capacities of over 100 MB became common, the disk data structures and algorithms in MS-DOS had to be modified to allow larger file systems. (Each FAT entry was expanded to 16 bits and later to 32 bits.) The initial file-system decisions were made for efficiency reasons; however, with the advent of MS-DOS Version 4, millions of computer users were inconvenienced when they had to switch to the new, larger file system. Sun's ZFS file system uses 128-bit pointers, which theoretically should never need to be extended. (The minimum mass of a device capable of storing 2^{128} bytes using atomic-level storage would be about 272 trillion kilograms.)

As another example, consider the evolution of Sun's Solaris operating system. Originally, many data structures were of fixed length, allocated at system startup. These structures included the process table and the open-file table. When the process table became full, no more processes could be created. When the file table became full, no more files could be opened. The system would fail to provide services to users. Table sizes could be increased only by recompiling the kernel and rebooting the system. Since the release of Solaris 2, almost all kernel structures have been allocated dynamically, eliminating these artificial limits on system performance. Of course, the algorithms that manipulate these tables are more complicated, and the operating system is a little slower because it must dynamically allocate and deallocate table entries; but that price is the usual one for more general functionality.

11.6.2 Performance

Even after the basic file-system algorithms have been selected, we can still improve performance in several ways. As will be discussed in Chapter 13, most disk controllers include local memory to form an on-board cache that is large enough to store entire tracks at a time. Once a seek is performed, the track is read into the disk cache starting at the sector under the disk head

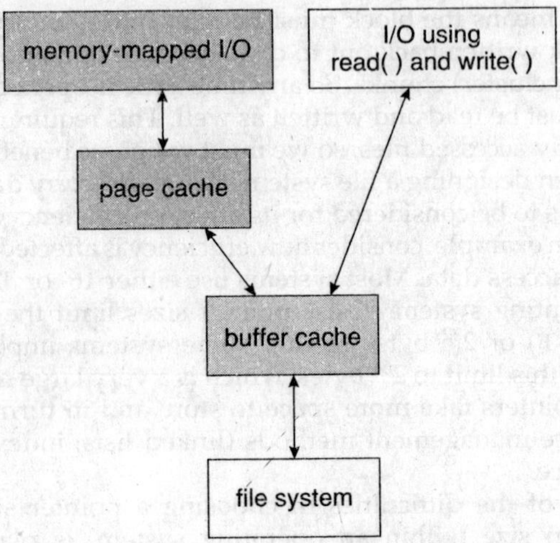

Figure 11.11 I/O without a unified buffer cache.

(reducing latency time). The disk controller then transfers any sector requests to the operating system. Once blocks make it from the disk controller into main memory, the operating system may cache the blocks there.

Some systems maintain a separate section of main memory for a **buffer cache**, where blocks are kept under the assumption that they will be used again shortly. Other systems cache file data using a **page cache**. The page cache uses virtual memory techniques to cache file data as pages rather than as file-system-oriented blocks. Caching file data using virtual addresses is far more efficient than caching through physical disk blocks, as accesses interface with virtual memory rather than the file system. Several systems—including Solaris, Linux, and Windows NT, 2000, and XP—use page caching to cache both process pages and file data. This is known as **unified virtual memory**.

Some versions of UNIX and Linux provide a **unified buffer cache**. To illustrate the benefits of the unified buffer cache, consider the two alternatives for opening and accessing a file. One approach is to use memory mapping (Section 9.7); the second is to use the standard system calls `read()` and `write()`. Without a unified buffer cache, we have a situation similar to Figure 11.11. Here, the `read()` and `write()` system calls go through the buffer cache. The memory-mapping call, however, requires using two caches—the page cache and the buffer cache. A memory mapping proceeds by reading in disk blocks from the file system and storing them in the buffer cache. Because the virtual memory system does not interface with the buffer cache, the contents of the file in the buffer cache must be copied into the page cache. This situation is known as **double caching** and requires caching file-system data twice. Not only does it waste memory but it also wastes significant CPU and I/O cycles due to the extra data movement within system memory. In addition, inconsistencies between the two caches can result in corrupt files. In contrast, when a unified buffer cache is provided, both memory mapping and the `read()` and `write()` system calls use the same page cache. This has the benefit of avoiding double

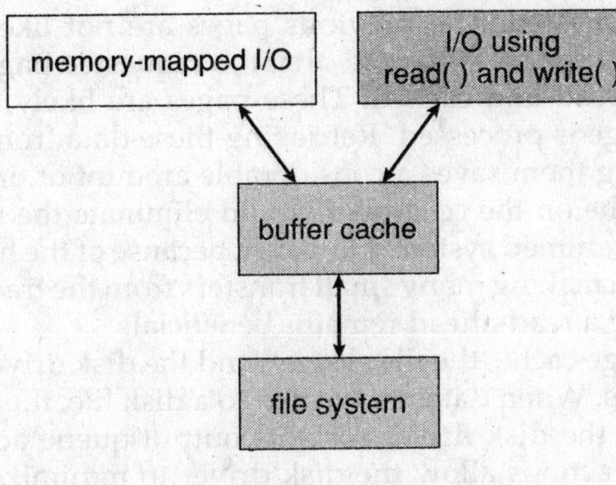

Figure 11.12 I/O using a unified buffer cache.

caching, and it allows the virtual memory system to manage file-system data. The unified buffer cache is shown in Figure 11.12.

Regardless of whether we are caching disk blocks or pages (or both), LRU (Section 9.4.4) seems a reasonable general-purpose algorithm for block or page replacement. However, the evolution of the Solaris page-caching algorithms reveals the difficulty in choosing an algorithm. Solaris allows processes and the page cache to share unused memory. Versions earlier than Solaris 2.5.1 made no distinction between allocating pages to a process and allocating them to the page cache. As a result, a system performing many I/O operations used most of the available memory for caching pages. Because of the high rates of I/O, the page scanner (Section 9.10.2) reclaimed pages from processes—rather than from the page cache—when free memory ran low. Solaris 2.6 and Solaris 7 optionally implemented *priority paging,* in which the page scanner gives priority to process pages over the page cache. Solaris 8 applied a fixed limit to process pages and the file-system page cache, preventing either from forcing the other out of memory. Solaris 9 and 10 again changed the algorithms to maximize memory use and minimize thrashing.

Another issue that can affect the performance of I/O is whether writes to the file system occur synchronously or asynchronously. **Synchronous writes** occur in the order in which the disk subsystem receives them, and the writes are not buffered. Thus, the calling routine must wait for the data to reach the disk drive before it can proceed. In an **asynchronous write**, the data are stored in the cache, and control returns to the caller. Asynchronous writes are done the majority of the time. However, metadata writes, among others, can be synchronous. Operating systems frequently include a flag in the open system call to allow a process to request that writes be performed synchronously. For example, databases use this feature for atomic transactions, to assure that data reach stable storage in the required order.

Some systems optimize their page cache by using different replacement algorithms, depending on the access type of the file. A file being read or written sequentially should not have its pages replaced in LRU order, because the most recently used page will be used last, or perhaps never again. Instead, sequential access can be optimized by techniques known as free-behind and read-ahead. **Free-behind** removes a page from the buffer as soon as the next page is requested. The previous pages are not likely to be used again and waste buffer space. With read-ahead, a requested page and several subsequent pages are read and cached. These pages are likely to be requested after the current page is processed. Retrieving these data from the disk in one transfer and caching them saves a considerable amount of time. One might think that a track cache on the controller would eliminate the need for read-ahead on a multiprogrammed system. However, because of the high latency and overhead involved in making many small transfers from the track cache to main memory, performing a read-ahead remains beneficial.

The page cache, the file system, and the disk drivers have some interesting interactions. When data are written to a disk file, the pages are buffered in the cache, and the disk driver sorts its output queue according to disk address. These two actions allow the disk driver to minimize disk-head seeks and to write data at times optimized for disk rotation. Unless synchronous writes are required, a process writing to disk simply writes into the cache, and the system asynchronously writes the data to disk when convenient. The user process sees very fast writes. When data are read from a disk file, the block I/O system does some read-ahead; however, writes are much more nearly asynchronous than are reads. Thus, output to the disk through the file system is often faster than is input for large transfers, counter to intuition.

11.7 Recovery

Files and directories are kept both in main memory and on disk, and care must be taken to ensure that a system failure does not result in loss of data or in data inconsistency. We deal with these issues in this section as well as how a system can recover from such a failure.

A system crash can cause inconsistencies among on-disk file-system data structures, such as directory structures, free-block pointers, and free FCB pointers. Many file systems apply changes to these structures in place. A typical operation, such as creating a file, can involve many structural changes within the file system on the disk. Directory structures are modified, FCBs are allocated, data blocks are allocated, and the free counts for all of these blocks are decreased. These changes can be interrupted by a crash, and inconsistencies among the structures can result. For example, the free FCB count might indicate that an FCB had been allocated, but the directory structure might not point to the FCB. Compounding this problem is the caching that operating systems do to optimize I/O performance. Some changes may go directly to disk, while others may be cached. If the cached changes do not reach disk before a crash occurs, more corruption is possible.

In addition to crashes, bugs in file-system implementation, disk controllers, and even user applications can corrupt a file system. File systems have varying methods to deal with corruption, depending on the file-system data structures and algorithms. We deal with these issues next.

11.7.1 Consistency Checking

Whatever the cause of corruption, a file system must first detect the problems and then correct them. For detection, a scan of all the metadata on each file system can confirm or deny the consistency of the system. Unfortunately, this scan can take minutes or hours and should occur every time the system boots. Alternatively, a file system can record its state within the file-system metadata. At the start of any metadata change, a status bit is set to indicate that the metadata is in flux. If all updates to the metadata complete successfully, the file system can clear that bit. If, however, the status bit remains set, a consistency checker is run.

The **consistency checker**—a systems program such as `fsck` in UNIX or `chkdsk` in Windows—compares the data in the directory structure with the data blocks on disk and tries to fix any inconsistencies it finds. The allocation and free-space-management algorithms dictate what types of problems the checker can find and how successful it will be in fixing them. For instance, if linked allocation is used and there is a link from any block to its next block, then the entire file can be reconstructed from the data blocks, and the directory structure can be recreated. In contrast, the loss of a directory entry on an indexed allocation system can be disastrous, because the data blocks have no knowledge of one another. For this reason, UNIX caches directory entries for reads; but any write that results in space allocation, or other metadata changes, is done synchronously, before the corresponding data blocks are written. Of course, problems can still occur if a synchronous write is interrupted by a crash.

11.7.2 Log-Structured File Systems

Computer scientists often find that algorithms and technologies originally used in one area are equally useful in other areas. Such is the case with the database log-based recovery algorithms described in Section 6.9.2. These logging algorithms have been applied successfully to the problem of consistency checking. The resulting implementations are known as **log-based transaction-oriented** (or **journaling**) file systems.

Note that with the consistency-checking approach discussed in the preceding section, we essentially allow structures to break and repair them on recovery. However, there are several problems with this approach. One is that the inconsistency may be irreparable. The consistency check may not be able to recover the structures, resulting in loss of files and even entire directories. Consistency checking can require human intervention to resolve conflicts, and that is inconvenient if no human is available. The system can remain unavailable until the human tells it how to proceed. Consistency checking also takes system and clock time. To check terabytes of data, hours of clock time may be required.

The solution to this problem is to apply log-based recovery techniques to file-system metadata updates. Both NTFS and the Veritas file system use this method, and it is included in recent versions of UFS on Solaris. In fact, it is becoming common on many operating systems.

Fundamentally, all metadata changes are written sequentially to a log. Each set of operations for performing a specific task is a **transaction**. Once the changes are written to this log, they are considered to be committed, and the system call can return to the user process, allowing it to continue execution. Meanwhile, these log entries are replayed across the actual file-system structures. As the changes are made, a pointer is updated to indicate which actions have completed and which are still incomplete. When an entire committed transaction is completed, it is removed from the log file, which is actually a circular buffer. A **circular buffer** writes to the end of its space and then continues at the beginning, overwriting older values as it goes. We would not want the buffer to write over data that had not yet been saved, so that scenario is avoided. The log may be in a separate section of the file system or even on a separate disk spindle. It is more efficient, but more complex, to have it under separate read and write heads, thereby decreasing head contention and seek times.

If the system crashes, the log file will contain zero or more transactions. Any transactions it contains were not completed to the file system, even though they were committed by the operating system, so they must now be completed. The transactions can be executed from the pointer until the work is complete so that the file-system structures remain consistent. The only problem occurs when a transaction was aborted—that is, was not committed before the system crashed. Any changes from such a transaction that were applied to the file system must be undone, again preserving the consistency of the file system. This recovery is all that is needed after a crash, eliminating any problems with consistency checking.

A side benefit of using logging on disk metadata updates is that those updates proceed much faster than when they are applied directly to the on-disk data structures. The reason for this improvement is found in the performance advantage of sequential I/O over random I/O. The costly synchronous random metadata writes are turned into much less costly synchronous sequential writes to the log-structured file system's logging area. Those changes in turn are replayed asynchronously via random writes to the appropriate structures. The overall result is a significant gain in performance of metadata-oriented operations, such as file creation and deletion.

11.7.3 Other Solutions

Another alternative to consistency checking is employed by Network Appliance's WAFL file system and Sun's ZFS file system. These systems never overwrite blocks with new data. Rather, a transaction writes all data and metadata changes to new blocks. When the transaction is complete, the metadata structures that pointed to the old versions of these blocks are updated to point to the new blocks. The file system can then remove the old pointers and the old blocks and make them available for reuse. If the old pointers and blocks are kept, a **snapshot** is created; the snapshot is a view of the file system before the last update took place. This solution should require no consistency checking if the pointer update is done atomically. WAFL does have a consistency checker, however, so some failure scenarios can still cause metadata corruption. (See 11.9 for details of the WAFL file system.)

Sun's ZFS takes an even more innovative approach to disk consistency. It never overwrites blocks, just as is the case with WAFL. However, ZFS goes further and provides check-summing of all metadata and data blocks. This solution (when combined with RAID) assures that data are always correct. ZFS therefore has no consistency checker. (More details on ZFS are found in Section 12.7.6.)

11.7.4 Backup and Restore

Magnetic disks sometimes fail, and care must be taken to ensure that the data lost in such a failure are not lost forever. To this end, system programs can be used to **back up** data from disk to another storage device, such as a floppy disk, magnetic tape, optical disk, or other hard disk. Recovery from the loss of an individual file, or of an entire disk, may then be a matter of **restoring** the data from backup.

To minimize the copying needed, we can use information from each file's directory entry. For instance, if the backup program knows when the last backup of a file was done, and the file's last write date in the directory indicates that the file has not changed since that date, then the file does not need to be copied again. A typical backup schedule may then be as follows:

- **Day 1**. Copy to a backup medium all files from the disk. This is called a **full backup**.
- **Day 2**. Copy to another medium all files changed since day 1. This is an **incremental backup**.
- **Day 3**. Copy to another medium all files changed since day 2.

.

.

.

- **Day** N. Copy to another medium all files changed since day $N-1$. Then go back to Day 1.

The new cycle can have its backup written over the previous set or onto a new set of backup media. In this manner, we can restore an entire disk by starting restores with the full backup and continuing through each of the incremental backups. Of course, the larger the value of N, the greater the number of media that must be read for a complete restore. An added advantage of this backup cycle is that we can restore any file accidentally deleted during the cycle by retrieving the deleted file from the backup of the previous day. The length of the cycle is a compromise between the amount of backup medium needed and the number of days back from which a restore can be done. To decrease the number of tapes that must be read to do a restore, an option is to perform a full backup and then each day back up all files that have changed since the full backup. In this way, a restore can be done via the most recent incremental backup and the full backup, with no other incremental backups needed. The trade-off is that more files will be modified each day, so each successive incremental backup involves more files and more backup media.

A user may notice that a particular file is missing or corrupted long after the damage was done. For this reason, we usually plan to take a full backup from time to time that will be saved "forever." It is a good idea to store these permanent backups far away from the regular backups to protect against hazard, such as a fire that destroys the computer and all the backups too. And if the backup cycle reuses media, we must take care not to reuse the media too many times—if the media wear out, it might not be possible to restore any data from the backups.

11.8 NFS

Network file systems are commonplace. They are typically integrated with the overall directory structure and interface of the client system. NFS is a good example of a widely used, well-implemented client–server network file system. Here, we use it as an example to explore the implementation details of network file systems.

NFS is both an implementation and a specification of a software system for accessing remote files across LANs (or even WANs). NFS is part of ONC+, which most UNIX vendors and some PC operating systems support. The implementation described here is part of the Solaris operating system, which is a modified version of UNIX SVR4 running on Sun workstations and other hardware. It uses either the TCP or UDP/IP protocol (depending on the interconnecting network). The specification and the implementation are intertwined in our description of NFS. Whenever detail is needed, we refer to the Sun implementation; whenever the description is general, it applies to the specification also.

There are multiple versions of NFS, with the latest being Version 4. Here, we describe Version 3, as that is the one most commonly deployed.

11.8.1 Overview

NFS views a set of interconnected workstations as a set of independent machines with independent file systems. The goal is to allow some degree of sharing among these file systems (on explicit request) in a transparent manner. Sharing is based on a client–server relationship. A machine may be, and often is, both a client and a server. Sharing is allowed between any pair of machines. To ensure machine independence, sharing of a remote file system affects only the client machine and no other machine.

So that a remote directory will be accessible in a transparent manner from a particular machine—say, from *M1*—a client of that machine must first carry out a mount operation. The semantics of the operation involve mounting a remote directory over a directory of a local file system. Once the mount operation is completed, the mounted directory looks like an integral subtree of the local file system, replacing the subtree descending from the local directory. The local directory becomes the name of the root of the newly mounted directory. Specification of the remote directory as an argument for the mount operation is not done transparently; the location (or host name) of the remote directory has to be provided. However, from then on, users on machine *M1* can access files in the remote directory in a totally transparent manner.

To illustrate file mounting, consider the file system depicted in Figure 11.13, where the triangles represent subtrees of directories that are of interest. The figure shows three independent file systems of machines named *U*, *S1*, and *S2*. At this point, on each machine, only the local files can be accessed. Figure 11.14(a) shows the effects of mounting `S1:/usr/shared` over `U:/usr/local`. This figure depicts the view users on *U* have of their file system. Notice that after the mount is complete, they can access any file within the `dir1` directory

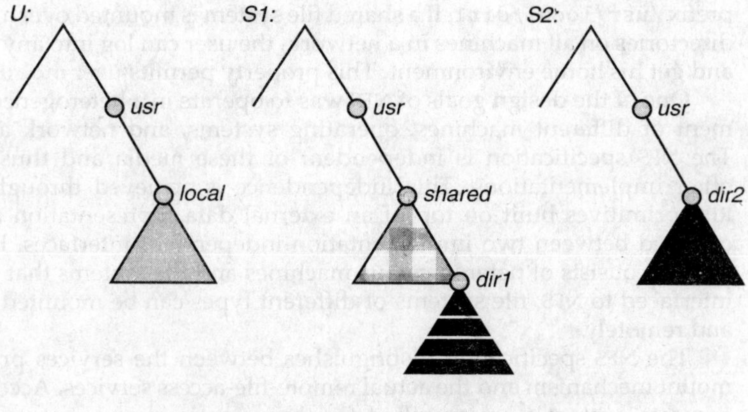

Figure 11.13 Three independent file systems.

using the prefix `/usr/local/dir1`. The original directory `/usr/local` on that machine is no longer visible.

Subject to access-rights accreditation, any file system, or any directory within a file system, can be mounted remotely on top of any local directory. Diskless workstations can even mount their own roots from servers. Cascading mounts are also permitted in some NFS implementations. That is, a file system can be mounted over another file system that is remotely mounted, not local. A machine is affected by only those mounts that it has itself invoked. Mounting a remote file system does not give the client access to other file systems that were, by chance, mounted over the former file system. Thus, the mount mechanism does not exhibit a transitivity property.

In Figure 11.14(b), we illustrate cascading mounts. The figure shows the result of mounting `S2:/usr/dir2` over `U:/usr/local/dir1`, which is already remotely mounted from *S1*. Users can access files within `dir2` on *U* using the

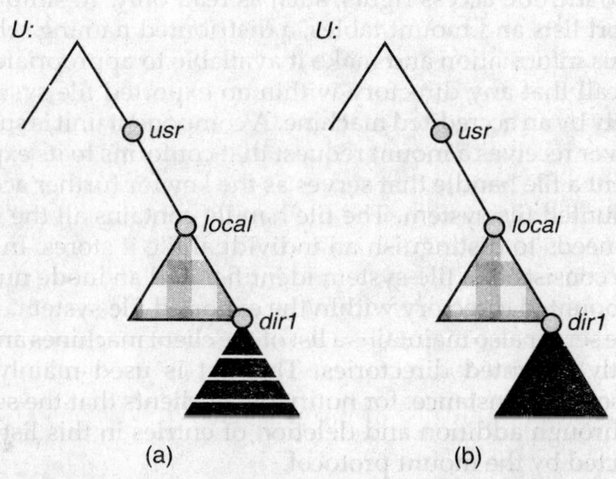

Figure 11.14 Mounting in NFS. (a) Mounts. (b) Cascading mounts.

prefix `/usr/local/dir1`. If a shared file system is mounted over a user's home directories on all machines in a network, the user can log into any workstation and get his home environment. This property permits **user mobility**.

One of the design goals of NFS was to operate in a heterogeneous environment of different machines, operating systems, and network architectures. The NFS specification is independent of these media and thus encourages other implementations. This independence is achieved through the use of RPC primitives built on top of an external data representation (XDR) protocol used between two implementation-independent interfaces. Hence, if the system consists of heterogeneous machines and file systems that are properly interfaced to NFS, file systems of different types can be mounted both locally and remotely.

The NFS specification distinguishes between the services provided by a mount mechanism and the actual remote-file-access services. Accordingly, two separate protocols are specified for these services: a mount protocol and a protocol for remote file accesses, the **NFS protocol**. The protocols are specified as sets of RPCs. These RPCs are the building blocks used to implement transparent remote file access.

11.8.2 The Mount Protocol

The **mount protocol** establishes the initial logical connection between a server and a client. In Sun's implementation, each machine has a server process, outside the kernel, performing the protocol functions.

A mount operation includes the name of the remote directory to be mounted and the name of the server machine storing it. The mount request is mapped to the corresponding RPC and is forwarded to the mount server running on the specific server machine. The server maintains an **export list** that specifies local file systems that it exports for mounting, along with names of machines that are permitted to mount them. (In Solaris, this list is the `/etc/dfs/dfstab`, which can be edited only by a superuser.) The specification can also include access rights, such as read only. To simplify the maintenance of export lists and mount tables, a distributed naming scheme can be used to hold this information and make it available to appropriate clients.

Recall that any directory within an exported file system can be mounted remotely by an accredited machine. A component unit is such a directory. When the server receives a mount request that conforms to its export list, it returns to the client a file handle that serves as the key for further accesses to files within the mounted file system. The file handle contains all the information that the server needs to distinguish an individual file it stores. In UNIX terms, the file handle consists of a file-system identifier and an inode number to identify the exact mounted directory within the exported file system.

The server also maintains a list of the client machines and the corresponding currently mounted directories. This list is used mainly for administrative purposes—for instance, for notifying all clients that the server is going down. Only through addition and deletion of entries in this list can the server state be affected by the mount protocol.

Usually, a system has a static mounting preconfiguration that is established at boot time (`/etc/vfstab` in Solaris); however, this layout can be modified. In addition to the actual mount procedure, the mount protocol includes several other procedures, such as unmount and return export list.

11.8.3 The NFS Protocol

The NFS protocol provides a set of RPCs for remote file operations. The procedures support the following operations:

- Searching for a file within a directory
- Reading a set of directory entries
- Manipulating links and directories
- Accessing file attributes
- Reading and writing files

These procedures can be invoked only after a file handle for the remotely mounted directory has been established.

The omission of `open()` and `close()` operations is intentional. A prominent feature of NFS servers is that they are *stateless*. Servers do not maintain information about their clients from one access to another. No parallels to UNIX's open-files table or file structures exist on the server side. Consequently, each request has to provide a full set of arguments, including a unique file identifier and an absolute offset inside the file for the appropriate operations. The resulting design is robust; no special measures need be taken to recover a server after a crash. File operations must be idempotent for this purpose. Every NFS request has a sequence number, allowing the server to determine if a request is duplicated or if any are missing.

Maintaining the list of clients that we mentioned seems to violate the statelessness of the server. However, this list is not essential for the correct operation of the client or the server, and hence it does not need to be restored after a server crash. Consequently, it might include inconsistent data and is treated as only a hint.

A further implication of the stateless-server philosophy and a result of the synchrony of an RPC is that modified data (including indirection and status blocks) must be committed to the server's disk before results are returned to the client. That is, a client can cache write blocks, but when it flushes them to the server, it assumes that they have reached the server's disks. The server must write all NFS data synchronously. Thus, a server crash and recovery will be invisible to a client; all blocks that the server is managing for the client will be intact. The consequent performance penalty can be large, because the advantages of caching are lost. Performance can be increased by using storage with its own nonvolatile cache (usually battery-backed-up memory). The disk controller acknowledges the disk write when the write is stored in the nonvolatile cache. In essence, the host sees a very fast synchronous write. These blocks remain intact even after system crash and are written from this stable storage to disk periodically.

A single NFS write procedure call is guaranteed to be atomic and is not intermixed with other write calls to the same file. The NFS protocol, however, does not provide concurrency-control mechanisms. A `write()` system call may

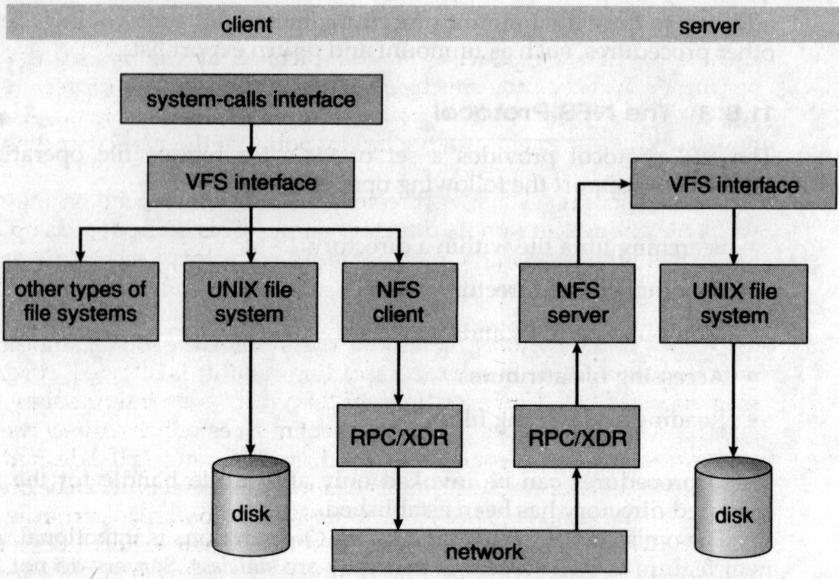

Figure 11.15 Schematic view of the NFS architecture.

be broken down into several RPC writes, because each NFS write or read call can contain up to 8 KB of data and UDP packets are limited to 1,500 bytes. As a result, two users writing to the same remote file may get their data intermixed. The claim is that, because lock management is inherently stateful, a service outside the NFS should provide locking (and Solaris does). Users are advised to coordinate access to shared files using mechanisms outside the scope of NFS.

NFS is integrated into the operating system via a VFS. As an illustration of the architecture, let's trace how an operation on an already open remote file is handled (follow the example in Figure 11.15). The client initiates the operation with a regular system call. The operating-system layer maps this call to a VFS operation on the appropriate vnode. The VFS layer identifies the file as a remote one and invokes the appropriate NFS procedure. An RPC call is made to the NFS service layer at the remote server. This call is reinjected to the VFS layer on the remote system, which finds that it is local and invokes the appropriate file-system operation. This path is retraced to return the result. An advantage of this architecture is that the client and the server are identical; thus, a machine may be a client, or a server, or both. The actual service on each server is performed by kernel threads.

11.8.4 Path-Name Translation

Path-name translation in NFS involves the parsing of a path name such as `/usr/local/dir1/file.txt` into separate directory entries, or components: (1) `usr`, (2) `local`, and (3) `dir1`. Path-name translation is done by breaking the path into component names and performing a separate NFS `lookup call` for every pair of component name and directory vnode. Once a mount point is crossed, every component lookup causes a separate RPC to the server. This expensive path-name-traversal scheme is needed, since the layout of each client's logical name space is unique, dictated by the mounts the client has performed. It would be much more efficient to hand a server a path name and receive a target vnode once a mount point is encountered. At any point, however, there might be another mount point for the particular client of which the stateless server is unaware.

So that lookup is fast, a directory-name-lookup cache on the client side holds the vnodes for remote directory names. This cache speeds up references to files with the same initial path name. The directory cache is discarded when attributes returned from the server do not match the attributes of the cached vnode.

Recall that mounting a remote file system on top of another already mounted remote file system (a cascading mount) is allowed in some implementations of NFS. However, a server cannot act as an intermediary between a client and another server. Instead, a client must establish a direct client–server connection with the second server by directly mounting the desired directory. When a client has a cascading mount, more than one server can be involved in a path-name traversal. However, each component lookup is performed between the original client and some server. Therefore, when a client does a lookup on a directory on which the server has mounted a file system, the client sees the underlying directory instead of the mounted directory.

11.8.5 Remote Operations

With the exception of opening and closing files, there is almost a one-to-one correspondence between the regular UNIX system calls for file operations and the NFS protocol RPCs. Thus, a remote file operation can be translated directly to the corresponding RPC. Conceptually, NFS adheres to the remote-service paradigm; but in practice, buffering and caching techniques are employed for the sake of performance. No direct correspondence exists between a remote operation and an RPC. Instead, file blocks and file attributes are fetched by the RPCs and are cached locally. Future remote operations use the cached data, subject to consistency constraints.

There are two caches: the file-attribute (inode-information) cache and the file-blocks cache. When a file is opened, the kernel checks with the remote server to determine whether to fetch or revalidate the cached attributes. The cached file blocks are used only if the corresponding cached attributes are up to date. The attribute cache is updated whenever new attributes arrive from the server. Cached attributes are, by default, discarded after 60 seconds. Both read-ahead and delayed-write techniques are used between the server and the client. Clients do not free delayed-write blocks until the server confirms that the data have been written to disk. Delayed-write is retained even when a file is opened concurrently, in conflicting modes. Hence, UNIX semantics (Section 10.5.3.1) are not preserved.

Tuning the system for performance makes it difficult to characterize the consistency semantics of NFS. New files created on a machine may not be visible elsewhere for 30 seconds. Furthermore, writes to a file at one site may or may not be visible at other sites that have this file open for reading. New opens of a file observe only the changes that have already been flushed to the server. Thus, NFS provides neither strict emulation of UNIX semantics nor the session semantics of Andrew (Section 10.5.3.2). In spite of these drawbacks, the utility and good performance of the mechanism make it the most widely used multi-vendor-distributed system in operation.

11.9 Example: The WAFL File System

Disk I/O has a huge impact on system performance. As a result, file-system design and implementation command quite a lot of attention from system designers. Some file systems are general purpose, in that they can provide reasonable performance and functionality for a wide variety of file sizes, file types, and I/O loads. Others are optimized for specific tasks in an attempt to provide better performance in those areas than general-purpose file systems. The WAFL file system from Network Appliance is an example of this sort of optimization. WAFL, the *write-anywhere file layout,* is a powerful, elegant file system optimized for random writes.

WAFL is used exclusively on network file servers produced by Network Appliance and so is meant for use as a distributed file system. It can provide files to clients via the NFS, CIFS, `ftp`, and `http` protocols, although it was designed just for NFS and CIFS. When many clients use these protocols to talk to a file server, the server may see a very large demand for random reads and an even larger demand for random writes. The NFS and CIFS protocols cache data from read operations, so writes are of the greatest concern to file-server creators.

WAFL is used on file servers that include an NVRAM cache for writes. The WAFL designers took advantage of running on a specific architecture to optimize the file system for random I/O, with a stable-storage cache in front. Ease of use is one of the guiding principles of WAFL, because it is designed to be used in an appliance. Its creators also designed it to include a new snapshot functionality that creates multiple read-only copies of the file system at different points in time, as we shall see.

The file system is similar to the Berkeley Fast File System, with many modifications. It is block-based and uses inodes to describe files. Each inode contains 16 pointers to blocks (or indirect blocks) belonging to the file described by the inode. Each file system has a root inode. All of the metadata lives in files: all inodes are in one file, the free-block map in another, and the free-inode

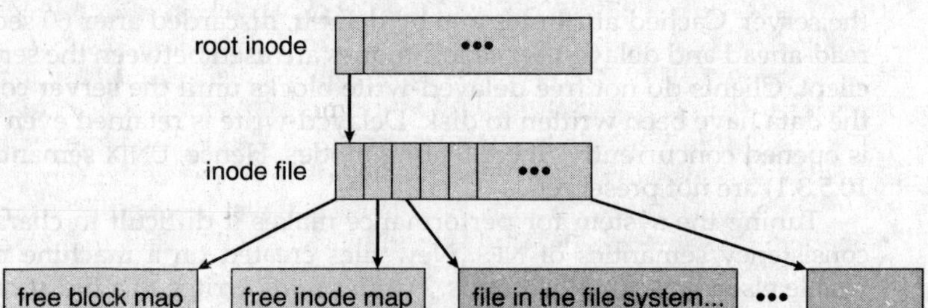

Figure 11.16 The WAFL file layout.

map in a third, as shown in Figure 11.16. Because these are standard files, the data blocks are not limited in location and can be placed anywhere. If a file system is expanded by addition of disks, the lengths of the metadata files are automatically expanded by the file system.

Thus, a WAFL file system is a tree of blocks with the root inode as its base. To take a snapshot, WAFL creates a copy of the root inode. Any file or metadata updates after that go to new blocks rather than overwriting their existing blocks. The new root inode points to metadata and data changed as a result of these writes. Meanwhile, the snapshot (the old root inode) still points to the old blocks, which have not been updated. It therefore provides access to the file system just as it was at the instant the snapshot was made—and takes very little disk space to do so! In essence, the extra disk space occupied by a snapshot consists of just the blocks that have been modified since the snapshot was taken.

An important change from more standard file systems is that the free-block map has more than one bit per block. It is a bitmap with a bit set for each snapshot that is using the block. When all snapshots that have been using the block are deleted, the bit map for that block is all zeros, and the block is free to be reused. Used blocks are never overwritten, so writes are very fast, because a write can occur at the free block nearest the current head location. There are many other performance optimizations in WAFL as well.

Many snapshots can exist simultaneously, so one can be taken each hour of the day and each day of the month. A user with access to these snapshots can access files as they were at any of the times the snapshots were taken. The snapshot facility is also useful for backups, testing, versioning, and so on. WAFL's snapshot facility is very efficient in that it does not even require that copy-on-write copies of each data block be taken before the block is modified. Other file systems provide snapshots, but frequently with less efficiency. WAFL snapshots are depicted in Figure 11.17.

Newer versions of WAFL actually allow read–write snapshots, known as **clones**. Clones are also efficient, using the same techniques as shapshots. In this case, a read-only snapshot captures the state of the file system, and a clone refers back to that read-only snapshot. Any writes to the clone are stored in new blocks, and the clone's pointers are updated to refer to the new blocks. The original snapshot is unmodified, still giving a view into the file system as it was before the clone was updated. Clones can also be promoted to replace the original file system; this involves throwing out all of the old pointers and any associated old blocks. Clones are useful for testing and upgrades, as the original version is left untouched and the clone deleted when the test is done or if the upgrade fails.

Another feature that naturally falls from the WAFL file system implementation is **replication**, the duplication and synchronization of a set of data over a network to another system. First, a snapshot of a WAFL file system is duplicated to another system. When another snapshot is taken on the source system, it is relatively easy to update the remote system just by sending over all blocks contained in the new snapshot. These blocks are the ones that have changed between the times the two snapshots were taken. The remote system adds these blocks to the file system and updates its pointers, and the new system then is a duplicate of the source system as of the time of the second snapshot. Repeating this process maintains the remote system as a nearly up-to-date copy of the first

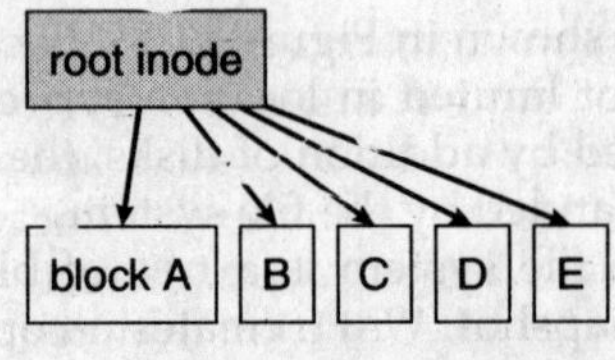

(a) Before a snapshot.

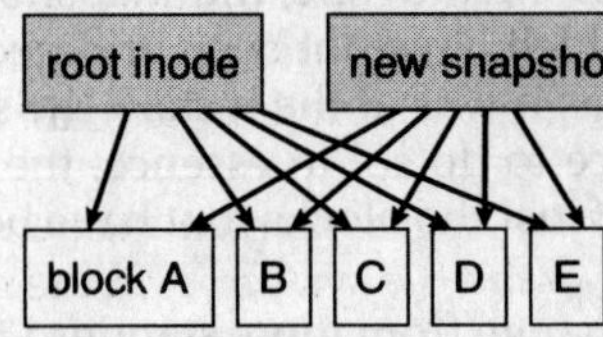

(b) After a snapshot, before any blocks change.

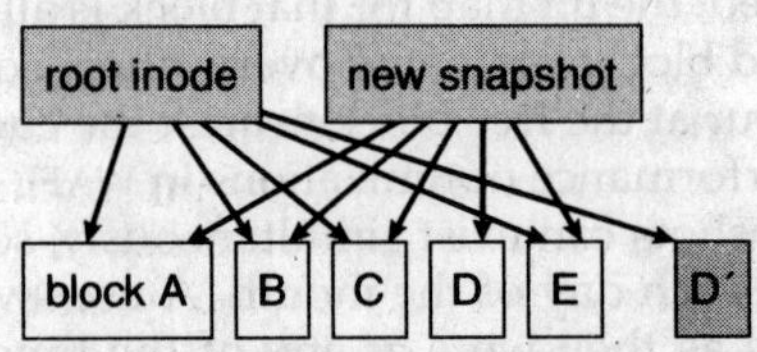

(c) After block D has changed to D´.

Figure 11.17 Snapshots in WAFL.

system. Such replication is used for disaster recovery. Should the first system be destroyed, most of its data are available for use on the remote system.

Finally, we should note that Sun's ZFS file system supports similarly efficient snapshots, clones, and replication.

11.10 Summary

The file system resides permanently on secondary storage, which is designed to hold a large amount of data permanently. The most common secondary-storage medium is the disk.

Physical disks may be segmented into partitions to control media use and to allow multiple, possibly varying, file systems on a single spindle. These file systems are mounted onto a logical file system architecture to make them available for use. File systems are often implemented in a layered or modular structure. The lower levels deal with the physical properties of storage devices. Upper levels deal with symbolic file names and logical properties of files. Intermediate levels map the logical file concepts into physical device properties.

Any file-system type can have different structures and algorithms. A VFS layer allows the upper layers to deal with each file-system type uniformly. Even remote file systems can be integrated into the system's directory structure and acted on by standard system calls via the VFS interface.

The various files can be allocated space on the disk in three ways: through contiguous, linked, or indexed allocation. Contiguous allocation can suffer from external fragmentation. Direct access is very inefficient with linked allocation. Indexed allocation may require substantial overhead for its index block. These algorithms can be optimized in many ways. Contiguous space can be enlarged through extents to increase flexibility and to decrease external fragmentation. Indexed allocation can be done in clusters of multiple blocks to increase throughput and to reduce the number of index entries needed. Indexing in large clusters is similar to contiguous allocation with extents.

Free-space allocation methods also influence the efficiency of disk-space use, the performance of the file system, and the reliability of secondary storage. The methods used include bit vectors and linked lists. Optimizations include grouping, counting, and the FAT, which places the linked list in one contiguous area.

Directory-management routines must consider efficiency, performance, and reliability. A hash table is a commonly used method, as it is fast and efficient. Unfortunately, damage to the table or a system crash can result in inconsistency between the directory information and the disk's contents. A consistency checker can be used to repair the damage. Operating-system backup tools allow disk data to be copied to tape, enabling the user to recover from data or even disk loss due to hardware failure, operating system bug, or user error

Network file systems, such as NFS, use client–server methodology to allow users to access files and directories from remote machines as if they were on local file systems. System calls on the client are translated into network protocols and retranslated into file-system operations on the server. Networking and multiple-client access create challenges in the areas of data consistency and performance.

Due to the fundamental role that file systems play in system operation, their performance and reliability are crucial. Techniques such as log structures and caching help improve performance, while log structures and RAID improve reliability. The WAFL file system is an example of optimization of performance to match a specific I/O load.

Exercises

11.1 In what situations would using memory as a RAM disk be more useful than using it as a disk cache?

11.2 Consider a file system that uses a modifed contiguous-allocation scheme with support for extents. A file is a collection of extents, with each extent corresponding to a contiguous set of blocks. A key issue in such systems is the degree of variability in the size of the extents. What are the advantages and disadvantages of the following schemes?

a. All extents are of the same size, and the size is predetermined.

b. Extents can be of any size and are allocated dynamically.

c. Extents can be of a few fixed sizes, and these sizes are predetermined.

11.3 Some file systems allow disk storage to be allocated at different levels of granularity. For instance, a file system could allocate 4 KB of disk space as a single 4-KB block or as eight 512-byte blocks. How could we take advantage of this flexibility to improve performance? What modifications would have to be made to the free-space management scheme in order to support this feature?

11.4 What are the advantages of the variant of linked allocation that uses a FAT to chain together the blocks of a file?

11.5 Consider a file currently consisting of 100 blocks. Assume that the file-control block (and the index block, in the case of indexed allocation) is already in memory. Calculate how many disk I/O operations are required for contiguous, linked, and indexed (single-level) allocation strategies, if, for one block, the following conditions hold. In the contiguous-allocation case, assume that there is no room to grow at the beginning but there is room to grow at the end. Also assume that the block information to be added is stored in memory.

a The block is added at the beginning.

b. The block is added in the middle.

c. The block is added at the end.

d. The block is removed from the beginning.

e. The block is removed from the middle.

f. The block is removed from the end.

11.6 Consider a file system that uses inodes to represent files. Disk blocks are 8 KB in size, and a pointer to a disk block requires 4 bytes. This file system has 12 direct disk blocks, as well as single, double, and triple indirect disk blocks. What is the maximum size of a file that can be stored in this file system?

11.7 Assume that in a particular augmentation of a remote-file-access protocol, each client maintains a name cache that caches translations from file names to corresponding file handles. What issues should we take into account in implementing the name cache?

11.8 Consider the following backup scheme:

- **Day 1**. Copy to a backup medium all files from the disk.
- **Day 2**. Copy to another medium all files changed since day 1.
- **Day 3**. Copy to another medium all files changed since day 1.

This differs from the schedule given in Section 11.7.4 by having all subsequent backups copy all files modified since the first full backup. What are the benefits of this system over the one in Section 11.7.4? What are the drawbacks? Are restore operations made easier or more difficult? Explain your answer.

11.9 Why must the bit map for file allocation be kept on mass storage, rather than in main memory?

11.10 Consider a file system on a disk that has both logical and physical block sizes of 512 bytes. Assume that the information about each file is already in memory. For each of the three allocation strategies (contiguous, linked, and indexed), answer these questions:

a. How is the logical-to-physical address mapping accomplished in this system? (For the indexed allocation, assume that a file is always less than 512 blocks long.)

b. If we are currently at logical block 10 (the last block accessed was block 10) and want to access logical block 4, how many physical blocks must be read from the disk?

11.11 Why is it advantageous to the user for an operating system to dynamically allocate its internal tables? What are the penalties to the operating system for doing so?

11.12 Explain why logging metadata updates ensures recovery of a file system after a file-system crash.

11.13 Fragmentation on a storage device can be eliminated by recompaction of the information. Typical disk devices do not have relocation or base registers (such as those used when memory is to be compacted), so how can we relocate files? Give three reasons why recompacting and relocation of files are often avoided.

11.14 Consider a system where free space is kept in a free-space list.

a. Suppose that the pointer to the free-space list is lost. Can the system reconstruct the free-space list? Explain your answer.

b. Consider a file system similar to the one used by UNIX with indexed allocation. How many disk I/O operations might be required to read the contents of a small local file at */a/b/c*? Assume that none of the disk blocks is currently being cached.

c. Suggest a scheme to ensure that the pointer is never lost as a result of memory failure.

11.15 One problem with contiguous allocation is that the user must preallocate enough space for each file. If the file grows to be larger than the space allocated for it, special actions must be taken. One solution to this problem is to define a file structure consisting of an initial contiguous area (of a specified size). If this area is filled, the operating system automatically defines an overflow area that is linked to the initial contiguous area. If the overflow area is filled, another overflow area is allocated. Compare this implementation of a file with the standard contiguous and linked implementations.

11.16 Discuss how performance optimizations for file systems might result in difficulties in maintaining the consistency of the systems in the event of computer crashes.

Bibliographical Notes

The MS-DOS FAT system is explained in Norton and Wilton [1988], and the OS/2 description can be found in Iacobucci [1988]. These operating systems use the Intel 8086 CPUs(Intel [1985b], Intel [1985a], Intel [1986], and Intel [1990]). IBM allocation methods are described in Deitel [1990]. The internals of the BSD UNIX system are covered in full in McKusick et al. [1996]. McVoy and Kleiman [1991] discusses optimizations of these methods made in Solaris. The Google file system is described in Ghemawat et al. [2003]. FUSE can be found at http://fuse.sourceforge.net/.

Disk file allocation based on the buddy system is covered in Koch [1987]. A file-organization scheme that guarantees retrieval in one access is described by Larson and Kajla [1984]. Log-structured file organizations for enhancing both performance and consistency are discussed in Rosenblum and Ousterhout [1991], Seltzer et al. [1993], and Seltzer et al. [1995]. Algorithms such as balanced trees (and much more) are covered by Knuth [1998] and Cormen et al. [2001]. The ZFS source code for space maps can be found at http://src.opensolaris.org/source/xref/onnv/onnv-gate/usr/src/uts/common/fs/zfs/space_map.c.

Disk caching is discussed by McKeon [1985] and Smith [1985]. Caching in the experimental Sprite operating system is described in Nelson et al. [1988]. General discussions concerning mass-storage technology are offered by Chi [1982] and Hoagland [1985]. Folk and Zoellick [1987] covers the gamut of file structures. Silvers [2000] discusses implementing the page cache in the NetBSD operating system.

The network file system (NFS) is discussed in Sandberg et al. [1985], Sandberg [1987], Sun [1990], and Callaghan [2000]. NFS Version 4 is a standard described at http://www.ietf.org/rfc/rfc3530.txt. The characteristics of workloads in distributed file systems are examined in Baker et al. [1991]. Ousterhout [1991] discusses the role of distributed state in networked file systems. Log-structured designs for networked file systems are proposed in Hartman and Ousterhout [1995] and Thekkath et al. [1997]. NFS and the UNIX file system (UFS) are described in Vahalia [1996] and Mauro and McDougall [2007]. The Windows NT file system, NTFS, is explained in Solomon [1998]. The Ext2 file system used in Linux is described in Bovet and Cesati [2002] and the WAFL file system in Hitz et al. [1995]. ZFS documentation can be found at http://www.opensolaris.org/os/community/ZFS/docs.

Secondary-Storage Structure

CHAPTER 12

The file system can be viewed logically as consisting of three parts. In Chapter 10, we examined the user and programmer interface to the file system. In Chapter 11, we described the internal data structures and algorithms used by the operating system to implement this interface. In this chapter, we discuss the lowest level of the file system: the secondary and tertiary storage structures. We first describe the physical structure of magenetic disks and magnetic tapes. We then describe disk-scheduling algorithms, which schedule the order of disk I/Os to improve performance. Next, we discuss disk formatting and management of boot blocks, damaged blocks, and swap space. We then examine secondary storage structure, covering disk reliability and stable-storage implementation. We conclude with a brief description of tertiary storage devices and the problems that arise when an operating system uses tertiary storage.

CHAPTER OBJECTIVES

- To describe the physical structure of secondary and tertiary storage devices and its effects on the uses of the devices.
- To explain the performance characteristics of mass-storage devices.
- To discuss operating-system services provided for mass storage, including RAID and HSM.

12.1 Overview of Mass-Storage Structure

In this section, we present a general overview of the physical structure of secondary and tertiary storage devices.

12.1.1 Magnetic Disks

Magnetic disks provide the bulk of secondary storage for modern computer systems. Conceptually, disks are relatively simple (Figure 12.1). Each disk **platter** has a flat circular shape, like a CD. Common platter diameters range

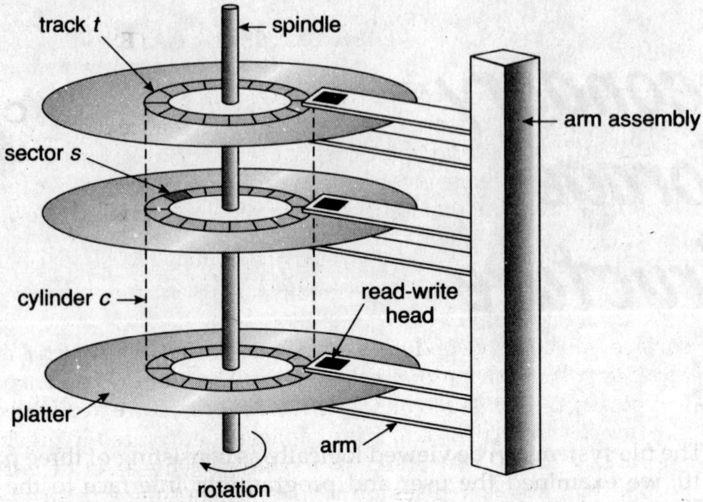

Figure 12.1 Moving-head disk mechanism.

from 1.8 to 5.25 inches. The two surfaces of a platter are covered with a magnetic material. We store information by recording it magnetically on the platters.

A read–write head "flies" just above each surface of every platter. The heads are attached to a **disk arm** that moves all the heads as a unit. The surface of a platter is logically divided into circular **tracks**, which are subdivided into **sectors**. The set of tracks that are at one arm position makes up a **cylinder**. There may be thousands of concentric cylinders in a disk drive, and each track may contain hundreds of sectors. The storage capacity of common disk drives is measured in gigabytes.

When the disk is in use, a drive motor spins it at high speed. Most drives rotate 60 to 200 times per second. Disk speed has two parts. The **transfer rate** is the rate at which data flow between the drive and the computer. The **positioning time**, sometimes called the **random-access time**, consists of the time necessary to move the disk arm to the desired cylinder, called the **seek time**, and the time necessary for the desired sector to rotate to the disk head, called the **rotational latency**. Typical disks can transfer several megabytes of data per second, and they have seek times and rotational latencies of several milliseconds.

Because the disk head flies on an extremely thin cushion of air (measured in microns), there is a danger that the head will make contact with the disk surface. Although the disk platters are coated with a thin protective layer, the head will sometimes damage the magnetic surface. This accident is called a **head crash**. A head crash normally cannot be repaired; the entire disk must be replaced.

A disk can be **removable**, allowing different disks to be mounted as needed. Removable magnetic disks generally consist of one platter, held in a plastic case to prevent damage while not in the disk drive. **Floppy disks** are inexpensive removable magnetic disks that have a soft plastic case containing a flexible platter. The head of a floppy-disk drive generally sits directly on the disk

DISK TRANSFER RATES

As with many aspects of computing, published performance numbers for disks are not the same as real-world performance numbers. Stated transfer rates are always lower than effective transfer rates, for example. The transfer rate may be the rate at which bits can be read from the magnetic media by the disk head, but that is different from the rate at which blocks are delivered to the operating system.

surface, so the drive is designed to rotate more slowly than a hard-disk drive to reduce the wear on the disk surface. The storage capacity of a floppy disk is typically only 1.44 MB or so. Removable disks are available that work much like normal hard disks and have capacities measured in gigabytes.

A disk drive is attached to a computer by a set of wires called an I/O bus. Several kinds of buses are available, including enhanced integrated drive electronics (EIDE), advanced technology attachment (ATA), serial ATA (SATA), universal serial bus (USB), fiber channel (FC), and small computer-systems interface (SCSI) buses. The data transfers on a bus are carried out by special electronic processors called controllers. The host controller is the controller at the computer end of the bus. A disk controller is built into each disk drive. To perform a disk I/O operation, the computer places a command into the host controller, typically using memory-mapped I/O ports, as described in Section 9.7.3. The host controller then sends the command via messages to the disk controller, and the disk controller operates the disk-drive hardware to carry out the command. Disk controllers usually have a built-in cache. Data transfer at the disk drive happens between the cache and the disk surface, and data transfer to the host, at fast electronic speeds, occurs between the cache and the host controller.

12.1.2 Magnetic Tapes

Magnetic tape was used as an early secondary-storage medium. Although it is relatively permanent and can hold large quantities of data, its access time is slow compared with that of main memory and magnetic disk. In addition, random access to magnetic tape is about a thousand times slower than random access to magnetic disk, so tapes are not very useful for secondary storage. Tapes are used mainly for backup, for storage of infrequently used information, and as a medium for transferring information from one system to another.

A tape is kept in a spool and is wound or rewound past a read–write head. Moving to the correct spot on a tape can take minutes, but once positioned, tape drives can write data at speeds comparable to disk drives. Tape capacities vary greatly, depending on the particular kind of tape drive. Typically, they store from 20 GB to 200 GB. Some have built-in compression that can more than double the effective storage. Tapes and their drivers are usually categorized by width, including 4, 8, and 19 millimeters and 1/4 and 1/2 inch. Some are named according to technology, such as LTO-2 and SDLT. Tape storage is further described in Section 12.9.

FIREWIRE

FireWire refers to an interface designed for connecting peripheral devices such as hard drives, DVD drives, and digital video cameras to a computer system. FireWire was first developed by Apple Computer and became the IEEE 1394 standard in 1995. The original FireWire standard provided bandwidth up to 400 megabits per second. Recently, a new standard—FireWire 2—has emerged and is identified by the IEEE 1394b standard. FireWire 2 provides double the data rate of the original FireWire—800 megabits per second.

12.2 Disk Structure

Modern disk drives are addressed as large one-dimensional arrays of **logical blocks**, where the logical block is the smallest unit of transfer. The size of a logical block is usually 512 bytes, although some disks can be **low-level formatted** to have a different logical block size, such as 1,024 bytes. This option is described in Section 12.5.1. The one-dimensional array of logical blocks is mapped onto the sectors of the disk sequentially. Sector 0 is the first sector of the first track on the outermost cylinder. The mapping proceeds in order through that track, then through the rest of the tracks in that cylinder, and then through the rest of the cylinders from outermost to innermost.

By using this mapping, we can—at least in theory—convert a logical block number into an old-style disk address that consists of a cylinder number, a track number within that cylinder, and a sector number within that track. In practice, it is difficult to perform this translation, for two reasons. First, most disks have some defective sectors, but the mapping hides this by substituting spare sectors from elsewhere on the disk. Second, the number of sectors per track is not a constant on some drives.

Let's look more closely at the second reason. On media that use **constant linear velocity (CLV)**, the density of bits per track is uniform. The farther a track is from the center of the disk, the greater its length, so the more sectors it can hold. As we move from outer zones to inner zones, the number of sectors per track decreases. Tracks in the outermost zone typically hold 40 percent more sectors than do tracks in the innermost zone. The drive increases its rotation speed as the head moves from the outer to the inner tracks to keep the same rate of data moving under the head. This method is used in CD-ROM and DVD-ROM drives. Alternatively, the disk rotation speed can stay constant; in this case, the density of bits decreases from inner tracks to outer tracks to keep the data rate constant. This method is used in hard disks and is known as **constant angular velocity (CAV)**.

The number of sectors per track has been increasing as disk technology improves, and the outer zone of a disk usually has several hundred sectors per track. Similarly, the number of cylinders per disk has been increasing; large disks have tens of thousands of cylinders.

12.3 Disk Attachment

Computers access disk storage in two ways. One way is via I/O ports (or **host-attached storage**); this is common on small systems. The other way is via a remote host in a distributed file system; this is referred to as **network-attached storage**.

12.3.1 Host-Attached Storage

Host-attached storage is storage accessed through local I/O ports. These ports use several technologies. The typical desktop PC uses an I/O bus architecture called IDE or ATA. This architecture supports a maximum of two drives per I/O bus. A newer, similar protocol that has simplified cabling is SATA. High-end workstations and servers generally use more sophisticated I/O architectures, such as SCSI and fiber channel (FC).

SCSI is a bus architecture. Its physical medium is usually a ribbon cable with a large number of conductors (typically 50 or 68). The SCSI protocol supports a maximum of 16 devices per bus. Generally, the devices include one controller card in the host (the **SCSI initiator**) and up to 15 storage devices (the **SCSI targets**). A SCSI disk is a common SCSI target, but the protocol provides the ability to address up to 8 **logical units** in each SCSI target. A typical use of logical unit addressing is to direct commands to components of a RAID array or components of a removable media library (such as a CD jukebox sending commands to the media-changer mechanism or to one of the drives).

FC is a high-speed serial architecture that can operate over optical fiber or over a four-conductor copper cable. It has two variants. One is a large switched fabric having a 24-bit address space. This variant is expected to dominate in the future and is the basis of **storage-area networks (SANs)**, discussed in Section 12.3.3. Because of the large address space and the switched nature of the communication, multiple hosts and storage devices can attach to the fabric, allowing great flexibility in I/O communication. The other FC variant is an **arbitrated loop (FC-AL)** that can address 126 devices (drives and controllers).

A wide variety of storage devices are suitable for use as host-attached storage. Among these are hard disk drives, RAID arrays, and CD, DVD, and tape drives. The I/O commands that initiate data transfers to a host-attached storage device are reads and writes of logical data blocks directed to specifically identified storage units (such as bus ID, SCSI ID, and target logical unit).

12.3.2 Network-Attached Storage

A network-attached storage (NAS) device is a special-purpose storage system that is accessed remotely over a data network (Figure 12.2). Clients access network-attached storage via a remote-procedure-call interface such as NFS for UNIX systems or CIFS for Windows machines. The remote procedure calls (RPCs) are carried via TCP or UDP over an IP network—usually the same local-area network (LAN) that carries all data traffic to the clients. The network-attached storage unit is usually implemented as a RAID array with software that implements the RPC interface. It is easiest to think of NAS as simply another storage-access protocol. For example, rather than using a SCSI device driver and SCSI protocols to access storage, a system using NAS would use RPC over TCP/IP.

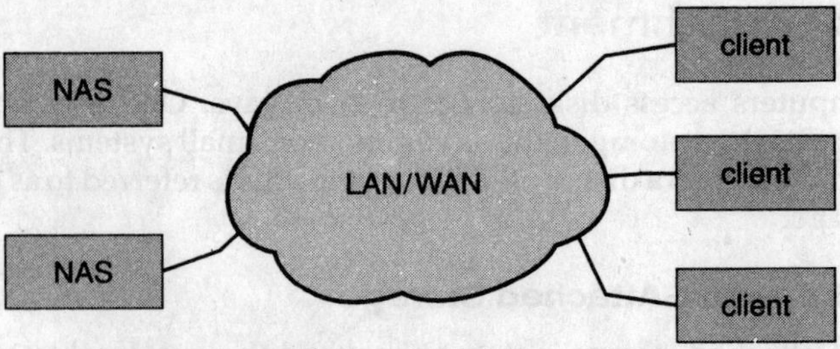

Figure 12.2 Network-attached storage.

Network-attached storage provides a convenient way for all the computers on a LAN to share a pool of storage with the same ease of naming and access enjoyed with local host-attached storage. However, it tends to be less efficient and have lower performance than some direct-attached storage options.

iSCSI is the latest network-attached storage protocol. In essence, it uses the IP network protocol to carry the SCSI protocol. Thus, networks—rather than SCSI cables—can be used as the interconnects between hosts and their storage. As a result, hosts can treat their storage as if it were directly attached, even if the storage is distant from the host.

12.3.3 Storage-Area Network

One drawback of network-attached storage systems is that the storage I/O operations consume bandwidth on the data network, thereby increasing the latency of network communication. This problem can be particularly acute in large client–server installations—the communication between servers and clients competes for bandwidth with the communication among servers and storage devices.

A storage-area network (SAN) is a private network (using storage protocols rather than networking protocols) connecting servers and storage units, as shown in Figure 12.3. The power of a SAN lies in its flexibility. Multiple hosts and multiple storage arrays can attach to the same SAN, and storage can be dynamically allocated to hosts. A SAN switch allows or prohibits access between the hosts and the storage. As one example, if a host is running low on disk space, the SAN can be configured to allocate more storage to that host. SANs make it possible for clusters of servers to share the same storage and for storage arrays to include multiple direct host connections. SANs typically have more ports, and less expensive ports, than storage arrays.

FC is the most common SAN interconnect, although the simplicity of iSCSI is increasing its use. An emerging alternative is a special-purpose bus architecture named InfiniBand, which provides hardware and software support for high-speed interconnection networks for servers and storage units.

12.4 Disk Scheduling

One of the responsibilities of the operating system is to use the hardware efficiently. For the disk drives, meeting this responsibility entails having

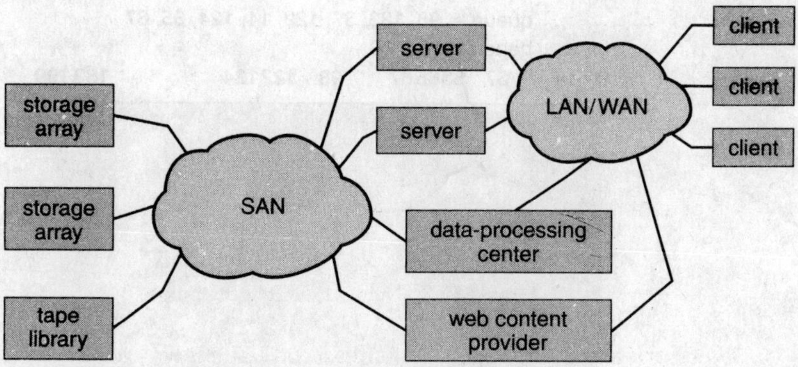

Figure 12.3 Storage-area network.

fast access time and large disk bandwidth. The access time has two major components (also see Section 12.1.1). The **seek time** is the time for the disk arm to move the heads to the cylinder containing the desired sector. The **rotational latency** is the additional time for the disk to rotate the desired sector to the disk head. The disk **bandwidth** is the total number of bytes transferred, divided by the total time between the first request for service and the completion of the last transfer. We can improve both the access time and the bandwidth by managing the order in which disk I/O requests are serviced.

Whenever a process needs I/O to or from the disk, it issues a system call to the operating system. The request specifies several pieces of information:

- Whether this operation is input or output
- What the disk address for the transfer is
- What the memory address for the transfer is
- What the number of sectors to be transferred is

If the desired disk drive and controller are available, the request can be serviced immediately. If the drive or controller is busy, any new requests for service will be placed in the queue of pending requests for that drive. For a multiprogramming system with many processes, the disk queue may often have several pending requests. Thus, when one request is completed, the operating system chooses which pending request to service next. How does the operating system make this choice? Any one of several disk-scheduling algorithms can be used, and we discuss them next.

12.4.1 FCFS Scheduling

The simplest form of disk scheduling is, of course, the first-come, first-served (FCFS) algorithm. This algorithm is intrinsically fair, but it generally does not provide the fastest service. Consider, for example, a disk queue with requests for I/O to blocks on cylinders

98, 183, 37, 122, 14, 124, 65, 67,

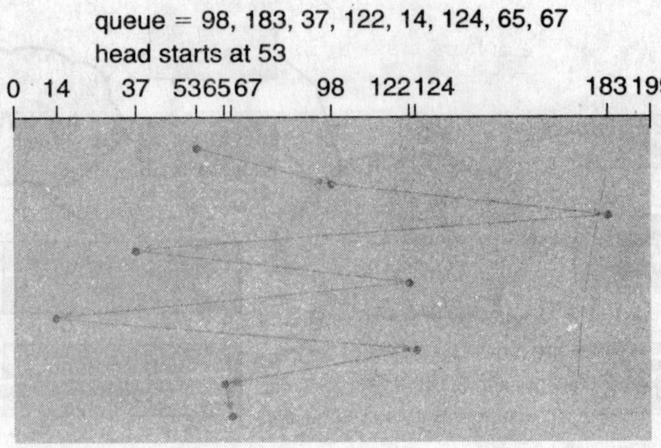

Figure 12.4 FCFS disk scheduling.

in that order. If the disk head is initially at cylinder 53, it will first move from 53 to 98, then to 183, 37, 122, 14, 124, 65, and finally to 67, for a total head movement of 640 cylinders. This schedule is diagrammed in Figure 12.4.

The wild swing from 122 to 14 and then back to 124 illustrates the problem with this schedule. If the requests for cylinders 37 and 14 could be serviced together, before or after the requests for 122 and 124, the total head movement could be decreased substantially, and performance could be thereby improved.

12.4.2 SSTF Scheduling

It seems reasonable to service all the requests close to the current head position before moving the head far away to service other requests. This assumption is the basis for the **shortest-seek-time-first (SSTF) algorithm**. The SSTF algorithm selects the request with the least seek time from the current head position. Since seek time increases with the number of cylinders traversed by the head, SSTF chooses the pending request closest to the current head position.

For our example request queue, the closest request to the initial head position (53) is at cylinder 65. Once we are at cylinder 65, the next closest request is at cylinder 67. From there, the request at cylinder 37 is closer than the one at 98, so 37 is served next. Continuing, we service the request at cylinder 14, then 98, 122, 124, and finally 183 (Figure 12.5). This scheduling method results in a total head movement of only 236 cylinders—little more than one-third of the distance needed for FCFS scheduling of this request queue. Clearly, this algorithm gives a substantial improvement in performance.

SSTF scheduling is essentially a form of shortest-job-first (SJF) scheduling; and like SJF scheduling, it may cause starvation of some requests. Remember that requests may arrive at any time. Suppose that we have two requests in the queue, for cylinders 14 and 186, and while the request from 14 is being serviced, a new request near 14 arrives. This new request will be serviced next, making the request at 186 wait. While this request is being serviced, another request close to 14 could arrive. In theory, a continual stream of requests near one another could cause the request for cylinder 186 to wait indefinitely.

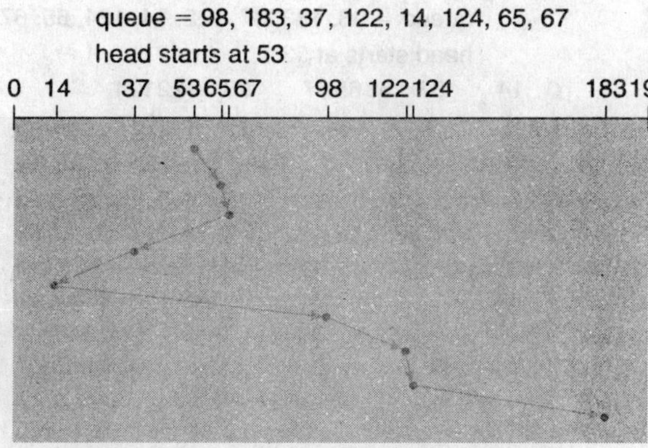

Figure 12.5 SSTF disk scheduling.

This scenario becomes increasingly likely as the pending-request queue grows longer.

Although the SSTF algorithm is a substantial improvement over the FCFS algorithm, it is not optimal. In the example, we can do better by moving the head from 53 to 37, even though the latter is not closest, and then to 14, before turning around to service 65, 67, 98, 122, 124, and 183. This strategy reduces the total head movement to 208 cylinders.

12.4.3 SCAN Scheduling

In the **SCAN algorithm**, the disk arm starts at one end of the disk and moves toward the other end, servicing requests as it reaches each cylinder, until it gets to the other end of the disk. At the other end, the direction of head movement is reversed, and servicing continues. The head continuously scans back and forth across the disk. The SCAN algorithm is sometimes called the **elevator algorithm**, since the disk arm behaves just like an elevator in a building, first servicing all the requests going up and then reversing to service requests the other way.

Let's return to our example to illustrate. Before applying SCAN to schedule the requests on cylinders 98, 183, 37, 122, 14, 124, 65, and 67, we need to know the direction of head movement in addition to the head's current position. Assuming that the disk arm is moving toward 0 and that the initial head position is again 53, the head will next service 37 and then 14. At cylinder 0, the arm will reverse and will move toward the other end of the disk, servicing the requests at 65, 67, 98, 122, 124, and 183 (Figure 12.6). If a request arrives in the queue just in front of the head, it will be serviced almost immediately; a request arriving just behind the head will have to wait until the arm moves to the end of the disk, reverses direction, and comes back.

Assuming a uniform distribution of requests for cylinders, consider the density of requests when the head reaches one end and reverses direction. At this point, relatively few requests are immediately in front of the head, since these cylinders have recently been serviced. The heaviest density of requests

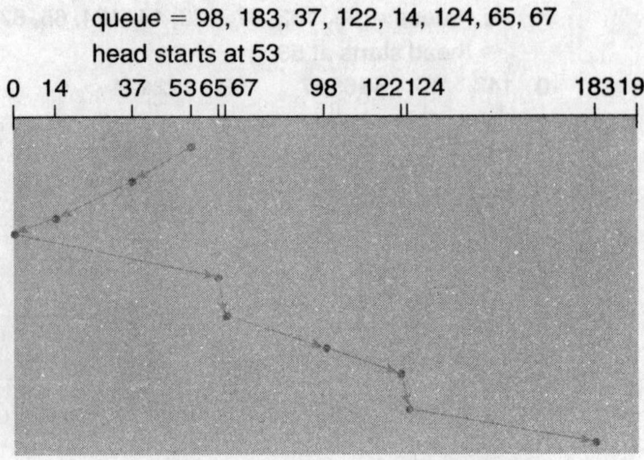

Figure 12.6 SCAN disk scheduling.

is at the other end of the disk. These requests have also waited the longest, so why not go there first? That is the idea of the next algorithm.

12.4.4 C-SCAN Scheduling

Circular SCAN (C-SCAN) scheduling is a variant of SCAN designed to provide a more uniform wait time. Like SCAN, C-SCAN moves the head from one end of the disk to the other, servicing requests along the way. When the head reaches the other end, however, it immediately returns to the beginning of the disk without servicing any requests on the return trip (Figure 12.7). The C-SCAN scheduling algorithm essentially treats the cylinders as a circular list that wraps around from the final cylinder to the first one.

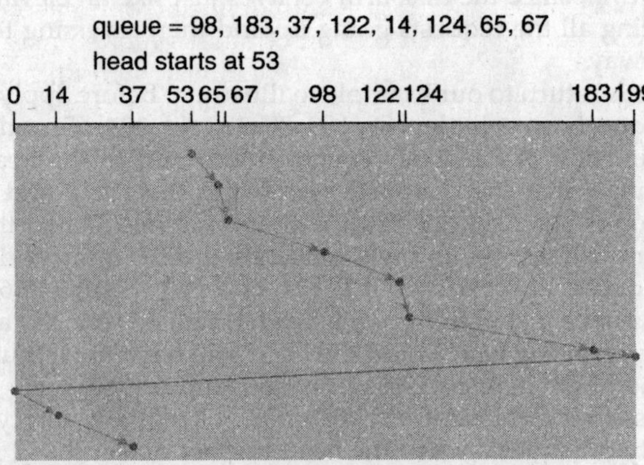

Figure 12.7 C-SCAN disk scheduling.

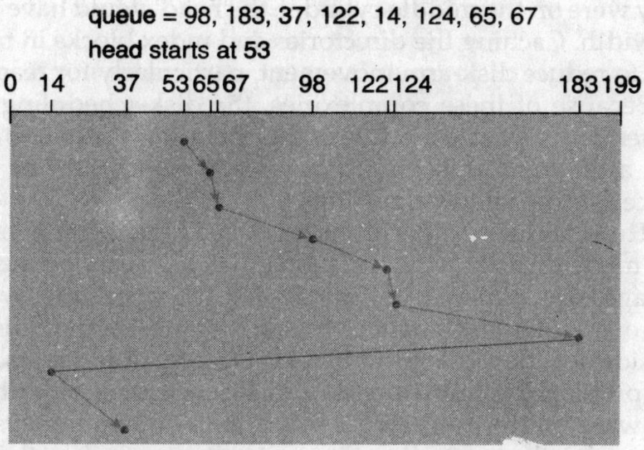

Figure 12.8 C-LOOK disk scheduling.

12.4.5 LOOK Scheduling

As we described them, both SCAN and C-SCAN move the disk arm across the full width of the disk. In practice, neither algorithm is often implemented this way. More commonly, the arm goes only as far as the final request in each direction. Then, it reverses direction immediately, without going all the way to the end of the disk. Versions of SCAN and C-SCAN that follow this pattern are called LOOK and **C-LOOK scheduling**, because they *look* for a request before continuing to move in a given direction (Figure 12.8).

12.4.6 Selection of a Disk-Scheduling Algorithm

Given so many disk-scheduling algorithms, how do we choose the best one? SSTF is common and has a natural appeal because it increases performance over FCFS. SCAN and C-SCAN perform better for systems that place a heavy load on the disk, because they are less likely to cause a starvation problem. For any particular list of requests, we can define an optimal order of retrieval, but the computation needed to find an optimal schedule may not justify the savings over SSTF or SCAN. With any scheduling algorithm, however, performance depends heavily on the number and types of requests. For instance, suppose that the queue usually has just one outstanding request. Then, all scheduling algorithms behave the same, because they have only one choice of where to move the disk head: they all behave like FCFS scheduling.

Requests for disk service can be greatly influenced by the file-allocation method. A program reading a contiguously allocated file will generate several requests that are close together on the disk, resulting in limited head movement. A linked or indexed file, in contrast, may include blocks that are widely scattered on the disk, resulting in greater head movement.

The location of directories and index blocks is also important. Since every file must be opened to be used, and opening a file requires searching the directory structure, the directories will be accessed frequently. Suppose that a directory entry is on the first cylinder and a file's data are on the final cylinder. In this case, the disk head has to move the entire width of the disk. If the directory entry were on the middle cylinder, the head would have to move only one-half the width. Caching the directories and index blocks in main memory can also help to reduce disk-arm movement, particularly for read requests.

Because of these complexities, the disk-scheduling algorithm should be written as a separate module of the operating system, so that it can be replaced with a different algorithm if necessary. Either SSTF or LOOK is a reasonable choice for the default algorithm.

The scheduling algorithms described here consider only the seek distances. For modern disks, the rotational latency can be nearly as large as the average seek time. It is difficult for the operating system to schedule for improved rotational latency, though, because modern disks do not disclose the physical location of logical blocks. Disk manufacturers have been alleviating this problem by implementing disk-scheduling algorithms in the controller hardware built into the disk drive. If the operating system sends a batch of requests to the controller, the controller can queue them and then schedule them to improve both the seek time and the rotational latency.

If I/O performance were the only consideration, the operating system would gladly turn over the responsibility of disk scheduling to the disk hardware. In practice, however, the operating system may have other constraints on the service order for requests. For instance, demand paging may take priority over application I/O, and writes are more urgent than reads if the cache is running out of free pages. Also, it may be desirable to guarantee the order of a set of disk writes to make the file system robust in the face of system crashes. Consider what could happen if the operating system allocated a disk page to a file and the application wrote data into that page before the operating system had a chance to flush the modified inode and free-space list back to disk. To accommodate such requirements, an operating system may choose to do its own disk scheduling and to spoon-feed the requests to the disk controller, one by one, for some types of I/O.

12.5 Disk Management

The operating system is responsible for several other aspects of disk management, too. Here we discuss disk initialization, booting from disk, and bad-block recovery.

12.5.1 Disk Formatting

A new magnetic disk is a blank slate: it is just a platter of a magnetic recording material. Before a disk can store data, it must be divided into sectors that the disk controller can read and write. This process is called **low-level formatting**, or **physical formatting**. Low-level formatting fills the disk with a special data structure for each sector. The data structure for a sector typically consists of a header, a data area (usually 512 bytes in size), and a trailer. The header and trailer contain information used by the disk controller, such as a sector number and an **error-correcting code (ECC)**. When the controller writes a sector of data during normal I/O, the ECC is updated with a value calculated from all the bytes in the data area. When the sector is read, the ECC is recalculated and compared with the stored value. If the stored and calculated numbers are different, this mismatch indicates that the data area of the sector has become corrupted and that the disk sector may be bad (Section 12.5.3). The ECC is an error-*correcting* code because it contains enough information, if only a few bits of data have been corrupted, to enable the controller to identify which bits have changed and calculate what their correct values should be. It then reports a recoverable **soft error**. The controller automatically does the ECC processing whenever a sector is read or written.

Most hard disks are low-level-formatted at the factory as a part of the manufacturing process. This formatting enables the manufacturer to test the disk and to initialize the mapping from logical block numbers to defect-free sectors on the disk. For many hard disks, when the disk controller is instructed to low-level-format the disk, it can also be told how many bytes of data space to leave between the header and trailer of all sectors. It is usually possible to choose among a few sizes, such as 256, 512, and 1,024 bytes. Formatting a disk with a larger sector size means that fewer sectors can fit on each track; but it also means that fewer headers and trailers are written on each track and more space is available for user data. Some operating systems can handle only a sector size of 512 bytes.

Before it can use a disk to hold files, the operating system still needs to record its own data structures on the disk. It does so in two steps. The first step is to **partition** the disk into one or more groups of cylinders. The operating system can treat each partition as though it were a separate disk. For instance, one partition can hold a copy of the operating system's executable code, while another holds user files. The second step is **logical formatting**, or creation of a file system. In this step, the operating system stores the initial file-system data structures onto the disk. These data structures may include maps of free and allocated space (a FAT or inodes) and an initial empty directory.

To increase efficiency, most file systems group blocks together into larger chunks, frequently called **clusters**. Disk I/O is done via blocks, but file system I/O is done via clusters, effectively assuring that I/O has more sequential-access and fewer random-access characteristics.

Some operating systems give special programs the ability to use a disk partition as a large sequential array of logical blocks, without any file-system data structures. This array is sometimes called the raw disk, and I/O to this array is termed raw I/O. For example, some database systems prefer raw I/O because it enables them to control the exact disk location where each database record is stored. Raw I/O bypasses all the file-system services, such as the buffer cache, file locking, prefetching, space allocation, file names, and directories. We can make certain applications more efficient by allowing them to implement their own special-purpose storage services on a raw partition, but most applications perform better when they use the regular file-system services.

12.5.2 Boot Block

For a computer to start running—for instance, when it is powered up or rebooted—it must have an initial program to run. This initial *bootstrap* program tends to be simple. It initializes all aspects of the system, from CPU registers to device controllers and the contents of main memory, and then starts the operating system. To do its job, the bootstrap program finds the operating-system kernel on disk, loads that kernel into memory, and jumps to an initial address to begin the operating-system execution.

For most computers, the bootstrap is stored in **read-only memory (ROM)**. This location is convenient, because ROM needs no initialization and is at a fixed location that the processor can start executing when powered up or reset. And, since ROM is read only, it cannot be infected by a computer virus. The problem is that changing this bootstrap code requires changing the ROM hardware chips. For this reason, most systems store a tiny bootstrap loader program in the boot ROM whose only job is to bring in a full bootstrap program from disk. The full bootstrap program can be changed easily: a new version is simply written onto the disk. The full bootstrap program is stored in the "boot blocks" at a fixed location on the disk. A disk that has a boot partition is called a **boot disk** or **system disk**.

The code in the boot ROM instructs the disk controller to read the boot blocks into memory (no device drivers are loaded at this point) and then starts executing that code. The full bootstrap program is more sophisticated than the bootstrap loader in the boot ROM; it is able to load the entire operating system from a non-fixed location on disk and to start the operating system running. Even so, the full bootstrap code may be small.

Let's consider as an example the boot process in Windows 2000. The Windows 2000 system places its boot code in the first sector on the hard disk (which it terms the **master boot record**, or **MBR**). Furthermore, Windows 2000 allows a hard disk to be divided into one or more partitions; one partition, identified as the **boot partition**, contains the operating system and device drivers. Booting begins in a Windows 2000 system by running code that is resident in the system's ROM memory. This code directs the system to read the boot code from the MBR. In addition to containing boot code, the MBR contains a table listing the partitions for the hard disk and a flag indicating which partition the system is to be booted from, as illustrated in Figure 12.9. Once the system identifies the boot partition, it reads the first sector from that partition (which is called the **boot sector**) and continues with the remainder of the boot process, which includes loading the various subsystems and system services.

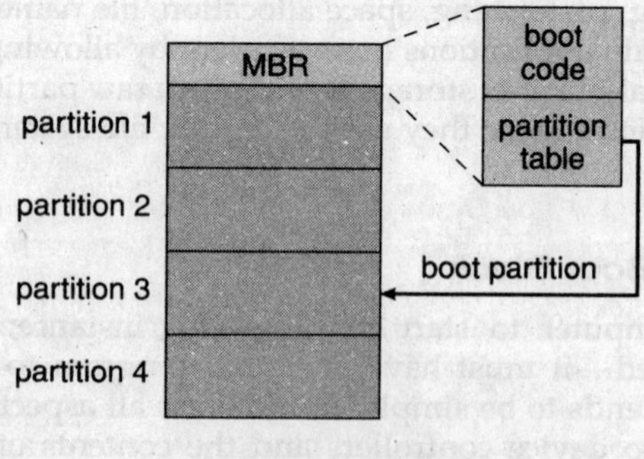

Figure 12.9 Booting from disk in Windows 2000.

12.5.3 Bad Blocks

Because disks have moving parts and small tolerances (recall that the disk head flies just above the disk surface), they are prone to failure. Sometimes the failure is complete; in this case, the disk needs to be replaced and its contents restored from backup media to the new disk. More frequently, one or more sectors become defective. Most disks even come from the factory with **bad blocks**. Depending on the disk and controller in use, these blocks are handled in a variety of ways.

On simple disks, such as some disks with IDE controllers, bad blocks are handled manually. For instance, the MS-DOS `format` command performs logical formatting and, as a part of the process, scans the disk to find bad blocks. If `format` finds a bad block, it writes a special value into the corresponding FAT entry to tell the allocation routines not to use that block. If blocks go bad during normal operation, a special program (such as `chkdsk`) must be run manually to search for the bad blocks and to lock them away. Data that resided on the bad blocks usually are lost.

More sophisticated disks, such as the SCSI disks used in high-end PCs and most workstations and servers, are smarter about bad-block recovery. The controller maintains a list of bad blocks on the disk. The list is initialized during the low-level formatting at the factory and is updated over the life of the disk. Low-level formatting also sets aside spare sectors not visible to the operating system. The controller can be told to replace each bad sector logically with one of the spare sectors. This scheme is known as **sector sparing** or **forwarding**.

A typical bad-sector transaction might be as follows:

- The operating system tries to read logical block 87.
- The controller calculates the ECC and finds that the sector is bad. It reports this finding to the operating system.
- The next time the system is rebooted, a special command is run to tell the SCSI controller to replace the bad sector with a spare.
- After that, whenever the system requests logical block 87, the request is translated into the replacement sector's address by the controller.

Note that such a redirection by the controller could invalidate any optimization by the operating system's disk-scheduling algorithm! For this reason, most disks are formatted to provide a few spare sectors in each cylinder and a spare cylinder as well. When a bad block is remapped, the controller uses a spare sector from the same cylinder, if possible.

As an alternative to sector sparing, some controllers can be instructed to replace a bad block by **sector slipping**. Here is an example: Suppose that logical block 17 becomes defective and the first available spare follows sector 202. Then, sector slipping remaps all the sectors from 17 to 202, moving them all down one spot. That is, sector 202 is copied into the spare, then sector 201 into 202, then 200 into 201, and so on, until sector 18 is copied into sector 19. Slipping the sectors in this way frees up the space of sector 18, so sector 17 can be mapped to it.

The replacement of a bad block generally is not totally automatic because the data in the bad block are usually lost. Soft errors may trigger a process in which a copy of the block data is made and the block is spared or slipped. An unrecoverable **hard error**, however, results in lost data. Whatever file was using that block must be repaired (for instance, by restoration from a backup tape), and that requires manual intervention.

12.6 Swap-Space Management

Swapping was first presented in Section 8.2, where we discussed moving entire processes between disk and main memory. Swapping in that setting occurs when the amount of physical memory reaches a critically low point and processes are moved from memory to swap space to free available memory. In practice, very few modern operating systems implement swapping in this fashion. Rather, systems now combine swapping with virtual memory techniques (Chapter 9) and swap pages, not necessarily entire processes. In fact, some systems now use the terms *swapping* and *paging* interchangeably, reflecting the merging of these two concepts.

Swap-space management is another low-level task of the operating system. Virtual memory uses disk space as an extension of main memory. Since disk access is much slower than memory access, using swap space significantly decreases system performance. The main goal for the design and implementation of swap space is to provide the best throughput for the virtual memory system. In this section, we discuss how swap space is used, where swap space is located on disk, and how swap space is managed.

12.6.1 Swap-Space Use

Swap space is used in various ways by different operating systems, depending on the memory-management algorithms in use. For instance, systems that implement swapping may use swap space to hold an entire process image, including the code and data segments. Paging systems may simply store pages that have been pushed out of main memory. The amount of swap space needed on a system can therefore vary from a few megabytes of disk space to gigabytes, depending on the amount of physical memory, the amount of virtual memory it is backing, and the way in which the virtual memory is used.

Note that it may be safer to overestimate than to underestimate the amount of swap space required, because if a system runs out of swap space it may be forced to abort processes or may crash entirely. Overestimation wastes disk space that could otherwise be used for files, but it does no other harm. Some systems recommend the amount to be set aside for swap space. Solaris, for example, suggests setting swap space equal to the amount by which virtual memory exceeds pageable physical memory. In the past, Linux has suggested setting swap space to double the amount of physical memory, although most Linux systems now use considerably less swap space. In fact, there is currently much debate in the Linux community about whether to set aside swap space at all!

Some operating systems—including Linux—allow the use of multiple swap spaces. These swap spaces are usually put on separate disks so that the load placed on the I/O system by paging and swapping can be spread over the system's I/O devices.

12.6.2 Swap-Space Location

A swap space can reside in one of two places: it can be carved out of the normal file system, or it can be in a separate disk partition. If the swap space is simply a large file within the file system, normal file-system routines can be used to create it, name it, and allocate its space. This approach, though easy to implement, is inefficient. Navigating the directory structure and the disk-allocation data structures takes time and (possibly) extra disk accesses. External fragmentation can greatly increase swapping times by forcing multiple seeks during reading or writing of a process image. We can improve performance by caching the block location information in physical memory and by using special tools to allocate physically contiguous blocks for the swap file, but the cost of traversing the file-system data structures remains.

Alternatively, swap space can be created in a separate **raw** partition. No file system or directory structure is placed in this space. Rather, a separate swap-space storage manager is used to allocate and deallocate the blocks from the raw partition. This manager uses algorithms optimized for speed rather than for storage efficiency, because swap space is accessed much more frequently than file systems (when it is used). Internal fragmentation may increase, but this trade-off is acceptable because the life of data in the swap space generally is much shorter than that of files in the file system. Since swap space is reinitialized at boot time, any fragmentation is short-lived. The raw-partition approach creates a fixed amount of swap space during disk partitioning. Adding more swap space requires either repartitioning the disk (which involves moving the other file-system partitions or destroying them and restoring them from backup) or adding another swap space elsewhere.

Some operating systems are flexible and can swap both in raw partitions and in file-system space. Linux is an example: the policy and implementation are separate, allowing the machine's administrator to decide which type of swapping to use. The trade-off is between the convenience of allocation and management in the file system and the performance of swapping in raw partitions.

12.6.3 Swap-Space Management: An Example

We can illustrate how swap space is used by following the evolution of swapping and paging in various UNIX systems. The traditional UNIX kernel started with an implementation of swapping that copied entire processes between contiguous disk regions and memory. UNIX later evolved to a combination of swapping and paging as paging hardware became available.

In Solaris 1 (SunOS), the designers changed standard UNIX methods to improve efficiency and reflect technological developments. When a process executes, text-segment pages containing code are brought in from the file system, accessed in main memory, and thrown away if selected for pageout. It is more efficient to reread a page from the file system than to write it to swap space and then reread it from there. Swap space is only used as a backing store for pages of **anonymous** memory, which includes memory allocated for the stack, heap, and uninitialized data of a process.

More changes were made in later versions of Solaris. The biggest change is that Solaris now allocates swap space only when a page is forced out of physical memory, rather than when the virtual memory page is first created.

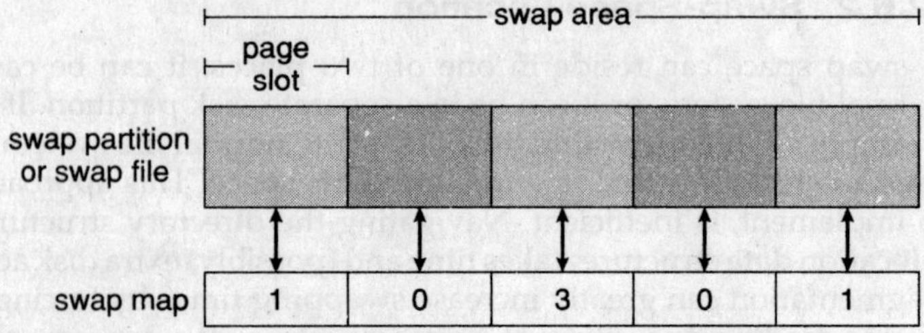

Figure 12.10 The data structures for swapping on Linux systems.

This scheme gives better performance on modern computers, which have more physical memory than older systems and tend to page less.

Linux is similar to Solaris in that swap space is only used for anonymous memory or for regions of memory shared by several processes. Linux allows one or more swap areas to be established. A swap area may be in either a swap file on a regular file system or a raw-swap-space partition. Each swap area consists of a series of 4-KB **page slots**, which are used to hold swapped pages. Associated with each swap area is a **swap map**—an array of integer counters, each corresponding to a page slot in the swap area. If the value of a counter is 0, the corresponding page slot is available. Values greater than 0 indicate that the page slot is occupied by a swapped page. The value of the counter indicates the number of mappings to the swapped page; for example, a value of 3 indicates that the swapped page is mapped to three different processes (which can occur if the swapped page is storing a region of memory shared by three processes). The data structures for swapping on Linux systems are shown in Figure 12.10.

12.7 RAID Structure

Disk drives have continued to get smaller and cheaper, so it is now economically feasible to attach many disks to a computer system. Having a large number of disks in a system presents opportunities for improving the rate at which data can be read or written, if the disks are operated in parallel. Furthermore, this setup offers the potential for improving the reliability of data storage, because redundant information can be stored on multiple disks. Thus, failure of one disk does not lead to loss of data. A variety of disk-organization techniques, collectively called **redundant arrays of independent disks** (**RAIDs**), are commonly used to address the performance and reliability issues.

In the past, RAIDs composed of small, cheap disks were viewed as a cost-effective alternative to large, expensive disks; today, RAIDs are used for their higher reliability and higher data-transfer rate, rather than for economic reasons. Hence, the *I* in *RAID*, which once stood for "inexpensive," now stands for "independent."

12.7.1 Improvement of Reliability via Redundancy

Let us first consider the reliability of RAIDs. The chance that some disk out of a set of *N* disks will fail is much higher than the chance that a specific single

> **STRUCTURING RAID**
>
> RAID storage can be structured in a variety of ways. For example, a system can have disks directly attached to its buses. In this case, the operating system or system software can implement RAID functionality. Alternatively, an intelligent host controller can control multiple attached disks and can implement RAID on those disks in hardware. Finally, a storage array, or RAID array, can be used. A RAID array is a standalone unit with its own controller, cache (usually), and disks. It is attached to the host via one or more standard ATA SCSI or FC controllers. This common setup allows any operating system and software without RAID functionality to have RAID-protected disks. It is even used on systems that do have RAID software layers because of its simplicity and flexibility.

disk will fail. Suppose that the mean time to failure of a single disk is 100,000 hours. Then the mean time to failure of some disk in an array of 100 disks will be 100,000/100 = 1,000 hours, or 41.66 days, which is not long at all! If we store only one copy of the data, then each disk failure will result in loss of a significant amount of data—and such a high rate of data loss is unacceptable.

The solution to the problem of reliability is to introduce redundancy; we store extra information that is not normally needed but that can be used in the event of failure of a disk to rebuild the lost information. Thus, even if a disk fails, data are not lost.

The simplest (but most expensive) approach to introducing redundancy is to duplicate every disk. This technique is called mirroring. With mirroring, a logical disk consists of two physical disks, and every write is carried out on both disks. The result is called a *mirrored volume*. If one of the disks in the volume fails, the data can be read from the other. Data will be lost only if the second disk fails before the first failed disk is replaced.

The mean time to failure of a mirrored volume—where *failure* is the loss of data— depends on two factors. One is the mean time to failure of the individual disks. The other is the mean time to repair, which is the time it takes (on average) to replace a failed disk and to restore the data on it. Suppose that the failures of the two disks are independent; that is, the failure of one disk is not connected to the failure of the other. Then, if the mean time to failure of a single disk is 100,000 hours and the mean time to repair is 10 hours, the mean time to data loss of a mirrored disk system is $100,000^2/(2 * 10) = 500 * 10^6$ hours, or 57,000 years!

You should be aware that the assumption of independence of disk failures is not valid. Power failures and natural disasters, such as earthquakes, fires, and floods, may result in damage to both disks at the same time. Also, manufacturing defects in a batch of disks can cause correlated failures. As disks age, the probability of failure grows, increasing the chance that a second disk will fail while the first is being repaired. In spite of all these considerations, however, mirrored-disk systems offer much higher reliability than do single-disk systems.

Power failures are a particular source of concern, since they occur far more frequently than do natural disasters. Even with mirroring of disks, if writes are in progress to the same block in both disks, and power fails before both blocks are fully written, the two blocks can be in an inconsistent state. One solution to this problem is to write one copy first, then the next. Another is to add a **nonvolatile RAM (NVRAM)** cache to the RAID array. This write-back cache is protected from data loss during power failures, so the write can be considered complete at that point, assuming the NVRAM has some kind of error protection and correction, such as ECC or mirroring.

12.7.2 Improvement in Performance via Parallelism

Now let's consider how parallel access to multiple disks improves performance. With disk mirroring, the rate at which read requests can be handled is doubled, since read requests can be sent to either disk (as long as both disks in a pair are functional, as is almost always the case). The transfer rate of each read is the same as in a single-disk system, but the number of reads per unit time has doubled.

With multiple disks, we can improve the transfer rate as well (or instead) by striping data across the disks. In its simplest form, **data striping** consists of splitting the bits of each byte across multiple disks; such striping is called **bit-level striping**. For example, if we have an array of eight disks, we write bit i of each byte to disk i. The array of eight disks can be treated as a single disk with sectors that are eight times the normal size and, more important, that have eight times the access rate. In such an organization, every disk participates in every access (read or write); so the number of accesses that can be processed per second is about the same as on a single disk, but each access can read eight times as many data in the same time as on a single disk.

Bit-level striping can be generalized to include a number of disks that either is a multiple of 8 or divides 8. For example, if we use an array of four disks, bits i and $4+i$ of each byte go to disk i. Further, striping need not occur at the bit level. In **block-level striping**, for instance, blocks of a file are striped across multiple disks; with n disks, block i of a file goes to disk $(i \bmod n)+1$. Other levels of striping, such as bytes of a sector or sectors of a block, also are possible. Block-level striping is the most common.

Parallelism in a disk system, as achieved through striping, has two main goals:

1. Increase the throughput of multiple small accesses (that is, page accesses) by load balancing.

2. Reduce the response time of large accesses.

12.7.3 RAID Levels

Mirroring provides high reliability, but it is expensive. Striping provides high data-transfer rates, but it does not improve reliability. Numerous schemes to provide redundancy at lower cost by using disk striping combined with "parity" bits (which we describe next) have been proposed. These schemes have different cost–performance trade-offs and are classified according to levels called **RAID levels**. We describe the various levels here; Figure 12.11 shows them pictorially (in the figure, P indicates error-correcting bits, and C

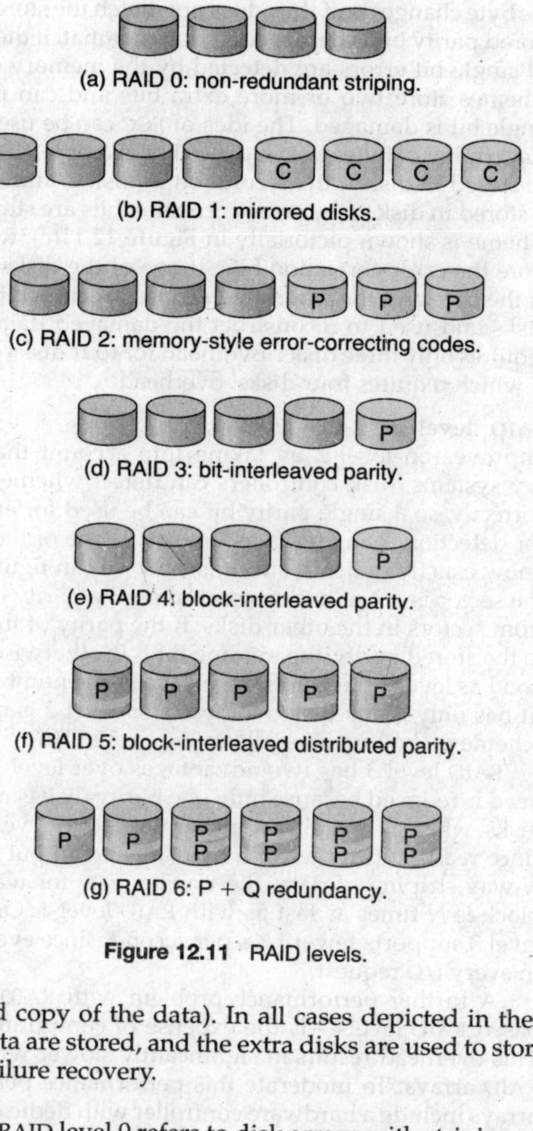

(a) RAID 0: non-redundant striping.

(b) RAID 1: mirrored disks.

(c) RAID 2: memory-style error-correcting codes.

(d) RAID 3: bit-interleaved parity.

(e) RAID 4: block-interleaved parity.

(f) RAID 5: block-interleaved distributed parity.

(g) RAID 6: P + Q redundancy.

Figure 12.11 RAID levels.

indicates a second copy of the data). In all cases depicted in the figure, four disks' worth of data are stored, and the extra disks are used to store redundant information for failure recovery.

- **RAID level 0**. RAID level 0 refers to disk arrays with striping at the level of blocks but without any redundancy (such as mirroring or parity bits), as shown in Figure 12.11(a).
- **RAID level 1**. RAID level 1 refers to disk mirroring. Figure 12.11(b) shows a mirrored organization.
- **RAID level 2**. RAID level 2 is also known as **memory-style error-correcting-code (ECC) organization**. Memory systems have long detected certain errors by using parity bits. Each byte in a memory system may have a parity bit associated with it that records whether the number of bits in the byte set to 1 is even (parity = 0) or odd (parity = 1). If one of the bits in the

byte is damaged (either a 1 becomes a 0, or a 0 becomes a 1), the parity of the byte changes and thus does not match the stored parity. Similarly, if the stored parity bit is damaged, it does not match the computed parity. Thus, all single-bit errors are detected by the memory system. Error-correcting schemes store two or more extra bits and can reconstruct the data if a single bit is damaged. The idea of ECC can be used directly in disk arrays via striping of bytes across disks. For example, the first bit of each byte can be stored in disk 1, the second bit in disk 2, and so on until the eighth bit is stored in disk 8; the error-correction bits are stored in further disks. This scheme is shown pictorially in Figure 12.11(c), where the disks labeled *P* store the error-correction bits. If one of the disks fails, the remaining bits of the byte and the associated error-correction bits can be read from other disks and used to reconstruct the damaged data. Note that RAID level 2 requires only three disks' overhead for four disks of data, unlike RAID level 1, which requires four disks' overhead.

- **RAID level 3**. RAID level 3, or **bit-interleaved parity organization**, improves on level 2 by taking into account the fact that, unlike memory systems, disk controllers can detect whether a sector has been read correctly, so a single parity bit can be used for error correction as well as for detection. The idea is as follows: If one of the sectors is damaged, we know exactly which sector it is, and we can figure out whether any bit in the sector is a 1 or a 0 by computing the parity of the corresponding bits from sectors in the other disks. If the parity of the remaining bits is equal to the stored parity, the missing bit is 0; otherwise, it is 1. RAID level 3 is as good as level 2 but is less expensive in the number of extra disks required (it has only a one-disk overhead), so level 2 is not used in practice. This scheme is shown pictorially in Figure 12.11(d).

  RAID level 3 has two advantages over level 1. First, the storage overhead is reduced because only one parity disk is needed for several regular disks, whereas one mirror disk is needed for every disk in level 1. Second, since reads and writes of a byte are spread out over multiple disks with *N*-way striping of data, the transfer rate for reading or writing a single block is *N* times as fast as with RAID level 1. On the negative side, RAID level 3 supports fewer I/Os per second, since every disk has to participate in every I/O request.

  A further performance problem with RAID 3—and with all parity-based RAID levels—is the expense of computing and writing the parity. This overhead results in significantly slower writes than with non-parity RAID arrays. To moderate this performance penalty, many RAID storage arrays include a hardware controller with dedicated parity hardware. This controller offloads the parity computation from the CPU to the array. The array has an NVRAM cache as well, to store the blocks while the parity is computed and to buffer the writes from the controller to the spindles. This combination can make parity RAID almost as fast as non-parity. In fact, a caching array doing parity RAID can outperform a non-caching non-parity RAID.

- **RAID level 4**. RAID level 4, or **block-interleaved parity organization**, uses block-level striping, as in RAID 0, and in addition keeps a parity block on a separate disk for corresponding blocks from *N* other disks. This scheme is diagramed in Figure 12.11(e). If one of the disks fails, the parity block can be used with the corresponding blocks from the other disks to restore the blocks of the failed disk.

A block read accesses only one disk, allowing other requests to be processed by the other disks. Thus, the data-transfer rate for each access is slower, but multiple read accesses can proceed in parallel, leading to a higher overall I/O rate. The transfer rates for large reads are high, since all the disks can be read in parallel; large writes also have high transfer rates, since the data and parity can be written in parallel.

Small independent writes cannot be performed in parallel. An operating-system write of data smaller than a block requires that the block be read, modified with the new data, and written back. The parity block has to be updated as well. This is known as the **read-modify-write cycle**. Thus, a single write requires four disk accesses: two to read the two old blocks and two to write the two new blocks.

WAFL (Chapter 11) uses RAID level 4 because this RAID level allows disks to be added to a RAID set seamlessly. If the added disks are initialized with blocks containing all zeros, then the parity value does not change, and the RAID set is still correct.

- **RAID level 5**. RAID level 5, or **block-interleaved distributed parity**, differs from level 4 by spreading data and parity among all $N+1$ disks, rather than storing data in N disks and parity in one disk. For each block, one of the disks stores the parity, and the others store data. For example, with an array of five disks, the parity for the nth block is stored in disk $(n \bmod 5)+1$; the nth blocks of the other four disks store actual data for that block. This setup is shown in Figure 12.11(f), where the Ps are distributed across all the disks. A parity block cannot store parity for blocks in the same disk, because a disk failure would result in loss of data as well as of parity, and hence the loss would not be recoverable. By spreading the parity across all the disks in the set, RAID 5 avoids potential overuse of a single parity disk, which can occur with RAID 4. RAID 5 is the most common parity RAID system.
- **RAID level 6**. RAID level 6, also called the **P + Q redundancy scheme**, is much like RAID level 5 but stores extra redundant information to guard against multiple disk failures. Instead of parity, error-correcting codes such as the **Reed–Solomon codes** are used. In the scheme shown in Figure 12.11(g), 2 bits of redundant data are stored for every 4 bits of data—compared with 1 parity bit in level 5—and the system can tolerate two disk failures.
- **RAID levels 0 + 1 and 1 + 0**. RAID level 0 + 1 refers to a combination of RAID levels 0 and 1. RAID 0 provides the performance, while RAID 1 provides the reliability. Generally, this level provides better performance than RAID 5. It is common in environments where both performance and reliability are important. Unfortunately, like RAID 1, it doubles the number of disks needed for storage, so it is also relatively expensive. In RAID 0 + 1, a set of disks are striped, and then the stripe is mirrored to another, equivalent stripe.

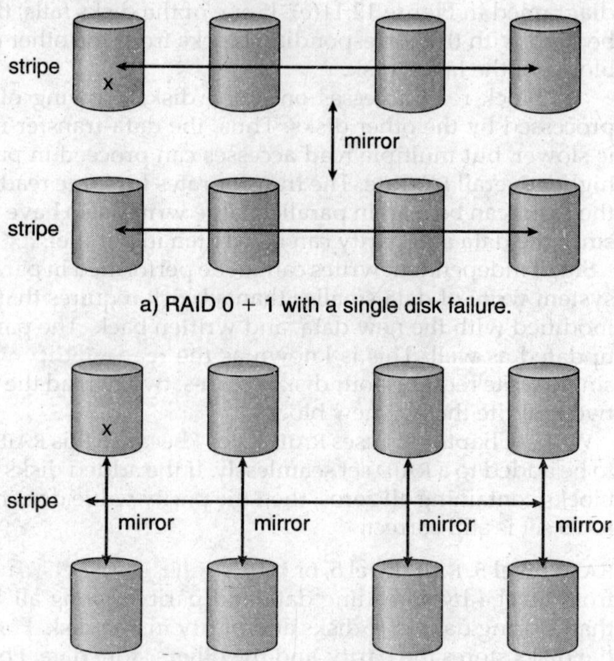

Figure 12.12 RAID 0 + 1 and 1 + 0.

Another RAID option that is becoming available commercially is RAID level 1 + 0, in which disks are mirrored in pairs and then the resulting mirrored pairs are striped. This scheme has some theoretical advantages over RAID 0 + 1. For example, if a single disk fails in RAID 0 + 1, an entire stripe is inaccessible, leaving only the other stripe available. With a failure in RAID 1 + 0, a single disk is unavailable, but the disk that mirrors it is still available, as are all the rest of the disks (Figure 12.12).

Numerous variations have been proposed to the basic RAID schemes described here. As a result, some confusion may exist about the exact definitions of the different RAID levels.

The implementation of RAID is another area of variation. Consider the following layers at which RAID can be implemented.

- Volume-management software can implement RAID within the kernel or at the system software layer. In this case, the storage hardware can provide a minimum of features and still be part of a full RAID solution. Parity RAID is fairly slow when implemented in software, so typically RAID 0, 1, or 0 + 1 is used.
- RAID can be implemented in the host bus-adapter (HBA) hardware. Only the disks directly connected to the HBA can be part of a given RAID set. This solution is low in cost but not very flexible.

- RAID can be implemented in the hardware of the storage array. The storage array can create RAID sets of various levels and can even slice these sets into smaller volumes, which are then presented to the operating system. The operating system need only implement the file system on each of the volumes. Arrays can have multiple connections available or can be part of a SAN, allowing multiple hosts to take advantage of the array's features.
- RAID can be implemented in the SAN interconnect layer by disk virtualization devices. In this case, a device sits between the hosts and the storage. It accepts commands from the servers and manages access to the storage. It could provide mirroring, for example, by writing each block to two separate storage devices.

Other features, such as snapshots and replication, can be implemented at each of these levels as well. **Replication** involves the automatic duplication of writes between separate sites for redundancy and disaster recovery. Replication can be synchronous or asynchronous. In synchronous replication, each block must be written locally and remotely before the write is considered complete, whereas in asynchronous replication, the writes are grouped together and written periodically. Asynchronous replication can result in data loss if the primary site fails, but it is faster and has no distance limitations.

The implementation of these features differs depending on the layer at which RAID is implemented. For example, if RAID is implemented in software, then each host may need to carry out and manage its own replication. If replication is implemented in the storage array or in the SAN interconnect, however, then whatever the host operating system or its features, the host's data can be replicated.

One other aspect of most RAID implementations is a hot spare disk or disks. A **hot spare** is not used for data but is configured to be used as a replacement in case of disk failure. For instance, a hot spare can be used to rebuild a mirrored pair should one of the disks in the pair fail. In this way, the RAID level can be reestablished automatically, without waiting for the failed disk to be replaced. Allocating more than one hot spare allows more than one failure to be repaired without human intervention.

12.7.4 Selecting a RAID Level

Given the many choices they have, how do system designers choose a RAID level? One consideration is rebuild performance. If a disk fails, the time needed to rebuild its data can be significant. This may be an important factor if a continuous supply of data is required, as it is in high-performance or interactive database systems. Furthermore, rebuild performance influences the mean time to failure.

Rebuild performance varies with the RAID level used. Rebuilding is easiest for RAID level 1, since data can be copied from another disk; for the other levels, we need to access all the other disks in the array to rebuild data in a failed disk. Rebuild times can be hours for RAID 5 rebuilds of large disk sets.

RAID level 0 is used in high-performance applications where data loss is not critical. RAID level 1 is popular for applications that require high reliability with fast recovery. RAID 0 + 1 and 1 + 0 are used where both performance and reliability are important—for example, for small databases. Due to RAID 1's

THE InServ STORAGE ARRAY

Innovation, in an effort to provide better, faster, and less expensive solutions, frequently blurs the lines that separated previous technologies. Consider the InServ storage array from 3Par. Unlike most other storage arrays, InServ does not require that a set of disks be configured at a specific RAID level. Rather, each disk is broken into 256-MB "chunklets." RAID is then applied at the chunklet level. A disk can thus participate in multiple and various RAID levels as its chunklets are used for multiple volumes.

InServ also provides snapshots similar to those created by the WAFL file system. The format of InServ snapshots can be read–write as well as read-only, allowing multiple hosts to mount copies of a given file system without needing their own copies of the entire file system. Any changes a host makes in its own copy are copy-on-write and so are not reflected in the other copies.

A further innovation is **utility storage**. Some file systems do not expand or shrink. On these systems, the original size is the only size, and any change requires copying data. An administrator can configure InServ to provide a host with a large amount of logical storage that initially occupies only a small amount of physical storage. As the host starts using the storage, unused disks are allocated to the host, up to the original logical level. The host thus can believe that it has a large fixed storage space, create its file systems there, and so on. Disks can be added or removed from the file system by InServ without the file systems noticing the change. This feature can reduce the number of drives needed by hosts, or at least delay the purchase of disks until they are really needed.

high space overhead, RAID level 5 is often preferred for storing large volumes of data. Level 6 is not supported currently by many RAID implementations, but it should offer better reliability than level 5.

RAID system designers and administrators of storage have to make several other decisions as well. For example, how many disks should be in a given RAID set? How many bits should be protected by each parity bit? If more disks are in an array, data-transfer rates are higher, but the system is more expensive. If more bits are protected by a parity bit, the space overhead due to parity bits is lower, but the chance that a second disk will fail before the first failed disk is repaired is greater, and that will result in data loss.

12.7.5 Extensions

The concepts of RAID have been generalized to other storage devices, including arrays of tapes, and even to the broadcast of data over wireless systems. When applied to arrays of tapes, RAID structures are able to recover data even if one of the tapes in an array is damaged. When applied to broadcast of data, a block of data is split into short units and is broadcast along with a parity unit; if one of the units is not received for any reason, it can be reconstructed from the other units. Commonly, tape-drive robots containing multiple tape drives will stripe data across all the drives to increase throughput and decrease backup time.

12.7.6 Problems with RAID

Unfortunately, RAID does not always assure that data are available for the operating system and its users. A pointer to a file could be wrong, for example, or pointers within the file structure could be wrong. Incomplete writes, if not properly recovered, could result in corrupt data. Some other process could accidentally write over a file system's structures, too. RAID protects against physical media errors, but not other hardware and software errors. As large as is the landscape of software and hardware bugs, that is how numerous are the potential perils for data on a system.

The Solaris ZFS file system takes an innovative approach to solving these problems through the use of **checksums** — a technique which is used to verify the integrity of data. ZFS maintains internal checksums of all blocks, including data and metadata. These checksums are not kept with the block that is being checksummed. Rather, they are stored with the pointer to that block. (See figure 12.13.) Consider an inode with pointers to its data. Within the inode is the checksum of each block of data. If there is a problem with the data, the checksum will be incorrect, and the file system will know about it. If the data are mirrored, and there is a block with a correct checksum and one with an incorrect checksum, ZFS will automatically update the bad block with the good one. Similarly, the directory entry that points to the inode has a checksum for the inode. Any problem in the inode is detected when the directory is accessed. This checksumming takes places throughout all ZFS structures, providing a much higher level of consistency, error detection, and error correction than is found in RAID disk sets or standard file systems. The extra overhead that is created by the checksum calculation and extra block read-modify-write cycles is not noticeable because the overall performance of ZFS is very fast.

Another issue with most RAID implementations is lack of flexibility. Consider a storage array with twenty disks divided into four sets of five disks. Each set of five disks is a RAID level 5 set. As a result, there are four separate

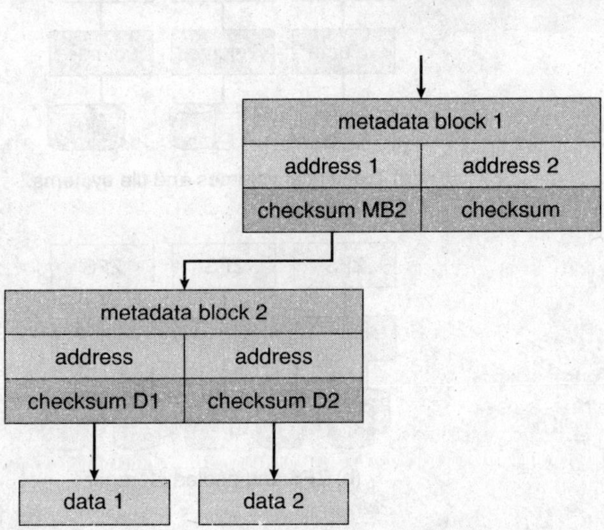

Figure 12.13 ZFS checksums all metadata and data.

volumes, each holding a file system. But what if one file system is too large to fit on a five-disk RAID level 5 set ? And what if another file system needs very little space? If such factors are known ahead of time, then the disks and volumes can be properly allocated. Very frequently, however, disk use and requirements change over time.

Even if the storage array allowed the entire set of twenty disks to be created as one large RAID set, other issues could arise. Several volumes of various sizes could be built on the set. But some volume managers do not allow us to change a volume's size. In that case, we would be left with the same issue described above—mismatched file-system sizes. Some volume managers allow size changes, but some file systems do not allow for file-system growth or shrinkage. The volumes could change sizes, but the file systems would need to be recreated to take advantage of those changes.

ZFS combines file-system management and volume management into a unit providing greater functionality than the traditional separation of those functions allows. Disks, or partitions of disks, are gathered together via RAID sets into **pools** of storage. A pool can hold one or more ZFS file systems. The entire pool's free space is available to all file systems within that pool. ZFS uses the memory model of "malloc" and "free" to allocate and release storage for each file system as blocks are used and freed within the file system. As a result, there are no artificial limits on storage use and no need to relocate file systems between volumes or resize volumes. ZFS provides quotas to limit the size of a file system and reservations to assure that a file system can grow by a specified amount, but those variables may be changed by the file system owner at any time. Figure 12.14(a) depicts traditional volumes and file systems, and Figure 12.14(b) shows the ZFS model.

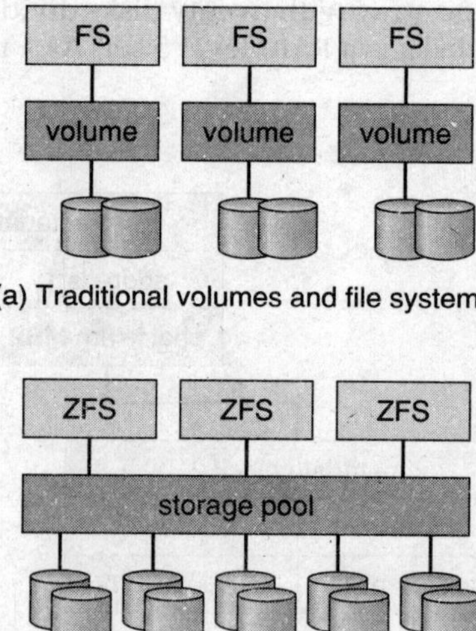

(a) Traditional volumes and file systems.

(b) ZFS and pooled storage.

Figure 12.14 (a) Traditional volumes and file systems. (b) A ZFS pool and file systems.

12.8 Stable-Storage Implementation

In Chapter 6, we introduced the write-ahead log, which requires the availability of stable storage. By definition, information residing in stable storage is *never* lost. To implement such storage, we need to replicate the required information on multiple storage devices (usually disks) with independent failure modes. We also need to coordinate the writing of updates in a way that guarantees that a failure during an update will not leave all the copies in a damaged state and that, when we are recovering from a failure, we can force all copies to a consistent and correct value, even if another failure occurs during the recovery. In this section, we discuss how to meet these needs.

A disk write results in one of three outcomes:

1. **Successful completion**. The data were written correctly on disk.
2. **Partial failure**. A failure occurred in the midst of transfer, so only some of the sectors were written with the new data, and the sector being written during the failure may have been corrupted.
3. **Total failure**. The failure occurred before the disk write started, so the previous data values on the disk remain intact.

Whenever a failure occurs during writing of a block, the system needs to detect it and invoke a recovery procedure to restore the block to a consistent state. To do that, the system must maintain two physical blocks for each logical block. An output operation is executed as follows:

1. Write the information onto the first physical block.
2. When the first write completes successfully, write the same information onto the second physical block.
3. Declare the operation complete only after the second write completes successfully.

During recovery from a failure, each pair of physical blocks is examined. If both are the same and no detectable error exists, then no further action is necessary. If one block contains a detectable error, then we replace its contents with the value of the other block. If neither block contains a detectable error, but the blocks differ in content, then we replace the content of the first block with that of the second. This recovery procedure ensures that a write to stable storage either succeeds completely or results in no change.

We can extend this procedure easily to allow the use of an arbitrarily large number of copies of each block of stable storage. Although having a large number of copies further reduces the probability of a failure, it is usually reasonable to simulate stable storage with only two copies. The data in stable storage are guaranteed to be safe unless a failure destroys all the copies.

Because waiting for disk writes to complete (synchronous I/O) is time consuming, many storage arrays add NVRAM as a cache. Since the memory is nonvolatile (it usually has battery power to back up the unit's power), it can be trusted to store the data en route to the disks. It is thus considered part of the stable storage. Writes to it are much faster than to disk, so performance is greatly improved.

12.9 Tertiary-Storage Structure

Would you buy a DVD or CD player that had one disk sealed inside? Of course not. You expect to use a DVD or CD player with many relatively inexpensive disks. On a computer as well, using many inexpensive cartridges with one drive lowers the overall cost. Low cost is the defining characteristic of tertiary storage, which we discuss in this section.

12.9.1 Tertiary-Storage Devices

Because cost is so important, in practice, tertiary storage is built with **removable media**. The most common examples are floppy disks, tapes, and read-only, write-once, and rewritable CDs and DVDs. Many any other kinds of tertiary-storage devices are available as well, including removable devices that store data in flash memory and interact with the computer system via a USB interface.

12.9.1.1 Removable Disks

Removable disks are one kind of tertiary storage. Floppy disks are an example of removable magnetic disks. They are made from a thin, flexible disk coated with magnetic material and enclosed in a protective plastic case. Although common floppy disks can hold only about 1 MB, similar technology is used for removable magnetic disks that hold more than 1 GB. Removable magnetic disks can be nearly as fast as hard disks, although the recording surface is at greater risk of damage from scratches.

A **magneto-optic disk** is another kind of removable disk. It records data on a rigid platter coated with magnetic material, but the recording technology is quite different from that for a magnetic disk. The magneto-optic head flies much farther from the disk surface than a magnetic disk head does, and the magnetic material is covered with a thick protective layer of plastic or glass. This arrangement makes the disk much more resistant to head crashes.

The magneto-optic disk drive has a coil that produces a magnetic field; at room temperature, the field is too large and too weak to magnetize a bit on the disk. To write a bit, the disk head flashes a laser beam at the disk surface. The laser is aimed at a tiny spot where a bit is to be written. The laser heats this spot, which makes the spot susceptible to the magnetic field. Now the large, weak magnetic field can record a tiny bit.

The magneto-optic head is too far from the disk surface to read the data by detecting the tiny magnetic fields in the way that the head of a hard disk does. Instead, the drive reads a bit using a property of laser light called the **Kerr effect**. When a laser beam is bounced off of a magnetic spot, the polarization of the laser beam is rotated clockwise or counterclockwise, depending on the orientation of the magnetic field. This rotation is what the head detects to read a bit.

Another category of removable disk is the **optical disk**. Optical disks do not use magnetism at all. Instead, they use special materials that can be altered by laser light to have relatively dark or bright spots. One example of optical-disk technology is the phase-change disk, which is coated with a material that can freeze into either a crystalline or an amorphous state. The crystalline state is more transparent, and hence a laser beam is brighter when it passes through the material and bounces off the reflective layer. The phase-change drive uses laser light at three different powers: low power to read data, medium power to erase the disk by melting and refreezing the recording medium into the crystalline state, and high power to melt the medium into the amorphous state to write to the disk. The most common examples of this technology are the re-recordable CD-RW and DVD-RW.

The kinds of disks just described can be used over and over. They are called read–write disks. In contrast, write-once, read-many-times (WORM) disks can be written only once. An old way to make a WORM disk is to manufacture a thin aluminum film sandwiched between two glass or plastic platters. To write a bit, the drive uses a laser light to burn a small hole through the aluminum. This burning cannot be reversed. Although it is possible to destroy the information on a WORM disk by burning holes everywhere, it is virtually impossible to alter data on the disk, because holes can only be added, and the ECC code associated with each sector is likely to detect such additions. WORM disks are considered durable and reliable because the metal layer is safely encapsulated between the protective glass or plastic platters and magnetic fields cannot damage the recording. A newer write-once technology records on an organic polymer dye instead of an aluminum layer; the dye absorbs laser light to form marks. This technology is used in the recordable CD-R and DVD-R.

Read-only disks, such as CD-ROM and DVD-ROM, come from the factory with the data prerecorded. They use technology similar to that of WORM disks (although the bits are pressed, not burned), and they are very durable.

Most removable disks are slower than their nonremovable counterparts. The writing process is slower, as are rotation and sometimes seek time.

12.9.1.2 Tapes

Magnetic tape is another type of removable medium. As a general rule, a tape holds more data than an optical or magnetic disk cartridge. Tape drives and disk drives have similar transfer rates. But random access to tape is much slower than a disk seek, because it requires a fast-forward or rewind operation that takes tens of seconds or even minutes.

Although a typical tape drive is more expensive than a typical disk drive, the price of a tape cartridge is lower than the price of the equivalent capacity of magnetic disks. So tape is an economical medium for purposes that do not require fast random access. Tapes are commonly used to hold backup copies of disk data. They are also used in large supercomputer centers to hold the enormous volumes of data used in scientific research and by large commercial enterprises.

Large tape installations typically use robotic tape changers that move tapes between tape drives and storage slots in a tape library. These mechanisms give the computer automated access to many tape cartridges.

A robotic tape library can lower the overall cost of data storage. A disk-resident file that will not be needed for a while can be archived to tape, where the cost per gigabyte is lower; if the file is needed in the future, the computer can stage it back into disk storage for active use. A robotic tape library is sometimes called near-line storage, since it is between the high performance of on-line magnetic disks and the low cost of off-line tapes sitting on shelves in a storage room.

12.9.1.3 Future Technology

In the future, other storage technologies may become important. Sometimes old technologies are used in new ways, as economics change or the technologies evolve. For example, solid-state disks, or SSDs, are growing in importance and becoming more common. Simply described, an SSD is a disk that is used like a hard drive. Depending on the memory technology used, it can be volatile or nonvolatile. The memory technology also affects performance. Nonvolatile SSDs have the same characteristics as traditional hard disks but can be more reliable because they have no moving parts and faster because they have no seek time or latency. In addition, they use less energy. However, they are more expensive per megabyte than traditional hard disks, have lower capacity than the larger hard disks, and may have shorter life-spans than hard disks; so their uses are limited. In one example, SSDs are being used in storage arrays to hold metadata which requires high-performance such as the journal of a journaling file system. SSDs are also being added to notebook computers to make them smaller, faster, and more energy efficient.

Another promising storage technology, holographic storage, uses laser light to record holographic photographs on special media. We can think of a hologram as a three-dimensional array of pixels. Each pixel represents one bit: 0 for black or 1 for white. And all the pixels in a hologram are transferred in one flash of laser light, so the data transfer rate is extremely high. With continued development, holographic storage may become commercially viable.

Another storage technology under active research is based on micro-electronic mechanical systems (MEMS). The idea is to apply the fabrication technologies that produce electronic chips to the manufacture of small data-storage machines. One proposal calls for the fabrication of an array of 10,000 tiny disk heads, with a square centimeter of magnetic storage material suspended above the array. When the storage material is moved lengthwise over the heads, each head accesses its own linear track of data on the material. The storage material can be shifted sideways slightly to enable all the heads to access their next track. Although it remains to be seen whether this technology can be successful, it may provide a nonvolatile data-storage technology that is faster than magnetic disk and cheaper than semiconductor DRAM.

Whether the storage medium is a removable magnetic disk, a DVD, or a magnetic tape, the operating system needs to provide several capabilities to use removable media for data storage. These capabilities are discussed in Section 12.9.2.

12.9.2 Operating-System Support

Two major jobs of an operating system are to manage physical devices and to present a virtual machine abstraction to applications. In this chapter, we have seen that, for hard disks, the operating system provides two abstractions. One is the raw device, which is just an array of data blocks. The other is a file system. For a file system on a magnetic disk, the operating system queues and schedules the interleaved requests from several applications. Now, we shall see how the operating system does its job when the storage media are removable.

12.9.2.1 Application Interface

Most operating systems can handle removable disks almost exactly as they do fixed disks. When a blank cartridge is inserted into the drive (or mounted), the cartridge must be formatted, and then an empty file system is generated on the disk. This file system is used just like a file system on a hard disk.

Tapes are often handled differently. The operating system usually presents a tape as a raw storage medium. An application does not open a file on the tape; it opens the whole tape drive as a raw device. Usually, the tape drive is then reserved for the exclusive use of that application until the application exits or closes the tape device. This exclusivity makes sense, because random access on a tape can take tens of seconds, or even a few minutes, so interleaving random accesses to tapes from more than one application would be likely to cause thrashing.

When the tape drive is presented as a raw device, the operating system does not provide file-system services. The application must decide how to use the array of blocks. For instance, a program that backs up a hard disk to tape might store a list of file names and sizes at the beginning of the tape and then copy the data of the files to the tape in that order.

It is easy to see the problems that can arise from this way of using tape. Since every application makes up its own rules for how to organize a tape, a tape full of data can generally be used only by the program that created it. For instance, even if we know that a backup tape contains a list of file names and file sizes followed by the file data, we will still find it difficult to use the tape. How exactly are the file names stored? Are the file sizes in binary or ASCII form? Are the files written one per block, or are they all concatenated in one tremendously long string of bytes? We do not even know the block size on the tape, because this variable is generally one that can be chosen separately for each block written.

For a disk drive, the basic operations are `read()`, `write()`, and `seek()`. Tape drives have a different set of basic operations. Instead of `seek()`, a tape drive uses the `locate()` operation. The tape `locate()` operation is more precise than the disk `seek()` operation, because it positions the tape to a specific logical block, rather than an entire track. Locating to block 0 is the same as rewinding the tape.

For most kinds of tape drives, it is possible to locate to any block that has been written on a tape. In a partly filled tape, however, it is not possible to locate into the empty space beyond the written area, because most tape drives do not manage their physical space in the same way disk drives do. For a disk drive, the sectors have a fixed size, and the formatting process must be used to place empty sectors in their final positions before any data can be written. Most tape drives have a variable block size, and the size of each block is determined on the fly, when that block is written. If an area of defective tape is encountered during writing, the bad area is skipped and the block is written again. This operation explains why it is not possible to locate into the empty space beyond the written area—the positions and numbers of the logical blocks have not yet been determined.

Most tape drives have a `read_position()` operation that returns the logical block number where the tape head is currently located. Many tape drives also support a `space()` operation for relative motion. So, for example, the operation `space(-2)` would locate backward over two logical blocks.

For most kinds of tape drives, writing a block has the side effect of logically erasing everything beyond the position of the write. In practice, this side effect means that most tape drives are append-only devices, because updating a block in the middle of the tape also effectively erases everything beyond that block. The tape drive implements this appending by placing an end-of-tape (EOT) mark after a block that is written. The drive refuses to locate past the EOT mark, but it is possible to locate to the EOT and then start writing. Doing so overwrites the old EOT mark and places a new one at the end of the new blocks just written.

In principle, a file system can be implemented on a tape. But many of the file-system data structures and algorithms would be different from those used for disks, because of the append-only property of tape.

12.9.2.2 File Naming

Another question that the operating system needs to handle is how to name files on removable media. For a fixed disk, naming is not difficult. On a PC, the file name consists of a drive letter followed by a path name. In UNIX, the file name does not contain a drive letter, but the mount table enables the operating system to discover on what drive the file is located. If the disk is removable, however, knowing what drive contained the cartridge at some time in the past does not mean knowing how to find the file. If every removable cartridge in the world had a different serial number, the name of a file on a removable device could be prefixed with the serial number, but to ensure that no two serial numbers are the same would require each one to be about 12 digits in length. Who could remember the names of her files if she had to memorize a 12-digit serial number for each one?

The problem becomes even more difficult when we want to write data on a removable cartridge on one computer and then use the cartridge in another computer. If both machines are of the same type and have the same kind of removable drive, the only difficulty is knowing the contents and data layout on the cartridge. But if the machines or drives are different, many additional problems can arise. Even if the drives are compatible, different computers may store bytes in different orders and may use different encodings for binary numbers and even for letters (such as ASCII on PCs versus EBCDIC on mainframes).

Today's operating systems generally leave the name-space problem unsolved for removable media and depend on applications and users to figure out how to access and interpret the data. Fortunately, a few kinds of removable media are so well standardized that all computers use them the same way. One example is the CD. Music CDs use a universal format that is understood by any CD drive. Data CDs are available in only a few different formats, so it is usual for a CD drive and the operating-system device driver to be programmed to handle all the common formats. DVD formats are also well standardized.

12.9.2.3 Hierarchical Storage Management

A **robotic jukebox** enables the computer to change the removable cartridge in a tape or disk drive without human assistance. Two major uses of this technology are for backups and hierarchical storage systems. The use of a jukebox for backups is simple: When one cartridge becomes full, the computer instructs the jukebox to switch to the next cartridge. Some jukeboxes hold tens of drives and thousands of cartridges, with robotic arms managing the movement of tapes to the drives.

A hierarchical storage system extends the storage hierarchy beyond primary memory and secondary storage (that is, magnetic disk) to incorporate tertiary storage. Tertiary storage is usually implemented as a jukebox of tapes or removable disks. This level of the storage hierarchy is larger, cheaper, and slower.

Although the virtual memory system can be extended in a straightforward manner to tertiary storage, this extension is rarely carried out in practice. The reason is that a retrieval from a jukebox can take tens of seconds or even minutes, and such a long delay is intolerable for demand paging and for other forms of virtual memory use.

The usual way to incorporate tertiary storage is to extend the file system. Small and frequently used files remain on magnetic disk, while large and old files that are not actively used are archived to the jukebox. In some file-archiving systems, the directory entry for the file continues to exist, but the contents of the file no longer occupy space in secondary storage. If an application tries to open the file, the `open()` system call is suspended until the file contents can be staged in from tertiary storage. When the contents are again available from magnetic disk, the `open()` operation returns control to the application, which proceeds to use the disk-resident copy of the data.

Today, **hierarchical storage management (HSM)** is usually found in installations that have large volumes of data that are used seldom, sporadically, or periodically. Current work in HSM includes extending it to provide full **information life-cycle management (ILM)**. Here, data move from disk to tape and back to disk, as needed, but are deleted on a schedule or according to policy. For example, some sites save e-mail for seven years but want to be sure that at the end of seven years it is destroyed. At that point, the data might be on disk, HSM tape, and backup tape. ILM centralizes knowledge of where the data are so that policies can be applied across all these locations.

12.9.3 Performance Issues

As with any component of the operating system, the three most important aspects of tertiary-storage performance are speed, reliability, and cost.

12.9.3.1 Speed

The speed of tertiary storage has two aspects: bandwidth and latency. We measure the bandwidth in bytes per second. The **sustained bandwidth** is the average data rate during a large transfer—that is, the number of bytes divided by the transfer time. The **effective bandwidth** calculates the average over the entire I/O time, including the time for `seek()` or `locate()` and any cartridge-switching time in a jukebox. In essence, the sustained bandwidth is the rate at which the data stream actually flows, and the effective bandwidth is the overall data rate provided by the drive. The *bandwidth of a drive* is generally understood to mean the sustained bandwidth.

For removable disks, the bandwidth ranges from a few megabytes per second for the slowest to over 40 MB per second for the fastest. Tapes have a similar range of bandwidths, from a few megabytes per second to over 30 MB per second.

The second aspect of speed is the **access latency**. By this performance measure, disks are much faster than tapes. Disk storage is essentially two-dimensional—all the bits are out in the open. A disk access simply moves the arm to the selected cylinder and waits for the rotational latency, which may take less than 5 milliseconds. By contrast, tape storage is three-dimensional. At any time, a small portion of the tape is accessible to the head, whereas most of the bits are buried below hundreds or thousands of layers of tape wound on the reel. A random access on tape requires winding the tape reels until the selected block reaches the tape head, which can take tens or hundreds of seconds. So we can generally say that random access within a tape cartridge is more than a thousand times slower than random access on disk.

If a jukebox is involved, the access latency can be significantly higher. For a removable disk to be changed, the drive must stop spinning, then the robotic arm must switch the disk cartridges, and then the drive must spin up the new cartridge. This operation takes several seconds—about a hundred times longer than the random-access time within one disk. So switching disks in a jukebox incurs a relatively high performance penalty.

For tapes, the robotic-arm time is about the same as for disks. But for tapes to be switched, the old tape generally must rewind before it can be ejected, and that operation can take as long as 4 minutes. And, after a new tape is loaded into the drive, many seconds can be required for the drive to calibrate itself to the tape and to prepare for I/O. Although a slow tape jukebox can have a tape-switch time of 1 or 2 minutes, this time is not enormously greater than the random-access time within one tape.

To generalize, we can say that random access in a disk jukebox has a latency of tens of seconds, whereas random access in a tape jukebox has a latency of hundreds of seconds; switching tapes is expensive, but switching disks is not. We must be careful not to overgeneralize, though. Some expensive tape jukeboxes can rewind, eject, load a new tape, and fast-forward to a random item of data all in less than 30 seconds.

If we pay attention to only the performance of the drives in a jukebox, the bandwidth and latency seem reasonable. But if we focus our attention on the cartridges instead, we find a terrible bottleneck. Consider first the bandwidth. The bandwidth-to-storage-capacity ratio of a robotic library is much less favorable than that of a fixed disk. To read all the data stored on a large hard disk could take about an hour. To read all the data stored in a large tape library could take years. The situation with respect to access latency is nearly as bad. To illustrate, if 100 requests are queued for a disk drive, the average waiting time will be about a second. If 100 requests are queued for a tape library, the average waiting time could be over an hour. The low cost of tertiary storage results from having many cheap cartridges share a few expensive drives. But a removable library is best devoted to the storage of infrequently used data, because the library can satisfy only a relatively small number of I/O requests per hour.

12.9.3.2 Reliability

Although we often think *good performance* means *high speed,* another important aspect of performance is *reliability.* If we try to read some data and are unable to do so because of a drive or media failure, for all practical purposes the access time is infinitely long and the bandwidth is infinitely small. So it is important to understand the reliability of removable media.

Removable magnetic disks are somewhat less reliable than are fixed hard disks, because they are more likely to be exposed to harmful environmental conditions such as dust, large changes in temperature and humidity, and mechanical forces such as shock and bending. Optical disks are considered very reliable, because the layer that stores the bits is protected by a transparent plastic or glass layer. The reliability of magnetic tape varies widely, depending on the kind of drive. Some inexpensive drives wear out tapes after a few dozen uses; other drives are gentle enough to allow millions of reuses. By comparison with a magnetic-disk head, the head in a magnetic-tape drive is a weak spot. A disk head flies above the media, but a tape head is in close contact with the tape. The scrubbing action of the tape can wear out the head after a few thousands or tens of thousands of hours.

In summary, we can say that a fixed-disk drive is likely to be more reliable than a removable-disk or tape drive, and an optical disk is likely to be more reliable than a magnetic disk or tape. But a fixed magnetic disk has one weakness. A head crash in a hard disk generally destroys the data, whereas the failure of a tape drive or optical-disk drive often leaves the data cartridge unharmed.

12.9.3.3 Cost

Storage cost is another important factor. Here is a concrete example of how removable media may lower the overall storage cost. Suppose that a hard disk that holds X GB has a price of \$200; of this amount, \$190 is for the housing, motor, and controller, and \$10 is for the magnetic platters. The storage cost for this disk is \$200/X per gigabyte. Now, suppose that we can manufacture the platters in a removable cartridge. For one drive and 10 cartridges, the total price is \$190 + \$100, and the capacity is 10X GB, so the storage cost is \$29/X per gigabyte. Even if it is a little more expensive to make a removable cartridge, the cost per gigabyte of removable storage may well be lower than the cost per gigabyte of a hard disk, because the expense of one drive is averaged with the low price of many removable cartridges.

Figures 12.15, 12.16, and 12.17 show cost trends per megabyte for DRAM memory, magnetic hard disks, and tape drives. The prices in the graphs are the lowest prices found in advertisements in various computer magazines and on the World Wide Web at the end of each year. These prices reflect the small-computer marketplace of the readership of these magazines, where prices are low by comparison with the mainframe and minicomputer markets. In the case of tape, the price is for a drive with one tape. The overall cost of tape storage becomes much lower as more tapes are purchased for use with the drive,

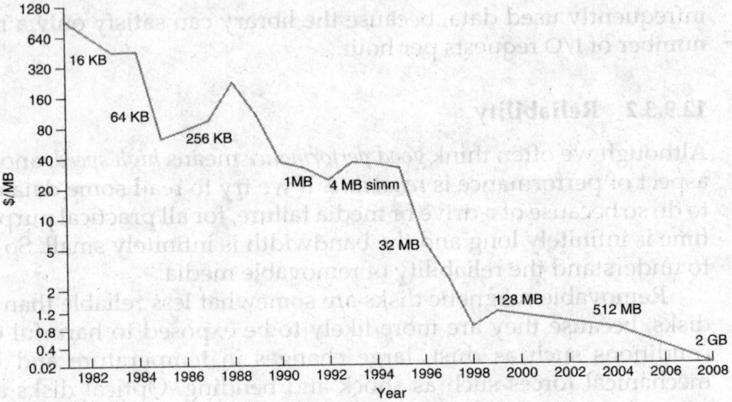

Figure 12.15 Price per megabyte of DRAM, from 1981 to 2008.

because the price of a tape is a small fraction of the price of the drive. However, in a huge tape library containing thousands of cartridges, the storage cost is dominated by the cost of the tape cartridges. As of 2004, the cost per GB of tape cartridges was around $.40.

As Figure 12.15 shows, the cost of DRAM fluctuates widely. In the period from 1981 to 2004, we can see three price crashes (around 1981, 1989, and 1996) as excess production caused a glut in the marketplace. We can also see two periods (around 1987 and 1993) where shortages in the marketplace caused significant price increases. In the case of hard disks (Figure 12.16), the price decline has been steadier. Tape-drive prices also fell steadily up to 1997 (Figure 12.17). Since 1997, the price per gigabyte of inexpensive tape drives has ceased its dramatic fall, although the price of mid-range tape technology (such as DAT/DDS) has continued to fall and is now approaching that of the

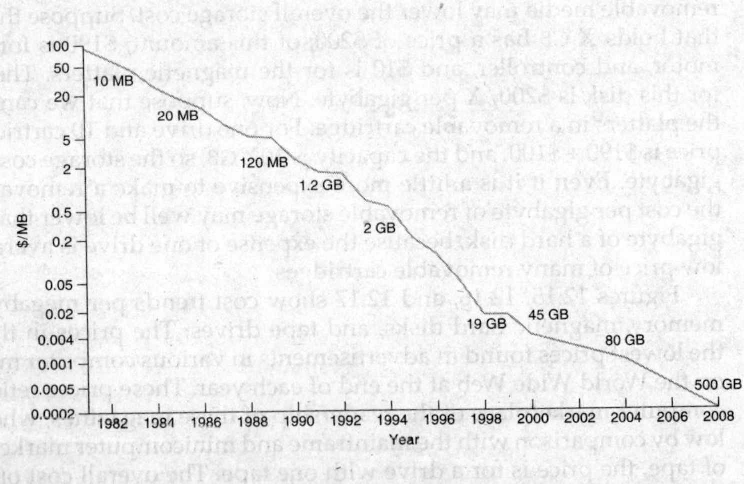

Figure 12.16 Price per megabyte of magnetic hard disk, from 1981 to 2008.

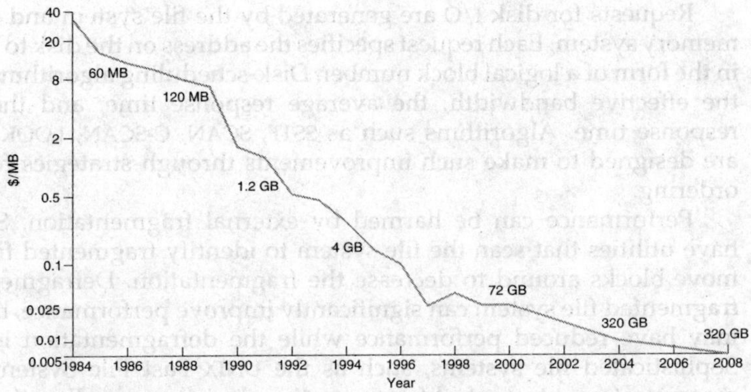

Figure 12.17 Price per megabyte of a tape drive, from 1984 to 2008.

inexpensive drives. Tape-drive prices are not shown for years prior to 1984, because, as mentioned, the magazines used in tracking prices are targeted to the small-computer marketplace, and tape drives were not widely used with small computers prior to 1984.

We can see from these graphs that the cost of storage has fallen dramatically. By comparing the graphs, we can also see that the price of disk storage has plummeted relative to the price of DRAM and tape.

The price per megabyte of magnetic disk storage improved by more than four orders of magnitude from 1981 to 2004, whereas the corresponding improvement for main memory was only three orders of magnitude. Main memory today is more expensive than disk storage by a factor of 100.

The price per megabyte dropped much more rapidly for disk drives than for tape drives as well. In fact, the price per megabyte of a magnetic disk drive is approaching that of a tape cartridge without the tape drive. Consequently, small- and medium-sized tape libraries have a higher storage cost than disk systems with equivalent capacity.

The dramatic fall in disk prices has largely rendered tertiary storage obsolete. We no longer have any tertiary storage technology that is orders of magnitude less expensive than magnetic disk. It appears that the revival of tertiary storage must await a revolutionary technology breakthrough. Meanwhile, tape storage will find its use mostly limited to purposes such as backups of disk drives and archival storage in enormous tape libraries that greatly exceed the practical storage capacity of large disk farms.

12.10 Summary

Disk drives are the major secondary-storage I/O devices on most computers. Most secondary storage devices are either magnetic disks or magnetic tapes. Modern disk drives are structured as large one-dimensional arrays of logical disk blocks. Generally, these logical blocks are 512 bytes in size. Disks may be attached to a computer system in one of two ways: (1) through the local I/O ports on the host computer or (2) through a network connection.

Requests for disk I/O are generated by the file system and by the virtual memory system. Each request specifies the address on the disk to be referenced, in the form of a logical block number. Disk-scheduling algorithms can improve the effective bandwidth, the average response time, and the variance in response time. Algorithms such as SSTF, SCAN, C-SCAN, LOOK, and C-LOOK are designed to make such improvements through strategies for disk-queue ordering.

Performance can be harmed by external fragmentation. Some systems have utilities that scan the file system to identify fragmented files; they then move blocks around to decrease the fragmentation. Defragmenting a badly fragmented file system can significantly improve performance, but the system may have reduced performance while the defragmentation is in progress. Sophisticated file systems, such as the UNIX Fast File System, incorporate many strategies to control fragmentation during space allocation so that disk reorganization is not needed.

The operating system manages the disk blocks. First, a disk must be low-level-formatted to create the sectors on the raw hardware—new disks usually come preformatted. Then, the disk is partitioned, file systems are created, and boot blocks are allocated to store the system's bootstrap program. Finally, when a block is corrupted, the system must have a way to lock out that block or to replace it logically with a spare.

Because an efficient swap space is a key to good performance, systems usually bypass the file system and use raw disk access for paging I/O. Some systems dedicate a raw disk partition to swap space, and others use a file within the file system instead. Still other systems allow the user or system administrator to make the decision by providing both options.

Because of the amount of storage required on large systems, disks are frequently made redundant via RAID algorithms. These algorithms allow more than one disk to be used for a given operation and allow continued operation and even automatic recovery in the face of a disk failure. RAID algorithms are organized into different levels; each level provides some combination of reliability and high transfer rates.

The write-ahead log scheme requires the availability of stable storage. To implement such storage, we need to replicate the needed information on multiple nonvolatile storage devices (usually disks) with independent failure modes. We also need to update the information in a controlled manner to ensure that we can recover the stable data after any failure during data transfer or recovery.

Tertiary storage is built from disk and tape drives that use removable media. Many different technologies are available, including magnetic tape, removable magnetic and magneto-optic disks, and optical disks.

For removable disks, the operating system generally provides the full services of a file-system interface, including space management and request-queue scheduling. For many operating systems, the name of a file on a removable cartridge is a combination of a drive name and a file name within that drive. This convention is simpler but potentially more confusing than is using a name that identifies a specific cartridge.

For tapes, the operating system generally provides only a raw interface. Many operating systems have no built-in support for jukeboxes. Jukebox support can be provided by a device driver or by a privileged application designed for backups or for HSM.

Three important aspects of performance are bandwidth, latency, and reliability. Many bandwidths are available for both disks and tapes, but the random-access latency for a tape is generally much greater than that for a disk. Switching cartridges in a jukebox is also relatively slow. Because a jukebox has a low ratio of drives to cartridges, reading a large fraction of the data in a jukebox can take a long time. Optical media, which protect the sensitive layer with a transparent coating, are generally more robust than magnetic media, which are more likely to expose the magnetic material to physical damage. Lastly, the cost of storage has decreased greatly in the past two decades, most notably for disk storage.

Exercises

12.1 What would be the effects on cost and performance if tape storage had the same areal density as disk storage? (*Areal density* is the number of gigabits per square inch.)

12.2 It is sometimes said that tape is a sequential-access medium, whereas a magnetic disk is a random-access medium. In fact, the suitability of a storage device for random access depends on the transfer size. The term *streaming transfer rate* denotes the rate for a data transfer that is underway, excluding the effect of access latency. By contrast, the *effective transfer rate* is the ratio of total bytes per total seconds, including overhead time such as access latency.

Suppose that, in a computer, the level-2 cache has an access latency of 8 nanoseconds and a streaming transfer rate of 800 megabytes per second, the main memory has an access latency of 60 nanoseconds and a streaming transfer rate of 80 megabytes per second, the magnetic disk has an access latency of 15 milliseconds and a streaming transfer rate of 5 megabytes per second, and a tape drive has an access latency of 60 seconds and a streaming transfer rate of 2 megabytes per seconds.

a. Random access causes the effective transfer rate of a device to decrease, because no data are transferred during the access time. For the disk described, what is the effective transfer rate if an average access is followed by a streaming transfer of (1) 512 bytes, (2) 8 kilobytes, (3) 1 megabyte, and (4) 16 megabytes?

b. The utilization of a device is the ratio of effective transfer rate to streaming transfer rate. Calculate the utilization of the disk drive for each of the four transfer sizes given in part a.

c. Suppose that a utilization of 25 percent (or higher) is considered acceptable. Using the performance figures given, compute the smallest transfer size for disk that gives acceptable utilization.

d. Complete the following sentence: A disk is a random-access device for transfers larger than ______ bytes and is a sequential-access device for smaller transfers.

e. Compute the minimum transfer sizes that give acceptable utilization for cache, memory, and tape.

f. When is a tape a random-access device, and when is it a sequential-access device?

12.3 The reliability of a hard-disk drive is typically described in terms of a quantity called *mean time between failures* (MTBF). Although this quantity is called a "time," the MTBF actually is measured in drive-hours per failure.

a. If a system contains 1,000 disk drives, each of which has a 750,000-hour MTBF, which of the following best describes how often a drive failure will occur in that disk farm: once per thousand years, once per century, once per decade, once per year, once per month, once per week, once per day, once per hour, once per minute, or once per second?

b. Mortality statistics indicate that, on the average, a U.S. resident has about 1 chance in 1,000 of dying between the ages of 20 and 21. Deduce the MTBF hours for 20-year-olds. Convert this figure from hours to years. What does this MTBF tell you about the expected lifetime of a 20-year-old?

c. The manufacturer guarantees a 1-million-hour MTBF for a certain model of disk drive. What can you conclude about the number of years for which one of these drives is under warranty?

12.4 Discuss how an operating system could maintain a free-space list for a tape-resident file system. Assume that the tape technology is append-only and that it uses EOT marks and `locate`, `space`, and `read position` commands as described in Section 12.9.2.1.

12.5 Imagine that a holographic storage drive has been invented. The drive costs $10,000 and has an average access time of 40 milliseconds. It uses a $100 cartridge the size of a CD. This cartridge holds 40,000 images, and each image is a square black-and-white picture with a resolution of $6,000 \times 6,000$ pixels (each pixel stores 1 bit). The drive can read or write one picture in 1 millisecond. Answer the following questions.

a. What would be some good uses for this device?

b. How would this device affect the I/O performance of a computing system?

c. What kinds of storage devices, if any, would become obsolete as a result of the invention of this device?

12.6 The term "Fast Wide SCSI-II" denotes a SCSI bus that operates at a data rate of 20 megabytes per second when it moves a packet of bytes between the host and a device. Suppose that a Fast Wide SCSI-II disk drive spins at 7,200 RPM, has a sector size of 512 bytes, and holds 160 sectors per track.

a. Estimate the sustained transfer rate of this drive in megabytes per second.

b. Suppose that the drive has 7,000 cylinders, 20 tracks per cylinder, a head-switch time (from one platter to another) of 0.5 millisecond, and an adjacent-cylinder seek time of 2 milliseconds. Use this additional information to give an accurate estimate of the sustained transfer rate for a huge transfer.

c. Suppose that the average seek time for the drive is 8 milliseconds. Estimate the I/O operations per second and the effective transfer rate for a random-access workload that reads individual sectors that are scattered across the disk.

d. Calculate the random-access I/O operations per second and transfer rate for I/O sizes of 4 kilobytes, 8 kilobytes, and 64 kilobytes.

e. If multiple requests are in the queue, a scheduling algorithm such as SCAN should be able to reduce the average seek distance. Suppose that a random-access workload is reading 8-kilobyte pages, the average queue length is 10, and the scheduling algorithm reduces the average seek time to 3 milliseconds. Now calculate the I/O operations per second and the effective transfer rate of the drive.

12.7 Compare the performance of write operations achieved by a RAID level 5 organization with that achieved by a RAID level 1 organization.

12.8 Suppose that a disk drive has 5,000 cylinders, numbered 0 to 4999. The drive is currently serving a request at cylinder 143, and the previous request was at cylinder 125. The queue of pending requests, in FIFO order, is:

86, 1470, 913, 1774, 948, 1509, 1022, 1750, 130

Starting from the current head position, what is the total distance (in cylinders) that the disk arm moves to satisfy all the pending requests for each of the following disk-scheduling algorithms?

a. FCFS

b. SSTF

c. SCAN
d. LOOK
e. C-SCAN
f. C-LOOK

12.9 Elementary physics states that when an object is subjected to a constant acceleration a, the relationship between distance d and time t is given by $d = \frac{1}{2}at^2$. Suppose that, during a seek, the disk in Exercise 12.8 accelerates the disk arm at a constant rate for the first half of the seek, then decelerates the disk arm at the same rate for the second half of the seek. Assume that the disk can perform a seek to an adjacent cylinder in 1 millisecond and a full-stroke seek over all 5,000 cylinders in 18 milliseconds.

a. The distance of a seek is the number of cylinders that the head moves. Explain why the seek time is proportional to the square root of the seek distance.

b. Write an equation for the seek time as a function of the seek distance. This equation should be of the form $t = x + y\sqrt{L}$, where t is the time in milliseconds and L is the seek distance in cylinders.

c. Calculate the total seek time for each of the schedules in Exercise 12.8. Determine which schedule is the fastest (has the smallest total seek time).

d. The *percentage speedup* is the time saved divided by the original time. What is the percentage speedup of the fastest schedule over FCFS?

12.10 The accelerating seek described in Exercise 12.9 is typical of hard-disk drives. By contrast, floppy disks (and many hard disks manufactured before the mid-1980s) typically seek at a fixed rate. Suppose that the disk in Exercise 12.9 has a constant-rate seek rather than a constant-acceleration seek, so the seek time is of the form $t = x + yL$, where t is the time in milliseconds and L is the seek distance. Suppose that the time to seek to an adjacent cylinder is 1 millisecond, as before, and the time to seek to each additional cylinder is 0.5 milliseconds.

a. Write an equation for this seek time as a function of the seek distance.

b. Using this seek-time function, calculate the total seek time for each of the schedules in Exercise 12.8. Is your answer the same as the one for Exercise 12.9(c)?

c. What is the percentage speedup of the fastest schedule over FCFS in this case?

12.11 Suppose that the disk in Exercise 12.9 rotates at 7,200 RPM.

a. What is the average rotational latency of this disk drive?

b. What seek distance can be covered in the time that you found for part a?

12.12 Suppose that a one-sided 5.25-inch optical-disk cartridge has an areal density of 1 gigabit per square inch. Further suppose that a magnetic tape has an areal density of 20 megabits per square inch and is 1/2 inch wide and 1,800 feet long. Calculate an estimate of the storage capacities of these two kinds of storage media. Suppose that an optical tape exists that has the same physical size as the magnetic tape but the same storage density as the optical disk. What volume of data could the optical tape hold? What would be a marketable price for the optical tape if the magnetic tape cost $25?

12.13 Write a program that simulates the disk-scheduling algorithms discussed in Section 12.4.

12.14 Why is rotational latency usually not considered in disk scheduling? How would you modify SSTF, SCAN, and C-SCAN to include latency optimization?

12.15 Remapping bad blocks by sector sparing or sector slipping can influence performance. Suppose that the drive in Exercise 12.6 has a total of 100 bad sectors at random locations and that each bad sector is mapped to a spare that is located on a different track within the same cylinder. Estimate the number of I/O operations per second and the effective transfer rate for a random-access workload consisting of 8-kilobyte reads, assuming a queue length of 1 (that is, the choice of scheduling algorithm is not a factor). What is the effect of a bad sector on performance?

12.16 Discuss the relative advantages and disadvantages of sector sparing and sector slipping.

12.17 Compare the performance of C-SCAN and SCAN scheduling, assuming a uniform distribution of requests. Consider the average response time (the time between the arrival of a request and the completion of that request's service), the variation in response time, and the effective bandwidth. How does performance depend on the relative sizes of seek time and rotational latency?

12.18 None of the disk-scheduling disciplines, except FCFS, is truly *fair* (starvation may occur).

a. Explain why this assertion is true.

b. Describe a way to modify algorithms such as SCAN to ensure fairness.

c. Explain why fairness is an important goal in a time-sharing system.

d. Give three or more examples of circumstances in which it is important that the operating system be *unfair* in serving I/O requests.

12.19 Consider a RAID level 5 organization comprising five disks, with the parity for sets of four blocks on four disks stored on the fifth disk. How many blocks are accessed in order to perform the following?

a. A write of one block of data

b. A write of seven continuous blocks of data

12.20 The operating system generally treats removable disks as shared file systems but assigns a tape drive to only one application at a time. Give three reasons that could explain this difference in treatment of disks and tapes. Describe the additional features that an operating system would need to support shared file-system access to a tape jukebox. Would the applications sharing the tape jukebox need any special properties, or could they use the files as though the files were disk-resident? Explain your answer.

12.21 How would use of a RAM disk affect your selection of a disk-scheduling algorithm? What factors would you need to consider? Do the same considerations apply to hard-disk scheduling, given that the file system stores recently used blocks in a buffer cache in main memory?

12.22 You can use simple estimates to compare the cost and performance of a terabyte storage system made entirely from disks with one that incorporates tertiary storage. Suppose that each magnetic disk holds 10 GB, costs $1,000, transfers 5 MB per second, and has an average access latency of 15 milliseconds. Also suppose that a tape library costs $10 per gigabyte, transfers 10 MB per second, and has an average access latency of 20 seconds. Compute the total cost, the maximum total data rate, and the average waiting time for a pure disk system. If you make any assumptions about the workload, describe and justify them. Now, suppose that 5 percent of the data are frequently used, so they must reside on disk, but the other 95 percent are archived in the tape library. Further suppose that the disk system handles 95 percent of the requests and the library handles the other 5 percent. What are the total cost, the maximum total data rate, and the average waiting time for this hierarchical storage system?

12.23 Assume that you have a mixed configuration comprising disks organized as RAID level 1 and RAID level 5 disks. Assume that the system has flexibility in deciding which disk organization to use for storing a particular file. Which files should be stored in the RAID level 1 disks and which in the RAID level 5 disks in order to optimize performance?

12.24 What are the tradeoffs involved in rereading code pages from the file system versus using swap space to store them?

12.25 Requests are not usually uniformly distributed. For example, we can expect a cylinder containing the file-system FAT or inodes to be accessed more frequently than a cylinder containing only files. Suppose you know that 50 percent of the requests are for a small, fixed number of cylinders.

a. Would any of the scheduling algorithms discussed in this chapter be particularly good for this case? Explain your answer.

b. Propose a disk-scheduling algorithm that gives even better performance by taking advantage of this "hot spot" on the disk.

c. File systems typically find data blocks via an indirection table, such as a FAT in DOS or inodes in UNIX. Describe one or more ways to take advantage of this indirection to improve disk performance.

12.26 Discuss the reasons why the operating system might require accurate information on how blocks are stored on a disk. How could the operating system improve file system performance with this knowledge?

12.27 In a disk jukebox, what would be the effect of having more open files than the number of drives in the jukebox?

12.28 Compare the throughput achieved by a RAID level 5 organization with that achieved by a RAID level 1 organization for the following:

a. Read operations on single blocks

b. Read operations on multiple contiguous blocks

12.29 Could a RAID level 1 organization achieve better performance for read requests than a RAID level 0 organization (with nonredundant striping of data)? If so, how?

Bibliographical Notes

Discussions of redundant arrays of independent disks (RAIDs) are presented by Patterson et al. [1988] and in the detailed survey of Chen et al. [1994]. Disk-system architectures for high-performance computing are discussed by Katz et al. [1989]. Enhancements to RAID systems are discussed in Wilkes et al. [1996] and Yu et al. [2000]. Teorey and Pinkerton [1972] present an early comparative analysis of disk-scheduling algorithms. They use simulations that model a disk for which seek time is linear in the number of cylinders crossed. For this disk, LOOK is a good choice for queue lengths below 140, and C-LOOK is good for queue lengths above 100. King [1990] describes ways to improve the seek time by moving the disk arm when the disk is otherwise idle. Seltzer et al. [1990] and Jacobson and Wilkes [1991] describe disk-scheduling algorithms that consider rotational latency in addition to seek time. Scheduling optimizations that exploit disk idle times are discussed in Lumb et al. [2000]. Worthington et al. [1994] discuss disk performance and show the negligible performance impact of defect management. The placement of hot data to improve seek times has been considered by Ruemmler and Wilkes [1991] and Akyurek and Salem [1993]. Ruemmler and Wilkes [1994] describe an accurate performance model for a modern disk drive. Worthington et al. [1995] tell how to determine low-level disk properties such as the zone structure, and this work is further advanced by Schindler and Gregory [1999]. Disk power management issues are discussed in Douglis et al. [1994], Douglis et al. [1995], Greenawalt [1994], and Golding et al. [1995].

The I/O size and randomness of the workload has a considerable influence on disk performance. Ousterhout et al. [1985] and Ruemmler and Wilkes [1993] report numerous interesting workload characteristics, including that most files are small, most newly created files are deleted soon thereafter, most files that are opened for reading are read sequentially in their entirety, and most seeks are short. McKusick et al. [1984] describe the Berkeley Fast File System (FFS), which uses many sophisticated techniques to obtain good performance for a wide variety of workloads. McVoy and Kleiman [1991] discuss further improvements to the basic FFS. Quinlan [1991] describes how to implement a file system on WORM storage with a magnetic disk cache; Richards [1990] discusses a file-system approach to tertiary storage. Maher et al. [1994] give an overview of the integration of distributed file systems and tertiary storage.

The concept of a storage hierarchy has been studied for more than thirty years. For instance, a 1970 paper by Mattson et al. [1970] describes a mathematical approach to predicting the performance of a storage hierarchy. Alt [1993] describes the accommodation of removable storage in a commercial operating system, and Miller and Katz [1993] describe the characteristics of tertiary-storage access in a supercomputing environment. Benjamin [1990] gives an overview of the massive storage requirements for the EOSDIS project at NASA. Management and use of network-attached disks and programmable disks are discussed in Gibson et al. [1997b], Gibson et al. [1997a], Riedel et al. [1998], and Lee and Thekkath [1996].

Holographic storage technology is the subject of an article by Psaltis and Mok [1995]; a collection of papers on this topic dating from 1963 has been assembled by Sincerbox [1994]. Asthana and Finkelstein [1995] describe several emerging storage technologies, including holographic storage, optical tape, and electron trapping. Toigo [2000] gives an in-depth description of modern disk technology and several potential future storage technologies.

CHAPTER 13

I/O Systems

The two main jobs of a computer are I/O and processing. In many cases, the main job is I/O, and the processing is merely incidental. For instance, when we browse a Web page or edit a file, our immediate interest is to read or enter some information, not to compute an answer.

The role of the operating system in computer I/O is to manage and control I/O operations and I/O devices. Although related topics appear in other chapters, here we bring together the pieces to paint a complete picture of I/O. First, we describe the basics of I/O hardware, because the nature of the hardware interface places constraints on the internal facilities of the operating system. Next, we discuss the I/O services provided by the operating system and the embodiment of these services in the application I/O interface. Then, we explain how the operating system bridges the gap between the hardware interface and the application interface. We also discuss the UNIX System V STREAMS mechanism, which enables an application to assemble pipelines of driver code dynamically. Finally, we discuss the performance aspects of I/O and the principles of operating-system design that improve I/O performance.

CHAPTER OBJECTIVES

- To explore the structure of an operating system's I/O subsystem.
- To discuss the principles and complexities of I/O hardware.
- To explain the performance aspects of I/O hardware and software.

13.1 Overview

The control of devices connected to the computer is a major concern of operating-system designers. Because I/O devices vary so widely in their function and speed (consider a mouse, a hard disk, and a CD-ROM jukebox), varied methods are needed to control them. These methods form the *I/O subsystem* of the kernel, which separates the rest of the kernel from the complexities of managing I/O devices.

I/O-device technology exhibits two conflicting trends. On the one hand, we see increasing standardization of software and hardware interfaces. This trend helps us to incorporate improved device generations into existing computers and operating systems. On the other hand, we see an increasingly broad variety of I/O devices. Some new devices are so unlike previous devices that it is a challenge to incorporate them into our computers and operating systems. This challenge is met by a combination of hardware and software techniques. The basic I/O hardware elements, such as ports, buses, and device controllers, accommodate a wide variety of I/O devices. To encapsulate the details and oddities of different devices, the kernel of an operating system is structured to use device-driver modules. The **device drivers** present a uniform device-access interface to the I/O subsystem, much as system calls provide a standard interface between the application and the operating system.

13.2 I/O Hardware

Computers operate a great many kinds of devices. Most fit into the general categories of storage devices (disks, tapes), transmission devices (network cards, modems), and human-interface devices (screen, keyboard, mouse). Other devices are more specialized, such as those involved in the steering of a military fighter jet or a space shuttle. In these aircraft, a human gives input to the flight computer via a joystick and foot pedals, and the computer sends output commands that cause motors to move rudders, flaps, and thrusters. Despite the incredible variety of I/O devices, though, we need only a few concepts to understand how the devices are attached and how the software can control the hardware.

A device communicates with a computer system by sending signals over a cable or even through the air. The device communicates with the machine via a connection point, or **port**—for example, a serial port. If devices use a common set of wires, the connection is called a *bus*. A **bus** is a set of wires and a rigidly defined protocol that specifies a set of messages that can be sent on the wires. In terms of the electronics, the messages are conveyed by patterns of electrical voltages applied to the wires with defined timings. When device *A* has a cable that plugs into device *B*, and device *B* has a cable that plugs into device *C*, and device *C* plugs into a port on the computer, this arrangement is called a **daisy chain**. A daisy chain usually operates as a bus.

Buses are used widely in computer architecture and vary in their signaling methods, speed, throughput, and connection methods. A typical PC bus structure appears in Figure 13.1. This figure shows a **PCI bus** (the common PC system bus) that connects the processor–memory subsystem to the fast devices and an **expansion bus** that connects relatively slow devices, such as the keyboard and serial and USB ports. In the upper-right portion of the figure, four disks are connected together on a SCSI bus plugged into a SCSI controller. Other common buses used to interconnect main parts of a computer include **PCI-X**, with throughput up to 4.3 GB; **PCI Express** (PCIe), with throughput up to 16 GB; and **HyperTransport**, with throughput up to 20 GB.

A **controller** is a collection of electronics that can operate a port, a bus, or a device. A serial-port controller is a simple device controller. It is a single chip (or portion of a chip) in the computer that controls the signals on the

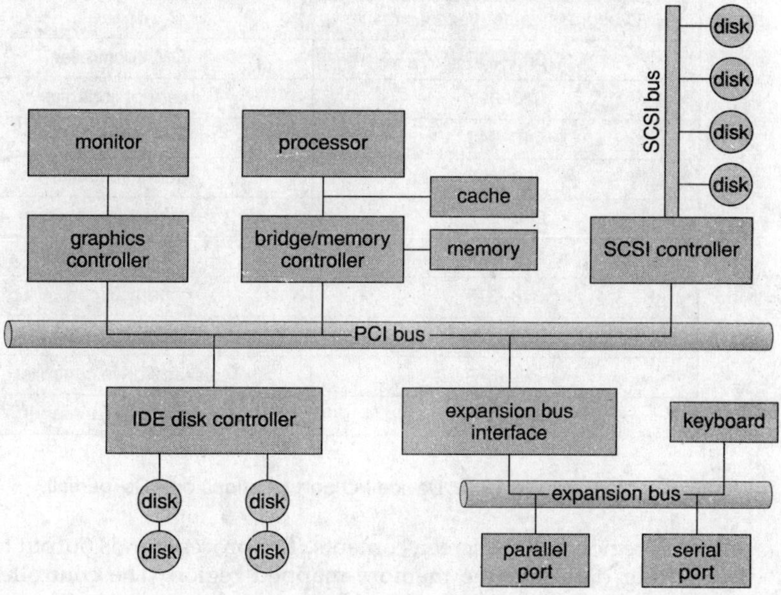

Figure 13.1 A typical PC bus structure.

wires of a serial port. By contrast, a SCSI bus controller is not simple. Because the SCSI protocol is complex, the SCSI bus controller is often implemented as a separate circuit board (or a **host adapter**) that plugs into the computer. It typically contains a processor, microcode, and some private memory to enable it to process the SCSI protocol messages. Some devices have their own built-in controllers. If you look at a disk drive, you will see a circuit board attached to one side. This board is the disk controller. It implements the disk side of the protocol for some kind of connection—SCSI or ATA, for instance. It has microcode and a processor to do many tasks, such as bad-sector mapping, prefetching, buffering, and caching.

How can the processor give commands and data to a controller to accomplish an I/O transfer? The short answer is that the controller has one or more registers for data and control signals. The processor communicates with the controller by reading and writing bit patterns in these registers. One way in which this communication can occur is through the use of special I/O instructions that specify the transfer of a byte or word to an I/O port address. The I/O instruction triggers bus lines to select the proper device and to move bits into or out of a device register. Alternatively, the device controller can support **memory-mapped I/O**. In this case, the device-control registers are mapped into the address space of the processor. The CPU executes I/O requests using the standard data-transfer instructions to read and write the device-control registers.

Some systems use both techniques. For instance, PCs use I/O instructions to control some devices and memory-mapped I/O to control others. Figure 13.2 shows the usual I/O port addresses for PCs. The graphics controller has I/O ports for basic control operations, but the controller has a large memory-

I/O address range (hexadecimal)	device
000–00F	DMA controller
020–021	interrupt controller
040–043	timer
200–20F	game controller
2F8–2FF	serial port (secondary)
320–32F	hard-disk controller
378–37F	parallel port
3D0–3DF	graphics controller
3F0–3F7	diskette-drive controller
3F8–3FF	serial port (primary)

Figure 13.2 Device I/O port locations on PCs (partial).

mapped region to hold screen contents. The process sends output to the screen by writing data into the memory-mapped region. The controller generates the screen image based on the contents of this memory. This technique is simple to use. Moreover, writing millions of bytes to the graphics memory is faster than issuing millions of I/O instructions. But the ease of writing to a memory-mapped I/O controller is offset by a disadvantage. Because a common type of software fault is a write through an incorrect pointer to an unintended region of memory, a memory-mapped device register is vulnerable to accidental modification. Of course, protected memory helps to reduce this risk.

An I/O port typically consists of four registers, called the (1) status, (2) control, (3) data-in, and (4) data-out registers.

- The **data-in register** is read by the host to get input.
- The **data-out register** is written by the host to send output.
- The **status register** contains bits that can be read by the host. These bits indicate states, such as whether the current command has completed, whether a byte is available to be read from the data-in register, and whether a device error has occurred.
- The **control register** can be written by the host to start a command or to change the mode of a device. For instance, a certain bit in the control register of a serial port chooses between full-duplex and half-duplex communication, another bit enables parity checking, a third bit sets the word length to 7 or 8 bits, and other bits select one of the speeds supported by the serial port.

The data registers are typically 1 to 4 bytes in size. Some controllers have FIFO chips that can hold several bytes of input or output data to expand the capacity of the controller beyond the size of the data register. A FIFO chip can hold a small burst of data until the device or host is able to receive those data.

13.2.1 Polling

The complete protocol for interaction between the host and a controller can be intricate, but the basic *handshaking* notion is simple. We explain handshaking with an example. Assume that 2 bits are used to coordinate the producer–consumer relationship between the controller and the host. The controller indicates its state through the *busy* bit in the *status* register. (Recall that to *set* a bit means to write a 1 into the bit and to *clear* a bit means to write a 0 into it.) The controller sets the *busy* bit when it is busy working and clears the *busy* bit when it is ready to accept the next command. The host signals its wishes via the *command-ready* bit in the *command* register. The host sets the *command-ready* bit when a command is available for the controller to execute. For this example, the host writes output through a port, coordinating with the controller by handshaking as follows.

1. The host repeatedly reads the *busy* bit until that bit becomes clear.
2. The host sets the *write* bit in the *command* register and writes a byte into the *data-out* register.
3. The host sets the *command-ready* bit.
4. When the controller notices that the *command-ready* bit is set, it sets the *busy* bit.
5. The controller reads the command register and sees the `write` command. It reads the *data-out* register to get the byte and does the I/O to the device.
6. The controller clears the *command-ready* bit, clears the *error* bit in the status register to indicate that the device I/O succeeded, and clears the *busy* bit to indicate that it is finished.

This loop is repeated for each byte.

In step 1, the host is **busy-waiting** or **polling**: it is in a loop, reading the *status* register over and over until the *busy* bit becomes clear. If the controller and device are fast, this method is a reasonable one. But if the wait may be long, the host should probably switch to another task. How, then, does the host know when the controller has become idle? For some devices, the host must service the device quickly, or data will be lost. For instance, when data are streaming in on a serial port or from a keyboard, the small buffer on the controller will overflow and data will be lost if the host waits too long before returning to read the bytes.

In many computer architectures, three CPU-instruction cycles are sufficient to poll a device: *read* a device register, *logical–and* to extract a status bit, and *branch* if not zero. Clearly, the basic polling operation is efficient. But polling becomes inefficient when it is attempted repeatedly yet rarely finds a device to be ready for service, while other useful CPU processing remains undone. In such instances, it may be more efficient to arrange for the hardware controller to notify the CPU when the device becomes ready for service, rather than to require the CPU to poll repeatedly for an I/O completion. The hardware mechanism that enables a device to notify the CPU is called an **interrupt**.

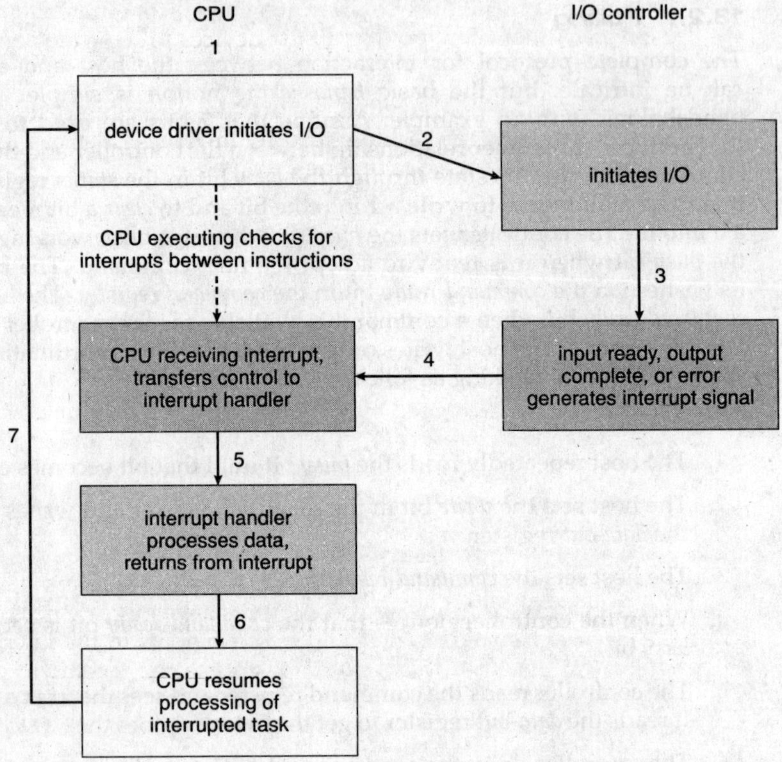

Figure 13.3 Interrupt-driven I/O cycle.

13.2.2 Interrupts

The basic interrupt mechanism works as follows. The CPU hardware has a wire called the **interrupt-request line** that the CPU senses after executing every instruction. When the CPU detects that a controller has asserted a signal on the interrupt-request line, the CPU performs a state save and jumps to the **interrupt-handler routine** at a fixed address in memory. The interrupt handler determines the cause of the interrupt, performs the necessary processing, performs a state restore, and executes a `return from interrupt` instruction to return the CPU to the execution state prior to the interrupt. We say that the device controller *raises* an interrupt by asserting a signal on the interrupt request line, the CPU *catches* the interrupt and *dispatches* it to the interrupt handler, and the handler *clears* the interrupt by servicing the device. Figure 13.3 summarizes the interrupt-driven I/O cycle.

This basic interrupt mechanism enables the CPU to respond to an asynchronous event, as when a device controller becomes ready for service. In a modern operating system, however, we need more sophisticated interrupt-handling features.

1. We need the ability to defer interrupt handling during critical processing.

2. We need an efficient way to dispatch to the proper interrupt handler for a device without first polling all the devices to see which one raised the interrupt.
3. We need multilevel interrupts, so that the operating system can distinguish between high- and low-priority interrupts and can respond with the appropriate degree of urgency.

In modern computer hardware, these three features are provided by the CPU and by the **interrupt-controller hardware**.

Most CPUs have two interrupt request lines. One is the **nonmaskable interrupt**, which is reserved for events such as unrecoverable memory errors. The second interrupt line is **maskable**: it can be turned off by the CPU before the execution of critical instruction sequences that must not be interrupted. The maskable interrupt is used by device controllers to request service.

The interrupt mechanism accepts an **address**—a number that selects a specific interrupt-handling routine from a small set. In most architectures, this address is an offset in a table called the **interrupt vector**. This vector contains the memory addresses of specialized interrupt handlers. The purpose of a vectored interrupt mechanism is to reduce the need for a single interrupt handler to search all possible sources of interrupts to determine which one needs service. In practice, however, computers have more devices (and, hence, interrupt handlers) than they have address elements in the interrupt vector. A common way to solve this problem is to use the technique of **interrupt chaining**, in which each element in the interrupt vector points to the head of a list of interrupt handlers. When an interrupt is raised, the handlers on the corresponding list are called one by one, until one is found that can service the request. This structure is a compromise between the overhead of a huge interrupt table and the inefficiency of dispatching to a single interrupt handler.

Figure 13.4 illustrates the design of the interrupt vector for the Intel Pentium processor. The events from 0 to 31, which are nonmaskable, are used to signal various error conditions. The events from 32 to 255, which are maskable, are used for purposes such as device-generated interrupts.

The interrupt mechanism also implements a system of **interrupt priority levels**. This mechanism enables the CPU to defer the handling of low-priority interrupts without masking off all interrupts and makes it possible for a high-priority interrupt to preempt the execution of a low-priority interrupt.

A modern operating system interacts with the interrupt mechanism in several ways. At boot time, the operating system probes the hardware buses to determine what devices are present and installs the corresponding interrupt handlers into the interrupt vector. During I/O, the various device controllers raise interrupts when they are ready for service. These interrupts signify that output has completed, or that input data are available, or that a failure has been detected. The interrupt mechanism is also used to handle a wide variety of **exceptions**, such as dividing by zero, accessing a protected or nonexistent memory address, or attempting to execute a privileged instruction from user mode. The events that trigger interrupts have a common property: they are occurrences that induce the CPU to execute an urgent, self-contained routine.

An operating system has other good uses for an efficient hardware and software mechanism that saves a small amount of processor state and then

vector number	description
0	divide error
1	debug exception
2	null interrupt
3	breakpoint
4	INTO-detected overflow
5	bound range exception
6	invalid opcode
7	device not available
8	double fault
9	coprocessor segment overrun (reserved)
10	invalid task state segment
11	segment not present
12	stack fault
13	general protection
14	page fault
15	(Intel reserved, do not use)
16	floating-point error
17	alignment check
18	machine check
19–31	(Intel reserved, do not use)
32–255	maskable interrupts

Figure 13.4 Intel Pentium processor event-vector table.

calls a privileged routine in the kernel. For example, many operating systems use the interrupt mechanism for virtual memory paging. A page fault is an exception that raises an interrupt. The interrupt suspends the current process and jumps to the page-fault handler in the kernel. This handler saves the state of the process, moves the process to the wait queue, performs page-cache management, schedules an I/O operation to fetch the page, schedules another process to resume execution, and then returns from the interrupt.

Another example is found in the implementation of system calls. Usually, a program uses library calls to issue system calls. The library routines check the arguments given by the application, build a data structure to convey the arguments to the kernel, and then execute a special instruction called a **software interrupt**, or **trap**. This instruction has an operand that identifies the desired kernel service. When a process executes the trap instruction, the interrupt hardware saves the state of the user code, switches to supervisor mode, and dispatches to the kernel routine that implements the requested service. The trap is given a relatively low interrupt priority compared with those assigned to device interrupts—executing a system call on behalf of an application is less urgent than servicing a device controller before its FIFO queue overflows and loses data.

Interrupts can also be used to manage the flow of control within the kernel. For example, consider the processing required to complete a disk read. One step is to copy data from kernel space to the user buffer. This copying is time consuming but not urgent—it should not block other high-priority interrupt handling. Another step is to start the next pending I/O for that disk drive. This step has higher priority. If the disks are to be used efficiently, we need to start the next I/O as soon as the previous one completes. Consequently, a *pair* of interrupt handlers implements the kernel code that completes a disk read. The high-priority handler records the I/O status, clears the device interrupt, starts the next pending I/O, and raises a low-priority interrupt to complete the work. Later, when the CPU is not occupied with high-priority work, the low-priority interrupt will be dispatched. The corresponding handler completes the user-level I/O by copying data from kernel buffers to the application space and then calling the scheduler to place the application on the ready queue.

A threaded kernel architecture is well suited to implement multiple interrupt priorities and to enforce the precedence of interrupt handling over background processing in kernel and application routines. We illustrate this point with the Solaris kernel. In Solaris, interrupt handlers are executed as kernel threads. A range of high priorities is reserved for these threads. These priorities give interrupt handlers precedence over application code and kernel housekeeping and implement the priority relationships among interrupt handlers. The priorities cause the Solaris thread scheduler to preempt low-priority interrupt handlers in favor of higher-priority ones, and the threaded implementation enables multiprocessor hardware to run several interrupt handlers concurrently. We describe the interrupt architecture of Windows XP and UNIX in Chapter 22 and Appendix A, respectively.

In summary, interrupts are used throughout modern operating systems to handle asynchronous events and to trap to supervisor-mode routines in the kernel. To enable the most urgent work to be done first, modern computers use a system of interrupt priorities. Device controllers, hardware faults, and system calls all raise interrupts to trigger kernel routines. Because interrupts are used so heavily for time-sensitive processing, efficient interrupt handling is required for good system performance.

13.2.3 Direct Memory Access

For a device that does large transfers, such as a disk drive, it seems wasteful to use an expensive general-purpose processor to watch status bits and to feed data into a controller register one byte at a time—a process termed **programmed I/O (PIO)**. Many computers avoid burdening the main CPU with PIO by offloading some of this work to a special-purpose processor called a **direct-memory-access (DMA) controller**. To initiate a DMA transfer, the host writes a DMA command block into memory. This block contains a pointer to the source of a transfer, a pointer to the destination of the transfer, and a count of the number of bytes to be transferred. The CPU writes the address of this command block to the DMA controller, then goes on with other work. The DMA controller proceeds to operate the memory bus directly, placing addresses on the bus to perform transfers without the help of the main CPU. A simple DMA controller is a standard component in PCs, and **bus-mastering I/O boards** for the PC usually contain their own high-speed DMA hardware.

Handshaking between the DMA controller and the device controller is performed via a pair of wires called `DMA-request` and `DMA-acknowledge`. The device controller places a signal on the `DMA-request` wire when a word of data is available for transfer. This signal causes the DMA controller to seize the memory bus, place the desired address on the memory-address wires, and place a signal on the DMA-acknowledge wire. When the device controller receives the DMA-acknowledge signal, it transfers the word of data to memory and removes the DMA-request signal.

When the entire transfer is finished, the DMA controller interrupts the CPU. This process is depicted in Figure 13.5. When the DMA controller seizes the memory bus, the CPU is momentarily prevented from accessing main memory, although it can still access data items in its primary and secondary caches. Although this **cycle stealing** can slow down the CPU computation, offloading the data-transfer work to a DMA controller generally improves the total system performance. Some computer architectures use physical memory addresses for DMA, but others perform **direct virtual memory access (DVMA)**, using virtual addresses that undergo translation to physical addresses. DVMA can perform a transfer between two memory-mapped devices without the intervention of the CPU or the use of main memory.

On protected-mode kernels, the operating system generally prevents processes from issuing device commands directly. This discipline protects data from access-control violations and also protects the system from erroneous use of device controllers that could cause a system crash. Instead, the operating system exports functions that a sufficiently privileged process can use to access low-level operations on the underlying hardware. On kernels without memory protection, processes can access device controllers directly. This direct access can be used to achieve high performance, since it can avoid kernel communication, context switches, and layers of kernel software. Unfortunately, it interferes with system security and stability. The trend in general-purpose operating systems is to protect memory and devices so that the system can try to guard against erroneous or malicious applications.

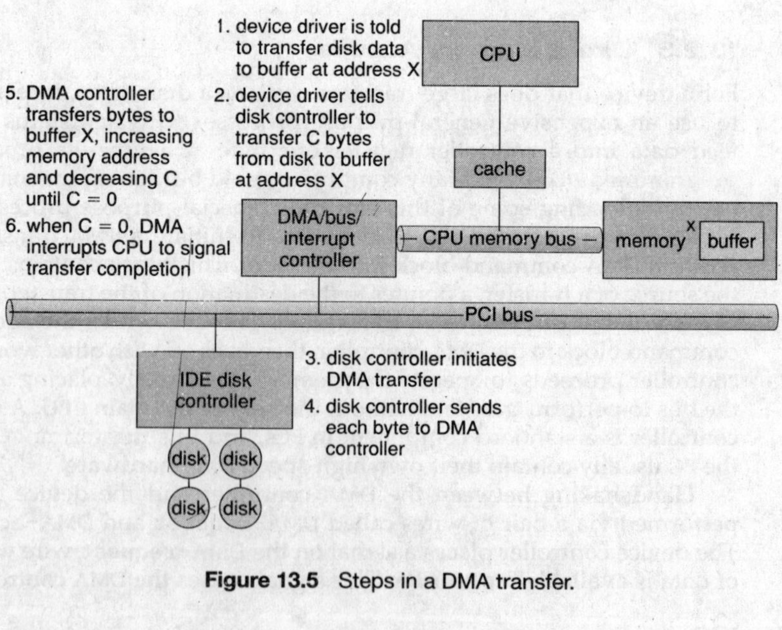

Figure 13.5 Steps in a DMA transfer.

13.2.4 I/O Hardware Summary

Although the hardware aspects of I/O are complex when considered at the level of detail of electronics-hardware design, the concepts that we have just described are sufficient to enable us to understand many I/O features of operating systems. Let's review the main concepts:

- A bus
- A controller
- An I/O port and its registers
- The handshaking relationship between the host and a device controller
- The execution of this handshaking in a polling loop or via interrupts
- The offloading of this work to a DMA controller for large transfers

We gave a basic example of the handshaking that takes place between a device controller and the host earlier in this section. In reality, the wide variety of available devices poses a problem for operating-system implementers. Each kind of device has its own set of capabilities, control-bit definitions, and protocols for interacting with the host—and they are all different. How can the operating system be designed so that we can attach new devices to the computer without rewriting the operating system? And when the devices vary so widely, how can the operating system give a convenient, uniform I/O interface to applications? We address those questions next.

13.3 Application I/O Interface

In this section, we discuss structuring techniques and interfaces for the operating system that enable I/O devices to be treated in a standard, uniform way. We explain, for instance, how an application can open a file on a disk without knowing what kind of disk it is and how new disks and other devices can be added to a computer without disruption of the operating system.

Like other complex software-engineering problems, the approach here involves abstraction, encapsulation, and software layering. Specifically, we can abstract away the detailed differences in I/O devices by identifying a few general kinds. Each general kind is accessed through a standardized set of functions—an **interface**. The differences are encapsulated in kernel modules called device drivers that internally are custom-tailored to specific devices but that export one of the standard interfaces. Figure 13.6 illustrates how the I/O-related portions of the kernel are structured in software layers.

The purpose of the device-driver layer is to hide the differences among device controllers from the I/O subsystem of the kernel, much as the I/O system calls encapsulate the behavior of devices in a few generic classes that hide hardware differences from applications. Making the I/O subsystem independent of the hardware simplifies the job of the operating-system developer. It also benefits the hardware manufacturers. They either design new devices to be compatible with an existing host controller interface (such as SCSI-2), or they write device drivers to interface the new hardware to popular

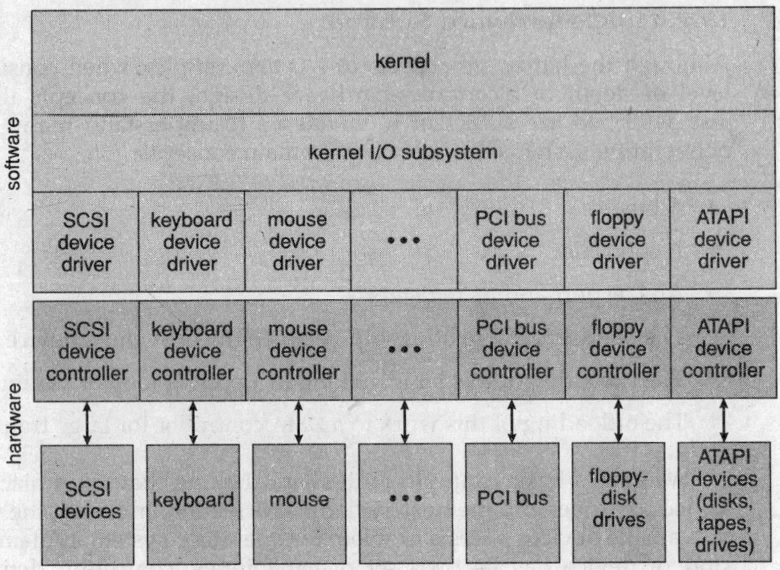

Figure 13.6 A kernel I/O structure.

operating systems. Thus, we can attach new peripherals to a computer without waiting for the operating-system vendor to develop support code.

Unfortunately for device-hardware manufacturers, each type of operating system has its own standards for the device-driver interface. A given device may ship with multiple device drivers—for instance, drivers for MS-DOS, Windows 95/98, Windows NT/2000, and Solaris. Devices vary on many dimensions, as illustrated in Figure 13.7.

- **Character-stream or block**. A character-stream device transfers bytes one by one, whereas a block device transfers a block of bytes as a unit.
- **Sequential or random access**. A sequential device transfers data in a fixed order determined by the device, whereas the user of a random-access device can instruct the device to seek to any of the available data storage locations.
- **Synchronous or asynchronous**. A synchronous device performs data transfers with predictable response times. An asynchronous device exhibits irregular or unpredictable response times.
- **Sharable or dedicated**. A sharable device can be used concurrently by several processes or threads; a dedicated device cannot.
- **Speed of operation**. Device speeds range from a few bytes per second to a few gigabytes per second.
- **Read–write, read only, or write only**. Some devices perform both input and output, but others support only one data transfer direction.

aspect	variation	example
data-transfer mode	character block	terminal disk
access method	sequential random	modem CD-ROM
transfer schedule	synchronous asynchronous	tape keyboard
sharing	dedicated sharable	tape keyboard
device speed	latency seek time transfer rate delay between operations	
I/O direction	read only write only read–write	CD-ROM graphics controller disk

Figure 13.7 Characteristics of I/O devices.

For the purpose of application access, many of these differences are hidden by the operating system, and the devices are grouped into a few conventional types. The resulting styles of device access have been found to be useful and broadly applicable. Although the exact system calls may differ across operating systems, the device categories are fairly standard. The major access conventions include block I/O, character-stream I/O, memory-mapped file access, and network sockets. Operating systems also provide special system calls to access a few additional devices, such as a time-of-day clock and a timer. Some operating systems provide a set of system calls for graphical display, video, and audio devices.

Most operating systems also have an **escape** (or **back door**) that transparently passes arbitrary commands from an application to a device driver. In UNIX, this system call is `ioctl()` (for "I/O control"). The `ioctl()` system call enables an application to access any functionality that can be implemented by any device driver, without the need to invent a new system call. The `ioctl()` system call has three arguments. The first is a file descriptor that connects the application to the driver by referring to a hardware device managed by that driver. The second is an integer that selects one of the commands implemented in the driver. The third is a pointer to an arbitrary data structure in memory that enables the application and driver to communicate any necessary control information or data.

13.3.1 Block and Character Devices

The **block-device interface** captures all the aspects necessary for accessing disk drives and other block-oriented devices. The device is expected to understand commands such as `read()` and `write()`; if it is a random-access device, it is also expected to have a `seek()` command to specify which block to transfer next.

Applications normally access such a device through a file-system interface. We can see that `read()`, `write()`, and `seek()` capture the essential behaviors of block-storage devices, so that applications are insulated from the low-level differences among those devices.

The operating system itself, as well as special applications such as database-management systems, may prefer to access a block device as a simple linear array of blocks. This mode of access is sometimes called **raw I/O**. If the application performs its own buffering, then using a file system would cause extra, unneeded buffering. Likewise, if an application provides its own locking of file blocks or regions, then any operating-system locking services would be redundant at the least and contradictory at the worst. To avoid these conflicts, raw-device access passes control of the device directly to the application, letting the operating system step out of the way. Unfortunately, no operating-system services are then performed on this device. A compromise that is becoming common is for the operating system to allow a mode of operation on a file that disables buffering and locking. In the UNIX world, this is called **direct I/O**.

Memory-mapped file access can be layered on top of block-device drivers. Rather than offering read and write operations, a memory-mapped interface provides access to disk storage via an array of bytes in main memory. The system call that maps a file into memory returns the virtual memory address that contains a copy of the file. The actual data transfers are performed only when needed to satisfy access to the memory image. Because the transfers are handled by the same mechanism as that used for demand-paged virtual memory access, memory-mapped I/O is efficient. Memory mapping is also convenient for programmers—access to a memory-mapped file is as simple as reading from and writing to memory. Operating systems that offer virtual memory commonly use the mapping interface for kernel services. For instance, to execute a program, the operating system maps the executable into memory and then transfers control to the entry address of the executable. The mapping interface is also commonly used for kernel access to swap space on disk.

A keyboard is an example of a device that is accessed through a **character-stream interface**. The basic system calls in this interface enable an application to `get()` or `put()` one character. On top of this interface, libraries can be built that offer line-at-a-time access, with buffering and editing services (for example, when a user types a backspace, the preceding character is removed from the input stream). This style of access is convenient for input devices such as keyboards, mice, and modems that produce data for input "spontaneously" —that is, at times that cannot necessarily be predicted by the application. This access style is also good for output devices such as printers and audio boards, which naturally fit the concept of a linear stream of bytes.

13.3.2 Network Devices

Because the performance and addressing characteristics of network I/O differ significantly from those of disk I/O, most operating systems provide a network I/O interface that is different from the `read()-write()-seek()` interface used for disks. One interface available in many operating systems, including UNIX and Windows NT, is the network **socket** interface.

Think of a wall socket for electricity: any electrical appliance can be plugged in. By analogy, the system calls in the socket interface enable an application to create a socket, to connect a local socket to a remote address (which plugs this application into a socket created by another application), to listen for any remote application to plug into the local socket, and to send and receive packets over the connection. To support the implementation of servers, the socket interface also provides a function called `select()` that manages a set of sockets. A call to `select()` returns information about which sockets have a packet waiting to be received and which sockets have room to accept a packet to be sent. The use of `select()` eliminates the polling and busy waiting that would otherwise be necessary for network I/O. These functions encapsulate the essential behaviors of networks, greatly facilitating the creation of distributed applications that can use any underlying network hardware and protocol stack.

Many other approaches to interprocess communication and network communication have been implemented. For instance, Windows NT provides one interface to the network interface card and a second interface to the network protocols (Appendix C.6). In UNIX, which has a long history as a proving ground for network technology, we find half-duplex pipes, full-duplex FIFOs, full-duplex STREAMS, message queues, and sockets. Information on UNIX networking is given in Appendix A.9.

13.3.3 Clocks and Timers

Most computers have hardware clocks and timers that provide three basic functions:

- Give the current time.
- Give the elapsed time.
- Set a timer to trigger operation *X* at time *T*.

These functions are used heavily by the operating system, as well as by time-sensitive applications. Unfortunately, the system calls that implement these functions are not standardized across operating systems.

The hardware to measure elapsed time and to trigger operations is called a **programmable interval timer**. It can be set to wait a certain amount of time and then generate an interrupt, and it can be set to do this once or to repeat the process to generate periodic interrupts. The scheduler uses this mechanism to generate an interrupt that will preempt a process at the end of its time slice. The disk I/O subsystem uses it to invoke the periodic flushing of dirty cache buffers to disk, and the network subsystem uses it to cancel operations that are proceeding too slowly because of network congestion or failures. The operating system may also provide an interface for user processes to use timers. The operating system can support more timer requests than the number of timer hardware channels by simulating virtual clocks. To do so, the kernel (or the timer device driver) maintains a list of interrupts wanted by its own routines and by user requests, sorted in earliest-time-first order. It sets the timer for the earliest time. When the timer interrupts, the kernel signals the requester and reloads the timer with the next earliest time.

On many computers, the interrupt rate generated by the hardware clock is between 18 and 60 ticks per second. This resolution is coarse, since a modern computer can execute hundreds of millions of instructions per second. The precision of triggers is limited by the coarse resolution of the timer, together with the overhead of maintaining virtual clocks. Furthermore, if the timer ticks are used to maintain the system time-of-day clock, the system clock can drift. In most computers, the hardware clock is constructed from a high-frequency counter. In some computers, the value of this counter can be read from a device register, in which case the counter can be considered a high-resolution clock. Although this clock does not generate interrupts, it offers accurate measurements of time intervals.

13.3.4 Blocking and Nonblocking I/O

Another aspect of the system-call interface relates to the choice between blocking I/O and nonblocking I/O. When an application issues a **blocking** system call, the execution of the application is suspended. The application is moved from the operating system's run queue to a wait queue. After the system call completes, the application is moved back to the run queue, where it is eligible to resume execution. When it resumes execution, it will receive the values returned by the system call. The physical actions performed by I/O devices are generally asynchronous—they take a varying or unpredictable amount of time. Nevertheless, most operating systems use blocking system calls for the application interface, because blocking application code is easier to understand than nonblocking application code.

Some user-level processes need **nonblocking** I/O. One example is a user interface that receives keyboard and mouse input while processing and displaying data on the screen. Another example is a video application that reads frames from a file on disk while simultaneously decompressing and displaying the output on the display.

One way an application writer can overlap execution with I/O is to write a multithreaded application. Some threads can perform blocking system calls, while others continue executing. The Solaris developers used this technique to implement a user-level library for asynchronous I/O, freeing the application writer from that task. Some operating systems provide nonblocking I/O system calls. A nonblocking call does not halt the execution of the application for an extended time. Instead, it returns quickly, with a return value that indicates how many bytes were transferred.

An alternative to a nonblocking system call is an asynchronous system call. An asynchronous call returns immediately, without waiting for the I/O to complete. The application continues to execute its code. The completion of the I/O at some future time is communicated to the application, either through the setting of some variable in the address space of the application or through the triggering of a signal or software interrupt or a call-back routine that is executed outside the linear control flow of the application. The difference between nonblocking and asynchronous system calls is that a nonblocking `read()` returns immediately with whatever data are available—the full number of bytes requested, fewer, or none at all. An asynchronous `read()` call requests a transfer that will be performed in its entirety but will complete at some future time. These two I/O methods are shown in Figure 13.8.

A good example of nonblocking behavior is the `select()` system call for network sockets. This system call takes an argument that specifies a maximum waiting time. By setting it to 0, an application can poll for network activity

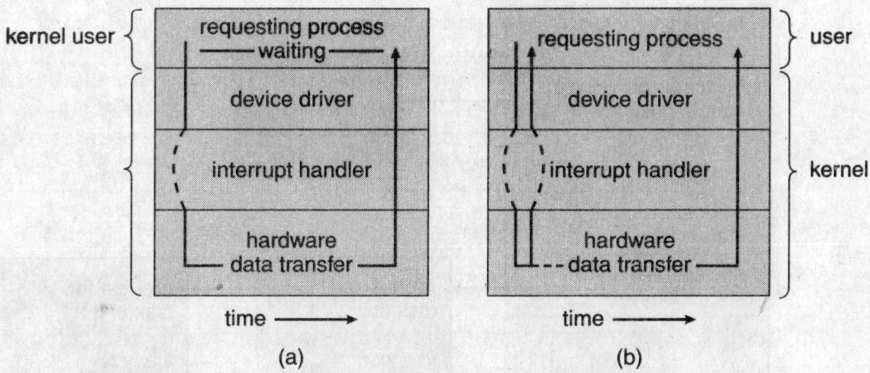

Figure 13.8 Two I/O methods: (a) synchronous and (b) asynchronous.

without blocking. But using `select()` introduces extra overhead, because the `select()` call only checks whether I/O is possible. For a data transfer, `select()` must be followed by some kind of `read()` or `write()` command. A variation on this approach, found in Mach, is a blocking multiple-read call. It specifies desired reads for several devices in one system call and returns as soon as any one of them completes.

13.4 Kernel I/O Subsystem

Kernels provide many services related to I/O. Several services—scheduling, buffering, caching, spooling, device reservation, and error handling—are provided by the kernel's I/O subsystem and build on the hardware and device-driver infrastructure. The I/O subsystem is also responsible for protecting itself from errant processes and malicious users.

13.4.1 I/O Scheduling

To schedule a set of I/O requests means to determine a good order in which to execute them. The order in which applications issue system calls rarely is the best choice. Scheduling can improve overall system performance, can share device access fairly among processes, and can reduce the average waiting time for I/O to complete. Here is a simple example to illustrate. Suppose that a disk arm is near the beginning of a disk and that three applications issue blocking read calls to that disk. Application 1 requests a block near the end of the disk, application 2 requests one near the beginning, and application 3 requests one in the middle of the disk. The operating system can reduce the distance that the disk arm travels by serving the applications in the order 2, 3, 1. Rearranging the order of service in this way is the essence of I/O scheduling.

Operating-system developers implement scheduling by maintaining a wait queue of requests for each device. When an application issues a blocking I/O system call, the request is placed on the queue for that device. The I/O scheduler rearranges the order of the queue to improve the overall system efficiency and the average response time experienced by applications. The operating

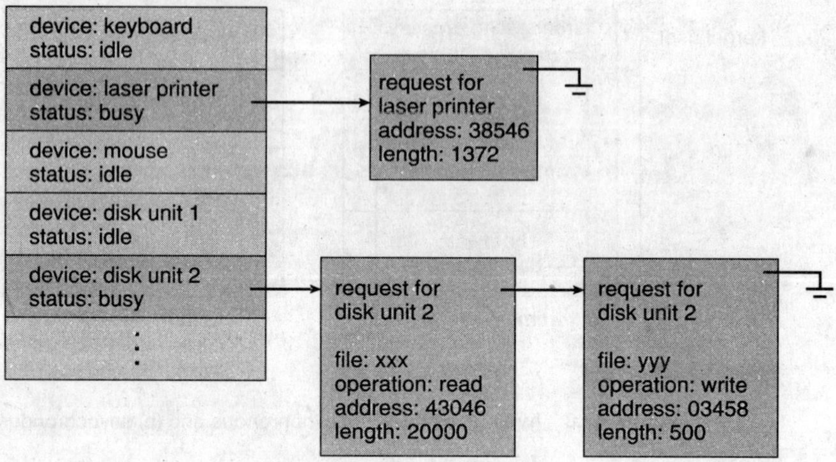

Figure 13.9 Device-status table.

system may also try to be fair, so that no one application receives especially poor service, or it may give priority service for delay-sensitive requests. For instance, requests from the virtual memory subsystem may take priority over application requests. Several scheduling algorithms for disk I/O are detailed in Section 12.4.

When a kernel supports asynchronous I/O, it must be able to keep track of many I/O requests at the same time. For this purpose, the operating system might attach the wait queue to a **device-status table**. The kernel manages this table, which contains an entry for each I/O device, as shown in Figure 13.9. Each table entry indicates the device's type, address, and state (not functioning, idle, or busy). If the device is busy with a request, the type of request and other parameters will be stored in the table entry for that device.

One way in which the I/O subsystem improves the efficiency of the computer is by scheduling I/O operations. Another way is by using storage space in main memory or on disk via techniques called buffering, caching, and spooling.

13.4.2 Buffering

A **buffer** is a memory area that stores data being transferred between two devices or between a device and an application. Buffering is done for three reasons. One reason is to cope with a speed mismatch between the producer and consumer of a data stream. Suppose, for example, that a file is being received via modem for storage on the hard disk. The modem is about a thousand times slower than the hard disk. So a buffer is created in main memory to accumulate the bytes received from the modem. When an entire buffer of data has arrived, the buffer can be written to disk in a single operation. Since the disk write is not instantaneous and the modem still needs a place to store additional incoming data, two buffers are used. After the modem fills the first buffer, the disk write is requested. The modem then starts to fill the second buffer while the first buffer is written to disk. By the time the modem has filled the second buffer, the disk write from the first one should have completed, so the modem can switch back to the first buffer while the disk writes the second one. This **double buffering** decouples the producer of data from the consumer, thus relaxing timing requirements between them. The need for this decoupling is illustrated in Figure 13.10, which lists the enormous differences in device speeds for typical computer hardware.

A second use of buffering is to provide adaptations for devices that have different data-transfer sizes. Such disparities are especially common in computer networking, where buffers are used widely for fragmentation and reassembly of messages. At the sending side, a large message is fragmented into small network packets. The packets are sent over the network, and the receiving side places them in a reassembly buffer to form an image of the source data.

A third use of buffering is to support copy semantics for application I/O. An example will clarify the meaning of "copy semantics." Suppose that an application has a buffer of data that it wishes to write to disk. It calls the `write()` system call, providing a pointer to the buffer and an integer specifying the number of bytes to write. After the system call returns, what happens if the application changes the contents of the buffer? With **copy semantics**, the version of the data written to disk is guaranteed to be the version at the time of the application system call, independent of any subsequent changes in the application's buffer. A simple way in which the operating system can guarantee copy semantics is for the `write()` system call to copy the application

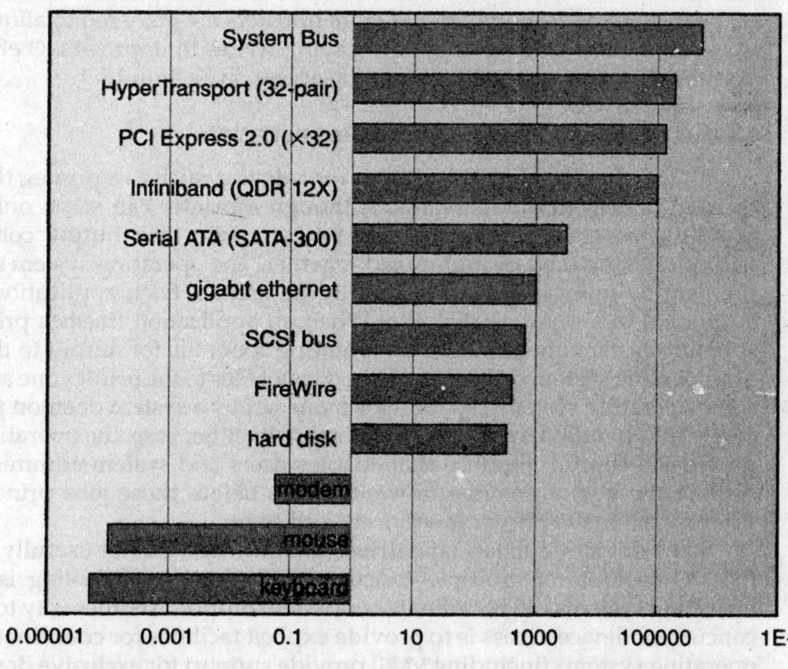

Figure 13.10 Sun Enterprise 6000 device-transfer rates (logarithmic).

data into a kernel buffer before returning control to the application. The disk write is performed from the kernel buffer, so that subsequent changes to the application buffer have no effect. Copying of data between kernel buffers and application data space is common in operating systems, despite the overhead that this operation introduces, because of the clean semantics. The same effect can be obtained more efficiently by clever use of virtual memory mapping and copy-on-write page protection.

13.4.3 Caching

A **cache** is a region of fast memory that holds copies of data. Access to the cached copy is more efficient than access to the original. For instance, the instructions of the currently running process are stored on disk, cached in physical memory, and copied again in the CPU's secondary and primary caches. The difference between a buffer and a cache is that a buffer may hold the only existing copy of a data item, whereas a cache, by definition, holds a copy on faster storage of an item that resides elsewhere.

Caching and buffering are distinct functions, but sometimes a region of memory can be used for both purposes. For instance, to preserve copy semantics and to enable efficient scheduling of disk I/O, the operating system uses buffers in main memory to hold disk data. These buffers are also used as a cache, to improve the I/O efficiency for files that are shared by applications or that are being written and reread rapidly. When the kernel receives a file I/O request, the kernel first accesses the buffer cache to see whether that region of the file is already available in main memory. If it is, a physical disk I/O can be avoided or deferred. Also, disk writes are accumulated in the buffer cache for several seconds, so that large transfers are gathered to allow efficient write schedules. This strategy of delaying writes to improve I/O efficiency is discussed, in the context of remote file access, in Section 17.3.

13.4.4 Spooling and Device Reservation

A **spool** is a buffer that holds output for a device, such as a printer, that cannot accept interleaved data streams. Although a printer can serve only one job at a time, several applications may wish to print their output concurrently, without having their output mixed together. The operating system solves this problem by intercepting all output to the printer. Each application's output is spooled to a separate disk file. When an application finishes printing, the spooling system queues the corresponding spool file for output to the printer. The spooling system copies the queued spool files to the printer one at a time. In some operating systems, spooling is managed by a system daemon process. In others, it is handled by an in-kernel thread. In either case, the operating system provides a control interface that enables users and system administrators to display the queue, remove unwanted jobs before those jobs print, suspend printing while the printer is serviced, and so on.

Some devices, such as tape drives and printers, cannot usefully multiplex the I/O requests of multiple concurrent applications. Spooling is one way operating systems can coordinate concurrent output. Another way to deal with concurrent device access is to provide explicit facilities for coordination. Some operating systems (including VMS) provide support for exclusive device access by enabling a process to allocate an idle device and to deallocate that device when it is no longer needed. Other operating systems enforce a limit of one open file handle to such a device. Many operating systems provide functions that enable processes to coordinate exclusive access among themselves. For instance, Windows NT provides system calls to wait until a device object becomes available. It also has a parameter to the `open()` system call that declares the types of access to be permitted to other concurrent threads. On these systems, it is up to the applications to avoid deadlock.

13.4.5 Error Handling

An operating system that uses protected memory can guard against many kinds of hardware and application errors, so that a complete system failure is not the usual result of each minor mechanical glitch. Devices and I/O transfers can fail in many ways, either for transient reasons, as when a network becomes overloaded, or for "permanent" reasons, as when a disk controller becomes defective. Operating systems can often compensate effectively for transient failures. For instance, a disk `read()` failure results in a `read()` retry, and a network `send()` error results in a `resend()`, if the protocol so specifies. Unfortunately, if an important component experiences a permanent failure, the operating system is unlikely to recover.

As a general rule, an I/O system call will return one bit of information about the status of the call, signifying either success or failure. In the UNIX operating system, an additional integer variable named `errno` is used to return an error code—one of about a hundred values—indicating the general nature of the failure (for example, argument out of range, bad pointer, or file not open). By contrast, some hardware can provide highly detailed error information, although many current operating systems are not designed to convey this information to the application. For instance, a failure of a SCSI device is reported by the SCSI protocol in three levels of detail: a **sense key** that identifies the general nature of the failure, such as a hardware error or an illegal request; an **additional sense code** that states the category of failure, such as a bad command parameter or a self-test failure; and an **additional sense-code qualifier** that gives even more detail, such as which command parameter was in error or which hardware subsystem failed its self-test. Further, many SCSI devices maintain internal pages of error-log information that can be requested by the host—but seldom are.

13.4.6 I/O Protection

Errors are closely related to the issue of protection. A user process may accidentally or purposely attempt to disrupt the normal operation of a system by attempting to issue illegal I/O instructions. We can use various mechanisms to ensure that such disruptions cannot take place in the system.

To prevent users from performing illegal I/O, we define all I/O instructions to be privileged instructions. Thus, users cannot issue I/O instructions directly; they must do it through the operating system. To do I/O, a user program executes a system call to request that the operating system perform I/O on its behalf (Figure 13.11). The operating system, executing in monitor mode, checks that the request is valid and, if it is, does the I/O requested. The operating system then returns to the user.

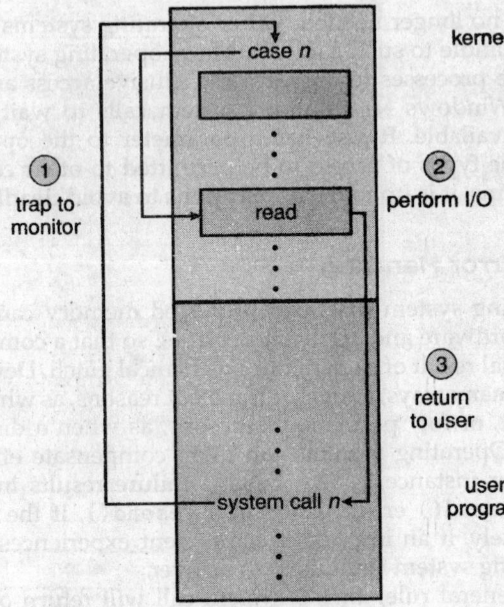

Figure 13.11 Use of a system call to perform I/O.

In addition, any memory-mapped and I/O port memory locations must be protected from user access by the memory-protection system. Note that a kernel cannot simply deny all user access. Most graphics games and video editing and playback software need direct access to memory-mapped graphics controller memory to speed the performance of the graphics, for example. The kernel might in this case provide a locking mechanism to allow a section of graphics memory (representing a window on screen) to be allocated to one process at a time.

13.4.7 Kernel Data Structures

The kernel needs to keep state information about the use of I/O components. It does so through a variety of in-kernel data structures, such as the open-file table structure from Section 11.1. The kernel uses many similar structures to track network connections, character-device communications, and other I/O activities.

UNIX provides file-system access to a variety of entities, such as user files, raw devices, and the address spaces of processes. Although each of these entities supports a `read()` operation, the semantics differ. For instance, to read a user file, the kernel needs to probe the buffer cache before deciding whether to perform a disk I/O. To read a raw disk, the kernel needs to ensure that the request size is a multiple of the disk sector size and is aligned on a sector boundary. To read a process image, it is merely necessary to copy data from memory. UNIX encapsulates these differences within a uniform structure by using an object-oriented technique. The open-file record, shown in

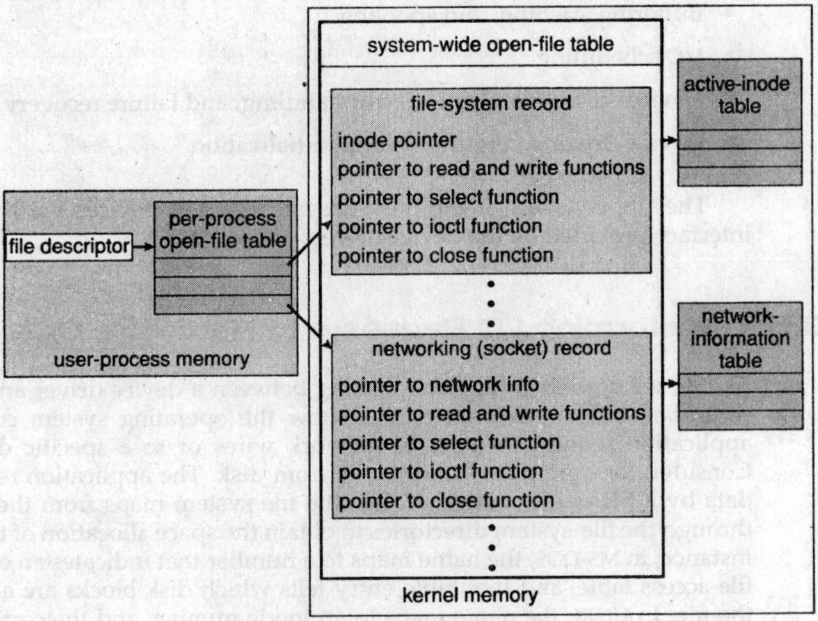

Figure 13.12 UNIX I/O kernel structure.

Figure 13.12, contains a dispatch table that holds pointers to the appropriate routines, depending on the type of file.

Some operating systems use object-oriented methods even more extensively. For instance, Windows NT uses a message-passing implementation for I/O. An I/O request is converted into a message that is sent through the kernel to the I/O manager and then to the device driver, each of which may change the message contents. For output, the message contains the data to be written. For input, the message contains a buffer to receive the data. The message-passing approach can add overhead, by comparison with procedural techniques that use shared data structures, but it simplifies the structure and design of the I/O system and adds flexibility.

13.4.8 Kernel I/O Subsystem Summary

In summary, the I/O subsystem coordinates an extensive collection of services that are available to applications and to other parts of the kernel. The I/O subsystem supervises these procedures:

- Management of the name space for files and devices
- Access control to files and devices
- Operation control (for example, a modem cannot `seek()`)
- File-system space allocation
- Device allocation

- Buffering, caching, and spooling
- I/O scheduling
- Device-status monitoring, error handling, and failure recovery
- Device-driver configuration and initialization

The upper levels of the I/O subsystem access devices via the uniform interface provided by the device drivers.

13.5 Transforming I/O Requests to Hardware Operations

Earlier, we described the handshaking between a device driver and a device controller, but we did not explain how the operating system connects an application request to a set of network wires or to a specific disk sector. Consider, for example, reading a file from disk. The application refers to the data by a file name. Within a disk, the file system maps from the file name through the file-system directories to obtain the space allocation of the file. For instance, in MS-DOS, the name maps to a number that indicates an entry in the file-access table, and that table entry tells which disk blocks are allocated to the file. In UNIX, the name maps to an inode number, and the corresponding inode contains the space-allocation information. But how is the connection made from the file name to the disk controller (the hardware port address or the memory-mapped controller registers)?

One method is that used by MS-DOS, a relatively simple operating system. The first part of an MS-DOS file name, preceding the colon, is a string that identifies a specific hardware device. For example, *c:* is the first part of every file name on the primary hard disk. The fact that *c:* represents the primary hard disk is built into the operating system; *c:* is mapped to a specific port address through a device table. Because of the colon separator, the device name space is separate from the file-system name space. This separation makes it easy for the operating system to associate extra functionality with each device. For instance, it is easy to invoke spooling on any files written to the printer.

If, instead, the device name space is incorporated in the regular file-system name space, as it is in UNIX, the normal file-system name services are provided automatically. If the file system provides ownership and access control to all file names, then devices have owners and access control. Since files are stored on devices, such an interface provides access to the I/O system at two levels. Names can be used to access the devices themselves or to access the files stored on the devices.

UNIX represents device names in the regular file-system name space. Unlike an MS-DOS file name, which has a colon separator, a UNIX path name has no clear separation of the device portion. In fact, no part of the path name is the name of a device. UNIX has a **mount table** that associates prefixes of path names with specific device names. To resolve a path name, UNIX looks up the name in the mount table to find the longest matching prefix; the corresponding entry in the mount table gives the device name. This device name also has the form of a name in the file-system name space. When UNIX looks up this name in the file-system directory structures, it finds not an inode number but a <*major,* *minor*> device number. The major device number identifies a device driver that should be called to handle I/O to this device. The minor device number is passed to the device driver to index into a device table. The corresponding device-table entry gives the port address or the memory-mapped address of the device controller.

Modern operating systems obtain significant flexibility from the multiple stages of lookup tables in the path between a request and a physical device controller. The mechanisms that pass requests between applications and drivers are general. Thus, we can introduce new devices and drivers into a computer without recompiling the kernel. In fact, some operating systems have the ability to load device drivers on demand. At boot time, the system first probes the hardware buses to determine what devices are present; it then loads in the necessary drivers, either immediately or when first required by an I/O request.

We next describe the typical life cycle of a blocking read request, as depicted in Figure 13.13. The figure suggests that an I/O operation requires a great many steps that together consume a tremendous number of CPU cycles.

1. A process issues a blocking `read()` system call to a file descriptor of a file that has been opened previously.
2. The system-call code in the kernel checks the parameters for correctness. In the case of input, if the data are already available in the buffer cache, the data are returned to the process, and the I/O request is completed.
3. Otherwise, a physical I/O must be performed. The process is removed from the run queue and is placed on the wait queue for the device, and the I/O request is scheduled. Eventually, the I/O subsystem sends the request to the device driver. Depending on the operating system, the request is sent via a subroutine call or an in-kernel message.
4. The device driver allocates kernel buffer space to receive the data and schedules the I/O. Eventually, the driver sends commands to the device controller by writing into the device-control registers.
5. The device controller operates the device hardware to perform the data transfer.
6. The driver may poll for status and data, or it may have set up a DMA transfer into kernel memory. We assume that the transfer is managed by a DMA controller, which generates an interrupt when the transfer completes.
7. The correct interrupt handler receives the interrupt via the interrupt-vector table, stores any necessary data, signals the device driver, and returns from the interrupt.
8. The device driver receives the signal, determines which I/O request has completed, determines the request's status, and signals the kernel I/O subsystem that the request has been completed.
9. The kernel transfers data or return codes to the address space of the requesting process and moves the process from the wait queue back to the ready queue.

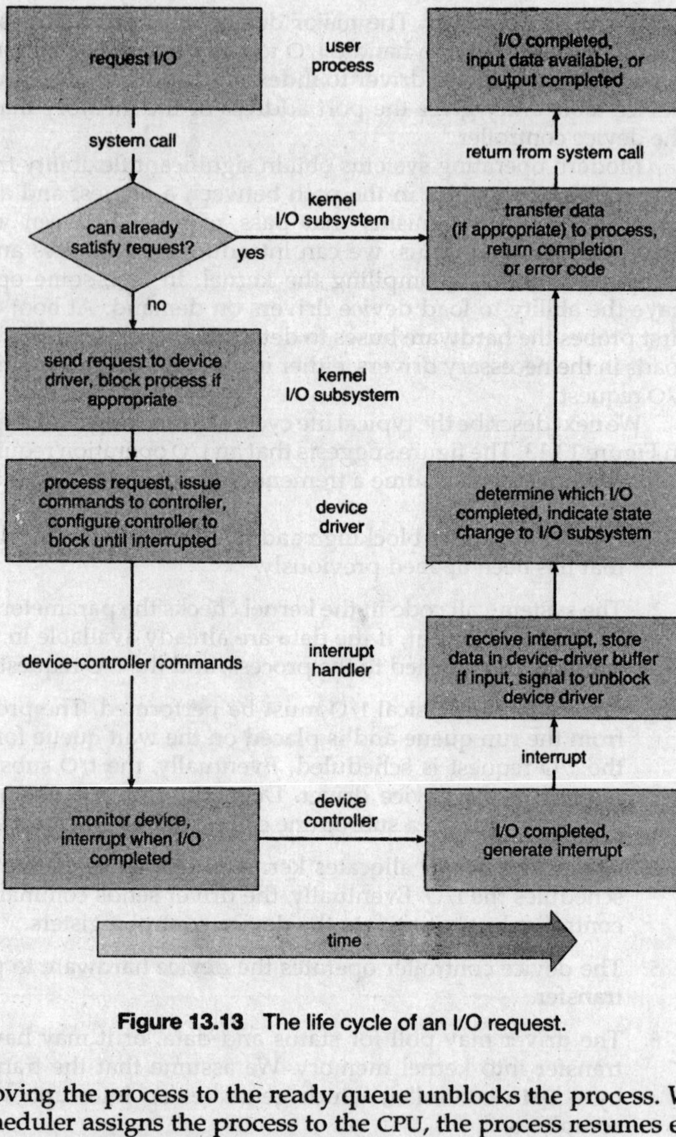

Figure 13.13 The life cycle of an I/O request.

10. Moving the process to the ready queue unblocks the process. When the scheduler assigns the process to the CPU, the process resumes execution at the completion of the system call.

13.6 STREAMS

UNIX System V has an interesting mechanism, called STREAMS, that enables an application to assemble pipelines of driver code dynamically. A stream is a full-duplex connection between a device driver and a user-level process. It consists of a stream head that interfaces with the user process, a driver end that controls the device, and zero or more stream modules between the stream

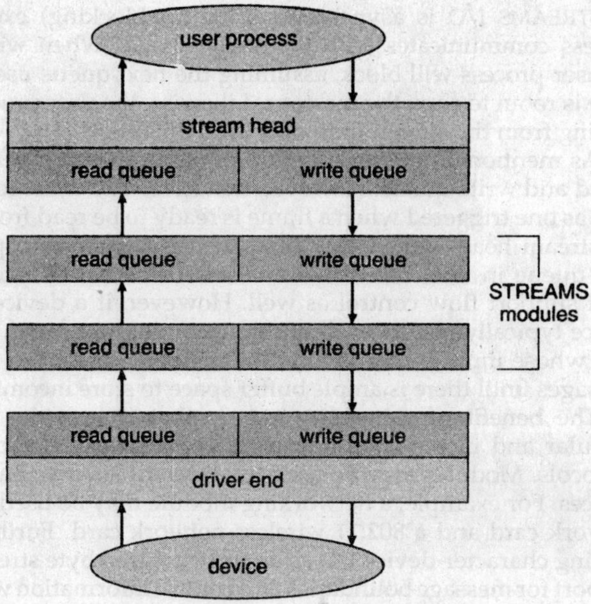

Figure 13.14 The STREAMS structure.

head and the driver end. Each of these components contains a pair of queues —a read queue and a write queue. Message passing is used to transfer data between queues. The STREAMS structure is shown in Figure 13.14.

Modules provide the functionality of STREAMS processing; they are *pushed* onto a stream by use of the `ioctl()` system call. For example, a process can open a serial-port device via a stream and can push on a module to handle input editing. Because messages are exchanged between queues in adjacent modules, a queue in one module may overflow an adjacent queue. To prevent this from occurring, a queue may support **flow control**. Without flow control, a queue accepts all messages and immediately sends them on to the queue in the adjacent module without buffering them. A queue supporting flow control buffers messages and does not accept messages without sufficient buffer space; this process involves exchanges of control messages between queues in adjacent modules.

A user process writes data to a device using either the `write()` or `putmsg()` system call. The `write()` system call writes raw data to the stream, whereas `putmsg()` allows the user process to specify a message. Regardless of the system call used by the user process, the stream head copies the data into a message and delivers it to the queue for the next module in line. This copying of messages continues until the message is copied to the driver end and hence the device. Similarly, the user process reads data from the stream head using either the `read()` or `getmsg()` system call. If `read()` is used, the stream head gets a message from its adjacent queue and returns ordinary data (an unstructured byte stream) to the process. If `getmsg()` is used, a message is returned to the process.

STREAMS I/O is asynchronous (or nonblocking) except when the user process communicates with the stream head. When writing to the stream, the user process will block, assuming the next queue uses flow control, until there is room to copy the message. Likewise, the user process will block when reading from the stream until data are available.

As mentioned, the driver end—like the stream head and modules—has a read and write queue. However, the driver end must respond to interrupts, such as one triggered when a frame is ready to be read from a network. Unlike the stream head, which may block if it is unable to copy a message to the next queue in line, the driver end must handle all incoming data. Drivers must support flow control as well. However, if a device's buffer is full, the device typically resorts to dropping incoming messages. Consider a network card whose input buffer is full. The network card must simply drop further messages until there is ample buffer space to store incoming messages.

The benefit of using STREAMS is that it provides a framework for a modular and incremental approach to writing device drivers and network protocols. Modules may be used by different streams and hence by different devices. For example, a networking module may be used by both an Ethernet network card and a 802.11 wireless network card. Furthermore, rather than treating character-device I/O as an unstructured byte stream, STREAMS allows support for message boundaries and control information when communicating between modules. Most UNIX variants support STREAMS, and it is the preferred method for writing protocols and device drivers. For example, System V UNIX and Solaris implement the socket mechanism using STREAMS.

13.7 Performance

I/O is a major factor in system performance. It places heavy demands on the CPU to execute device-driver code and to schedule processes fairly and efficiently as they block and unblock. The resulting context switches stress the CPU and its hardware caches. I/O also exposes any inefficiencies in the interrupt-handling mechanisms in the kernel. In addition, I/O loads down the memory bus during data copies between controllers and physical memory and again during copies between kernel buffers and application data space. Coping gracefully with all these demands is one of the major concerns of a computer architect.

Although modern computers can handle many thousands of interrupts per second, interrupt handling is a relatively expensive task. Each interrupt causes the system to perform a state change, to execute the interrupt handler, and then to restore state. Programmed I/O can be more efficient than interrupt-driven I/O, if the number of cycles spent in busy waiting is not excessive. An I/O completion typically unblocks a process, leading to the full overhead of a context switch.

Network traffic can also cause a high context-switch rate. Consider, for instance, a remote login from one machine to another. Each character typed on the local machine must be transported to the remote machine. On the local machine, the character is typed; a keyboard interrupt is generated; and the character is passed through the interrupt handler to the device driver, to the kernel, and then to the user process. The user process issues a network I/O system call to send the character to the remote machine. The character then flows into the local kernel, through the network layers that construct a network packet, and into the network device driver. The network device driver transfers the packet to the network controller, which sends the character and generates an interrupt. The interrupt is passed back up through the kernel to cause the network I/O system call to complete.

Now, the remote system's network hardware receives the packet, and an interrupt is generated. The character is unpacked from the network protocols and is given to the appropriate network daemon. The network daemon identifies which remote login session is involved and passes the packet to the appropriate subdaemon for that session. Throughout this flow, there are context switches and state switches (Figure 13.15). Usually, the receiver echoes the character back to the sender; that approach doubles the work.

To eliminate the context switches involved in moving each character between daemons and the kernel, the Solaris developers reimplemented the **telnet** daemon using in-kernel threads. Sun estimates that this improvement

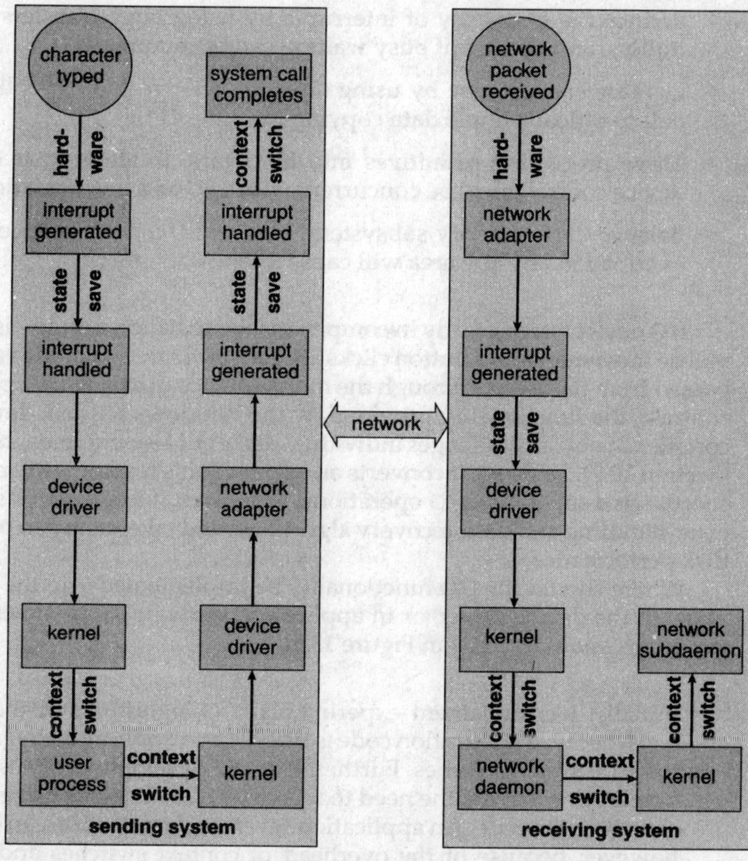

Figure 13.15 Intercomputer communications.

increased the maximum number of network logins from a few hundred to a few thousand on a large server.

Other systems use separate front-end processors for terminal I/O to reduce the interrupt burden on the main CPU. For instance, a terminal concentrator can multiplex the traffic from hundreds of remote terminals into one port on a large computer. An I/O channel is a dedicated, special-purpose CPU found in mainframes and in other high-end systems. The job of a channel is to offload I/O work from the main CPU. The idea is that the channels keep the data flowing smoothly, while the main CPU remains free to process the data. Like the device controllers and DMA controllers found in smaller computers, a channel can process more general and sophisticated programs, so channels can be tuned for particular workloads.

We can employ several principles to improve the efficiency of I/O:

- Reduce the number of context switches.
- Reduce the number of times that data must be copied in memory while passing between device and application.
- Reduce the frequency of interrupts by using large transfers, smart controllers, and polling (if busy waiting can be minimized).
- Increase concurrency by using DMA-knowledgeable controllers or channels to offload simple data copying from the CPU.
- Move processing primitives into hardware, to allow their operation in device controllers to be concurrent with CPU and bus operation.
- Balance CPU, memory subsystem, bus, and I/O performance, because an overload in any one area will cause idleness in others.

I/O devices vary greatly in complexity. For instance, a mouse is simple. The mouse movements and button clicks are converted into numeric values that are passed from hardware, through the mouse device driver, to the application. By contrast, the functionality provided by the Windows NT disk device driver is complex. It not only manages individual disks but also implements RAID arrays (Section 12.7). To do so, it converts an application's read or write request into a coordinated set of disk I/O operations. Moreover, it implements sophisticated error-handling and data-recovery algorithms and takes many steps to optimize disk performance.

Where should the I/O functionality be implemented—in the device hardware, in the device driver, or in application software? Sometimes we observe the progression depicted in Figure 13.16.

- Initially, we implement experimental I/O algorithms at the application level, because application code is flexible and application bugs are unlikely to cause system crashes. Furthermore, by developing code at the application level, we avoid the need to reboot or reload device drivers after every change to the code. An application-level implementation can be inefficient, however, because of the overhead of context switches and because the application cannot take advantage of internal kernel data structures and

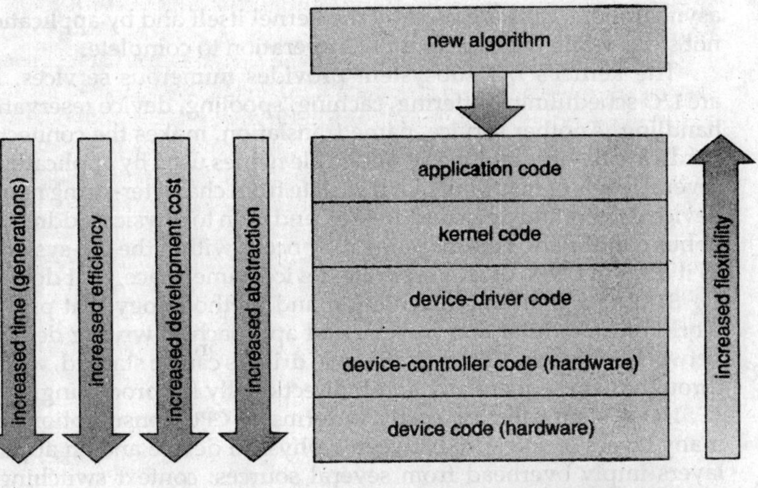

Figure 13.16 Device functionality progression.

kernel functionality (such as efficient in-kernel messaging, threading, and locking).

- When an application-level algorithm has demonstrated its worth, we may reimplement it in the kernel. This can improve performance, but the development effort is more challenging, because an operating-system kernel is a large, complex software system. Moreover, an in-kernel implementation must be thoroughly debugged to avoid data corruption and system crashes.

- The highest performance may be obtained through a specialized implementation in hardware, either in the device or in the controller. The disadvantages of a hardware implementation include the difficulty and expense of making further improvements or of fixing bugs, the increased development time (months rather than days), and the decreased flexibility. For instance, a hardware RAID controller may not provide any means for the kernel to influence the order or location of individual block reads and writes, even if the kernel has special information about the workload that would enable it to improve the I/O performance.

13.8 Summary

The basic hardware elements involved in I/O are buses, device controllers, and the devices themselves. The work of moving data between devices and main memory is performed by the CPU as programmed I/O or is offloaded to a DMA controller. The kernel module that controls a device is a device driver. The system-call interface provided to applications is designed to handle several basic categories of hardware, including block devices, character devices, memory-mapped files, network sockets, and programmed interval timers. The system calls usually block the processes that issue them, but nonblocking and asynchronous calls are used by the kernel itself and by applications that must not sleep while waiting for an I/O operation to complete.

The kernel's I/O subsystem provides numerous services. Among these are I/O scheduling, buffering, caching, spooling, device reservation, and error handling. Another service, name translation, makes the connections between hardware devices and the symbolic file names used by applications. It involves several levels of mapping that translate from character-string names, to specific device drivers and device addresses, and then to physical addresses of I/O ports or bus controllers. This mapping may occur within the file-system name space, as it does in UNIX, or in a separate device name space, as it does in MS-DOS.

STREAMS is an implementation and methodology that provides a framework for a modular and incremental approach to writing device drivers and network protocols. Through streams, drivers can be stacked, with data passing through them sequentially and bidirectionally for processing.

I/O system calls are costly in terms of CPU consumption because of the many layers of software between a physical device and an application. These layers imply overhead from several sources: context switching to cross the kernel's protection boundary, signal and interrupt handling to service the I/O devices, and the load on the CPU and memory system to copy data between kernel buffers and application space.

Exercises

13.1 Write (in pseudocode) an implementation of virtual clocks, including the queueing and management of timer requests for the kernel and applications. Assume that the hardware provides three timer channels.

13.2 What are the advantages and disadvantages of supporting memory-mapped I/O to device control registers?

13.3 Typically, at the completion of a device I/O, a single interrupt is raised and appropriately handled by the host processor. In certain settings, however, the code that is to be executed at the completion of the I/O can be broken into two separate pieces. The first piece executes immediately after the I/O completes and schedules a second interrupt for the remaining piece of code to be executed at a later time. What is the purpose of using this strategy in the design of interrupt handlers?

13.4 Why might a system use interrupt-driven I/O to manage a single serial port and polling I/O to manage a front-end processor, such as a terminal concentrator?

13.5 What are the various kinds of performance overhead associated with servicing an interrupt?

13.6 UNIX coordinates the activities of the kernel I/O components by manipulating shared in-kernel data structures, whereas Windows NT uses object-oriented message passing between kernel I/O components. Discuss three pros and three cons of each approach.

13.7 In most multiprogrammed systems, user programs access memory through virtual addresses, while the operating system uses raw physical addresses to access memory. What are the implications of this design for the initiation of I/O operations by the user program and their execution by the operating system?

13.8 Polling for an I/O completion can waste a large number of CPU cycles if the processor iterates a busy-waiting loop many times before the I/O completes. But if the I/O device is ready for service, polling can be much more efficient than is catching and dispatching an interrupt. Describe a hybrid strategy that combines polling, sleeping, and interrupts for I/O device service. For each of these three strategies (pure polling, pure interrupts, hybrid), describe a computing environment in which that strategy is more efficient than is either of the others.

13.9 Consider the following I/O scenarios on a single-user PC:

a. A mouse used with a graphical user interface

b. A tape drive on a multitasking operating system (with no device preallocation available)

c. A disk drive containing user files

d. A graphics card with direct bus connection, accessible through memory-mapped I/O

For each of these scenarios, would you design the operating system to use buffering, spooling, caching, or a combination? Would you use polled I/O or interrupt-driven I/O? Give reasons for your choices.

13.10 The example of handshaking in Section 13.2 used 2 bits: a busy bit and a command-ready bit. Is it possible to implement this handshaking with only 1 bit? If it is, describe the protocol. If it is not, explain why 1 bit is insufficient.

13.11 Discuss the advantages and disadvantages of guaranteeing reliable transfer of data between modules in the STREAMS abstraction.

13.12 Some DMA controllers support direct virtual memory access, where the targets of I/O operations are specified as virtual addresses and a translation from virtual to physical address is performed during the DMA. How does this design complicate the design of the DMA controller? What are the advantages of providing such functionality?

13.13 Why is it important to scale up system-bus and device speeds as CPU speed increases?

13.14 When multiple interrupts from different devices appear at about the same time, a priority scheme could be used to determine the order in which the interrupts would be serviced. Discuss what issues need to be considered in assigning priorities to different interrupts.

13.15 Describe three circumstances under which blocking I/O should be used. Describe three circumstances under which nonblocking I/O should be used. Why not just implement nonblocking I/O and have processes busy-wait until their devices are ready?

Bibliographical Notes

Vahalia [1996] provides a good overview of I/O and networking in UNIX. Leffler et al. [1989] detail the I/O structures and methods employed in BSD UNIX. Milenkovic [1987] discusses the complexity of I/O methods and implementation. The use and programming of the various interprocess-communication and network protocols in UNIX are explored in Stevens [1992]. Brain [1996] documents the Windows NT application interface. The I/O implementation in the sample MINIX operating system is described in Tanenbaum and Woodhull [1997]. Custer [1994] includes detailed information on the NT message-passing implementation of I/O.

For details of hardware-level I/O handling and memory-mapping functionality, processor reference manuals (Motorola [1993] and Intel [1993]) are among the best sources. Hennessy and Patterson [2002] describe multiprocessor systems and cache-consistency issues. Tanenbaum [1990] describes hardware I/O design at a low level, and Sargent and Shoemaker [1995] provide a programmer's guide to low-level PC hardware and software. The IBM PC device I/O address map is given in IBM [1983]. The March 1994 issue of *IEEE Computer* is devoted to I/O hardware and software. Rago [1993] provides a good discussion of STREAMS.

Part Six

Protection and Security

Protection mechanisms control access to a system by limiting the types of file access permitted to users. In addition, protection must ensure that only processes that have gained proper authorization from the operating system can operate on memory segments, the CPU, and other resources.

Protection is provided by a mechanism that controls the access of programs, processes, or users to the resources defined by a computer system. This mechanism must provide a means for specifying the controls to be imposed, together with a means of enforcing them.

Security ensures the authentication of system users to protect the integrity of the information stored in the system (both data and code), as well as the physical resources of the computer system. The security system prevents unauthorized access, malicious destruction or alteration of data, and accidental introduction of inconsistency.

CHAPTER 14

System Protection

The processes in an operating system must be protected from one another's activities. To provide such protection, we can use various mechanisms to ensure that only processes that have gained proper authorization from the operating system can operate on the files, memory segments, CPU, and other resources of a system.

Protection refers to a mechanism for controlling the access of programs, processes, or users to the resources defined by a computer system. This mechanism must provide a means for specifying the controls to be imposed, together with a means of enforcement. We distinguish between protection and security, which is a measure of confidence that the integrity of a system and its data will be preserved. In this chapter, we focus on protection. Security assurance is a much broader topic, and we address it in Chapter 15.

CHAPTER OBJECTIVES

- To discuss the goals and principles of protection in a modern computer system.
- To explain how protection domains, combined with an access matrix, are used to specify the resources a process may access.
- To examine capability- and language-based protection systems.

14.1 Goals of Protection

As computer systems have become more sophisticated and pervasive in their applications, the need to protect their integrity has also grown. Protection was originally conceived as an adjunct to multiprogramming operating systems, so that untrustworthy users might safely share a common logical name space, such as a directory of files, or share a common physical name space, such as memory. Modern protection concepts have evolved to increase the reliability of any complex system that makes use of shared resources.

We need to provide protection for several reasons. The most obvious is the need to prevent the mischievous, intentional violation of an access restriction by a user. Of more general importance, however, is the need to ensure that each program component active in a system uses system resources only in ways consistent with stated policies. This requirement is an absolute one for a reliable system.

Protection can improve reliability by detecting latent errors at the interfaces between component subsystems. Early detection of interface errors can often prevent contamination of a healthy subsystem by a malfunctioning subsystem. Also, an unprotected resource cannot defend against use (or misuse) by an unauthorized or incompetent user. A protection-oriented system provides means to distinguish between authorized and unauthorized usage.

The role of protection in a computer system is to provide a mechanism for the enforcement of the policies governing resource use. These policies can be established in a variety of ways. Some are fixed in the design of the system, while others are formulated by the management of a system. Still others are defined by the individual users to protect their own files and programs. A protection system must have the flexibility to enforce a variety of policies.

Policies for resource use may vary by application, and they may change over time. For these reasons, protection is no longer the concern solely of the designer of an operating system. The application programmer needs to use protection mechanisms as well, to guard resources created and supported by an application subsystem against misuse. In this chapter, we describe the protection mechanisms the operating system should provide, but application designers can use them as well in designing their own protection software.

Note that *mechanisms* are distinct from *policies*. Mechanisms determine *how* something will be done; policies decide *what* will be done. The separation of policy and mechanism is important for flexibility. Policies are likely to change from place to place or time to time. In the worst case, every change in policy would require a change in the underlying mechanism. Using general mechanisms enables us to avoid such a situation.

14.2 Principles of Protection

Frequently, a guiding principle can be used throughout a project, such as the design of an operating system. Following this principle simplifies design decisions and keeps the system consistent and easy to understand. A key, time-tested guiding principle for protection is the **principle of least privilege**. It dictates that programs, users, and even systems be given just enough privileges to perform their tasks.

Consider the analogy of a security guard with a passkey. If this key allows the guard into just the public areas that she guards, then misuse of the key will result in minimal damage. If, however, the passkey allows access to all areas, then damage from its being lost, stolen, misused, copied, or otherwise compromised will be much greater.

An operating system following the principle of least privilege implements its features, programs, system calls, and data structures so that failure or compromise of a component does the minimum damage and allows the minimum damage to be done. The overflow of a buffer in a system daemon might cause the daemon process to fail, for example, but should not allow the execution of code from the daemon process's stack that would enable a remote user to gain maximum privileges and access to the entire system (as happens too often today).

Such an operating system also provides system calls and services that allow applications to be written with fine-grained access controls. It provides mechanisms to enable privileges when they are needed and to disable them when they are not needed. Also beneficial is the creation of audit trails for all privileged function access. The audit trail allows the programmer, systems administrator, or law-enforcement officer to trace all protection and security activities on the system.

Managing users with the principle of least privilege entails creating a separate account for each user, with just the privileges that the user needs. An operator who needs to mount tapes and back up files on the system has access to just those commands and files needed to accomplish the job. Some systems implement role-based access control (RBAC) to provide this functionality.

Computers implemented in a computing facility under the principle of least privilege can be limited to running specific services, accessing specific remote hosts via specific services, and doing so during specific times. Typically, these restrictions are implemented through enabling or disabling each service and through using access control lists, as described in Sections 10.6.2 and 14.6.

The principle of least privilege can help produce a more secure computing environment. Unfortunately, it frequently does not. For example, Windows 2000 has a complex protection scheme at its core and yet has many security holes. By comparison, Solaris is considered relatively secure, even though it is a variant of UNIX, which historically was designed with little protection in mind. One reason for the difference may be that Windows 2000 has more lines of code and more services than Solaris and thus has more to secure and protect. Another reason could be that the protection scheme in Windows 2000 is incomplete or protects the wrong aspects of the operating system, leaving other areas vulnerable.

14.3 Domain of Protection

A computer system is a collection of processes and objects. By *objects*, we mean both **hardware objects** (such as the CPU, memory segments, printers, disks, and tape drives) and **software objects** (such as files, programs, and semaphores). Each object has a unique name that differentiates it from all other objects in the system, and each can be accessed only through well-defined and meaningful operations. Objects are essentially abstract data types.

The operations that are possible may depend on the object. For example, on a CPU, we can only execute. Memory segments can be read and written, whereas a CD-ROM or DVD-ROM can only be read. Tape drives can be read, written, and rewound. Data files can be created, opened, read, written, closed, and deleted; program files can be read, written, executed, and deleted.

A process should be allowed to access only those resources for which it has authorization. Furthermore, at any time, a process should be able to access only those resources that it currently requires to complete its task. This second requirement, commonly referred to as the *need-to-know* principle, is useful in limiting the amount of damage a faulty process can cause in the system. For example, when process p invokes procedure $A()$, the procedure should be allowed to access only its own variables and the formal parameters passed to it; it should not be able to access all the variables of process *p*. Similarly, consider the case in which process *p* invokes a compiler to compile a particular file. The compiler should not be able to access files arbitrarily but should have access only to a well-defined subset of files (such as the source file, listing file, and so on) related to the file to be compiled. Conversely, the compiler may have private files used for accounting or optimization purposes that process *p* should not be able to access. The need-to-know principle is similar to the principle of least privilege discussed in Section 14.2 in that the goals of protection are to minimize the risks of possible security violations.

14.3.1 Domain Structure

To facilitate the scheme just described, a process operates within a **protection domain**, which specifies the resources that the process may access. Each domain defines a set of objects and the types of operations that may be invoked on each object. The ability to execute an operation on an object is an **access right**. A domain is a collection of access rights, each of which is an ordered pair *<object-name, rights-set>*. For example, if domain *D* has the access right *<file F*, {read,write}>, then a process executing in domain *D* can both read and write file *F*; it cannot, however, perform any other operation on that object.

Domains do not need to be disjoint; they may share access rights. For example, in Figure 14.1, we have three domains: D_1, D_2, and D_3. The access right <O_4, {print}> is shared by D_2 and D_3, implying that a process executing in either of these two domains can print object O_4. Note that a process must be executing in domain D_1 to read and write object O_1, while only processes in domain D_3 may execute object O_1.

The association between a process and a domain may be either **static**, if the set of resources available to the process is fixed throughout the process's lifetime, or **dynamic**. As might be expected, establishing dynamic protection domains is more complicated than establishing static protection domains.

If the association between processes and domains is fixed, and we want to adhere to the need-to-know principle, then a mechanism must be available to change the content of a domain. The reason stems from the fact that a process may execute in two different phases and may, for example, need read access in one phase and write access in another. If a domain is static, we must define the domain to include both read and write access. However, this arrangement provides more rights than are needed in each of the two phases, since we have read access in the phase where we need only write access, and vice versa. Thus, the need-to-know principle is violated. We must allow the contents of

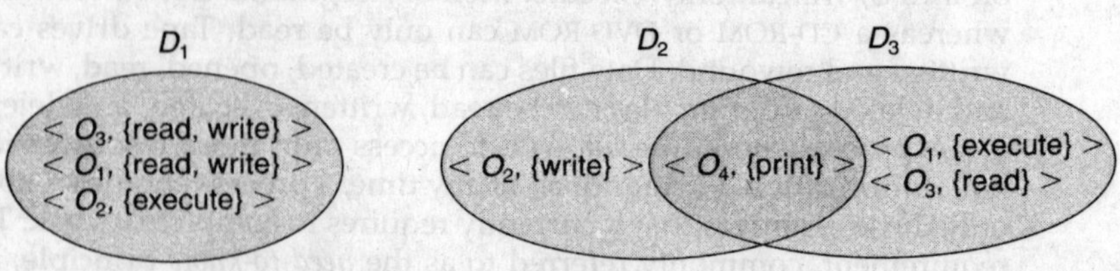

Figure 14.1 System with three protection domains.

a domain to be modified so that the domain always reflects the minimum necessary access rights.

If the association is dynamic, a mechanism is available to allow **domain switching**, enabling the process to switch from one domain to another. We may also want to allow the content of a domain to be changed. If we cannot change the content of a domain, we can provide the same effect by creating a new domain with the changed content and switching to that new domain when we want to change the domain content.

A domain can be realized in a variety of ways:

- Each *user* may be a domain. In this case, the set of objects that can be accessed depends on the identity of the user. Domain switching occurs when the user is changed—generally when one user logs out and another user logs in.
- Each *process* may be a domain. In this case, the set of objects that can be accessed depends on the identity of the process. Domain switching occurs when one process sends a message to another process and then waits for a response.
- Each *procedure* may be a domain. In this case, the set of objects that can be accessed corresponds to the local variables defined within the procedure. Domain switching occurs when a procedure call is made.

We discuss domain switching in greater detail in Section 14.4.

Consider the standard dual-mode (monitor–user mode) model of operating-system execution. When a process executes in monitor mode, it can execute privileged instructions and thus gain complete control of the computer system. In contrast, when a process executes in user mode, it can invoke only nonprivileged instructions. Consequently, it can execute only within its predefined memory space. These two modes protect the operating system (executing in monitor domain) from the user processes (executing in user domain). In a multiprogrammed operating system, two protection domains are insufficient, since users also want to be protected from one another. Therefore, a more elaborate scheme is needed. We illustrate such a scheme by examining two influential operating systems—UNIX and MULTICS—to see how they implement these concepts.

14.3.2 An Example: UNIX

In the UNIX operating system, a domain is associated with the user. Switching the domain corresponds to changing the user identification temporarily. This change is accomplished through the file system as follows. An owner identification and a domain bit (known as the *setuid bit*) are associated with each file. When the setuid bit is *on*, and a user executes that file, the user ID is set to that of the owner of the file; when the bit is *off*, however, the user ID does not change. For example, when a user *A* (that is, a user with *userID* = *A*) starts executing a file owned by *B*, whose associated domain bit is *off*, the *userID* of the process is set to *A*. When the setuid bit is *on*, the userID is set to that of the owner of the file: *B*. When the process exits, this temporary userID change ends.

Other methods are used to change domains in operating systems in which user IDs are used for domain definition, because almost all systems need to provide such a mechanism. This mechanism is used when an otherwise privileged facility needs to be made available to the general user population. For instance, it might be desirable to allow users to access a network without letting them write their own networking programs. In such a case, on a UNIX system, the setuid bit on a networking program would be set, causing the user ID to change when the program was run. The user ID would change to that of a user with network access privilege (such as *root*, the most powerful user ID). One problem with this method is that if a user manages to create a file with user ID *root* and with its setuid bit *on*, that user can become *root* and do anything and everything on the system. The setuid mechanism is discussed further in Appendix A.

An alternative to this method used in other operating systems is to place privileged programs in a special directory. The operating system would be designed to change the user ID of any program run from this directory, either to the equivalent of *root* or to the user ID of the owner of the directory. This eliminates one security problem with setuid programs in which crackers create and hide such programs for later use (using obscure file or directory names). This method is less flexible than that used in UNIX, however.

Even more restrictive, and thus more protective, are systems that simply do not allow a change of user ID. In these instances, special techniques must be used to allow users access to privileged facilities. For instance, a **daemon process** may be started at boot time and run as a special user ID. Users then run a separate program, which sends requests to this process whenever they need to use the facility. This method is used by the TOPS-20 operating system.

In any of these systems, great care must be taken in writing privileged programs. Any oversight can result in a total lack of protection on the system. Generally, these programs are the first to be attacked by people trying to break into a system; unfortunately, the attackers are frequently successful. For example, security has been breached on many UNIX systems because of the setuid feature. We discuss security in Chapter 15.

14.3.3 An Example: MULTICS

In the MULTICS system, the protection domains are organized hierarchically into a ring structure. Each ring corresponds to a single domain (Figure 14.2). The rings are numbered from 0 to 7. Let D_i and D_j be any two domain rings. If $j < i$, then D_i is a subset of D_j. That is, a process executing in domain D_j has more privileges than does a process executing in domain D_i. A process executing in domain D_0 has the most privileges. If only two rings exist, this scheme is equivalent to the monitor–user mode of execution, where monitor mode corresponds to D_0 and user mode corresponds to D_1.

MULTICS has a segmented address space; each segment is a file, and each segment is associated with one of the rings. A segment description includes an entry that identifies the ring number. In addition, it includes three access bits to control reading, writing, and execution. The association between segments and rings is a policy decision with which we are not concerned here.

A *current-ring-number* counter is associated with each process, identifying the ring in which the process is executing currently. When a process is executing

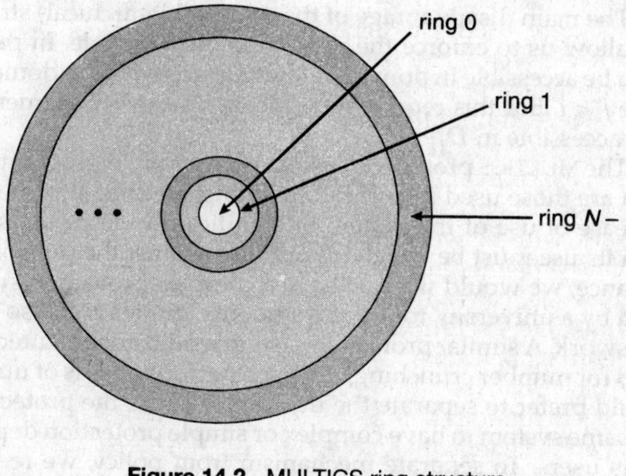

Figure 14.2 MULTICS ring structure

in ring i, it cannot access a segment associated with ring j ($j < i$). It can access a segment associated with ring k ($k \geq i$). The type of access, however, is restricted according to the access bits associated with that segment.

Domain switching in MULTICS occurs when a process crosses from one ring to another by calling a procedure in a different ring. Obviously, this switch must be done in a controlled manner; otherwise, a process could start executing in ring 0, and no protection would be provided. To allow controlled domain switching, we modify the ring field of the segment descriptor to include the following:

- **Access bracket**. A pair of integers, $b1$ and $b2$, such that $b1 \leq b2$.
- **Limit**. An integer $b3$ such that $b3 > b2$.
- **List of gates**. Identifies the entry points (or gates) at which the segments may be called.

If a process executing in ring i calls a procedure (or segment) with access bracket ($b1$,$b2$), then the call is allowed if $b1 \leq i \leq b2$, and the current ring number of the process remains i. Otherwise, a trap to the operating system occurs, and the situation is handled as follows:

- If $i < b1$, then the call is allowed to occur, because we have a transfer to a ring (or domain) with fewer privileges. However, if parameters are passed that refer to segments in a lower ring (that is, segments not accessible to the called procedure), then these segments must be copied into an area that can be accessed by the called procedure.
- If $i > b2$, then the call is allowed to occur only if $b3$ is greater than or equal to i and the call has been directed to one of the designated entry points in the list of gates. This scheme allows processes with limited access rights to call procedures in lower rings that have more access rights, but only in a carefully controlled manner.

The main disadvantage of the ring (or hierarchical) structure is that it does not allow us to enforce the need-to-know principle. In particular, if an object must be accessible in domain D_j but not accessible in domain D_i, then we must have $j < i$. But this requirement means that every segment accessible in D_i is also accessible in D_j.

The MULTICS protection system is generally more complex and less efficient than are those used in current operating systems. If protection interferes with the ease of use of the system or significantly decreases system performance, then its use must be weighed carefully against the purpose of the system. For instance, we would want to have a complex protection system on a computer used by a university to process students' grades and also used by students for classwork. A similar protection system would not be suited to a computer being used for number crunching, in which performance is of utmost importance. We would prefer to separate the mechanism from the protection policy, allowing the same system to have complex or simple protection depending on the needs of its users. To separate mechanism from policy, we require a more general model of protection.

14.4 Access Matrix

Our model of protection can be viewed abstractly as a matrix, called an **access matrix**. The rows of the access matrix represent domains, and the columns represent objects. Each entry in the matrix consists of a set of access rights. Because the column defines objects explicitly, we can omit the object name from the access right. The entry `access`(i,j) defines the set of operations that a process executing in domain D_i can invoke on object O_j.

To illustrate these concepts, we consider the access matrix shown in Figure 14.3. There are four domains and four objects—three files (F_1, F_2, F_3) and one laser printer. A process executing in domain D_1 can read files F_1 and F_3. A process executing in domain D_4 has the same privileges as one executing in domain D_1; but in addition, it can also write onto files F_1 and F_3. Note that the laser printer can be accessed only by a process executing in domain D_2.

The access-matrix scheme provides us with the mechanism for specifying a variety of policies. The mechanism consists of implementing the access

domain \ object	F_1	F_2	F_3	printer
D_1	read		read	
D_2				print
D_3		read	execute	
D_4	read write		read write	

Figure 14.3 Access matrix.

matrix and ensuring that the semantic properties we have outlined hold. More specifically, we must ensure that a process executing in domain D_i can access only those objects specified in row i, and then only as allowed by the access-matrix entries.

The access matrix can implement policy decisions concerning protection. The policy decisions involve which rights should be included in the (i,j)th entry. We must also decide the domain in which each process executes. This last policy is usually decided by the operating system.

The users normally decide the contents of the access-matrix entries. When a user creates a new object O_j, the column O_j is added to the access matrix with the appropriate initialization entries, as dictated by the creator. The user may decide to enter some rights in some entries in column j and other rights in other entries, as needed.

The access matrix provides an appropriate mechanism for defining and implementing strict control for both the static and dynamic association between processes and domains. When we switch a process from one domain to another, we are executing an operation (`switch`) on an object (the domain). We can control domain switching by including domains among the objects of the access matrix. Similarly, when we change the content of the access matrix, we are performing an operation on an object: the access matrix. Again, we can control these changes by including the access matrix itself as an object. Actually, since each entry in the access matrix may be modified individually, we must consider each entry in the access matrix as an object to be protected. Now, we need to consider only the operations possible on these new objects (domains and the access matrix) and decide how we want processes to be able to execute these operations.

Processes should be able to switch from one domain to another. Switching from domain D_i to domain D_j is allowed if and only if the access right `switch` ∈ `access`(i, j). Thus, in Figure 14.4, a process executing in domain D_2 can switch to domain D_3 or to domain D_4. A process in domain D_4 can switch to D_1, and one in domain D_1 can switch to D_2.

Allowing controlled change in the contents of the access-matrix entries requires three additional operations: `copy`, `owner`, and `control`. We examine these operations next.

domain \ object	F_1	F_2	F_3	laser printer	D_1	D_2	D_3	D_4
D_1	read		read			switch		
D_2				print			switch	switch
D_3		read	execute					
D_4	read write		read write		switch			

Figure 14.4 Access matrix of Figure 14.3 with domains as objects.

domain \ object	F_1	F_2	F_3
D_1	execute		write*
D_2	execute	read*	execute
D_3	execute		

(a)

domain \ object	F_1	F_2	F_3
D_1	execute		write*
D_2	execute	read*	execute
D_3	execute	read	

(b)

Figure 14.5 Access matrix with *copy* rights.

The ability to copy an access right from one domain (or row) of the access matrix to another is denoted by an asterisk (*) appended to the access right. The *copy* right allows the access right to be copied only within the column (that is, for the object) for which the right is defined. For example, in Figure 14.5(a), a process executing in domain D_2 can copy the read operation into any entry associated with file F_2. Hence, the access matrix of Figure 14.5(a) can be modified to the access matrix shown in Figure 14.5(b).

This scheme has two variants:

1. A right is copied from `access(i,j)` to `access(k,j)`; it is then removed from `access(i,j)`. This action is a *transfer* of a right, rather than a copy.

2. Propagation of the *copy* right may be limited. That is, when the right R^* is copied from `access(i,j)` to `access(k,j)`, only the right R (not R^*) is created. A process executing in domain D_k cannot further copy the right R.

A system may select only one of these three *copy* rights, or it may provide all three by identifying them as separate rights: *copy*, *transfer*, and *limited copy*.

We also need a mechanism to allow addition of new rights and removal of some rights. The *owner* right controls these operations. If `access(i,j)` includes the *owner* right, then a process executing in domain D_i can add and remove any right in any entry in column j. For example, in Figure 14.6(a), domain D_1 is the owner of F_1 and thus can add and delete any valid right in column F_1. Similarly, domain D_2 is the owner of F_2 and F_3 and thus can add and remove any valid right within these two columns. Thus, the access matrix of Figure 14.6(a) can be modified to the access matrix shown in Figure 14.6(b).

domain \ object	F_1	F_2	F_3
D_1	owner execute		write
D_2		read* owner	read* owner write
D_3	execute		

(a)

domain \ object	F_1	F_2	F_3
D_1	owner execute		write
D_2		owner read* write*	read* owner write
D_3		write	write

(b)

Figure 14.6 Access matrix with *owner* rights.

The *copy* and *owner* rights allow a process to change the entries in a column. A mechanism is also needed to change the entries in a row. The *control* right is applicable only to domain objects. If `access`(i, j) includes the *control* right, then a process executing in domain D_i can remove any access right from row j. For example, suppose that, in Figure 14.4, we include the *control* right in `access`$(D_2,\ D_4)$. Then, a process executing in domain D_2 could modify domain D_4, as shown in Figure 14.7.

domain \ object	F_1	F_2	F_3	laser printer	D_1	D_2	D_3	D_4
D_1	read		read			switch		
D_2				print			switch	switch control
D_3		read	execute					
D_4	write		write		switch			

Figure 14.7 Modified access matrix of Figure 14.4.

The *copy* and *owner* rights provide us with a mechanism to limit the propagation of access rights. However, they do not give us the appropriate tools for preventing the propagation (or disclosure) of information. The problem of guaranteeing that no information initially held in an object can migrate outside of its execution environment is called the confinement problem. This problem is in general unsolvable (see the bibliographical notes at the end of the chapter).

These operations on the domains and the access matrix are not in themselves important, but they illustrate the ability of the access-matrix model to allow the implementation and control of dynamic protection requirements. New objects and new domains can be created dynamically and included in the access-matrix model. However, we have shown only that the basic mechanism exists; system designers and users must make the policy decisions concerning which domains are to have access to which objects in which ways.

14.5 Implementation of Access Matrix

How can the access matrix be implemented effectively? In general, the matrix will be sparse; that is, most of the entries will be empty. Although data-structure techniques are available for representing sparse matrices, they are not particularly useful for this application, because of the way in which the protection facility is used. Here, we first describe several methods of implementing the access matrix and then compare the methods.

14.5.1 Global Table

The simplest implementation of the access matrix is a global table consisting of a set of ordered triples <*domain, object, rights-set*>. Whenever an operation M is executed on an object O_j within domain D_i, the global table is searched for a triple $<D_i, O_j, R_k>$, with $M \in R_k$. If this triple is found, the operation is allowed to continue; otherwise, an exception (or error) condition is raised.

This implementation suffers from several drawbacks. The table is usually large and thus cannot be kept in main memory, so additional I/O is needed. Virtual memory techniques are often used for managing this table. In addition, it is difficult to take advantage of special groupings of objects or domains. For example, if everyone can read a particular object, this object must have a separate entry in every domain.

14.5.2 Access Lists for Objects

Each column in the access matrix can be implemented as an access list for one object, as described in Section 10.6.2. Obviously, the empty entries can be discarded. The resulting list for each object consists of ordered pairs <*domain, rights-set*>, which define all domains with a nonempty set of access rights for that object.

This approach can be extended easily to define a list plus a *default* set of access rights. When an operation M on an object O_j is attempted in domain D_i, we search the access list for object O_j, looking for an entry $<D_i, R_k>$ with $M \in R_k$. If the entry is found, we allow the operation; if it is not, we check the default set. If M is in the default set, we allow the access. Otherwise, access is denied, and an exception condition occurs. For efficiency, we may check the default set first and then search the access list.

14.5.3 Capability Lists for Domains

Rather than associating the columns of the access matrix with the objects as access lists, we can associate each row with its domain. A **capability list** for a domain is a list of objects together with the operations allowed on those objects. An object is often represented by its physical name or address, called a **capability**. To execute operation M on object O_j, the process executes the operation M, specifying the capability (or pointer) for object O_j as a parameter. Simple **possession** of the capability means that access is allowed.

The capability list is associated with a domain, but it is never directly accessible to a process executing in that domain. Rather, the capability list is itself a protected object, maintained by the operating system and accessed by the user only indirectly. Capability-based protection relies on the fact that the capabilities are never allowed to migrate into any address space directly accessible by a user process (where they could be modified). If all capabilities are secure, the object they protect is also secure against unauthorized access.

Capabilities were originally proposed as a kind of secure pointer, to meet the need for resource protection that was foreseen as multiprogrammed computer systems came of age. The idea of an inherently protected pointer provides a foundation for protection that can be extended up to the applications level.

To provide inherent protection, we must distinguish capabilities from other kinds of objects, and they must be interpreted by an abstract machine on which higher-level programs run. Capabilities are usually distinguished from other data in one of two ways:

- Each object has a **tag** to denote whether it is a capability or accessible data. The tags themselves must not be directly accessible by an application program. Hardware or firmware support may be used to enforce this restriction. Although only one bit is necessary to distinguish between capabilities and other objects, more bits are often used. This extension allows all objects to be tagged with their types by the hardware. Thus, the hardware can distinguish integers, floating-point numbers, pointers, Booleans, characters, instructions, capabilities, and uninitialized values by their tags.
- Alternatively, the address space associated with a program can be split into two parts. One part is accessible to the program and contains the program's normal data and instructions. The other part, containing the capability list, is accessible only by the operating system. A segmented memory space (Section 8.6) is useful to support this approach.

Several capability-based protection systems have been developed; we describe them briefly in Section 14.8. The Mach operating system also uses a version of capability-based protection; it is described in Appendix B.

14.5.4 A Lock–Key Mechanism

The lock–key scheme is a compromise between access lists and capability lists. Each object has a list of unique bit patterns, called locks. Similarly, each domain has a list of unique bit patterns, called keys. A process executing in a domain can access an object only if that domain has a key that matches one of the locks of the object.

As with capability lists, the list of keys for a domain must be managed by the operating system on behalf of the domain. Users are not allowed to examine or modify the list of keys (or locks) directly.

14.5.5 Comparison

As you might expect, choosing a technique for implementing an access matrix involves various trade-offs. Using a global table is simple; however, the table can be quite large and often cannot take advantage of special groupings of objects or domains. Access lists correspond directly to the needs of users. When a user creates an object, he can specify which domains can access the object, as well as what operations are allowed. However, because access-rights information for a particular domain is not localized, determining the set of access rights for each domain is difficult. In addition, every access to the object must be checked, requiring a search of the access list. In a large system with long access lists, this search can be time consuming.

Capability lists do not correspond directly to the needs of users; they are useful, however, for localizing information for a given process. The process attempting access must present a capability for that access. Then, the protection system needs only to verify that the capability is valid. Revocation of capabilities, however, may be inefficient (Section 14.7).

The lock–key mechanism, as mentioned, is a compromise between access lists and capability lists. The mechanism can be both effective and flexible, depending on the length of the keys. The keys can be passed freely from domain to domain. In addition, access privileges can be effectively revoked by the simple technique of changing some of the locks associated with the object (Section 14.7).

Most systems use a combination of access lists and capabilities. When a process first tries to access an object, the access list is searched. If access is denied, an exception condition occurs. Otherwise, a capability is created and attached to the process. Additional references use the capability to demonstrate swiftly that access is allowed. After the last access, the capability is destroyed. This strategy is used in the MULTICS system and in the CAL system.

As an example of how such a strategy works, consider a file system in which each file has an associated access list. When a process opens a file, the directory structure is searched to find the file, access permission is checked, and buffers are allocated. All this information is recorded in a new entry in a file table associated with the process. The operation returns an index into this table for the newly opened file. All operations on the file are made by specification of the index into the file table. The entry in the file table then points to the file and its buffers. When the file is closed, the file-table entry is deleted. Since the file table is maintained by the operating system, the user cannot accidentally corrupt it. Thus, the user can access only those files that have been opened.

Since access is checked when the file is opened, protection is ensured. This strategy is used in the UNIX system.

The right to access *must* still be checked on each access, and the file-table entry has a capability only for the allowed operations. If a file is opened for reading, then a capability for read access is placed in the file-table entry. If an attempt is made to write onto the file, the system identifies this protection violation by comparing the requested operation with the capability in the file-table entry.

14.6 Access Control

In Section 10.6.2, we described how access controls can be used on files within a file system. Each file and directory are assigned an owner, a group, or possibly a list of users, and for each of those entities, access-control information is assigned. A similar function can be added to other aspects of a computer system. A good example of this is found in Solaris 10.

Solaris 10 advances the protection available in the Sun Microsystems operating system by explicitly adding the principle of least privilege via **role-based access control (RBAC)**. This facility revolves around privileges. A privilege is the right to execute a system call or to use an option within that system call (such as opening a file with write access). Privileges can be assigned to processes, limiting them to exactly the access they need to perform their work. Privileges and programs can also be assigned to roles. Users are assigned roles or can take roles based on passwords to the roles. In this way, a user can take a role that enables a privilege, allowing the user to run a program to accomplish a specific task, as depicted in Figure 14.8. This implementation of privileges decreases the security risk associated with superusers and setuid programs.

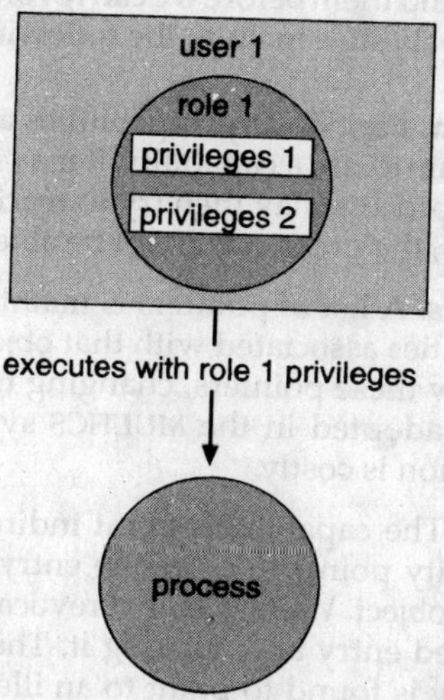

Figure 14.8 Role-based access control in Solaris 10.

Notice that this facility is similar to the access matrix described in Section 14.4. This relationship is further explored in the exercises at the end of the chapter.

14.7 Revocation of Access Rights

In a dynamic protection system, we may sometimes need to revoke access rights to objects shared by different users. Various questions about revocation may arise:

- **Immediate versus delayed**. Does revocation occur immediately, or is it delayed? If revocation is delayed, can we find out when it will take place?
- **Selective versus general**. When an access right to an object is revoked, does it affect *all* the users who have an access right to that object, or can we specify a select group of users whose access rights should be revoked?
- **Partial versus total**. Can a subset of the rights associated with an object be revoked, or must we revoke all access rights for this object?
- **Temporary versus permanent**. Can access be revoked permanently (that is, the revoked access right will never again be available), or can access be revoked and later be obtained again?

With an access-list scheme, revocation is easy. The access list is searched for any access rights to be revoked, and they are deleted from the list. Revocation is immediate and can be general or selective, total or partial, and permanent or temporary.

Capabilities, however, present a much more difficult revocation problem, as mentioned earlier. Since the capabilities are distributed throughout the system, we must find them before we can revoke them. Schemes that implement revocation for capabilities include the following:

- **Reacquisition**. Periodically, capabilities are deleted from each domain. If a process wants to use a capability, it may find that that capability has been deleted. The process may then try to reacquire the capability. If access has been revoked, the process will not be able to reacquire the capability.
- **Back-pointers**. A list of pointers is maintained with each object, pointing to all capabilities associated with that object. When revocation is required, we can follow these pointers, changing the capabilities as necessary. This scheme was adopted in the MULTICS system. It is quite general, but its implementation is costly.
- **Indirection**. The capabilities point indirectly, not directly, to the objects. Each capability points to a unique entry in a global table, which in turn points to the object. We implement revocation by searching the global table for the desired entry and deleting it. Then, when an access is attempted, the capability is found to point to an illegal table entry. Table entries can be reused for other capabilities without difficulty, since both the capability and the table entry contain the unique name of the object. The object for a

capability and its table entry must match. This scheme was adopted in the CAL system. It does not allow selective revocation.

- **Keys**. A key is a unique bit pattern that can be associated with a capability. This key is defined when the capability is created, and it can be neither modified nor inspected by the process that owns the capability. A **master key** is associated with each object; it can be defined or replaced with the `set-key` operation. When a capability is created, the current value of the master key is associated with the capability. When the capability is exercised, its key is compared with the master key. If the keys match, the operation is allowed to continue; otherwise, an exception condition is raised. Revocation replaces the master key with a new value via the `set-key` operation, invalidating all previous capabilities for this object.

  This scheme does not allow selective revocation, since only one master key is associated with each object. If we associate a list of keys with each object, then selective revocation can be implemented. Finally, we can group all keys into one global table of keys. A capability is valid only if its key matches some key in the global table. We implement revocation by removing the matching key from the table. With this scheme, a key can be associated with several objects, and several keys can be associated with each object, providing maximum flexibility.

  In key-based schemes, the operations of defining keys, inserting them into lists, and deleting them from lists should not be available to all users. In particular, it would be reasonable to allow only the owner of an object to set the keys for that object. This choice, however, is a policy decision that the protection system can implement but should not define.

14.8 Capability-Based Systems

In this section, we survey two capability-based protection systems. These systems differ in their complexity and in the types of policies that can be implemented on them. Neither system is widely used, but both provide interesting proving grounds for protection theories.

14.8.1 An Example: Hydra

Hydra is a capability-based protection system that provides considerable flexibility. The system implements a fixed set of possible access rights, including such basic forms of access as the right to read, write, or execute a memory segment. In addition, a user (of the protection system) can declare other rights. The interpretation of user-defined rights is performed solely by the user's program, but the system provides access protection for the use of these rights, as well as for the use of system-defined rights. These facilities constitute a significant development in protection technology.

Operations on objects are defined procedurally. The procedures that implement such operations are themselves a form of object, and they are accessed indirectly by capabilities. The names of user-defined procedures must be identified to the protection system if it is to deal with objects of the user-defined type. When the definition of an object is made known to Hydra, the names of operations on the type become **auxiliary rights**. Auxiliary rights can be described in a capability for an instance of the type. For a process to perform an operation on a typed object, the capability it holds for that object must contain the name of the operation being invoked among its auxiliary rights. This restriction enables discrimination of access rights to be made on an instance-by-instance and process-by-process basis.

Hydra also provides **rights amplification**. This scheme allows a procedure to be certified as *trustworthy* to act on a formal parameter of a specified type on behalf of any process that holds a right to execute the procedure. The rights held by a trustworthy procedure are independent of, and may exceed, the rights held by the calling process. However, such a procedure must not be regarded as universally trustworthy (the procedure is not allowed to act on other types, for instance), and the trustworthiness must not be extended to any other procedures or program segments that might be executed by a process.

Amplification allows implementation procedures access to the representation variables of an abstract data type. If a process holds a capability to a typed object *A*, for instance, this capability may include an auxiliary right to invoke some operation *P* but does not include any of the so-called kernel rights, such as read, write, or execute, on the segment that represents *A*. Such a capability gives a process a means of indirect access (through the operation *P*) to the representation of *A*, but only for specific purposes.

When a process invokes the operation *P* on an object *A*, however, the capability for access to *A* may be amplified as control passes to the code body of *P*. This amplification may be necessary to allow *P* the right to access the storage segment representing *A* so as to implement the operation that *P* defines on the abstract data type. The code body of *P* may be allowed to read or to write to the segment of *A* directly, even though the calling process cannot. On return from *P*, the capability for *A* is restored to its original, unamplified state. This case is a typical one in which the rights held by a process for access to a protected segment must change dynamically, depending on the task to be performed. The dynamic adjustment of rights is performed to guarantee consistency of a programmer-defined abstraction. Amplification of rights can be stated explicitly in the declaration of an abstract type to the Hydra operating system.

When a user passes an object as an argument to a procedure, we may need to ensure that the procedure cannot modify the object. We can implement this restriction readily by passing an access right that does not have the modification (write) right. However, if amplification may occur, the right to modify may be reinstated. Thus, the user-protection requirement can be circumvented. In general, of course, a user may trust that a procedure performs its task correctly. This assumption is not always correct, however, because of hardware or software errors. Hydra solves this problem by restricting amplifications.

The procedure-call mechanism of Hydra was designed as a direct solution to the *problem of mutually suspicious subsystems*. This problem is defined as follows. Suppose that a program is provided that can be invoked as a service by a number of different users (for example, a sort routine, a compiler, a game). When users invoke this service program, they take the risk that the program will malfunction and will either damage the given data or retain some access right to the data to be used (without authority) later. Similarly, the service program may have some private files (for accounting purposes, for example) that should not be accessed directly by the calling user program. Hydra provides mechanisms for directly dealing with this problem.

A Hydra subsystem is built on top of its protection kernel and may require protection of its own components. A subsystem interacts with the kernel through calls on a set of kernel-defined primitives that define access rights to resources defined by the subsystem. The subsystem designer can define policies for use of these resources by user processes, but the policies are enforceable by use of the standard access protection afforded by the capability system.

Programmers can make direct use of the protection system after acquainting themselves with its features in the appropriate reference manual. Hydra provides a large library of system-defined procedures that can be called by user programs. Programmers can explicitly incorporate calls on these system procedures into their program code or can use a program translator that has been interfaced to Hydra.

14.8.2 An Example: Cambridge CAP System

A different approach to capability-based protection has been taken in the design of the Cambridge CAP system. CAP's capability system is simpler and superficially less powerful than that of Hydra. However, closer examination shows that it, too, can be used to provide secure protection of user-defined objects. CAP has two kinds of capabilities. The ordinary kind is called a **data capability**. It can be used to provide access to objects, but the only rights provided are the standard read, write, and execute of the individual storage segments associated with the object. Data capabilities are interpreted by microcode in the CAP machine.

The second kind of capability is the so-called **software capability**, which is protected, but not interpreted, by the CAP microcode. It is interpreted by a *protected* (that is, privileged) procedure, which may be written by an application programmer as part of a subsystem. A particular kind of rights amplification is associated with a protected procedure. When executing the code body of such a procedure, a process temporarily acquires the right to read or write the contents of a software capability itself. This specific kind of rights amplification corresponds to an implementation of the `seal` and `unseal` primitives on capabilities. Of course, this privilege is still subject to type verification to ensure that only software capabilities for a specified abstract type are passed to any such procedure. Universal trust is not placed in any code other than the CAP machine's microcode. (See Bibliographical Notes for references.)

The interpretation of a software capability is left completely to the subsystem, through the protected procedures it contains. This scheme allows a variety of protection policies to be implemented. Although programmers can define their own protected procedures (any of which might be incorrect), the security of the overall system cannot be compromised. The basic protection system will not allow an unverified, user-defined, protected procedure access to any storage segments (or capabilities) that do not belong to the protection environment in which it resides. The most serious consequence of an insecure protected procedure is a protection breakdown of the subsystem for which that procedure has responsibility.

The designers of the CAP system have noted that the use of software capabilities allowed them to realize considerable economies in formulating and implementing protection policies commensurate with the requirements of abstract resources. However, subsystem designers who want to make use of this facility cannot simply study a reference manual, as is the case with Hydra. Instead, they must learn the principles and techniques of protection, since the system provides them with no library of procedures.

14.9 Language-Based Protection

To the degree that protection is provided in existing computer systems, it is usually achieved through an operating-system kernel, which acts as a security agent to inspect and validate each attempt to access a protected resource. Since comprehensive access validation may be a source of considerable overhead, either we must give it hardware support to reduce the cost of each validation or we must allow the system designer to compromise the goals of protection. Satisfying all these goals is difficult if the flexibility to implement protection policies is restricted by the support mechanisms provided or if protection environments are made larger than necessary to secure greater operational efficiency.

As operating systems have become more complex, and particularly as they have attempted to provide higher-level user interfaces, the goals of protection have become much more refined. The designers of protection systems have drawn heavily on ideas that originated in programming languages and especially on the concepts of abstract data types and objects. Protection systems are now concerned not only with the identity of a resource to which access is attempted but also with the functional nature of that access. In the newest protection systems, concern for the function to be invoked extends beyond a set of system-defined functions, such as standard file-access methods, to include functions that may be user-defined as well.

Policies for resource use may also vary, depending on the application, and they may be subject to change over time. For these reasons, protection can no longer be considered a matter of concern only to the designer of an operating system. It should also be available as a tool for use by the application designer, so that resources of an applications subsystem can be guarded against tampering or the influence of an error.

14.9.1 Compiler-Based Enforcement

At this point, programming languages enter the picture. Specifying the desired control of access to a shared resource in a system is making a declarative statement about the resource. This kind of statement can be integrated into a language by an extension of its typing facility. When protection is declared along with data typing, the designer of each subsystem can specify its requirements for protection, as well as its need for use of other resources in a system. Such a specification should be given directly as a program is composed, and in the language in which the program itself is stated. This approach has several significant advantages:

1. Protection needs are simply declared, rather than programmed as a sequence of calls on procedures of an operating system.

2. Protection requirements can be stated independently of the facilities provided by a particular operating system.

3. The means for enforcement need not be provided by the designer of a subsystem.

4. A declarative notation is natural because access privileges are closely related to the linguistic concept of data type.

A variety of techniques can be provided by a programming-language implementation to enforce protection, but any of these must depend on some degree of support from an underlying machine and its operating system. For example, suppose a language is used to generate code to run on the Cambridge CAP system. On this system, every storage reference made on the underlying hardware occurs indirectly through a capability. This restriction prevents any process from accessing a resource outside of its protection environment at any time. However, a program may impose arbitrary restrictions on how a resource can be used during execution of a particular code segment. We can implement such restrictions most readily by using the software capabilities provided by CAP. A language implementation might provide standard protected procedures to interpret software capabilities that would realize the protection policies that could be specified in the language. This scheme puts policy specification at the disposal of the programmers, while freeing them from implementing its enforcement.

Even if a system does not provide a protection kernel as powerful as those of Hydra or CAP, mechanisms are still available for implementing protection specifications given in a programming language. The principal distinction is that the *security* of this protection will not be as great as that supported by a protection kernel, because the mechanism must rely on more assumptions about the operational state of the system. A compiler can separate references for which it can certify that no protection violation could occur from those for which a violation might be possible, and it can treat them differently. The security provided by this form of protection rests on the assumption that the code generated by the compiler will not be modified prior to or during its execution.

What, then, are the relative merits of enforcement based solely on a kernel, as opposed to enforcement provided largely by a compiler?

- **Security**. Enforcement by a kernel provides a greater degree of security of the protection system itself than does the generation of protection-checking code by a compiler. In a compiler-supported scheme, security rests on correctness of the translator, on some underlying mechanism of storage management that protects the segments from which compiled code is executed, and, ultimately, on the security of files from which a program is loaded. Some of these considerations also apply to a software-supported protection kernel, but to a lesser degree, since the kernel may reside in fixed physical storage segments and may be loaded only from a designated file. With a tagged-capability system, in which all address computation is performed either by hardware or by a fixed microprogram, even greater security is possible. Hardware-supported protection is also relatively immune to protection violations that might occur as a result of either hardware or system software malfunction.

- **Flexibility**. There are limits to the flexibility of a protection kernel in implementing a user-defined policy, although it may supply adequate facilities for the system to provide enforcement of its own policies. With a programming language, protection policy can be declared and enforcement provided as needed by an implementation. If a language does not provide sufficient flexibility, it can be extended or replaced with less disturbance of a system in service than would be caused by the modification of an operating-system kernel.

- **Efficiency**. The greatest efficiency is obtained when enforcement of protection is supported directly by hardware (or microcode). Insofar as software support is required, language-based enforcement has the advantage that static access enforcement can be verified off-line at compile time. Also, since an intelligent compiler can tailor the enforcement mechanism to meet the specified need, the fixed overhead of kernel calls can often be avoided.

In summary, the specification of protection in a programming language allows the high-level description of policies for the allocation and use of resources. A language implementation can provide software for protection enforcement when automatic hardware-supported checking is unavailable. In addition, it can interpret protection specifications to generate calls on whatever protection system is provided by the hardware and the operating system.

One way of making protection available to the application program is through the use of a software capability that could be used as an object of computation. Inherent in this concept is the idea that certain program components might have the privilege of creating or examining these software capabilities. A capability-creating program would be able to execute a primitive operation that would seal a data structure, rendering the latter's contents inaccessible to any program components that did not hold either the seal or the unseal privilege. Such components might copy the data structure or pass its address to other program components, but they could not gain access to its contents. The reason for introducing such software capabilities is to bring a protection mechanism into the programming language. The only problem with the concept as proposed is that the use of the `seal` and `unseal` operations takes a procedural approach to specifying protection. A nonprocedural or declarative notation seems a preferable way to make protection available to the application programmer.

What is needed is a safe, dynamic access-control mechanism for distributing capabilities to system resources among user processes. To contribute to the overall reliability of a system, the access-control mechanism should be safe to use. To be useful in practice, it should also be reasonably efficient. This requirement has led to the development of a number of language constructs that allow the programmer to declare various restrictions on the use of a specific managed resource. (See the Bibliographical Notes for appropriate references.) These constructs provide mechanisms for three functions:

1. Distributing capabilities safely and efficiently among customer processes. In particular, mechanisms ensure that a user process will use the managed resource only if it was granted a capability to that resource.
2. Specifying the type of operations that a particular process may invoke on an allocated resource (for example, a reader of a file should be allowed only to read the file, whereas a writer should be able both to read and to write). It should not be necessary to grant the same set of rights to every user process, and it should be impossible for a process to enlarge its set of access rights, except with the authorization of the access-control mechanism.
3. Specifying the order in which a particular process may invoke the various operations of a resource (for example, a file must be opened before it can be read). It should be possible to give two processes different restrictions on the order in which they can invoke the operations of the allocated resource.

The incorporation of protection concepts into programming languages, as a practical tool for system design, is in its infancy. Protection will likely become a matter of greater concern to the designers of new systems with distributed architectures and increasingly stringent requirements on data security. Then the importance of suitable language notations in which to express protection requirements will be recognized more widely.

14.9.2 Protection in Java

Because Java was designed to run in a distributed environment, the Java virtual machine—or JVM—has many built-in protection mechanisms. Java programs are composed of **classes**, each of which is a collection of data fields and functions (called **methods**) that operate on those fields. The JVM loads a class in response to a request to create instances (or objects) of that class. One of the most novel and useful features of Java is its support for dynamically loading untrusted classes over a network and for executing mutually distrusting classes within the same JVM.

Because of these capabilities of Java, protection is a paramount concern. Classes running in the same JVM may be from different sources and may not be equally trusted. As a result, enforcing protection at the granularity of the JVM process is insufficient. Intuitively, whether a request to open a file should be allowed will generally depend on which class has requested the open. The operating system lacks this knowledge.

Thus, such protection decisions are handled within the JVM. When the JVM loads a class, it assigns the class to a protection domain that gives the permissions of that class. The protection domain to which the class is assigned depends on the URL from which the class was loaded and any digital signatures on the class file. (Digital signatures are covered in Section 15.4.1.3.) A configurable policy file determines the permissions granted to the domain (and its classes). For example, classes loaded from a trusted server might be placed in a protection domain that allows them to access files in the user's home directory, whereas classes loaded from an untrusted server might have no file access permissions at all.

It can be complicated for the JVM to determine what class is responsible for a request to access a protected resource. Accesses are often performed indirectly, through system libraries or other classes. For example, consider a class that is not allowed to open network connections. It could call a system library to request the load of the contents of a URL. The JVM must decide whether or not to open a network connection for this request. But which class should be used to determine if the connection should be allowed, the application or the system library?

The philosophy adopted in Java is to require the library class to explicitly permit a network connection. More generally, in order to access a protected resource, some method in the calling sequence that resulted in the request must explicitly assert the privilege to access the resource. By doing so, this method *takes responsibility* for the request; presumably, it will also perform whatever checks are necessary to ensure the safety of the request. Of course, not every method is allowed to assert a privilege; a method can assert a privilege only if its class is in a protection domain that is itself allowed to exercise the privilege.

This implementation approach is called **stack inspection**. Every thread in the JVM has an associated stack of its ongoing method invocations. When a caller may not be trusted, a method executes an access request within a `doPrivileged` block to perform the access to a protected resource directly or indirectly. `doPrivileged()` is a static method in the `AccessController` class that is passed a class with a `run()` method to invoke. When the `doPrivileged` block is entered, the stack frame for this method is annotated to indicate this fact. Then, the contents of the block are executed. When an access to a protected resource is subsequently requested, either by this method or a method it calls, a call to `checkPermissions()` is used to invoke stack inspection to determine if the request should be allowed. The inspection examines stack frames on the calling thread's stack, starting from the most recently added frame and working toward the oldest. If a stack frame is first found that has the `doPrivileged()` annotation, then `checkPermissions()` returns immediately and silently, allowing the access. If a stack frame is first found for which access is disallowed based on the protection domain of the method's class, then `checkPermissions()` throws an `AccessControlException`. If the stack inspection exhausts the stack without finding either type of frame, then whether access is allowed depends on the implementation (for example, some implementations of the JVM may allow access, while other implementations may disallow it).

Stack inspection is illustrated in Figure 14.9. Here, the `gui()` method of a class in the *untrusted applet* protection domain performs two operations, first a `get()` and then an `open()`. The former is an invocation of the `get()` method of a class in the *URL loader* protection domain, which is permitted to `open()` sessions to sites in the `lucent.com` domain, in particular a proxy server `proxy.lucent.com` for retrieving URLs. For this reason, the untrusted applet's `get()` invocation will succeed: the `checkPermissions()` call in the networking library encounters the stack frame of the `get()` method, which performed its `open()` in a `doPrivileged` block. However, the untrusted applet's `open()` invocation will result in an exception, because the `checkPermissions()` call finds no `doPrivileged` annotation before encountering the stack frame of the `gui()` method.

protection domain:	untrusted applet	URL loader	networking
socket permission:	none	*.lucent.com:80, connect	any

class:	gui:
	...
	get(url);
	open(addr);
	...
		get(URL u):
		...
		doPrivileged {
		open('proxy.lucent.com:80');
		}
		<request u from proxy>
		...
			open(Addr a):
			...
			checkPermission
			(a, connect);
			connect (a);
			...

Figure 14.9 Stack inspection.

Of course, for stack inspection to work, a program must be unable to modify the annotations on its own stack frame or to do other manipulations of stack inspection. This is one of the most important differences between Java and many other languages (including C++). A Java program cannot directly access memory; it can manipulate only an object for which it has a reference. References cannot be forged, and the manipulations are made only through well-defined interfaces. Compliance is enforced through a sophisticated collection of load-time and run-time checks. As a result, an object cannot manipulate its run-time stack, because it cannot get a reference to the stack or other components of the protection system.

More generally, Java's load-time and run-time checks enforce **type safety** of Java classes. Type safety ensures that classes cannot treat integers as pointers, write past the end of an array, or otherwise access memory in arbitrary ways. Rather, a program can access an object only via the methods defined on that object by its class. This is the foundation of Java protection, since it enables a class to effectively **encapsulate** and protect its data and methods from other classes loaded in the same JVM. For example, a variable can be defined as `private` so that only the class that contains it can access it or `protected` so that it can be accessed only by the class that contains it, subclasses of that class, or classes in the same package. Type safety ensures that these restrictions can be enforced.

14.10 Summary

Computer systems contain many objects, and they need to be protected from misuse. Objects may be hardware (such as memory, CPU time, and I/O devices) or software (such as files, programs, and semaphores). An access right is permission to perform an operation on an object. A domain is a set of access rights. Processes execute in domains and may use any of the access rights in the domain to access and manipulate objects. During its lifetime, a process may be either bound to a protection domain or allowed to switch from one domain to another.

The access matrix is a general model of protection that provides a mechanism for protection without imposing a particular protection policy on the system or its users. The separation of policy and mechanism is an important design property.

The access matrix is sparse. It is normally implemented either as access lists associated with each object or as capability lists associated with each domain. We can include dynamic protection in the access-matrix model by considering domains and the access matrix itself as objects. Revocation of access rights in a dynamic protection model is typically easier to implement with an access-list scheme than with a capability list.

Real systems are much more limited than the general model and tend to provide protection only for files. UNIX is representative, providing read, write, and execution protection separately for the owner, group, and general public for each file. MULTICS uses a ring structure in addition to file access. Hydra, the Cambridge CAP system, and Mach are capability systems that extend protection to user-defined software objects. Solaris 10 implements the principle of least privilege via role-based access control, a form of the access matrix.

Language-based protection provides finer-grained arbitration of requests and privileges than the operating system is able to provide. For example, a single Java JVM can run several threads, each in a different protection class. It enforces the resource requests through sophisticated stack inspection and via the type safety of the language.

Exercises

14.1 Consider a computer system in which "computer games" can be played by students only between 10 P.M. and 6 A.M., by faculty members between 5 P.M. and 8 A.M., and by the computer center staff at all times. Suggest a scheme for implementing this policy efficiently.

14.2 The RC 4000 system, among others, has defined a tree of processes (called a *process tree*) such that all the descendants of a process can be given resources (objects) and access rights by their ancestors only. Thus, a descendant can never have the ability to do anything that its ancestors cannot do. The root of the tree is the operating system, which has the ability to do anything. Assume the set of access rights is represented by an access matrix, A. $A(x,y)$ defines the access rights of process x to object y. If x is a descendant of z, what is the relationship between $A(x,y)$ and $A(z,y)$ for an arbitrary object y?

14.3 How are the access-matrix facility and the role-based access-control facility similar? How do they differ?

14.4 Discuss the need for rights amplification in Hydra. How does this practice compare with the cross-ring calls in a ring-protection scheme?

14.5 Explain why a capability-based system such as Hydra provides greater flexibility than the ring-protection scheme in enforcing protection policies.

14.6 Consider the ring-protection scheme in MULTICS. If we were to implement the system calls of a typical operating system and store them in a segment associated with ring 0, what should be the values stored in the ring field of the segment descriptor? What happens during a system call when a process executing in a higher-numbered ring invokes a procedure in ring 0?

14.7 Discuss the strengths and weaknesses of implementing an access matrix using capabilities that are associated with domains.

14.8 Discuss the strengths and weaknesses of implementing an access matrix using access lists that are associated with objects.

14.9 The access-control matrix can be used to determine whether a process can switch from, say, domain A to domain B and enjoy the access privileges of domain B. Is this approach equivalent to including the access privileges of domain B in those of domain A?

14.10 How can systems that implement the principle of least privilege still have protection failures that lead to security violations?

14.11 How does the principle of least privilege aid in the creation of protection systems?

14.12 What protection problems may arise if a shared stack is used for parameter passing?

14.13 If all the access rights to an object are deleted, the object can no longer be accessed. At this point, the object should also be deleted, and the space it occupies should be returned to the system. Suggest an efficient implementation of this scheme.

14.14 Discuss which of the following systems allow module designers to enforce the need-to-know principle.

a. The MULTICS ring-protection scheme

b. Hydra's capabilities

c. JVM's stack-inspection scheme

14.15 Consider a computing environment where a unique number is associated with each process and each object in the system. Suppose that we allow a process with number n to access an object with number m only if $n > m$. What type of protection structure do we have?

14.16 What is the need-to-know principle? Why is it important for a protection system to adhere to this principle?

14.17 What hardware features does a computer system need for efficient capability manipulation? Can these features be used for memory protection?

14.18 Describe how the Java protection model would be compromised if a Java program were allowed to directly alter the annotations of its stack frame.

14.19 A Burroughs B7000/B6000 MCP file can be tagged as sensitive data. When such a file is deleted, its storage area is overwritten by some random bits. For what purpose would such a scheme be useful?

Bibliographical Notes

The access-matrix model of protection between domains and objects was developed by Lampson [1969] and Lampson [1971]. Popek [1974] and Saltzer and Schroeder [1975] provided excellent surveys on the subject of protection. Harrison et al. [1976] used a formal version of this model to enable them to prove properties of a protection system mathematically.

The concept of a capability evolved from Iliffe's and Jodeit's *codewords*, which were implemented in the Rice University computer (Iliffe and Jodeit [1962]). The term *capability* was introduced by Dennis and Horn [1966].

The Hydra system was described by Wulf et al. [1981]. The CAP system was described by Needham and Walker [1977]. Organick [1972] discussed the MULTICS ring-protection system.

Revocation was discussed by Redell and Fabry [1974], Cohen and Jefferson [1975], and Ekanadham and Bernstein [1979]. The principle of separation of policy and mechanism was advocated by the designer of Hydra (Levin et al. [1975]). The confinement problem was first discussed by Lampson [1973] and was further examined by Lipner [1975].

The use of higher-level languages for specifying access control was suggested first by Morris [1973], who proposed the use of the `seal` and `unseal` operations discussed in Section 14.9. Kieburtz and Silberschatz [1978], Kieburtz and Silberschatz [1983], and McGraw and Andrews [1979] proposed various language constructs for dealing with general dynamic-resource-management schemes. Jones and Liskov [1978] considered how a static access-control scheme can be incorporated in a programming language that supports abstract data types. The use of minimal operating-system support to enforce protection was advocated by the Exokernel Project (Ganger et al. [2002], Kaashoek et al. [1997]).

Extensibility of system code through language-based protection mechanisms was discussed in Bershad et al. [1995]. Other techniques for enforcing protection include sandboxing (Goldberg et al. [1996]) and software fault isolation (Wahbe et al. [1993b]). The issues of lowering the overhead associated with protection costs and enabling user-level access to networking devices were discussed in McCanne and Jacobson [1993] and Basu et al. [1995].

More detailed analyses of stack inspection, including comparisons with other approaches to Java security, can be found in Wallach et al. [1997] and Gong et al. [1997].

CHAPTER 15

System Security

Protection, as we discussed in Chapter 14, is strictly an *internal* problem: How do we provide controlled access to programs and data stored in a computer system? **Security**, on the other hand, requires not only an adequate protection system but also consideration of the *external* environment within which the system operates. A protection system is ineffective if user authentication is compromised or a program is run by an unauthorized user.

Computer resources must be guarded against unauthorized access, malicious destruction or alteration, and accidental introduction of inconsistency. These resources include information stored in the system (both data and code), as well as the CPU, memory, disks, tapes, and networking that are the computer. In this chapter, we start by examining ways in which resources may be accidentally or purposely misused. We then explore a key security enabler —cryptography. Finally, we look at mechanisms to guard against or detect attacks.

CHAPTER OBJECTIVES

- To discuss security threats and attacks.
- To explain the fundamentals of encryption, authentication, and hashing.
- To examine the uses of cryptography in computing.
- To describe various countermeasures to security attacks.

15.1 The Security Problem

In many applications, ensuring the security of the computer system is worth considerable effort. Large commercial systems containing payroll or other financial data are inviting targets to thieves. Systems that contain data pertaining to corporate operations may be of interest to unscrupulous competitors. Furthermore, loss of such data, whether by accident or fraud, can seriously impair the ability of the corporation to function.

In Chapter 14, we discussed mechanisms that the operating system can provide (with appropriate aid from the hardware) that allow users to protect their resources, including programs and data. These mechanisms work well only as long as the users conform to the intended use of and access to these resources. We say that a system is **secure** if its resources are used and accessed as intended under all circumstances. Unfortunately, total security cannot be achieved. Nonetheless, we must have mechanisms to make security breaches a rare occurrence, rather than the norm.

Security violations (or misuse) of the system can be categorized as intentional (malicious) or accidental. It is easier to protect against accidental misuse than against malicious misuse. For the most part, protection mechanisms are the core of protection from accidents. The following list includes several forms of accidental and malicious security violations. We should note that in our discussion of security, we use the terms *intruder* and *cracker* for those attempting to breach security. In addition, a **threat** is the potential for a security violation, such as the discovery of a vulnerability, whereas an **attack** is the attempt to break security.

- **Breach of confidentiality**. This type of violation involves unauthorized reading of data (or theft of information). Typically, a breach of confidentiality is the goal of an intruder. Capturing secret data from a system or a data stream, such as credit-card information or identity information for identity theft, can result directly in money for the intruder.
- **Breach of integrity**. This violation involves unauthorized modification of data. Such attacks can, for example, result in passing of liability to an innocent party or modification of the source code of an important commercial application.
- **Breach of availability**. This violation involves unauthorized destruction of data. Some crackers would rather wreak havoc and gain status or bragging rights than gain financially. Web-site defacement is a common example of this type of security breach.
- **Theft of service**. This violation involves unauthorized use of resources. For example, an intruder (or intrusion program) may install a daemon on a system that acts as a file server.
- **Denial of service.** This violation involves preventing legitimate use of the system. **Denial-of-service**, or **DOS**, attacks are sometimes accidental. The original Internet worm turned into a DOS attack when a bug failed to delay its rapid spread. We discuss DOS attacks further in Section 15.3.3.

Attackers use several standard methods in their attempts to breach security. The most common is **masquerading**, in which one participant in a communication pretends to be someone else (another host or another person). By masquerading, attackers breach **authentication**, the correctness of identification; they can then gain access that they would not normally be allowed or escalate their privileges—obtain privileges to which they would not normally be entitled. Another common attack is to replay a captured exchange of data. A **replay attack** consists of the malicious or fraudulent repeat of a valid data transmission. Sometimes the replay comprises the entire attack—for example, in a repeat of a request to transfer money. But frequently it is done along with **message modification**, again to escalate privileges. Consider

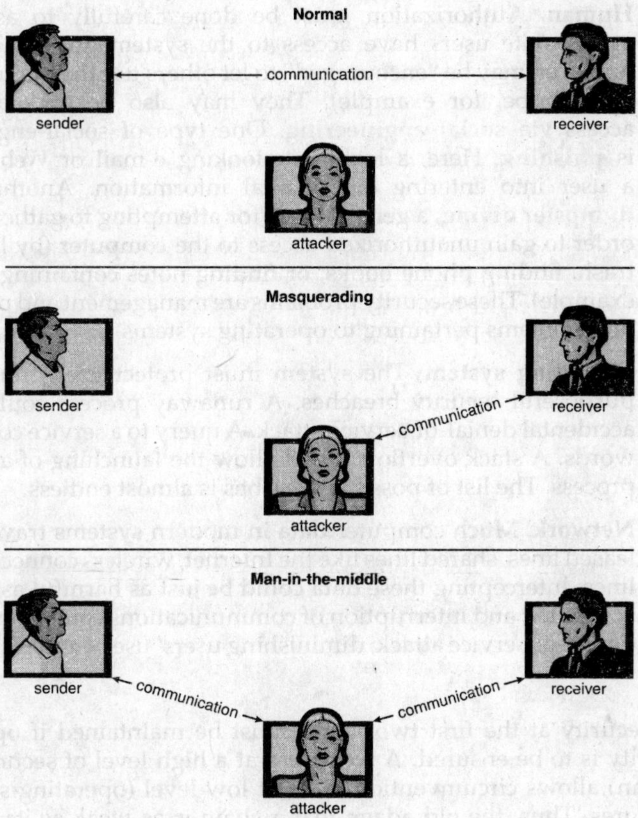

Figure 15.1 Standard security attacks.

the damage that could be done if a request for authentication had a legitimate user's information replaced with an unauthorized user's. Yet another kind of attack is the **man-in-the-middle attack**, in which an attacker sits in the data flow of a communication, masquerading as the sender to the receiver, and vice versa. In a network communication, a man-in-the-middle attack may be preceded by a **session hijacking**, in which an active communication session is intercepted. Several attack methods are depicted in Figure 15.1.

As we have already suggested, absolute protection of the system from malicious abuse is not possible, but the cost to the perpetrator can be made sufficiently high to deter most intruders. In some cases, such as a denial-of-service attack, it is preferable to prevent the attack but sufficient to detect the attack so that countermeasures can be taken.

To protect a system, we must take security measures at four levels:

1. **Physical**. The site or sites containing the computer systems must be physically secured against armed or surreptitious entry by intruders. Both the machine rooms and the terminals or workstations that have access to the machines must be secured.

2. **Human**. Authorization must be done carefully to assure that only appropriate users have access to the system. Even authorized users, however, may be "encouraged" to let others use their access (in exchange for a bribe, for example). They may also be tricked into allowing access via **social engineering**. One type of social-engineering attack is **phishing**. Here, a legitimate-looking e-mail or Web page misleads a user into entering confidential information. Another technique is **dumpster diving**, a general term for attempting to gather information in order to gain unauthorized access to the computer (by looking through trash, finding phone books, or finding notes containing passwords, for example). These security problems are management and personnel issues, not problems pertaining to operating systems.

3. **Operating system**. The system must protect itself from accidental or purposeful security breaches. A runaway process could constitute an accidental denial-of-service attack. A query to a service could reveal passwords. A stack overflow could allow the launching of an unauthorized process. The list of possible breaches is almost endless.

4. **Network**. Much computer data in modern systems travels over private leased lines, shared lines like the Internet, wireless connections, or dial-up lines. Intercepting these data could be just as harmful as breaking into a computer; and interruption of communications could constitute a remote denial-of-service attack, diminishing users' use of and trust in the system.

Security at the first two levels must be maintained if operating-system security is to be ensured. A weakness at a high level of security (physical or human) allows circumvention of strict low-level (operating-system) security measures. Thus, the old adage that a chain is as weak as its weakest link is especially true of system security. All of these aspects must be addressed for security to be maintained.

Furthermore, the system must provide protection (Chapter 14) to allow the implementation of security features. Without the ability to authorize users and processes, to control their access, and to log their activities, it would be impossible for an operating system to implement security measures or to run securely. Hardware protection features are needed to support an overall protection scheme. For example, a system without memory protection cannot be secure. New hardware features are allowing systems to be made more secure, as we shall discuss.

Unfortunately, little in security is straightforward. As intruders exploit security vulnerabilities, security countermeasures are created and deployed. This causes intruders to become more sophisticated in their attacks. For example, recent security incidents include the use of spyware to provide a conduit for spam through innocent systems (we discuss this practice in Section 15.2). This cat-and-mouse game is likely to continue, with more security tools needed to block the escalating intruder techniques and activities.

In the remainder of this chapter, we address security at the network and operating-system levels. Security at the physical and human levels, although important, is for the most part beyond the scope of this text. Security within the operating system and between operating systems is implemented in several ways, ranging from passwords for authentication through guarding against viruses to detecting intrusions. We start with an exploration of security threats.

15.2 Program Threats

Processes, along with the kernel, are the only means of accomplishing work on a computer. Therefore, writing a program that creates a breach of security, or causing a normal process to change its behavior and create a breach, is a common goal of crackers. In fact, even most nonprogram security events have as their goal causing a program threat. For example, while it is useful to log in to a system without authorization, it is quite a lot more useful to leave behind a **back-door** daemon that provides information or allows easy access even if the original exploit is blocked. In this section, we describe common methods by which programs cause security breaches. Note that there is considerable variation in the naming conventions of security holes and that we use the most common or descriptive terms.

15.2.1 Trojan Horse

Many systems have mechanisms for allowing programs written by users to be executed by other users. If these programs are executed in a domain that provides the access rights of the executing user, the other users may misuse these rights. A text-editor program, for example, may include code to search the file to be edited for certain keywords. If any are found, the entire file may be copied to a special area accessible to the creator of the text editor. A code segment that misuses its environment is called a **Trojan horse**. Long search paths, such as are common on UNIX systems, exacerbate the Trojan-horse problem. The search path lists the set of directories to search when an ambiguous program name is given. The path is searched for a file of that name, and the file is executed. All the directories in such a search path must be secure, or a Trojan horse could be slipped into the user's path and executed accidentally.

For instance, consider the use of the "." character in a search path. The "." tells the shell to include the current directory in the search. Thus, if a user has "." in her search path, has set her current directory to a friend's directory, and enters the name of a normal system command, the command may be executed from the friend's directory instead. The program would run within the user's domain, allowing the program to do anything that the user is allowed to do, including deleting the user's files, for instance.

A variation of the Trojan horse is a program that emulates a login program. An unsuspecting user starts to log in at a terminal and notices that he has apparently mistyped his password. He tries again and is successful. What has happened is that his authentication key and password have been stolen by the login emulator, which was left running on the terminal by the thief. The emulator stored away the password, printed out a login error message, and exited; the user was then provided with a genuine login prompt. This type of attack can be defeated by having the operating system print a usage message at the end of an interactive session or by a non-trappable key sequence, such as the `control-alt-delete` combination used by all modern Windows operating systems.

Another variation on the Trojan horse is **spyware**. Spyware sometimes accompanies a program that the user has chosen to install. Most frequently, it comes along with freeware or shareware programs, but sometimes it is included with commercial software. The goal of spyware is to download ads to display on the user's system, create **pop-up browser windows** when certain sites are visited, or capture information from the user's system and return it to a central site. This latter practice is an example of a general category of attacks known as **covert channels**, in which surreptitious communication occurs. For example, the installation of an innocuous-seeming program on a Windows system could result in the loading of a spyware daemon. The spyware could contact a central site, be given a message and a list of recipient addresses, and deliver the spam message to those users from the Windows machine. This process continues until the user discovers the spyware. Frequently, the spyware is not discovered. In 2004, it was estimated that 80 percent of spam was being delivered by this method. This theft of service is not even considered a crime in most countries!

Spyware is a micro example of a macro problem: violation of the principle of least privilege. Under most circumstances, a user of an operating system does not need to install network daemons. Such daemons are installed via two mistakes. First, a user may run with more privileges than necessary (for example, as the administrator), allowing programs that she runs to have more access to the system than is necessary. This is a case of human error—a common security weakness. Second, an operating system may allow by default more privileges than a normal user needs. This is a case of poor operating-system design decisions. An operating system (and, indeed, software in general) should allow fine-grained control of access and security, but it must also be easy to manage and understand. Inconvenient or inadequate security measures are bound to be circumvented, causing an overall weakening of the security they were designed to implement.

15.2.2 Trap Door

The designer of a program or system might leave a hole in the software that only he is capable of using. This type of security breach (or **trap door**) was shown in the movie *War Games*. For instance, the code might check for a specific user ID or password, and it might circumvent normal security procedures. Programmers have been arrested for embezzling from banks by including rounding errors in their code and having the occasional half-cent credited to their accounts. This account crediting can add up to a large amount of money, considering the number of transactions that a large bank executes.

A clever trap door could be included in a compiler. The compiler could generate standard object code as well as a trap door, regardless of the source code being compiled. This activity is particularly nefarious, since a search of the source code of the program will not reveal any problems. Only the source code of the compiler would contain the information.

Trap doors pose a difficult problem because, to detect them, we have to analyze all the source code for all components of a system. Given that software systems may consist of millions of lines of code, this analysis is not done frequently, and frequently it is not done at all!

15.2.3 Logic Bomb

Consider a program that initiates a security incident only under certain circumstances. It would be hard to detect because under normal operations, there would be no security hole. However, when a predefined set of parameters were met, the security hole would be created. This scenario is known as a **logic bomb**. A programmer, for example, might write code to detect whether she was still employed; if that check failed, a daemon could be spawned to allow remote access, or code could be launched to cause damage to the site.

15.2.4 Stack and Buffer Overflow

The stack- or buffer-overflow attack is the most common way for an attacker outside the system, on a network or dial-up connection, to gain unauthorized access to the target system. An authorized user of the system may also use this exploit for privilege escalation.

Essentially, the attack exploits a bug in a program. The bug can be a simple case of poor programming, in which the programmer neglected to code bounds checking on an input field. In this case, the attacker sends more data than the program was expecting. By using trial and error, or by examining the source code of the attacked program if it is available, the attacker determines the vulnerability and writes a program to do the following:

1. Overflow an input field, command-line argument, or input buffer—for example, on a network daemon—until it writes into the stack.
2. Overwrite the current return address on the stack with the address of the exploit code loaded in step 3.
3. Write a simple set of code for the next space in the stack that includes the commands that the attacker wishes to execute—for instance, spawn a shell.

The result of this attack program's execution will be a root shell or other privileged command execution.

For instance, if a Web-page form expects a user name to be entered into a field, the attacker could send the user name, plus extra characters to overflow the buffer and reach the stack, plus a new return address to load onto the stack, plus the code the attacker wants to run. When the buffer-reading subroutine returns from execution, the return address is the exploit code, and the code is run.

Let's look at a buffer-overflow exploit in more detail. Consider the simple C program shown in Figure 15.2. This program creates a character array of size `BUFFER_SIZE` and copies the contents of the parameter provided on the command line—`argv[1]`. As long as the size of this parameter is less than `BUFFER_SIZE` (we need one byte to store the null terminator), this program works properly. But consider what happens if the parameter provided on the command line is longer than `BUFFER_SIZE`. In this scenario, the `strcpy()` function will begin copying from `argv[1]` until it encounters a null terminator (\0) or until the program crashes. Thus, this program suffers from a potential buffer-overflow problem in which copied data overflow the `buffer` array.

```
#include <stdio.h>
#define BUFFER_SIZE 256

int main(int argc, char *argv[])
{
   char buffer[BUFFER_SIZE];

   if (argc < 2)
      return -1;
   else {
      strcpy(buffer,argv[1]);
      return 0;
   }
}
```

Figure 15.2 C program with buffer-overflow condition.

Note that a careful programmer could have performed bounds checking on the size of argv[1] by using the strncpy() function rather than strcpy(), replacing the line "strcpy(buffer, argv[1]);" with "strncpy(buffer, argv[1], sizeof(buffer)-1);". Unfortunately, good bounds checking is the exception rather than the norm.

Furthermore, lack of bounds checking is not the only possible cause of the behavior of the program in Figure 15.2. The program could instead have been carefully designed to compromise the integrity of the system. We now consider the possible security vulnerabilities of a buffer overflow.

When a function is invoked in a typical computer architecture, the variables defined locally to the function (sometimes known as **automatic variables**), the parameters passed to the function, and the address to which control returns once the function exits are stored in a **stack frame**. The layout for a typical stack frame is shown in Figure 15.3. Examining the stack frame from top to bottom, we first see the parameters passed to the function, followed by any automatic variables declared in the function. We next see the **frame pointer**, which is the address of the beginning of the stack frame. Finally, we have the return

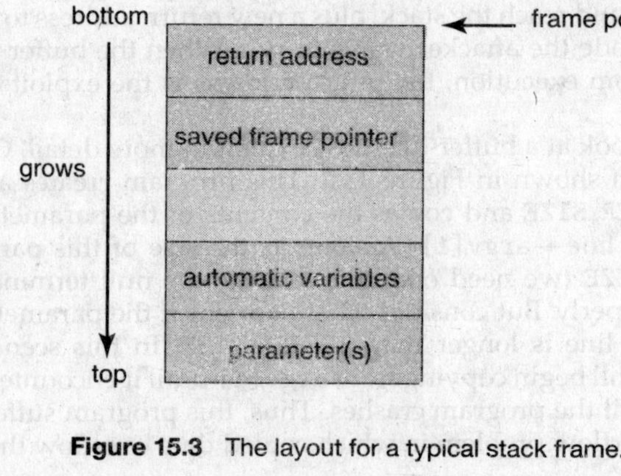

Figure 15.3 The layout for a typical stack frame.

address, which specifies where to return control once the function exits. The frame pointer must be saved on the stack, as the value of the stack pointer can vary during the function call; the saved frame pointer allows relative access to parameters and automatic variables.

Given this standard memory layout, a cracker could execute a buffer-overflow attack. Her goal is to replace the return address in the stack frame so that it now points to the code segment containing the attacking program.

The programmer first writes a short code segment such as the following:

```
#include <stdio.h>

int main(int argc, char *argv[])
{
    execvp(''\bin\sh'',''\bin \sh'', NULL);
    return 0;
}
```

Using the `execvp()` system call, this code segment creates a shell process. If the program being attacked runs with system-wide permissions, this newly created shell will gain complete access to the system. Of course, the code segment could do anything allowed by the privileges of the attacked process. This code segment is then compiled so that the assembly language instructions can be modified. The primary modification is to remove unnecessary features in the code, thereby reducing the code size so that it can fit into a stack frame. This assembled code fragment is now a binary sequence that will be at the heart of the attack.

Refer again to the program shown in Figure 15.2. Let's assume that when the `main()` function is called in that program, the stack frame appears as shown in Figure 15.4(a). Using a debugger, the programmer then finds the

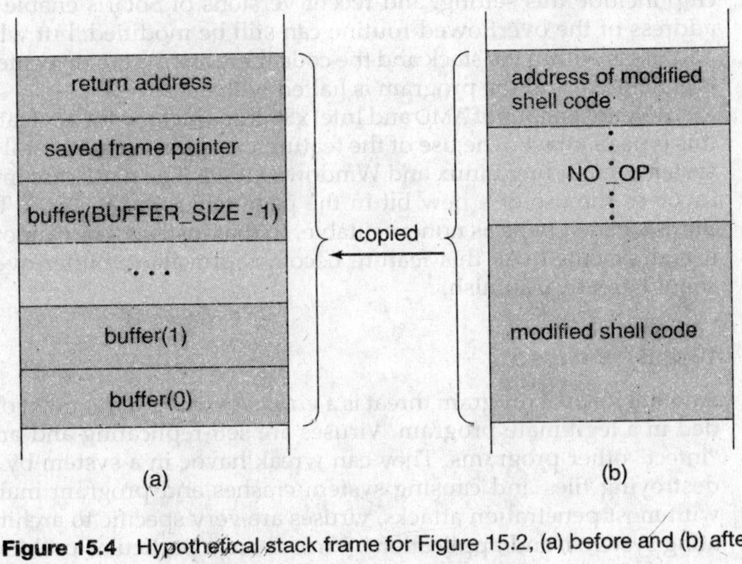

Figure 15.4 Hypothetical stack frame for Figure 15.2, (a) before and (b) after.

address of `buffer[0]` in the stack. That address is the location of the code the attacker wants executed. The binary sequence is appended with the necessary amount of NO-OP instructions (for NO-`OPeration`) to fill the stack frame up to the location of the return address; and the location of `buffer[0]`, the new return address, is added. The attack is complete when the attacker gives this constructed binary sequence as input to the process. The process then copies the binary sequence from `argv[1]` to position `buffer[0]` in the stack frame. Now, when control returns from `main()`, instead of returning to the location specified by the old value of the return address, we return to the modified shell code, which runs with the access rights of the attacked process! Figure 15.4(b) contains the modified shell code.

There are many ways to exploit potential buffer-overflow problems. In this example, we considered the possibility that the program being attacked—the code shown in Figure 15.2—ran with system-wide permissions. However, the code segment that runs once the value of the return address has been modified might perform any type of malicious act, such as deleting files, opening network ports for further exploitation, and so on.

This example buffer-overflow attack reveals that considerable knowledge and programming skill are needed to recognize exploitable code and then to exploit it. Unfortunately, it does not take great programmers to launch security attacks. Rather, one cracker can determine the bug and then write an exploit. Anyone with rudimentary computer skills and access to the exploit—a so-called **script kiddie**—can then try to launch the attack at target systems.

The buffer-overflow attack is especially pernicious because it can be run between systems and can travel over allowed communication channels. Such attacks can occur within protocols that are expected to be used to communicate with the target machine, and they can therefore be hard to detect and prevent. They can even bypass the security added by firewalls (Section 15.7).

One solution to this problem is for the CPU to have a feature that disallows execution of code in a stack section of memory. Recent versions of Sun's SPARC chip include this setting, and recent versions of Solaris enable it. The return address of the overflowed routine can still be modified; but when the return address is within the stack and the code there attempts to execute, an exception is generated, and the program is halted with an error.

Recent versions of AMD and Intel x86 chips include the NX feature to prevent this type of attack. The use of the feature is supported in several x86 operating systems, including Linux and Windows XP SP2. The hardware implementation involves the use of a new bit in the page tables of the CPUs. This bit marks the associated page as nonexecutable, so that instructions cannot be read from it and executed. As this feature becomes prevalent, buffer-overflow attacks should greatly diminish.

15.2.5 Viruses

Another form of program threat is a **virus**. A virus is a fragment of code embedded in a legitimate program. Viruses are self-replicating and are designed to "infect" other programs. They can wreak havoc in a system by modifying or destroying files and causing system crashes and program malfunctions. As with most penetration attacks, viruses are very specific to architectures, operating systems, and applications. Viruses are a particular problem for users of

PCs. UNIX and other multiuser operating systems generally are not susceptible to viruses because the executable programs are protected from writing by the operating system. Even if a virus does infect such a program, its powers usually are limited because other aspects of the system are protected.

Viruses are usually borne via e-mail, with spam the most common vector. They can also spread when users download viral programs from Internet file-sharing services or exchange infected disks.

Another common form of virus transmission uses Microsoft Office files, such as Microsoft Word documents. These documents can contain *macros* (or Visual Basic programs) that programs in the Office suite (Word, PowerPoint, and Excel) will execute automatically. Because these programs run under the user's own account, the macros can run largely unconstrained (for example, deleting user files at will). Commonly, the virus will also e-mail itself to others in the user's contact list. Here is a code sample that shows the simplicity of writing a Visual Basic macro that a virus could use to format the hard drive of a Windows computer as soon as the file containing the macro was opened:

```
Sub AutoOpen()
Dim oFS
   Set oFS = CreateObject(''Scripting.FileSystemObject'')
   vs = Shell(''c: command.com /k format c:'',vbHide)
End Sub
```

How do viruses work? Once a virus reaches a target machine, a program known as a **virus dropper** inserts the virus into the system. The virus dropper is usually a Trojan horse, executed for other reasons but installing the virus as its core activity. Once installed, the virus may do any one of a number of things. There are literally thousands of viruses, but they fall into several main categories. Note that many viruses belong to more than one category.

- **File**. A standard file virus infects a system by appending itself to a file. It changes the start of the program so that execution jumps to its code. After it executes, it returns control to the program so that its execution is not noticed. File viruses are sometimes known as parasitic viruses, as they leave no full files behind and leave the host program still functional.
- **Boot**. A boot virus infects the boot sector of the system, executing every time the system is booted and before the operating system is loaded. It watches for other bootable media (that is, floppy disks) and infects them. These viruses are also known as memory viruses, because they do not appear in the file system. Figure 15.5 shows how a boot virus works.
- **Macro**. Most viruses are written in a low-level language, such as assembly or C. Macro viruses are written in a high-level language, such as Visual Basic. These viruses are triggered when a program capable of executing the macro is run. For example, a macro virus could be contained in a spreadsheet file.
- **Source code**. A source code virus looks for source code and modifies it to include the virus and to help spread the virus.

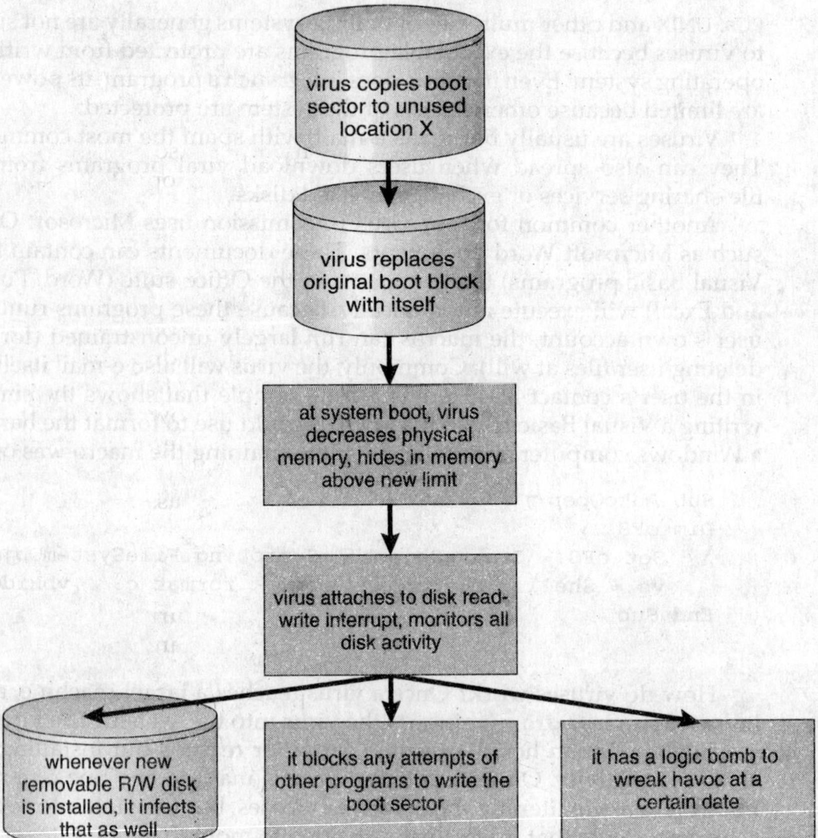

Figure 15.5 A boot-sector computer virus.

- **Polymorphic**. A polymorphic virus changes each time it is installed to avoid detection by antivirus software. The changes do not affect the virus's functionality but rather change the virus's signature. A **virus signature** is a pattern that can be used to identify a virus, typically a series of bytes that make up the virus code.
- **Encrypted**. An encrypted virus includes decryption code along with the encrypted virus, again to avoid detection. The virus first decrypts and then executes.
- **Stealth**. This tricky virus attempts to avoid detection by modifying parts of the system that could be used to detect it. For example, it could modify the `read` system call so that if the file it has modified is read, the original form of the code is returned rather than the infected code.
- **Tunneling**. This virus attempts to bypass detection by an antivirus scanner by installing itself in the interrupt-handler chain. Similar viruses install themselves in device drivers.

- **Multipartite**. A virus of this type is able to infect multiple parts of a system, including boot sectors, memory, and files. This makes it difficult to detect and contain.
- **Armored**. An armored virus is coded to make it hard for antivirus researchers to unravel and understand. It can also be compressed to avoid detection and disinfection. In addition, virus droppers and other full files that are part of a virus infestation are frequently hidden via file attributes or unviewable file names.

This vast variety of viruses is likely to continue to grow. In fact, in 2004 a new and widespread virus was detected. It exploited three separate bugs for its operation. This virus started by infecting hundreds of Windows servers (including many trusted sites) running Microsoft Internet Information Server (IIS). Any vulnerable Microsoft Explorer Web browser visiting those sites received a browser virus with any download. The browser virus installed several back-door programs, including a **keystroke logger**, which records all things entered on the keyboard (including passwords and credit-card numbers). It also installed a daemon to allow unlimited remote access by an intruder and another that allowed an intruder to route spam through the infected desktop computer.

Generally, viruses are the most disruptive security attacks; and because they are effective, they will continue to be written and to spread. Among the active debates within the computing community is whether a **monoculture**, in which many systems run the same hardware, operating system, and/or application software, is increasing the threat of and damage caused by security intrusions. This monoculture supposedly consists of Microsoft products, and part of the debate concerns whether such a monoculture even exists today.

15.3 System and Network Threats

Program threats typically use a breakdown in the protection mechanisms of a system to attack programs. In contrast, system and network threats involve the abuse of services and network connections. System and network threats create a situation in which operating-system resources and user files are misused. Sometimes a system and network attack is used to launch a program attack, and vice versa.

The more **open** an operating system is—the more services it has enabled and the more functions it allows—the more likely it is that a bug is available to exploit. Increasingly, operating systems strive to be **secure by default**. For example, Solaris 10 moved from a model in which many services (FTP, telnet, and others) were enabled by default when the system was installed to a model in which almost all services are disabled at installation time and must specifically be enabled by system administrators. Such changes reduce the system's **attack surface**—the set of ways in which an attacker can try to break into the system.

In the remainder of this section, we discuss some examples of system and network threats, including worms, port scanning, and denial-of-service attacks. It is important to note that masquerading and replay attacks are also commonly launched over networks between systems. In fact, these attacks are more effective and harder to counter when multiple systems are involved. For example, within a computer, the operating system usually can determine the sender and receiver of a message. Even if the sender changes to the ID of someone else, there may be a record of that ID change. When multiple systems are involved, especially systems controlled by attackers, then such tracing is much more difficult.

In general, we can say that sharing secrets (to prove identity and as keys to encryption) is required for authentication and encryption, and sharing secrets is easier in environments (such as a single operating system) in which secure sharing methods exist. These methods include shared memory and interprocess communications. Creating secure communication and authentication is discussed in Sections 15.4 and 15.5.

15.3.1 Worms

A **worm** is a process that uses the **spawn** mechanism to ravage system performance. The worm spawns copies of itself, using up system resources and perhaps locking out all other processes. On computer networks, worms are particularly potent, since they may reproduce themselves among systems and thus shut down an entire network. Such an event occurred in 1988 to UNIX systems on the Internet, causing the loss of system and system-administrator time worth millions of dollars.

At the close of the workday on November 2, 1988, Robert Tappan Morris, Jr., a first-year Cornell graduate student, unleashed a worm program on one or more hosts connected to the Internet. Targeting Sun Microsystems' Sun 3 workstations and VAX computers running variants of Version 4 BSD UNIX, the worm quickly spread over great distances; within a few hours of its release, it had consumed system resources to the point of bringing down the infected machines.

Although Robert Morris designed the self-replicating program for rapid reproduction and distribution, some of the features of the UNIX networking environment provided the means to propagate the worm throughout the system. It is likely that Morris chose for initial infection an Internet host left open for and accessible to outside users. From there, the worm program exploited flaws in the UNIX operating system's security routines and took advantage of UNIX utilities that simplify resource sharing in local-area networks to gain unauthorized access to thousands of other connected sites. Morris's methods of attack are outlined next.

The worm was made up of two programs, a **grappling hook** (also called a **bootstrap** or **vector**) program and the main program. Named *l1.c*, the grappling hook consisted of 99 lines of C code compiled and run on each machine it accessed. Once established on the computer system under attack, the grappling hook connected to the machine where it originated and uploaded a copy of the main worm onto the *hooked* system (Figure 15.6). The main program proceeded to search for other machines to which the newly infected system could connect easily. In these actions, Morris exploited the UNIX networking utility `rsh` for easy remote task execution. By setting up special files that list host–login name pairs, users can omit entering a password each time they access a remote account on the paired list. The worm searched these special files for site names

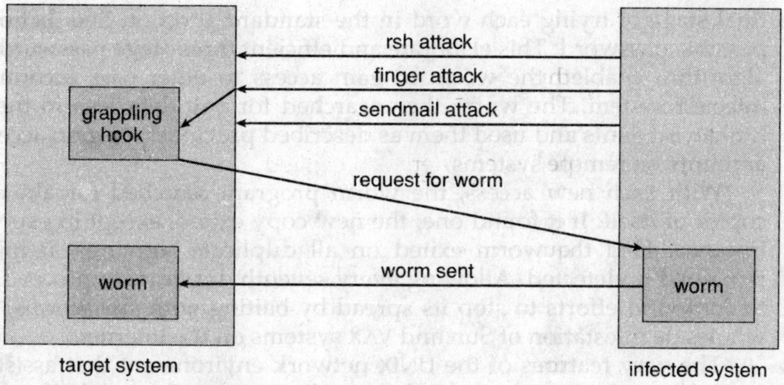

Figure 15.6 The Morris Internet worm.

that would allow remote execution without a password. Where remote shells were established, the worm program was uploaded and began executing anew.

The attack via remote access was one of three infection methods built into the worm. The other two methods involved operating-system bugs in the UNIX `finger` and `sendmail` programs.

The `finger` utility functions as an electronic telephone directory; the command

```
finger user-name@hostname
```

returns a person's real and login names along with other information that the user may have provided, such as office and home address and telephone number, research plan, or clever quotation. `Finger` runs as a background process (or daemon) at each BSD site and responds to queries throughout the Internet. The worm executed a buffer-overflow attack on `finger`. The program queried `finger` with a 536-byte string crafted to exceed the buffer allocated for input and to overwrite the stack frame. Instead of returning to the *main* routine where it resided before Morris's call, the `finger` daemon was routed to a procedure within the invading 536-byte string now residing on the stack. The new procedure executed `/bin/sh`, which, if successful, gave the worm a remote shell on the machine under attack.

The bug exploited in `sendmail` also involved using a daemon process for malicious entry. `sendmail` sends, receives, and routes electronic mail. Debugging code in the utility permits testers to verify and display the state of the mail system. The debugging option was useful to system administrators and was often left on. Morris included in his attack arsenal a call to `debug` that —instead of specifying a user address, as would be normal in testing—issued a set of commands that mailed and executed a copy of the grappling-hook program.

Once in place, the main worm systematically attempted to discover user passwords. It began by trying simple cases of no password or passwords constructed of account–user-name combinations, then used comparisons with an internal dictionary of 432 favorite password choices, and then went to the final stage of trying each word in the standard UNIX on-line dictionary as a possible password. This elaborate and efficient three-stage password-cracking algorithm enabled the worm to gain access to other user accounts on the infected system. The worm then searched for `rsh` data files in these newly broken accounts and used them as described previously to gain access to user accounts on remote systems.

With each new access, the worm program searched for already active copies of itself. If it found one, the new copy exited, except in every seventh instance. Had the worm exited on all duplicate sightings, it might have remained undetected. Allowing every seventh duplicate to proceed (possibly to confound efforts to stop its spread by baiting with *fake* worms) created a wholesale infestation of Sun and VAX systems on the Internet.

The very features of the UNIX network environment that assisted in the worm's propagation also helped to stop its advance. Ease of electronic communication, mechanisms to copy source and binary files to remote machines, and access to both source code and human expertise allowed cooperative efforts to develop solutions quickly. By the evening of the next day, November 3, methods of halting the invading program were circulated to system administrators via the Internet. Within days, specific software patches for the exploited security flaws were available.

Why did Morris unleash the worm? The action has been characterized as both a harmless prank gone awry and a serious criminal offense. Based on the complexity of the attack, it is unlikely that the worm's release or the scope of its spread was unintentional. The worm program took elaborate steps to cover its tracks and to repel efforts to stop its spread. Yet the program contained no code aimed at damaging or destroying the systems on which it ran. The author clearly had the expertise to include such commands; in fact, data structures were present in the bootstrap code that could have been used to transfer Trojan-horse or virus programs. The behavior of the program may lead to interesting observations, but it does not provide a sound basis for inferring motive. What is not open to speculation, however, is the legal outcome: A federal court convicted Morris and handed down a sentence of three years' probation, 400 hours of community service, and a $10,000 fine. Morris's legal costs probably exceeded $100,000.

Security experts continue to evaluate methods to decrease or eliminate worms. A more recent event, though, shows that worms are still a fact of life on the Internet. It also shows that as the Internet grows, the damage that even "harmless" worms can do also grows and can be significant. This example occurred during August 2003. The fifth version of the "Sobig" worm, more properly known as "W32.Sobig.F@mm," was released by persons at this time unknown. It was the fastest-spreading worm released to date, at its peak infecting hundreds of thousands of computers and one in seventeen e-mail messages on the Internet. It clogged e-mail inboxes, slowed networks, and took a huge number of hours to clean up.

Sobig.F was launched by being uploaded to a pornography newsgroup via an account created with a stolen credit card. It was disguised as a photo. The virus targeted Microsoft Windows systems and used its own SMTP engine to e-mail itself to all the addresses found on an infected system. It used a variety of subject lines to help avoid detection, including "Thank You!" "Your details," and "Re: Approved." It also used a random address on the host as the "From:"

address, making it difficult to determine from the message which machine was the infected source. Sobig.F included an attachment for the target e-mail reader to click on, again with a variety of names. If this payload was executed, it stored a program called WINPPR32.EXE in the default Windows directory, along with a text file. It also modified the Windows registry.

The code included in the attachment was also programmed to periodically attempt to connect to one of twenty servers and download and execute a program from them. Fortunately, the servers were disabled before the code could be downloaded. The content of the program from these servers has not yet been determined. If the code was malevolent, untold damage to a vast number of machines could have resulted.

15.3.2 Port Scanning

Port scanning is not an attack but rather a means for a cracker to detect a system's vulnerabilities to attack. Port scanning typically is automated, involving a tool that attempts to create a TCP/IP connection to a specific port or a range of ports. For example, suppose there is a known vulnerability (or bug) in `sendmail`. A cracker could launch a port scanner to try to connect, say, to port 25 of a particular system or to a range of systems. If the connection was successful, the cracker (or tool) could attempt to communicate with the answering service to determine if the service was indeed `sendmail` and, if so, if it was the version with the bug.

Now imagine a tool in which each bug of every service of every operating system was encoded. The tool could attempt to connect to every port of one or more systems. For every service that answered, it could try to use each known bug. Frequently, the bugs are buffer overflows, allowing the creation of a privileged command shell on the system. From there, of course, the cracker could install Trojan horses, back-door programs, and so on.

There is no such tool, but there are tools that perform subsets of that functionality. For example, `nmap` (from http://www.insecure.org/nmap/) is a very versatile open-source utility for network exploration and security auditing. When pointed at a target, it will determine what services are running, including application names and versions. It can identify the host operating system. It can also provide information about defenses, such as what firewalls are defending the target. It does not exploit any known bugs.

`Nessus` (from http://www.nessus.org/) performs a similar function, but it has a database of bugs and their exploits. It can scan a range of systems, determine the services running on those systems, and attempt to attack all appropriate bugs. It generates reports about the results. It does not perform the final step of exploiting the found bugs, but a knowledgeable cracker or a script kiddie could.

Because port scans are detectable (Section 15.6.3), they frequently are launched from **zombie systems**. Such systems are previously compromised, independent systems that are serving their owners while being used for nefarious purposes, including denial-of-service attacks and spam relay. Zombies make crackers particularly difficult to prosecute because determining the source of the attack and the person that launched it is challenging. This is one of many reasons for securing "inconsequential" systems, not just systems containing "valuable" information or services.

15.3.3 Denial of Service

As mentioned earlier, denial-of-service attacks are aimed not at gaining information or stealing resources but rather at disrupting legitimate use of a system or facility. Most such attacks involve systems that the attacker has not penetrated. Indeed, launching an attack that prevents legitimate use is frequently easier than breaking into a machine or facility.

Denial-of-service attacks are generally network based. They fall into two categories. Attacks in the first category use so many facility resources that, in essence, no useful work can be done. For example, a Web-site click could download a Java applet that proceeds to use all available CPU time or to pop up windows infinitely. The second category involves disrupting the network of the facility. There have been several successful denial-of-service attacks of this kind against major Web sites. These attacks result from abuse of some of the fundamental functionality of TCP/IP. For instance, if the attacker sends the part of the protocol that says "I want to start a TCP connection," but never follows with the standard "The connection is now complete," the result can be partially started TCP sessions. If enough of these sessions are launched, they can eat up all the network resources of the system, disabling any further legitimate TCP connections. Such attacks, which can last hours or days, have caused partial or full failure of attempts to use the target facility. The attacks are usually stopped at the network level until the operating systems can be updated to reduce their vulnerability.

Generally, it is impossible to prevent denial-of-service attacks. The attacks use the same mechanisms as normal operation. Even more difficult to prevent and resolve are **distributed denial-of-service attacks (DDOS)**. These attacks are launched from multiple sites at once, toward a common target, typically by zombies. DDOS attacks have become more common and are sometimes associated with blackmail attempts. A site comes under attack, and the attackers offer to halt the attack in exchange for money.

Sometimes a site does not even know it is under attack. It can be difficult to determine whether a system slowdown is an attack or just a surge in system use. Consider that a successful advertising campaign that greatly increases traffic to a site could be considered a DDOS.

There are other interesting aspects of DOS attacks. For example, if an authentication algorithm locks an account for a period of time after several incorrect attempts to access the account, then an attacker could cause all authentication to be blocked by purposely making incorrect attempts to access all accounts. Similarly, a firewall that automatically blocks certain kinds of traffic could be induced to block that traffic when it should not. These examples suggest that programmers and systems managers need to fully understand the algorithms and technologies they are deploying. Finally, computer science classes are notorious sources of accidental system DOS attacks. Consider the first programming exercises in which students learn to create subprocesses or threads. A common bug involves spawning subprocesses infinitely. The system's free memory and CPU resources don't stand a chance.

15.4 Cryptography as a Security Tool

There are many defenses against computer attacks, running the gamut from methodology to technology. The broadest tool available to system designers and users is cryptography. In this section, we discuss the details of cryptography and its use in computer security.

In an isolated computer, the operating system can reliably determine the sender and recipient of all interprocess communication, since it controls all communication channels in the computer. In a network of computers, the situation is quite different. A networked computer receives bits *from the wire* with no immediate and reliable way of determining what machine or application sent those bits. Similarly, the computer sends bits onto the network with no way of knowing who might eventually receive them.

Commonly, network addresses are used to infer the potential senders and receivers of network messages. Network packets arrive with a source address, such as an IP address. And when a computer sends a message, it names the intended receiver by specifying a destination address. However, for applications where security matters, we are asking for trouble if we assume that the source or destination address of a packet reliably determines who sent or received that packet. A rogue computer can send a message with a falsified source address, and numerous computers other than the one specified by the destination address can (and typically do) receive a packet. For example, all of the routers on the way to the destination will receive the packet, too. How, then, is an operating system to decide whether to grant a request when it cannot trust the named source of the request? And how is it supposed to provide protection for a request or data when it cannot determine who will receive the response or message contents it sends over the network?

It is generally considered infeasible to build a network of any scale in which the source and destination addresses of packets can be *trusted* in this sense. Therefore, the only alternative is somehow to eliminate the need to trust the network. This is the job of cryptography. Abstractly, **cryptography** is used to constrain the potential senders and/or receivers of a message. Modern cryptography is based on secrets called **keys** that are selectively distributed to computers in a network and used to process messages. Cryptography enables a recipient of a message to verify that the message was created by some computer possessing a certain key—the key is the *source* of the message. Similarly, a sender can encode its message so that only a computer with a certain key can decode the message, so that the key becomes the *destination*. Unlike network addresses, however, keys are designed so that it is not computationally feasible to derive them from the messages they were used to generate or from any other public information. Thus, they provide a much more trustworthy means of constraining senders and receivers of messages. Note that cryptography is a field of study unto itself, with large and small complexities and subtleties. Here, we explore the most important aspects of the parts of cryptography that pertain to operating systems.

15.4.1 Encryption

Because it solves a wide variety of communication security problems, **encryption** is used frequently in many aspects of modern computing. Encryption is a means for constraining the possible receivers of a message. An encryption algorithm enables the sender of a message to ensure that only a computer possessing a certain key can read the message. Encryption of messages is an ancient practice, of course, and there have been many encryption algorithms, dating back to ancient times. In this section, we describe important modern encryption principles and algorithms.

Figure 15.7 shows an example of two users communicating securely over an insecure channel. We refer to this figure throughout the section. Note that the key exchange can take place directly between the two parties or via a trusted third party (that is, a certificate authority), as discussed in Section 15.4.1.4.

An encryption algorithm consists of the following components:

- A set K of keys.
- A set M of messages.
- A set C of ciphertexts.
- A function $E : K \rightarrow (M \rightarrow C)$. That is, for each $k \in K$, $E(k)$ is a function for generating ciphertexts from messages. Both E and $E(k)$ for any k should be efficiently computable functions.
- A function $D : K \rightarrow (C \rightarrow M)$. That is, for each $k \in K$, $D(k)$ is a function for generating messages from ciphertexts. Both D and $D(k)$ for any k should be efficiently computable functions.

An encryption algorithm must provide this essential property: given a ciphertext $c \in C$, a computer can compute m such that $E(k)(m) = c$ only if it possesses

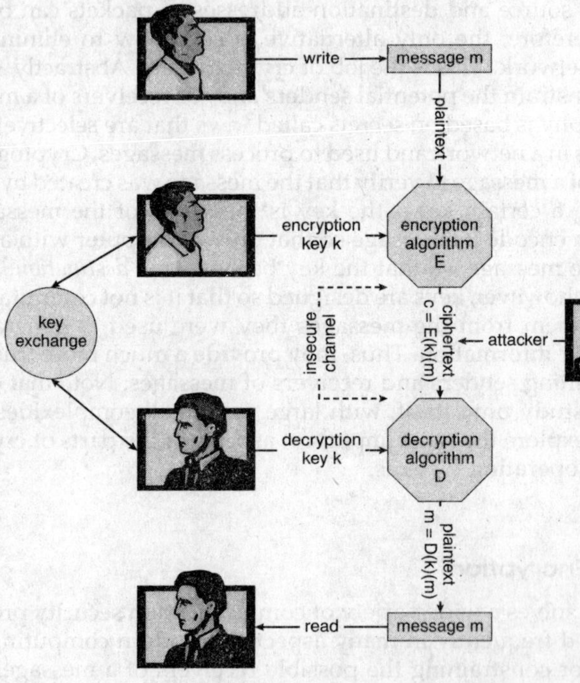

Figure 15.7 A secure communication over an insecure medium.

$D(k)$. Thus, a computer holding $D(k)$ can decrypt ciphertexts to the plaintexts used to produce them, but a computer not holding $D(k)$ cannot decrypt ciphertexts. Since ciphertexts are generally exposed (for example, sent on a network), it is important that it be infeasible to derive $D(k)$ from the ciphertexts.

There are two main types of encryption algorithms: symmetric and asymmetric. We discuss both types in the following sections.

15.4.1.1 Symmetric Encryption

In a **symmetric encryption algorithm**, the same key is used to encrypt and to decrypt. That is, $E(k)$ can be derived from $D(k)$, and vice versa. Therefore, the secrecy of $E(k)$ must be protected to the same extent as that of $D(k)$.

For the past several decades, the most commonly used symmetric encryption algorithm in the United States for civilian applications has been the **data-encryption standard (DES)** adopted by the National Institute of Standards and Technology (NIST). DES works by taking a 64-bit value and a 56-bit key and performing a series of transformations. These transformations are based on substitution and permutation operations, as is generally the case for symmetric encryption transformations. Some of the transformations are **black-box transformations**, in that their algorithms are hidden. In fact, these so-called "S-boxes" are classified by the United States government. Messages longer than 64 bits are broken into 64-bit chunks. Because DES works on a chunk of bits at a time, is known as a **block cipher**. If the same key is used for encrypting an extended amount of data, it becomes vulnerable to attack. Consider, for example, that the same source block would result in the same ciphertext if the same key and encryption algorithm were used. Therefore, the chunks are not just encrypted but also exclusive-or'ed (XORed) with the previous ciphertext block before encryption. This is known as **cipher-block chaining**.

DES is now considered insecure for many applications because its keys can be exhaustively searched with moderate computing resources. Rather than giving up on DES, though, NIST created a modification called **triple DES**, in which the DES algorithm is repeated three times (two encryptions and one decryption) on the same plaintext using two or three keys—for example, $c = E(k_3)(D(k_2)(E(K_1)(m)))$. When three keys are used, the effective key length is 168 bits. Triple DES is in widespread use today.

In 2001, NIST adopted a new encryption algorithm, called the **advanced encryption standard (AES)**, to replace DES. AES is another symmetric block cipher. It can use key lengths of 128, 192, and 256 bits and works on 128-bit blocks. It works by performing 10 to 14 rounds of transformations on a matrix formed from a block. Generally, the algorithm is compact and efficient.

Several other symmetric block encryption algorithms in use today bear mentioning. The **twofish** algorithm is fast, compact, and easy to implement. It can use a variable key length of up to 256 bits and works on 128-bit blocks. **RC5** can vary in key length, number of transformations, and block size. Because it uses only basic computational operations, it can run on a wide variety of CPUs.

RC4 is perhaps the most common stream cipher. A **stream cipher** is designed to encrypt and decrypt a stream of bytes or bits rather than a block. This is useful when the length of a communication would make a block cipher too slow. The key is input into a pseudo–random-bit generator, which is an algorithm that attempts to produce random bits. The output of the generator when fed a key is a keystream. A **keystream** is an infinite set of keys that can be used for the input plaintext stream. RC4 is used in encrypting steams of data, such as in WEP, the wireless LAN protocol. It is also used in communications between Web browsers and Web servers, as we discuss below. Unfortunately, RC4 as used in WEP (IEEE standard 802.11) has been found to be breakable in a reasonable amount of computer time. In fact, RC4 itself has vulnerabilities.

15.4.1.2 Asymmetric Encryption

In an **asymmetric encryption algorithm**, there are different encryption and decryption keys. Here, we describe one such algorithm, known as *RSA* after the names of its inventors (Rivest, Shamir, and Adleman). The RSA cipher is a block-cipher public-key algorithm and is the most widely used asymmetrical algorithm. Asymmetrical algorithms based on elliptical curves are gaining ground, however, because the key length of such an algorithm can be shorter for the same amount of cryptographic strength.

It is computationally infeasible to derive $D(k_d, N)$ from $E(k_e, N)$, and so $E(k_e, N)$ need not be kept secret and can be widely disseminated; thus, $E(k_e, N)$ (or just k_e) is the **public key** and $D(k_d, N)$ (or just k_d) is the **private key**. N is the

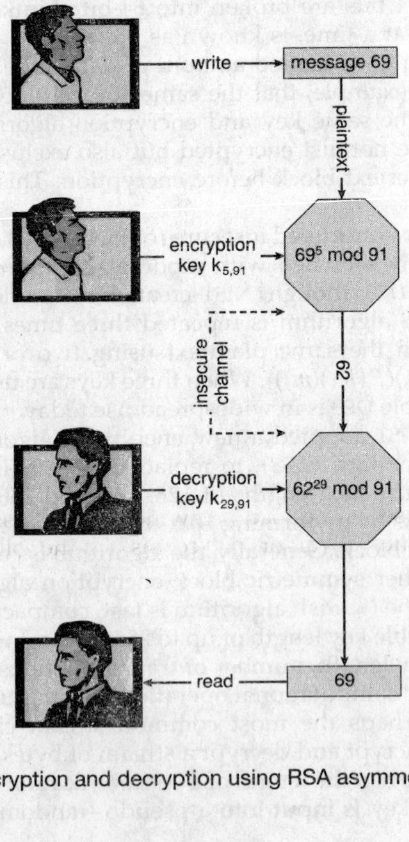

Figure 15.8 Encryption and decryption using RSA asymmetric cryptography.

product of two large, randomly chosen prime numbers p and q (for example, p and q are 512 bits each). The encryption algorithm is $E(k_e, N)(m) = m^{k_e} \bmod N$, where k_e satisfies $k_e k_d \bmod (p-1)(q-1) = 1$. The decryption algorithm is then $D(k_d, N)(c) = c^{k_d} \bmod N$.

An example using small values is shown in Figure 15.8. In this example, we make $p = 7$ and $q = 13$. We then calculate $N = 7*13 = 91$ and $(p-1)(q-1) = 72$. We next select k_e relatively prime to 72 and < 72, yielding 5. Finally, we calculate k_d such that $k_e k_d \bmod 72 = 1$, yielding 29. We now have our keys: the public key, $k_e, N = 5, 91$, and the private key, $k_d, N = 29, 91$. Encrypting the message 69 with the public key results in the message 62, which is then decoded by the receiver via the private key.

The use of asymmetric encryption begins with the publication of the public key of the destination. For bidirectional communication, the source also must publish its public key. "Publication" can be as simple as handing over an electronic copy of the key, or it can be more complex. The private key (or "secret key") must be jealously guarded, as anyone holding that key can decrypt any message created by the matching public key.

We should note that the seemingly small difference in key use between asymmetric and symmetric cryptography is quite large in practice. Asymmetric cryptography is based on mathematical functions rather than transformations, making it much more computationally expensive to execute. It is much faster for a computer to encode and decode ciphertext by using the usual symmetric algorithms than by using asymmetric algorithms. Why, then, use an asymmetric algorithm? In truth, these algorithms are not used for general-purpose encryption of large amounts of data. However, they are used not only for encryption of small amounts of data but also for authentication, confidentiality, and key distribution, as we show in the following sections.

15.4.1.3 Authentication

We have seen that encryption offers a way of constraining the set of possible receivers of a message. Constraining the set of potential senders of a message is called **authentication**. Authentication is thus complementary to encryption. In fact, sometimes their functions overlap. Consider that an encrypted message can also prove the identity of the sender. For example, if $D(k_d, N)(E(k_e, N)(m))$ produces a valid message, then we know that the creator of the message must hold k_e. Authentication is also useful for proving that a message has not been modified. In this section, we discuss authentication as a constraint on possible receivers of a message. Note that this sort of authentication is similar to but distinct from user authentication, which we discuss in Section 15.5.

An authentication algorithm consists of the following components:

- A set K of keys.
- A set M of messages.
- A set A of authenticators.
- A function $S : K \rightarrow (M \rightarrow A)$. That is, for each $k \in K$, $S(k)$ is a function for generating authenticators from messages. Both S and $S(k)$ for any k should be efficiently computable functions.

- A function $V : K \rightarrow (M \times A \rightarrow \{\texttt{true}, \texttt{false}\})$. That is, for each $k \in K$, $V(k)$ is a function for verifying authenticators on messages. Both V and $V(k)$ for any k should be efficiently computable functions.

The critical property that an authentication algorithm must possess is this: for a message m, a computer can generate an authenticator $a \in A$ such that $V(k)(m, a) = \texttt{true}$ only if it possesses $S(k)$. Thus, a computer holding $S(k)$ can generate authenticators on messages so that any computer possessing $V(k)$ can verify them. However, a computer not holding $S(k)$ cannot generate authenticators on messages that can be verified using $V(k)$. Since authenticators are generally exposed (for example, sent on a network with the messages themselves), it must not be feasible to derive $S(k)$ from the authenticators.

Just as there are two types of encryption algorithms, there are two main varieties of authentication algorithms. The first step in understanding these algorithms is to explore hash functions. A **hash function** $H(m)$ creates a small, fixed-sized block of data, known as a **message digest** or **hash value**, from a message m. Hash functions work by taking a message in n-bit blocks and processing the blocks to produce an n-bit hash. H must be collision resistant on m—that is, it must be infeasible to find an $m' \neq m$ such that $H(m) = H(m')$. Now, if $H(m) = H(m')$, we know that $m = m'$—that is, we know that the message has not been modified. Common message-digest functions include **MD5**, which produces a 128-bit hash, and **SHA-1**, which outputs a 160-bit hash. Message digests are useful for detecting changed messages but are not useful as authenticators. For example, $H(m)$ can be sent along with a message; but if H is known, then someone could modify m and recompute $H(m)$, and the message modification would not be detected. Therefore, an authentication algorithm takes the message digest and encrypts it.

The first main type of authentication algorithm uses symmetric encryption. In a **message-authentication code (MAC)**, a cryptographic checksum is generated from the message using a secret key. Knowledge of $V(k)$ and knowledge of $S(k)$ are equivalent: one can be derived from the other, so k must be kept secret. A simple example of a MAC defines $S(k)(m) = f(k, H(m))$, where f is a function that is one-way on its first argument (that is, k cannot be derived from $f(k, H(m))$). Because of the collision resistance in the hash function, we are reasonably assured that no other message could create the same MAC. A suitable verification algorithm is then $V(k)(m, a) \equiv (f(k, m) = a)$. Note that k is needed to compute both $S(k)$ and $V(k)$, so anyone able to compute one can compute the other.

The second main type of authentication algorithm is a **digital-signature algorithm**, and the authenticators thus produced are called **digital signatures**. In a digital-signature algorithm, it is computationally infeasible to derive $S(k_s)$ from $V(k_v)$; in particular, V is a one-way function. Thus, k_v is the public key and k_s is the private key.

Consider as an example the RSA digital-signature algorithm. It is similar to the RSA encryption algorithm, but the key use is reversed. The digital signature of a message is derived by computing $S(k_s)(m) = H(m)^{k_s} \bmod N$. The key k_s again is a pair $\langle d, N \rangle$, where N is the product of two large, randomly chosen prime numbers p and q. The verification algorithm is then $V(k_v)(m, a) \equiv (a^{k_v} \bmod N = H(m))$, where k_v satisfies $k_v k_s \bmod (p-1)(q-1) = 1$.

If encryption can prove the identity of the sender of a message, then why do we need separate authentication algorithms? There are three primary reasons.

- Authentication algorithms generally require fewer computations (with the notable exception of RSA digital signatures). Over large amounts of plaintext, this efficiency can make a huge difference in resource use and the time needed to authenticate a message.
- The authenticator of a message is almost always shorter than the message and its ciphertext. This improves space use and transmission time efficiency.
- Sometimes, we want authentication but not confidentiality. For example, a company could provide a software patch and could "sign" that patch to prove that it came from the company and that it hasn't been modified.

Authentication is a component of many aspects of security. For example, it is the core of **nonrepudiation**, which supplies proof that an entity performed an action. A typical example of nonrepudiation involves the filling out of electronic forms as an alternative to the signing of paper contracts. Nonrepudiation assures that a person filling out an electronic form cannot deny that he did so.

15.4.1.4 Key Distribution

Certainly, a good part of the battle between cryptographers (those inventing ciphers) and cryptanalysts (those trying to break them) involves keys. With symmetric algorithms, both parties need the key, and no one else should have it. The delivery of the symmetric key is a huge challenge. Sometimes it is performed **out-of-band**—say, via a paper document or a conversation. These methods do not scale well, however. Also consider the key-management challenge. Suppose a user wanted to communicate with N other users privately. That user would need N keys and, for more security, would need to change those keys frequently.

These are the very reasons for efforts to create asymmetric key algorithms. Not only can the keys be exchanged in public, but a given user needs only one private key, no matter how many other people she wants to communicate with. There is still the matter of managing a public key for each party to be communicated with, but since public keys need not be secured, simple storage can be used for that **key ring**.

Unfortunately, even the distribution of public keys requires some care. Consider the man-in-the-middle attack shown in Figure 15.9. Here, the person who wants to receive an encrypted message sends out his public key, but an attacker also sends her "bad" public key (which matches her private key). The person who wants to send the encrypted message knows no better and so uses the bad key to encrypt the message. The attacker then happily decrypts it.

The problem is one of authentication—what we need is proof of who (or what) owns a public key. One way to solve that problem involves the use of digital certificates. A **digital certificate** is a public key digitally signed by a trusted party. The trusted party receives proof of identification from some entity

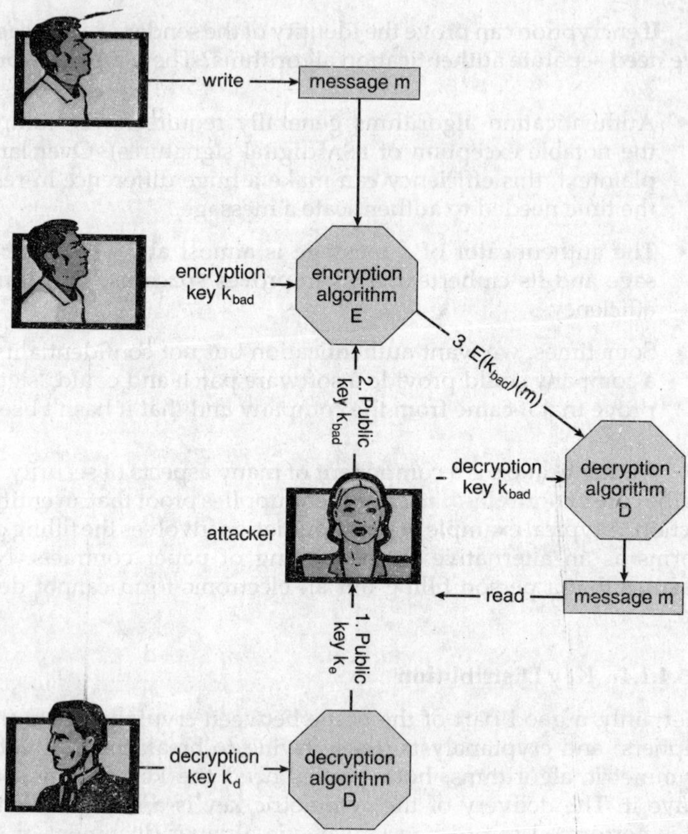

Figure 15.9 A man-in-the-middle attack on asymmetric cryptography.

and certifies that the public key belongs to that entity. But how do we know we can trust the certifier? These **certificate authorities** have their public keys included within Web browsers (and other consumers of certificates) before they are distributed. The certificate authorities can then vouch for other authorities (digitally signing the public keys of these other authorities), and so on, creating a web of trust. The certificates can be distributed in a standard X.509 digital certificate format that can be parsed by computer. This scheme is used for secure Web communication, as we discuss in Section 15.4.3.

15.4.2 Implementation of Cryptography

Network protocols are typically organized in **layers**, each layer acting as a client of the one below it. That is, when one protocol generates a message to send to its protocol peer on another machine, it hands its message to the protocol below it in the network-protocol stack for delivery to its peer on that machine. For example, in an IP network, TCP (a *transport-layer* protocol) acts as a client of IP (a *network-layer* protocol): TCP packets are passed down to IP for delivery to the TCP peer at the other end of the TCP connection. IP encapsulates the TCP packet in an IP packet, which it similarly passes down to the *data-link layer* to be transmitted across the network to its IP peer on the destination computer. This IP peer then delivers the TCP packet up to the TCP peer on that machine. All in all, the **ISO Reference Model**, which has been almost universally adopted as a model for data networking, defines seven such protocol layers. (You will read more about the ISO model of networking in Chapter 16; Figure 16.6 shows a diagram of the model.)

Cryptography can be inserted at almost any layer in the ISO model. SSL (Section 15.4.3), for example, provides security at the transport layer. Network-layer security generally has been standardized on **IPSec**, which defines IP packet formats that allow the insertion of authenticators and the encryption of packet contents. It uses symmetric encryption and uses the **IKE** protocol for key exchange. IPSec is becoming widely used as the basis for **virtual private networks** (**VPNs**), in which all traffic between two IPSec endpoints is encrypted to make a private network out of one that may otherwise be public. Numerous protocols also have been developed for use by applications, but then the applications themselves must be coded to implement security.

Where is cryptographic protection best placed in a protocol stack? In general, there is no definitive answer. On the one hand, more protocols benefit from protections placed lower in the stack. For example, since IP packets encapsulate TCP packets, encryption of IP packets (using IPSec, for example) also hides the contents of the encapsulated TCP packets. Similarly, authenticators on IP packets detect the modification of contained TCP header information.

On the other hand, protection at lower layers in the protocol stack may give insufficient protection to higher-layer protocols. For example, an application server that runs over IPSec might be able to authenticate the client computers from which requests are received. However, to authenticate a user at a client computer, the server may need to use an application-level protocol—for example, the user may be required to type a password. Also consider the problem of e-mail. E-mail delivered via the industry standard SMTP protocol is stored and forwarded, frequently multiple times, before it is delivered. Each of these transmissions could go over a secure or an insecure network. For e-mail to be secure, the e-mail message needs to be encrypted so that its security is independent of the transports that carry it.

15.4.3 An Example: SSL

SSL 3.0 is a cryptographic protocol that enables two computers to communicate securely—that is, so that each can limit the sender and receiver of messages to the other. It is perhaps the most commonly used cryptographic protocol on the Internet today, since it is the standard protocol by which Web browsers communicate securely with Web servers. For completeness, we should note that SSL was designed by Netscape and that it evolved into the industry standard TLS protocol. In this discussion, we use SSL to mean both SSL and TLS.

SSL is a complex protocol with many options. Here, we present only a single variation of it, and even then in a very simplified and abstract form, so as to maintain focus on its use of cryptographic primitives. What we are about to see is a complex dance in which asymmetric cryptography is used so that a client and a server can establish a secure **session key** that can be used for symmetric encryption of the session between the two—all of this while avoiding man-in-the-middle and replay attacks. For added cryptographic strength, the session keys are forgotten once a session is completed. Another communication between the two will require generation of new session keys.

The SSL protocol is initiated by a **client** c to communicate securely with a **server**. Prior to the protocol's use, the server s is assumed to have obtained a certificate, denoted cert_s, from certification authority CA. This certificate is a structure containing the following:

- Various attributes attrs of the server, such as its unique *distinguished* name and its *common* (DNS) name
- The identity of a public encryption algorithm $E()$ for the server
- The public key k_e of this server
- A validity interval interval during which the certificate should be considered valid
- A digital signature a on the above information made by the CA—that is, $a = S(k_{CA})(\langle \text{attrs}, E(k_e), \text{interval} \rangle)$

In addition, prior to the protocol's use, the client is presumed to have obtained the public verification algorithm $V(k_{CA})$ for CA. In the case of the Web, the user's browser is shipped from its vendor containing the verification algorithms and public keys of certain certification authorities. The user can add or delete these for certification authorities as she chooses.

When c connects to s, it sends a 28-byte random value n_c to the server, which responds with a random value n_s of its own, plus its certificate cert_s. The client verifies that $V(k_{CA})(\langle \text{attrs}, E(k_e), \text{interval}\rangle, a) = \text{true}$ and that the current time is in the validity interval interval. If both of these tests are satisfied, the server has proved its identity. Then the client generates a random 46-byte **premaster secret** pms and sends $\text{cpms} = E(k_s)(\text{pms})$ to the server. The server recovers $\text{pms} = D(k_d)(\text{cpms})$. Now both the client and the server are in possession of n_c, n_s, and pms, and each can compute a shared 48-byte **master secret** $\text{ms} = f(n_c, n_s, \text{pms})$, where f is a one-way and collision-resistant function. Only the server and client can compute ms, since only they know pms. Moreover, the dependence of ms on n_c and n_s ensures that ms is a *fresh* value—that is, a session key that has not been used in a previous communication. At this point, the client and the server both compute the following keys from the ms:

- A symmetric encryption key k_{cs}^{crypt} for encrypting messages from the client to the server
- A symmetric encryption key k_{sc}^{crypt} for encrypting messages from the server to the client
- A MAC generation key k_{cs}^{mac} for generating authenticators on messages from the client to the server
- A MAC generation key k_{sc}^{mac} for generating authenticators on messages from the server to the client

To send a message m to the server, the client sends

$$c = E(k_{cs}^{\text{crypt}})(\langle m, S(k_{cs}^{\text{mac}})(m)\rangle).$$

Upon receiving c, the server recovers

$$\langle m, a\rangle = D(k_{cs}^{\text{crypt}})(c)$$

and accepts m if $V(k_{cs}^{\text{mac}})(m, a) = \text{true}$. Similarly, to send a message m to the client, the server sends

$$c = E(k_{sc}^{\text{crypt}})(\langle m, S(k_{sc}^{\text{mac}})(m)\rangle)$$

and the client recovers

$$\langle m, a\rangle = D(k_{sc}^{\text{crypt}})(c)$$

and accepts m if $V(k_{sc}^{\text{mac}})(m, a) = \text{true}$.

This protocol enables the server to limit the recipients of its messages to the client that generated pms and to limit the senders of the messages it accepts to that same client. Similarly, the client can limit the recipients of the messages it sends and the senders of the messages it accepts to the party that knows $S(k_d)$ (that is, the party that can decrypt cpms). In many applications, such as Web transactions, the client needs to verify the identity of the party that knows $S(k_d)$. This is one purpose of the certificate cert_s; in particular, the attrs field contains information that the client can use to determine the identity—for example, the domain name—of the server with which it is communicating. For applications in which the server also needs information about the client, SSL supports an option by which a client can send a certificate to the server.

In addition to its use on the Internet, SSL is being used for a wide variety of tasks. For example, IPSec VPNs now have a competitor in SSL VPNs. IPSec is good for point-to-point encryption of traffic—say, between two company offices. SSL VPNs are more flexible but not as efficient, so they might be used between an individual employee working remotely and the corporate office.

15.5 User Authentication

Our earlier discussion of authentication involves messages and sessions. But what about users? If a system cannot authenticate a user, then authenticating that a message came from that user is pointless. Thus, a major security problem for operating systems is **user authentication**. The protection system depends on the ability to identify the programs and processes currently executing, which in turn depends on the ability to identify each user of the system. Users normally identify themselves. How do we determine whether a user's identity is authentic? Generally, user authentication is based on one or more of three things: the user's possession of something (a key or card), the user's knowledge of something (a user identifier and password), and/or an attribute of the user (fingerprint, retina pattern, or signature).

15.5.1 Passwords

The most common approach to authenticating a user identity is the use of **passwords**. When the user identifies herself by user ID or account name, she is asked for a password. If the user-supplied password matches the password stored in the system, the system assumes that the account is being accessed by the owner of that account.

Passwords are often used to protect objects in the computer system, in the absence of more complete protection schemes. They can be considered a special case of either keys or capabilities. For instance, a password may be associated with each resource (such as a file). Whenever a request is made to use the resource, the password must be given. If the password is correct, access is granted. Different passwords may be associated with different access rights. For example, different passwords may be used for reading files, appending files, and updating files.

In practice, most systems require only one password for a user to gain full rights. Although more passwords theoretically would be more secure, such systems tend not to be implemented due to the classic trade-off between security and convenience. If security makes something inconvenient, then the security is frequently bypassed or otherwise circumvented.

15.5.2 Password Vulnerabilities

Passwords are extremely common because they are easy to understand and use. Unfortunately, passwords can often be guessed, accidentally exposed, sniffed, or illegally transferred from an authorized user to an unauthorized one, as we show next.

There are two common ways to guess a password. One way is for the intruder (either human or program) to know the user or to have information about the user. All too frequently, people use obvious information (such as the names of their cats or spouses) as their passwords. The other way is to use brute force, trying enumeration—or all possible combinations of valid password characters (letters, numbers, and punctuation on some systems)—until the password is found. Short passwords are especially vulnerable to this method. For example, a four-character password provides only 10,000 variations. On average, guessing 5,000 times would produce a correct hit. A program that could try a password every millisecond would take only about 5 seconds to guess a four-character password. Enumeration is less successful where systems allow longer passwords that include both uppercase and lowercase letters, along with numbers and all punctuation characters. Of course, users must take advantage of the large password space and must not, for example, use only lowercase letters.

In addition to being guessed, passwords can be exposed as a result of visual or electronic monitoring. An intruder can look over the shoulder of a user (**shoulder surfing**) when the user is logging in and can learn the password easily by watching the keyboard. Alternatively, anyone with access to the network on which a computer resides can seamlessly add a network monitor, allowing him to watch all data being transferred on the network (**sniffing**), including user IDs and passwords. Encrypting the data stream containing the password solves this problem. Even such a system could have passwords stolen, however. For example, if a file is used to contain the passwords, it could be copied for off-system analysis. Or consider a Trojan-horse program installed on the system that captures every keystroke before sending it on to the application.

Exposure is a particularly severe problem if the password is written down where it can be read or lost. As we shall see, some systems force users to select hard-to-remember or long passwords, which may cause a user to record the password or to reuse it. As a result, such systems provide much less security than systems that allow users to select easy passwords!

The final type of password compromise, illegal transfer, is the result of human nature. Most computer installations have a rule that forbids users to share accounts. This rule is sometimes implemented for accounting reasons but is often aimed at improving security. For instance, suppose one user ID is shared by several users, and a security breach occurs from that user ID. It is impossible to know who was using the ID at the time the break occurred or even whether the user was an authorized one. With one user per user ID, any user can be questioned directly about use of the account; in addition, the user might notice something different about the account and detect the break-in. Sometimes, users break account-sharing rules to help friends or to circumvent accounting, and this behavior can result in a system's being accessed by unauthorized users—possibly harmful ones.

Passwords can be either generated by the system or selected by a user. System-generated passwords may be difficult to remember, and thus users may write them down. As mentioned, however, user-selected passwords are often easy to guess (the user's name or favorite car, for example). Some systems will check a proposed password for ease of guessing or cracking before accepting it. At some sites, administrators occasionally check user passwords and notify a user if his password is easy to guess. Some systems also *age* passwords, forcing users to change their passwords at regular intervals (every three months, for instance). This method is not foolproof either, because users can easily toggle between two passwords. The solution, as implemented on some systems, is to record a password history for each user. For instance, the system could record the last N passwords and not allow their reuse.

Several variants on these simple password schemes can be used. For example, the password can be changed more frequently. In the extreme, the password is changed from session to session. A new password is selected (either by the system or by the user) at the end of *each* session, and that password must be used for the next session. In such a case, even if a password is misused, it can be used only once. When the legitimate user tries to use a now-invalid password at the next session, he discovers the security violation. Steps can then be taken to repair the breached security.

15.5.3 Encrypted Passwords

One problem with all these approaches is the difficulty of keeping the password secret within the computer. How can the system store a password securely yet allow its use for authentication when the user presents her password? The UNIX system uses encryption to avoid the necessity of keeping its password list secret. Each user has a password. The system contains a function that is extremely difficult—the designers hope impossible—to invert but is simple to compute. That is, given a value x, it is easy to compute the function value $f(x)$. Given a function value $f(x)$, however, it is impossible to compute x. This function is used to encode all passwords. Only encoded passwords are stored. When a user presents a password, it is encoded and compared against the stored encoded password. Even if the stored encoded password is seen, it cannot be decoded, so the password cannot be determined. Thus, the password file does not need to be kept secret. The function $f(x)$ is typically an encryption algorithm that has been designed and tested rigorously.

The flaw in this method is that the system no longer has control over the passwords. Although the passwords are encrypted, anyone with a copy of the password file can run fast encryption routines against it—encrypting each word in a dictionary, for instance, and comparing the results against the passwords. If the user has selected a password that is also a word in the dictionary, the password is cracked. On sufficiently fast computers, or even on clusters of slow computers, such a comparison may take only a few hours. Furthermore, because UNIX systems use a well-known encryption algorithm, a cracker might keep a cache of passwords that have been cracked previously. For these reasons, new versions of UNIX store the encrypted password entries in a file readable only by the **superuser**. The programs that compare a presented password to the stored password run `setuid` to root; so they can read this file, but other users cannot. They also include a "salt," or recorded random number, in the encryption algorithm. The salt is added to the password to ensure that if two plaintext passwords are the same, they result in different ciphertexts.

Another weakness in the UNIX password methods is that many UNIX systems treat only the first eight characters as significant. It is therefore extremely important for users to take advantage of the available password space. To avoid the dictionary encryption method, some systems disallow the use of dictionary words as passwords. A good technique is to generate your password by using the first letter of each word of an easily remembered phrase using both upper and lower characters with a number or punctuation mark thrown in for good measure. For example, the phrase "My mother's name is Katherine" might yield the password "Mmn.isK!". The password is hard to crack but easy for the user to remember.

15.5.4 One-Time Passwords

To avoid the problems of password sniffing and shoulder surfing, a system could use a set of **paired passwords**. When a session begins, the system randomly selects and presents one part of a password pair; the user must supply the other part. In this system, the user is **challenged** and must **respond** with the correct answer to that challenge.

This approach can be generalized to the use of an algorithm as a password. The algorithm might be an integer function, for example. The system selects a random integer and presents it to the user. The user applies a function and replies with the correct result. The system also applies the function. If the two results match, access is allowed.

Such algorithmic passwords are not susceptible to reuse; that is, a user can type in a password, and no entity intercepting that password will be able to reuse it. In this scheme, the system and the user share a secret. The secret is never transmitted over a medium that allows exposure. Rather, the secret is used as input to the function, along with a shared seed. A **seed** is a random number or alphanumeric sequence. The seed is the authentication challenge from the computer. The secret and the seed are used as input to the function $f(secret, seed)$. The result of this function is transmitted as the password to the computer. Because the computer also knows the secret and the seed, it can perform the same computation. If the results match, the user is authenticated. The next time the user needs to be authenticated, another seed is generated, and the same steps ensue. This time, the password is different.

In this **one-time password** system, the password is different in each instance. Anyone capturing the password from one session and trying to reuse it in another session will fail. One-time passwords are among the only ways to prevent improper authentication due to password exposure.

One-time password systems are implemented in various ways. Commercial implementations, such as SecurID, use hardware calculators. Most of these calculators are shaped like a credit card, a key-chain dangle, or a USB device; they include a display and may or may not also have a keypad. Some use the current time as the random seed. Others require the user to enter the shared secret, also known as a **personal identification number** or **PIN**, on the keypad. The display then shows the one-time password. The use of both a one-time password generator and a PIN is one form of **two-factor authentication**. Two different types of components are needed in this case. Two-factor authentication offers far better authentication protection than single-factor authentication.

Another variation on one-time passwords uses a **code book**, or **one-time pad**, which is a list of single-use passwords. Each password on the list is used once and then is crossed out or erased. The commonly used S/Key system uses either a software calculator or a code book based on these calculations as a source of one-time passwords. Of course, the user must protect his code book.

15.5.5 Biometrics

Yet another variation on the use of passwords for authentication involves the use of biometric measures. Palm- or hand-readers are commonly used to secure physical access—for example, access to a data center. These readers match stored parameters against what is being read from hand-reader pads. The parameters can include a temperature map, as well as finger length, finger width, and line patterns. These devices are currently too large and expensive to be used for normal computer authentication.

Fingerprint readers have become accurate and cost-effective and should become more common in the future. These devices read finger ridge patterns and convert them into a sequence of numbers. Over time, they can store a set of sequences to adjust for the location of the finger on the reading pad and other factors. Software can then scan a finger on the pad and compare its features with these stored sequences to determine if they match. Of course, multiple users can have profiles stored, and the scanner can differentiate among them. A very accurate two-factor authentication scheme can result from requiring a password as well as a user name and fingerprint scan. If this information is encrypted in transit, the system can be very resistant to spoofing or replay attack.

Multifactor authentication is better still. Consider how strong authentication can be with a USB device that must be plugged into the system, a PIN, and a fingerprint scan. Except for the user's having to place her finger on a pad and plug the USB into the system, this authentication method is no less convenient that using normal passwords. Recall, though, that strong authentication by itself is not sufficient to guarantee the ID of the user. An authenticated session can still be hijacked if it is not encrypted.

15.6 Implementing Security Defenses

Just as there are myriad threats to system and network security, there are many security solutions. The solutions run the gamut from improved user education, through technology, to writing bug-free software. Most security professionals subscribe to the theory of **defense in depth**, which states that more layers of defense are better than fewer layers. Of course, this theory applies to any kind of security. Consider the security of a house without a door lock, with a door lock, and with a lock and an alarm. In this section, we look at the major methods, tools, and techniques that can be used to improve resistance to threats.

15.6.1 Security Policy

The first step toward improving the security of any aspect of computing is to have a **security policy**. Policies vary widely but generally include a statement of what is being secured. For example, a policy might state that all outside-accessible applications must have a code review before being deployed, or that users should not share their passwords, or that all connection points between a company and the outside must have port scans run every six months. Without a policy in place, it is impossible for users and administrators to know what is permissible, what is required, and what is not allowed. The policy is a road map to security, and if a site is trying to move from less secure to more secure, it needs a map to know how to get there.

Once the security policy is in place, the people it affects should know it well. It should be their guide. The policy should also be a **living document** that is reviewed and updated periodically to ensure that it is still pertinent and still followed.

15.6.2 Vulnerability Assessment

How can we determine whether a security policy has been correctly implemented? The best way is to execute a vulnerability assessment. Such assessments can cover broad ground, from social engineering through risk assessment to port scans. **Risk assessment**, for example, endeavors to value the assets of the entity in question (a program, a management team, a system, or a facility) and determine the odds that a security incident will affect the entity and decrease its value. When the odds of suffering a loss and the amount of the potential loss are known, a value can be placed on trying to secure the entity.

The core activity of most vulnerability assessments is a **penetration test**, in which the entity is scanned for known vulnerabilities. Because this book is concerned with operating systems and the software that runs on them, we concentrate on those aspects of vulnerability assessment.

Vulnerability scans typically are done at times when computer use is relatively low, to minimize their impact. When appropriate, they are done on test systems rather than production systems, because they can induce unhappy behavior from the target systems or network devices.

A scan within an individual system can check a variety of aspects of the system:

- Short or easy-to-guess passwords
- Unauthorized privileged programs, such as *setuid* programs
- Unauthorized programs in system directories
- Unexpectedly long-running processes
- Improper directory protections on user and system directories
- Improper protections on system data files, such as the password file, device drivers, or the operating-system kernel itself
- Dangerous entries in the program search path (for example, the Trojan horse discussed in Section 15.2.1)
- Changes to system programs detected with checksum values
- Unexpected or hidden network daemons

Any problems found by a security scan can be either fixed automatically or reported to the managers of the system.

Networked computers are much more susceptible to security attacks than are standalone systems. Rather than attacks from a known set of access points, such as directly connected terminals, we face attacks from an unknown and large set of access points—a potentially severe security problem. To a lesser extent, systems connected to telephone lines via modems are also more exposed.

In fact, the U.S. government considers a system to be only as secure as its most far-reaching connection. For instance, a top-secret system may be accessed only from within a building also considered top-secret. The system loses its top-secret rating if any form of communication can occur outside that environment. Some government facilities take extreme security precautions. The connectors that plug a terminal into the secure computer are locked in a safe in the office when the terminal is not in use. A person must have proper ID to gain access to the building and her office, must know a physical lock combination, and must know authentication information for the computer itself to gain access to the computer—an example of multifactor authentication.

Unfortunately for systems administrators and computer-security professionals, it is frequently impossible to lock a machine in a room and disallow all remote access. For instance, the Internet network currently connects millions of computers. It is becoming a mission-critical, indispensable resource for many companies and individuals. If you consider the Internet a club, then, as in any club with millions of members, there are many good members and some bad members. The bad members have many tools they can use to attempt to gain access to the interconnected computers, just as Morris did with his worm.

Vulnerability scans can be applied to networks to address some of the problems with network security. The scans search a network for ports that respond to a request. If services are enabled that should not be, access to them can be blocked, or they can be disabled. The scans then determine the details of the application listening on that port and try to determine if it has any known vulnerabilities. Testing those vulnerabilities can determine if the system is misconfigured or lacks needed patches.

Finally, though, consider the use of port scanners in the hands of a cracker rather than someone trying to improve security. These tools could help crackers find vulnerabilities to attack. (Fortunately, it is possible to detect port scans through anomaly detection, as we discuss next.) It is a general challenge to security that the same tools can be used for good and for harm. In fact, some people advocate **security through obscurity**, stating that no tools should be written to test security, because such tools can be used to find (and exploit) security holes. Others believe that this approach to security is not a valid one, pointing out, for example, that crackers could write their own tools. It seems reasonable that security through obscurity be considered one of the layers of security only so long as it is not the only layer. For example, a company could publish its entire network configuration; but keeping that information secret makes it harder for intruders to know what to attack or to determine what might be detected. Even here, though, a company assuming that such information will remain a secret has a false sense of security.

15.6.3 Intrusion Detection

Securing systems and facilities is intimately linked to intrusion detection. **Intrusion detection**, as its name suggests, strives to detect attempted or successful intrusions into computer systems and to initiate appropriate responses to the intrusions. Intrusion detection encompasses a wide array of techniques that vary on a number of axes, including the following:

- The time at which detection occurs. Detection can occur in real time (while the intrusion is occurring) or after the fact.
- The types of inputs examined to detect intrusive activity. These may include user-shell commands, process system calls, and network packet headers or contents. Some forms of intrusion might be detected only by correlating information from several such sources.
- The range of response capabilities. Simple forms of response include alerting an administrator to the potential intrusion or somehow halting the potentially intrusive activity—for example, killing a process engaged in such activity. In a sophisticated form of response, a system might transparently divert an intruder's activity to a **honeypot**—a false resource exposed to the attacker. The resource appears real to the attacker and enables the system to monitor and gain information about the attack.

These degrees of freedom in the design space for detecting intrusions have yielded a wide range of solutions, known as **intrusion-detection systems** (**IDSs**) and **intrusion-prevention systems** (**IDPs**). IDS systems raise an alarm when an intrusion is detected, while IDP systems act as routers, passing traffic unless an intrusion is detected (at which point that traffic is blocked).

But just what constitutes an intrusion? Defining a suitable specification of intrusion turns out to be quite difficult, and thus automatic IDSs and IDPs today typically settle for one of two less ambitious approaches. In the first, called **signature-based detection**, system input or network traffic is examined for specific behavior patterns (or **signatures**) known to indicate attacks. A simple example of signature-based detection is scanning network packets for the string */etc/passwd/* targeted for a UNIX system. Another example is virus-detection software, which scans binaries or network packets for known viruses.

The second approach, typically called **anomaly detection**, attempts through various techniques to detect anomalous behavior within computer systems. Of course, not all anomalous system activity indicates an intrusion, but the presumption is that intrusions often induce anomalous behavior. An example of anomaly detection is monitoring system calls of a daemon process to detect whether the system-call behavior deviates from normal patterns, possibly indicating that a buffer overflow has been exploited in the daemon to corrupt its behavior. Another example is monitoring shell commands to detect anomalous commands for a given user or detecting an anomalous login time for a user, either of which may indicate that an attacker has succeeded in gaining access to that user's account.

Signature-based detection and anomaly detection can be viewed as two sides of the same coin: Signature-based detection attempts to characterize dangerous behaviors and to detect when one of these behaviors occurs, whereas anomaly detection attempts to characterize normal (or nondangerous) behaviors and to detect when something other than these behaviors occurs.

These different approaches yield IDSs and IDPs with very different properties, however. In particular, anomaly detection can find previously unknown methods of intrusion (so-called **zero-day attacks**). Signature-based detection, in contrast, will identify only known attacks that can be codified in a recognizable pattern. Thus, new attacks that were not contemplated when the signatures were generated will evade signature-based detection. This problem is well known to vendors of virus-detection software, who must release new signatures with great frequency as new viruses are detected manually.

Anomaly detection is not necessarily superior to signature-based detection, however. Indeed, a significant challenge for systems that attempt anomaly detection is to benchmark "normal" system behavior accurately. If the system has already been penetrated when it is benchmarked, then the intrusive activity may be included in the "normal" benchmark. Even if the system is benchmarked cleanly, without influence from intrusive behavior, the benchmark must give a fairly complete picture of normal behavior. Otherwise, the number of **false positives** (false alarms) or, worse, **false negatives** (missed intrusions) will be excessive.

To illustrate the impact of even a marginally high rate of false alarms, consider an installation consisting of a hundred UNIX workstations from which security-relevant events are recorded for purposes of intrusion detection. A small installation such as this could easily generate a million audit records per day. Only one or two might be worthy of an administrator's investigation. If we suppose, optimistically, that each actual attack is reflected in ten audit records, we can roughly compute the rate of occurrence of audit records reflecting truly intrusive activity as follows:

$$\frac{2\frac{\text{intrusions}}{\text{day}} \cdot 10\frac{\text{records}}{\text{intrusion}}}{10^6\frac{\text{records}}{\text{day}}} = 0.00002.$$

Interpreting this as a "probability of occurrence of intrusive records," we denote it as $P(I)$; that is, event I is the occurrence of a record reflecting truly intrusive behavior. Since $P(I) = 0.00002$, we also know that $P(\neg I) = 1 - P(I) = 0.99998$. Now we let A denote the raising of an alarm by an IDS. An accurate IDS should maximize both $P(I|A)$ and $P(\neg I|\neg A)$—that is, the probabilities that an alarm indicates an intrusion and that no alarm indicates no intrusion. Focusing on $P(I|A)$ for the moment, we can compute it using **Bayes' theorem**:

$$P(I|A) = \frac{P(I) \cdot P(A|I)}{P(I) \cdot P(A|I) + P(\neg I) \cdot P(A|\neg I)}$$

$$= \frac{0.00002 \cdot P(A|I)}{0.00002 \cdot P(A|I) + 0.99998 \cdot P(A|\neg I)}$$

Now consider the impact of the false-alarm rate $P(A|\neg I)$ on $P(I|A)$. Even with a very good true-alarm rate of $P(A|I) = 0.8$, a seemingly good false-alarm rate of $P(A|\neg I) = 0.0001$ yields $P(I|A) \approx 0.14$. That is, fewer than one in every seven alarms indicates a real intrusion! In systems where a security administrator investigates each alarm, a high rate of false alarms—called a "Christmas tree effect"—is exceedingly wasteful and will quickly teach the administrator to ignore alarms.

This example illustrates a general principle for IDSs and IDPs: For usability, they must offer an extremely low false-alarm rate. Achieving a sufficiently low false-alarm rate is an especially serious challenge for anomaly-detection systems, as mentioned, because of the difficulties of adequately benchmarking normal system behavior. However, research continues to improve anomaly-detection techniques. Intrusion detection software is evolving to implement signatures, anomaly algorithms, and other algorithms and to combine the results to arrive at a more accurate anomaly-detection rate.

15.6.4 Virus Protection

As we have seen, viruses can and do wreak havoc on systems. Protection from viruses thus is an important security concern. Antivirus programs are often used to provide this protection. Some of these programs are effective against only particular known viruses. They work by searching all the programs on a system for the specific pattern of instructions known to make up the virus. When they find a known pattern, they remove the instructions, **disinfecting** the program. Antivirus programs may have catalogs of thousands of viruses for which they search.

Both viruses and antivirus software continue to become more sophisticated. Some viruses modify themselves as they infect other software to avoid the basic pattern-match approach of antivirus programs. Antivirus programs in turn now look for families of patterns rather than a single pattern to identify a virus. In fact, some antivirus programs implement a variety of detection algorithms. They can decompress compressed viruses before checking for a signature. Some also look for process anomalies. A process opening an executable file for writing is suspicious, for example, unless it is a compiler. Another popular technique is to run a program in a **sandbox**, which is a controlled or emulated

THE TRIPWIRE FILE SYSTEM

An example of an anomaly-detection tool is the **Tripwire file system** integrity-checking tool for UNIX, developed at Purdue University. Tripwire operates on the premise that many intrusions result in modification of system directories and files. For example, an attacker might modify the system programs, perhaps inserting copies with Trojan horses, or might insert new programs into directories commonly found in user-shell search paths. Or an intruder might remove system log files to cover his tracks. Tripwire is a tool to monitor file systems for added, deleted, or changed files and to alert system administrators to these modifications.

The operation of Tripwire is controlled by a configuration file `tw.config` that enumerates the directories and files to be monitored for changes, deletions, or additions. Each entry in this configuration file includes a selection mask to specify the file attributes (inode attributes) that will be monitored for changes. For example, the selection mask might specify that a file's permissions be monitored but its access time be ignored. In addition, the selection mask can instruct that the file be monitored for changes. Monitoring the hash of a file for changes is as good as monitoring the file itself, but storing hashes of files requires far less room than copying the files themselves.

When run initially, Tripwire takes as input the `tw.config` file and computes a signature for each file or directory consisting of its monitored attributes (inode attributes and hash values). These signatures are stored in a database. When run subsequently, Tripwire inputs both `tw.config` and the previously stored database, recomputes the signature for each file or directory named in `tw.config`, and compares this signature with the signature (if any) in the previously computed database. Events reported to an administrator include any monitored file or directory whose signature differs from that in the database (a changed file), any file or directory in a monitored directory for which a signature does not exist in the database (an added file), and any signature in the database for which the corresponding file or directory no longer exists (a deleted file).

Although effective for a wide class of attacks, Tripwire does have limitations. Perhaps the most obvious is the need to protect the Tripwire program and its associated files, especially the database file, from unauthorized modification. For this reason, Tripwire and its associated files should be stored on some tamper-proof medium, such as a write-protected disk or a secure server where logins can be tightly controlled. Unfortunately, this makes it less convenient to update the database after authorized updates to monitored directories and files. A second limitation is that some security-relevant files—for example, system log files—are *supposed* to change over time, and Tripwire does not provide a way to distinguish between an authorized and an unauthorized change. So, for example, an attack that modifies (without deleting) a system log that would normally change anyway would escape Tripwire's detection capabilities. The best Tripwire can do in this case is to detect certain obvious inconsistencies (for example, a shrinking log file). Free and commercial versions of Tripwire are available from http://tripwire.org and http://tripwire.com.

section of the system. The antivirus software analyzes the behavior of the code in the sandbox before letting it run unmonitored. Some antivirus programs also put up a complete shield rather than just scanning files within a file system. They search boot sectors, memory, inbound and outbound e-mail, files as they are downloaded, files on removable devices or media, and so on.

The best protection against computer viruses is prevention, or the practice of **safe computing**. Purchasing unopened software from vendors and avoiding free or pirated copies from public sources or disk exchange offer the safest route to preventing infection. However, even new copies of legitimate software applications are not immune to virus infection: in a few cases, disgruntled employees of a software company have infected the master copies of software programs to do economic harm to the company. For macro viruses, one defense is to exchange Microsoft Word documents in an alternative file format called **rich text format (RTF)**. Unlike the native Word format, RTF does not include the capability to attach macros.

Another defense is to avoid opening any e-mail attachments from unknown users. Unfortunately, history has shown that e-mail vulnerabilities appear as fast as they are fixed. For example, in 2000, the *love bug* virus became very widespread by traveling in e-mail messages that pretended to be love notes sent by friends of the receivers. Once a receiver opened the attached Visual Basic script, the virus propagated by sending itself to the first addresses in the receiver's e-mail contact list. Fortunately, except for clogging e-mail systems and users' inboxes, it was relatively harmless. It did, however, effectively negate the defensive strategy of opening attachments only from people known to the receiver. A more effective defense method is to avoid opening any e-mail attachment that contains executable code. Some companies now enforce this as policy by removing all incoming attachments to e-mail messages.

Another safeguard, although it does not prevent infection, does permit early detection. A user must begin by completely reformatting the hard disk, especially the boot sector, which is often targeted for viral attack. Only secure software is uploaded, and a signature of each program is taken via a secure message-digest computation. The resulting filename and associated message-digest list must then be kept free from unauthorized access. Periodically, or each time a program is run, the operating system recomputes the signature and compares it with the signature on the original list; any differences serve as a warning of possible infection. This technique can be combined with others. For example, a high-overhead antivirus scan, such as a sandbox, can be used; and if a program passes the test, a signature can be created for it. If the signatures match the next time the program is run, it does not need to be virus-scanned again.

15.6.5 Auditing, Accounting, and Logging

Auditing, accounting, and logging can decrease system performance, but they are useful in several areas, including security. Logging can be general or specific. All system-call executions can be logged for analysis of program behavior (or misbehavior). More typically, suspicious events are logged. Authentication failures and authorization failures can tell us quite a lot about break-in attempts.

Accounting is another potential tool in a security administrator's kit. It can be used to find performance changes, which in turn can reveal security problems. One of the early UNIX computer break-ins was detected by Cliff Stoll when he was examining accounting logs and spotted an anomaly.

15.7 Firewalling to Protect Systems and Networks

We turn next to the question of how a trusted computer can be connected safely to an untrustworthy network. One solution is the use of a firewall to separate trusted and untrusted systems. A **firewall** is a computer, appliance, or router that sits between the trusted and the untrusted. A network firewall limits network access between the two **security domains** and monitors and logs all connections. It can also limit connections based on source or destination address, source or destination port, or direction of the connection. For instance, Web servers use HTTP to communicate with Web browsers. A firewall therefore may allow only HTTP to pass from all hosts outside the firewall to the Web server within the firewall. The Morris Internet worm used the `finger` protocol to break into computers, so `finger` would not be allowed to pass, for example.

In fact, a network firewall can separate a network into multiple domains. A common implementation has the Internet as the untrusted domain; a semitrusted and semisecure network, called the **demilitarized zone (DMZ)**, as another domain; and a company's computers as a third domain (Figure 15.10). Connections are allowed from the Internet to the DMZ computers and from the company computers to the Internet but are not allowed from the Internet or DMZ computers to the company computers. Optionally, controlled communications may be allowed between the DMZ and one company computer or more. For instance, a Web server on the DMZ may need to query a database server on the corporate network. With a firewall, however, access is contained, and any DMZ systems that are broken into still are unable to access the company computers.

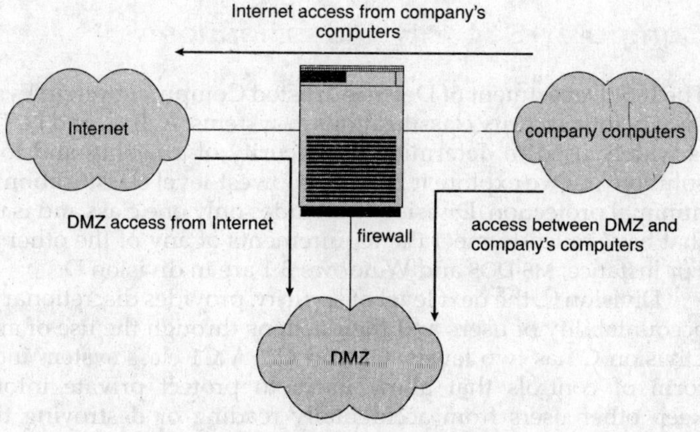

Figure 15.10 Domain separation via firewall.

Of course, a firewall itself must be secure and attack-proof; otherwise, its ability to secure connections can be compromised. Furthermore, firewalls do not prevent attacks that **tunnel**, or travel within protocols or connections that the firewall allows. A buffer-overflow attack to a Web server will not be stopped by the firewall, for example, because the HTTP connection is allowed; it is the contents of the HTTP connection that house the attack. Likewise, denial-of-service attacks can affect firewalls as much as any other machines. Another vulnerability of firewalls is **spoofing**, in which an unauthorized host pretends to be an authorized host by meeting some authorization criterion. For example, if a firewall rule allows a connection from a host and identifies that host by its IP address, then another host could send packets using that same address and be allowed through the firewall.

In addition to the most common network firewalls, there are other, newer kinds of firewalls, each with its pros and cons. A **personal firewall** is a software layer either included with the operating system or added as an application. Rather than limiting communication between security domains, it limits communication to (and possibly from) a given host. A user could add a personal firewall to her PC so that a Trojan horse would be denied access to the network to which the PC is connected, for example. An **application proxy firewall** understands the protocols that applications speak across the network. For example, SMTP is used for mail transfer. An application proxy accepts a connection just as an SMTP server would and then initiates a connection to the original destination SMTP server. It can monitor the traffic as it forwards the message, watching for and disabling illegal commands, attempts to exploit bugs, and so on. Some firewalls are designed for one specific protocol. An **XML firewall**, for example, has the specific purpose of analyzing XML traffic and blocking disallowed or malformed XML. **System-call firewalls** sit between applications and the kernel, monitoring system-call execution. For example, in Solaris 10, the "least privilege" feature implements a list of more than fifty system calls that processes may or may not be allowed to make. A process that does not need to spawn other processes can have that ability taken away, for instance.

15.8 Computer-Security Classifications

The U.S. Department of Defense Trusted Computer System Evaluation Criteria specify four security classifications in systems: A, B, C, and D. This specification is widely used to determine the security of a facility and to model security solutions, so we explore it here. The lowest-level classification is division D, or minimal protection. Division D includes only one class and is used for systems that have failed to meet the requirements of any of the other security classes. For instance, MS-DOS and Windows 3.1 are in division D.

Division C, the next level of security, provides discretionary protection and accountability of users and their actions through the use of audit capabilities. Division C has two levels: C1 and C2. A C1-class system incorporates some form of controls that allow users to protect private information and to keep other users from accidentally reading or destroying their data. A C1 environment is one in which cooperating users access data at the same levels of sensitivity. Most versions of UNIX are C1 class.

The total of all protection systems within a computer system (hardware, software, firmware) that correctly enforce a security policy is known as a **trusted computer base (TCB)**. The TCB of a C1 system controls access between users and files by allowing the user to specify and control sharing of objects by named individuals or defined groups. In addition, the TCB requires that the users identify themselves before they start any activities that the TCB is expected to mediate. This identification is accomplished via a protected mechanism or password; the TCB protects the authentication data so that they are inaccessible to unauthorized users.

A C2-class system adds an individual-level access control to the requirements of a C1 system. For example, access rights of a file can be specified to the level of a single individual. In addition, the system administrator can selectively audit the actions of any one or more users based on individual identity. The TCB also protects itself from modification of its code or data structures. In addition, no information produced by a prior user is available to another user who accesses a storage object that has been released back to the system. Some special, secure versions of UNIX have been certified at the C2 level.

Division-B mandatory-protection systems have all the properties of a class-C2 system; in addition, they attach a sensitivity label to each object. The B1-class TCB maintains the security label of each object in the system; the label is used for decisions pertaining to mandatory access control. For example, a user at the confidential level could not access a file at the more sensitive secret level. The TCB also denotes the sensitivity level at the top and bottom of each page of any human-readable output. In addition to the normal user-name–password authentication information, the TCB also maintains the clearance and authorizations of individual users and will support at least two levels of security. These levels are hierarchical, so that a user may access any objects that carry sensitivity labels equal to or lower than his security clearance. For example, a secret-level user could access a file at the confidential level in the absence of other access controls. Processes are also isolated through the use of distinct address spaces.

A B2-class system extends the sensitivity labels to each system resource, such as storage objects. Physical devices are assigned minimum and maximum security levels that the system uses to enforce constraints imposed by the physical environments in which the devices are located. In addition, a B2 system supports covert channels and the auditing of events that could lead to the exploitation of a covert channel.

A B3-class system allows the creation of access-control lists that denote users or groups *not* granted access to a given named object. The TCB also contains a mechanism to monitor events that may indicate a violation of security policy. The mechanism notifies the security administrator and, if necessary, terminates the event in the least disruptive manner.

The highest-level classification is division A. Architecturally, a class-A1 system is functionally equivalent to a B3 system, but it uses formal design specifications and verification techniques, granting a high degree of assurance that the TCB has been implemented correctly. A system beyond class A1 might be designed and developed in a trusted facility by trusted personnel.

The use of a TCB merely ensures that the system can enforce aspects of a security policy; the TCB does not specify what the policy should be. Typically, a given computing environment develops a security policy for **certification** and has the plan **accredited** by a security agency, such as the National Computer Security Center. Certain computing environments may require other certification, such as that supplied by TEMPEST, which guards against electronic eavesdropping. For example, a TEMPEST-certified system has terminals that are shielded to prevent electromagnetic fields from escaping. This shielding ensures that equipment outside the room or building where the terminal is housed cannot detect what information is being displayed by the terminal.

15.9 An Example: Windows XP

Microsoft Windows XP is a general-purpose operating system designed to support a variety of security features and methods. In this section, we examine features that Windows XP uses to perform security functions. For more information and background on Windows XP, see Chapter 22.

The Windows XP security model is based on the notion of **user accounts**. Windows XP allows the creation of any number of user accounts, which can be grouped in any manner. Access to system objects can then be permitted or denied as desired. Users are identified to the system by a *unique* security ID. When a user logs on, Windows XP creates a **security access token** that includes the security ID for the user, security IDs for any groups of which the user is a member, and a list of any special privileges that the user has. Examples of special privileges include backing up files and directories, shutting down the computer, logging on interactively, and changing the system clock. Every process that Windows XP runs on behalf of a user will receive a copy of the access token. The system uses the security IDs in the access token to permit or deny access to system objects whenever the user, or a process on behalf of the user, attempts to access the object. Authentication of a user account is typically accomplished via a user name and password, although the modular design of Windows XP allows the development of custom authentication packages. For example, a retinal (or eye) scanner might be used to verify that the user is who she says she is.

Windows XP uses the idea of a subject to ensure that programs run by a user do not get greater access to the system than the user is authorized to have. A **subject** is used to track and manage permissions for each program that a user runs; it is composed of the user's access token and the program acting on behalf of the user. Since Windows XP operates with a client–server model, two classes of subjects are used to control access: simple subjects and server subjects. An example of a **simple subject** is the typical application program that a user executes after she logs on. The simple subject is assigned a **security context** based on the security access token of the user. A **server subject** is a process implemented as a protected server that uses the security context of the client when acting on the client's behalf.

As mentioned in Section 15.7, auditing is a useful security technique. Windows XP has built-in auditing that allows many common security threats to be monitored. Examples include failure auditing for login and logoff events to detect random password break-ins, success auditing for login and logoff events to detect login activity at strange hours, success and failure write-access auditing for executable files to track a virus outbreak, and success and failure auditing for file access to detect access to sensitive files.

Security attributes of an object in Windows XP are described by a **security descriptor**. The security descriptor contains the security ID of the owner of the object (who can change the access permissions), a group security ID used only by the POSIX subsystem, a discretionary access-control list that identifies which users or groups are allowed (and which are not allowed) access, and a system access-control list that controls which auditing messages the system will generate. For example, the security descriptor of the file *foo.bar* might have owner avi and this discretionary access-control list:

- avi—all access
- group cs—read–write access
- user cliff—no access

In addition, it might have a system access-control list of audit writes by everyone.

An access-control list is composed of access-control entries that contain the security ID of the individual and an access mask that defines all possible actions on the object, with a value of AccessAllowed or AccessDenied for each action. Files in Windows XP may have the following access types: `ReadData`, `WriteData`, `AppendData`, `Execute`, `ReadExtendedAttribute`, `WriteExtendedAttribute`, `ReadAttributes`, and `WriteAttributes`. We can see how this allows a fine degree of control over access to objects.

Windows XP classifies objects as either container objects or noncontainer objects. **Container objects**, such as directories, can logically contain other objects. By default, when an object is created within a container object, the new object inherits permissions from the parent object. Similarly, if the user copies a file from one directory to a new directory, the file will inherit the permissions of the destination directory. **Noncontainer objects** inherit no other permissions. Furthermore, if a permission is changed on a directory, the new permissions do not automatically apply to existing files and subdirectories; the user may explicitly apply them if she so desires.

The system administrator can prohibit printing to a printer on the system for all or part of a day and can use the Windows XP Performance Monitor to help her spot approaching problems. In general, Windows XP does a good job of providing features to help ensure a secure computing environment. Many of these features are not enabled by default, however, which may be one reason for the myriad security breaches on Windows XP systems. Another reason is the vast number of services Windows XP starts at system boot time and the number of applications that typically are installed on a Windows XP system. For a real multiuser environment, the system administrator should formulate a security plan and implement it, using the features that Windows XP provides and other security tools.

15.10 Summary

Protection is an internal problem. Security, in contrast, must consider both the computer system and the environment—people, buildings, businesses, valuable objects, and threats—within which the system is used.

The data stored in the computer system must be protected from unauthorized access, malicious destruction or alteration, and accidental introduction of inconsistency. It is easier to protect against accidental loss of data consistency than to protect against malicious access to the data. Absolute protection of the information stored in a computer system from malicious abuse is not possible; but the cost to the perpetrator can be made sufficiently high to deter most, if not all, attempts to access that information without proper authority.

Several types of attacks can be launched against programs and against individual computers or the masses. Stack- and buffer-overflow techniques allow successful attackers to change their level of system access. Viruses and worms are self-perpetuating, sometimes infecting thousands of computers. Denial-of-service attacks prevent legitimate use of target systems.

Encryption limits the domain of receivers of data, while authentication limits the domain of senders. Encryption is used to provide confidentiality of data being stored or transferred. Symmetric encryption requires a shared key, while asymmetric encryption provides a public key and a private key. Authentication, when combined with hashing, can prove that data have not been changed.

User authentication methods are used to identify legitimate users of a system. In addition to standard user-name and password protection, several authentication methods are used. One-time passwords, for example, change from session to session to avoid replay attacks. Two-factor authentication requires two forms of authentication, such as a hardware calculator with an activation PIN. Multifactor authentication uses three or more forms. These methods greatly decrease the chance of authentication forgery.

Methods of preventing or detecting security incidents include intrusion-detection systems, antivirus software, auditing and logging of system events, monitoring of system software changes, system-call monitoring, and firewalls.

Exercises

15.1 Argue for or against the judicial sentence handed down against Robert Morris, Jr., for his creation and execution of the Internet worm discussed in Section 15.3.1.

15.2 Discuss a means by which managers of systems connected to the Internet could design their systems to limit or eliminate the damage done by worms. What are the drawbacks of making the change that you suggest?

15.3 What commonly used computer programs are prone to man-in-the-middle attacks? Discuss solutions for preventing this form of attack.

15.4 The UNIX program COPS scans a given system for possible security holes and alerts the user to possible problems. What are two potential hazards of using such a system for security? How can these problems be limited or eliminated?

15.5 Make a list of six security concerns for a bank's computer system. For each item on your list, state whether this concern relates to physical, human, or operating-system security.

15.6 An experimental addition to UNIX allows a user to connect a **watchdog** program to a file. The watchdog is invoked whenever a program requests access to the file. The watchdog then either grants or denies access to the file. Discuss two pros and two cons of using watchdogs for security.

15.7 Discuss how the asymmetric encryption algorithm can be used to achieve the following goals.

a. Authentication: the receiver knows that only the sender could have generated the message.

b. Secrecy: only the receiver can decrypt the message.

c. Authentication and secrecy: only the receiver can decrypt the message, and the receiver knows that only the sender could have generated the message.

15.8 Why doesn't $D(k_e, N)(E(k_d, N)(m))$ provide authentication of the sender? To what uses can such an encryption be put?

15.9 Consider a system that generates 10 million audit records per day. Also assume that there are on average 10 attacks per day on this system and that each such attack is reflected in 20 records. If the intrusion-detection system has a true-alarm rate of 0.6 and a false-alarm rate of 0.0005, what percentage of alarms generated by the system correspond to real intrusions?

15.10 What is the purpose of using a "salt" along with the user-provided password? Where should the "salt" be stored, and how should it be used?

Bibliographical Notes

General discussions concerning security are given by Hsiao et al. [1979], Landwehr [1981], Denning [1982], Pfleeger and Pfleeger [2003], Tanenbaum 2003, and Russell and Gangemi [1991]. Also of general interest is the text by Lobel [1986]. Computer networking is discussed in Kurose and Ross [2005].

Issues concerning the design and verification of secure systems are discussed by Rushby [1981] and by Silverman [1983]. A security kernel for a multiprocessor microcomputer is described by Schell [1983]. A distributed secure system is described by Rushby and Randell [1983].

Morris and Thompson [1979] discuss password security. Morshedian [1986] presents methods to fight password pirates. Password authentication with insecure communications is considered by Lamport [1981]. The issue of password cracking is examined by Seely [1989]. Computer break-ins are discussed by Lehmann [1987] and by Reid [1987]. Issues related to trusting computer programs are discussed in Thompson [1984].

Discussions concerning UNIX security are offered by Grampp and Morris [1984], Wood and Kochan [1985], Farrow [1986b], Farrow [1986a], Filipski and Hanko [1986], Hecht et al. [1988], Kramer [1988], and Garfinkel et al. [2003]. Bershad and Pinkerton [1988] present the watchdog extension to BSD UNIX. The COPS security-scanning package for UNIX was written by Farmer at Purdue University. It is available to users on the Internet via the FTP program from host ftp.uu.net in directory /pub/security/cops.

Spafford [1989] presents a detailed technical discussion of the Internet worm. The Spafford article appears with three others in a special section on the Morris Internet worm in *Communications of the ACM* (Volume 32, Number 6, June 1989).

Security problems associated with the TCP/IP protocol suite are described in Bellovin [1989]. The mechanisms commonly used to prevent such attacks are discussed in Cheswick et al. [2003]. Another approach to protecting networks from insider attacks is to secure topology or route discovery. Kent et al. [2000], Hu et al. [2002], Zapata and Asokan [2002], and Hu and Perrig [2004] present solutions for secure routing. Savage et al. [2000] examine the distributed denial-of-service attack and propose IP trace-back solutions to address the problem. Perlman [1988] proposes an approach to diagnose faults when the network contains malicious routers.

Information about viruses and worms can be found at http://www.viruslist.com, as well as in Ludwig [1998] and Ludwig [2002]. Other Web sites containing up-to-date security information include http://www.trusecure.com and httpd://www.eeye.com. A paper on the dangers of a computer monoculture can be found at http://www.ccianet.org/papers/cyberinsecurity.pdf.

Diffie and Hellman [1976] and Diffie and Hellman [1979] were the first researchers to propose the use of the public-key encryption scheme. The algorithm presented in Section 15.4.1 is based on the public-key encryption scheme; it was developed by Rivest et al. [1978]. Lempel [1979], Simmons [1979], Denning and Denning [1979], Gifford [1982], Denning [1982], Ahituv et al. [1987], Schneier [1996], and Stallings [2003] explore the use of cryptography in computer systems. Discussions concerning protection of digital signatures are offered by Akl [1983], Davies [1983], Denning [1983], and Denning [1984].

The U.S. government is, of course, concerned about security. The *Department of Defense Trusted Computer System Evaluation Criteria* (DoD [1985]), known also as the *Orange Book,* describes a set of security levels and the features that an operating system must have to qualify for each security rating. Reading it is a good starting point for understanding security concerns. The *Microsoft Windows NT Workstation Resource Kit* (Microsoft [1996]) describes the security model of NT and how to use that model.

The RSA algorithm is presented in Rivest et al. [1978]. Information about NIST's AES activities can be found at http://www.nist.gov/aes/; information about other cryptographic standards for the United States can also be found at that site. More complete coverage of SSL 3.0 can be found at http://home.netscape.com/eng/ssl3/. In 1999, SSL 3.0 was modified slightly and presented in an IETF Request for Comments (RFC) under the name TLS.

The example in Section 15.6.3 illustrating the impact of false-alarm rate on the effectiveness of IDSs is based on Axelsson [1999]. The description of Tripwire in Section 15.6.5 is based on Kim and Spafford [1993]. Research into system-call-based anomaly detection is described in Forrest et al. [1996].

Part Seven

Distributed Systems

A distributed system is a collection of processors that do not share memory or a clock. Instead, each processor has its own local memory, and the processors communicate with one another through communication lines such as local-area or wide-area networks. The processors in a distributed system vary in size and function. Such systems may include small handheld or real-time devices, personal computers, workstations, and large mainframe computer systems.

A distributed file system is a file-service system whose users, servers, and storage devices are dispersed among the sites of a distributed system. Accordingly, service activity has to be carried out across the network; instead of a single centralized data repository, there are multiple independent storage devices.

The benefits of a distributed system include giving users access to the resources maintained by the system and thereby speeding up computation and improving data availability and reliability. Because a system is distributed, however, it must provide mechanisms for process synchronization and communication, for dealing with the deadlock problem, and for handling failures that are not encountered in a centralized system.

CHAPTER 16

Distributed Operating Systems

A distributed system is a collection of processors that do not share memory or a clock. Instead, each processor has its own local memory. The processors communicate with one another through various communication networks, such as high-speed buses or telephone lines. In this chapter, we discuss the general structure of distributed systems and the networks that interconnect them. We contrast the main differences in operating-system design between these systems and centralized systems. In Chapter 17, we go on to discuss distributed file systems. Then, in Chapter 18, we describe the methods necessary for distributed operating systems to coordinate their actions.

CHAPTER OBJECTIVES

- To provide a high-level overview of distributed systems and the networks that interconnect them.
- To discuss the general structure of distributed operating systems.

16.1 Motivation

A **distributed system** is a collection of loosely coupled processors interconnected by a communication network. From the point of view of a specific processor in a distributed system, the rest of the processors and their respective resources are remote, whereas its own resources are local.

The processors in a distributed system may vary in size and function. They may include small microprocessors, workstations, minicomputers, and large general-purpose computer systems. These processors are referred to by a number of names, such as *sites*, *nodes*, *computers*, *machines*, and *hosts*, depending on the context in which they are mentioned. We mainly use *site* to indicate the location of a machine and *host* to refer to a specific system at a site. Generally, one host at one site, the *server*, has a resource that another host at another site, the *client* (or user), would like to use. A general structure of a distributed system is shown in Figure 16.1.

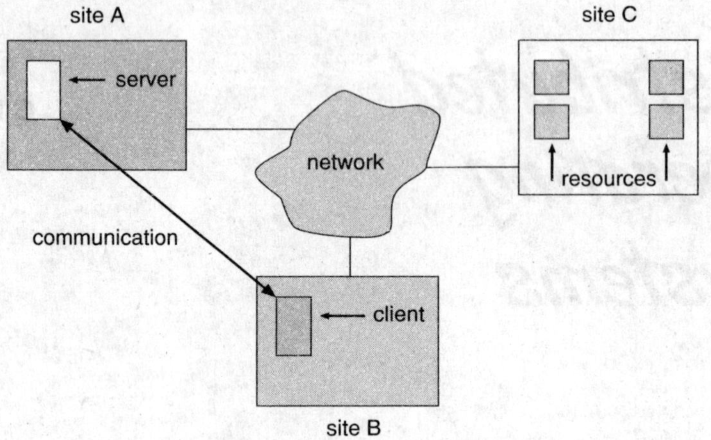

Figure 16.1 A distributed system.

There are four major reasons for building distributed systems: *resource sharing*, *computation speedup*, *reliability*, and *communication*. In this section, we briefly discuss each of them.

16.1.1 Resource Sharing

If a number of different sites (with different capabilities) are connected to one another, then a user at one site may be able to use the resources available at another. For example, a user at site A may be using a laser printer located at site B. Meanwhile, a user at B may access a file that resides at A. In general, **resource sharing** in a distributed system provides mechanisms for sharing files at remote sites, processing information in a distributed database, printing files at remote sites, using remote specialized hardware devices (such as a high-speed array processor), and performing other operations.

16.1.2 Computation Speedup

If a particular computation can be partitioned into subcomputations that can run concurrently, then a distributed system allows us to distribute the subcomputations among the various sites; the subcomputations can be run concurrently and thus provide **computation speedup**. In addition, if a particular site is currently overloaded with jobs, some of them can be moved to other, lightly loaded sites. This movement of jobs is called **load sharing**. Automated load sharing, in which the distributed operating system automatically moves jobs, is not yet common in commercial systems.

16.1.3 Reliability

If one site fails in a distributed system, the remaining sites can continue operating, giving the system better reliability. If the system is composed of multiple large autonomous installations (that is, general-purpose computers), the failure of one of them should not affect the rest. If, however, the system is composed of small machines, each of which is responsible for some crucial system function (such as terminal character I/O or the file system), then a single failure may halt the operation of the whole system. In general, with enough redundancy (in both hardware and data), the system can continue operation, even if some of its sites have failed.

The failure of a site must be detected by the system, and appropriate action may be needed to recover from the failure. The system must no longer use the services of that site. In addition, if the function of the failed site can be taken over by another site, the system must ensure that the transfer of function occurs correctly. Finally, when the failed site recovers or is repaired, mechanisms must be available to integrate it back into the system smoothly. As we shall see in Chapters 17 and 18, these actions present difficult problems that have many possible solutions.

16.1.4 Communication

When several sites are connected to one another by a communication network, users at the various sites have the opportunity to exchange information. At a low level, **messages** are passed between systems, much as messages are passed between processes in the single-computer message system discussed in Section 3.4. Given message passing, all the higher-level functionality found in standalone systems can be expanded to encompass the distributed system. Such functions include file transfer, login, mail, and remote procedure calls (RPCs).

The advantage of a distributed system is that these functions can be carried out over great distances. Two people at geographically distant sites can collaborate on a project, for example. By transferring the files of the project, logging in to each other's remote systems to run programs, and exchanging mail to coordinate the work, users minimize the limitations inherent in long-distance work. We wrote this book by collaborating in such a manner.

The advantages of distributed systems have resulted in an industry-wide trend toward **downsizing**. Many companies are replacing their mainframes with networks of workstations or personal computers. Companies get a bigger bang for the buck (that is, better functionality for the cost), more flexibility in locating resources and expanding facilities, better user interfaces, and easier maintenance.

16.2 Types of Network-based Operating Systems

In this section, we describe the two general categories of network-oriented operating systems: network operating systems and distributed operating systems. Network operating systems are simpler to implement but generally more difficult for users to access and utilize than are distributed operating systems, which provide more features.

16.2.1 Network Operating Systems

A **network operating system** provides an environment in which users, who are aware of the multiplicity of machines, can access remote resources by either logging in to the appropriate remote machine or transferring data from the remote machine to their own machines.

16.2.1.1 Remote Login

An important function of a network operating system is to allow users to log in remotely. The Internet provides the **telnet** facility for this purpose. To illustrate this facility, lets suppose that a user at Westminster College wishes to compute on "cs.yale.edu," a computer that is located at Yale University. To do so, the user must have a valid account on that machine. To log in remotely, the user issues the command

```
telnet cs.yale.edu
```

This command results in the formation of a socket connection between the local machine at Westminster College and the "cs.yale.edu" computer. After this connection has been established, the networking software creates a transparent, bidirectional link so that all characters entered by the user are sent to a process on "cs.yale.edu" and all the output from that process is sent back to the user. The process on the remote machine asks the user for a login name and a password. Once the correct information has been received, the process acts as a proxy for the user, who can compute on the remote machine just as any local user can.

16.2.1.2 Remote File Transfer

Another major function of a network operating system is to provide a mechanism for **remote file transfer** from one machine to another. In such an environment, each computer maintains its own local file system. If a user at one site (say, "cs.uvm.edu") wants to access a file located on another computer (say, "cs.yale.edu"), then the file must be copied explicitly from the computer at Yale to the computer at the University of Vermont.

The Internet provides a mechanism for such a transfer with the file transfer protocol (FTP) program. Suppose that a user on "cs.uvm.edu" wants to copy a Java program `Server.java` that resides on "cs.yale.edu." The user must first invoke the FTP program by executing

```
ftp cs.yale.edu
```

The program then asks the user for a login name and a password. Once the correct information has been received, the user must connect to the subdirectory where the file `Server.java` resides and then copy the file by executing

```
get Server.java
```

In this scheme, the file location is not transparent to the user; users must know exactly where each file is. Moreover, there is no real file sharing, because a user can only *copy* a file from one site to another. Thus, several copies of the same file may exist, resulting in a waste of space. In addition, if these copies are modified, the various copies will be inconsistent.

Notice that, in our example, the user at the University of Vermont must have login permission on "cs.yale.edu." FTP also provides a way to allow a user who does not have an account on the Yale computer to copy files remotely. This remote copying is accomplished through the "anonymous FTP" method, which works as follows. The file to be copied (that is, `Server.java`) must be placed in a special subdirectory (say, *ftp*) with the protection set to allow the public to read the file. A user who wishes to copy the file uses the `ftp` command as before. When the user is asked for the login name, the user supplies the name "anonymous" and an arbitrary password.

Once anonymous login is accomplished, care must be taken by the system to ensure that this partially authorized user does not access inappropriate files. Generally, the user is allowed to access only those files that are in the directory tree of user "anonymous." Any files placed here are accessible to any anonymous users, subject to the usual file-protection scheme used on that machine. Anonymous users, however, cannot access files outside of this directory tree.

Implementation of the FTP mechanism is similar to telnet implementation. A daemon on the remote site watches for requests to connect to the system's FTP port. Login authentication is accomplished, and the user is allowed to execute commands remotely. Unlike the telnet daemon, which executes any command for the user, the FTP daemon responds only to a predefined set of file-related commands. These include the following:

- `get`—Transfer a file from the remote machine to the local machine.
- `put`—Transfer from the local machine to the remote machine.
- `ls` or `dir`—List files in the current directory on the remote machine.
- `cd`—Change the current directory on the remote machine.

There are also various commands to change transfer modes (for binary or ASCII files) and to determine connection status.

An important point about telnet and FTP is that they require the user to change paradigms. FTP requires the user to know a command set entirely different from the normal operating-system commands. Telnet requires a smaller shift: the user must know appropriate commands on the remote system. For instance, a user on a Windows machine who telnets to a UNIX machine must switch to UNIX commands for the duration of the telnet session. Facilities are more convenient for users if they do not require the use of a different set of commands. Distributed operating systems are designed to address this problem.

16.2.2 Distributed Operating Systems

In a distributed operating system, users access remote resources in the same way they access local resources. Data and process migration from one site to another is under the control of the distributed operating system.

16.2.2.1 Data Migration

Suppose a user on site A wants to access data (such as a file) that reside at site B. The system can transfer the data by one of two basic methods. One approach to **data migration** is to transfer the entire file to site A. From that point on, all access to the file is local. When the user no longer needs access to the file, a copy of the file (if it has been modified) is sent back to site B. Even if only a modest change has been made to a large file, all the data must be transferred. This mechanism can be thought of as an automated FTP system. This approach was used in the Andrew file system, as we discuss in Chapter 17, but it was found to be too inefficient.

The other approach is to transfer to site A only those portions of the file that are actually *necessary* for the immediate task. If another portion is required later, another transfer will take place. When the user no longer wants to access the file, any part of it that has been modified must be sent back to site B. (Note the similarity to demand paging.) The Sun Microsystems network file system (NFS) protocol uses this method (Chapter 17), as do newer versions of Andrew. The Microsoft SMB protocol (running on top of either TCP/IP or the Microsoft NetBEUI protocol) also allows file sharing over a network. SMB is described in Appendix C.6.1.

Clearly, if only a small part of a large file is being accessed, the latter approach is preferable. If significant portions of the file are being accessed, however, it is more efficient to copy the entire file. In both methods, data migration includes more than the mere transfer of data from one site to another. The system must also perform various data translations if the two sites involved are not directly compatible (for instance, if they use different character-code representations or represent integers with a different number or order of bits).

16.2.2.2 Computation Migration

In some circumstances, we may want to transfer the computation, rather than the data, across the system; this approach is called **computation migration**. For example, consider a job that needs to access various large files that reside at different sites, to obtain a summary of those files. It would be more efficient to access the files at the sites where they reside and return the desired results to the site that initiated the computation. Generally, if the time to transfer the data is longer than the time to execute the remote command, the remote command should be used.

Such a computation can be carried out in different ways. Suppose that process P wants to access a file at site A. Access to the file is carried out at site A and could be initiated by an RPC. An RPC uses a **datagram protocol** (UDP on the Internet) to execute a routine on a remote system (Section 3.6.2). Process P invokes a predefined procedure at site A. The procedure executes appropriately and then returns the results to P.

Alternatively, process P can send a *message* to site A. The operating system at site A then creates a new process Q whose function is to carry out the designated task. When process Q completes its execution, it sends the needed result back to P via the message system. In this scheme, process P may execute concurrently with process Q; in fact, it may have several processes running concurrently on several sites.

Either method could be used to access several files residing at various sites. One RPC might result in the invocation of another RPC or even in the transfer of messages to another site. Similarly, process Q could, during the course of its execution, send a message to another site, which in turn would create another process. This process might either send a message back to Q or repeat the cycle.

16.2.2.3 Process Migration

A logical extension of computation migration is **process migration**. When a process is submitted for execution, it is not always executed at the site at which it is initiated. The entire process, or parts of it, may be executed at different sites. This scheme may be used for several reasons:

- **Load balancing**. The processes (or subprocesses) may be distributed across the network to even the workload.
- **Computation speedup**. If a single process can be divided into a number of subprocesses that can run concurrently on different sites, then the total process turnaround time can be reduced.
- **Hardware preference**. The process may have characteristics that make it more suitable for execution on some specialized processor (such as matrix inversion on an array processor) rather than on a microprocessor.
- **Software preference**. The process may require software that is available at only a particular site, and either the software cannot be moved, or it is less expensive to move the process.
- **Data access**. Just as in computation migration, if the data being used in the computation are numerous, it may be more efficient to have a process run remotely than to transfer all the data.

We use two complementary techniques to move processes in a computer network. In the first, the system can attempt to hide the fact that the process has migrated from the client. This scheme has the advantage that the user does not need to code her program explicitly to accomplish the migration. This method is usually employed for achieving load balancing and computation speedup among homogeneous systems, as they do not need user input to help them execute programs remotely.

The other approach is to allow (or require) the user to specify explicitly how the process should migrate. This method is usually employed when the process must be moved to satisfy a hardware or software preference.

You have probably realized that the Web has many aspects of a distributed-computing environment. Certainly it provides data migration (between a Web server and a Web client). It also provides computation migration. For instance, a Web client could trigger a database operation on a Web server. Finally, with Java, it provides a form of process migration: Java applets are sent from the server to the client, where they are executed. A network operating system provides most of these features, but a distributed operating system makes them seamless and easily accessible. The result is a powerful and easy-to-use facility—one of the reasons for the huge growth of the World Wide Web.

16.3 Network Structure

There are basically two types of networks: **local-area networks (LAN)** and **wide-area networks (WAN)**. The main difference between the two is the way in which they are geographically distributed. Local-area networks are composed of processors distributed over small areas (such as a single building or a number of adjacent buildings), whereas wide-area networks are composed of a number of autonomous processors distributed over a large area (such as the United States). These differences imply major variations in the speed and reliability of the communications networks, and they are reflected in the distributed operating-system design.

16.3.1 Local-Area Networks

Local-area networks emerged in the early 1970s as a substitute for large mainframe computer systems. For many enterprises, it is more economical to have a number of small computers, each with its own self-contained applications, than to have a single large system. Because each small computer is likely to need a full complement of peripheral devices (such as disks and printers), and because some form of data sharing is likely to occur in a single enterprise, it was a natural step to connect these small systems into a network.

LANs, as mentioned, are usually designed to cover a small geographical area (such as a single building or a few adjacent buildings) and are generally used in an office environment. All the sites in such systems are close to one another, so the communication links tend to have a higher speed and lower error rate than do their counterparts in wide-area networks. High-quality (expensive) cables are needed to attain this higher speed and reliability. It is also possible to use the cable exclusively for data network traffic. Over longer distances, the cost of using high-quality cable is enormous, and the exclusive use of the cable tends to be prohibitively expensive.

The most common links in a local-area network are twisted-pair and fiber-optic cabling. The most common configurations are multiaccess bus, ring, and star networks. Communication speeds range from 1 megabit per second, for networks such as AppleTalk, infrared, and the new Bluetooth local radio network, to 1 gigabit per second for gigabit Ethernet. Ten megabits per second is the speed of **10BaseT Ethernet**. **100BaseT Ethernet** requires a higher-quality cable but runs at 100 megabits per second and is common. Also growing is the use of optical-fiber–based FDDI networking. The FDDI network is token-based and runs at over 100 megabits per second.

A typical LAN may consist of a number of different computers (from mainframes to laptops or PDAs), various shared peripheral devices (such as laser printers and magnetic-tape drives), and one or more gateways (specialized processors) that provide access to other networks (Figure 16.2). An Ethernet scheme is commonly used to construct LANs. An Ethernet network has no central controller, because it is a multiaccess bus, so new hosts can be added easily to the network. The Ethernet protocol is defined by the IEEE 802.3 standard.

There has been significant growth in using the wireless spectrum for designing local-area networks. Wireless (or *WiFi*) networks allow constructing a network using only a wireless router for transmitting signals between hosts. Each host has a wireless adapter networking card which allows it to join and use the wireless network. However, where Ethernet systems often run at 100 megabits per second, WiFi networks typically run at slower speeds. There are

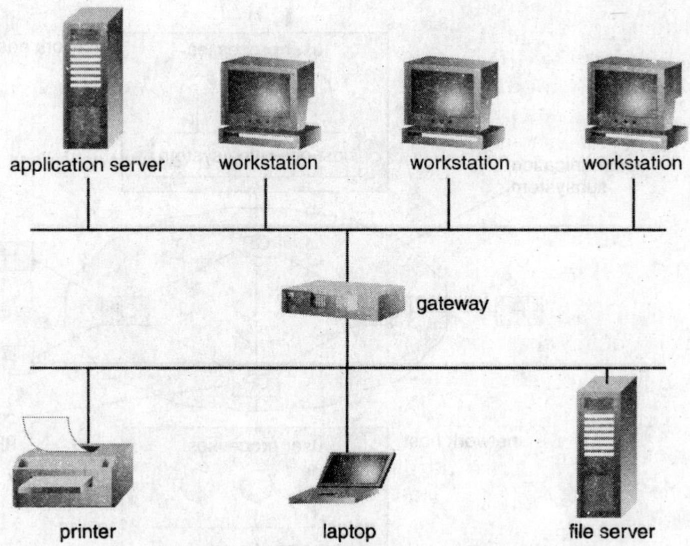

Figure 16.2 Local-area network.

several IEEE standards for wireless networks: 802.11g can theoretically run at 54 megabits per second, although in practice data rates are often less than half that amount. The recent 802.11n standard provides theoretically much higher data rates than 802.11g, although in actual practice 802.11n networks have typical data rates of around 75 megabits per second. Data rates of wireless networks are heavily influenced by the distance between the wireless router and the host as well as interference in the wireless spectrum. Wireless networks often have a physical advantage over wired Ethernet networks as no cabling needs to be run to connect communicating hosts. As a result, wireless networks are popular in homes as well as public areas such as libraries and Internet cafes.

16.3.2 Wide-Area Networks

Wide-area networks emerged in the late 1960s, mainly as an academic research project to provide efficient communication among sites, allowing hardware and software to be shared conveniently and economically by a wide community of users. The first WAN to be designed and developed was the *Arpanet*. Begun in 1968, the Arpanet has grown from a four-site experimental network to a worldwide network of networks, the Internet, comprising millions of computer systems.

Because the sites in a WAN are physically distributed over a large geographical area, the communication links are, by default, relatively slow and unreliable. Typical links are telephone lines, leased (dedicated data) lines, microwave links, and satellite channels. These communication links are controlled by special **communication processors** (Figure 16.3), which are responsible for defining the interface through which the sites communicate over the network, as well as for transferring information among the various sites.

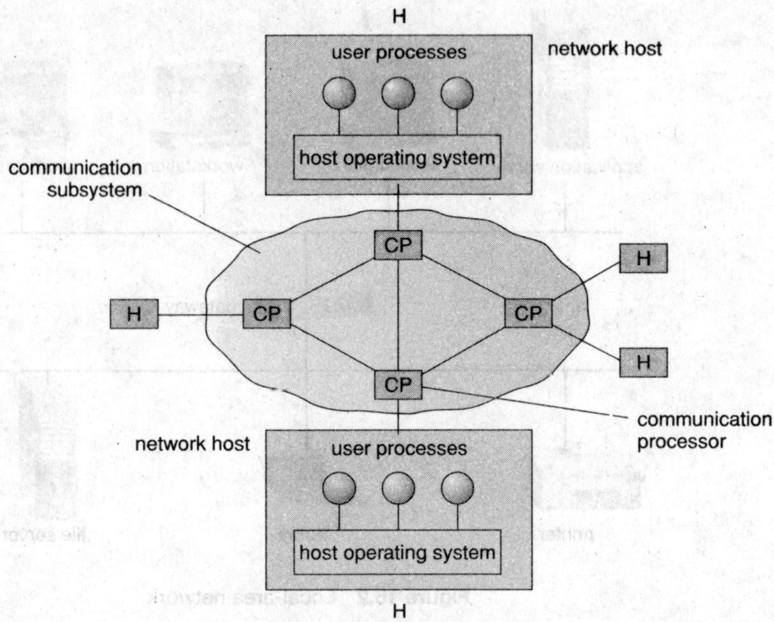

Figure 16.3 Communication processors in a wide-area network.

For example, the Internet WAN enables hosts at geographically separated sites to communicate with one another. The host computers typically differ from one another in type, speed, word length, operating system, and so on. Hosts are generally on LANs, which are, in turn, connected to the Internet via regional networks. The regional networks, such as NSFnet in the northeast United States, are interlinked with **routers** (Section 16.5.2) to form the worldwide network. Connections between networks frequently use a telephone-system service called T1, which provides a transfer rate of 1.544 megabits per second over a leased line. For sites requiring faster Internet access, T1s are collected into multiple-T1 units that work in parallel to provide more throughput. For instance, a T3 is composed of 28 T1 connections and has a transfer rate of 45 megabits per second. The routers control the path each message takes through the net. This routing may be either dynamic, to increase communication efficiency, or static, to reduce security risks or to allow communication charges to be computed.

Other WANs use standard telephone lines as their primary means of communication. **Modems** are devices that accept digital data from the computer side and convert it to the analog signals that the telephone system uses. A modem at the destination site converts the analog signal back to digital form, and the destination receives the data. The UNIX news network, UUCP, allows systems to communicate with each other at predetermined times, via modems, to exchange messages. The messages are then routed to other nearby systems and in this way either are propagated to all hosts on the network (public messages) or are transferred to specific destinations (private messages). WANs are generally slower than LANs; their transmission rates range from 1,200 bits per second to over 1 megabit per second. UUCP has been superseded by PPP, the point-to-point protocol. PPP functions over modem connections, allowing home computers to be fully connected to the Internet.

16.4 Network Topology

The sites in a distributed system can be connected physically in a variety of ways. Each configuration has advantages and disadvantages. We can compare the configurations by using the following criteria:

- **Installation cost**. The cost of physically linking the sites in the system
- **Communication cost**. The cost in time and money to send a message from site A to site B
- **Availability**. The extent to which data can be accessed despite the failure of some links or sites

The various topologies are depicted in Figure 16.4 as graphs whose nodes correspond to sites. An edge from node A to node B corresponds to a direct communication link between the two sites. In a fully connected network, each site is directly connected to every other site. However, the number of links grows as the square of the number of sites, resulting in a huge installation cost. Therefore, fully connected networks are impractical in any large system.

In a partially connected network, direct links exist between some—but not all—pairs of sites. Hence, the installation cost of such a configuration is lower than that of the fully connected network. However, if two sites A and B are not directly connected, messages from one to the other must be routed through a sequence of communication links. This requirement results in a higher communication cost.

If a communication link fails, messages that would have been transmitted across the link must be rerouted. In some cases, another route through the network may be found, so that the messages are able to reach their destination. In other cases, a failure may mean that no connection exists between some pair (or pairs) of sites. When a system is split into two (or more) unconnected subsystems, it is partitioned. Under this definition, a subsystem (or partition) may consist of a single node.

The various partially connected network types include tree-structured networks, ring networks, and star networks, as shown in Figure 16.4. These types have different failure characteristics and installation and communication costs. Installation and communication costs are relatively low for a tree-structured network. However, the failure of a single link in such a network can result in the network's becoming partitioned. In a ring network, at least two links must fail for partition to occur. Thus, the ring network has a higher degree of availability than does a tree-structured network. However, the communication cost is high, since a message may have to cross a large number of links. In a star network, the failure of a single link results in a network partition, but one of the partitions has only a single site. Such a partition can be treated as a single-site failure. The star network also has a low communication cost, since each site is at most two links away from every other site. However,

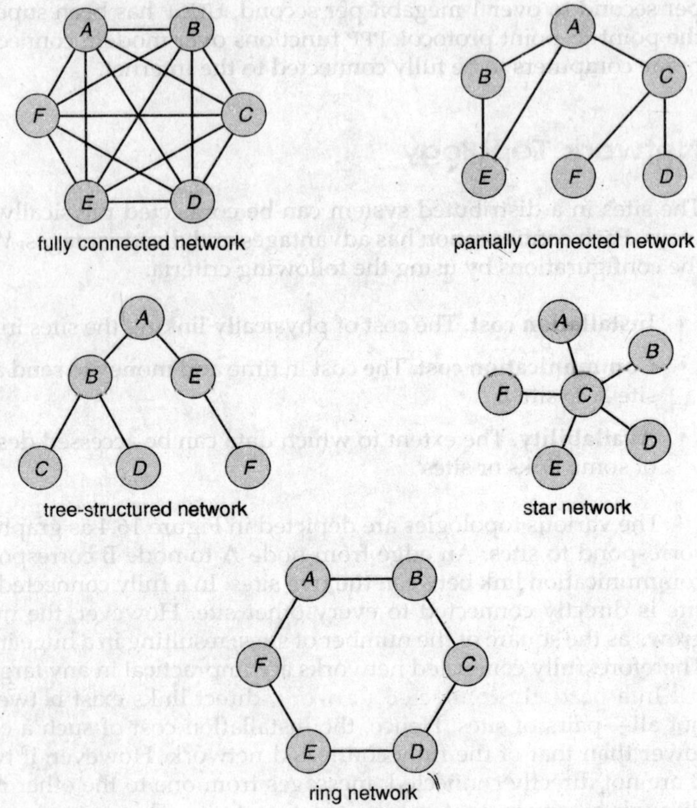

Figure 16.4 Network topology.

if the central site fails, all the sites in the system become disconnected from one another.

16.5 Communication Structure

Now that we have discussed the physical aspects of networking, we turn to the internal workings. The designer of a communication network must address five basic issues:

- **Naming and name resolution**. How do two processes locate each other to communicate?
- **Routing strategies**. How are messages sent through the network?
- **Packet strategies**. Are packets sent individually or as a sequence?
- **Connection strategies**. How do two processes send a sequence of messages?

- **Contention**. How do we resolve conflicting demands for the network's use, given that it is a shared resource?

In the following sections, we elaborate on each of these issues.

16.5.1 Naming and Name Resolution

The first component of network communication is the naming of the systems in the network. For a process at site A to exchange information with a process at site B, each must be able to specify the other. Within a computer system, each process has a process identifier, and messages may be addressed with the process identifier. Because networked systems share no memory, however, a host within the system initially has no knowledge about the processes on other hosts.

To solve this problem, processes on remote systems are generally identified by the pair <host name, identifier>, where *host name* is a name unique within the network and *identifier* may be a process identifier or other unique number within that host. A *host name* is usually an alphanumeric identifier, rather than a number, to make it easier for users to specify. For instance, site A might have hosts named *homer, marge, bart,* and *lisa. Bart* is certainly easier to remember than is *12814831100*.

Names are convenient for humans to use, but computers prefer numbers for speed and simplicity. For this reason, there must be a mechanism to **resolve** the host name into a **host-id** that describes the destination system to the networking hardware. This mechanism is similar to the name-to-address binding that occurs during program compilation, linking, loading, and execution (Chapter 8). In the case of host names, two possibilities exist. First, every host may have a data file containing the names and addresses of all the other hosts reachable on the network (similar to binding at compile time). The problem with this model is that adding or removing a host from the network requires updating the data files on all the hosts. The alternative is to distribute the information among systems on the network. The network must then use a protocol to distribute and retrieve the information. This scheme is like execution-time binding. The first method was the one originally used on the Internet; as the Internet grew, however, it became untenable, so the second method, the **domain-name system (DNS)**, is now in use.

DNS specifies the naming structure of the hosts, as well as name-to-address resolution. Hosts on the Internet are logically addressed with multipart names known as IP addresses. The parts of an IP address progress from the most specific to the most general part, with periods separating the fields. For instance, *bob.cs.brown.edu* refers to host *bob* in the Department of Computer Science at Brown University within the top-level domain *edu*. (Other top-level domains include *com* for commercial sites and *org* for organizations, as well as a domain for each country connected to the network, for systems specified by country rather than organization type.) Generally, the system resolves addresses by examining the host-name components in reverse order. Each component has a **name server**—simply a process on a system—that accepts a name and returns the address of the name server responsible for that name. As the final step, the name server for the host in question is contacted, and a host-id is returned. For example, a request made by a process on system A to communicate with *bob.cs.brown.edu* would result in the following steps:

1. The kernel of system A issues a request to the name server for the *edu* domain, asking for the address of the name server for *brown.edu*. The name server for the *edu* domain must be at a known address, so that it can be queried.

2. The *edu* name server returns the address of the host on which the *brown.edu* name server resides.

3. The kernel on system A then queries the name server at this address and asks about *cs.brown.edu*.

4. An address is returned; and a request to that address for *bob.cs.brown.edu* now, finally, returns an **Internet address** host-id for that host (for example, 128.148.31.100).

This protocol may seem inefficient, but local caches are usually kept by each name server to speed the process. For example, the *edu* name server would have *brown.edu* in its cache and would inform system A that it could resolve two portions of the name, returning a pointer to the *cs.brown.edu* name server. Of course, the contents of these caches must be refreshed over time in case the name server is moved or its address changes. In fact, this service is so important that many optimizations have occurred in the protocol, as well as many safeguards. Consider what would happen if the primary *edu* name server crashed. It is possible that no *edu* hosts would be able to have their addresses resolved, making them all unreachable! The solution is to use secondary, back-up name servers that duplicate the contents of the primary servers.

Before the domain-name service was introduced, all hosts on the Internet needed to have copies of a file that contained the names and addresses of each host on the network. All changes to this file had to be registered at one site (host SRI-NIC), and periodically all hosts had to copy the updated file from SRI-NIC to be able to contact new systems or find hosts whose addresses had changed. Under the domain-name service, each name-server site is responsible for updating the host information for that domain. For instance, any host changes at Brown University are the responsibility of the name server for *brown.edu* and need not be reported anywhere else. DNS lookups will automatically retrieve the updated information because they will contact *brown.edu* directly. Within domains, there can be autonomous subdomains to further distribute the responsibility for host-name and host-id changes.

Java provides the necessary API to design a program that maps IP names to IP addresses. The program shown in Figure 16.5 is passed an IP name (such as *bob.cs.brown.edu*) on the command line and either outputs the IP address of the host or returns a message indicating that the host name could not be resolved. An `InetAddress` is a Java class representing an IP name or address. The static method `getByName()` belonging to the `InetAddress` class is passed a string representation of an IP name, and it returns the corresponding `InetAddress`. The program then invokes the `getHostAddress()` method, which internally uses DNS to look up the IP address of the designated host.

Generally, the operating system is responsible for accepting from its processes a message destined for <host name, identifier> and for transferring that message to the appropriate host. The kernel on the destination host is then responsible for transferring the message to the process named by the identifier. This exchange is by no means trivial; it is described in Section 16.5.4.

```
/**
 * Usage: java DNSLookUp <IP name>
 * i.e. java DNSLookUp www.wiley.com
 */
public class DNSLookUp {
  public static void main(String[] args) {
    InetAddress hostAddress;

    try {
      hostAddress = InetAddress.getByName(args[0]);
      System.out.println(hostAddress.getHostAddress());
    }
    catch (UnknownHostException uhe) {
      System.err.println("Unknown host: " + args[0]);
    }
  }
}
```

Figure 16.5 Java program illustrating a DNS lookup.

16.5.2 Routing Strategies

When a process at site A wants to communicate with a process at site B, how is the message sent? If there is only one physical path from A to B (such as in a star or tree-structured network), the message must be sent through that path. However, if there are multiple physical paths from A to B, then several routing options exist. Each site has a routing table indicating the alternative paths that can be used to send a message to other sites. The table may include information about the speed and cost of the various communication paths, and it may be updated as necessary, either manually or via programs that exchange routing information. The three most common routing schemes are fixed routing, virtual routing, and dynamic routing.

- **Fixed routing**. A path from A to B is specified in advance and does not change unless a hardware failure disables it. Usually, the shortest path is chosen, so that communication costs are minimized.
- **Virtual routing**. A path from A to B is fixed for the duration of one session. Different sessions involving messages from A to B may use different paths. A session could be as short as a file transfer or as long as a remote-login period.
- **Dynamic routing**. The path used to send a message from site A to site B is chosen only when the message is sent. Because the decision is made dynamically, separate messages may be assigned different paths. Site A will make a decision to send the message to site C; C, in turn, will decide to send it to site D, and so on. Eventually, a site will deliver the message to B. Usually, a site sends a message to another site on whatever link is the least used at that particular time.

There are tradeoffs among these three schemes. Fixed routing cannot adapt to link failures or load changes. In other words, if a path has been established between A and B, the messages must be sent along this path, even if the path is down or is used more heavily than another possible path. We can partially remedy this problem by using virtual routing and can avoid it completely by using dynamic routing. Fixed routing and virtual routing ensure that messages from A to B will be delivered in the order in which they were sent. In dynamic routing, messages may arrive out of order. We can remedy this problem by appending a sequence number to each message.

Dynamic routing is the most complicated to set up and run; however, it is the best way to manage routing in complicated environments. UNIX provides both fixed routing for use on hosts within simple networks and dynamic routing for complicated network environments. It is also possible to mix the two. Within a site, the hosts may just need to know how to reach the system that connects the local network to other networks (such as company-wide networks or the Internet). Such a node is known as a **gateway**. Each individual host has a static route to the gateway, although the gateway itself uses dynamic routing to reach any host on the rest of the network.

A router is the entity within the computer network responsible for routing messages. A router can be a host computer with routing software or a special-purpose device. Either way, a router must have at least two network connections, or else it would have nowhere to route messages. A router decides whether any given message needs to be passed from the network on which it is received to any other network connected to the router. It makes this determination by examining the destination Internet address of the message. The router checks its tables to determine the location of the destination host, or at least of the network to which it will send the message toward the destination host. In the case of static routing, this table is changed only by manual update (a new file is loaded onto the router). With dynamic routing, a **routing protocol** is used between routers to inform them of network changes and to allow them to update their routing tables automatically. Gateways and routers typically are dedicated hardware devices that run code out of firmware.

16.5.3 Packet Strategies

Messages generally vary in length. To simplify the system design, we commonly implement communication with fixed-length messages called **packets**, **frames**, or **datagrams**. A communication implemented in one packet can be sent to its destination in a **connectionless message**. A connectionless message can be **unreliable**, in which case the sender has no guarantee that, and cannot tell whether, the packet reached its destination. Alternatively, the packet can be **reliable**; usually, in this case, a packet is returned from the destination indicating that the packet arrived. (Of course, the return packet could be lost along the way.) If a message is too long to fit within one packet, or if the packets need to flow back and forth between the two communicators, a connection is established to allow the reliable exchange of multiple packets.

16.5.4 Connection Strategies

Once messages are able to reach their destinations, processes can institute **communications sessions** to exchange information. Pairs of processes that want to communicate over the network can be connected in a number of ways.

The three most common schemes are circuit switching, message switching, and packet switching.

- **Circuit switching**. If two processes want to communicate, a permanent physical link is established between them. This link is allocated for the duration of the communication session, and no other process can use that link during this period (even if the two processes are not actively communicating for a while). This scheme is similar to that used in the telephone system. Once a communication line has been opened between two parties (that is, party A calls party B), no one else can use this circuit until the communication is terminated explicitly (for example, when the parties hang up).
- **Message switching**. If two processes want to communicate, a temporary link is established for the duration of one message transfer. Physical links are allocated dynamically among correspondents as needed and are allocated for only short periods. Each message is a block of data with system information—such as the source, the destination, and error-correction codes (ECC)—that allows the communication network to deliver the message to the destination correctly. This scheme is similar to the post-office mailing system. Each letter is a message that contains both the destination address and source (return) address. Many messages (from different users) can be shipped over the same link.
- **Packet switching**. One logical message may have to be divided into a number of packets. Each packet may be sent to its destination separately, and each therefore must include a source and a destination address with its data. Furthermore, the various packets may take different paths through the network. The packets must be reassembled into messages as they arrive. Note that it is not harmful for data to be broken into packets, possibly routed separately, and reassembled at the destination. Breaking up an audio signal (say, a telephone communication), in contrast, could cause great confusion if it was not done carefully.

There are obvious tradeoffs among these schemes. Circuit switching requires substantial set-up time and may waste network bandwidth, but it incurs less overhead for shipping each message. Conversely, message and packet switching require less set-up time but incur more overhead per message. Also, in packet switching, each message must be divided into packets and later reassembled. Packet switching is the method most commonly used on data networks because it makes the best use of network bandwidth.

16.5.5 Contention

Depending on the network topology, a link may connect more than two sites in the computer network, and several of these sites may want to transmit information over a link simultaneously. This situation occurs mainly in a ring or multiaccess bus network. In this case, the transmitted information may become scrambled. If it does, it must be discarded; and the sites must be notified about the problem so that they can retransmit the information. If no special provisions are made, this situation may be repeated, resulting in degraded performance.

Several techniques have been developed to avoid repeated collisions, including collision detection and token passing.

- **CSMA/CD**. Before transmitting a message over a link, a site must listen to determine whether another message is currently being transmitted over that link; this technique is called **carrier sense with multiple access (CSMA)**. If the link is free, the site can start transmitting. Otherwise, it must wait (and continue to listen) until the link is free. If two or more sites begin transmitting at exactly the same time (each thinking that no other site is using the link), then they will register a **collision detection (CD)** and will stop transmitting. Each site will try again after some random time interval. The main problem with this approach is that, when the system is very busy, many collisions may occur, and thus performance may be degraded. Nevertheless, CSMA/CD has been used successfully in the Ethernet system, the most common local area network system. One strategy for limiting the number of collisions is to limit the number of hosts per Ethernet network. Adding more hosts to a congested network could result in poor network throughput. As systems get faster, they are able to send more packets per time segment. As a result, the number of systems per Ethernet network generally is decreasing so that networking performance is kept reasonable.
- **Token passing**. A unique message type, known as a **token**, continuously circulates in the system (usually a ring structure). A site that wants to transmit information must wait until the token arrives. It then removes the token from the ring and begins to transmit its messages. When the site completes its round of message passing, it retransmits the token. This action, in turn, allows another site to receive and remove the token and to start its message transmission. If the token gets lost, the system must detect the loss and generate a new token. It usually does that by declaring an **election** to choose a unique site where a new token will be generated. Later, in Section 18.6, we present one election algorithm. A token-passing scheme has been adopted by the IBM and HP/Apollo systems. The benefit of a token-passing network is that performance is constant. Adding new sites to a network may lengthen the waiting time for a token, but it will not cause a large performance decrease, as may happen on Ethernet. On lightly loaded networks, however, Ethernet is more efficient, because systems can send messages at any time.

16.6 Communication Protocols

When we are designing a communication network, we must deal with the inherent complexity of coordinating asynchronous operations communicating in a potentially slow and error-prone environment. In addition, the systems on the network must agree on a protocol or a set of protocols for determining host names, locating hosts on the network, establishing connections, and so on. We can simplify the design problem (and related implementation) by partitioning the problem into multiple layers. Each layer on one system communicates with the equivalent layer on other systems. Typically, each layer has its own protocols, and communication takes place between peer layers

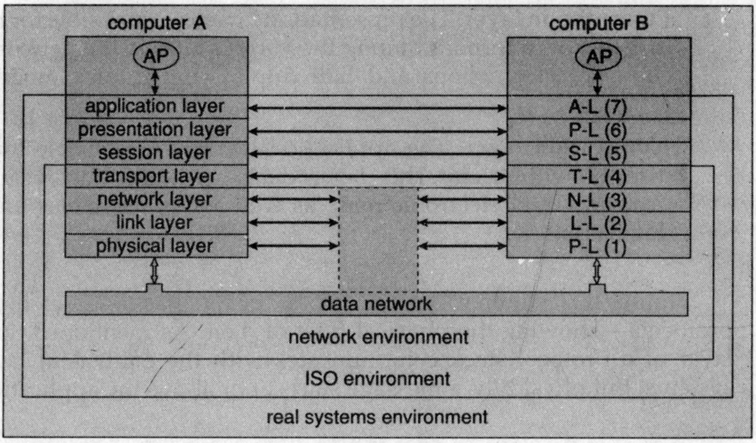

Figure 16.6 Two computers communicating via the ISO network model.

using a specific protocol. The protocols may be implemented in hardware or software. For instance, Figure 16.6 shows the logical communications between two computers, with the three lowest-level layers implemented in hardware. Following the International Standards Organization (ISO), we refer to the layers as follows:

1. **Physical layer**. The physical layer is responsible for handling both the mechanical and the electrical details of the physical transmission of a bit stream. At the physical layer, the communicating systems must agree on the electrical representation of a binary 0 and 1, so that when data are sent as a stream of electrical signals, the receiver is able to interpret the data properly as binary data. This layer is implemented in the hardware of the networking device.

2. **Data-link layer**. The data-link layer is responsible for handling *frames*, or fixed-length parts of packets, including any error detection and recovery that occurs in the physical layer.

3. **Network layer**. The network layer is responsible for providing connections and for routing packets in the communication network, including handling the addresses of outgoing packets, decoding the addresses of incoming packets, and maintaining routing information for proper response to changing load levels. Routers work at this layer.

4. **Transport layer**. The transport layer is responsible for low-level access to the network and for transfer of messages between clients, including partitioning messages into packets, maintaining packet order, controlling flow, and generating physical addresses.

5. **Session layer**. The session layer is responsible for implementing sessions, or process-to-process communication protocols. Typically, these protocols are the actual communications for remote logins and for file and mail transfers.

6. **Presentation layer**. The presentation layer is responsible for resolving the differences in formats among the various sites in the network, including character conversions and half duplex–full duplex modes (character echoing).

7. **Application layer**. The application layer is responsible for interacting directly with users. This layer deals with file transfer, remote-login protocols, and electronic mail, as well as with schemas for distributed databases.

Figure 16.7 summarizes the ISO protocol stack—a set of cooperating protocols—showing the physical flow of data. As mentioned, logically each layer of a protocol stack communicates with the equivalent layer on other systems. But physically, a message starts at or above the application layer and

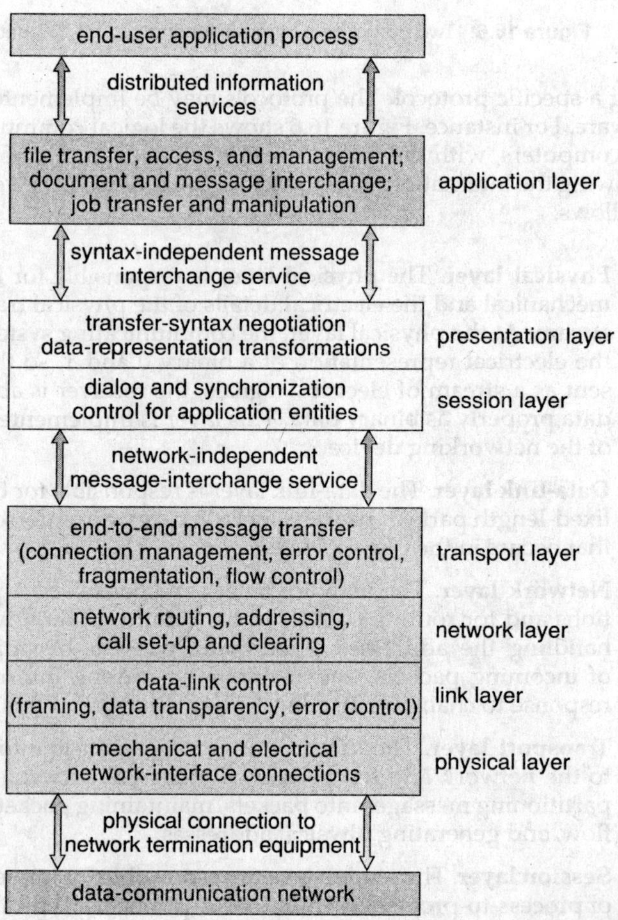

Figure 16.7 The ISO protocol stack.

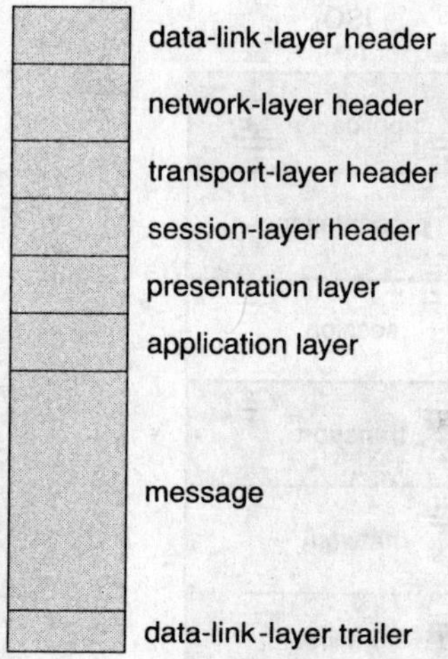

Figure 16.8 An ISO network message.

is passed through each lower level in turn. Each layer may modify the message and include message-header data for the equivalent layer on the receiving side. Ultimately, the message reaches the data-network layer and is transferred as one or more packets (Figure 16.8). The data-link layer of the target system receives these data, and the message is moved up through the protocol stack; it is analyzed, modified, and stripped of headers as it progresses. It finally reaches the application layer for use by the receiving process.

The ISO model formalizes some of the earlier work done in network protocols but was developed in the late 1970s and is currently not in widespread use. Perhaps the most widely adopted protocol stack is the TCP/IP model, which has been adopted by virtually all Internet sites. The TCP/IP protocol stack has fewer layers than does the ISO model. Theoretically, because it combines several functions in each layer, it is more difficult to implement but more efficient than ISO networking. The relationship between the ISO and TCP/IP models is shown in Figure 16.9. The TCP/IP application layer identifies several protocols in widespread use in the Internet, including HTTP, FTP, Telnet, DNS, and SMTP. The transport layer identifies the unreliable, connectionless **user datagram protocol** (**UDP**) and the reliable, connection-oriented **transmission control protocol** (**TCP**). The Internet protocol (**IP**) is responsible for routing IP datagrams through the Internet. The TCP/IP model does not formally identify a link or physical layer, allowing TCP/IP traffic to run across any physical network. In Section 16.9, we consider the TCP/IP model running over an Ethernet network.

Security should be a concern in the design and implementation of any modern communication protocol. Both strong authentication and encryption are needed for secure communication. Strong authentication ensures that the sender and receiver of a communication are who or what they are supposed to be. Encryption protects the contents of the communication from eavesdropping. Weak authentication and clear-text communication are still very common, however, for a variety of reasons. When most of the

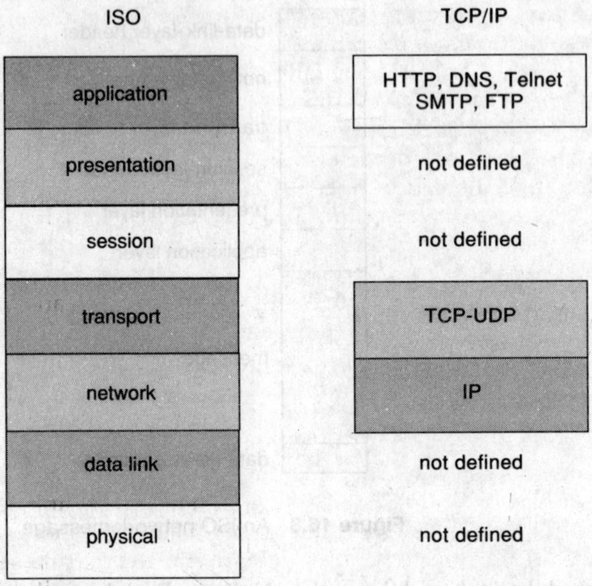

Figure 16.9 The ISO and TCP/IP protocol stacks.

common protocols were designed, security was frequently less important than performance, simplicity, and efficiency.

Strong authentication requires a multistep handshake protocol or authentication devices, adding complexity to a protocol. Modern CPUs can efficiently perform encryption, and systems frequently offload encryption to separate cryptography processors, so system performance is not compromised. Long-distance communication can be made secure by authenticating the endpoints and encrypting the stream of packets in a virtual private network, as discussed in 15.4.2. LAN communication remains unencrypted at most sites, but protocols such as NFS Version 4, which includes strong native authentication and encryption, should help improve even LAN security.

16.7 Robustness

A distributed system may suffer from various types of hardware failure. The failure of a link, the failure of a site, and the loss of a message are the most common types. To ensure that the system is robust, we must detect any of these failures, reconfigure the system so that computation can continue, and recover when a site or a link is repaired.

16.7.1 Failure Detection

In an environment with no shared memory, we are generally unable to differentiate among link failure, site failure, and message loss. We can usually detect only that one of these failures has occurred. Once a failure has been detected, appropriate action must be taken. What action is appropriate depends on the particular application.

To detect link and site failure, we use a **handshaking** procedure. Suppose that sites A and B have a direct physical link between them. At fixed intervals, the sites send each other an *I-am-up* message. If site A does not receive this message within a predetermined time period, it can assume that site B has failed, that the link between A and B has failed, or that the message from B has been lost. At this point, site A has two choices. It can wait for another time period to receive an *I-am-up* message from B, or it can send an *Are-you-up?* message to B.

If time goes by and site A still has not received an *I-am-up* message, or if site A has sent an *Are-you-up?* message and has not received a reply, the procedure can be repeated. Again, the only conclusion that site A can draw safely is that some type of failure has occurred.

Site A can try to differentiate between link failure and site failure by sending an *Are-you-up?* message to B by another route (if one exists). If and when B receives this message, it immediately replies positively. This positive reply tells A that B is up and that the failure is in the direct link between them. Since we do not know in advance how long it will take the message to travel from A to B and back, we must use a **time-out scheme**. At the time A sends the *Are-you-up?* message, it specifies a time interval during which it is willing to wait for the reply from B. If A receives the reply message within that time interval, then it can safely conclude that B is up. If not, however (that is, if a time-out occurs), then A may conclude only that one or more of the following situations has occurred:

- Site B is down.
- The direct link (if one exists) from A to B is down.
- The alternative path from A to B is down.
- The message has been lost.

Site A cannot, however, determine which of these events has occurred.

16.7.2 Reconfiguration

Suppose that site A has discovered, through the mechanism described in the previous section, that a failure has occurred. It must then initiate a procedure that will allow the system to reconfigure and to continue its normal mode of operation.

- If a direct link from A to B has failed, this information must be broadcast to every site in the system, so that the various routing tables can be updated accordingly.
- If the system believes that a site has failed (because that site can be reached no longer), then all sites in the system must be so notified, so that they will no longer attempt to use the services of the failed site. The failure of a site that serves as a central coordinator for some activity (such as deadlock detection) requires the election of a new coordinator. Similarly, if the failed

site is part of a logical ring, then a new logical ring must be constructed. Note that, if the site has not failed (that is, if it is up but cannot be reached), then we may have the undesirable situation in which two sites serve as the coordinator. When the network is partitioned, the two coordinators (each for its own partition) may initiate conflicting actions. For example, if the coordinators are responsible for implementing mutual exclusion, we may have a situation in which two processes are executing simultaneously in their critical sections.

16.7.3 Recovery from Failure

When a failed link or site is repaired, it must be integrated into the system gracefully and smoothly.

- Suppose that a link between A and B has failed. When it is repaired, both A and B must be notified. We can accomplish this notification by continuously repeating the handshaking procedure described in Section 16.7.1.
- Suppose that site B has failed. When it recovers, it must notify all other sites that it is up again. Site B then may have to receive information from the other sites to update its local tables; for example, it may need routing-table information, a list of sites that are down, or undelivered messages and mail. If the site has not failed but simply could not be reached, then this information is still required.

16.7.4 Fault Tolerance

A distributed system must tolerate a certain level of failure and continue to function normally when faced with various types of failures. Making a facility fault tolerant starts at the protocol level, as described above, but continues through all aspects of the system. We use the term *fault tolerance* in a broad sense. Communication faults, machine failures (of type *fail-stop* where the machine stops before performing an erroneous operation that is visible to other processors), storage-device crashes, and decays of storage media should all be tolerated to some extent. A **fault-tolerant system** should continue to function, perhaps in a degraded form, when faced with such failures. The degradation can be in performance, in functionality, or in both. It should be proportional, however, to the failures that caused it. A system that grinds to a halt when only one of its components fails is certainly not fault tolerant.

Unfortunately, fault tolerance can be difficult and expensive to implement. At the network layer, multiple redundant communication paths and network devices such as switches and routers are needed to avoid a communication failure. A storage failure can cause loss of the operating system, applications, or data. Storage units can include redundant hardware components that automatically take over from each other in case of failure. In addition, RAID systems can ensure continued access to the data even in the event of one or more disk failures (Section 12.7).

A system failure without redundancy can cause an application or an entire facility to stop operation. The most simple system failure involves a system running only stateless applications. These applications can be restarted without compromising the operation; so as long as the applications can run on more than one computer (node), operation can continue. Such a facility is commonly known as a **compute cluster** because it is computation-centric.

In contrast, data-centric systems involve running applications that access and modify shared data. As a result, data-centric computing facilities are more difficult to make fault tolerant. They require failure-monitoring software and special infrastructure. For instance, **high-availability clusters** such as Veritas Cluster and Sun Cluster include two or more computers and a set of shared disks. Any given application can be stored on the computers or on the shared disk, but the data must be stored on the shared disk. The running application's node has exclusive access to the application's data on disk. The application is monitored by the cluster software, and if it fails it is automatically restarted. If it cannot be restarted, or if the entire computer fails, the node's exclusive access to the application's data is terminated and is granted to another node in the cluster. The application is restarted on that new node. The application loses whatever state information was in the failed system's memory but can continue based on whatever state it last wrote to the shared disk. From a user's point of view, a service was interrupted and then restarted, possibly with some data missing.

Specific applications may improve on this functionality by implementing lock management along with clustering. With lock management (Section 18.4.1), the application can run on multiple nodes and can use the same data on shared disks concurrently. Clustered databases frequently implement this functionality. If a node fails, transactions can continue on other nodes, and users notice no interruption of service, as long as the client is able to automatically locate the other nodes in the cluster. Any noncommitted transactions on the failed node are lost, but again, client applications can be designed to retry noncommitted transactions if they detect a failure of their database node.

16.8 Design Issues

Making the multiplicity of processors and storage devices **transparent** to the users has been a key challenge to many designers. Ideally, a distributed system should look to its users like a conventional, centralized system. The user interface of a transparent distributed system should not distinguish between local and remote resources. That is, users should be able to access remote resources as though these resources were local, and the distributed system should be responsible for locating the resources and for arranging for the appropriate interaction.

Another aspect of transparency is user mobility. It would be convenient to allow users to log into any machine in the system rather than forcing them to use a specific machine. A transparent distributed system facilitates user mobility by bringing over the user's environment (for example, home directory) to wherever he logs in. Both the Andrew file system from CMU and Project Athena from MIT provide this functionality on a large scale; NFS can provide it on a smaller scale.

Still another issue is **scalability**—the capability of a system to adapt to increased service load. Systems have bounded resources and can become completely saturated under increased load. For example, with respect to a file system, saturation occurs either when a server's CPU runs at a high utilization rate or when disks are almost full. Scalability is a relative property, but it can be measured accurately. A scalable system reacts more gracefully to increased load than does a nonscalable one. First, its performance degrades more moderately; and second, its resources reach a saturated state later. Even perfect design cannot accommodate an ever-growing load. Adding new resources might solve the problem, but it might generate additional indirect load on other resources (for example, adding machines to a distributed system can clog the network and increase service loads). Even worse, expanding the system can call for expensive design modifications. A scalable system should have the potential to grow without these problems. In a distributed system, the ability to scale up gracefully is of special importance, since expanding the network by adding new machines or interconnecting two networks is commonplacc. In short, a scalable design should withstand high service load, accommodate growth of the user community, and enable simple integration of added resources.

Scalability is related to fault tolerance, discussed earlier. A heavily loaded component can become paralyzed and behave like a faulty component. Also, shifting the load from a faulty component to that component's backup can saturate the latter. Generally, having spare resources is essential for ensuring reliability as well as for handling peak loads gracefully. An inherent advantage of a distributed system is a potential for fault tolerance and scalability because of the multiplicity of resources. However, inappropriate design can obscure this potential. Fault-tolerance and scalability considerations call for a design demonstrating distribution of control and data.

Very large-scale distributed systems, to a great extent, are still only theoretical. No magic guidelines ensure the scalability of a system. It is easier to point out why current designs are *not* scalable. We next discuss several designs that pose problems and propose possible solutions, all in the context of scalability.

One principle for designing very large-scale systems is that the service demand from any component of the system should be bounded by a constant that is independent of the number of nodes in the system. Any service mechanism whose load demand is proportional to the size of the system is destined to become clogged once the system grows beyond a certain size. Adding more resources will not alleviate such a problem. The capacity of this mechanism simply limits the growth of the system.

Another principle concerns centralization. Central control schemes and central resources should not be used to build scalable (and fault-tolerant) systems. Examples of centralized entities are central authentication servers, central naming servers, and central file servers. Centralization is a form of functional asymmetry among machines constituting the system. The ideal alternative is a functionally symmetric configuration; that is, all the component machines have an equal role in the operation of the system, and hence each machine has some degree of autonomy. Practically, it is virtually impossible to comply with such a principle. For instance, incorporating diskless machines violates functional symmetry, since the workstations depend on a central disk. However, autonomy and symmetry are important goals to which we should aspire.

Deciding on the process structure of the server is a major problem in the design of any service. Servers are supposed to operate efficiently in peak periods, when hundreds of active clients need to be served simultaneously. A single-process server is certainly not a good choice, since whenever a request necessitates disk I/O, the whole service will be blocked. Assigning a process for each client is a better choice; however, the expense of frequent context switches between the processes must be considered. A related problem occurs because all the server processes need to share information.

One of the best solutions for the server architecture is the use of lightweight processes, or threads, which we discuss in Chapter 4. We can think of a group of lightweight processes as multiple threads of control associated with some shared resources. Usually, a lightweight process is not bound to a particular client. Instead, it serves single requests of different clients. Scheduling of threads can be preemptive or nonpreemptive. If threads are allowed to run to completion (nonpreemptive), then their shared data do not need to be protected explicitly. Otherwise, some explicit locking mechanism must be used. Clearly, some form of lightweight-process scheme is essential if servers are to be scalable.

16.9 An Example: Networking

We now return to the name-resolution issue raised in Section 16.5.1 and examine its operation with respect to the TCP/IP protocol stack on the Internet. We consider the processing needed to transfer a packet between hosts on different Ethernet networks.

In a TCP/IP network, every host has a name and an associated IP address (or host-id). Both of these strings must be unique; and so that the name space can be managed, they are segmented. The name is hierarchical (as explained in Section 16.5.1), describing the host name and then the organization with which the host is associated. The host-id is split into a network number and a host number. The proportion of the split varies, depending on the size of the network. Once the Internet administrators assign a network number, the site with that number is free to assign host-ids.

The sending system checks its routing tables to locate a router to send the frame on its way. The routers use the network part of the host-id to transfer the packet from its source network to the destination network. The destination system then receives the packet. The packet may be a complete message, or it may just be a component of a message, with more packets needed before the message can be reassembled and passed to the TCP/UDP layer for transmission to the destination process.

Now we know how a packet moves from its source network to its destination. Within a network, how does a packet move from sender (host or router) to receiver? Every Ethernet device has a unique byte number, called the **medium access control (MAC) address**, assigned to it for addressing. Two devices on a LAN communicate with each other only with this number. If a system needs to send data to another system, the networking software generates an **address resolution protocol (ARP)** packet containing the IP address of the destination system. This packet is **broadcast** to all other systems on that Ethernet network.

A broadcast uses a special network address (usually, the maximum address) to signal that all hosts should receive and process the packet. The broadcast is not re-sent by gateways, so only systems on the local network receive it. Only the system whose IP address matches the IP address of the ARP request responds and sends back its MAC address to the system that initiated the query. For efficiency, the host caches the IP–MAC address pair in an internal table. The cache entries are **aged**, so that an entry is eventually removed from the cache if an access to that system is not required within a given time. In this way, hosts that are removed from a network are eventually *forgotten*. For added performance, ARP entries for heavily used hosts may be hardwired in the ARP cache.

Once an Ethernet device has announced its host-id and address, communication can begin. A process may specify the name of a host with which to communicate. Networking software takes that name and determines the IP address of the target, using a DNS lookup. The message is passed from the application layer, through the software layers, and to the hardware layer. At the hardware layer, the packet (or packets) has the Ethernet address at its start; a trailer indicates the end of the packet and contains a **checksum** for detection of packet damage (Figure 16.10). The packet is placed on the network by the Ethernet device. The data section of the packet may contain some or all of the data of the original message, but it may also contain some of the upper-level headers that compose the message. In other words, all parts of the original message must be sent from source to destination, and all headers above the 802.3 layer (data-link layer) are included as data in the Ethernet packets.

If the destination is on the same local network as the source, the system can look in its ARP cache, find the Ethernet address of the host, and place the packet on the wire. The destination Ethernet device then sees its address in the packet and reads in the packet, passing it up the protocol stack.

If the destination system is on a network different from that of the source, the source system finds an appropriate router on its network and sends the packet there. Routers then pass the packet along the WAN until it reaches its

bytes		
7	preamble—start of packet	each byte pattern 10101010
1	start of frame delimiter	pattern 10101011
2 or 6	destination address	Ethernet address or broadcast
2 or 6	source address	Ethernet address
2	length of data section	length in bytes
0–1500	data	message data
0–46	pad (optional)	message must be > 63 bytes long
4	frame checksum	for error detection

Figure 16.10 An Ethernet packet.

destination network. The router that connects the destination network checks its ARP cache, finds the Ethernet number of the destination, and sends the packet to that host. Through all of these transfers, the data-link-layer header may change as the Ethernet address of the next router in the chain is used, but the other headers of the packet remain the same until the packet is received and processed by the protocol stack and finally passed to the receiving process by the kernel.

16.10 Summary

A distributed system is a collection of processors that do not share memory or a clock. Instead, each processor has its own local memory, and the processors communicate with one another through various communication lines, such as high-speed buses and telephone lines. The processors in a distributed system vary in size and function. They may include small microprocessors, workstations, minicomputers, and large general-purpose computer systems.

The processors in the system are connected through a communication network, which can be configured in a number of ways. The network may be fully or partially connected. It may be a tree, a star, a ring, or a multiaccess bus. The communication-network design must include routing and connection strategies, and it must solve the problems of contention and security.

A distributed system provides the user with access to the resources the system provides. Access to a shared resource can be provided by data migration, computation migration, or process migration.

Protocol stacks, as specified by network layering models, "massage" the message, adding information to it to ensure that it reaches its destination. A naming system (such as DNS) must be used to translate from a host name to a network address, and another protocol (such as ARP) may be needed to translate the network number to a network device address (an Ethernet address, for instance). If systems are located on separate networks, routers are needed to pass packets from source network to destination network.

A distributed system may suffer from various types of hardware failure. For a distributed system to be fault tolerant, it must detect hardware failures and reconfigure the system. When the failure is repaired, the system must be reconfigured again.

Exercises

16.1 What are the advantages of using dedicated hardware devices for routers and gateways? What are the disadvantages of using these devices compared with using general-purpose computers?

16.2 Why would it be a bad idea for gateways to pass broadcast packets between networks? What would be the advantages of doing so?

16.3 Consider a network layer that senses collisions and retransmits immediately on detection of a collision. What problems could arise with this strategy? How could they be rectified?

16.4 Even though the ISO model of networking specifies seven layers of functionality, most computer systems use fewer layers to implement a network. Why do they use fewer layers? What problems could the use of fewer layers cause?

16.5 The lower layers of the ISO network model provide datagram service, with no delivery guarantees for messages. A transport-layer protocol such as TCP is used to provide reliability. Discuss the advantages and disadvantages of supporting reliable message delivery at the lowest possible layer.

16.6 What are the advantages and the disadvantages of making the computer network transparent to the user?

16.7 Under what circumstances is a token-passing network more effective than an Ethernet network?

16.8 Process migration within a heterogeneous network is usually impossible, given the differences in architectures and operating systems. Describe a method for process migration across different architectures running:

a. The same operating system

b. Different operating systems

16.9 Contrast the various network topologies in terms of the following attributes:

a. Reliability

b. Available bandwidth for concurrent communications

c. Installation cost

d. Load balance in routing responsibilities

16.10 How does using a dynamic routing strategy affect application behavior? For what type of applications is it beneficial to use virtual routing instead of dynamic routing?

16.11 The original HTTP protocol used TCP/IP as the underlying network protocol. For each page, graphic, or applet, a separate TCP session was constructed, used, and torn down. Because of the overhead of building and destroying TCP/IP connections, performance problems resulted from this implementation method. Would using UDP rather than TCP be a good alternative? What other changes could you make to improve HTTP performance?

16.12 What are the advantages and disadvantages of using circuit switching? For what kinds of applications is circuit switching a viable strategy?

16.13 In what ways is using a name server better than using static host tables? What problems or complications are associated with name servers? What methods could you use to decrease the amount of traffic name servers generate to satisfy translation requests?

16.14 Of what use is an address-resolution protocol? Why is it better to use such a protocol than to make each host read each packet to determine that packet's destination? Does a token-passing network need such a protocol? Explain your answer.

16.15 What is the difference between computation migration and process migration? Which is easier to implement, and why?

16.16 Run the program shown in Figure 16.5 and determine the IP addresses of the following host names:

- www.wiley.com
- www.cs.yale.edu
- www.apple.com
- www.westminstercollege.edu
- www.ietf.org

16.17 To build a robust distributed system, you must know what kinds of failures can occur.

a. List three possible types of failure in a distributed system.

b. Specify which of the entries in your list also are applicable to a centralized system.

16.18 Explain why doubling the speed of the systems on an Ethernet segment may result in decreased network performance. What changes could help solve this problem?

16.19 Name servers are organized in a hierarchical manner. What is the purpose of using a hierarchical organization?

16.20 Consider a distributed system with two sites, A and B. Consider whether site A can distinguish among the following:

a. B goes down.

b. The link between A and B goes down.

c. B is extremely overloaded, and its response time is 100 times longer than normal.

What implications does your answer have for recovery in distributed systems?

Bibliographical Notes

Tanenbaum [2003], Stallings [2000a], and Kurose and Ross [2005] provide general overviews of computer networks. Williams [2001] covers computer networking from a computer-architecture viewpoint.

The Internet and its protocols are described in Comer [1999] and Comer [2000]. Coverage of TCP/IP can be found in Stevens [1994] and Stevens [1995].

UNIX network programming is described thoroughly in Stevens [1997] and Stevens [1998].

Discussions concerning distributed operating-system structures have been offered by Coulouris et al. [2001] and Tanenbaum and van Steen [2002].

Load balancing and load sharing are discussed by Harchol-Balter and Downey [1997] and Vee and Hsu [2000]. Harish and Owens [1999] describes load-balancing DNS servers. Process migration is discussed by Jul et al. [1988], Douglis and Ousterhout [1991], Han and Ghosh [1998], and Milojicic et al. [2000]. Issues relating to a distributed virtual machine for distributed systems are examined in Sirer et al. [1999].

Distributed File Systems

CHAPTER 17

In the previous chapter, we discussed network construction and the low-level protocols needed to transfer messages between systems. Now we examine one use of this infrastructure. A **distributed file system (DFS)** is a distributed implementation of the classical time-sharing model of a file system, where multiple users share files and storage resources (Chapter 11). The purpose of a DFS is to support the same kind of sharing when the files are physically dispersed among the sites of a distributed system.

In this chapter, we describe how a DFS can be designed and implemented. First, we discuss common concepts on which DFSs are based. Then, we illustrate our concepts by examining one influential DFS—the Andrew file system (AFS).

CHAPTER OBJECTIVES

- To explain the naming mechanism that provides location transparency and independence.
- To describe the various methods for accessing distributed files.
- To contrast stateful and stateless distributed file servers.
- To show how replication of files on different machines in a distributed file system is a useful redundancy for improving availability.
- To introduce the Andrew file system (AFS) as an example of a distributed file system.

17.1 Background

As we noted in the preceding chapter, a distributed system is a collection of loosely coupled computers interconnected by a communication network. These computers can share physically dispersed files by using a distributed file system (DFS). In this chapter, we use the term *DFS* to mean distributed file systems in general, not the commercial Transarc DFS product; we refer to the latter as *Transarc DFS*. Also, NFS refers to NFS Version 3, unless otherwise noted.

To explain the structure of a DFS, we need to define the terms *service, server,* and *client*. A **service** is a software entity running on one or more machines and providing a particular type of function to clients. A **server** is the service software running on a single machine. A **client** is a process that can invoke a service using a set of operations that form its **client interface**. Sometimes a lower-level interface is defined for the actual cross-machine interaction; it is the **intermachine interface**.

Using this terminology, we say that a file system provides file services to clients. A client interface for a file service is formed by a set of primitive file operations, such as create a file, delete a file, read from a file, and write to a file. The primary hardware component that a file server controls is a set of local secondary-storage devices (usually, magnetic disks) on which files are stored and from which they are retrieved according to the clients' requests.

A DFS is a file system whose clients, servers, and storage devices are dispersed among the machines of a distributed system. Accordingly, service activity has to be carried out across the network. Instead of a single centralized data repository, the system frequently has multiple and independent storage devices. As you will see, the concrete configuration and implementation of a DFS may vary from system to system. In some configurations, servers run on dedicated machines; in others, a machine can be both a server and a client. A DFS can be implemented as part of a distributed operating system or, alternatively, by a software layer whose task is to manage the communication between conventional operating systems and file systems. The distinctive features of a DFS are the multiplicity and autonomy of clients and servers in the system.

Ideally, a DFS should appear to its clients to be a conventional, centralized file system. The multiplicity and dispersion of its servers and storage devices should be made invisible. That is, the client interface of a DFS should not distinguish between local and remote files. It is up to the DFS to locate the files and to arrange for the transport of the data. A **transparent** DFS facilitates user mobility by bringing a user's environment (that is, home directory) to wherever the user logs in.

The most important performance measure of a DFS is the amount of time needed to satisfy service requests. In conventional systems, this time consists of disk-access time and a small amount of CPU-processing time. In a DFS, however, a remote access has the additional overhead attributed to the distributed structure. This overhead includes the time to deliver the request to a server, as well as the time to get the response across the network back to the client. For each direction, in addition to the transfer of the information, there is the CPU overhead of running the communication protocol software. The performance of a DFS can be viewed as another dimension of the DFS's transparency. That is, the performance of an ideal DFS would be comparable to that of a conventional file system.

The fact that a DFS manages a set of dispersed storage devices is the DFS's key distinguishing feature. The overall storage space managed by a DFS is composed of different and remotely located smaller storage spaces. Usually, these constituent storage spaces correspond to sets of files. A **component unit** is the smallest set of files that can be stored on a single machine, independently from other units. All files belonging to the same component unit must reside in the same location.

17.2 Naming and Transparency

Naming is a mapping between logical and physical objects. For instance, users deal with logical data objects represented by file names, whereas the system manipulates physical blocks of data stored on disk tracks. Usually, a user refers to a file by a textual name. The latter is mapped to a lower-level numerical identifier that in turn is mapped to disk blocks. This multilevel mapping provides users with an abstraction of a file that hides the details of how and where on the disk the file is stored.

In a transparent DFS, a new dimension is added to the abstraction: that of hiding where in the network the file is located. In a conventional file system, the range of the naming mapping is an address within a disk. In a DFS, this range is expanded to include the specific machine on whose disk the file is stored. Going one step further with the concept of treating files as abstractions leads to the possibility of file replication. Given a file name, the mapping returns a set of the locations of this file's replicas. In this abstraction, both the existence of multiple copies and their locations are hidden.

17.2.1 Naming Structures

We need to differentiate two related notions regarding name mappings in a DFS:

1. Location transparency. The name of a file does not reveal any hint of the file's physical storage location.

2. Location independence. The name of a file does not need to be changed when the file's physical storage location changes.

Both definitions relate to the level of naming discussed previously, since files have different names at different levels (that is, user-level textual names and system-level numerical identifiers). A location-independent naming scheme is a dynamic mapping, since it can map the same file name to different locations at two different times. Therefore, location independence is a stronger property than is location transparency.

In practice, most of the current DFSs provide a static, location-transparent mapping for user-level names. These systems, however, do not support file migration; that is, changing the location of a file automatically is impossible. Hence, the notion of location independence is irrelevant for these systems. Files are associated permanently with a specific set of disk blocks. Files and disks can be moved between machines manually, but file migration implies an automatic, operating-system-initiated action. Only AFS and a few experimental file systems support location independence and file mobility. AFS supports file mobility mainly for administrative purposes. A protocol provides migration of AFS component units to satisfy high-level user requests, without changing either the user-level names or the low-level names of the corresponding files.

A few aspects can further differentiate location independence and static location transparency:

- Divorce of data from location, as exhibited by location independence, provides a better abstraction for files. A file name should denote the file's most significant attributes, which are its contents rather than its location. Location-independent files can be viewed as logical data containers that are not attached to a specific storage location. If only static location transparency is supported, the file name still denotes a specific, although hidden, set of physical disk blocks.

- Static location transparency provides users with a convenient way to share data. Users can share remote files by simply naming the files in a location-transparent manner, as though the files were local. Nevertheless, sharing the storage space is cumbersome, because logical names are still statically attached to physical storage devices. Location independence promotes sharing the storage space itself, as well as the data objects. When files can be mobilized, the overall, system-wide storage space looks like a single virtual resource. A possible benefit of such a view is the ability to balance the utilization of disks across the system.
- Location independence separates the naming hierarchy from the storage-devices hierarchy and from the intercomputer structure. By contrast, if static location transparency is used (although names are transparent), we can easily expose the correspondence between component units and machines. The machines are configured in a pattern similar to the naming structure. This configuration may restrict the architecture of the system unnecessarily and conflict with other considerations. A server in charge of a root directory is an example of a structure that is dictated by the naming hierarchy and contradicts decentralization guidelines.

Once the separation of name and location has been completed, clients can access files residing on remote server systems. In fact, these clients may be **diskless** and rely on servers to provide all files, including the operating-system kernel. Special protocols are needed for the boot sequence, however. Consider the problem of getting the kernel to a diskless workstation. The diskless workstation has no kernel, so it cannot use the DFS code to retrieve the kernel. Instead, a special boot protocol, stored in read-only memory (ROM) on the client, is invoked. It enables networking and retrieves only one special file (the kernel or boot code) from a fixed location. Once the kernel is copied over the network and loaded, its DFS makes all the other operating-system files available. The advantages of diskless clients are many, including lower cost (because the client machines require no disks) and greater convenience (when an operating-system upgrade occurs, only the server needs to be modified). The disadvantages are the added complexity of the boot protocols and the performance loss resulting from the use of a network rather than a local disk.

The current trend is for clients to use both local disks and remote file servers. Operating systems and networking software are stored locally; file systems containing user data—and possibly applications—are stored on remote file systems. Some client systems may store commonly used applications, such as word processors and Web browsers, on the local file system as well. Other, less commonly used applications may be **pushed** from the remote file server to the client on demand. The main reason for providing clients with local file systems rather than pure diskless systems is that disk drives are rapidly increasing in capacity and decreasing in cost, with new generations appearing every year or so. The same cannot be said for networks, which evolve every few years.

Overall, systems are growing more quickly than are networks, so extra work is needed to limit network access to improve system throughput.

17.2.2 Naming Schemes

There are three main approaches to naming schemes in a DFS. In the simplest approach, a file is identified by some combination of its host name and local name, which guarantees a unique system-wide name. In Ibis, for instance, a file is identified uniquely by the name *host:local-name,* where *local-name* is a UNIX-like path. This naming scheme is neither location transparent nor location independent. Nevertheless, the same file operations can be used for both local and remote files. The DFS is structured as a collection of isolated component units, each of which is an entire conventional file system. In this first approach, component units remain isolated, although means are provided to refer to a remote file. We do not consider this scheme any further in this text.

The second approach was popularized by Sun's network file system, NFS. NFS is the file-system component of ONC+, a networking package supported by many UNIX vendors. NFS provides a means to attach remote directories to local directories, thus giving the appearance of a coherent directory tree. Early NFS versions allowed only previously mounted remote directories to be accessed transparently. With the advent of the **automount** feature, mounts are done on demand, based on a table of mount points and file-structure names. Components are integrated to support transparent sharing, although this integration is limited and is not uniform, because each machine may attach different remote directories to its tree. The resulting structure is versatile.

We can achieve total integration of the component file systems by using the third approach. Here, a single global name structure spans all the files in the system. Ideally, the composed file-system structure is the same as the structure of a conventional file system. In practice, however, the many special files (for example, UNIX device files and machine-specific binary directories) make this goal difficult to attain.

To evaluate naming structures, we look at their **administrative complexity**. The most complex and most difficult-to-maintain structure is the NFS structure. Because any remote directory can be attached anywhere onto the local directory tree, the resulting hierarchy can be highly unstructured. If a server becomes unavailable, some arbitrary set of directories on different machines becomes unavailable. In addition, a separate accreditation mechanism controls which machine is allowed to attach which directory to its tree. Thus, a user might be able to access a remote directory tree on one client but be denied access on another client.

17.2.3 Implementation Techniques

Implementation of transparent naming requires a provision for the mapping of a file name to the associated location. To keep this mapping manageable, we must aggregate sets of files into component units and provide the mapping on a component-unit basis rather than on a single-file basis. This aggregation serves administrative purposes as well. UNIX-like systems use the hierarchical directory tree to provide name-to-location mapping and to aggregate files recursively into directories.

To enhance the availability of the crucial mapping information, we can use replication, local caching, or both. As we noted, location independence means that the mapping changes over time; hence, replicating the mapping makes a simple yet consistent update of this information impossible. A technique to overcome this obstacle is to introduce low-level **location-independent file identifiers**. Textual file names are mapped to lower-level file identifiers that indicate to which component unit the file belongs. These identifiers are still location independent. They can be replicated and cached freely without being invalidated by migration of component units. The inevitable price is the need for a second level of mapping, which maps component units to locations and needs a simple yet consistent update mechanism. Implementing UNIX-like directory trees using these low-level, location-independent identifiers makes the whole hierarchy invariant under component-unit migration. The only aspect that does change is the component-unit location mapping.

A common way to implement low-level identifiers is to use structured names. These names are bit strings that usually have two parts. The first part identifies the component unit to which the file belongs; the second part identifies the particular file within the unit. Variants with more parts are possible. The invariant of structured names, however, is that individual parts of the name are unique at all times only within the context of the rest of the parts. We can obtain uniqueness at all times by taking care not to reuse a name that is still in use, by adding sufficiently more bits (this method is used in AFS), or by using a timestamp as one part of the name (as done in Apollo Domain). Another way to view this process is that we are taking a location-transparent system, such as Ibis, and adding another level of abstraction to produce a location-independent naming scheme.

Aggregating files into component units and using lower-level location-independent file identifiers are techniques exemplified in AFS.

17.3 Remote File Access

Consider a user who requests access to a remote file. The server storing the file has been located by the naming scheme, and now the actual data transfer must take place.

One way to achieve this transfer is through a **remote-service mechanism**, whereby requests for accesses are delivered to the server, the server machine performs the accesses, and their results are forwarded back to the user. One of the most common ways of implementing remote service is the remote procedure call (RPC) paradigm, which we discussed in Chapter 3. A direct analogy exists between disk-access methods in conventional file systems and the remote-service method in a DFS: using the remote-service method is analogous to performing a disk access for each access request.

To ensure reasonable performance of a remote-service mechanism, we can use a form of caching. In conventional file systems, the rationale for caching is to reduce disk I/O (thereby increasing performance), whereas in DFSs, the goal is to reduce both network traffic and disk I/O. In the following discussion, we describe the implementation of caching in a DFS and contrast it with the basic remote-service paradigm.

17.3.1 Basic Caching Scheme

The concept of caching is simple. If the data needed to satisfy the access request are not already cached, then a copy of those data is brought from the server to the client system. Accesses are performed on the cached copy. The idea is to retain recently accessed disk blocks in the cache, so that repeated accesses to the same information can be handled locally, without additional network traffic. A replacement policy (for example, the least-recently-used algorithm) keeps the cache size bounded. No direct correspondence exists between accesses and traffic to the server. Files are still identified with one master copy residing at the server machine, but copies (or parts) of the file are scattered in different caches. When a cached copy is modified, the changes need to be reflected on the master copy to preserve the relevant consistency semantics. The problem of keeping the cached copies consistent with the master file is the **cache-consistency problem**, which we discuss in Section 17.3.4. DFS caching could just as easily be called **network virtual memory**; it acts similarly to demand-paged virtual memory, except that the backing store usually is not a local disk but rather a remote server. NFS allows the swap space to be mounted remotely, so it actually can implement virtual memory over a network, notwithstanding the resulting performance penalty.

The granularity of the cached data in a DFS can vary from blocks of a file to an entire file. Usually, more data are cached than are needed to satisfy a single access, so that many accesses can be served by the cached data. This procedure is much like disk read-ahead (Section 11.6.2). AFS caches files in large chunks (64 KB). The other systems discussed in this chapter support caching of individual blocks driven by client demand. Increasing the caching unit increases the hit ratio, but it also increases the miss penalty, because each miss requires more data to be transferred. It increases the potential for consistency problems as well. Selecting the unit of caching involves considering parameters such as the network transfer unit and the RPC protocol service unit (if an RPC protocol is used). The network transfer unit (for Ethernet, a packet) is about 1.5 KB, so larger units of cached data need to be disassembled for delivery and reassembled on reception.

Block size and total cache size are obviously of importance for block-caching schemes. In UNIX-like systems, common block sizes are 4 KB and 8 KB. For large caches (over 1 MB), large block sizes (over 8 KB) are beneficial. For smaller caches, large block sizes are less beneficial because they result in fewer blocks in the cache and a lower hit ratio.

17.3.2 Cache Location

Where should the cached data be stored—on disk or in main memory? Disk caches have one clear advantage over main-memory caches: they are reliable. Modifications to cached data are lost in a crash if the cache is kept in volatile memory. Moreover, if the cached data are kept on disk, they are still there during recovery, and there is no need to fetch them again. Main-memory caches have several advantages of their own, however:

- Main-memory caches permit workstations to be diskless.
- Data can be accessed more quickly from a cache in main memory than from one on a disk.

- Technology is moving toward larger and less expensive memory. The resulting performance speedup is predicted to outweigh the advantages of disk caches.
- The server caches (used to speed up disk I/O) will be in main memory regardless of where user caches are located; if we use main-memory caches on the user machine, too, we can build a single caching mechanism for use by both servers and users.

Many remote-access implementations can be thought of as hybrids of caching and remote service. In NFS, for instance, the implementation is based on remote service but is augmented with client- and server-side memory caching for performance. Similarly, Sprite's implementation is based on caching; but under certain circumstances, a remote-service method is adopted. Thus, to evaluate the two methods, we must evaluate the degree to which either method is emphasized.

The NFS protocol and most implementations do not provide disk caching. Recent Solaris implementations of NFS (Solaris 2.6 and beyond) include a client-side disk-caching option, the **cachefs** file system. Once the NFS client reads blocks of a file from the server, it caches them in memory as well as on disk. If the memory copy is flushed, or even if the system reboots, the disk cache is referenced. If a needed block is neither in memory nor in the cachefs disk cache, an RPC is sent to the server to retrieve the block, and the block is written into the disk cache as well as stored in the memory cache for client use.

17.3.3 Cache-Update Policy

The policy used to write modified data blocks back to the server's master copy has a critical effect on the system's performance and reliability. The simplest policy is to write data through to disk as soon as they are placed in any cache. The advantage of a **write-through policy** is reliability: little information is lost when a client system crashes. However, this policy requires each write access to wait until the information is sent to the server, so it causes poor write performance. Caching with write-through is equivalent to using remote service for write accesses and exploiting caching only for read accesses.

An alternative is the **delayed-write policy**, also known as **write-back caching**, where we delay updates to the master copy. Modifications are written to the cache and then are written through to the server at a later time. This policy has two advantages over write-through. First, because writes are made to the cache, write accesses complete much more quickly. Second, data may be overwritten before they are written back, in which case only the last update needs to be written at all. Unfortunately, delayed-write schemes introduce reliability problems, since unwritten data are lost whenever a user machine crashes.

Variations of the delayed-write policy differ in when modified data blocks are flushed to the server. One alternative is to flush a block when it is about to be ejected from the client's cache. This option can result in good performance, but some blocks can reside in the client's cache a long time before they are written back to the server. A compromise between this alternative and the write-through policy is to scan the cache at regular intervals and to flush blocks that have been modified since the most recent scan, just as UNIX scans

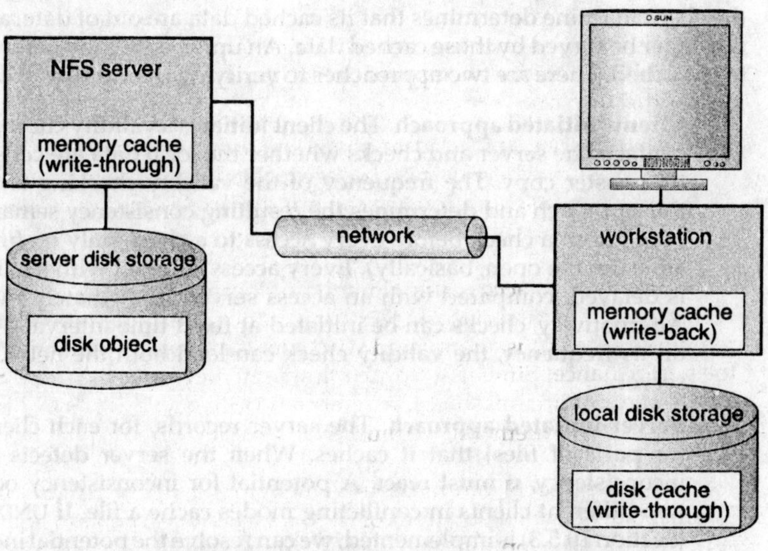

Figure 17.1 Cachefs and its use of caching.

its local cache. Sprite uses this policy with a 30-second interval. NFS uses the policy for file data, but once a write is issued to the server during a cache flush, the write must reach the server's disk before it is considered complete. NFS treats metadata (directory data and file-attribute data) differently. Any metadata changes are issued synchronously to the server. Thus, file-structure loss and directory-structure corruption are avoided when a client or the server crashes.

For NFS with cachefs, writes are also written to the local disk cache area when they are written to the server, to keep all copies consistent. Thus, NFS with cachefs improves performance over standard NFS on a read request with a cachefs cache hit but decreases performance for read or write requests with a cache miss. As with all caches, it is vital to have a high cache hit rate to gain performance. Figure 17.1 shows how cachefs uses write-through and write-back caching.

Yet another variation on delayed write is to write data back to the server when the file is closed. This **write-on-close policy** is used in AFS. In the case of files that are open for short periods or are modified rarely, this policy does not significantly reduce network traffic. In addition, the write-on-close policy requires the closing process to delay while the file is written through, which reduces the performance advantages of delayed writes. For files that are open for long periods and are modified frequently, however, the performance advantages of this policy over delayed write with more frequent flushing are apparent.

17.3.4 Consistency

A client machine is faced with the problem of deciding whether a locally cached copy of the data is consistent with the master copy (and hence can be used). If the client machine determines that its cached data are out of date, accesses can no longer be served by those cached data. An up-to-date copy of the data needs to be cached. There are two approaches to verifying the validity of cached data:

1. **Client-initiated approach**. The client initiates a validity check, in which it contacts the server and checks whether the local data are consistent with the master copy. The frequency of the validity checking is the crux of this approach and determines the resulting consistency semantics. It can range from a check before every access to a check only on first access to a file (on file open, basically). Every access coupled with a validity check is delayed, compared with an access served immediately by the cache. Alternatively, checks can be initiated at fixed time intervals. Depending on its frequency, the validity check can load both the network and the server.

2. **Server-initiated approach**. The server records, for each client, the files (or parts of files) that it caches. When the server detects a potential inconsistency, it must react. A potential for inconsistency occurs when two different clients in conflicting modes cache a file. If UNIX semantics (Section 10.5.3) is implemented, we can resolve the potential inconsistency by having the server play an active role. The server must be notified whenever a file is opened, and the intended mode (read or write) must be indicated for every open. The server can then act when it detects that a file has been opened simultaneously in conflicting modes by disabling caching for that particular file. Actually, disabling caching results in switching to a remote-service mode of operation.

17.3.5 A Comparison of Caching and Remote Service

Essentially, the choice between caching and remote service trades off potentially increased performance with decreased simplicity. We evaluate this tradeoff by listing the advantages and disadvantages of the two methods:

- When caching is used, the local cache can handle a substantial number of the remote accesses efficiently. Capitalizing on locality in file-access patterns makes caching even more attractive. Thus, most of the remote accesses will be served as fast as will local ones. Moreover, servers are contacted only occasionally, rather than for each access. Consequently, server load and network traffic are reduced, and the potential for scalability is enhanced. By contrast, when the remote-service method is used, every remote access is handled across the network. The penalty in network traffic, server load, and performance is obvious.

- Total network overhead is lower for transmitting big chunks of data (as is done in caching) than for transmitting series of responses to specific requests (as in the remote-service method). Furthermore, disk-access routines on the server may be better optimized if it is known that requests will always be for large, contiguous segments of data rather than for random disk blocks.

- The cache-consistency problem is the major drawback of caching. When access patterns exhibit infrequent writes, caching is superior. However, when writes are frequent, the mechanisms employed to overcome the consistency problem incur substantial overhead in terms of performance, network traffic, and server load.

- So that caching will confer a benefit, execution should be carried out on machines that have either local disks or large main memories. Remote access on diskless, small-memory-capacity machines should be done through the remote-service method.
- In caching, since data are transferred en masse between the server and the client, rather than in response to the specific needs of a file operation, the lower-level intermachine interface is different from the upper-level user interface. The remote-service paradigm, in contrast, is just an extension of the local file-system interface across the network. Thus, the intermachine interface mirrors the user interface.

17.4 Stateful versus Stateless Service

There are two approaches for storing server-side information when a client accesses remote files: either the server tracks each file being accessed by each client, or it simply provides blocks as they are requested by the client without knowledge of how those blocks are used. In the former case, the service provided is *stateful;* in the latter case, it is *stateless.*

The typical scenario involving a stateful file service is as follows: A client must perform an `open()` operation on a file before accessing that file. The server fetches information about the file from its disk, stores it in its memory, and gives the client a connection identifier that is unique to the client and the open file. (In UNIX terms, the server fetches the inode and gives the client a file descriptor, which serves as an index to an in-core table of inodes.) This identifier is used for subsequent accesses until the session ends. A stateful service is characterized as a connection between the client and the server during a session. Either on closing the file or through a garbage-collection mechanism, the server must reclaim the main-memory space used by clients that are no longer active. The key point regarding fault tolerance in a stateful service approach is that the server keeps main-memory information about its clients. AFS is a stateful file service.

A stateless file service avoids state information by making each request self-contained. That is, each request identifies the file and the position in the file (for read and write accesses) in full. The server does not need to keep a table of open files in main memory, although it usually does so for efficiency reasons. Moreover, there is no need to establish and terminate a connection through `open()` and `close()` operations. They are totally redundant, since each file operation stands on its own and is not considered part of a session. A client process would open a file, and that open would not result in the sending of a remote message. Reads and writes would take place as remote messages (or cache lookups). The final close by the client would again result in only a local operation. NFS is a stateless file service.

The advantage of a stateful over a stateless service is increased performance. File information is cached in main memory and can be accessed easily via the connection identifier, thereby saving disk accesses. In addition, a stateful server knows whether a file is open for sequential access and can therefore read ahead the next blocks. Stateless servers cannot do so, since they have no knowledge of the purpose of the client's requests.

The distinction between stateful and stateless service becomes more evident when we consider the effects of a crash that occurs during a service activity. A stateful server loses all its volatile state in a crash. Ensuring the graceful recovery of such a server involves restoring this state, usually by a recovery protocol based on a dialog with clients. Less graceful recovery requires that the operations that were underway when the crash occurred be aborted. A different problem is caused by client failures. The server needs to become aware of such failures so that it can reclaim space allocated to record the state of crashed client processes. This phenomenon is sometimes referred to as **orphan detection and elimination.**

A stateless computer server avoids these problems, since a newly reincarnated server can respond to a self-contained request without any difficulty. Therefore, the effects of server failures and recovery are almost unnoticeable. There is no difference between a slow server and a recovering server from a client's point of view. The client keeps retransmitting its request if it receives no response.

The penalty for using the robust stateless service is longer request messages and slower processing of requests, since there is no in-core information to speed the processing. In addition, stateless service imposes additional constraints on the design of the DFS. First, since each request identifies the target file, a uniform, system-wide, low-level naming scheme should be used. Translating remote to local names for each request would cause even slower processing of the requests. Second, since clients retransmit requests for file operations, these operations must be idempotent; that is, each operation must have the same effect and return the same output if executed several times consecutively. Self-contained read and write accesses are idempotent, as long as they use an absolute byte count to indicate the position within the file they access and do not rely on an incremental offset (as is done in UNIX `read()` and `write()` system calls). However, we must be careful when implementing destructive operations (such as deleting a file) to make them idempotent, too.

In some environments, a stateful service is a necessity. If the server employs the server-initiated method for cache validation, it cannot provide stateless service, since it maintains a record of which files are cached by which clients.

The way UNIX uses file descriptors and implicit offsets is inherently stateful. Servers must maintain tables to map the file descriptors to inodes and must store the current offset within a file. This requirement is why NFS, which employs a stateless service, does not use file descriptors and does include an explicit offset in every access.

17.5 File Replication

Replication of files on different machines in a distributed file system is a useful redundancy for improving availability. Multimachine replication can benefit performance too: selecting a nearby replica to serve an access request results in shorter service time.

The basic requirement of a replication scheme is that different replicas of the same file reside on failure-independent machines. That is, the availability

NFS V4

Our coverage of NFS thus far has only considered Version 3 (or V3) NFS. The most recent NFS standard is Version 4 (V4), and it differs fundamentally from previous versions. The most significant change is that the protocol is now *stateful*, meaning that the server maintains the state of the client session from the time the remote file is opened until it is closed. Thus, the NFS protocol now provides `open()` and `close()` operations; previous versions of NFS (which are stateless) provide no such operations. Furthermore, previous versions specify separate protocols for mounting remote file systems and for locking remote files. V4 provides all of these features under a single protocol. In particular, the *mount* protocol was eliminated, allowing NFS to work with network firewalls. The *mount* protocol was a notorious security hole in NFS implementations.

Additionally, V4 has enhanced the ability of clients to cache file data locally. This feature improves the performance of the distributed file system, as clients are able to resolve more file accesses from the local cache rather than having to go through the server. V4 allows clients to request file locks from servers as well. If the server grants the request, the client maintains the lock until it is released or its lease expires. (Clients are also permitted to renew existing leases.) Traditionally, UNIX-based systems provide advisory file locking, whereas Windows operating systems use mandatory locking. To allow NFS to work well with non-UNIX systems, V4 now provides mandatory locking as well. The new locking and caching mechanisms are based on the concept of **delegation**, whereby the server delegates responsibilities for a file's lock and contents to the client that requested the lock. That delegated client maintains in cache the current version of the file, and other clients can ask that delegated client for lock access and file contents until the delegated client relinquishes the lock and delegation.

Finally, whereas previous versions of NFS are based on the UDP network protocol, V4 is based on TCP, which allows it to better adjust to varying traffic loads on the network. Delegating these responsibilities to clients reduces the load on the server and improves cache coherency.

of one replica is not affected by the availability of the rest of the replicas. This obvious requirement implies that replication management is inherently a location-opaque activity. Provisions for placing a replica on a particular machine must be available.

It is desirable to hide the details of replication from users. Mapping a replicated file name to a particular replica is the task of the naming scheme. The existence of replicas should be invisible to higher levels. At lower levels, however, the replicas must be distinguished from one another by different lower-level names. Another transparency requirement is providing replication control at higher levels. Replication control includes determination of the degree of replication and of the placement of replicas. Under certain circumstances, we may want to expose these details to users. Locus, for instance, provides users and system administrators with mechanisms to control the replication scheme.

The main problem associated with replicas is updating. From a user's point of view, replicas of a file denote the same logical entity, and thus an update to any replica must be reflected on all other replicas. More precisely, the relevant consistency semantics must be preserved when accesses to replicas are viewed as virtual accesses to the replicas' logical files. If consistency is not of primary importance, it can be sacrificed for availability and performance. In this fundamental tradeoff in the area of fault tolerance, the choice is between preserving consistency at all costs, thereby creating a potential for indefinite blocking, and sacrificing consistency under some (we hope, rare) circumstances for the sake of guaranteed progress. Locus, for example, employs replication extensively and sacrifices consistency in the case of network partition for the sake of availability of files for read and write accesses.

Ibis uses a variation of the primary-copy approach. The domain of the name mapping is a pair *<primary-replica-identifier, local-replica-identifier>*. If no local replica exists, a special value is used. Thus, the mapping is relative to a machine. If the local replica is the primary one, the pair contains two identical identifiers. Ibis supports demand replication, an automatic replication-control policy similar to whole-file caching. Under demand replication, reading of a nonlocal replica causes it to be cached locally, thereby generating a new nonprimary replica. Updates are performed only on the primary copy and cause all other replicas to be invalidated through the sending of appropriate messages. Atomic and serialized invalidation of all nonprimary replicas is not guaranteed. Hence, a stale replica may be considered valid. To satisfy remote write accesses, we migrate the primary copy to the requesting machine.

17.6 An Example: AFS

Andrew is a distributed computing environment designed and implemented at Carnegie Mellon University. The Andrew file system (AFS) constitutes the underlying information-sharing mechanism among clients of the environment. The Transarc Corporation took over development of AFS and then was purchased by IBM. IBM has since produced several commercial implementations of AFS. AFS was subsequently chosen as the DFS for an industry coalition; the result was Transarc DFS, part of the distributed computing environment (DCE) from the OSF organization.

In 2000, IBM's Transarc Lab announced that AFS would be an open-source product (termed OpenAFS) available under the IBM public license, and Transarc DFS was canceled as a commercial product. OpenAFS is available under most commercial versions of UNIX as well as Linux and Microsoft Windows systems. Many UNIX vendors, as well as Microsoft, support the DCE system and its DFS, which is based on AFS, and work is ongoing to make DCE a cross-platform, universally accepted DFS. As AFS and Transarc DFS are very similar, we describe AFS throughout this section, unless Transarc DFS is named specifically.

AFS seeks to solve many of the problems of the simpler DFSs, such as NFS, and is arguably the most feature-rich nonexperimental DFS. It features a uniform name space, location-independent file sharing, client-side caching with cache consistency, and secure authentication via Kerberos. It also includes server-side caching in the form of replicas, with high availability through automatic switchover to a replica if the source server is unavailable. One of the most formidable attributes of AFS is scalability: the Andrew system is targeted to span over 5,000 workstations. Between AFS and Transarc DFS, there are hundreds of implementations worldwide.

17.6.1 Overview

AFS distinguishes between *client machines* (sometimes referred to as *workstations*) and dedicated *server machines*. Servers and clients originally ran only 4.2 BSD UNIX, but AFS has been ported to many operating systems. The clients and servers are interconnected by a network of LANs or WANs.

Clients are presented with a partitioned space of file names: a local name space and a shared name space. Dedicated servers, collectively called *Vice* after the name of the software they run, present the shared name space to the clients as a homogeneous, identical, and location-transparent file hierarchy. The local name space is the root file system of a workstation, from which the shared name space descends. Workstations run the *Virtue* protocol to communicate with Vice, and each is required to have a local disk where it stores its local name space. Servers collectively are responsible for the storage and management of the shared name space. The local name space is small, is distinct for each workstation, and contains system programs essential for autonomous operation and better performance. Also local are temporary files and files that the workstation owner, for privacy reasons, explicitly wants to store locally.

Viewed at a finer granularity, clients and servers are structured in clusters interconnected by a WAN. Each cluster consists of a collection of workstations on a LAN and a representative of Vice called a cluster server, and each cluster is connected to the WAN by a router. The decomposition into clusters is done primarily to address the problem of scale. For optimal performance, workstations should use the server on their own cluster most of the time, thereby making cross-cluster file references relatively infrequent.

The file-system architecture is also based on considerations of scale. The basic heuristic is to offload work from the servers to the clients, in light of experience indicating that server CPU speed is the system's bottleneck. Following this heuristic, the key mechanism for remote file operations is to cache files in large chunks (64 KB). This feature reduces file-open latency and allows reads and writes to be directed to the cached copy without frequently involving the servers.

Briefly, here are a few additional issues in the design of AFS:

- **Client mobility**. Clients are able to access any file in the shared name space from any workstation. A client may notice some initial performance degradation due to the caching of files when accessing files from a workstation other than the usual one.

- **Security**. The Vice interface is considered the boundary of trustworthiness, because no client programs are executed on Vice machines. Authentication and secure-transmission functions are provided as part of a connection-based communication package based on the RPC paradigm. After mutual authentication, a Vice server and a client communicate via encrypted messages. Encryption is performed by hardware devices or (more slowly) in software. Information about clients and groups is stored in a protection database replicated at each server.

- **Protection**. AFS provides access lists for protecting directories and the regular UNIX bits for file protection. The access list may contain information about those users allowed to access a directory, as well as information about those users *not* allowed to access it. Thus, it is simple to specify that everyone except, say, Jim can access a directory. AFS supports the access types read, write, lookup, insert, administer, lock, and delete.

- **Heterogeneity**. Defining a clear interface to Vice is a key for integration of diverse workstation hardware and operating systems. So that heterogeneity is facilitated, some files in the local */bin* directory are symbolic links pointing to machine-specific executable files residing in Vice.

17.6.2 The Shared Name Space

AFS's shared name space is made up of component units called volumes. The volumes are unusually small component units. Typically, they are associated with the files of a single client. Few volumes reside within a single disk partition, and they may grow (up to a quota) and shrink in size. Conceptually, volumes are glued together by a mechanism similar to the UNIX mount mechanism. However, the granularity difference is significant, since in UNIX only an entire disk partition (containing a file system) can be mounted. Volumes are a key administrative unit and play a vital role in identifying and locating an individual file.

A Vice file or directory is identified by a low-level identifier called a fid. Each AFS directory entry maps a path-name component to a fid. A fid is 96 bits long and has three equal-length components: a *volume number*, a *vnode number*, and a *uniquifier*. The vnode number is used as an index into an array containing the inodes of files in a single volume. The uniquifier allows reuse of vnode numbers, thereby keeping certain data structures compact. Fids are location transparent; therefore, file movements from server to server do not invalidate cached directory contents.

Location information is kept on a volume basis in a volume-location database replicated on each server. A client can identify the location of every volume in the system by querying this database. The aggregation of files into volumes makes it possible to keep the location database at a manageable size.

To balance the available disk space and utilization of servers, volumes need to be migrated among disk partitions and servers. When a volume is shipped to its new location, its original server is left with temporary forwarding information, so that the location database need not be updated synchronously. While the volume is being transferred, the original server can still handle updates, which are shipped later to the new server. At some point, the volume is briefly disabled so that the recent modifications can be processed; then, the new volume becomes available again at the new site. The volume-movement operation is atomic; if either server crashes, the operation is aborted.

Read-only replication at the granularity of an entire volume is supported for system-executable files and for seldom-updated files in the upper levels of the Vice name space. The volume-location database specifies the server containing the only read–write copy of a volume and a list of read-only replication sites.

17.6.3 File Operations and Consistency Semantics

The fundamental architectural principle in AFS is the caching of entire files from servers. Accordingly, a client workstation interacts with Vice servers only during opening and closing of files, and even this interaction is not always necessary. Reading and writing files do not cause remote interaction (in contrast to the remote-service method). This key distinction has far-reaching ramifications for performance, as well as for semantics of file operations.

The operating system on each workstation intercepts file-system calls and forwards them to a client-level process on that workstation. This process, called *Venus,* caches files from Vice when they are opened and stores modified copies of files back on the servers from which they came when they are closed. Venus may contact Vice only when a file is opened or closed; reading and writing of individual bytes of a file are performed directly on the cached copy and bypass Venus. As a result, writes at some sites are not visible immediately at other sites.

Caching is further exploited for future opens of the cached file. Venus assumes that cached entries (files or directories) are valid unless notified otherwise. Therefore, Venus does not need to contact Vice on a file open to validate the cached copy. The mechanism to support this policy, called callback, dramatically reduces the number of cache-validation requests received by servers. It works as follows. When a client caches a file or a directory, the server updates its state information to record this caching. We say that the client has a callback on that file. The server notifies the client before allowing another client to modify the file. In such a case, we say that the server removes the callback on the file for the former client. A client can use a cached file for open purposes only when the file has a callback. If a client closes a file after modifying it, all other clients caching this file lose their callbacks. Therefore, when these clients open the file later, they have to get the new version from the server.

Reading and writing bytes of a file are done directly by the kernel without Venus's intervention on the cached copy. Venus regains control when the file is closed. If the file has been modified locally, it updates the file on the appropriate server. Thus, the only occasions on which Venus contacts Vice servers are on opens of files that either are not in the cache or have had their callback revoked and on closes of locally modified files.

Basically, AFS implements session semantics. The only exceptions are file operations other than the primitive read and write (such as protection changes at the directory level), which are visible everywhere on the network immediately after the operation completes.

In spite of the callback mechanism, a small amount of cached validation traffic is still present, usually to replace callbacks lost because of machine or network failures. When a workstation is rebooted, Venus considers all cached files and directories suspect, and it generates a cache-validation request for the first use of each such entry.

The callback mechanism forces each server to maintain callback information and each client to maintain validity information. If the amount of callback information maintained by a server is excessive, the server can break callbacks and reclaim some storage by unilaterally notifying clients and revoking the validity of their cached files. If the callback state maintained by Venus gets out of sync with the corresponding state maintained by the servers, some inconsistency may result.

Venus also caches contents of directories and symbolic links, for path-name translation. Each component in the path name is fetched, and a callback is established for it if it is not already cached or if the client does not have a callback on it. Venus does lookups on the fetched directories locally, using fids. No requests are forwarded from one server to another. At the end of a path-name traversal, all the intermediate directories and the target file are in the cache with callbacks on them. Future open calls to this file will involve no network communication at all, unless a callback is broken on a component of the path name.

The only exception to the caching policy is a modification to a directory that is made directly on the server responsible for that directory for reasons of integrity. The Vice interface has well-defined operations for such purposes. Venus reflects the changes in its cached copy to avoid re-fetching the directory.

17.6.4 Implementation

Client processes are interfaced to a UNIX kernel with the usual set of system calls. The kernel is modified slightly to detect references to Vice files in the relevant operations and to forward the requests to the client-level Venus process at the workstation.

Venus carries out path-name translation component by component, as described above. It has a mapping cache that associates volumes to server locations in order to avoid server interrogation for an already known volume location. If a volume is not present in this cache, Venus contacts any server to which it already has a connection, requests the location information, and enters that information into the mapping cache. Unless Venus already has a connection to the server, it establishes a new connection. It then uses this connection to fetch the file or directory. Connection establishment is needed for authentication and security purposes. When a target file is found and cached, a copy is created on the local disk. Venus then returns to the kernel, which opens the cached copy and returns its handle to the client process.

The UNIX file system is used as a low-level storage system for both AFS servers and clients. The client cache is a local directory on the workstation's disk. Within this directory are files whose names are placeholders for cache entries. Both Venus and server processes access UNIX files directly by the latter's inodes to avoid the expensive path-name-to-inode translation routine (*namei*). Because the internal inode interface is not visible to client-level processes (both Venus and server processes are client-level processes), an appropriate set of additional system calls was added. DFS uses its own journaling file system to improve performance and reliability over UFS.

Venus manages two separate caches: one for status and the other for data. It uses a simple least-recently-used (LRU) algorithm to keep each of them bounded in size. When a file is flushed from the cache, Venus notifies the appropriate server to remove the callback for this file. The status cache is kept in virtual memory to allow rapid servicing of `stat()` (file-status-returning) system calls. The data cache is resident on the local disk, but the UNIX I/O buffering mechanism does some caching of disk blocks in memory that is transparent to Venus.

A single client-level process on each file server services all file requests from clients. This process uses a lightweight-process package with non-preemptible scheduling to service many client requests concurrently. The RPC package is integrated with the lightweight-process package, thereby allowing the file server to concurrently make or service one RPC per lightweight process. The RPC package is built on top of a low-level datagram abstraction. Whole-file transfer is implemented as a side effect of the RPC calls. One RPC connection exists per client, but there is no a priori binding of lightweight processes to these connections. Instead, a pool of lightweight processes services client requests on all connections. The use of a single multithreaded server process allows the caching of data structures needed to service requests. On the negative side, a crash of a single server process has the disastrous effect of paralyzing this particular server.

17.7 Summary

A DFS is a file-service system whose clients, servers, and storage devices are dispersed among the sites of a distributed system. Accordingly, service activity has to be carried out across the network; instead of a single centralized data repository, there are multiple independent storage devices.

Ideally, a DFS should look to its clients like a conventional, centralized file system. The multiplicity and dispersion of its servers and storage devices should be made transparent. That is, the client interface of a DFS should not distinguish between local and remote files. It is up to the DFS to locate the files and to arrange for the transport of the data. A transparent DFS facilitates client mobility by bringing the client's environment to the site where the client logs in.

There are several approaches to naming schemes in a DFS. In the simplest approach, files are named by some combination of their host name and local name, which guarantees a unique system-wide name. Another approach, popularized by NFS, provides a means to attach remote directories to local directories, thus giving the appearance of a coherent directory tree.

Requests to access a remote file are usually handled by two complementary methods. With remote service, requests for accesses are delivered to the server. The server machine performs the accesses, and their results are forwarded back to the client. With caching, if the data needed to satisfy the access request are not already cached, then a copy of the data is brought from the server to the client. Accesses are performed on the cached copy. The idea is to retain recently accessed disk blocks in the cache, so that repeated accesses to the same information can be handled locally, without additional network traffic. A replacement policy is used to keep the cache size bounded. The problem of keeping the cached copies consistent with the master file is the cache-consistency problem.

There are two approaches to server-side information. Either the server tracks each file the client accesses, or it simply provides blocks as the client requests them without knowledge of their use. These approaches are the stateful versus stateless service paradigms.

Replication of files on different machines is a useful redundancy for improving availability. Multimachine replication can benefit performance, too, since selecting a nearby replica to serve an access request results in shorter service time.

AFS is a feature-rich DFS characterized by location independence and location transparency. It also imposes significant consistency semantics. Caching and replication are used to improve performance.

Exercises

17.1 Discuss whether AFS and NFS provide the following: (a) location transparency and (b) location independence.

17.2 Discuss whether clients in the following systems can obtain inconsistent or stale data from the file server and, if so, under what scenarios this could occur.

a. AFS

b. Sprite

c. NFS

17.3 Consider AFS, which is a stateful distributed file system. What actions need to be performed to recover from a server crash in order to preserve the consistency guaranteed by the system?

17.4 Discuss the advantages and disadvantages of path-name translation in which the client ships the entire path to the server requesting a translation for the entire path name of the file.

17.5 Under what circumstances would a client prefer a location-transparent DFS? Under what circumstances would she prefer a location-independent DFS? Discuss the reasons for these preferences.

17.6 Which of the example DFSs discussed in this chapter would handle a large, multiclient database application most efficiently? Explain your answer.

17.7 What are the benefits of mapping objects into virtual memory, as Apollo Domain does? What are the drawbacks?

17.8 Compare and contrast the techniques of caching disk blocks locally, on a client system, and remotely, on a server.

17.9 What aspects of a distributed system would you select for a system running on a totally reliable network?

Bibliographical Notes

Consistency and recovery control for replicated files are examined by Davcev and Burkhard [1985]. Management of replicated files in a UNIX environment is covered by Brereton [1986] and Purdin et al. [1987]. Wah [1984] discusses the issue of file placement on distributed computer systems. A detailed survey of mainly centralized file servers appears in Svobodova [1984].

Sun's network file system (NFS) is described by Callaghan [2000] and Sandberg et al. [1985]. The AFS system is discussed by Morris et al. [1986], Howard et al. [1988], and Satyanarayanan [1990]. Information about OpenAFS is available from http://www.openafs.org

Many different and interesting DFSs are not covered in detail in this text, including UNIX United, Sprite, and Locus. UNIX United is described by Brownbridge et al. [1982]. The Locus system is discussed by Popek and Walker [1985]. The Sprite system is described by Ousterhout et al. [1988] and Nelson et al. [1988]. Distributed file systems for mobile storage devices are discussed in Kistler and Satyanarayanan [1992] and Sobti et al. [2004]. Considerable research has also been performed on cluster-based distributed file systems (Anderson et al. [1995], Lee and Thekkath [1996], Thekkath et al. [1997], and Anderson et al. [2000]). Distributed storage systems for large-scale, wide-area settings are presented in Dabek et al. [2001] and Kubiatowicz et al. [2000].

CHAPTER 18

Distributed Synchronization

In Chapter 6, we described various mechanisms that allow processes to synchronize their actions. We also discussed a number of schemes to ensure the atomicity of a transaction that executes either in isolation or concurrently with other transactions. In Chapter 7, we described various methods that an operating system can use to deal with the deadlock problem. In this chapter, we examine how centralized synchronization mechanisms can be extended to a distributed environment. We also discuss methods for handling deadlocks in a distributed system.

CHAPTER OBJECTIVES

- To describe various methods for achieving mutual exclusion in a distributed system.
- To explain how atomic transactions can be implemented in a distributed system.
- To show how some of the concurrency-control schemes discussed in Chapter 6 can be modified for use in a distributed environment.
- To present schemes for handling deadlock prevention, deadlock avoidance, and deadlock detection in a distributed system.

18.1 Event Ordering

In a centralized system, we can always determine the order in which two events occurred, since the system has a single common memory and clock. Many applications may require us to determine order. For example, in a resource-allocation scheme, we specify that a resource can be used only *after* the resource has been granted. A distributed system, however, has no common memory and no common clock. Therefore, it is sometimes impossible to say which of two events occurred first. The *happened-before* relation, discussed next, is only a partial ordering of the events in distributed systems. Since the ability to define a total ordering is crucial in many applications, we present a distributed algorithm for extending the *happened-before* relation to a consistent total ordering of all the events in the system.

18.1.1 The Happened-Before Relation

Since we are considering only sequential processes, all events executed in a single process are totally ordered. Also, by the law of causality, a message can be received only after it has been sent. Therefore, we can define the *happened-before* relation (denoted by →) on a set of events as follows (assuming that sending and receiving a message constitutes an event):

1. If A and B are events in the same process, and A was executed before B, then A → B.
2. If A is the event of sending a message by one process and B is the event of receiving that message by another process, then A → B.
3. If A → B and B → C, then A → C.

Since an event cannot happen before itself, the → relation is an irreflexive partial ordering.

If two events, A and B, are not related by the → relation (that is, A did not happen before B, and B did not happen before A), then we say that these two events were executed concurrently. In this case, neither event can causally affect the other. If, however, A → B, then it is possible for event A to affect event B causally.

A space–time diagram, such as that in Figure 18.1, can best illustrate the definitions of concurrency and *happened-before*. The horizontal direction represents space (that is, different processes), and the vertical direction represents time. The labeled vertical lines denote processes (or processors). The labeled dots denote events. A wavy line denotes a message sent from one process to another. Events are concurrent if and only if no path exists between them.

For example, these are some of the events related by the *happened-before* relation in Figure 18.1:

$$p_1 \rightarrow q_2$$
$$r_0 \rightarrow q_4$$
$$q_3 \rightarrow r_4$$
$$p_1 \rightarrow q_4 \text{ (since } p_1 \rightarrow q_2 \text{ and } q_2 \rightarrow q_4\text{)}$$

These are some of the concurrent events in the system:

q_0 and p_2
r_0 and q_3
r_0 and p_3
q_3 and p_3

We cannot know which of two concurrent events, such as q_0 and p_2, happened first. However, since neither event can affect the other (there is no way for one of them to know whether the other has occurred yet), it is not important which

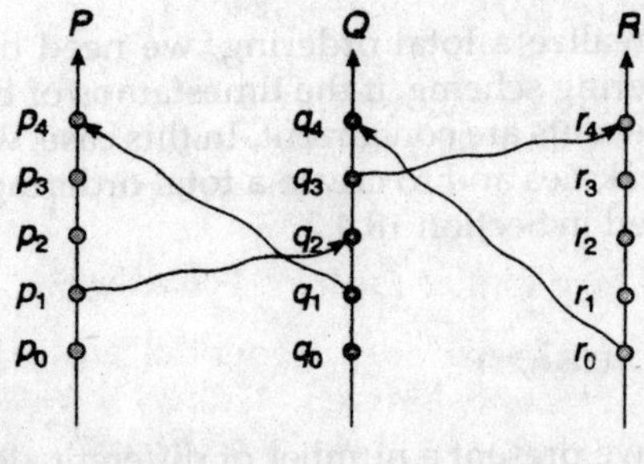

Figure 18.1 Relative time for three concurrent processes.

happened first. It is important only that any processes that care about the order of two concurrent events agree on some order.

18.1.2 Implementation

To determine that an event A happened before an event B, we need either a common clock or a set of perfectly synchronized clocks. Since neither of these is available in a distributed system, we must define the *happened-before* relation without the use of physical clocks.

First we associate with each system event a **timestamp**. We can then define the **global ordering** requirement: for every pair of events A and B, if A → B, then the timestamp of A is less than the timestamp of B. (Below, we will see that the converse need not be true.)

How do we enforce the global ordering requirement in a distributed environment? We define within *each* process P_i a **logical clock**, LC_i. The logical clock can be implemented as a simple counter incremented between any two successive events executed within a process. Since the logical clock has a **monotonically** increasing value, it assigns a unique number to every event, and if an event A occurs before event B in process P_i, then $LC_i(A) < LC_i(B)$. The timestamp for an event is the value of the logical clock for that event. This scheme ensures that for any two events in the same process the global ordering requirement is met.

Unfortunately, this scheme does not ensure that the global ordering requirement is met across processes. To illustrate the problem, consider two processes P_1 and P_2 that communicate with each other. Suppose that P_1 sends a message to P_2 (event A) with $LC_1(A) = 200$, and P_2 receives the message (event B) with $LC_2(B) = 195$ (because the processor for P_2 is slower than the processor for P_1, its logical clock ticks more slowly). This situation violates our requirement, since A → B but the timestamp of A is greater than the timestamp of B.

To resolve this difficulty, we require a process to advance its logical clock when it receives a message whose timestamp is greater than the current value of its logical clock. In particular, if process P_i receives a message (event B) with timestamp t and $LC_i(B) \leq t$, then it should advance its clock so that $LC_i(B) = t + 1$. Thus, in our example, when P_2 receives the message from P_1, it will advance its logical clock so that $LC_2(B) = 201$.

Finally, to realize a total ordering, we need only observe that, with our timestamp-ordering scheme, if the timestamps of two events, A and B, are the same, then the events are concurrent. In this case, we may use process identity numbers to break ties and to create a total ordering. The use of timestamps is further discussed in Section 18.4.2.

18.2 Mutual Exclusion

In this section, we present a number of different algorithms for implementing mutual exclusion in a distributed environment. We assume that the system consists of n processes, each of which resides at a different processor. To simplify our discussion, we assume that processes are numbered uniquely from 1 to n and that a one-to-one mapping exists between processes and processors (that is, each process has its own processor).

18.2.1 Centralized Approach

In a centralized approach to providing mutual exclusion, one of the processes in the system is chosen to coordinate the entry to the critical section. Each process that wants to invoke mutual exclusion sends a *request* message to the coordinator. When the process receives a *reply* message from the coordinator, it can enter its critical section. After exiting its critical section, the process sends a *release* message to the coordinator and proceeds with its execution.

On receiving a *request* message, the coordinator checks to see whether some other process is in its critical section. If no process is in its critical section, the coordinator immediately sends back a *reply* message. Otherwise, the request is queued. When the coordinator receives a *release* message, it removes one of the *request* messages from the queue (in accordance with some scheduling algorithm) and sends a *reply* message to the requesting process.

It should be clear that this algorithm ensures mutual exclusion. In addition, if the scheduling policy within the coordinator is fair—such as first-come, first-served (FCFS) scheduling—no starvation can occur. This scheme requires three messages per critical-section entry: a *request*, a *reply*, and a *release*.

If the coordinator process fails, then a new process must take its place. In Section 18.6, we describe some algorithms for electing a unique new coordinator. Once a new coordinator has been elected, it must poll all the processes in the system to reconstruct its *request* queue. Once the queue has been constructed, the computation can resume.

18.2.2 Fully Distributed Approach

If we want to distribute the decision making across the entire system, then the solution is far more complicated. One approach, described next, uses an algorithm based on the event-ordering scheme described in Section 18.1.

When a process P_i wants to enter its critical section, it generates a new timestamp, *TS*, and sends the message *request*(P_i, *TS*) to all processes in the system (including itself). On receiving a *request* message, a process may reply immediately (that is, send a *reply* message back to P_i), or it may defer sending a reply back (because it is already in its critical section, for example). A process that has received a *reply* message from all other processes in the system can enter its critical section, queueing incoming requests and deferring them. After exiting its critical section, the process sends *reply* messages to all its deferred requests.

The decision whether process P_i replies immediately to a *request*(P_j, TS) message or defers its reply is based on three factors:

1. If process P_i is in its critical section, then it defers its reply to P_j.
2. If process P_i does *not* want to enter its critical section, then it sends a reply immediately to P_j.
3. If process P_i wants to enter its critical section but has not yet entered it, then it compares its own *request* timestamp with the timestamp of the incoming request made by process P_j. If its own *request* timestamp is greater than that of the incoming request, then it sends a reply immediately to P_j (P_j asked first). Otherwise, the reply is deferred.

This algorithm exhibits the following desirable behavior:

- Mutual exclusion is obtained.
- Freedom from deadlock is ensured.
- Freedom from starvation is ensured, since entry to the critical section is scheduled according to the timestamp ordering. The timestamp ordering ensures that processes are served in FCFS order.
- The number of messages per critical-section entry is $2 \times (n-1)$. This number represents the minimum number of required messages per critical-section entry when processes act independently and concurrently.

To illustrate how the algorithm functions, we consider a system consisting of processes P_1, P_2, and P_3. Suppose that processes P_1 and P_3 want to enter their critical sections. Process P_1 then sends a message *request* (P_1, timestamp = 10) to processes P_2 and P_3, while process P_3 sends a message *request* (P_3, timestamp = 4) to processes P_1 and P_2. (The timestamps 4 and 10 were obtained from the logical clocks described in Section 18.1.) When process P_2 receives these *request* messages, it replies immediately. When process P_1 receives the *request* from process P_3, it replies immediately, since the timestamp (10) on its own *request* message is greater than the timestamp (4) for process P_3. When process P_3 receives the *request* message from process P_1, it defers its reply, since the timestamp (4) on its *request* message is less than the timestamp (10) for the message from process P_1. On receiving replies from both process P_1 and process P_2, process P_3 can enter its critical section. After exiting its critical section, process P_3 sends a reply to process P_1, which can then enter its critical section.

Because this scheme requires the participation of all the processes in the system, it has three undesirable consequences:

1. The processes need to know the identity of all other processes in the system. When a new process joins the group of processes participating in the mutual-exclusion algorithm, the following actions need to be taken:

a. The process must receive the names of all the other processes in the group.

b. The name cf the new process must be distributed to all the other processes in the group.

This task is not as trivial as it may seem, since some *request* and *reply* messages may be circulating in the system when the new process joins the group. The interested reader is referred to the bibliographical notes at the end of the chapter.

2. If one process fails, then the entire scheme collapses. We can resolve this difficulty by continuously monitoring the state of all processes in the system. If one process fails, then all other processes are notified, so that they will no longer send *request* messages to the failed process. When a process recovers, it must initiate the procedure that allows it to rejoin the group.

3. Processes that have not entered their critical section must pause frequently to assure other processes that they intend to enter the critical section.

Because of these difficulties, this protocol is best suited for small, stable sets of cooperating processes.

18.2.3 Token-Passing Approach

Another method of providing mutual exclusion is to circulate a token among the processes in the system. A **token** is a special type of message that is passed from process to process. Possession of the token entitles the holder to enter the critical section. Since there is only a single token, only one process can be in its critical section at a time.

We assume that the processes in the system are *logically* organized in a **ring structure**. The physical communication network need not be a ring. As long as the processes are connected to one another, it is possible to implement a logical ring. To implement mutual exclusion, we pass the token around the ring. When a process receives the token, it may enter its critical section, keeping the token. After the process exits its critical section, the token is passed around again. If the process receiving the token does not want to enter its critical section, it passes the token to its neighbor. This scheme is similar to algorithm 1 in Chapter 6, but a token is substituted for a shared variable.

If the ring is unidirectional, freedom from starvation is ensured. The number of messages required to implement mutual exclusion may vary from one message per entry, in the case of high contention (that is, every process wants to enter its critical section), to an infinite number of messages, in the case of low contention (that is, no process wants to enter its critical section).

Two types of failure must be considered. First, if the token is lost, an election must be called to generate a new token. Second, if a process fails, a new logical ring must be established. In Section 18.6, we present an election algorithm; others are possible. The development of an algorithm for reconstructing the ring is left to you in Exercise 18.4.

18.3 Atomicity

In Chapter 6, we introduced the concept of an atomic transaction, which is a program unit that must be executed **atomically**. That is, either all the operations associated with it are executed to completion, or none are performed. When we are dealing with a distributed system, ensuring the atomicity of a transaction becomes much more complicated than in a centralized system. This difficulty occurs because several sites may be participating in the execution of a single transaction. The failure of one of these sites, or the failure of a communication link connecting the sites, may result in erroneous computations.

Ensuring that the execution of transactions in the distributed system preserves atomicity is the function of the **transaction coordinator**. Each site has its own local transaction coordinator, which is responsible for coordinating the execution of all the transactions initiated at that site. For each such transaction, the coordinator is responsible for the following:

- Starting the execution of the transaction
- Breaking the transaction into a number of subtransactions and distributing these subtransactions to the appropriate sites for execution
- Coordinating the termination of the transaction, which may result in the transactions being committed at all sites or aborted at all sites

We assume that each local site maintains a log for recovery purposes.

18.3.1 The Two-Phase Commit Protocol

For atomicity to be ensured, all the sites in which a transaction T has executed must agree on the final outcome of the execution. T must either commit at all sites, or it must abort at all sites. To ensure this property, the transaction coordinator of T must execute a **commit protocol**. Among the simplest and most widely used commit protocols is the **two-phase commit (2PC) protocol**, which we discuss next.

Assume that T is a transaction initiated at site S_i and that the transaction coordinator at S_i is C_i. When T completes its execution—that is, when all the sites at which T has executed inform C_i that T has completed—then C_i starts the 2PC protocol.

- **Phase 1**. C_i adds the record <prepare T> to the log and forces the record onto stable storage. It then sends a *prepare (T)* message to all the sites at which T has executed. On receiving the message, the transaction manager at each of these sites determines whether it is willing to commit its portion of T. If the answer is *no*, it adds a record <no T> to the log, and then it responds by sending an *abort (T)* message to C_i. If the answer is *yes*, it adds a record <ready T> to the log and forces all the log records corresponding to T onto stable storage. The transaction manager then replies with a *ready (T)* message to C_i.
- **Phase 2**. When C_i has received responses to the *prepare (T)* message from all the sites, or when a pre-specified interval of time has elapsed since the *prepare (T)* message was sent out, C_i can determine whether the transaction

T can be committed or aborted. Transaction T can be committed if C_i has received a *ready (T)* message from all the participating sites. Otherwise, transaction T must be aborted. Depending on the verdict, either a record <commit T> or a record <abort T> is added to the log and forced onto stable storage. At this point, the fate of the transaction has been sealed. Following this, the coordinator sends either a *commit (T)* or an *abort (T)* message to all participating sites. When a site receives that message, it records the message in the log.

A site at which T has executed can unconditionally abort T at any time prior to its sending the message *ready (T)* to the coordinator. The *ready (T)* message is, in effect, a promise by a site to follow the coordinator's order to commit T or to abort T. A site can make such a promise only when the needed information is stored in stable storage. Otherwise, if the site crashes after sending *ready (T)*, it may be unable to make good on its promise.

Since unanimity is required to commit a transaction, the fate of T is sealed as soon as at least one site responds with *abort (T)*. Note that the coordinator site S_i can decide unilaterally to abort T, as it is one of the sites at which T has executed. The final verdict regarding T is determined at the time the coordinator writes that verdict (commit or abort) to the log and forces it to stable storage.

In some implementations of the 2PC protocol, a site sends an *acknowledge (T)* message to the coordinator at the end of the second phase of the protocol. When the coordinator has received the *acknowledge (T)* message from all the sites, it adds the record <complete T> to the log.

18.3.2 Failure Handling in 2PC

We now examine in detail how 2PC responds to various types of failures. As we shall see, one major disadvantage of the 2PC protocol is that coordinator failure may result in blocking, and a decision either to commit or to abort T may have to be postponed until the coordinator recovers.

18.3.2.1 Failure of a Participating Site

When a participating site S_k recovers from a failure, it must examine its log to determine the fate of those transactions that were in the midst of execution when the failure occurred. Suppose that T is one such transaction. How will S_k deal with T? We consider each of the possible alternatives:

- The log contains a <commit T> record. In this case, the site executes `redo`(T).
- The log contains an <abort T> record. In this case, the site executes `undo`(T).
- The log contains a <ready T> record. In this case, the site must consult C_i to determine the fate of T. If C_i is up, it tells S_k whether T committed or aborted. In the former case, it executes `redo`(T); in the latter case, it executes `undo`(T). If C_i is down, S_k must try to find out the fate of T from other sites. It does so by sending a *query-status (T)* message to all the sites in the system. On receiving such a message, a site must consult

its log to determine whether T has executed there and, if so, whether T committed or aborted. It then notifies S_k about this outcome. If no site has the appropriate information (that is, whether T committed or aborted), then S_k can neither abort nor commit T. The decision concerning T is postponed until S_k can obtain the needed information. Thus, S_k must periodically resend the *query-status (T)* message to the other sites. It does so until a site responds with the needed information. The site at which C_i resides always has this information.

- The log contains no control records (abort, commit, ready) concerning T. The absence of control records implies that S_k failed before responding to the *prepare (T)* message from C_i. Since the failure of S_k means that it could not have sent such a response, by our algorithm, C_i must have aborted T. Hence, S_k must execute undo(T).

18.3.2.2 Failure of the Coordinator

If the coordinator fails in the midst of the execution of the commit protocol for transaction T, then the participating sites must decide the fate of T. We shall see that, in certain cases, the participating sites cannot decide whether to commit or abort T, and therefore these sites must wait for the recovery of the failed coordinator.

- If an active site contains a <commit T> record in its log, then T must be committed.
- If an active site contains an <abort T> record in its log, then T must be aborted.
- If some active site does *not* contain a <ready T> record in its log, then the failed coordinator C_i cannot have decided to commit T. We can draw this conclusion because a site that does not have a <ready T> record in its log cannot have sent a *ready (T)* message to C_i. However, the coordinator may have decided to abort T. Rather than wait for C_i to recover, it is preferable to abort T in this case.
- If none of the preceding cases holds, then all the active sites must have a <ready T> record in their logs, but no additional control records (such as <abort T> or <commit T>). Since the coordinator has failed, it is impossible to determine whether a decision has been made—or, if so, what that decision is—until the coordinator recovers. Thus, the active sites must wait for C_i to recover. As long as the fate of T remains in doubt, T may continue to hold system resources. For example, if locking is used, T may hold locks on data at active sites. Such a situation is undesirable because hours or days may pass before C_i is again active. During this time, other transactions may be forced to wait for T. As a result, data are unavailable not only on the failed site (C_i) but on active sites as well. The amount of unavailable data increases as the downtime of C_i grows. This situation is called the *blocking* problem, because T is blocked pending the recovery of site C_i.

18.3.2.3 Failure of the Network

When a link fails, the messages in the process of being routed through the link do not arrive at their destinations intact. From the viewpoint of the sites connected throughout that link, the other sites appear to have failed. Thus, our previous schemes apply here as well.

When a number of links fail, the network may partition. In this case, two possibilities exist. The coordinator and all its participants may remain in one partition; in this case, the failure has no effect on the commit protocol. Alternatively, the coordinator and its participants may belong to several partitions; in this case, messages between the participant and the coordinator are lost, reducing the case to a link failure.

18.4 Concurrency Control

We move next to the issue of concurrency control. In this section, we show how certain of the concurrency-control schemes discussed in Chapter 6 can be modified for use in a distributed environment.

The transaction manager of a distributed database system manages the execution of those transactions (or subtransactions) that access data stored in a local site. Each such transaction may be either a local transaction (that is, a transaction that executes only at that site) or part of a global transaction (that is, a transaction that executes at several sites). Each transaction manager is responsible for maintaining a log for recovery purposes and for participating in an appropriate concurrency-control scheme to coordinate the concurrent execution of the transactions executing at that site. As we shall see, the concurrency schemes described in Chapter 6 need to be modified to accommodate the distribution of transactions.

18.4.1 Locking Protocols

The two-phase locking protocols described in Chapter 6 can be used in a distributed environment. The only change needed is in the way the lock manager is implemented. Here, we present several possible schemes. The first deals with the case where no data replication is allowed. The others apply to the more general case where data can be replicated in several sites. As in Chapter 6, we assume the existence of the shared and exclusive lock modes.

18.4.1.1 Nonreplicated Scheme

If no data are replicated in the system, then the locking schemes described in Section 6.9 can be applied as follows: Each site maintains a local lock manager whose function is to administer the lock and unlock requests for those data items stored in that site. When a transaction wishes to lock data item Q at site S_i, it simply sends a message to the lock manager at site S_i requesting a lock (in a particular lock mode). If data item Q is locked in an incompatible mode, then the request is delayed until that request can be granted. Once it has been determined that the lock request can be granted, the lock manager sends a message back to the initiator indicating that the lock request has been granted.

This scheme has the advantage of simple implementation. It requires two message transfers for handling lock requests and one message transfer for handling unlock requests. However, deadlock handling is more complex. Since the lock and unlock requests are no longer made at a single site, the various deadlock-handling algorithms discussed in Chapter 7 must be modified; these modifications are discussed in Section 18.5.

18.4.1.2 Single-Coordinator Approach

Several concurrency-control schemes can be used in systems that allow data replication. Under the single-coordinator approach, the system maintains a *single* lock manager that resides in a *single* chosen site—say, S_i. All lock and unlock requests are made at site S_i. When a transaction needs to lock a data item, it sends a lock request to S_i. The lock manager determines whether the lock can be granted immediately. If so, it sends a message to that effect to the site at which the lock request was initiated. Otherwise, the request is delayed until it can be granted; and at that time, a message is sent to the site at which the lock request was initiated. The transaction can read the data item from *any* one of the sites at which a replica of the data item resides. In the case of a `write` operation, all the sites where a replica of the data item resides must be involved in the writing.

The scheme has the following advantages:

- **Simple implementation**. This scheme requires two messages for handling lock requests and one message for handling unlock requests.
- **Simple deadlock handling**. Since all lock and unlock requests are made at one site, the deadlock-handling algorithms discussed in Chapter 7 can be applied directly to this environment.

The disadvantages of the scheme include the following:

- **Bottleneck**. The site S_i becomes a bottleneck, since all requests must be processed there.
- **Vulnerability**. If the site S_i fails, the concurrency controller is lost. Either processing must stop or a recovery scheme must be used.

A compromise between these advantages and disadvantages can be achieved through a **multiple-coordinator approach**, in which the lock-manager function is distributed over several sites. Each lock manager administers the lock and unlock requests for a subset of the data items. This distribution reduces the degree to which the coordinator is a bottleneck, but it complicates deadlock handling, since the lock and unlock requests are not made at a single site.

18.4.1.3 Majority Protocol

The majority protocol is a modification of the nonreplicated data scheme presented earlier. The system maintains a lock manager at each site. Each manager controls the locks for all the data or replicas of data stored at that site. When a transaction wishes to lock a data item Q that is replicated in n different sites, it must send a lock request to more than one-half of the n sites in which Q is stored. Each lock manager determines whether the lock can be granted immediately (as far as it is concerned). As before, the response is delayed until the request can be granted. The transaction does not operate on Q until it has successfully obtained a lock on a majority of the replicas of Q

This scheme deals with replicated data in a decentralized manner, thus avoiding the drawbacks of central control. However, it suffers from its own disadvantages:

- **Implementation**. The majority protocol is more complicated to implement than the previous schemes. It requires $2(n/2 + 1)$ messages for handling lock requests and $(n/2 + 1)$ messages for handling unlock requests.
- **Deadlock handling**. Since the lock and unlock requests are not made at one site, the deadlock-handling algorithms must be modified (Section 18.5). In addition, a deadlock can occur even if only one data item is being locked. To illustrate, consider a system with four sites and full replication. Suppose that transactions T_1 and T_2 wish to lock data item Q in exclusive mode. Transaction T_1 may succeed in locking Q at sites S_1 and S_3, while transaction T_2 may succeed in locking Q at sites S_2 and S_4. Each then must wait to acquire the third lock, and hence a deadlock has occurred.

18.4.1.4 Biased Protocol

The biased protocol is similar to the majority protocol. The difference is that requests for shared locks are given more favorable treatment than are requests for exclusive locks. The system maintains a lock manager at each site. Each manager manages the locks for all the data items stored at that site. Shared and exclusive locks are handled differently.

- **Shared locks**. When a transaction needs to lock data item Q, it simply requests a lock on Q from the lock manager at one site containing a replica of Q
- **Exclusive locks**. When a transaction needs to lock data item Q, it requests a lock on Q from the lock manager at each site containing a replica of Q

As before, the response to the request is delayed until the request can be granted.

The scheme has the advantage of imposing less overhead on read operations than does the majority protocol. This advantage is especially significant in common cases in which the frequency of reads is much greater than the frequency of writes. However, the additional overhead on writes is a disadvantage. Furthermore, the biased protocol shares the majority protocol's disadvantage of complexity in handling deadlock

18.4.1.5 Primary Copy

Yet another alternative is to choose one of the replicas as the primary copy. Thus, for each data item Q, the primary copy of Q must reside in precisely one site, which we call the *primary site of* Q. When a transaction needs to lock a data item Q, it requests a lock at the primary site of Q. Again, the response to the request is delayed until the request can be granted.

This scheme enables us to handle concurrency control for replicated data in much the same way as for unreplicated data. Implementation of the method is simple. However, if the primary site of Q fails, Q is inaccessible even though other sites containing a replica may be accessible.

18.4.2 Timestamping

The principal idea behind the timestamping scheme discussed in Section 6.9 is that each transaction is given a *unique* timestamp, which is used to decide the serialization order. Our first task, then, in generalizing the centralized scheme to a distributed scheme is to develop a method for generating unique timestamps. Our previous protocols can then be applied directly to the nonreplicated environment.

18.4.2.1 Generation of Unique Timestamps

Two primary methods are used to generate unique timestamps; one is centralized, and one is distributed. In the centralized scheme, a single site is chosen for distributing the timestamps. The site can use a logical counter or its own local clock for this purpose.

In the distributed scheme, each site generates a local unique timestamp using either a logical counter or the local clock. The global unique timestamp is obtained by concatenation of the local unique timestamp with the site identifier, which must also be unique (Figure 18.2). The order of concatenation is important! We use the site identifier in the least significant position to ensure that the global timestamps generated in one site are not always greater than those generated in another site. Compare this technique for generating unique timestamps with the one presented in Section 18.1.2 for generating unique names.

We may still have a problem if one site generates local timestamps at a faster rate than do other sites. In such a case, the fast site's logical counter will be larger than those of other sites. Therefore, all timestamps generated by the fast site will be larger than those generated by other sites. A mechanism is needed to ensure that local timestamps are generated fairly across the system. To accomplish the fair generation of timestamps, we define within each site S_i a logical clock (LC_i), which generates the local timestamp (see Section 18.1.2). To ensure that the various logical clocks are synchronized, we require that a site

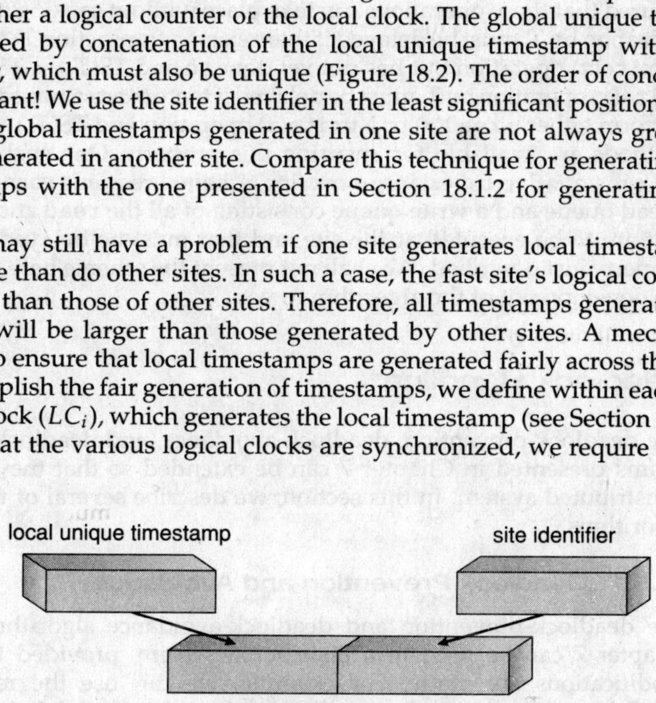

Figure 18.2 Generation of unique timestamps.

S_i advance its logical clock whenever a transaction T_i with timestamp $<x,y>$ visits that site and x is greater than the current value of LC_i. In this case, site S_i advances its logical clock to the value $x + 1$.

If the system clock is used to generate timestamps, then timestamps are assigned fairly, provided that no site has a system clock that runs fast or slow. Since clocks may not be perfectly accurate, a technique similar to that used for logical clocks must be used to ensure that no clock gets far ahead or far behind another clock.

18.4.2.2 Timestamp-Ordering Scheme

The basic timestamp scheme introduced in Section 6.9.4.3 can be extended in a straightforward manner to a distributed system. As in the centralized case, cascading rollbacks may result if no mechanism is used to prevent a transaction from reading a data item value that is not yet committed. To eliminate cascading rollbacks, we can combine the basic timestamp scheme of Section 6.9 with the 2PC protocol of Section 18.3 to obtain a protocol that ensures serializability with no cascading rollbacks. We leave the development of such an algorithm to you.

The basic timestamp scheme just described suffers from the undesirable property that conflicts between transactions are resolved through rollbacks, rather than through waits. To alleviate this problem, we can buffer the various `read` and `write` operations (that is, *delay* them) until a time when we are assured that these operations can take place without causing aborts. A `read`(x) operation by T_i must be delayed if there exists a transaction T_j that will perform a `write`(x) operation but has not yet done so and $TS(T_j) < TS(T_i)$. Similarly, a `write`(x) operation by T_i must be delayed if there exists a transaction T_j that will perform either a `read`(x) or a `write`(x) operation and $TS(T_j) < TS(T_i)$. Various methods are available for ensuring this property. One such method, called the **conservative timestamp-ordering scheme**, requires each site to maintain a read queue and a write queue consisting of all the `read` and `write` requests that are to be executed at the site and that must be delayed to preserve the property just described. We shall not present the scheme here. Again, we leave the development of the algorithm to you.

18.5 Deadlock Handling

The deadlock-prevention, deadlock-avoidance, and deadlock-detection algorithms presented in Chapter 7 can be extended so that they can be used in a distributed system. In this section, we describe several of these distributed algorithms.

18.5.1 Deadlock Prevention and Avoidance

The deadlock-prevention and deadlock-avoidance algorithms presented in Chapter 7 can be used in a distributed system, provided that appropriate modifications are made. For example, we can use the resource-ordering deadlock-prevention technique by simply defining a global ordering among the system resources. That is, all resources in the entire system are assigned unique numbers, and a process may request a resource (at any processor) with unique number i only if it is not holding a resource with a unique number greater than i. Similarly, we can use the banker's algorithm in a distributed system by designating one of the processes in the system (the *banker*) as the process that maintains the information necessary to carry out the banker's algorithm. Every resource request must be channeled through the banker.

The global resource-ordering deadlock-prevention scheme is simple to implement in a distributed environment and requires little overhead. The banker's algorithm can also be implemented easily, but it may require too much overhead. The banker may become a bottleneck, since the number of messages to and from the banker may be large. Thus, the banker's scheme does not seem to be of practical use in a distributed system.

We turn next to a new deadlock-prevention scheme based on a timestamp-ordering approach with resource preemption. Although this approach can handle any deadlock situation that may arise in a distributed system, for simplicity we consider only the case of a single instance of each resource type.

To control the preemption, we assign a unique priority number to each process. These numbers are used to decide whether a process P_i should wait for a process P_j. For example, we can let P_i wait for P_j if P_i has a priority higher than that of P_j; otherwise, P_i is rolled back. This scheme prevents deadlocks because, for every edge $P_i \rightarrow P_j$ in the wait-for graph, P_i has a higher priority than P_j. Thus, a cycle cannot exist.

One difficulty with this scheme is the possibility of starvation. Some processes with extremely low priorities may always be rolled back. This difficulty can be avoided through the use of timestamps. Each process in the system is assigned a unique timestamp when it is created. Two complementary deadlock-prevention schemes using timestamps have been proposed:

1. **The wait–die scheme**. This approach is based on a nonpreemptive technique. When process P_i requests a resource currently held by P_j, P_i is allowed to wait only if it has a smaller timestamp than does P_j (that is, P_i is older than P_j). Otherwise, P_i is rolled back (dies). For example, suppose that processes P_1, P_2, and P_3 have timestamps 5, 10, and 15, respectively. If P_1 requests a resource held by P_2, P_1 will wait. If P_3 requests a resource held by P_2, P_3 will be rolled back.

2. **The wound–wait scheme**. This approach is based on a preemptive technique and is a counterpart to the wait–die approach. When process P_i requests a resource currently held by P_j, P_i is allowed to wait only if it has a larger timestamp than does P_j (that is, P_i is younger than P_j). Otherwise, P_j is rolled back (P_j is *wounded* by P_i). Returning to our previous example, with processes P_1, P_2, and P_3, if P_1 requests a resource held by P_2, then the resource will be preempted from P_2, and P_2 will be rolled back. If P_3 requests a resource held by P_2, then P_3 will wait.

Both schemes can avoid starvation provided that, when a process is rolled back, it is *not* assigned a new timestamp. Since timestamps always increase, a process that is rolled back will eventually have the smallest timestamp. Thus, it will not be rolled back again. There are, however, significant differences in the way the two schemes operate.

- In the wait–die scheme, an older process must wait for a younger one to release its resource. Thus, the older the process gets, the more it tends to wait. By contrast, in the wound–wait scheme, an older process never waits for a younger process.
- In the wait–die scheme, if a process P_i dies and is rolled back because it has requested a resource held by process P_j, then P_i may reissue the same sequence of requests when it is restarted. If the resource is still held by P_j, then P_i will die again. Thus, P_i may die several times before acquiring the needed resource. Contrast this series of events with what happens in the wound–wait scheme. Process P_i is wounded and rolled back because P_j has requested a resource it holds. When P_i is restarted and requests the resource now being held by P_j, P_i waits. Thus, fewer rollbacks occur in the wound–wait scheme.

The major problem with both schemes is that unnecessary rollbacks may occur.

18.5.2 Deadlock Detection

The deadlock-prevention algorithm may preempt resources even if no deadlock has occurred. To prevent unnecessary preemptions, we can use a deadlock-detection algorithm. We construct a wait-for graph describing the resource-allocation state. Since we are assuming only a single resource of each type, a cycle in the wait-for graph represents a deadlock.

The main problem in a distributed system is deciding how to maintain the wait-for graph. We illustrate this problem by describing several common techniques to deal with this issue. These schemes require each site to keep a *local* wait-for graph. The nodes of the graph correspond to all the processes (local as well as nonlocal) currently holding or requesting any of the resources local to that site. For example, in Figure 18.3 we have a system consisting of two sites, each maintaining its local wait-for graph. Note that processes P_2 and P_3 appear in both graphs, indicating that the processes have requested resources at both sites.

These local wait-for graphs are constructed in the usual manner for local processes and resources. When a process P_i in site S_1 needs a resource held by process P_j in site S_2, a request message is sent by P_i to site S_2. The edge $P_i \rightarrow P_j$ is then inserted in the local wait-for graph of site S_2.

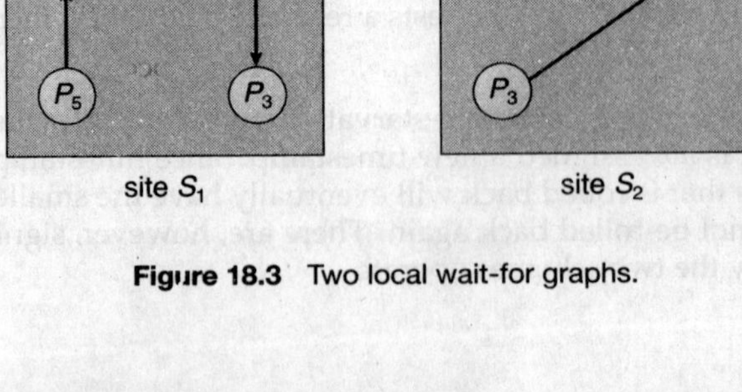

Figure 18.3 Two local wait-for graphs.

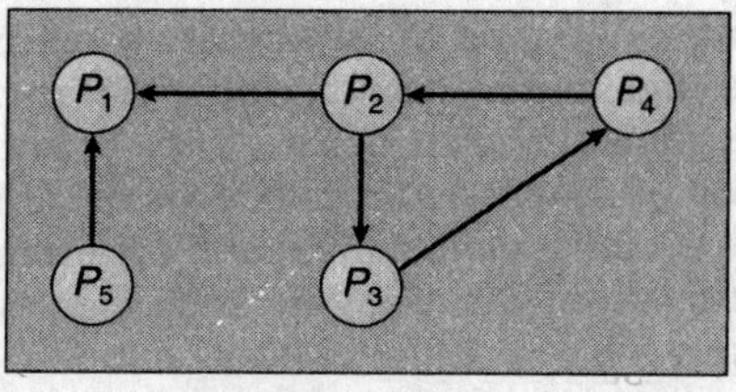

Figure 18.4 Global wait-for graph for Figure 18.3.

Clearly, if any local wait-for graph has a cycle, deadlock has occurred. The fact that we find no cycles in any of the local wait-for graphs does not mean that there are no deadlocks, however. To illustrate this problem, we consider the system depicted in Figure 18.3. Each wait-for graph is acyclic; nevertheless, a deadlock exists in the system. To prove that a deadlock has not occurred, we must show that the **union** of all local graphs is acyclic. The graph (Figure 18.4) that we obtain from the union of the two wait-for graphs of Figure 18.3 does indeed contain a cycle, implying that the system is in a deadlocked state.

A number of methods are available to organize the wait-for graph in a distributed system. We describe several common schemes here.

18.5.2.1 Centralized Approach

In the centralized approach, a global wait-for graph is constructed as the union of all the local wait-for graphs. It is maintained in a *single* process: the **deadlock-detection coordinator**. Since there is communication delay in the system, we must distinguish between two types of wait-for graphs. The *real* graph describes the real but unknown state of the system at any point in time, as would be seen by an omniscient observer. The *constructed* graph is an approximation generated by the coordinator during the execution of its algorithm. The constructed graph must be generated so that, whenever the detection algorithm is invoked, the reported results are correct. By *correct* we mean the following:

- If a deadlock exists, then it is reported properly.
- If a deadlock is reported, then the system is indeed in a deadlocked state.

As we shall show, it is not easy to construct such correct algorithms.

The wait-for graph may be constructed at three different points in time:

1. Whenever a new edge is inserted in or removed from one of the local wait-for graphs
2. Periodically, when a number of changes have occurred in a wait-for graph
3. Whenever the deadlock-detection coordinator needs to invoke the cycle-detection algorithm

When the deadlock-detection algorithm is invoked, the coordinator searches its global graph. If a cycle is found, a *victim* is selected to be rolled back. The coordinator must notify all the sites that a particular process has been selected as victim. The sites, in turn, roll back the victim process.

Next, we consider each of the three graph-construction options listed above. With option 1, whenever an edge is either inserted in or removed from a local graph, the local site must also send a message to the coordinator to notify it of this modification. On receiving such a message, the coordinator updates its global graph.

Alternatively (option 2), a site can send a number of such changes in a single message periodically. Returning to our previous example, the coordinator process will maintain the global wait-for graph as depicted in Figure 18.4. When site S_2 inserts the edge $P_3 \rightarrow P_4$ in its local wait-for graph, it also sends a message to the coordinator. Similarly, when site S_1 deletes the edge $P_5 \rightarrow P_1$ because P_1 has released a resource that was requested by P_5, an appropriate message is sent to the coordinator.

Note that no matter which of these two options is used, unnecessary rollbacks may occur, as a result of two situations:

1. **False cycles** may exist in the global wait-for graph. To illustrate this point, we consider a snapshot of the system as depicted in Figure 18.5. Suppose that P_2 releases the resource it is holding in site S_1, resulting in the deletion of the edge $P_1 \rightarrow P_2$ in site S_1. Process P_2 then requests a resource held by P_3 at site S_2, resulting in the addition of the edge $P_2 \rightarrow P_3$ in site S_2. If the *insert* $P_2 \rightarrow P_3$ message from site S_2 arrives before the *delete* $P_1 \rightarrow P_2$ message from site S_1, the coordinator may discover the false cycle $P_1 \rightarrow P_2 \rightarrow P_3 \rightarrow P_1$ after the *insert* (but before the *delete*). Deadlock recovery may be initiated, although no deadlock has occurred.

2. Unnecessary rollbacks may also result when a deadlock has indeed occurred and a victim has been picked, but *at the same time* one of the processes has been aborted for reasons unrelated to the deadlock (as when a process has exceeded its allocated time). For example, suppose that site S_1 in Figure 18.3 decides to abort P_2. At the same time, the coordinator has discovered a cycle and picked P_3 as a victim. Both P_2 and P_3 are now rolled back, although only P_2 needed to be rolled back.

Now consider a centralized deadlock-detection algorithm using option 3 that detects all deadlocks that actually occur and does not detect false deadlocks. To avoid the report of false deadlocks, we require that requests

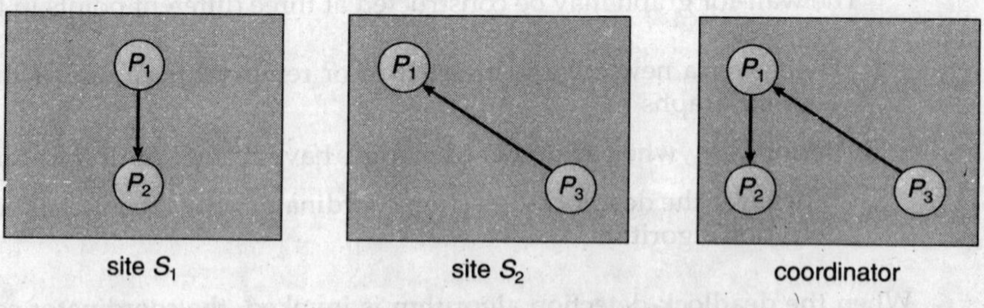

Figure 18.5 Local and global wait-for graphs.

from different sites be appended with unique identifiers (or timestamps). When process P_i, at site S_1, requests a resource from P_j, at site S_2, a request message with timestamp TS is sent. The edge $P_i \rightarrow P_j$ with the label TS is inserted in the local wait-for graph of S_1. This edge is inserted in the local wait-for graph of site S_2 only if site S_2 has received the request message and cannot immediately grant the requested resource. A request from P_i to P_j in the same site is handled in the usual manner; no timestamps are associated with the edge $P_i \rightarrow P_j$.

The detection algorithm is as follows:

1. The controller sends an initiating message to each site in the system.
2. On receiving this message, a site sends its local wait-for graph to the coordinator. Each of these wait-for graphs contains all the local information the site has about the state of the real graph. The graph reflects an instantaneous state of the site, but it is not synchronized with respect to any other site.
3. When the controller has received a reply from each site, it constructs a graph as follows:

   a. The constructed graph contains a vertex for every process in the system.

   b. The graph has an edge $P_i \rightarrow P_j$ *if and only if* there is an edge $P_i \rightarrow P_j$ in one of the wait-for graphs *or* an edge $P_i \rightarrow P_j$ with some label TS in more than one wait-for graph.

If the constructed graph contains a cycle, then the system is in a deadlocked state. If the constructed graph does not contain a cycle, then the system was not in a deadlocked state when the detection algorithm was invoked as resu of the initiating messages sent by the coordinator (in step 1).

18.5.2.2 Fully Distributed Approach

In the **fully distributed deadlock-detection algorithm**, all controllers share equally the responsibility for detecting deadlock. Every site constructs a wait-for graph that represents a part of the total graph, depending on the dynamic behavior of the system. The idea is that, if a deadlock exists, a cycle will appear in at least one of the partial graphs. We present one such algorithm, which involves construction of partial graphs in every site.

Each site maintains its own local wait-for graph. A local wait-for graph in this scheme differs from the one described earlier in that we add one additional node P_{ex} to the graph. An arc $P_i \rightarrow P_{ex}$ exists in the graph if P_i is waiting for a data item in another site being held by *any* process. Similarly, an arc $P_{ex} \rightarrow P_j$ exists in the graph if a process at another site is waiting to acquire a resource currently being held by P_j in this local site.

To illustrate this situation, we consider again the two local wait-for graphs of Figure 18.3. The addition of the node P_{ex} in both graphs results in the local wait-for graphs shown in Figure 18.6.

If a local wait-for graph contains a cycle that does not involve node P_{ex}, then the system is in a deadlocked state. If, however, a local graph contains a cycle involving P_{ex}, then this implies the *possibility* of a deadlock.

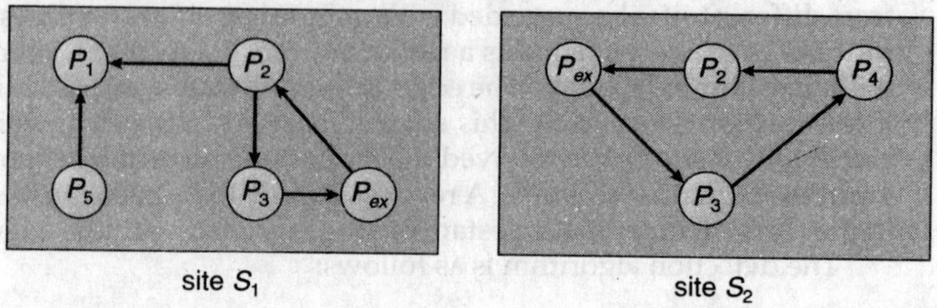

Figure 18.6 Augmented local wait-for graphs from Figure 18.3.

To ascertain whether a deadlock does exist, we must invoke a distributed deadlock-detection algorithm.

Suppose that, at site S_i, the local wait-for graph contains a cycle involving node P_{ex}. This cycle must be of the form

$$P_{ex} \rightarrow P_{k_1} \rightarrow P_{k_2} \rightarrow \ldots \rightarrow P_{k_n} \rightarrow P_{ex},$$

which indicates that process P_{k_n} in site S_i is waiting to acquire a data item located in some other site—say, S_j. On discovering this cycle, site S_i sends to site S_j a deadlock-detection message containing information about that cycle.

When site S_j receives this deadlock-detection message, it updates its local wait-for graph with the new information. Then it searches the newly constructed wait-for graph for a cycle not involving P_{ex}. If one exists, a deadlock is found, and an appropriate recovery scheme is invoked. If a cycle involving P_{ex} is discovered, then S_j transmits a deadlock-detection message to the appropriate site—say, S_k. Site S_k, in return, repeats the procedure. Thus, after a finite number of rounds, either a deadlock is discovered or the deadlock-detection computation halts.

To illustrate this procedure, we consider the local wait-for graphs of Figure 18.6. Suppose that site S_1 discovers the cycle

$$P_{ex} \rightarrow P_2 \rightarrow P_3 \rightarrow P_{ex}.$$

Since P_3 is waiting to acquire a data item in site S_2, a deadlock-detection message describing that cycle is transmitted from site S_1 to site S_2. When site S_2 receives this message, it updates its local wait-for graph, obtaining the wait-for graph of Figure 18.7. This graph contains the cycle

$$P_2 \rightarrow P_3 \rightarrow P_4 \rightarrow P_2,$$

which does not include node P_{ex}. Therefore, the system is in a deadlocked state, and an appropriate recovery scheme must be invoked.

Note that the outcome would be the same if site S_2 discovered the cycle first in its local wait-for graph and sent the deadlock-detection message to site S_1. In the worst case, both sites will discover the cycle at about the same time, and two deadlock-detection messages will be sent: one by S_1 to S_2 and another by S_2 to S_1. This situation results in unnecessary message transfer and overhead in updating the two local wait-for graphs and searching for cycles in both graphs.

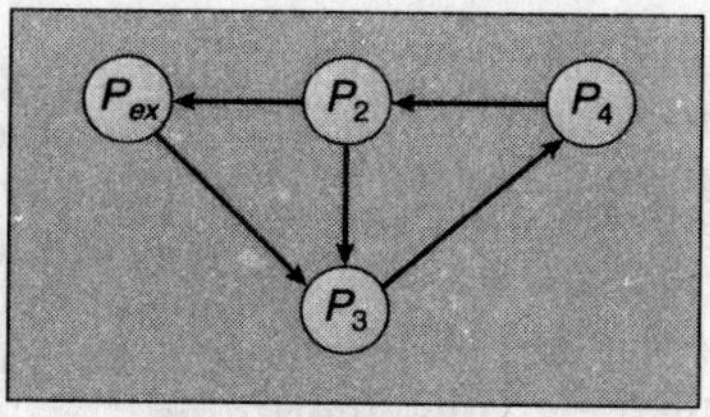

Figure 18.7 Augmented local wait-for graph in site S_2 of Figure 18.6.

To reduce message traffic, we assign to each process P_i a unique identifier, which we denote $ID(P_i)$. When site S_k discovers that its local wait-for graph contains a cycle involving node P_{ex} of the form

$$P_{ex} \rightarrow P_{K_1} \rightarrow P_{K_2} \rightarrow \ldots \rightarrow P_{K_n} \rightarrow P_{ex},$$

it sends a deadlock-detection message to another site only if

$$ID(P_{K_n}) < ID(P_{K_1}).$$

Otherwise, site S_k continues its normal execution, leaving the burden of initiating the deadlock-detection algorithm to some other site.

To illustrate this scheme, we consider again the wait-for graphs maintained at sites S_1 and S_2 as shown in Figure 18.6. Suppose that

$$ID(P_1) < ID(P_2) < ID(P_3) < ID(P_4).$$

Suppose both sites discover these local cycles at about the same time. The cycle in site S_1 is of the form

$$P_{ex} \rightarrow P_2 \rightarrow P_3 \rightarrow P_{ex}.$$

Since $ID(P_3) > ID(P_2)$, site S_1 does not send a deadlock-detection message to site S_2.

The cycle in site S_2 is of the form

$$P_{ex} \rightarrow P_3 \rightarrow P_4 \rightarrow P_2 \rightarrow P_{ex}.$$

Since $ID(P_2) < ID(P_3)$, site S_2 does send a deadlock-detection message to site S_1, which, on receiving the message, updates its local wait-for graph. Site S_1 then searches for a cycle in the graph and discovers that the system is in a deadlocked state.

18.6 Election Algorithms

As we pointed out in Section 18.3, many distributed algorithms employ a coordinator process that performs functions needed by the other processes in the system. These functions include enforcing mutual exclusion, maintaining a global wait-for graph for deadlock detection, replacing a lost token, and controlling an input or output device in the system. If the coordinator process fails due to the failure of the site at which it resides, the system can continue execution only by restarting a new copy of the coordinator on some other site. The algorithms that determine where a new copy of the coordinator should be restarted are called **election algorithms**.

Election algorithms assume that a unique priority number is associated with each active process in the system. For ease of notation, we assume that the priority number of process P_i is i. To simplify our discussion, we assume a one-to-one correspondence between processes and sites and thus refer to both as processes. The coordinator is always the process with the largest priority number. Hence, when a coordinator fails, the algorithm must elect that active process with the largest priority number. This number must be sent to each active process in the system. In addition, the algorithm must provide a mechanism for a recovered process to identify the current coordinator.

In this section, we present examples of election algorithms for two different configurations of distributed systems. The first algorithm applies to systems where every process can send a message to every other process in the system. The second algorithm applies to systems organized as a ring (logically or physically). Both algorithms require n^2 messages for an election, where n is the number of processes in the system. We assume that a process that has failed knows on recovery that it has indeed failed and thus takes appropriate actions to rejoin the set of active processes.

18.6.1 The Bully Algorithm

Suppose that process P_i sends a request that is not answered by the coordinator within a time interval T. In this situation, it is assumed that the coordinator has failed, and P_i tries to elect itself as the new coordinator. This task is completed through the following algorithm.

Process P_i sends an election message to every process with a higher priority number. Process P_i then waits for a time interval T for an answer from any one of these processes.

If no response is received within time T, P_i assumes that all processes with numbers greater than i have failed and elects itself the new coordinator. Process P_i restarts a new copy of the coordinator and sends a message to inform all active processes with priority numbers less than i that P_i is the new coordinator.

However, if an answer is received, P_i begins a time interval T', waiting to receive a message informing it that a process with a higher priority number has been elected. (That is, some other process is electing itself coordinator and should report the results within time T'.) If no message is received within T', then the process with a higher number is assumed to have failed, and process P_i should restart the algorithm.

If P_i is not the coordinator, then, at any time during execution, P_i may receive one of the following two messages from process P_j:

1. P_j is the new coordinator ($j > i$). Process P_i, in turn, records this information.

2. P_j has started an election ($j < i$). Process P_i sends a response to P_j and begins its own election algorithm, provided that P_i has not already initiated such an election.

The process that completes its algorithm has the highest number and is elected as the coordinator. It has sent its number to all active processes with lower numbers. After a failed process recovers, it immediately begins execution of the same algorithm. If there are no active processes with higher numbers, the recovered process forces all processes with lower numbers to let it become the coordinator process, even if there is a currently active coordinator with a lower number. For this reason, the algorithm is termed the **bully algorithm**.

We can demonstrate the operation of the algorithm with a simple example of a system consisting of processes P_1 through P_4. The operations are as follows:

1. All processes are active; P_4 is the coordinator process.
2. P_1 and P_4 fail. P_2 determines that P_4 has failed by sending a request that is not answered within time T. P_2 then begins its election algorithm by sending a request to P_3.
3. P_3 receives the request, responds to P_2, and begins its own algorithm by sending an election request to P_4.
4. P_2 receives P_3's response and begins waiting for an interval T'.
5. P_4 does not respond within an interval T, so P_3 elects itself the new coordinator and sends the number 3 to P_2 and P_1. (P_1 does not receive the number, since it has failed.)
6. Later, when P_1 recovers, it sends an election request to P_2, P_3, and P_4.
7. P_2 and P_3 respond to P_1 and begin their own election algorithms. P_3 will again be elected, through the same events as before.
8. Finally, P_4 recovers and notifies P_1, P_2, and P_3 that it is the current coordinator. (P_4 sends no election requests, since it is the process with the highest number in the system.)

18.6.2 The Ring Algorithm

The **ring algorithm** assumes that the links between processes are unidirectional and that each process sends its messages to the neighbor on the right. The main data structure used by the algorithm is the **active list**, a list that contains the priority numbers of all active processes in the system when the algorithm ends; each process maintains its own active list. The algorithm works as follows:

1. If process P_i detects a coordinator failure, it creates a new active list that is initially empty. It then sends a message *elect*(i) to its neighbor on the right and adds the number i to its active list.

2. If P_i receives a message *elect*(j) from the process on the left, it must respond in one of three ways:

   a. If this is the first *elect* message it has seen or sent, P_i creates a new active list with the numbers i and j. It then sends the message *elect*(i), followed by the message *elect*(j).

   b. If $i \neq j$—that is, if the message received does not contain P_i's number—then P_i adds j to its active list and forwards the message to its neighbor on the right.

   c. If $i = j$—that is, if P_i receives the message *elect*(i)—then the active list for P_i now contains the numbers of all the active processes in the system. Process P_i can now determine the largest number in the active list to identify the new coordinator process.

This algorithm does not specify how a recovering process determines the number of the current coordinator process. One solution requires a recovering process to send an inquiry message. This message is forwarded around the ring to the current coordinator, which in turn sends a reply containing its number.

18.7 Reaching Agreement

For a system to be reliable, we need a mechanism that allows a set of processes to agree on a common *value*. Such an agreement may not take place, for several reasons. First, the communication medium may be faulty, resulting in lost or garbled messages. Second, the processes themselves may be faulty, resulting in unpredictable process behavior. The best we can hope for in this case is that processes fail in a clean way, stopping their execution without deviating from their normal execution pattern. In the worst case, processes may send garbled or incorrect messages to other processes or even collaborate with other failed processes in an attempt to destroy the integrity of the system.

The **Byzantine generals problem** provides an analogy for this situation. Several divisions of the Byzantine army, each commanded by its own general, surround an enemy camp. The Byzantine generals must reach agreement on whether or not to attack the enemy at dawn. It is crucial that all generals agree, since an attack by only some of the divisions would result in defeat. The various divisions are geographically dispersed, and the generals can communicate with one another only via messengers who run from camp to camp. The generals may not be able to reach agreement for at least two major reasons:

1. Messengers may get caught by the enemy and thus may be unable to deliver their messages. This situation corresponds to unreliable communication in a computer system and is discussed further in Section 18.7.1.

2. Generals may be *traitors*, trying to prevent the *loyal* generals from reaching an agreement. This situation corresponds to faulty processes in a computer system and is discussed further in Section 18.7.2.

18.7.1 Unreliable Communications

Let us first assume that, if processes fail, they do so in a clean way and that the communication medium is unreliable. Suppose that process P_i at site S_1, which has sent a message to process P_j at site S_2, needs to know whether P_j has received the message so that it can decide how to proceed with its computation. For example, P_i may decide to compute a function *foo* if P_j has received its message or to compute a function *boo* if P_j has not received the message (because of some hardware failure).

To detect failures, we can use a **time-out scheme** similar to the one described in Section 16.7.1. When P_i sends out a message, it also specifies a time interval during which it is willing to wait for an acknowledgment message from P_j. When P_j receives the message, it immediately sends an acknowledgment to P_i. If P_i receives the acknowledgment message within the specified time interval, it can safely conclude that P_j has received its message. If, however, a time-out occurs, then P_i needs to retransmit its message and wait for an acknowledgment. This procedure continues until P_i either gets the acknowledgment message back or is notified by the system that site S_2 is down. In the first case, it will compute *foo;* in the latter case, it will compute *boo*. Note that, if these are the only two viable alternatives, P_i must wait until it has been notified that one of the situations has occurred.

Suppose now that P_j also needs to know that P_i has received its acknowledgment message, so that it can decide how to proceed with its computation. For example, P_j may want to compute *foo* only if it is assured that P_i got its acknowledgment. In other words, P_i and P_j will compute *foo* if and only if both have agreed on it. It turns out that, in the presence of failure, it is not possible to accomplish this task. More precisely, it is not possible in a distributed environment for processes P_i and P_j to agree completely on their respective states.

To prove this claim, let us suppose that a minimal sequence of message transfers exists such that, after the messages have been delivered, both processes agree to compute *foo*. Let m' be the last message sent by P_i to P_j. Since P_i does not know whether its message will arrive at P_j (since the message may be lost due to a failure), P_i will execute *foo* regardless of the outcome of the message delivery. Thus, m' could be removed from the sequence without affecting the decision procedure. Hence, the original sequence was not minimal, contradicting our assumption and showing that there is no sequence. The processes can never be sure that both will compute *foo*.

18.7.2 Faulty Processes

Now let us assume that the communication medium is reliable but that processes can fail in unpredictable ways. Consider a system of n processes, of which no more than m are faulty. Suppose that each process P_i has some private value of V_i. We wish to devise an algorithm that allows each nonfaulty process P_i to construct a vector $X_i = (A_{i,1}, A_{i,2}, ..., A_{i,n})$ such that the following conditions exist:

1. If P_j is a nonfaulty process, then $A_{i,j} = V_j$.
2. If P_i and P_j are both nonfaulty processes, then $X_i = X_j$.

There are many solutions to this problem, and they share the following properties:

1. A correct algorithm can be devised only if $n \geq 3 \times m + 1$.
2. The worst-case delay for reaching agreement is proportionate to $m + 1$ message-passing delays.
3. The number of messages required for reaching agreement is large. No single process is trustworthy, so all processes must collect all information and make their own decisions.

Rather than presenting a general solution, which would be complicated, we present an algorithm for the simple case where $m = 1$ and $n = 4$. The algorithm requires two rounds of information exchange:

1. Each process sends its private value to the other three processes.
2. Each process sends the information it has obtained in the first round to all other processes.

A faulty process obviously may refuse to send messages. In this case, a nonfaulty process can choose an arbitrary value and pretend that the value was sent by the faulty process.

Once these two rounds are completed, a nonfaulty process P_i can construct its vector $X_i = (A_{i,1}, A_{i,2}, A_{i,3}, A_{i,4})$ as follows:

1. $A_{i,i} = V_i$.
2. For $j \neq i$, if at least two of the three values reported for process P_j (in the two rounds of exchange) agree, then the majority value is used to set the value of $A_{i,j}$. Otherwise, a default value—say, *nil*—is used to set the value of $A_{i,j}$.

18.8 Summary

In a distributed system with no common memory and no common clock, it is sometimes impossible to determine the exact order in which two events occur. The *happened-before* relation is only a partial ordering of the events in a distributed system. Timestamps can be used to provide a consistent event ordering.

Mutual exclusion in a distributed environment can be implemented in a variety of ways. In a centralized approach, one of the processes in the system is chosen to coordinate the entry to the critical section. In the fully distributed approach, the decision making is distributed across the entire system. A distributed algorithm, which is applicable to ring-structured networks, is the token-passing approach.

For atomicity to be ensured, all the sites in which a transaction T has executed must agree on the final outcome of the execution. T either commits at all sites or aborts at all sites. To ensure this property, the transaction coordinator of T must execute a commit protocol. The most widely used commit protocol is the 2PC protocol.

The various concurrency-control schemes that can be used in a centralized system can be modified for use in a distributed environment. In the case of locking protocols, we need only change the way the lock manager is implemented. In the case of timestamping and validation schemes, the only change needed is the development of a mechanism for generating unique global timestamps. The mechanism can either concatenate a local timestamp with the site identification or advance local clocks whenever a message arrives that has a larger timestamp.

The primary method for dealing with deadlocks in a distributed environment is deadlock detection. The main problem is deciding how to maintain the wait-for graph. Methods for organizing the wait-for graph include a centralized approach and a fully distributed approach.

Some distributed algorithms require the use of a coordinator. If the coordinator fails because of the failure of the site at which it resides, the system can continue execution only by restarting a new copy of the coordinator on some other site. It can do so by maintaining a backup coordinator that is ready to assume responsibility if the coordinator fails. Another approach is to choose the new coordinator after the coordinator has failed. The algorithms that determine where a new copy of the coordinator should be restarted are called election algorithms. Two algorithms, the bully algorithm and the ring algorithm, can be used to elect a new coordinator in case of failures.

Exercises

18.1 Why is deadlock detection much more expensive in a distributed environment than in a centralized environment?

18.2 Consider a *hierarchical* deadlock-detection algorithm in which the global wait-for graph is distributed over a number of different *controllers,* which are organized in a tree. Each non-leaf controller maintains a wait-for graph that contains relevant information from the graphs of the controllers in the subtree below it. In particular, let S_A, S_B, and S_C be controllers such that S_C is the lowest common ancestor of S_A and S_B (S_C must be unique, since we are dealing with a tree). Suppose that node T_i appears in the local wait-for graph of controllers S_A and S_B. Then T_i must also appear in the local wait-for graph of

- Controller S_C
- Every controller in the path from S_C to S_A
- Every controller in the path from S_C to S_B

In addition, if T_i and T_j appear in the wait-for graph of controller S_D and there exists a path from T_i to T_j in the wait-for graph of one of the children of S_D, then an edge $T_i \rightarrow T_j$ must be in the wait-for graph of S_D.

Show that, if a cycle exists in any of the wait-for graphs, then the system is deadlocked.

18.3 Your company is building a computer network, and you are asked to develop a scheme for dealing with the deadlock problem.

a. Would you use a deadlock-detection scheme or a deadlock-prevention scheme?

b. If you used a deadlock-prevention scheme, which one would you use? Explain your choice.

c. If you used a deadlock-detection scheme, which one would you use? Explain your choice.

18.4 Derive an election algorithm for bidirectional rings that is more efficient than the one presented in this chapter. How many messages are needed for n processes?

18.5 Your company is building a computer network, and you are asked to write an algorithm for achieving distributed mutual exclusion. Which scheme will you use? Explain your choice.

18.6 Consider the following failure model for faulty processors. Processors follow the prescribed protocol but may fail at unexpected points in time. When processors fail, they simply stop functioning and do not continue to participate in the distributed system. Given such a failure model, design an algorithm for reaching agreement among a set of processors. Discuss the conditions under which agreement could be reached.

18.7 Under what circumstances does the wait–die scheme perform better than the wound–wait scheme for granting resources to concurrently executing transactions?

18.8 Consider a failure that occurs during 2PC for a transaction. For each possible failure, explain how 2PC ensures transaction atomicity despite the failure.

18.9 The logical clock timestamp scheme presented in this chapter provides the following guarantee: if event A happens before event B, then the timestamp of A is smaller than the timestamp of B. Note, however, that we cannot order two events based only on their timestamps. The fact that an event C has a timestamp that is smaller than the timestamp of event D does not necessarily mean that event C happened before event D; C and D could be concurrent events in the system. Discuss ways in which the logical clock timestamp scheme could be extended to distinguish concurrent events from events that can be ordered by the *happened-before* relation.

Bibliographical Notes

The distributed algorithm for extending the *happened-before* relation to a consistent total ordering of all the events in the system was developed by Lamport [1978b]. Further discussions of using logical time to characterize the behavior of distributed systems can be found in Fidge [1991], Raynal and

Singhal [1996], Babaoglu and Marzullo [1993], Schwarz and Mattern [1994], and Mattern [1988].

The first general algorithm for implementing mutual exclusion in a distributed environment was also developed by Lamport [1978b]. Lamport's scheme requires $3 \times (n - 1)$ messages per critical-section entry. Subsequently, Ricart and Agrawala [1981] proposed a distributed algorithm that requires only $2 \times (n - 1)$ messages. Their algorithm is presented in Section 18.2.2. A square-root algorithm for distributed mutual exclusion is described by Maekawa [1985]. The token-passing algorithm for ring-structured systems presented in Section 18.2.3 was developed by Lann [1977]. Carvalho and Roucairol [1983] discusses mutual exclusion in computer networks, and Agrawal and Abbadi [1991] describes an efficient and fault-tolerant solution of distributed mutual exclusion. A simple taxonomy for distributed mutual-exclusion algorithms is presented by Raynal [1991].

The issue of distributed synchronization is discussed by Reed and Kanodia [1979] (shared-memory environment), Lamport [1978b], Lamport [1978a], and Schneider [1982] (totally disjoint processes). A distributed solution to the dining-philosophers problem is presented by Chang [1980].

The 2PC protocol was developed by Lampson and Sturgis [1976] and Gray [1978]. Two modified versions of 2PC, called presume commit and presume abort, reduce the overhead of 2PC by defining default assumptions regarding the fate of transactions (Mohan and Lindsay [1983]).

Papers dealing with the problems of implementing the transaction concept in a distributed database were presented by Gray [1981], Traiger et al. [1982], and Spector and Schwarz [1983]. Bernstein et al. [1987] offer comprehensive discussions of distributed concurrency control. Rosenkrantz et al. [1978] report on the timestamp distributed deadlock-prevention algorithm. The fully distributed deadlock-detection scheme presented in Section 18.5.2 was developed by Obermarck [1982]. The hierarchical deadlock-detection scheme of Exercise 18.1 appears in Menasce and Muntz [1979]. Knapp [1987] and Singhal [1989] offer surveys of deadlock detection in distributed systems. Deadlocks can also be detected by taking global snapshots of a distributed system, as discussed in Chandy and Lamport [1985].

The Byzantine generals problem is discussed by Lamport et al. [1982] and Pease et al. [1980]. The bully algorithm is presented by Garcia-Molina [1982], and the election algorithm for a ring-structured system was written by Lann [1977].

Part Eight

Special-Purpose Systems

Our coverage of operating-system issues thus far has focused mainly on general-purpose computing systems. There are, however, special-purpose systems with requirements different from those of many of the systems we have described.

A *real-time system* is a computer system that requires not only that computed results be correct but also that the results be produced within a specified deadline period. Results produced after the deadline has passed—even if correct—may be of no real value. For such systems, many traditional operating-system scheduling algorithms must be modified to meet the stringent timing deadlines.

A *multimedia system* must be able to handle not only conventional data, such as text files, programs, and word-processing documents, but also multimedia data. Multimedia data consist of continuous-media data (audio and video) as well as conventional data. Continuous-media data—such as frames of video—must be delivered according to certain time restrictions (for example, 30 frames per second). The demands of handling continuous-media data require significant changes in operating-system structure, most notably in memory, disk, and network management.

CHAPTER 19

Real-Time Systems

Our coverage of operating-system issues thus far has focused mainly on general-purpose computing systems (for example, desktop and server systems). We now turn our attention to real-time computing systems. The requirements of real-time systems differ from those of many of the systems we have described, largely because real-time systems must produce results within certain time limits. In this chapter, we provide an overview of real-time computer systems and describe how real-time operating systems must be constructed to meet the stringent timing requirements of these systems.

CHAPTER OBJECTIVES

- To explain the timing requirements of real-time systems.
- To distinguish between hard and soft real-time systems.
- To discuss the defining characteristics of real-time systems.
- To describe scheduling algorithms for hard real-time systems.

19.1 Overview

A **real-time system** is a computer system that requires not only that the computing results be "correct" but also that the results be produced within a specified deadline period. Results produced after the deadline has passed—even if correct—may be of no real value. To illustrate, consider an autonomous robot that delivers mail in an office complex. If its vision-control system identifies a wall *after* the robot has walked into it, despite correctly identifying the wall, the system has not met its requirement. Contrast this timing requirement with the much less strict demands of other systems. In an interactive desktop computer system, it is desirable to provide a quick response time to the interactive user, but it is not mandatory to do so. Some systems—such as a batch-processing system—may have no timing requirements whatsoever.

Real-time systems executing on traditional computer hardware are used in a wide range of applications. In addition, many real-time systems are embedded in "specialized devices," such as ordinary home appliances (for example, microwave ovens and dishwashers), consumer digital devices (for example, cameras and MP3 players), and communication devices (for example, cellular telephones and Blackberry handheld devices). They are also present in larger entities, such as automobiles and airplanes. An **embedded system** is a computing device that is part of a larger system in which the presence of a computing device is often not obvious to the user.

To illustrate, consider an embedded system for controlling a home dishwasher. The embedded system may allow various options for scheduling the operation of the dishwasher—the water temperature, the type of cleaning (light or heavy), even a timer indicating when the dishwasher is to start. Most likely, the user of the dishwasher is unaware that there is in fact a computer embedded in the appliance. As another example, consider an embedded system controlling antilock brakes in an automobile. Each wheel in the automobile has a sensor detecting how much sliding and traction are occurring, and each sensor continually sends its data to the system controller. Taking the results from these sensors, the controller tells the braking mechanism in each wheel how much braking pressure to apply. Again, to the user (in this instance, the driver of the automobile), the presence of an embedded computer system may not be apparent. It is important to note, however, that not all embedded systems are real-time. For example, an embedded system controlling a home furnace may have no real-time requirements whatsoever.

Some real-time systems are identified as **safety-critical systems**. In a safety-critical system, incorrect operation—usually due to a missed deadline—results in some sort of "catastrophe." Examples of safety-critical systems include weapons systems, antilock brake systems, flight-management systems, and health-related embedded systems, such as pacemakers. In these scenarios, the real-time system *must* respond to events by the specified deadlines; otherwise, serious injury—or worse—might occur. However, a significant majority of embedded systems do not qualify as safety-critical, including FAX machines, microwave ovens, wristwatches, and networking devices such as switches and routers. For these devices, missing deadline requirements results in nothing more than perhaps an unhappy user.

Real-time computing is of two types: hard and soft. A **hard real-time system** has the most stringent requirements, guaranteeing that critical real-time tasks be completed within their deadlines. Safety-critical systems are typically hard real-time systems. A **soft real-time system** is less restrictive, simply providing that a critical real-time task will receive priority over other tasks and that it will retain that priority until it completes. Many commercial operating systems—as well as Linux—provide soft real-time support.

19.2 System Characteristics

In this section, we explore the characteristics of real-time systems and address issues related to designing both soft and hard real-time operating systems.

The following characteristics are typical of many real-time systems:

- Single purpose
- Small size

- Inexpensively mass-produced
- Specific timing requirements

We next examine each of these characteristics.

Unlike PCs, which are put to many uses, a real-time system typically serves only a single purpose, such as controlling antilock brakes or delivering music on an MP3 player. It is unlikely that a real-time system controlling an airliner's navigation system will also play DVDs! The design of a real-time operating system reflects its single-purpose nature and is often quite simple.

Many real-time systems exist in environments where physical space is constrained. Consider the amount of space available in a wristwatch or a microwave oven—it is considerably less than what is available in a desktop computer. As a result of space constraints, most real-time systems lack both the CPU processing power and the amount of memory available in standard desktop PCs. Whereas most contemporary desktop and server systems use 32- or 64-bit processors, many real-time systems run on 8- or 16-bit processors. Similarly, a desktop PC might have several gigabytes of physical memory, whereas a real-time system might have less than a megabyte. We refer to the amount of memory required to run the operating system and its applications as the **footprint** of a system. Because the amount of memory is limited, most real-time operating systems must have small footprints.

Next, consider where many real-time systems are implemented: they are often found in home appliances and consumer devices. Devices such as digital cameras, microwave ovens, and thermostats are mass-produced in very cost-conscious environments. Thus, the microprocessors for real-time systems must also be inexpensively mass-produced.

One technique for reducing the cost of an embedded controller is to use an alternative technique for organizing the components of the computer system. Rather than organizing the computer around the structure shown in Figure 19.1, where buses provide the mechanism interconnecting individual components, many embedded system controllers use a strategy known as system-on-chip (SOC). Here, the CPU, memory (including cache), memory-

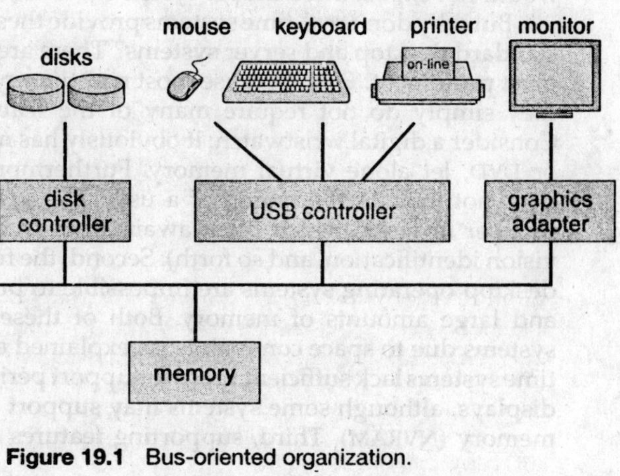

Figure 19.1 Bus-oriented organization.

management-unit (MMU), and any attached peripheral ports, such as USB ports, are contained in a single integrated circuit. The SOC strategy is typically less expensive than the bus-oriented organization of Figure 19.1.

We turn now to the final characteristic identified above for real-time systems: specific timing requirements. It is, in fact, the defining characteristic of such systems. Accordingly, the primary task of both hard and soft real-time operating systems is to support the timing requirements of real-time tasks, and the remainder of this chapter focuses on this issue. Real-time operating systems meet timing requirements by using scheduling algorithms that give real-time processes the highest scheduling priorities. Furthermore, schedulers must ensure that the priority of a real-time task does not degrade over time. Another technique for addressing timing requirements is by minimizing the response time to events such as interrupts.

19.3 Features of Real-Time Kernels

In this section, we discuss the features necessary for designing an operating system that supports real-time processes. Before we begin, though, let's consider what is typically *not* needed for a real-time system. We begin by examining several features provided in many of the operating systems discussed so far in this text, including Linux, UNIX, and the various versions of Windows. These systems typically provide support for the following:

- A variety of peripheral devices, such as graphical displays, CD drives, and DVD drives
- Protection and security mechanisms
- Multiple users

Supporting these features often results in a sophisticated—and large—kernel. For example, Windows XP has over forty million lines of source code. In contrast, a typical real-time operating system usually has a very simple design, often written in thousands rather than millions of lines of source code. We would not expect these simple systems to include the features listed above.

But why don't real-time systems provide these features, which are crucial to standard desktop and server systems? There are several reasons, but three are most prominent. First, because most real-time systems serve a single purpose, they simply do not require many of the features found in a desktop PC. Consider a digital wristwatch: it obviously has no need to support a disk drive or DVD, let alone virtual memory. Furthermore, a typical real-time system does not include the notion of a user. The system simply supports a small number of tasks, which often await input from hardware devices (sensors, vision identification, and so forth). Second, the features supported by standard desktop operating systems are impossible to provide without fast processors and large amounts of memory. Both of these are unavailable in real-time systems due to space constraints, as explained earlier. In addition, many real-time systems lack sufficient space to support peripheral disk drives or graphical displays, although some systems may support file systems using nonvolatile memory (NVRAM). Third, supporting features common in standard desktop

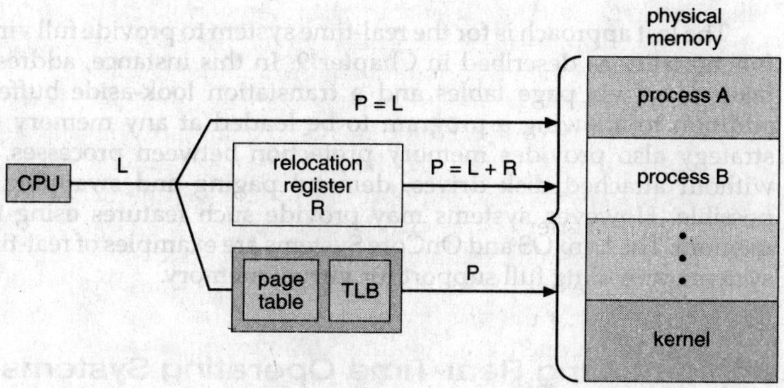

Figure 19.2 Address translation in real-time systems.

computing environments would greatly increase the cost of real-time systems, which could make such systems economically impractical.

Additional considerations arise when we consider virtual memory in a real-time system. Providing virtual memory features as described in Chapter 9 requires that the system include a memory-management unit (MMU) for translating logical to physical addresses. However, MMUs typically increase the cost and power consumption of the system. In addition, the time required to translate logical addresses to physical addresses—especially in the case of a translation look-aside buffer (TLB) miss—may be prohibitive in a hard real-time environment. In the following discussion, we examine several approaches for translating addresses in real-time systems.

Figure 19.2 illustrates three different strategies for managing address translation available to designers of real-time operating systems. In this scenario, the CPU generates logical address L, which must be mapped to physical address P. The first approach is to bypass logical addresses and have the CPU generate physical addresses directly. This technique—known as **real-addressing mode**—does not employ virtual memory techniques and is effectively stating that P equals L. One problem with real-addressing mode is the absence of memory protection between processes. Real-addressing mode may also require that programmers specify the physical location where their programs are loaded into memory. However, the benefit of this approach is that the system is quite fast, as no time is spent on address translation. Real-addressing mode is quite common in embedded systems with hard real-time constraints. In fact, some real-time operating systems running on microprocessors containing an MMU actually disable the MMU to gain the performance benefit of referencing physical addresses directly.

A second strategy for translating addresses is to use an approach similar to the dynamic relocation register shown in Figure 8.4. In this scenario, a relocation register R is set to the memory location where a program is loaded. The physical address P is generated by adding the contents of the relocation register R to L. Some real-time systems configure the MMU to perform this way. The obvious benefit of this strategy is that the MMU can easily translate logical addresses to physical addresses using $P = L + R$. However, this system still suffers from a lack of memory protection between processes.

The last approach is for the real-time system to provide full virtual memory functionality as described in Chapter 9. In this instance, address translation takes place via page tables and a translation look-aside buffer, or TLB. In addition to allowing a program to be loaded at any memory location, this strategy also provides memory protection between processes. For systems without attached disk drives, demand paging and swapping may not be possible. However, systems may provide such features using NVRAM flash memory. The LynxOS and OnCore Systems are examples of real-time operating systems providing full support for virtual memory.

19.4 Implementing Real-Time Operating Systems

Keeping in mind the many possible variations, we now identify the features necessary for implementing a real-time operating system. This list is by no means absolute; some systems provide more features than we list below, while other systems provide fewer.

- Preemptive, priority-based scheduling
- Preemptive kernel
- Minimized latency

One notable feature we omit from this list is networking support. However, deciding whether to support networking protocols such as TCP/IP is simple: if the real-time system must be connected to a network, the operating system must provide networking capabilities. For example, a system that gathers real-time data and transmits it to a server must obviously include networking features. Alternatively, a self-contained embedded system requiring no interaction with other computer systems has no obvious networking requirement.

In the remainder of this section, we examine the basic requirements listed above and identify how they can be implemented in a real-time operating system.

19.4.1 Priority-Based Scheduling

The most important feature of a real-time operating system is to respond immediately to a real-time process as soon as that process requires the CPU. As a result, the scheduler for a real-time operating system must support a priority-based algorithm with preemption. Recall that priority-based scheduling algorithms assign each process a priority based on its importance; more important tasks are assigned higher priorities than those deemed less important. If the scheduler also supports preemption, a process currently running on the CPU will be preempted if a higher-priority process becomes available to run.

Preemptive, priority-based scheduling algorithms are discussed in detail in Chapter 5, where we also present examples of the soft real-time scheduling features of the Solaris, Windows XP, and Linux operating systems. Each of these systems assigns real-time processes the highest scheduling priority. For example, Windows XP has 32 different priority levels; the highest levels—priority values 16 to 31—are reserved for real-time processes. Solaris and Linux have similar prioritization schemes.

Note, however, that providing a preemptive, priority-based scheduler only guarantees soft real-time functionality. Hard real-time systems must further guarantee that real-time tasks will be serviced in accord with their deadline requirements, and making such guarantees may require additional scheduling features. In Section 19.5, we cover scheduling algorithms appropriate for hard real-time systems.

19.4.2 Preemptive Kernels

Nonpreemptive kernels disallow preemption of a process running in kernel mode; a kernel-mode process will run until it exits kernel mode, blocks, or voluntarily yields control of the CPU. In contrast, a preemptive kernel allows the preemption of a task running in kernel mode. Designing preemptive kernels can be quite difficult, and traditional user-oriented applications such as spreadsheets, word processors, and Web browsers typically do not require such quick response times. As a result, some commercial desktop operating systems—such as Windows XP—are nonpreemptive.

However, to meet the timing requirements of real-time systems—in particular, hard real-time systems—preemptive kernels are mandatory. Otherwise, a real-time task might have to wait an arbitrarily long period of time while another task was active in the kernel.

There are various strategies for making a kernel preemptible. One approach is to insert **preemption points** in long-duration system calls. A preemption point checks to see whether a high-priority process needs to be run. If so, a context switch takes place. Then, when the high-priority process terminates, the interrupted process continues with the system call. Preemption points can be placed only at *safe* locations in the kernel—that is, only where kernel data structures are not being modified. A second strategy for making a kernel preemptible is through the use of synchronization mechanisms, discussed in Chapter 6. With this method, the kernel can always be preemptible, because any kernel data being updated are protected from modification by the high-priority process.

19.4.3 Minimizing Latency

Consider the event-driven nature of a real-time system. The system is typically waiting for an event in real time to occur. Events may arise either in software—as when a timer expires—or in hardware—as when a remote-controlled vehicle detects that it is approaching an obstruction. When an event occurs, the system must respond to and service it as quickly as possible. We refer to **event latency** as the amount of time that elapses from when an event occurs to when it is serviced (Figure 19.3).

Usually, different events have different latency requirements. For example, the latency requirement for an antilock brake system might be three to five milliseconds, meaning that from the time a wheel first detects that it is sliding, the system controlling the antilock brakes has three to five milliseconds to respond to and control the situation. Any response that takes longer might result in the automobile's veering out of control. In contrast, an embedded

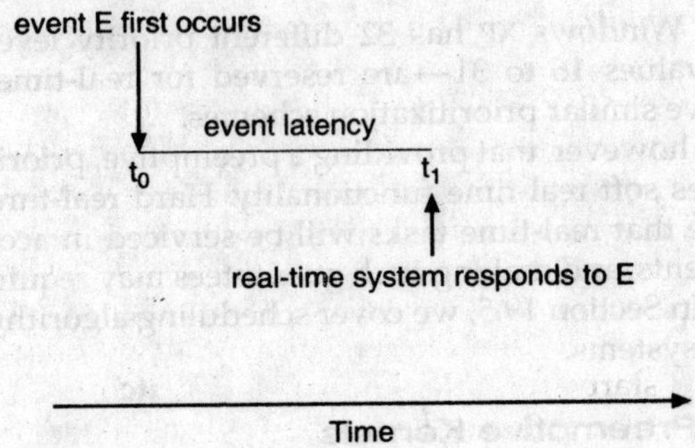

Figure 19.3 Event latency.

system controlling radar in an airliner might tolerate a latency period of several seconds.

Two types of latencies affect the performance of real-time systems:

1. Interrupt latency
2. Dispatch latency

Interrupt latency refers to the period of time from the arrival of an interrupt at the CPU to the start of the routine that services the interrupt. When an interrupt occurs, the operating system must first complete the instruction it is executing and determine the type of interrupt that occurred. It must then save the state of the current process before servicing the interrupt using the specific interrupt service routine (ISR). The total time required to perform these tasks is the interrupt latency (Figure 19.4). Obviously, it is crucial for real-time

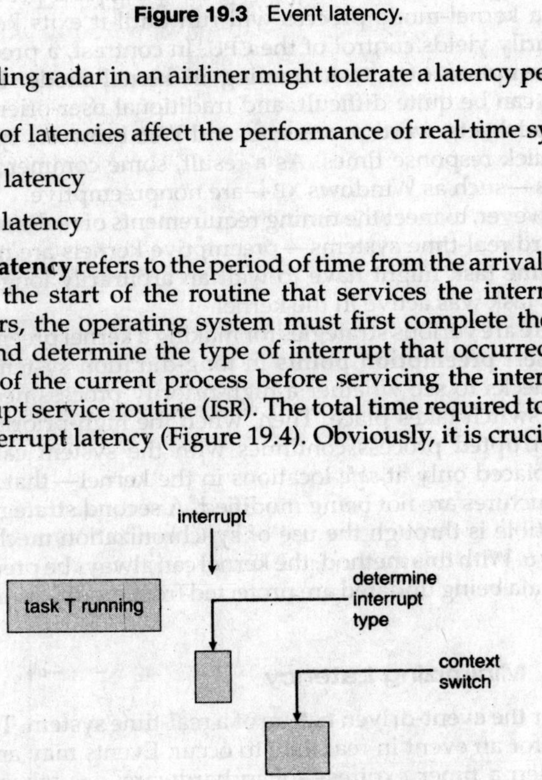

Figure 19.4 Interrupt latency.

operating systems to minimize interrupt latency to ensure that real-time tasks receive immediate attention.

One important factor contributing to interrupt latency is the amount of time interrupts may be disabled while kernel data structures are being updated. Real-time operating systems require that interrupts be disabled for very short periods of time. However, for hard real-time systems, interrupt latency must not only be minimized, it must in fact be bounded to guarantee the deterministic behavior required of hard real-time kernels.

The amount of time required for the scheduling dispatcher to stop one process and start another is known as **dispatch latency**. Providing real-time tasks with immediate access to the CPU mandates that real-time operating systems minimize this latency. The most effective technique for keeping dispatch latency low is to provide preemptive kernels.

In Figure 19.5, we diagram the makeup of dispatch latency. The **conflict phase** of dispatch latency has two components:

1. Preemption of any process running in the kernel
2. Release by low-priority processes of resources needed by a high-priority process

As an example, in Solaris, the dispatch latency with preemption disabled is over a hundred milliseconds. With preemption enabled, it is reduced to less than a millisecond.

One issue that can affect dispatch latency arises when a higher-priority process needs to read or modify kernel data that are currently being accessed by a lower-priority process—or a chain of lower-priority processes. As kernel

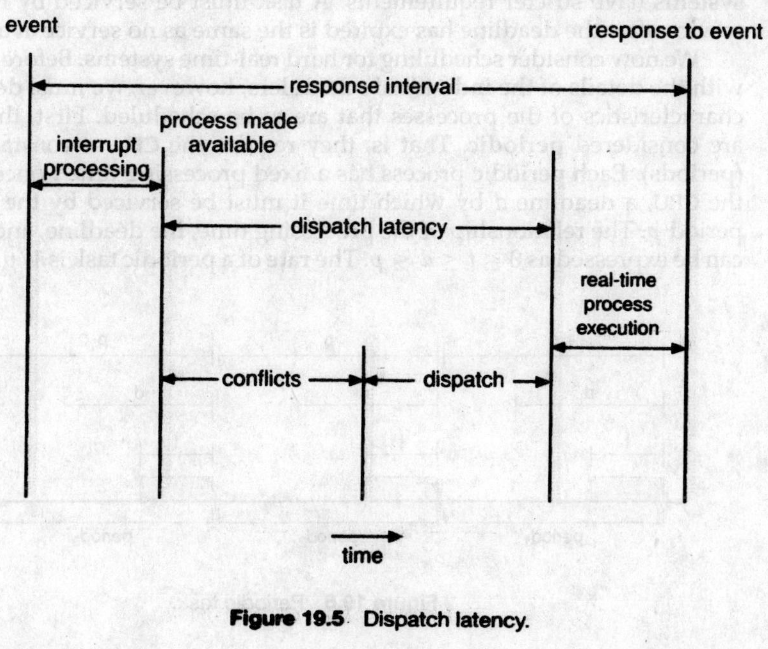

Figure 19.5 Dispatch latency.

data are typically protected with a lock, the higher-priority process will have to wait for a lower-priority one to finish with the resource. The situation becomes more complicated if the lower-priority process is preempted in favor of yet another process with a higher priority. As an example, assume we have three processes, L, M, and H, whose priorities follow the order $L < M < H$. Also assume that process H requires resource R, which is currently being accessed by process L. Ordinarily, process H would wait for L to finish using resource R. However, now suppose that process M becomes runnable, thereby preempting process L. Indirectly, a process with a lower priority—process M—has affected how long process H must wait for L to relinquish resource R.

This problem, known as **priority inversion**, can be solved by use of the **priority-inheritance protocol**. According to this protocol, all processes that are accessing resources needed by a higher-priority process inherit the higher priority until they are finished with the resources in question. When they are finished, their priorities revert to their original values. In the example above, a priority-inheritance protocol allows process L to temporarily inherit the priority of process H, thereby preventing process M from preempting its execution. When process L has finished using resource R, it relinquishes its inherited priority from H and assumes its original priority. As resource R is now available, process H—not M—will run next.

19.5 Real-Time CPU Scheduling

Our coverage of scheduling so far has focused primarily on soft real-time systems. As mentioned, though, scheduling for such systems provides no guarantee on when a critical process will be scheduled; it guarantees only that the process will be given preference over noncritical processes. Hard real-time systems have stricter requirements. A task must be serviced by its deadline; service after the deadline has expired is the same as no service at all.

We now consider scheduling for hard real-time systems. Before we proceed with the details of the individual schedulers, however, we must define certain characteristics of the processes that are to be scheduled. First, the processes are considered **periodic**. That is, they require the CPU at constant intervals (periods). Each periodic process has a fixed processing time t once it acquires the CPU, a deadline d by which time it must be serviced by the CPU, and a period p. The relationship of the processing time, the deadline, and the period can be expressed as $0 \leq t \leq d \leq p$. The **rate** of a periodic task is $1/p$. Figure 19.6

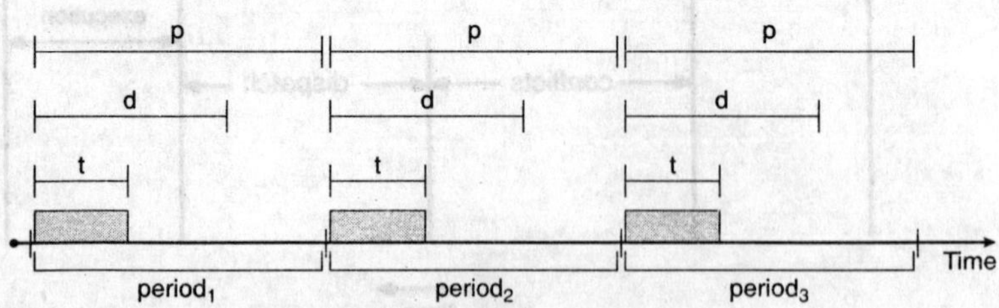

Figure 19.6 Periodic task.

illustrates the execution of a periodic process over time. Schedulers can take advantage of this relationship and assign priorities according to the deadline or rate requirements of a periodic process.

What is unusual about this form of scheduling is that a process may have to announce its deadline requirements to the scheduler. Then, using a technique known as an **admission-control** algorithm, the scheduler either admits the process, guaranteeing that the process will complete on time, or rejects the request as impossible if it cannot guarantee that the task will be serviced by its deadline.

In the following sections, we explore scheduling algorithms that address the deadline requirements of hard real-time systems.

19.5.1 Rate-Monotonic Scheduling

The **rate-monotonic** scheduling algorithm schedules periodic tasks using a static priority policy with preemption. If a lower-priority process is running and a higher-priority process becomes available to run, it will preempt the lower-priority process. Upon entering the system, each periodic task is assigned a priority inversely based on its period. The shorter the period, the higher the priority; the longer the period, the lower the priority. The rationale behind this policy is to assign a higher priority to tasks that require the CPU more often. Furthermore, rate-monotonic scheduling assumes that the processing time of a periodic process is the same for each CPU burst. That is, every time a process acquires the CPU, the duration of its CPU burst is the same.

Let's consider an example. We have two processes P_1 and P_2. The periods for P_1 and P_2 are 50 and 100, respectively—that is, $p_1 = 50$ and $p_2 = 100$. The processing times are $t_1 = 20$ for P_1 and $t_2 = 35$ for P_2. The deadline for each process requires that it complete its CPU burst by the start of its next period.

We must first ask ourselves whether it is possible to schedule these tasks so that each meets its deadlines. If we measure the CPU utilization of a process P_i as the ratio of its burst to its period—t_i/p_i—the CPU utilization of P_1 is $20/50 = 0.40$ and that of P_2 is $35/100 = 0.35$, for a total CPU utilization of 75 percent. Therefore, it seems we can schedule these tasks in such a way that both meet their deadlines and still leave the CPU with available cycles.

First, suppose we assign P_2 a higher priority than P_1. The execution of P_1 and P_2 is shown in Figure 19.7. As we can see, P_2 starts execution first and completes at time 35. At this point, P_1 starts; it completes its CPU burst at time 55. However, the first deadline for P_1 was at time 50, so the scheduler has caused P_1 to miss its deadline.

Now suppose we use rate-monotonic scheduling, in which we assign P_1 a higher priority than P_2, since the period of P_1 is shorter than that of P_2.

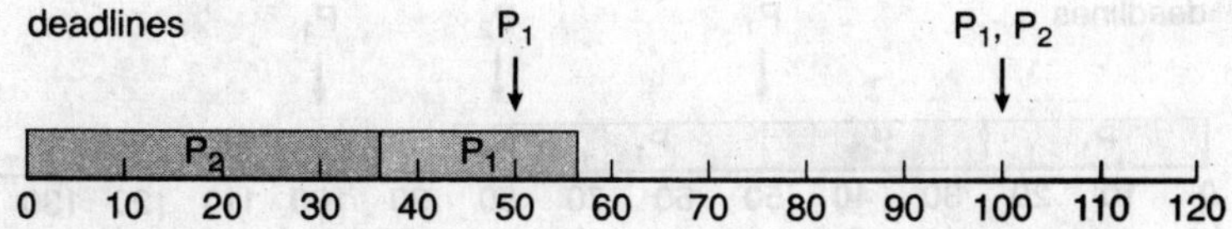

Figure 19.7 Scheduling of tasks when P_2 has a higher priority than P_1.

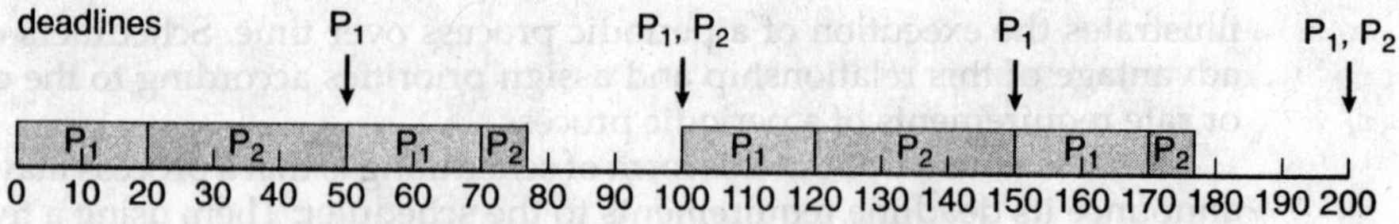

Figure 19.8 Rate-monotonic scheduling.

The execution of these processes is shown in Figure 19.8. P_1 starts first and completes its CPU burst at time 20, thereby meeting its first deadline. P_2 starts running at this point and runs until time 50. At this time, it is preempted by P_1, although it still has 5 milliseconds remaining in its CPU burst. P_1 completes its CPU burst at time 70, at which point the scheduler resumes P_2. P_2 completes its CPU burst at time 75, also meeting its first deadline. The system is idle until time 100, when P_1 is scheduled again.

Rate-monotonic scheduling is considered optimal in that if a set of processes cannot be scheduled by this algorithm, it cannot be scheduled by any other algorithm that assigns static priorities. Let's next examine a set of processes that cannot be scheduled using the rate-monotonic algorithm. Assume that process P_1 has a period of $p_1 = 50$ and a CPU burst of $t_1 = 25$. For P_2, the corresponding values are $p_2 = 80$ and $t_2 = 35$. Rate-monotonic scheduling would assign process P_1 a higher priority, as it has the shorter period. The total CPU utilization of the two processes is $(25/50)+(35/80) = 0.94$, and it therefore seems logical that the two processes could be scheduled and still leave the CPU with 6 percent available time. Figure 19.9 shows the scheduling of processes P_1 and P_2. Initially, P_1 runs until it completes its CPU burst at time 25. Process P_2 then begins running and runs until time 50, when it is preempted by P_1. At this point, P_2 still has 10 milliseconds remaining in its CPU burst. Process P_1 runs until time 75; consequently, P_2 misses the deadline for completion of its CPU burst at time 80.

Despite being optimal, then, rate-monotonic scheduling has a limitation: CPU utilization is bounded, and it is not always possible to fully maximize CPU resources. The worst-case CPU utilization for scheduling N processes is

$$2(2^{1/n} - 1).$$

With one process in the system, CPU utilization is 100 percent, but it falls to approximately 69 percent as the number of processes approaches infinity. With two processes, CPU utilization is bounded at about 83 percent. Combined CPU utilization for the two processes scheduled in Figures 19.7 and 19.8 is 75 percent; therefore, the rate-monotonic scheduling algorithm is guaranteed to schedule

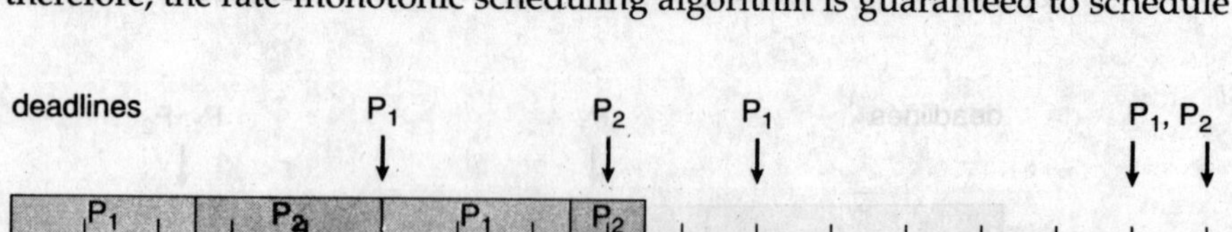

Figure 19.9 Missing deadlines with rate-monotonic scheduling.

them so that they can meet their deadlines. For the two processes scheduled in Figure 19.9, combined CPU utilization is approximately 94 percent; therefore, rate-monotonic scheduling cannot guarantee that they can be scheduled so that they meet their deadlines.

19.5.2 Earliest-Deadline-First Scheduling

Earliest-deadline-first (EDF) scheduling dynamically assigns priorities according to deadline. The earlier the deadline, the higher the priority; the later the deadline, the lower the priority. Under the EDF policy, when a process becomes runnable, it must announce its deadline requirements to the system. Priorities may have to be adjusted to reflect the deadline of the newly runnable process. Note how this differs from rate-monotonic scheduling, where priorities are fixed.

To illustrate EDF scheduling, we again schedule the processes shown in Figure 19.9, which failed to meet deadline requirements under rate-monotonic scheduling. Recall that P_1 has values of $p_1 = 50$ and $t_1 = 25$ and that P_2 has values of $p_2 = 80$ and $t_2 = 35$. The EDF scheduling of these processes is shown in Figure 19.10. Process P_1 has the earliest deadline, so its initial priority is higher than that of process P_2. Process P_2 begins running at the end of the CPU burst for P_1. However, whereas rate-monotonic scheduling allows P_1 to preempt P_2 at the beginning of its next period at time 50, EDF scheduling allows process P_2 to continue running. P_2 now has a higher priority than P_1 because its next deadline (at time 80) is earlier than that of P_1 (at time 100). Thus, both P_1 and P_2 meet their first deadlines. Process P_1 again begins running at time 60 and completes its second CPU burst at time 85, also meeting its second deadline at time 100. P_2 begins running at this point, only to be preempted by P_1 at the start of its next period at time 100. P_2 is preempted because P_1 has an earlier deadline (time 150) than P_2 (time 160). At time 125, P_1 completes its CPU burst and P_2 resumes execution, finishing at time 145 and meeting its deadline as well. The system is idle until time 150, when P_1 is scheduled to run once again.

Unlike the rate-monotonic algorithm, EDF scheduling does not require that processes be periodic, nor must a process require a constant amount of CPU time per burst. The only requirement is that a process announce its deadline to the scheduler when it becomes runnable. The appeal of EDF scheduling is that it is theoretically optimal—theoretically, it can schedule processes so that each process can meet its deadline requirements and CPU utilization will be 100 percent. In practice, however, it is impossible to achieve this level of CPU utilization due to the cost of context switching between processes and interrupt handling.

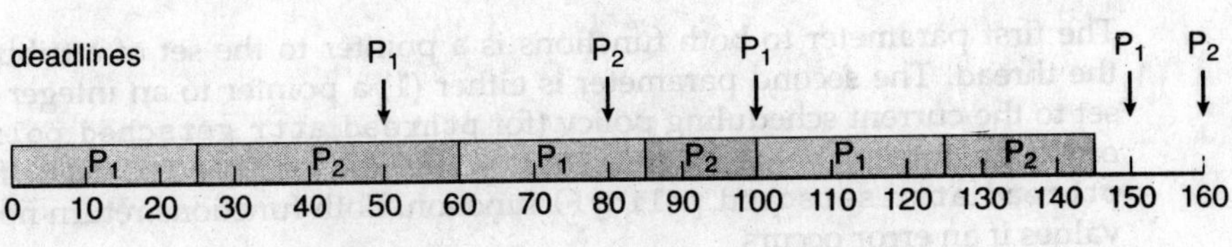

Figure 19.10 Earliest-deadline-first scheduling.

19.5.3 Proportional Share Scheduling

Proportional share schedulers operate by allocating T shares among all applications. An application can receive N shares of time, thus ensuring that the application will have N/T of the total processor time. As an example, assume that a total of $T = 100$ shares is to be divided among three processes, A, B, and C. A is assigned 50 shares, B is assigned 15 shares, and C is assigned 20 shares. This scheme ensures that A will have 50 percent of total processor time, B will have 15 percent, and C will have 20 percent.

Proportional share schedulers must work in conjunction with an admission control policy to guarantee that an application receives its allocated shares of time. An admission control policy will only admit a client requesting a particular number of shares if sufficient shares are available. In our current example, we have allocated $50 + 15 + 20 = 85$ shares of the total of 100 shares. If a new process D requested 30 shares, the admission controller would deny D entry into the system.

19.5.4 Pthread Scheduling

The POSIX standard also provides extensions for real-time computing—POSIX.1b. In this section, we cover some of the POSIX Pthread API related to scheduling real-time threads. Pthreads defines two scheduling classes for real-time threads:

- SCHED_FIFO
- SCHED_RR

SCHED_FIFO schedules threads according to a first-come, first-served policy using a FIFO queue as outlined in Section 5.3.1. However, there is no time slicing among threads of equal priority. Therefore, the highest-priority real-time thread at the front of the FIFO queue will be granted the CPU until it terminates or blocks. SCHED_RR (for round-robin) is similar to SCHED_FIFO except that it provides time slicing among threads of equal priority. Pthreads provides an additional scheduling class—SCHED_OTHER—but its implementation is undefined and system specific; it may behave differently on different systems.

The Pthread API specifies the following two functions for getting and setting the scheduling policy:

- `pthread_attr_getsched_policy(pthread_attr_t *attr, int *policy)`
- `pthread_attr_setsched_policy(pthread_attr_t *attr, int policy)`

The first parameter to both functions is a pointer to the set of attributes for the thread. The second parameter is either (1) a pointer to an integer that is set to the current scheduling policy (for `pthread_attr_getsched_policy()`) or (2) an integer value (SCHED_FIFO, SCHED_RR, or SCHED_OTHER) for the `pthread_attr_setsched_policy()` function. Both functions return non-zero values if an error occurs.

```
#include <pthread.h>
#include <stdio.h>
#define NUM_THREADS 5

int main(int argc, char *argv[])
{
   int i, policy;
   pthread_t tid[NUM_THREADS];
   pthread_attr_t attr;

   /* get the default attributes */
   pthread_attr_init(&attr);

   /* get the current scheduling policy */
   if (pthread_attr_getschedpolicy(&attr, &policy) != 0)
     fprintf(stderr, "Unable to get policy.\n");
   else {
     if (policy == SCHED_OTHER)
      printf("SCHED_OTHER\n");
     else if (policy == SCHED_RR)
      printf("SCHED_RR\n");
     else if (policy == SCHED_FIFO)
      printf("SCHED_FIFO\n");
   }

   /* set the scheduling policy - FIFO, RR, or OTHER */
   if (pthread_attr_setschedpolicy(&attr, SCHED_OTHER) != 0)
     fprintf(stderr, "Unable to set policy.\n");

   /* create the threads */
   for (i = 0; i < NUM_THREADS; i++)
      pthread_create(&tid[i],&attr,runner,NULL);

   /* now join on each thread */
   for (i = 0; i < NUM_THREADS; i++)
     pthread_join(tid[i], NULL);
}

/* Each thread will begin control in this function */
void *runner(void *param)
{
   /* do some work ... */

   pthread_exit(0);
}
```

Figure 19.11 Pthread scheduling API.

In Figure 19.11, we illustrate a Pthread program using this API. This program first determines the current scheduling policy and then sets the scheduling algorithm to SCHED_OTHER.

19.6 An Example: VxWorks 5.x

In this section, we describe VxWorks, a popular real-time operating system providing hard real-time support. VxWorks, commercially developed by Wind River Systems, is widely used in automobiles, consumer and industrial devices, and networking equipment such as switches and routers. VxWorks is also used to control the two rovers—*Spirit* and *Opportunity*—that began exploring the planet Mars in 2004.

The organization of VxWorks is shown in Figure 19.12. VxWorks is centered on the *Wind* microkernel. Recall from our discussion in Section 2.7.3 that microkernels are designed so that the operating-system kernel provides a bare minimum of features; additional utilities, such as networking, file systems, and graphics, are provided in libraries outside of the kernel. This approach offers many benefits, including minimizing the size of the kernel—a desirable feature for an embedded system requiring a small footprint.

The Wind microkernel supports the following basic features:

- **Processes**. The Wind microkernel provides support for individual processes and threads (using the Pthread API). However, similar to Linux, VxWorks does not distinguish between processes and threads, instead referring to both as **tasks**.

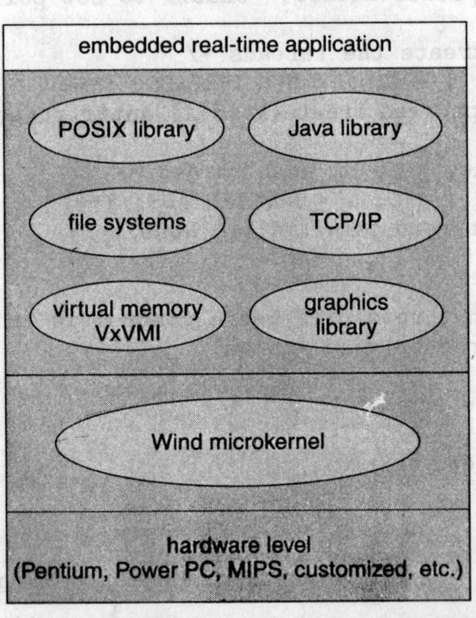

Figure 19.12 The organization of VxWorks.

REAL-TIME LINUX

The Linux operating system is being used increasingly in real-time environments. We have already covered its soft real-time scheduling features (Section 5.6.3), whereby real-time tasks are assigned the highest priority in the system. Additional features in the 2.6 release of the kernel make Linux even more suitable for embedded systems. These features include a fully preemptive kernel and a more efficient scheduling algorithm, which runs in $O(1)$ time regardless of the number of tasks active in the system. The 2.6 release also makes it easier to port Linux to different hardware architectures by dividing the kernel into modular components.

Another strategy for integrating Linux into real-time environments involves combining the Linux operating system with a small real-time kernel, thereby providing a system that acts as both a general-purpose and a real-time system. This is the approach taken by the RTLinux operating system. In RTLinux, the standard Linux kernel runs as a task in a small real-time operating system. The real-time kernel handles all interrupts—directing each interrupt to a handler in the standard kernel or to an interrupt handler in the real-time kernel. Furthermore, RTLinux prevents the standard Linux kernel from ever disabling interrupts, thus ensuring that it cannot add latency to the real-time system. RTLinux also provides different scheduling policies, including rate-monotonic scheduling (Section 19.5.1) and earliest-deadline-first scheduling (Section 19.5.2).

- **Scheduling**. The Wind microkernel provides two separate scheduling models: preemptive scheduling and nonpreemptive round-robin scheduling with 256 different priority levels. The scheduler also supports the POSIX API for real-time threads, covered in Section 19.5.4.
- **Interrupts**. The Wind microkernel also manages interrupts. To support hard real-time requirements, interrupt and dispatch latency times are bounded.
- **Interprocess communication**. The Wind microkernel provides both shared memory and message passing as mechanisms for communication between separate tasks. It also allows tasks to communicate using a technique known as **pipes**—a mechanism that behaves in the same way as a FIFO queue but allows tasks to communicate by writing to a special file, the pipe. To protect data shared by separate tasks, VxWorks provides semaphores and mutex locks with a priority inheritance protocol to prevent priority inversion.

Outside the microkernel, VxWorks includes several component libraries that provide support for POSIX, Java, TCP/IP networking, and the like. All components are optional, allowing the designer of an embedded system to customize the system according to its specific needs. For example, if networking is not required, the TCP/IP library can be excluded from the image of the operating system. This strategy allows the operating-system designer to include only required features, thereby minimizing the size—or footprint—of the operating system.

VxWorks takes an interesting approach to memory management, supporting two levels of virtual memory. The first level, which is quite simple, allows for control of the cache on a per-page basis. This policy enables an application to specify certain pages as non-cacheable. When data are being shared by separate tasks running on a multiprocessor architecture, it is possible that shared data can reside in separate caches local to individual processors. Unless an architecture supports a cache-coherency policy to ensure that the same data residing in two caches will not be different, such shared data should not be cached and should instead reside only in main memory so that all tasks maintain a consistent view of the data.

The second level of virtual memory requires the optional virtual memory component VxVMI (Figure 19.12), along with processor support for a memory-management unit (MMU). When this optional component is loaded on a system with an MMU, VxWorks allows a task to mark certain data areas as *private.* A data area marked as private may only be accessed by the task it belongs to. Furthermore, VxWorks allows pages containing kernel code along with the interrupt vector to be declared as read-only. This is useful, as VxWorks does not distinguish between user and kernel modes; all applications run in kernel mode, giving an application access to the entire address space of the system.

19.7 Summary

A real-time system is a computer system requiring that results arrive within a deadline period; results arriving after the deadline has passed are useless. Many real-time systems are embedded in consumer and industrial devices. There are two types of real-time systems: soft and hard real-time systems. Soft real-time systems are the least restrictive, assigning real-time tasks higher scheduling priority than other tasks. Hard real-time systems must guarantee that real-time tasks are serviced within their deadline periods. In addition to strict timing requirements, real-time systems can further be characterized as having only a single purpose and running on small, inexpensive devices.

To meet timing requirements, real-time operating systems must employ various techniques. The scheduler for a real-time operating system must support a priority-based algorithm with preemption. Furthermore, the operating system must allow tasks running in the kernel to be preempted in favor of higher-priority real-time tasks. Real-time operating systems also address specific timing issues by minimizing both interrupt and dispatch latency.

Real-time scheduling algorithms include rate-monotonic and earliest-deadline-first scheduling. Rate-monotonic scheduling assigns tasks that require the CPU more often a higher priority than tasks that require the CPU less often. Earliest-deadline-first scheduling assigns priority according to upcoming deadlines—the earlier the deadline, the higher the priority. Proportional share scheduling uses the technique of dividing up processor time into shares and assigning each process a number of shares, thus guaranteeing each process its proportional share of CPU time. The Pthread API provides various features for scheduling real-time threads as well.

Exercises

19.1 Explain why interrupt and dispatch latency times must be bounded in a hard real-time system.

19.2 Identify whether hard or soft real-time scheduling is more appropriate in the following environments:

a. Thermostat in a household

b. Control system for a nuclear power plant

c. Fuel economy system in an automobile

d. Landing system in a jet airliner

19.3 Consider two processes, P_1 and P_2, where $p_1 = 50$, $t_1 = 25$, $p_2 = 75$, and $t_2 = 30$.

a. Can these two processes be scheduled using rate-monotonic scheduling? Illustrate your answer using a Gantt chart such as the ones in Figures 19.7–19.10.

b. Illustrate the scheduling of these two processes using earliest-deadline-first (EDF) scheduling.

19.4 Discuss ways in which the priority inversion problem could be addressed in a real-time system. Also discuss whether the solutions could be implemented within the context of a proportional share scheduler.

19.5 Under what circumstances is rate-monotonic scheduling inferior to earliest-deadline-first scheduling in meeting the deadlines associated with processes?

Bibliographical Notes

The scheduling algorithms for hard real-time systems, such as rate monotonic scheduling and earliest-deadline-first scheduling, are presented in Liu and Layland [1973]. Other scheduling algorithms and extensions to previous algorithms are presented in Jensen et al. [1985], Lehoczky et al. [1989], Audsley et al. [1991], Mok [1983], and Stoica et al. [1996]. Mok [1983] describes a dynamic priority-assignment algorithm called least-laxity-first scheduling. Stoica et al. [1996] analyze the proportional share algorithm. Useful information regarding various popular operating systems used in embedded systems can be obtained from http://rtlinux.org, http://windriver.com, and http://qnx.com. Future directions and important research issues in the field of embedded systems are discussed in a research article by Stankovic [1996].

CHAPTER 20

Multimedia Systems

In earlier chapters, we generally concerned ourselves with how operating systems handle conventional data, such as text files, programs, binaries, word-processing documents, and spreadsheets. However, operating systems may have to handle other kinds of data as well. A relatively recent trend in technology is the incorporation of multimedia data into computer systems. Multimedia data consist of continuous-media (audio and video) data as well as conventional files. Continuous-media data differ from conventional data in that continuous-media data—such as frames of video—must be delivered (streamed) according to certain time restrictions (for example, 30 frames per second). In this chapter, we explore the demands of continuous-media data. We also discuss in more detail how such data differ from conventional data and how these differences affect the design of operating systems that support the requirements of multimedia systems.

CHAPTER OBJECTIVES

- To identify the characteristics of multimedia data.
- To examine several algorithms used to compress multimedia data.
- To explore the operating-system requirements of multimedia data, including CPU and disk scheduling and network management.

20.1 What Is Multimedia?

The term *multimedia* describes a wide range of applications that are in popular use today. These include audio and video files such as MP3 audio files, DVD movies, and short video clips of movie previews or news stories downloaded over the Internet. Multimedia applications also include live webcasts (broadcast over the World Wide Web) of speeches or sporting events and even live webcams that allow a viewer in Manhattan to observe customers at a cafe in Paris. Multimedia applications need not be either audio or video; rather, a multimedia application often includes a combination of both. For example, a movie may consist of separate audio and video tracks.

Nor must multimedia applications be delivered only to desktop personal computers. Increasingly, they are being directed toward smaller devices, including personal digital assistants (PDAs) and cellular telephones. For example, a stock trader may have stock quotes delivered in real time to her PDA.

In this section, we explore several characteristics of multimedia systems and examine how multimedia files can be delivered from a server to a client system. We also look at common standards for representing multimedia video and audio files.

20.1.1 Media Delivery

Multimedia data are stored in the file system just like any other data. The major difference between a regular file and a multimedia file is that the multimedia file must be accessed at a specific rate, whereas accessing the regular file requires no special timing. Let's use video as an example of what we mean by "rate." Video is represented by a series of images, formally known as **frames**, that are displayed in rapid succession. The faster the frames are displayed, the smoother the video appears. In general, a rate of 24 to 30 frames per second is necessary for video to appear smooth to human eyes. (The eye retains the image of each frame for a short time after it has been presented, a characteristic known as **persistence of vision**. A rate of 24 to 30 frames per second is fast enough to appear continuous.) A rate lower than 24 frames per second will result in a choppy-looking presentation. The video file must be accessed from the file system at a rate consistent with the rate at which the video is being displayed. We refer to data with associated rate requirements as **continuous-media data**.

Multimedia data may be delivered to a client either from the local file system or from a remote server. When the data are delivered from the local file system, we refer to the delivery as **local playback**. Examples include watching a DVD on a laptop computer or listening to an MP3 audio file on a handheld MP3 player. In these cases, the data comprise a regular file that is stored on the local file system and played back (that is, viewed or listened to) from that system.

Multimedia files may also be stored on a remote server and delivered to a client across a network using a technique known as **streaming**. A client may be a personal computer or a smaller device such as a handheld computer, PDA, or cellular telephone. Data from live continuous media—such as live webcams—are also streamed from a server to clients.

There are two types of streaming techniques: progressive download and real-time streaming. With a **progressive download**, a media file containing audio or video is downloaded and stored on the client's local file system. As the file is being downloaded, the client is able to play back the media file without having to wait for the file to be downloaded in its entirety. Because the media file is ultimately stored on the client system, progressive download is most useful for relatively small media files, such as short video clips.

Real-time streaming differs from progressive download in that the media file is streamed to the client but is only played—and not stored—by the client. Because the media file is not stored on the client system, real-time streaming is preferable to progressive download for media files that might be too large for storage on the system, such as long videos and Internet radio and TV broadcasts.

Both progressive download and real-time streaming may allow a client to move to different points in the stream, just as you can use the fast-forward and rewind operations on a DVD controller to move to different points in the DVD disc. For example, we could move to the end of a 5-minute streaming video or replay a certain section of a movie clip. The ability to move around within the media stream is known as **random access**.

Two types of real-time streaming are available: live streaming and on-demand streaming. **Live streaming** is used to deliver an event, such as a concert or a lecture, live as it is actually occurring. A radio program broadcast over the Internet is an example of a live real-time stream. In fact, one of the authors of this text regularly listens to a favorite radio station from Vermont while at his home in Utah as it is streamed live over the Internet. Live real-time streaming is also used for applications such as live webcams and video conferencing. Due to its live delivery, this type of real-time streaming does not allow clients random access to different points in the media stream. In addition, live delivery means that a client who wishes to view (or listen to) a particular live stream already in progress will "join" the session "late," thereby missing earlier portions of the stream. The same thing happens with a live TV or radio broadcast. If you start watching the 7:00 P.M. news at 7:10 P.M., you will have missed the first 10 minutes of the broadcast.

On-demand streaming is used to deliver media streams such as full-length movies and archived lectures. The difference between live and on-demand streaming is that on-demand streaming does not take place as the event is occurring. Thus, for example, whereas watching a live stream is like watching a news broadcast on TV, watching an on-demand stream is like viewing a movie on a DVD player at some convenient time—there is no notion of arriving late. Depending on the type of on-demand streaming, a client may or may not have random access to the stream.

Examples of well-known streaming media products include RealPlayer, Apple QuickTime, and Windows Media Player. These products include both servers that stream the media and client media players that are used for playback.

20.1.2 Characteristics of Multimedia Systems

The demands of multimedia systems are unlike the demands of traditional applications. In general, multimedia systems may have the following characteristics:

1. Multimedia files can be quite large. For example, a 100-minute MPEG-1 video file requires approximately 1.125 GB of storage space; 100 minutes of high-definition television (HDTV) requires approximately 15 GB of storage. A server storing hundreds or thousands of digital video files may thus require several terabytes of storage.

2. Continuous media may require very high data rates. Consider digital video, in which a frame of color video is displayed at a resolution of 800×600. If we use 24 bits to represent the color of each pixel (which allows us to have 2^{24}, or roughly 16 million, different colors), a single

frame requires $800 \times 600 \times 24 = 11,520,000$ bits of data. If the frames are displayed at a rate of 30 frames per second, a bandwidth in excess of 345 Mbps is required.

3. Multimedia applications are sensitive to timing delays during playback. Once a continuous-media file is delivered to a client, delivery must continue at a certain rate during playback of the media; otherwise, the listener or viewer will be subjected to pauses during the presentation.

20.1.3 Operating-System Issues

For a computer system to deliver continuous-media data, it must guarantee the specific rate and timing requirements—also known as **quality of service**, or QoS, requirements—of continuous media.

Providing these QoS guarantees affects several components in a computer system and influences such operating-system issues as CPU scheduling, disk scheduling, and network management. Specific examples include the following:

1. Compression and decoding may require significant CPU processing.
2. Multimedia tasks must be scheduled with certain priorities to ensure meeting the deadline requirements of continuous media.
3. Similarly, file systems must be efficient to meet the rate requirements of continuous media.
4. Network protocols must support bandwidth requirements while minimizing delay and jitter (which we discuss further later in the chapter).

In later sections, we explore these and several other issues related to QoS. First, however, we provide an overview of various techniques for compressing multimedia data. As suggested above, compression makes significant demands on the CPU.

20.2 Compression

Because of the size and rate requirements of multimedia systems, multimedia files are often compressed from their original form to a much smaller form. Once a file has been compressed, it takes up less space for storage and can be delivered to a client more quickly. Compression is particularly important when the content is being streamed across a network connection. In discussing file compression, we often refer to the **compression ratio**, which is the ratio of the original file size to the size of the compressed file. For example, an 800-KB file that is compressed to 100 KB has a compression ratio of 8:1.

Once a file has been compressed (**encoded**), it must be decompressed (**decoded**) before it can be accessed. A feature of the algorithm used to compress the file affects the later decompression. Compression algorithms are classified as either **lossy** or **lossless**. With lossy compression, some of the original data are lost when the file is decoded, whereas lossless compression ensures that the compressed file can always be restored to its original form. In general, lossy techniques provide much higher compression ratios. Obviously, though, only certain types of data can tolerate lossy compression—namely, images, audio, and video. Lossy compression algorithms often work by eliminating certain data, such as very high or low frequencies that a human ear cannot detect. Some lossy compression algorithms used on video operate by storing only the differences between successive frames. Lossless algorithms are used for compressing text files, such as computer programs (for example, **zipping** files), because we want to restore these compressed files to their original state.

A number of different lossy compression schemes for continuous-media data are commercially available. In this section, we cover one used by the Moving Picture Experts Group, better known as MPEG.

MPEG refers to a set of file formats and compression standards for digital video. Because digital video often contains an audio portion as well, each of the standards is divided into three layers. Layers 3 and 2 apply to the audio and video portions of the media file. Layer 1, known as the **systems layer**, contains timing information to allow the MPEG player to multiplex the audio and video portions so that they are synchronized during playback. There are three major MPEG standards: MPEG-1, MPEG-2, and MPEG-4.

MPEG-1 is used for digital video and its associated audio stream. The resolution of MPEG-1 is 352 × 240 at 30 frames per second with a bit rate of up to 1.5 Mbps. This provides a quality slightly lower than that of conventional VCR videos. MP3 audio files (a popular medium for storing music) use the audio layer (layer 3) of MPEG-1. For video, MPEG-1 can achieve a compression ratio of up to 200:1, although in practice compression ratios are much lower. Because MPEG-1 does not require high data rates, it is often used to download short video clips over the Internet.

MPEG-2 provides better quality than MPEG-1 and is used for compressing DVD movies and digital television (including high-definition television, or HDTV). MPEG-2 identifies a number of levels and profiles of video compression. The **level** refers to the resolution of the video; the **profile** characterizes the video's quality. In general, the higher the level of resolution and the better the quality of the video, the higher the required data rate. Typical bit rates for MPEG-2 encoded files are 1.5 Mbps to 15 Mbps. Because MPEG-2 requires higher rates, it is often unsuitable for delivery of video across a network and is generally used for local playback.

MPEG-4 is the most recent of the standards and is used to transmit audio, video, and graphics, including two-dimensional and three-dimensional animation layers. Animation makes it possible for end users to interact with the file during playback. For example, a potential home buyer can download an MPEG-4 file and take a virtual tour through a home she is considering purchasing, moving from room to room as she chooses. Another appealing feature of MPEG-4 is that it provides a scalable level of quality, allowing delivery over relatively slow network connections such as 56-Kbps modems or over high-speed local area networks with rates of several megabits per second. Furthermore, by providing a scalable level of quality, MPEG-4 audio and video files can be delivered to wireless devices, including handheld computers, PDAs, and cell phones.

All three MPEG standards discussed here perform lossy compression to achieve high compression ratios. The fundamental idea behind MPEG compression is to store the differences between successive frames. We do not cover further details of how MPEG performs compression but rather encourage the interested reader to consult the bibliographical notes at the end of this chapter.

20.3 Requirements of Multimedia Kernels

As a result of the characteristics described in Section 20.1.2, multimedia applications often require levels of service from the operating system that differ from the requirements of traditional applications, such as word processors, compilers, and spreadsheets. Timing and rate requirements are perhaps the issues of foremost concern, as the playback of audio and video data demands that the data be delivered within a certain deadline and at a continuous, fixed rate. Traditional applications typically do not have such time and rate constraints.

Tasks that request data at constant intervals—or **periods**—are known as **periodic processes**. For example, an MPEG-1 video might require a rate of 30 frames per second during playback. Maintaining this rate requires that a frame be delivered approximately every $1/30^{th}$, or 3.34 hundredths, of a second. To put this in the context of deadlines, let's assume that frame F_j succeeds frame F_i in the video playback and that frame F_i was displayed at time T_0. The deadline for displaying frame F_j is 3.34 hundredths of a second after time T_0. If the operating system is unable to display the frame by this deadline, the frame will be omitted from the stream.

As mentioned earlier, rate requirements and deadlines are known as quality of service (QoS) requirements. There are three QoS levels:

1. **Best-effort service**. The system makes a best-effort attempt to satisfy the requirements; however, no guarantees are made.
2. **Soft QoS**. This level treats different types of traffic in different ways, giving certain traffic streams higher priority than other streams. However, just as with best-effort service, no guarantees are made.
3. **Hard QoS**. The quality-of-service requirements are guaranteed.

Traditional operating systems—the systems we have discussed in this text so far—typically provide only best-effort service and rely on **overprovisioning**; that is, they simply assume that the total amount of resources available will tend to be larger than a worst-case workload would demand. If demand exceeds resource capacity, manual intervention must take place, and a process (or several processes) must be removed from the system. However next-generation multimedia systems cannot make such assumptions. These systems must provide continuous-media applications with the guarantees made possible by hard QoS. Therefore, in the remainder of this discussion, when we refer to QoS, we mean hard QoS. Next, we explore various techniques that enable multimedia systems to provide such service-level guarantees.

There are a number of parameters defining QoS for multimedia applications, including the following:

- **Throughput.** Throughput is the total amount of work done during a certain interval. For multimedia applications, throughput is the required data rate.
- **Delay.** Delay refers to the elapsed time from when a request is first submitted to when the desired result is produced. For example, the time from when a client requests a media stream to when the stream is delivered is the delay.
- **Jitter.** Jitter is related to delay; but whereas delay refers to the time a client must wait to receive a stream, jitter refers to delays that occur during playback of the stream. Certain multimedia applications, such as on-demand real-time streaming, can tolerate this sort of delay. Jitter is generally considered unacceptable for continuous-media applications, however, because it may mean long pauses—or lost frames—during playback. Clients can often compensate for jitter by buffering a certain amount of data—say, 5 seconds' worth—before beginning playback.
- **Reliability.** Reliability refers to how errors are handled during transmission and processing of continuous media. Errors may occur due to lost packets in the network or processing delays by the CPU. In these—and other—scenarios, errors cannot be corrected, since packets typically arrive too late to be useful.

The quality of service may be **negotiated** between the client and the server. For example, continuous-media data may be compressed at different levels of quality: the higher the quality, the higher the required data rate. A client may negotiate a specific data rate with a server, thus agreeing to a certain level of quality during playback. Furthermore, many media players allow the client to configure the player according to the speed of the client's connection to the network. This allows a client to receive a streaming service at a data rate specific to a particular connection. Thus, the client is negotiating quality of service with the content provider.

To provide QoS guarantees, operating systems often use **admission control**, which is simply the practice of admitting a request for service only if the server has sufficient resources to satisfy the request. We see admission control quite often in our everyday lives. For example, a movie theater only admits as many customers as it has seats in the theater. (There are also many situations in everyday life where admission control is not practiced but would be desirable!) If no admission-control policy is used in a multimedia environment, the demands on the system might become so great that the system becomes unable to meet its QoS guarantees.

In Chapter 6, we discussed using semaphores as a method of implementing a simple admission-control policy. In this scenario, there exist a finite number of nonshareable resources. When a resource is requested, we grant the request only if sufficient resources are available; otherwise, the requesting process must wait until a resource becomes available. We can use semaphores to implement an admission-control policy by first initializing a semaphore to the number of resources available. Every request for a resource is made through a `wait()` operation on the semaphore; a resource is released with an invocation of `signal()` on the semaphore. Once all resources are in use, subsequent calls to `wait()` block until there is a corresponding `signal()`.

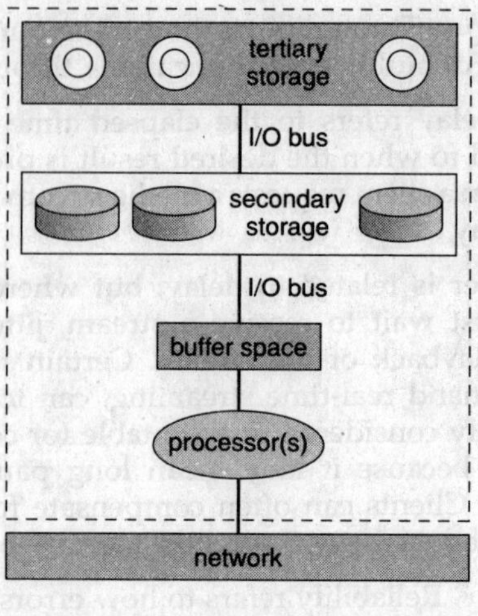

Figure 20.1 Resources on a file server.

A common technique for implementing admission control is to use **resource reservations**. For example, resources on a file server may include the CPU, memory, file system, devices, and network (Figure 20.1). Note that resources may be either exclusive or shared and that there may be either single or multiple instances of each resource type. To use a resource, a client must make a reservation request for the resource in advance. If the request cannot be granted, the reservation is denied. An admission-control scheme assigns a **resource manager** to each type of resource. Requests for resources have associated QoS requirements—for example, required data rates. When a request for a resource arrives, the resource manager determines if the resource can meet the QoS demands of the request. If it cannot, the request may be rejected, or a lower level of QoS may be negotiated between the client and the server. If the request is accepted, the resource manager reserves the resources for the requesting client, thus assuring the client that the desired QoS requirements will be met. In Section 20.7.2, we examine the admission-control algorithm used to ensure QoS guarantees in the CineBlitz multimedia storage server.

20.4 CPU Scheduling

In Chapter 19, which covers real-time systems, we distinguished between **soft real-time systems** and **hard real-time systems**. Soft real-time systems simply give scheduling priority to critical processes. A soft real-time system ensures that a critical process will be given preference over a noncritical process but provides no guarantee as to when the critical process will be scheduled. A typical requirement of continuous media, however, is that data must be delivered to a client by a certain deadline; data that do not arrive by the deadline are unusable. Multimedia systems thus require hard real-time scheduling to ensure that a critical task will be serviced within a guaranteed period of time.

Another scheduling issue concerns whether a scheduling algorithm uses **static priority** or **dynamic priority**—a distinction first discussed in Chapter 5. The difference between the two is that the priority of a process will remain unchanged if the scheduler assigns it a static priority. Scheduling algorithms that assign dynamic priorities allow priorities to change over time. Most operating systems use dynamic priorities when scheduling non-real-time tasks with the intention of giving higher priority to interactive processes. However, when scheduling real-time tasks, most systems assign static priorities, as the design of the scheduler is less complex.

Several of the real-time scheduling strategies discussed in Section 19.5 can be used to meet the rate and deadline QoS requirements of continuous-media applications.

20.5 Disk Scheduling

We first discussed disk scheduling in Chapter 12. There, we focused primarily on systems that handle conventional data; for these systems, the scheduling goals are fairness and throughput. As a result, most traditional disk schedulers employ some form of the SCAN (Section 12.4.3) or C-SCAN (Section 12.4.4) algorithm.

Continuous-media files, however, have two constraints that conventional data files generally do not have: timing deadlines and rate requirements. These two constraints must be satisfied to preserve QoS guarantees, and disk-scheduling algorithms must be optimized for the constraints. Unfortunately, these two constraints are often in conflict. Continuous-media files typically require very high disk-bandwidth rates to satisfy their data-rate requirements. Because disks have relatively low transfer rates and relatively high latency rates, disk schedulers must reduce the latency times to ensure high bandwidth. However, reducing latency times may result in a scheduling policy that does not prioritize according to deadlines. In this section, we explore two disk-scheduling algorithms that meet the QoS requirements for continuous-media systems.

20.5.1 Earliest-Deadline-First Scheduling

We first presented the earliest-deadline-first (EDF) algorithm in Section 19.5.2 as an example of a CPU-scheduling algorithm that assigns priorities according to deadlines. EDF can also be used as a disk-scheduling algorithm; in this context, EDF uses a queue to order requests according to the time each request must be completed (its deadline). EDF is similar to shortest-seek-time-first (SSTF), discussed in Section 12.4.2, except that instead of servicing the request closest to the current cylinder, we service requests according to deadline—the request with the closest deadline is serviced first.

A problem with this approach is that servicing requests strictly according to deadline may result in higher seek times, since the disk heads may move randomly throughout the disk without any regard to their current position. For example, suppose a disk head is currently at cylinder 75 and the queue of cylinders (ordered according to deadlines) is 98, 183, 105. Under strict EDF scheduling, the disk head will move from 75, to 98, to 183, and then back to

105. Note that the head passes over cylinder 105 as it travels from 98 to 183. It is possible that the disk scheduler could have serviced the request for cylinder 105 en route to cylinder 183 and still preserved the deadline requirement for cylinder 183.

20.5.2 SCAN-EDF Scheduling

The fundamental problem with strict EDF scheduling is that it ignores the position of the read–write heads of the disk; it is possible that the heads will swing wildly to and fro across the disk, leading to unacceptable seek times that negatively affect disk throughput. Recall that this is the same issue faced with FCFS scheduling (Section 12.4.1). In the context of CPU scheduling, we can address this issue by adopting SCAN scheduling, wherein the disk arm moves in one direction across the disk, servicing requests according to their proximity to the current cylinder. Once the disk arm reaches the end of the disk, it begins moving in the reverse direction. This strategy optimizes seek times.

SCAN-EDF is a hybrid algorithm that combines EDF with SCAN scheduling. SCAN-EDF starts with EDF ordering but services requests with the same deadline using SCAN order. What if several requests have different deadlines that are relatively close together? In this case, SCAN-EDF may batch requests, using SCAN ordering to service requests in the same batch. There are many techniques for batching requests with similar deadlines; the only requirement is that reordering requests within a batch must not prevent a request from being serviced by its deadline. If deadlines are equally distributed, batches can be organized in groups of a certain size—say, 10 requests per batch.

Another approach is to batch requests whose deadlines fall within a given time threshold—say, 100 milliseconds. Let's consider an example in which we batch requests in this way. Assume we have the following requests, each with a specified deadline (in milliseconds) and a requested cylinder:

request	deadline	cylinder
A	150	25
B	201	112
C	399	95
D	94	31
E	295	185
F	78	85
G	165	150
H	125	101
I	300	85
J	210	90

Suppose we are at $time_0$, the cylinder currently being serviced is 50, and the disk head is moving toward cylinder 51. According to our batching scheme, requests D and F will be in the first batch; A, G, and H in batch 2; B, E, and J in batch 3; and C and I in the last batch. Requests within each batch will be ordered according to SCAN order. Thus, in batch 1, we will first service request F and then request D. Note that we are moving downward in cylinder numbers, from 85 to 31. In batch 2, we first service request A; then the heads begin moving upward in cylinders, servicing requests H and then G. Batch 3 is serviced in the order E, B, J. Requests I and C are serviced in the final batch.

20.6 Network Management

Perhaps the foremost QoS issue with multimedia systems concerns preserving rate requirements. For example, if a client wishes to view a video compressed with MPEG-1, the quality of service greatly depends on the system's ability to deliver the frames at the required rate.

Our coverage of issues such as CPU- and disk-scheduling algorithms has focused on how these techniques can be used to better meet the quality-of-service requirements of multimedia applications. However, if the media file is being streamed over a network—perhaps the Internet—issues relating to how the network delivers the multimedia data can also significantly affect how QoS demands are met. In this section, we explore several network issues related to the unique demands of continuous media.

Before we proceed, it is worth noting that computer networks in general —and the Internet in particular— currently do not provide network protocols that can ensure the delivery of data with timing requirements. (There are some proprietary protocols—notably those running on Cisco routers—that do allow certain network traffic to be prioritized to meet QoS requirements. Such proprietary protocols are not generalized for use across the Internet and therefore do not apply to our discussion.)

When data are routed across a network, it is likely that the transmission will encounter congestion, delays, and other network traffic issues—issues that are beyond the control of the originator of the data. For multimedia data with timing requirements, any timing issues must be synchronized between the end hosts: the server delivering the content and the client playing it back.

One protocol that addresses timing issues is the **real-time transport protocol** (RTP). RTP is an Internet standard for delivering real-time data, including audio and video. It can be used for transporting media formats such as MP3 audio files and video files compressed using MPEG. RTP does not provide any QoS guarantees; rather, it provides features that allow a receiver to remove jitter introduced by delays and congestion in the network.

In following sections, we consider two other approaches for handling the unique requirements of continuous media.

20.6.1 Unicasting and Multicasting

In general, there are three methods for delivering content from a server to a client across a network:

- **Unicasting**. The server delivers the content to a single client. If the content is being delivered to more than one client, the server must establish a separate unicast for each client.

- **Broadcasting**. The server delivers the content to all clients, regardless of whether they wish to receive the content or not.
- **Multicasting**. The server delivers the content to a group of receivers that indicate they wish to receive the content; this method lies somewhere between unicasting and broadcasting.

An issue with unicast delivery is that the server must establish a separate unicast session for each client. This seems especially wasteful for live real-time streaming, where the server must make several copies of the same content, one for each client. Obviously, broadcasting is not always appropriate, as not all clients may wish to receive the stream. (Suffice it to say that broadcasting is typically only used across local area networks and is not possible across the public Internet.)

Multicasting appears to be a reasonable compromise, since it allows the server to deliver a single copy of the content to all clients indicating that they wish to receive it. The difficulty with multicasting from a practical standpoint is that the clients must be physically close to the server or to intermediate routers that relay the content from the originating server. If the route from the server to the client must cross intermediate routers, the routers must also support multicasting. If these conditions are not met, the delays incurred during routing may result in violation of the timing requirements of the continuous media. In the worst case, if a client is connected to an intermediate router that does not support multicasting, the client will be unable to receive the multicast stream at all!

Currently, most streaming media are delivered across unicast channels; however, multicasting is used in various areas where the organization of the server and clients is known in advance. For example, a corporation with several sites across a country may be able to ensure that all sites are connected to multicasting routers and are within reasonable physical proximity to the routers. The organization will then be able to deliver a presentation from the chief executive officer using multicasting.

20.6.2 Real-Time Streaming Protocol

In Section 20.1.1, we described some features of streaming media. As we noted there, users may be able to randomly access a media stream, perhaps replaying or pausing, as they would with a DVD controller. How is this possible?

To answer this question, let's consider how streaming media are delivered to clients. One approach is to stream the media from a standard Web server using the hypertext transport protocol, or HTTP—the protocol used to deliver documents from a Web server. Quite often, clients use a **media player**, such as QuickTime, RealPlayer, or Windows Media Player, to play back media streamed from a standard Web server. Typically, the client first requests a **metafile**, which contains the location (possibly identified by a uniform resource locator, or URL) of the streaming media file. This metafile is delivered to the client's Web browser, and the browser then starts the appropriate media player according to the type of media specified by the metafile. For example, a Real Audio stream would require the RealPlayer, while the Windows Media Player would be used to play back streaming Windows media. The media player then contacts the Web server and requests the streaming media. The stream

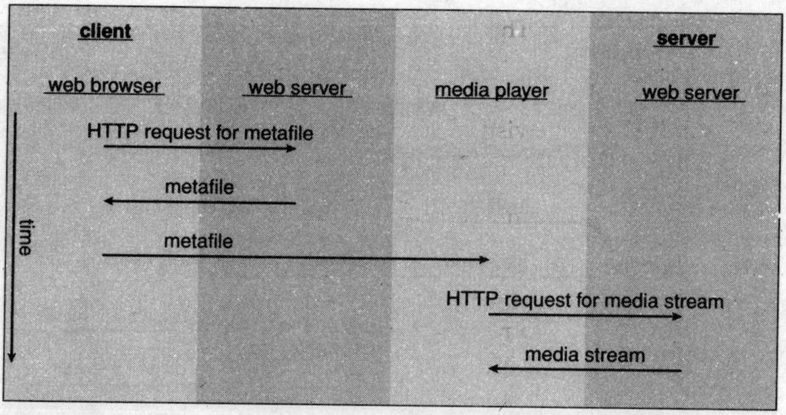

Figure 20.2 Streaming media from a conventional Web server.

is delivered from the Web server to the media player using standard HTTP requests. This process is outlined in Figure 20.2.

The problem with delivering streaming media from a standard Web server is that HTTP is considered a **stateless** protocol; thus, a Web server does not maintain the state (or status) of its connection with a client. As a result, it is difficult for a client to pause during the delivery of streaming media content, since pausing would require the Web server to know where in the stream to begin when the client wished to resume playback.

An alternative strategy is to use a specialized streaming server that is designed specifically for streaming media. One protocol designed for communication between streaming servers and media players is known as the **real-time streaming protocol**, or **RTSP**. The significant advantage RTSP provides over HTTP is a stateful connection between the client and the server, which allows the client to pause or seek to random positions in the stream during playback. Delivery of streaming media using RTSP is similar to delivery using HTTP (Figure 20.2) in that the metafile is delivered using a conventional Web server. However, rather than a Web server, the streaming media is delivered from a streaming server using the RTSP protocol. The operation of RTSP is shown in Figure 20.3.

RTSP defines several commands as part of its protocol; these commands are sent from a client to an RTSP streaming server. The commands include the following:

- SETUP. The server allocates resources for a client session.
- PLAY. The server delivers a stream to a client session established from a SETUP command.
- PAUSE. The server suspends delivery of a stream but maintains the resources for the session.
- TEARDOWN. The server breaks down the connection and frees up resources allocated for the session.

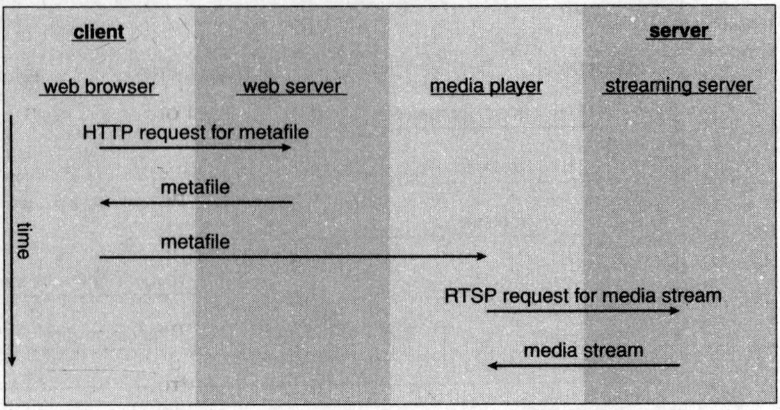

Figure 20.3 Real-time streaming protocol (RTSP).

The commands can be illustrated with a state machine for the server, as shown in Figure 20.4. As you can see in the figure, the RTSP server may be in one of three states: **init**, **ready**, and **playing**. Transitions between these three states are triggered when the server receives one of the RTSP commands from the client.

Using RTSP rather than HTTP for streaming media offers several other advantages, but they are primarily related to networking issues and are therefore beyond the scope of this text. We encourage interested readers to consult the bibliographical notes at the end of this chapter for sources of further information.

20.7 An Example: CineBlitz

The CineBlitz multimedia storage server is a high-performance media server that supports both continuous media with rate requirements (such as video and audio) and conventional data with no associated rate requirements (such as text and images). CineBlitz refers to clients with rate requirements as **real-time clients**, whereas **non-real-time clients** have no rate constraints. CineBlitz guarantees to meet the rate requirements of real-time clients by implementing an admission controller, admitting a client only if there are sufficient resources to allow data retrieval at the required rate. In this section, we explore the CineBlitz disk-scheduling and admission-control algorithms.

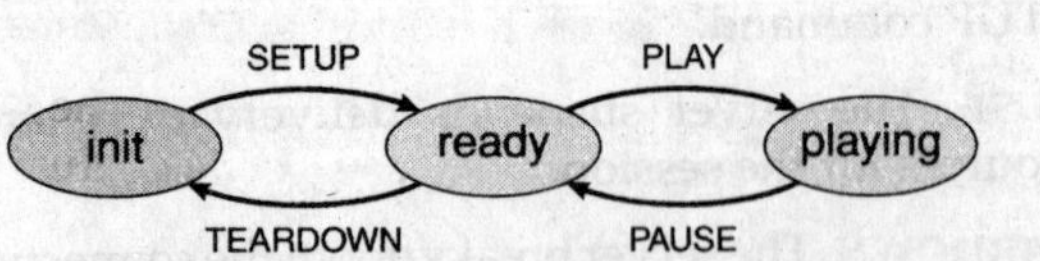

Figure 20.4 Finite-state machine representing RTSP.

20.7.1 Disk Scheduling

The CineBlitz disk scheduler services requests in cycles. At the beginning of each service cycle, requests are placed in C-SCAN order (Section 12.4.4). Recall from our earlier discussions of C-SCAN that the disk heads move from one end of the disk to the other. However, rather than reversing direction when they reach the end of the disk, as in pure SCAN disk scheduling (Section 12.4.3), the disk heads move back to the beginning of the disk.

20.7.2 Admission Control

The admission-control algorithm in CineBlitz must monitor requests from both real-time and non-real-time clients, ensuring that both classes of clients receive service. Furthermore, the admission controller must provide the rate guarantees required by real-time clients. To ensure fairness, only a fraction p of time is reserved for real-time clients, while the remainder, $1 - p$, is set aside for non-real-time clients. Here, we explore the admission controller for real-time clients only; thus, the term *client* refers to a real-time client.

The admission controller in CineBlitz monitors various system resources, such as disk bandwidth and disk latency, while keeping track of available buffer space. The CineBlitz admission controller admits a client only if there is enough available disk bandwidth and buffer space to retrieve data for the client at its required rate.

CineBlitz queues requests for continuous media files, where $R_1, R_2, R_3, ..., R_n$ are the requests and r_i is the required data rate for a given request R_i. Requests in the queue are served in cyclic order in rounds of time-length T (T being tpically measured in seconds). The scheme is using a technique known as double buffering, wherein a buffer is allocated for each request R_i of size $2 \times T \times r_i$.

During each cycle I, the server must, for each request R_j:

1. Retrieve the data from disk to buffer (I mod 2).
2. Transfer data from the (($I + 1$) mod 2) buffer to the client.

This process is illustrated in Figure 20.5. For N clients, the total buffer space B required is

$$\sum_{i=1}^{N} 2 \times T \times r_i \le B. \tag{20.1}$$

The fundamental idea behind the admission controller in CineBlitz is to bound requests for entry into the queue according to the following criteria:

1. The service time for each request is first estimated.
2. A request is admitted only if the sum of the estimated service times for all admitted requests does not exceed the duration of service cycle T.

Let $T \times r_i$ bits be retrieved during a cycle for each real-time client R_i with rate r_i. If $R_1, R_2, ..., R_n$ are the clients currently active in the system, then the admission controller must ensure that the total time for retrieving $T \times r_1, T \times r_2, ..., T \times r_n$

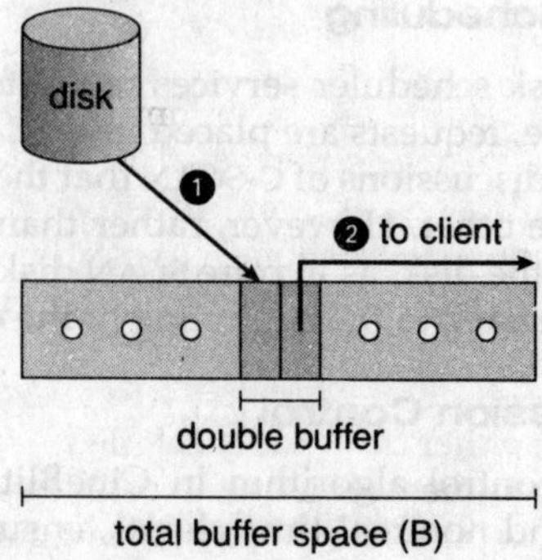

Figure 20.5 Double buffering in CineBlitz.

bits for the corresponding real-time clients does not exceed T. We explore the details of this admission policy in the remainder of this section.

If b is the size of a disk block, then the maximum number of disk blocks that can be retrieved for request R_k during each cycle is $\lceil (T \times r_k)/b \rceil + 1$. The 1 in this formula comes from the fact that, if $T \times r_k$ is less than b, then it is possible for $T \times r_k$ bits to span the last portion of one disk block and the beginning of another, causing two blocks to be retrieved. We know that the retrieval of a disk block involves (a) a seek to the track containing the block and (b) the rotational delay as the data in the desired track arrive under the disk head. As described, CineBlitz uses a C-SCAN disk-scheduling algorithm, so disk blocks are retrieved in the sorted order of their positions on the disk.

If t_{seek} and t_{rot} refer to the worst-case seek and rotational delay times, the maximum latency incurred for servicing N requests is

$$2 \times t_{seek} + \sum_{i=1}^{N} \left(\lceil \frac{T \times r_i}{b} \rceil + 1 \right) \times t_{rot}. \tag{20.2}$$

In this equation, the $2 \times t_{seek}$ component refers to the maximum disk-seek latency incurred in a cycle. The second component reflects the sum of the retrievals of the disk blocks multiplied by the worst-case rotational delay.

If the transfer rate of the disk is r_{disk}, then the time to transfer $T \times r_k$ bits of data for request R_k is $(T \times r_k)/r_{disk}$. As a result, the total time for retrieving $T \times r_1, T \times r_2, ..., T \times r_n$ bits for requests $R_1, R_2, ..., R_n$ is the sum of equation 20.2 and

$$\sum_{i=1}^{N} \frac{T \times r_i}{r_{disk}} \tag{20.3}$$

Therefore, the admission controller in CineBlitz only admits a new client R_i if at least $2 \times T \times r_i$ bits of free buffer space are available for the client and the following equation is satisfied:

$$2 \times t_{seek} + \sum_{i=1}^{N} \left(\lceil \frac{T \times r_i}{b} \rceil + 1 \right) \times t_{rot} + \sum_{i=1}^{N} \frac{T \times r_i}{r_{disk}} \leq T. \tag{20.4}$$

20.8 Summary

Multimedia applications are in common use in modern computer systems. Multimedia files include video and audio files, which may be delivered to systems such as desktop computers, personal digital assistants, and cell phones. The primary distinction between multimedia data and conventional data is that multimedia data have specific rate and deadline requirements. Because multimedia files have specific timing requirements, the data must often be compressed before delivery to a client for playback. Multimedia data may be delivered either from the local file system or from a multimedia server across a network connection using a technique known as streaming.

The timing requirements of multimedia data are known as quality-of-service requirements, and conventional operating systems often cannot make quality-of-service guarantees. To provide quality of service, multimedia systems must provide a form of admission control whereby a system accepts a request only if it can meet the quality-of-service level specified by the request. Providing quality-of-service guarantees requires evaluating how an operating system performs CPU scheduling, disk scheduling, and network management. Both CPU and disk scheduling typically use the deadline requirements of a continuous-media task as a scheduling criterion. Network management requires the use of protocols that handle delay and jitter caused by the network as well as allowing a client to pause or move to different positions in the stream during playback.

Exercises

20.1 Explain why the traditional Internet protocols for transmitting data are not sufficient to provide the quality-of-service guarantees required for a multimedia system. Discuss what changes are required to provide the QoS guarantees.

20.2 Contrast unicasting, multicasting, and broadcasting as techniques for delivering content across a computer network.

20.3 Assume that we wish to compress a digital video file using MPEG-1 technology. The target bit rate is 1.5 Mbps. If the video is displayed at a resolution of 352×240 at 30 frames per second using 24 bits to represent each color, what is the necessary compression ratio to achieve the desired bit rate?

20.4 Assume that a digital video file is being displayed at a rate of 30 frames per second; the resolution of each frame is 640×480, and 24 bits are being used to represent each color. Assuming that no compression is being used, what is the bandwidth necessary to deliver this file? Next, assuming that the file has been compressed at a ratio of 200 : 1, what is the bandwidth necessary to deliver the compressed file?

20.5 A multimedia application consists of a set containing 100 images, 10 minutes of video, and 10 minutes of audio. The compressed sizes of the images, video, and audio are 500 MB, 550 MB, and 8 MB, respectively. The images were compressed at a ratio of 15 : 1, and the video and audio were compressed at 200 : 1 and 10 : 1, respectively. What were the sizes of the images, video, and audio before compression?

20.6 Which of the following types of real-time streaming applications can tolerate delay? Which can tolerate jitter?

- Live real-time streaming
- On-demand real-time streaming

20.7 Distinguish between progressive download and real-time streaming.

20.8 The following table contains a number of requests with their associated deadlines and cylinders. Requests with deadlines occurring within 100 milliseconds of each other will be batched. The disk head is currently at cylinder 94 and is moving toward cylinder 95. If SCAN-EDF disk scheduling is used, how are the requests batched together, and what is the order of requests within each batch?

request	deadline	cylinder
R1	57	77
R2	300	95
R3	250	25
R4	88	28
R5	85	100
R6	110	90
R7	299	50
R8	300	77
R9	120	12
R10	212	2

20.9 Repeat Exercise 20.8, but this time batch requests that have deadlines occurring within 75 milliseconds of each other.

20.10 What operating principle is used by the CineBlitz system in performing admission control for requests for media files?

20.11 Consider two processes, P_1 and P_2, where $p_1 = 50$, $t_1 = 25$, $p_2 = 75$, and $t_2 = 30$.

a. Can these two processes be scheduled using rate-monotonic scheduling? Illustrate your answer using a Gantt chart.

b. Illustrate the scheduling of these two processes using earliest-deadline-first (EDF) scheduling.

Bibliographical Notes

Fuhrt [1994] provides a general overview of multimedia systems. Topics related to the delivery of multimedia through networks can be found in Kurose and Ross [2005]. Operating-system support for multimedia is discussed in Steinmetz [1995] and Leslie et al. [1996]. Resource management for resources such as processing capability and memory buffers is discussed in Mercer et al. [1994] and Druschel and Peterson [1993]. Reddy and Wyllie [1994] give a good overview of issues relating to the use of I/O in a multimedia system. Discussions regarding the appropriate programming model for developing multimedia applications are presented in Regehr et al. [2000]. An admission control system for a rate-monotonic scheduler is considered in Lauzac et al. [2003]. Bolosky et al. [1997] present a system for serving video data and discuss the schedule-management issues that arise in such a system. The details of a real-time streaming protocol can be found at http://www.rtsp.org. Tudor [1995] gives a tutorial on MPEG-2. A tutorial on video compression techniques can be found at http://www.wave-report.com/tutorials/VC.htm.

Part Nine

Case Studies

We can now integrate the concepts described in this book by describing real operating systems. Two such systems are covered in great detail—Linux and Windows XP. We chose Linux for several reasons: It is popular, it is freely available, and it represents a full-featured UNIX system. This gives a student of operating systems an opportunity to read—and modify—*real* operating-system source code.

We also cover Windows XP in great detail. This recent operating system from Microsoft is gaining popularity, not only in the stand-alone-machine market, but also in the workgroup–server market. We chose Windows XP because it provides an opportunity for us to study a modern operating system that has a design and implementation drastically different from those of UNIX.

In addition, we briefly discuss other highly influential operating systems. We have chosen the order of presentation to highlight the similarities and differences among the systems; it is not strictly chronological and does not reflect the relative importance of the systems.

Finally, we provide on-line coverage of three other systems. The FreeBSD system is another UNIX system. However, whereas Linux combines features from several UNIX systems, FreeBSD is based on the BSD model of UNIX. FreeBSD source code, like Linux source code, is freely available. The Mach operating system is a modern operating system that provides compatibility with BSD UNIX. Windows is another modern operating system from Microsoft for Intel Pentium and later microprocessors; it is compatible with MS-DOS and Microsoft Windows applications.

CHAPTER 21

The Linux System

This chapter presents an in-depth examination of the Linux operating system. By examining a complete, real system, we can see how the concepts we have discussed relate both to one another and to practice.

Linux is a version of UNIX that has gained popularity in recent years. In this chapter, we look at the history and development of Linux and cover the user and programmer interfaces that Linux presents—interfaces that owe a great deal to the UNIX tradition. We also discuss the internal methods by which Linux implements these interfaces. Linux is a rapidly evolving operating system. This chapter describes developments through the Linux 2.6 kernel, which was released in late 2003.

CHAPTER OBJECTIVES

- To explore the history of the UNIX operating system from which Linux is derived and the principles upon which Linux is designed.
- To examine the Linux process model and illustrate how Linux schedules processes and provides interprocess communication.
- To look at memory management in Linux.
- To explore how Linux implements file systems and manages I/O devices.

21.1 Linux History

Linux looks and feels much like any other UNIX system; indeed, UNIX compatibility has been a major design goal of the Linux project. However, Linux is much younger than most UNIX systems. Its development began in 1991, when a Finnish student, Linus Torvalds, wrote and christened Linux, a small but self-contained kernel for the 80386 processor, the first true 32-bit processor in Intel's range of PC-compatible CPUs.

Early in its development, the Linux source code was made available free on the Internet. As a result, Linux's history has been one of collaboration by many users from all around the world, corresponding almost exclusively over the Internet. From an initial kernel that partially implemented a small subset of the UNIX system services, the Linux system has grown to include much UNIX functionality.

In its early days, Linux development revolved largely around the central operating-system kernel—the core, privileged executive that manages all system resources and that interacts directly with the computer hardware. We need much more than this kernel to produce a full operating system, of course. It is useful to make the distinction between the Linux kernel and a Linux system. The **Linux kernel** is an entirely original piece of software developed from scratch by the Linux community. The **Linux system**, as we know it today, includes a multitude of components, some written from scratch, others borrowed from other development projects, and still others created in collaboration with other teams.

The basic Linux system is a standard environment for applications and user programming, but it does not enforce any standard means of managing the available functionality as a whole. As Linux has matured, a need has arisen for another layer of functionality on top of the Linux system. This need has been met by various Linux distributions. A **Linux distribution** includes all the standard components of the Linux system, plus a set of administrative tools to simplify the initial installation and subsequent upgrading of Linux and to manage installation and removal of other packages on the system. A modern distribution also typically includes tools for management of file systems, creation and management of user accounts, administration of networks, Web browsers, word processors, and so on.

21.1.1 The Linux Kernel

The first Linux kernel released to the public was Version 0.01, dated May 14, 1991. It had no networking, ran only on 80386-compatible Intel processors and PC hardware, and had extremely limited device-driver support. The virtual memory subsystem was also fairly basic and included no support for memory-mapped files; however, even this early incarnation supported shared pages with copy-on-write. The only file system supported was the Minix file system—the first Linux kernels were cross-developed on a Minix platform. However, the kernel did implement proper UNIX processes with protected address spaces.

The next milestone version, Linux 1.0, was released on March 14, 1994. This release culminated three years of rapid development of the Linux kernel. Perhaps the single biggest new feature was networking: 1.0 included support for UNIX's standard TCP/IP networking protocols, as well as a BSD-compatible socket interface for networking programming. Device-driver support was added for running IP over an Ethernet or (using PPP or SLIP protocols) over serial lines or modems.

The 1.0 kernel also included a new, much enhanced file system without the limitations of the original Minix file system and supported a range of SCSI controllers for high-performance disk access. The developers extended the virtual memory subsystem to support paging to swap files and memory mapping of arbitrary files (but only read-only memory mapping was implemented in 1.0).

A range of extra hardware support was also included in this release. Although still restricted to the Intel PC platform, hardware support had grown to include floppy-disk and CD-ROM devices, as well as sound cards, a range of mice, and international keyboards. Floating-point emulation was provided in the kernel for 80386 users who had no 80387 math coprocessor; System V UNIX-style **interprocess communication (IPC)**, including shared memory, semaphores, and message queues, was implemented. Simple support for dynamically loadable and unloadable kernel modules was supplied as well.

At this point, development started on the 1.1 kernel stream, but numerous bug-fix patches were released subsequently against 1.0. A pattern was adopted as the standard numbering convention for Linux kernels. Kernels with an odd minor-version number, such as 1.1, 1.3, and 2.1, are **development kernels**; even-numbered minor-version numbers are stable **production kernels**. Updates against the stable kernels are intended only as remedial versions, whereas the development kernels may include newer and relatively untested functionality.

In March 1995, the 1.2 kernel was released. This release did not offer nearly the same improvement in functionality as the 1.0 release, but it did support a much wider variety of hardware, including the new PCI hardware bus architecture. Developers added another PC-specific feature—support for the 80386 CPU's virtual 8086 mode—to allow emulation of the DOS operating system for PC computers. They also updated the networking stack to provide support for the IPX protocol and made the IP implementation more complete by including accounting and firewalling functionality.

The 1.2 kernel was the final PC-only Linux kernel. The source distribution for Linux 1.2 included partially implemented support for SPARC, Alpha, and MIPS CPUs, but full integration of these other architectures did not begin until after the 1.2 stable kernel was released.

The Linux 1.2 release concentrated on wider hardware support and more complete implementations of existing functionality. Much new functionality was under development at the time, but integration of the new code into the main kernel source code had been deferred until after the stable 1.2 kernel had been released. As a result, the 1.3 development stream saw a great deal of new functionality added to the kernel.

This work was finally released as Linux 2.0 in June 1996. This release was given a major version-number increment on account of two major new capabilities: support for multiple architectures, including a 64-bit native Alpha port, and support for multiprocessor architectures. Linux distributions based on 2.0 are also available for the Motorola 68000-series processors and for Sun's SPARC systems. A derived version of Linux running on top of the Mach microkernel also runs on PC and PowerMac systems.

The changes in 2.0 did not stop there. The memory-management code was substantially improved to provide a unified cache for file-system data independent of the caching of block devices. As a result of this change, the kernel offered greatly increased file-system and virtual memory performance. For the first time, file-system caching was extended to networked file systems, and writable memory-mapped regions also were supported.

The 2.0 kernel also included much improved TCP/IP performance, and a number of new networking protocols were added, including AppleTalk, AX.25 amateur radio networking, and ISDN support. The ability to mount remote netware and SMB (Microsoft LanManager) network volumes was added.

Other major improvements in 2.0 were support for internal kernel threads, for handling dependencies between loadable modules, and for automatic loading of modules on demand. Dynamic configuration of the kernel at run time was much improved through a new, standardized configuration interface.

Additional new features included file-system quotas and POSIX-compatible real-time process-scheduling classes.

Improvements continued with the release of Linux 2.2 in January 1999. A port for UltraSPARC systems was added. Networking was enhanced with more flexible firewalling, better routing and traffic management, and support for TCP large window and selective acks. Acorn, Apple, and NT disks could now be read, and NFS was enhanced and a kernel-mode NFS daemon added. Signal handling, interrupts, and some I/O were locked at a finer level than before to improve symmetric multiprocessor (SMP) performance.

Advances in the 2.4 and 2.6 releases of the kernel include increased support for SMP systems, journaling file systems, and enhancements to the memory-management system. The process scheduler was modified in Version 2.6, providing an efficient $O(1)$ scheduling algorithm. In addition, the Linux 2.6 kernel is now preemptive, allowing a process to be preempted while running in kernel mode.

21.1.2 The Linux System

In many ways, the Linux kernel forms the core of the Linux project, but other components make up the complete Linux operating system. Whereas the Linux kernel is composed entirely of code written from scratch specifically for the Linux project, much of the supporting software that makes up the Linux system is not exclusive to Linux but is common to a number of UNIX-like operating systems. In particular, Linux uses many tools developed as part of Berkeley's BSD operating system, MIT's X Window System, and the Free Software Foundation's GNU project.

This sharing of tools has worked in both directions. The main system libraries of Linux were originated by the GNU project, but the Linux community greatly improved the libraries by addressing omissions, inefficiencies, and bugs. Other components, such as the GNU C compiler (gcc), were already of sufficiently high quality to be used directly in Linux. The networking-administration tools under Linux were derived from code first developed for 4.3 BSD, but more recent BSD derivatives, such as FreeBSD, have borrowed code from Linux in return. Examples include the Intel floating-point-emulation math library and the PC sound-hardware device drivers.

The Linux system as a whole is maintained by a loose network of developers collaborating over the Internet, with small groups or individuals having responsibility for maintaining the integrity of specific components. A small number of public Internet file-transfer-protocol (FTP) archive sites act as de facto standard repositories for these components. The File System Hierarchy Standard document is also maintained by the Linux community as a means of ensuring compatibility across the various system components. This standard specifies the overall layout of a standard Linux file system; it determines under which directory names configuration files, libraries, system binaries, and run-time data files should be stored.

21.1.3 Linux Distributions

In theory, anybody can install a Linux system by fetching the latest revisions of the necessary system components from the FTP sites and compiling them. In Linux's early days, this operation was often precisely what a Linux user had to carry out. As Linux has matured, however, various individuals and groups have attempted to make this job less painful by providing standard, precompiled sets of packages for easy installation.

These collections, or distributions, include much more than just the basic Linux system. They typically include extra system-installation and management utilities, as well as precompiled and ready-to-install packages of many of the common UNIX tools, such as news servers, Web browsers, text-processing and editing tools, and even games.

The first distributions managed these packages by simply providing a means of unpacking all the files into the appropriate places. One of the important contributions of modern distributions, however, is advanced package management. Today's Linux distributions include a package-tracking database that allows packages to be installed, upgraded, or removed painlessly.

The SLS distribution, dating back to the early days of Linux, was the first collection of Linux packages that was recognizable as a complete distribution. Although it could be installed as a single entity, SLS lacked the package-management tools now expected of Linux distributions. The Slackware distribution represented a great improvement in overall quality, even though it also had poor package management; in fact, it is still one of the most widely installed distributions in the Linux community.

Since Slackware's release, many commercial and noncommercial Linux distributions have become available. Red Hat and Debian are particularly popular distributions; the first comes from a commercial Linux support company and the second from the free-software Linux community. Other commercially supported versions of Linux include distributions from Caldera, Craftworks, and WorkGroup Solutions. A large Linux following in Germany has resulted in several dedicated German-language distributions, including versions from SuSE and Unifix. There are too many Linux distributions in circulation for us to list all of them here. The variety of distributions does not prohibit compatibility across Linux distributions, however. The RPM package file format is used, or at least understood, by the majority of distributions, and commercial applications distributed in this format can be installed and run on any distribution that can accept RPM files.

21.1.4 Linux Licensing

The Linux kernel is distributed under the GNU general public license (GPL), the terms of which are set out by the Free Software Foundation. Linux is not public-domain software. Public domain implies that the authors have waived copyright rights in the software, but copyright rights in Linux code are still held by the code's various authors. Linux is *free* software, however, in the sense that people can copy it, modify it, use it in any manner they want, and give away their own copies, without any restrictions.

The main implications of Linux's licensing terms are that nobody using Linux, or creating a derivative of Linux (a legitimate exercise), can make the derived product proprietary. Software released under the GPL cannot be redistributed as a binary-only product. If you release software that includes any components covered by the GPL, then, under the GPL, you must make source code available alongside any binary distributions. (This restriction does not prohibit making—or even selling—binary-only software distributions, as long as anybody who receives binaries is also given the opportunity to get source code for a reasonable distribution charge.)

21.2 Design Principles

In its overall design, Linux resembles any other traditional, nonmicrokernel UNIX implementation. It is a multiuser, multitasking system with a full set of UNIX-compatible tools. Linux's file system adheres to traditional UNIX semantics, and the standard UNIX networking model is implemented fully. The internal details of Linux's design have been influenced heavily by the history of this operating system's development.

Although Linux runs on a wide variety of platforms, it was developed exclusively on PC architecture. A great deal of that early development was carried out by individual enthusiasts, rather than by well-funded development or research facilities, so from the start Linux attempted to squeeze as much functionality as possible from limited resources. Today, Linux can run happily on a multiprocessor machine with hundreds of megabytes of main memory and many gigabytes of disk space, but it is still capable of operating usefully in under 4 MB of RAM.

As PCs became more powerful and as memory and hard disks became cheaper, the original, minimalist Linux kernels grew to implement more UNIX functionality. Speed and efficiency are still important design goals, but much recent and current work on Linux has concentrated on a third major design goal: standardization. One of the prices paid for the diversity of UNIX implementations currently available is that source code written for one may not necessarily compile or run correctly on another. Even when the same system calls are present on two different UNIX systems, they do not necessarily behave in exactly the same way. The POSIX standards comprise a set of specifications for different aspects of operating-system behavior. There are POSIX documents for common operating-system functionality and for extensions such as process threads and real-time operations. Linux is designed to be compliant with the relevant POSIX documents; at least two Linux distributions have achieved official POSIX certification.

Because it gives standard interfaces to both the programmer and the user, Linux presents few surprises to anybody familiar with UNIX. We do not detail these interfaces here. The sections on the programmer interface (Section A.3) and user interface (Section A.4) of BSD apply equally well to Linux. By default, however, the Linux programming interface adheres to SVR4 UNIX semantics, rather than to BSD behavior. A separate set of libraries is available to implement BSD semantics in places where the two behaviors differ significantly.

Many other standards exist in the UNIX world, but full certification of Linux with respect to these standards is sometimes slowed because certification is often available only for a fee, and the expense involved in certifying an operating system's compliance with most standards is substantial. However, supporting a wide base of applications is important for any operating system, so implementation of standards is a major goal for Linux development, even if the implementation is not formally certified. In addition to the basic POSIX standard, Linux currently supports the POSIX threading extensions—Pthreads—and a subset of the POSIX extensions for real-time process control.

21.2.1 Components of a Linux System

The Linux system is composed of three main bodies of code, in line with most traditional UNIX implementations:

1. **Kernel**. The kernel is responsible for maintaining all the important abstractions of the operating system, including such things as virtual memory and processes.
2. **System libraries**. The system libraries define a standard set of functions through which applications can interact with the kernel. These functions implement much of the operating-system functionality that does not need the full privileges of kernel code.
3. **System utilities**. The system utilities are programs that perform individual, specialized management tasks. Some system utilities may be invoked just once to initialize and configure some aspect of the system; others—known as *daemons* in UNIX terminology—may run permanently, handling such tasks as responding to incoming network connections, accepting logon requests from terminals, and updating log files.

Figure 21.1 illustrates the various components that make up a full Linux system. The most important distinction here is between the kernel and everything else. All the kernel code executes in the processor's privileged mode with full access to all the physical resources of the computer. Linux refers to this privileged mode as **kernel mode**. Under Linux, no user-mode code is built into the kernel. Any operating-system-support code that does not need to run in kernel mode is placed into the system libraries instead.

Although various modern operating systems have adopted a message-passing architecture for their kernel internals, Linux retains UNIX's historical model: the kernel is created as a single, monolithic binary. The main reason is to improve performance. Because all kernel code and data structures are kept in a single address space, no context switches are necessary when a process calls an operating-system function or when a hardware interrupt is delivered.

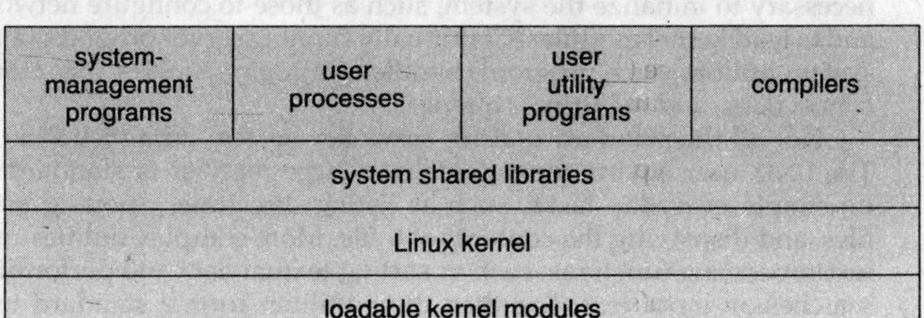

Figure 21.1 Components of the Linux system.

This single address space contains not only the core scheduling and virtual memory code but *all* kernel code, including all device drivers, file systems, and networking code.

Even though all the kernel components share this same melting pot, there is still room for modularity. In the same way that user applications can load shared libraries at run time to pull in a needed piece of code, so the Linux kernel can load (and unload) modules dynamically at run time. The kernel does not necessarily need to know in advance which modules may be loaded —they are truly independent loadable components.

The Linux kernel forms the core of the Linux operating system. It provides all the functionality necessary to run processes, and it provides system services to give arbitrated and protected access to hardware resources. The kernel implements all the features required to qualify as an operating system. On its own, however, the operating system provided by the Linux kernel looks nothing like a UNIX system. It is missing many of the extra features of UNIX, and the features that it does provide are not necessarily in the format in which a UNIX application expects them to appear. The operating-system interface visible to running applications is not maintained directly by the kernel. Rather, applications make calls to the system libraries, which in turn call the operating-system services as necessary.

The system libraries provide many types of functionality. At the simplest level, they allow applications to make kernel-system service requests. Making a system call involves transferring control from unprivileged user mode to privileged kernel mode; the details of this transfer vary from architecture to architecture. The libraries take care of collecting the system-call arguments and, if necessary, arranging those arguments in the special form necessary to make the system call.

The libraries may also provide more complex versions of the basic system calls. For example, the C language's buffered file-handling functions are all implemented in the system libraries, providing more advanced control of file I/O than the basic kernel system calls. The libraries also provide routines that do not correspond to system calls at all, such as sorting algorithms, mathematical functions, and string-manipulation routines. All the functions necessary to support the running of UNIX or POSIX applications are implemented here in the system libraries.

The Linux system includes a wide variety of user-mode programs—both system utilities and user utilities. The system utilities include all the programs necessary to initialize the system, such as those to configure network devices and to load kernel modules. Continually running server programs also count as system utilities; such programs handle user login requests, incoming network connections, and the printer queues.

Not all the standard utilities serve key system-administration functions. The UNIX user environment contains a large number of standard utilities to do simple everyday tasks, such as listing directories, moving and deleting files, and displaying the contents of a file. More complex utilities can perform text-processing functions, such as sorting textual data and performing pattern searches on input text. Together, these utilities form a standard tool set that users can expect on any UNIX system; although they do not perform any operating-system function, they are an important part of the basic Linux system.

21.3 Kernel Modules

The Linux kernel has the ability to load and unload arbitrary sections of kernel code on demand. These loadable kernel modules run in privileged kernel mode and as a consequence have full access to all the hardware capabilities of the machine on which they run. In theory, there is no restriction on what a kernel module is allowed to do; typically, a module might implement a device driver, a file system, or a networking protocol.

Kernel modules are convenient for several reasons. Linux's source code is free, so anybody wanting to write kernel code is able to compile a modified kernel and to reboot to load that new functionality; however, recompiling, relinking, and reloading the entire kernel is a cumbersome cycle to undertake when you are developing a new driver. If you use kernel modules, you do not have to make a new kernel to test a new driver—the driver can be compiled on its own and loaded into the already-running kernel. Of course, once a new driver is written, it can be distributed as a module so that other users can benefit from it without having to rebuild their kernels.

This latter point has another implication. Because it is covered by the GPL license, the Linux kernel cannot be released with proprietary components added to it, unless those new components are also released under the GPL and the source code for them is made available on demand. The kernel's module interface allows third parties to write and distribute, on their own terms, device drivers or file systems that could not be distributed under the GPL.

Kernel modules allow a Linux system to be set up with a standard minimal kernel, without any extra device drivers built in. Any device drivers that the user needs can be either loaded explicitly by the system at startup or loaded automatically by the system on demand and unloaded when not in use. For example, a CD-ROM driver might be loaded when a CD is mounted and unloaded from memory when the CD is dismounted from the file system.

The module support under Linux has three components:

1. The **module management** allows modules to be loaded into memory and to talk to the rest of the kernel.
2. The **driver registration** allows modules to tell the rest of the kernel that a new driver has become available.
3. A **conflict-resolution mechanism** allows different device drivers to reserve hardware resources and to protect those resources from accidental use by another driver.

21.3.1 Module Management

Loading a module requires more than just loading its binary contents into kernel memory. The system must also make sure that any references the module makes to kernel symbols or entry points are updated to point to the correct locations in the kernel's address space. Linux deals with this reference updating by splitting the job of module loading into two separate sections: the management of sections of module code in kernel memory and the handling of symbols that modules are allowed to reference.

Linux maintains an internal symbol table in the kernel. This symbol table does not contain the full set of symbols defined in the kernel during the latter's compilation; rather, a symbol must be exported explicitly by the kernel. The set of exported symbols constitutes a well-defined interface by which a module can interact with the kernel.

Although exporting symbols from a kernel function requires an explicit request by the programmer, no special effort is needed to import those symbols into a module. A module writer just uses the standard external linking of the C language: Any external symbols referenced by the module but not declared by it are simply marked as unresolved in the final module binary produced by the compiler. When a module is to be loaded into the kernel, a system utility first scans the module for these unresolved references. All symbols that still need to be resolved are looked up in the kernel's symbol table, and the correct addresses of those symbols in the currently running kernel are substituted into the module's code. Only then is the module passed to the kernel for loading. If the system utility cannot resolve any references in the module by looking them up in the kernel's symbol table, then the module is rejected.

The loading of the module is performed in two stages. First, the module-loader utility asks the kernel to reserve a continuous area of virtual kernel memory for the module. The kernel returns the address of the memory allocated, and the loader utility can use this address to relocate the module's machine code to the correct loading address. A second system call then passes the module, plus any symbol table that the new module wants to export, to the kernel. The module itself is now copied verbatim into the previously allocated space, and the kernel's symbol table is updated with the new symbols for possible use by other modules not yet loaded.

The final module-management component is the module requestor. The kernel defines a communication interface to which a module-management program can connect. With this connection established, the kernel will inform the management process whenever a process requests a device driver, file system, or network service that is not currently loaded and will give the manager the opportunity to load that service. The original service request will complete once the module is loaded. The manager process regularly queries the kernel to see whether a dynamically loaded module is still in use and unloads that module when it is no longer actively needed.

21.3.2 Driver Registration

Once a module is loaded, it remains no more than an isolated region of memory until it lets the rest of the kernel know what new functionality it provides. The kernel maintains dynamic tables of all known drivers and provides a set of routines to allow drivers to be added to or removed from these tables at any time. The kernel makes sure that it calls a module's startup routine when that module is loaded and calls the module's cleanup routine before that module is unloaded: these routines are responsible for registering the module's functionality.

A module may register many types of drivers and may register more than one driver if it wishes. For example, a device driver might want to register two separate mechanisms for accessing the device. Registration tables include the following items:

- **Device drivers**. These drivers include character devices (such as printers, terminals, and mice), block devices (including all disk drives), and network interface devices.

- **File systems**. The file system may be anything that implements Linux's virtual-file-system calling routines. It might implement a format for storing files on a disk, but it might equally well be a network file system, such as NFS, or a virtual file system whose contents are generated on demand, such as Linux's `/proc` file system.

- **Network protocols**. A module may implement an entire networking protocol, such as IPX, or simply a new set of packet-filtering rules for a network firewall.

- **Binary format**. This format specifies a way of recognizing, and loading, a new type of executable file.

In addition, a module can register a new set of entries in the *sysctl* and */proc* tables, to allow that module to be configured dynamically (Section 21.7.4).

21.3.3 Conflict Resolution

Commercial UNIX implementations are usually sold to run on a vendor's own hardware. One advantage of a single-supplier solution is that the software vendor has a good idea about what hardware configurations are possible. PC hardware, however, comes in a vast number of configurations, with large numbers of possible drivers for devices such as network cards, SCSI controllers, and video display adapters. The problem of managing the hardware configuration becomes more severe when modular device drivers are supported, since the currently active set of devices becomes dynamically variable.

Linux provides a central conflict-resolution mechanism to help arbitrate access to certain hardware resources. Its aims are as follows:

- To prevent modules from clashing over access to hardware resources

- To prevent autoprobes—device-driver probes that auto-detect device configuration—from interfering with existing device drivers

- To resolve conflicts among multiple drivers trying to access the same hardware—for example, as when both the parallel printer driver and the parallel-line IP (PLIP) network driver try to talk to the parallel printer port

To these ends, the kernel maintains lists of allocated hardware resources. The PC has a limited number of possible I/O ports (addresses in its hardware I/O address space), interrupt lines, and DMA channels. When any device driver wants to access such a resource, it is expected to reserve the resource with the kernel database first. This requirement incidentally allows the system administrator to determine exactly which resources have been allocated by which driver at any given point.

A module is expected to use this mechanism to reserve in advance any hardware resources that it expects to use. If the reservation is rejected because the resource is not present or is already in use, then it is up to the module to decide how to proceed. It may fail its initialization and request that it be unloaded if it cannot continue, or it may carry on, using alternative hardware resources.

21.4 Process Management

A process is the basic context within which all user-requested activity is serviced within the operating system. To be compatible with other UNIX systems, Linux must use a process model similar to those of other versions of UNIX. Linux operates differently from UNIX in a few key places, however. In this section, we review the traditional UNIX process model (Section A.3.2) and introduce Linux's own threading model.

21.4.1 The fork() and exec() Process Model

The basic principle of UNIX process management is to separate two operations: the creation of a process and the running of a new program. A new process is created by the `fork()` system call, and a new program is run after a call to `exec()`. These are two distinctly separate functions. A new process may be created with `fork()` without a new program being run—the new subprocess simply continues to execute exactly the same program that the first (parent) process was running. Equally, running a new program does not require that a new process be created first: any process may call `exec()` at any time. The currently running program is immediately terminated, and the new program starts executing in the context of the existing process.

This model has the advantage of great simplicity. It is not necessary to specify every detail of the environment of a new program in the system call that runs that program; the new program simply runs in its existing environment. If a parent process wishes to modify the environment in which a new program is to be run, it can fork and then, still running the original program in a child process, make any system calls it requires to modify that child process before finally executing the new program.

Under UNIX, then, a process encompasses all the information that the operating system must maintain to track the context of a single execution of a single program. Under Linux, we can break down this context into a number of specific sections. Broadly, process properties fall into three groups: the process identity, environment, and context.

21.4.1.1 Process Identity

A process identity consists mainly of the following items:

- **Process ID (PID)**. Each process has a unique identifier. The PID is used to specify the process to the operating system when an application makes a system call to signal, modify, or wait for the process. Additional identifiers associate the process with a process group (typically, a tree of processes `fork`ed by a single user command) and login session.
- **Credentials**. Each process must have an associated user ID and one or more group IDs (user groups are discussed in Section 10.6.2) that determine the rights of a process to access system resources and files.

- **Personality**. Process personalities are not traditionally found on UNIX systems, but under Linux each process has an associated personality identifier that can slightly modify the semantics of certain system calls. Personalities are primarily used by emulation libraries to request that system calls be compatible with certain varieties of UNIX.

Most of these identifiers are under the limited control of the process itself. The process group and session identifiers can be changed if the process wants to start a new group or session. Its credentials can be changed, subject to appropriate security checks. However, the primary PID of a process is unchangeable and uniquely identifies that process until termination.

21.4.1.2 Process Environment

A process's environment is inherited from its parent and is composed of two null-terminated vectors: the argument vector and the environment vector. The **argument vector** simply lists the command-line arguments used to invoke the running program; it conventionally starts with the name of the program itself. The **environment vector** is a list of "NAME=VALUE" pairs that associates named environment variables with arbitrary textual values. The environment is not held in kernel memory but is stored in the process's own user-mode address space as the first datum at the top of the process's stack.

The argument and environment vectors are not altered when a new process is created; the new child process will inherit the environment that its parent possesses. However, a completely new environment is set up when a new program is invoked. On calling `exec()`, a process must supply the environment for the new program. The kernel passes these environment variables to the next program, replacing the process's current environment. The kernel otherwise leaves the environment and command-line vectors alone—their interpretation is left entirely to the user-mode libraries and applications.

The passing of environment variables from one process to the next and the inheriting of these variables by the children of a process provide flexible ways to pass information to components of the user-mode system software. Various important environment variables have conventional meanings to related parts of the system software. For example, the `TERM` variable is set up to name the type of terminal connected to a user's login session; many programs use this variable to determine how to perform operations on the user's display, such as moving the cursor and scrolling a region of text. Programs with multilingual support use the `LANG` variable to determine in which language to display system messages for programs that include multilingual support.

The environment-variable mechanism custom-tailors the operating system on a per-process basis, rather than for the system as a whole. Users can choose their own languages or select their own editors independently of one another.

21.4.1.3 Process Context

The process identity and environment properties are usually set up when a process is created and not changed until that process exits. A process may choose to change some aspects of its identity if it needs to do so, or it may alter its environment. In contrast, process context is the state of the running program at any one time; it changes constantly. Process context includes the following parts:

- **Scheduling context**. The most important part of the process context is its scheduling context—the information that the scheduler needs to suspend and restart the process. This information includes saved copies of all the process's registers. Floating-point registers are stored separately and are restored only when needed, so that processes that do not use floating-point arithmetic do not incur the overhead of saving that state. The scheduling context also includes information about scheduling priority and about any outstanding signals waiting to be delivered to the process. A key part of the scheduling context is the process's kernel stack, a separate area of kernel memory reserved for use exclusively by kernel-mode code. Both system calls and interrupts that occur while the process is executing will use this stack.
- **Accounting**. The kernel maintains accounting information about the resources currently being consumed by each process and the total resources consumed by the process in its entire lifetime so far.
- **File table**. The file table is an array of pointers to kernel file structures. When making file-I/O system calls, processes refer to files by their index into this table.
- **File-system context**. Whereas the file table lists the existing open files, the file-system context applies to requests to open new files. The current root and default directories to be used for new file searches are stored here.
- **Signal-handler table**. UNIX systems can deliver asynchronous signals to a process in response to various external events. The signal-handler table defines the routine in the process's address space to be called when a specific signal arrives.
- **Virtual memory context**. The virtual memory context describes the full contents of a process's private address space; we discuss it in Section 21.6.

21.4.2 Processes and Threads

Linux provides the `fork()` system call with the traditional functionality of duplicating a process. Linux also provides the ability to create threads using the `clone()` system call. However, Linux does not distinguish between processes and threads. In fact, Linux generally uses the term *task*—rather than *process* or *thread*—when referring to a flow of control within a program. When `clone()` is invoked, it is passed a set of flags that determine how much sharing is to take place between the parent and child tasks. Some of these flags are:

flag	meaning
`CLONE_FS`	File-system information is shared.
`CLONE_VM`	The same memory space is shared.
`CLONE_SIGHAND`	Signal handlers are shared.
`CLONE_FILES`	The set of open files is shared.

Thus, if `clone()` is passed the flags `CLONE_FS`, `CLONE_VM`, `CLONE_SIGHAND`, and `CLONE_FILES`, the parent and child tasks will share the same file-system information (such as the current working directory), the same memory space, the same signal handlers, and the same set of open files. Using `clone()` in this fashion is equivalent to creating a thread in other systems, since the parent task shares most of its resources with its child task. However, if none of these flags is set when `clone()` is invoked, no sharing takes place, resulting in functionality similar to the `fork()` system call.

The lack of distinction between processes and threads is possible because Linux does not hold a process's entire context within the main process data structure; rather, it holds the context within independent subcontexts. Thus, a process's file-system context, file-descriptor table, signal-handler table, and virtual memory context are held in separate data structures. The process data structure simply contains pointers to these other structures, so any number of processes can easily share a subcontext by pointing to the same subcontext.

The arguments to the `clone()` system call tell it which subcontexts to copy, and which to share, when it creates a new process. The new process always is given a new identity and a new scheduling context. According to the arguments passed, however, it may either create new subcontext data structures initialized to be copies of the parent's or set up the new process to use the same subcontext data structures being used by the parent. The `fork()` system call is nothing more than a special case of `clone()` that copies all subcontexts, sharing none.

21.5 Scheduling

Scheduling is the job of allocating CPU time to different tasks within an operating system. Normally, we think of scheduling as being the running and interrupting of processes, but another aspect of scheduling is also important to Linux: the running of the various kernel tasks. Kernel tasks encompass both tasks that are requested by a running process and tasks that execute internally on behalf of a device driver.

21.5.1 Process Scheduling

Linux has two separate process-scheduling algorithms. One is a time-sharing algorithm for fair, preemptive scheduling among multiple processes; the other is designed for real-time tasks, where absolute priorities are more important than fairness.

The scheduling algorithm used for routine time-sharing tasks received a major overhaul with Version 2.5 of the kernel. Earlier versions of the Linux kernel ran a variation of the traditional UNIX scheduling algorithm, which does not provide adequate support for SMP systems and does not scale well as the number of tasks on the system grows. The overhaul of the Linux scheduler with Version 2.5 of the kernel provides a scheduling algorithm that runs in constant time—known as $O(1)$—regardless of the number of tasks on the system. The new scheduler also provides increased support for SMP, including processor affinity and load balancing, as well as maintaining fairness and support for interactive tasks.

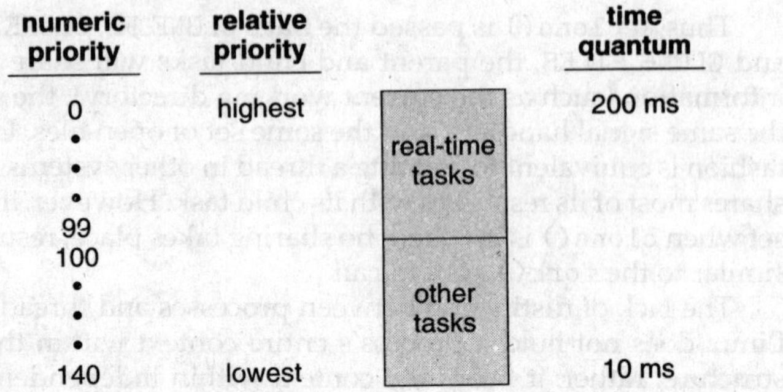

Figure 21.2 The relationship between priorities and time-slice length.

The Linux scheduler is a preemptive, priority-based algorithm with two separate priority ranges: a **real-time** range from 0 to 99 and a **nice** value ranging from 100 to 140. These two ranges map into a global priority scheme whereby numerically lower values indicate higher priorities.

Unlike schedulers for many other systems, the Linux scheduler assigns higher-priority tasks longer time quanta and lower-priority tasks shorter time quanta. Because of the unique nature of the scheduler, this is appropriate for Linux, as we shall soon see. The relationship between priorities and time-slice length is shown in Figure 21.2.

A runnable task is considered eligible for execution on the CPU so long as it has time remaining in its time slice. When a task has exhausted its time slice, it is considered **expired** and is not eligible for execution again until all other tasks have also exhausted their time quanta. The kernel maintains a list of all runnable tasks in a **runqueue** data structure. Because of its support for SMP, each processor maintains its own runqueue and schedules itself independently. Each runqueue contains two priority arrays—**active** and **expired**. The active array contains all tasks with time remaining in their time slices, and the expired array contains all expired tasks. Each of these priority arrays includes a list of tasks indexed according to priority (Figure 21.3). The scheduler chooses the task with the highest priority from the active array for execution on the CPU. On multiprocessor machines, this means that each processor is scheduling the highest-priority task from its own runqueue structure. When all tasks have exhausted their time slices (that is, the active array is empty), the two priority arrays are exchanged as the expired array becomes the active array and vice-versa.

Tasks are assigned dynamic priorities that are based on the *nice* value plus or minus a value up to the value 5. Whether a value is added to or subtracted from a task's *nice* value depends on the interactivity of the task. A task's interactivity is determined by how long it has been sleeping while waiting for I/O. Tasks that are more interactive typically have longer sleep times and therefore are more likely to have adjustments closer to -5, as the scheduler favors such interactive tasks. Conversely, tasks with shorter sleep times are often CPU-bound and thus will have their priorities lowered.

A task's dynamic priority is recalculated when the task has exhausted its time quantum and is to be moved to the expired array. Thus, when the two

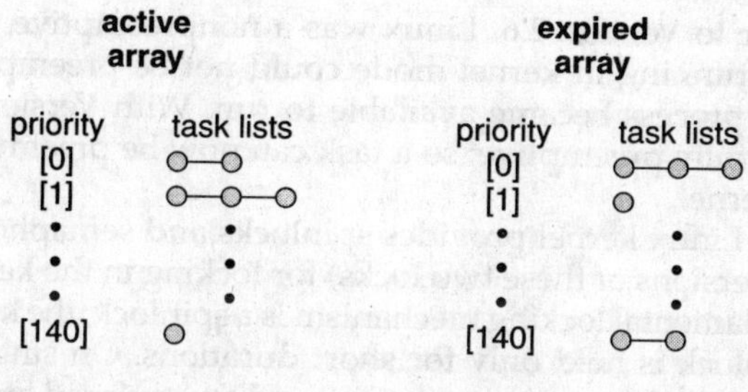

Figure 21.3 List of tasks indexed according to priority.

arrays are exchanged, all tasks in the new active array have been assigned new priorities and corresponding time slices.

Linux's real-time scheduling is simpler still. Linux implements the two real-time scheduling classes required by POSIX.1b: first-come, first-served (FCFS) and round-robin (Sections 5.3.1 and 5.3.4, respectively). In both cases, each process has a priority in addition to its scheduling class. Processes with different priorities can compete with one another to some extent in time-sharing scheduling; in real-time scheduling, however, the scheduler always runs the process with the highest priority. Among processes of equal priority, it runs the process that has been waiting longest. The only difference between FCFS and round-robin scheduling is that FCFS processes continue to run until they either exit or block, whereas a round-robin process will be preempted after a while and will be moved to the end of the scheduling queue, so round-robin processes of equal priority will automatically time-share among themselves. Unlike routine time-sharing tasks, real-time tasks are assigned static priorities.

Linux's real-time scheduling is soft—rather than hard—real time. The scheduler offers strict guarantees about the relative priorities of real-time processes, but the kernel does not offer any guarantees about how quickly a real-time process will be scheduled once that process becomes runnable.

21.5.2 Kernel Synchronization

The way the kernel schedules its own operations is fundamentally different from the way it schedules processes. A request for kernel-mode execution can occur in two ways. A running program may request an operating-system service, either explicitly via a system call or implicitly—for example, when a page fault occurs. Alternatively, a device controller may deliver a hardware interrupt that causes the CPU to start executing a kernel-defined handler for that interrupt.

The problem posed to the kernel is that all these tasks may try to access the same internal data structures. If one kernel task is in the middle of accessing some data structure when an interrupt service routine executes, then that service routine cannot access or modify the same data without risking data corruption. This fact relates to the idea of critical sections—portions of code that access shared data and that must not be allowed to execute concurrently. As a result, kernel synchronization involves much more than just process scheduling. A framework is required that allows kernel tasks to run without violating the integrity of shared data.

Prior to Version 2.6, Linux was a nonpreemptive kernel, meaning that a process running in kernel mode could not be preempted—even if a higher-priority process became available to run. With Version 2.6, the Linux kernel became fully preemptive; so a task can now be preempted when it is running in the kernel.

The Linux kernel provides spinlocks and semaphores (as well as reader–writer versions of these two locks) for locking in the kernel. On SMP machines, the fundamental locking mechanism is a spinlock; the kernel is designed so that the spinlock is held only for short durations. On single-processor machines, spinlocks are inappropriate for use and are replaced by enabling and disabling kernel preemption. That is, on single-processor machines, rather than holding a spinlock, the task disables kernel preemption. When the task would otherwise release the spinlock, it enables kernel preemption. This pattern is summarized below:

single processor	multiple processors
Disable kernel preemption.	Acquire spin lock.
Enable kernel preemption.	Release spin lock.

Linux uses an interesting approach to disable and enable kernel preemption. It provides two simple system calls—`preempt_disable()` and `preempt_enable()`—for disabling and enabling kernel preemption. However, in addition, the kernel is not preemptible if a kernel-mode task is holding a lock. To enforce this rule, each task in the system has a `thread-info` structure that includes the field `preempt_count`, which is a counter indicating the number of locks being held by the task. The counter is incremented when a lock is acquired and decremented when a lock is released. If the value of `preempt_count` for the task currently running is greater than zero, it is not safe to preempt the kernel, as this task currently holds a lock. If the count is zero, the kernel can safely be interrupted, assuming there are no outstanding calls to `preempt_disable()`.

Spinlocks—along with enabling and disabling of kernel preemption—are used in the kernel only when the lock is held for short durations. When a lock must be held for longer periods, semaphores are used.

The second protection technique used by Linux applies to critical sections that occur in interrupt service routines. The basic tool is the processor's interrupt-control hardware. By disabling interrupts (or using spinlocks) during a critical section, the kernel guarantees that it can proceed without the risk of concurrent access to shared data structures.

However, there is a penalty for disabling interrupts. On most hardware architectures, interrupt enable and disable instructions are expensive. Furthermore, as long as interrupts remain disabled, all I/O is suspended, and any device waiting for servicing will have to wait until interrupts are reenabled; so performance degrades. The Linux kernel uses a synchronization architecture that allows long critical sections to run for their entire duration without having interrupts disabled. This ability is especially useful in the networking code. An interrupt in a network device driver can signal the arrival of an entire network packet, which may result in a great deal of code being executed to disassemble, route, and forward that packet within the interrupt service routine.

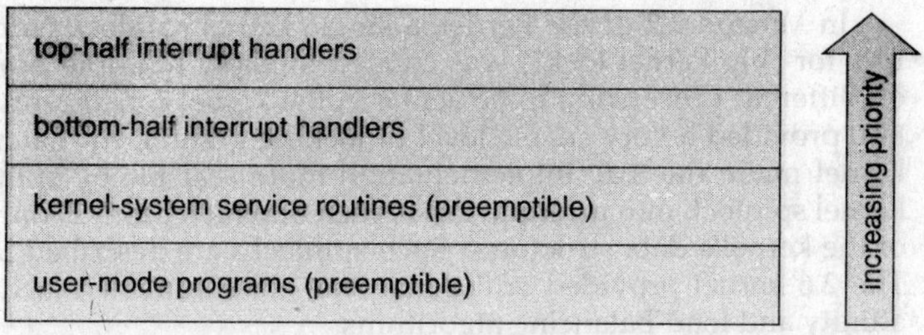

Figure 21.4 Interrupt protection levels.

Linux implements this architecture by separating interrupt service routines into two sections: the top half and the bottom half. The **top half** is a normal interrupt service routine that runs with recursive interrupts disabled; interrupts of a higher priority may interrupt the routine, but interrupts of the same or lower priority are disabled. The **bottom half** of a service routine is run, with all interrupts enabled, by a miniature scheduler that ensures that bottom halves never interrupt themselves. The bottom-half scheduler is invoked automatically whenever an interrupt service routine exits.

This separation means that the kernel can complete any complex processing that has to be done in response to an interrupt without worrying about being interrupted itself. If another interrupt occurs while a bottom half is executing, then that interrupt can request that the same bottom half execute, but the execution will be deferred until the one currently running completes. Each execution of the bottom half can be interrupted by a top half but can never be interrupted by a similar bottom half.

The top-half/bottom-half architecture is completed by a mechanism for disabling selected bottom halves while executing normal, foreground kernel code. The kernel can code critical sections easily using this system. Interrupt handlers can code their critical sections as bottom halves; and when the foreground kernel wants to enter a critical section, it can disable any relevant bottom halves to prevent any other critical sections from interrupting it. At the end of the critical section, the kernel can reenable the bottom halves and run any bottom-half tasks that have been queued by top-half interrupt service routines during the critical section.

Figure 21.4 summarizes the various levels of interrupt protection within the kernel. Each level may be interrupted by code running at a higher level but will never be interrupted by code running at the same or a lower level; except for user-mode code, user processes can always be preempted by another process when a time-sharing scheduling interrupt occurs.

21.5.3 Symmetric Multiprocessing

The Linux 2.0 kernel was the first stable Linux kernel to support **symmetric multiprocessor (SMP)** hardware, allowing separate processes to execute in parallel on separate processors. Originally, the implementation of SMP imposed the restriction that only one processor at a time could be executing kernel-mode code.

In Version 2.2 of the kernel, a single kernel spinlock (sometimes termed **BKL** for "big kernel lock") was created to allow multiple processes (running on different processors) to be active in the kernel concurrently. However, the BKL provided a very coarse level of locking granularity. Later releases of the kernel made the SMP implementation more scalable by splitting this single kernel spinlock into multiple locks, each of which protects only a small subset of the kernel's data structures. Such spinlocks are described in Section 21.5.2. The 2.6 kernel provided additional SMP enhancements, including processor affinity and load-balancing algorithms.

21.6 Memory Management

Memory management under Linux has two components. The first deals with allocating and freeing physical memory—pages, groups of pages, and small blocks of memory. The second handles virtual memory, which is memory mapped into the address space of running processes. In this section, we describe these two components and then examine the mechanisms by which the loadable components of a new program are brought into a process's virtual memory in response to an `exec()` system call.

21.6.1 Management of Physical Memory

Due to specific hardware characteristics, Linux separates physical memory into three different **zones**, or regions:

- ZONE_DMA
- ZONE_NORMAL
- ZONE_HIGHMEM

These zones are architecture specific. For example, on the Intel 80x86 architecture, certain ISA (industry standard architecture) devices can only access the lower 16 MB of physical memory using DMA. On these systems, the first 16 MB of physical memory comprise ZONE_DMA. ZONE_NORMAL identifies physical memory that is mapped to the CPU's address space. This zone is used for most routine memory requests. For architectures that do not limit what DMA can access, ZONE_DMA is not present, and ZONE_NORMAL is used. Finally, ZONE_HIGHMEM (for "high memory") refers to physical memory that is not mapped into the kernel address space. For example, on the 32-bit Intel architecture (where 2^{32} provides a 4-GB address space), the kernel is mapped into the first 896 MB of the address space; the remaining memory is referred to as **high memory** and is allocated from ZONE_HIGHMEM. The relationship of zones and physical addresses on the Intel 80x86 architecture is shown in Figure 21.5. The kernel maintains a list of free pages for each zone. When a request for physical memory arrives, the kernel satisfies the request using the appropriate zone.

The primary physical-memory manager in the Linux kernel is the **page allocator**. Each zone has its own allocator, which is responsible for allocating and freeing all physical pages for the zone and is capable of allocating ranges

zone	physical memory
ZONE_DMA	< 16 MB
ZONE_NORMAL	16 .. 896 MB
ZONE_HIGHMEM	> 896 MB

Figure 21.5 Relationship of zones and physical addresses on the Intel 80x86.

of physically contiguous pages on request. The allocator uses a **buddy system** (Section 9.8.1) to keep track of available physical pages. In this scheme, adjacent units of allocatable memory are paired together (hence its name). Each allocatable memory region has an adjacent partner (or buddy). Whenever two allocated partner regions are freed up, they are combined to form a larger region—a *buddy heap*. That larger region also has a partner, with which it can combine to form a still larger free region. Conversely, if a small memory request cannot be satisfied by allocation of an existing small free region, then a larger free region will be subdivided into two partners to satisfy the request. Separate linked lists are used to record the free memory regions of each allowable size; under Linux, the smallest size allocatable under this mechanism is a single physical page. Figure 21.6 shows an example of buddy-heap allocation. A 4-KB region is being allocated, but the smallest available region is 16 KB. The region is broken up recursively until a piece of the desired size is available.

Ultimately, all memory allocations in the Linux kernel are made either statically, by drivers that reserve a contiguous area of memory during system boot time, or dynamically, by the page allocator. However, kernel functions do not have to use the basic allocator to reserve memory. Several specialized memory-management subsystems use the underlying page allocator to manage their own pools of memory. The most important are the virtual memory system, described in Section 21.6.2; the `kmalloc()` variable-length allocator; the slab allocator, used for allocating memory for kernel data structures; and the page cache, used for caching pages belonging to files.

Many components of the Linux operating system need to allocate entire pages on request, but often smaller blocks of memory are required. The kernel

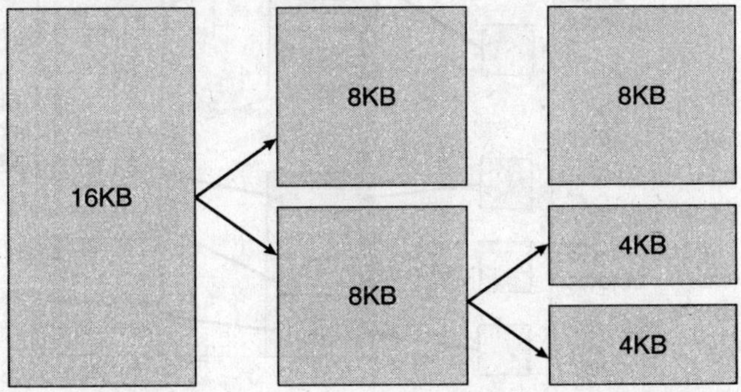

Figure 21.6 Splitting of memory in the buddy system.

provides an additional allocator for arbitrary-sized requests, where the size of a request is not known in advance and may be only a few bytes. Analogous to the C language's `malloc()` function, this `kmalloc()` service allocates entire pages on demand but then splits them into smaller pieces. The kernel maintains lists of pages in use by the `kmalloc()` service. Allocating memory involves determining the appropriate list and either taking the first free piece available on the list or allocating a new page and splitting it up. Memory regions claimed by the `kmalloc()` system are allocated permanently until they are freed explicitly; the `kmalloc()` system cannot reallocate or reclaim these regions in response to memory shortages.

Another strategy adopted by Linux for allocating kernel memory is known as slab allocation. A **slab** is used for allocating memory for kernel data structures and is made up of one or more physically contiguous pages. A **cache** consists of one or more slabs. There is a single cache for each unique kernel data structure —a cache for the data structure representing process descriptors, a cache for file objects, a cache for semaphores, and so forth. Each cache is populated with **objects** that are instantiations of the kernel data structure the cache represents. For example, the cache representing semaphores stores instances of semaphore objects, and the cache representing process descriptors stores instances of process descriptor objects. The relationship among slabs, caches, and objects is shown in Figure 21.7. The figure shows two kernel objects 3 KB in size and three objects 7 KB in size. These objects are stored in the respective caches for 3-KB and 7-KB objects.

The slab-allocation algorithm uses caches to store kernel objects. When a cache is created, a number of objects are allocated to the cache. The number of objects in the cache depends on the size of the associated slab. For example, a 12-KB slab (made up of three contiguous 4-KB pages) could store six 2-KB objects. Initially, all the objects in the cache are marked as **free**. When a new object for a kernel data structure is needed, the allocator can assign any free

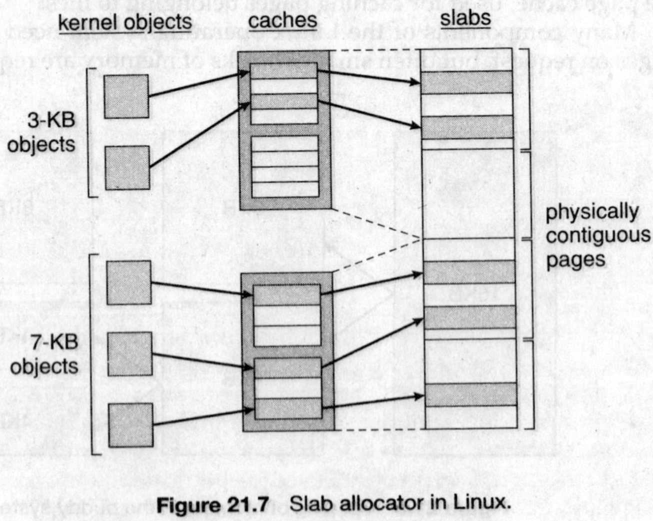

Figure 21.7 Slab allocator in Linux.

object from the cache to satisfy the request. The object assigned from the cache is marked as **used**.

Let's consider a scenario in which the kernel requests memory from the slab allocator for an object representing a process descriptor. In Linux systems, a process descriptor is of the type `struct task_struct`, which requires approximately 1.7 KB of memory. When the Linux kernel creates a new task, it requests the necessary memory for the `struct task_struct` object from its cache. The cache will fulfill the request using a `struct task_struct` object that has already been allocated in a slab and is marked as free.

In Linux, a slab may be in one of three possible states:

1. **Full**. All objects in the slab are marked as used.
2. **Empty**. All objects in the slab are marked as free.
3. **Partial**. The slab consists of both used and free objects.

The slab allocator first attempts to satisfy the request with a free object in a partial slab. If none exist, a free object is assigned from an empty slab. If no empty slabs are available, a new slab is allocated from contiguous physical pages and assigned to a cache; memory for the object is allocated from this slab.

Two other main subsystems in Linux do their own management of physical pages: the page cache and the virtual memory system. These systems are closely related to one another. The **page cache** is the kernel's main cache for block devices (Section 21.8.1) and memory-mapped files and is the main mechanism through which I/O to these devices is performed. Both the native Linux disk-based file systems and the NFS networked file system use the page cache. The page cache stores entire pages of file contents and is not limited to block devices; it can also cache networked data. The virtual memory system manages the contents of each process's virtual address space. These two systems interact closely with one another because reading a page of data into the page cache requires mapping pages in the page cache using the virtual memory system. In the following section, we look at the virtual memory system in greater detail.

21.6.2 Virtual Memory

The Linux virtual memory system is responsible for maintaining the address space visible to each process. It creates pages of virtual memory on demand and manages loading those pages from disk and swapping them back out to disk as required. Under Linux, the virtual memory manager maintains two separate views of a process's address space: as a set of separate regions and as a set of pages.

The first view of an address space is the logical view, describing instructions that the virtual memory system has received concerning the layout of the address space. In this view, the address space consists of a set of non-overlapping regions, each region representing a continuous, page-aligned subset of the address space. Each region is described internally by a single `vm_area_struct` structure that defines the properties of the region, including the process's read, write, and execute permissions in the region as well as information about any files associated with the region. The regions for each address space are linked into a balanced binary tree to allow fast lookup of the region corresponding to any virtual address.

The kernel also maintains a second, physical view of each address space. This view is stored in the hardware page tables for the process. The page-table entries identify the exact current location of each page of virtual memory, whether it is on disk or in physical memory. The physical view is managed by a set of routines, which are invoked from the kernel's software-interrupt handlers whenever a process tries to access a page that is not currently present in the page tables. Each `vm_area_struct` in the address-space description contains a field that points to a table of functions that implement the key page-management functions for any given virtual memory region. All requests to read or write an unavailable page are eventually dispatched to the appropriate handler in the function table for the `vm_area_struct`, so that the central memory-management routines do not have to know the details of managing each possible type of memory region.

21.6.2.1 Virtual Memory Regions

Linux implements several types of virtual memory regions. One property that characterizes virtual memory is the backing store for the region, which describes where the pages for the region come from. Most memory regions are backed either by a file or by nothing. A region backed by nothing is the simplest type of virtual memory region. Such a region represents **demand-zero memory**: when a process tries to read a page in such a region, it is simply given back a page of memory filled with zeros.

A region backed by a file acts as a viewport onto a section of that file. Whenever the process tries to access a page within that region, the page table is filled with the address of a page within the kernel's page cache corresponding to the appropriate offset in the file. The same page of physical memory is used by both the page cache and the process's page tables, so any changes made to the file by the file system are immediately visible to any processes that have mapped that file into their address space. Any number of processes can map the same region of the same file, and they will all end up using the same page of physical memory for the purpose.

A virtual memory region is also defined by its reaction to writes. The mapping of a region into the process's address space can be either *private* or *shared*. If a process writes to a privately mapped region, then the pager detects that a copy-on-write is necessary to keep the changes local to the process. In contrast, writes to a shared region result in updating of the object mapped into that region, so that the change will be visible immediately to any other process that is mapping that object.

21.6.2.2 Lifetime of a Virtual Address Space

The kernel will create a new virtual address space in two situations: when a process runs a new program with the `exec()` system call and when a new process is created by the `fork()` system call. The first case is easy. When a new program is executed, the process is given a new, completely empty virtual address space. It is up to the routines for loading the program to populate the address space with virtual memory regions.

The second case, creating a new process with `fork()`, involves creating a complete copy of the existing process's virtual address space. The kernel copies the parent process's `vm_area_struct` descriptors, then creates a new set of page tables for the child. The parent's page tables are copied directly into the child's, and the reference count of each page covered is incremented; thus, after the fork, the parent and child share the same physical pages of memory in their address spaces.

A special case occurs when the copying operation reaches a virtual memory region that is mapped privately. Any pages to which the parent process has written within such a region are private, and subsequent changes to these pages by either the parent or the child must not update the page in the other process's address space. When the page-table entries for such regions are copied, they are set to be read only and are marked for copy-on-write. As long as neither process modifies these pages, the two processes share the same page of physical memory. However, if either process tries to modify a copy-on-write page, the reference count on the page is checked. If the page is still shared, then the process copies the page's contents to a brand-new page of physical memory and uses its copy instead. This mechanism ensures that private data pages are shared between processes whenever possible; copies are made only when absolutely necessary.

21.6.2.3 Swapping and Paging

An important task for a virtual memory system is to relocate pages of memory from physical memory out to disk when that memory is needed. Early UNIX systems performed this relocation by swapping out the contents of entire processes at once, but modern versions of UNIX rely more on paging—the movement of individual pages of virtual memory between physical memory and disk. Linux does not implement whole-process swapping; it uses the newer paging mechanism exclusively.

The paging system can be divided into two sections. First, the **policy algorithm** decides which pages to write out to disk and when to write them. Second, the **paging mechanism** carries out the transfer and pages data back into physical memory when they are needed again.

Linux's **pageout policy** uses a modified version of the standard clock (or second-chance) algorithm described in Section 9.4.5.2. Under Linux, a multiple-pass clock is used, and every page has an *age* that is adjusted on each pass of the clock. The age is more precisely a measure of the page's youthfulness, or how much activity the page has seen recently. Frequently accessed pages will attain a higher age value, but the age of infrequently accessed pages will drop toward zero with each pass. This age valuing allows the pager to select pages to page out based on a least frequently used (LFU) policy.

The paging mechanism supports paging both to dedicated swap devices and partitions and to normal files, although swapping to a file is significantly slower due to the extra overhead incurred by the file system. Blocks are allocated from the swap devices according to a bitmap of used blocks, which is maintained in physical memory at all times. The allocator uses a next-fit algorithm to try to write out pages to continuous runs of disk blocks for improved performance. The allocator records the fact that a page has been paged out to disk by using a feature of the page tables on modern processors:

the page-table entry's page-not-present bit is set, allowing the rest of the page-table entry to be filled with an index identifying where the page has been written.

21.6.2.4 Kernel Virtual Memory

Linux reserves for its own internal use a constant, architecture-dependent region of the virtual address space of every process. The page-table entries that map to these kernel pages are marked as protected, so that the pages are not visible or modifiable when the processor is running in user mode. This kernel virtual memory area contains two regions. The first is a static area that contains page-table references to every available physical page of memory in the system, so that a simple translation from physical to virtual addresses occurs when kernel code is run. The core of the kernel, along with all pages allocated by the normal page allocator, resides in this region.

The remainder of the kernel's reserved section of address space is not reserved for any specific purpose. Page-table entries in this address range can be modified by the kernel to point to any other areas of memory. The kernel provides a pair of facilities that allow processes to use this virtual memory. The `vmalloc()` function allocates an arbitrary number of physical pages of memory that may not be physically contiguous into a single region of virtually contiguous kernel memory. The `vremap()` function maps a sequence of virtual addresses to point to an area of memory used by a device driver for memory-mapped I/O.

21.6.3 Execution and Loading of User Programs

The Linux kernel's execution of user programs is triggered by a call to the `exec()` system call. This `exec()` call commands the kernel to run a new program within the current process, completely overwriting the current execution context with the initial context of the new program. The first job of this system service is to verify that the calling process has permission rights to the file being executed. Once that matter has been checked, the kernel invokes a loader routine to start running the program. The loader does not necessarily load the contents of the program file into physical memory, but it does at least set up the mapping of the program into virtual memory.

There is no single routine in Linux for loading a new program. Instead, Linux maintains a table of possible loader functions, and it gives each such function the opportunity to try loading the given file when an `exec()` system call is made. The initial reason for this loader table was that, between the releases of the 1.0 and 1.2 kernels, the standard format for Linux's binary files was changed. Older Linux kernels understood the `a.out` format for binary files—a relatively simple format common on older UNIX systems. Newer Linux systems use the more modern **ELF** format, now supported by most current UNIX implementations. ELF has a number of advantages over `a.out`, including flexibility and extensibility. New sections can be added to an ELF binary (for example, to add extra debugging information) without causing the loader routines to become confused. By allowing registration of multiple loader routines, Linux can easily support the ELF and `a.out` binary formats in a single running system.

In Sections 21.6.3.1 and 21.6.3.2, we concentrate exclusively on the loading and running of ELF-format binaries. The procedure for loading a.out binaries is simpler but is similar in operation.

21.6.3.1 Mapping of Programs into Memory

Under Linux, the binary loader does not load a binary file into physical memory. Rather, the pages of the binary file are mapped into regions of virtual memory. Only when the program tries to access a given page will a page fault result in the loading of that page into physical memory using demand paging.

It is the responsibility of the kernel's binary loader to set up the initial memory mapping. An ELF-format binary file consists of a header followed by several page-aligned sections. The ELF loader works by reading the header and mapping the sections of the file into separate regions of virtual memory.

Figure 21.8 shows the typical layout of memory regions set up by the ELF loader. In a reserved region at one end of the address space sits the kernel, in its own privileged region of virtual memory inaccessible to normal user-mode programs. The rest of virtual memory is available to applications, which can use the kernel's memory-mapping functions to create regions that map a portion of a file or that are available for application data.

The loader's job is to set up the initial memory mapping to allow the execution of the program to start. The regions that need to be initialized include the stack and the program's text and data regions.

The stack is created at the top of the user-mode virtual memory; it grows downward toward lower-numbered addresses. It includes copies of the arguments and environment variables given to the program in the `exec()` system call. The other regions are created near the bottom end of virtual memory. The sections of the binary file that contain program text or read-only

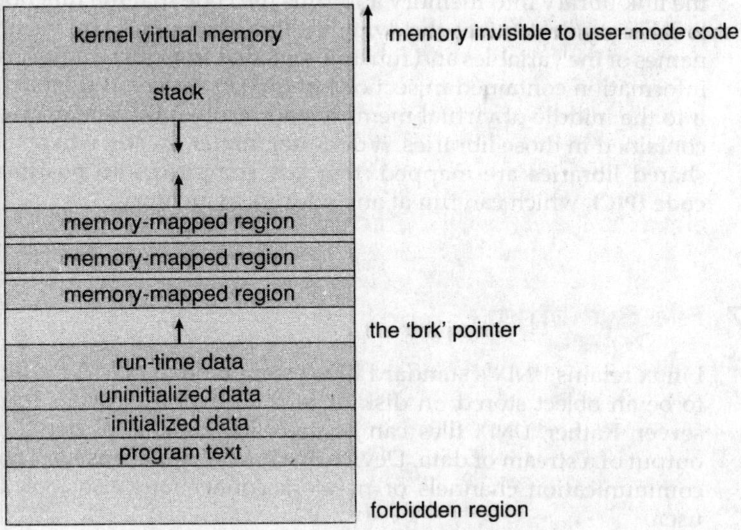

Figure 21.8 Memory layout for ELF programs.

data are mapped into memory as a write-protected region. Writable initialized data are mapped next; then any uninitialized data are mapped in as a private demand-zero region.

Directly beyond these fixed-sized regions is a variable-sized region that programs can expand as needed to hold data allocated at run time. Each process has a pointer, `brk`, that points to the current extent of this data region, and processes can extend or contract their `brk` region with a single system call —`sbrk()`.

Once these mappings have been set up, the loader initializes the process's program-counter register with the starting point recorded in the ELF header, and the process can be scheduled.

21.6.3.2 Static and Dynamic Linking

Once the program has been loaded and has started running, all the necessary contents of the binary file have been loaded into the process's virtual address space. However, most programs also need to run functions from the system libraries, and these library functions must also be loaded. In the simplest case, the necessary library functions are embedded directly in the program's executable binary file. Such a program is statically linked to its libraries, and statically linked executables can commence running as soon as they are loaded.

The main disadvantage of static linking is that every program generated must contain copies of exactly the same common system library functions. It is much more efficient, in terms of both physical memory and disk-space usage, to load the system libraries into memory only once. Dynamic linking allows this single loading to happen.

Linux implements dynamic linking in user mode through a special linker library. Every dynamically linked program contains a small, statically linked function that is called when the program starts. This static function just maps the link library into memory and runs the code that the function contains. The link library determines the dynamic libraries required by the program and the names of the variables and functions needed from those libraries by reading the information contained in sections of the ELF binary. It then maps the libraries into the middle of virtual memory and resolves the references to the symbols contained in those libraries. It does not matter exactly where in memory these shared libraries are mapped: they are compiled into **position-independent code (PIC)**, which can run at any address in memory.

21.7 File Systems

Linux retains UNIX's standard file-system model. In UNIX, a file does not have to be an object stored on disk or fetched over a network from a remote file server. Rather, UNIX files can be anything capable of handling the input or output of a stream of data. Device drivers can appear as files, and interprocess-communication channels or network connections also look like files to the user.

The Linux kernel handles all these types of files by hiding the implementation details of any single file type behind a layer of software, the virtual file system (VFS). Here, we first cover the virtual file system and then discuss the standard Linux file system—ext2fs.

21.7.1 The Virtual File System

The Linux VFS is designed around object-oriented principles. It has two components: a set of definitions that specify what file-system objects are allowed to look like and a layer of software to manipulate the objects. The VFS defines four main object types:

- An **inode object** represents an individual file.
- A **file object** represents an open file.
- A **superblock object** represents an entire file system.
- A **dentry object** represents an individual directory entry.

For each of these four object types, the VFS defines a set of operations. Every object of one of these types contains a pointer to a function table. The function table lists the addresses of the actual functions that implement the defined operations for that object. For example, an abbreviated API for some of the file object's operations includes:

- `int open(. . .)` — Open a file.
- `ssize_t read(. . .)` — Read from a file.
- `ssize_t write(. . .)` — Write to a file.
- `int mmap(. . .)` — Memory-map a file.

The complete definition of the file object is specified in the `struct file_operations`, which is located in the file `/usr/include/linux/fs.h`. An implementation of the file object (for a specific file type) is required to implement each function specified in the definition of the file object.

The VFS software layer can perform an operation on one of the file-system objects by calling the appropriate function from the object's function table, without having to know in advance exactly what kind of object it is dealing with. The VFS does not know, or care, whether an inode represents a networked file, a disk file, a network socket, or a directory file. The appropriate function for that file's `read()` operation will always be at the same place in its function table, and the VFS software layer will call that function without caring how the data are actually read.

The inode and file objects are the mechanisms used to access files. An inode object is a data structure containing pointers to the disk blocks that contain the actual file contents, and a file object represents a point of access to the data in an open file. A process cannot access an inode's contents without first obtaining a file object pointing to the inode. The file object keeps track of where in the file the process is currently reading or writing, to keep track of sequential file I/O. It also remembers whether the process asked for write permissions when the file was opened and tracks the process's activity if necessary to perform adaptive read-ahead, fetching file data into memory before the process requests the data, to improve performance.

File objects typically belong to a single process, but inode objects do not. Even when a file is no longer being used by any processes, its inode object may still be cached by the VFS to improve performance if the file is used again in the near future. All cached file data are linked onto a list in the file's inode object. The inode also maintains standard information about each file, such as the owner, size, and time most recently modified.

Directory files are dealt with slightly differently from other files. The UNIX programming interface defines a number of operations on directories, such as creating, deleting, and renaming a file in a directory. The system calls for these directory operations do not require that the user open the files concerned, unlike the case for reading or writing data. The VFS therefore defines these directory operations in the inode object, rather than in the file object.

The superblock object represents a connected set of files that form a self-contained file system. The operating-system kernel maintains a single superblock object for each disk device mounted as a file system and for each networked file system currently connected. The main responsibility of the superblock object is to provide access to inodes. The VFS identifies every inode by a unique file-system/inode number pair, and it finds the inode corresponding to a particular inode number by asking the superblock object to return the inode with that number.

Finally, a dentry object represents a directory entry that may include the name of a directory in the path name of a file (such as `/usr`) or the actual file (such as `stdio.h`). For example, the file `/usr/include/stdio.h` contains the directory entries (1) `/`, (2) `usr`, (3) `include`, and (4) `stdio.h`. Each one of these values is represented by a separate dentry object.

As an example of how dentry objects are used, consider the situation in which a process wishes to open the file with the pathname `/usr/include/stdio.h` using an editor. Because Linux treats directory names as files, translating this path requires first obtaining the inode for the root—`/`. The operating system must then read through this file to obtain the inode for the file `include`. It must continue this process until it obtains the inode for the file `stdio.h`. Because path-name translation can be a time-consuming task, Linux maintains a cache of dentry objects, which is consulted during path-name translation. Obtaining the inode from the dentry cache is considerably faster than having to read the on-disk file.

21.7.2 The Linux ext2fs File System

The standard on-disk file system used by Linux is called **ext2fs**, for historical reasons. Linux was originally programmed with a Minix-compatible file system, to ease exchanging data with the Minix development system, but that file system was severely restricted by 14-character file-name limits and a maximum file-system size of 64 MB. The Minix file system was superseded by a new file system, which was christened the **extended file system (extfs)**. A later redesign of this file system to improve performance and scalability and to add a few missing features led to the **second extended file system (ext2fs)**.

Linuxs ext2fs has much in common with the BSD Fast File System (FFS) (Section A.7.7). It uses a similar mechanism for locating the data blocks belonging to a specific file, storing data-block pointers in indirect blocks throughout the file system with up to three levels of indirection. As in FFS, directory files are stored on disk just like normal files, although their contents are interpreted differently. Each block in a directory file consists of a linked list of entries; each entry contains the length of the entry, the name of a file, and the inode number of the inode to which that entry refers.

The main differences between ext2fs and FFS lie in their disk-allocation policies. In FFS, the disk is allocated to files in blocks of 8 KB. These blocks are subdivided into fragments of 1 KB for storage of small files or partially filled blocks at the ends of files. In contrast, ext2fs does not use fragments at all but performs all its allocations in smaller units. The default block size on ext2fs is 1 KB, although 2-KB and 4-KB blocks are also supported.

To maintain high performance, the operating system must try to perform I/O operations in large chunks whenever possible by clustering physically adjacent I/O requests. Clustering reduces the per-request overhead incurred by device drivers, disks, and disk-controller hardware. A 1-KB I/O request size is too small to maintain good performance, so ext2fs uses allocation policies designed to place logically adjacent blocks of a file into physically adjacent blocks on disk, so that it can submit an I/O request for several disk blocks as a single operation.

The ext2fs allocation policy comes in two parts. As in FFS, an ext2fs file system is partitioned into multiple **block groups**. FFS uses the similar concept of **cylinder groups**, where each group corresponds to a single cylinder of a physical disk. However, modern disk-drive technology packs sectors onto the disk at different densities, and thus with different cylinder sizes, depending on how far the disk head is from the center of the disk. Therefore, fixed-sized cylinder groups do not necessarily correspond to the disk's geometry.

When allocating a file, ext2fs must first select the block group for that file. For data blocks, it attempts to allocate the file to the block group to which the file's inode has been allocated. For inode allocations, it selects the block group in which the file's parent directory resides, for nondirectory files. Directory files are not kept together but rather are dispersed throughout the available block groups. These policies are designed not only to keep related information within the same block group but also to spread out the disk load among the disk's block groups to reduce the fragmentation of any one area of the disk.

Within a block group, ext2fs tries to keep allocations physically contiguous if possible, reducing fragmentation if it can. It maintains a bitmap of all free blocks in a block group. When allocating the first blocks for a new file, it starts searching for a free block from the beginning of the block group; when extending a file, it continues the search from the block most recently allocated to the file. The search is performed in two stages. First, ext2fs searches for an entire free byte in the bitmap; if it fails to find one, it looks for any free bit. The search for free bytes aims to allocate disk space in chunks of at least eight blocks where possible.

Once a free block has been identified, the search is extended backward until an allocated block is encountered. When a free byte is found in the bitmap, this backward extension prevents ext2fs from leaving a hole between the most recently allocated block in the previous nonzero byte and the zero byte found. Once the next block to be allocated has been found by either bit or byte search, ext2fs extends the allocation forward for up to eight blocks and **preallocates**

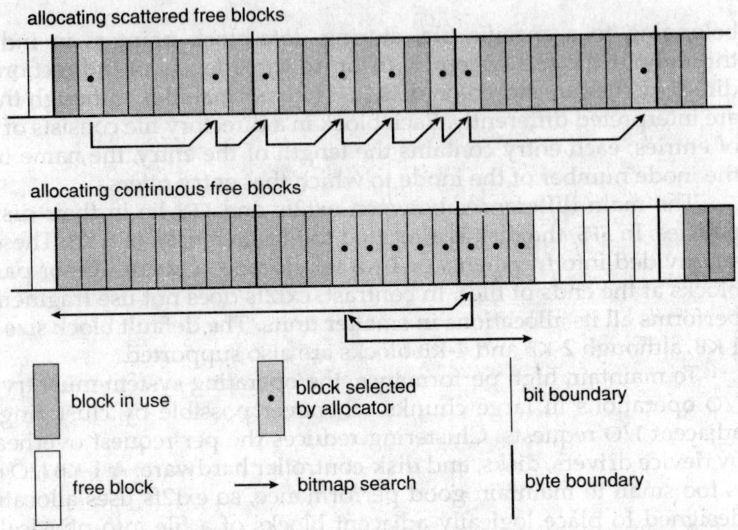

Figure 21.9 ext2fs block-allocation policies.

these extra blocks to the file. This preallocation helps to reduce fragmentation during interleaved writes to separate files and also reduces the CPU cost of disk allocation by allocating multiple blocks simultaneously. The preallocated blocks are returned to the free-space bitmap when the file is closed.

Figure 21.9 illustrates the allocation policies. Each row represents a sequence of set and unset bits in an allocation bitmap, indicating used and free blocks on disk. In the first case, if we can find any free blocks sufficiently near the start of the search, then we allocate them no matter how fragmented they may be. The fragmentation is partially compensated for by the fact that the blocks are close together and can probably all be read without any disk seeks, and allocating them all to one file is better in the long run than allocating isolated blocks to separate files once large free areas become scarce on disk. In the second case, we have not immediately found a free block close by, so we search forward for an entire free byte in the bitmap. If we allocated that byte as a whole, we would end up creating a fragmented area of free space between it and the allocation preceding it, so before allocating we back up to make this allocation flush with the allocation preceding it, and then we allocate forward to satisfy the default allocation of eight blocks.

21.7.3 Journaling

One popular feature in a file system is **journaling**, whereby modifications to the file system are sequentially written to a journal. A set of operations that performs a specific task is a **transaction**. Once a transaction is written to the journal, it is considered to be committed, and the system call modifying the file system (`write()`) can return to the user process, allowing it to continue execution. Meanwhile, the journal entries relating to the transaction are replayed across the actual file-system structures. As the changes are made, a pointer is updated to indicate which actions have completed and which are still incomplete. When an entire committed transaction is completed, it is removed from the journal. The journal, which is actually a circular buffer, may be in a separate section of the file system, or it may even be on a separate disk spindle. It is more efficient, but more complex, to have it under separate read–write heads, thereby decreasing head contention and seek times.

If the system crashes, some transactions may remain in the journal. Those transactions were never completed to the file system even though they were committed by the operating system, so they must be completed once the system recovers. The transactions can be executed from the pointer until the work is complete, and the file-system structures remain consistent. The only problem occurs when a transaction has been aborted—that is, it was not committed before the system crashed. Any changes from those transactions that were applied to the file system must be undone, again preserving the consistency of the file system. This recovery is all that is needed after a crash, eliminating all problems with consistency checking.

Journaling file systems are also typically faster than non-journaling systems, as updates proceed much faster when they are applied to the in-memory journal rather than directly to the on-disk data structures. The reason for this improvement is found in the performance advantage of sequential I/O over random I/O. Costly synchronous random writes to the file system are turned into much less costly synchronous sequential writes to the file system's journal. Those changes in turn are replayed asynchronously via random writes to the appropriate structures. The overall result is a significant gain in performance of file-system metadata-oriented operations, such as file creation and deletion.

Journaling is not provided in ext2fs. It is provided, however, in another common file system available for Linux systems, **ext3**, which is based on ext2fs.

21.7.4 The Linux Process File System

The flexibility of the Linux VFS enables us to implement a file system that does not store data persistently at all but rather provides an interface to some other functionality. The Linux **process file system**, known as the `/proc` file system, is an example of a file system whose contents are not actually stored anywhere but are computed on demand according to user file I/O requests.

A `/proc` file system is not unique to Linux. SVR4 UNIX introduced a `/proc` file system as an efficient interface to the kernel's process debugging support. Each subdirectory of the file system corresponded not to a directory on any disk but rather to an active process on the current system. A listing of the file system reveals one directory per process, with the directory name being the ASCII decimal representation of the process's unique process identifier (PID).

Linux implements such a `/proc` file system but extends it greatly by adding a number of extra directories and text files under the file system's root directory. These new entries correspond to various statistics about the kernel and the associated loaded drivers. The `/proc` file system provides a way for programs to access this information as plain text files; the standard UNIX user environment provides powerful tools to process such files. For example, in the past, the traditional UNIX ps command for listing the states of all running processes has been implemented as a privileged process that reads the process state directly from the kernel's virtual memory. Under Linux, this command is implemented as an entirely unprivileged program that simply parses and formats the information from /proc.

The /proc file system must implement two things: a directory structure and the file contents within. Because a UNIX file system is defined as a set of file and directory inodes identified by their inode numbers, the /proc file system must define a unique and persistent inode number for each directory and the associated files. Once such a mapping exists, the file system can use this inode number to identify just what operation is required when a user tries to read from a particular file inode or to perform a lookup in a particular directory inode. When data are read from one of these files, the /proc file system will collect the appropriate information, format it into textual form, and place it into the requesting process's read buffer.

The mapping from inode number to information type splits the inode number into two fields. In Linux, a PID is 16 bits wide, but an inode number is 32 bits. The top 16 bits of the inode number are interpreted as a PID, and the remaining bits define what type of information is being requested about that process.

A PID of zero is not valid, so a zero PID field in the inode number is taken to mean that this inode contains global—rather than process-specific—information. Separate global files exist in /proc to report information such as the kernel version, free memory, performance statistics, and drivers currently running.

Not all the inode numbers in this range are reserved. The kernel can allocate new /proc inode mappings dynamically, maintaining a bitmap of allocated inode numbers. It also maintains a tree data structure of registered global /proc file-system entries. Each entry contains the file's inode number, file name, and access permissions, along with the special functions used to generate the file's contents. Drivers can register and deregister entries in this tree at any time, and a special section of the tree—appearing under the */proc/sys* directory—is reserved for kernel variables. Files under this tree are managed by a set of common handlers that allow both reading and writing of these variables, so a system administrator can tune the value of kernel parameters simply by writing the new desired values out in ASCII decimal to the appropriate file.

To allow efficient access to these variables from within applications, the */proc/sys* subtree is made available through a special system call, sysctl(), that reads and writes the same variables in binary, rather than in text, without the overhead of the file system. sysctl() is not an extra facility; it simply reads the /proc dynamic entry tree to identify the variables to which the application is referring.

21.8 Input and Output

To the user, the I/O system in Linux looks much like that in any UNIX system. That is, to the extent possible, all device drivers appear as normal files. Users can open an access channel to a device in the same way they opens any other file—devices can appear as objects within the file system. The system administrator can create special files within a file system that contain references to a specific device driver, and a user opening such a file will be able to read from and write to the device referenced. By using the normal file-protection

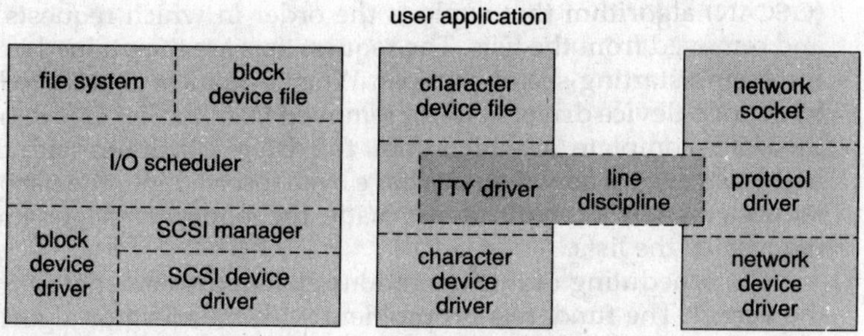

Figure 21.10 Device-driver block structure.

system, which determines who can access which file, the administrator can set access permissions for each device.

Linux splits all devices into three classes: block devices, character devices, and network devices. Figure 21.10 illustrates the overall structure of the device-driver system.

Block devices include all devices that allow random access to completely independent, fixed-sized blocks of data, including hard disks and floppy disks, CD-ROMs, and flash memory. Block devices are typically used to store file systems, but direct access to a block device is also allowed so that programs can create and repair the file system that the device contains. Applications can also access these block devices directly if they wish; for example, a database application may prefer to perform its own, fine-tuned laying out of data onto the disk, rather than using the general-purpose file system.

Character devices include most other devices, such as mice and keyboards. The fundamental difference between block and character devices is random access—block devices may be accessed randomly, while character devices are only accessed serially. For example, seeking to a certain position in a file might be supported for a DVD but makes no sense to a pointing device such as a mouse.

Network devices are dealt with differently from block and character devices. Users cannot directly transfer data to network devices; instead, they must communicate indirectly by opening a connection to the kernel's networking subsystem. We discuss the interface to network devices separately in Section 21.10.

21.8.1 Block Devices

Block devices provide the main interface to all disk devices in a system. Performance is particularly important for disks, and the block-device system must provide functionality to ensure that disk access is as fast as possible. This functionality is achieved through the scheduling of I/O operations.

In the context of block devices, a **block** represents the unit with which the kernel performs I/O. When a block is read into memory, it is stored in a **buffer**. The **request manager** is the layer of software that manages the reading and writing of buffer contents to and from a block-device driver.

A separate list of requests is kept for each block-device driver. Traditionally, these requests have been scheduled according to a unidirectional-elevator

(C-SCAN) algorithm that exploits the order in which requests are inserted in and removed from the lists. The request lists are maintained in sorted order of increasing starting-sector number. When a request is accepted for processing by a block-device driver, it is not removed from the list. It is removed only after the I/O is complete, at which point the driver continues with the next request in the list, even if new requests have been inserted into the list before the active request. As new I/O requests are made, the request manager attempts to merge requests in the lists.

The scheduling of I/O operations changed somewhat with Version 2.6 of the kernel. The fundamental problem with the elevator algorithm is that I/O operations concentrated in a specific region of the disk can result in starvation of requests that need to occur in other regions of the disk. The **deadline I/O scheduler** used in Version 2.6 works similarly to the elevator algorithm except that it also associates a deadline with each request, thus addressing the starvation issue. By default, the deadline for read requests is 0.5 second, and that for write requests is 5 seconds. The deadline scheduler maintains a **sorted queue** of pending I/O operations ordered by sector number. However, it also maintains two other queues—a **read queue** for read operations and a **write queue** for write operations. These two queues are ordered according to deadline. Every I/O request is placed in both the sorted queue and either the read or the write queue, as appropriate. Ordinarily, I/O operations occur from the sorted queue. However, if a deadline expires for a request in either the read or the write queue, I/O operations are scheduled from the queue containing the expired request. This policy ensures that an I/O operation will wait no longer than its expiration time.

21.8.2 Character Devices

A character-device driver can be almost any device driver that does not offer random access to fixed blocks of data. Any character-device drivers registered to the Linux kernel must also register a set of functions that implement the file I/O operations that the driver can handle. The kernel performs almost no preprocessing of a file read or write request to a character device; it simply passes the request to the device in question and lets the device deal with the request.

The main exception to this rule is the special subset of character-device drivers that implement terminal devices. The kernel maintains a standard interface to these drivers by means of a set of `tty_struct` structures. Each of these structures provides buffering and flow control on the data stream from the terminal device and feeds those data to a line discipline.

A **line discipline** is an interpreter for the information from the terminal device. The most common line discipline is the `tty` discipline, which glues the terminal's data stream onto the standard input and output streams of a user's running processes, allowing those processes to communicate directly with the user's terminal. This job is complicated by the fact that several such processes may be running simultaneously, and the `tty` line discipline is responsible for attaching and detaching the terminal's input and output from the various processes connected to it as those processes are suspended or awakened by the user.

Other line disciplines also are implemented that have nothing to do with I/O to a user process. The PPP and SLIP networking protocols are ways of encoding a networking connection over a terminal device such as a serial line. These protocols are implemented under Linux as drivers that at one end appear to the terminal system as line disciplines and at the other end appear to the networking system as network-device drivers. After one of these line disciplines has been enabled on a terminal device, any data appearing on that terminal will be routed directly to the appropriate network-device driver.

21.9 Interprocess Communication

Linux provides a rich environment for processes to communicate with each other. Communication may be just a matter of letting another process know that some event has occurred, or it may involve transferring data from one process to another.

21.9.1 Synchronization and Signals

The standard Linux mechanism for informing a process that an event has occurred is the **signal**. Signals can be sent from any process to any other process, with restrictions on signals sent to processes owned by another user. However, a limited number of signals are available, and they cannot carry information. Only the fact that a signal has occurred is available to a process. Signals are not generated only by processes. The kernel also generates signals internally; for example, it can send a signal to a server process when data arrive on a network channel, to a parent process when a child terminates, or to a waiting process when a timer expires.

Internally, the Linux kernel does not use signals to communicate with processes running in kernel mode. If a kernel-mode process is expecting an event to occur, it will not normally use signals to receive notification of that event. Rather, communication about incoming asynchronous events within the kernel takes place through the use of scheduling states and `wait_queue` structures. These mechanisms allow kernel-mode processes to inform one another about relevant events, and they also allow events to be generated by device drivers or by the networking system. Whenever a process wants to wait for some event to complete, it places itself on a **wait queue** associated with that event and tells the scheduler that it is no longer eligible for execution. Once the event has completed, it will wake up every process on the wait queue. This procedure allows multiple processes to wait for a single event. For example, if several processes are trying to read a file from a disk, then they will all be awakened once the data have been read into memory successfully.

Although signals have always been the main mechanism for communicating asynchronous events among processes, Linux also implements the semaphore mechanism of System V UNIX. A process can wait on a semaphore as easily as it can wait for a signal, but semaphores have two advantages: Large numbers of semaphores can be shared among multiple independent processes, and operations on multiple semaphores can be performed atomically. Internally, the standard Linux wait queue mechanism synchronizes processes that are communicating with semaphores.

21.9.2 Passing of Data Among Processes

Linux offers several mechanisms for passing data among processes. The standard UNIX pipe mechanism allows a child process to inherit a communication channel from its parent; data written to one end of the pipe can be read at the other. Under Linux, pipes appear as just another type of inode to virtual-file-system software, and each pipe has a pair of wait queues to synchronize the reader and writer. UNIX also defines a set of networking facilities that can send streams of data to both local and remote processes. Networking is covered in Section 21.10.

Another process communications method, shared memory, offers an extremely fast way to communicate large or small amounts of data. Any data written by one process to a shared memory region can be read immediately by any other process that has mapped that region into its address space. The main disadvantage of shared memory is that, on its own, it offers no synchronization. A process can neither ask the operating system whether a piece of shared memory has been written to nor suspend execution until such a write occurs. Shared memory becomes particularly powerful when used in conjunction with another interprocess-communication mechanism that provides the missing synchronization.

A shared-memory region in Linux is a persistent object that can be created or deleted by processes. Such an object is treated as though it were a small, independent address space. The Linux paging algorithms can elect to page out to disk shared-memory pages, just as they can page out a process's data pages. The shared-memory object acts as a backing store for shared-memory regions, just as a file can act as a backing store for a memory-mapped memory region. When a file is mapped into a virtual-address-space region, then any page faults that occur cause the appropriate page of the file to be mapped into virtual memory. Similarly, shared-memory mappings direct page faults to map in pages from a persistent shared-memory object. Also just as for files, shared-memory objects remember their contents even if no processes are currently mapping them into virtual memory.

21.10 Network Structure

Networking is a key area of functionality for Linux. Not only does Linux support the standard Internet protocols used for most UNIX-to-UNIX communications, but it also implements a number of protocols native to other, non-UNIX operating systems. In particular, since Linux was originally implemented primarily on PCs, rather than on large workstations or on server-class systems, it supports many of the protocols typically used on PC networks, such as AppleTalk and IPX.

Internally, networking in the Linux kernel is implemented by three layers of software:

1. The socket interface
2. Protocol drivers
3. Network-device drivers

User applications perform all networking requests through the socket interface. This interface is designed to look like the 4.3 BSD socket layer, so that any programs designed to make use of Berkeley sockets will run on Linux without any source-code changes. This interface is described in Section A.9.1. The BSD socket interface is sufficiently general to represent network addresses for a wide range of networking protocols. This single interface is used in Linux to access not just those protocols implemented on standard BSD systems but all the protocols supported by the system.

The next layer of software is the protocol stack, which is similar in organization to BSD's own framework. Whenever any networking data arrive at this layer, either from an application's socket or from a network-device driver, the data are expected to have been tagged with an identifier specifying which network protocol they contain. Protocols can communicate with one another if they desire; for example, within the Internet protocol set, separate protocols manage routing, error reporting, and reliable retransmission of lost data.

The protocol layer may rewrite packets, create new packets, split or reassemble packets into fragments, or simply discard incoming data. Ultimately, once the protocol layer has finished processing a set of packets, it passes them on, upward to the socket interface if the data are destined for a local connection or downward to a device driver if the data need to be transmitted remotely. The protocol layer decides to which socket or device it will send the packet.

All communication between the layers of the networking stack is performed by passing single `skbuff` (socket buffer) structures. Each of these structures contains a set of pointers into a single continuous area of memory, representing a buffer inside which network packets can be constructed. The valid data in a `skbuff` do not need to start at the beginning of the `skbuff`'s buffer, and they do not need to run to the end. The networking code can add data to or trim data from either end of the packet, as long as the result still fits into the `skbuff`. This capacity is especially important on modern microprocessors, where improvements in CPU speed have far outstripped the performance of main memory. The `skbuff` architecture allows flexibility in manipulating packet headers and checksums while avoiding any unnecessary data copying.

The most important set of protocols in the Linux networking system is the TCP/IP protocol suite. This suite comprises a number of separate protocols. The IP protocol implements routing between different hosts anywhere on the network. On top of the routing protocol are built the UDP, TCP, and ICMP protocols. The UDP protocol carries arbitrary individual datagrams between hosts. The TCP protocol implements reliable connections between hosts with guaranteed in-order delivery of packets and automatic retransmission of lost data. The ICMP protocol is used to carry various error and status messages between hosts.

Each packet (`skbuff`) arriving at the networking stack's protocol software is expected to be already tagged with an internal identifier indicating the protocol to which the packet is relevant. Different networking-device drivers encode the protocol type in different ways; thus, the protocol for incoming data must be identified in the device driver. The device driver uses a hash table of known networking-protocol identifiers to look up the appropriate protocol and passes the packet to that protocol. New protocols can be added to the hash table as kernel-loadable modules.

Incoming IP packets are delivered to the IP driver. The job of this layer is to perform routing. After deciding where the packet is to be sent, the IP driver forwards the packet to the appropriate internal protocol driver to be delivered locally or injects it back into a selected network-device-driver queue to be forwarded to another host. It performs the routing decision using two tables: the persistent forwarding information base (FIB) and a cache of recent routing decisions. The FIB holds routing-configuration information and can specify routes based either on a specific destination address or on a wildcard representing multiple destinations. The FIB is organized as a set of hash tables indexed by destination address; the tables representing the most specific routes are always searched first. Successful lookups from this table are added to the route-caching table, which caches routes only by specific destination; no wildcards are stored in the cache, so lookups can be made quickly. An entry in the route cache expires after a fixed period with no hits.

At various stages, the IP software passes packets to a separate section of code for **firewall management**—selective filtering of packets according to arbitrary criteria, usually for security purposes. The firewall manager maintains a number of separate **firewall chains** and allows a `skbuff` to be matched against any chain. Chains are reserved for separate purposes: one is used for forwarded packets, one for packets being input to this host, and one for data generated at this host. Each chain is held as an ordered list of rules, where a rule specifies one of a number of possible firewall-decision functions plus some arbitrary data for matching purposes.

Two other functions performed by the IP driver are disassembly and reassembly of large packets. If an outgoing packet is too large to be queued to a device, it is simply split up into smaller **fragments**, which are all queued to the driver. At the receiving host, these fragments must be reassembled. The IP driver maintains an `ipfrag` object for each fragment awaiting reassembly and an `ipq` for each datagram being assembled. Incoming fragments are matched against each known `ipq`. If a match is found, the fragment is added to it; otherwise, a new `ipq` is created. Once the final fragment has arrived for a `ipq`, a completely new `skbuff` is constructed to hold the new packet, and this packet is passed back into the IP driver.

Packets identified by the IP as destined for this host are passed on to one of the other protocol drivers. The UDP and TCP protocols share a means of associating packets with source and destination sockets: each connected pair of sockets is uniquely identified by its source and destination addresses and by the source and destination port numbers. The socket lists are linked to hash tables keyed on these four address–port values for socket lookup on incoming packets. The TCP protocol has to deal with unreliable connections, so it maintains ordered lists of unacknowledged outgoing packets to retransmit after a timeout and of incoming out-of-order packets to be presented to the socket when the missing data have arrived.

21.11 Security

Linux's security model is closely related to typical UNIX security mechanisms. The security concerns can be classified in two groups:

1. **Authentication**. Making sure that nobody can access the system without first proving that she has entry rights
2. **Access control**. Providing a mechanism for checking whether a user has the right to access a certain object and preventing access to objects as required

21.11.1 Authentication

Authentication in UNIX has typically been performed through the use of a publicly readable password file. A user's password is combined with a random "salt" value, and the result is encoded with a one-way transformation function and stored in the password file. The use of the one-way function means that the original password cannot be deduced from the password file except by trial and error. When a user presents a password to the system, the password is recombined with the salt value stored in the password file and passed through the same one-way transformation. If the result matches the contents of the password file, then the password is accepted.

Historically, UNIX implementations of this mechanism have had several problems. Passwords were often limited to eight characters, and the number of possible salt values was so low that an attacker could easily combine a dictionary of commonly used passwords with every possible salt value and have a good chance of matching one or more passwords in the password file, gaining unauthorized access to any accounts compromised as a result. Extensions to the password mechanism have been introduced that keep the encrypted password secret in a file that is not publicly readable, that allow longer passwords, or that use more secure methods of encoding the password. Other authentication mechanisms have been introduced that limit the times during which a user is permitted to connect to the system. Also, mechanisms exist to distribute authentication information to all the related systems in a network.

A new security mechanism has been developed by UNIX vendors to address authentication problems. The **pluggable authentication modules (PAM)** system is based on a shared library that can be used by any system component that needs to authenticate users. An implementation of this system is available under Linux. PAM allows authentication modules to be loaded on demand as specified in a system-wide configuration file. If a new authentication mechanism is added at a later date, it can be added to the configuration file, and all system components will immediately be able to take advantage of it. PAM modules can specify authentication methods, account restrictions, session-setup functions, and password-changing functions (so that, when users change their passwords, all the necessary authentication mechanisms can be updated at once).

21.11.2 Access Control

Access control under UNIX systems, including Linux, is performed through the use of unique numeric identifiers. A user identifier (UID) identifies a single user or a single set of access rights. A group identifier (GID) is an extra identifier that can be used to identify rights belonging to more than one user.

Access control is applied to various objects in the system. Every file available in the system is protected by the standard access-control mechanism. In addition, other shared objects, such as shared-memory sections and semaphores, employ the same access system.

Every object in a UNIX system under user and group access control has a single UID and a single GID associated with it. User processes also have a single UID, but they may have more than one GID. If a process's UID matches the UID of an object, then the process has **user rights** or **owner rights** to that object. If the UIDs do not match but any GID of the process matches the object's GID, then **group rights** are conferred; otherwise, the process has **world rights** to the object.

Linux performs access control by assigning objects a **protection mask** that specifies which access modes—read, write, or execute—are to be granted to processes with owner, group, or world access. Thus, the owner of an object might have full read, write, and execute access to a file; other users in a certain group might be given read access but denied write access; and everybody else might be given no access at all.

The only exception is the privileged **root** UID. A process with this special UID is granted automatic access to any object in the system, bypassing normal access checks. Such processes are also granted permission to perform privileged operations, such as reading any physical memory or opening reserved network sockets. This mechanism allows the kernel to prevent normal users from accessing these resources: most of the kernel's key internal resources are implicitly owned by the root UID.

Linux implements the standard UNIX `setuid` mechanism described in Section A.3.2. This mechanism allows a program to run with privileges different from those of the user running the program. For example, the `lpr` program (which submits a job to a print queue) has access to the system's print queues even if the user running that program does not. The UNIX implementation of `setuid` distinguishes between a process's *real* and *effective* UID. The real UID is that of the user running the program; the effective UID is that of the file's owner.

Under Linux, this mechanism is augmented in two ways. First, Linux implements the POSIX specification's `saved user-id` mechanism, which allows a process to drop and reacquire its effective UID repeatedly. For security reasons, a program may want to perform most of its operations in a safe mode, waiving the privileges granted by its `setuid` status; but it may wish to perform selected operations with all its privileges. Standard UNIX implementations achieve this capacity only by swapping the real and effective UIDs; the previous effective UID is remembered, but the program's real UID does not always correspond to the UID of the user running the program. Saved UIDs allow a process to set its effective UID to its real UID and then back to the previous value of its effective UID without having to modify the real UID at any time.

The second enhancement provided by Linux is the addition of a process characteristic that grants just a subset of the rights of the effective UID. The **fsuid** and **fsgid** process properties are used when access rights are granted to files. The appropriate property is set every time the effective UID or GID is set. However, the fsuid and fsgid can be set independently of the effective ids, allowing a process to access files on behalf of another user without taking on the identity of that other user in any other way. Specifically, server processes can use this mechanism to serve files to a certain user without becoming vulnerable to being killed or suspended by that user.

Finally, Linux provides a mechanism for flexible passing of rights from one program to another—a mechanism that has become common in modern versions of UNIX. When a local network socket has been set up between any two processes on the system, either of those processes may send to the other process a file descriptor for one of its open files; the other process receives a duplicate file descriptor for the same file. This mechanism allows a client to pass access to a single file selectively to some server process without granting that process any other privileges. For example, it is no longer necessary for a print server to be able to read all the files of a user who submits a new print job; the print client can simply pass the server file descriptors for any files to be printed, denying the server access to any of the user's other files.

21.12 Summary

Linux is a modern, free operating system based on UNIX standards. It has been designed to run efficiently and reliably on common PC hardware; it also runs on a variety of other platforms. It provides a programming interface and user interface compatible with standard UNIX systems and can run a large number of UNIX applications, including an increasing number of commercially supported applications.

Linux has not evolved in a vacuum. A complete Linux system includes many components that were developed independently of Linux. The core Linux operating-system kernel is entirely original, but it allows much existing free UNIX software to run, resulting in an entire UNIX-compatible operating system free from proprietary code.

The Linux kernel is implemented as a traditional monolithic kernel for performance reasons, but it is modular enough in design to allow most drivers to be dynamically loaded and unloaded at run time.

Linux is a multiuser system, providing protection between processes and running multiple processes according to a time-sharing scheduler. Newly created processes can share selective parts of their execution environment with their parent processes, allowing multithreaded programming. Interprocess communication is supported by both System V mechanisms—message queues, semaphores, and shared memory—and BSD's socket interface. Multiple networking protocols can be accessed simultaneously through the socket interface.

The memory-management system uses page sharing and copy-on-write to minimize the duplication of data shared by different processes. Pages are loaded on demand when they are first referenced and are paged back out to backing store according to an LFU algorithm if physical memory needs to be reclaimed.

To the user, the file system appears as a hierarchical directory tree that obeys UNIX semantics. Internally, Linux uses an abstraction layer to manage multiple file systems. Device-oriented, networked, and virtual file systems are supported. Device-oriented file systems access disk storage through a page cache that is unified with the virtual memory system.

Exercises

21.1 What are the advantages and disadvantages of making only some of the symbols defined inside a kernel accessible to a loadable kernel module?

21.2 The Linux scheduler implements *soft* real-time scheduling. What features necessary for certain real-time programming tasks are missing? How might they be added to the kernel?

21.3 In what ways does the Linux setuid feature differ from the setuid feature in standard Unix?

21.4 What socket type should be used to implement an intercomputer file-transfer program? What type should be used for a program that periodically tests to see whether another computer is up on the network? Explain your answer.

21.5 What scenarios would cause a page of memory to be mapped into a user program's address space with the copy-on-write attribute enabled?

21.6 What extra costs are incurred in the creation and scheduling of a process, compared with the cost of a cloned thread?

21.7 Linux runs on a variety of hardware platforms. What steps must Linux developers take to ensure that the system is portable to different processors and memory-management architectures and to minimize the amount of architecture-specific kernel code?

21.8 Multithreading is a commonly used programming technique. Describe three different ways to implement threads, and compare these three methods with the Linux clone() mechanism. When might using each alternative mechanism be better or worse than using clones?

21.9 The Linux source code is freely and widely available over the Internet and from CD-ROM vendors. What are three implications of this availability for the security of the Linux system?

21.10 Under what circumstances would a user process request an operation that results in the allocation of a demand-zero memory region?

21.11 What are the primary goals of the conflict-resolution mechanism used by the Linux kernel for loading kernel modules?

21.12 What are the advantages and disadvantages of writing an operating system in a high-level language, such as C?

21.13 In Linux, shared libraries perform many operations central to the operating system. What is the advantage of keeping this functionality out of the kernel? Are there any drawbacks? Explain your answer.

21.14 The Linux kernel does not allow paging out of kernel memory. What effect does this restriction have on the kernel's design? What are two advantages and two disadvantages of this design decision?

21.15 The directory structure of a Linux operating system could include files corresponding to several different file systems, including the Linux /proc file system. How might the need to support different file-system types affect the structure of the Linux kernel?

21.16 Would you classify Linux threads as user-level threads or as kernel-level threads? Support your answer with the appropriate arguments.

21.17 At one time, UNIX systems used disk-layout optimizations based on the rotation position of disk data, but modern implementations, including Linux, simply optimize for sequential data access. Why do they do so? Of what hardware characteristics does sequential access take advantage? Why is rotational optimization no longer so useful?

21.18 Discuss how the clone() operation supported by Linux is used to support both processes and threads.

21.19 In what circumstances is the system-call sequence `fork()` `exec()` most appropriate? When is `vfork()` preferable?

Bibliographical Notes

The Linux system is a product of the Internet; as a result, much of the available documentation on Linux is available in some form on the Internet. The following key sites reference most of the useful information available:

- The Linux Cross-Reference Pages (http://lxr.linux.no/) maintain current listings of the Linux kernel, browsable via the Web and fully cross-referenced.
- Linux-HQ (http://www.linuxhq.com/) provides a large amount of information relating to the Linux 2.x kernels. This site also includes links to the home pages of most Linux distributions, as well as archives of the major mailing lists.
- The Linux Documentation Project (http://sunsite.unc.edu/linux/) lists many books on Linux that are available in source format as part of the Linux Documentation Project. The project also hosts the Linux *How-To* guides, which contain hints and tips relating to aspects of Linux.
- The *Kernel Hackers' Guide* is an Internet-based guide to kernel internals in general. This constantly expanding site is located at http://www.redhat.com:8080/HyperNews/get/khg.html.
- The Kernel Newbies website (http://www.kernelnewbies.org/) provides a resource for introducing the Linux kernel to newcomers.

Many mailing lists devoted to Linux are also available. The most important are maintained by a mailing-list manager that can be reached at the e-mail address `majordomo@vger.rutgers.edu`. Send e-mail to this address with the single line "help" in the mail's body for information on how to access the list server and to subscribe to any lists.

Finally, the Linux system itself can be obtained over the Internet. Complete Linux distributions can be obtained from the home sites of the companies concerned, and the Linux community also maintains archives of current system components at several places on the Internet. The most important are these:

- ftp://tsx-11.mit.edu/pub/linux/
- ftp://sunsite.unc.edu/pub/Linux/
- ftp://linux.kernel.org/pub/linux/

In addition to investigating Internet resources, you can read about the internals of the Linux kernel in Bovet and Cesati [2002] and Love [2004].

CHAPTER 22

Windows XP

The Microsoft Windows XP operating system is a 32-/64-bit preemptive multitasking operating system for AMD K6/K7, Intel IA32/IA64, and later microprocessors. The successor to Windows NT and Windows 2000, Windows XP is also intended to replace the Windows 95/98 operating system. In this chapter, we discuss the key goals of Windows XP, the layered architecture of the system that has made it so easy to use, the file system, the networking features, and the programming interface.

CHAPTER OBJECTIVES

- To explore the principles underlying Windows XP's design and the specific components of the system.
- To explain how Windows XP can run programs designed for other operating systems.
- To provide a detailed discussion of the Windows XP file system.
- To illustrate the networking protocols supported in Windows XP.
- To describe the interface available to system and application programmers.

22.1 History

In the mid-1980s, Microsoft and IBM cooperated to develop the OS/2 operating system, which was written in assembly language for single-processor Intel 80286 systems. In 1988, Microsoft decided to make a fresh start and to develop a "new technology" (or NT) portable operating system that supported both the OS/2 and POSIX application-programming interfaces (APIs). In October 1988, Dave Cutler, the architect of the DEC VAX/VMS operating system, was hired and given the charter of building this new operating system.

Originally, the team planned to use the OS/2 API as NTs native environment, but during development, NT was changed to use the 32-bit Windows API (or Win32 API), reflecting the popularity of Windows 3.0. The first versions of NT were Windows NT 3.1 and Windows NT 3.1 Advanced Server. (At that time,

16-bit Windows was at version 3.1.) Windows NT Version 4.0 adopted the Windows 95 user interface and incorporated Internet Web-server and Web-browser software. In addition, user-interface routines and all graphics code were moved into the kernel to improve performance, with the side effect of decreased system reliability. Although previous versions of NT had been ported to other microprocessor architectures, the Windows 2000 version, released in February 2000, supported only Intel (and compatible) processors due to marketplace factors. Windows 2000 incorporated significant changes. It added Active Directory (an X.500-based directory service), better networking and laptop support, support for plug-and-play devices, a distributed file system, and support for more processors and more memory.

In October 2001, Windows XP was released as both an update to the Windows 2000 desktop operating system and a replacement for Windows 95/98. In 2002, the server versions of Windows XP became available (called Windows .Net Server). Windows XP updated the graphical user interface (GUI) with a visual design that took advantage of more recent hardware advances and many new ease-of-use features. Numerous features were added to automatically repair problems in applications and the operating system itself. As a result of these changes, Windows XP provides better networking and device experience (including zero-configuration wireless, instant messaging, streaming media, and digital photography/video), dramatic performance improvements for both the desktop and large multiprocessors, and better reliability and security than earlier Windows operating systems.

Windows XP uses a client–server architecture (like Mach) to implement multiple operating-system personalities, such as Win32 API and POSIX, with user-level processes called subsystems. The subsystem architecture allows enhancements to be made to one operating-system personality without affecting the application compatibility of any others.

Windows XP is a multiuser operating system, supporting simultaneous access through distributed services or through multiple instances of the graphical user interface via the Windows terminal server. The server versions of Windows XP support simultaneous terminal server sessions from Windows desktop systems. The desktop versions of terminal server multiplex the keyboard, mouse, and monitor between virtual terminal sessions for each logged-on user. This feature, called fast user switching, allows users to preempt each other at the console of a PC without having to log off and onto the system.

Windows XP was the first version of Windows to ship a 64-bit version. The native NT file system (NTFS) and many of the Win32 APIs have always used 64-bit integers where appropriate—so the major extension to 64-bit in Windows XP was support for large addresses.

There are two desktop versions of Windows XP. Windows XP Professional is the premium desktop system for power users at work and at home. Windows XP Personal provides the reliability and ease of use of Windows XP but lacks the more advanced features needed to work seamlessly with Active Directory or run POSIX applications.

The members of the Windows .Net Server family use the same core components as the desktop versions but add a range of features needed for uses such as webserver farms, print/file servers, clustered systems, and large datacenter machines. The large datacenter machines can have up to 64 GB of memory and 32 processors on IA32 systems and 128 GB and 64 processors on IA64 systems.

22.2 Design Principles

Microsoft's design goals for Windows XP included security, reliability, Windows and POSIX application compatibility, high performance, extensibility, portability, and international support. We discuss each of these goals in the following sections.

22.2.1 Security

Windows XP **security** goals required more than just adherence to the design standards that had enabled Windows NT 4.0 to receive a C-2 security classification from the U.S. government (which signifies a moderate level of protection from defective software and malicious attacks). Extensive code review and testing were combined with sophisticated automatic analysis tools to identify and investigate potential defects that might represent security vulnerabilities.

22.2.2 Reliability

Windows 2000 was the most reliable, stable operating system Microsoft had ever shipped to that point. Much of this reliability came from maturity in the source code, extensive stress testing of the system, and automatic detection of many serious errors in drivers. The **reliability** requirements for Windows XP were even more stringent. Microsoft used extensive manual and automatic code review to identify over 63,000 lines in the source files that might contain issues not detected by testing and then set about reviewing each area to verify that the code was indeed correct.

Windows XP extended driver verification to catch more subtle bugs, improved the facilities for catching programming errors in user-level code, and subjected third-party applications, drivers, and devices to a rigorous certification process. Furthermore, Windows XP added facilities for monitoring the health of the PC, including downloading fixes for problems before they are encountered by users. The perceived reliability of Windows XP was also improved by making the graphical user interface easier to use through better visual design, simpler menus, and measured improvements in the ease with which users can discover how to perform common tasks.

22.2.3 Windows and POSIX Application Compatibility

As mentioned, Windows XP was not only an update of Windows 2000 but also a replacement for Windows 95/98. Windows 2000 focused primarily on compatibility for business applications. The requirements for Windows XP included a much higher compatibility with the consumer applications that ran on Windows 95/98. **Application compatibility** is difficult to achieve because each application checks for a particular version of Windows, may depend to some extent on the quirks of the implementation of APIs, may have latent application bugs that were masked in the previous system, and so forth.

Windows XP introduced a compatibility layer that falls between applications and the Win32 APIs. This layer makes Windows XP look (almost) bug-for-bug compatible with previous versions of Windows. Windows XP, like earlier NT releases, maintains support for running many 16-bit applications using a *thunking*, or conversion, layer that translates 16-bit API calls into equivalent 32-bit calls. Similarly, the 64-bit version of Windows XP provides a thunking layer that translates 32-bit API calls into native 64-bit calls. In addition, POSIX support in Windows XP was much improved by a new POSIX subsystem called Interix. Most available UNIX-compatible software compiles and runs under Interix without modification.

22.2.4 High Performance

Windows XP was designed to provide **high performance** on desktop systems (which are largely constrained by I/O performance), server systems (where the CPU is often the bottleneck), and large multithreaded and multiprocessor environments (where locking and cache-line management are keys to scalability). To satisfy performance requirements, NT used a variety of techniques, such as asynchronous I/O, optimized protocols for networks, kernel-based graphics, and sophisticated caching of file-system data. The memory-management and synchronization algorithms were designed with an awareness of the performance considerations related to cache lines and multiprocessors.

Windows XP further improved performance by reducing the code-path length in critical functions, using better algorithms and per-processor data structures, using memory coloring for NUMA (non-uniform memory access) machines, and implementing more scalable locking protocols, such as queued spinlocks. The new locking protocols helped reduce system bus cycles and included lock-free lists and queues, atomic read–modify–write operations (like interlocked increment), and other advanced locking techniques.

The subsystems that constitute Windows XP communicate with one another efficiently through a local procedure call (LPC) facility that provides high-performance message passing. Except while executing in the kernel dispatcher, threads in the subsystems of Windows XP can be preempted by higher-priority threads. Thus, the system responds quickly to external events. In addition, Windows XP was designed for symmetrical multiprocessing; on a multiprocessor computer, several threads can run at the same time.

22.2.5 Extensibility

Extensibility refers to the capacity of an operating system to keep up with advances in computing technology. To facilitate change over time, the developers implemented Windows XP using a layered architecture. The Windows XP executive runs in kernel or protected mode and provides the basic system services. On top of the executive, several server subsystems operate in user mode. Among them are **environmental subsystems** that emulate different operating systems. Thus, programs written for MS-DOS, Microsoft Windows, and POSIX all run on Windows XP in the appropriate environment. (See Section 22.4 for more information on environmental subsystems.) Because of the modular structure, additional environmental subsystems can be added without affecting the executive. In addition, Windows XP uses loadable drivers in the I/O system, so new file systems, new kinds of I/O devices, and new kinds of networking can be added while the system is running. Windows XP uses a client–server model like the Mach operating system and supports distributed processing by remote procedure calls (RPCs) as defined by the Open Software Foundation.

22.2.6 Portability

An operating system is **portable** if it can be moved from one hardware architecture to another with relatively few changes. Windows XP was designed to be portable. Like the UNIX operating system, Windows XP is written primarily in C and C++. Most processor-dependent code is isolated in a dynamic link library (DLL) called the **hardware-abstraction layer (HAL)**. A DLL is a file that is mapped into a process's address space in such a way that any functions in the DLL appear to be part of the process. The upper layers of the Windows XP kernel depend on the HAL interfaces rather than on the underlying hardware, bolstering Windows XP portability. The HAL manipulates hardware directly, isolating the rest of Windows XP from hardware differences among the platforms on which it runs.

Although for market reasons Windows 2000 shipped only on Intel IA32-compatible platforms, it was also tested on IA32 and DEC Alpha platforms until just prior to release to ensure portability. Windows XP runs on IA32-compatible and IA64 processors. Microsoft recognizes the importance of multiplatform development and testing, since, as a practical matter, maintaining portability is a matter of "use it or lose it."

22.2.7 International Support

Windows XP was also designed for **international** and **multinational** use. It provides support for different locales via the **national-language-support (NLS) API**. The NLS API provides specialized routines to format dates, time, and money in accordance with national customs. String comparisons are specialized to account for varying character sets. UNICODE is Windows XP's native character code. Windows XP supports ANSI characters by converting them to UNICODE characters before manipulating them (8-bit to 16-bit conversion). System text strings are kept in resource files that can be replaced to localize the system for different languages. Multiple locales can be used concurrently, which is important to multilingual individuals and businesses.

22.3 System Components

The architecture of Windows XP is a layered system of modules, as shown in Figure 22.1. The main layers are the HAL, the kernel, and the executive, all of which run in protected mode, and a collection of subsystems and services that run in user mode. The user-mode subsystems fall into two categories: the environmental subsystems, which emulate different operating systems, and the **protection subsystems**, which provide security functions. One of the chief advantages of this type of architecture is that interactions between modules are kept simple. The remainder of this section describes these layers and subsystems.

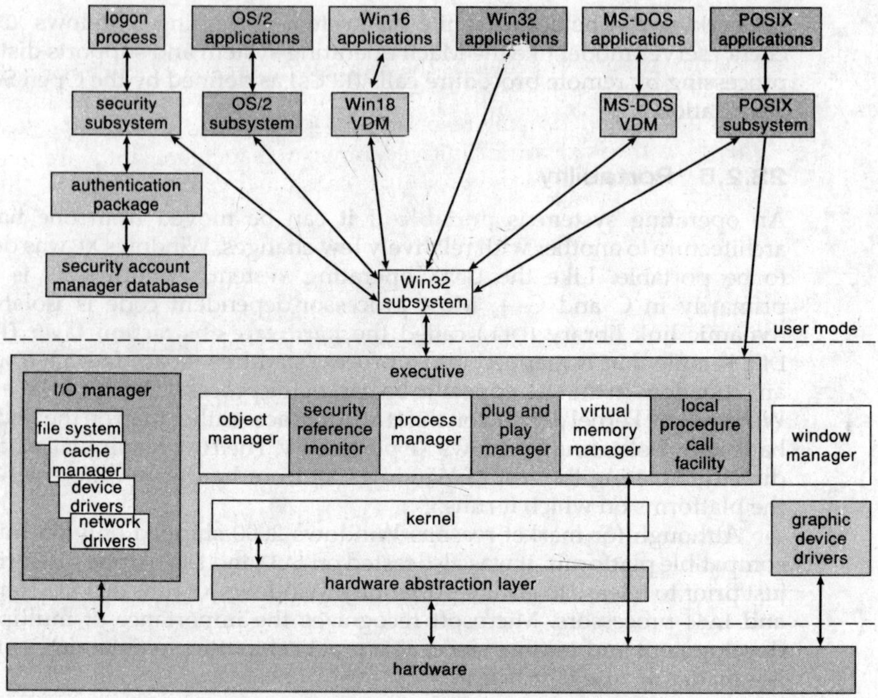

Figure 22.1 Windows XP block diagram.

22.3.1 Hardware-Abstraction Layer

The HAL is the layer of software that hides hardware differences from upper levels of the operating system, to help make Windows XP portable. The HAL exports a virtual machine interface that is used by the kernel dispatcher, the executive, and the device drivers. One advantage of this approach is that only a single version of each device driver is required—it runs on all hardware platforms without porting the driver code. The HAL also provides support for symmetric multiprocessing. Device drivers map devices and access them directly, but the administrative details of mapping memory, configuring I/O buses, setting up DMA, and coping with motherboard-specific facilities are all provided by the HAL interfaces.

22.3.2 Kernel

The kernel of Windows XP has four main responsibilities: thread scheduling, interrupt and exception handling, low-level processor synchronization, and recovery after a power failure. The kernel is object oriented. An *object type* in Windows 2000 is a system-defined data type that has a set of attributes (data values) and a set of methods (for example, functions or operations). An *object* is an instance of an object type. The kernel performs its job by using a set of kernel objects whose attributes store the kernel data and whose methods perform the kernel activities.

22.3.2.1 Kernel Dispatcher

The kernel dispatcher provides the foundation for the executive and the subsystems. Most of the dispatcher is never paged out of memory, and its execution is never preempted. Its main responsibilities are thread scheduling, implementation of synchronization primitives, timer management, software interrupts (asynchronous and deferred procedure calls), and exception dispatching.

22.3.2.2 Threads and Scheduling

Like many other modern operating systems, Windows XP uses processes and threads for executable code. Each process has one or more threads, and each thread has its own scheduling state, including actual priority, processor affinity, and CPU-usage information.

There are six possible thread states: ready, standby, running, waiting, transition, and terminated. **Ready** indicates that the thread is waiting to run. The highest-priority ready thread is moved to the **standby** state, which means it is the next thread to run. In a multiprocessor system, each process keeps one thread in a standby state. A thread is **running** when it is executing on a processor. It runs until it is preempted by a higher-priority thread, until it terminates, until its allotted execution time (**quantum**) ends, or until it blocks on a dispatcher object, such as an event signaling I/O completion. A thread is in the **waiting** state when it is waiting for a dispatcher object to be signaled. A new thread is in the **transition** state while it waits for resources necessary for execution. A thread enters the **terminated** state when it finishes execution.

The dispatcher uses a 32-level priority scheme to determine the order of thread execution. Priorities are divided into two classes: variable class and real-time class. The variable class contains threads having priorities from 0 to 15, and the real-time class contains threads with priorities ranging from 16 to 31. The dispatcher uses a queue for each scheduling priority and traverses the set of queues from highest to lowest until it finds a thread that is ready to run. If a thread has a particular processor affinity but that processor is not available, the dispatcher skips past it and continues looking for a ready thread that is willing to run on the available processor. If no ready thread is found, the dispatcher executes a special thread called the idle thread.

When a thread's time quantum runs out, the clock interrupt queues a quantum-end deferred procedure call (DPC) to the processor in order to reschedule the processor. If the preempted thread is in the variable-priority class, its priority is lowered. The priority is never lowered below the base priority. Lowering the thread's priority tends to limit the CPU consumption of compute-bound threads. When a variable-priority thread is released from a wait operation, the dispatcher boosts the priority. The amount of the boost depends on the device for which the thread was waiting; for example, a thread waiting for keyboard I/O would get a large priority increase, whereas a thread waiting for a disk operation would get a moderate one. This strategy tends to give good response times to interactive threads using a mouse and windows. It also enables I/O-bound threads to keep the I/O devices busy while permitting compute-bound threads to use spare CPU cycles in the background. This strategy is used by several time-sharing operating systems, including UNIX. In addition, the thread associated with the user's active GUI window receives a priority boost to enhance its response time.

Scheduling occurs when a thread enters the ready or wait state, when a thread terminates, or when an application changes a thread's priority or processor affinity. If a higher-priority real-time thread becomes ready while a lower-priority thread is running, the lower-priority thread is preempted. This preemption gives a real-time thread preferential access to the CPU when the thread needs such access. Windows XP is not a hard real-time operating system, however, because it does not guarantee that a real-time thread will start to execute within a particular time limit.

22.3.2.3 Implementation of Synchronization Primitives

Key operating-system data structures are managed as objects using common facilities for allocation, reference counting, and security. **Dispatcher objects** control dispatching and synchronization in the system.

Examples of these objects include the following:

- The **event object** is used to record an event occurrence and to synchronize this occurrence with some action. Notification events signal all waiting threads, and synchronization events signal a single waiting thread.
- The **mutant** provides kernel-mode or user-mode mutual exclusion with the notion of ownership.
- The **mutex**, available only in kernel mode, provides deadlock-free mutual exclusion.
- The Defsemaphore object acts as a counter or gate to control the number of threads that access a resource.
- The **thread object** is the entity that is scheduled by the kernel dispatcher and is associated with a **process object**, which encapsulates a virtual address space.
- The **timer object** is used to keep track of time and to signal timeouts when operations take too long and need to be interrupted or when a periodic activity needs to be scheduled.

Many of the dispatcher objects are accessed from user mode via an open operation that returns a handle. The user-mode code polls or waits on handles to synchronize with other threads as well as with the operating system (see Section 22.7.1).

22.3.2.4 Software Interrupts: Asynchronous and Deferred Procedure Calls

The dispatcher implements two types of software interrupts: asynchronous procedure calls and deferred procedure calls. An asynchronous procedure call (APC) breaks into an executing thread and calls a procedure. APCs are used to begin execution of new threads, terminate processes, and deliver notification that an asynchronous I/O has completed. APCs are queued to specific threads and allow the system to execute both system and user code within a process's context.

Deferred procedure calls (DPCs) are used to postpone interrupt processing. After handling all blocked device-interrupt processes, the interrupt service routine (ISR) schedules the remaining processing by queuing a DPC. The dispatcher schedules software interrupts at a lower priority than the device interrupts so that DPCs do not block other ISRs. In addition to deferring device-interrupt processing, the dispatcher uses DPCs to process timer expirations and to preempt thread execution at the end of the scheduling quantum.

Execution of DPCs prevents threads from being scheduled on the current processor and also keeps APCs from signaling the completion of I/O. This is done so that completion of DPC routines does not take an extended amount of time. As an alternative, the dispatcher maintains a pool of worker threads. ISRs and DPCs queue work items to the worker threads. DPC routines are restricted so that they cannot take page faults (be paged out of memory), call system services, or take any other action that might possibly result in an attempt to block execution of a dispatcher object. Unlike APCs, DPC routines make no assumptions about what process context the processor is executing.

22.3.2.5 Exceptions and Interrupts

The kernel dispatcher also provides trap handling for exceptions and interrupts generated by hardware or software. Windows XP defines several architecture-independent exceptions, including:

- Memory-access violation
- Integer overflow
- Floating-point overflow or underflow
- Integer divide by zero
- Floating-point divide by zero
- Illegal instruction
- Data misalignment
- Privileged instruction
- Page-read error
- Access violation
- Paging file quota exceeded
- Debugger breakpoint
- Debugger single step

The trap handlers deal with simple exceptions. Elaborate exception handling is performed by the kernel's exception dispatcher. The **exception dispatcher** creates an exception record containing the reason for the exception and finds an exception handler to deal with it.

When an exception occurs in kernel mode, the exception dispatcher simply calls a routine to locate the exception handler. If no handler is found, a fatal system error occurs and the user is left with the infamous "blue screen of death" that signifies system failure.

Exception handling is more complex for user-mode processes, because an environmental subsystem (such as the POSIX system) sets up a debugger port and an exception port for every process it creates. If a debugger port is registered, the exception handler sends the exception to the port. If the debugger port is not found or does not handle that exception, the dispatcher attempts to find an appropriate exception handler. If no handler is found, the debugger is called again to catch the error for debugging. If no debugger is running, a message is sent to the process's exception port to give the environmental subsystem a chance to translate the exception. For example, the POSIX environment translates Windows XP exception messages into POSIX signals before sending them to the thread that caused the exception. Finally, if nothing else works, the kernel simply terminates the process containing the thread that caused the exception.

The interrupt dispatcher in the kernel handles interrupts by calling either an interrupt service routine (ISR) supplied by a device driver or a kernel trap-handler routine. The interrupt is represented by an interrupt object that contains all the information needed to handle the interrupt. Using an interrupt object makes it easy to associate interrupt-service routines with an interrupt without having to access the interrupt hardware directly.

Different processor architectures, such as Intel and DEC Alpha, have different types and numbers of interrupts. For portability, the interrupt dispatcher maps the hardware interrupts into a standard set. The interrupts are prioritized and are serviced in priority order. There are 32 interrupt request levels (**IRQLs**) in Windows XP. Eight are reserved for use by the kernel; the remaining 24 represent hardware interrupts via the HAL (although most IA32 systems use only 16). The Windows XP interrupts are defined in Figure 22.2.

The kernel uses an **interrupt-dispatch table** to bind each interrupt level to a service routine. In a multiprocessor computer, Windows XP keeps a separate interrupt-dispatch table for each processor, and each processor's IRQL can be set independently to mask out interrupts. All interrupts that occur at a level equal to or less than the IRQL of a processor are blocked until the IRQL is lowered by a kernel-level thread or by an ISR returning from interrupt processing. Windows XP takes advantage of this property and uses software interrupts to deliver APCs and DPCs, to perform system functions such as synchronizing threads with I/O completion, to start thread dispatches, and to handle timers.

interrupt levels	types of interrupts
31	machine check or bus error
30	power fail
29	interprocessor notification (request another processor to act; e.g., dispatch a process or update the TLB)
28	clock (used to keep track of time)
27	profile
3–26	traditional PC IRQ hardware interrupts
2	dispatch and deferred procedure call (DPC) (kernel)
1	asynchronous procedure call (APC)
0	passive

Figure 22.2 Windows XP interrupt request levels.

22.3.3 Executive

The Windows XP executive provides a set of services that all environmental subsystems use. The services are grouped as follows: object manager, virtual memory manager, process manager, local procedure call facility, I/O manager, cache manager, security reference monitor, plug-and-play and power managers, registry, and booting.

22.3.3.1 Object Manager

For managing kernel-mode entities, Windows XP uses a generic set of interfaces that are manipulated by user-mode programs. Windows XP calls these entities *objects*, and the executive component that manipulates them is the **object manager**. Each process has an object table containing entries that track the objects used by the process. User-mode code accesses these objects using an opaque value called a *handle* that is returned by many APIs. Object handles can also be created by duplicating an existing handle, either from the same process or from a different process. Examples of objects are semaphores, mutexes, events, processes, and threads. These are all *dispatcher objects*. Threads can block in the kernel dispatcher waiting for any of these objects to be signaled. The process, thread, and virtual memory APIs use process and thread handles to identify the process or thread to be operated on. Other examples of objects include files, sections, ports, and various internal I/O objects. File objects are used to maintain the open state of files and devices. Sections are used to map files. Open files are described in terms of file objects. Local-communication endpoints are implemented as port objects.

The object manager maintains the Windows XP internal name space. In contrast to UNIX, which roots the system name space in the file system, Windows XP uses an abstract name space and connects the file systems as devices.

The object manager provides interfaces for defining both object types and object instances, translating names to objects, maintaining the abstract name space (through internal directories and symbolic links), and managing object creation and deletion. Objects are typically managed through the use of reference counts in protected-mode code and handles in user-mode code. However, some kernel-mode components use the same APIs as user-mode code and thus use handles to manipulate objects. If a handle needs to exist beyond the lifetime of the current process, it is marked as a kernel handle and stored in the object table for the system process. The abstract name space does not persist across reboots but is built up from configuration information stored in the system registry, plug-and-play device discovery, and creation of objects by system components.

The Windows XP executive allows any object to be given a **name**. One process may create a named object, while a second process opens a handle to the object and shares it with the first process. Processes can also share objects by duplicating handles between processes, in which case the objects need not be named.

A name can be either permanent or temporary. A permanent name represents an entity, such as a disk drive, that remains even if no process is accessing it. A temporary name exists only while a process holds a handle to the object.

Object names are structured like file path names in MS-DOS and UNIX. Name space directories are represented by a directory object that contains the names of all the objects in the directory. The object name space is extended by the addition of device objects representing volumes containing file systems.

Objects are manipulated by a set of virtual functions with implementations provided for each object type: `create()`, `open()`, `close()`, `delete()`, `query_name()`, `parse()`, and `security()`. The latter three functions may need some explanation:

- `query_name()` is called when a thread has a reference to an object but wants to know the object's name.
- `parse()` is used by the object manager to search for an object given the object's name.
- `security()` is called to make security checks on all object operations, such as when a process opens or closes an object, makes changes to the security descriptor, or duplicates a handle for an object.

The parse procedure is used to extend the abstract name space to include files. The translation of a path name to a file object begins at the root of the abstract name space. Path-name components are separated by whack characters (\) rather than the slashes (/) used in UNIX. Each component is looked up in the current parse directory of the name space. Internal nodes within the name space are either directories or symbolic links. If a leaf object is found and there are no path-name components remaining, the leaf object is returned. Otherwise, the leaf object's parse procedure is invoked with the remaining path name.

Parse procedures are only used with a small number of objects belonging to the Windows GUI, the configuration manager (registry), and—most notably—device objects representing file systems. The parse procedure for the device object type allocates a file object and initiates an open or create I/O operation on the file system. If successful, the file object fields are filled in to describe the file.

In summary, the path name to a file is used to traverse the object-manager namespace, translating the original absolute path name into a (device object, relative path name) pair. This pair is then passed to the file system via the I/O manager, which fills in the file object. The file object itself has no name but is referred to by a handle.

UNIX file systems have symbolic links that permit multiple nicknames—or aliases—for the same file. The symbolic-link object implemented by the Windows XP object manager is used within the abstract name space, not to provide files with aliases. Even so, symbolic links are very useful. They are used to organize the name space, similar to the organization of the `/devices` directory in UNIX. They are also used to map standard MS-DOS drive letters to drive names. Drive letters are symbolic links that can be remapped to suit the convenience of the user or administrator.

Drive letters are one place where the abstract name space in Windows XP is not global. Each logged-on user has his or her own set of drive letters so that users can avoid interfering with one another. In contrast, terminal server sessions share all processes within a session. `BaseNamedObjects` contain the named objects created by most applications.

Although the name space is not directly visible across a network, the object manager's `parse()` method is used to help access a named object on another system. When a process attempts to open an object that resides on a remote computer, the object manager calls the parse method for the device object corresponding to a network redirector. This results in an I/O operation that accesses the file across the network.

As mentioned, objects are instances of an **object type**. The object type specifies how instances are to be allocated, the definitions of the data fields, and the implementation of the standard set of virtual functions used for all objects. These functions implement operations such as mapping names to objects, closing and deleting, and applying security.

The object manager keeps track of two counts for each object. The pointer count is the number of distinct references made to an object. Protected-mode code that refers to objects must keep a reference on the objects to ensure that an object is not deleted while in use. The handle count is the number of handle table entries referring to an object. Each handle is also reflected in the reference count.

When a handle for an object is closed, the object's close routine is called. In the case of file objects, this call causes the I/O manager to do a cleanup operation at the close of the last handle. The cleanup operation tells the file system that the file is no longer accessed by user mode so that sharing restrictions, range locks, and other states specific to the corresponding open routine can be removed.

Each handle close removes a reference from the pointer count, but internal system components may retain additional references. When the final reference is removed, the object's delete procedure is called. Again using file objects as an example, the delete procedure causes the I/O manager to send the file system a close operation on the file object. This causes the file system to deallocate any internal data structures that were allocated for the file object.

After the delete procedure for a temporary object completes, the object is deleted from memory. The object manager can make an object permanent (at least with respect to the current boot of the system) by taking an extra reference against the object. Thus, permanent objects are not deleted even when the last reference outside the object manager is removed. When a permanent object is made temporary again, the object manager removes the extra reference. If this was the last reference, the object is deleted. Permanent objects are rare, used mostly for devices, drive-letter mappings, and the directory and symbolic link objects.

The job of the object manager is to supervise the use of all managed objects. When a thread wants to use an object, it calls the object manager's `open()` method to get a reference to the object. If the object is being opened from a user-mode API, the reference is inserted into the process's object table, and a handle is returned.

A process gets a handle by creating an object, by opening an existing object, by receiving a duplicated handle from another process, or by inheriting a handle from a **parent process**, similar to the way a UNIX process gets a file descriptor. These handles are all stored in the process's **object table**. An entry in the object table contains the object's access rights and states whether the handle should be inherited by **child processes**. When a process terminates, Windows XP automatically closes all the process's open handles.

Handles are a standardized interface to all kinds of objects. Like a file descriptor in UNIX, an object handle is an identifier unique to a process that confers the ability to access and manipulate a system resource. Handles can be duplicated within a process or between processes. The latter case is used when child processes are created and when out-of-process execution contexts are implemented.

Since the object manager is the only entity that generates object handles, it is the natural place to check security. The object manager checks whether a process has the right to access an object when the process tries to open the object. The object manager also enforces quotas, such as the maximum amount of memory a process may use, by charging a process for the memory occupied by all its referenced objects and refusing to allocate more memory when the accumulated charges exceed the process's quota.

When the login process authenticates a user, an access token is attached to the user's process. The access token contains information such as the security ID, group IDs, privileges, primary group, and default access-control list. The services and objects a user can access are determined by these attributes.

The token that controls access is associated with the thread making the access. Normally, the thread token is missing and defaults to the process token, but services often need to execute code on behalf of their clients. Windows XP allows threads to impersonate a client temporarily by using a client's token. Thus, the thread token is not necessarily the same as the process token.

In Windows XP, each object is protected by an access-control list that contains the security IDs and access rights granted. When a thread attempts to access an object, the system compares the security ID in the thread's access token with the object's access-control list to determine whether access should be permitted. The check is performed only when an object is opened, so it is not possible to deny access after the open occurs. Operating-system components executing in kernel mode bypass the access check, since kernel-mode code is assumed to be trusted. Therefore, kernel-mode code must avoid security vulnerabilities, such as leaving checks disabled while creating a user-mode-accessible handle in an untrusted process.

Generally, the creator of the object determines the access-control list for the object. If none is explicitly supplied, one may be set to a default by the object type's open routine, or a default list may be obtained from the user's access-token object.

The access token has a field that controls auditing of object accesses. Operations that are being audited are logged to the system's security log with an identification of the user. An administrator monitors this log to discover attempts to break into the system or to access protected objects.

22.3.3.2 Virtual Memory Manager

The executive component that manages the virtual address space, physical memory allocation, and paging is the **virtual memory (VM) manager**. The design of the VM manager assumes that the underlying hardware supports virtual-to-physical mapping, a paging mechanism, and transparent cache coherence on multiprocessor systems, as well as allowing multiple page-table entries to map to the same physical page frame. The VM manager in Windows XP uses a page-based management scheme with a page size of 4 KB on

IA32-compatible processors and 8 KB on the IA64. Pages of data allocated to a process that are not in physical memory are either stored in the **paging files** on disk or mapped directly to a regular file on a local or remote file system. Pages can also be marked zero-fill-on-demand, which fills the page with zeros before they are allocated, thus erasing the previous contents.

On IA32 processors, each process has a 4-GB virtual address space. The upper 2 GB are mostly identical for all processes and are used by Windows XP in kernel mode to access the operating-system code and data structures. Key areas of the kernel-mode region that are not identical for all processes are the **page-table self-map**, **hyperspace**, and **session space**. The hardware references a process's page tables using physical page-frame numbers. The VM manager maps the page tables into a single 4-MB region in the process's address space so they are accessed through virtual addresses. Hyperspace maps the current process's working-set information into the kernel-mode address space.

Session space is used to share the Win32 and other session-specific drivers among all the processes in the same terminal-server session, rather than all the processes in the system. The lower 2 GB are specific to each process and are accessible by both user- and kernel-mode threads. Certain configurations of Windows XP reserve only 1 GB for operating-system use, allowing a process to use 3 GB of address space. Running the system in 3-GB mode drastically reduces the amount of data caching in the kernel. However, for large applications that manage their own I/O, such as SQL databases, the advantage of a larger user-mode address space may be worth the loss of caching.

The Windows XP VM manager uses a two-step process to allocate user memory. The first step *reserves* a portion of the process's virtual address space. The second step *commits* the allocation by assigning virtual memory space (physical memory or space in the paging files). Windows XP limits the amount of virtual memory space a process consumes by enforcing a quota on committed memory. A process decommits memory that it is no longer using to free up virtual memory for use by other processes. The APIs used to reserve virtual addresses and commit virtual memory take a handle on a process object as a parameter. This allows one process to control the virtual memory of another. Environmental subsystems manage the memory of their client processes in this way.

For performance, the VM manager allows a privileged process to lock selected pages in physical memory, thus ensuring that the pages are not paged out to the paging file. Processes also allocate raw physical memory and then map regions into its virtual address space. IA32 processors with the physical address extension (PAE) feature can have up to 64 GB of physical memory on a system. This memory cannot all be mapped in a process's address space at once, but Windows XP makes it available using the address windowing extension (AWE) APIs, which allocate physical memory and then map regions of virtual addresses in the process's address space onto part of the physical memory. The AWE facility is used primarily by very large applications such as the SQL database.

Windows XP implements shared memory by defining a **section object**. After getting a handle to a section object, a process maps the memory portion it needs into its address space. This portion is called a **view**. A process redefines its view of an object to gain access to the entire object, one region at a time.

A process can control the use of a shared-memory section object in many ways. The maximum size of a section can be bounded. The section can be backed by disk space either in the system-paging file or in a regular file (a **memory-mapped file**). A section can be *based*, meaning the section appears at the same virtual address for all processes attempting to access it. Finally, the memory protection of pages in the section can be set to read-only, read–write, read–write–execute, execute-only, no access, or copy-on-write. Let's look more closely at the last two of these protection settings:

- A *no-access page* raises an exception if accessed; the exception is used, for example, to check whether a faulty program iterates beyond the end of an array. Both the user-mode memory allocator and the special kernel allocator used by the device verifier can be configured to map each allocation onto the end of a page followed by a no-access page to detect buffer overruns.
- The *copy-on-write mechanism* enables the VM manager to use physical memory more efficiently. When two processes want independent copies of an object, the VM manager places a single shared copy into virtual memory and activates the copy-on-write property for that region of memory. If one of the processes tries to modify data in a copy-on-write page, the VM manager makes a private copy of the page for the process.

The virtual address translation in Windows XP uses a multilevel page table. For IA32 processors without the physical address extensions enabled, each process has a **page directory** that contains 1,024 **page-directory entries (PDEs)** 4 bytes in size. Each PDE points to a **page table** that contains 1,024 **page-table entries (PTEs)** 4 bytes in size. Each PTE points to a 4-KB **page frame** in physical memory. The total size of all page tables for a process is 4 MB, so the VM manager pages out individual tables to disk when necessary. See Figure 22.3 for a diagram of this structure.

The page directory and page tables are referenced by the hardware via physical addresses. To improve performance, the VM manager self-maps the page directory and page tables into a 4-MB region of virtual addresses. The self-map allows the VM manager to translate a virtual address into the corresponding PDE or PTE without additional memory accesses. When a process context is changed, a single page-directory entry must be changed to map the new process's page tables. For a variety of reasons, the hardware requires that each page directory or page table occupy a single page. Thus, the number of PDEs or PTEs that fit in a page determine how virtual addresses are translated.

We next consider how virtual addresses are translated into physical addresses on IA32-compatible processors (without PAE enabled). A 10-bit value can represent all the values from 0 to 1,023. Thus, a 10-bit value can select any entry in the page directory or in a page table. This property is used when a virtual address pointer is translated to a byte address in physical memory. A 32-bit virtual-memory address is split into three values, as shown in Figure 22.4. The first 10 bits of the virtual address are used as an index into the page directory. This address selects one page-directory entry (PDE), which contains the physical page frame of a page table. The memory-management unit (MMU) uses the next 10 bits of the virtual address to select a PTE from the page table.

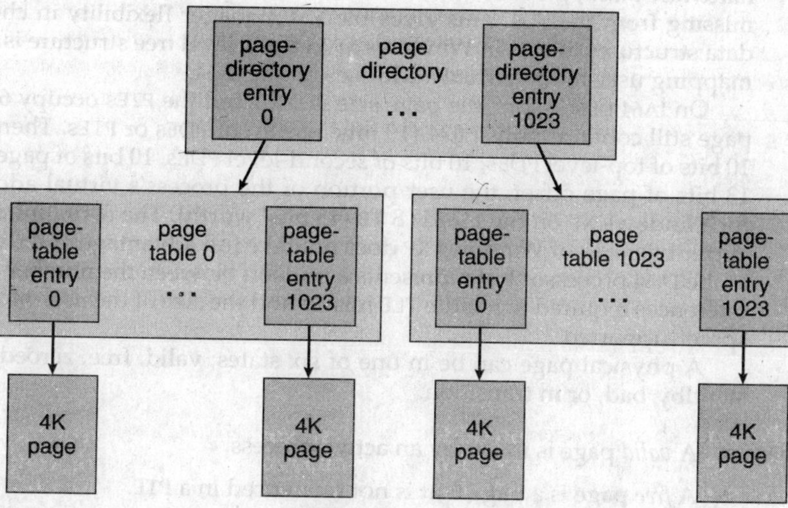

Figure 22.3 Page table layout.

The PTE specifies a page frame in physical memory. The remaining 12 bits of the virtual address are the offset of a specific byte in the page frame. The MMU creates a pointer to the specific byte in physical memory by concatenating the 20 bits from the PTE with the lower 12 bits from the virtual address. Thus, the 32-bit PTE has 12 bits to describe the state of the physical page. The IA32 hardware reserves 3 bits for use by the operating system. The rest of the bits specify whether the page has been accessed or written, the caching attributes, the access mode, whether the page is global, and whether the PTE is valid.

IA32 processors running with PAE enabled use 64-bit PDEs and PTEs in order to represent the larger 24-bit page-frame number field. Thus, the second-level page directories and the page tables contain only 512 PDEs and PTEs, respectively. To provide 4 GB of virtual address space requires an extra level of page directory containing four PDEs. Translation of a 32-bit virtual address uses 2 bits for the top-level directory index and 9 bits for each of the second-level page directories and the page tables.

To avoid the overhead of translating every virtual address by looking up the PDE and PTE, processors use a **translation-lookaside buffer (TLB)**, which contains an associative memory cache for mapping virtual pages to PTEs. Unlike the IA32 architecture, in which the TLB is maintained by the

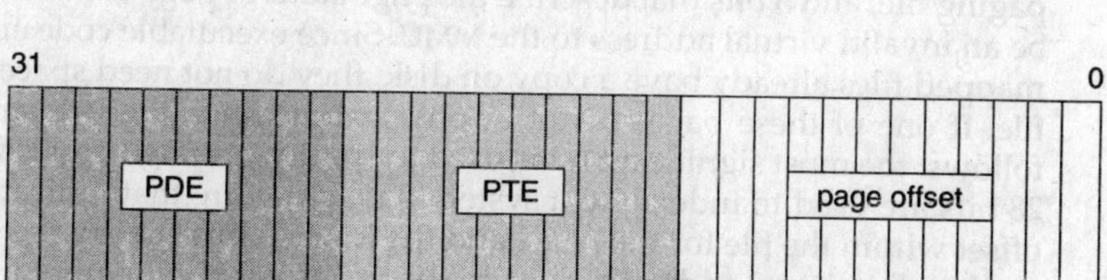

Figure 22.4 Virtual-to-physical address translation on IA32.

hardware MMU, the IA64 invokes a software-trap routine to supply translations missing from the TLB. This gives the VM manager flexibility in choosing the data structures to use. In Windows XP, a three-level tree structure is chosen for mapping user-mode virtual addresses on the IA64.

On IA64 processors, the page size is 8 KB, but the PTEs occupy 64 bits, so a page still contains only 1,024 (10 bits' worth) of PDEs or PTEs. Therefore, with 10 bits of top-level PDEs, 10 bits of second-level PDEs, 10 bits of page table, and 13 bits of page offset, the user portion of the process's virtual address space for Windows XP on the IA64 is 8 TB (43 bits' worth). The 8-TB limitation in the current version of Windows XP does not take full advantage of the capabilities of the IA64 processor but represents a tradeoff between the number of memory references required to handle TLB misses and the size of the user-mode address space supported.

A physical page can be in one of six states: valid, free, zeroed, modified, standby, bad, or in transition.

- A *valid* page is in use by an active process.
- A *free* page is a page that is not referenced in a PTE.
- A *zeroed* page is a free page that has been zeroed out and is ready for immediate use to satisfy zero-on-demand faults.
- A *modified* page has been written by a process and must be sent to the disk before it is allocated for another process.
- A *standby* page is a copy of information already stored on disk. Standby pages can be pages that were not modified, modified pages that have already been written to the disk, or pages that were prefetched to exploit locality.
- A *bad* page is unusable because a hardware error has been detected.
- Finally, a *transition* page is on its way in from disk to a page frame allocated in physical memory.

When the valid bit in a PTE is zero, the VM manager defines the format of the other bits. Invalid pages can have a number of states represented by bits in the PTE. Page-file pages that have never been faulted in are marked zero-on-demand. Files mapped through section objects encode a pointer to that section object. Pages that have been written to the page file contain enough information to find the page on disk, and so forth.

The actual structure of the page-file PTE is shown in Figure 22.5. The PTE contains 5 bits for page protection, 20 bits for page-file offset, 4 bits to select the paging file, and 3 bits that describe the page state. A page-file PTE is marked to be an invalid virtual address to the MMU. Since executable code and memory-mapped files already have a copy on disk, they do not need space in a paging file. If one of these pages is not in physical memory, the PTE structure is as follows: the most significant bit is used to specify the page protection, the next 28 bits are used to index into a system data structure that indicates a file and offset within the file for the page, and the lower 3 bits specify the page state.

Invalid virtual addresses can also be in a number of temporary states that are part of the paging algorithms. When a page is removed from a processs

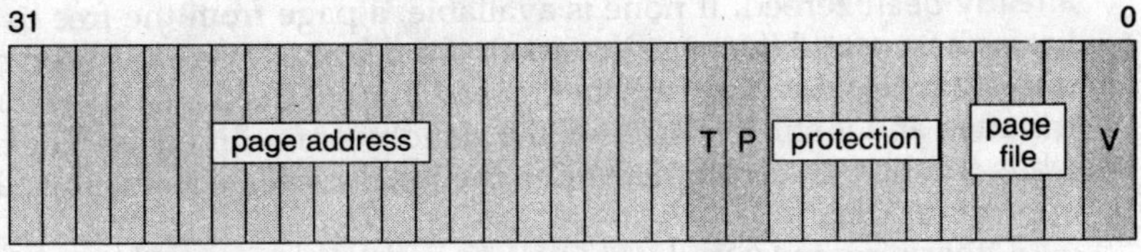

Figure 22.5 Page-file page-table entry. The valid bit is zero.

working set, it is moved either to the modified list (to be written to disk) or directly to the standby list. If written to the standby list, the page is reclaimed without being read from disk if it is needed again before it is moved to the free list. When possible, the VM manager uses idle CPU cycles to zero pages on the free list and move them to the zeroed list. Transition pages have been allocated a physical page and are awaiting the completion of the paging I/O before the PTE is marked as valid.

Windows XP uses section objects to describe pages that are sharable between processes. Each process has its own set of virtual page tables, but the section object also includes a set of page tables containing the master (or prototype) PTEs. When a PTE in a process page table is marked valid, it points to the physical page frame containing the page, as it must on IA32 processors, where the hardware MMU reads the page tables directly from memory. But when a shared page is made invalid, the PTE is edited to point to the prototype PTE associated with the section object.

The page tables associated with a section object are virtual insofar as they are created and trimmed as needed. The only prototype PTEs needed are those that describe pages for which there is a currently mapped view. This greatly improves performance and allows more efficient use of kernel virtual addresses.

The prototype PTE contains the page-frame address and the protection and state bits. Thus, the first access by a process to a shared page generates a page fault. After the first access, further accesses are performed in the normal manner. If a process writes to a copy-on-write page marked read-only in the PTE, the VM manager makes a copy of the page and marks the PTE writable, and the process effectively does not have a shared page any longer. Shared pages never appear in the page file but are instead found in the file system.

The VM manager keeps track of all pages of physical memory in a **page-frame database**. There is one entry for every page of physical memory in the system. The entry points to the PTE, which in turn points to the page frame, so the VM manager can maintain the state of the page. Page frames not referenced by a valid PTE are linked to lists according to page type, such as zeroed, modified, or free.

If a shared physical page is marked as valid for any process, the page cannot be removed from memory. The VM manager keeps a count of valid PTEs for each page in the page-frame database. When the count goes to zero, the physical page can be reused once its contents have been written back to disk (if it was marked dirty).

When a page fault occurs, the VM manager finds a physical page to hold the data. For zero-on-demand pages, the first choice is to find a page that has already been zeroed. If none is available, a page from the free list or standby list is chosen, and the page is zeroed. If the faulted page has been marked as in transition, it is either already being read in from disk or has been unmapped or trimmed and is still available on the standby or modified list. The thread either waits for the I/O to complete or, in the latter cases, reclaims the page from the appropriate list.

Otherwise, an I/O must be issued to read the page in from the paging file or file system. The VM manager tries to allocate an available page from either the free list or the standby list. Pages in the modified list cannot be used until they have been written back to disk and transferred to the standby list. If no pages are available, the thread blocks until the working-set manager trims pages from memory or until a page in physical memory is unmapped by a process.

Windows XP uses a per-process first-in, first-out (FIFO) replacement policy to take pages from processes as appropriate. When a process is started, it is assigned a default minimum working-set size of 50 pages. Windows XP monitors the page faulting of each process that is at its minimum working-set size and adjusts the working-set size accordingly. The VM manager replaces and trims pages in the working set of a process according to their age. The age of a page is determined by how many trimming cycles have occurred without the PTE. Trimmed pages are moved to the standby or modified list, depending on whether the modified bit is set in the page's PTE.

The VM manager does not fault in only the page immediately needed. Research shows that the memory referencing of a thread tends to have a **locality** property; when a page is used, it is likely that adjacent pages will be referenced in the near future. (Think of iterating over an array or fetching sequential instructions that form the executable code for a thread.) Because of locality, when the VM manager faults in a page, it also faults in a few adjacent pages. This prefetching tends to reduce the total number of page faults. Writes are also clustered to reduce the number of independent I/O operations.

In addition to managing committed memory, the VM manager manages each process's reserved memory, or virtual address space. Each process has an associated splay tree that describes the ranges of virtual addresses in use and what the uses are. This allows the VM manager to fault in page tables as needed. If the PTE for a faulting address does not exist, the VM manager searches for the address in the process's tree of **virtual address descriptors (VADs)** and uses this information to fill in the missing PTE and retrieve the page. In some cases, a page-table page itself may not exist; such a page must be transparently allocated and initialized by the VM manager.

22.3.3.3 Process Manager

The Windows XP process manager provides services for creating, deleting, and using processes, threads, and jobs. It has no knowledge about parent–child relationships or process hierarchies; those refinements are left to the particular environmental subsystem that owns the process. The process manager is also not involved in the scheduling of processes, other than setting the priorities and affinities in processes and threads when they are created. Thread scheduling takes place in the kernel dispatcher.

Each process contains one or more threads. Processes themselves can be collected into large units called **job objects**; the use of job objects allows limits to be placed on CPU usage, working-set size, and processor affinities that control multiple processes at once. Job objects are used to manage large data-center machines.

An example of process creation in the Win32 API environment is as follows:

1. A Win32 API application calls `CreateProcess()`.
2. A message is sent to the Win32 API subsystem to notify it that the process is being created.
3. `CreateProcess()` in the original process then calls an API in the process manager of the NT executive to actually create the process.
4. The process manager calls the object manager to create a process object and returns the object handle to Win32 API.
5. Win32 API calls the process manager again to create a thread for the process and returns handles to the new process and thread.

The Windows XP APIs for manipulating virtual memory and threads and for duplicating handles take a process handle, so subsystems can perform operations on behalf of a new process without having to execute directly in the new process's context. Once a new process is created, the initial thread is created, and an asynchronous procedure call is delivered to the thread to prompt the start of execution at the user-mode image loader. The loader is an ntdll.dll, which is a link library automatically mapped into every newly created process. Windows XP also supports a UNIX fork() style of process creation in order to support the POSIX environmental subsystem. Although the Win32 API environment calls the process manager from the client process, POSIX uses the cross-process natuie of the Windows XP APIs to create the new process from within the subsystem process.

The process manager also implements the queuing and delivery of asynchronous procedure calls (APCs) to threads. APCs are used by the system to initiate thread execution, complete I/O, terminate threads and processes, and attach debuggers. User-mode code can also queue an APC to a thread for delivery of signal-like notifications. To support POSIX, the process manager provides APIs that send alerts to threads to unblock them from system calls.

The debugger support in the process manager includes the capability to suspend and resume threads and to create threads that begin in a suspended mode. There are also process-manager APIs that get and set a thread's register context and access another process's virtual memory.

Threads can be created in the current process; they can also be injected into another process. Within the executive, existing threads can temporarily attach to another process. This method is used by worker threads that need to execute in the context of the process originating a work request.

The process manager also supports impersonation. A thread running in a process with a security token belonging to one user can set a thread-specific token belonging to another user. This facility is fundamental to the client–server computing model, where services need to act on behalf of a variety of clients with different security IDs.

22.3.3.4 Local Procedure Call Facility

The implementation of Windows XP uses a client–server model. The environmental subsystems are servers that implement particular operating-system personalities. The client–server model is used for implementing a variety of operating-system services besides the environmental subsystems. Security management, printer spooling, Web services, network file systems, plug-and-play, and many other features are implemented using this model. To reduce the memory footprint, multiple services are often collected into a few processes, which then rely on the user-mode thread-pool facilities to share threads and wait for messages (see Section 22.3.3.3).

The operating system uses the local procedure call (LPC) facility to pass requests and results between client and server processes within a single machine. In particular, LPC is used to request services from the various Windows XP subsystems. LPC is similar in many respects to the RPC mechanisms used by many operating systems for distributed processing across networks, but LPC is optimized for use within a single system. The Windows XP implementation of Open Software Foundation (OSF) RPC often uses LPC as a transport on the local machine.

LPC is a message-passing mechanism. The server process publishes a globally visible connection-port object. When a client wants services from a subsystem, it opens a handle to the subsystem's connection-port object and sends a connection request to the port. The server creates a channel and returns a handle to the client. The channel consists of a pair of private communication ports: one for client-to-server messages and the other for server-to-client messages. Communication channels support a callback mechanism, so the client and server can accept requests when they would normally be expecting a reply.

When an LPC channel is created, one of three message-passing techniques must be specified.

1. The first technique is suitable for small messages (up to a few hundred bytes). In this case, the port's message queue is used as intermediate storage, and the messages are copied from one process to the other.
2. The second technique is for larger messages. In this case, a shared-memory section object is created for the channel. Messages sent through the port's message queue contain a pointer and size information referring to the section object. This avoids the need to copy large messages. The sender places data into the shared section, and the receiver views them directly.
3. The third technique uses APIs that read and write directly into a process's address space. The LPC provides functions and synchronization so that a server can access the data in a client.

The Win32 API window manager uses its own form of message passing, which is independent of the executive LPC facilities. When a client asks for a connection that uses window-manager messaging, the server sets up three objects: (1) a dedicated server thread to handle requests, (2) a 64-KB section object, and (3) an event-pair object. An *event-pair object* is a synchronization object used by the Win32 API subsystem to provide notification when the client thread has copied a message to the Win32 API server, or vice versa. The section object passes the messages, and the event-pair object performs synchronization.

Window-manager messaging has several advantages:

- The section object eliminates message copying, since it represents a region of shared memory.
- The event-pair object eliminates the overhead of using the port object to pass messages containing pointers and lengths.
- The dedicated server thread eliminates the overhead of determining which client thread is calling the server, since there is one server thread per client thread.
- The kernel gives scheduling preference to these dedicated server threads to improve performance.

22.3.3.5 I/O Manager

The I/O manager is responsible for file systems, device drivers, and network drivers. It keeps track of which device drivers, filter drivers, and file systems are loaded, and it also manages buffers for I/O requests. It works with the VM manager to provide memory-mapped file I/O and controls the Windows XP cache manager, which handles caching for the entire I/O system. The I/O manager is fundamentally asynchronous, providing synchronous I/O by explicitly waiting for an I/O operation to complete. The I/O manager provides several models of asynchronous I/O completion, including setting of events, delivery of APCs to initiating threads, and use of I/O completion ports, which allow a single thread to process I/O completions from many other threads.

Device drivers are arranged in a list for each device (called a driver or I/O stack). The I/O manager converts the requests it receives into a standard form called an I/O request packet (IRP). It then forwards the IRP to the first driver in the stack for processing. After a driver processes the IRP, it calls the I/O manager either to forward the IRP to the next driver in the stack or, if all processing is finished, to complete the operation on the IRP.

The I/O request may be completed in a context different from the one in which it was made. For example, if a driver is performing its part of an I/O operation and is forced to block for an extended time, it may queue the IRP to a worker thread to continue processing in the system context. In the original thread, the driver returns a status indicating that the I/O request is pending so that the thread can continue executing in parallel with the I/O operation. An IRP may also be processed in interrupt-service routines and completed in an arbitrary context. Because some final processing may need to take place in the context that initiated the I/O, the I/O manager uses an APC to do final I/O-completion processing in the context of the originating thread.

The stack model is very flexible. As a driver stack is built, various drivers have the opportunity to insert themselves into the stack as filter drivers. Filter drivers can examine and potentially modify each I/O operation. Mount management, partition management, and disk striping and mirroring are all examples of functionality implemented using filter drivers that execute beneath the file system in the stack. File-system filter drivers execute above the file system and have been used to implement functionalities such as hierarchical storage management, single instancing of files for remote boot, and dynamic format conversion. Third parties also use file-system filter drivers to implement virus detection.

Device drivers for Windows XP are written to the Windows Driver Model (WDM) specification. This model lays out all the requirements for device drivers, including how to layer filter drivers, share common code for handling power and plug-and-play requests, build correct cancellation logic, and so forth.

Because of the richness of the WDM, writing a full WDM device driver for each new hardware device can involve an excessive amount of work. Fortunately, the port/miniport model makes it unnecessary to do this. Within a class of similar devices, such as audio drivers, SCSI devices, or Ethernet controllers, each instance of a device shares a common driver for that class, called a **port driver**. The port driver implements the standard operations for the class and then calls device-specific routines in the device's **miniport driver** to implement device-specific functionality.

22.3.3.6 Cache Manager

In many operating systems, caching is done by the file system. Instead, Windows XP provides a centralized caching facility. The **cache manager** works closely with the VM manager to provide cache services for all components under the control of the I/O manager. Caching in Windows XP is based on files rather than raw blocks.

The size of the cache changes dynamically according to how much free memory is available in the system. Recall that the upper 2 GB of a process's address space comprise the system area; it is available in the context of all processes. The VM manager allocates up to one-half of this space to the system cache. The cache manager maps files into this address space and uses the capabilities of the VM manager to handle file I/O.

The cache is divided into blocks of 256 KB. Each cache block can hold a view (that is, a memory-mapped region) of a file. Each cache block is described by a **virtual address control block (VACB)** that stores the virtual address and file offset for the view, as well as the number of processes using the view. The VACBs reside in a single array maintained by the cache manager.

For each open file, the cache manager maintains a separate VACB index array that describes the caching for the entire file. This array has an entry for each 256-KB chunk of the file; so, for instance, a 2-MB file would have an 8-entry VACB index array. An entry in the VACB index array points to the VACB if that portion of the file is in the cache; it is null otherwise. When the I/O manager receives a file's user-level read request, the I/O manager sends an IRP to the device-driver stack on which the file resides. The file system attempts to look up the requested data in the cache manager (unless the request specifically asks for a noncached read). The cache manager calculates which entry of that file's VACB index array corresponds to the byte offset of the request. The entry either points to the view in the cache or is invalid. If it is invalid, the cache manager allocates a cache block (and the corresponding entry in the VACB array) and maps the view into the cache block. The cache manager then attempts to copy data from the mapped file to the caller's buffer. If the copy succeeds, the operation is completed.

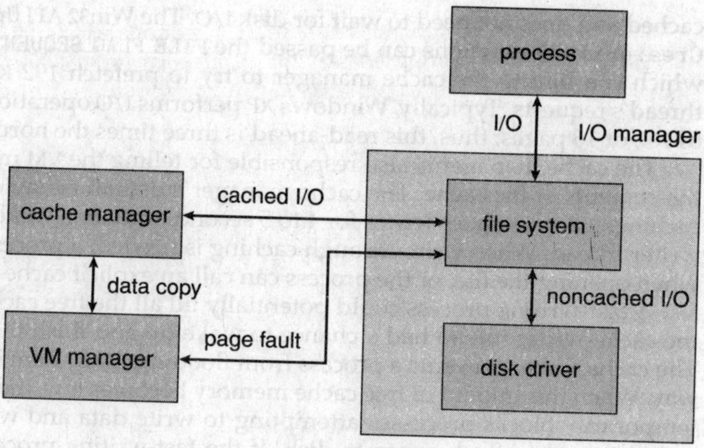

Figure 22.6 File I/O.

If the copy fails, it does so because of a page fault, which causes the VM manager to send a noncached read request to the I/O manager. The I/O manager sends another request down the driver stack, this time requesting a *paging* operation, which bypasses the cache manager and reads the data from the file directly into the page allocated for the cache manager. Upon completion, the VACB is set to point at the page. The data, now in the cache, are copied to the caller's buffer, and the original I/O request is completed. Figure 22.6 shows an overview of these operations.

When possible, for synchronous operations on cached files, I/O is handled by the **fast I/O mechanism**. This mechanism parallels the normal IRP-based I/O but calls into the driver stack directly rather than passing down an IRP. Because no IRP is involved, the operation should not block for an extended period of time and cannot be queued to a worker thread. Therefore, when the operation reaches the file system and calls the cache manager, the operation fails if the information is not already in cache. The I/O manager then attempts the operation using the normal IRP path.

A kernel-level read operation is similar, except that the data can be accessed directly from the cache, rather than being copied to a buffer in user space. To use file-system metadata (data structures that describe the file system), the kernel uses the cache manager's mapping interface to read the metadata. To modify the metadata, the file system uses the cache manager's pinning interface. **Pinning** a page locks the page into a physical-memory page frame so that the VM manager cannot move or page out the page. After updating the metadata, the file system asks the cache manager to unpin the page. A modified page is marked dirty, and so the VM manager flushes the page to disk. The metadata are stored in a regular file.

To improve performance, the cache manager keeps a small history of read requests and from this history attempts to predict future requests. If the cache manager finds a pattern in the previous three requests, such as sequential access forward or backward, it prefetches data into the cache before the next request is submitted by the application. In this way, the application finds its data already cached and does not need to wait for disk I/O. The Win32 API `OpenFile()` and `CreateFile()` functions can be passed the `FILE_FLAG_SEQUENTIAL_SCAN` flag, which is a hint to the cache manager to try to prefetch 192 KB ahead of the thread's requests. Typically, Windows XP performs I/O operations in chunks of 64 KB, or 16 pages; thus, this read-ahead is three times the normal amount.

The cache manager is also responsible for telling the VM manager to flush the contents of the cache. The cache manager's default behavior is write-back caching: it accumulates writes for 4 to 5 seconds and then wakes up the cache-writer thread. When write-through caching is needed, a process can set a flag when opening the file, or the process can call an explicit cache-flush function.

A fast-writing process could potentially fill all the free cache pages before the cache-writer thread had a chance to wake up and flush the pages to disk. The cache writer prevents a process from flooding the system in the following way. When the amount of free cache memory becomes low, the cache manager temporarily blocks processes attempting to write data and wakes the cache-writer thread to flush pages to disk. If the fast-writing process is actually a network redirector for a network file system, blocking it for too long could cause network transfers to time out and be retransmitted. This retransmission would waste network bandwidth. To prevent such waste, network redirectors can instruct the cache manager to limit the backlog of writes in the cache.

Because a network file system needs to move data between a disk and the network interface, the cache manager also provides a DMA interface to move the data directly. Moving data directly avoids the need to copy data through an intermediate buffer.

22.3.3.7 Security Reference Monitor

Centralizing management of system entities in the object manager enables Windows XP to use a uniform mechanism to perform run-time access validation and audit checks for every user-accessible entity in the system. Whenever a process opens a handle to an object, the **security reference monitor (SRM)** checks the process's security token and the object's access-control list to see whether the process has the necessary rights.

The SRM is also responsible for manipulating the privileges in security tokens. Special privileges are required for users to perform backup or restore operations on file systems, debug processes, and so forth. Tokens can also be marked as being restricted in their privileges so that they cannot access objects that are available to most users. Restricted tokens are primarily used to restrict the damage that can be done by execution of untrusted code.

Another responsibility of the SRM is logging security audit events. A C-2 security rating requires that the system have the ability to detect and log all attempts to access system resources so that it is easier to trace attempts at unauthorized access. Because the SRM is responsible for making access checks, it generates most of the audit records in the security-event log.

22.3.3.8 Plug-and-Play and Power Managers

The operating system uses the **plug-and-play (PnP) manager** to recognize and adapt to changes in the hardware configuration. For PnP to work, both the device and the driver must support the PnP standard. The PnP manager automatically recognizes installed devices and detects changes in devices as the system operates. The manager also keeps track of resources used by a device, as well as potential resources that could be used, and takes care of loading the appropriate drivers. This management of hardware resources—primarily interrupts and I/O memory ranges—has the goal of determining a hardware configuration in which all devices are able to operate.

For example, if device B can use interrupt 5 and device A can use 5 or 7, then the PnP manager will assign 5 to B and 7 to A. In previous versions, the user might have had to remove device A and reconfigure it to use interrupt 7 before installing device B. The user thus had to study system resources before installing new hardware and had to determine which devices were using which hardware resources. The proliferation of PCMCIA cards, laptop docks, and USB, IEEE 1394, Infiniband, and other hot-pluggable devices also dictates the support of dynamically configurable resources.

The PnP manager handles dynamic reconfiguration as follows. First, it gets a list of devices from each bus driver (for example, PCI, USB). It loads the installed driver (or installs one, if necessary) and sends an `add-device` request to the appropriate driver for each device. The PnP manager figures out the optimal resource assignments and sends a `start-device` request to each driver, along with the resource assignment for the device. If a device needs to be reconfigured, the PnP manager sends a `query-stop` request, which asks the driver whether the device can be temporarily disabled. If the driver can disable the device, then all pending operations are completed, and new operations are prevented from starting. Next, the PnP manager sends a `stop` request; it can then reconfigure the device with another `start-device` request.

The PnP manager also supports other requests, such as `query-remove`. This request, which is used when the user is getting ready to eject a PCCARD device, operates in a fashion similar to `query-stop`. The `surprise-remove` request is used when a device fails or, more likely, when a user removes a PCCARD device without stopping it first. The `remove` request tells the driver to stop using the device and release all resources allocated to it.

Windows XP supports sophisticated power management. Although this feature is useful for home systems to reduce power consumption, it is primarily useful in promoting ease of use (quicker access) and extending the battery life of laptops. The system and individual devices can be moved to low-power mode (called standby or sleep mode) when not in use, so the battery is primarily directed at physical memory (RAM) data retention. The system can turn itself back on when packets are received from the network, a phone line to a modem rings, or a user opens a laptop or pushes a soft power button. Windows XP can also *hibernate* a system by storing physical memory contents to disk, completely shutting down the machine, and then restoring the system at a later point before execution continues.

Further strategies for reducing power consumption are supported as well. Rather than allowing it to spin in a processor loop when the CPU is idle, Windows XP moves the system to a state requiring lower power consumption. If the CPU is underutilized, Windows XP reduces the CPU clock speed, which can save significant power.

22.3.3.9 Registry

Windows XP keeps much of its configuration information in an internal database called the **registry**. A registry database is called a **hive**. There are separate hives for system information, default user preferences, software installation, and security. Because the information in the system hive is required to boot the system, the registry manager is implemented as a component of the executive.

Every time the system successfully boots, it saves the system hive as *last known good*. If the user installs software, such as a device driver, that produces a system-hive configuration that will not boot, the user can usually boot using the last-known-good configuration.

Damage to the system hive from installing third-party applications and drivers is so common that Windows XP has a component called **system restore** that periodically saves the hives, as well as other software states like driver executables and configuration files, so that the system can be restored to a previously working state in cases where the system boots but no longer operates as expected.

22.3.3.10 Booting

The booting of a Windows XP PC begins when the hardware powers on and the BIOS begins executing from ROM. The BIOS identifies the **system device** to be booted and loads and executes the bootstrap loader from the front of the disk. This loader knows enough about the file-system format to load the NTLDR program from the root directory of the system device. NTLDR is used to determine which **boot device** contains the operating system. Next, the NTLDR loads in the HAL library, the kernel, and the system hive from the boot device. From the system hive, it determines what device drivers are needed to boot the system (the *boot drivers*) and loads them. Finally, NTLDR begins kernel execution.

The kernel initializes the system and creates two processes. The **system process** contains all the internal worker threads and never executes in user mode. The first user-mode process created is SMSS, which is similar to the INIT (initialization) process in UNIX. SMSS does further initialization of the system, including establishing the paging files and loading device drivers, and creates the WINLOGON and CSRSS processes. CSRSS is the Win32 API subsystem. WINLOGON brings up the rest of the system, including the LSASS security subsystem and the remaining services needed to run the system.

The system optimizes the boot process by pre-loading files from disk based on previous boots of the system. Disk access patterns at boot are also used to lay out system files on disk to reduce the number of I/O operations required. The processes required to start the system are reduced by grouping services into one process. All of these approaches contribute to a dramatic reduction in system boot time. Of course, system boot time is less important than it once was because of the sleep and hibernation capabilities of Windows XP, which allow users to power down their computers and then quickly resume where they left off.

22.4 Environmental Subsystems

Environmental subsystems are user-mode processes layered over the native Windows XP executive services to enable Windows XP to run programs developed for other operating systems, including 16-bit Windows, MS-DOS, and POSIX. Each environmental subsystem provides a single application environment.

Windows XP uses the Win32 API subsystem as the main operating environment, and thus this subsystem starts all processes. When an application is executed, the Win32 API subsystem calls the VM manager to load the application's executable code. The memory manager returns a status to Win32 indicating the type of executable. If it is not a native Win32 API executable, the Win32 API environment checks whether the appropriate environmental subsystem is running; if the subsystem is not running, it is started as a user-mode process. The subsystem then takes control over the application startup.

The environmental subsystems use the LPC facility to provide operating-system services to client processes. The Windows XP subsystem architecture keeps applications from mixing API routines from different environments. For instance, a Win32 API application cannot make a POSIX system call, because only one environmental subsystem can be associated with each process.

Since each subsystem is run as a separate user-mode process, a crash in one has no effect on other processes. The exception is Win32 API, which provides all keyboard, mouse, and graphical display capabilities. If it fails, the system is effectively disabled and requires a reboot.

The Win32 API environment categorizes applications as either graphical or character based, where a *character-based application* is one that thinks interactive output goes to a character-based (command) window. Win32 API transforms the output of a character-based application to a graphical representation in the command window. This transformation is easy: whenever an output routine is called, the environmental subsystem calls a Win32 routine to display the text. Since the Win32 API environment performs this function for all character-based windows, it can transfer screen text between windows via the clipboard. This transformation works for MS-DOS applications, as well as for POSIX command-line applications.

22.4.1 MS-DOS Environment

The MS-DOS environment does not have the complexity of the other Windows XP environmental subsystems. It is provided by a Win32 API application called the **virtual DOS machine (VDM)**. Since the VDM is a user-mode process, it is paged and dispatched like any other Windows XP application. The VDM has an **instruction-execution unit** to execute or emulate Intel 486 instructions. The VDM also provides routines to emulate the MS-DOS ROM BIOS and "int 21" software-interrupt services and has virtual device drivers for the screen, keyboard, and communication ports. The VDM is based on MS-DOS 5.0 source code; it allocates at least 620 KB of memory to the application.

The Windows XP command shell is a program that creates a window that looks like an MS-DOS environment. It can run both 16-bit and 32-bit executables. When an MS-DOS application is run, the command shell starts a VDM process to execute the program.

If Windows XP is running on a IA32-compatible processor, MS-DOS graphical applications run in full-screen mode, and character applications can run full screen or in a window. Not all MS-DOS applications run under the VDM. For example, some MS-DOS applications access the disk hardware directly, so they fail to run on Windows XP because disk access is restricted to protect the file system. In general, MS-DOS applications that directly access hardware will fail to operate under Windows XP.

Since MS-DOS is not a multitasking environment, some applications have been written in such a way as to "hog" the CPU. For instance, the use of busy loops can cause time delays or pauses in execution. The scheduler in the kernel dispatcher detects such delays and automatically throttles the CPU usage, but this may cause the offending application to operate incorrectly.

22.4.2 16-Bit Windows Environment

The Win16 execution environment is provided by a VDM that incorporates additional software called *Windows on Windows* (WOW32 for 16-bit applications); this software provides the Windows 3.1 kernel routines and stub routines for window-manager and graphical-device-interface (GDI) functions. The stub routines call the appropriate Win32 API subroutines—converting, or *thunking*, 16-bit addresses into 32-bit addresses. Applications that rely on the internal structure of the 16-bit window manager or GDI may not work, because the underlying Win32 API implementation is, of course, different from true 16-bit Windows.

WOW32 can multitask with other processes on Windows XP, but it resembles Windows 3.1 in many ways. Only one Win16 application can run at a time, all applications are single threaded and reside in the same address space, and all share the same input queue. These features imply that an application that stops receiving input will block all the other Win16 applications, just as in Windows 3.x, and one Win16 application can crash other Win16 applications by corrupting the address space. The user can enable multiple Win16 environments to coexist, however, by using the command *start /separate win16application* from the command line.

There are relatively few 16-bit applications that users need to continue to run on Windows XP, but some of them include common installation (setup) programs. Thus, the WOW32 environment continues to exist primarily because a number of 32-bit applications cannot be installed on Windows XP without it.

22.4.3 32-Bit Windows Environment on IA64

The native environment for Windows on IA64 uses 64-bit addresses and the native IA64 instruction set. To execute IA32 programs in this environment requires a thunking layer to translate 32-bit Win32 API calls into the corresponding 64-bit calls—just as 16-bit applications require translation on IA32 systems. Thus, 64-bit Windows supports the WOW64 environment. The implementations of 32-bit and 64-bit Windows are essentially identical, and the IA64 processor provides direct execution of IA32 instructions, so WOW64 achieves a higher level of compatibility than WOW32.

22.4.4 Win32 Environment

As mentioned earlier, the main subsystem in Windows XP is the Win32 API, which runs Win32 API applications and manages all keyboard, mouse, and screen I/O. Since it is the controlling environment, it is designed to be extremely robust. Several features of the Win32 API contribute to this robustness. Unlike processes in the Win16 environment, each Win32 process has its own input queue. The window manager dispatches all input on the system to the appropriate process's input queue, so a failed process does not block input to other processes.

The Windows XP kernel also provides preemptive multitasking, which enables the user to terminate applications that have failed or are no longer needed. The Win32 API also validates all objects before using them, to prevent crashes that could otherwise occur if an application tried to use an invalid or wrong handle. The Win32 API subsystem verifies the type of the object to which a handle points before using the object. The reference counts kept by the object manager prevent objects from being deleted while they are still being used and prevent their use after they have been deleted.

To achieve a high level of compatibility with Windows 95/98 systems, Windows XP allows users to specify that individual applications be run using a **shim layer**, which modifies the Win32 API to better approximate the behavior expected by old applications. For example, some applications expect to see a particular version of the system and fail on new versions. Frequently, applications have latent bugs that become exposed due to changes in the implementation. Running an application with the Windows 95/98 shims enabled causes the system to provide behavior much closer to Windows 95/98—though with reduced performance and limited interoperability with other applications.

22.4.5 POSIX Subsystem

The POSIX subsystem is designed to run POSIX applications written to follow the POSIX standard, which is based on the UNIX model. POSIX applications can be started by the Win32 API subsystem or by another POSIX application. POSIX applications use the POSIX subsystem server `PSXSS.EXE`, the POSIX dynamic link library `PSXDLL.DLL`, and the POSIX console session manager `POSIX.EXE`.

Although the POSIX standard does not specify printing, POSIX applications can use printers transparently via the Windows XP redirection mechanism. POSIX applications have access to any file system on the Windows XP system; the POSIX environment enforces UNIX-like permissions on directory trees.

Due to scheduling issues, the POSIX system in Windows XP does not ship with the system but is available separately for professional desktop systems and servers. It provides a much higher level of compatibility with UNIX applications than previous versions of NT. Of the commonly available UNIX applications, most compile and run without change with the latest version of Interix.

22.4.6 Logon and Security Subsystems

Before a user can access objects on Windows XP, that user must be authenticated by the logon service, WINLOGON. WINLOGON is responsible for responding to the secure attention sequence (Control-Alt-Delete). The secure attention sequence is a required mechanism for keeping an application from acting as a Trojan horse. Only WINLOGON can intercept this sequence in order to put up a logon screen, change passwords, and lock the workstation. To be authenticated, a user must have an account and provide the password for that account. Alternatively, a user logs on by using a smart card and personal identification number, subject to the security policies in effect for the domain.

The local security authority subsystem (LSASS) is the process that generates access tokens to represent users on the system. It calls an **authentication package** to perform authentication using information from the logon subsystem or network server. Typically, the authentication package simply looks up the account information in a local database and checks to see that the password is correct. The security subsystem then generates the access token for the user ID containing the appropriate privileges, quota limits, and group IDs. Whenever the user attempts to access an object in the system, such as by opening a handle to the object, the access token is passed to the security reference monitor, which checks privileges and quotas. The default authentication package for Windows XP domains is Kerberos. LSASS also has the responsibility for implementing security policy, such as strong passwords; for authenticating users; and for performing encryption of data and keys.

22.5 File System

Historically, MS-DOS systems have used the file-allocation table (FAT) file system. The 16-bit FAT file system has several shortcomings, including internal fragmentation, a size limitation of 2 GB, and a lack of access protection for files. The 32-bit FAT file system has solved the size and fragmentation problems, but its performance and features are still weak by comparison with modern file systems. The NTFS file system is much better. It was designed to include many features, including data recovery, security, fault tolerance, large files and file systems, multiple data streams, UNICODE names, sparse files, encryption, journaling, volume shadow copies, and file compression.

Windows XP uses NTFS as its basic file system, and we focus on it here. Windows XP continues to use FAT16, however, to read floppies and other removable media. And despite the advantages of NTFS, FAT32 continues to be important for interoperability of media with Windows 95/98 systems. Windows XP supports additional file-system types for the common formats used for CD and DVD media.

22.5.1 NTFS Internal Layout

The fundamental entity in NTFS is a volume. A volume is created by the Windows XP logical disk management utility and is based on a logical disk partition. A volume may occupy a portion of a disk, may occupy an entire disk, or may span several disks.

NTFS does not deal with individual sectors of a disk but instead uses clusters as the units of disk allocation. A **cluster** is a number of disk sectors that is a power of 2. The cluster size is configured when an NTFS file system is formatted. The default cluster size is the sector size for volumes up to 512 MB, 1 KB for volumes up to 1 GB, 2 KB for volumes up to 2 GB, and 4 KB for larger volumes. This cluster size is much smaller than that for the 16-bit FAT file system, and the small size reduces the amount of internal fragmentation. As an example, consider a 1.6-GB disk with 16,000 files. If you use a FAT-16 file system, 400 MB may be lost to internal fragmentation because the cluster size is 32 KB. Under NTFS, only 17 MB would be lost when storing the same files.

NTFS uses **logical cluster numbers (LCNs)** as disk addresses. It assigns them by numbering clusters from the beginning of the disk to the end. Using this scheme, the system can calculate a physical disk offset (in bytes) by multiplying the LCN by the cluster size.

A file in NTFS is not a simple byte stream as it is in MS-DOS or UNIX; rather, it is a structured object consisting of typed **attributes**. Each attribute of a file is an independent byte stream that can be created, deleted, read, and written. Some attribute types are standard for all files, including the file name (or names, if the file has aliases, such as an MS-DOS shortname), the creation time, and the security descriptor that specifies access control. User data is stored in *data attributes*.

Most traditional data files have an *unnamed* data attribute that contains all the file's data. However, additional data streams can be created with explicit names. For instance, in Macintosh files stored on a Windows XP server, the resource fork is a named data stream. The IProp interfaces of the Component Object Model (COM) use a named data stream to store properties on ordinary files, including thumbnails of images. In general, attributes may be added as necessary and are accessed using a *file-name:attribute* syntax. NTFS returns the size of the unnamed attribute only in response to file-query operations, such as when running the `dir` command.

Every file in NTFS is described by one or more records in an array stored in a special file called the master file table (MFT). The size of a record is determined when the file system is created; it ranges from 1 to 4 KB. Small attributes are stored in the MFT record itself and are called **resident attributes**. Large attributes, such as the unnamed bulk data, are called **nonresident attributes** and are stored in one or more contiguous **extents** on the disk; a pointer to each extent is stored in the MFT record. For a small file, even the data attribute may fit inside the MFT record. If a file has many attributes—or if it is highly fragmented, so that many pointers are needed to point to all the fragments—one record in the MFT might not be large enough. In this case, the file is described by a record called the **base file record**, which contains pointers to overflow records that hold the additional pointers and attributes.

Each file in an NTFS volume has a unique ID called a **file reference**. The file reference is a 64-bit quantity that consists of a 48-bit file number and a 16-bit sequence number. The file number is the record number (that is, the array slot) in the MFT that describes the file. The sequence number is incremented every time an MFT entry is reused. The sequence number enables NTFS to perform internal consistency checks, such as catching a stale reference to a deleted file after the MFT entry has been reused for a new file.

22.5.1.1 NTFS B+ Tree

As in MS-DOS and UNIX, the NTFS namespace is organized as a hierarchy of directories. Each directory uses a data structure called a **B+ tree** to store an index of the file names in that directory. In a B+ tree, the length of every path from the root of the tree to a leaf is the same, and the cost of reorganizing the tree is eliminated. The **index root** of a directory contains the top level of the B+ tree. For a large directory, this top level contains pointers to disk extents that hold the remainder of the tree. Each entry in the directory contains the name and file reference of the file, as well as a copy of the update timestamp and file size taken from the file's resident attributes in the MFT. Copies of this information are stored in the directory, so a directory listing can be efficiently generated. Because all the file names, sizes, and update times are available from the directory itself, there is no need to gather these attributes from the MFT entries for each of the files.

22.5.1.2 NTFS Metadata

The NTFS volume's metadata are all stored in files. The first file is the MFT. The second file, which is used during recovery if the MFT is damaged, contains a copy of the first 16 entries of the MFT. The next few files are also special in purpose. They include the files described below.

- The **log file** records all metadata updates to the file system.
- The **volume file** contains the name of the volume, the version of NTFS that formatted the volume, and a bit that tells whether the volume may have been corrupted and needs to be checked for consistency.
- The **attribute-definition table** indicates which attribute types are used in the volume and what operations can be performed on each of them.
- The **root directory** is the top-level directory in the file-system hierarchy.
- The **bitmap file** indicates which clusters on a volume are allocated to files and which are free.
- The **boot file** contains the startup code for Windows XP and must be located at a particular disk address so that it can be found easily by a simple ROM bootstrap loader. The boot file also contains the physical address of the MFT.
- The **bad-cluster file** keeps track of any bad areas on the volume; NTFS uses this record for error recovery.

22.5.2 Recovery

In many simple file systems, a power failure at the wrong time can damage the file-system data structures so severely that the entire volume is scrambled. Many versions of UNIX store redundant metadata on the disk, and they recover from crashes by using the `fsck` program to check all the file-system data structures and restore them forcibly to a consistent state. Restoring them often involves deleting damaged files and freeing data clusters that had been written with user data but not properly recorded in the file system's metadata structures. This checking can be a slow process and can cause the loss of significant amounts of data.

NTFS takes a different approach to file-system robustness. In NTFS, all file-system data-structure updates are performed inside transactions. Before a data structure is altered, the transaction writes a log record that contains redo and undo information; after the data structure has been changed, the transaction writes a commit record to the log to signify that the transaction succeeded.

After a crash, the system can restore the file-system data structures to a consistent state by processing the log records, first redoing the operations for committed transactions and then undoing the operations for transactions that did not commit successfully before the crash. Periodically (usually every 5 seconds), a checkpoint record is written to the log. The system does not need log records prior to the checkpoint to recover from a crash. They can be discarded, so the log file does not grow without bounds. The first time after system startup that an NTFS volume is accessed, NTFS automatically performs file-system recovery.

This scheme does not guarantee that all the user-file contents are correct after a crash; it ensures only that the file-system data structures (the metadata files) are undamaged and reflect some consistent state that existed prior to the crash. It would be possible to extend the transaction scheme to cover user files, and Microsoft may do so in the future.

The log is stored in the third metadata file at the beginning of the volume. It is created with a fixed maximum size when the file system is formatted. It has two sections: the **logging area**, which is a circular queue of log records, and the **restart area**, which holds context information, such as the position in the logging area where NTFS should start reading during a recovery. In fact, the restart area holds two copies of its information, so recovery is still possible if one copy is damaged during the crash.

The logging functionality is provided by the Windows XP **log-file service**. In addition to writing the log records and performing recovery actions, the log-file service keeps track of the free space in the log file. If the free space gets too low, the log-file service queues pending transactions, and NTFS halts all new I/O operations. After the in-progress operations complete, NTFS calls the cache manager to flush all data and then resets the log file and performs the queued transactions.

22.5.3 Security

The security of an NTFS volume is derived from the Windows XP object model. Each NTFS file references a security descriptor, which contains the access token of the owner of the file, and an access-control list, which states the access privileges granted to each user having access to the file.

In normal operation, NTFS does not enforce permissions on traversal of directories in file path names. However, for compatibility with POSIX, these checks can be enabled. Traversal checks are inherently more expensive, since modern parsing of file path names uses prefix matching rather than component-by-component opening of directory names.

22.5.4 Volume Management and Fault Tolerance

`FtDisk` is the fault-tolerant disk driver for Windows XP. When installed, it provides several ways to combine multiple disk drives into one logical volume so as to improve performance, capacity, or reliability.

22.5.4.1 Volume Set

One way to combine multiple disks is to concatenate them logically to form a large logical volume, as shown in Figure 22.7. In Windows XP, this logical

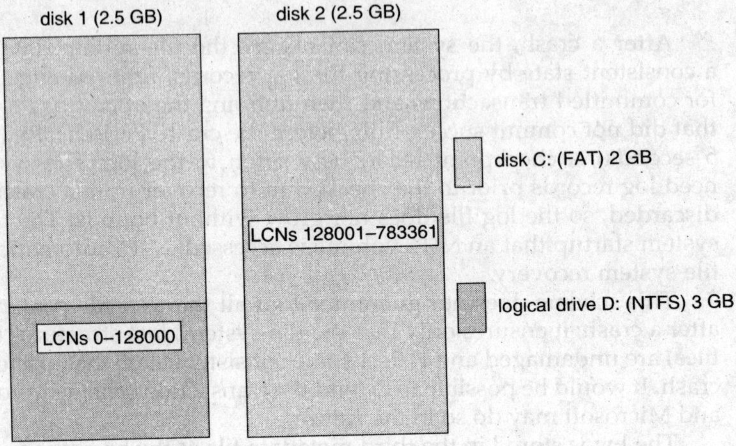

Figure 22.7 Volume set on two drives.

volume, called a **volume set**, can consist of up to 32 physical partitions. A volume set that contains an NTFS volume can be extended without disturbance of the data already stored in the file system. The bitmap metadata on the NTFS volume are simply extended to cover the newly added space. NTFS continues to use the same LCN mechanism that it uses for a single physical disk, and the `FtDisk` driver supplies the mapping from a logical-volume offset to the offset on one particular disk.

22.5.4.2 Stripe Set

Another way to combine multiple physical partitions is to interleave their blocks in round-robin fashion to form a **stripe set**, as shown in Figure 22.8. This scheme is also called RAID level 0, or **disk striping**. `FtDisk` uses a stripe size of 64 KB. The first 64 KB of the logical volume are stored in the first

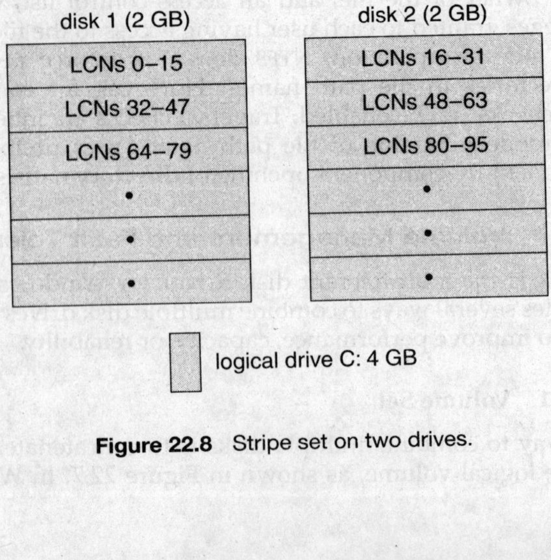

Figure 22.8 Stripe set on two drives.

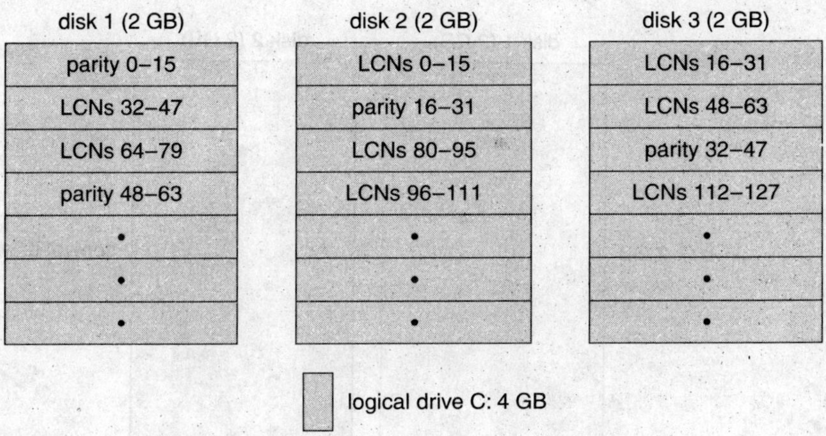

Figure 22.9 Stripe set with parity on three drives.

physical partition, the second 64 KB in the second physical partition, and so on, until each partition has contributed 64 KB of space. Then, the allocation wraps around to the first disk, allocating the second 64-KB block. A stripe set forms one large logical volume, but the physical layout can improve the I/O bandwidth, because, for a large I/O, all the disks can transfer data in parallel.

22.5.4.3 Stripe Set with Parity

A variation of this idea is the **stripe set with parity**, which is shown in Figure 22.9. This scheme is also called RAID level 5. Suppose that a stripe set has eight disks. Seven of the disks will store data stripes, with one data stripe on each disk, and the eighth disk will store a parity stripe for each data stripe. The parity stripe contains the byte-wise `exclusive or` of the data stripes. If any one of the eight stripes is destroyed, the system can reconstruct the data by calculating the `exclusive or` of the remaining seven. This ability to reconstruct data makes the disk array much less likely to lose data in case of a disk failure.

Notice that an update to one data stripe also requires recalculation of the parity stripe. Seven concurrent writes to seven different data stripes thus require updates to seven parity stripes. If the parity stripes were all on the same disk, that disk could have seven times the I/O load of the data disks. To avoid creating this bottleneck, we spread the parity stripes over all the disks by assigning them in round-robin style. To build a stripe set with parity, we need a minimum of three equal-sized partitions located on three separate disks.

22.5.4.4 Disk Mirroring

An even more robust scheme is called **disk mirroring**, or RAID level 1; it is depicted in Figure 22.10. A **mirror set** comprises two equal-sized partitions on two disks. When an application writes data to a mirror set, FtDisk writes the data to both partitions, so that the data contents of the two partitions are identical. If one partition fails, FtDisk has another copy safely stored on the mirror. Mirror sets can also improve performance, because read requests can

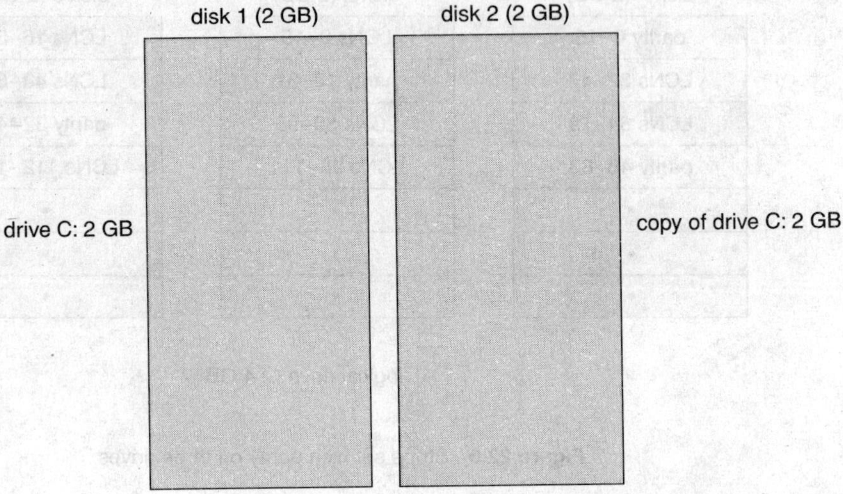

Figure 22.10 Mirror set on two drives.

be split between the two mirrors, giving each mirror half of the workload. To protect against the failure of a disk controller, we can attach the two disks of a mirror set to two separate disk controllers. This arrangement is called a **duplex set**.

22.5.4.5 Sector Sparing and Cluster Remapping

To deal with disk sectors that go bad, `FtDisk` uses a hardware technique called sector sparing, and NTFS uses a software technique called cluster remapping. **Sector sparing** is a hardware capability provided by many disk drives. When a disk drive is formatted, it creates a map from logical block numbers to good sectors on the disk. It also leaves extra sectors unmapped, as spares. If a sector fails, `FtDisk` instructs the disk drive to substitute a spare. **Cluster remapping** is a software technique performed by the file system. If a disk block goes bad, NTFS substitutes a different, unallocated block by changing any affected pointers in the MFT. NTFS also makes a note that the bad block should never be allocated to any file.

When a disk block goes bad, the usual outcome is a data loss. But sector sparing or cluster remapping can be combined with fault-tolerant volumes to mask the failure of a disk block. If a read fails, the system reconstructs the missing data by reading the mirror or by calculating the `exclusive or` parity in a stripe set with parity. The reconstructed data are stored in a new location that is obtained by sector sparing or cluster remapping.

22.5.5 Compression and Encryption

NTFS can perform data compression on individual files or on all data files in a directory. To compress a file, NTFS divides the file's data into **compression units**, which are blocks of 16 contiguous clusters. When a compression unit is written, a data-compression algorithm is applied. If the result fits into fewer than 16 clusters, the compressed version is stored. When reading, NTFS can determine whether data have been compressed: if they have been, the length of the stored compression unit is less than 16 clusters. To improve performance when reading contiguous compression units, NTFS prefetches and decompresses ahead of the application requests.

For sparse files or files that contain mostly zeros, NTFS uses another technique to save space. Clusters that contain only zeros because they have never been written are not actually allocated or stored on disk. Instead, gaps are left in the sequence of virtual-cluster numbers stored in the MFT entry for the file. When reading a file, if NTFS finds a gap in the virtual-cluster numbers, it just zero-fills that portion of the caller's buffer. This technique is also used by UNIX.

NTFS supports encryption of files. Individual files or entire directories can be specified for encryption. The security system manages the keys used, and a key-recovery service is available to retrieve lost keys.

22.5.6 Mount Points

Mount points are a form of symbolic link specific to directories on NTFS. They provide a mechanism for organizing disk volumes that is more flexible than the use of global names (like drive letters). A mount point is implemented as a symbolic link with associated data that contain the true volume name. Ultimately, mount points will supplant drive letters completely, but there will be a long transition due to the dependence of many applications on the drive-letter scheme.

22.5.7 Change Journal

NTFS keeps a journal describing all changes that have been made to the file system. User-mode services can receive notifications of changes to the journal and then identify what files have changed. The content-indexing service uses the change journal to identify files that need to be re-indexed. The file-replication service uses it to identify files that need to be replicated across the network.

22.5.8 Volume Shadow Copies

Windows XP implements the capability of bringing a volume to a known state and then creating a shadow copy that can be used to back up a consistent view of the volume. Making a shadow copy of a volume is a form of copy-on-write, where blocks modified after the shadow copy is created are stored in their original form in the copy. To achieve a consistent state for the volume requires the cooperation of applications, since the system cannot know when the data used by the application are in a stable state from which the application could be safely restarted.

The server version of Windows XP uses shadow copies to efficiently maintain old versions of files stored on file servers. This allows users to see documents stored on file servers as they existed at earlier points in time. The user can use this feature to recover files that were accidentally deleted or simply to look at a previous version of the file, all without pulling out a backup tape.

22.6 Networking

Windows XP supports both peer-to-peer and client–server networking. It also has facilities for network management. The networking components in Windows XP provide data transport, interprocess communication, file sharing across a network, and the ability to send print jobs to remote printers.

22.6.1 Network Interfaces

To describe networking in Windows XP, we must first mention two of the internal networking interfaces: the **network device interface specification (NDIS)** and the **transport driver interface (TDI)**. The NDIS interface was developed in 1989 by Microsoft and 3Com to separate network adapters from transport protocols so that either could be changed without affecting the other. NDIS resides at the interface between the data-link and network layers in the ISO model and enables many protocols to operate over many different network adapters. In terms of the ISO model, the TDI is the interface between the transport layer (layer 4) and the session layer (layer 5). This interface enables any session-layer component to use any available transport mechanism. (Similar reasoning led to the streams mechanism in UNIX.) The TDI supports both connection-based and connectionless transport and has functions to send any type of data.

22.6.2 Protocols

Windows XP implements transport protocols as drivers. These drivers can be loaded and unloaded from the system dynamically, although in practice the system typically has to be rebooted after a change. Windows XP comes with several networking protocols. Next, we discuss a number of the protocols supported in Windows XP to provide a variety of network functionality.

22.6.2.1 Server-Message Block

The **server-message-block (SMB)** protocol was first introduced in MS-DOS 3.1. The system uses the protocol to send I/O requests over the network. The SMB protocol has four message types. `Session control` messages are commands that start and end a redirector connection to a shared resource at the server. A redirector uses `File` messages to access files at the server. `Printer` messages are used to send data to a remote print queue and to receive status information from the queue, and `Message` messages are used to communicate with another workstation. The SMB protocol was published as the **Common Internet File System** (CIFS) and is supported on a number of operating systems.

22.6.2.2 Network Basic Input/Output System

The **network basic input/output system (NetBIOS)** is a hardware-abstraction interface for networks, analogous to the BIOS hardware-abstraction interface devised for PCs running MS-DOS. NetBIOS, developed in the early 1980s, has become a standard network-programming interface. NetBIOS is used to establish logical names on the network; to establish logical connections, or **sessions**, between two logical names on the network; and to support reliable data transfer for a session via either NetBIOS or SMB requests.

22.6.2.3 NetBIOS Extended User Interface

The NetBIOSextended user interface (NetBEUI) was introduced by IBM in 1985 as a simple, efficient networking protocol for up to 254 machines. It is the default protocol for Windows 95 peer networking and for Windows for Workgroups. Windows XP uses NetBEUI when it wants to share resources with these networks. Among the limitations of NetBEUI are that it uses the actual name of a computer as the address and that it does not support routing.

22.6.2.4 Transmission Control Protocol/Internet Protocol

The transmission control protocol/Internet protocol (TCP/IP) suite that is used on the Internet has become the de facto standard networking infrastructure. Windows XP uses TCP/IP to connect to a wide variety of operating systems and hardware platforms. The Windows XP TCP/IP package includes the simple network-management protocol (SNM), dynamic host-configuration protocol (DHCP), Windows Internet name service (WINS), and NetBIOS support.

22.6.2.5 Point-to-Point Tunneling Protocol

The point-to-point tunneling protocol (PPTP) is a protocol provided by Windows XP to communicate between remote-access server modules running on Windows XP server machines and other client systems that are connected over the Internet. The remote-access servers can encrypt data sent over the connection, and they support multi-protocol virtual private networks (VPNs) over the Internet.

22.6.2.6 Novell NetWare Protocols

The Novell NetWare protocols (IPX datagram service on the SPX transport layer) are widely used for PC LANs. The Windows XP NWLink protocol connects the NetBIOS to NetWare networks. In combination with a redirector (such as Microsoft's Client Service for NetWare or Novell's NetWare Client for Windows), this protocol enables a Windows XP client to connect to a NetWare server.

22.6.2.7 Web-Distributed Authoring and Versioning Protocol

Web-distributed authoring and versioning (WebDAV) is an http-based protocol for collaborative authoring across a network. Windows XP builds a WebDAV redirector into the file system. Building this support directly into the file system enables WebDAV to work with other features, such as encryption. Personal files can now be stored securely in a public place.

22.6.2.8 AppleTalk Protocol

The AppleTalk protocol was designed as a low-cost connection by Apple to allow Macintosh computers to share files. Windows XP systems can share files and printers with Macintosh computers via AppleTalk if a Windows XP server on the network is running the Windows Services for Macintosh package.

22.6.3 Distributed-Processing Mechanisms

Although Windows XP is not a distributed operating system, it does support distributed applications. Mechanisms that support distributed processing on Windows XP include NetBIOS, named pipes and mailslots, Windows sockets, RPCs, the Microsoft Interface Definition Language, and COM.

22.6.3.1 NetBIOS

In Windows XP, NetBIOS applications can communicate over the network using NetBEUI, NWLink, or TCP/IP.

22.6.3.2 Named Pipes

Named pipes are a connection-oriented messaging mechanism. Named pipes were originally developed as a high-level interface to NetBIOS connections over the network. A process can also use named pipes to communicate with other processes on the same machine. Since named pipes are accessed through the file-system interface, the security mechanisms used for file objects also apply to named pipes.

The format of pipe names follows the **uniform naming convention** (UNC). A UNC name looks like a typical remote file name. The format is `\\server_name\share_name\x\y\z`, where `server_name` identifies a server on the network; `share_name` identifies any resource that is made available to network users, such as directories, files, named pipes, and printers; and `\x\y\z` is a normal file path name.

22.6.3.3 Mailslots

Mailslots are a connectionless messaging mechanism. They are unreliable when accessed across the network, in that a message sent to a mailslot may be lost before the intended recipient receives it. Mailslots are used for broadcast applications, such as finding components on the network; they are also used by the Windows computer browser service.

22.6.3.4 Winsock

Winsock is the Windows XP sockets API. Winsock is a session-layer interface that is largely compatible with UNIX sockets but has some added Windows XP extensions. It provides a standardized interface to many transport protocols that may have different addressing schemes, so that any Winsock application can run on any Winsock-compliant protocol stack.

22.6.3.5 Remote Procedure Calls

A remote procedure call (RPC) is a client–server mechanism that enables an application on one machine to make a procedure call to code on another machine. The client calls a local procedure—a stub routine—which packs its arguments into a message and sends them across the network to a particular server process. The client-side stub routine then blocks. Meanwhile, the server unpacks the message, calls the procedure, packs the return results into a message, and sends them back to the client stub. The client stub unblocks, receives the message, unpacks the results of the RPC, and returns them to the caller. This packing of arguments is sometimes called **marshalling**.

The Windows XP RPC mechanism follows the widely used distributed-computing-environment standard for RPC messages, so programs written to use Windows XP RPCs are highly portable. The RPC standard is detailed. It hides many of the architectural differences among computers, such as the sizes of binary numbers and the order of bytes and bits in computer words, by specifying standard data formats for RPC messages.

Windows XP can send RPC messages using NetBIOS, or Winsock on TCP/IP networks, or named pipes on LAN Manager networks. The LPC facility, discussed earlier, is similar to RPC, except that in the case of LPC the messages are passed between two processes running on the same computer.

22.6.3.6 Microsoft Interface Definition Language

It is tedious and error-prone to write the code to marshal and transmit arguments in the standard format, to unmarshal and execute the remote procedure, to marshal and send the return results, and to unmarshal and return them to the caller. Fortunately, however, much of this code can be generated automatically from a simple description of the arguments and return results.

Windows XP provides the **Microsoft Interface Definition Language** to describe the remote procedure names, arguments, and results. The compiler for this language generates header files that declare the stubs for the remote procedures, as well as the data types for the arguments and return-value messages. It also generates source code for the stub routines used at the client side and for an unmarshaller and dispatcher at the server side. When the application is linked, the stub routines are included. When the application executes the RPC stub, the generated code handles the rest.

22.6.3.7 Component Object Model

The **component object model (COM)** is a mechanism for interprocess communication that was developed for Windows. COM objects provide a well-defined interface to manipulate the data in the object. For instance, COM is the infrastructure used by Microsoft's **object linking and embedding (OLE)** technology for inserting spreadsheets into Microsoft Word documents. Windows XP has a distributed extension called **DCOM** that can be used over a network utilizing RPC to provide a transparent method of developing distributed applications.

22.6.4 Redirectors and Servers

In Windows XP, an application can use the Windows XP I/O API to access files from a remote computer as though they were local, provided that the remote computer is running a CIFS server, such as is provided by Windows XP and earlier Windows systems. A **redirector** is the client-side object that forwards I/O requests to remote files, where they are satisfied by a server. For performance and security, the redirectors and servers run in kernel mode.

In more detail, access to a remote file occurs as follows:

1. The application calls the I/O manager to request that a file be opened with a file name in the standard UNC format.

2. The I/O manager builds an I/O request packet, as described in Section 22.3.3.5.

3. The I/O manager recognizes that the access is for a remote file and calls a driver called a **multiple universal-naming- convention provider (MUP)**.

4. The MUP sends the I/O request packet asynchronously to all registered redirectors.

5. A redirector that can satisfy the request responds to the MUP. To avoid asking all the redirectors the same question in the future, the MUP uses a cache to remember which redirector can handle this file.

6. The redirector sends the network request to the remote system.

7. The remote-system network drivers receive the request and pass it to the server driver.

8. The server driver hands the request to the proper local file-system driver.

9. The proper device driver is called to access the data.

10. The results are returned to the server driver, which sends the data back to the requesting redirector. The redirector then returns the data to the calling application via the I/O manager.

A similar process occurs for applications that use the Win32 API network API, rather than the UNC services, except that a module called a *multi-provider router* is used instead of a MUP.

For portability, redirectors and servers use the TDI API for network transport. The requests themselves are expressed in a higher-level protocol, which by default is the SMB protocol mentioned in Section 22.6.2. The list of redirectors is maintained in the system registry database.

22.6.4.1 Distributed File System

UNC names are not always convenient, because multiple file servers may be available to serve the same content, and UNC names explicitly include the name of the server. Windows XP supports a **distributed file system (DFS)** protocol that allows a network administrator to serve up files from multiple servers using a single distributed name space.

22.6.4.2 Folder Redirection and Client-Side Caching

To improve the PC experience for business users who frequently switch among computers, Windows XP allows administrators to give users **roaming profiles**, which keep users' preferences and other settings on servers. **Folder redirection** is then used to automatically store a user's documents and other files on a server.

This works well until one of the computers is no longer attached to the network, as when a user takes a laptop onto an airplane. To give users off-line access to their redirected files, Windows XP uses **client-side caching (CSC)**. CSC is used when the computer is online to keep copies of the server files on the local machine for better performance. The files are pushed up to the server as they are changed. If the computer becomes disconnected, the files are still available, and the update of the server is deferred until the next time the computer is online.

22.6.5 Domains

Many networked environments have natural groups of users, such as students in a computer laboratory at school or employees in one department in a business. Frequently, we want all the members of the group to be able to access shared resources on their various computers in the group. To manage the global access rights within such groups, Windows XP uses the concept of a domain. Previously, these domains had no relationship whatsoever to the domain-name system (DNS) that maps Internet host names to IP addresses. Now, however, they are closely related.

Specifically, a Windows XP domain is a group of Windows XP workstations and servers that share a common security policy and user database. Since Windows XP now uses the Kerberos protocol for trust and authentication, a Windows XP domain is the same thing as a Kerberos realm. Previous versions of NT used the idea of primary and backup domain controllers; now all servers in a domain are domain controllers. In addition, previous versions required the setup of one-way trusts between domains. Windows XP uses a hierarchical approach based on DNS and allows transitive trusts that can flow up and down the hierarchy. This approach reduces the number of trusts required for n domains from $n * (n - 1)$ to $O(n)$. The workstations in the domain trust the domain controller to give correct information about the access rights of each user (via the user's access token). All users retain the ability to restrict access to their own workstations, however, no matter what any domain controller may say.

22.6.5.1 Domain Trees and Forests

Because a business may have many departments and a school may have many classes, it is often necessary to manage multiple domains within a single organization. A **domain tree** is a contiguous DNS naming hierarchy for managing multiple domains. For example, *bell-labs.com* might be the root of the tree, with *research.bell-labs.com* and *pez.bell-labs.com* as children—domains *research* and *pez*. A **forest** is a set of noncontiguous names. An example would be the trees *bell-labs.com* and *lucent.com*. A forest may be made up of only one domain tree, however.

22.6.5.2 Trust Relationships

Trust relationships may be set up between domains in three ways: one-way, transitive, and cross-link. Versions of NT through 4.0 allowed only one-way trusts. A **one-way trust** is exactly what its name implies: domain A is told it can trust domain B. However, B will not trust A unless another relationship is configured. Under a **transitive trust**, if A trusts B and B trusts C, then A, B, and C all trust one another, since transitive trusts are two-way by default. Transitive trusts are enabled by default for new domains in a tree and can be configured only among domains within a forest. The third type, a **cross-link trust**, is useful to cut down on authentication traffic. Suppose that domains A and B are leaf nodes and that users in A often use resources in B. If a standard transitive trust is used, authentication requests must traverse up to the common ancestor of the two leaf nodes; but if A and B have a cross-linking trust, the authentications are sent directly to the other node.

22.6.6 Active Directory

Active Directory is the Windows XP implementation of **lightweight directory-access protocol (LDAP)** services. Active Directory stores the topology information about the domain, keeps the domain-based user and group accounts and passwords, and provides a domain-based store for technologies like **group policies** and **intellimirror**.

Administrators use group policies to establish uniform standards for desktop preferences and software. For many corporate information-technology groups, uniformity drastically reduces the cost of computing. Intellimirror is used in conjunction with group policies to specify what software should be available to each class of user, even automatically installing it on demand from a corporate server.

22.6.7 Name Resolution in TCP/IP Networks

On an IP network, **name resolution** is the process of converting a computer name to an IP address, such as resolving *www.bell-labs.com* to 135.104.1.14. Windows XP provides several methods of name resolution, including Windows Internet name service (WINS), broadcast-name resolution, domain-name system (DNS), a hosts file, and an LMHOSTS file. Most of these methods are used by many operating systems, so we describe only WINS here.

Under WINS, two or more WINS servers maintain a dynamic database of name-to-IP address bindings, along with client software to query the servers. At least two servers are used, so that the WINS service can survive a server failure and so that the name-resolution workload can be spread over multiple machines.

WINS uses the dynamic host-configuration protocol (DHCP). DHCP updates address configurations automatically in the WINS database, without user or administrator intervention, as follows. When a DHCP client starts up, it broadcasts a `discover` message. Each DHCP server that receives the message replies with an `offer` message that contains an IP address and configuration information for the client. The client chooses one of the configurations and sends a `request` message to the selected DHCP server. The DHCP server responds with the IP address and configuration information it gave previously and with a **lease** for that address. The lease gives the client the right to use the IP address for a specified period of time. When the lease time is half expired, the client attempts to renew the lease for the address. If the lease is not renewed, the client must obtain a new one.

22.7 Programmer Interface

The Win32 API is the fundamental interface to the capabilities of Windows XP. This section describes five main aspects of the Win32 API: access to kernel objects, sharing of objects between processes, process management, interprocess communication, and memory management.

```
SECURITY_ATTRIBUTES sa;
sa.nlength = sizeof(sa);
sa.lpSecurityDescriptor = NULL;
sa.bInheritHandle = TRUE;
Handle a_semaphore = CreateSemaphore(&sa, 1, 1, NULL);
char comand_line[132];
ostrstream ostring(command_line, sizeof(command_line));
ostring << a_semaphore << ends;
CreateProcess("another_process.exe", command_line,
    NULL, NULL, TRUE, . . .);
```

Figure 22.11 Code enabling a child to share an object by inheriting a handle.

22.7.1 Access to Kernel Objects

The Windows XP kernel provides many services that application programs can use. Application programs obtain these services by manipulating kernel objects. A process gains access to a kernel object named XXX by calling the CreateXXX function to open a handle to XXX. This handle is unique to the process. Depending on which object is being opened, if the Create() function fails, it may return 0, or it may return a special constant named INVALID_HANDLE_VALUE. A process can close any handle by calling the CloseHandle() function, and the system may delete the object if the count of processes using the object drops to 0.

22.7.2 Sharing Objects between Processes

Windows XP provides three ways to share objects between processes. The first way is for a child process to inherit a handle to the object. When the parent calls the CreateXXX function, the parent supplies a SECURITIES_ATTRIBUTES structure with the bInheritHandle field set to TRUE. This field creates an inheritable handle. Next, the child process is created, passing a value of TRUE to the CreateProcess() function's bInheritHandle argument. Figure 22.11 shows a code sample that creates a semaphore handle inherited by a child process.

Assuming the child process knows which handles are shared, the parent and child can achieve interprocess communication through the shared objects. In the example in Figure 22.11, the child process gets the value of the handle from the first command-line argument and then shares the semaphore with the parent process.

The second way to share objects is for one process to give the object a name when the object is created and for the second process to open the name. This method has two drawbacks: Windows XP does not provide a way to check whether an object with the chosen name already exists, and the object name space is global, without regard to the object type. For instance, two applications may create an object named *pipe* when two distinct—and possibly different—objects are desired.

Named objects have the advantage that unrelated processes can readily share them. The first process calls one of the CreateXXX functions and supplies a name in the lpszName parameter. The second process gets a handle to share

```
// Process A
. . .
HANDLE a_semaphore = CreateSemaphore(NULL, 1, 1, "MySEM1");
. . .
// Process B
. . .
HANDLE b_semaphore = OpenSemaphore(SEMAPHORE_ALL_ACCESS,
  FALSE, "MySEM1");
. . .
```

Figure 22.12 Code for sharing an object by name lookup.

the object by calling OpenXXX() (or CreateXXX) with the same name, as shown in the example of Figure 22.12.

The third way to share objects is via the DuplicateHandle() function. This method requires some other method of interprocess communication to pass the duplicated handle. Given a handle to a process and the value of a handle within that process, a second process can get a handle to the same object and thus share it. An example of this method is shown in Figure 22.13.

22.7.3 Process Management

In Windows XP, a **process** is an executing instance of an application, and a **thread** is a unit of code that can be scheduled by the operating system. Thus, a process contains one or more threads. A process is started when some other process calls the CreateProcess() routine. This routine loads any dynamic link libraries used by the process and creates a **primary thread**. Additional threads can be created by the CreateThread() function. Each

```
// Process A wants to give Process B access to a semaphore

// Process A
HANDLE a_semaphore = CreateSemaphore(NULL, 1, 1, NULL);
// send the value of the semaphore to Process B
// using a message or shared memory object
. . .

// Process B
HANDLE process_a = OpenProcess(PROCESS_ALL_ACCESS, FALSE,
   process_id_of_A);
HANDLE b_semaphore;
DuplicateHandle(process_a, a_semaphore,
  GetCurrentProcess(), &b_semaphore,
  0, FALSE, DUPLICATE_SAME_ACCESS);
// use b_semaphore to access the semaphore
. . .
```

Figure 22.13 Code for sharing an object by passing a handle.

thread is created with its own stack, which defaults to 1 MB unless specified otherwise in an argument to CreateThread(). Because some C run-time functions maintain state in static variables, such as errno, a multithread application needs to guard against unsynchronized access. The wrapper function beginthreadex() provides appropriate synchronization.

22.7.3.1 Instance Handles

Every dynamic link library or executable file loaded into the address space of a process is identified by an instance handle. The value of the instance handle is actually the virtual address where the file is loaded. An application can get the handle to a module in its address space by passing the name of the module to GetModuleHandle(). If NULL is passed as the name, the base address of the process is returned. The lowest 64 KB of the address space are not used, so a faulty program that tries to de-reference a NULL pointer gets an access violation.

Priorities in the Win32 API environment are based on the Windows XP scheduling model, but not all priority values may be chosen. Win32 API uses four priority classes:

1. IDLE_PRIORITY_CLASS (priority level 4)
2. NORMAL_PRIORITY_CLASS (priority level 8)
3. HIGH_PRIORITY_CLASS (priority level 13)
4. REALTIME_PRIORITY_CLASS (priority level 24)

Processes are typically members of the NORMAL_PRIORITY_CLASS unless the parent of the process was of the IDLE_PRIORITY_CLASS or another class was specified when CreateProcess was called. The priority class of a process can be changed with the SetPriorityClass() function or by passing of an argument to the START command. For example, the command START /REALTIME cbserver.exe would run the cbserver program in the REALTIME_PRIORITY_CLASS. Only users with the *increase scheduling priority* privilege can move a process into the REALTIME_PRIORITY_CLASS. Administrators and power users have this privilege by default.

22.7.3.2 Scheduling Rule

When a user is running an interactive program, the system needs to provide especially good performance for the process. For this reason, Windows XP has a special scheduling rule for processes in the NORMAL_PRIORITY_CLASS. Windows XP distinguishes between the foreground process that is currently selected on the screen and the background processes that are not currently selected. When a process moves into the foreground, Windows XP increases the scheduling quantum by some factor—typically by 3. (This factor can be changed via the performance option in the system section of the control panel.) This increase gives the foreground process three times longer to run before a time-sharing preemption occurs.

22.7.3.3 Thread Priorities

A thread starts with an initial priority determined by its class. The priority can be altered by the SetThreadPriority() function. This function takes an argument that specifies a priority relative to the base priority of its class:

- THREAD_PRIORITY_LOWEST: base − 2
- THREAD_PRIORITY_BELOW_NORMAL: base − 1
- THREAD_PRIORITY_NORMAL: base + 0
- THREAD_PRIORITY_ABOVE_NORMAL: base + 1
- THREAD_PRIORITY_HIGHEST: base + 2

Two other designations are also used to adjust the priority. Recall from Section 22.3.2.1 that the kernel has two priority classes: 16–31 for the real-time class and 0–15 for the variable-priority class. THREAD_PRIORITY_IDLE sets the priority to 16 for real-time threads and to 1 for variable-priority threads. THREAD_PRIORITY_TIME_CRITICAL sets the priority to 31 for real-time threads and to 15 for variable-priority threads.

As we discussed in Section 22.3.2.1, the kernel adjusts the priority of a thread dynamically depending on whether the thread is I/O bound or CPU bound. The Win32 API provides a method to disable this adjustment via SetProcessPriorityBoost() and SetThreadPriorityBoost() functions.

22.7.3.4 Thread Synchronization

A thread can be created in a **suspended state**; the thread does not execute until another thread makes it eligible via the ResumeThread() function. The SuspendThread() function does the opposite. These functions set a counter so that if a thread is suspended twice, it must be resumed twice before it can run. To synchronize the concurrent access to shared objects by threads, the kernel provides synchronization objects, such as semaphores and mutexes.

In addition, synchronization of threads can be achieved by use of the WaitForSingleObject() and WaitForMultipleObjects() functions. Another method of synchronization in the Win32 API is the critical section. A critical section is a synchronized region of code that can be executed by only one thread at a time. A thread establishes a critical section by calling InitializeCriticalSection(). The application must call EnterCriticalSection() before entering the critical section and LeaveCriticalSection() after exiting. These two routines guarantee that, if multiple threads attempt to enter the critical section concurrently, only one thread at a time will be permitted to proceed; the others will wait in the EnterCriticalSection() routine. The critical-section mechanism is faster than using kernel-synchronization objects because it does not allocate kernel objects until it first encounters contention for the critical section.

22.7.3.5 Fibers

A **fiber** is user-mode code that is scheduled according to a user-defined scheduling algorithm. A process may have multiple fibers in it, just as it may have multiple threads. A major difference between threads and fibers is that whereas threads can execute concurrently, only one fiber at a time is permitted to execute, even on multiprocessor hardware. This mechanism is included in Windows XP to facilitate the porting of those legacy UNIX applications that were written for a fiber-execution model.

The system creates a fiber by calling either `ConvertThreadToFiber()` or `CreateFiber()`. The primary difference between these functions is that `CreateFiber()` does not begin executing the fiber that was created. To begin execution, the application must call `SwitchToFiber()`. The application can terminate a fiber by calling `DeleteFiber()`.

22.7.3.6 Thread Pool

Repeated creation and deletion of threads can be expensive for applications and services that perform small amounts of work in each instantiation. The thread pool provides user-mode programs with three services: a queue to which work requests may be submitted (via the `QueueUserWorkItem()` API), an API that can be used to bind callbacks to waitable handles (`RegisterWaitForSingleObject()`), and APIs to bind callbacks to timeouts (`CreateTimerQueue()` and `CreateTimerQueueTimer()`).

The thread pool's goal is to increase performance. Threads are relatively expensive, and a processor can only be executing one thing at a time no matter how many threads are used. The thread pool attempts to reduce the number of outstanding threads by slightly delaying work requests (reusing each thread for many requests) while providing enough threads to effectively utilize the machine's CPUs. The wait and timer-callback APIs allow the thread pool to further reduce the number of threads in a process, using far fewer threads than would be necessary if a process were to devote one thread to servicing each waitable handle or timeout.

22.7.4 Interprocess Communication

Win32 API applications handle interprocess communication in several ways. One way is by sharing kernel objects. Another way is by passing messages, an approach that is particularly popular for Windows GUI applications. One thread can send a message to another thread or to a window by calling `PostMessage()`, `PostThreadMessage()`, `SendMessage()`, `SendThreadMessage()`, or `SendMessageCallback()`. *Posting* a message and *sending* a message differ in this way: The post routines are asynchronous; they return immediately, and the calling thread does not know when the message is actually delivered. The send routines are synchronous; they block the caller until the message has been delivered and processed.

In addition to sending a message, a thread can send data with the message. Since processes have separate address spaces, the data must be copied. The system copies data by calling `SendMessage()` to send a message of type `WM_COPYDATA` with a `COPYDATASTRUCT` data structure that contains the length and address of the data to be transferred. When the message is sent, Windows XP copies the data to a new block of memory and gives the virtual address of the new block to the receiving process.

Unlike threads in the 16-bit Windows environment, every Win32 API thread has its own input queue from which it receives messages. (All input is received

```
// allocate 16 MB at the top of our address space
void *buf = VirtualAlloc(0, 0x1000000, MEM_RESERVE | MEM_TOP_DOWN,
   PAGE_READWRITE);
// commit the upper 8 MB of the allocated space
VirtualAlloc(buf + 0x800000, 0x800000, MEM_COMMIT, PAGE_READWRITE);
// do something with the memory
. . .
// now decommit the memory
VirtualFree(buf + 0x800000, 0x800000, MEM_DECOMMIT);
// release all of the allocated address space
VirtualFree(buf, 0, MEM_RELEASE);
```

Figure 22.14 Code fragments for allocating virtual memory.

via messages.) This structure is more reliable than the shared input queue of 16-bit Windows, because, with separate queues, it is no longer possible for one stuck application to block input to the other applications. If a Win32 API application does not call `GetMessage()` to handle events on its input queue, the queue fills up; and after about five seconds, the system marks the application as "Not Responding".

22.7.5 Memory Management

The Win32 API provides several ways for an application to use memory: virtual memory, memory-mapped files, heaps, and thread-local storage.

22.7.5.1 Virtual Memory

An application calls `VirtualAlloc()` to reserve or commit virtual memory and `VirtualFree()` to decommit or release the memory. These functions enable the application to specify the virtual address at which the memory is allocated. They operate on multiples of the memory page size, and the starting address of an allocated region must be greater than 0x10000. Examples of these functions appear in Figure 22.14.

A process may lock some of its committed pages into physical memory by calling `VirtualLock()`. The maximum number of pages a process can lock is 30, unless the process first calls `SetProcessWorkingSetSize()` to increase the maximum working-set size.

22.7.5.2 Memory-Mapping Files

Another way for an application to use memory is by memory-mapping a file into its address space. Memory mapping is also a convenient way for two processes to share memory: both processes map the same file into their virtual memory. Memory mapping is a multistage process, as you can see in the example in Figure 22.15.

If a process wants to map some address space just to share a memory region with another process, no file is needed. The process calls `Create-FileMapping()` with a file handle of `0xffffffff` and a particular size. The resulting file-mapping object can be shared by inheritance, by name lookup, or by duplication.

```
// open the file or create it if it does not exist
HANDLE hfile = CreateFile("somefile", GENERIC_READ | GENERIC_WRITE,
   FILE_SHARE_READ | FILE_SHARE_WRITE, NULL,
   OPEN_ALWAYS, FILE_ATTRIBUTE_NORMAL, NULL);
// create the file mapping 8 MB in size
HANDLE hmap = CreateFileMapping(hfile, PAGE_READWRITE,
   SEC_COMMIT, 0, 0x800000, "SHM_1");
// now get a view of the space mapped
void *buf = MapViewOfFile(hmap, FILE_MAP_ALL_ACCESS,
   0, 0, 0, 0x800000);
// do something with the mapped file
. . .
// now unmap the file
UnMapViewOfFile(buf);
CloseHandle(hmap);
CloseHandle(hfile);
```

Figure 22.15 Code fragments for memory mapping of a file.

22.7.5.3 Heaps

Heaps provide a third way for applications to use memory. A heap in the Win32 environment is a region of reserved address space. When a Win32 API process is initialized, it is created with a 1-MB **default heap**. Since many Win32 API functions use the default heap, access to the heap is synchronized to protect the heap's space-allocation data structures from being damaged by concurrent updates by multiple threads.

Win32 API provides several heap-management functions so that a process can allocate and manage a private heap. These functions are `HeapCreate()`, `HeapAlloc()`, `HeapRealloc()`, `HeapSize()`, `HeapFree()`, and `HeapDestroy()`. The Win32 API also provides the `HeapLock()` and `HeapUnlock()` functions to enable a thread to gain exclusive access to a heap. Unlike `VirtualLock()`, these functions perform only synchronization; they do not lock pages into physical memory.

22.7.5.4 Thread-Local Storage

The fourth way for applications to use memory is through a thread-local storage mechanism. Functions that rely on global or static data typically fail to work properly in a multithreaded environment. For instance, the C run-time function `strtok()` uses a static variable to keep track of its current position while parsing a string. For two concurrent threads to execute `strtok()` correctly, they need separate *current position* variables. The thread-local storage mechanism allocates global storage on a per-thread basis. It provides both dynamic and static methods of creating thread-local storage. The dynamic method is illustrated in Figure 22.16.

To use a thread-local static variable, the application declares the variable as follows to ensure that every thread has its own private copy:

```
_declspec(thread) DWORD cur_pos = 0;
```

```
// reserve a slot for a variable
DWORD var_index = T1sAlloc();
// set it to the value 10
T1sSetValue(var_index, 10);
// get the value
int var T1sGetValue(var_index);
// release the index
T1sFree(var_index);
```

Figure 22.16 Code for dynamic thread-local storage.

22.8 Summary

Microsoft designed Windows XP to be an extensible, portable operating system —one able to take advantage of new techniques and hardware. Windows XP supports multiple operating environments and symmetric multiprocessing, including both 32-bit and 64-bit processors and NUMA computers. The use of kernel objects to provide basic services, along with support for client–server computing, enables Windows XP to support a wide variety of application environments. For instance, Windows XP can run programs compiled for MS-DOS, Win16, Windows 95, Windows XP, and POSIX. It provides virtual memory, integrated caching, and preemptive scheduling. Windows XP supports a security model stronger than those of previous Microsoft operating systems and includes internationalization features. Windows XP runs on a wide variety of computers, so users can choose and upgrade hardware to match their budgets and performance requirements without needing to alter the applications they run.

Exercises

22.1 Describe the booting process for a Windows XP system.

22.2 What is a process, and how is it managed in Windows XP?

22.3 Describe some of the ways in which an application can use memory via the Windows32 API.

22.4 Describe a useful application of the no-access page facility provided in Windows XP.

22.5 Under what circumstances would one use the deferred procedure calls facility in Windows XP?

22.6 Describe the three main architectural layers of Windows XP.

22.7 What is the purpose of the Win16 execution environment? What limitations are imposed on the programs executing inside this environment? What are the protection guarantees provided between different applications executing inside the Win16 environment? What are the protection guarantees provided between an application executing inside the Win16 environment and a 32-bit application?

22.8 What is the fiber abstraction provided by Windows XP? How does it differ from the threads abstraction?

22.9 Describe two user-mode processes that enable Windows XP to run programs developed for other operating systems.

22.10 Describe the management scheme of the virtual memory manager. How does the VM manager improve performance?

22.11 Describe the three techniques used for communicating data in a local procedure call. What settings are most conducive to the application of the different message-passing techniques?

22.12 How does NTFS handle data structures? How does NTFS recover from a system crash? What is guaranteed after a recovery takes place?

22.13 Describe two user-mode processes that Windows XP provides to enable it to run programs developed for other operating systems.

22.14 What is the job of the object manager?

22.15 The IA64 processors contain registers that can be used to address a 64-bit address space. However, Windows XP limits the address space of user programs to 8 TB, which corresponds to 43 bits' worth. Why was this decision made?

22.16 How does the NTFS directory structure differ from the directory structure used in UNIX operating systems?

22.17 What are the responsibilities of the I/O manager?

22.18 What manages caching in Windows XP? How is caching managed?

22.19 What is a handle, and how does a process obtain a handle?

Bibliographical Notes

Solomon and Russinovich [2000] give an overview of Windows XP and considerable technical detail about system internals and components. Tate [2000] is a good reference on using Windows XP. The Microsoft Windows XP Server Resource Kit (Microsoft [2000b]) is a six-volume set helpful for using and deploying Windows XP. The Microsoft Developer Network Library (Microsoft [2000a]), issued quarterly, supplies a wealth of information on Windows XP and other Microsoft products.

Iseminger [2000] provides a good reference on the Windows XP Active Directory. Richter [1997] gives a detailed discussion on writing programs that use the Win32 API. Silberschatz et al. [2001] contains a good discussion of B+ trees.

Influential Operating Systems

CHAPTER 23

Now that you understand the fundamental concepts of operating systems (CPU scheduling, memory management, processes, and so on), we are in a position to examine how these concepts have been applied in several older and highly influential operating systems. Some of them (such as the XDS-940 and the THE system) were one-of-a-kind systems; others (such as OS/360) are widely used. The order of presentation highlights the similarities and differences of the systems; it is not strictly chronological or ordered by importance. The serious student of operating systems should be familiar with all these systems.

As we describe early systems, we include references to further reading. The papers, written by the designers of the systems, are important both for their technical content and for their style and flavor.

CHAPTER OBJECTIVES

- To explain how operating-system features migrate over time from large computer systems to smaller ones.
- To discuss the features of several historically important operating systems.

23.1 Feature Migration

One reason to study early architectures and operating systems is that a feature that once ran only on huge systems may eventually have made its way into very small systems. Indeed, an examination of operating systems for mainframes and microcomputers shows that many features once available only on mainframes have been adopted for microcomputers. The same operating-system concepts are thus appropriate for various classes of computers: mainframes, minicomputers, microcomputers, and handhelds. To understand modern operating systems, then, you need to recognize the theme of feature migration and the long history of many operating-system features, as shown in figure 23.1.

A good example of feature migration started with the Multiplexed Information and Computing Services (MULTICS) operating system. MULTICS was developed from 1965 to 1970 at the Massachusetts Institute of Technology () as

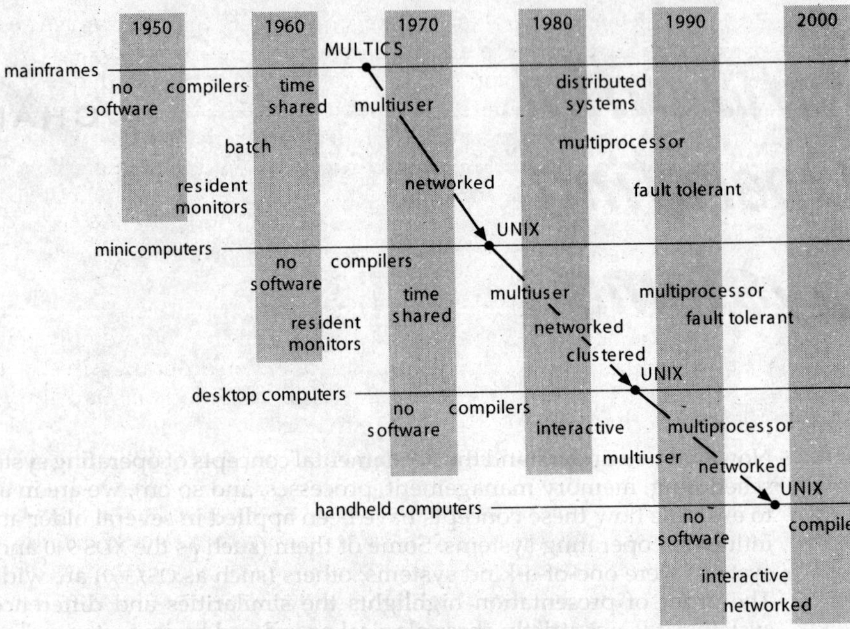

Figure 23.1 Migration of operating-system concepts and features.

a computing **utility**. It ran on a large, complex mainframe computer (the GE 645). Many of the ideas that were developed for MULTICS were subsequently used at Bell Laboratories (one of the original partners in the development of MULTICS) in the design of UNIX. The UNIX operating system was designed around 1970 for a PDP-11 minicomputer. Around 1980, the features of UNIX became the basis for UNIX-like operating systems on microcomputers; and these features are included in several more recent operating systems for microcomputers, such as Microsoft Windows, Windows XP, and the Mac OS X operating system. Linux includes some of these same features, and they can now be found on PDAs.

23.2 Early Systems

We turn our attention now to a historical overview of early computer systems. We should note that the history of computing starts far before "computers" with looms and calculators, as described in Frah [2001] and shown graphically in Frauenfelder [2005]. We begin our discussion, however, with the computers of the twentieth century.

Before the 1940s, computing devices were designed and implemented to perform specific, fixed tasks. Modifying one of those tasks required a great deal of effort and manual labor. All that changed in the 1940s when Alan Turing and John von Neumann (and colleagues), both separately and together, worked on the idea of a more general-purpose **stored program** computer. Such a machine has both a program store and a data store, where the program store provides instructions about what to do to the data.

This fundamental computer concept quickly generated a number of general-purpose computers, but much of the history of these machines is blurred by time and the secrecy of their development during World War II. It is likely that the first working stored-program general-purpose computer was the Manchester Mark 1, which ran successfully in 1949. The first commercial computer was its offspring, the Ferranti Mark 1, which went on sale in 1951. These early computing efforts are described by Rojas and Hashagen [2000] and Ceruzzi [1998].

Early computers were physically enormous machines run from consoles. The programmer, who was also the operator of the computer system, would write a program and then would operate the program directly from the operator's console. First, the program would be loaded manually into memory from the front panel switches (one instruction at a time), from paper tape, or from punched cards. Then the appropriate buttons would be pushed to set the starting address and to start the execution of the program. As the program ran, the programmer/operator could monitor its execution by the display lights on the console. If errors were discovered, the programmer could halt the program, examine the contents of memory and registers, and debug the program directly from the console. Output was printed or was punched onto paper tape or cards for later printing.

23.2.1 Dedicated Computer Systems

As time went on, additional software and hardware were developed. Card readers, line printers, and magnetic tape became commonplace. Assemblers, loaders, and linkers were designed to ease the programming task. Libraries of common functions were created. Common functions could then be copied into a new program without having to be written again, providing software reusability.

The routines that performed I/O were especially important. Each new I/O device had its own characteristics, requiring careful programming. A special subroutine—called a device driver—was written for each I/O device. A device driver knows how the buffers, flags, registers, control bits, and status bits for a particular device should be used. Each type of device has its own driver. A simple task, such as reading a character from a paper-tape reader, might involve complex sequences of device-specific operations. Rather than writing the necessary code every time, the device driver was simply used from the library.

Later, compilers for FORTRAN, COBOL, and other languages appeared, making the programming task much easier but the operation of the computer more complex. To prepare a FORTRAN program for execution, for example, the programmer would first need to load the FORTRAN compiler into the computer. The compiler was normally kept on magnetic tape, so the proper tape would need to be mounted on a tape drive. The program would be read through the card reader and written onto another tape. The FORTRAN compiler produced assembly-language output, which then had to be assembled. This procedure required mounting another tape with the assembler. The output of the assembler would need to be linked to supporting library routines. Finally, the binary object form of the program would be ready to execute. It could be loaded into memory and debugged from the console, as before.

A significant amount of **set-up time** could be involved in the running of a job. Each job consisted of many separate steps:

1. Loading the FORTRAN compiler tape
2. Running the compiler
3. Unloading the compiler tape
4. Loading the assembler tape
5. Running the assembler
6. Unloading the assembler tape
7. Loading the object program
8. Running the object program

If an error occurred during any step, the programmer/operator might have to start over at the beginning. Each job step might involve the loading and unloading of magnetic tapes, paper tapes, and punch cards.

The job set-up time was a real problem. While tapes were being mounted or the programmer was operating the console, the CPU sat idle. Remember that, in the early days, few computers were available, and they were expensive. A computer might have cost millions of dollars, not including the operational costs of power, cooling, programmers, and so on. Thus, computer time was extremely valuable, and owners wanted their computers to be used as much as possible. They needed high **utilization** to get as much as they could from their investments.

23.2.2 Shared Computer Systems

The solution was twofold. First, a professional computer operator was hired. The programmer no longer operated the machine. As soon as one job was finished, the operator could start the next. Since the operator had more experience with mounting tapes than a programmer, set-up time was reduced. The programmer provided whatever cards or tapes were needed, as well as a short description of how the job was to be run. Of course, the operator could not debug an incorrect program at the console, since the operator would not understand the program. Therefore, in the case of program error, a dump of memory and registers was taken, and the programmer had to debug from the dump. Dumping the memory and registers allowed the operator to continue immediately with the next job but left the programmer with the more difficult debugging problem.

Second, jobs with similar needs were batched together and run through the computer as a group to reduce set-up time. For instance, suppose the operator received one FORTRAN job, one COBOL job, and another FORTRAN job. If she ran them in that order, she would have to set up for FORTRAN (load the compiler tapes and so on), then set up for COBOL, and then set up for FORTRAN again. If she ran the two FORTRAN programs as a batch, however, she could set up only once for FORTRAN, saving operator time.

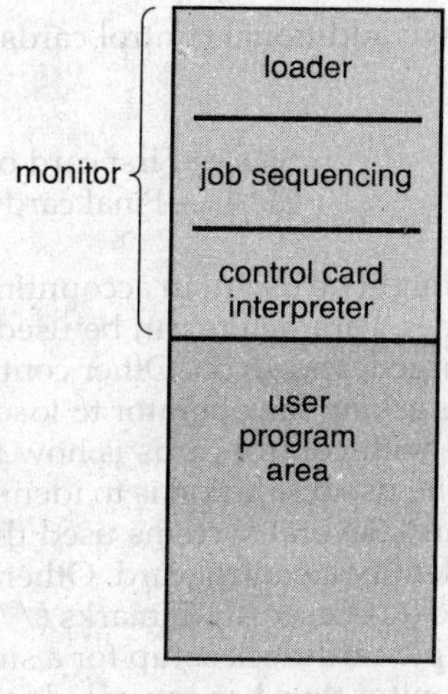

Figure 23.2 Memory layout for a resident monitor.

But there were still problems. For example, when a job stopped, the operator would have to notice that it had stopped (by observing the console), determine *why* it stopped (normal or abnormal termination), dump memory and register (if necessary), load the appropriate device with the next job, and restart the computer. During this transition from one job to the next, the CPU sat idle.

To overcome this idle time, people developed **automatic job sequencing**; with this technique, the first rudimentary operating systems were created. A small program, called a **resident monitor**, was created to transfer control automatically from one job to the next (Figure 23.2). The resident monitor is always in memory (or *resident*).

When the computer was turned on, the resident monitor was invoked, and it would transfer control to a program. When the program terminated, it would return control to the resident monitor, which would then go on to the next program. Thus, the resident monitor would automatically sequence from one program to another and from one job to another.

But how would the resident monitor know which program to execute? Previously, the operator had been given a short description of what programs were to be run on what data. **Control cards** were introduced to provide this information directly to the monitor. The idea is simple. In addition to the program or data for a job, the programmer included the control cards, which contained directives to the resident monitor indicating what program to run. For example, a normal user program might require one of three programs to run: the FORTRAN compiler (FTN), the assembler (ASM), or the user's program (RUN). We could use a separate control card for each of these:

$FTN—Execute the FORTRAN compiler.
$ASM—Execute the assembler.
$RUN—Execute the user program.

These cards tell the resident monitor which program to run.

We can use two additional control cards to define the boundaries of each job:

$JOB—First card of a job
$END—Final card of a job

These two cards might be useful in accounting for the machine resources used by the programmer. Parameters can be used to define the job name, account number to be charged, and so on. Other control cards can be defined for other functions, such as asking the operator to load or unload a tape.

One problem with control cards is how to distinguish them from data or program cards. The usual solution is to identify them by a special character or pattern on the card. Several systems used the dollar-sign character ($) in the first column to identify a control card. Others used a different code. IBM's Job Control Language (JCL) used slash marks (//) in the first two columns. Figure 23.3 shows a sample card-deck setup for a simple batch system.

A resident monitor thus has several identifiable parts:

- The **control-card interpreter** is responsible for reading and carrying out the instructions on the cards at the point of execution.
- The **loader** is invoked by the control-card interpreter to load system programs and application programs into memory at intervals.
- The **device drivers** are used by both the control-card interpreter and the loader for the system's I/O devices. Often, the system and application programs are linked to these same device drivers, providing continuity in their operation, as well as saving memory space and programming time.

These batch systems work fairly well. The resident monitor provides automatic job sequencing as indicated by the control cards. When a control card indicates that a program is to be run, the monitor loads the program into memory and transfers control to it. When the program completes, it

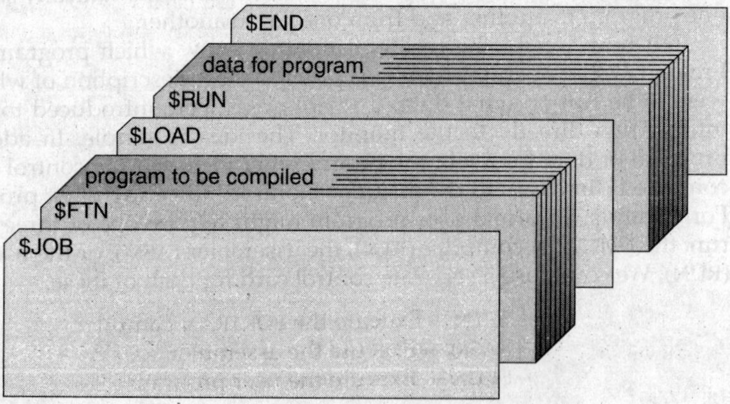

Figure 23.3 Card deck for a simple batch system.

transfers control back to the monitor, which reads the next control card, loads the appropriate program, and so on. This cycle is repeated until all control cards are interpreted for the job. Then the monitor automatically continues with the next job.

The switch to batch systems with automatic job sequencing was made to improve performance. The problem, quite simply, is that humans are considerably slower than the computer. Consequently, it is desirable to replace human operation with operating-system software. Automatic job sequencing eliminates the need for human set-up time and job sequencing.

Even with this arrangement, however, the CPU is often idle. The problem is the speed of the mechanical I/O devices, which are intrinsically slower than electronic devices. Even a slow CPU works in the microsecond range, with thousands of instructions executed per second. A fast card reader, in contrast, might read 1,200 cards per minute (or 20 cards per second). Thus, the difference in speed between the CPU and its I/O devices may be three orders of magnitude or more. Over time, of course, improvements in technology resulted in faster I/O devices. Unfortunately, CPU speeds increased even faster, so that the problem was not only unresolved but also exacerbated.

23.2.3 Overlapped I/O

One common solution to the I/O problem was to replace slow card readers (input devices) and line printers (output devices) with magnetic-tape units. Most computer systems in the late 1950s and early 1960s were batch systems reading from card readers and writing to line printers or card punches. The CPU did not read directly from cards, however; instead, the cards were first copied onto a magnetic tape via a separate device. When the tape was sufficiently full, it was taken down and carried over to the computer. When a card was needed for input to a program, the equivalent record was read from the tape. Similarly, output was written to the tape, and the contents of the tape were printed later. The card readers and line printers were operated *off-line*, rather than by the main computer (Figure 23.4).

An obvious advantage of off-line operation was that the main computer was no longer constrained by the speed of the card readers and line printers but was limited only by the speed of the much faster magnetic tape units.

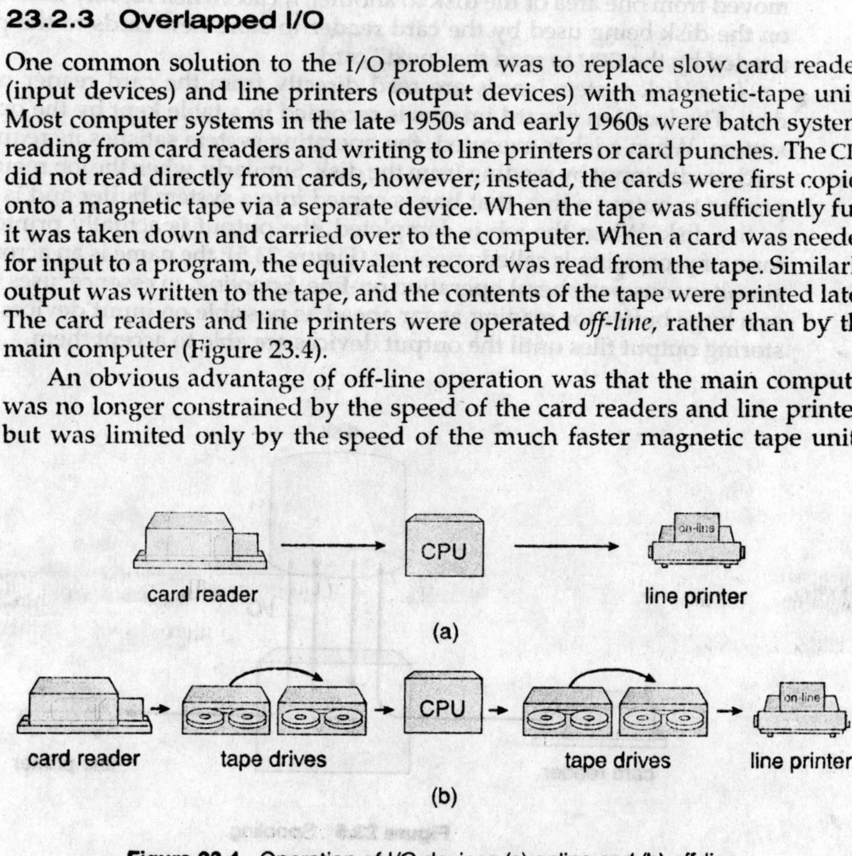

Figure 23.4 Operation of I/O devices (a) online and (b) off-line.

The technique of using magnetic tape for all I/O could be applied with any similar equipment (such as card readers, card punches, plotters, paper tape, and printers).

The real gain in off-line operation comes from the possibility of using multiple reader-to-tape and tape-to-printer systems for one CPU. If the CPU can process input twice as fast as the reader can read cards, then two readers working simultaneously can produce enough tape to keep the CPU busy. There is a disadvantage, too, however—a longer delay in getting a particular job run. The job must first be read onto tape. Then it must wait until enough additional jobs are read onto the tape to "fill" it. The tape must then be rewound, unloaded, hand-carried to the CPU, and mounted on a free tape drive. This process is not unreasonable for batch systems, of course. Many similar jobs can be batched onto a tape before it is taken to the computer.

Although off-line preparation of jobs continued for some time, it was quickly replaced in most systems. Disk systems became widely available and greatly improved on off-line operation. The problem with tape systems was that the card reader could not write onto one end of the tape while the CPU read from the other. The entire tape had to be written before it was rewound and read, because tapes are by nature **sequential-access devices**. Disk systems eliminated this problem by being **random-access devices**. Because the head is moved from one area of the disk to another, it can switch rapidly from the area on the disk being used by the card reader to store new cards to the position needed by the CPU to read the "next" card.

In a disk system, cards are read directly from the card reader onto the disk. The location of card images is recorded in a table kept by the operating system. When a job is executed, the operating system satisfies its requests for card-reader input by reading from the disk. Similarly, when the job requests the printer to output a line, that line is copied into a system buffer and is written to the disk. When the job is completed, the output is actually printed. This form of processing is called **spooling** (Figure 23.5); the name is an acronym for simultaneous peripheral operation on-line. Spooling, in essence, uses the disk as a huge buffer for reading as far ahead as possible on input devices and for storing output files until the output devices are able to accept them.

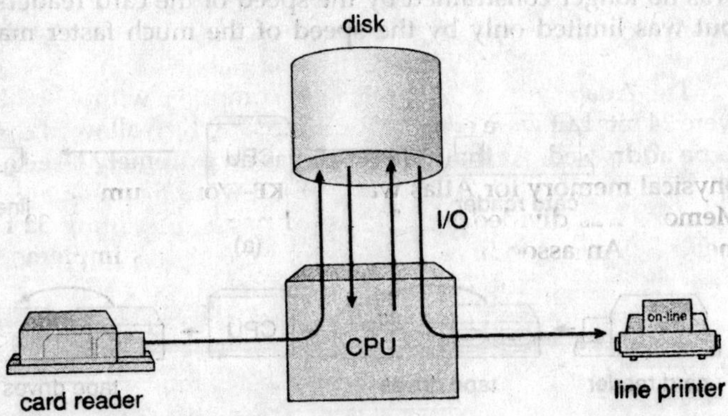

Figure 23.5 Spooling.

Spooling is also used for processing data at remote sites. The CPU sends the data via communication paths to a remote printer (or accepts an entire input job from a remote card reader). The remote processing is done at its own speed, with no CPU intervention. The CPU just needs to be notified when the processing is completed, so that it can spool the next batch of data.

Spooling overlaps the I/O of one job with the computation of other jobs. Even in a simple system, the spooler may be reading the input of one job while printing the output of a different job. During this time, still another job (or other jobs) may be executed, reading its "cards" from disk and "printing" its output lines onto the disk.

Spooling has a direct beneficial effect on the performance of the system. For the cost of some disk space and a few tables, the computation of one job and the I/O of other jobs can take place at the same time. Thus, spooling can keep both the CPU and the I/O devices working at much higher rates. Spooling leads naturally to multiprogramming, which is the foundation of all modern operating systems.

23.3 Atlas

The Atlas operating system (Kilburn et al. [1961], Howarth et al. [1961]) was designed at the University of Manchester in England in the late 1950s and early 1960s. Many of its basic features that were novel at the time have become standard parts of modern operating systems. Device drivers were a major part of the system. In addition, system calls were added by a set of special instructions called *extra codes*.

Atlas was a batch operating system with spooling. Spooling allowed the system to schedule jobs according to the availability of peripheral devices, such as magnetic tape units, paper tape readers, paper tape punches, line printers, card readers, and card punches.

The most remarkable feature of Atlas, however, was its memory management. Core memory was new and expensive at the time. Many computers, like the IBM 650, used a drum for primary memory. The Atlas system used a drum for its main memory, but it had a small amount of core memory that was used as a cache for the drum. Demand paging was used to transfer information between core memory and the drum automatically.

The Atlas system used a British computer with 48-bit words. Addresses were 24 bits but were encoded in decimal, which allowed only 1 million words to be addressed. At that time, this was an extremely large address space. The physical memory for Atlas was a 98-KB-word drum and 16-KB words of core. Memory was divided into 512-word pages, providing 32 frames in physical memory. An associative memory of 32 registers implemented the mapping from a virtual address to a physical address.

If a page fault occurred, a page-replacement algorithm was invoked. One memory frame was always kept empty, so that a drum transfer could start immediately. The page-replacement algorithm attempted to predict future memory-accessing behavior based on past behavior. A reference bit for each frame was set whenever the frame was accessed. The reference bits were read into memory every 1,024 instructions, and the last 32 values of these bits were retained. This history was used to define the time since the most recent reference (t_1) and the interval between the last two references (t_2). Pages were chosen for replacement in the following order:

1. Any page with $t_1 > t_2 + 1$; such a page is considered to be no longer in use.
2. If $t_1 \leq t_2$ for all pages, then replace the page with the largest $t_2 - t_1$.

The page-replacement algorithm assumes that programs access memory in loops. If the time between the last two references is t_2, then another reference is expected t_2 time units later. If a reference does not occur ($t_1 > t_2$), it is assumed that the page is no longer being used, and the page is replaced. If all pages are still in use, then the page that will not be needed for the longest time is replaced. The time to the next reference is expected to be $t_2 - t_1$.

23.4 XDS-940

The XDS-940 operating system (Lichtenberger and Pirtle [1965]) was designed at the University of California at Berkeley. Like the Atlas system, it used paging for memory management. Unlike the Atlas system, it was a time-shared system. The paging was used only for relocation; it was not used for demand paging. The virtual memory of any user process was made up of 16-KB words, whereas the physical memory was made up of 64-KB words. Each page was made up of 2-KB words. The page table was kept in registers. Since physical memory was larger than virtual memory, several user processes could be in memory at the same time. The number of users could be increased by sharing of pages when the pages contained read-only reentrant code. Processes were kept on a drum and were swapped in and out of memory as necessary.

The XDS-940 system was constructed from a modified XDS-930. The modifications were typical of the changes made to a basic computer to allow an operating system to be written properly. A user-monitor mode was added. Certain instructions, such as I/O and halt, were defined to be privileged. An attempt to execute a privileged instruction in user mode would trap to the operating system.

A system-call instruction was added to the user-mode instruction set. This instruction was used to create new resources, such as files, allowing the operating system to manage the physical resources. Files, for example, were allocated in 256-word blocks on the drum. A bit map was used to manage free drum blocks. Each file had an index block with pointers to the actual data blocks. Index blocks were chained together.

The XDS-940 system also provided system calls to allow processes to create, start, suspend, and destroy subprocesses. A programmer could construct a system of processes. Separate processes could share memory for communication and synchronization. Process creation defined a tree structure, where a process is the root and its subprocesses are nodes below it in the tree. Each of the subprocesses could, in turn, create more subprocesses.

23.5 THE

The THE operating system (Dijkstra [1968], McKeag and Wilson [1976]) was designed at the Technische Hogeschool at Eindhoven in the Netherlands. It was a batch system running on a Dutch computer, the EL X8, with 32 KB of 27-bit words. The system was mainly noted for its clean design, particularly its layer structure, and its use of a set of concurrent processes employing semaphores for synchronization.

Unlike those in the XDS-940 system, however, the set of processes in the THE system was static. The operating system itself was designed as a set of cooperating processes. In addition, five user processes were created that served as the active agents to compile, execute, and print user programs. When one job was finished, the process would return to the input queue to select another job.

A priority CPU-scheduling algorithm was used. The priorities were recomputed every 2 seconds and were inversely proportional to the amount of CPU time used recently (in the last 8 to 10 seconds). This scheme gave higher priority to I/O-bound processes and to new processes.

Memory management was limited by the lack of hardware support. However, since the system was limited and user programs could be written only in Algol, a software paging scheme was used. The Algol compiler automatically generated calls to system routines, which made sure the requested information was in memory, swapping if necessary. The backing store was a 512-KB-word drum. A 512-word page was used, with an LRU page-replacement strategy.

Another major concern of the THE system was deadlock control. The banker's algorithm was used to provide deadlock avoidance.

Closely related to the THE system is the Venus system (Liskov [1972]). The Venus system was also a layer-structured design, using semaphores to synchronize processes. The lower levels of the design were implemented in microcode, however, providing a much faster system. The memory management was changed to paged-segmented memory. The system was also designed as a time-sharing system, rather than a batch system.

23.6 RC 4000

The RC 4000 system, like the THE system, was notable primarily for its design concepts. It was designed for the Danish 4000 computer by Regnecentralen, particularly by Brinch-Hansen (Brinch-Hansen [1970], Brinch-Hansen [1973]). The objective was not to design a batch system, or a time-sharing system, or any other specific system. Rather, the goal was to create an operating-system nucleus, or kernel, on which a complete operating system could be built. Thus, the system structure was layered, and only the lower levels—comprising the kernel—were provided.

The kernel supported a collection of concurrent processes. A round-robin CPU scheduler was used. Although processes could share memory, the primary communication and synchronization mechanism was the message system provided by the kernel. Processes could communicate with each other by exchanging fixed-sized messages of eight words in length. All messages were stored in buffers from a common buffer pool. When a message buffer was no longer required, it was returned to the common pool.

A message queue was associated with each process. It contained all the messages that had been sent to that process but had not yet been received. Messages were removed from the queue in FIFO order. The system supported four primitive operations, which were executed atomically:

- **send-message** (**in** *receiver*, **in** *message*, **out** *buffer*)
- **wait-message** (**out** *sender*, **out** *message*, **out** *buffer*)
- **send-answer** (**out** *result*, **in** *message*, **in** *buffer*)
- **wait-answer** (**out** *result*, **out** *message*, **in** *buffer*)

The last two operations allowed processes to exchange several messages at a time.

These primitives required that a process service its message queue in FIFO order and that it block itself while other processes were handling its messages. To remove these restrictions, the developers provided two additional communication primitives that allowed a process to wait for the arrival of the next message or to answer and service its queue in any order:

- **wait-event** (**in** *previous-buffer*, **out** *next-buffer*, **out** *result*)
- **get-event** (**out** *buffer*)

I/O devices were also treated as processes. The device drivers were code that converted the device interrupts and registers into messages. Thus, a process would write to a terminal by sending that terminal a message. The device driver would receive the message and output the character to the terminal. An input character would interrupt the system and transfer to a device driver. The device driver would create a message from the input character and send it to a waiting process.

23.7 CTSS

The Compatible Time-Sharing System (CTSS) (Corbato et al. [1962]) was designed at MIT as an experimental time-sharing system. It was implemented on an IBM 7090 and eventually supported up to 32 interactive users. The users were provided with a set of interactive commands that allowed them to manipulate files and to compile and run programs through a terminal.

The 7090 had a 32-KB memory made up of 36-bit words. The monitor used 5-KB words, leaving 27 KB for the users. User memory images were swapped between memory and a fast drum. CPU scheduling employed a multilevel-feedback-queue algorithm. The time quantum for level i was $2 * i$ time units. If a program did not finish its CPU burst in one time quantum, it was moved down to the next level of the queue, giving it twice as much time. The program at the highest level (with the shortest quantum) was run first. The initial level of a program was determined by its size, so that the time quantum was at least as long as the swap time.

CTSS was extremely successful and was in use as late as 1972. Although it was limited, it succeeded in demonstrating that time sharing was a convenient and practical mode of computing. One result of CTSS was increased development of time-sharing systems. Another result was the development of MULTICS.

23.8 MULTICS

The MULTICS operating system (Corbato and Vyssotsky [1965], Organick [1972]) was designed at MIT as a natural extension of CTSS. CTSS and other early time-sharing systems were so successful that they created an immediate desire to proceed quickly to bigger and better systems. As larger computers became available, the designers of CTSS set out to create a time-sharing utility. Computing service would be provided like electrical power. Large computer systems would be connected by telephone wires to terminals in offices and homes throughout a city. The operating system would be a time-shared system running continuously with a vast file system of shared programs and data.

MULTICS was designed by a team from MIT, GE (which later sold its computer department to Honeywell), and Bell Laboratories (which dropped out of the project in 1969). The basic GE 635 computer was modified to a new computer system called the GE 645, mainly by the addition of paged-segmentation memory hardware.

In MULTICS, a virtual address was composed of an 18-bit segment number and a 16-bit word offset. The segments were then paged in 1-KB-word pages. The second-chance page-replacement algorithm was used.

The segmented virtual address space was merged into the file system; each segment was a file. Segments were addressed by the name of the file. The file system itself was a multilevel tree structure, allowing users to create their own subdirectory structures.

Like CTSS, MULTICS used a multilevel feedback queue for CPU scheduling. Protection was accomplished through an access list associated with each file and a set of protection rings for executing processes. The system, which was written almost entirely in PL/1, comprised about 300,000 lines of code. It was extended to a multiprocessor system, allowing a CPU to be taken out of service for maintenance while the system continued running.

23.9 IBM OS/360

The longest line of operating-system development is undoubtedly that of IBM computers. The early IBM computers, such as the IBM 7090 and the IBM 7094, are prime examples of the development of common I/O subroutines, followed by development of a resident monitor, privileged instructions, memory protection, and simple batch processing. These systems were developed separately, often at independent sites. As a result, IBM was faced with many different computers, with different languages and different system software.

The IBM/360 was designed to alter this situation. The IBM/360 was designed as a family of computers spanning the complete range from small business machines to large scientific machines. Only one set of software would be needed for these systems, which all used the same operating system: OS/360 (Mealy et al. [1966]). This arrangement was intended to reduce maintenance problems for IBM and to allow users to move programs and applications freely from one IBM system to another.

Unfortunately, OS/360 tried to be all things for all people. As a result, it did none of its tasks especially well. The file system included a type field that defined the type of each file, and different file types were defined for fixed-length and variable-length records and for blocked and unblocked files. Contiguous allocation was used, so the user had to guess the size of each output file. The Job Control Language (JCL) added parameters for every possible option, making it incomprehensible to the average user.

The memory-management routines were hampered by the architecture. Although a base-register addressing mode was used, the program could access and modify the base register, so that absolute addresses were generated by the CPU. This arrangement prevented dynamic relocation; the program was bound to physical memory at load time. Two separate versions of the operating system were produced: OS/MFT used fixed regions and OS/MVT used variable regions.

The system was written in assembly language by thousands of programmers, resulting in millions of lines of code. The operating system itself required large amounts of memory for its code and tables. Operating-system overhead often consumed one-half of the total CPU cycles. Over the years, new versions were released to add new features and to fix errors. However, fixing one error often caused another in some remote part of the system, so that the number of known errors in the system remained fairly constant.

Virtual memory was added to OS/360 with the change to the IBM 370 architecture. The underlying hardware provided a segmented-paged virtual memory. New versions of OS used this hardware in different ways. OS/VS1 created one large virtual address space and ran OS/MFT in that virtual memory. Thus, the operating system itself was paged, as well as user programs. OS/VS2 Release 1 ran OS/MVT in virtual memory. Finally, OS/VS2 Release 2, which is now called MVS, provided each user with his own virtual memory.

MVS is still basically a batch operating system. The CTSS system was run on an IBM 7094, but the developers at MIT decided that the address space of the 360, IBM's successor to the 7094, was too small for MULTICS, so they switched vendors. IBM then decided to create its own time-sharing system, TSS/360 (Lett and Konigsford [1968]). Like MULTICS, TSS/360 was supposed to be a large, time-shared utility. The basic 360 architecture was modified in the model 67 to provide virtual memory. Several sites purchased the 360/67 in anticipation of TSS/360.

TSS/360 was delayed, however, so other time-sharing systems were developed as temporary systems until TSS/360 was available. A time-sharing option (TSO) was added to OS/360. IBM's Cambridge Scientific Center developed CMS as a single-user system and CP/67 to provide a virtual machine to run it on (Meyer and Seawright [1970], Parmelee et al. [1972]).

When TSS/360 was eventually delivered, it was a failure. It was too large and too slow. As a result, no site would switch from its temporary system to TSS/360. Today, time sharing on IBM systems is largely provided either by TSO under MVS or by CMS under CP/67 (renamed VM).

Neither TSS/360 nor MULTICS achieved commercial success. What went wrong? Part of the problem was that these advanced systems were too large and too complex to be understood. Another problem was the assumption that computing power would be available from a large, remote source. Minicomputers came along and decreased the need for large monolithic systems. They were followed by workstations and then personal computers, which put computing power closer and closer to the end users.

23.10 TOPS-20

DEC created many influential computer systems during its history. Probably the most famous operating system associated with DEC is VMS (Kenah et al. [1988]), a popular business-oriented system that is still in use today as OpenVMS, a product of Hewlett-Packard. But perhaps the most influential of DEC's operating systems was TOPS-20.

TOPS-20 started life as a research project at Bolt, Beranek, and Newman (BBN) around 1970. BBN took the business-oriented DEC PDP-10 computer running TOPS-10, added a hardware memory paging system to implement virtual memory, and wrote a new operating system for that computer to take advantage of the new hardware features. The result was TENEX (Bobrow et al. [1972]), a general-purpose timesharing system. DEC then purchased the rights to TENEX and created a new computer with a built-in hardware pager. The resulting system was the DECSYSTEM-20 and the TOPS-20 operating system. Figure 23.6 is a photo of the BBN pager. Notice that it was the size of a standard data-center "19-inch" rack. Such a rack can hold hundreds of CPUs (each containing a hardware pager) today.

TOPS-20 had an advanced command-line interpreter that provided help as needed to users. That, in combination with the power of the computer and its reasonable price, made the DECSYSTEM-20 the most popular time-sharing system of its time. In 1984, DEC stopped work on its line of 36-bit PDP-10 computers to concentrate on 32-bit VAX systems running VMS.

23.11 CP/M and MS/DOS

Early hobbyist computers were typically built from kits and ran a single program at a time. The systems evolved into more advanced systems as computer components improved. An early "standard" operating system for these computers of the 1970s was CP/M, short for Control Program/Monitor, written by Gary Kindall of Digital Research, Inc. CP/M ran primarily on the first "personal computer" CPU, the 8-bit Intel 8080. CP/M originally supported only 64 KB of memory and ran only one program at a time. Of course, it was text-based, with a command interpreter. The command interpreter resembled those in other operating systems of the time, such as the TOPS-10 from DEC.

When IBM entered the personal computer business, it decided to have Bill Gates and company write a new operating system for its 16-bit CPU of choice—the Intel 8086. This operating system, MS-DOS, was similar to CP/M but had a richer set of built-in commands, again mostly modeled after TOPS-10. MS-DOS became the most popular personal-computer operating system of its time, starting in 1981 and continuing development until 2000. It supported 640 KB of memory, with the ability to address "extended" and "expanded"

Figure 23.6 The BBN hardware-pager addition to the PDP-10.

memory to get somewhat beyond that limit. It lacked fundamental current operating-system features, however, especially protected memory.

23.12 Macintosh Operating System and Windows

With the advent of 16-bit CPUs, operating systems for personal computers could become more advanced, feature rich, and usable. The Apple Macintosh computer was arguably the first computer with a GUI designed for home users (Apple [1987]). It was certainly the most successful for a while, starting at its launch in 1984. It used a mouse for screen pointing and selecting and came with many utility programs that took advantage of the new user interface. Hard-disk drives were relatively expensive in 1984, so it came only with a 400-KB-capacity floppy drive by default.

The original Mac OS ran only on Apple computers and slowly was eclipsed by Microsoft Windows (starting with Version 1.0 in 1985), which was licensed to run on many different computers from a multitude of companies. As microprocessor CPUs evolved to 32-bit chips with advanced features, such as protected memory and context switching, these operating systems added features that had previously been found only on mainframes and minicomputers. Over time, personal computers became as powerful as those systems and more useful for many purposes. Minicomputers died out, replaced by general and special-purpose "servers." Although personal computers continue to increase in capacity and performance, servers tend to stay ahead of them in amount of memory, disk space, and number and speed of available CPUs. Today, servers typically run in data centers or machine rooms, while personal computers sit on or next to desks and talk to each other and servers across a network.

The desktop rivalry between Apple and Microsoft continues today, with new versions of Windows and Mac OS trying to outdo each other in features, usability, and application functionality. Other operating systems, such as AmigaOS and OS/2, have appeared over time but have not been long-term competitors to the two leading desktop operating systems. Meanwhile, Linux in its many forms continues to gain in popularity among more technical users—and even with nontechnical users on systems like the One Laptop per Child (OLPC) children's connected computer network (`http://laptop.org/`).

For more information on these operating systems and their history, see Freiberger and Swaine [2000].

23.13 Mach

The Mach operating system traces its ancestry to the Accent operating system developed at Carnegie Mellon University (CMU) (Rashid and Robertson [1981]). Mach's communication system and philosophy are derived from Accent, but many other significant portions of the system (for example, the virtual memory system and task and thread management) were developed from scratch (Rashid [1986], Tevanian et al. [1989], and Accetta et al. [1986]). The Mach scheduler was described in detail by Tevanian et al. [1987a] and Black [1990]. An early version of the Mach shared-memory and memory-mapping system was presented by Tevanian et al. [1987b].

The Mach operating system was designed with the following three critical goals in mind:

1. Emulate 4.3BSD UNIX so that the executable files from a UNIX system can run correctly under Mach.

2. Be a modern operating system that supports many memory models, as well as parallel and distributed computing.

3. Have a kernel that is simpler and easier to modify than is 4.3BSD.

Mach's development followed an evolutionary path from BSD UNIX systems. Mach code was initially developed inside the 4.2BSD kernel, with BSD kernel components replaced by Mach components as the Mach components were completed. The BSD components were updated to 4.3BSD when that became available. By 1986, the virtual memory and communication subsystems were running on the DEC VAX computer family, including multiprocessor versions of the VAX. Versions for the IBM RT/PC and for SUN 3 workstations followed shortly. Then, 1987 saw the completion of the Encore Multimax and Sequent Balance multiprocessor versions, including task and thread support, as well as the first official releases of the system, Release 0 and Release 1.

Through Release 2, Mach provided compatibility with the corresponding BSD systems by including much of BSD's code in the kernel. The new features and capabilities of Mach made the kernels in these releases larger than the corresponding BSD kernels. Mach 3 moved the BSD code outside the kernel, leaving a much smaller microkernel. This system implements only basic Mach features in the kernel; all UNIX-specific code has been evicted to run in user-mode servers. Excluding UNIX-specific code from the kernel allows the replacement of BSD with another operating system or the simultaneous execution of multiple operating-system interfaces on top of the microkernel. In addition to BSD, user-mode implementations have been developed for DOS, the Macintosh operating system, and OSF/1. This approach has similarities to the virtual machine concept, but here the virtual machine is defined by software (the Mach kernel interface), rather than by hardware. With Release 3.0, Mach became available on a wide variety of systems, including single- processor SUN, Intel, IBM, and DEC machines and multiprocessor DEC, Sequent, and Encore systems.

Mach was propelled to the forefront of industry attention when the Open Software Foundation (OSF) announced in 1989 that it would use Mach 2.5 as the basis for its new operating system, OSF/1. (Mach 2.5 was also the basis for the operating system on the NeXT workstation, the brainchild of Steve Jobs, of Apple Computer fame.) The initial release of OSF/1 occurred a year later, and this system competed with UNIX System V, Release 4, the operating system of choice at that time among UNIX International (UI) members. OSF members included key technological companies such as IBM, DEC, and HP. OSF has since changed its direction, and only DEC UNIX is based on the Mach kernel.

Unlike UNIX, which was developed without regard for multiprocessing, Mach incorporates multiprocessing support throughout. This support is also exceedingly flexible, ranging from shared-memory systems to systems with no memory shared between processors. Mach uses lightweight processes, in the form of multiple threads of execution within one task (or address space), to support multiprocessing and parallel computation. Its extensive use of messages as the only communication method ensures that protection mechanisms are complete and efficient. By integrating messages with the virtual memory system, Mach also ensures that messages can be handled efficiently. Finally, by having the virtual memory system use messages to communicate with the daemons managing the backing store, Mach provides great flexibility in the design and implementation of these memory-object-managing tasks. By providing low-level, or primitive, system calls from which more complex functions can be built, Mach reduces the size of the kernel while permitting operating-system emulation at the user level, much like IBM's virtual-machine systems.

Some previous editions of *Operating System Concepts* included an entire chapter on Mach. This chapter, as it appeared in the fourth edition, is available on the Web (`http://www.os-book.com`).

23.14 Other Systems

There are, of course, other operating systems, and most of them have interesting properties. The MCP operating system for the Burroughs computer family (McKeag and Wilson [1976]) was the first to be written in a system-programming language. It supported segmentation and multiple CPUs. The SCOPE operating system for the CDC 6600 (McKeag and Wilson [1976]) was also a multi-CPU system. The coordination and synchronization of the multiple processes were surprisingly well designed.

History is littered with operating systems that suited a purpose for a time (be it a long or a short time) and then, when faded, were replaced by operating systems that had more features, supported newer hardware, were easier to use, or were better marketed. We are sure this trend will continue in the future.

Exercises

23.1 Consider the page replacement algorithm used by Atlas. In what ways is it different from the clock algorithm discussed in Section 9.4.5.2?

23.2 Consider the multilevel feedback queue used by CTSS and MULTICS. Suppose a program consistently uses seven time units every time it is scheduled before it performs an I/O operation and blocks. How many time units are allocated to this program when it is scheduled for execution at different points in time?

23.3 What optimizations were used to minimize the discrepancy between CPU and I/O speeds on early computer systems?

23.4 What conclusions can be drawn about the evolution of operating systems? What causes some operating systems to gain in popularity and others to fade?

Bibliography

[Accetta et al. 1986] M. Accetta, R. Baron, W. Bolosky, D. B. Golub, R. Rashid, A. Tevanian, and M. Young, "Mach: A New Kernel Foundation for UNIX Development", *Proceedings of the Summer USENIX Conference* (1986), pages 93–112.

[Adl-Tabatabai et al. 2007] A.-R. Adl-Tabatabai, C. Kozyrakis, and B. Saha, "Unlocking Concurrency", *Queue*, Volume 4, Number 10 (2007), pages 24–33.

[Agrawal and Abbadi 1991] D. P. Agrawal and A. E. Abbadi, "An Efficient and Fault-Tolerant Solution of Distributed Mutual Exclusion", *ACM Transactions on Computer Systems*, Volume 9, Number 1 (1991), pages 1–20.

[Agre 2003] P. E. Agre, "P2P and the Promise of Internet Equality", *Communications of the ACM*, Volume 46, Number 2 (2003), pages 39–42.

[Ahituv et al. 1987] N. Ahituv, Y. Lapid, and S. Neumann, "Processing Encrypted Data", *Communications of the ACM*, Volume 30, Number 9 (1987), pages 777–780.

[Ahmed 2000] I. Ahmed, "Cluster Computing: A Glance at Recent Events", *IEEE Concurrency*, Volume 8, Number 1 (2000).

[Akl 1983] S. G. Akl, "Digital Signatures: A Tutorial Survey", *Computer*, Volume 16, Number 2 (1983), pages 15–24.

[Akyurek and Salem 1993] S. Akyurek and K. Salem, "Adaptive Block Rearrangement", *Proceedings of the International Conference on Data Engineering* (1993), pages 182–189.

[Alt 1993] H. Alt, "Removable Media in Solaris", *Proceedings of the Winter USENIX Conference* (1993), pages 281–287.

[Anderson 1990] T. E. Anderson, "The Performance of Spin Lock Alternatives for Shared-Money Multiprocessors", *IEEE Trans. Parallel Distrib. Syst.*, Volume 1, Number 1 (1990), pages 6–16.

[Anderson et al. 1989] T. E. Anderson, E. D. Lazowska, and H. M. Levy, "The Performance Implications of Thread Management Alternatives for Shared-Memory Multiprocessors", *IEEE Transactions on Computers*, Volume 38, Number 12 (1989), pages 1631–1644.

[Anderson et al. 1991] T. E. Anderson, B. N. Bershad, E. D. Lazowska, and H. M. Levy, "Scheduler Activations: Effective Kernel Support for the User-Level Management of Parallelism", *Proceedings of the ACM Symposium on Operating Systems Principles* (1991), pages 95–109.

[Anderson et al. 1995] T. E. Anderson, M. D. Dahlin, J. M. Neefe, D. A. Patterson, D. S. Roselli, and R. Y. Wang, "Serverless Network File Systems", *Proceedings of the ACM Symposium on Operating Systems Principles* (1995), pages 109–126.

[Anderson et al. 2000] D. Anderson, J. Chase, and A. Vahdat, "Interposed Request Routing for Scalable Network Storage", *Proceedings of the Fourth Symposium on Operating Systems Design and Implementation* (2000).

[Apple 1987] *Apple Technical Introduction to the Macintosh Family*. Addison-Wesley (1987).

[Asthana and Finkelstein 1995] P. Asthana and B. Finkelstein, "Superdense Optical Storage", *IEEE Spectrum*, Volume 32, Number 8 (1995), pages 25–31.

[Audsley et al. 1991] N. C. Audsley, A. Burns, M. F. Richardson, and A. J. Wellings, "Hard Real-Time Scheduling: The Deadline Monotonic Approach", *Proceedings of the IEEE Workshop on Real-Time Operating Systems and Software* (1991).

[Axelsson 1999] S. Axelsson, "The Base-Rate Fallacy and Its Implications for Intrusion Detection". *Proceedings of the ACM Conference on Computer and Communications Security* (1999), pages 1–7.

[Babaoglu and Marzullo 1993] O. Babaoglu and K. Marzullo. "Consistent Global States of Distributed Systems: Fundamental Concepts and Mechanisms", pages 55–96. Addison-Wesley (1993).

[Bach 1987] M. J. Bach, *The Design of the UNIX Operating System*, Prentice Hall (1987).

[Back et al. 2000] G. Back, P. Tullman, L. Stoller, W. C. Hsieh, and J. Lepreau, "Techniques for the Design of Java Operating Systems", *2000 USENIX Annual Technical Conference* (2000).

[Baker et al. 1991] M. G. Baker, J. H. Hartman, M. D. Kupfer, K. W. Shirriff, and J. K. Ousterhout, "Measurements of a Distributed File System", *Proceedings of the ACM Symposium on Operating Systems Principles* (1991), pages 198–212.

[Balakrishnan et al. 2003] H. Balakrishnan, M. F. Kaashoek, D. Karger, R. Morris, and I. Stoica, "Looking up Data in P2P Systems", *Communications of the ACM*, Volume 46, Number 2 (2003), pages 43–48.

[Baldwin 2002] J. Baldwin, "Locking in the Multithreaded FreeBSD Kernel", *USENIX BSD* (2002).

[Barnes 1993] G. Barnes, "A Method for Implementing Lock-Free Shared Data Structures", *Proceedings of the ACM Symposium on Parallel Algorithms and Architectures* (1993), pages 261–270.

[Barrera 1991] J. S. Barrera, "A Fast Mach Network IPC Implementation", *Proceedings of the USENIX Mach Symposium* (1991), pages 1–12.

[Basu et al. 1995] A. Basu, V. Buch, W. Vogels, and T. von Eicken, "U-Net: A User-Level Network Interface for Parallel and Distributed Computing", *Proceedings of the ACM Symposium on Operating Systems Principles* (1995).

[Bays 1977] C. Bays, "A Comparison of Next-Fit, First-Fit and Best-Fit", *Communications of the ACM*, Volume 20, Number 3 (1977), pages 191–192.

[Belady 1966] L. A. Belady, "A Study of Replacement Algorithms for a Virtual-Storage Computer", *IBM Systems Journal*, Volume 5, Number 2 (1966), pages 78–101.

[Belady et al. 1969] L. A. Belady, R. A. Nelson, and G. S. Shedler, "An Anomaly in Space-Time Characteristics of Certain Programs Running in a Paging Machine", *Communications of the ACM*, Volume 12, Number 6 (1969), pages 349–353.

[Bellovin 1989] S. M. Bellovin, "Security Problems in the TCP/IP Protocol Suite", *Computer Communications Review*, Volume 19:2, (1989), pages 32–48.

[Ben-Ari 1990] M. Ben-Ari, *Principles of Concurrent and Distributed Programming*, Prentice Hall (1990).

[Benjamin 1990] C. D. Benjamin, "The Role of Optical Storage Technology for NASA", *Proceedings, Storage and Retrieval Systems and Applications* (1990), pages 10–17.

[Bernstein and Goodman 1980] P. A. Bernstein and N. Goodman, "Time-Stamp-Based Algorithms for Concurrency Control in Distributed Database Systems", *Proceedings of the International Conference on Very Large Databases* (1980), pages 285–300.

[Bernstein et al. 1987] A. Bernstein, V. Hadzilacos, and N. Goodman, *Concurrency Control and Recovery in Database Systems*, Addison-Wesley (1987).

[Bershad 1993] B. Bershad, "Practical Considerations for Non-Blocking Concurrent Objects", *IEEE International Conference on Distributed Computing Systems* (1993), pages 264–273.

[Bershad and Pinkerton 1988] B. N. Bershad and C. B. Pinkerton, "Watchdogs: Extending the Unix File System", *Proceedings of the Winter USENIX Conference* (1988).

[Bershad et al. 1990] B. N. Bershad, T. E. Anderson, E. D. Lazowska, and H. M. Levy, "Lightweight Remote Procedure Call", *ACM Transactions on Computer Systems*, Volume 8, Number 1 (1990), pages 37–55.

[Bershad et al. 1995] B. N. Bershad, S. Savage, P. Pardyak, E. G. Sirer, M. Fiuczynski, D. Becker, S. Eggers, and C. Chambers, "Extensibility, Safety and Performance in the SPIN Operating System", *Proceedings of the ACM Symposium on Operating Systems Principles* (1995), pages 267–284.

[Beveridge and Wiener 1997] J. Beveridge and R. Wiener, *Mutlithreading Applications in Win32*, Addison-Wesley (1997).

[Binding 1985] C. Binding, "Cheap Concurrency in C", *SIGPLAN Notices*, Volume 20, Number 9 (1985), pages 21–27.

[Birrell 1989] A. D. Birrell, "An Introduction to Programming with Threads", Technical report, DEC-SRC (1989).

[Birrell and Nelson 1984] A. D. Birrell and B. J. Nelson, "Implementing Remote Procedure Calls", *ACM Transactions on Computer Systems*, Volume 2, Number 1 (1984), pages 39–59.

[Blaauw and Brooks 1997] G. Blaauw and F. Brooks, *Computer Architecture: Concepts and Evolution*, Addison-Wesley (1997).

[Black 1990] D. L. Black, "Scheduling Support for Concurrency and Parallelism in the Mach Operating System", *IEEE Computer*, Volume 23, Number 5 (1990), pages 35–43.

[Bobrow et al. 1972] D. G. Bobrow, J. D. Burchfiel, D. L. Murphy, and R. S. Tomlinson, "TENEX, a Paged Time Sharing System for the PDP-10", *Communications of the ACM*, Volume 15, Number 3 (1972).

[Bolosky et al. 1997] W. J. Bolosky, R. P. Fitzgerald, and J. R. Douceur, "Distributed Schedule Management in the Tiger Video Fileserver", *Proceedings of the ACM Symposium on Operating Systems Principles* (1997), pages 212–223.

[Bonwick 1994] J. Bonwick, "The Slab Allocator: An Object-Caching Kernel Memory Allocator", *USENIX Summer* (1994), pages 87–98.

[Bonwick and Adams 2001] J. Bonwick and J. Adams, "Magazines and Vmem: Extending the Slab Allocator to Many CPUs and Arbitrary Resources", *Proceedings of the 2001 USENIX Annual Technical Conference* (2001).

[Bovet and Cesati 2002] D. P. Bovet and M. Cesati, *Understanding the Linux Kernel, Second Edition*, O'Reilly & Associates (2002).

[Bovet and Cesati 2006] D. Bovet and M. Cesati, *Understanding the Linux Kernel, Third Edition*, O'Reilly & Associates (2006).

[Brain 1996] M. Brain, *Win32 System Services, Second Edition*, Prentice Hall (1996).

[Brent 1989] R. Brent, "Efficient Implementation of the First-Fit Strategy for Dynamic Storage Allocation", *ACM Transactions on Programming Languages and Systems*, Volume 11, Number 3 (1989), pages 388–403.

[Brereton 1986] O. P. Brereton, "Management of Replicated Files in a UNIX Environment", *Software —Practice and Experience*, Volume 16, (1986), pages 771–780.

[Brinch-Hansen 1970] P. Brinch-Hansen, "The Nucleus of a Multiprogramming System", *Communications of the ACM*, Volume 13, Number 4 (1970), pages 238–241 and 250.

[Brinch-Hansen 1972] P. Brinch-Hansen, "Structured Multiprogramming", *Communications of the ACM*, Volume 15, Number 7 (1972), pages 574–578.

[Brinch-Hansen 1973] P. Brinch-Hansen, *Operating System Principles*, Prentice Hall (1973).

[Brookshear 2003] J. G. Brookshear, *Computer Science: An Overview, Seventh Edition*, Addison-Wesley (2003).

[Brownbridge et al. 1982] D. R. Brownbridge, L. F. Marshall, and B. Randell, "The Newcastle Connection or UNIXes of the World Unite!", *Software—Practice and Experience*, Volume 12, Number 12 (1982), pages 1147–1162.

[Burns 1978] J. E. Burns, "Mutual Exclusion with Linear Waiting Using Binary Shared Variables", *SIGACT News*, Volume 10, Number 2 (1978), pages 42–47.

[Butenhof 1997] D. Butenhof, *Programming with POSIX Threads*, Addison-Wesley (1997).

[Buyya 1999] R. Buyya, *High Performance Cluster Computing: Architectures and Systems*, Prentice Hall (1999).

[Callaghan 2000] B. Callaghan, *NFS Illustrated*, Addison-Wesley (2000).

[Cantrill et al. 2004] B. M. Cantrill, M. W. Shapiro, and A. H. Leventhal, "Dynamic Instrumation of Production Systems", *2004 USENIX Annual Technical Conference* (2004).

[Carr and Hennessy 1981] W. R. Carr and J. L. Hennessy, "WSClock—A Simple and Effective Algorithm for Virtual Memory Management", *Proceedings of the ACM Symposium on Operating Systems Principles* (1981), pages 87–95.

[Carvalho and Roucairol 1983] O. S. Carvalho and G. Roucairol, "On Mutual Exclusion in Computer Networks", *Communications of the ACM*, Volume 26, Number 2 (1983), pages 146–147.

[Ceruzzi 1998] P. E. Ceruzzi, *A History of Modern Computing*, MIT Press (1998).

[Chandy and Lamport 1985] K. M. Chandy and L. Lamport, "Distributed Snapshots: Determining Global States of Distributed Systems", *ACM Transactions on Computer Systems*, Volume 3, Number 1 (1985), pages 63–75.

[Chang 1980] E. Chang, "N-Philosophers: An Exercise in Distributed Control", *Computer Networks*, Volume 4, Number 2 (1980), pages 71–76.

[Chang and Mergen 1988] A. Chang and M. F. Mergen, "801 Storage: Architecture and Programming", *ACM Transactions on Computer Systems*, Volume 6, Number 1 (1988), pages 28–50.

[Chase et al. 1994] J. S. Chase, H. M. Levy, M. J. Feeley, and E. D. Lazowska, "Sharing and Protection in a Single-Address-Space Operating System", *ACM Transactions on Computer Systems*, Volume 12, Number 4 (1994), pages 271–307.

[Chen et al. 1994] P. M. Chen, E. K. Lee, G. A. Gibson, R. H. Katz, and D. A. Patterson, "RAID: High-Performance, Reliable Secondary Storage", *ACM Computing Surveys*, Volume 26, Number 2 (1994), pages 145–185.

[Cheriton 1988] D. Cheriton, "The V Distributed System", *Communications of the ACM*, Volume 31, Number 3 (1988), pages 314–333.

[Cheriton et al. 1979] D. R. Cheriton, M. A. Malcolm, L. S. Melen, and G. R. Sager, "Thoth, a Portable Real-Time Operating System", *Communications of the ACM*, Volume 22, Number 2 (1979), pages 105–115.

[Cheswick et al. 2003] W. Cheswick, S. Bellovin, and A. Rubin, *Firewalls and Internet Security: Repelling the Wily Hacker*, second edition, Addison-Wesley (2003).

[Cheung and Loong 1995] W. H. Cheung and A. H. S. Loong, "Exploring Issues of Operating Systems Structuring: From Microkernel to Extensible Systems", *Operating Systems Review*, Volume 29, Number 4 (1995), pages 4–16.

[Chi 1982] C. S. Chi, "Advances in Computer Mass Storage Technology", *Computer*, Volume 15, Number 5 (1982), pages 60–74.

[Coffman et al. 1971] E. G. Coffman, M. J. Elphick, and A. Shoshani, "System Deadlocks", *Computing Surveys*, Volume 3, Number 2 (1971), pages 67–78.

[Cohen and Jefferson 1975] E. S. Cohen and D. Jefferson, "Protection in the Hydra Operating System", *Proceedings of the ACM Symposium on Operating Systems Principles* (1975), pages 141–160.

[Cohen and Woodring 1997] A. Cohen and M. Woodring, *Win32 Multithreaded Programming*, O'Reilly & Associates (1997).

[Comer 1999] D. Comer, *Internetworking with TCP/IP, Volume II, Third Edition*, Prentice Hall (1999).

[Comer 2000] D. Comer, *Internetworking with TCP/IP, Volume I, Fourth Edition*, Prentice Hall (2000).

[Corbato and Vyssotsky 1965] F. J. Corbato and V. A. Vyssotsky, "Introduction and Overview of the MULTICS System", *Proceedings of the AFIPS Fall Joint Computer Conference* (1965), pages 185–196.

[Corbato et al. 1962] F. J. Corbato, M. Merwin-Daggett, and R. C. Daley, "An Experimental Time-Sharing System", *Proceedings of the AFIPS Fall Joint Computer Conference* (1962), pages 335–344.

[Cormen et al. 2001] T. H. Cormen, C. E. Leiserson, R. L. Rivest, and C. Stein, *Introduction to Algorithms, Second Edition*, MIT Press (2001).

[Coulouris et al. 2001] G. Coulouris, J. Dollimore, and T. Kindberg, *Distributed Systems Concepts and Designs, Third Edition*, Addison Wesley (2001).

[Courtois et al. 1971] P. J. Courtois, F. Heymans, and D. L. Parnas, "Concurrent Control with 'Readers' and 'Writers'", *Communications of the ACM*, Volume 14, Number 10 (1971), pages 667–668.

[Culler et al. 1998] D. E. Culler, J. P. Singh, and A. Gupta, *Parallel Computer Architecture: A Hardware/Software Approach*, Morgan Kaufmann Publishers Inc. (1998).

[Custer 1994] H. Custer, *Inside the Windows NT File System*, Microsoft Press (1994).

[Dabek et al. 2001] F. Dabek, M. F. Kaashoek, D. Karger, R. Morris, and I. Stoica, "Wide-Area Cooperative Storage with CFS", *Proceedings of the ACM Symposium on Operating Systems Principles* (2001), pages 202–215.

[Daley and Dennis 1967] R. C. Daley and J. B. Dennis, "Virtual Memory, Processes, and Sharing in Multics", *Proceedings of the ACM Symposium on Operating Systems Principles* (1967), pages 121–128.

[Davcev and Burkhard 1985] D. Davcev and W. A. Burkhard, "Consistency and Recovery Control for Replicated Files", *Proceedings of the ACM Symposium on Operating Systems Principles* (1985), pages 87–96.

[Davies 1983] D. W. Davies, "Applying the RSA Digital Signature to Electronic Mail", *Computer*, Volume 16, Number 2 (1983), pages 55–62.

[deBruijn 1967] N. G. deBruijn, "Additional Comments on a Problem in Concurrent Programming and Control", *Communications of the ACM*, Volume 10, Number 3 (1967), pages 137–138.

[Deitel 1990] H. M. Deitel, *An Introduction to Operating Systems, Second Edition*, Addison-Wesley (1990).

[Denning 1968] P. J. Denning, "The Working Set Model for Program Behavior", *Communications of the ACM*, Volume 11, Number 5 (1968), pages 323–333.

[Denning 1980] P. J. Denning, "Working Sets Past and Present', *IEEE Transactions on Software Engineering*, Volume SE-6, Number 1 (1980), pages 64–84.

[Denning 1982] D. E. Denning, *Cryptography and Data Security*, Addison-Wesley (1982).

[Denning 1983] D. E. Denning, "Protecting Public Keys and Signature Keys", *Computer*, Volume 16, Number 2 (1983), pages 27–35.

[Denning 1984] D. E. Denning, "Digital Signatures with RSA and Other Public-Key Cryptosystems", *Communications of the ACM*, Volume 27, Number 4 (1984), pages 388–392.

[Denning and Denning 1979] D. E. Denning and P. J. Denning, "Data Security", *ACM Computing Surveys*, Volume 11, Number 3 (1979), pages 227–249.

[Dennis 1965] J. B. Dennis, "Segmentation and the Design of Multiprogrammed Computer Systems", *Communications of the ACM*, Volume 8, Number 4 (1965), pages 589–602.

[Dennis and Horn 1966] J. B. Dennis and E. C. V. Horn, "Programming Semantics for Multiprogrammed Computations", *Communications of the ACM*, Volume 9, Number 3 (1966), pages 143–155.

[Di Pietro and Mancini 2003] R. Di Pietro and L. V. Mancini, "Security and Privacy Issues of Handheld and Wearable Wireless Devices", *Communications of the ACM*, Volume 46, Number 9 (2003), pages 74–79.

[Diffie and Hellman 1976] W. Diffie and M. E. Hellman, "New Directions in Cryptography", *IEEE Transactions on Information Theory*, Volume 22, Number 6 (1976), pages 644–654.

[Diffie and Hellman 1979] W. Diffie and M. E. Hellman, "Privacy and Authentication", *Proceedings of the IEEE* (1979), pages 397–427.

[Dijkstra 1965a] E. W. Dijkstra, "Cooperating Sequential Processes", Technical report, Technological University, Eindhoven, the Netherlands (1965).

[Dijkstra 1965b] E. W. Dijkstra, "Solution of a Problem in Concurrent Programming Control", *Communications of the ACM*, Volume 8, Number 9 (1965), page 569.

[Dijkstra 1968] E. W. Dijkstra, "The Structure of the THE Multiprogramming System", *Communications of the ACM*, Volume 11, Number 5 (1968), pages 341–346.

[Dijkstra 1971] E. W. Dijkstra, "Hierarchical Ordering of Sequential Processes", *Acta Informatica*, Volume 1, Number 2 (1971), pages 115–138.

[DoD 1985] *Trusted Computer System Evaluation Criteria.* Department of Defense (1985).

[Dougan et al. 1999] C. Dougan, P. Mackerras, and V. Yodaiken, "Optimizing the Idle Task and Other MMU Tricks", *Proceedings of the Symposium on Operating System Design and Implementation* (1999).

[Douglis and Ousterhout 1991] F. Douglis and J. K. Ousterhout, "Transparent Process Migration: Design Alternatives and the Sprite Implementation", *Software—Practice and Experience*, Volume 21, Number 8 (1991), pages 757–785.

[Douglis et al. 1994] F. Douglis, F. Kaashoek, K. Li, R. Caceres, B. Marsh, and J. A. Tauber, "Storage Alternatives for Mobile Computers", *Proceedings of the Symposium on Operating Systems Design and Implementation* (1994), pages 25–37.

[Douglis et al. 1995] F. Douglis, P. Krishnan, and B. Bershad, "Adaptive Disk Spin-Down Policies for Mobile Computers", *Proceedings of the USENIX Symposium on Mobile and Location Independent Computing* (1995), pages 121–137.

[Druschel and Peterson 1993] P. Druschel and L. L. Peterson, "Fbufs: A High-Bandwidth Cross-Domain Transfer Facility", *Proceedings of the ACM Symposium on Operating Systems Principles* (1993), pages 189–202.

[Eastlake 1999] D. Eastlake, "Domain Name System Security Extensions", *Network Working Group, Request for Comments: 2535* (1999).

[Eisenberg and McGuire 1972] M. A. Eisenberg and M. R. McGuire, "Further Comments on Dijkstra's Concurrent Programming Control Problem", *Communications of the ACM*, Volume 15, Number 11 (1972), page 999.

[Ekanadham and Bernstein 1979] K. Ekanadham and A. J. Bernstein, "Conditional Capabilities", *IEEE Transactions on Software Engineering*, Volume SE-5, Number 5 (1979), pages 458–464.

[Engelschall 2000] R. Engelschall, "Portable Multithreading: The Signal Stack Trick For User-Space Thread Creation", *Proceedings of the 2000 USENIX Annual Technical Conference* (2000).

[Eswaran et al. 1976] K. P. Eswaran, J. N. Gray, R. A. Lorie, and I. L. Traiger, "The Notions of Consistency and Predicate Locks in a Database System", *Communications of the ACM*, Volume 19, Number 11 (1976), pages 624–633.

[Fang et al. 2001] Z. Fang, L. Zhang, J. B. Carter, W. C. Hsieh, and S. A. McKee, "Reevaluating Online Superpage Promotion with Hardware Support", *Proceedings of the International Symposium on High-Performance Computer Architecture*, Volume 50, Number 5 (2001).

[Farrow 1986a] R. Farrow, "Security for Superusers, or How to Break the UNIX System", *UNIX World* (May 1986), pages 65–70.

[Farrow 1986b] R. Farrow, "Security Issues and Strategies for Users", *UNIX World* (April 1986), pages 65–71.

[Fidge 1991] C. Fidge, "Logical Time in Distributed Computing Systems", *Computer*, Volume 24, Number 8 (1991), pages 28–33.

[Filipski and Hanko 1986] A. Filipski and J. Hanko, "Making UNIX Secure", *Byte* (April 1986), pages 113–128.

[Fisher 1981] J. A. Fisher, "Trace Scheduling: A Technique for Global Microcode Compaction", *IEEE Transactions on Computers*, Volume 30, Number 7 (1981), pages 478–490.

[Folk and Zoellick 1987] M. J. Folk and B. Zoellick, *File Structures*, Addison-Wesley (1987).

[Forrest et al. 1996] S. Forrest, S. A. Hofmeyr, and T. A. Longstaff, "A Sense of Self for UNIX Processes", *Proceedings of the IEEE Symposium on Security and Privacy* (1996), pages 120–128.

[Fortier 1989] P. J. Fortier, *Handbook of LAN Technology*, McGraw-Hill (1989).

[Frah 2001] G. Frah, *The Universal History of Computing*, John Wiley and Sons (2001).

[Frauenfelder 2005] M. Frauenfelder, *The Computer—An Illustrated History*, Carlton Books (2005).

[Freedman 1983] D. H. Freedman, "Searching for Denser Disks", *Infosystems* (1983), page 56.

[Freiberger and Swaine 2000] P. Freiberger and M. Swaine, *Fire in the Valley—The Making of the Personal Computer*, McGraw-Hill (2000).

[Fuhrt 1994] B. Fuhrt, "Multimedia Systems: An Overview", *IEEE MultiMedia*, Volume 1, Number 1 (1994), pages 47–59.

[Fujitani 1984] L. Fujitani, "Laser Optical Disk: The Coming Revolution in On-Line Storage", *Communications of the ACM*, Volume 27, Number 6 (1984), pages 546–554.

[Gait 1988] J. Gait, "The Optical File Cabinet: A Random-Access File System for Write-On Optical Disks", *Computer*, Volume 21, Number 6 (1988).

[Ganapathy and Schimmel 1998] N. Ganapathy and C. Schimmel, "General Purpose Operating System Support for Multiple Page Sizes", *Proceedings of the USENIX Technical Conference* (1998).

[Ganger et al. 2002] G. R. Ganger, D. R. Engler, M. F. Kaashoek, H. M. Briceno, R. Hunt, and T. Pinckney, "Fast and Flexible Application-Level Networking on Exokernel Systems", *ACM Transactions on Computer Systems*, Volume 20, Number 1 (2002), pages 49–83.

[Garcia-Molina 1982] H. Garcia-Molina, "Elections in Distributed Computing Systems", *IEEE Transactions on Computers*, Volume C-31, Number 1 (1982).

[Garfinkel et al. 2003] S. Garfinkel, G. Spafford, and A. Schwartz, *Practical UNIX & Internet Security*, O'Reilly & Associates (2003).

[Ghemawat et al. 2003] S. Ghemawat, H. Gobioff, and S.-T. Leung, "The Google File System", *Proceedings of the ACM Symposium on Operating Systems Principles* (2003).

[Gibson et al. 1997a] G. Gibson, D. Nagle, K. Amiri, F. Chang, H. Gobioff, E. Riedel, D. Rochberg, and J. Zelenka, "Filesystems for Network-Attached Secure Disks", Technical report, Carnegie-Mellon University (1997).

[Gibson et al. 1997b] G. A. Gibson, D. Nagle, K. Amiri, F. W. Chang, E. M. Feinberg, H. Gobioff, C. Lee, B. Ozceri, E. Riedel, D. Rochberg, and J. Zelenka, "File Server Scaling with Network-Attached Secure Disks", *Measurement and Modeling of Computer Systems* (1997), pages 272–284.

[Gifford 1982] D. K. Gifford, "Cryptographic Sealing for Information Secrecy and Authentication", *Communications of the ACM*, Volume 25, Number 4 (1982), pages 274–286.

[Goetz et al. 2006] B. Goetz, T. Peirls, J. Bloch, J. Bowbeer, D. Holmes, and D. Lea, *Java Concurrency in Practice*, Addison-Wesley (2006).

[Goldberg et al. 1996] I. Goldberg, D. Wagner, R. Thomas, and E. A. Brewer, "A Secure Environment for Untrusted Helper Applications", *Proceedings of the 6th Usenix Security Symposium* (1996).

[Golden and Pechura 1986] D. Golden and M. Pechura, "The Structure of Microcomputer File Systems", *Communications of the ACM*, Volume 29, Number 3 (1986), pages 222–230.

[Golding et al. 1995] R. A. Golding, P. B. II, C. Staelin, T. Sullivan, and J. Wilkes, "Idleness is Not Sloth", *USENIX Winter* (1995), pages 201–212.

[Golm et al. 2002] M. Golm, M. Felser, C. Wawersich, and J. Kleinoder, "The JX Operating System", *2002 USENIX Annual Technical Conference* (2002).

[Gong 2002] L. Gong, "Peer-to-Peer Networks in Action", *IEEE Internet Computing*, Volume 6, Number 1 (2002).

[Gong et al. 1997] L. Gong, M. Mueller, H. Prafullchandra, and R. Schemers, "Going Beyond the Sandbox: An Overview of the New Security Architecture in the Java Development Kit 1.2", *Proceedings of the USENIX Symposium on Internet Technologies and Systems* (1997).

[Goodman et al. 1989] J. R. Goodman, M. K. Vernon, and P. J. Woest, "Efficient Synchronization Primitives for Large-Scale Cache-Coherent Multiprocessors", *Proceedings of the International Conference on Architectural Support for Programming Languages and Operating Systems* (1989), pages 64–75.

[Gosling et al. 1996] J. Gosling, B. Joy, and G. Steele, *The Java Language Specification*, Addison-Wesley (1996).

[Govindan and Anderson 1991] R. Govindan and D. P. Anderson, "Scheduling and IPC Mechanisms for Continuous Media", *Proceedings of the ACM Symposium on Operating Systems Principles* (1991), pages 68–80.

[Grampp and Morris 1984] F. T. Grampp and R. H. Morris, "UNIX Operating-System Security", *AT&T Bell Laboratories Technical Journal*, Volume 63, Number 8 (1984), pages 1649–1672.

[Gray 1978] J. N. Gray, "Notes on Data Base Operating Systems", in **[Bayer et al. 1978]** (1978), pages 393–481.

[Gray 1981] J. N. Gray, "The Transaction Concept: Virtues and Limitations", *Proceedings of the International Conference on Very Large Databases* (1981), pages 144–154.

[Gray 1997] J. Gray, *Interprocess Communications in UNIX*, Prentice Hall (1997).

[Gray et al. 1981] J. N. Gray, P. R. McJones, and M. Blasgen, "The Recovery Manager of the System R Database Manager", *ACM Computing Surveys*, Volume 13, Number 2 (1981), pages 223–242.

[Greenawalt 1994] P. Greenawalt, "Modeling Power Management for Hard Disks", *Proceedings of the Symposium on Modeling and Simulation of Computer Telecommunication Systems* (1994), pages 62–66.

[Grosshans 1986] D. Grosshans, *File Systems Design and Implementation*, Prentice Hall (1986).

[Habermann 1969] A. N. Habermann, "Prevention of System Deadlocks", *Communications of the ACM*, Volume 12, Number 7 (1969), pages 373–377, 385.

[Hall et al. 1996] L. Hall, D. Shmoys, and J. Wein, "Scheduling To Minimize Average Completion Time: Off-line and On-line Algorithms", *SODA: ACM-SIAM Symposium on Discrete Algorithms* (1996).

[Hamacher et al. 2002] C. Hamacher, Z. Vranesic, and S. Zaky, *Computer Organization, Fifth Edition*, McGraw-Hill (2002).

[Han and Ghosh 1998] K. Han and S. Ghosh, "A Comparative Analysis of Virtual Versus Physical Process-Migration Strategies for Distributed Modeling and Simulation of Mobile Computing Networks", *Wireless Networks*, Volume 4, Number 5 (1998), pages 365–378.

[Harchol-Balter and Downey 1997] M. Harchol-Balter and A. B. Downey, "Exploiting Process Lifetime Distributions for Dynamic Load Balancing", *ACM Transactions on Computer Systems*, Volume 15, Number 3 (1997), pages 253–285.

[Harish and Owens 1999] V. C. Harish and B. Owens, "Dynamic Load Balancing DNS", *Linux Journal*, Volume 1999, Number 64 (1999).

[Harker et al. 1981] J. M. Harker, D. W. Brede, R. E. Pattison, G. R. Santana, and L. G. Taft, "A Quarter Century of Disk File Innovation", *IBM Journal of Research and Development*, Volume 25, Number 5 (1981), pages 677–689.

[Harold 2005] E. R. Harold, *Java Network Programming, Third Edition*, O'Reilly & Associates (2005).

[Harrison et al. 1976] M. A. Harrison, W. L. Ruzzo, and J. D. Ullman, "Protection in Operating Systems", *Communications of the ACM*, Volume 19, Number 8 (1976), pages 461–471.

[Hart 2005] J. M. Hart, *Windows System Programming, Third Edition*, Addison-Wesley (2005).

[Hartman and Ousterhout 1995] J. H. Hartman and J. K. Ousterhout, "The Zebra Striped Network File System", *ACM Transactions on Computer Systems*, Volume 13, Number 3 (1995), pages 274–310.

[Havender 1968] J. W. Havender, "Avoiding Deadlock in Multitasking Systems", *IBM Systems Journal*, Volume 7, Number 2 (1968), pages 74–84.

[Hecht et al. 1988] M. S. Hecht, A. Johri, R. Aditham, and T. J. Wei, "Experience Adding C2 Security Features to UNIX", *Proceedings of the Summer USENIX Conference* (1988), pages 133–146.

[Hennessy and Patterson 2002] J. L. Hennessy and D. A. Patterson, *Computer Architecture: A Quantitative Approach, Third Edition*, Morgan Kaufmann Publishers (2002).

[Hennessy and Patterson 2007] J. Hennessy and D. Patterson, *Computer Architecture: A Quantitative Approach, Fourth Edition*, Morgan Kaufmann (2007).

[Henry 1984] G. Henry, "The Fair Share Scheduler", *AT&T Bell Laboratories Technical Journal* (1984).

[Herlihy 1993] M. Herlihy, "A Methodology for Implementing Highly Concurrent Data Objects", *ACM Transactions on Programming Languages and Systems*, Volume 15, Number 5 (1993), pages 745–770.

[Herlihy and Moss 1993] M. Herlihy and J. E. B. Moss, "Transactional Memory: Architectural Support For Lock-Free Data Structures", *Proceedings of the Twentieth Annual International Symposium on Computer Architecture* (1993).

[Hitz et al. 1995] D. Hitz, J. Lau, and M. Malcolm, "File System Design for an NFS File Server Appliance", Technical report, NetApp (http://www.netapp.com/tech_library/3002.html) (1995).

[Hoagland 1985] A. S. Hoagland, "Information Storage Technology—A Look at the Future", *Computer*, Volume 18, Number 7 (1985), pages 60–68.

[Hoare 1972] C. A. R. Hoare, "Towards a Theory of Parallel Programming", in **[Hoare and Perrott 1972]** (1972), pages 61–71.

[Hoare 1974] C. A. R. Hoare, "Monitors: An Operating System Structuring Concept", *Communications of the ACM*, Volume 17, Number 10 (1974), pages 549–557.

[Holt 1971] R. C. Holt, "Comments on Prevention of System Deadlocks", *Communications of the ACM*, Volume 14, Number 1 (1971), pages 36–38.

[Holt 1972] R. C. Holt, "Some Deadlock Properties of Computer Systems", *Computing Surveys*, Volume 4, Number 3 (1972), pages 179–196.

[Holub 2000] A. Holub, *Taming Java Threads*, Apress (2000).

[Howard et al. 1988] J. H. Howard, M. L. Kazar, S. G. Menees, D. A. Nichols, M. Satyanarayanan and R. N. Sidebotham, "Scale and Performance in a Distributed File System", *ACM Transactions on Computer Systems*, Volume 6, Number 1 (1988), pages 55–81.

[Howarth et al. 1961] D. J. Howarth, R. B. Payne, and F. H. Sumner, "The Manchester University Atlas Operating System, Part II: User's Description", *Computer Journal*, Volume 4, Number 3 (1961), pages 226–229.

[Hsiao et al. 1979] D. K. Hsiao, D. S. Kerr, and S. E. Madnick, *Computer Security*, Academic Press (1979).

[Hu and Perrig 2004] Y.-C. Hu and A. Perrig, "SPV: A Secure Path Vector Routing Scheme for Securing BGP", *Proceedings of ACM SIGCOMM Conference on Data Communication* (2004).

[Hu et al. 2002] Y.-C. Hu, A. Perrig, and D. Johnson, "Ariadne: A Secure On-Demand Routing Protocol for Ad Hoc Networks", *Proceedings of the Annual International Conference on Mobile Computing and Networking* (2002).

[Hyman 1985] D. Hyman, *The Columbus Chicken Statute and More Bonehead Legislation*, S. Greene Press (1985).

[Iacobucci 1988] E. Iacobucci, *OS/2 Programmer's Guide*, Osborne McGraw-Hill (1988).

[IBM 1983] *Technical Reference*. IBM Corporation (1983).

[Iliffe and Jodeit 1962] J. K. Iliffe and J. G. Jodeit, "A Dynamic Storage Allocation System", *Computer Journal*, Volume 5, Number 3 (1962), pages 200–209.

[Intel 1985a] *iAPX 286 Programmer's Reference Manual*. Intel Corporation (1985).

[Intel 1985b] *iAPX 86/88, 186/188 User's Manual Programmer's Reference*. Intel Corporation (1985).

[Intel 1986] *iAPX 386 Programmer's Reference Manual*. Intel Corporation (1986).

[Intel 1990] *i486 Microprocessor Programmer's Reference Manual*. Intel Corporation (1990).

[Intel 1993] *Pentium Processor User's Manual, Volume 3: Architecture and Programming Manual*. Intel Corporation (1993).

[Iseminger 2000] D. Iseminger, *Active Directory Services for Microsoft Windows 2000. Technical Reference*, Microsoft Press (2000).

[Jacob and Mudge 1997] B. Jacob and T. Mudge, "Software-Managed Address Translation", *Proceedings of the International Symposium on High Performance Computer Architecture and Implementation* (1997).

[Jacob and Mudge 1998a] B. Jacob and T. Mudge, "Virtual Memory in Contemporary Microprocessors", *IEEE Micro Magazine*, Volume 18, (1998), pages 60–75.

[Jacob and Mudge 1998b] B. Jacob and T. Mudge, "Virtual Memory: Issues of Implementation", *IEEE Computer Magazine*, Volume 31, Number 6 (1998), pages 33–43.

[Jacob and Mudge 2001] B. Jacob and T. Mudge, "Uniprocessor Virtual Memory Without TLBs", *IEEE Transactions on Computers*, Volume 50, Number 5 (2001).

[Jacobson and Wilkes 1991] D. M. Jacobson and J. Wilkes, "Disk Scheduling Algorithms Based on Rotational Position", Technical report, Hewlett-Packard Laboratories (1991).

[Jensen et al. 1985] E. D. Jensen, C. D. Locke, and H. Tokuda, "A Time-Driven Scheduling Model for Real-Time Operating Systems", *Proceedings of the IEEE Real-Time Systems Symposium* (1985), pages 112–122.

[Johnstone and Wilson 1998] M. S. Johnstone and P. R. Wilson, "The Memory Fragmentation Problem: Solved?", *Proceedings of the First International Symposium on Memory Management* (1998), pages 26–36.

[Jones and Liskov 1978] A. K. Jones and B. H. Liskov, "A Language Extension for Expressing Constraints on Data Access", *Communications of the ACM*, Volume 21, Number 5 (1978), pages 358–367.

[Jul et al. 1988] E. Jul, H. Levy, N. Hutchinson, and A. Black, "Fine-Grained Mobility in the Emerald System", *ACM Transactions on Computer Systems*, Volume 6, Number 1 (1988), pages 109–133.

[Kaashoek et al. 1997] M. F. Kaashoek, D. R. Engler, G. R. Ganger, H. M. Briceno, R. Hunt, D. Mazieres, T. Pinckney, R. Grimm, J. Jannotti, and K. Mackenzie, "Application Performance and Flexibility on Exokernel Systems", *Proceedings of the ACM Symposium on Operating Systems Principles* (1997), pages 52–65.

[Katz et al. 1989] R. H. Katz, G. A. Gibson, and D. A. Patterson, "Disk System Architectures for High Performance Computing", *Proceedings of the IEEE* (1989).

[Kay and Lauder 1988] J. Kay and P. Lauder, "A Fair Share Scheduler", *Communications of the ACM*, Volume 31, Number 1 (1988), pages 44–55.

[Kenah et al. 1988] L. J. Kenah, R. E. Goldenberg, and S. F. Bate, *VAX/VMS Internals and Data Structures*, Digital Press (1988).

[Kent et al. 2000] S. Kent, C. Lynn, and K. Seo, "Secure Border Gateway Protocol (Secure-BGP)", *IEEE Journal on Selected Areas in Communications*, Volume 18, Number 4 (2000), pages 582–592.

[Kenville 1982] R. F. Kenville, "Optical Disk Data Storage", *Computer*, Volume 15, Number 7 (1982), pages 21–26.

[Kessels 1977] J. L. W. Kessels, "An Alternative to Event Queues for Synchronization in Monitors", *Communications of the ACM*, Volume 20, Number 7 (1977), pages 500–503.

[Kieburtz and Silberschatz 1978] R. B. Kieburtz and A. Silberschatz, "Capability Managers", *IEEE Transactions on Software Engineering*, Volume SE-4, Number 6 (1978), pages 467–477.

[Kieburtz and Silberschatz 1983] R. B. Kieburtz and A. Silberschatz, "Access Right Expressions", *ACM Transactions on Programming Languages and Systems*, Volume 5, Number 1 (1983), pages 78–96.

[Kilburn et al. 1961] T. Kilburn, D. J. Howarth, R. B. Payne, and F. H. Sumner, "The Manchester University Atlas Operating System, Part I: Internal Organization", *Computer Journal*, Volume 4, Number 3 (1961), pages 222–225.

[Kim and Spafford 1993] G. H. Kim and E. H. Spafford, "The Design and Implementation of Tripwire: A File System Integrity Checker", Technical report, Purdue University (1993).

[King 1990] R. P. King, "Disk Arm Movement in Anticipation of Future Requests", *ACM Transactions on Computer Systems*, Volume 8, Number 3 (1990), pages 214–229.

[Kistler and Satyanarayanan 1992] J. Kistler and M. Satyanarayanan, "Disconnected Operation in the Coda File System", *ACM Transactions on Computer Systems*, Volume 10, Number 1 (1992), pages 3–25.

[Kleinrock 1975] L. Kleinrock, *Queueing Systems, Volume II: Computer Applications*, Wiley-Interscience (1975).

[Knapp 1987] E. Knapp, "Deadlock Detection in Distributed Databases", *Computing Surveys*, Volume 19, Number 4 (1987), pages 303–328.

[Knowlton 1965] K. C. Knowlton, "A Fast Storage Allocator", *Communications of the ACM*, Volume 8, Number 10 (1965), pages 623–624.

[Knuth 1966] D. E. Knuth, "Additional Comments on a Problem in Concurrent Programming Control", *Communications of the ACM*, Volume 9, Number 5 (1966), pages 321–322.

[Knuth 1973] D. E. Knuth, *The Art of Computer Programming, Volume 1: Fundamental Algorithms, Second Edition*, Addison-Wesley (1973).

[Knuth 1998] D. E. Knuth, *The Art of Computer Programming, Volume 3: Sorting and Searching, Second Edition*, Addison-Wesley (1998).

[Koch 1987] P. D. L. Koch, "Disk File Allocation Based on the Buddy System", *ACM Transactions on Computer Systems*, Volume 5, Number 4 (1987), pages 352–370.

[Kongetira et al. 2005] P. Kongetira, K. Aingaran, and K. Olukotun, "Niagara: A 32-Way Multithreaded SPARC Processor", *IEEE Micro Magazine*, Volume 25, Number 2 (2005), pages 21–29.

[Kopetz and Reisinger 1993] H. Kopetz and J. Reisinger, "The Non-Blocking Write Protocol NBW: A Solution to a Real-Time Synchronisation Problem", *IEEE Real-Time Systems Symposium* (1993), pages 131–137.

[Kosaraju 1973] S. Kosaraju, "Limitations of Dijkstra's Semaphore Primitives and Petri Nets", *Operating Systems Review*, Volume 7, Number 4 (1973), pages 122–126.

[Kozierok 2005] C. Kozierok, *The TCP/IP Guide*, No Starch Press (2005).

[Kramer 1988] S. M. Kramer, "Retaining SUID Programs in a Secure UNIX", *Proceedings of the Summer USENIX Conference* (1988), pages 107–118.

[Kubiatowicz et al. 2000] J. Kubiatowicz, D. Bindel, Y. Chen, S. Czerwinski, P. Eaton, D. Geels, R. Gummadi, S. Rhea, H. Weatherspoon, W. Weimer, C. Wells, and B. Zhao, "OceanStore: An Architecture for Global-Scale Persistent Storage", *Proc. of Architectural Support for Programming Languages and Operating Systems* (2000).

[Kurose and Ross 2005] J. Kurose and K. Ross, *Computer Networking—A Top-Down Approach Featuring the Internet, Third Edition*, Addison-Wesley (2005).

[Lamport 1974] L. Lamport, "A New Solution of Dijkstra's Concurrent Programming Problem", *Communications of the ACM*, Volume 17, Number 8 (1974), pages 453–455.

[Lamport 1976] L. Lamport, "Synchronization of Independent Processes", *Acta Informatica*, Volume 7, Number 1 (1976), pages 15–34.

[Lamport 1977] L. Lamport, "Concurrent Reading and Writing", *Communications of the ACM*, Volume 20, Number 11 (1977), pages 806–811.

[Lamport 1978a] L. Lamport, "The Implementation of Reliable Distributed Multiprocess Systems", *Computer Networks*, Volume 2, Number 2 (1978), pages 95–114.

[Lamport 1978b] L. Lamport, "Time, Clocks and the Ordering of Events in a Distributed System", *Communications of the ACM*, Volume 21, Number 7 (1978), pages 558–565.

[Lamport 1981] L. Lamport, "Password Authentication with Insecure Communications", *Communications of the ACM*, Volume 24, Number 11 (1981), pages 770–772.

[Lamport 1986] L. Lamport, "The Mutual Exclusion Problem", *Communications of the ACM*, Volume 33, Number 2 (1986), pages 313–348.

[Lamport 1987] L. Lamport, "A Fast Mutual Exclusion Algorithm", *ACM Transactions on Computer Systems*, Volume 5, Number 1 (1987), pages 1–11.

[Lamport 1991] L. Lamport, "The Mutual Exclusion Problem Has Been Solved", *Communications of the ACM*, Volume 34, Number 1 (1991), page 110.

[Lamport et al. 1982] L. Lamport, R. Shostak, and M. Pease, "The Byzantine Generals Problem", *ACM Transactions on Programming Languages and Systems*, Volume 4, Number 3 (1982), pages 382–401.

[Lampson 1969] B. W. Lampson, "Dynamic Protection Structures", *Proceedings of the AFIPS Fall Joint Computer Conference* (1969), pages 27–38.

[Lampson 1971] B. W. Lampson, "Protection", *Proceedings of the Fifth Annual Princeton Conference on Information Systems Science* (1971), pages 437–443.

[Lampson 1973] B. W. Lampson, "A Note on the Confinement Problem", *Communications of the ACM*, Volume 10, Number 16 (1973), pages 613–615.

[Lampson and Redell 1979] B. W. Lampson and D. D. Redell, "Experience with Processes and Monitors in Mesa", *Proceedings of the 7th ACM Symposium on Operating Systems Principles (SOSP)* (1979), pages 43–44.

[Lampson and Sturgis 1976] B. Lampson and H. Sturgis, "Crash Recovery in a Distributed Data Storage System", Technical report, Xerox Research Center (1976).

[Landwehr 1981] C. E. Landwehr, "Formal Models of Computer Security", *Computing Surveys*, Volume 13, Number 3 (1981), pages 247–278.

[Lann 1977] G. L. Lann, "Distributed Systems—Toward a Formal Approach", *Proceedings of the IFIP Congress* (1977), pages 155–160.

[Larson and Kajla 1984] P. Larson and A. Kajla, "File Organization: Implementation of a Method Guaranteeing Retrieval in One Access", *Communications of the ACM*, Volume 27, Number 7 (1984), pages 670–677.

[Lauzac et al. 2003] S. Lauzac, R. Melhem, and D. Mosse, "An Improved Rate-Monotonic Admission Control and Its Applications", *IEEE Transactions on Computers*, Volume 52, Number 3 (2003).

[Lee 2003] J. Lee, "An End-User Perspective on File-Sharing Systems", *Communications of the ACM*, Volume 46, Number 2 (2003), pages 49–53.

[Lee and Thekkath 1996] E. K. Lee and C. A. Thekkath, "Petal: Distributed Virtual Disks", *Proceedings of the Seventh International Conference on Architectural Support for Programming Languages and Operating Systems* (1996), pages 84–92.

[Leffler et al. 1989] S. J. Leffler, M. K. McKusick, M. J. Karels, and J. S. Quarterman, *The Design and Implementation of the 4.3BSD UNIX Operating System*, Addison-Wesley (1989).

[Lehmann 1987] F. Lehmann, "Computer Break-Ins", *Communications of the ACM*, Volume 30, Number 7 (1987), pages 584–585.

[Lehoczky et al. 1989] J. Lehoczky, L. Sha, and Y. Ding, "The Rate Monotonic Scheduling Algorithm: Exact Characterization and Average Case Behaviour", *Proceedings of 10th IEEE Real-Time Systems Symposium* (1989).

[Lempel 1979] A. Lempel, "Cryptology in Transition", *Computing Surveys*, Volume 11, Number 4 (1979), pages 286–303.

[Leslie et al. 1996] I. M. Leslie, D. McAuley, R. Black, T. Roscoe, P. T. Barham, D. Evers, R. Fairbairns, and E. Hyden, "The Design and Implementation of an Operating System to Support Distributed Multimedia Applications", *IEEE Journal of Selected Areas in Communications*, Volume 14, Number 7 (1996), pages 1280–1297.

[Lett and Konigsford 1968] A. L. Lett and W. L. Konigsford, "TSS/360: A Time-Shared Operating System", *Proceedings of the AFIPS Fall Joint Computer Conference* (1968), pages 15–28.

[Levin et al. 1975] R. Levin, E. S. Cohen, W. M. Corwin, F. J. Pollack, and W. A. Wulf, "Policy/Mechanism Separation in Hydra", *Proceedings of the ACM Symposium on Operating Systems Principles* (1975), pages 132–140.

[Levine 2003] G. Levine, "Defining Deadlock", *Operating Systems Review*, Volume 37, Number 1 (2003).

[Levy 1994] S. Levy, *Hackers*, Penguin Books (1994).

[Lewis and Berg 1998] B. Lewis and D. Berg, *Multithreaded Programming with Pthreads*, Sun Microsystems Press (1998).

[Lewis and Berg 2000] B. Lewis and D. Berg, *Multithreaded Programming with Java Technology*, Sun Microsystems Press (2000).

[Lichtenberger and Pirtle 1965] W. W. Lichtenberger and M. W. Pirtle, "A Facility for Experimentation in Man-Machine Interaction", *Proceedings of the AFIPS Fall Joint Computer Conference* (1965), pages 589–598.

[Lindholm and Yellin 1999] T. Lindholm and F. Yellin, *The Java Virtual Machine Specification, Second Edition*, Addison-Wesley (1999).

[Ling et al. 2000] Y. Ling, T. Mullen, and X. Lin, "Analysis of Optimal Thread Pool Size", *Operating System Review*, Volume 34, Number 2 (2000).

[Lipner 1975] S. Lipner, "A Comment on the Confinement Problem", *Operating System Review*, Volume 9, Number 5 (1975), pages 192–196.

[Lipton 1974] R. Lipton, *On Synchronization Primitive Systems*. PhD thesis, Carnegie-Mellon University (1974).

[Liskov 1972] B. H. Liskov, "The Design of the Venus Operating System", *Communications of the ACM*, Volume 15, Number 3 (1972), pages 144–149.

[Liu and Layland 1973] C. L. Liu and J. W. Layland, "Scheduling Algorithms for Multiprogramming in a Hard Real-Time Environment", *Communications of the ACM*, Volume 20, Number 1 (1973), pages 46–61.

[Lobel 1986] J. Lobel, *Foiling the System Breakers: Computer Security and Access Control*, McGraw-Hill (1986).

[Loo 2003] A. W. Loo, "The Future of Peer-to-Peer Computing", *Communications of the ACM*, Volume 46, Number 9 (2003), pages 56–61.

[Love 2004] R. Love, *Linux Kernel Development*, Developer's Library (2004).

[Love 2005] R. Love, *Linux Kernel Development, Second Edition*, Developer's Library (2005).

[Lowney et al. 1993] P. G. Lowney, S. M. Freudenberger, T. J. Karzes, W. D. Lichtenstein, R. P. Nix, J. S. O'Donnell, and J. C. Ruttenberg, "The Multiflow Trace Scheduling Compiler". *Journal of Supercomputing*, Volume 7, Number 1-2 (1993), pages 51–142.

[Ludwig 1998] M. Ludwig, *The Giant Black Book of Computer Viruses, Second Edition*, American Eagle Publications (1998).

[Ludwig 2002] M. Ludwig, *The Little Black Book of Email Viruses*, American Eagle Publications (2002).

[Lumb et al. 2000] C. Lumb, J. Schindler, G. R. Ganger, D. F. Nagle, and E. Riedel, "Towards Higher Disk Head Utilization: Extracting Free Bandwidth From Busy Disk Drives", *Symposium on Operating Systems Design and Implementation* (2000).

[Maekawa 1985] M. Maekawa, "A Square Root Algorithm for Mutual Exclusion in Decentralized Systems", *ACM Transactions on Computer Systems*, Volume 3, Number 2 (1985), pages 145–159.

[Maher et al. 1994] C. Maher, J. S. Goldick, C. Kerby, and B. Zumach, "The Integration of Distributed File Systems and Mass Storage Systems", *Proceedings of the IEEE Symposium on Mass Storage Systems* (1994), pages 27–31.

[Marsh et al. 1991] B. D. Marsh, M. L. Scott, T. J. LeBlanc, and E. P. Markatos, "First-Class User-Level Threads", *Proceedings of the 13th ACM Symposium on Operating Systems Principle* (1991), pages 110–121.

[Mattern 1988] F. Mattern, "Virtual Time and Global States of Distributed Systems", *Workshop on Parallel and Distributed Algorithms* (1988).

[Mattson et al. 1970] R. L. Mattson, J. Gecsei, D. R. Slutz, and I. L. Traiger, "Evaluation Techniques for Storage Hierarchies", *IBM Systems Journal*, Volume 9, Number 2 (1970), pages 78–117.

[Mauro and McDougall 2007] J. Mauro and R. McDougall, *Solaris Internals: Core Kernel Architecture*, Prentice Hall (2007).

[McCanne and Jacobson 1993] S. McCanne and V. Jacobson, "The BSD Packet Filter: A New Architecture for User-level Packet Capture", *USENIX Winter* (1993), pages 259–270.

[McDougall and Laudon 2006] R. McDougall and J. Laudon, "Multi-Core Processors are Here", *USENIX ;login: The USENIX Magazine*, Volume 31, Number 5 (2006), pages 32–39.

[McDougall and Mauro 2007] R. McDougall and J. Mauro, *Solaris Internals, Second Edition*, Prentice Hall (2007).

[McGraw and Andrews 1979] J. R. McGraw and G. R. Andrews, "Access Control in Parallel Programs", *IEEE Transactions on Software Engineering*, Volume SE-5, Number 1 (1979), pages 1–9.

[McKeag and Wilson 1976] R. M. McKeag and R. Wilson, *Studies in Operating Systems*, Academic Press (1976).

[McKeon 1985] B. McKeon, "An Algorithm for Disk Caching with Limited Memory", *Byte*, Volume 10, Number 9 (1985), pages 129–138.

[McKusick and Neville-Neil 2005] M. K. McKusick and G. V. Neville-Neil, *The Design and Implementation of the FreeBSD UNIX Operating System*, Addison Wesley (2005).

[McKusick et al. 1984] M. K. McKusick, W. N. Joy, S. J. Leffler, and R. S. Fabry, "A Fast File System for UNIX", *ACM Transactions on Computer Systems*, Volume 2, Number 3 (1984), pages 181–197.

[McKusick et al. 1996] M. K. McKusick, K. Bostic, and M. J. Karels, *The Design and Implementation of the 4.4 BSD UNIX Operating System*, John Wiley and Sons (1996).

[McNairy and Bhatia 2005] C. McNairy and R. Bhatia, "Montecito: A Dual-Core, Dual-Threaded Itanium Processor", *IEEE Micro Magazine*, Volume 25, Number 2 (2005), pages 10–20.

[McVoy and Kleiman 1991] L. W. McVoy and S. R. Kleiman, "Extent-like Performance from a UNIX File System", *Proceedings of the Winter USENIX Conference* (1991), pages 33–44.

[Mealy et al. 1966] G. H. Mealy, B. I. Witt, and W. A. Clark, "The Functional Structure of OS/360", *IBM Systems Journal*, Volume 5, Number 1 (1966).

[Mellor-Crummey and Scott 1991] J. M. Mellor-Crummey and M. L. Scott, "Algorithms for Scalable Synchronization on Shared-Memory Multiprocessors", *ACM Transactions on Computer Systems*, Volume 9, Number 1 (1991), pages 21–65.

[Menasce and Muntz 1979] D. Menasce and R. R. Muntz, "Locking and Deadlock Detection in Distributed Data Bases", *IEEE Transactions on Software Engineering*, Volume SE-5, Number 3 (1979), pages 195–202.

[Mercer et al. 1994] C. W. Mercer, S. Savage, and H. Tokuda, "Processor Capacity Reserves: Operating System Support for Multimedia Applications", *International Conference on Multimedia Computing and Systems* (1994), pages 90–99.

[Meyer and Seawright 1970] R. A. Meyer and L. H. Seawright, "A Virtual Machine Time-Sharing System", *IBM Systems Journal*, Volume 9, Number 3 (1970), pages 199–218.

[Microsoft 1986] *Microsoft MS-DOS User's Reference and Microsoft MS-DOS Programmer's Reference*. Microsoft Press (1986).

[Microsoft 1996] *Microsoft Windows NT Workstation Resource Kit*. Microsoft Press (1996).

[Microsoft 2000a] *Microsoft Developer Network Development Library*. Microsoft Press (2000).

[Microsoft 2000b] *Microsoft Windows 2000 Server Resource Kit*. Microsoft Press (2000).

[Milenkovic 1987] M. Milenkovic, *Operating Systems: Concepts and Design*, McGraw-Hill (1987).

[Miller and Katz 1993] E. L. Miller and R. H. Katz, "An Analysis of File Migration in a UNIX Supercomputing Environment", *Proceedings of the Winter USENIX Conference* (1993), pages 421–434.

[Milojicic et al. 2000] D. S. Milojicic, F. Douglis, Y. Paindaveine, R. Wheeler, and S. Zhou, "Process Migration", *ACM Computing Surveys*, Volume 32, Number 3 (2000), pages 241–299.

[Mockapetris 1987] P. Mockapetris, "Domain Names—Concepts and Facilities", *Network Working Group, Request for Comments: 1034* (1987).

[Mohan and Lindsay 1983] C. Mohan and B. Lindsay, "Efficient Commit Protocols for the Tree of Processes Model of Distributed Transactions", *Proceedings of the ACM Symposium on Principles of Database Systems* (1983).

[Mok 1983] A. K. Mok, *Fundamental Design Problems of Distributed Systems for the Hard Real-Time Environment*. PhD thesis, Massachusetts Institute of Technology, MA (1983).

[Morris 1973] J. H. Morris, "Protection in Programming Languages", *Communications of the ACM*, Volume 16, Number 1 (1973), pages 15–21.

[Morris and Thompson 1979] R. Morris and K. Thompson, "Password Security: A Case History", *Communications of the ACM*, Volume 22, Number 11 (1979), pages 594–597.

[Morris et al. 1986] J. H. Morris, M. Satyanarayanan, M. H. Conner, J. H. Howard, D. S. H. Rosenthal, and F. D. Smith, "Andrew: A Distributed Personal Computing Environment", *Communications of the ACM*, Volume 29, Number 3 (1986), pages 184–201.

[Morshedian 1986] D. Morshedian, "How to Fight Password Pirates", *Computer*, Volume 19, Number 1 (1986).

[Motorola 1993] *PowerPC 601 RISC Microprocessor User's Manual*. Motorola Inc. (1993).

[Mullender 1993] S. Mullender, *Distributed Systems, Third Edition*, Addison-Wesley (1993).

[Myers and Beigl 2003] B. Myers and M. Beigl, "Handheld Computing", *Computer*, Volume 36, Number 9 (2003), pages 27–29.

[Navarro et al. 2002] J. Navarro, S. Lyer, P. Druschel, and A. Cox, "Practical, Transparent Operating System Support for Superpages", *Proceedings of the USENIX Symposium on Operating Systems Design and Implementation* (2002).

[Needham and Walker 1977] R. M. Needham and R. D. H. Walker, "The Cambridge CAP Computer and Its Protection System", *Proceedings of the Sixth Symposium on Operating System Principles* (1977), pages 1–10.

[Nelson et al. 1988] M. Nelson, B. Welch, and J. K. Ousterhout, "Caching in the Sprite Network File System", *ACM Transactions on Computer Systems*, Volume 6, Number 1 (1988), pages 134–154.

[Norton and Wilton 1988] P. Norton and R. Wilton, *The New Peter Norton Programmer's Guide to the IBM PC & PS/2*, Microsoft Press (1988).

[Nutt 2004] G. Nutt, *Operating Systems: A Modern Perspective, Third Edition*, Addison-Wesley (2004).

[Oaks and Wong 1999] S. Oaks and H. Wong, *Java Threads, Second Edition*, O'Reilly & Associates (1999).

[Obermarck 1982] R. Obermarck, "Distributed Deadlock Detection Algorithm", *ACM Transactions on Database Systems*, Volume 7, Number 2 (1982), pages 187–208.

[O'Leary and Kitts 1985] B. T. O'Leary and D. L. Kitts, "Optical Device for a Mass Storage System", *Computer*, Volume 18, Number 7 (1985).

[Olsen and Kenley 1989] R. P. Olsen and G. Kenley, "Virtual Optical Disks Solve the On-Line Storage Crunch", *Computer Design*, Volume 28, Number 1 (1989), pages 93–96.

[Organick 1972] E. I. Organick, *The Multics System: An Examination of Its Structure*, MIT Press (1972).

[Ortiz 2001] S. Ortiz, "Embedded OSs Gain the Inside Track", *Computer*, Volume 34, Number 11 (2001).

[Ousterhout 1991] J. Ousterhout. "The Role of Distributed State". In CMU Computer Science: a 25th Anniversary Commemorative (1991), R. F. Rashid, Ed., Addison-Wesley (1991).

[Ousterhout et al. 1985] J. K. Ousterhout, H. D. Costa, D. Harrison, J. A. Kunze, M. Kupfer, and J. G. Thompson, "A Trace-Driven Analysis of the UNIX 4.2 BSD File System", *Proceedings of the ACM Symposium on Operating Systems Principles* (1985), pages 15–24.

[Ousterhout et al. 1988] J. K. Ousterhout, A. R. Cherenson, F. Douglis, M. N. Nelson, and B. B. Welch, "The Sprite Network-Operating System", *Computer*, Volume 21, Number 2 (1988), pages 23–36.

[Parameswaran et al. 2001] M. Parameswaran, A. Susarla, and A. B. Whinston, "P2P Networking: An Information-Sharing Alternative", *Computer*, Volume 34, Number 7 (2001).

[Parmelee et al. 1972] R. P. Parmelee, T. I. Peterson, C. C. Tillman, and D. Hatfield, "Virtual Storage and Virtual Machine Concepts", *IBM Systems Journal*, Volume 11, Number 2 (1972), pages 99–130.

[Parnas 1975] D. L. Parnas, "On a Solution to the Cigarette Smokers' Problem Without Conditional Statements", *Communications of the ACM*, Volume 18, Number 3 (1975), pages 181–183.

[Patil 1971] S. Patil, "Limitations and Capabilities of Dijkstra's Semaphore Primitives for Coordination Among Processes", Technical report, Massachusetts Institute of Technology (1971).

[Patterson et al. 1988] D. A. Patterson, G. Gibson, and R. H. Katz, "A Case for Redundant Arrays of Inexpensive Disks (RAID)", *Proceedings of the ACM SIGMOD International Conference on the Management of Data* (1988).

[Pease et al. 1980] M. Pease, R. Shostak, and L. Lamport, "Reaching Agreement in the Presence of Faults", *Communications of the ACM*, Volume 27, Number 2 (1980), pages 228–234.

[Pechura and Schoeffler 1983] M. A. Pechura and J. D. Schoeffler, "Estimating File Access Time of Floppy Disks", *Communications of the ACM*, Volume 26, Number 10 (1983), pages 754–763.

[Perlman 1988] R. Perlman, *Network Layer Protocols with Byzantine Robustness*. PhD thesis, Massachusetts Institute of Technology (1988).

[Peterson 1981] G. L. Peterson, "Myths About the Mutual Exclusion Problem", *Information Processing Letters*, Volume 12, Number 3 (1981).

[Peterson and Norman 1977] J. L. Peterson and T. A. Norman, "Buddy Systems", *Communications of the ACM*, Volume 20, Number 6 (1977), pages 421–431.

[Pfleeger and Pfleeger 2003] C. Pfleeger and S. Pfleeger, *Security in Computing, Third Edition*, Prentice Hall (2003).

[Philbin et al. 1996] J. Philbin, J. Edler, O. J. Anshus, C. C. Douglas, and K. Li, "Thread Scheduling for Cache Locality", *Architectural Support for Programming Languages and Operating Systems* (1996), pages 60–71.

[Pinilla and Gill 2003] R. Pinilla and M. Gill, "JVM: Platform Independent vs. Performance Dependent", *Operating System Review* (2003).

[Popek 1974] G. J. Popek, "Protection Structures", *Computer*, Volume 7, Number 6 (1974), pages 22–33.

[Popek and Walker 1985] G. Popek and B. Walker, editors, *The LOCUS Distributed System Architecture*, MIT Press (1985).

[Prieve and Fabry 1976] B. G. Prieve and R. S. Fabry, "VMIN—An Optimal Variable Space Page-Replacement Algorithm", *Communications of the ACM*, Volume 19, Number 5 (1976), pages 295–297.

[Psaltis and Mok 1995] D. Psaltis and F. Mok, "Holographic Memories", *Scientific American*, Volume 273, Number 5 (1995), pages 70–76.

[Purdin et al. 1987] T. D. M. Purdin, R. D. Schlichting, and G. R. Andrews, "A File Replication Facility for Berkeley UNIX", *Software—Practice and Experience*, Volume 17, (1987), pages 923–940.

[Purdom, Jr. and Stigler 1970] P. W. Purdom, Jr. and S. M. Stigler, "Statistical Properties of the Buddy System", *J. ACM*, Volume 17, Number 4 (1970), pages 683–697.

[Quinlan 1991] S. Quinlan, "A Cached WORM", *Software—Practice and Experience*, Volume 21, Number 12 (1991), pages 1289–1299.

[Rago 1993] S. Rago, *UNIX System V Network Programming*, Addison-Wesley (1993).

[Rashid 1986] R. F. Rashid, "From RIG to Accent to Mach: The Evolution of a Network Operating System", *Proceedings of the ACM/IEEE Computer Society, Fall Joint Computer Conference* (1986).

[Rashid and Robertson 1981] R. Rashid and G. Robertson, "Accent: A Communication-Oriented Network Operating System Kernel", *Proceedings of the ACM Symposium on Operating System Principles* (1981).

[Raymond 1999] E. S. Raymond, *The Cathedral & the Bazaar*, O'Reilly & Associates (1999).

[Raynal 1986] M. Raynal, *Algorithms for Mutual Exclusion*, MIT Press (1986).

[Raynal 1991] M. Raynal, "A Simple Taxonomy for Distributed Mutual Exclusion Algorithms", *Operating Systems Review*, Volume 25, Number 1 (1991), pages 47–50.

[Raynal and Singhal 1996] M. Raynal and M. Singhal, "Logical Time: Capturing Causality in Distributed Systems", *Computer*, Volume 29, Number 2 (1996), pages 49–56.

[Reddy and Wyllie 1994] A. L. N. Reddy and J. C. Wyllie, "I/O issues in a Multimedia System", *Computer*, Volume 27, Number 3 (1994), pages 69–74.

[Redell and Fabry 1974] D. D. Redell and R. S. Fabry, "Selective Revocation of Capabilities", *Proceedings of the IRIA International Workshop on Protection in Operating Systems* (1974), pages 197–210.

[Redell et al. 1980] D. D. Redell, Y. K. Dalal, T. R. Horsley, H. C. Lauer, W. C. Lynch, P. R. McJones, H. G. Murray, and S. P. Purcell, "Pilot: An Operating System for a Personal Computer", *Communications of the ACM*, Volume 23, Number 2 (1980), pages 81–92.

[Reed 1983] D. P. Reed, "Implementing Atomic Actions on Decentralized Data", *ACM Transactions on Computer Systems*, Volume 1, Number 1 (1983), pages 3–23.

[Reed and Kanodia 1979] D. P. Reed and R. K. Kanodia, "Synchronization with Eventcounts and Sequences", *Communications of the ACM*, Volume 22, Number 2 (1979), pages 115–123.

[Regehr et al. 2000] J. Regehr, M. B. Jones, and J. A. Stankovic, "Operating System Support for Multimedia: The Programming Model Matters", Technical report, Microsoft Research (2000).

[Reid 1987] B. Reid, "Reflections on Some Recent Widespread Computer Break-Ins", *Communications of the ACM*, Volume 30, Number 2 (1987), pages 103–105.

[Ricart and Agrawala 1981] G. Ricart and A. K. Agrawala, "An Optimal Algorithm for Mutual Exclusion in Computer Networks", *Communications of the ACM*, Volume 24, Number 1 (1981), pages 9–17.

[Richards 1990] A. E. Richards, "A File System Approach for Integrating Removable Media Devices and Jukeboxes", *Optical Information Systems*, Volume 10, Number 5 (1990), pages 270–274.

[Richter 1997] J. Richter, *Advanced Windows*, Microsoft Press (1997).

[Riedel et al. 1998] E. Riedel, G. A. Gibson, and C. Faloutsos, "Active Storage for Large-Scale Data Mining and Multimedia", *Proceedings of 24th International Conference on Very Large Data Bases* (1998), pages 62–73.

[Ripeanu et al. 2002] M. Ripeanu, A. Immnitchi, and I. Foster, "Mapping the Gnutella Network", *IEEE Internet Computing*, Volume 6, Number 1 (2002).

[Rivest et al. 1978] R. L. Rivest, A. Shamir, and L. Adleman, "On Digital Signatures and Public Key Cryptosystems", *Communications of the ACM*, Volume 21, Number 2 (1978), pages 120–126.

[Robbins and Robbins 2003] K. Robbins and S. Robbins, *Unix Systems Programming: Communication, Concurrency and Threads, Second Edition*, Prentice Hall (2003).

[Roberson 2003] J. Roberson, "ULE: A Modern Scheduler For FreeBSD", *Proceedings of the USENIX BSDCon Conference* (2003).

[Rodeheffer and Schroeder 1991] T. L. Rodeheffer and M. D. Schroeder, "Automatic Reconfiguration in Autonet", *Proceedings of the ACM Symposium on Operating Systems Principles* (1991), pages 183–97.

[Rojas and Hashagen 2000] R. Rojas and U. Hashagen, *The First Computers—History and Architectures*, MIT Press (2000).

[Rosenblum and Ousterhout 1991] M. Rosenblum and J. K. Ousterhout, "The Design and Implementation of a Log-Structured File System", *Proceedings of the ACM Symposium on Operating Systems Principles* (1991), pages 1–15.

[Rosenkrantz et al. 1978] D. J. Rosenkrantz, R. E. Stearns, and P. M. Lewis, "System Level Concurrency Control for Distributed Database Systems", *ACM Transactions on Database Systems*, Volume 3, Number 2 (1978), pages 178–198.

[Ruemmler and Wilkes 1991] C. Ruemmler and J. Wilkes, "Disk Shuffling", Technical report (1991).

[Ruemmler and Wilkes 1993] C. Ruemmler and J. Wilkes, "Unix Disk Access Patterns", *Proceedings of the Winter USENIX Conference* (1993), pages 405–420.

[Ruemmler and Wilkes 1994] C. Ruemmler and J. Wilkes, "An Introduction to Disk Drive Modeling", *Computer*, Volume 27, Number 3 (1994), pages 17–29.

[Rushby 1981] J. M. Rushby, "Design and Verification of Secure Systems", *Proceedings of the ACM Symposium on Operating Systems Principles* (1981), pages 12–21.

[Rushby and Randell 1983] J. Rushby and B. Randell, "A Distributed Secure System", *Computer*, Volume 16, Number 7 (1983), pages 55–67.

[Russell and Gangemi 1991] D. Russell and G. T. Gangemi, *Computer Security Basics*, O'Reilly & Associates (1991).

[Russinovich and Solomon 2005] M. E. Russinovich and D. A. Solomon, *Microsoft Windows Internals, Fourth Edition*, Microsoft Press (2005).

[Saltzer and Schroeder 1975] J. H. Saltzer and M. D. Schroeder, "The Protection of Information in Computer Systems", *Proceedings of the IEEE* (1975), pages 1278–1308.

[Sandberg 1987] R. Sandberg, *The Sun Network File System: Design, Implementation and Experience*, Sun Microsystems (1987).

[Sandberg et al. 1985] R. Sandberg, D. Goldberg, S. Kleiman, D. Walsh, and B. Lyon, "Design and Implementation of the Sun Network Filesystem", *Proceedings of the Summer USENIX Conference* (1985), pages 119–130.

[Sargent and Shoemaker 1995] M. Sargent and R. Shoemaker, *The Personal Computer from the Inside Out, Third Edition*, Addison-Wesley (1995).

[Sarisky 1983] L. Sarisky, "Will Removable Hard Disks Replace the Floppy?", *Byte* (1983), pages 110–117.

[Satyanarayanan 1990] M. Satyanarayanan, "Scalable, Secure and Highly Available Distributed File Access", *Computer*, Volume 23, Number 5 (1990), pages 9–21.

[Savage et al. 2000] S. Savage, D. Wetherall, A. R. Karlin, and T. Anderson, "Practical Network Support for IP Traceback", *Proceedings of ACM SIGCOMM Conference on Data Communication* (2000), pages 295–306.

[Schell 1983] R. R. Schell, "A Security Kernel for a Multiprocessor Microcomputer", *Computer* (1983), pages 47–53.

[Schindler and Gregory 1999] J. Schindler and G. Gregory, "Automated Disk Drive Characterization", Technical report (1999).

[Schlichting and Schneider 1982] R. D. Schlichting and F. B. Schneider, "Understanding and Using Asynchronous Message Passing Primitives", *Proceedings of the Symposium on Principles of Distributed Computing* (1982), pages 141–147.

[Schneider 1982] F. B. Schneider, "Synchronization in Distributed Programs", *ACM Transactions on Programming Languages and Systems*, Volume 4, Number 2 (1982), pages 125–148.

[Schneier 1996] B. Schneier, *Applied Cryptography, Second Edition*, John Wiley and Sons (1996).

[Schrage 1967] L. E. Schrage, "The Queue M/G/I with Feedback to Lower Priority Queues", *Management Science*, Volume 13, (1967), pages 466–474.

[Schwarz and Mattern 1994] R. Schwarz and F. Mattern, "Detecting Causal Relationships in Distributed Computations: In Search of the Holy Grail", *Distributed Computing*, Volume 7, Number 3 (1994), pages 149–174.

[Seely 1989] D. Seely, "Password Cracking: A Game of Wits", *Communications of the ACM*, Volume 32, Number 6 (1989), pages 700–704.

[Seltzer et al. 1990] M. Seltzer, P. Chen, and J. Ousterhout, "Disk Scheduling Revisited", *Proceedings of the Winter USENIX Conference* (1990), pages 313–323.

[Seltzer et al. 1993] M. I. Seltzer, K. Bostic, M. K. McKusick, and C. Staelin, "An Implementation of a Log-Structured File System for UNIX", *USENIX Winter* (1993), pages 307–326.

[Seltzer et al. 1995] M. I. Seltzer, K. A. Smith, H. Balakrishnan, J. Chang, S. McMains, and V. N. Padmanabhan, "File System Logging Versus Clustering: A Performance Comparison", *USENIX Winter* (1995), pages 249–264.

[Shrivastava and Panzieri 1982] S. K. Shrivastava and F. Panzieri, "The Design of a Reliable Remote Procedure Call Mechanism", *IEEE Transactions on Computers*, Volume C-31, Number 7 (1982), pages 692–697.

[Siddha et al. 2007] S. Siddha, V. Pallipadi, and A. Mallick, "Process Scheduling Challenges in the Era of Multi-Core Processors", *Intel Technology Journal*, Volume 11, (2007).

[Silberschatz et al. 2001] A. Silberschatz, H. F. Korth, and S. Sudarshan, *Database System Concepts, Fourth Edition*, McGraw-Hill (2001).

[Silverman 1983] J. M. Silverman, "Reflections on the Verification of the Security of an Operating System Kernel", *Proceedings of the ACM Symposium on Operating Systems Principles* (1983), pages 143–154.

[Silvers 2000] C. Silvers, "UBC: An Efficient Unified I/O and Memory Caching Subsystem for NetBSD", *USENIX Annual Technical Conference—FREENIX Track* (2000).

[Simmons 1979] G. J. Simmons, "Symmetric and Asymmetric Encryption", *Computing Surveys*, Volume 11, Number 4 (1979), pages 304–330.

[Sincerbox 1994] G. T. Sincerbox, editor, *Selected Papers on Holographic Storage*, Optical Engineering Press (1994).

[Singh 2007] A. Singh, *Mac OS X Internals : A Systems Approach*, Addison-Wesley (2007).

[Singhal 1989] M. Singhal, "Deadlock Detection in Distributed Systems", *Computer*, Volume 22, Number 11 (1989), pages 37–48.

[Sirer et al. 1999] E. G. Sirer, R. Grimm, A. J. Gregory, and B. N. Bershad, "Design and Implementation of a Distributed Virtual Machine for Networked Computers", *Symposium on Operating Systems Principles* (1999), pages 202–216.

[Smith 1982] A. J. Smith, "Cache Memories", *ACM Computing Surveys*, Volume 14, Number 3 (1982), pages 473–530.

[Smith 1985] A. J. Smith, "Disk Cache-Miss Ratio Analysis and Design Considerations", *ACM Transactions on Computer Systems*, Volume 3, Number 3 (1985), pages 161–203.

[Sobti et al. 2004] S. Sobti, N. Garg, F. Zheng, J. Lai, Y. Shao, C. Zhang, E. Ziskind, A. Krishnamurthy, and R. Wang, "Segank: A Distributed Mobile Storage System", *Proceedings of the Third USENIX Conference on File and Storage Technologies* (2004).

[Solomon 1998] D. A. Solomon, *Inside Windows NT, Second Edition*, Microsoft Press (1998).

[Solomon and Russinovich 2000] D. A. Solomon and M. E. Russinovich, *Inside Microsoft Windows 2000, Third Edition*, Microsoft Press (2000).

[Spafford 1989] E. H. Spafford, "The Internet Worm: Crisis and Aftermath", *Communications of the ACM*, Volume 32, Number 6 (1989), pages 678–687.

[Spector and Schwarz 1983] A. Z. Spector and P. M. Schwarz, "Transactions: A Construct for Reliable Distributed Computing", *ACM SIGOPS Operating Systems Review*, Volume 17, Number 2 (1983), pages 18–35.

[Stallings 2000a] W. Stallings, *Local and Metropolitan Area Networks*, Prentice Hall (2000).

[Stallings 2000b] W. Stallings, *Operating Systems, Fourth Edition*, Prentice Hall (2000).

[Stallings 2003] W. Stallings, *Cryptography and Network Security: Principles and Practice, Third Edition*, Prentice Hall (2003).

[Stankovic 1982] J. S. Stankovic, "Software Communication Mechanisms: Procedure Calls Versus Messages", *Computer*, Volume 15, Number 4 (1982).

[Stankovic 1996] J. A. Stankovic, "Strategic Directions in Real-Time and Embedded Systems", *ACM Computing Surveys*, Volume 28, Number 4 (1996), pages 751–763.

[Staunstrup 1982] J. Staunstrup, "Message Passing Communication Versus Procedure Call Communication", *Software—Practice and Experience*, Volume 12, Number 3 (1982), pages 223–234.

[Steinmetz 1995] R. Steinmetz, "Analyzing the Multimedia Operating System", *IEEE MultiMedia*, Volume 2, Number 1 (1995), pages 68–84.

[Stephenson 1983] C. J. Stephenson, "Fast Fits: A New Method for Dynamic Storage Allocation", *Proceedings of the Ninth Symposium on Operating Systems Principles* (1983), pages 30–32.

[Stevens 1992] R. Stevens, *Advanced Programming in the UNIX Environment*, Addison-Wesley (1992).

[Stevens 1994] R. Stevens, *TCP/IP Illustrated Volume 1: The Protocols*, Addison-Wesley (1994).

[Stevens 1995] R. Stevens, *TCP/IP Illustrated, Volume 2: The Implementation*, Addison-Wesley (1995).

[Stevens 1997] W. R. Stevens, *UNIX Network Programming—Volume I*, Prentice Hall (1997).

[Stevens 1998] W. R. Stevens, *UNIX Network Programming—Volume II*, Prentice Hall (1998).

[Stevens 1999] W. R. Stevens, *UNIX Network Programming Interprocess Communications—Volume 2*, Prentice Hall (1999).

[Stoica et al. 1996] I. Stoica, H. Abdel-Wahab, K. Jeffay, S. Baruah, J. Gehrke, and G. Plaxton, "A Proportional Share Resource Allocation Algorithm for Real-Time, Time-Shared Systems", *IEEE Real-Time Systems Symposium* (1996).

[Stokes 2007] J. Stokes, *Inside the Machine*, No Starch Press (2007).

[Su 1982] Z. Su, "A Distributed System for Internet Name Service", *Network Working Group, Request for Comments: 830* (1982).

[Sugerman et al. 2001] J. Sugerman, G. Venkitachalam, and B. Lim, "Virtualizing I/O Devices on VMware Workstation's Hosted Virtual Machine Monitor", *2001 USENIX Annual Technical Conference* (2001).

[Sun 1990] *Network Programming Guide*. Sun Microsystems (1990).

[Svobodova 1984] L. Svobodova, "File Servers for Network-Based Distributed Systems", *ACM Computing Surveys*, Volume 16, Number 4 (1984), pages 353–398.

[Talluri et al. 1995] M. Talluri, M. D. Hill, and Y. A. Khalidi, "A New Page Table for 64-bit Address Spaces", *Proceedings of the ACM Symposium on Operating Systems Principles* (1995).

[Tamches and Miller 1999] A. Tamches and B. P. Miller, "Fine-Grained Dynamic Instrumentation of Commodity Operating System Kernels", *USENIX Symposium on Operating Systems Design and Implementation* (1999).

[Tanenbaum 1990] A. S. Tanenbaum, *Structured Computer Organization, Third Edition*, Prentice Hall (1990).

[Tanenbaum 2001] A. S. Tanenbaum, *Modern Operating Systems*, Prentice Hall (2001).

[Tanenbaum 2003] A. S. Tanenbaum, *Computer Networks, Fourth Edition*, Prentice Hall (2003).

[Tanenbaum and Van Renesse 1985] A. S. Tanenbaum and R. Van Renesse, "Distributed Operating Systems", *ACM Computing Surveys*, Volume 17, Number 4 (1985), pages 419–470.

[Tanenbaum and van Steen 2002] A. Tanenbaum and M. van Steen, *Distributed Systems: Principles and Paradigms*, Prentice Hall (2002).

[Tanenbaum and Woodhull 1997] A. S. Tanenbaum and A. S. Woodhull, *Operating System Design and Implementation, Second Edition*, Prentice Hall (1997).

[Tate 2000] S. Tate, *Windows 2000 Essential Reference*, New Riders (2000).

[Tay and Ananda 1990] B. H. Tay and A. L. Ananda, "A Survey of Remote Procedure Calls", *Operating Systems Review*, Volume 24, Number 3 (1990), pages 68–79.

[Teorey and Pinkerton 1972] T. J. Teorey and T. B. Pinkerton, "A Comparative Analysis of Disk Scheduling Policies", *Communications of the ACM*, Volume 15, Number 3 (1972), pages 177–184.

[Tevanian et al. 1987a] A. Tevanian, Jr., R. F. Rashid, D. B. Golub, D. L. Black, E. Cooper, and M. W. Young, "Mach Threads and the Unix Kernel: The Battle for Control", *Proceedings of the Summer USENIX Conference* (1987).

[Tevanian et al. 1987b] A. Tevanian, Jr., R. F. Rashid, M. W. Young, D. B. Golub, M. R. Thompson, W. Bolosky, and R. Sanzi, "A UNIX Interface for Shared Memory and Memory Mapped Files Under Mach", Technical report, Carnegie-Mellon University (1987).

[Tevanian et al. 1989] A. Tevanian, Jr., and B. Smith, "Mach: The Model for Future Unix", *Byte* (1989).

[Thekkath et al. 1997] C. A. Thekkath, T. Mann, and E. K. Lee, "Frangipani: A Scalable Distributed File System", *Symposium on Operating Systems Principles* (1997), pages 224–237.

[Thompson 1984] K. Thompson, "Reflections on Trusting Trust", *Communications of ACM*, Volume 27, Number 8 (1984), pages 761–763.

[Thorn 1997] T. Thorn, "Programming Languages for Mobile Code", *ACM Computing Surveys*, Volume 29, Number 3 (1997), pages 213–239.

[Toigo 2000] J. Toigo, "Avoiding a Data Crunch", *Scientific American*, Volume 282, Number 5 (2000), pages 58–74.

[Traiger et al. 1982] I. L. Traiger, J. N. Gray, C. A. Galtieri, and B. G. Lindsay, "Transactions and Consistency in Distributed Database Management Systems", *ACM Transactions on Database Systems*, Volume 7, Number 3 (1982), pages 323–342.

[Tudor 1995] P. N. Tudor. "MPEG-2 Video Compression Tutorial". IEEE Coloquium on MPEG-2—What it Is and What it Isn't (1995).

[Vahalia 1996] U. Vahalia, *Unix Internals: The New Frontiers*, Prentice Hall (1996).

[Vee and Hsu 2000] V. Vee and W. Hsu, ""Locality-Preserving Load-Balancing Mechanisms for Synchronous Simulations on Shared-Memory Multiprocessors", *Proceedings of the Fourteenth Workshop on Parallel and Distributed Simulation* (2000), pages 131–138.

[Venners 1998] B. Venners, *Inside the Java Virtual Machine*, McGraw-Hill (1998).

[Wah 1984] B. W. Wah, "File Placement on Distributed Computer Systems", *Computer*, Volume 17, Number 1 (1984), pages 23–32.

[Wahbe et al. 1993a] R. Wahbe, S. Lucco, T. E. Anderson, and S. L. Graham, "Efficient Software-Based Fault Isolation", *ACM SIGOPS Operating Systems Review*, Volume 27, Number 5 (1993), pages 203–216.

[Wahbe et al. 1993b] R. Wahbe, S. Lucco, T. E. Anderson, and S. L. Graham, "Efficient Software-Based Fault Isolation", *ACM SIGOPS Operating Systems Review*, Volume 27, Number 5 (1993), pages 203–216.

[Wallach et al. 1997] D. S. Wallach, D. Balfanz, D. Dean, and E. W. Felten, "Extensible Security Architectures for Java", *Proceedings of the ACM Symposium on Operating Systems Principles* (1997).

[Wilkes et al. 1996] J. Wilkes, R. Golding, C. Staelin, and T. Sullivan, "The HP AutoRAID Hierarchical Storage System", *ACM Transactions on Computer Systems*, Volume 14, Number 1 (1996), pages 108–136.

[Williams 2001] R. Williams, *Computer Systems Architecture—A Networking Approach*, Addison-Wesley (2001).

[Williams 2002] N. Williams, "An Implementation of Scheduler Activations on the NetBSD Operating System", *2002 USENIX Annual Technical Conference, FREENIX Track* (2002).

[Wilson et al. 1995] P. R. Wilson, M. S. Johnstone, M. Neely, and D. Boles, "Dynamic Storage Allocation: A Survey and Critical Review", *Proceedings of the International Workshop on Memory Management* (1995), pages 1–116.

[Wolf 2003] W. Wolf, "A Decade of Hardware/Software Codesign", *Computer*, Volume 36, Number 4 (2003), pages 38–43.

[Wood and Kochan 1985] P. Wood and S. Kochan, *UNIX System Security*, Hayden (1985).

[Woodside 1986] C. Woodside, "Controllability of Computer Performance Tradeoffs Obtained Using Controlled-Share Queue Schedulers", *IEEE Transactions on Software Engineering*, Volume SE-12, Number 10 (1986), pages 1041–1048.

[Worthington et al. 1994] B. L. Worthington, G. R. Ganger, and Y. N. Patt, "Scheduling Algorithms for Modern Disk Drives", *Proceedings of the ACM Sigmetrics Conference on Measurement and Modeling of Computer Systems* (1994), pages 241–251.

[Worthington et al. 1995] B. L. Worthington, G. R. Ganger, Y. N. Patt, and J. Wilkes, "On-Line Extraction of SCSI Disk Drive Parameters", *Proceedings of the ACM Sigmetrics Conference on Measurement and Modeling of Computer Systems* (1995), pages 146–156.

[Wulf 1969] W. A. Wulf, "Performance Monitors for Multiprogramming Systems", *Proceedings of the ACM Symposium on Operating Systems Principles* (1969), pages 175–181.

[Wulf et al. 1981] W. A. Wulf, R. Levin, and S. P. Harbison, *Hydra/C.mmp: An Experimental Computer System*, McGraw-Hill (1981).

[Yeong et al. 1995] W. Yeong, T. Howes, and S. Kille, "Lightweight Directory Access Protocol", *Network Working Group, Request for Comments: 1777* (1995).

[Young et al. 1987] M. Young, A. Tevanian, R. Rashid, D. Golub, and J. Eppinger, "The Duality of Memory and Communication in the Implementation of a Multiprocessor Operating System", *Proceedings of the ACM Symposium on Operating Systems Principles* (1987), pages 63–76.

[Yu et al. 2000] X. Yu, B. Gum, Y. Chen, R. Y. Wang, K. Li, A. Krishnamurthy, and T. E. Anderson, "Trading Capacity for Performance in a Disk Array", *Proceedings of the 2000 Symposium on Operating Systems Design and Implementation* (2000), pages 243–258.

[Zabatta and Young 1998] F. Zabatta and K. Young, "A Thread Performance Comparison: Windows NT and Solaris on a Symmetric Multiprocessor", *Proceedings of the 2nd USENIX Windows NT Symposium* (1998).

[Zapata and Asokan 2002] M. Zapata and N. Asokan, "Securing Ad Hoc Routing Protocols", *Proc. 2002 ACM Workshop on Wireless Security* (2002).

Credits

Figure 3.9: From Iaccobucci, *OS/2 Programmer's Guide*, © 1988, McGraw-Hill, Inc., New York, New York. Figure 1.7, p. 20. Reprinted with permission of the publisher.

Figure 6.8: From Khanna/Sebree/Zolnowsky, "Realtime Scheduling in SunOS 5.0," Proceedings of Winter USENIX, January 1992, San Francisco, California. Derived with permission of the authors.

Figure 6.10 adapted with permission from Sun Microsystems, Inc.

Figure 9.21: From *80386 Programmer's Reference Manual*, Figure 5-12, p. 5-12. Reprinted by permission of Intel Corporation, Copyright / Intel Corporation 1986.

Figure 10.16: From *IBM Systems Journal*, Vol. 10, No. 3, © 1971, International Business Machines Corporation. Reprinted by permission of IBM Corporation.

Figure 12.9: From Leffler/McKusick/Karels/Quarterman, *The Design and Implementation of the 4.3BSD UNIX Operating System*, © 1989 by Addison-Wesley Publishing Co., Inc., Reading, Massachusetts. Figure 7.6, p. 196. Reprinted with permission of the publisher.

Figure 13.9: From *Pentium Processor User's Manual: Architecture and Programming Manual*, Volume 3, Copyright 1993. Reprinted by permission of Intel Corporation.

Figures 15.4, 15.5, and 15.7: From Halsall, *Data Communications, Computer Networks, and Open Systems, Third Edition*, © 1992, Addison-Wesley Publishing Co., Inc., Reading, Massachusetts. Figure 1.9, p. 14, Figure 1.10, p. 15, and Figure 1.11, p. 18. Reprinted with permission of the publisher.

Sections of chapter 7 and 17 from Silberschatz/Korth, *Database System Concepts, Third Edition*, Copyright 1997, McGraw-Hill, Inc., New York, New York. Section 13.5, p. 451-454, 14.1.1, p. 471-742, 14.1.3, p. 476-479, 14.2, p. 482-485, 15.2.1, p. 512-513, 15.4, p. 517-518, 15.4.3, p. 523-524, 18.7, p. 613-617, 18.8, p. 617-622. Reprinted with permission of the publisher.

Figure A.1: From Quarterman/Wilhelm, *UNIX, POSIX and Open Systems: The Open Standards Puzzle*, © 1993, by Addison-Wesley Publishing Co., Inc. Reading, Massachusetts. Figure 2.1, p. 31. Reprinted with permission of the publisher.

Timeline information for the back end papers was assembled: From a variety of sources, which include "The History of Electronic Computing," compiled and edited by Marc Rettig, Association for Computing Machinery, Inc. (ACM), New York, New York, and Shedroff/Hutto/Fromm, Understanding Computers, © 1992, Vivid Publishing, distributed by SYBEX, San Francisco, California.

Index

Q

R

S